Enhanced Network+ Guide To Networks

Enhanced Edition

Tamara Dean

THOMSON

COURSE TECHNOLOGY

Australia • Canada • Mexico • Singapore • Spain • United Kingdom • United States

THOMSON
───────★───────™
COURSE TECHNOLOGY

Enhanced Network+ Guide to Networks, Enhanced Edition
is published by Course Technology.

Senior Editor:
Lisa Egan

Developmental Editor:
Ann Shaffer

Composition Designer:
GEX Publishing Services

Publisher, Senior Vice President:
Kristen Duerr

Quality Assurance Manager:
John Bosco

Text Designer:
GEX Publishing Services

Senior Editor:
Will Pitkin III

Quality Assurance Tester:
Nicole Ashton

Cover Designer:
Efrat Reis

Product Manager:
Amy Lyon

Product Manager:
Tim Gleeson

Marketing Manager:
Jason "Dusty" Sakos

Production Editor:
Elena Montillo

Manufacturing:
Alexander Schall

CONTENTS AT A GLANCE

TABLE OF CONTENTS

CHAPTER 5
PHYSICAL AND LOGICAL TOPOLOGIES 177

CHAPTER 16

MANAGING NETWORK DESIGN AND IMPLEMENTATION 809

NETWORK+ COURSEPREP/EXAM GUIDE

PREFACE

Knowing how to install, configure, and troubleshoot a computer network is a highly marketable and exciting skill. This book covers a wide range of material about networking, from assessments of careers in networking to discussions of local area networks, wide area networks, protocols, topologies, transmission media, and security. It not only introduces a variety of concepts, but also provides in-depth examinations of the most significant aspects of networking, such as the TCP/IP protocol suite. In addition to explaining concepts, each chapter includes several real-world examples of networking issues from a professional's standpoint, making the book a practical learning tool.

The Exam Guide content included in this Enhanced Edition prepares students for the Network+ Exam from CompTIA. Individual chapters discuss the following topics:

Chapters 1, 2, and 3 provide an introduction to networking fundamentals, including networking standards organizations, the OSI Model, and networking protocols.

Chapter 4 builds on the fundamentals introduced in earlier chapters by explaining data transmission methods and transmission media, such as twisted-pair copper wiring and fiber optic cabling.

Chapter 5 discusses the variety of physical and logical topologies used in local area networks.

Chapters 6 examines the physical components of a network, including network interface cards, hubs, routers, bridges, and switches. In Chapter 6, you will find several photos portraying typical networking equipment.

Chapter 7 expands on your knowledge of local area networks by examining wide area networking topologies and transmission methods.

Chapters 8, 9, and 10 introduce the most popular network operating systems: Windows 2000, NetWare, and UNIX.

Chapter 11 provides a detailed examination of the components and uses of the TCP/IP protocol suite, the most popular protocol in use on contemporary networks.

Chapters 12 and 13 approach the tasks of troubleshooting and maintaining networks in a logical, practical manner. Once you have learned how networks operate and how to create them, you will need to know how to fix and maintain them.

Chapters 14 and 15 consider how to keep the network safe in the face of dangers such as power flaws, hardware or software failures, and security breaches. In Chapter 15, you will also learn about firewalls, encryption, and how to implement an enterprise-wide security policy.

Chapter 16 brings together all of your knowledge about networking by tackling a network implementation project. This chapter includes tips on project planning specifically for technical endeavors.

The five appendices at the end of this book serve as references for the networking professional. Appendix A provides a complete listing of the Network + certification exam objectives, including what percentage of the exam's content they represent. Appendix B offers a practice exam containing questions similar in content and presentation to those you will find on the Network+ examination. Appendix C provides a visual connector reference chart for quick identification of connectors and plugs used in networking. Appendix D gives examples of forms that you can use while planning, installing, and troubleshooting your network. Appendix E expands on what you learned about networking hardware by providing pictures of a typical networking professional's tools.

THE INTENDED AUDIENCE

This book is intended to serve the needs of professionals who are interested in mastering broad, vendor-independent networking concepts. In particular, it will help those professionals who are seeking to pass the Computing Technology Industry Association's Network+ certification exam. For more information on Network+ certification, visit CompTIA's web site at *www.comptia.org*. The text and pedagogical features are designed to provide a truly interactive learning experience, preparing you for the challenges of the highly dynamic networking industry. In addition to the information presented in the text, each chapter includes Hands-on Projects that take you through various tasks in a step-by-step fashion. Each chapter also contains a running case study that places you in the role of problem solver, requiring you to use concepts presented in the chapter so as to achieve a successful solution.

FEATURES

To aid you in fully understanding networking concepts, this book includes many features designed to enhance your learning experience.

- **Chapter Objectives.** Each chapter begins with a detailed list of the concepts to be mastered within that chapter. This list provides you with both a quick reference to the chapter's contents and a useful study aid.

- **Illustrations and Tables.** Numerous illustrations of server screens and components help you visualize common setup steps, theories, and concepts. In addition, the many tables included provide details and comparisons of both practical and theoretical information.

- **Hands-on Projects.** Although it is important to understand the theory behind networking technology, nothing can improve upon real-world experience. To this end, along with theoretical explanations, each chapter provides numerous Hands-on Projects aimed at providing you with practical implementation experience.

- **Chapter Summaries.** Each chapter's text is followed by a summary of the concepts introduced in that chapter. These summaries provide a helpful way to recap and revisit the ideas covered in each chapter.
- **Review Questions.** The end-of-chapter assessment begins with a set of review questions that reinforce the ideas introduced in each chapter. Answering these questions will ensure that you have mastered the important concepts.
- **Case Projects.** Located at the end of each chapter are several cases. In these extensive exercises, you implement the skills and knowledge gained in the chapter through real design and implementation scenarios.
- **CoursePrep Exam Guide.** Provides the information you need to master each exam objective. The Exam Guide devotes an entire two-page spread to each certification objective. In addition, there are practice questions for each objective.

TEXT AND GRAPHIC CONVENTIONS

Wherever appropriate, additional information and exercises have been added to this book to help you better understand the topic at hand. Icons throughout the text alert you to additional materials. The icons used in this textbook are described below.

The Note icon draws your attention to additional helpful material related to the subject being described.

Each hands-on activity in this book is preceded by the Hands-On icon and a description of the exercise that follows.

Tips based on the authors' experience provide extra information about how to attack a problem or what to do in real-world situations.

The cautions warn you about potential mistakes or problems and explains how to avoid them.

Case Project icons mark case projects, which are more involved, scenario-based assignments. In these extensive case examples, you are asked to implement independently what you have learned.

INSTRUCTOR'S MATERIALS

The following additional materials are available when this book is used in a classroom setting. All of the supplements available with this book are provided to the instructor on a single CD-ROM.

Electronic Instructor's Manual. The Instructor's Manual that accompanies this textbook includes the following items:

- Additional instructional material to assist in class preparation, including suggestions for lecture topics, suggested lab activities, tips on setting up a lab for the hands-on assignments, and solutions to all end-of-chapter materials

ExamView Test Bank. This cutting-edge Windows-based testing software helps instructors design and administer tests and pretests. In addition to generating tests that can be printed and administered, this full-featured program has an online testing component that allows students to take tests at the computer and have their exams automatically graded.

PowerPoint presentations. This book comes with a set of Microsoft PowerPoint slides for each chapter. These slides are meant to be used as a teaching aid for classroom presentations, to be made available to students on the network for chapter review, or to be printed for classroom distribution. Instructors are also at liberty to add their own slides for other topics introduced.

CoursePrep® Test Prep Software. Network+ test preparation software is included on CD and mimics the exam environment so you can practice for exam day.

Text on CD. An electronic copy of the entire text is included on CD.

ACKNOWLEDGMENTS

As with any large undertaking, this book is the result of many contributions and collaborative efforts. I could not have persevered without the help of friends, family, fellow networking professionals, and Course Technology staff. Thanks to Kristen Duerr, Publisher and Senior Vice President, for her continued enthusiasm and support for the project. Thanks to Stephen Solomon, Managing Editor, for his dedication and business expertise. Lisa Egan, Senior Product Manager at Course Technology, was a champion at minding the production and development details, maintaining communication between all parties, and acting as an advocate and liaison. With the second edition, I am again deeply grateful to Ann Shaffer, developmental editor and friend, for being a constant cheerleader, confidante, and stickler, all in the right proportions. Nothing vaguely vague survived her edits. Thanks also to substitute Developmental Editor and Packers fan Lisa Ruffolo for stepping in when we needed her talents. Thanks to Elena Montillo, Production Editor, and to the copyeditors, who include the people at Foxxe Editorial and Robin Flynn, who fabulously minded the details and polished the final drafts for production. Thanks to John Bosco for his phenomenal technical reviews and forthright commentary. Credit goes to the Course Technology quality assurance staff who checked my work at every step. Kudos to the reviewers who carefully read the drafts and took the time to suggest better, more accurate alternatives.

Peter Beauregard	Westfield Vocational Technical High School
Judson Miers	DeVry Training, Kansas City
Randall Perry	Davenport University
David Pope	Ozarks Technical Community College
Bob Pierson	Northwestern Michigan College
Jeffery Richardson	Westfield Vocational Technical High School
Sara Robben	DeVry Training, Kansas City

For additional help with technical material, I'm grateful to my smart, generous colleagues Jim Berbee, Tom Callaci, Peyton Engel, Dan Geisler, Nancy Gibson, Michael Grice, David Klann, Sara Koehler, Katie McCullough, Tom Pendergast, Jerry Steinhauer, and Craig Weinhold. Thanks also to Paul and Janet Dean, scientists and teachers both, for their encouragement, pedagogical advice, and technical bent.

PHOTO CREDITS

Figure 6-3	Courtesy of 3Com Corporation
Figure 6-4	Courtesy of Belkin Components
Figure 6-5	Courtesy of Xircom, Inc.
Figure 6-6	Courtesy of Raylink
	Courtesy of Cisco Systems, Inc.
Figure 6-7	1) Courtesy of 3Com Corporation
	2) Courtesy of CNet Technology, Inc.
	3) Courtesy of Intel Corporation
Figure 6-8	1) Courtesy of IBM Corporation
	2) Courtesy of 3Com Corporation
Figure 6-9	Courtesy of Hewlett-Packard Company
Figure 6-16	Courtesy of Cisco Systems, Inc.
Figure 6-19	1) Courtesy of 3Com Corporation
	2) Courtesy of Intel Corporation
Figure 6-20	1) Courtesy of Cabletron Systems
	2) Courtesy of Nortel Networks
Figure 6-23	1) Courtesy of Cabletron Systems

Figure 6-25   1) Courtesy of Cabletron Systems
                     2) Courtesy of Lucent Technology
                     3) Courtesy of Cisco Systems, Inc.
Figure 6-27   Courtesy of Cisco Systems, Inc.
Figure 7-10   Courtesy of Paradyne Corporation
Figure 7-11   Courtesy of Motorola
Figure 12-6   Courtesy of Agilent Technologies
Figure 12-7   Courtesy of Microtest, Inc.
Figure 12-8   Courtesy of Fluke Networks
Figure 14-1   Courtesy of APC Corporation
Figure 14-2   Courtesy of Best Power
Figure 14-17   Courtesy of Imation
Figure 15-3   Courtesy of Cisco Systems, Inc.

CHAPTER 1

AN INTRODUCTION TO NETWORKING

After reading this chapter and completing the exercises, you will be able to:

➤ List the advantages of networked computing relative to standalone computing

➤ Identify the elements of a network

➤ Describe several specific uses for a network

➤ Distinguish between client/server and peer-to-peer networks

➤ Identify some of the certifications available to networking professionals

➤ Identify the kinds of nontechnical, or "soft," skills that will help you succeed as a networking professional

---

ON THE JOB

I never intended to be a networking professional. In high school my greatest love was reading, so I decided to study literature in college. I only used computers for writing term papers and e-mail. When I graduated from college, I don't think I even knew what a network was. With an English degree, I tried to find interesting jobs, and occasionally I did, but usually I wound up as a temp answering phones and typing all day.

One of the more interesting temporary jobs I had was at a pharmaceutical company, setting up laptop computers for their sales force. I installed software, tested the software, then shipped the machines to their owners. Soon I became fascinated with the hardware inside the machines and performed small repairs such as swapping out memory chips or fixing a keyboard connector. After I learned about PCs, I became more and more curious about the network: for example, how the laptop users picked up their e-mail while they were travelling. And before I knew it, I was supporting these users and troubleshooting the network problems that affected them. Because there was no one else around to help them, I had to learn quickly and without much formal training.

Since that time I've taken classes to fill in what I couldn't learn on the job. I've also met a lot of networking professionals who, like me, never intended to be in this field. In fact, very few of my colleagues have computer science degrees: some studied Music, Film, Microbiology, Russian, Meteorology, Math, Accounting, Mechanical Engineering, and the list goes on. We're all proof that you may wind up doing something entirely different from what you planned, but that you may enjoy it more than you imagined.

Lisa Stefanik
Abbotsford Information Networks

Loosely defined, a **network** is a group of computers and other devices (such as printers) that are connected by some type of transmission media, usually wire or cable. The variations on the hardware, software, transmission media, and design of networks, however, are nearly infinite. Networks may consist of two computers connected by a cable in a home office or several thousand computers connected across the world via a combination of cable, phone lines, and satellite links. In addition to connecting personal computers, networks may link together mainframe computers, modems, CD-ROMs, printers, plotters, fax machines, and phone systems. They may communicate through copper wires, fiber-optic cable, radio waves, infrared, or satellite links.

All networks offer advantages relative to using a **standalone computer** (a personal computer that uses programs and data only from its local disks). Most importantly, networks enable multiple users to share devices and data that, collectively, are referred to as the networks' **resources**. For any organization, sharing devices saves money. For example, rather than buying 20 printers for 20 staff members, you can buy one printer and have those 20 staff members share it over a network. Sharing devices also saves time. For example, it's faster for co-workers to share data over a network than to copy data to a disk and transport it from one computer to another—an outdated method commonly referred to as **sneakernet** (presumably because people wore sneakers when walking from computer to computer). Before networks, transferring data via floppy disks (illustrated in Figure 1-1) was the only possible way to share data.

Figure 1-1   Data sharing before the advent of networks

Another advantage to networks is that they allow you to manage, or administer, hardware and software on multiple computers from one central location. Imagine you work in the Information Technology (IT) department of a multinational insurance company and must verify that each of 5000 insurance agents across the world uses the same version of WordPerfect. Without a network you could never keep up! Networks, along with network management software, allow you to manage computers in your office or around the world from one computer. The computer on which you are actually working is referred to as the **local computer**. The computer that you are controlling or working on via the network is referred to as the **remote computer**. Because they allow you to share devices and administer computers centrally, networks increase productivity. It's not surprising, then, that most businesses depend on their networks to stay competitive.

The simplest form of a network is a **peer-to-peer network**. In a peer-to-peer network computers communicate directly with other computers on a single segment of cable and share each others' data and devices, such as printers or CD-ROM drives. By default, no computer in a peer-to-peer network has more authority than another, and every computer can use resources from every other computer. Most computers in a peer-to-peer network are general-purpose personal computers that are not designed to handle heavy processing loads.

The primary advantage to using peer-to-peer networks is that they are simple to configure. For this reason, they are often used in environments where technical expertise is scarce. Peer-to-peer networks are also less expensive to set up and maintain than other types of networks. This fact makes them suitable for environments where saving money is critical. However, peer-to-peer networks are not very flexible. Once a peer-to-peer network is established, adding or changing significant elements of the network may be difficult. Peer-to-peer networks are also not very secure—meaning that data and other resources shared by network users can be easily discovered and used by unauthorized people. Finally, traditional peer-to-peer networks are not practical for connecting more than a handful of computers, because they do not necessarily centralize resources. For example, if your computer is part of a peer-to-peer network that includes five other computers, and each computer user stores his or her spreadsheets and word-processing files on his or her own hard disk, whenever your colleagues want to edit your files, they must attach to your machine on the network. If one colleague saves a changed version of one of your spreadsheets on her hard disk, you'll find it difficult to keep track of which version is the most current. As you can imagine, the more computers you add to a peer-to-peer network, the more difficult it becomes to find and track resources. Figure 1-2 shows an example of a peer-to-peer network.

Desktop computer   Desktop computer   Desktop computer

Desktop computer   Desktop computer

Figure 1-2   A simple peer-to-peer network

One way to establish a peer-to-peer network is by manipulating Windows 98 or Windows 2000 file-sharing controls. Peer-to-peer networks do not require a special network operating system such as Microsoft Windows 2000 Server or Novell NetWare. Instead, each user on this type of network can modify the properties of his or her desktop operating system to allow others to read and edit files on that particular computer's hard disk. Because access depends on many different users, it typically isn't uniform and may not be secure.

The peer-to-peer network is a very simple example of a local area network. As its name suggests, a **local area network (LAN)** is a network of computers and other devices that is confined to a relatively small space, such as one building or even one office. Small LANs became popular in businesses in the early 1980s. Today's LANs are typically larger and more complex than the peer-to-peer network in the previous example.

LANs involving many computers are usually server-based. On a **server-based network**, special computers, known as **servers**, process data for and facilitate communication between the other computers on the network, which are known as **clients**. Clients usually take the form of desktop computers, known as **workstations**. A network that uses a server to enable clients to share data, data storage space, and devices, is known as a **client/server network**. Because this is the most popular type of network, most of the networking concepts covered in this book and on the Net+ exam pertain to client/server networks.

The server's main job is to allow clients to share resources. To function as a server, a computer must be running a network operating system, such as Microsoft Windows 2000 Server, Novell NetWare, or UNIX. (By contrast, a standalone computer, or a client computer, uses a simpler operating system, such as Windows 98 or Windows 2000 Professional.) A **network operating system (NOS)** is special software designed to manage data and other resources on a server for a number of clients. Network operating systems also provide the ability to manage network security, network users and groups, protocols, and networked applications.

When designing a network, an engineer typically follows a plan, or model, which specifies the relationships between the various computers in the network. The term **client/server architecture** refers to a networking model in which clients (typically desktop PCs) use a central server to share applications, devices, and data. Every computer on a client/server network acts as a client or a server, and some computers may act as both. Clients on a network can still run applications from and save data to their local hard disk; a server, on the other hand, offers the option of using shared applications and data. Typically, clients on a client/server network do not communicate directly with each other, but rather use the server as an intermediate step in communications.

Usually, servers are more powerful computers than those found on a user's desktop. They may even be equipped with special hardware designed to provide network management functions beyond that provided by the network operating system. Figure 1-3 depicts a simple LAN that incorporates a server.

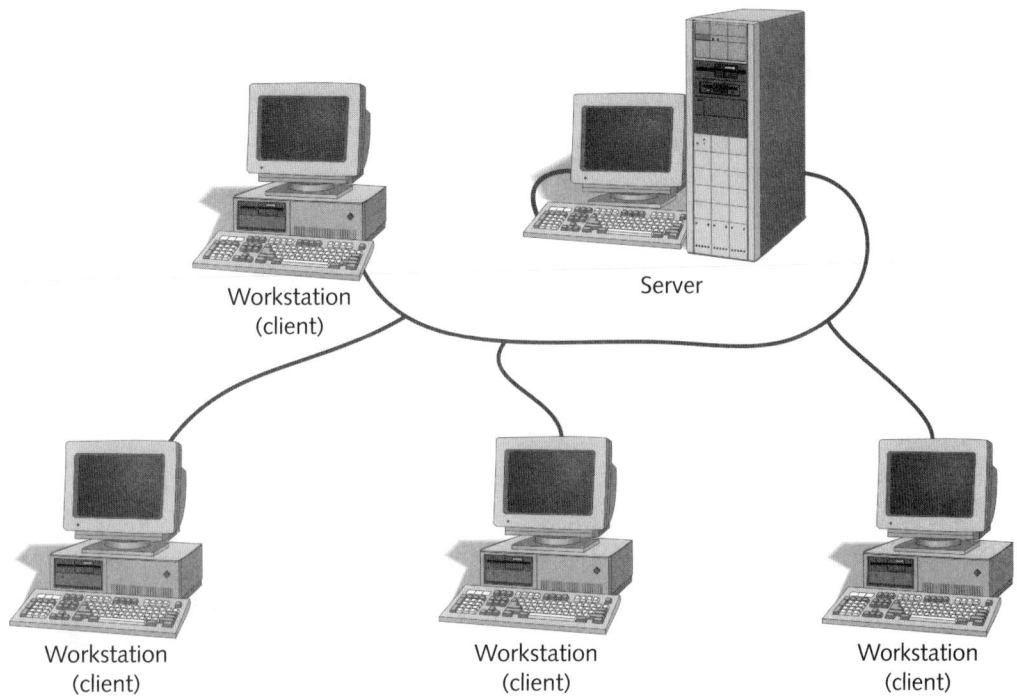

Figure 1-3   LAN with a file server

Networks are usually more complex than the simple LAN example in Figure 1-3. Often separate LANs are interconnected and rely on several servers running many different applications and managing resources other than data. For example, a single network may connect 15 servers, 200 workstations, 3 fax machines, 5 CD-ROM devices, 2 mainframes, and 7 scanners. Figure 1-4 depicts a more complex network.

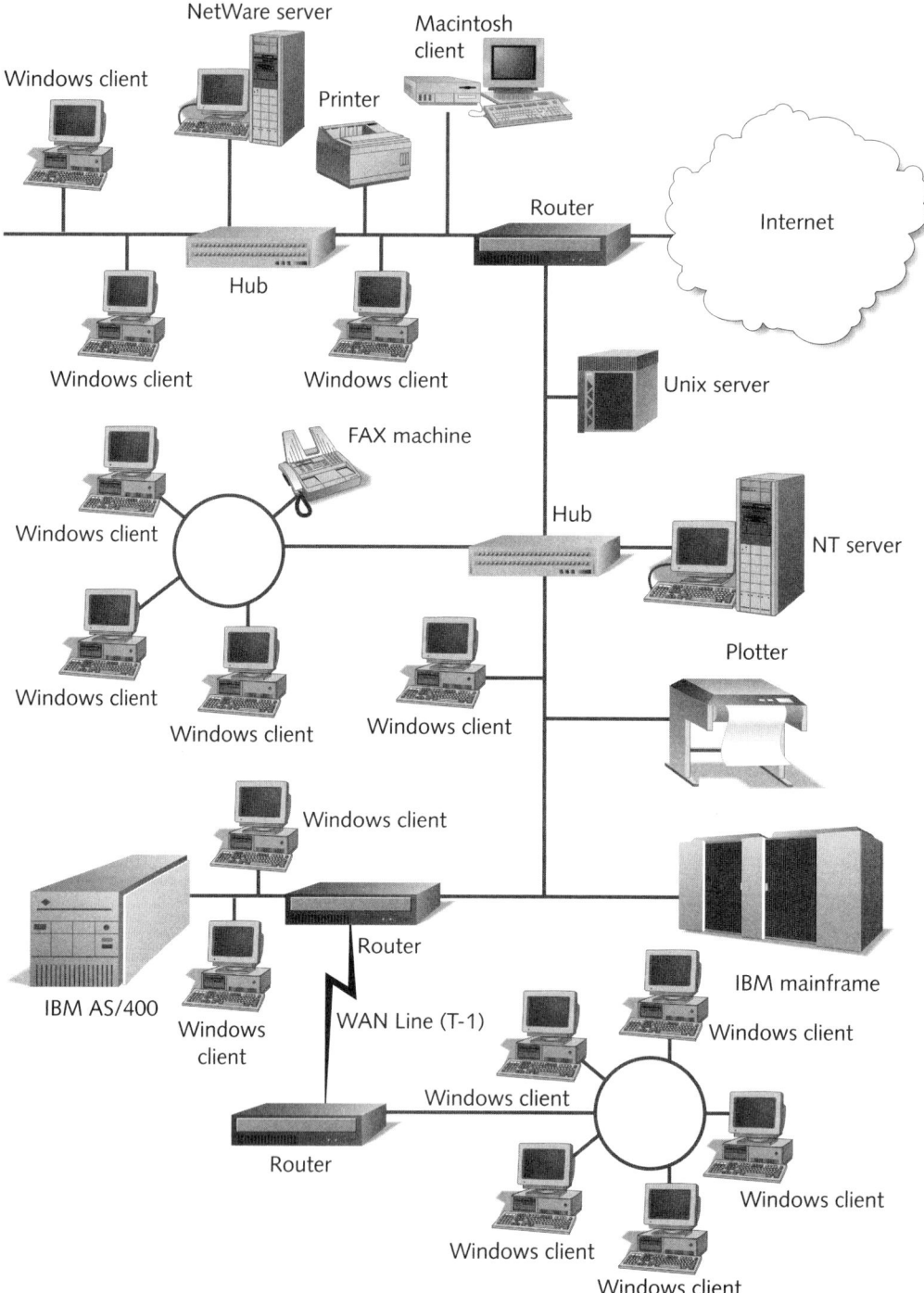

Figure 1-4   An example of a complex network

Don't worry if the network in Figure 1-4 looks overwhelming to you right now. As you progress through this book, you will learn about every part of this diagram. In the process, you will learn to integrate these pieces so as to create a variety of networks that are reliable, secure, and manageable.

The following list describes advantages of server-based networks relative to peer-to-peer networks:

- User login accounts and passwords for anyone on a server-based network can be assigned in one place.

- Access to multiple shared resources (such as data files or printers) can be centrally granted, by a single user or groups of users.

- Servers are optimized to handle heavy processing loads and dedicated to handling requests from clients.

- Because of their efficient processing and larger disk storage, servers can connect more than a handful of computers on a network.

Networks may extend beyond the boundaries of a building. A network that connects clients and servers in multiple buildings within a limited geographic area, for example, a handful of government offices surrounding a state capitol is known as a **metropolitan area network (MAN)**. A network that connects two or more geographically distinct LANs is called a **wide area network (WAN)**. Imagine you work for a nationwide software reseller that keeps its software inventory in warehouses in Topeka, Kansas, and Panama City, Florida. Suppose also that your office is located in New York. When a customer calls and asks whether you have 70 copies of Lotus Notes available to ship overnight, you need to check the inventory database located on servers at both the Topeka and Panama City warehouses. To access these servers, you would connect to the warehouses through a WAN link, then log on to their servers.

In fact, most organizations use WANs to connect separate offices, whether the offices are across town or across the world from each other. The **Internet** is an example of a very intricate and extensive WAN that spans the globe. Because they carry data over longer distances than LANs, WANs require slightly different technology and transmission media. WANs will be covered in detail in Chapter 7. Figure 1-5 depicts a simple WAN design.

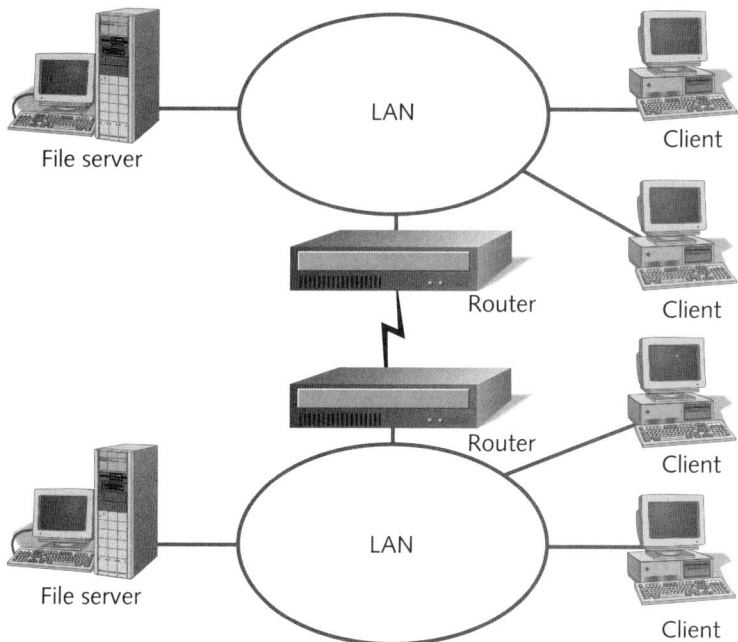

Figure 1-5   A simple WAN

ELEMENTS COMMON TO ALL SERVER-BASED NETWORKS

You have learned that networks—no matter how simple or how complex—provide some benefits over standalone computers. They also share terminology and common building blocks, some of which you've already encountered. The following list provides a more complete rundown of basic elements common to all server-based networks. You will learn more about these topics throughout this book.

- *Client.* A computer on the network that requests resources or services from another computer on a network. In some cases, a client could also act as a server. The term "client" may also refer to the human **user** of a client workstation.

- *Server.* A computer on the network that manages shared resources. Servers usually have more processing power, memory, and hard disk space than clients. They run network operating software that can manage not only data, but also users, groups, security, and applications on the network.

- *Workstation.* A desktop computer, which may or may not be connected to a network. Most clients are workstation computers.

- *Network interface card (NIC).* The device that enables a workstation to connect to the network and communicate with other computers. Several companies (such as 3Com, IBM, Intel, SMC, and Xircom) manufacture NICs, which come with a variety of specifications that are tailored to the requirements of the workstation and the network. Figure 1-6 shows a typical workstation NIC.

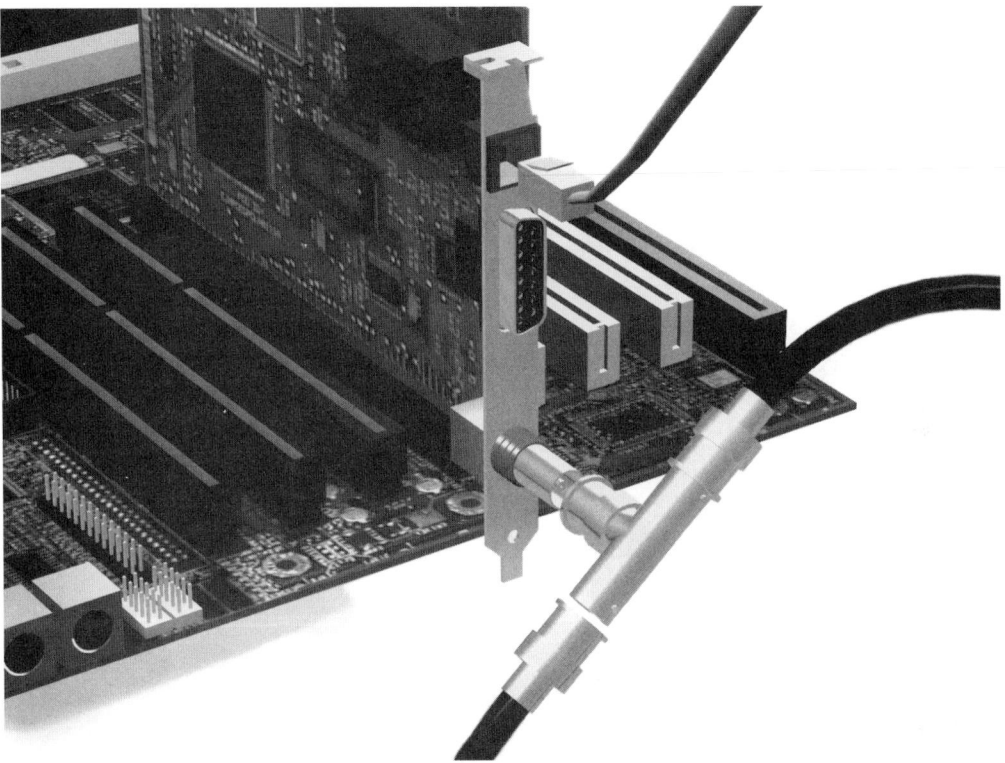

Figure 1-6   A network interface card (NIC)

 Because different PCs and network types require different kinds of network interface cards, you cannot assume that a NIC that works in one workstation will work in another.

- *Network operating system (NOS).* The software that runs on a server and enables the server to manage data, users, groups, security, applications, and other networking functions. The most popular network operating systems are Microsoft Windows NT, Windows 2000, Novell NetWare, and UNIX.

- *Host.* A server that manages shared resources.

- *Node.* A client, server, or other device that can communicate over a network and that is identified by a unique identifying number, known as its network address.

- *Topology.* The physical layout of a computer network. Topologies vary according to the needs of the organization and available hardware and expertise.

Networks are usually arranged in a ring, bus, or star formation; hybrid combinations of these patterns are also possible. Figure 1-7 illustrates the most common network topologies, which you must understand to design and troubleshoot networks. (You will learn about topologies in detail in Chapter 5.)

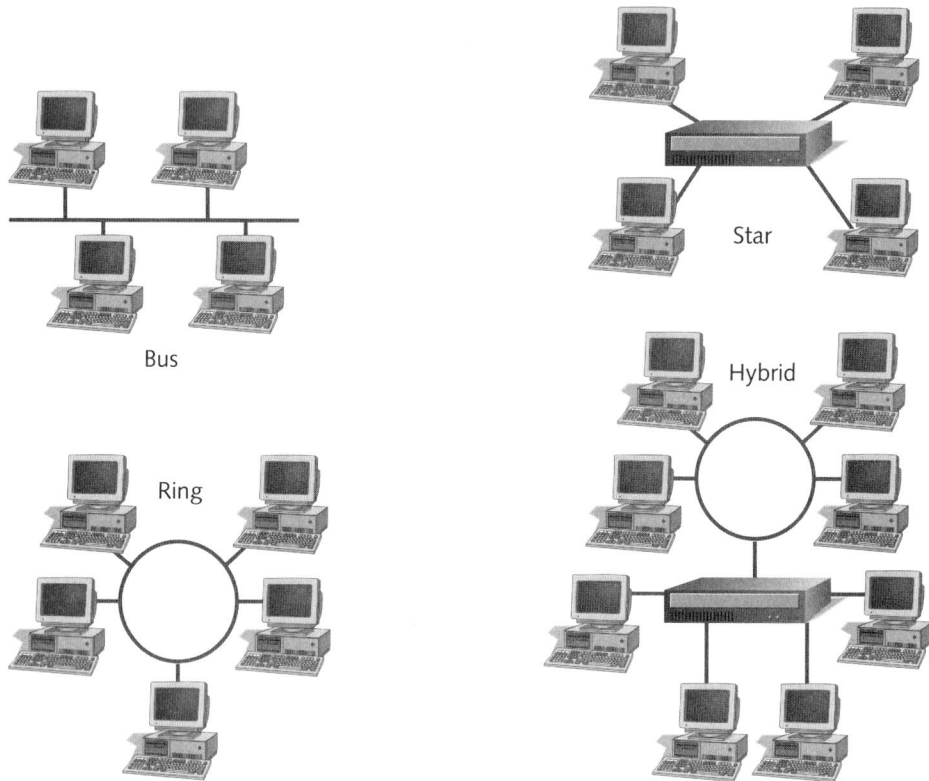

Figure 1-7 Commonly used network topologies

- *Protocol.* The rules that the network uses to transfer data. Protocols ensure that data are transferred whole, in sequence, and without error from one node on the network to another. To effectively maintain and manage a network, you must have a thorough understanding of network protocols. You will learn about network protocols in Chapter 3.

- *Data packets.* The distinct units of data that are transmitted from one computer on a network to another. Data packets are also known as datagrams, protocol data units (PDU), frames, or cells, depending on the context. You will learn more about data packets in Chapters 2 and 3.

- *Addressing.* The scheme for assigning a unique identifying number to every workstation and device on the network. The type of addressing used depends on the network's protocols and network operating system. It is important that each computer on a network have a unique **address** so that data can be transmitted reliably to and from that computer. You will learn more about network addressing in Chapters 2 and 3.

- *Transmission media.* The means through which data are transmitted and received. Transmission media may be physical, such as wire or cable, or atmospheric (wireless), such as radio waves. You will learn more about transmission media in Chapter 4. Figure 1-8 shows several examples of transmission media.

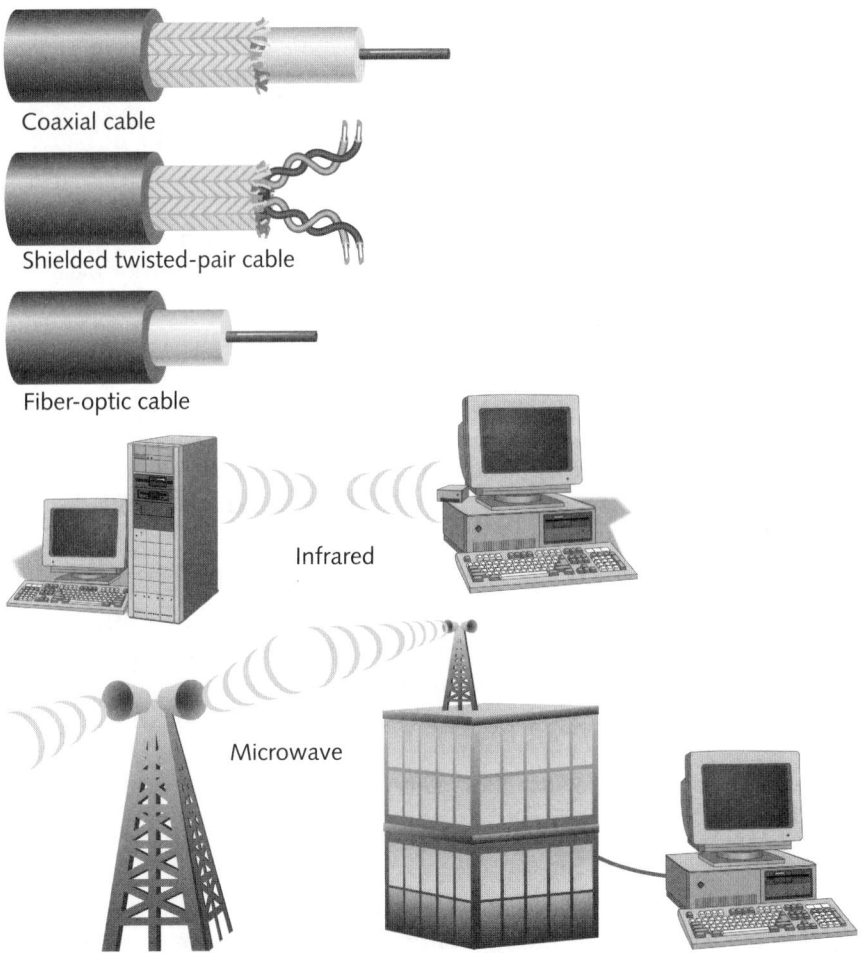

Coaxial cable

Shielded twisted-pair cable

Fiber-optic cable

Infrared

Microwave

Figure 1-8   Examples of network transmission media

Now that you are familiar with basic network terminology, you are ready to appreciate the many uses of computer networks.

HOW NETWORKS ARE USED

The features provided by a network are usually referred to as **services**. Any network manager will tell you that the network service with the highest visibility is e-mail. If your company's e-mail system fails, users will notice within minutes—and they will not be shy about informing you of the failure. Although e-mail may be the most visible network service, other services are just as vital. Printer sharing, file sharing, Internet access, remote dial-in capabilities, mainframe communication, and management services are all critical business functions provided through networks. In large organizations, separate servers may be dedicated to performing each of these functions. In offices with only a few users and little network traffic, one server may perform all functions.

File and Print Services

File services refer to the capability of a server to share data files, applications (such as word-processing programs or spreadsheets), and disk storage space. File services accounted for the first use of networks and remain the foundation of networking today, for a number of reasons. A server that provides file services is called a **file server**. As mentioned earlier, it's easier and faster to store shared data at a central location than to copy files to a disk and then pass the disks around. Data stored at a central location are also more secure because, as the network administrator, you can take charge of backing up this data, rather than relying on individual users to make their own copies. In addition, using a file server to run applications for multiple users requires that fewer copies of the application be purchased and results in less maintenance work for the network administrator.

Using **print services** to share printers across a network also saves time and money. A high-capacity printer costs thousands of dollars, but can simultaneously print jobs for an entire department, thereby eliminating the need to buy a desktop printer for each worker. With one printer, less time is spent on maintenance and management. If a shared printer fails, the network administrator can diagnose the problem from a workstation anywhere on the network using the network operating system's printer control functions. Often, the administrator can solve the problem without even visiting the printer.

Communications Services

A network's communications services allow remote users to connect to the network (usually through a phone line and modem). (The term **remote user** refers to a person working on a computer in a different geographical location from the LAN's server.) Less frequently, communications services allow network users to connect to machines outside the network. Network operating systems such as Windows 2000 and NetWare include built-in communications services. In Windows 2000, the communications software is known as Remote Access Server (RAS). In NetWare, it is called Network Access Server (NAS). Both enable users to dial into a **communications server**, or the server running these communications services, then log in to the network and take advantage of any network features, just as if they were logged in to a workstation in the server's home office.

Businesses and other organizations commonly use communications services to provide LAN access for workers at home, workers on the road, and workers at small satellite offices where WAN connections are not cost-effective. In addition, they may use communications services to allow staff from other organizations (such as a software or hardware vendor) to help diagnose a network problem. For example, suppose you work for a clothing manufacturer that uses embroidery software to sew insignias on shirts and hats. You are an expert on networking, but less adept with the automated embroidery software. When the software causes problems, you turn to the software vendor for help. If that software company is located in Australia, however, it's much easier and cheaper to allow the vendor's technician to dial in to your network through a communications server and remotely diagnose the software than to fly the technician to your office.

Communications servers are also referred to as **access servers** or **remote access servers**. It's important to remember that these servers—no matter which platform (hardware or operating system software) they run on—allow external users to use network resources and devices just as if they were logged in to a workstation in the office. From a remote location, users can print files to shared printers, log in to IBM mainframe hosts, retrieve mail from an internal messaging system, or run queries on internal databases. Because they can be accessed by the world outside the local network, communications servers necessitate strict security measures.

Mail Services

Mail services coordinate the storage and transfer of e-mail between users on a network. Users depend on e-mail for fast, convenient communication both within and outside the organization. In addition to sending, receiving, and storing mail, however, mail services can include e-mail routing capabilities (for example, forwarding a message to a supervisor automatically if a technical support representative has not opened that message within 15 minutes of receiving it), notification, scheduling, document management, and gateways to other mail servers. (A **gateway** is a combination of software and hardware that enables two different kinds of networks to exchange data.) Mail services can run on several kinds of systems; they may be connected to the Internet or may be isolated within an organization. Examples of mail services software include Microsoft's Exchange Server, NetWare's GroupWise, and Lotus's cc:Mail. Mail services are the most visible networking functions to users. As a result, their client interfaces (that is, the part of the software with which the user interacts) are usually well developed and easy to use. Also, because of their heavy use, mail services require a significant commitment of technical support and administration resources.

Internet Services

Gone are the days when businesses could remain competitive by using isolated local area networks. Today, global communication and data exchange is essential. The Internet, as the most far-reaching network in the world, has become a necessary tool. You have probably connected to the Internet already without knowing or caring about all of the services running behind the scenes. Once you establish a connection, your workstation and its accompanying servers must run standard protocols to use the Internet's features. **Internet services** include World Wide Web servers and browsers, file transfer capabilities, Internet addressing schemes, security filters, and a means for directly logging into other computers on the Internet. Internet services are a broad category of network functions; reflecting their growing importance, entire books have been devoted to them. You will learn more about Internet services in Chapter 11.

Management Services

When networks were small, they could be managed easily by a single network administrator and the network operating system's internal functions. For instance, suppose a user called to report a problem logging on to the network. The administrator diagnosed the problem as an addressing conflict (that is, two workstations having the same network address). In a very small network, the conflicting workstations might be located right around the corner from each other, and one address could be changed quickly. In another example, if a manager needed to report the number of copies of Lotus 1-2-3 in use in a certain department, the network administrator could probably get the desired information by just walking through the department and checking the various workstations.

As networks grow larger and more complex, however, they become more difficult to manage. To keep track of a large network, you need to employ special network management services. Network **management services** centrally administer and simplify complicated management tasks on the network, such as making sure that no more than 20 workstations are using WordPerfect at one time. Some organizations dedicate a number of servers to network management functions, with each server performing only one or two unique services.

Numerous services fall under the category of network management. Some of the most important services include the following:

- *Traffic monitoring and control.* Determining how much **traffic** (that is, data transmission and processing activity) is taking place on a network or network segment and notifying administrators when a segment becomes overloaded. A **segment** is a part of a LAN that is logically separated from other parts of the LAN and that shares a fixed amount of traffic capacity. In general, the larger the network, the more critical it is to monitor traffic.

- *Load balancing.* Distributing processing activity evenly across a network so that no single device becomes overwhelmed. Load balancing is especially important for networks where it's difficult to predict the number of requests that will be issued to a server, as is the case with Web servers.

- *Hardware diagnosis and failure alert.* Determining when a network component fails and automatically notifying the network administrator through e-mail or paging.

- *Asset management.* Collecting and storing data on the number and types of software and hardware assets (or resources) in an organization's network. The data collection process, in which each network client is examined electronically, takes place automatically. In the past, these data were typically gathered manually from paper records and typed into spreadsheet forms.

- *License tracking.* Determining how many copies of a single application are currently in use on the network. This information is important for legal reasons, as the concern over illegal software copying and excessive usage grows.

- *Security auditing.* Evaluating what security measures are currently in force and notifying the network administrator if a security breach occurs.

- *Software distribution.* Automatically transferring a data file or program from the server to a client on the network. Software distribution can be initiated from either the server or the client. Several options are available when distributing software, such as warning users about updates, writing changes to a workstation's system files, and restarting the workstation after the update.

- *Address management.* Centrally managing a finite number of network addresses for an entire LAN. Usually this task can be accomplished without touching the client workstations.

- *Backup and restoration of data.* Copying (or **backing up**) critical data files to a secure storage area and then **restoring** (or retrieving) data if the original files are lost or deleted. Often backups are performed according to a formulaic schedule. Backup and data restoration services provide centralized management of data backup on multiple servers and on-demand restoration of files and directories.

Network management services will be covered in depth in Chapters 12 through 13 of this book. For now, it is enough to be aware of the variety of services and the importance of this growing area of networking.

BECOMING A NETWORKING PROFESSIONAL

Examine the classified ad section of any newspaper, and you will probably find more ads for computer professionals than any other kind of skilled worker. Of course, the level of expertise required for each of these jobs differs. Some companies simply need "warm bodies" to ensure that a mainframe's tape backup doesn't fail during the night; other companies are looking for people to plan their information technology strategies.

Needless to say, the more varied your skills, the better your chances for landing a lucrative and interesting job in networking. To prepare yourself to enter this job market, you should master a number of general networking skills. Only then should you pick a few areas that interest you and study those specialties. Hone your communication and teamwork skills, and stay abreast of emerging technologies. Consider the tremendous advantages of attaining professional certification and getting to know others in your field. The following sections offer suggestions on how to approach a career in networking.

Mastering the Technical Challenges

Although computer networking is a varied field, some general technical skills will serve you well no matter which specialty you choose. Because you are already interested in computers, you probably enjoy an aptitude for logical and analytical thinking. You may also want to acquire these skills:

- Installing, configuring, and troubleshooting network server software
- Installing, configuring, and troubleshooting network server hardware
- Installing, configuring, and troubleshooting network client software
- Installing, configuring, and troubleshooting network client hardware
- Understanding the characteristics of different transmission media
- Understanding network design
- Understanding network protocols
- Understanding how users interact with the network

Because you can expand your networking knowledge in almost any direction, you should pay attention to the general skills that interest you most, then pick one or two of those areas and concentrate on them. If you try to become a specialist in everything at once, you are likely to become frustrated. The following specialties are currently in high demand:

- Network security
- Internet and intranet design
- Network management
- Voice/data integration
- Remote and mobile computing
- Data integrity and fault tolerance
- In-depth knowledge of Microsoft networking products
- In-depth knowledge of NetWare networking products
- In-depth knowledge of router configuration and management

Determine what method of learning works best for you. A small classroom with an experienced instructor and a hands-on projects lab is an excellent learning environment, because there you can ask questions and learn by doing. Many colleges offer courses or continuing education on networking topics. You may also want to enroll at a computer training center. These training centers can be found in every metropolitan area and even many small towns. If you are pursuing certification, make sure the training center you choose is authorized to provide training for that certification. Most computer training centers also operate a Web site that provides information on their course schedule, fees, and qualifications. Some of these sites even offer online class registration.

Another great way to improve your technical skills is by gaining practical experience. There is no substitute for hands-on experience when it comes to networking hardware and software skills. If you don't already work in an Information Technology department, try to find a position that puts you in that environment, even if it isn't your dream job. Volunteer a few hours a week if necessary. Once you are surrounded with other information technology professionals and encounter real-life situations, you will have the opportunity to expand your skills by practicing and asking questions of more experienced staff. On the Web, you can find a number of searchable online job boards and recruiter sites. The placement office at your local college or university can also connect you with job opportunities.

If you already work in an Information Technology department, you should pay close attention to the technical issues and trends, experiment, and ask lots of questions.

If your organization offers a mentoring program, participate in it. If not, find an unofficial mentor among your experienced colleagues who is willing to spend extra time explaining technical details to you. Chances are, your colleague will be honored to be chosen and eager to help.

Developing Your "Soft Skills"

Knowing how to configure a router or install Windows 2000 will serve you well, but without advanced soft skills, you cannot excel in the networking field. The term **soft skills** refers to those skills that are not easily measurable, such as customer relations, oral and written communications, dependability, teamwork, and leadership abilities. Some of these soft skills might appear to be advantages in any profession, but they are especially important when you must work in teams, in challenging technical circumstances and under tight deadlines—characteristics that apply to most networking projects. For this reason, soft skills merit closer examination.

- *Customer relations.* Perhaps one of the most important soft skills, customer relations involve an ability to listen to customers' frustrations and desires and then empathize, respond, and guide customers to their goals without acting arrogant. Bear in mind that some of your customers will not appreciate or enjoy technology as much as you do, and they will value your patience as you help them. The better your customer relations, the more respected and in demand you will be as a network professional.

- *Oral and written communications.* You may understand the most complicated technical details about a network, but if you cannot communicate them to colleagues and clients, the significance of your knowledge is diminished. Imagine that you are a networking consultant who is competing with another firm to overhaul a metropolitan school district's network, a project that could generate $10 million in business for your company. You may have designed the best solution and have it clearly mapped out in your head, but your plan is useless if you can't convey it. The members of the school board will accept whichever proposal makes the most sense to them—that is, the proposal whose suggestions and justifications are plainly communicated.

- *Dependability.* This characteristic will help you in any career. However, in the field of networking, where breakdowns or glitches can occur at any time of day or night and only a limited number of individuals have the expertise to fix them, being dependable is critical. Your career will benefit when you are the one who is available to address a problem, even if you don't always know the answer immediately.

- *Teamwork.* Individual computer professionals often have strong preferences for a certain type of hardware or software. And some technical people like to think that they have all of the answers. For these and other reasons, teamwork in Information Technology departments is often lacking. To be the best networking professional in your department, you must be open to new ideas, encourage cooperation among your colleagues, and allow others to help you and make suggestions.

- *Leadership abilities.* As a networking professional, you will sometimes need to make difficult or unpopular decisions under pressure. You may need to persuade opinionated colleagues to try a new product, tell a group of angry users that what they want is not possible, or manage a project with nearly impossible budgetary and time restrictions. In all of these situations, you will benefit from having strong leadership skills.

Once your career in networking begins, you will discover which soft skills you already possess and which ones you need to cultivate. The important thing is that you realize the importance of these attributes and are willing to devote the time necessary to develop them.

Pursuing Certification

Certification is the process of mastering material pertaining to a particular hardware system, operating system, programming language, or other software program, then proving your mastery by passing a series of exams. Certification programs are developed and administered either by a manufacturer or a professional organization such as the **Computing Technology Industry Association (CompTIA)**. You can pursue a number of different certifications, depending on your specialty interest. For example, if you want to become a PC technician, you should attain **A+** certification. If you want to specialize in Microsoft product support and development, you should pursue **Microsoft Certified Systems Engineer (MCSE)** certification. If you want to specialize in Novell networking product support and administration, you should pursue **Certified NetWare Engineer (CNE)** certification. If you want to prove a mastery of many aspects of networking, you should choose to become Network+ certified. **Network+ (Net+)** is a professional certification established by CompTIA that verifies broad, vendor-independent networking technology skills such as an understanding of protocols, topologies, networking hardware, and network troubleshooting. Net+ may also be a stepping stone to more advanced certifications. For example, Novell now accepts Net+ certification as a substitute for its Networking Technologies exam for candidates pursuing CNE status. The material in this book addresses the knowledge objectives required to qualify for Net+ certification.

Certification is a popular career development tool for job seekers and a measure of an employee's qualifications for employers. Following are a list of benefits you can expect after becoming certified:

- *Better salary.* Professionals with certification can usually ask for higher salaries than those who aren't certified. Employers will also want to retain certified employees, especially if they helped pay for their training, and will offer incentives to keep certified professionals at the company.

- *Greater opportunities.* Certification may qualify you for additional degrees or more advanced technical positions.

- *Professional respect.* Once you have proved your skills with a product or system, your colleagues and clients will have great respect for your ability to solve problems with that system or product. They will therefore feel confident asking you for help.

- *Access to better support.* Many manufacturers reward certified professionals with less expensive, more detailed, and more direct access to their technical support.

One potential drawback of some certifications is the number of people attaining them—so many that they now have less value. Currently, hundreds of thousands of networking professionals have acquired the MCSE certification. When only tens of thousands of people had MCSEs, employers were willing to pay substantially higher salaries to workers with that certification than they are now. Other kinds of certifications, such as Cisco's Certified Internetworking Engineer (CCIE) program, require candidates to pass lab exams. These kinds of certifications, because they require rigorous proof of knowledge, are very highly respected.

Finding a Job in Networking

With the proper credentials and demonstrated technical knowledge, you will qualify for a multitude of positions in networking. For this reason, you can and must be selective when searching for a job. Following are some ways to research your possibilities:

- *Search the Web.* Because your job will deal directly with technology, it makes sense that you should use technology to find it. Companies in the computer industry recruit intensively on the Web, either through searchable job databases or through links on their company Web sites. Unlike firms in other industries, these companies typically do not mind (and might prefer) receiving résumés and letters through e-mail. Most job database Web sites do not charge for their services or require you to register with them. Table 1-1 lists a few of these Web sites, some of which are devoted exclusively to posting information technology positions. The table provides just a sample of the best-known job databases on the Web; you could probably find hundreds more.

Table 1-1   Web sites with job databases

Web Site Location	Description and Emphasis
www.informationweek.com/career3	InformationWeek's "Best Jobs": an IT career site with links to job searches, career advice, salary surveys, and training sites
www.hotjobs.com	HotJobs: a searchable site for job seekers and employers from around the world and from many different industries
www.careerweb.com	Career Web: a searchable site for job seekers and employers from around the United States and from many different industries
www.monster.com	The Monster Board: a searchable site for job seekers and employers from around the world and from many different industries
www.ajb.dni.us	America's Job Bank: a searchable site for job seekers and employers from around the world and from many different industries
www.headhunter.net	Headhunter.net: a searchable site for job seekers and employers from around the United States and from many different industries
www.careerbuilder.com	Career Builder: a list of links to numerous searchable job databases and other career resources

- *Read the paper.* An obvious place to look for jobs is the classified ad section of your local newspaper. Papers with large distributions often devote a section of their classified ads to careers in computing. Highlight the ads that sound interesting to you, even if you don't have all of the qualifications cited by the employer. In some ads, employers will list every skill they could possibly want a new hire to have, but they don't truly expect one person to have all of them.

- *Visit a career center.* Regardless of whether you are a registered university or college student, you can use career center services to find a list of job openings in your area. Companies that are hiring pay much attention to the collegiate career centers because of the number of job seekers served by these centers. Visit the college or university campus nearest you and search through its career center listings.

- *Network.* Find like-minded professionals with whom you can discuss job possibilities. You may meet these individuals through training classes, conferences, professional organizations, or career fairs. Let them know that you're looking for a job and specify exactly what kind of job you want. If they can't suggest any leads for you, ask these people if they have other colleagues who might.

- *Attend career fairs.* Most metropolitan areas host career fairs for job seekers in the information technology field, and some large companies host their own job fairs. Even if you aren't sure you want to work for any of the companies represented at a job fair, attend the job fair to research the market. You can find out which skills are in high demand in your area and which types of companies are hiring the most networking professionals. You can also meet other people in your field who may offer valuable advice based on their employment experience.

Joining Professional Associations

At some point in your life, you have probably belonged to a club or organization. You know, therefore, that the benefits of joining can vary, depending on many factors. In the best case, joining an organization can connect you with people who have similar interests, provide new opportunities for learning, allow you to access specialized information, and give you more tangible assets such as free goods. Specifically, a networking professional organization might offer its own journal, technical workshops and conferences, free software, pre-release software, and access to expensive hardware labs. Some associations even offer health insurance benefits to their members.

You can choose from several prominent professional organizations in the field of networking. Because the field has grown so quickly and because so many areas in which to specialize exist, however, no single professional organization stands out as the most advantageous or highly respected. You will have to decide whether an organization is appropriate for you. Among other things, you will want to consider the organization's number of members, membership benefits, membership dues, technical emphasis, and whether it hosts a local chapter. You may also want to find a professional association that caters to your demographic group (such as Women in Technology International, if you are female). Table 1-2 lists a number of professional organizations and their Web sites.

Table 1-2   Web sites of networking organizations

Professional Organization	Emphasis	Web Site
Network Professional Association	All disciplines, all groups	www.npa.org
Association for Computing Machinery (ACM)	All disciplines, all groups	www.acm.org
IEEE Computer Society	Advanced computing, all groups	www.computer.org
Network and Systems Professionals Association	All disciplines, all groups	www.naspa.net
Information Technology Association of America	All disciplines, all groups	www.itaa.org
Chinese Information and Networking Association	All disciplines, Chinese Americans	www.cina.org
Women in Technology International	All disciplines, women	www.witi.com

CHAPTER SUMMARY

❑ A network is a group of computers and other devices that are connected by some type of transmission media, usually wire or cable.

❑ Networks may consist of two computers connected by a cable in a home office or several thousand computers connected across the world. In addition to connecting personal computers, they may incorporate mainframe computers, modems, CD-ROMs, printers, plotters, fax machines, or phone systems. Computers on a network may communicate through cables, wires, radio waves, infrared, or satellite links.

❑ All networks provide advantages relative to a standalone personal computer. Most importantly, networks enable multiple users to share devices and data. They also allow for centralized administration of hardware and software.

❑ The simplest form of a network still used today connects a handful of computers through one cable and uses peer-to-peer communication. Peer-to-peer communication enables computers to talk directly to other computers on a single segment of cable, without any computer having more authority than another.

❑ A local area network (LAN) is a network of computers and other devices that is confined to a relatively small space, such as one building or even one office. A peer-to-peer network is a simple example of a LAN. More complex LANs are server-based and rely on a central file server to manage resources.

❑ A network that connects two or more geographically distinct LANs is called a wide area network (WAN).

❑ All server-based networks share some common elements, including clients, servers, workstations, transmission media, protocols, addressing, topology, network interface cards, data packets, network operating systems, hosts, and nodes.

❑ The physical layout of a computer network is called a topology. Topologies are usually arranged in a ring, bus, or star formation; hybrid combinations of these patterns are also possible. You must understand topologies to design and troubleshoot networks.

❑ Network protocols are the rules that the network uses to transfer data. Protocols ensure that data are transferred whole, in sequence, and without error from one node on the network to another. To effectively maintain and manage a network, you must have a thorough understanding of network protocols.

❑ Although e-mail is the most visible network service, networks also provide services for printing, file sharing, Internet access, remote dial-in capabilities, mainframe communication, and management services.

❑ File and print services provide the foundation for networking. They enable multiple users to share data, applications, storage areas, and printers.

❑ Networks use communications services to allow remote users to connect to the network (usually through a phone line and modem) or network users to connect to machines outside the network. Communications servers are also called access servers or remote access servers.

❑ Mail services allow users on a network to exchange and store e-mail. Many mail packages also provide routing, scheduling, notification, document management, and gateways to other mail systems.

❑ Internet services such as World Wide Web servers and browsers, file transfer capabilities, addressing schemes, and security filters enable organizations to connect to and use the global Internet.

❑ Network management services centrally administer and simplify complicated management tasks on the network. Some organizations dedicate a number of servers to network management functions, with each server performing only one or two unique services.

❑ Networking professionals are currently in great demand. The more varied your skills, the better your chances for landing a lucrative and interesting job in networking. To prepare yourself, you should master a number of broad networking skills. Only then should you pick a few areas that interest you and study those specialties. Hone your communication and teamwork skills, and stay abreast of emerging technologies. Consider the tremendous advantages of attaining professional certification and get to know members of your field.

❑ Certification is the process of mastering material pertaining to a particular hardware system, operating system, programming language, or other software program, then proving your mastery by passing a series of exams. The benefits of certification include a better salary, more job opportunities, greater professional respect, and better access to technical support.

❑ To excel in the field of networking, you should hone your soft skills, such as leadership abilities, written and oral communication, a professional attitude, dependability, and customer relations.

❐ With the proper credentials, you can easily find a job in networking. To find the *best* job, you should perform research using the newspaper classified ads, searchable job databases on the Web, networking with colleagues, a nearby college career center, and career fairs.

❐ Joining an association for networking professionals can connect you with like-minded people, give you access to workshops and other educational materials, allow you to receive discounted or free software, and maybe even provide insurance benefits. Before joining an association, make sure its emphasis is appropriate for you and that you will be able to use its membership benefits.

KEY TERMS

A+ — Professional certification established by CompTIA that verifies knowledge about PC operation, repair, and management.

access server — See *communications server*.

address — A number that uniquely identifies each workstation and device on a network. Without unique addresses, computers on the network could not reliably communicate.

address management — Centrally administering a finite number of network addresses for an entire LAN. Usually this task can be accomplished without touching the client workstations.

addressing — The scheme for assigning a unique identifying number to every workstation and device on the network. The type of addressing used on a network depends on its protocols and network operating system.

asset management — Collecting and storing data on the number and types of software and hardware assets in an organization's network. The data collection is automated by electronically examining each network client from a server.

backup — The process of copying critical data files to a secure storage area. Often backups are performed according to a formulaic schedule.

certification — The process of mastering material pertaining to a particular hardware system, operating system, programming language, or other software program, then proving your mastery by passing a series of exams.

Certified NetWare Engineer (CNE) — Professional certification established by Novell that demonstrates an in-depth understanding of Novell's networking software, including NetWare.

client — A computer on the network that requests resources or services from another computer on a network. In some cases, a client could also act as a server. The term "client" may also refer to the user of a client workstation.

client/server architecture — The model of networking in which clients (typically desktop PCs) use a central server to share data, data storage space, and devices.

client/server network — A network based on the client/server architecture.

communications server — A server that runs communications services such as Windows NT's RAS or NetWare's NAS, also known as an access server or remote access server.

Computing Technology Industry Association (CompTIA) — An association of computer resellers, manufacturers, and training companies that sets industry-wide standards for computer professionals. CompTIA established and sponsors the A+ and Network+ (Net+) certifications.

data packet — A discreet unit of information sent from one computer on a network to another.

file server — A specialized server that enables clients to share applications and data across the network.

file services — The function of a file server that allows users to share data files, applications, and storage areas.

gateway — A combination of hardware and software that enables two different kinds of networks to exchange data.

host — A type of computer that enables resource sharing by other computers on the same network.

Internet — A complex WAN that connects LANs around the globe.

Internet services — Services that enable a network to communicate with the Internet, including World Wide Web servers and browsers, file transfer capabilities, Internet addressing schemes, security filters, and a means for directly logging on to other computers.

license tracking — Determining how many copies of a single application are currently in use on the network.

load balancing — Distributing processing activity evenly across a network so that no single device is overwhelmed.

local area network (LAN) — A network of computers and other devices that is confined to a relatively small space, such as one building or even one office.

local computer — The computer on which you are actually working (as opposed to a remote computer).

mail services — Network services that manage the storage and transfer of e-mail between users on a network. In addition to sending, receiving, and storing mail, mail services can include intelligent e-mail routing capabilities, notification, scheduling, indexing, document libraries, and gateways to other mail servers.

management services — Network services that centrally administer and simplify complicated management tasks on the network. Examples of management services include license tracking, security auditing, asset management, addressing management, software distribution, traffic monitoring, load balancing, and hardware diagnosis.

metropolitan area network (MAN) — A network that connects clients and servers in multiple buildings within a limited geographic area. For example, a network connecting multiple city government buildings around the city's center.

Microsoft Certified Systems Engineer (MCSE) — A professional certification established by Microsoft that demonstrates in-depth knowledge about Microsoft's products, including Windows 98 and Windows 2000.

network — A group of computers and other devices (such as printers) that are connected by some type of transmission media, usually wire or cable.

Network+ (Net+) — Professional certification established by CompTIA that verifies broad, vendor-independent networking technology skills such as an understanding of protocols, topologies, networking hardware, and network troubleshooting.

network interface card (NIC) — The device that enables a workstation to connect to the network and communicate with other computers. NICs are manufactured by several different companies and come with a variety of specifications that are tailored to the workstation's and the network's requirements.

network operating system (NOS) — The software that runs on a server and enables the server to manage data, users, groups, security, applications, and other networking functions. The most popular network operating systems are Microsoft's Windows NT, Windows 2000, UNIX, and Novell's NetWare.

node — A computer or other device connected to a network which has a unique address and is capable of sending or receiving data.

peer-to-peer communication — A simple means of networking computers using a single cable. In peer-to-peer communication, no single computer has more authority than another and each computer can share its resources with other computers.

peer-to-peer network — A network in which computers communicate directly with other computers on a single segment of cable and share each others' data and devices. By default, no computer in a peer-to-peer network has more authority than another, and every computer can use resources from every other computer.

print services — The network service that allows printers to be shared by several users on a network.

protocol — The rules that the network uses to transfer data. Protocols ensure that data are transferred whole, in sequence, and without error from one node on the network to another.

remote access server — See *communications server.*

remote computer — The computer that you are controlling or working on via a network connection.

remote user — A person working on a computer in a different geographical location from the LAN's server.

resources — The devices, data, and data storage space provided by a computer, whether standalone or shared.

restore — The process of retrieving files from a backup if the original files are lost or deleted.

security auditing — Evaluating security measures currently in place on a network and notifying the network administrator if a security breach occurs.

segment — A part of a LAN that is logically separated from other parts of the LAN and that shares a fixed amount of traffic capacity.

server — A computer on the network that manages shared resources. Servers usually have more processing power, memory, and hard disk space than clients. They run network operating software that can manage not only data, but also users, groups, security, and applications on the network.

server-based network — A network that uses special computers, known as servers, to process data for and facilitate communication between the other computers on the network. See *client/server network*.

services — The features provided by a network.

sneakernet — The only means of exchanging data without using a network. Sneakernet requires that data be copied from a computer to a floppy disk, carried (presumably by someone wearing sneakers) to another computer, then copied from the floppy disk onto the second computer.

soft skills — Skills such as customer relations, leadership ability, and dependability, which are not easily measured, but are nevertheless important in a networking career.

software distribution — The process of automatically transferring a data file or program from the server to a client on the network.

standalone computer — A computer that uses programs and data only from its local disks and that is not connected to a network.

topology — The physical layout of a computer network.

traffic — The data transmission and processing activity taking place on a computer network at any given time.

traffic monitoring — Determining how much processing activity is taking place on a network or network segment and notifying administrators when a segment becomes overloaded.

transmission media — The means through which data are transmitted and received. Transmission media may be physical, such as wire or cable, or atmospheric (wireless), such as radio waves.

user — A person who uses a computer.

wide area network (WAN) — A network that spans a large distance and connects two or more LANs.

workstation — A computer that typically runs a desktop operating system and connects to a network.

REVIEW QUESTIONS

1. What resources do networks *not* enable workstations to share?

   a. data

   b. passwords

   c. printers

   d. fax machines

2. A server-based network can:

   a. allow multiple users to share applications

   b. allow multiple users to access each other's workstations

   c. allow multiple users to share floppy disks

   d. allow multiple users to share phone lines

3. What is the simplest form of a network still in use today?

   a. server-based networking

   b. thin client networking

   c. host-to-host networking

   d. peer-to-peer networking

4. Servers usually possess the same amount of memory and hard disk capacity as workstations. True or False?

5. What is the primary function of a file server on a network?

   a. It routes traffic between two or more LAN segments.

   b. It monitors how many people are logged on to a wide area network.

   c. It supplies error messages when unauthorized users try to access the network.

   d. It manages shared resources such as spreadsheet and word-processing files.

6. What is the primary difference between LANs and WANs?

   a. the distance they span

   b. the type of servers they use

   c. the type of data they transmit

   d. the transmission speed they can achieve

7. Any two computers can use the same network interface card to connect to the network. True or False?

8. Why is it important to make sure that each workstation on a network has a unique network address?

   a. to enable users to move from one workstation to another and still find their data

   b. to enable the workstation to communicate with the server and other networked workstations

   c. to enable the workstation to request priority processing from the file server

   d. to enable the user to identify his or her machine to technical support representatives

9. A shared HP Laserjet 6P could be considered a network node. True or False?

10. Which of the following is not a network topology?

   a. star

   b. bus

   c. cube

   d. ring

11. Which of the following is not true about peer-to-peer networks?

    a. They are typically very secure.

    b. They are typically inexpensive.

    c. They are typically easy to set up.

    d. They do not depend on a file server.

12. In addition to message storage and transfer, what additional function might a mail server provide?

    a. mail text search and replace

    b. address book creation

    c. mail gateways to other systems

    d. mail attachment conversion

13. Which of the following could not be considered a network management service?

    a. automated software distribution

    b. license tracking

    c. traffic control

    d. dial-up access authentication

14. Security is a concern when using communications servers on a network because:

    a. communications servers enable computers to dial into a network, thereby opening the network up to the outside world

    b. communications servers have poor password enforcement capabilities, so they rely on users to choose good passwords

    c. communications servers cannot accept encrypted data transfers, requiring users to transmit plain text to and from the network

    d. communications servers are difficult to understand and support, so many networks are using them incorrectly and perhaps insecurely

15. Which of the following services does not belong to the Internet services group of networked functions?

    a. World Wide Web browser service

    b. file transfer service

    c. Internet addressing services

    d. load balancing traffic on multiple Internet connections

16. One function that network protocols serve is to ensure that data are delivered in the correct sequence. True or False?

17. Name three specialties within the networking field that are in high demand.

18. Soft skills are probably not necessary in which of the following on-the-job scenarios?

    a. An angry customer fumes at you because you inform him that you do not have access to his mail account and cannot look up a message he sent three weeks ago.

    b. The server on which you're working continually hangs up while rebooting, and you can't find a bootable floppy disk.

    c. One of your software suppliers insists she never received an order that you faxed to her twice in the last week, and you need the software now.

    d. For several hours one morning, your network had problems that prevented any users from logging on, and now your supervisor is asking you why you didn't fix the problem sooner.

19. Which of the following is probably not a benefit of attaining professional certification?

    a. a better-paying job

    b. faster access to technical support

    c. never having to attend additional training courses

    d. more respect from technical colleagues

20. To find the best possible job in networking, what sources would you investigate?

HANDS-ON PROJECTS

Project 1-1

During your career in networking, you will frequently need to interpret network diagrams, if not design them yourself. This exercise is the first of several in this book that give you practice in drawing network diagrams.

On a separate piece of paper, draw a simple diagram of a network composed of 12 clients, 2 shared printers, 2 file servers, and a mainframe host. This network should use the bus topology.

After you have drawn a simple network based on the bus topology, try drawing the same type of network with a ring topology.

Project 1-2

Even before you are ready to look for a job in networking, you should be familiar with the kinds of employers who are looking for information systems professionals and the skills that they desire. The more research you do, the better prepared you will be when you begin job hunting in earnest. This exercise will familiarize you with searching job databases on the Web. To complete this project you need a computer with access to the Internet.

The steps in this project matched the Web sites mentioned at the time this book was published. If you notice discrepancies, look for similar links and follow the same general steps.

1. Access the Internet and go to www.monster.com.

2. From The Monster Board's home page, click **Search Jobs**.

3. Ignore the Location Search and Category Search options, and scroll down to the Keyword Search text box. Type **network administrator**, then click the **Search Jobs** button. How many jobs were returned by the search?

4. Click the first 15 job postings, one after the other, to display the job descriptions. On a separate piece of paper, note how many require or recommend each technical proficiency listed below.

   ❑ NetWare   ❑ Internet Services

   ❑ Windows 2000   ❑ Bridges, routers, or gateways

   ❑ Macintosh   ❑ Network security

   ❑ UNIX   ❑ Printers

   ❑ TCP/IP   ❑ WANs

5. For each proficiency, calculate the percentage of jobs that require it.

6. How many of the position descriptions mention A+, Net+, MCSE, CCIE, or CNE certification?

7. Return to the job search page, verify that "network administrator" still appears in the Keyword "Search" (see step 3) text box, then use the Location Search list box to select the metropolitan areas in your state. How many jobs did the search return? Which areas have the most job openings?

8. Return to the "job" (see step 7) search page. In the Keyword Search text box replace "network administrator" with "manager," deselect any locations in the Location Search list box, select **Information Technology** in the Job Category Search list box, then click the **Search Jobs** button.

9. How many jobs did the search return?

10. Examine the first 15 jobs. On a separate piece of paper, note the number of these jobs that require the "soft skills" listed below.

    ❑ Leadership   ❑ Teamwork

    ❑ Oral/written communication ❑ Supervision

    ❑ Customer relations   ❑ Motivation (of yourself and others)

11. Continue to search The Monster Board, choosing keywords or categories for specialty areas of networking that appeal to you. Some examples might be network security, voice/data integration, or router configuration.

12. As you read the job descriptions, jot down terms and skills that are new to you, then look up their definitions in the glossary of this text.

Project 1-3

If you intend to pursue the Net+ certification, you should familiarize yourself with the Net+ exam objectives. Although these objectives are mentioned in the pertinent chapters of this book and summarized in Appendix A, you can learn more about them at the CompTIA (Computing Technology Industry Association) organization's Web site. In this exercise, you will explore CompTIA's Web site.

1. Access the Internet and go to www.comptia.org.

2. Click **Certification** to view information about the different computer certifications that CompTIA sponsors.

3. Click **Network+** to view more information about the Net+ certification. What kind of prior experience does CompTIA suggest for those aspiring to obtain Net+ certification?

4. Choose the **All About Network+** option near the bottom of the page to learn more about this certification. A new browser window opens.

5. In the new window, click **Objectives**.

6. Among other things, this page describes how different skills are weighted in the Net+ exam. For example, questions about networking technology security account for approximately 6% of all exam questions. What percentage of the exam questions pertains to TCP/IP fundamentals? What percentage of the exam questions pertains to troubleshooting the network?

7. Click your browser's Back button to return to the All About Network+ page.

8. Click on **Industry Acceptance** to view how Net+ is regarded by different networking vendors. What other certifications might passing the Net+ exam prepare you for?

9. One feature of the Net+ examination is its company-neutral approach, meaning that it does not focus solely on any one vendor's networking products. How might this neutrality benefit your networking career?

CASE PROJECTS

1. You have been asked by Thrift Towne, a local charity retail organization, to install a network in its downtown office. It currently has four PCs running Windows 98, with the following specifications:

   □ 486/66 MHz processor, 200 MB hard drive, 16 MB RAM

   □ 486/233 MHz processor, 500 MB hard drive, 32 MB RAM

   □ Pentium 233 MHz processor, 2.5 GB hard drive, 64 MB RAM

   □ Pentium II 533 MHz processor, 16 GB hard drive, 128 MB RAM

   Thrift Towne's owners are not very concerned about security, because the network will share only inventory information (customers remain anonymous and are not tracked). Thrift Towne uses volunteers to run its stores, and the volunteers are not technical experts. In addition, Thrift Towne doesn't have much money to spend on this project. The owners have asked for a simple, inexpensive solution. What type of network would you recommend and why? What role (or roles) would you assign to each of the four workstations and any other equipment you recommend? What type of upgrades might the workstations require to make your solution work?

2. Your work at Thrift Towne was so successful that you are asked to provide networking advice to a chain of ice cream stores called Scoops. Scoops already has a server-based network. The server that holds the company's inventory, ordering, sales, time tracking, and employee information and provides an Internet connection is located at their store across the street from Thrift Towne. Three other Scoops stores in town connect to a modem on the central server through dial-in phone lines. Scoops is having problems with heavy traffic and slow server response at 8:00 A.M. and 3:00 P.M. each day. They don't exactly know where the traffic originates or what type of traffic it is. They also don't know whether the two heavy traffic times every day warrant a change in their connection methods. What kind of services do you suggest will help them assess their traffic situation and provide answers about possible network expansion? What types of things can they find out? What other kinds of services might they also use, given their network configuration?

3. The owners of Thrift Towne and Scoops were so impressed with your networking abilities that they recommended you apply for a network administrator position in one of the city government offices. You applied for the job and got an interview. Although you think the interview was successful, the city's Director of Planning unfortunately didn't offer you the job because he didn't think you were qualified. In particular, he wanted you to have more hands-on experience with enterprise-wide networks. What can you do to gain that experience to make sure you don't miss another great opportunity?

CHAPTER 2

NETWORKING STANDARDS AND THE OSI MODEL

After reading this chapter and completing the exercises, you will be able to:

➤ Identify organizations that set standards for networking

➤ Explain the layers of the OSI Model

➤ Describe specific networking services within each layer of the OSI Model

➤ Explain how two systems communicate through the OSI Model

➤ Discuss the structure and purpose of data frames

➤ Describe the two types of addressing contained in the OSI Model

ON THE JOB

When I first heard about the OSI Model, I had already been working as a networking technician for a few months. I thought I knew all about NICs and cabling, but I didn't know the OSI layer to which they belonged. When someone tried to teach me about the OSI Model, I thought it was baloney. The more I learned, however, the more I realized I didn't understand. For example, once a colleague and I tried to figure out why a networked printer wasn't printing. He insisted that it was a "Layer 3 problem." I didn't know what he meant, so I couldn't agree or disagree. From the symptoms, I thought that the printer was probably experiencing an addressing conflict with another device. The printer worked for a while, but after we restarted it, the network didn't recognize it. I didn't know whether this error was a Layer 3 problem; not wanting to sound foolish, I didn't say anything at all. Luckily, an addressing conflict is exactly what my colleague meant by a "Layer 3 problem," and he quickly fixed the problem.

You can be sure that I quietly figured out what "Layer 3" meant shortly after that incident. Since then, I've noticed that an increasing number of people refer to networking hardware, applications, or problems by the OSI Model layer involved. For instance, one networking hardware manufacturer's slogan is "Providing solutions for Layers 1–3." The company doesn't even have to mention the OSI Model, because anyone involved in networking understands the message.

These days we take for granted that servers and clients from different hardware manufacturers, such as Compaq, IBM, Dell, and Hewlett-Packard, will work together. Before the OSI Model, no standard existed, which meant that computing professionals could not assume any kind of compatibility between different manufacturers' hardware and software. Believe it or not, the OSI Model has made our lives easier.

Andy Zimmerman
MedTech Data Systems

When trying to grasp a new theoretical concept, it often helps to form a picture of that concept in your mind. In the field of chemistry, for example, even though you can't see a water molecule, you can represent it with a simple drawing of two hydrogen atoms and one oxygen atom. Similarly, in the field of networking, even though you can't see the communication that occurs between two nodes on a network, you can use a model to depict how the communication takes place. The model commonly used to describe network communications is called the Open Systems Interconnection (OSI) Model.

In this chapter, you will learn about the standards organizations that have helped create the various models (such as the OSI Model) used in networking. Next, you'll be introduced to the seven layers of the OSI Model and learn how they interact. You will then take a closer look at what goes on in each layer. Finally, you will learn to apply those details to a practical networking environment. Granted, learning the OSI Model is not the most exciting part of becoming a networking expert. Unless you understand it thoroughly, however, you will never become an expert.

Networking Standards Organizations

Standards are documented agreements containing technical specifications or other precise criteria that stipulate how a particular product or service should be designed or performed. Many different industries use standards to ensure that products, processes, and services suit their purpose. For example, when plastics manufacturers test their products for flexibility, the tests must adhere to strict American National Standards Institute (ANSI) specifications so that the results can be accurately compared with other manufacturers' results. If manufacturers didn't use the same ANSI test, one company might test flexibility by pulling on the plastic, while one might test flexibility by poking it. The flexibility numbers that each manufacturer obtained, even for the same type of plastic, would then be completely different, and consumers could not compare the two products' flexibility.

Because of the wide variety of hardware and software in use today, standards are especially important in the world of networking. Without standards, you could not design a network because one piece of hardware might not work properly with another. Likewise, one software program might not be able to communicate with another. For example, if one manufacturer designed a network cable with a 1-centimeter-wide plug and another company manufactured a wall plate with a 0.8-centimeter-wide opening, you would not be able to insert the cable into the wall plate.

Because the computer industry grew so quickly out of several technical traditions, many different organizations evolved to oversee its standards. In some cases, a few organizations are responsible for a single aspect of networking. For example, both ANSI and ITU are involved in setting standards for Integrated Services Digital Network (ISDN) communications. While ANSI prescribes the kind of hardware that the consumer needs to accept an ISDN connection, ITU prescribes how the ISDN link will ensure that data arrive in the correct sequence, among other things. A complete list of the standards that regulate computers and networking would fill an encyclopedia. At a minimum, you should be familiar with the handful of significant groups that set the standards referenced by manuals, articles, and books. These groups are responsible for establishing the future of networking.

ANSI

ANSI (American National Standards Institute) is an organization composed of more than 1000 representatives from industry and government who together determine standards for the electronics industry in addition to other fields, such as chemical and nuclear engineering, health and safety, and construction. ANSI also represents the United States in setting international standards. This organization does not dictate that manufacturers comply with its standards, but requests them to comply voluntarily. Of course, manufacturers and developers benefit from compliance, because compliance assures potential customers that the systems are reliable and can be integrated with an existing infrastructure. New electronic equipment and methods must undergo rigorous testing to prove they are worthy of ANSI's approval.

An example of an ANSI standard is ANSI T1.240-1998, "Telecommunications— Operations, Administration, Maintenance, and Provisioning (OAM&P)—Generic Network Information Model for Interfaces between Operations Systems and Network Elements." You can purchase ANSI standards documents online from ANSI's Web site (*www.ansi.org*) or find them at a university or public library. You need not read complete ANSI standards to be a competent networking professional, but you should understand the breadth and significance of ANSI's influence.

EIA

EIA (Electronic Industries Alliance) is a trade organization composed of representatives from electronics manufacturing firms across the United States. EIA began as the Radio Manufacturers Association (RMA) in 1924; over time, it evolved to include manufacturers of televisions, semiconductors, computers, and networking devices. This group not only sets standards for its members, but also helps write ANSI standards and lobbies for legislation favorable to the growth of the computer and electronics industry.

EIA is divided into several subgroups: the Telecommunications Industry Association (TIA); the Consumer Electronics Manufacturers Association (CEMA); the Electronic Components, Assemblies, and Materials Association (ECA); the JEDEC (Joint Electron Device Engineering Council); Solid State Technology Association; the Government Division; and the Electronic Information Group (EIG). In addition to lobbying and setting standards, each specialized group sponsors conferences, exhibitions, and forums in its area of interest. You can find out more about EIA from its Web site: *www.eia.org*.

IEEE

The **IEEE (Institute of Electrical and Electronic Engineers)**, or "I-triple-E," is an international society composed of engineering professionals. Its goals are to promote development and education in the electrical engineering and computer science fields. To this end, IEEE hosts numerous symposia, conferences, and local chapter meetings and publishes papers designed to educate members on technological advances. It also maintains a

standards board that establishes its own standards for the electronics and computer industry and contributes to the work of other standards-setting bodies, such as ANSI.

IEEE technical papers and standards are highly respected in the networking profession.
Among other places, you will find references to IEEE standards in the manuals that
accompany network interface cards. Following are just a few examples of IEEE standards: "Information Technology Year 2000 Test Methods," "Virtual Bridged Local Area
Networks," and "Software Project Management Plans." Hundreds more are currently in
use. You can order these documents online from IEEE's Web site (*www.ieee.org*) or find
them in a university or public library.

ISO

ISO (International Organization for Standardization) is a collection of standards
organizations representing 130 countries; its headquarters is located in Geneva,
Switzerland. ISO's goal is to establish international technological standards to facilitate
global exchange of information and barrier-free trade. Given the organization's full
name, you might assume it should be called "IOS," but "ISO" is not meant to be an
acronym. In fact, "iso" is the Greek word for "equal." Using this term conveys the organization's dedication to standards.

ISO's authority is not limited to the information-processing and communications industry, but also applies to the fields of textiles, packaging, distribution of goods, energy production and utilization, shipbuilding, and banking and financial services. The universal
agreements on screw threads, bank cards, and even the names for currencies are all products of ISO's work. In fact, only about 500 of ISO's nearly 12,000 standards apply to
computer-related products and functions. International electronics and electrical engineering standards are separately established by the International Electrotechnical
Commission (IEC), a similar international standards body. All of ISO's information technology standards are designed in tandem with the IEC. You can find out more about
ISO at its Web page: *www.iso.ch*.

ITU

The **ITU (International Telecommunication Union)** is a specialized United
Nations agency that regulates international telecommunications, including radio and TV
frequencies, satellite and telephony specifications, networking infrastructure, and tariffs
applied to global communications. It also provides developing countries with technical
expertise and equipment to advance those nations' technological bases.

The ITU was founded in Paris in 1865. It became part of the United Nations in 1947
and relocated to Geneva, Switzerland. Its standards arm contains members from 188
countries and publishes detailed policy and standards documents that can be found on its
Web site: *www.itu.int*. Typically, ITU's documents pertain more to global telecommunications issues than to industry technical specifications. Some examples of ITU documents

are "Communications for Rural and Remote Areas," "Telecommunication Support for the Protection of the Environment," and "The International Frequency List."

The ITU used to be called the CCITT, or Consultative Committee on International Telegraph and Telephony. You may still see references to CCITT standards in manuals and texts.

THE OSI MODEL

In the early 1980s, ISO began work on a universal set of specifications that would enable computer platforms across the world to communicate openly. The organization created a helpful model for understanding and developing computer-to-computer communications. This model, called the **Open Systems Interconnection (OSI) Model**, divides networking architecture into seven layers: Physical, Data Link, Network, Transport, Session, Presentation, and Application. Each layer has its own set of functions and interacts with the layers directly above and below it. At the top, the Application layer interacts with the software you use (such as a word-processing or spreadsheet program). At the bottom of the OSI Model are the networking cables and connectors that carry signals. Generally speaking, every layer in between the top and bottom layers ensures that data are delivered in a readable, error-free, and properly sequenced format.

The combination of a network's building blocks is often described as its "architecture." The use of the term "architecture" in the networking field reflects the fact that, like a building, a network contains many distinct but integrated elements: the cabling, servers, protocols, clients, applications, NICs, and so on. A professional involved in network design is sometimes called a **network architect**.

The OSI Model is a theoretical representation of what happens between two nodes on a network. It does not prescribe the type of hardware or software that should support each layer. Nor does it describe how software programs interact with other software programs or how software programs interact with humans. Everything you will learn about networking can be associated with a layer of this model, however, so you should know not only the names of the layers, but also their functions and the way in which the layers interact. Figure 2-1 depicts the OSI Model and its layers.

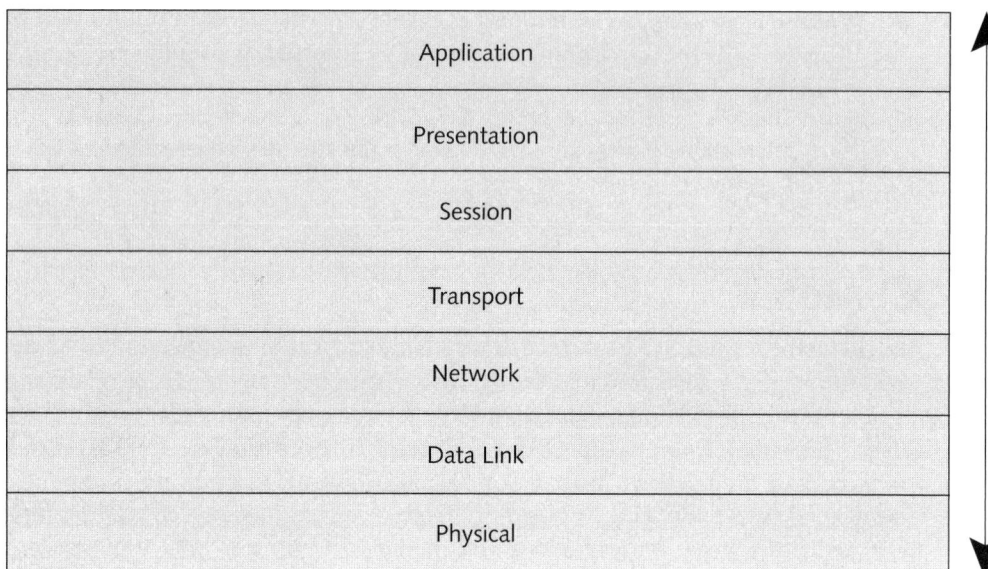

Figure 2-1   The OSI Model

 Networking professionals typically devise their own mnemonics for remembering the seven layers of the OSI Model. One strategy is to make a sentence using words that begin with the same first letter of each layer, starting with the Physical layer and ending with the Application layer. For example, you might choose to remember the phrase "Phil Donahue Never Televises Sick People Anymore." If the mnemonic phrase you create is quirky or unexpected, you'll probably remember it more easily.

Physical Layer

The **Physical layer** is the lowest, or first, layer of the OSI Model. This layer contains the physical networking medium, such as cabling, connectors, and repeaters. Protocols at the Physical layer generate and detect voltage so as to transmit and receive signals carrying data. When you install a NIC in your desktop PC, you are establishing the foundation that allows the computer to be networked. In other words, you are providing a Physical layer. The Physical layer sets the data transmission rate and monitors data error rates, though it does not provide error correction services. Physical network problems, such as a severed wire, affect the Physical layer. Similarly, if you insert a NIC but fail to seat it deeply enough in the computer's circuit board, your computer will experience network problems at the Physical layer.

The IEEE has set standards for protocols used at the Physical layer. In particular, the IEEE 802 standards specify how data is handled by Ethernet and Token Ring networks (see Chapter 3). The terms "Layer 1 protocols" and "Physical layer protocols" refer to the standards that dictate how the electrical signals are amplified and transmitted over the wire. Devices that operate at the Physical layer include repeaters and hubs. NICs operate at both the Physical layer and at the Data Link layer (discussed next). You will learn more about Physical layer devices and their operation in Chapters 4 and 6.

Data Link Layer

The second layer of the OSI Model, the **Data Link layer**, controls communications between the Network layer and the Physical layer. Its primary function is to divide data it receives from the Network layer into distinct frames that can then be transmitted by the Physical layer. A **frame** is a structured package for moving data that includes not only the raw data, or "payload," but also the sender's and receiver's network addresses, and error checking and control information. The addresses tell the network where to deliver the frame, whereas the error checking and control information ensure that the frame arrives without any problems.

It may be helpful to envision data frames as trains with many cars. Some of these cars may not be necessary, and the amount of cargo carried by each train will vary, but every train needs an engine and a caboose. Just as different kinds of trains may position their cars in slightly different arrangements, different kinds of frames may arrange their components differently. Figure 2-2 shows a simplified picture of a data frame. Each component of this frame is essential and common to all types of frames. Ethernet and Token Ring frames and their components will be described in detail later in this chapter.

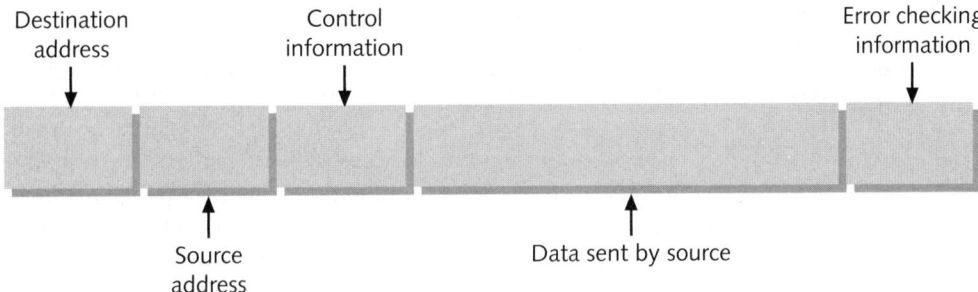

Figure 2-2   A simplified data frame

To fully understand the function of the Data Link layer, pretend for a moment that computers communicate as humans do. You might be in a large classroom full of noisy students and need to ask the teacher a question. Your teacher's name is Ms. Jones. To get your message through, you might say, "Ms. Jones? Can you explain more about the effects of railroads on commerce in the mid-nineteenth century?" In this example, you are the sender (in a busy network) and you have addressed your recipient, Ms. Jones, just as the Data Link layer addresses another computer on the network. In addition, you have formatted your thought as a question, just as the Data Link layer formats data into frames that can be interpreted by receiving computers.

What happens if the room is so noisy that Ms. Jones hears only part of your question? For example, she might receive "on commerce in the late-nineteenth century?" This kind of error can happen in network communications as well (because of electrical interference or wiring problems). The Data Link layer's job is to find out that information has been dropped and ask the first computer to retransmit its message—just as in a classroom setting Ms. Jones might say, "I didn't hear you. Can you repeat the question?" The Data Link layer accomplishes this task through a process called error checking. Later in this chapter, you will learn more about error checking.

In general, the sender's Data Link layer waits for acknowledgment from the receiver that data was received correctly. If the sender does not get this acknowledgment, its Data Link layer gives instruction to retransmit the information. The Data Link layer does not try to figure out what went wrong in the transmission. Similarly, as in a busy classroom, Ms. Jones will probably say, "Pardon me?" rather than, "It sounds as if you might have a question about railroads, and I heard only the last part of it, which dealt with commerce, so I assume you are asking about commerce and railroads; is that correct?" Obviously, the former method is more efficient for both the sender and the receiver.

Another communications mishap that might occur in a noisy classroom or on a busy network is a glut of communication requests. For example, at the end of class, 20 people might ask Ms. Jones 20 different questions at once. Of course, she can't pay attention to all of them simultaneously. She will probably say, "One person at a time, please," then point to one student who asked a question. This situation is analogous to what the Data Link layer does for the Physical layer. One node on a network (a server, for example) may receive multiple requests that include many frames of data each. The Data Link layer controls the flow of this information, allowing the NIC to process data without error.

The Data Link layer functions independently of the type of Physical layer used by the network and its nodes. It also doesn't care whether you are running WordPerfect or Excel or using the Internet. Connectivity devices, such as bridges and switches, work in the Data Link layer, because they decode frames and use the frame information to transmit data to its correct recipient. Ethernet is an example of a Data Link layer technology. Chapters 3 and 6 both discuss elements of the Data Link layer.

Network Layer

The primary function of the **Network layer**, the third layer in the OSI Model, is to translate network addresses into their physical counterparts and decide how to route data from the sender to the receiver. For example, a computer might have a network address of 10.34.99.12 (if it's using the TCP/IP protocol) and a physical address of 0060973E97F3. In the classroom example, this addressing scheme is like saying that "Ms. Jones" and "U.S. citizen with Social Security number 123-45-6789" are the same person. Even though there may be other people named "Ms. Jones" in the United States, only one person has the Social Security number 123-45-6789. Within the confines of your classroom, however, there is only one Ms. Jones, so you can be certain the correct person will respond when you say, "Ms. Jones?"

2

The Network layer determines the best path from point A on one network to point B on another network by factoring in delivery priorities, network congestion, quality of service, and cost of alternative routes. Because the Network layer handles routing, **routers**—the devices that connect network segments and intelligently direct data— belong in the Network layer. In networking, the term "to **route**" means to direct data based on addressing, patterns of usage, and availability. Chapter 6 explains routers and their functions in detail.

Transport Layer

The **Transport layer** is primarily responsible for ensuring that data are transferred from point A to point B (which may or may not be on the same network segment) reliably, in the correct sequence, and without errors. The Transport layer may be considered the most important layer in the OSI Model because without it, data could not be verified or interpreted by their recipients. Transport protocols also handle **flow control**, or the method of gauging the appropriate rate of transmission based on how fast the recipient can accept data.

In addition, Transport layer services break arbitrarily long packets into the maximum size that the type of network in use can handle. For example, Ethernet networks cannot accept packets larger than 1500 bytes. **Segmentation** refers to the process of decreasing the size of the data units when moving data from part of a network that can handle larger data units to part of a network that can handle only smaller data units. This process is just like the process of breaking down words into recognizable syllables that a small child uses when learning to read. **Reassembly** is the process of reconstructing the segmented data units. To continue the reading analogy, when a child understands the separate syllables, he can combine them into a word—that is, reassemble the parts into a whole.

The segmentation that takes place in the Transport layer of the OSI Model has nothing to do with network segmentation, which was introduced in Chapter 1 and will be described in more detail in Chapter 4. Segmentation in the Transport layer refers to a reduction in the size of the data frames, while network segmentation refers to the separation of a network into smaller logical or physical pieces.

When the sending node's Transport layer services divide its data into smaller pieces, they assign a sequence number to each piece, so that the data can be reassembled in the correct order by the receiving node's Transport layer services. This process is called **sequencing**.

To understand how sequencing works, consider the classroom example again. Suppose you asked the question, "Ms. Jones? How did poor farming techniques contribute to the Dust Bowl?" but that the words arrived at Ms. Jones's ear as "poor farming techniques Ms. Jones? how did to the Dust Bowl? contribute." On a network, the Transport layer would recognize this disorder and rearrange the data pieces so that they make sense. In addition, the Transport layer sends an **acknowledgment (ACK)** to notify the sender that data were received correctly. If the data contained errors, the Transport layer would request that the sender retransmit the data. Also, if the data weren't acknowledged within a given time period, the sender's Transport layer would consider the data lost and retransmit them.

One service that works in the Transport layer is TCP (Transmission Control Protocol) of the TCP/IP protocol suite. Another Transport layer service is SPX (Sequence Packet Exchange) of the IPX/SPX protocol suite. You will learn more about these and other Transport layer services in Chapter 3.

Session Layer

The **Session layer** is responsible for establishing and maintaining communication between two nodes on the network. The term **session** refers to a connection for data exchange between two parties; it is most often used in the context of terminal and mainframe communications, in which the **terminal** is a device with little (if any) of its own processing or disk capacity that depends on a host to supply it with applications and data processing services. Among the Session layer's functions are establishing and keeping alive the communications link for the duration of the session, synchronizing the dialog between the two nodes, determining whether communications have been cut off, and, if so, figuring out where to restart transmission. Often you will hear the Session layer called the "traffic cop" of network communications. When you dial your Internet service provider (ISP) to connect to the Internet, the Session layer services at your ISP's server, and on your PC client, negotiate the connection. If your phone line is accidentally pulled out of the wall jack, the Session layer on your end will detect the loss of a connection and initiate attempts to reconnect.

The Session layer also sets the terms of communication by deciding which node will communicate first and how long a node can communicate. In this sense, the Session layer acts as a judge in a debate competition. For example, if you were a member of a debate team and had two minutes to state your opening argument, the judge might signal you after one and a half minutes that you have only 30 seconds remaining. If you tried to interrupt a member of the opposing debate team, he would tell you to wait your turn. Finally, the Session layer monitors the identification of session participants, ensuring that only the authorized nodes can access the session.

Presentation Layer

The **Presentation layer** serves as a translator between the application and the network. At the Presentation layer, data become formatted in a schema that the network can understand; this format varies with the type of network used. The Presentation layer also manages data encryption and decryption, such as the scrambling of system passwords. For example, if you look up your bank account status on the Internet, you are using a secure connection, and your account data will be encrypted before they are transmitted.

2

On your end of the network, the Presentation layer will decrypt the data as they are received. In addition, Presentation layer protocols code and decode graphics and file format information.

Application Layer

The top, or seventh, layer of the OSI Model is the Application layer. The **Application layer** provides interfaces to the software that enable programs to use network services. The term "Application layer" does not refer to a particular software application, such as Microsoft Word, running on the network. Instead, some of the services provided by the Application layer include file transfer, file management, and message handling for electronic mail. For example, if you are running Microsoft Word on a network and choose to open a file, your request for that data is transferred from Microsoft Word to the network by the Application layer.

The part of Microsoft Word that handles this request is its application program interface (API). An **application program interface** is a routine (a set of instructions) that allows a program to interact with the operating system. APIs belong to the Application layer of the OSI Model. Programmers use APIs to establish links between their code and the operating system. An example of an API used in a network environment is **Microsoft Message Queueing (MSMQ)**. MSMQ stores messages sent between nodes in queues and then forwards them to their destinations based on when the link to the recipient becomes available. As a result, programs can run independently of whether the data's destination is connected to the network when the messages are sent.

APPLYING THE OSI MODEL

Now that you have been introduced to the seven layers of the OSI Model, you can take a closer look at exactly how the layers interact. For reference, Table 2-1 summarizes the functions of the seven OSI Model layers.

Table 2-1　Functions of the OSI layers

OSI Layer	Function
Application	Transfers information from program to program
Presentation	Handles text formatting and displays code conversion
Session	Establishes, maintains, and coordinates communication
Transport	Ensures accurate delivery of data
Network	Determines transport routes and handles the transfer of messages
Data Link	Codes, addresses, and transmits information
Physical	Manages hardware connections

Communication Between Two Systems

An exemplary process to trace through the OSI Model layers is the retrieval of a message file from the server. Once you log in to the network and start your mail program, you can choose to pick up your mail. At that point, the Application layer recognizes your choice and formulates a request for data from a remote node (in this case, the mail server). The Application layer transfers the request to the Presentation layer.

The Presentation layer first determines whether and how it should format or encrypt the data request received from the Application layer. After it has made that determination, it adds any translation or codes required to implement that formatting and then passes your request on to the Session layer.

The Session layer picks up your formatted request and assigns a data token to it. A **token** is a special control frame that indicates to the rest of the network that you have the right to transmit data. (Remember that the Session layer acts as the "traffic cop" for communications between nodes.) The Session layer then passes your data to the Transport layer.

At the Transport layer, your data and the control information it has accumulated thus far are broken down into manageable chunks of data and prepared to be packaged in frames at the Data Link layer. If the data is too large to fit in one frame, the Transport layer subdivides it into several smaller blocks and assigns sequence identifiers to each block. This layer then passes the data blocks, one at a time, to the Network layer.

The Network layer adds addressing information to the data it receives from the Transport layer, so that subsequent layers will know the source and the destination of the data. It then passes the data blocks, with their addressing identifications, to the Data Link layer.

At the Data Link layer, the data blocks are packaged into individual frames. As you have learned, a frame is a structured format for transmitting small blocks of data. Using frames reduces the possibility of lost data or errors on the network, because each frame has its own built-in error check. This error checking algorithm, also known as the **Frame Check Sequence (FCS)**, is inserted at the end of the frame by the Data Link layer. In addition, the Data Link layer adds a header to the frame that incorporates destination and source addresses assigned by the Network layer. (Frame types and specifications are discussed in more detail in the next section.) The Data Link layer then passes the frames to the Physical layer.

Finally, your request for your mail message hits the NIC at the Physical layer. The Physical layer does not interpret the frame or add information to the frame; it simply delivers the data to the cabling and sends it across the network. Once the data arrives at the Physical layer of the remote system, the mail server's Data Link layer begins to unravel your request, reversing the process just described, until it responds to your request with its own transmission, beginning from its Application layer. Figure 2-3 shows how data is transferred from your system to the server, then back to your system through the OSI Model.

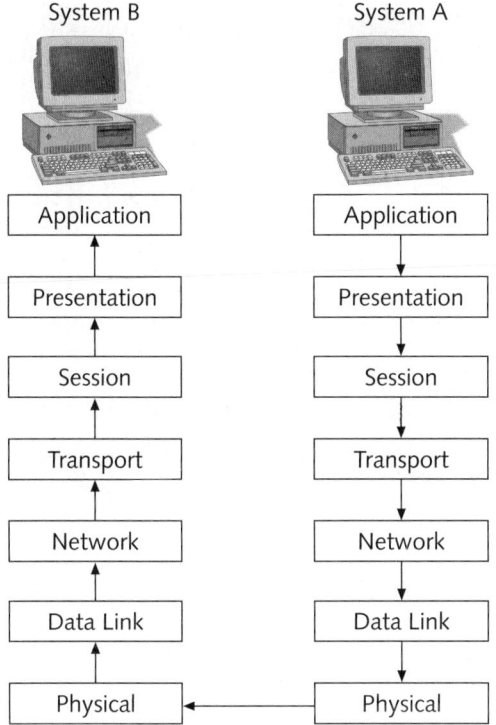

Figure 2-3   Data transfer between two systems

In the preceding example, you learned that every successive layer in the OSI Model—beginning with the Application layer and ending with the Physical layer—adds some control, formatting, or addressing information to the data it handles. The receiving system then interprets and uses the added information as it reverses the process, passing data from the Physical layer back up to the Application layer. Between your initial software request and the network cable, your blocks of data grow larger as they accumulate more handling information. Figure 2-4 depicts the transformation of data as it travels through the OSI Model layers.

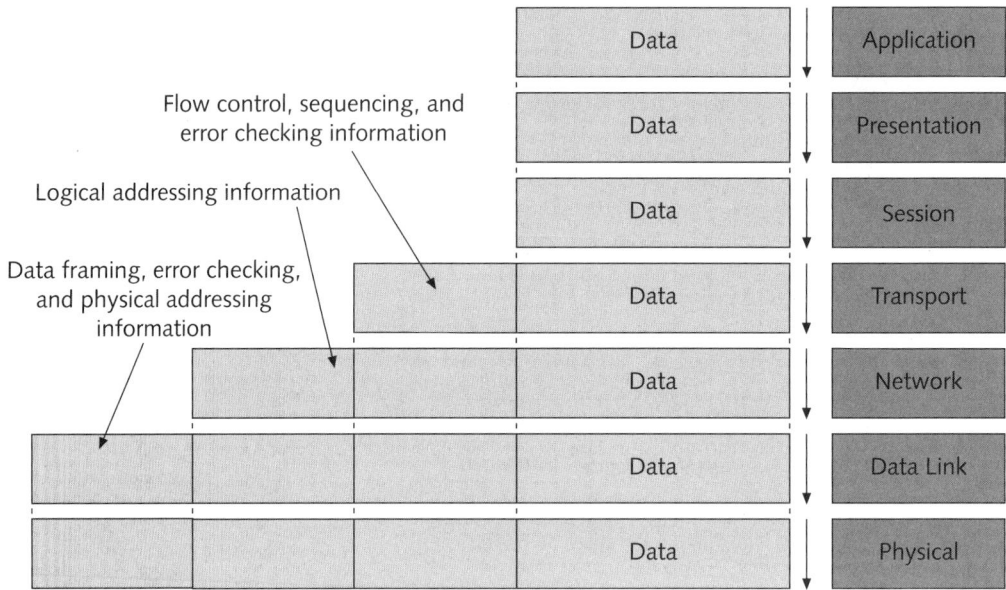

Figure 2-4   Data transformed through the OSI Model

Frame Specifications

Figure 2-2 introduced the basic structure of a data frame. In reality, frames are composed of several smaller components, or fields. The characteristics of these components depend on the type of network on which the frames run and on the standards that they must follow. The two major categories of frame types, Ethernet and Token Ring, correspond to the two most commonly used network technologies.

Ethernet is a networking technology originally developed at Xerox in the early 1970s and improved by Digital Equipment Corporation, Intel, and Xerox. Today, four types of Ethernet technology are used on LANs, with each type being governed by a set of IEEE standards. Ethernet LANs can transmit data at different rates and on a multitude of networking media. Ethernet is covered in detail in Chapter 5.

Token Ring is a networking technology developed by IBM in the 1980s. It relies upon direct links between nodes and a ring topology, passing around tokens that allow nodes to transmit data. Token Ring technology will be discussed in detail in Chapter 5.

Each frame type is unique and will not interact with different frame types on the network, because routers cannot support more than one frame type per physical interface. You can, however, work with multiple protocols on a network while using only one frame type. For example, you can run both IPX/SPX and TCP/IP on an Ethernet network. Although you can conceivably transmit both Token Ring and Ethernet frames on a network, Ethernet interfaces cannot interpret Token Ring frames, and vice versa. Normally, LANs use *either* Ethernet or Token Ring. On the other hand, many LANs run both TCP/IP *and* IPX/SPX.

It's important to know what frame type (or types) your network environment requires. You will use this information when installing network operating systems, configuring servers and client workstations, installing NICs, troubleshooting network problems and purchasing network equipment. It's also important to know what constitutes the frame. The following sections describe two typical frame types, Ethernet 802.3 and Token Ring 802.5.

A Typical Ethernet Frame

Figure 2-5 depicts a typical Ethernet frame as specified by the IEEE **802.3** standard.

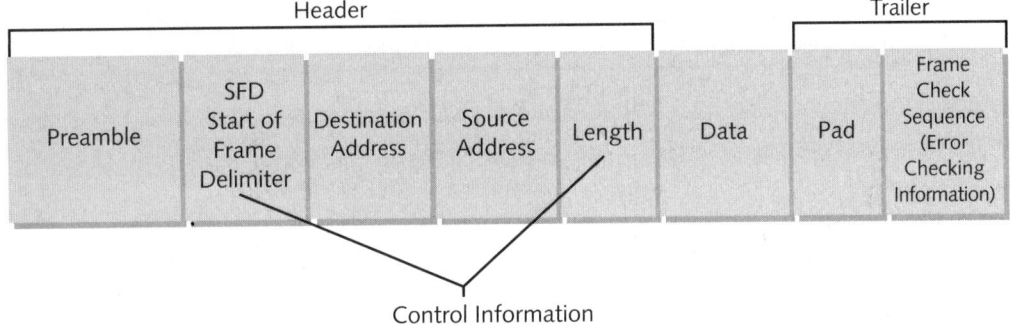

Figure 2-5   Ethernet frame as specified by the IEEE 802.3 standard

The components of the Ethernet 802.3 frame are described in the following list:

- *Preamble*—Marks the beginning of the entire frame, providing a signal that essentially announces to the network that data is en route. Because this field is part of the communications process, a preamble typically isn't included when calculating the size of a frame.

- *Start of Frame Delimiter (SFD)*—Indicates the beginning of the addressing frame.

- *Destination Address*—Contains the destination node address.

- *Source Address*—Contains the address of the originating node.

- *Length (LEN)*—Indicates the length of the packet.

- *Data*—Contains the data, or segmented part of that data, transmitted from the originating node.

- *Pad*—Used to increase the size of the frame to its minimum size requirement of 46 bytes.

- *Frame Check Sequence (FCS)*—Provides an algorithm to determine whether the data were received correctly. The most commonly used algorithm is called **Cyclic Redundancy Check (CRC)**, so you may also see this field called "CRC."

Chapter 5 provides more detail on this type of Ethernet frame. Chapter 5 also covers the other three Ethernet frame types.

A Typical Token Ring Frame

Figure 2-6 depicts a typical Token Ring frame, which is specified in the IEEE **802.5** standard. Note that some of its characteristics match those of the Ethernet frame, but significant differences arise in how the control information is handled.

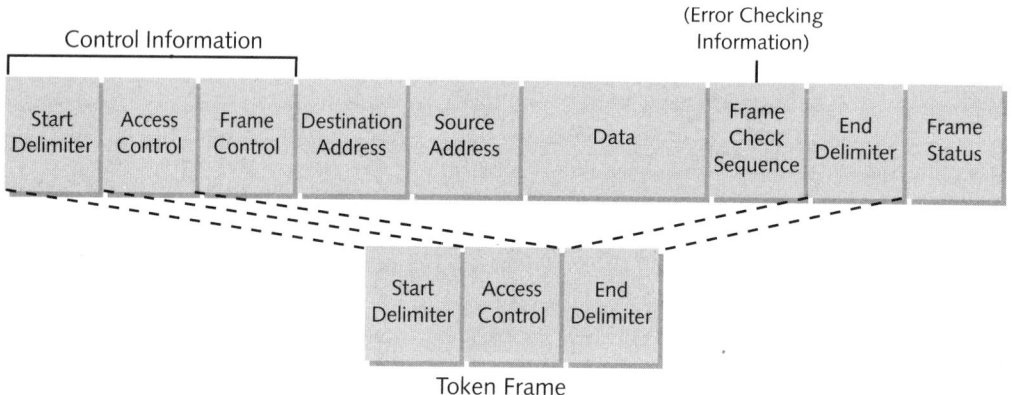

Figure 2-6   A typical Token Ring frame

The following list describes the components of the typical Token Ring frame:

- *Start Delimiter (SD)*—Signifies the beginning of the packet. It is one of three fields that compose the Token Ring frame.

- *Access Control (AC)*—Contains information about the priority of the frame. It is the second of three fields that compose the Token Ring frame.

- *Frame Control (FC)*—Defines the type of frame; used in the Frame Check Sequence.

- *Destination Address*—Contains the destination node address.

- *Source Address*—Contains the address of the originating node.

- *Data*—Contains the data transmitted from the originating node. May also contain routing and management information.

- *Frame Check Sequence (FCS)*—Used to check the integrity of the frame.

- *End Delimiter (ED)*—Indicates the end of the frame. It is the third field that composes the Token Ring frame.

- *Frame Status (FS)*—Indicates whether the destination node recognized and correctly copied the frame, or whether the destination node was not available.

Token Ring networks and frame types will be covered in more detail in Chapter 5.

Addressing Through the Layers

In Chapter 1, you learned that addressing is a system for assigning unique identification numbers to each node on a network. In this chapter, you learned that addressing is interpreted at the network layer of the OSI Model. In fact, each node on a network can be identified by two types of addresses: Network layer addresses and Data Link layer addresses.

Data Link layer addresses are fixed numbers associated with the networking hardware; they are usually assigned at the factory. These addresses are also called **MAC addresses**, after the **Media Access Control (MAC) sublayer**, which lies within the Data Link layer and appends the physical address of the destination to the data frame. MAC addresses are guaranteed to be unique because industry standards (established and maintained by IEEE) specify which numbers each manufacturer can use. For example, Ethernet NICs manufactured by the 3Com Corporation begin with the six-character sequence "00608C," while Ethernet NICs manufactured by Intel begin with "00AA00." The part of the MAC address that is unique to a particular vendor is called the **Block ID**. Some manufacturers have several different Block IDs. The remaining six characters in the sequence are added at the factory, based on the NIC's model and manufacture date, and collectively form the **Device ID**. An example of a Device ID assigned by a manufacturer might be 005499. The combination of the Block ID and Device ID result in a unique, 12-digit MAC address of 00608C005499. Networks rely upon unique MAC addressing to transmit data to their correct destination.

Data Link layer—or MAC—addresses are also called physical addresses or hardware addresses.

Network layer addresses, which reside at the network level of the OSI Model, follow a hierarchical addressing scheme and can be assigned through operating system software. They are hierarchical because they contain subsets of data that incrementally narrow down the location of a node, just as your home address is hierarchical because it provides a country, state, zip code, city, street, house number, and person's name. Network Layer addresses, therefore, are more useful to internetworking devices such as routers, because they make sorting data more logical. Network layer address formats differ depending on which protocols the network uses. Chapter 3 covers the addressing rules for the different protocols.

Network layer addresses are also called logical addresses or virtual addresses.

IEEE Networking Specifications

In addition to frame types, the IEEE networking specifications apply to connectivity, networking media, error checking algorithms, encryption, emerging technologies, and more. All of these specifications fall under the IEEE's "Project 802," an effort to standardize physical elements of a network. IEEE developed these standards before the OSI Model was standardized by ISO, but IEEE's 802 standards can be applied to the layers of the OSI Model. Table 2-2 describes the IEEE 802 specifications. You should be familiar with the topics that each standard covers. The Network+ certification exam includes questions about IEEE 802 specifications.

Table 2-2   IEEE 802 standards

Standard	Name	Explanation
802.1	Internetworking	Covers routing, bridging, and internetwork communications
802.2	Logical Link Control	Relates to error and flow control over data frames
802.3	Ethernet LAN	Covers all forms of Ethernet media and interfaces
802.4	Token Bus LAN	Covers all forms of Token Bus media and interfaces
802.5	Token Ring LAN	Covers all forms of Token Ring media and interfaces
802.6	Metropolitan Area Network (MAN)	Covers MAN technologies, addressing, and services
802.7	Broadband Technical Advisory Group	Covers broadband networking media, interfaces, and other equipment
802.8	Fiber-Optic Technical Advisory Group	Covers use of fiber-optic media and technologies for various networking types
802.9	Integrated Voice/Data Networks	Covers integration of voice and data traffic over a single network medium
802.10	Network Security	Covers network access controls, encryption, certification, and other security topics
802.11	Wireless Networks	Standards for wireless networking for many different broadcast frequencies and usage techniques
802.12	High-Speed Networking	Covers a variety of 100Mbps-plus technologies, including 100BASEVG-AnyLAN

To accommodate shared access for multiple network nodes (as opposed to simple point-to-point communication), the IEEE expanded the OSI Model by separating the Data Link layer into two sublayers: the Logical Link Control (LLC) sublayer and the Media Access Control (MAC) sublayer. The **LLC**, the upper sublayer in the Data Link layer, provides a common interface and supplies reliability and flow control services. The **MAC**, the lower sublayer of the Data Link layer, actually appends the physical address of the destination computer onto the data frame. IEEE's specifications for Ethernet and

2

Token Ring technology (found in Table 2-2) apply to the MAC sublayer of the Data Link layer. Figure 2-7 shows how the IEEE subdivided the Data Link layer.

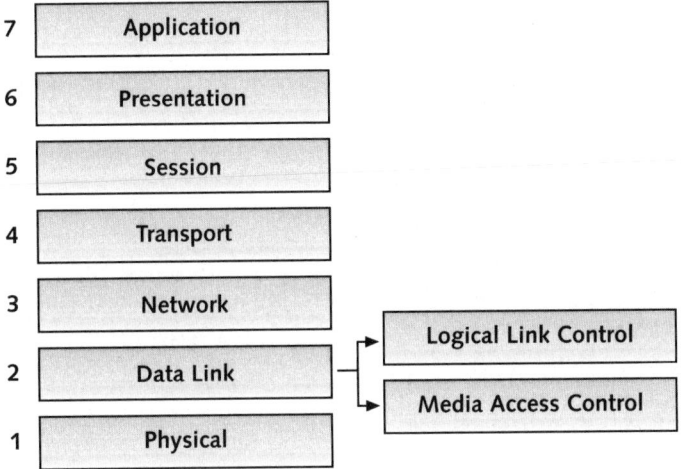

Figure 2-7   The Logical Link Control and Media Access Control sublayers

CHAPTER SUMMARY

- ❑ Standards are documented agreements containing technical specifications or other precise criteria that are used as guidelines to ensure that materials, products, processes, and services suit their purpose. Without standards, you could not design a network because your hardware would not fit together and your programs could not communicate with each other.

- ❑ A complete compilation of standards that apply to the networking and computer industries would fill an encyclopedia. Some of the significant standards organizations are ANSI (American National Standards Institute), EIA (Electronic Industries Alliance), IEEE (Institute of Electrical and Electronic Engineers), ISO (International Organization for Standardization), and ITU (International Telecommunications Union, formerly called the CCITT).

- ❑ In the early 1980s, ISO began work on a universal set of specifications that would enable computer platforms across the world to communicate openly. The result was a helpful model for understanding and developing computer-to-computer communication. This model, called the Open Systems Interconnection (OSI) Model, divides networking architecture into seven layers: Physical, Data Link, Network, Transport, Session, Presentation, and Application. Each layer has its own set of functions and interacts with the layers directly above and below it.

- ❑ The Physical layer is the lowest, or first, layer of the OSI Model. It contains the physical networking medium, such as cabling, connectors, and repeaters. Protocols at the Physical layer generate and detect voltage so as to transmit and receive signals carrying data. The Physical layer sets the data transmission rate and monitors data error rates, though it does not provide error correction.

❑ The second layer of the OSI Model, the Data Link layer, bridges the networking media with the abstract software and data streams. Its primary function is to divide data it receives from the Network layer into frames that can then be transmitted by the Physical layer. Connectivity devices such as bridges and switches work in the Data Link layer, because they decode frames and use the frame information to transmit data to its correct recipient.

❑ The Network layer, the third OSI Model layer, manages addressing and routing data based on addressing, patterns of usage, and availability. Routers belong to the Network layer because they use this information to intelligently direct data from sender to receiver. The Network layer is also responsible for segmentation and reassembly of packets.

❑ The Transport layer is primarily responsible for ensuring that data are transferred from point A to point B (which may or may not be on the same network segment) reliably and without errors. For example, the Transport layer ensures that data are sent and received in the same order, or sequence. It also establishes the level of packet error checking.

❑ The Session layer establishes and maintains communication between two nodes on the network. It can be considered the "traffic cop" of network communications. The term "session" refers to a connection for data exchange between two parties; it is most often used in the context of terminal and mainframe communications.

❑ The Presentation layer, the sixth OSI Model layer, serves as a translator between the application and the network. At the Presentation layer, data are formatted in a schema that the network can understand; this format varies with the type of network used. The Presentation layer also manages data encryption and decryption, such as the scrambling of system passwords.

❑ The top, or seventh, layer of the OSI Model is the Application layer. It provides interfaces to the software that enable it to use network services. Some of the services provided by the Application layer include file transfer, file management, and message handling for electronic mail.

❑ A data request from a software program is received by the Application layer services and is transferred down through the layers of the OSI Model until it reaches the Physical layer, or the network cable. At that point, data are sent to their destination over the wire, and the Physical layer services at the destination send it back up through the layers of the OSI Model until it reaches the Application layer.

❑ Data frames, also known simply as "frames," are small blocks of data with control, addressing, and handling information attached to them. Frames are composed of several smaller components. The characteristics of these components depend on the type of network on which the frames run and the standards that they must follow. The two major categories of frame types, Ethernet and Token Ring, correspond to the two most commonly used network technologies.

□ Each node on a network can be identified by two types of addresses: Network layer addresses and Data Link layer addresses. Data Link layer addresses are hardwired into the networking device, and are also called physical, MAC, or hardware addresses. Network layer addresses, also called logical or virtual addresses, are assigned to devices through operating software. These logical addresses are composed of hierarchical information, so they can be easily interpreted by routers and used to direct data to their destinations.

□ In addition to frame types, the IEEE networking specifications apply to connectivity, networking media, error checking algorithms, encryption, emerging technologies, and more. All of these specifications fall under the IEEE's Project 802, an effort to standardize the elements of networking.

□ The IEEE expanded the OSI Model by separating the Data Link layer into two sublayers: the Logical Link Control (LLC) sublayer and the Medium Access Control (MAC) sublayer. The LLC, the upper sublayer in the Data Link layer, provides a common interface and supplies reliability and flow control services. The MAC, the lower sublayer of the Data Link layer, actually appends the physical address of the destination computer onto the data frame.

KEY TERMS

802.3 — The IEEE standard for Ethernet networking devices and data handling.

802.4 — The IEEE standard for Token Bus networking devices and data handling.

802.5 — The IEEE standard for Token Ring networking devices and data handling.

802.6 — The IEEE standard for Metropolitan Area Network (MAN) networking.

802.10 — The IEEE standard that describes network access controls, encryption, certification, and other security topics.

802.11 — The IEEE standard for wireless networking.

acknowledgment (ACK) — A response generated at the Transport layer of the OSI Model that confirms to a sender that its frame was received.

ANSI (American National Standards Institute) — An organization composed of more than 1000 representatives from industry and government who together determine standards for the electronics industry in addition to other fields, such as chemical and nuclear engineering, health and safety, and construction.

Application layer — The seventh layer of the OSI Model. The Application layer provides interfaces to the software that enable programs to use network services.

application programming interface (API) — A routine (or set of instructions) that allows a program to interact with the operating system. APIs belong to the Application layer of the OSI Model.

Block ID — The first set of six characters that make up the MAC address and that are unique to a particular vendor.

Cyclic Redundancy Check (CRC) — An algorithm used to verify the accuracy of data contained in a data frame.

Data Link layer — The second layer in the OSI Model. The Data Link layer bridges the networking media with the Network layer. Its primary function is to divide the data it receives from the Network layer into frames that can then be transmitted by the Physical layer.

Data Link layer address — See *MAC address*.

Device ID — The second set of six characters that make up a network device's MAC address. The Device ID, which is added at the factory, is based on the device's model and manufacture date.

EIA (Electronic Industries Alliance) — A trade organization composed of representatives from electronics manufacturing firms across the United States.

Ethernet — A networking technology originally developed at Xerox in 1970 and improved by Digital Equipment Corporation, Intel, and Xerox. Today, four types of Ethernet technology are used on LANs, with each type being governed by a set of IEEE standards.

flow control — A method of gauging the appropriate rate of data transmission based on how fast the recipient can accept data.

frame — A package for data that includes not only the raw data, or "payload," but also the sender's and receiver's network addresses and control information.

Frame Check Sequence (FCS) — The field in a frame responsible for ensuring that data carried by the frame arrives intact. It uses an algorithm, such as CRC, to accomplish this verification.

IEEE (Institute of Electrical and Electronic Engineers) — An international society composed of engineering professionals. Its goals are to promote development and education in the electrical engineering and computer science fields.

ISO (International Organization for Standardization) — A collection of standards organizations representing 130 countries with headquarters located in Geneva, Switzerland. Its goal is to establish international technological standards to facilitate the global exchange of information and barrier-free trade.

ITU (International Telecommunication Union) — A United Nations agency that regulates international telecommunications, including radio and TV frequencies, satellite and telephony specifications, networking infrastructure, and tariffs applied to global communication. It also provides developing countries with technical expertise and equipment to advance these nations' technological bases.

logical address — See *Network layer addresses*.

Logical Link Control (LLC) sublayer — The upper sublayer in the Data Link layer. The LLC provides a common interface and supplies reliability and flow control services.

2

MAC address — A number that uniquely identifies a network node. The manufacturer hard-codes the MAC address on the NIC. This address is composed of the Block ID and Device ID.

Media Access Control (MAC) sublayer — The lower sublayer of the Data Link layer. The MAC appends the physical address of the destination computer onto the frame.

Microsoft Message Queueing (MSMQ) — An API used in a network environment. MSMQ stores messages sent between nodes in queues then forwards them to their destination based on when the link to the recipient is available.

network address — See *Network layer addresses.*

network architect — A professional who designs networks, performing tasks that range from choosing basic components (such as cabling type) to figuring out how to make those components work together (by, for example, choosing the correct protocols).

Network layer — The third layer in the OSI Model. The Network layer translates network addresses into their physical counterparts and decides how to route data from the sender to the receiver.

Network layer addresses — Addresses that reside at the Network level of the OSI Model, follow a hierarchical addressing scheme, and can be assigned through operating system software.

Open Systems Interconnection (OSI) Model — A model for understanding and developing computer-to-computer communication developed in the 1980s by ISO. It divides networking architecture into seven layers: Physical, Data Link, Network, Transport, Session, Presentation, and Application.

physical address — See *MAC address.*

Physical layer — The lowest, or first, layer of the OSI Model. The Physical layer contains the physical networking media, such as cabling and connectors.

Presentation layer — The sixth layer of the OSI Model. The Presentation layer serves as a translator between the application and the network. Here data are formatted in a schema that the network can understand, with the format varying according to the type of network used. The Presentation layer also manages data encryption and decryption, such as the scrambling of system passwords.

reassembly — The process of reconstructing data units that have been segmented.

route — To direct data between networks based on addressing, patterns of usage, and availability of network segments.

routers — Devices that connect network segments and intelligently direct data based on information contained in the data frame.

segmentation — The process of decreasing the size of data units when moving data from a network segment that can handle larger data units to a network segment that can handle only smaller data units.

sequencing — The process of assigning a placeholder to each piece of a data block to allow the receiving node's Transport layer to reassemble the data in the correct order.

session — A connection for data exchange between two parties. The term "session" is most often used in the context of terminal and mainframe communications.

Session layer — The fifth layer in the OSI Model. The Session layer establishes and maintains communication between two nodes on the network. It can be considered the "traffic cop" for network communications.

standards — Documented agreements containing technical specifications or other precise criteria that are used as guidelines to ensure that materials, products, processes, and services suit their intended purpose.

terminal — A device with little (if any) of its own processing or disk capacity that depends on a host to supply it with applications and data-processing services.

token — A special control frame that indicates to the rest of the network that a particular node has the right to transmit data.

Token Ring — A networking technology developed by IBM in the 1980s. It relies upon direct links between nodes and a ring topology, using tokens to allow nodes to transmit data.

Transport layer — The fourth layer of the OSI Model. The Transport layer is primarily responsible for ensuring that data are transferred from point A to point B (which may or may not be on the same network segment) reliably and without errors.

REVIEW QUESTIONS

1. Which international standards organization is part of the United Nations?
   a. IEEE
   b. ITU
   c. ISO
   d. ANSI

2. What does "ISO" stand for?
   a. Institute for Standards Organization
   b. International Standards Organization
   c. International Organization for Standardization
   d. International Statisticians Organization

3. Which organization represents the United States in ISO?
   a. ANSI
   b. ITU
   c. IEEE
   d. EIA

2

4. Which technology is standardized in the IEEE 802.5 specification?

   a. network security

   b. Token Ring LANs

   c. wireless networks

   d. Ethernet LANs

5. Which technology is standardized in the IEEE 802.3 specification?

   a. network security

   b. Token Ring LANs

   c. wireless networks

   d. Ethernet LANs

6. Which layer of the OSI Model provides file transfer services?

   a. Application layer

   b. Data Link layer

   c. Transport layer

   d. Presentation layer

7. Netscape is an example of a program that runs in the Application layer. True or False?

8. Which layer of the OSI Model establishes the rules of communication between two nodes?

   a. Transport layer

   b. Session layer

   c. Data Link layer

   d. Presentation layer

9. In which layer of the OSI Model do switches and bridges belong?

   a. Data Link layer

   b. Transport layer

   c. Network layer

   d. Session layer

10. In which layer of the OSI Model do routers belong?

    a. Data Link layer

    b. Transport layer

    c. Network layer

    d. Physical layer

11. In which two layers of the OSI Model do NICs belong?

    a. Presentation and Application layer

    b. Transport and Network layer

    c. Network and Data Link layer

    d. Physical and Data Link layer

12. Which standards organization developed the OSI Model?

    a. IEEE

    b. ITU

    c. OSI

    d. ISO

13. Under what circumstances would the Network layer use segmentation?

    a. when too many data frames are flooding into a receiving node's NIC

    b. when the network is transmitting too many incorrect frames

    c. when the destination node cannot accept the size of the data blocks transmitted by the source node

    d. when the source node requests that data blocks be segmented for faster processing

14. Generating and detecting voltage so as to transmit and receive signals carrying data is the responsibility of which OSI Model layer?

    a. Transport layer

    b. Session layer

    c. Presentation layer

    d. Physical layer

15. Flow control is the process of making sure data frames are received in the correct order. True or False?

16. What is the purpose of a token in a token-passing network?

    a. It indicates to the rest of the network that one node has the right to transmit data.

    b. It indicates to the rest of the network that one node is busy and cannot receive traffic.

    c. It indicates to the rest of the network that a broadcast message is about to be sent.

    d. It indicates to the rest of the network that one node is causing transmission errors for the rest of the network.

2

17. If you use a password to log in to your Microsoft Exchange program, which layer of the OSI Model would decode your password?

a. Application layer

b. Session layer

c. Presentation layer

d. Network layer

18. Which layer of the OSI Model handles error checking and retransmission of bad data?

a. Transport layer

b. Network layer

c. Session layer

d. Physical layer

19. What are the differences between MAC addresses and Network layer addresses?

20. One frame type will not interact with another frame type on the network. True or False?

21. Which of the following types of addresses follow a hierarchical format?

a. Physical layer addresses

b. MAC addresses

c. Network layer addresses

d. Data Link layer addresses

22. Which of the following is not a field found in an Ethernet 802.3 data frame?

a. path selector

b. destination address

c. source address

d. length

23. Token Ring technology was originally developed by which company?

a. Hewlett-Packard

b. IBM

c. Cisco

d. 3Com

24. Which of the following is not a field found in a Token Ring data frame?

a. frame status

b. source address

c. destination address

d. pad

25. A single frame type can support only one kind of protocol. True or False?

26. What are the sublayers of the Data Link layer as defined in the IEEE 802 standards?

    a. Logical Link Control sublayer and Media Access Control sublayer

    b. Transport Control sublayer and Media Access Control sublayer

    c. Logical Link Control sublayer and Physical Addressing sublayer

    d. Transport Control sublayer and Data Link Control sublayer

27. Describe the functions of the two Data Link layer sublayers.

28. What is the purpose of a router?

29. What part of the MAC address is unique to each vendor?

    a. the destination ID

    b. the Block ID

    c. the physical node ID

    d. the segment ID

30. IEEE has standardized four Ethernet frame types. True or False?

HANDS-ON PROJECTS

Project 2-1

To better understand the impact IEEE has on networking standards, it is helpful to look at some of the specifications developed by IEEE. This exercise will guide you through the process of searching for IEEE specifications on the Web. To complete this project, you need a computer with access to the Internet.

1. Access the Internet and go to www.standards.ieee.org.

2. On the Standards page, click the **IEEE Standards Online** link.

3. Under the heading "IEEE Standards Online Subscriptions," click the **SEARCH** link.

4. The IEEE Standards Online Search Web page appears.

5. Beneath the search text box, click **Advanced** to access advanced search options.

6. Type **Ethernet** in the text box below the first search parameter line.

7. Leave the other options on the search page as they are, then click **seek** to execute your search.

8. Note how many abstracts your search returned. For those abstracts that give designation numbers, note the numbers as well.

9. What was the date of the last 802.3 CSMA/CD standards revision? Why do you suppose this standard would be updated so frequently?

Project 2-2

2

When supporting computers on a network, you will often need to change the network properties on client workstations. You may perform this task when you first set up a machine or later, if it is having problems or if the network specifications have changed. This exercise introduces you to the process of finding and changing network properties on a client workstation. You will need to be familiar with this process not only to be a successful networking professional, but also to qualify for Net+ certification.

This project requires a desktop computer client running Windows 2000 Professional and both the TCP/IP and IPX/SPX protocols connected to a Windows 2000 server running on an Ethernet network. (You will learn more about the TCP/IP and IPX/SPX protocols in Chapter 3.)

1. On the Windows 2000 Professional computer, click **Start**, point to **Settings**, then click **Network and Dial-up Connections**. The Network and Dial-up Connections window opens.

2. Right-click **Local Area Connection** and then click **Properties** in the shortcut menu. The Local Area Connection Properties dialog box appears.

3. Scroll down the list of installed components until you find the NWLink IPX/SPX/NetBIOS-Compatible Transport Protocol, then double-click this service to see its properties.

4. Note your workstation's current Ethernet frame type. Click the down arrow next to the frame type setting to view other frame type options.

5. Change the frame type value to **Ethernet SNAP**, then click OK to save your change.

6. Click **OK** again to close the Local Area Connection Properties dialog box.

7. To make sure the changes have taken effect, reboot your computer.

8. Note what happens after you restart your computer and try to connect to the network. Do you have trouble making a connection, or does the network accept your login ID and password? Why or why not?

9. To ensure that your workstation will function properly on the network once again, you should restore your original frame type settings. To do so, repeat Steps 1 through 4. In the Frame type properties list, select the original frame type you noted in Step 5.

10. Click **OK** to save your change, then click **OK** to continue.

11. To make sure the changes have taken effect, reboot your computer.

Project 2-3

You will need to know how to find and interpret MAC addresses when supporting networks. In this exercise, you will discover two ways of finding your computer's MAC address, also known as its physical address, or sometimes, its adapter address. For this exercise you will need a workstation running the Windows 2000 Professional operating system and the TCP/IP protocols connected to a Windows 2000 server. You will also need a screwdriver that fits the workstation's cover screws, if the computer's cover is attached with screws.

1. On the Windows 2000 Professional computer, click **Start**, point to **Programs**, point to **Accessories**, and then click **Command Prompt**. The Command Prompt window opens with a cursor blinking at the C:\> prompt.

2. Type **ipconfig/all** then press **Enter**. A list of your Windows 2000 IP Configuration and Ethernet adapter Local Area Connection parameters appears. This includes your workstation's TCP/IP properties, as well as its MAC address.

3. Search the list for the Physical Address parameter. This 12-digit hexadecimal number is your NIC's MAC address.

4. Type **exit** and press Enter to close the Command Prompt window.

5. Log off the network and shut down your workstation.

6. If necessary, use the screwdriver to remove the screws that secure the workstation's housing. Ask your instructor for help if you can't find the correct screws. Usually there are three to five screws. In some cases, a computer housing may use no screws.

7. Remove the cover from the rest of the CPU.

8. If a cable is connected to your NIC, remove the cable.

9. With the computer open, remove the screw that holds the NIC in place. Gently remove the NIC from its place in the computer's motherboard.

10. In most cases, a NIC's MAC address is printed on a small white sticker attached to the NIC; alternatively, it may be stamped directly on the NIC itself. Find the MAC address and compare it to the one you discovered in Step 3.

11. Reinsert the NIC into its slot so that it is secure and replace the screw that holds it in.

12. Replace the computer's cover and the screws that fasten it to the CPU.

CASE PROJECTS

1. You are a networking professional who works in a college computer lab. The computers run only the TCP/IP protocol on an Ethernet network, and all computers use 3Com NICs. Many beginning computer science students use this lab for homework; you help them access the network and troubleshoot problems with their connections on a daily basis. One day a student begins tampering with his computer; when he restarts the computer, it alerts him that it can't find the network. In a step-by-step fashion, explain the approach you take to find and fix the problem.

   (Your drive letter may vary, depending on how you installed Windows 2000 Professional.)

2. The same student is curious about how a Web site appears on his computer screen. On a separate piece of paper, draw and explain the process that occurs between a client and a server when requesting a Web page, using the OSI Model as a reference. Explain to the student why each step is important and how it contributes to data arriving in the correct place without errors.

3. The student appreciates the time you spent explaining what happens to the data as it moves through the OSI Model layers, but he wonders why he should ever care about the OSI Model or data frames. He says he wants to become a network architect and concern himself with routers, switches, and cabling. The student indicates that he doesn't care about the little details like packets. In response, draw a picture of an Ethernet data frame and identify its fields. Describe how these fields can affect a network's design and networking in general.

3

NETWORK PROTOCOLS

After reading this chapter and completing the exercises, you will be able to:

➤ Identify the characteristics of TCP/IP, IPX/SPX, NetBIOS, and AppleTalk

➤ Understand the position of network protocols in the OSI Model

➤ Identify the core protocols of each protocol suite and its functions

➤ Understand each protocol's addressing scheme

➤ Install protocols on Windows 98 and Windows 2000 clients

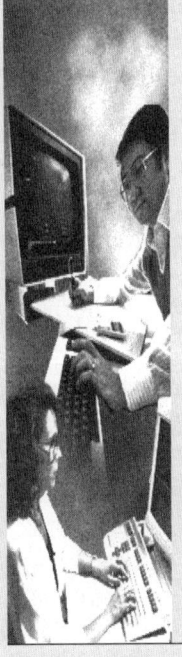

ON THE JOB

I work for a company that remotely monitors network environments for other companies. We gather statistics on everything from when a server goes down to when the humidity in a data center drops too low. We use this data to alert our clients to situations that may affect their networks and their bottom lines.

One evening our network monitoring system received a steady stream of alerts from one of our client's networks, indicating that something was wrong. Upon further investigation, I traced the alerts to a server that, for some reason, was not responding to requests. This server provided the main Web site for retail customers, so any downtime meant lost revenue for our client. I tried pinging the server by name, and indeed, it did not respond. Then I tried pinging its IP address, and I did receive a response—but not from the server. Instead, the response was from a workstation also located at the client site.

I called the client's network administrator and told him what I had discovered. He located the workstation that was responding to the IP address. Although this IP address was supposed to belong to the server, a new employee had inadvertently assigned his own workstation this IP address. Some time after the employee did so, the server had been rebooted and could not use its given IP address. Thus, it was not responding to any requests. The client's network administrator immediately disconnected the offending workstation from the network and rebooted the Web server so that it could once again use its correct IP address.

Roger DuRocher
Full Control Systems

As you learned in Chapter 1, a **protocol** is a rule that governs how networks communicate. Protocols define the standards for communication between network devices. Without protocols, devices could not interpret the signals sent by other devices, and data would go nowhere. Unfortunately, you cannot turn on a file server, add some clients, and expect the protocols to work their magic. Instead, you must first understand which protocol suits your network environment. Then you must install and configure protocols on file servers and clients and test your configuration.

In this chapter, you will learn about the most commonly used networking protocols, their components, and their functions. This chapter is not an exhaustive study of protocols, but rather a practical guide to applying them. At the end of the chapter, you will have the opportunity to read about some realistic networking scenarios pertaining to protocols and devise your own solutions. As protocols form the foundation of network communications, you must fully understand them to manage a network effectively.

INTRODUCTION TO PROTOCOLS

In Chapter 2, you learned about the tasks associated with each layer of the OSI Model. These tasks are actually carried out by network protocols. In the networking industry, the term "protocol" is often used to refer to a group, or suite, of individual protocols that work together. The protocols within a suite are assigned different tasks, such as data translation, data handling, error checking, and addressing; they correspond to different layers of the OSI Model. In the sections that follow, you will learn about the four major networking protocol suites—TCP/IP, IPX/SPX, NetBIOS, and AppleTalk—and see how their components correspond to the layers of the OSI Model. You must understand these protocols to qualify for Net+ certification. Pay particular attention to the TCP/IP discussions, because the Net+ certification exam emphasizes TCP/IP knowledge.

The protocol (or protocol suite) you use will depend on many factors, including the existing network operating environment, your organization's technical expertise, and your network's security and speed requirements. Protocols vary according to their speed, transmission efficiency, utilization of resources, ease of setup, compatibility, and ability to travel between one LAN segment and another. Protocols that can span more than one LAN segment are **routable**, because they carry Network layer and addressing information that can be interpreted by a router. Not all protocols are routable, however.

In addition to the size of the network, you will need to consider its interconnection requirements, data security needs, and the technical expertise of personnel who manage the network. Many networks use more than one kind of protocol because they have a mixed hardware or software infrastructure, so it is not only important to know about each protocol, but also to understand how they work together. A network that uses more than one protocol is called a **multiprotocol network**. Multiprotocol networks are common in businesses whose LANs are well established and have evolved from legacy systems to newer, more efficient networks.

As you read in this chapter about the most commonly used protocols, keep in mind that you may occasionally encounter additional protocols (such as SNA or DLC) on a network. The more flexible and robust protocols described in this chapter are gradually replacing these older protocols. TCP/IP is by far the most commonly used of the major protocols, followed by IPX/SPX, then NetBIOS and AppleTalk. In the next section, you'll begin by learning about the most popular of the four—TCP/IP.

TRANSMISSION CONTROL PROTOCOL/INTERNET PROTOCOL (TCP/IP)

3

TCP/IP is not simply one protocol, but rather a suite of small, specialized protocols—including TCP, IP, UDP, ARP, ICMP, and others—called **subprotocols**. Most network administrators refer to the entire group as "TCP/IP," or sometimes simply "IP." TCP/IP's roots lie with the U.S. Department of Defense, which developed the precursor to TCP/IP for its Advanced Research Projects Agency network (ARPAnet) in the late 1960s. Thanks to its low cost and its ability to communicate between a multitude of dissimilar platforms, TCP/IP has grown extremely popular. It is a de facto standard on the Internet and is fast becoming the protocol of choice on LANs. The latest network operating systems (such as NetWare 5.x and Windows 2000) use TCP/IP as their default protocol.

One of the greatest advantages to using TCP/IP relates to its status as a routable protocol, which means that it carries network addressing information that can be interpreted by routers. TCP/IP is also a flexible protocol, running on any combination of network operating systems or network media. Because of its flexibility, however, TCP/IP may require significant configuration.

TCP/IP is a broad topic with numerous theoretical, historical, and practical aspects. Because it is such an important protocol, it is covered in even more detail in Chapter 11. If you want to become an expert on TCP/IP, you should invest in a book or study guide solely devoted to this suite of protocols.

TCP/IP Compared to the OSI Model

The TCP/IP suite of protocols can be divided into four layers that roughly correspond to the seven layers of the OSI Model, as depicted in Figure 3-1 and described in the following list. (Unlike the OSI model, which was standardized by ISO, the TCP/IP model is an informal reference. Because there is no universal standard for the TCP/IP model, you may also find it represented as either five layers.)

OSI Model	TCP/IP Model
Application	Application
Presentation	Application
Session	Application
Transport	Transport
Network	Internet
Data Link	Network Interface
Physical	Network Interface

Figure 3-1   TCP/IP compared to the OSI Model

- *Application layer*—Roughly equivalent to the Application, Presentation, and Session layers of the OSI Model. Applications gain access to the network through this layer, via protocols such as the File Transfer Protocol (FTP), Trivial File Transfer Protocol (TFTP), Hypertext Transfer Protocol (HTTP), Simple Mail Transfer Protocol (SMTP), and Dynamic Host Configuration Protocol (DHCP).

- *Transport layer*—Roughly corresponds to the Transport layer of the OSI Model. This layer holds the Transmission Control Protocol (TCP) and User Datagram Protocol (UDP), which provide flow control, error checking, and sequencing. All service requests use one of these protocols.

- *Internet layer*—Equivalent to the Network layer of the OSI Model. This layer holds the Internet Protocol (IP), Internet Control Message Protocol (ICMP), Internet Group Message Protocol (IGMP), and Address Resolution Protocol (ARP). These protocols handle message routing and host address resolution.

- *Network Interface layer*—Roughly equivalent to the Data Link and Physical layers of the OSI Model. This layer handles the formatting of data and transmission to the network wire.

The TCP/IP Core Protocols

Certain subprotocols of the TCP/IP suite, called **TCP/IP core protocols**, operate in the Transport or Network layers of the OSI Model and provide basic services to the protocols in other layers of the four-layer model. As you might guess, TCP and IP are the most significant core protocols in the TCP/IP suite. These, plus some other core protocols are discussed below.

Internet Protocol (IP)

The **Internet Protocol (IP)** belongs to the Internet layer of the TCP/IP Model and provides information about how and where data should be delivered. IP is the subprotocol that enables TCP/IP to **internetwork**—that is, to traverse more than one LAN segment and more than one type of network through a router. In an internetwork, the individual networks that are joined together are called subnetworks, or **subnets**. Using subnets is an important part of TCP/IP networking.

 The following sections describe the IP subprotocol as it is used in IP version 4 (IPv4), the original version that was used for nearly 20 years and is still used by most networks today. A newer version of the IP subprotocol, called IP version 6 (IPv6), will soon replace IPv4.

The IP portion of a data frame is called an **IP datagram**. The IP datagram acts as an envelope for data and contains information necessary for routers to transfer data between subnets. The length of the IP datagram including its header and data cannot exceed 65,535 bytes. The components of an IPv4 IP datagram header are described in the following list and depicted in Figure 3-2.

■ *Version*—Identifies the version number of the protocol. The receiving work-station looks at this field first to determine whether it can read the incoming data. If it cannot, it will reject the packet. Rejection rarely occurs, however, because most TCP/IP networks use IP version 4 (IPv4). A more sophisticated IP version, called IP version 6 (IPv6), has been developed and will be implemented in coming years.

■ *Internet header length (IHL)*—Identifies the number of 4-byte (or 32-bit) blocks in the IP header. The most common header length comprises five groupings, as the minimum length of an IP header is 20 4-byte blocks. This field is important because it indicates to the receiving node where data will begin (immediately after the header ends).

■ *Type of service (ToS)*—Tells IP how to process the incoming datagram by indicating the data's speed, priority, or reliability.

■ *Total length*—Identifies the total length of the IP datagram, including the header and data, in bytes.

■ *Identification*—Identifies the message to which a datagram belongs and enables the receiving node to reassemble fragmented, or segmented, messages. This field and the following two fields, flags and fragment offset, assist in segmentation and reassembly of packets.

■ *Flags: don't fragment (DF) or more fragments (MF)*—Indicates whether a message is fragmented and, if it is fragmented, whether the datagram is the last in the fragment.

■ *Fragment offset*—Identifies where the datagram fragment belongs in the incoming set of fragments.

■ *Time to live (TTL)*—Indicates the maximum time, in seconds, that a datagram can remain on the network before it is discarded. TTL also corresponds to number of router hops that a datagram can go through; each time a datagram passes through a machine, another second is taken off its TTL, regardless of whether the machine took a whole second to process the data.

■ *Protocol*—Identifies the type of Transport layer protocol that will receive the datagram (for example, TCP or UDP).

■ *Header checksum*—Determines whether the IP header has been corrupted.

■ *Source IP address*—Identifies the full IP address of the source node.

■ *Destination IP address*—Indicates the full IP address of the destination node.

■ *Options*—May contain optional routing and timing information.

■ *Padding*—Contains filler information to ensure that the header is a multiple of 32 bits. The size of this field may vary.

■ *Data*—Includes the data originally sent by the source node, plus TCP information.

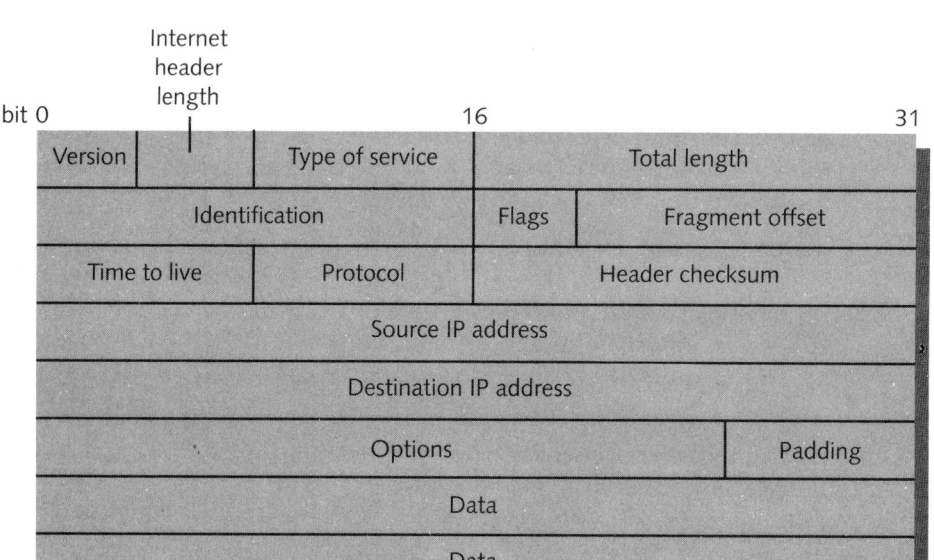

Figure 3-2   Components of an IP datagram

IP is an unreliable, **connectionless** protocol, which means that it does not guarantee delivery of data. Higher-level protocols of the TCP/IP suite, however, can use IP information to ensure that data packets are delivered to the right addresses. Note that the IP datagram does contain one checksum component, the header checksum, which verifies only the integrity of the routing information in the IP header. If the checksum accompanying the message does not have the proper value when the packet is received, then the packet is presumed to be corrupt and is discarded; at that point, a new packet is sent.

Transmission Control Protocol (TCP)

The **Transmission Control Protocol (TCP)** belongs to the Transport layer of the TCP/IP suite and provides reliable data delivery services. TCP is a **connection–oriented** subprotocol, which means that a connection must be established between communicating nodes before this protocol will transmit data. TCP sits on top of the IP subprotocol and compensates for IP's reliability deficiencies by providing checksum, flow control, and sequencing information. If an application relied only on IP to transmit data, IP would send packets indiscriminately, without checking whether the destination node is offline, for example, or whether the data becomes corrupt during transmission. TCP, on the other hand, contains several components that ensure data reliability. The fields of the **TCP segment**, the entity that becomes encapsulated by the IP datagram, are described in the following list. Figure 3-3 depicts a TCP segment and its fields.

- *Source port*—Indicates the port number at the source node. A **port** is the address on a host where an application makes itself available to incoming data. One example of a port is port 80, which is typically used to accept Web page requests. You will learn more about ports in Chapter 11.

- *Destination port*—Indicates the port number at the destination node.

- *Sequence number*—Identifies the data segment's position in the stream of data segments already sent.

- *Acknowledgment number (ACK)*—Confirms receipt of the data via a return message to the sender.

- *TCP header length*—Indicates the length of the TCP header.

- *Codes*—Includes flags that signal special conditions—for example, if a message is urgent, or if the source node wants to request a connection or terminate a connection.

- *Sliding-window size*—Indicates how many blocks of data the receiving machine can accept.

- *Checksum*—Allows the receiving node to determine whether the TCP segment became corrupted during transmission.

- *Urgent pointer*—Can indicate a location in the data where urgent data resides.

- *Options*—Used to specify special options.

- *Padding*—Contains filler information to ensure that the size of the TCP header is a multiple of 32 bits.

- *Data*—Contains data originally sent by the source node.

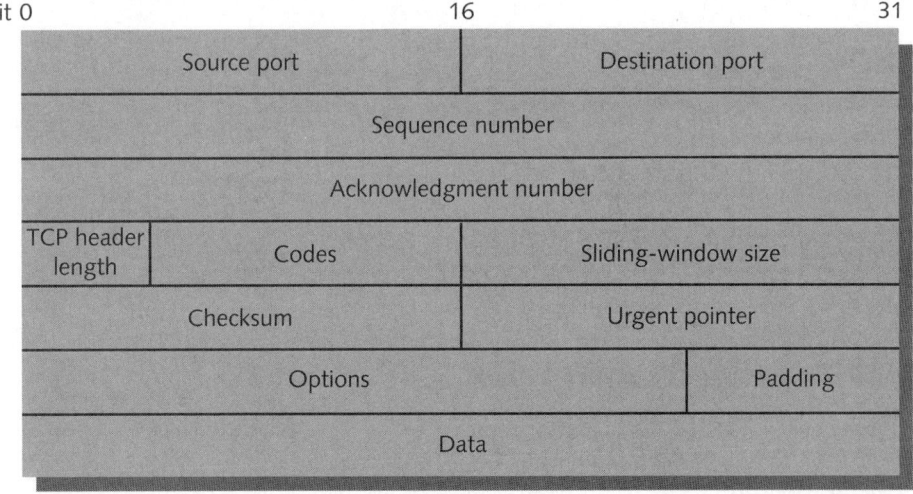

Figure 3-3   A TCP segment

User Datagram Protocol (UDP)

The **User Datagram Protocol (UDP)**, like TCP, sits in the Transport layer, between the Internet layer and the Application layer of the TCP/IP model. Unlike TCP, however, UDP is a connectionless transport service. UDP offers no assurance that packets will be received in the correct sequence. In fact, this protocol does not guarantee that the packets will be received at all. Furthermore, it provides no error checking or sequence numbering. Nevertheless, UDP's lack of sophistication makes it more efficient than TCP and renders it useful in situations where data must be transferred quickly, such as live audio or video transmissions over the Internet. In these cases, TCP—with its acknowledgments, checksums, and flow control mechanisms—would add too much overhead to the transmission and bog it down. In contrast to TCP's 10 fields, the UDP header contains only four fields: source port, destination port, length, and checksum.

Internet Control Message Protocol (ICMP)

Whereas IP ensures that packets reach the correct destination, **Internet Control Message Protocol (ICMP)** notifies the sender when something goes wrong in the transmission process and the packets are not delivered. ICMP sits between IP and TCP in the Internet layer of the TCP/IP model and does not provide error control. Instead, it simply reports which networks are unreachable and which packets have been discarded because the allotted time for their delivery (their TTL) expired. ICMP is used by diagnostic utilities such as PING and TRACERT, which are described in Chapter 11.

Address Resolution Protocol (ARP)

Address Resolution Protocol (ARP) is an Internet layer protocol that obtains the MAC (physical) address of a host, or node, then creates a local database that maps the MAC address to the host's IP (logical) address. ARP works very closely with IP, because IP must have the address of a destination host before it can direct data to it. If one host needs to know the MAC address of another host on the same subnet, the first host sends a broadcast message to the network through ARP that essentially says, "Will the computer with the IP address AA.BB.CC.DD please send me its MAC address?" The host on the local subnet that has the IP address AA.BB.CC.DD then broadcasts a reply that contains the physical address of the destination host. To make ARP more efficient, computers save recognized IP-to-MAC address mappings in a cache, so they don't have to broadcast redundant requests.

The TCP/IP Application Layer Protocols

In addition to the core Transport and Internet layer protocols, TCP/IP encompasses several Application layer protocols. These protocols work over TCP or UDP and IP, translating user requests into a format the network can read. The following list describes the most commonly used Application layer protocols:

- *Telnet*—A terminal emulation protocol used to log on to remote hosts using the TCP/IP protocol suite. Often Telnet is used to connect two dissimilar systems (such as PCs and UNIX machines). Through Telnet, you can control a remote host over LANs and WANs such as the Internet. For example, network managers can use Telnet to log on to their company's routers from home and modify the router's configuration.

■ *File Transfer Protocol (FTP)*—A protocol used to send and receive files via TCP/IP. FTP is a client/server protocol in which the host running the FTP server portion accepts commands from another host running the FTP client portion. It comes with a set of very simple commands that make up its user interface.

■ *Simple Mail Transfer Protocol (SMTP)*—The protocol responsible for moving messages from one e-mail server to another over the Internet and other TCP/IP-based networks. SMTP uses a simple request-and-response mechanism to move messages and relies upon more sophisticated protocols, such as the Post Office Protocol (POP), to keep track of storing and forwarding messages.

■ *Simple Network Management Protocol (SNMP)*—A communication protocol used to manage devices on a TCP/IP network. To use SNMP, each device on the network runs an agent that collects information about that device. SNMP transports the collected information to a central database. Many network management programs use SNMP.

You will learn about more Application layer TCP/IP protocols in Chapter 11.

Addressing in TCP/IP

As you learned in Chapter 1, each node on a network must have a unique identifying number called an address. You have also learned that networks recognize two kinds of addresses: logical and physical (or MAC) addresses. MAC addresses are assigned to a device's network interface card at the factory by its manufacturer, but logical addresses depend on rules set by the protocol standards. In the TCP/IP protocol suite, IP is the core protocol responsible for logical addressing. For this reason, addresses on TCP/IP networks are sometimes called "**IP addresses**." IP addresses are assigned and used according to very specific parameters.

Each IP address is a unique 32-bit number, divided into four **octets**, or 8-bit bytes, that are separated by periods. An example of a valid IP address is 144.92.43.178. An IP address contains two types of information: network and host. The first octet identifies the network class. Three types of network classes exist: Class A, Class B, and Class C. Table 3-1 summarizes the three commonly used classes of TCP/IP networks.

Table 3-1   Commonly used TCP/IP classes

Network Class	Beginning Octet	Number of Networks	Host Addresses per Network
A	1–126	126	16,777,214
B	128–191	>16,000	65,534
C	192–223	>2,000,000	254

Although 8 bits have 256 possible combinations, only the numbers 1 through 254 can be used to identify networks and hosts. The numbers 0 and 255 are reserved for **broadcasts**, or transmissions to all stations on a network.

All nodes on a Class A network share the first octet of their IP numbers, a number between 1 and 126. Nodes on a Class B network share the first two octets, and their IP addresses begin with a number between 128 and 191. Class C network IP numbers share the first three octets, with their first octet being a number between 192 and 223. For example, nodes with the following IP addresses may belong to the same Class A network: 23.78.110.109, 23.164.32.97, 23.48.112.43, and 23.108.37.22. Nodes with the following IP addresses may belong to the same Class B network: 168.34.88.29, 168.34.55.41, 168.34.73.49, and 168.34.205.113. Nodes with the following addresses may belong to the same Class C network: 204.139.118.7, 204.139.118.54, 204.139.118.14, and 204.139.118.31.

Because only 126 Class A networks are available on the Internet, most Class A networks have already been reserved by large corporations or governments. In addition, some IP addresses are reserved for network functions, like broadcasts, and cannot be assigned to machines or devices. Notice that 127 is not a valid first octet for any IP number. The range of addresses beginning with 127 is reserved for loopback information, with the IP address 127.0.0.1 being called a **loopback address**. When you try to contact this IP number, you are actually communicating with your own machine. This address can prove useful when you must troubleshoot problems with a workstation's TCP/IP communications. If you receive a positive response from the loopback test, you know that the TCP/IP protocols are installed and in use on your workstation.

To ensure that every Internet-connected device has a unique IP address, organizations across the globe rely on centralized authorities. In early Internet history, a non-profit group called the **Internet Assigned Numbers Authority (IANA)** kept records of available and reserved IP addresses and determined how addresses were doled out. Starting in 1997, IANA coordinated its efforts with three **Regional Internet Registries (RIRs)**: ARIN (American Registry for Internet Numbers), APNIC (Asia Pacific Network Information Centre), and RIPE (Réseaux IP Européens). An RIR is a not-for-profit agency that manages the distribution of IP addresses to private and public entities. In the late 1990s, the U.S. Department of Commerce, which funded IANA, decided to overhaul IP addressing and domain name management. The DOC recommended the formation of the **Internet Corporation for Assigned Names and Numbers (ICANN)**, a private, non-profit corporation. ICANN is now ultimately responsible for IP addressing and domain name management. Technically speaking, however, IANA continues to perform the system administration.

Individuals and businesses typically obtain IP addresses from their ISPs. An ISP, in turn, arranges with its RIR for the right to use certain IP addresses on its network. The RIR would have obtained its right to dole out those addresses from ICANN. In addition, the RIR would have coordinated with IANA to ensure that the addresses are associated with devices connected to the ISP's network. Alternatively, if a business's network sits behind a firewall, the administrator could devise her own IP addressing scheme without adhering to ICANN standards. A **firewall** is a specialized computer (often a type of router) that selectively filters or blocks traffic between networks. It is commonly used to protect businesses with a presence on the Web. (You will learn more about firewalls and other network security measures in Chapter 15.) For example, you could use a firewall to protect the Jan's Jams network from security breaches related to e-commerce transactions on its Web site. A firewall isolates the network from the Internet at large. As a result, valid IP addresses aren't required within the network. If your office machines aren't really using valid IP addresses, however, how will your staff get through the firewall and onto the Internet? When staff members request access to machines outside your office LAN, they must be assigned valid Internet IP addresses at the firewall.

Isolating a network behind a firewall and then using your own address scheme provide useful management benefits. (For example, if you ran a large LAN, you could assign all machines on the third floor of an office building addresses beginning with 10.3.) In addition, this scheme allows an organization to use more IP addresses than it could if it assigned ICANN-sanctioned numbers to each machine.

A secondary number, known as a subnet mask, is also assigned as part of the TCP/IP configuration process. A subnet mask allows large networks to be subdivided into smaller subnetworks known as subnets. The subnet mask identifies to the network software which addresses appear on the same local network and which addresses need to be contacted through a router. Subnetting is a complex, but highly useful aspect of TCP/IP networking. Chapter 11 explains subnetting in more detail.

Recall from Chapter 1 that a host is any machine on a network that enables resource sharing. All individual computers connected through a TCP/IP network can be called **hosts**. This idea represents a slightly different interpretation of the term "host," because probably not all computers on a TCP/IP network will facilitate resource sharing (though theoretically, they could).

IP address data are sent across the network in binary form, with each of the four octets consisting of eight bits. For example, the IP address 131.127.3.22 is the same as the binary number 10000011 01111111 00000011 00010110. Converting from the dotted decimal notation to binary number is a simple process when you use a scientific calculator, such as the one available with the Windows 2000 operating system.

To convert the first octet (131) of the IP address above to a binary number:

1. On a Windows 2000 computer, click **Start**, point to **Programs**, point to **Accessories**, then click **Calculator**.
2. Click **View**, then click **Scientific**. Make sure that the **Dec option button** is selected.
3. Type **131**, then click the **Bin option button**. The binary equivalent of the number 131, 10000011, appears in the display window.

You can reverse this process to convert a binary number to a decimal number.

Every host on a network must have a unique number, as duplicate addresses will cause problems on a network. If you add a host to a network and its IP address is already in use by another host on the subnet, an error message will be generated on the new client and its TCP/IP services will be disabled. The existing host may also receive an error message, but can continue to function normally.

You can assign IP addresses manually, by modifying the client workstation's TCP/IP properties. A manually assigned IP address is called a **static IP address** because it does not change automatically. It changes only when you reconfigure the client's TCP/IP properties. Alternatively, you can have IP addresses assigned automatically through the **Dynamic Host Configuration Protocol (DHCP)**, an Application layer protocol in the TCP/IP suite. Most networks provide the capability of dynamically assigning IP addresses.

You must take care to avoid assigning duplicate addresses. For example, suppose you spend an afternoon manually assigning IP addresses to 50 Windows 2000 Professional machines in a computer lab. After the forty-eighth machine, you feel tired and mistakenly give the same IP address, 198.5.77.207, to machines 49 and 50. The next day, a student uses computer 49 to pick up her e-mail. A few minutes later, a student turns on computer 50. When he tries to connect to the network, he receives an error message effectively saying that "IP address 198.5.77.207 is being used by 08-AF-82-01-44-CE," where 08-AF-82-01-44-CE is the MAC address of computer 49. The student at computer 50 cannot proceed until either computer 49 is shut down or changes its IP address or until he changes the IP address of computer 50.

Using a DHCP server to assign IP addresses can almost completely eliminate duplicate-addressing problems. (DHCP is described in detail in Chapter 11.) You can envision DHCP as a kind of resource manager for IP addresses. To understand how it works, think of how a health club attendant might hand out towels. When you arrive at the club, the attendant at the desk hands you a towel. You don't care which towel it is, because all towels are the same. You use the towel while you're at the club, then return it when you no longer need it. While you have possession of the towel, no one else can use it. Once you return the towel, it will be returned to the group of towels that the attendant might hand out to other health club members.

Both Windows 2000 and Windows 98 workstations allow users to view their current IP addresses. To view your current IP information on a Windows 98 workstation connected to a network:

1. Click **Start**, then click **Run**. The Run dialog box opens.

2. Type **winipcfg** in the Open text box.

3. Click **OK**. An IP Configuration window containing four numbers appears. The IP address appears second in the list of numbers.

4. To view more information about your network addressing, click the **More Info** button at the lower-right corner of the IP Configuration window. A larger IP

Configuration window appears, as shown in Figure 3-4. Some examples of additional information you can find are the host name, DNS server and DHCP server address.

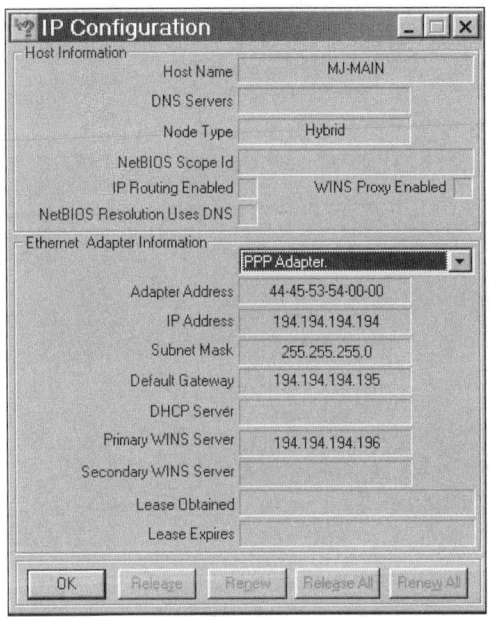

Figure 3-4   An example of an IP Configuration window

    5. Click **OK** to close the IP Configuration window.

To view your current IP address from a workstation running Windows 2000:

    1. Click **Start**, then click **Run**. The Run dialog box opens.

    2. In the Open text box, type **command**, then click **OK**. The Command Prompt window opens.

    3. At the DOS prompt, type **ipconfig /all**. Your workstation's IP address information is displayed, similar to the information shown in Figure 3-5.

In addition to using IP addresses, TCP/IP networks use names for networks and hosts, so as to make them more easily identifiable to humans. Each host (computer on a TCP/IP network) requires a host name. Each network must have a network name, also known as a **domain name**. If, while viewing the IP configuration window on your Windows 98 workstation, you click the More Info button, you would see your workstation's host name and domain name in the very first field at the top of the IP configuration window, under the Host Information section.

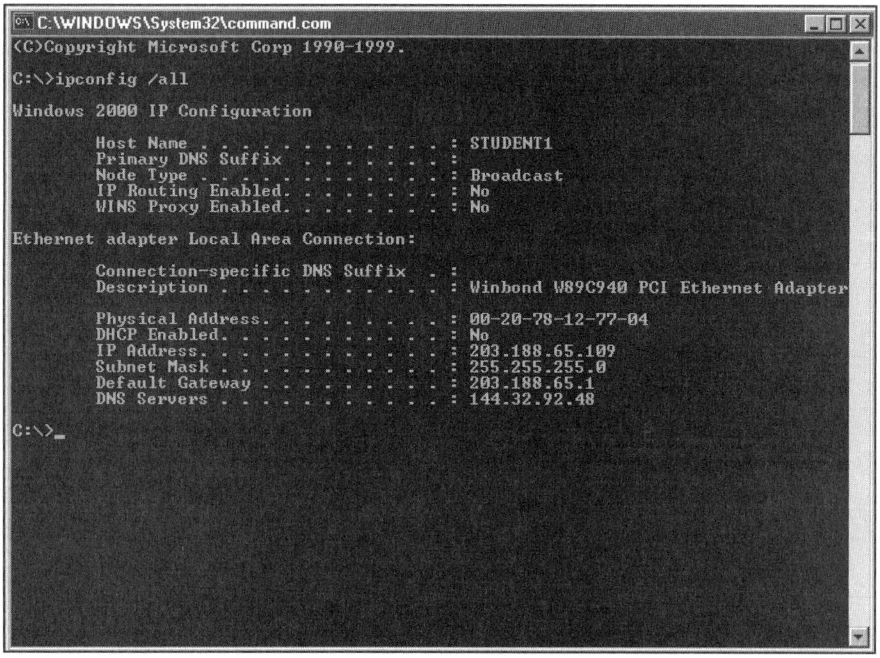

Figure 3-5   IP address information on a Windows 2000 workstation

Together, the host name and domain name constitute the **fully qualified domain name (FQDN).** For example, your host name might be student1 while your domain name is sacc.tec.ca.us. Therefore, your fully qualified domain name would be student1.sacc.tec.ca.us. Other users on a TCP/IP network, such as the Internet, would identify you by this name, and other machines would associate your IP address with this name. Your host name, "student1," is a field the network administrator configures on the computer (see the Installing Protocols section later in this chapter). The rest of the name, "sacc.tec.ca.us," is the network's domain name. Domain names must follow strict rules and depend on a domain name server to resolve network addresses with the domain name assigned to them.

Chapter 11 covers TCP/IP naming services in more detail. For now, it is enough to know that every node on a TCP/IP network requires a unique host name plus a domain name to communicate over the Internet.

IPX/SPX

Internetwork Packet Exchange/Sequenced Packet Exchange (IPX/SPX) is a protocol originally developed by Xerox, then modified and adopted by Novell in the 1980s for its NetWare network operating system. IPX/SPX is required to ensure the interoperability of LANs running NetWare versions 3.2 and lower and can be used with LANs running higher versions of the NetWare operating system. Other network operating systems, such as Windows 2000, and workstation operating systems, such as

Windows 98, can use IPX/SPX to internetwork with Novell NetWare systems. In the Windows 2000 network operating system, IPX/SPX is called NWLink.

IPX/SPX, like TCP/IP, is a combination of protocols that reside at different layers of the OSI Model. Also like TCP/IP, IPX/SPX carries network addressing information, so it is routable.

IPX/SPX Compared to the OSI Model

IPX/SPX contains a number of subprotocols that belong to different layers of the OSI Model. It does not contain as many subprotocols as TCP/IP, however. For this reason, it is not typically assigned its own model of communications. The IPX/SPX subprotocols roughly correspond to the OSI Model as shown in Figure 3-6. Notice that IPX corresponds to the Network layer of the OSI Model and SPX corresponds to the Transport layer. Later in this chapter, you will be introduced to the higher-level IPX/SPX protocols, including NCP, SAP, and RIP.

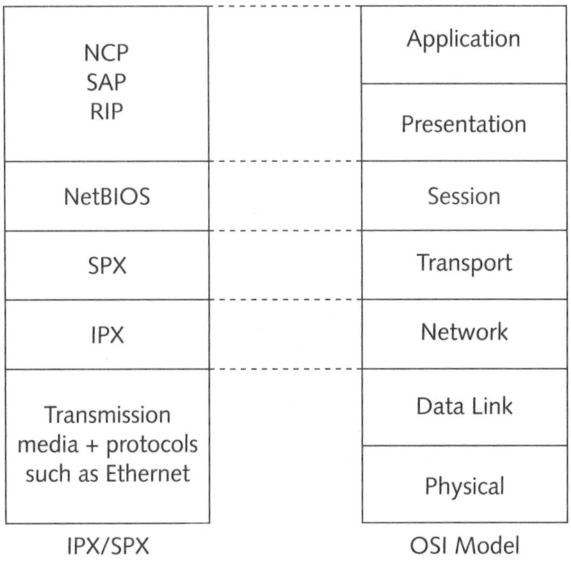

IPX/SPX	OSI Model
NCP SAP RIP	Application
	Presentation
NetBIOS	Session
SPX	Transport
IPX	Network
Transmission media + protocols such as Ethernet	Data Link
	Physical

Figure 3-6   IPX/SPX compared to the OSI Model

IPX/SPX Core Protocols

The core protocols of IPX/SPX provide services at the Transport and Network layers of the OSI Model. As you might guess, the most important subprotocols are IPX and SPX. These and other core protocols are explained following.

IPX

Internetwork Packet Exchange (IPX) operates at the Network layer of the OSI Model and provides routing and internetwork services, similar to IP in the TCP/IP suite. Like IP, IPX also uses datagrams to transport data. IPX is a connectionless service because it does not require a session to be established before it transmits, and it does not guarantee that data will be delivered in sequence or without errors. In summary, it is an efficient subprotocol with limited capabilities. All IPX/SPX communication relies upon IPX, however, and upper-layer protocols handle the functions that IPX cannot perform. The elements of an IPX datagram are described in the following list, and its structure is illustrated in Figure 3-7.

- *Checksum*—Provides integrity checking for the IPX datagram, or packet.

- *Packet length*—Identifies the length of the complete IPX packet in bytes.

- *Transport control*—Tracks the number of routers that a packet has passed through (similar to the TTL parameter in IP). IPX/SPX packets are discarded by the sixteenth router they encounter.

- *Packet type*—Defines the service offered or required by the packet.

- *Destination Network*—Indicates the network address of the destination network.

- *Destination node address*—Indicates the node address of the destination node (that is, its MAC address).

- *Destination socket*—Refers to the process address on the destination node. A **socket** is a logical address assigned to a specific process running on a computer. Some sockets are reserved for operating system functions.

- *Source network*—Indicates the network address of the source network.

- *Source node address*—Indicates the node address of the source node, equivalent to its MAC address.

- *Source socket*—Indicates the socket address of the process running on the source node.

- *Data*—Contains data originally sent by the source and the SPX packet.

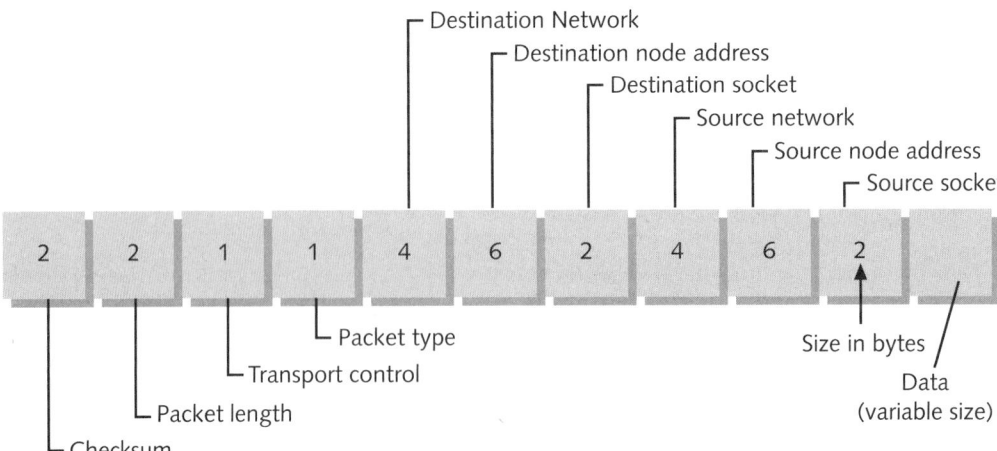

Figure 3-7   Components of an IPX datagram

SPX

Sequenced Packet Exchange (SPX) belongs to the Transport layer of the OSI Model. It works in tandem with IPX to ensure that data are received whole, in sequence, and error free. SPX, like TCP in the TCP/IP suite, is a connection-oriented protocol and therefore must verify that a session has been established with the destination node before it will transmit data. It can detect whether a packet was not received in its entirety. If it discovers a packet has been lost or corrupted, SPX will resend the packet.

The SPX information is enveloped by IPX. That is, its fields sit inside the data field of the IPX datagram, as depicted in Figure 3-8.

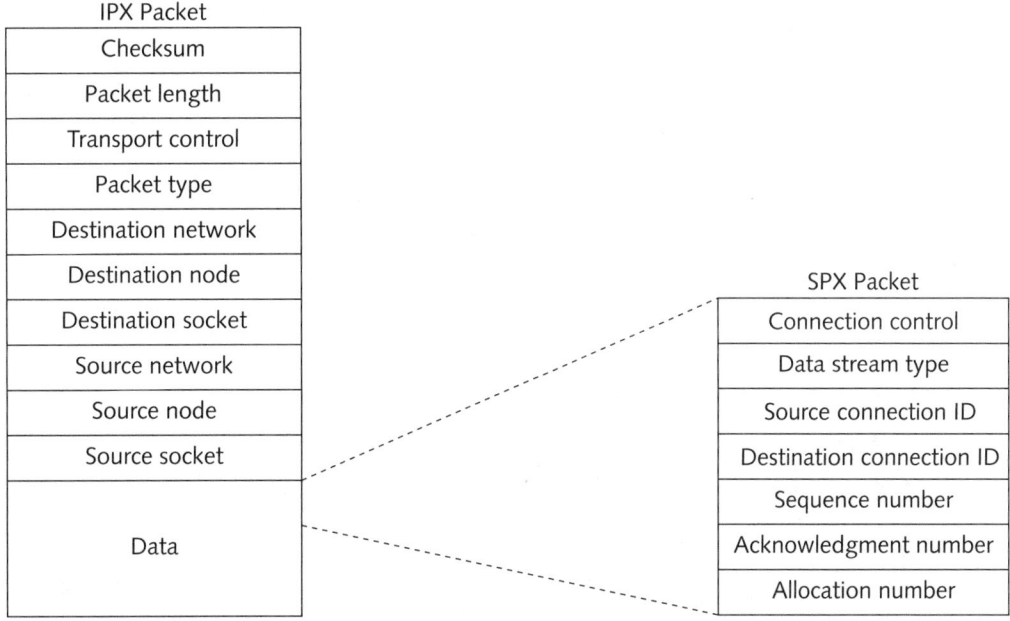

Figure 3-8   SPX packet encapsulated by an IPX packet

The SPX packet, like the TCP segment, contains a number of fields to ensure data reliability. An SPX packet consists of a 42-byte header followed by 0 to 534 bytes of data. An SPX packet can be as small as 42 bytes (the size of its header) or as large as 576 bytes. The following list describes each field in an SPX packet and its function:

- *Connection control*—Indicates whether the packet is a system or application packet.

- *Data stream type*—Indicates the type of data found in the packet—for example, whether the packet is the beginning or the end of a data stream.

- *Source connection ID*—Identifies the source node.

- *Destination connection ID*—Identifies the destination node.

- *Sequence number*—Indicates the number of packets exchanged in one direction on the connection.

- *Acknowledgment number*—Identifies the sequence number of the next packet that an SPX connection expects to receive.

- *Allocation number*—Used to manage flow control between communicating applications.

Service Advertising Protocol (SAP)

The **Service Advertising Protocol (SAP)** works in the Application, Presentation, and Session layers of the OSI Model and runs directly over IPX. NetWare servers and routers use SAP to advertise to the entire network which services they can provide. For example, a server that functions as a print server might use SAP to effectively announce to every node on the network, "I'm available to help you print." By default, SAP broadcasts occur every 60 seconds. Because SAP uses the broadcast mode to transmit its information, it may generate a great deal of unnecessary traffic on the network, slowing down other, more important transmissions. One way to reduce this traffic is to increase the time between SAP broadcasts from 60 seconds to a few minutes.

Once devices have advertised their availability through SAP, SAP servers maintain a database of device names correlated with their IPX addresses. When a client needs to request a service from a particular device, the client queries the SAP database and the database then provides the IPX address for the desired device. In this way, the protocol frees users from having to know the IPX addresses of other servers and workstations on their network.

On networks that use NetWare Directory Services (NDS), which is discussed in detail in Chapter 9, SAP may not be necessary because NDS will point clients to the necessary service. For example, rather than having a server advertise through SAP every 60 seconds that it can perform printer services, NDS can point clients directly to that server when the client needs to print.

NetWare Core Protocol (NCP)

The **NetWare Core Protocol (NCP)** handles requests for services, such as printing and file access, between clients and servers. NCP works over IPX and within the Presentation and Session layers of the OSI Model. In essence, NCP acts as a translator between the workstation's operating system and the NetWare operating system. It uses a request-and-response mechanism to accomplish its translation; that is, once a client asks it to request a service, it notifies the server that a request is pending. NCP then waits for the server to acknowledge the request before it allows the workstation to transmit data. Although this exchange results in high reliability, it also generates extra traffic and may add to congestion on networks, such as WANs, that use routers.

Addressing in IPX/SPX

Maintaining network addresses for clients running IPX/SPX is easier than maintaining addresses for TCP/IP networks, because IPX/SPX networks primarily rely on the MAC address for each workstation (although addressing for IPX/SPX servers can be somewhat more complex). Just as with TCP/IP networks, IPX/SPX networks require that each node on a network be assigned a unique address to avoid communication conflicts. Because IPX is the component of the protocol that handles addressing, addresses on an IPX/SPX network are called **IPX addresses**. IPX addresses contain two parts: the network address (also known as the **external network number**) and the node address.

The network administrator establishes a network address when installing the NetWare operating system software on a server. The network address must be an 8-bit hexadecimal address, which means that each of its bits can have a value of either 0–9 or A–F. An example of a valid network address is 000008A2. The network address then becomes the first part of the IPX address on all nodes that use the particular server as their primary server.

> The address 00000000 is a null value and cannot be used as a network address. The address FFFFFFFF is a broadcast address and also cannot be assigned as a network address.

The second part of an IPX address, the node address, is equal to the network device's MAC address. Because every network interface card should have a unique MAC address, no possibility of duplicating IPX addresses exists under this system. In addition, the use of MAC addresses means that you need not configure addresses for the IPX/SPX protocol on each client workstation. Instead, they are already defined by the NIC. Adding a MAC address to the network address example used previously, a complete IPX address for a workstation on the network might be 000008A2:0060973E97F3.

Imagine you are the administrator for a building's NetWare 3.11 network with one server and 40 connected workstations, plus five printers. Your network is connected to six other networks on a large corporate campus. A colleague alerts you that one of the Accounting department's four workstations is generating excessive error messages. You need to determine the malfunctioning workstation's IPX address before you can disconnect it from the server. Because you installed the network originally, you know that your network address is 0000AAAA. The workstation's address must therefore begin with 0000AAAA (addresses for workstations coming from networks elsewhere on campus will begin with a different sequence). You also know that the Accounting department's computers contain NICs manufactured by Compaq. You look up the manufacturer's Ethernet code (the first part of the MAC address) and find that it is 00805F. In the list of currently attached workstations, you find only one IPX address that matches the pattern beginning with 0000AAAA:00805F—a machine with the full address of 0000AAAA:00805F059822. You can correctly assume that it is the faulty Accounting workstation.

In addition to the network and node addresses, processes running on IPX-enabled workstations are identified by socket addresses. When a process needs to communicate on the network, it requests that a socket number be assigned to it. Any packets addressed to that socket are passed on to the corresponding process. This approach enables nodes to route communications between their own sockets. An example of a socket address is 456h; Novell has reserved this particular socket for its diagnostics process. Socket addresses are appended to IPX addresses, so an example of a complete IPX address for a socket would be 000008A2:0060973E97F3:456h.

To view your Windows 98 or Windows 2000 workstation's IPX address while connected to a NetWare server running version 4.0 or higher:

1. Click **Start**, then click **Run**. The Run dialog box opens.

2. In the Open text box, type **command**, then click **OK**. The Command Prompt window opens.

3. Change directories to a drive letter you have mapped to the network (for example, typing the command F: will work on most networks.)

4. At the DOS prompt, type **nlist user-XXXXX /a** where "XXXXX" is your NetWare logon ID. (The nlist command in NetWare is a listing command, while user defines the kind of information that you want to list and the /a parameter indicates that you want to see the address for the specified user.) As a result of this command, you see the user ID you specified along with its corresponding IPX address.

To view your Windows 98 or Windows 2000 workstation's IPX address while connected to a NetWare server running a version lower than 4.0:

1. Click **Start**, then click **Run**. The Run dialog box opens.

2. In the Open text box, type **command**, then click **OK**. The Command Prompt window opens.

3. At the DOS prompt, type **userlist user=XXXXX /a** where XXXXX is your NetWare logon ID. In NetWare versions lower than 4.0, the userlist command performs the same function as the nlist command in NetWare versions 4.0 and higher. You see the user ID you specified along with its corresponding IPX address.

NETBIOS AND NETBEUI

NetBIOS (Network Basic Input Output System) is a protocol originally designed for IBM to provide Transport and Session layer services for applications running on small, homogenous networks. Early versions of NetBIOS did not specify a standard Transport layer frame, and networks that used NetBIOS were not necessarily compatible. However, when Microsoft adopted IBM's NetBIOS as its foundation protocol—initially for networks using LAN Manager or Windows for Workgroups—it added a standard framing component called the **NetBIOS Enhanced User Interface** (**NetBEUI**; pronounced, "net-bóo-ee"). On small networks, NetBEUI is a fast and efficient protocol that consumes few network resources, provides excellent error correction, and requires little configuration. It can support only 254 connections, however, and does not allow for good security. Furthermore, because NetBEUI frames include only Data Link layer (or MAC) addresses and not Network layer addresses, it is not routable. On the other hand, because NetBEUI does not use Network layer headers and trailers, it operates more efficiently. If necessary, NetBEUI can be encapsulated by other protocols, such as TCP/IP, then routed, but in many cases, the preferred method would be to migrate a NetBEUI network to a network running TCP/IP. Thus, this protocol is not suitable for large networks. Today NetBEUI is most commonly used in small Microsoft-based networks to integrate legacy, peer-to-peer networks. In newer Microsoft-based networks, TCP/IP has become the protocol of choice because it is more flexible and scalable than NetBEUI.

NetBIOS and NetBEUI Compared to the OSI Model

Because neither NetBIOS nor NetBEUI provides services at all layers of the OSI Model, both are commonly paired with other protocol suites, such as IPX/SPX or TCP/IP when placed in the OSI Model. Figure 3-9 shows how NetBIOS and NetBEUI fit into the OSI Model.

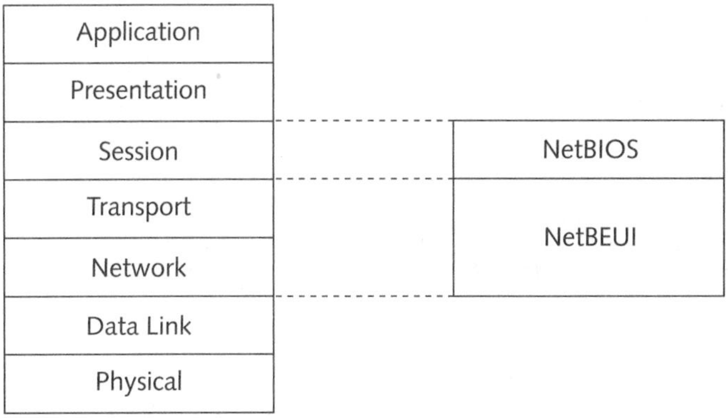

Figure 3-9   NetBIOS/NetBEUI compared to the OSI Model

NetBIOS Addressing

You have learned that NetBIOS does not contain a Network layer and therefore cannot be routed. To transmit data between network nodes, however, NetBIOS needs to reach each workstation. For this reason, network administrators must assign a NetBIOS name to each workstation. The NetBIOS name can consist of any combination of 16 or fewer alphanumeric characters (the only exception is that you cannot begin a NetBIOS name with an asterisk). Once NetBIOS has found a workstation's NetBIOS name, it will discover the workstation's MAC address and then use this address in further communications with the workstation. For example, a valid NetBIOS name is MY_COMPUTER. You might use NetBIOS names when troubleshooting problems on a NetBIOS network.

On networks running both TCP/IP and NetBIOS, it is simplest to make the NetBIOS name identical to the TCP/IP host name.

To view the NetBIOS name of a computer running the Windows 2000 operating system:

1. Click **Start**, point to **Settings**, then click **Control Panel**. The Control Panel window opens.

2. Double-click the **System** Icon. The System Properties dialog box opens.

3. Click the **Network Identification** tab. As shown in Figure 3-10, the first item in the Identification tab is the full computer name. The full computer name is the same as the workstation's NetBIOS name.

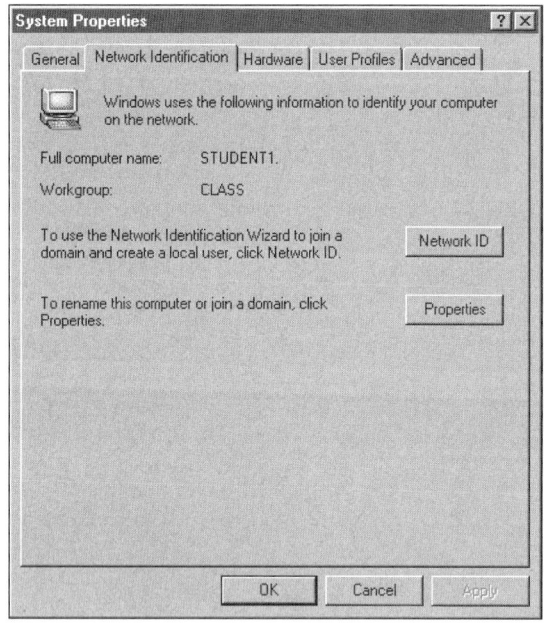

Figure 3-10   Network Identification tab in the System Properties dialog box

APPLETALK

Businesses and institutions involved in art or education, such as advertising agencies, elementary schools, and graphic designers, often use Apple Macintosh computers. **AppleTalk** is the protocol suite used to interconnect Macintosh computers. Although AppleTalk was originally designed to support peer-to-peer networking among

Macintoshes, it can now be routed between network segments and integrated with NetWare- or Microsoft-based networks.

An AppleTalk network is separated into logical groups of computers called **AppleTalk zones**. Each network can contain multiple zones, but each node can belong to only one zone. AppleTalk zones enable users to share file and printer resources on one another's Macintoshes. Zone names are not subject to the same strict naming conventions that TCP/IP and IPX/SPX networks must follow. Instead, zone names typically describe a department or other group of users who share files. An example of a zone name is "Sales and Marketing."

Although Apple has improved AppleTalk's ability to use different network models and span network segments, it remains unsuited to large LANs or WANs. Even Apple has begun supporting the TCP/IP protocol to integrate Macintoshes with other networks, including the Internet.

AppleTalk Compared to the OSI Model

AppleTalk is a complete protocol suite containing services that fit into each layer of the OSI Model, as depicted in Figure 3-11.

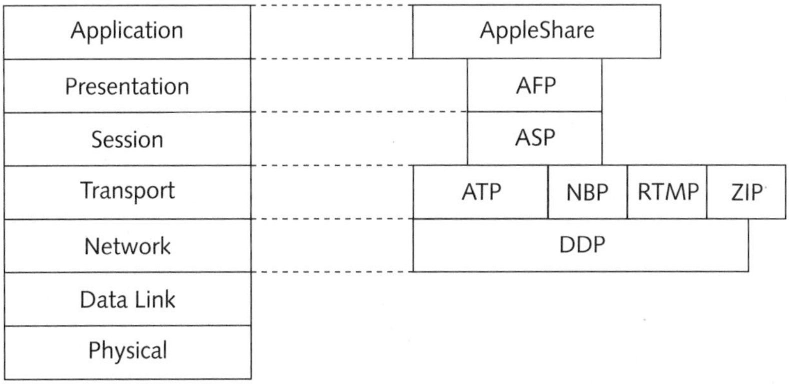

Application		AppleShare			
Presentation		AFP			
Session		ASP			
Transport		ATP	NBP	RTMP	ZIP
Network		DDP			
Data Link					
Physical					

Figure 3-11   The AppleTalk protocol compared to the OSI Model

The AppleTalk subprotocols that are significant for node-to-node communications are described in the following list:

- *AppleShare*—Provides file sharing services, print queueing services, password access to files or folders, and user accounting information.

- *AppleTalk Filing Protocol (AFP)*—Provides transparent access to files on both local and remote systems.

- *AppleTalk Session Protocol (ASP)*—Establishes and maintains connections between nodes and servers.

- *AppleTalk Transaction Protocol (ATP)*—Ensures reliable delivery of data by checking connections between nodes, checking packet sequence, and retransmitting any data packets that become lost.

- *Name Binding Protocol (NBP)*—Translates human-readable node names into numeric AppleTalk addresses.

- *Routing Table Maintenance Protocol (RTMP)*—Maintains a routing table of AppleTalk zones and their networks, and uses ZIP to manage data in the routing table.

- *Zone Information Protocol (ZIP)*—Updates zone information maps that tie zones to their networks for routing purposes.

- *Datagram Delivery Protocol (DDP)*—Assigns an AppleTalk node's address upon start-up and manages addressing for communications between AppleTalk nodes.

Addressing in AppleTalk

You have learned that AppleTalk uses zones and that zone names can be plain words or numbers with no restrictions. In addition to zone names, AppleTalk uses node IDs and network numbers to identify computers on a network.

An **AppleTalk node ID** is a unique 8-bit or 16-bit number that identifies a computer on an AppleTalk network. AppleTalk assigns a node ID to each workstation when the workstation first connects to the network. The ID is randomly chosen from a group of currently available addresses. Once a device has obtained an address, it stores it for later use.

An **AppleTalk network number** is a unique 16-bit number that identifies the network to which a node is connected. Its use allows nodes from several different networks to communicate.

AppleTalk addressing is simple because it allows you to identify a group of shared addresses from the server. When clients attach to that server they pick up an address, thus eliminating the need to configure addresses on each separate workstation.

INSTALLING PROTOCOLS

The protocols you install will depend on which operating system you are running. This section describes how to install the most commonly used protocols on Windows 98 and Windows 2000 client workstations. Chapters 8 and 9 discuss installing and configuring protocols on the two of the most commonly used network operating systems, NetWare 5.x and Windows 2000.

Installation is merely the first step in making protocols work. After they are installed, you must bind them to the NICs and services they will run on or with. **Binding** is the process of assigning one network component to work with another. Once you install a protocol on a Windows 2000 or Windows 98 workstation, it binds itself automatically to the NICs

3

and services it finds on the computer. However, depending on the computer's version of Windows, you may have to restart the machine for the bindings to take effect. For optimal network performance, you should install and bind only those protocols that you absolutely need. For example, a Windows 2000 server will attempt to use bound protocols in the order in which they appear in the protocol listing until it finds the correct one for the response at hand. This approach wastes processing time, making it more efficient to bind only the protocols you need.

Installing Protocols on a Windows 2000 Professional Workstation

The following exercise shows you how to install the NetBEUI protocol on a Windows 2000 Professional workstation (note that TCP/IP would normally be already installed with the operating system, while NetBEUI would not). The process of installing other protocols on a Windows 2000 Professional workstation is identical.

1. Log on to the workstation as an Administrator.

2. Click **Start**, point to **Settings**, then click **Network and Dial-up Connections**.

3. Right-click the **Local Area Connection** icon and click **Properties** in the shortcut menu. The Properties dialog box opens.

4. Click **Install**. The Select Network Component Type dialog box opens.

5. Click **Protocol** in the list of Network Component Types.

6. Click **Add**. The Select Network Protocol dialog box opens.

7. In the list of network protocols, click **NetBEUI Protocol**, then click **OK**.

   Notice that NetBEUI now appears in the list of network components.

8. Click **Close**. The Local Area Connection Properties dialog box closes and your change is saved.

9. To verify that the protocol was installed, click **Start**, point to **Settings**, then click **Network and Dial-up Connections**.

10. Right-click the **Local Area Connection** icon and click **Properties**. The Properties dialog box appears.

11. Verify that NetBEUI Protocol appears in the list of installed protocols.

12. Click **Cancel** to close the Network dialog box.

On a Windows 2000 workstation, you can install any other protocol in the same manner as you installed the NetBEUI protocol. Although the NetBEUI protocol requires no further configuration, usually you must configure the AppleTalk and TCP/IP protocols after installing them. Chapter 11 covers TCP/IP configuration in detail.

Installing Protocols on a Windows 98 Workstation

The following exercise shows you how to install the TCP/IP protocol on a Windows 98 workstation (it assumes that you have either previously removed the TCP/IP protocol or are installing it again; Windows 98 installations include the TCP/IP protocol by default).

1. Right-click the **Network Neighborhood** icon, then click **Properties**.

2. Verify that the **Configuration** tab is selected.

3. Click **Add**. The Select Network Component Type window opens.

4. Double-click **Protocol**. The Select Network Protocol window opens.

5. In the list of manufacturers, click **Microsoft**.

6. In the list of protocols, click **TCP/IP**.

7. Click **OK**, and then click **OK** again.

8. If TCP/IP is not already installed on your workstation, you will be prompted to restart your workstation to allow the changes to take effect. Click **Yes** to restart your workstation.

9. To verify that the protocol was installed, right-click the **Network Neighborhood** icon, then click **Properties**.

10. Verify that the **Configuration** tab is selected. One of the items in the list of services, clients, and protocols should be TCP/IP.

11. Click **Cancel** to close the Network properties window.

You can add other protocols to your Windows 98 workstation in the same manner. Although usually you do not need to configure IPX/SPX or NetBEUI after installation, you must configure TCP/IP unless you are using DHCP. Chapter 11 covers TCP/IP configuration in detail.

It is possible to bind multiple protocols to the same network adapter. In fact, this is necessary on networks that use more than one type of protocol. In addition, a workstation may have multiple NICs, in which case several different protocols might be bound to each NIC. What's more, the same protocol may be configured differently on different NICs. For example, let's say you managed a NetWare server that contained two NICs and provided both TCP/IP and IPX/SPX communications to many clients. After installing the TCP/IP protocol on the server, you would need to configure TCP/IP separately for each NIC using the network operating system's protocol configuration utility. Similarly, you would need to configure IPX/SPX separately for each NIC. If you did not configure the protocols for each NIC separately, clients would not know which NIC to address when sending and receiving information to and from the server.

CHAPTER SUMMARY

- ❏ Protocols define the standards for communication between nodes on a network. The term *protocol*, in networking, can refer to a group, or suite, of individual protocols that work together to accomplish data translation, data handling, error checking, and addressing.

- ❏ Protocols vary by speed, transmission efficiency, utilization of resources, ease of setup, compatibility, and ability to travel between one LAN segment and another. Protocols that can span more than one LAN segment are routable, because they carry Network layer and addressing information that can be interpreted by a router.

- ❏ The most commonly used protocols are TCP/IP, IPX/SPX, NetBIOS, and AppleTalk. You may also find other, outdated protocols in use, such as SNA and DLC.

- ❏ A network that uses more than one protocol is called a multiprotocol network. Multiprotocol networks are common in businesses with well-established LANs that have evolved from a legacy system to a newer, more efficient one.

- ❏ TCP/IP is fast becoming the most popular network protocol because of its low cost and its ability to communicate between a multitude of dissimilar platforms. It is a de facto standard on the Internet and is commonly the protocol of choice on LANs. TCP/IP is routable and flexible.

- ❏ The TCP/IP suite of protocols can be divided into four layers that roughly correspond to the seven layers of the OSI Model: the Application layer, the Transport layer, the Internet layer, and the Network Interface layer.

- ❏ The TCP/IP core protocols operate in the Transport or Network layers of the OSI Model, where they provide communications between hosts on a network. The most significant core protocols in the TCP/IP suite are IP and TCP.

- ❏ The Internet Protocol (IP) belongs to the Internet layer of the TCP/IP Model and provides information about how and where data should be delivered. IP is the subprotocol that enables TCP/IP to internetwork—that is, to traverse more than one LAN segment and more than one type of network through a router.

- ❏ The Transmission Control Protocol (TCP) belongs to the Transport layer of the TCP/IP suite and provides reliable data delivery services. TCP is a connection-oriented subprotocol, which means that it requires a connection to be established between communicating nodes before it will transmit data. TCP sits on top of the IP subprotocol and compensates for IP's reliability deficiencies with its checksum, flow control, and sequencing information.

- ❏ The User Datagram Protocol (UDP), like TCP, sits in the Transport layer, between the Internet layer and the Application layer of the TCP/IP Model. Unlike TCP, however, UDP is a connectionless transport service. It offers no error checking and no assurance that packets will be received in the correct sequence. UDP's lack of sophistication actually makes it more efficient than TCP and useful in situations where data must be transferred quickly, such as live audio or video transmissions over the Internet.

3

❏ Internet Control Message Protocol (ICMP), another TCP/IP core protocol, notifies the sender that something has gone wrong in the transmission process and that packets were not delivered. ICMP sits between IP and TCP in the Internet layer of the TCP/IP Model and reports which networks are unreachable and which packets have been discarded because the allotted time for their delivery has expired.

❏ The Address Resolution Protocol (ARP) belongs to the Internet layer of the TCP/IP Model. It obtains the MAC (physical) address of a host, or node, then creates a local database that maps the MAC address to the host's IP (logical) address.

❏ The TCP/IP suite includes a number of useful Application layer protocols, such as Telnet, FTP, SMTP, and SNMP.

❏ Each IP address is a unique 32-bit number, divided into four octets that are separated by periods. An example of a valid IP address is 144.92.43.178. An IP address contains two types of information: network and host.

❏ All nodes on a Class A network share the first octet of their IP numbers, a number between 1 and 126. Nodes on a Class B network share the first two octets, and all their IP addresses begin with a number between 128 and 191. Class C network IP numbers share the first three octets, with their first octet being a number between 192 and 223.

❏ The range of addresses beginning with 127 is reserved for loopback information. The IP address 127.0.0.1 is called a loopback address. When you try to contact this IP number, you actually communicate with your own machine. This address is useful for troubleshooting problems with a workstation's TCP/IP communications.

❏ Every host on a network must have a unique number, as duplicate addresses will cause problems. If a host is added to a network and its IP address is already assigned to another host on the subnet, an error message will be generated on the new client and its TCP/IP services will be disabled. The existing host may also receive an error message, but can continue to function normally.

❏ Although you may assign IP addresses manually, you must take care to avoid assigning duplicate addresses. IP addresses assigned manually are called static IP addresses. Most networks provide the capability of dynamically assigning IP addresses through the Dynamic Host Configuration Protocol (DHCP) protocol, an Application layer protocol in the TCP/IP suite. Using a DHCP server to assign IP addresses can nearly eliminate duplicate-addressing problems.

❏ Internetwork Packet Exchange/Sequenced Packet Exchange (IPX/SPX) is a protocol originally developed by Xerox, then modified and adopted by Novell in the 1980s for its NetWare network operating system. IPX/SPX is required for interoperability with LANs running NetWare versions 3.2 and lower; it can also be used with LANs running higher versions of the NetWare operating system. IPX/SPX, like TCP/IP, is a suite of protocols that reside at different layers of the OSI Model. Also like TCP/IP, IPX/SPX carries network addressing information, so it is routable.

❑ The core protocols of IPX/SPX provide services at the Transport and Network layers of the OSI Model. Its most important subprotocols are IPX and SPX.

❑ Internetwork Packet Exchange (IPX) operates at the Network layer of the OSI Model and provides routing and internetwork services, similar to IP in the TCP/IP suite. IPX uses datagrams to transport data. This protocol is a connectionless service because it does not require a session to be established before it transmits data, and it does not guarantee that data will be delivered in sequence or without errors. It is an efficient subprotocol with limited capabilities.

❑ Sequenced Packet Exchange (SPX) belongs to the Transport layer of the OSI Model. It works in tandem with IPX to ensure that data are received whole, in sequence, and error free. SPX is a connection-oriented protocol and therefore must verify that a session has been established with the destination node before it will transmit data. It can detect whether a packet was not received in its entirety; if it discovers that a packet has been lost or corrupted, SPX will resend the packet.

❑ The Service Advertising Protocol (SAP) works in the Application, Presentation, Session, and Transport layers of the OSI Model and runs directly over IPX. NetWare servers and routers use SAP to advertise to the entire network which services they can provide.

❑ The NetWare Core Protocol (NCP) handles requests for services, such as printing and file access, between clients and servers. NCP works over IPX and within the Presentation and Session layers of the OSI Model. It acts as a translator between the workstation's operating system and the NetWare operating system.

❑ Because IPX is the component of the protocol that handles addressing, addresses on an IPX/SPX network are called IPX addresses. IPX addresses contain two parts: the network address and the node address. The network address must be an 8-bit hexadecimal address, which means that each of its bits can have a value of either 0–9 or A–F. The second part of an IPX address, the node address, is equal to the network device's MAC address.

❑ NetBIOS (Network Basic Input Output System) is a protocol originally designed for IBM to provide Transport and Session layer services for applications running on small, homogenous networks.

❑ Microsoft adopted IBM's NetBIOS as its foundation protocol, initially for networks using LAN Manager or Windows for Workgroups, but then added an Application layer component on top of NetBIOS called the NetBIOS Enhanced User Interface (NetBEUI). NetBEUI is a fast and efficient protocol that consumes few network resources, provides excellent error correction, and requires little configuration. It can support only 254 connections, however, and does not allow for good security. Furthermore, because NetBEUI lacks a Network layer, it is not routable and therefore not suitable for large networks.

❑ To transmit data between network nodes, NetBIOS needs to know how to reach each workstation. For this reason, network administrators must assign a NetBIOS name to each workstation. The NetBIOS name can be any combination of 16 or fewer alphanumeric characters (although you cannot begin a NetBIOS name with an asterisk). Once NetBIOS has found a workstation's NetBIOS name, it will discover the workstation's MAC address and then use this address in further communications with the workstation.

❑ AppleTalk is the protocol suite used to interconnect Macintosh computers. Although AppleTalk was originally designed to support peer-to-peer networking among Macintoshes, it can now be routed between network segments and integrated with NetWare- or Microsoft-based networks.

❑ An AppleTalk network is separated into logical groups of computers called AppleTalk zones. Each network can contain multiple zones, but each node can belong to only one zone. AppleTalk zones enable users to share file and printer resources on one another's Macintoshes. Zone names typically describe a department or other group of users who share files.

❑ Although Apple has improved AppleTalk's ability to use different network models and span network segments, it remains unsuited to large LANs or WANs. Even Apple has begun supporting the TCP/IP protocol to integrate Macintoshes with other networks, including the Internet.

❑ In addition to zone names, AppleTalk uses node IDs and network numbers to identify computers on a network. An AppleTalk node ID is a unique 8- or 16-bit number that identifies a computer on an AppleTalk network. AppleTalk assigns a node ID to each workstation when the workstation connects to the network. An AppleTalk network number is a unique 16-bit number that identifies the network to which a node is connected. AppleTalk addressing can be managed centrally from the server.

❑ Although some protocols, such as NetBIOS, require no configuration after they are installed, more complex protocols, such as TCP/IP, do require configuration.

KEY TERMS

Address Resolution Protocol (ARP) — A core protocol in the TCP/IP suite that belongs in the Internet layer. It obtains the MAC (physical) address of a host, or node, and then creates a local database that maps the MAC address to the host's IP (logical) address.

AppleTalk — The protocol suite used to interconnect Macintosh computers. Although AppleTalk was originally designed to support peer-to-peer networking among Macintoshes, it can now be routed between network segments and integrated with NetWare- or Microsoft-based networks.

AppleTalk network number — A unique 16-bit number that identifies the network to which an AppleTalk node is connected.

3

AppleTalk node ID — A unique 8-bit or 16-bit (if you are using extended networking, in which a network can have multiple addresses and support multiple zones) number that identifies a computer on an AppleTalk network.

AppleTalk zone — Logical groups of computers defined on an AppleTalk network.

binding — The process of assigning one network component to work with another.

broadcast — A transmission to all stations on a network.

connection-oriented — A feature of some protocols that requires the establishment of a connection between communicating nodes before the protocol will transmit data.

connectionless — A feature of some protocols that allows the protocol to service a request without requiring a verified session and without guaranteeing delivery of data.

domain name — The symbolic name that identifies a group of IP addresses. Usually, a domain name is associated with a company or other type of organization, such as a university or military unit.

Dynamic Host Configuration Protocol (DHCP) — An Application layer protocol in the TCP/IP suite that manages the dynamic distribution of IP addresses on a network. Using DHCP to assign IP addresses can nearly eliminate duplicate-addressing problems.

external network number — Another term for the network address portion of an IPX/SPX address.

File Transfer Protocol (FTP) — An Application layer protocol used to send and receive files via TCP/IP.

firewall — A specialized device (typically a router, but possibly only a PC running special software) that selectively filters or blocks traffic between networks. A firewall may be strictly hardware-based, or it may involve a combination of hardware and software.

fully qualified domain name (FQDN) — In TCP/IP addressing, the combination of a host and domain name that together uniquely identify a device.

host — A computer connected to a network that uses the TCP/IP protocol.

Internet Assigned Numbers Authority (IANA) — A non-profit, U.S. government-funded group that was established at the University of Southern California and charged with managing IP address allocation and the domain name system. The oversight for many IANA's functions was given to ICANN in 1998; however, IANA continues to perform Internet addressing and domain name system administration.

Internet Control Message Protocol (ICMP) — A core protocol in the TCP/IP suite that notifies the sender that something has gone wrong in the transmission process and that packets were not delivered.

Internet Corporation for Assigned Names and Numbers (ICANN) — The non-profit corporation currently designated by the U.S. government to maintain and assign IP addresses.

Internet Protocol (IP) — A core protocol in the TCP/IP suite that belongs to the Internet layer of the TCP/IP model and provides information about how and where data should be delivered. IP is the subprotocol that enables TCP/IP to internetwork.

internetwork — To traverse more than one LAN segment and more than one type of network through a router.

Internetwork Packet Exchange (IPX) — A core protocol of the IPX/SPX suite that operates at the Network layer of the OSI Model and provides routing and internetwork services, similar to IP in the TCP/IP suite.

Internetwork Packet Exchange/Sequenced Packet Exchange (IPX/SPX) — A protocol originally developed by Xerox, then modified and adopted by Novell in the 1980s for the NetWare network operating system.

IP address — A logical address used in TCP/IP networking. This unique 32-bit number is divided into four groups of octets, or 8-bit bytes, that are separated by periods.

IP datagram — The IP portion of a TCP/IP frame that acts as an envelope for data, holding information necessary for routers to transfer data between subnets.

IPX address — An address assigned to a device on an IPX/SPX network.

loopback address — An IP address reserved for communicating from a node to itself (used mostly for testing purposes). The value of the loopback address is always 127.0.0.1.

multiprotocol network — A network that uses more than one protocol.

NetBIOS Enhanced User Interface (NetBEUI) — Microsoft's adaptation of the IBM NetBIOS protocol. NetBEUI expands on NetBIOS by adding an Application layer component. NetBEUI is a fast and efficient protocol that consumes few network resources, provides excellent error correction and requires little configuration.

NetWare Core Protocol (NCP) — One of the core protocols of the IPX/SPX suite. NCP handles requests for services, such as printing and file access, between clients and servers.

Network Basic Input Output System (NetBIOS) — A protocol designed by IBM to provide Transport and Session layer services for applications running on small, homogeneous networks.

octet — One of the four 8-bit bytes that are separated by periods and together make up an IP address.

port — The address on a host where an application makes itself available to incoming data.

protocol — The rules a network uses to transfer data. Protocols ensure that data is transferred whole, in sequence, and without error from one node on the network to another.

Regional Internet Registry (RIR) — A not-for-profit agency that manages the distribution of IP addresses to private and public entities. ARIN is the RIR for North, Central, and South America and sub-Saharan Africa. APNIC is the RIR for Asia and the Pacific region. RIPE is the RIR for Europe and North Africa.

routable — Protocols that can span more than one LAN segment because they carry Network layer and addressing information that can be interpreted by a router.

routing protocols — Protocols that assist routers in efficiently managing information flow.

Sequenced Packet Exchange (SPX) — One of the core protocols in the IPX/SPX suite. SPX belongs to the Transport layer of the OSI Model and works in tandem with IPX to ensure that data are received whole, in sequence, and error free.

Service Advertising Protocol (SAP) — A core protocol in the IPX/SPX suite that works in the Application, Presentation, Session, and Transport layers of the OSI Model and runs directly over IPX. NetWare servers and routers use SAP to advertise to the entire network which services they can provide.

3

Simple Mail Transfer Protocol (SMTP) — The protocol responsible for moving messages from one e-mail server to another over the Internet and other TCP/IP-based networks.

Simple Network Management Protocol (SNMP) — A communication protocol used to manage devices on a TCP/IP network.

socket — A logical address assigned to a specific process running on a computer. Some sockets are reserved for operating system functions.

static IP address — An IP address that is manually assigned to a device.

subnets — In an internetwork, the individual networks that are joined together by routers.

subprotocols — Small, specialized protocols that work together and belong to a protocol suite.

TCP segment — The portion of a TCP/IP packet that holds TCP data fields and becomes encapsulated by the IP datagram.

TCP/IP core protocols — The subprotocols of the TCP/IP suite.

Telnet — A terminal emulation protocol used to log on to remote hosts using the TCP/IP protocol. Telnet resides in the Application layer of the TCP/IP suite.

Transmission Control Protocol (TCP) — A core protocol of the TCP/IP suite. TCP belongs to the Transport layer and provides reliable data delivery services.

User Datagram Protocol (UDP) — A core protocol in the TCP/IP suite that sits in the Transport layer, between the Internet layer and the Application layer of the TCP/IP model. UDP is a connectionless transport service.

REVIEW QUESTIONS

1. What characteristics make a protocol routable?

   a. MAC sublayer addresses that can be interpreted by a server

   b. Network layer and addressing information that can be interpreted by a router

   c. Logical Link sublayer address information that can be interpreted by a hub

   d. Transport layer flow control information that can be interpreted by a router

2. Which layer in the TCP/IP model of network communications roughly corresponds to the Physical and Data Link layers of the OSI Model?

   a. Network Interface layer

   b. Internet layer

   c. Transport layer

   d. Application layer

3. To which layer of the TCP/IP model does the IP protocol belong?

    a. Network Interface layer

    b. Internet layer

    c. Transport layer

    d. Application layer

4. To which layer of the TCP/IP model does the TCP protocol belong?

    a. Network Interface layer

    b. Internet layer

    c. Transport layer

    d. Application layer

5. What is the function of ARP?

    a. to acknowledge that a data frame was received

    b. to obtain the IP address of a host, then map that IP address to a registered domain name

    c. to measure the number of dropped packets in a single transmission

    d. to obtain the MAC address of a host, and then map the MAC address to the host's IP address

6. Which TCP/IP utility might you use to connect to a UNIX host from your PC over the network?

    a. SNMP

    b. SMTP

    c. Telnet

    d. hup

7. What does SMTP stand for?

    a. Simple Mail Transfer Protocol

    b. Simple Message Transport Protocol

    c. Simple Media Transfer Protocol

    d. Simple Message Tracking Protocol

8. Which version of IP are most TCP/IP networks currently using?

    a. 3.0

    b. 4.0

    c. 5.0

    d. 6.0

9. Why might an application be better served by UDP than TCP?

10. An IP address consists of 4 bytes. True or False?

11. Which technique is used to break large TCP/IP-based networks into smaller logical segments?

   a. subnetting

   b. subclassing

   c. reverse lookups

   d. domain transfers

12. On which Class network would you find the workstation that uses the following IP address: 193.12.176.55?

   a. A

   b. B

   c. C

   d. D

13. Which of the following is the loopback address?

   a. 1.1.1.1

   b. 255.255.255.0

   c. 1.0.1.0

   d. 127.0.0.1

14. Which of the following is an alternative to configuring each workstation on a network with its own IP address?

   a. DHCP

   b. SNMP

   c. RARP

   d. TFTP

15. What kind of network operating system requires IPX/SPX?

   a. Windows 2000 Server

   b. UNIX

   c. NetWare version 3.2 or lower

   d. NetWare versions higher than 3.2

16. Which IPX/SPX core protocol provides data reliability services?

   a. IPX

   b. SPX

   c. NCP

   d. SAP

17. The node address portion of an IPX/SPX address is equivalent to what other address?

    a. MAC address

    b. IP address

    c. Data Link layer address

    d. Network address

18. What function is performed by the time to live (in IP) and the transport control (in IPX) fields?

19. Which of the following is not a valid network address for a NetWare server?

    a. F290F45A

    b. AAAAAAAA

    c. 23AK80A3

    d. 01010101

20. Why wouldn't you want to use NetBEUI for Internet connections (pick two reasons)?

    a. It's not routable.

    b. It's not secure.

    c. It's not reliable.

    d. It's not efficient.

21. Why are hosts on a TCP/IP network assigned host names?

22. IPX/SPX is not a routable protocol. True or False?

23. Macintosh computers can be integrated with Microsoft-based networks. True or False?

24. On a Windows 2000 workstation, how would you find your computer's NetBIOS name?

    a. Click Start, click Run, and type ipconfig /all.

    b. Click Start, click Settings, click Network and Dial-Up Connections, then right-click on the LAN Connection icon.

    c. Double-click My Computer, click General, and note the computer identification text.

    d. Click Start, click Settings, click Control Panel, then double-click the System icon. In the System Properties window, click the Identification tab.

25. Which AppleTalk protocol ensures reliable data delivery?

    a. NCP

    b. ZIP

    c. DDP

    d. ATP

3

26. What is a logically defined group of workstations called on an AppleTalk network?

    a. an AppleTalk zone

    b. an AppleTalk domain

    c. an AppleTalk segment

    d. an AppleTalk universe

27. On a Windows 2000 workstation, after you install the NWLink (IPX/SPX) protocol, you need not modify its network address to use it. True or False?

28. On a Windows 98 workstation, what is the default setting for the IP address in the TCP/IP protocol properties?

    a. Obtain IP address automatically

    b. Specify an IP address

    c. Enable NetBIOS over TCP/IP

    d. Enable WINS resolution

29. What information does the winipcfg command (run from a Windows 98 workstation) give you?

30. How many protocols can you install on a single Windows 98 workstation?

    a. 2

    b. 3

    c. 4

    d. as many as you want

HANDS-ON PROJECTS

You can detect protocols and test their effects through a variety of ways. The Hands-on Projects that follow add to what you have learned about protocols thus far, and form the basis for protocol troubleshooting and more in-depth analysis of the TCP/IP protocol in Chapter 11.

Project 3-1

This project requires a workstation running Windows 2000 Professional that has the TCP/IP protocol installed and that is connected to a Windows 2000 server with Internet access. It introduces the PING (Packet Internet Groper) utility, which can be used to verify that TCP/IP is running, configured correctly, and communicating with the network. A ping test is typically the first thing network professionals try when troubleshooting a TCP/IP connection problem. The process of sending out a signal is known as pinging. You can ping either an IP address or a host name. (You will learn more about PING and other diagnostic TCP/IP utilities in Chapter 11.)

  1. Click **Start**, then click **Run**. The Run dialog box opens.

  2. In the Open text box, type **command**, then click **OK**. The Command Prompt window opens.

3. At the DOS prompt, type **PING 127.0.0.1**. (Remember that 127.0.0.1 is the loopback address.) If your workstation is properly connected to the network, you should see a screen that contains five lines. The first line will read "Pinging 127.0.0.1 with 32 bytes of data." Following that you will see four lines that begin "Reply from 127.0.0.1." If you do not see four positive reply lines, or if you see four lines with the words "Request timed out," check the syntax of your ping command. If you typed the command correctly, check the status of your TCP/IP protocol. Is it installed and bound to your NIC? To reinstall TCP/IP, follow the steps mentioned earlier in this chapter for installing protocols.

4. At the end of each of the four reply lines, a TTL value appears. What is the value of the TTL and what does this number represent? Because you received these replies to your loopback ping test, you know that your TCP/IP services are installed correctly and bound to your NIC. The loopback test, however, doesn't indicate whether your TCP/IP services are operating correctly to grant you access to the network. In the next step, you will try a ping test that can help you determine whether your TCP/IP services are operating successfully.

5. At the DOS prompt, type **PING www.yahoo.com**.

6. What was the response? If you received a "Request timed out" message, why might you have received it? If you received a valid response, with four lines of replies, note the TTL. Why does it differ from the TTL observed when you pinged the loopback address?

7. Type **exit** at the MS DOS prompt to close the window.

Project 3-2

This project requires a Windows 2000 Professional workstation that is connected to a Windows 2000 network and has the TCP/IP protocol installed. In this project, you will uninstall the TCP/IP protocol, try the PING test again, then reinstall the TCP/IP protocol.

1. Log on to the workstation as an Administrator.

2. Click **Start**, point to **Settings**, then click **Network and Dial-up Connections**.

3. Right-click the **Local Area Connection** icon and then click **Properties** in the shortcut menu. The Properties dialog box opens, as shown in Figure 3-12.

4. Click **Internet Protocol (TCP/IP)** in the list of components, then click **Uninstall**.

5. Click **Yes** when asked to confirm the deletion.

6. You are prompted to restart your workstation to allow the changes to take effect.

7. Click **Yes** to restart your workstation.

8. When your workstation restarts, do you see any error messages? If so, write them on a separate piece of paper, then choose to ignore the errors and continue the start-up process.

9. Log on to the workstation as an Administrator again, and try pinging the loopback address as you did in Project 3-1. How did your workstation respond?

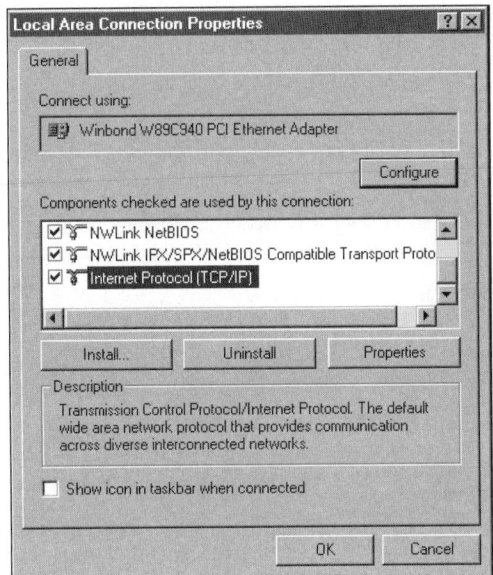

Figure 3-12   Local Area Connection Properties dialog box

10. Repeat steps 1, 2, and 3 from this project.

11. Verify that the the Local Area Connection Properties dialog box is open, and then click **Install**. The Select Network Component Type dialog box opens.

12. Click **Protocol**, then click **Add**. The Select Network Protocol dialog box opens.

13. In the list of protocols, click **Internet Protocol (TCP/IP)** and click **OK**.

14. Click **Close** to install the TCP/IP protocol. The Local Area Connection Properties dialog box closes.

15. Try pinging the loopback address once more. How does your workstation respond?

Project 3-3

In this project, you will exercise your knowledge about data frames and datagrams. Because these structures form the basis of all networking, it's important that you be able to visualize and understand their components. You will need a pencil and paper to complete this project.

1. Pretend that you are a device on a network with the node address of 05 73 AC 22 and you want to send 8 bytes of data to another device on the network that has the node address 22 A0 F3 D1. You are on an Ethernet network with an external network address of 00 00 20 20. Draw a picture of the IPX/SPX datagram that will carry your data. Name the parts of the datagram and fill in the values that you can (for example, addresses, size, and packet type).

2. Pretend that you are the same device as in Step 1 sending 8 bytes of data to the same second device on the same network; this time, however, you're sending the information with the TCP/IP protocol. Your IP address is 209.122.38.7 and the second device's IP address is 209.122.38.9. Draw a picture of the TCP/IP datagram that will carry your data. Name the parts of the datagram and fill in the values that you can (for example, addresses, length, and protocol type).

CASE PROJECTS

1. As a consultant for the First National Bank of Monroe, you have been asked to solve a problem on the bank's network that began on Monday. According to the bank manager, at the beginning of each day two of the 16 tellers have been unable to log on to the network. Two other tellers occasionally experience problems at the beginning of the day, but not if they get to work before everyone else. They receive an error that says something like "another machine is using that name." When you arrive at the bank, the college intern who has been setting up the machines tells you that he is using a program called Ghost to clone all PCs from a single disk image. In other words, an exact copy of one machine's software, operating system, and its properties has been copied to all of the computers. All of the PCs are brand new, are running Windows 98, and use the same hardware and software. First National Bank's network consists of two Windows 2000 servers and runs both TCP/IP and NetBIOS/NetBEUI protocols. It uses DHCP to allocate TCP/IP addresses. What might be preventing the two tellers from logging on to the network in the morning?

2. First National Bank's president congratulates you on quickly solving the problem. She then shares the information that she's about to make an offer to buy Monroe's other bank, Metropolitan Savings. She's worried that the two banks' networks won't integrate easily. She isn't sure what kinds of servers or workstations are used by the other bank, but Metropolitan Savings' manager mentioned something about a network that relies on the Internet. What can you tell her about integrating the two systems? What protocols would you recommend that she use or continue to use to facilitate the integration process?

3. Six months later, First National Bank has successfully consolidated the networks at its original location and at its new acquisition. Business is booming, and the bank is investigating the possibility of allowing customers to check their account balances from the Web. However, the bank's president tells you the bank doesn't have its own connection to the Internet at this time. She understands that she needs to obtain IP addresses for all of her machines. But, she says, they are already using IP addresses internally and they work well without having to pay ICANN for new IP addresses. Would you recommend leaving the bank's IP addressing as is or changing it? How do you suggest that the bank obtain Internet access? What concerns would you bring up with regard to allowing customers access to their account information off the Web? How might Internet access affect the bank's internal LAN?

CHAPTER 4

TRANSMISSION BASICS AND NETWORKING MEDIA

After reading this chapter and completing the exercises, you will be able to:

➤ Explain data transmission concepts including full-duplexing, attenuation, and noise

➤ Describe the physical characteristics of coaxial cable, STP, UTP, and fiber-optic media

➤ Compare the benefits and limitations of different networking media

➤ Identify the best practices for cabling buildings and work areas

➤ Describe methods of transmitting data through the atmosphere

---

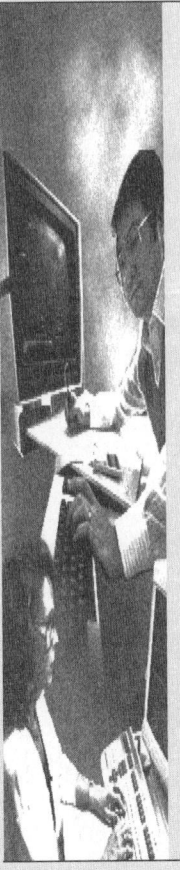

ON THE JOB

I was once asked to test the quality of various network-monitoring software packages. Our test lab had all the latest new equipment to mimic the client's LAN: managed stacks of 100-MHz hubs, powerful Intel-based servers with RAID subsystems, and nicely configured workstations. We also had the best surge arrestors available and an excellent UPS system.

Installation of the operating systems went well, but the results from the various management programs were unreliable. It soon became apparent that the lab contained bad hardware; the logs of traffic on the server NICs showed too many errors for a busy LAN—let alone an isolated test LAN. Internal diagnostics programs said that the cards were okay. When I generated as much traffic as I could through the new hubs, using a laptop with a new NIC, I found no errors.

What was next? I had checked the system's entire Physical layer—except for the LAN's wires. When testing the hubs, I had used the new cable that came with my new NIC. I visually double-checked the termination patterns to verify that I had a proper TIA-568 CAT5 cable. A continuity test also showed the cables to be correct.

Finally, I decided to reterminate the cable ends. As soon as I snipped off the ends and exposed the wires, it became apparent that the cable was CAT3 at best! In fact, our company was color-coding cables, using one color for one purpose. It had ordered several large spools from the same vendor—but the vendor did not check the wire before shipping it. The green twisted-pair cable used for my project was not stamped with a CAT5 verification and was not of the same quality as the other cable in the shipment.

Quality cable is as critical as quality memory or RAID subsystems. Termination of cable can be poorly done, however, leading to intermittent, difficult-to-trace problems. As little as 1 inch of untwisted wire at cable ends can reduce the capacity of a wire set from 150 MHz to 30 MHz! In my case, a CAT5 test on a high-quality cable tester would have detected the cable problem. I've learned my lesson. When odd problems arise on high-speed connections, I head for our company's sophisticated cable and fiber tester.

Tom Callaci
Berbee Information Networks, Inc.

Just as highways and streets provide the foundation for automobile travel, networking media provide the physical foundation of data transmission. As you know, networking media reside at the lowest layer of the OSI Model. The first networks transmitted data over thick, heavy coaxial cables.

Today, most networking media resemble telephone cords, with their flexible outsides and twisted copper wire inside. Because networks now demand more speed, versatility, and reliability, however, networking media are changing. Modern networks may incorporate not only copper wiring, but also fiber-optic cables, infrared, radio waves, and possibly other media.

Before you can fully understand network communications, you must understand how data are transmitted. You should also be familiar with the characteristics of various networking media. Although network users take data transmission for granted, giving little thought to how their e-mail messages or files move from point A to point B, you need to understand this process thoroughly. This chapter discusses the details of data transmission. You'll learn what it takes to make data transmission dependable and how to correct some common transmission problems.

TRANSMISSION BASICS

In data networking, the term **transmission** has two meanings. First, it can refer to the process of issuing data signals on a medium. It can also refer to the progress of data signals over a medium from one point to another. Long ago, people transmitted information across distances via smoke or fire signals. Needless to say, many different types of data transmission have evolved since that time. The transmission techniques in use on today's networks are complex and varied. In the following sections you will learn about some fundamental characteristics that define today's data transmission. In later chapters you will learn about more subtle and specific differences between types of data transmission.

Analog and Digital Signaling

One important characteristic of data transmission is the type of signaling involved. On a data network, information can be transmitted via one of two signaling methods: analog or digital. Both types of signals are generated by electrical current, the pressure of which is measured in **volts**. The strength of an electrical signal is directly proportional to its voltage. Thus, when network engineers talk about the strength of an analog or digital signal, they often refer to the signal's **voltage**.

The essential difference between analog and digital signals is the way voltage creates and sustains the signal. In **analog** signals, voltage varies continuously. In **digital** signals, voltage turns off and on repeatedly, pulsing from zero voltage to a specific positive voltage. An analog signal's voltage appears as a continuous wave when graphed over time, as shown in Figure 4-1.

Because voltage is varied and imprecise in analog signals, analog transmission is more susceptible to transmission flaws such as noise (discussed later) than digital signals. To understand this concept, think of two tin cans connected by a wire. When you speak into one of the tin cans, you produce analog sound waves that vibrate over the wire until they reach the tin can at the other end. These sound waves are merely approximations of your voice, and they are significantly affected by the quality of the wire. For example, if you try the tin can experiment with a pure copper wire, your voice will arrive at the other end sounding clearer than if you used fishing line, because copper conducts sound better than plastic. Regardless of which medium you use, however, the sound waves will become distorted as they traverse the wire, arriving at the second tin can at least a little muddled. This vulnerability makes analog transmission less precise than digital transmission.

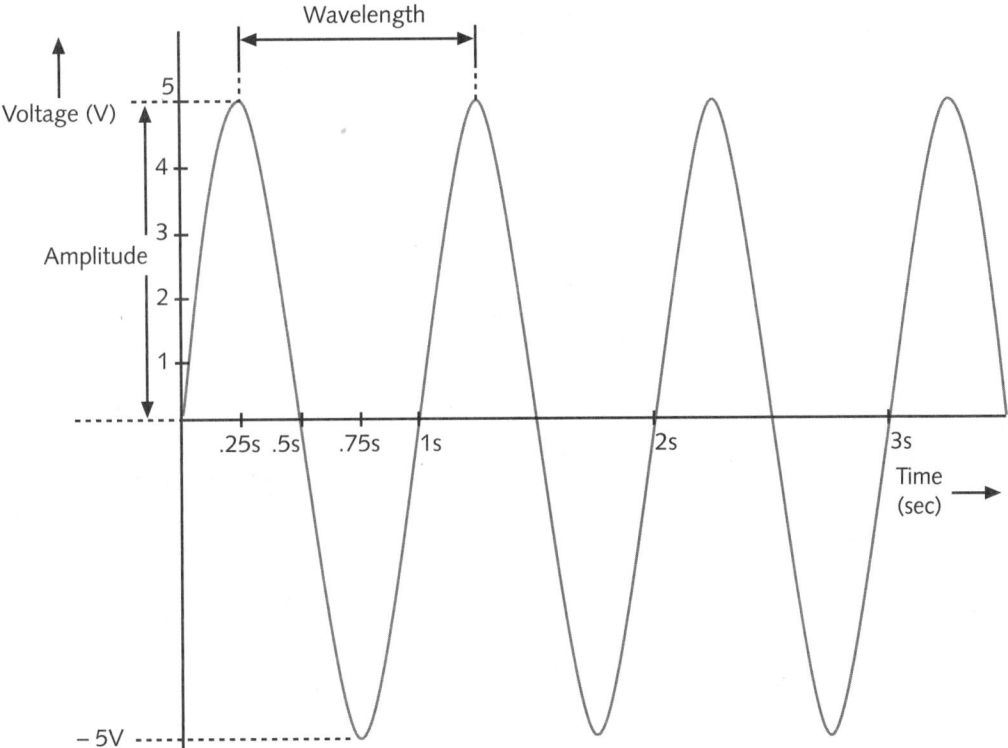

Figure 4-1   An example of an analog signal

An analog signal, like other waveforms, is characterized by four fundamental properties: amplitude, frequency, wavelength, and phase. A wave's **amplitude** is a measure of its strength at any given point in time. On a wave graph, the amplitude is essentially the height of the wave. In Figure 4-1, for example, the wave has an amplitude of 5 volts at .25 seconds and an amplitude of 0 volts at .5 seconds, and an amplitude of –5 volts at .75 seconds.

Whereas amplitude indicates an analog signal's strength, **frequency** is the number of times that a signal's amplitude cycles from its starting point to its highest or lowest amplitude, then to its lowest or highest amplitude and back to its starting amplitude over a fixed period of time. Frequency is expressed in cycles per second, or **hertz (Hz)**, named after German physicist Heinrich Hertz, who experimented with electromagnetic waves in the late nineteenth century. For example, in Figure 4-1 the wave cycles to its highest then lowest amplitude and returns to its starting point once in 1 second. Thus, the frequency of that wave would be 1 cycle per second, or 1 Hz—which, as it turns out, is an extremely low frequency. Frequencies used to convey speech over telephone wires fall in the 300 to 3300 Hz range. An FM radio station may use a frequency between 850,000 Hz (or 850 KHz) and 108,000,000 Hz (or 108 MHz) to transmit its signal through the air. You will learn more about radio frequencies used in networking later in this chapter.

The distance between corresponding points on a wave's cycle is called its **wavelength**, as shown in Figure 4-1. Wavelengths are expressed in meters or feet. A wave's wavelength is inversely proportional to its frequency. In other words, the higher the frequency, the shorter the wavelength. For example, a wave with a frequency of 1,000,000 cycles per second (1MHz) has a wavelength of 300 meters, while a wave with a frequency of 2,000,000 Hz (2 MHz) has a wavelength of 150 meters.

The term **phase** refers to the progress of a wave over time in relationship to a fixed point. An analogy will help to clarify this concept. Imagine that you and a friend are walking on the beach, both of you dragging a stick through the sand, swinging it from right to left in a wave pattern. Assume that both of you swing your sticks the same distance to the right and left (amplitude), and also assume that you are walking at the same rate (frequency). If you and your friend begin at the same spot, your waves will have equivalent phases. If, however, your friend starts one foot in front of you, even though she is dragging her stick the same distance to the left and right and walking at the same pace, your waves will not look identical because their maximum heights will not line up. That is, their phases will differ. Figure 4-2 illustrates the concept of phase.

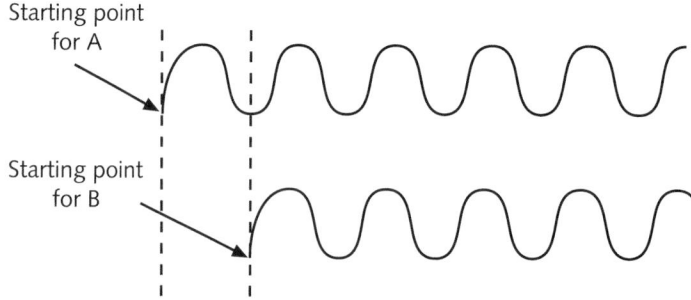

Figure 4-2   Phase differences

So far you have learned about wave properties applied to a very simple, single-frequency wave. However, voices and instruments emit a complex composite of fundamental tones whose frequencies and amplitudes rapidly vary. Figure 4-3 provides an example of an analog signal of a person speaking a full sentence. Because each person's voice patterns vary, a representation of the signal you generate when speaking the same sentence would look somewhat different.

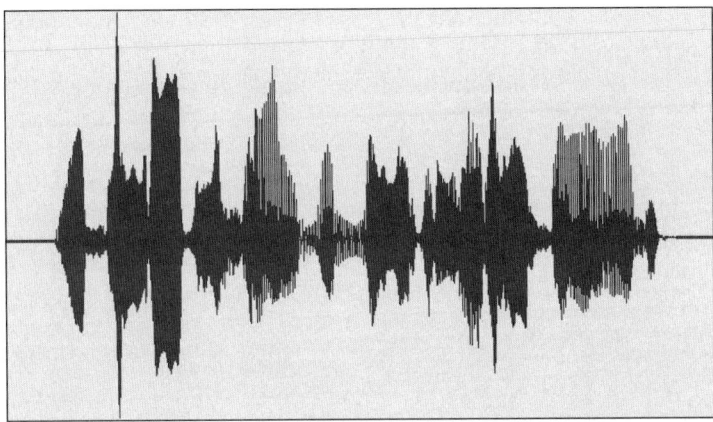

Figure 4-3   A complex analog signal representing human speech

One benefit to analog signals is that, because they are more variable than digital signals, they can convey greater subtleties. For example, think of the difference between your voice and the digital voice of an automated teller machine or a digital answering machine. These digital voices have a poorer quality than your own voice—that is, they sound "like machines." They can't convey the subtle changes in inflection that you expect in a human voice.

Now contrast the analog signals pictured in Figures 4-1 through 4-3 to a digital signal, as shown in Figure 4-4. Digital signals are composed of pulses of precise, positive voltages and zero voltages. A pulse of positive voltage represents a 1. A pulse of zero voltage (in other words, the lack of any voltage) represents a 0. As in any **binary** system, these 1s and 0s combine to encode information. Every pulse in the digital signal is called a binary digit, or **bit**. A bit can have only one of two possible values: 1 or 0. Eight bits together form a **byte**. In broad terms, one byte carries one piece of information. For example, the byte "01111001" means "121" on a digital network. As you learned in Chapter 3, in the case of TCP/IP addressing, a byte is also known as an octet.

Because digital transmission involves sending and receiving only a pattern of 1s and 0s, represented by precise pulses, it is more reliable than analog transmission, which relies on variable waves. In addition, **noise**, or any type of interference that may degrade a signal affects digital transmission less severely. On the other hand, digital transmission requires many pulses to transmit the same amount of information that an analog signal can transmit with a single wave. For example, you might convey the word "one" with a few waves in analog format; in digital format, however, the same message would require 8 bits (00000001), or eight separate pulses. Nevertheless, the high reliability of digital transmission makes this extra signaling worthwhile. In the end, digital transmission is more efficient than analog transmission, because it causes fewer errors and, therefore, requires less overhead to compensate for errors.

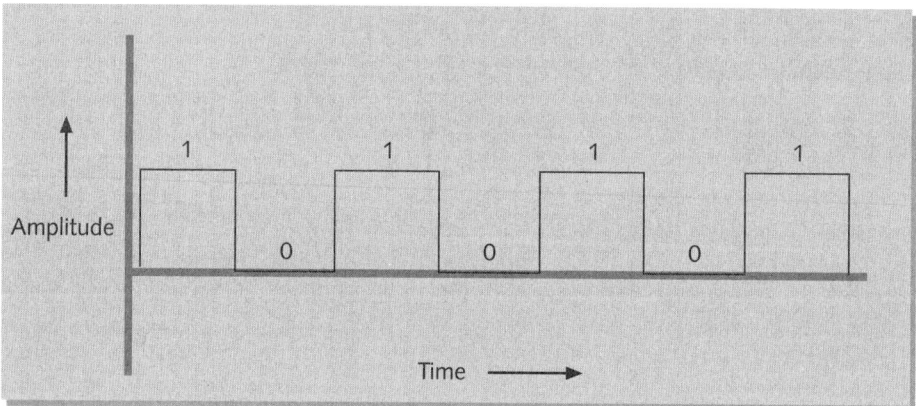

Figure 4-4   An example of a digital signal

 Overhead is a term used by networking professionals to describe the nondata information that must accompany data in order for a signal to be properly routed and interpreted by the network. Overhead is also used in other professions to describe what must be done in addition to a stated task in order to accomplish that task. For example, suppose you want a loan from your bank. The task you wish to accomplish is simply obtaining a certain amount of money. However, you must first talk with a bank employee and complete an application. The bank employee then must run a credit check to make sure you are a safe risk. The credit check may require the cooperation of other financial institutions. If the loan is very large, it may require the involvement of other bank employees. After more paperwork, and a review process, the loan will be approved. Next the bank will issue you a check. Its employees will also update your personal account information. Most of these steps do not equal giving you money. Instead, they contribute to the overhead of obtaining money. Data transmission overhead is an important networking concept when analyzing a network's performance, because, when all other factors are equal, the more overhead a transmission requires, the longer it will take to reach its destination.

It is important to understand that in both the analog and digital worlds, a variety of signaling techniques are used. For each different technique, standards (established by professional organizations such as IEEE or government organizations such as the FCC) dictate what type of transmitter, communications channel, and receiver should be used. For example, the type of transmitter (NIC) used for computers on a LAN and the way in which this transmitter manipulates electric current to produce signals is different from the transmitter and signaling techniques used on a satellite dish. While not all signaling methods are covered in this book, you will learn about the most common methods used for data networking.

Data Modulation

Most networks rely exclusively on digital transmissions. One situation in which you are likely to employ analog signals to transmit data is when you use a modem to connect two systems. The modem may transmit signals in analog over the phone lines, but the signals must be converted into digital signals by the modem at the receiving computer. The word **modem** reflects this device's function as a *modulator/demodulator*—that is, it modulates digital signals into analog signals at the transmitting end, then demodulates analog signals into digital signals at the receiving end. (You will learn more about modem communications in Chapter 7.)

Data modulation is a technology used to modify analog signals in order to make them suitable for carrying data over a communication path. In **modulation**, a simple wave, called a carrier wave, is combined with another analog signal to produce a unique signal that gets transmitted from one node to another. The carrier wave has preset properties (including frequency, amplitude, and phase). Its purpose is merely to help convey information; in other words, it does not represent information. Another signal, known as the information or data wave, is added to the carrier wave. When the information wave is added, it modifies one property of the carrier wave (for example, the frequency, amplitude, or phase). The result is a new, blended signal that contains properties of both the carrier wave and added data. When the signal reaches its destination, the receiver separates the data from the carrier wave.

Modulation can be used to make a signal conform to a specific pathway, as in the case of **frequency modulation (FM)** radio, in which the data must travel along a particular frequency. Modulation may also be used to issue multiple signals to the same communications channel and prevent the signals from interfering with one another. In frequency modulation, the frequency of the carrier signal is modified by the application of the data signal. Figure 4-5 depicts an unaltered carrier wave, a data wave, and the combined wave as modified through frequency modulation. (In **amplitude modulation (AM)**, the amplitude of the carrier signal is modified by the application of the data signal.) Later in this book you will learn about networking technologies, such as DSL, that make use of modulation.

Transmission Direction

Data transmission, whether analog or digital, may also be characterized by the direction in which the signals travel over the media.

Simplex, Half-Duplex and Duplex

In cases where signals may travel in only one direction, the transmission is considered **simplex**. For example, a football coach calling out orders to his team through a megaphone is using simplex communication. In this example, the coach's voice is the signal, and it travels in only one direction—away from the megaphone's mouthpiece and toward the team. Simplex is sometimes called one-way, or unidirectional, communication.

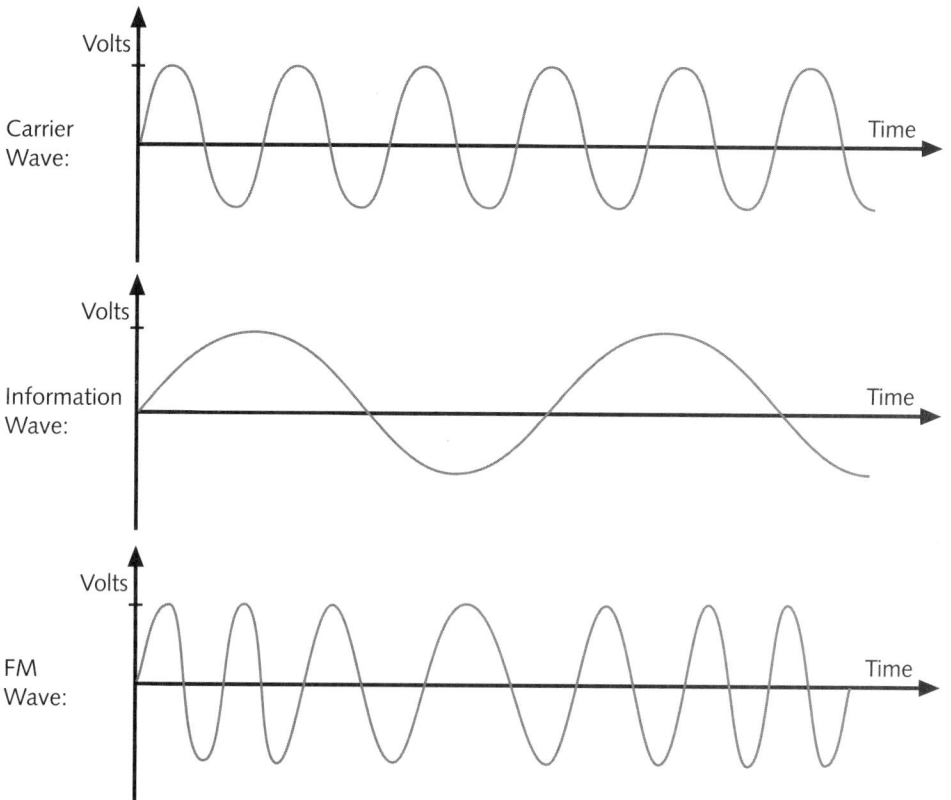

Figure 4-5   A carrier wave modified by frequency modulation

In **half-duplex** transmission signals may travel in both directions over a medium but in only one direction at a time. Half-duplex systems contain only one channel for communication, and that channel must be shared for multiple nodes to exchange information. For example, an apartment's intercom system that requires you to press a "talk" button in order to allow your voice to be transmitted over the wire uses half-duplex transmission. If you visit a friend's apartment building, you press the "talk" button to send your voice signals to their apartment. When your friend responds, he presses the "talk" button in his apartment to send his voice signal in the opposite direction over the wire to the speaker in the lobby where you wait. If you press the "talk" button while he's talking, you will not be able to hear his voice transmission. In a similar manner, some networks operate with only half-duplex capability over their wires.

When signals are free to travel in both directions over a medium simultaneously, the transmission is considered **full-duplex**. Full-duplex may also be called bidirectional transmission or sometimes, simply **duplex**. When you call a friend on the telephone, your connection is an example of a full-duplex transmission, because your voice signals can be transmitted to your friend at the same time your friend's voice signals are transmitted in the opposite direction to you. In other words, both of you can talk and hear each other simultaneously.

Full-duplex transmission is also used on data networks. For example, modern Ethernet networks use full-duplex. In this situation, full-duplex transmission uses multiple channels on the same medium. A **channel** is a distinct communication path between two or more nodes, much as a lane is a distinct transportation path on a freeway. Channels may be separated either logically or physically. You will learn about logically separate channels in the next section. An example of physically separate channels occurs when one wire within a network cable is be used for transmission while another wire is used for reception. In this example, while each separate wire in the medium allows half-duplex transmission, when combined in a cable they form a medium that provides full-duplex transmission. Full-duplex capability increases the speed with which data can travel over a network. In some cases—for example, telephone service over the Internet—full-duplex data networks are a requirement. Figure 4-6 compares simplex, half-duplex, and full-duplex transmissions.

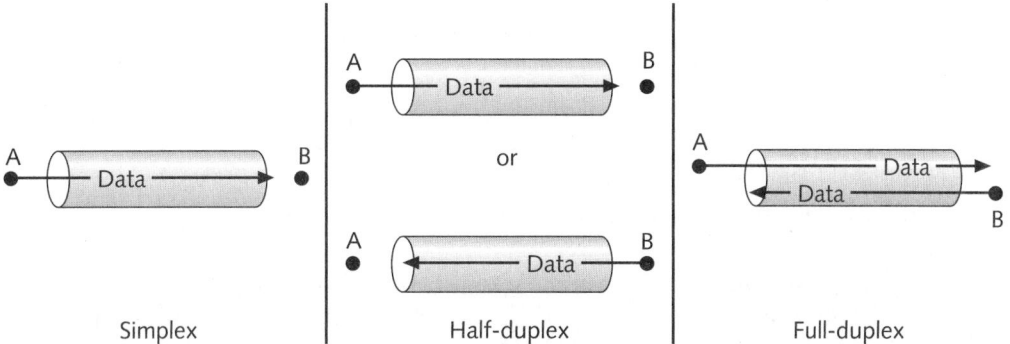

Figure 4-6   Simplex, half-duplex, and full-duplex transmission

Many network devices, such as modems and NICs, allow you to specify whether the device should use half- or full-duplex communication. It's important to know what type of transmission a network supports before installing network devices on that network. If you configure a computer's NIC to use full-duplex while the rest of the network is using half-duplex, for example, that computer will not be able to communicate on the network. Network hardware settings are explained in more detail in Chapter 6.

Multiplexing

A form of transmission that allows multiple signals to travel simultaneously over one medium is known as **multiplexing**. In order to accommodate multiple signals, the single medium is logically separated into multiple channels, or **subchannels**. There are many different types of multiplexing, and the type used in any given situation depends on what the media, transmission and reception equipment can handle. For each type of multiplexing, a device that can combine many signals on a channel, a **multiplexer (mux)**, is required at the sending end of the channel. At the receiving end, a **demultiplexer (demux)** separates the combined signals and regenerates them in their original form.

Multiplexing is commonly used on networks to increase the amount of data that can be transmitted in a given time span. For example, one type of multiplexing, **time division multiplexing (TDM)**, divides a channel into multiple intervals of time, or time slots. It then assigns a separate time slot to every node on the network and in that time slot, carries data from that node. For example, if five stations are connected to a network over one wire, five different time slots would be established in the communications channel. Workstation A may be assigned time slot 1, workstation B time slot 2, workstation C time slot 3, and so on. Time slots are reserved for their designated nodes no matter whether the node has data to transmit or not. If a node does not have data to send, nothing will be sent during its time slot. This arrangement can be inefficient if some nodes on the network rarely send data. Figure 4-7 shows a simple TDM model.

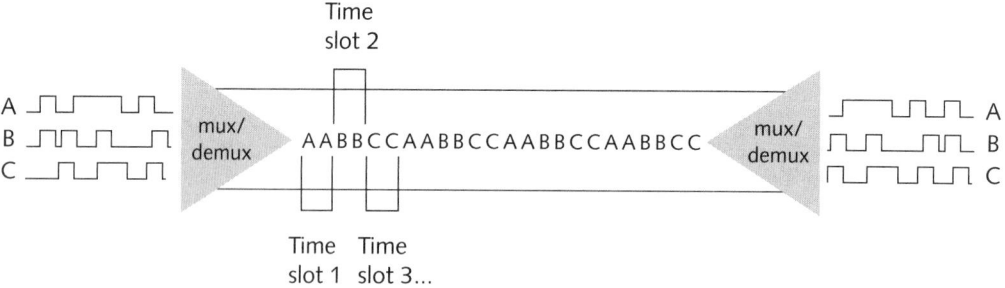

Figure 4-7   Time division multiplexing

Statistical multiplexing is similar to time division multiplexing, but rather than assigning a separate slot to each node in succession, it assigns slots to nodes according to priority and need. This method is more efficient than TDM because in statistical multiplexing time slots are unlikely to remain empty. To begin with, statistical multiplexing, like TDM, assigns one time slot per node. However, if a node doesn't use its time slot, statistical multiplexing devices will recognize that and assign its slot to another node that needs to send data. The contention for slots may be arbitrated according to use or priority or even more sophisticated factors, depending on the network. Most importantly, statistical multiplexing allows networks to maximize available bandwidth. Figure 4-8 depicts a simple statistical multiplexing system.

Figure 4-8 Statistical multiplexing

Wavelength division multiplexing (WDM) is a relatively new technology used only with fiber-optic cable. In fiber-optic transmission, data is represented as pulses of light (you will learn more about how this occurs later in this chapter). WDM enables one fiber-optic connection to carry multiple light signals simultaneously. Each carrier signal in WDM is assigned a different wavelength, which equates to its own separate subchannel. The wavelength of each carrier signal is then modulated with a data signal. In this manner multiple signals can be simultaneously transmitted in the same direction over a length of fiber. In fact, using WDM, a single fiber can transmit as many as 2 million telephone conversations.

Depending on the type of equipment and fiber used, WDM may send multiplexed signals in one direction or two directions simultaneously. At the transmitting end, an WDM wave is created by a **fiber-optic modem (FOM)** and at the receiving end, an FOM separates the multiplexed signals into individual signals according to their different wavelengths, as shown in Figure 4-9. In between, the multiple signals may need to be regenerated to carry over long distances, but with lightwave technology, this is simple to do.

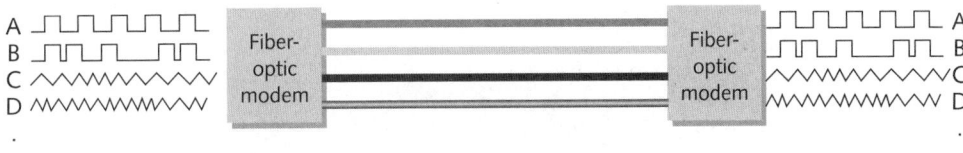

Figure 4-9 Wavelength division multiplexing

Time division multiplexing, statistical multiplexing, and wavelength division multiplexing are most often used in high-bandwidth or long-distance networks such as WANs. You will learn more about transmission technologies that use multiplexing in Chapter 7.

Relationships Between Nodes

So far you have learned about two important characteristics of data transmission: the type of signaling (analog or digital) and the direction in which the signal travels (simplex, half-duplex, duplex, or multiplex). Another important characteristic is the number of senders and receivers, as well as the relationship between them. In general, data communications may involve a single transmitter with one or more receivers, or multiple transmitters with one or more receivers. The remainder of this section introduces the most common relationships between transmitters and receivers.

When a data transmission involves one transmitter and one receiver, it is considered a **point-to-point** transmission. An office building in Dallas exchanging data with another office in St. Louis over a WAN connection is an example of point-to-point transmission. In this case, the sender only transmits data that is intended to be used by a specific receiver. By contrast, **broadcast** transmission involves one transmitter and multiple receivers. For example, a TV station indiscriminately transmitting a signal from its tower to thousands of homes with TVs uses broadcast transmission. A broadcast transmission sends data to any and all receivers, without regard for which receiver can use it. Broadcast transmissions are frequently used on networks because they are simple and quick. They are used to identify certain nodes, to send data to certain nodes (even though every node is capable of picking up the transmitted data, only the destination node will actually do it), and to send announcements to all nodes. Another example of network broadcast transmission is sending video signals to multiple viewers on a network. When used over the Web, this type of broadcast transmission is called **Webcasting**. Figure 4-10 contrasts point-to-point and broadcast transmissions.

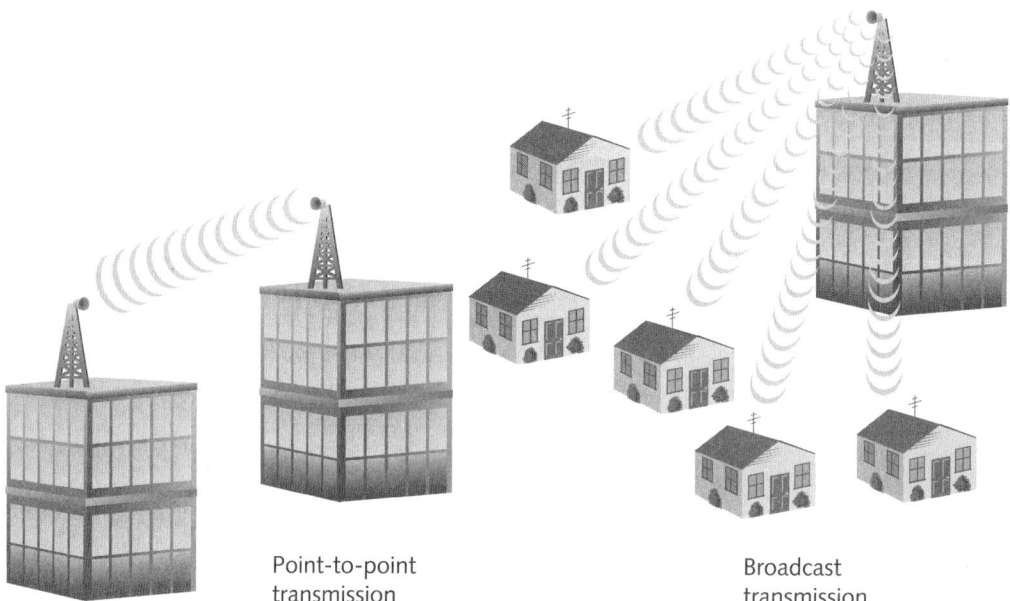

Point-to-point
transmission

Broadcast
transmission

Figure 4-10   Point-to-point versus broadcast transmission

Throughput and Bandwidth

The data transmission characteristic most frequently discussed and analyzed by networking professionals is throughput. **Throughput** is the measure of how much data is transmitted during a given period of time. It may also be called **capacity** or bandwidth (though as you will learn, bandwidth is technically different from throughput). Throughput is commonly expressed as a quantity of bits transmitted per second, with prefixes used to designate different throughput amounts. For example, the prefix "kilo" combined with the word "bit" (as in "kilobit") indicates a 1000 bits per second. Rather than talking about a transmission speed of 1000 bits per second, you would typically say the speed was 1 kilobit per second. Table 4-1 summarizes the terminology and abbreviations used when discussing different throughput amounts. As an example, a typical modem connecting a home PC to the Internet would probably be rated for a maximum throughput of 56.6 Kbps. A very fast LAN might transport up to 1 Gbps of data. The most common contemporary networks achieve throughputs between 10 and 100 Mbps.

Table 4-1   Throughput measures

Quantity	Prefix	Complete Example	Abbreviation
1 bit per second	n/a	1 bit per second	bps
1000 bits per second	kilo	1 kilobit per second	Kbps
1,000,000 bits per second	mega	1 megabit per second	Mbps
1,000,000,000 bits per second	giga	1 gigabit per second	Gbps
1,000,000,000,000 bits per second	tera	1 terabit per second	Tbps

Be careful not to confuse bits and bytes when discussing throughput. Although data storage quantities are typically expressed in multiples of bytes, data transmission quantities (in other words, throughput) are more commonly expressed in multiples of bits per second. Recall that one byte equals 8 bits. When representing different data quantities, a small "b" represents bits, while a capital "B" represents bytes. To put this into context, a modem may transmit data at 56.6 Kbps (kilobits per second); a data file may be 56 KB (kilobytes) in size.

Often, the term "bandwidth" is used interchangeably with throughput, and in fact, this may be the case on the Network+ certification exam. Bandwidth and throughput are similar concepts, but strictly speaking, **bandwidth** is a measure of the difference between the highest and lowest frequencies that a medium can transmit. This range of frequencies, which is expressed in Hz, is directly related to throughput. For example, if the FCC told you that you could transmit a radio signal between 870 and 880 MHz, your allotted bandwidth would be 10 MHz. Because higher frequencies can transmit more data in a given period of time than lower frequencies, bandwidth and throughput are directly related. The higher the bandwidth, the higher the throughput. Later in this chapter, you will discover the throughput characteristics of the most common networking media.

Baseband and Broadband

Baseband is a transmission form in which (typically) digital signals are sent through direct current (DC) pulses applied to the wire. This direct current requires exclusive use of the wire's capacity. As a result, baseband systems can transmit only one signal, or one channel, at a time. Every device on a baseband system shares the same channel. When one node is transmitting data on a baseband system, all other nodes on the network must wait for that transmission to end before they can send data. Baseband transmission supports bidirectional signal flow, which means that computers can both send and receive information on the same length of wire.

Ethernet is an example of a baseband system found on many LANs. In Ethernet (which is described in detail in Chapter 5), each device on a network can transmit over the wire—but only one device at a time. For example, if you want to save a file to the server, your NIC submits your request to use the wire; if no other device is using the wire to transmit data at that time, your workstation can go ahead. If the wire is in use, you must wait and try again later. Of course, this retrying process happens so quickly that you, as the user, may not even notice the wait.

Broadband is a form of transmission in which signals are modulated as radiofrequency (RF) analog pulses that use different frequency ranges. Unlike baseband, broadband technology does not involve digital pulses. Nevertheless, the use of multiple frequencies enables a broadband system to access several channels and, therefore, carry much more data than a baseband system.

As you may know, broadband transmission is used to bring cable TV to your home. Your cable TV connection can carry at least 25 times as much data as a typical baseband system (like Ethernet) carries, including many different broadcast frequencies (channels). In traditional broadband systems, signals travel in only one direction. Therefore, broadband cabling must provide a separate wire for the transmission and the receipt of data. (Because most TV cable provides only one wire, it cannot be used for transmitting data out of your home without some modification. In Chapter 7, you will learn more about using cable to provide Internet access.) Broadband transmission is generally more expensive than baseband transmission because of the extra hardware involved. On the other hand, broadband systems can span longer distances than baseband.

In the field of networking, some terms have more than one meaning, depending on their context. "Broadband" is one of those terms. The "broadband" described in this chapter is the transmission system that carries RF signals across multiple channels on a coaxial cable, as used by cable TV. This definition was the original meaning of broadband. In the discussion of WANs in Chapter 7, the term "broadband" refers to networks that use digital signaling and have very high transmission rates, such as Asynchronous Transfer Mode (ATM) networks.

Transmission Flaws

Both analog and digital signals are susceptible to degradation between the time they are issued by a transmitter and the time they are received. One of the most common transmission flaws affecting data signals is noise. As you learned earlier in this chapter, noise is interference from external sources that may degrade or distort a signal. Many different types of noise may affect transmission. Most of these are caused by one of two electromagnetic phenomenon: **electromagnetic interference (EMI)** or **radiofrequency interference (RFI)**. Both EMI and RFI are waves that emanate from electrical devices or cables carrying electricity. Motors, power lines, televisions, copiers, fluorescent lights, and other sources of electrical activity (including a severe thunderstorm) can cause both EMI and RFI. RFI may also be caused by strong broadcast signals from radio or TV towers. The extent to which noise affects a signal is influenced by the transmission media used to carry the signal. Wireless transmission is typically more susceptible to noise than wireline transmission.

You may be familiar with noise if you have talked on a phone and heard a hissing sound in the background or if you've tried to tune into a distant radio station while driving under strong power lines. When noise affects analog signals, this distortion can result in the incorrect transmission of data, just as if static on the phone line prevented you from hearing the person on the other end of the line. Figure 4-11 shows an analog signal affected by noise.

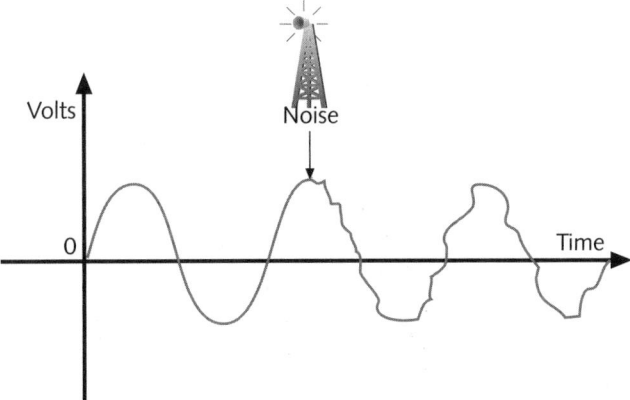

Figure 4-11   An analog signal distorted by noise

While noise affects digital signals, it affects them less severely than analog signals. As shown in Figure 4-12, a digital signal distorted by noise can still be interpreted as a pattern of 1s and 0s.

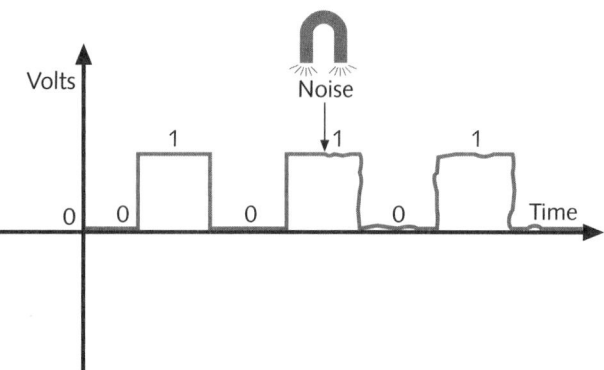

Figure 4-12   A digital signal distorted by noise

Another transmission flaw is **attenuation**, or the loss of a signal's strength as it travels away from its source. In order to compensate for attenuation, both analog and digital signals are strengthened en route to travel farther. However, the technology used to strengthen an analog signal is different from that used to strengthen a digital signal. Analog signals pass through an **amplifier**, an electronic device that increases the voltage, or power, of the signals. When an analog signal is amplified, the noise that it has accumulated is also amplified. This indiscriminate amplification causes the analog signal to progressively worsen. After multiple amplifications, an analog signal may become difficult to decipher. Figure 4-13 shows an analog signal distorted by noise and then amplified once.

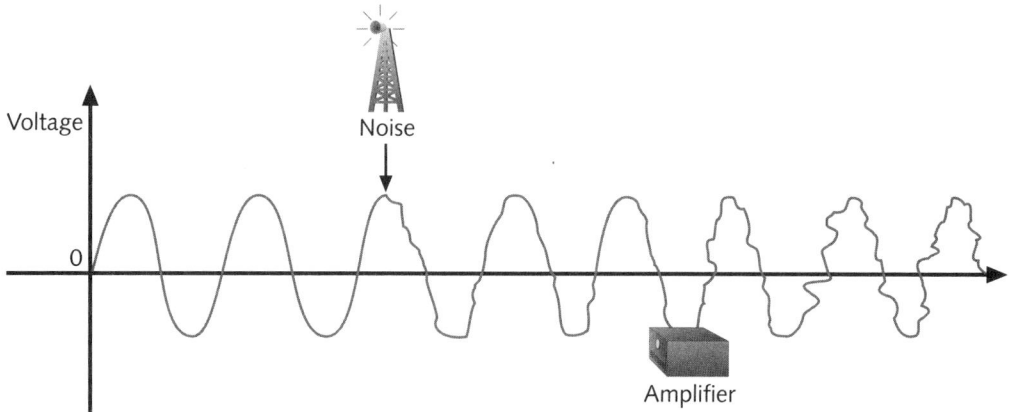

Figure 4-13   An analog signal distorted by noise, and then amplified

When digital signals are repeated, they are actually retransmitted in their original, pure form, without any noise. This process is known as **regeneration**. A device that regenerates a digital signal is called a **repeater**. Figure 4-14 shows a digital signal distorted by noise and then regenerated by a repeater.

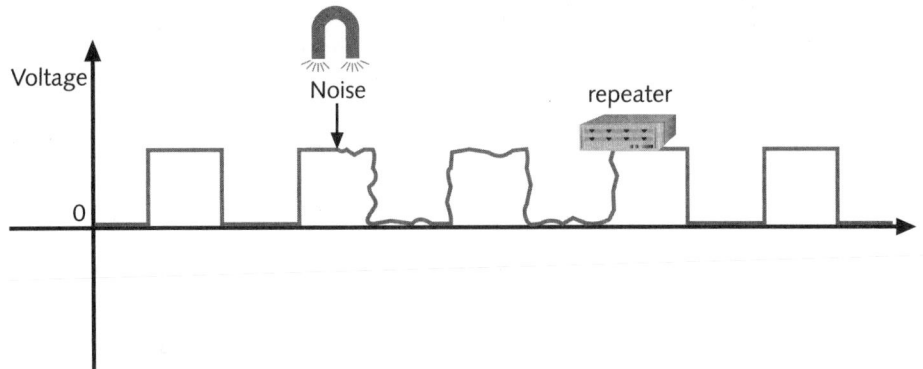

Figure 4-14   A digital signal distorted by noise, and then repeated

Amplifiers and repeaters belong to the Physical layer of the OSI Model. Both are used to extend the length of a network. Since most networks are digital, however, data signals are almost always boosted by repeaters. You will learn more about repeaters in Chapter 6.

MEDIA CHARACTERISTICS

Now that you are familiar with variations in data signaling, you are ready to understand the transmission media, or the physical or atmospheric paths that these signals traverse. When deciding which kind of transmission media to use, you must match your networking needs with the characteristics of the media. This section describes the characteristics of all types of media. Later, you will learn about the various types of media, and how to choose the appropriate media for your network.

Generally speaking, you must consider five characteristics when choosing a data transfer media: throughput, cost, size and scalability, connectors, and noise immunity. Of course, every networking situation varies; what is significant for one organization may not matter to another. You need to decide what matters most to your organization.

Throughput

Perhaps the most significant factor in choosing a transmission medium is throughput. The physical nature of every transmission medium determines its potential throughput. For example, the laws of physics limit how fast electricity can travel over copper wire, just as they limit how much water can travel through a 1-inch-diameter hose. If you try to direct more water through the 1-inch-diameter hose than it can handle, you will wind up with water splashing back at you or a ruptured hose. Similarly, if you try to push more data through a copper wire than it can handle, the result will be lost data and data errors. Noise and devices connected to the transmission medium can further limit throughput. A noisy circuit spends more time compensating for the noise and, therefore, has fewer resources available for transmitting data.

Cost

The cost implications of transmission media are difficult to pinpoint. While a vendor might quote you the cost per foot of a new type of network cabling, you might have to upgrade some expensive hardware on your network in order to use that type of cabling. Thus, the cost of that cabling would really include more than just the cost of the cabling itself. Not only do media costs depend on the hardware that already exists in a network, but they also depend on the length of your network and the cost of labor in your area (unless you plan to install the cable yourself). The following variables can all influence the final cost of implementing a certain type of media:

- *Cost of installation*—Can you install the media yourself, or must you hire contractors to do it? Will you need to move walls or build new conduits or closets? Will you need to lease lines from a service provider?

- *Cost of new infrastructure versus reusing existing infrastructure*—Can you use existing wiring? In some cases, for example, installing all new Category 7 UTP wiring may not pay off if you can use existing Category 5 UTP wiring. If you replace only part of your infrastructure, will it be easily integrated with the existing media?

- *Cost of maintenance and support*—Reuse of an existing cabling infrastructure does not save any money if it is in constant need of repair or enhancement. Also, if you use an unfamiliar media type, it may cost more to hire a technician to service it. Will you be able to service the media yourself, or must you hire contractors to service it?

- *Cost of a lower transmission rate affecting productivity*—If you save money by reusing existing slower lines, are you incurring costs by reducing productivity? In other words, are you making staff wait longer to save and print reports or exchange e-mail?

- *Cost of obsolescence*—Are you choosing media that may become passing fads, requiring rapid replacement? Will you be able to find reasonably priced connectivity hardware that will be compatible with your chosen media for years to come?

Size and Scalability

Three specifications determine the size and scalability of networking media: maximum nodes per segment, maximum segment length, and maximum network length. In cabling, each of these specifications is based on a physical characteristic of the wire. The maximum number of nodes per segment depends on the attenuation. Each device added to a network segment increases the signal's attenuation slightly. To ensure a clear, strong signal, you must limit the number of nodes on a segment.

The length of a network segment is also limited because of attenuation. After a certain distance, a signal loses so much strength that it cannot be accurately interpreted. Before this deterioration occurs, a repeater on the network must retransmit and amplify the signal. The maximum distance that a signal can travel and still be accurately interpreted equals the maximum segment length. Beyond this length, data loss is apt to occur. As with the maximum number of nodes per segment, maximum segment length varies between different cabling types.

In an ideal world, networks could transmit data instantaneously between sender and receiver, no matter how far apart the two were. Unfortunately, we don't live in an ideal world, and every network is subjected to a delay between the transmission of a signal and its eventual receipt. For example, when you press a key on your computer to save a file to the network, the file's data must travel through your NIC, the network wire, a hub or possibly a switch or router, more cabling, and the server's NIC before it lands on the server's hard disk. Although electrons travel rapidly, they still have to travel, and a brief delay takes place between the moment you press the key and the moment the server accepts the data. This delay is called **latency**.

The length of the cable involved affects latency, as does the existence of any intervening connectivity device, such as a router. The effects of latency become a problem only when a receiving node is expecting some type of communication, such as the rest of a data stream it has begun to accept. If that node does not receive the rest of the data stream, it assumes that no more data is coming. This assumption causes transmission errors on a network. When you connect multiple network segments, you increase the latency in the network. To constrain the latency and avoid its associated errors, each type of cabling is rated for a maximum number of connected network segments.

Connectors

Connectors are the pieces of hardware that connect the wire to the network device, be it a file server, workstation, switch, or printer. Every networking medium requires a specific kind of connector. The type of connectors you use will affect the cost of installing and maintaining the network, the ease of adding new segments or nodes to the network, and the technical expertise required to maintain the network. For example, connectors used with UTP wiring (which look like large telephone wire connectors) are much simpler to insert and replace than are the connectors used with coaxial cabling. UTP wiring connectors are also less expensive and can be used for a variety of cabling designs. You will learn more about the connectors required by different media in this chapter.

Noise Immunity

As you learned earlier, noise (such as EMI from fluorescent lights or motors) can distort data signals. The extent to which noise affects a signal depends partly on the transmission media. Some types of media are more susceptible to noise than others. For example, if you were to issue data signals on a bare copper wire, those signals would be more susceptible to degradation by external EMI sources than signals traveling over a copper wire surrounded by insulation. The type of media least susceptible to noise is fiber-optic cable, because it does not use electric current, but light waves, to conduct signals. In this chapter you will learn how each medium compares in its resistance to noise.

On most networks, noise is an ever-present threat, so you should take measures to limit its impact on your network. For example, you should install cabling well away from powerful electromagnetic forces. If your environment still leaves your network vulnerable, you should choose a type of transmission media that guards the signal-carrying wire from noise. As a general rule, thicker cables are less susceptible to noise, as are cables coated with a protective shielding. It is also possible to use antinoise algorithms to protect data from being corrupted by noise. If these measures don't ward off interference, you may need to use a metal **conduit**, or pipeline, to contain and further protect the cabling.

Now that you understand data transmission and the factors to consider when choosing a transmission medium, you are ready to learn about different types of networking cabling. To qualify for Net+ certification, you must know the characteristics and limitations of each type of cabling, how to install and design a network with each type, and how to provide for future network growth with each cabling option.

 The terms "wire" and "cable" are used synonymously in some situations. Strictly speaking, however, "wire" is a subset of "cabling," because the "cabling" category may also include fiber-optic cable, which is almost never called "wire." The exact meaning of the term "wire" depends on context. For example, if you said, in a somewhat casual way, "We had 6 gigs of data go over the wire last night," you would be referring to whatever transmission media helped carry the data—whether fiber, radio waves, coax, or UTP.

COAXIAL CABLE

Coaxial cable, called "coax" for short, was the foundation for Ethernet networks in the 1980s and remained a popular transmission medium for many years. Over time, however, twisted-pair cabling has replaced coax in most modern LANs. Coaxial cable consists of a central copper core surrounded by an insulator, a braided metal shielding, called

braiding, and an outer cover, called the **sheath** or jacket. Figure 4-15 depicts a typical coaxial cable. The copper core carries the electromagnetic signal, and the braided metal shielding acts as both a shield against noise and a ground for the signal. The insulator layer usually consists of a plastic material such as polyvinyl chloride (PVC) or Teflon. It protects the copper core from the metal shielding, because if the two made contact, the wire would short-circuit. The jacket, which protects the cable from physical damage, may be PVC or a more expensive, fire-resistant plastic.

4

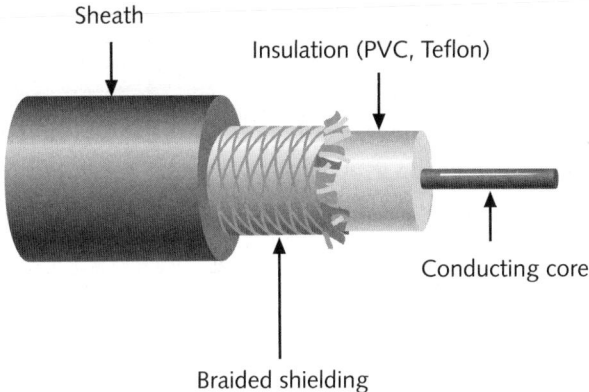

Sheath

Insulation (PVC, Teflon)

Conducting core

Braided shielding

Figure 4-15   Coaxial cable

Because of its insulation and protective braiding, coaxial cable has a high resistance to interference from noise. It can also carry signals farther than twisted-pair cabling before amplification of the signals becomes necessary, although not as far as fiber-optic cabling. On the other hand, coaxial cable is more expensive than twisted-pair cable because it requires significantly more raw materials (such as copper for the core, Teflon for the insulation, and so on) to manufacture. Coaxial cable is also less desirable than twisted-pair because it supports lower throughput.

Coaxial cabling comes in many specifications, although you are likely to see only two or three types of coax in use today. In any case, all types have been assigned an RG specification number. (RG stands for "radio guide," which is appropriate because coaxial cabling is used to guide radiofrequencies in broadband transmission.) The significant differences between the cable types lie in the materials used for their center cores, which in turn influence their impedance (or the resistance that contributes to controlling the signal, as expressed in ohms), throughput, and typical usage. Table 4-2 lists the specifications for several types of coaxial cable. The two with which you should be familiar are RG-58A/U (Thinnet) and RG-8 (Thicknet). As you can see, additional types of coaxial cabling exist (in fact, hundreds more than are represented here), but these are not typically used for data networking.

Table 4-2   Some types of coaxial cable

Designation	Type	Impedance (in ohms)	Description
RG-8	Thickwire	50	Solid core; used for Thicknet LANs
RG-58/U	Thinwire	53.5	Solid copper core; similar to RG-58A/U, but due to insufficient shielding should not be used on Thinnet LANs
RG-58A/U	Thinwire	50	Stranded copper core; used for standard Thinnet LANs
RG-58C/U	Thinwire	50	Military version of RG-58A/U used on Thinnet LANs
RG-59/U	CATV	75	Used for cable TV connections
RG-6 and RG-59	Thickwire	93	Used for IBM 3270 terminals and ARCNet (a nearly obsolete type of network)

RG-6 and RG-59 are the cabling specifications used for cable TV transmission. Because of their different impedance characteristics, you cannot use these types of cables for data networks, even though they might fit your connectors.

Thicknet (10Base5)

Thicknet cabling, also called **thickwire Ethernet**, is a rigid coaxial cable approximately 1-cm thick used for the original Ethernet networks. Because it is often covered with a yellow sheath, Thicknet is sometimes called "yellow Ethernet" or "yellow garden hose." IEEE designates Thicknet as **10Base5** Ethernet. The "10" represents its throughput of 10 Mbps, the "Base" stands for baseband transmission, and the "5" represents the maximum segment length of a Thicknet cable, which is 500 m. You will almost never find Thicknet on new networks, but you may find it on older networks, where it is used to connect one data closet to another as part of the network backbone. A **backbone** is essentially a network of networks; you can think of it as the main route through which data on a network travels. The following is a summary of Thicknet's characteristics:

- *Throughput*—According to the IEEE 802.3 standard, Thicknet transmits data at a maximum rate of 10 Mbps. It can only be used for baseband transmission.

- *Cost*—Thicknet is less expensive than fiber-optic cable, but more expensive than other types of coaxial cabling, such as Thinnet.

- *Connector*—Thicknet networks can include a few different types of connectors, which are very different from those used on modern networks. A **vampire tap**, a connector that pierces a hole in the wire, thus completing a connection between the metal tooth in the vampire tap and the copper core of the coaxial cable, joins the network cable with a transceiver. The word **transceiver** derives from its function as both a *trans*mitter and re*ceiver* of signals. Since a transceiver is concerned with applying signals to the wire, it belongs in the Physical layer of the OSI Model. Many different types of transceivers exist in networking. On modern (twisted-pair) networks, transceivers are typically built into the NIC. But in the case of Thicknet networking, the transceiver is a separate device and may also be called a **media access unit (MAU)**. A **drop cable**, which connects a networked node to the transceiver, is pictured in Figure 4-16.

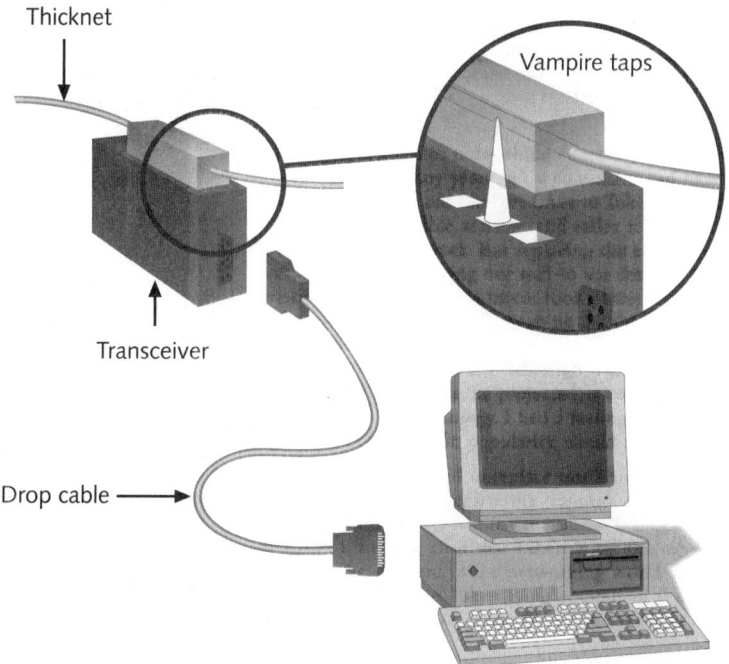

Figure 4-16   Thicknet cable transceiver with detail of a vampire tap

In a Thicknet network, a node's Ethernet interface, a port on the device's NIC, is connected with the drop cable via an AUI connector or an n-series connector. **AUI (Attachment Unit Interface)** is an Ethernet standard that establishes physical specifications for connecting coaxial cables with transceivers and networked nodes. The AUI standard calls for male connectors with 15 pins to connect to the MAU, and female connectors with openings for 15 pins to connect to the network node's Ethernet interface, as shown in Figure 4-17. An AUI connector may also be called a DIX or DB-15 connector. **DIX** stands for Digital, Intel, and Xerox, the three companies that together pioneered Thicknet technology. **DB-15** is a more general term for connectors that use 15 metal pins to complete a connection between devices. "DB" stands for "data bus," while the number "15" indicates how many pins are used to make the connection.

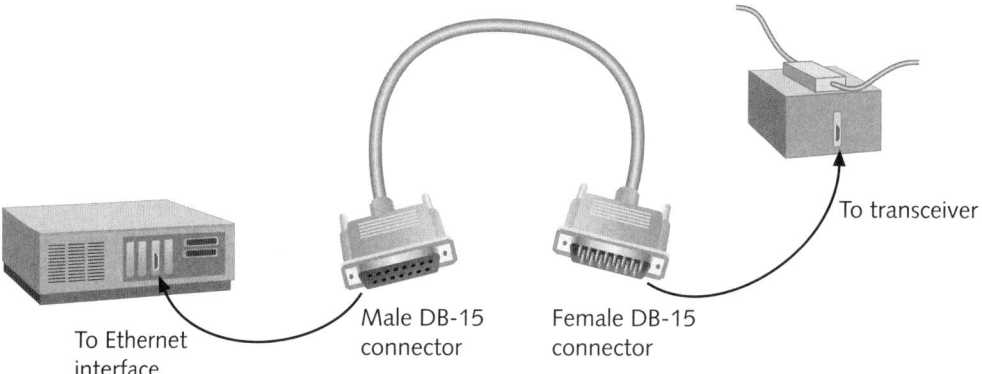

To transceiver

To Ethernet interface

Male DB-15 connector

Female DB-15 connector

Figure 4-17   AUI connectors

The second type of connector that may be used between a transceiver and a network node (though less frequently) is an **n-series connector** (or **n connector**), as shown in Figure 4-18. In this type of connector, a screw-and-barrel arrangement securely connects coaxial cable segments and devices.

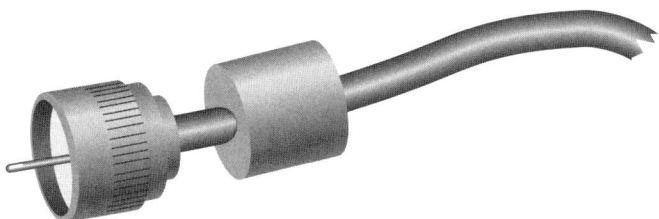

Figure 4-18   N-series connector

- *Noise immunity*—Because of its wide diameter and excellent shielding, Thicknet has the highest resistance to noise of any of the commonly used types of network wiring.

■ *Size and scalability*—Because Thicknet has high resistance to noise, it allows data to travel for longer distances than other types of cabling. Its maximum segment length is 500 m, or approximately 1640 feet. Thicknet standards allow for no more than 100 MAUs per segment, and therefore allow a maximum of 100 nodes per segment. Its maximum network length is 1500 m. To minimize the possibility of interference between stations, network devices should be separated by at least 2.5 m.

Thicknet is rarely used on modern networks because of its significant disadvantages. First, this type of cable is difficult to manage. Its rigidity makes it hard to handle and install. Second, it does not allow for network advances because high-speed data transmission cannot run on Thicknet. Although it is less expensive and more resistant to noise than many of the currently popular transmission media, Thicknet is essentially an obsolete technology.

Thinnet (10Base2)

Thinnet, also known as **thin Ethernet**, was the most popular medium for Ethernet LANs in the 1980s. Like Thicknet, Thinnet is rarely used on modern networks, although you may encounter it on networks installed in the 1980s or on newer small office or home office LANs. IEEE has designated Thinnet as 10Base2 Ethernet, with the "10" representing its data transmission rate of 10 Mbps, the "Base" representing the fact that it uses baseband transmission, and the "2" representing its maximum segment length of 185 (or roughly 200) m. Because of its black sheath, Thinnet may also be called "black Ethernet." Thinnet's cable diameter is approximately 0.64 cm, which makes it more flexible and easier to handle and install than Thicknet. More of Thinnet's characteristics are covered in the following list:

■ *Throughput*—Thinnet can transmit data at a maximum rate of 10 Mbps, via baseband transmission.

■ *Cost*—Thinnet is less expensive than Thicknet and fiber-optic cable, but more expensive than twisted-pair wiring. Prefabricated cables are available for approximately $1/foot. For this reason, Thinnet is sometimes called "cheapnet."

■ *Connector*—Thinnet connects the wire to network devices with **BNC T-connectors**, as shown in Figure 4-19. A BNC T-connector with three open ends attaches to the Ethernet interface card at the base of the "T" and to the Thinnet cable at its two sides so as to allow the signal in and out of the NIC. The origin of the acronym "BNC" is somewhat muddy, but probably stands for British Naval Connector. **BNC barrel connectors** (with only two open ends) are used to join two Thinnet cable segments together, as shown in Figure 4-19.

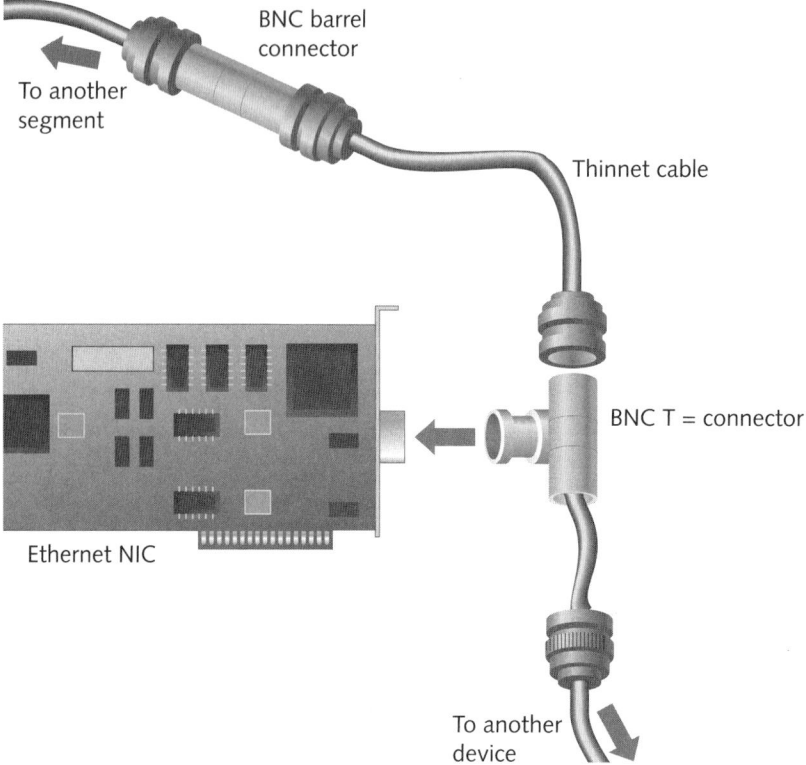

Figure 4-19   Thinnet BNC connectors

- *Size and scalability*— Thinnet allows a maximum of 185 m per network segment, as shown in Figure 4-20. This length is less than that available with Thicknet, because Thinnet's resistance to noise is not as strong. For the same reason, Thinnet can accommodate a maximum of only 30 nodes per segment. Its total maximum network length is slightly more than 550 m. To minimize interference, devices on a Thinnet network should be separated by at least 0.5 m.

- *Noise immunity*—Because of its insulation and shielding, Thinnet is more resistant to noise than twisted-pair wiring. It is not as resistant as Thicknet, however.

Thinnet is occasionally used on modern networks, but more often you will see it on networks installed in the 1980s. Its major advantages are its very low cost and relative ease of use. Because twisted-pair wiring can carry more data and has come down in price, Thinnet has become almost obsolete.

Both Thicknet and Thinnet coaxial cable rely on the bus topology (described in detail in Chapter 5). Recall from Chapter 1 that a topology describes the layout of nodes on a network. In a bus topology, nodes share one, uninterrupted channel. Networks using the bus topology must be terminated at both ends. Without terminators, signals on a bus network would travel endlessly between the two ends of the network, a phenomenon known as **signal bounce**. Figure 4-20 depicts a 10Base2 network using a bus topology.

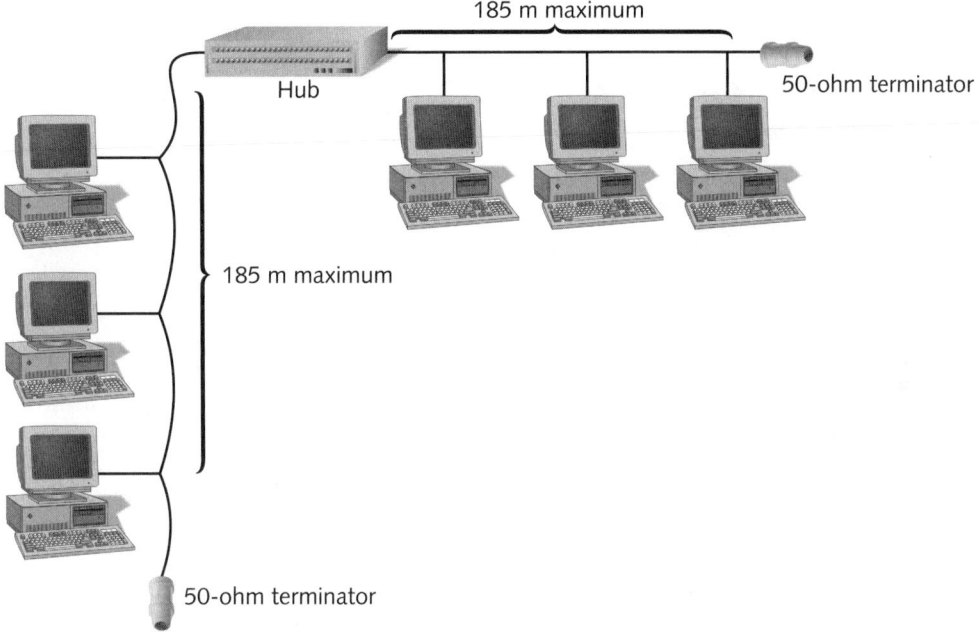

4

Figure 4-20   A 10Base2 Ethernet network

Thicknet and Thinnet cable both require 50-ohm resistors terminating either end of the network. These cables must also be grounded at one end. If you ground a coaxial network at both ends, or if you don't ground it at all, the network will generate intermittent data transmission errors.

TWISTED-PAIR CABLE

Twisted-pair (TP) cable is similar to telephone wiring and consists of color-coded pairs of insulated copper wires, each with a diameter of 0.4 to 0.8 mm, or 22-24 AWG (American Wire Gauge) standard copper wires. The wires are twisted around each other to form pairs and all the pairs are encased in a plastic sheath, as shown in Figure 4-21. The twists in the wire help to reduce the effects of crosstalk. **Crosstalk**, which is measured in decibels (dB), occurs when signals traveling on nearby wire pairs infringe on another pair's signal. If you envision the wire pairs in a single cable as couples in an elevator, you can imagine how one couple speaking very loudly might impair the other couple's ability to converse. Because they are twisted around each other, the release of current from one wire cancels out the release of current from the adjacent wire. Another form of crosstalk, called

alien crosstalk, can occur when signals from an adjacent cable (as opposed to adjacent wires) interfere with another cable's transmission. Alien crosstalk becomes a real threat when network administrators bundle more cables into smaller conduits.

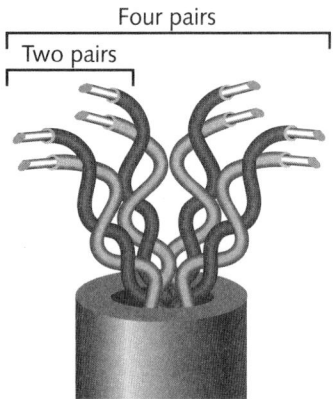

Figure 4-21   Twisted-pair cable

The more twists per inch in a pair of wires, the more resistant the pair will be to all forms of noise. Higher-quality, more expensive twisted-pair cable contains more twists per foot. The number of twists per meter or foot is known as the **twist ratio**. Because twisting the wire pairs more tightly requires more cable, however, a high twist ratio can result in greater attenuation. For optimal performance, cable manufacturers must strike a balance between crosstalk and attenuation reduction.

Because twisted-pair is used in such a wide variety of environments and for a variety of purposes, it comes in hundreds of different designs. These designs vary in their twist ratio, the number of wire pairs that they contain, the grade of copper used, the type of shielding (if any), and the materials used for shielding, among other things. A twisted-pair cable may contain from 1 to 4200 wire pairs. Early network cables incorporated two wire pairs: one pair dedicated to sending data and one pair dedicated to receiving data. Modern networks typically use cables containing four wire pairs, with more than one wire pair both sending and transmitting data simultaneously.

In 1991, two standards organizations, TIA (Telecommunications Industry Association) and EIA (Electronic Industries Alliance), finalized their specifications for twisted-pair wiring in a standard called TIA/EIA 568. Since then, TIA has become part of EIA, and this new body has continually revised the international standards for new and modified transmission media. Its standards now cover cabling media, design, and installation specifications. The TIA/EIA 568 standard divides twisted-pair wiring into several categories. Thus you will hear twisted-pair referred to as CAT (category) 1, 2, 3, 4, 5, 6, and now, CAT7. All of these cables fall under the TIA/EIA 568 standard. Modern LANs most frequently use CAT5 or higher wiring.

Twisted-pair cable is the most common form of cabling found on LANs today. It is relatively inexpensive, flexible, and easy to install, and it can span a significant distance before requiring a repeater (though not as far as coax). Twisted-pair cable easily accommodates several different topologies, although it is most often implemented in star or star-hybrid topologies. Furthermore, twisted-pair can handle the faster networking transmission rates currently being employed. Due to its wide acceptance, it will probably be updated to handle the even faster rates that will emerge in the future. One drawback to twisted-pair is that, because of its flexibility, it is more prone to physical damage than coaxial cable. This problem is a minor factor given its many advantages over coax. All twisted-pair cable falls into one of two categories: shielded twisted-pair (STP) or unshielded twisted-pair (UTP).

Shielded Twisted-Pair (STP)

As the name implies, **shielded twisted-pair (STP)** cable consists of twisted wire pairs that are not only individually insulated, but also surrounded by a shielding made of a metallic substance such as foil. Some STP use a braided metal shielding. The shielding acts as a barrier to external electromagnetic forces, thus preventing them from affecting the signals traveling over the wire inside the shielding. The shielding may be grounded to enhance its protective effect. The effectiveness of STP's shield depends on the level and type of environmental noise, the thickness and material used for the shield, the grounding mechanism, and the symmetry and consistency of the shielding. Figure 4-22 depicts an STP cable.

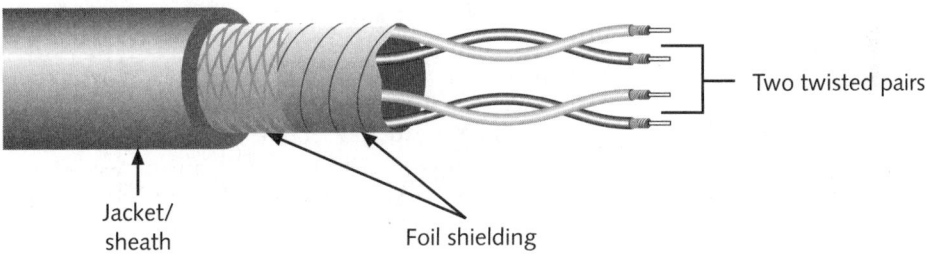

Two twisted pairs

Jacket/
sheath

Foil shielding

Figure 4-22   STP cable

Unshielded Twisted-Pair (UTP)

Unshielded twisted-pair (UTP) cabling consists of one or more insulated wire pairs encased in a plastic sheath. As its name implies, UTP does not contain additional shielding for the twisted pairs. As a result, UTP is both less expensive and less resistant to noise than STP. Figure 4-23 depicts a typical UTP cable.

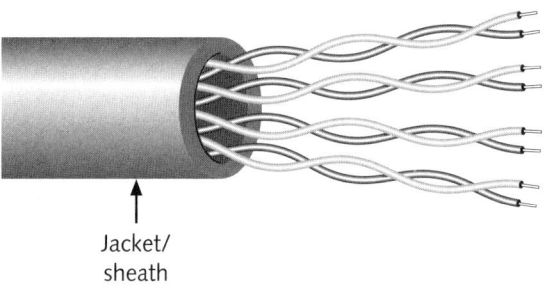

Jacket/
sheath

Figure 4-23   UTP cable

Earlier, you learned that the TIA/EIA consortium designated standards for twisted-pair wiring. To manage network cabling, you need to be familiar with the standards that may be used on modern networks, particularly CAT3 and CAT5 or higher.

- *Category 1 (CAT1)*—A form of UTP that contains two wire pairs. CAT1 is suitable for voice communications but not for data. With advanced signaling techniques, it can carry up to 128 kilobits per second (Kbps) of data.

- *Category 2 (CAT2)*—A form of UTP that contains four wire pairs and can carry up to 4 Mbps of data. CAT2 is rarely found on modern networks, however, because most systems require higher throughput.

- *Category 3 (CAT3)*—A form of UTP that contains four wire pairs and can carry up to 10 Mbps of data with a possible bandwidth of 16 MHz. CAT3 has typically been used for 10 Mbps Ethernet or 4 Mbps Token Ring networks. Network administrators are gradually replacing their existing CAT3 cabling with CAT5 to accommodate higher throughput.

- *Category 4 (CAT4)*—A form of UTP that contains four wire pairs and can support up to 16 Mbps throughput. CAT4 may be used for 16 Mbps Token Ring or 10 Mbps Ethernet networks. It is guaranteed for signals as high as 20 MHz and provides more protection against crosstalk and attenuation than CAT1, CAT2, or CAT3.

- *Category 5 (CAT5)*—The most popular form of UTP for new network installations and upgrades to Fast Ethernet. CAT5 contains four wire pairs and supports up to 100 Mbps throughput and a 100 MHz signal rate. In addition to 100 Mbps Ethernet, CAT5 wiring can support other fast networking technologies. Figure 4-24 depicts a typical CAT5 UTP cable with its twisted pairs untwisted, allowing you to see their matched color coding. For example, the wire that is colored solid orange is twisted around the wire that is part orange and part white to form the pair responsible for transmitting data.

 It can be difficult to tell the difference between four-pair CAT3 cables and four-pair CAT5 cables. However, some visual clues can help. On CAT5 cable, the jacket is usually stamped with the manufacturer's name and cable type, including the CAT5 specification. A cable whose jacket has no markings is often CAT3. Also, pairs in CAT5 cables have a significantly higher twist ratio than pairs in CAT3 cables. Although CAT3 pairs might be twisted as few as three times per foot, CAT5 pairs are twisted at least 12 times per foot. Other clues, such as the date of installation (old cable is more likely CAT3), looseness of the jacket (CAT3's jacket is typically looser than CAT5's), and the extent to which pairs are untwisted before a termination (CAT5 can tolerate only a small amount of untwisting) are also helpful, though less definitive.

- *Enhanced Category 5 (CAT5e)*—A higher-grade version of CAT5 wiring that contains high-quality copper, offers a high twist ratio, and uses advanced methods for reducing crosstalk. Enhanced CAT5 can support a signaling rate as high as 200 MHz, double the capability of regular CAT5.

■ *Category 6 (CAT6)*—A twisted-pair cable that contains four wire pairs, each wrapped in foil insulation. Additional foil insulation covers the bundle of wire pairs, and a fire-resistant plastic sheath covers the second foil layer. The foil insulation provides excellent resistance to crosstalk and enables CAT6 to support at least six times the throughput supported by regular CAT5. Because it is new and because most network technologies cannot exploit its superlative capacity, CAT6 is rarely encountered in today's networks.

■ *Category 7 (CAT7)*—A twisted-pair cable that contains multiple wire pairs, each surrounded by its own shielding, then packaged in additional shielding beneath the jacket. While standards have not yet been finalized for CAT7, some cable supply companies are selling it, and organizations are installing it. One advantage to CAT7 cabling is that it can support signal rates up to 1 GHz. However, it requires different connectors than other versions of UTP because its twisted pairs must be more isolated from each other to ward off crosstalk. Because of its added shielding, CAT7 cabling is also larger and less flexible than other versions of UTP cable. For the same reasons that CAT6 is not typically found on modern networks, CAT7 is also rare; but it will likely become popular as the final standard is released and networks are upgraded.

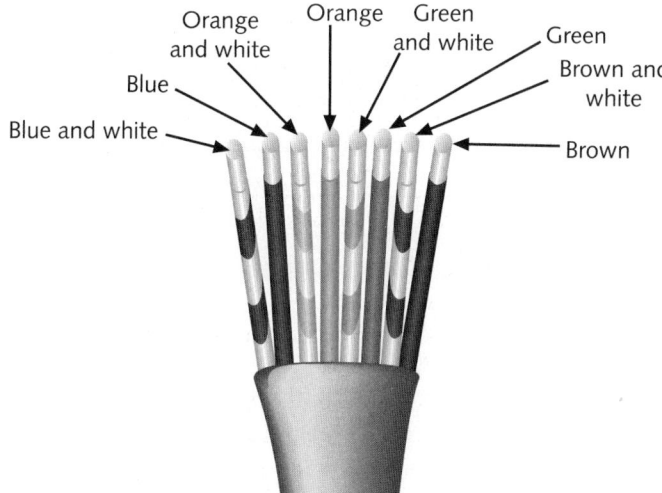

Figure 4-24   A CAT5 UTP cable

UTP cabling may be used with any one of several IEEE Physical layer networking standards. Recall that IEEE standards specify how signals are transmitted to the media. The following sections describe these standards, which you must understand in order to obtain Network+ certification.

10BaseT

10BaseT is a popular Ethernet networking standard that replaced the older 10Base2 and 10Base5 technologies. The "10" represents its maximum throughput of 10Mbps, the "Base" indicates that it uses baseband transmission, and the "T" stands for twisted pair, the medium it uses. On a 10BaseT network, one pair of wires in the UTP cable is used for transmission, while a second pair of wires is used for reception. By using two pairs of wires, 10BaseT networks use full-duplex transmission. A 10BaseT network requires CAT3 or higher UTP.

Nodes on a 10BaseT Ethernet network connect to a central hub or repeater in a star fashion. As is typical of a star topology, a single network cable connects only two devices. This characteristic makes 10BaseT networks more fault-tolerant than 10Base2 or 10Base5, both of which use the bus topology. It also means that 10BaseT networks are easier to troubleshoot because you can isolate problems more readily when every device has a separate connection to the LAN. Figure 4-25 depicts a small 10BaseT Ethernet network.

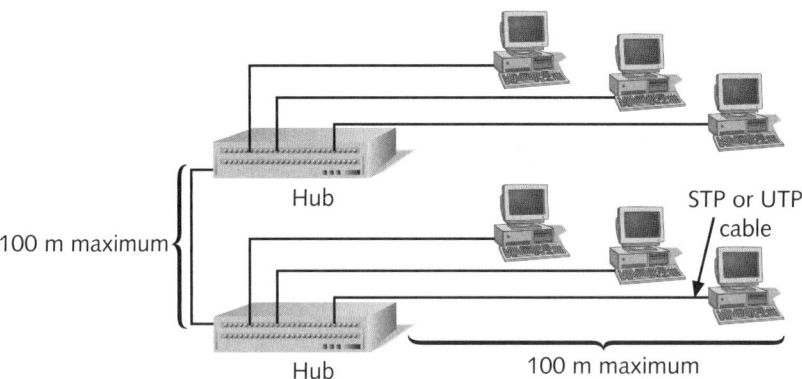

Figure 4-25   A 10BaseT Ethernet network

10BaseT, like 10Base2 and 10Base5, is also subject to a distance limitation. The maximum distance that a 10BaseT segment can traverse is 100 meters. To go beyond that distance, Ethernet star segments must be connected by additional hubs or switches to form more complex topologies (discussed in the next chapter). This arrangement can connect a maximum of five sequential network segments. Figure 4-26 illustrates how 10BaseT segments can be interconnected to form an enterprise-wide network. An **enterprise-wide network** is one that spans an entire organization and often services the needs of many diverse users. It may include many locations (as a WAN), or it may be confined to one location but include many different departments, floors, and network segments.

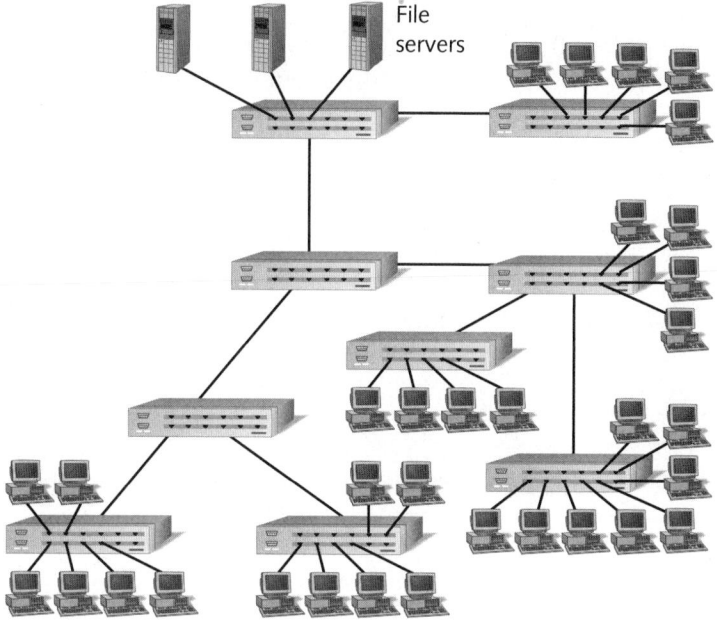

4

Figure 4-26   Interconnected 10BaseT segments

100BaseT

As networks become larger and handle heavier traffic, Ethernet's longstanding 10 Mbps limitation becomes a bottleneck that detrimentally affects response time. The need for faster LANs that can use the same infrastructure as the popular 10BaseT technology has been met by **100BaseT**, also known as **Fast Ethernet**. 100BaseT, specified in the IEEE 802.3u standard, enables LANs to run at a 100-Mbps data transfer rate, a tenfold increase from that provided by 10BaseT, without requiring a significant investment in new infrastructure. 100BaseT uses baseband transmission and the same, star topology as 10BaseT. It also uses the same RJ-45 data connectors. Depending on the type of 100BaseT technology used, it may require CAT3 or CAT5 or higher UTP.

As with 10BaseT, nodes on a 100BaseT network are configured in a star topology and the length between an end node and the hub for 100BaseT networks cannot exceed 100 meters. Multiple hubs can be connected on buses to extend the network, but 100BaseT buses can practically support a maximum of three network segments connected with two hubs.

Two 100BaseT specifications—100BaseT4 and 100BaseTX—have competed for popularity as organizations move to 100-Mbps technology. The difference between these technologies relates primarily to the way they achieve the 100-Mbps transmission rate, which affects their cabling requirements.

- **100BaseTX**—This is the version you are most likely to encounter. It achieves its speed by sending the signal 10 times faster and condensing the time between digital pulses as well as the time a station must wait and listen for a signal. 100BaseTX requires CAT 5 or higher unshielded twisted-pair cabling. Within the cable, it uses the same two pairs of wire for transmitting and receiving data that 10BaseT uses. Therefore, like 10BaseT, 100BaseTX is also capable of full-duplex transmission. Full duplexing can potentially double the bandwidth of a 100BaseT network to 200 Mbps.

- **100BaseT4**—This version is differentiated from 100BaseTX in that it uses all four pairs of wires in a UTP cable, and, therefore, can use lower-cost CAT 3 wiring. It achieves its speed by breaking the 100-Mbps data stream into three streams of 33-Mbps each. These three streams are sent over three pairs of wire in the cable. However, because 100BaseT4 technology uses all four wire pairs for unidirectional signaling, it cannot support full duplexing. One reason 100BaseT4 is less popular than 100BaseTX is because it cannot support full duplexing.

 You cannot mix 100BaseTX and 100BaseT4 on a single network segment. For example, if you purchase a hub designed for 100BaseTX transmission, you cannot use NICs designed for 100BaseT4 transmission to connect to that hub.

100BaseVG

A cousin of the Ethernet 100 Mbps technologies is **100BaseVG**, also called **100VG-AnyLAN**. The "VG" stands for voice grade. 100BaseVG, which was originally developed by Hewlett-Packard and AT&T, is now governed by IEEE standard 802.12. A significant difference between 100BaseVG and 100BaseT is the way in which they allow network nodes to transmit data on the network. 100BaseVG employs a more efficient and accurate process that allows it to better serve networks that carry audio, video, or other time-sensitive data (explaining the "voice grade" specification). However, this technology also requires more sophisticated NICs and connectivity devices than 100BaseT networks use. You will learn more about this technology in the following chapter.

Another disadvantage of 100BaseVG is that the time the hub takes to process each request reduces the network's overall performance, so that it cannot usually match the speed of a 100BaseT network. Also, 100BaseVG uses all four wire pairs in a UTP cable, and, therefore, cannot take advantage of full duplexing, which can potentially double a network's bandwidth. For these reasons, and because compatible equipment may be hard to find, 100BaseVG is not widely implemented.

Comparing STP and UTP

STP and UTP share several characteristics. The following list highlights their similarities and differences.

- *Throughput*—STP and UTP can both transmit data up to 100 Mbps (and with newer technology, potentially higher), depending on the grade of cabling and the transmission method in use.

- *Cost*—STP and UTP vary in cost, depending on the grade of copper used, the category rating, and any enhancements. Typically, STP is more expensive than UTP because it contains more materials and it has a lower demand. High-grade UTP, however, can be very expensive. For example, CAT6 costs more per foot than regular CAT5 cabling. As new types of cabling are released, they initially cost significantly more than older types of cabling. However, as they remain on the market and become more widely accepted, their price drops.

- *Connector*—STP and UTP use **RJ-45** connectors and data jacks, which look similar to telephone connectors and jacks. "RJ" stands for registered jack. Figure 4-27 shows a close-up of an RJ-45 connector for a cable containing four wire pairs. The section on "Installing Cable" later in this chapter describes the use of RJ-45 connectors and data jacks in more detail.

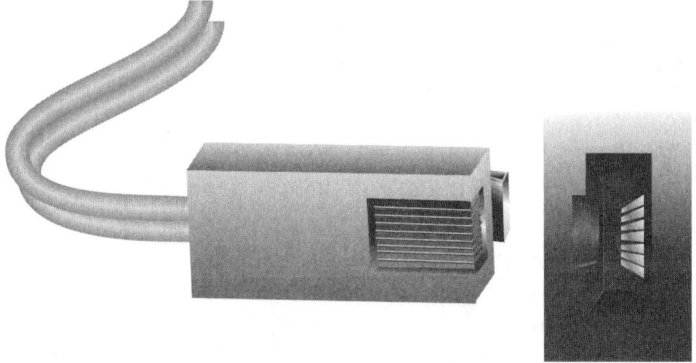

Figure 4-27   An RJ-45 connector

- *Noise immunity*—Because of its shielding, STP is more noise-resistant than UTP is. On the other hand, UTP may use filtering and balancing techniques to offset the effects of noise.

- *Size and scalability*—The maximum segment length for both STP and UTP is 100 m, or 328 feet. This span is less than that available with coaxial cable because twisted-pair is more susceptible to environmental noise. Twisted-pair can accommodate a maximum of only 1024 nodes per logical segment. Its maximum network length depends on the type of signaling used, as discussed in the following section.

FIBER-OPTIC CABLE

Fiber-optic cable, or simply *fiber*, contains one or several glass fibers at its center, or **core**. Data are transmitted via pulsing light sent from a laser or light-emitting diode (LED) through the central fibers. Surrounding the fibers is a layer of glass called **cladding.** The cladding glass is a different density from the glass in the strands. It acts as a mirror, reflecting light back to the core in patterns that vary depending on the trans-mission mode. This reflection allows the fiber to bend around corners without diminish-ing the integrity of the light-based signal. Outside the cladding, a plastic buffer protects the glass cladding and core. Since it is opaque, it also absorbs any light that might escape. To prevent the cable from stretching, and to further protect the inner core, strands of Kevlar (an advanced polymeric fiber) surround the plastic buffer. Finally, a plastic sheath covers the strands of Kevlar. Figure 4-28 shows the different layers of a fiber-optic cable.

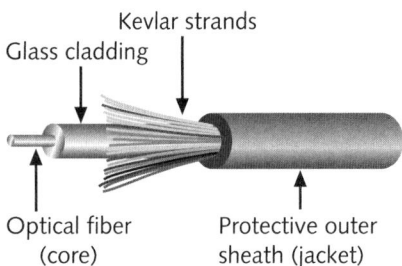

Figure 4-28   A fiber-optic cable

Like twisted-pair cable, fiber comes in a number of different types. Fiber cable variations fall into two categories: single-mode and multimode. **Single-mode fiber** uses a narrow core (less than 10 microns in diameter) through which light generated by a laser travels over one path, reflecting very little. Because it reflects little, the light does not disperse as the signal travels along the fiber. This continuity allows single mode fiber to accommodate high band-widths and long distances (without requiring repeaters). Single-mode fiber may be used to connect a carrier's two facilities. However, it costs too much to be considered for use on typ-ical data networks. **Multimode fiber** contains a core with a larger diameter than single-mode fiber (between 50 and 100 microns in diameter) over which many pulses of light generated by a light emitting diode (LED) travel at different angles. Because light is being reflected many different ways in a multimode fiber cable, the waves become less easily dis-tinguishable the longer they travel. Thus, multimode fiber is best suited for shorter distances than single-mode fiber. It is commonly found on cables that connect a router to a switch or a server on the backbone of a network. Figure 4-29 graphically depicts the differences between single-mode and multimode fiber.

Because of its reliability, fiber is currently used primarily as a cable that connects the many segments of a network. Experts predict, however, that it will replace UTP as the primary means of bringing data to the desktop within the next decade. Fiber-optic cable provides the benefits of nearly unlimited throughput, very high resistance to noise, and excellent security. Because fiber does not conduct electricity like copper wire, it does not emit a current. As a result, the signals it carries stay within the fiber and cannot eas-ily be picked up except at the destination node. Copper, on the other hand, generates a signal that can be monitored by taps into the network. Fiber can also carry signals for longer distances than can coax or twisted-pair cable. In addition, you can use longer lengths of fiber with fewer repeaters than on a copper-based network. Finally, fiber is widely accepted by the high-speed networking industry. Thus, industry groups are establishing standards to ensure that fiber networking equipment from multiple manufacturers can be integrated without difficulty.

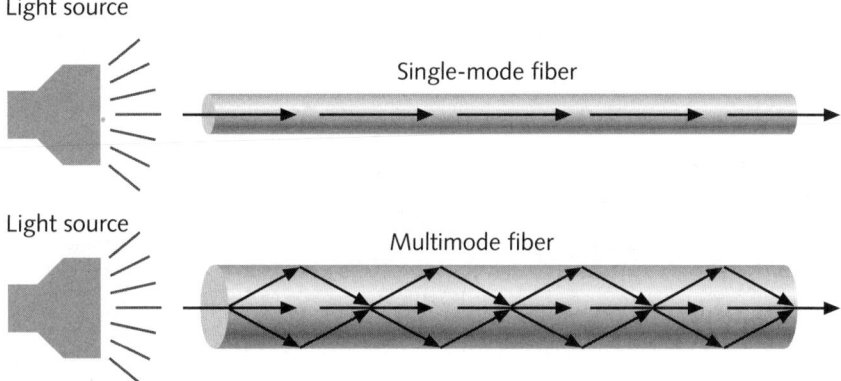

Figure 4-29   Single-mode and multimode fiber-optic cables

The most significant drawback to the use of fiber is its high cost. Another disadvantage is that fiber can transmit data in only one direction at a time; to overcome this drawback, each cable must contain two strands—one to send data and one to receive it. Finally, unlike copper wiring, fiber is difficult to splice, which means quickly repairing a cable in the field (given little time or resources) is difficult if not impossible. Fiber's characteristics are summarized following.

- *Throughput*—Fiber has proved reliable in transmitting data at rates as high as 1 gigabit (or 1000 megabits) per second. With further improvements expected, fiber will probably surpass that limit in the future. Fiber's amazing throughput is partly due to the physics of light traveling over glass. Unlike electrical pulses traveling over copper, the light experiences virtually no resistance and, therefore, can be reliably transmitted at faster rates than electrical pulses. In fact, a pure glass strand can accept up to 1 billion laser light pulses per second. Because of its high cost, however, fiber is currently found almost exclusively on backbone lengths. Nevertheless, its high throughput capability also makes it suitable for applications that generate a great deal of traffic, such as video or audio conferencing.

- *Cost*—Fiber is the most expensive type of cable. The cost of running fiber to every desktop is currently prohibitive; consequently, fiber is typically used only for long-distance transmission or network backbones that must bear extraordinary amounts of traffic. Not only is the cable itself more expensive than metal cabling, but fiber-optic NICs and hubs can cost as much as five times more than NICs and hubs designed for UTP networks. In addition, hiring skilled fiber cable installers costs more than hiring twisted-pair cable installers.

■ *Connector*—With fiber cabling, you can use any of 10 different types of connectors. Figure 4-30 shows two popular connector types, an ST connector and an SC connector. For short connections, such as 2-foot cable between a router and a patch panel, you should consider purchasing fiber cables with the connectors pre-installed. For longer connections, either you or the technician who installs your fiber can attach the connectors to the cable.

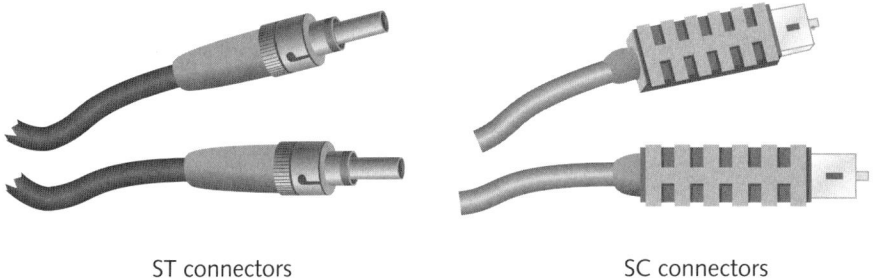

ST connectors   SC connectors

Figure 4-30   ST and SC fiber connectors

■ *Noise immunity*—Since fiber does not conduct electrical current to transmit signals, it is unaffected by either EMI or RFI. Its impressive noise resistance is one reason why fiber can span such long distances before it requires repeaters to regenerate its signal.

■ *Size and scalability*—Network segments made from fiber can span 100 m. Overall network lengths vary depending on the type of fiber-optic cable used. For multimode fiber, TIA/EIA recommends a segment limit of 2 km. For single-mode fiber, the limit is 3 km. Although signals transmitted over fiber do not suffer interference, they do experience **optical loss**, or the degradation of the light signal. Optical loss accrues over long distances and grows with every connection point in the fiber network. Dust or oil in a connection (for example, from people handling the fiber while splicing it) can further exacerbate optical loss.

Like twisted-pair and coaxial cabling, fiber-optic cabling comes in a number of different varieties, depending on its intended use and the manufacturer. For example, one type of fiber-optic cabling, the D series, is used for underground conduits to high-volume telecommunications carriers (such as AT&T or Global Crossing). This cable may contain as many as 1000 fibers and be heavily sheathed to prevent damage caused by rodents gnawing on it. At the other end of the spectrum, fiber-optic patch cables for use on LANs may contain only two strands of fiber and be pliable enough to bend easily around corners.

Just as with twisted-pair and coaxial cabling, IEEE has established Physical layer standards for networks that use fiber-optic cable. Two of the most important standards are described below.

10BaseF

In the **10BaseF** standard, the "10" represents its maximum throughput of 10 Mbps, "Base" indicates its use of baseband transmission, and "F" indicates that it relies on a medium of fiber-optic cable. In fact there are at least three different kinds of 10BaseF. All require two strands of multimode fiber. One strand is used for data transmission and one strand is used for reception, making 10BaseF a full-duplex technology. All versions of 10BaseF also require ST type of connectors on their patch cables, NICs, and connectivity devices. The maximum segment length for 10BaseF may be 1000 or 2000 meters, depending on the version used. It may contain no more than two repeaters per network. Like 10BaseT, 10BaseF makes use of the star topology, with its repeaters connected through a bus.

Since 10BaseF involves (expensive) fiber and achieves merely 10 Mbps throughput (whereas the fiber medium is capable of much higher throughput), it is not commonly found on modern networks.

100BaseFX

The **100BaseFX** standard specifies a network capable of 100-Mbps throughput that uses baseband transmission and fiber-optic cabling. Like 10BaseF, 100BaseFX requires multimode fiber containing at least two strands of fiber. One strand is used for data transmission, while the other strand is used for reception, making 100BaseFX a full-duplex technology. 100BaseFX networks require one of several types of connectors, including the two most popular connectors, SC and ST. Its maximum segment length is 400 meters, with a maximum of two repeaters allowed to connect segments. The 100BaseFX standard uses a star topology, with its repeaters connected through a bus.

100BaseFX, like 100BaseT, is also considered "Fast Ethernet." Organizations switching, or migrating, from UTP to fiber media can combine 100BaseTX and 100BaseFX within one network. In order to do this, connectivity devices must have both RJ-45 and SC or ST ports. Alternately, a 100BaseTX to 100BaseFX media converter may be used at any point in the network to interconnect the different media and convert the signals of one standard to signals that work with the other standard.

 In Ethernet technology, the most common network speeds are 10 Mbps and 100 Mbps. Actual data transfer rates on a network will vary, just as you might average 25 miles per gallon (mpg) driving your car to work and back, even though the manufacturer rates the car's gas mileage at 30 mpg.

PHYSICAL LAYER NETWORKING STANDARDS

In order to obtain Network+ certification, you must be familiar with the different characteristics and limitations of each physical networking medium discussed in this chapter. To put this information in context, Table 4-3 summarizes the characteristics and limitations for Physical layer networking standards, including Ethernet networks that use coaxial cable, twisted-pair cable, and fiber-optic cable.

Table 4-3   Physical layer networking standards

Standard	Maximum Transmission Speed (Mbps)	Maximum Distance per Segment (m)	Physical Media	Simple Physical Topology Used
10Base5	10	500	Thick coaxial cable	Bus
10Base2	10	185	Thin coaxial cable	Bus
10BaseT	10	100	Unshielded twisted-pair	Star
100BaseTX	100	100	Unshielded twisted-pair	Star
100BaseT4	100	100	Unshielded twisted-pair	Star
100BaseVG	100	100	Unshielded twisted-pair	Star
10BaseF	10	1000 or 2000, depending on version	Multimode fiber	Star
100BaseFX	100	400	Multimode fiber	Star

Some networks may use more than one type of physical media. For instance, 100BaseTX could run on fiber, even though the minimum standard is unshielded twisted-pair cabling. The latest unshielded twisted-pair may be able to carry data at 1Gbps, albeit with severe distance limitations, so fiber is recommended.

CABLE DESIGN AND MANAGEMENT

For a long time, organizations took their **cable plant**—the hardware that makes up the enterprise-wide cabling system—for granted. Because of increasing traffic demands and business's increasing reliance on networks, however, organizations must now actively manage their physical infrastructure. Proactive cable design and management make moves and expansion smoother and limit productivity losses due to Physical layer problems. Although it doesn't get as much attention as asset management or security concerns, cable management is a significant element of a sound network management strategy.

In 1991, TIA/EIA released its joint 568 Commercial Building Wiring Standard, also known as **structured cabling**, for uniform, enterprise-wide, multivendor cabling systems. Structured cabling suggests how networking media can best be installed to maximize performance and minimize upkeep. Structured cabling specifies standards without regard for the type of media or transmission technology used on the network. In other words, it is designed to work just as well for 10BaseT networks as it does for 100BaseFX networks. Structured cabling is based on a hierarchical design that divides cabling into six subsystems, described in the following list. You should be familiar with the principles of structured cabling before you attempt to design, install, or troubleshoot an organization's cable plant. Figure 4-31 illustrates how the six subsystems fit together.

4

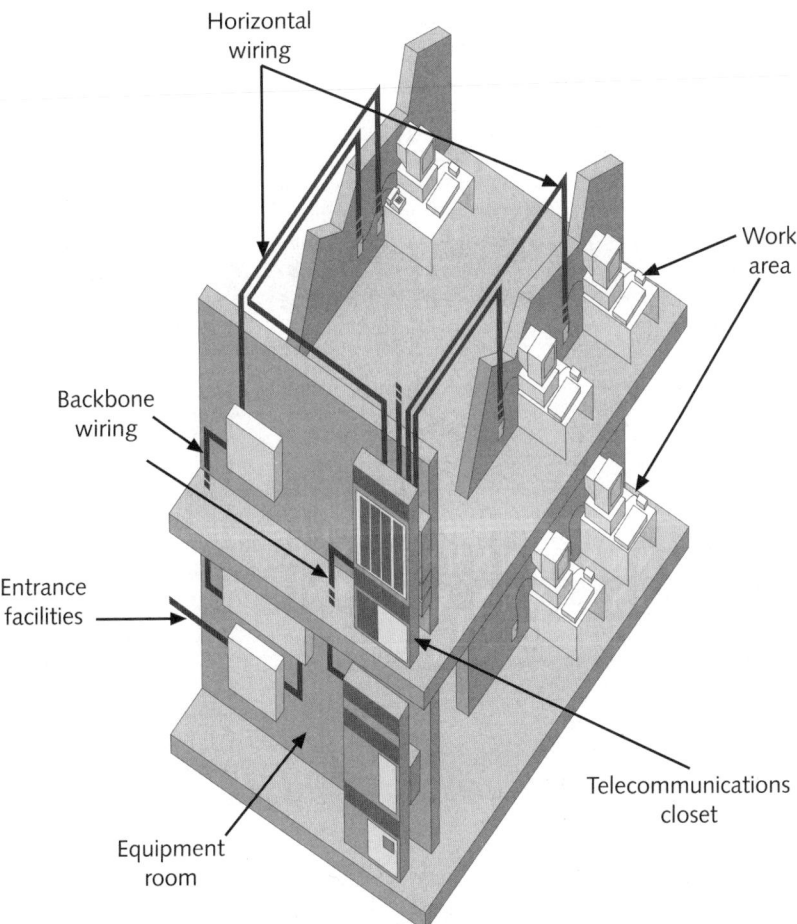

Horizontal wiring

Work area

Backbone wiring

Entrance facilities

Telecommunications closet

Equipment room

Figure 4-31   TIA/EIA structured cabling subsystems

- *Entrance facilities*—The point at which a building's internal cabling plant begins. The entrance facility separates LANs from WANs and designates where the telecommunications service carrier (whether it's a local phone company, dedicated, or long-distance carrier) accepts responsibility for the (external) wire.

- *Backbone wiring*—As you learned earlier, a backbone is essentially a network of networks. Backbone wiring provides interconnection between telecommunications closets, equipment rooms, and entrance facilities. On a campus-wide network, the backbone includes not only vertical connectors between floors, or **risers**, and cabling between equipment rooms, but also cabling between buildings. You will learn more about backbone topology and design in Chapter 5. The TIA/EIA standard designates distance limitations for backbones of varying cable types, as specified in Table 4-4. On modern networks, backbones are usually composed of fiber-optic or UTP cable. The cross connect is the central connection point for the backbone wiring.

Table 4-4   TIA/EIA specifications for backbone cabling

Cable Type	Cross-Connects to Telecommunications Room	Equipment Room to Telecommunications Room	Cross-Connects to Equipment Room
UTP	800 m (voice specification)	500 m	300 m
Single-mode fiber	3000 m	500 m	1500 m
Multimode fiber	2000 m	500 m	1500 m

- *Equipment room*—The location where significant networking hardware, such as servers and mainframe hosts, resides. Cabling to equipment rooms usually connects telecommunications closets. On a campus-wide network, each building may have its own equipment room.

- *Telecommunications closet*—A "telco room" that contains connectivity for groups of workstations in its area, plus cross connections to equipment rooms. Large organizations may have several telco rooms per floor. Telecommunications closets typically house patch panels, punch-down blocks, hubs or switches, and possibly other connectivity hardware. A **punch-down block** is a panel of data receptors into which horizontal cabling from the workstations is inserted. If used, a **patch panel** is a wall-mounted panel of data receptors into which patch cables from the punch-down block are inserted. Figure 4-32 shows examples of a punch-down block and a patch panel. Finally, patch cables connect the patch panel to the hub or switch. Because telecommunications closets are usually small, enclosed spaces, good cooling and ventilation systems are important to maintaining a constant temperature in telco rooms.

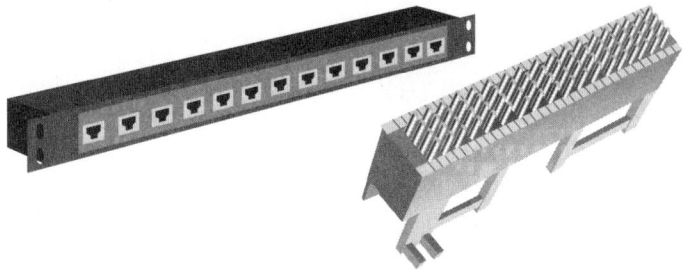

Figure 4-32   Patch panel (left) and punch-down block (right)

■ *Horizontal wiring*—Wiring that connects workstations to the closest telecommunications closet. TIA/EIA recognizes three possible cabling types for horizontal wiring: STP, UTP, or fiber-optic. The maximum allowable distance for horizontal wiring is 100 m. This span includes 90 m to connect a data jack on the wall to the telecommunications closet plus a maximum of 10 m to connect a workstation to the data jack on the wall. Figure 4-33 depicts a horizontal wiring configuration.

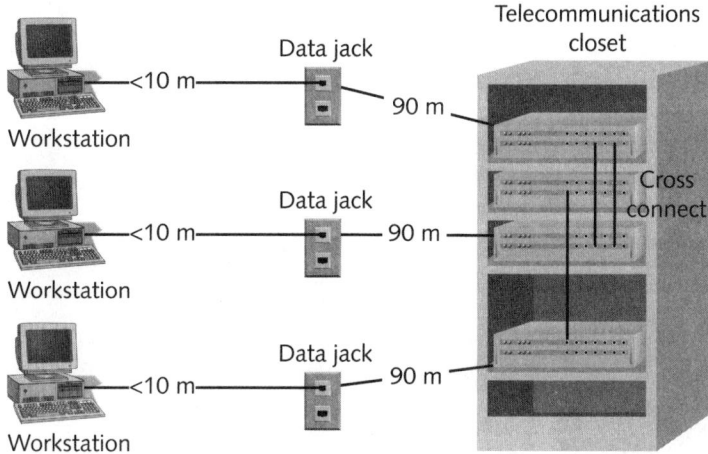

Figure 4-33   Horizontal wiring

■ *Work area*—An area that encompasses all patch cables and horizontal wiring necessary to connect workstations, printers, and other network devices from their NICs to the telecommunications closet. A **patch cable** is a relatively short section (usually between 3 and 25 feet long) of twisted-pair cabling with connectors on both ends that connects network devices to data outlets. The TIA/EIA standard calls for each wall jack to contain at least one voice and one data outlet, as pictured in Figure 4-34. Realistically, you will encounter a variety of wall jacks. For example, in a student computer lab lacking phones, a wall jack with a combination of voice and data outlets is unnecessary.

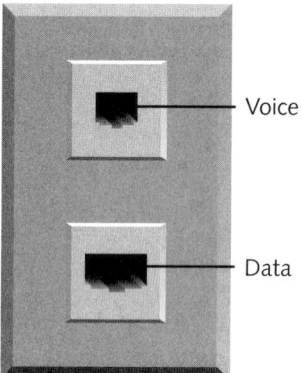

Figure 4-34   A standard TIA/EIA wall jack

Figure 4-35 depicts one possible example of a structured cabling hierarchy. The TIA/EIA standard dictates that a single hierarchy contain no more than two levels of cross-connection wiring.

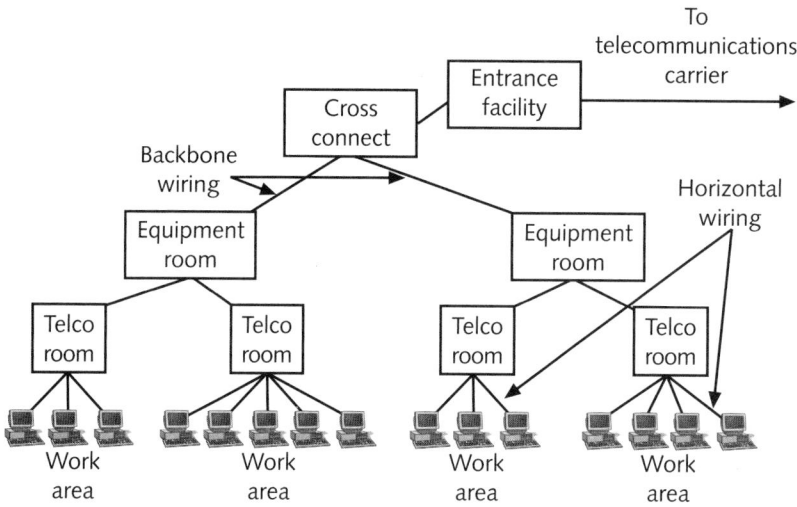

Figure 4-35   A structured cabling hierarchy

Adhering to standard cabling hierarchies is only part of a smart cable management strategy. You or your network manager should also specify standards for the types of cable used by your organization and maintain a list of approved cabling vendors. Keep a supply room stocked with spare parts so that you can easily and quickly replace defective parts.

Create documentation for your cabling plant, including the locations, lengths, and grades of installed cable. Label every data jack, punch-down block, and connector. Use color-coded cables for different purposes (cables can be purchased in a variety of sheath colors). For example, you might want to use pink for patch cables, green for horizontal wiring, and gray for vertical (backbone) wiring. Keep your documentation in a centrally accessible location and be certain to update it as you change the network. The more you document, the easier it will be to move or add cable segments.

Finally, plan for how your cabling plant will lend itself to growth. For example, if your organization is rapidly expanding, consider replacing your backbone with fiber and leave plenty of space in your telecommunications closets for more racks.

As you will most likely work with twisted-pair cable, the next section explains how to install this type of cabling from the server to the desktop.

INSTALLING CABLE

So far, you have read about the variety of cables used in networking and the limitations inherent in each. You may worry that with hundreds of varieties of cable, choosing the correct one and making it work with your network is next to impossible. The good news is that if you follow both the manufacturers' installation guidelines and the TIA/EIA standards, you are almost guaranteed success. Many network problems can be traced to poor cable installation techniques. For example, if you don't crimp twisted-pair wires in the correct position in an RJ-45 connector, the cable will fail to transmit or receive data (or both—in which case, the cable will not function at all). Installing the wrong grade of cable can either cause your network to fail or render it more susceptible to damage (for example, using typical, inexpensive twisted-pair cable in areas that might be susceptible to fire damage).

With networks moving to faster transmission speeds, adhering to installation guidelines is a more critical concern than ever. A Category 5 UTP segment that flawlessly transmits data at 10 Mbps may suffer data loss when pushed to 100 Mbps. In addition, some cable manufacturers will not honor warranties if their cables were improperly installed. This section outlines the most common method of installing UTP cable and points out cabling mistakes that can lead to network instability.

In the previous section, you learned about the six subsystems of the TIA/EIA structured cabling standard. A typical UTP network uses a modular setup to distinguish between cables at each subsystem. Figure 4-36 provides an overview of a modular cabling installation.

In this example, patch cables connect network devices (such as a workstation) to the wall jacks. Longer cables connect wire from the wall jack to a punch-down block in the telecommunications closet. From the punch-down block, patch cables bring the connection into a patch panel. From the patch panel, more patch cables connect to the hub or switch, which in turn connects to the equipment room or to the backbone, depending on the scale of the network. All of these sections of cable make network moves and additions easier. Believe it or not, they also keep the telecommunications closet organized.

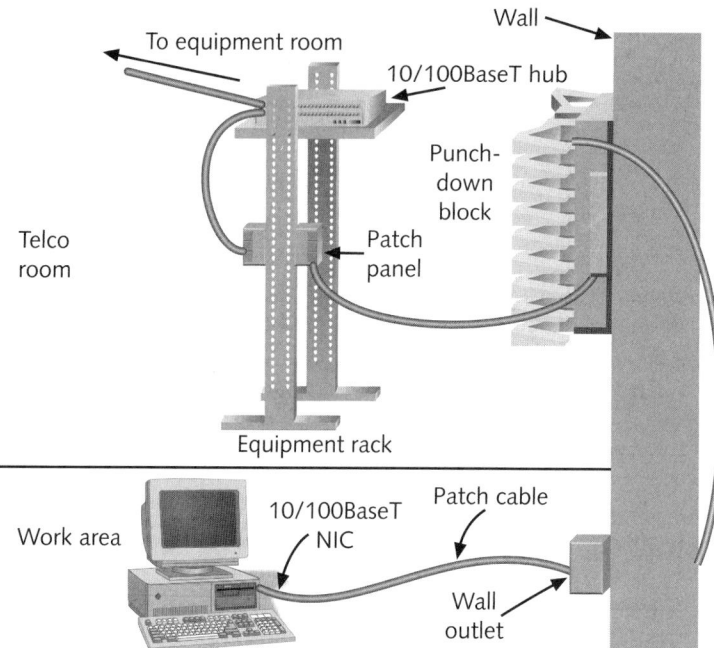

Figure 4-36   A typical UTP cabling installation

Although you may never have to make your own patch cables, you might have to repair one in a pinch. Table 4-5 explains how the pins in an RJ-45 connector correspond to the wires in a UTP cable. For example, in wire pair number 2, the green and the green and white striped wires are wound around each other. In this pair, the green wire transmits data from the device, while the green and white striped wire receives data from the network. The method of UTP coding described in Table 4-5 follows the TIA/EIA T568A wiring standard, the most popular wiring standard currently in use for networks. Another standard, the TIA/EIA T568B standard, is similar but the wire pairs colored orange and orange striped plus green and green striped are reversed. Yet another coding scheme has been established by IEEE. It typically doesn't matter which scheme you choose, but to avoid confusion and potential transmission errors you should ensure that you cable all wiring on your LAN according to one standard. In Project 4-2 at the end of this chapter, you will have the opportunity to create your own patch cable following these guidelines. Be advised, however, that any imperfection in how you fasten the wires in the connector will prevent the cable from working.

Table 4-5   Pin numbers and color codes for an RJ-45 connector

Pin Number	Pair Number	Use	Color
1	3	Transmit	White with green stripe
2	3	Receive	Green
3	2	Transmit	White with orange stripe
4	1	Receive	Blue
5	1	Transmit	White with blue stripe
6	2	Receive	Orange
7	4	Transmit	White with brown stripe
8	4	Receive	Brown

The type of patch cable detailed above is called a **straight-through cable**, so named because the terminations at both ends are identical, allowing the wires to pass "straight through." However, in some cases you may want to change the pin locations of some wires. One example is when you want to connect two network devices without using a connectivity device. This can be accomplished through the use of a **crossover cable**, a patch cable in which the terminations locations of the transmit and receive wires on one end of the cable are reversed, as shown in Figure 4–37. (Note that in the figure, T equals Transmit and R equals Receive.) Crossover cables can be useful in troubleshooting network problems when you suspect that a single device's networking hardware or software might be at fault.

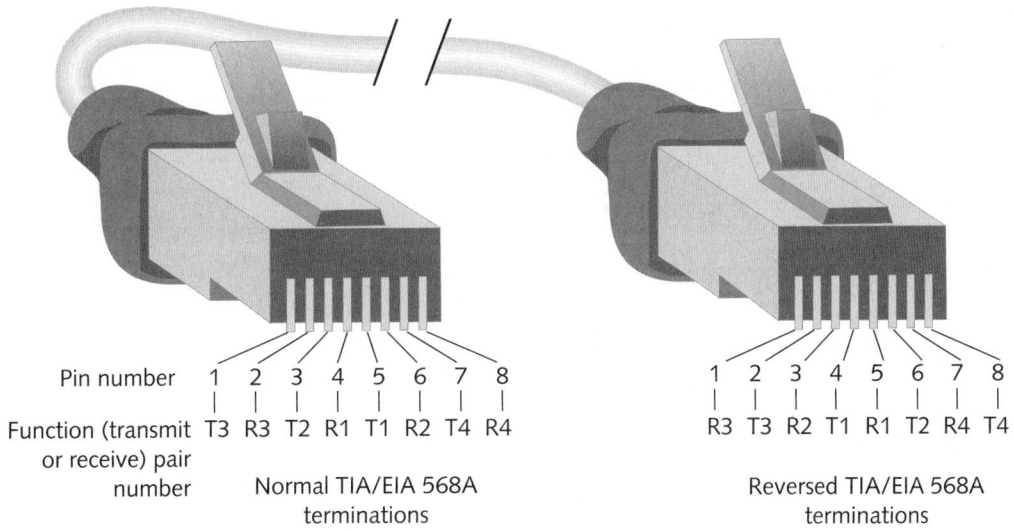

Figure 4-37   RJ-45 terminations on a crossover

The art of proper cabling could fill an entire book. If you plan to specialize in cable installation, design, or maintenance, you should invest in a reference dedicated to this topic. As a network professional, you will likely occasionally add new cables to a room or telecommunications closet, repair defective cable ends, or install a data outlet. Following are some cable installation tips that will help prevent Physical layer failures:

- Do not untwist twisted-pair cables more than one-half inch before inserting them into the punch-down block.

- Do not strip off more than 1 inch of insulation from the copper wire in twisted-pair cables.

- Pay attention to the bend radius limitations for the type of cable you are installing. **Bend radius** is the radius of the maximum arc into which you can loop a cable before you will impair data transmission. Generally, a twisted-pair cable's bend radius is equal to or greater than four times the diameter of the cable. Be careful not to exceed it.

- Test each segment of cabling as you install it with a cable tester. This practice will prevent you from later having to track down errors in multiple, long stretches of cable.

- Use only cable ties to cinch groups of cables together. In addition, avoid cinching cables so tightly that you squeeze their outer covering, a practice that leads to difficult-to-diagnose data errors.

- Avoid laying cable across the floor where it might sustain damage from rolling chairs or foot traffic. If you must take this tack, cover the cable with a cable protector.

- Install cable at least 3 feet away from fluorescent lights or other sources of EMI.

- Always leave slack in cable runs. Stringing cable too tightly risks connectivity and data transmission problems.

- If you run cable in the **plenum**, the area above the ceiling tile or below the subflooring, make sure the cable sheath is plenum-rated and consult with local electric installation codes to be certain you are installing it correctly. A plenum-rated cable is more fire-resistant than other cables, and its sheath will not release noxious fumes if it does start to burn.

- Pay attention to grounding requirements and follow them religiously.

Do not lay cable where animals or children can access it. Cases of squirrels or rabbits chewing through UTP are more common than you might think.

ATMOSPHERIC TRANSMISSION MEDIA

The earth's atmosphere provides an intangible means of transporting data over networks. For decades, radio and TV stations have used the atmosphere to transport information via analog signals. The atmosphere is also capable of carrying digital signals. Networks that transmit signals through the atmosphere are known as **wireless** networks. Wireless LANs typically use infrared or radiofrequency (RF) signaling. These transmission media are suited to very specialized network environments. For example, inventory control personnel who drive through large warehouses to record inventory data benefit from the mobility of wireless networking. In addition to infrared and RF transmission, microwave and satellite links can be used to transport data through the atmosphere.

4

Infrared Transmission

Infrared networks use infrared light signals to transmit data through space, not unlike the way a television remote control sends signals across the room. Networks may use two types of infrared transmission: direct or indirect.

Direct infrared transmission depends on the transmitter and receiver remaining within the line of sight of each other. Just as you cannot switch TV channels with your remote control from behind a wall, so you cannot transmit data through direct infrared between two computers that don't have a clear atmospheric path between them. This "line of sight" limitation prevents widespread use of direct infrared in modern networking environments. On the other hand, the same requirement makes direct infrared more secure than many other transmission methods. When signals are limited to a specific pathway, they become difficult to intercept.

Currently, direct infrared transmission is most often used for communications between devices in the same room. For example, wireless printer connections use direct infrared transmission, as do some synchronizing features of palmtop PCs. Infrared ports are almost standard on business laptop PCs. Many desktop PCs also come equipped with infrared ports.

In **indirect infrared transmission**, signals bounce off walls, ceilings, and any other objects in their path. Because indirect infrared signals are not confined to a specific pathway, this means of transmitting data is not very secure.

Infrared pathways can carry data at rates that rival fiber-optic cable's throughput. Infrared has been proven to function at 100 Mbps, but could probably carry even more traffic. It can span distances up to 1000 m, which is nearly as far as multimode fiber.

RF Transmission

Radiofrequency (RF) transmission relies on signals broadcast over specific frequencies, in the same manner as radio and TV broadcasts. At certain frequencies, RF can penetrate walls, making it the best wireless solution for networks that must transmit data through or around walls, ceilings, and other obstacles. This same characteristic permits easy interception of most types of RF transmissions. Therefore, RF should not be used in environments where data security is important.

In addition, RF is very susceptible to interference and, therefore, would not be a good medium for EMI-saturated locations such as factory floors. Because RF signals can easily interfere with each other, frequencies must be licensed from the Federal Communications Commission (FCC). Neither the frequency nor the geographic location where the frequency is transmitted can be altered without violating the terms of the license. Makers of RF computer and networking components must, therefore, obtain licenses for specific frequencies in different geographic locations. The licensing procedure ensures that nearby systems will not operate at the same frequencies and interfere with each other's signals.

The two most common RF technologies are **narrowband**, which concentrates significant RF energy at a single frequency, and **spread spectrum**, which uses a lower-level signal distributed over several frequencies simultaneously. Although narrowband RF can be easily intercepted and is, therefore, not suited for sensitive data transfer, spread spectrum RF is quite secure. Both types of RF offer a moderate throughput, ranging as high as 10 Mbps.

The U.S. Navy uses spread spectrum RF networking in a most intriguing way. Its ships travel in groups and communicate with each other across the water using RF and satellite network links. Because their transmissions must remain secure, they use spread spectrum RF rather than narrowband RF.

CHOOSING THE RIGHT TRANSMISSION MEDIUM

Now that you have read about the characteristics, benefits, and disadvantages of all types of network transmission media, you need to consider how to evaluate them in terms of realistic network environments. The following list summarizes the majority of environmental factors you must take into account and suggests appropriate transmission media for the various conditions. Most environments will contain a combination of these factors; you must therefore weigh the significance of each against the cost of your optimal solution.

- *Areas of high EMI or RFI*—If the environment houses a number of electrical power sources, you will want to use the most noise-resistant medium possible. Thick Ethernet and fiber-optic cable are the most noise-resistant media currently available.

- *Corners and small spaces*—If the environment requires that cable bend around tight corners or through small spaces, you should use the most flexible medium possible. STP and UTP are both very flexible.

- *Distance*—If the environment requires long stretches of transmission, you might want to consider fiber-optic or wireless media. You can use twisted-pair and coaxial media, but they are more susceptible to attenuation and interference and will require the use of repeaters.

- *Security*—If your organization is concerned about wire taps, you will want to choose the transmission media with the highest security. Fiber-optic, direct infrared, and spread spectrum RF media are excellent choices for this environment.

- *Existing infrastructure*—If you are adding cable to an existing cable plant, you will need to consider how it will interact with existing cabling and connectivity hardware. The media you choose should be tailored to your organization's previously installed equipment.

■ *Growth*—Find out how your organization plans to expand its network and consider future applications, traffic, and geographic expansion when designing its cable plant. In this instance, the medium you choose should be tailored to your organization's needs.

4

CHAPTER SUMMARY

❏ Information can be transmitted via two methods: analog or digital. Analog signals are continuous waves that result in variable and inexact transmission. Digital signals are based on electrical or light pulses that represent information encoded in binary form.

❏ In half-duplex transmission, signals may travel in both directions over a medium but in only one direction at a time. When signals may travel in both directions over a medium simultaneously, the transmission is considered full-duplex.

❏ A form of transmission that allows multiple signals to simultaneously travel over one medium is known as multiplexing. In multiplexing, the single medium is logically separated into multiple channels, or subchannels.

❏ Throughput is the amount of data that the medium can transmit during a given period of time. Throughput is usually measured in bits per second. The physical nature of every transmission medium determines its potential throughput.

❏ Baseband is a form of transmission in which digital signals are sent through direct current pulses applied to the wire. Baseband systems can transmit only one signal, or one channel, at a time. Broadband, on the other hand, uses modulated analog frequencies to transmit multiple signals over the same wire.

❏ Noise is interference that distorts an analog or digital signal. It may be caused by electrical sources, such as power lines, fluorescent lights, copiers, and microwave ovens, or by broadcast signals.

❏ Analog and digital signals both suffer attenuation, or loss of signal, as they travel farther from their sources. To compensate, analog signals are amplified, and digital signals are regenerated through repeaters. Digital signals can be regenerated without any noise they might have accumulated; analog signals, on the other hand, are amplified along with the accompanying noise.

❏ When considering media cost, you must calculate not only the cost of the physical medium, but also the cost of installation, connectivity hardware, maintenance, obsolescence, and productivity gained or lost as a result of a medium's capacity.

❏ Three specifications dictate the size and scalability of networking media: maximum nodes per segment, maximum segment length, and maximum network length.

❏ After a certain distance, a signal attenuates so much that it cannot be accurately interpreted. Thus, a repeater on the network must retransmit and amplify the signal. The maximum distance that a signal can travel and still be accurately interpreted equals the maximum segment length.

❏ Every network is susceptible to a delay between the transmission of a signal and its receipt. This delay is called latency. The length of the cable contributes to latency, as does the presence of any intervening connectivity device, such as a router.

❏ Connectors are the pieces of hardware that connect the wire to the network device, be it a file server, workstation, switch, or printer. Every networking medium requires a specific kind of connector.

❏ Coaxial cable consists of a central copper core surrounded by a plastic insulator, a braided metal shielding called braiding, and an outer plastic cover called the sheath. The copper core carries the electromagnetic signal, and the braiding acts as both a shield against noise and a ground for the signal. The insulator layer protects the copper core from the metal shielding. The sheath protects the cable from physical damage.

❏ Thicknet cabling, also called thickwire Ethernet, is a rigid coaxial cable approximately 1 cm thick that was used for the original Ethernet networks. IEEE has designated Thicknet as 10Base5 Ethernet. The "10" represents its throughput of 10 Mbps, the "Base" stands for baseband transmission, and the "5" represents the maximum segment length of a Thicknet cable, 500 m.

❏ Most Thicknet networks use AUI (also known as DB-15 or DIX) connectors on drop cables to connect network nodes to transceivers known as MAUs (media access units).

❏ Thinnet, also known as Thin Ethernet, or 10Base2 was the most popular medium for Ethernet LANs in the 1980s, but is rarely used on modern networks. The "10" represents its data transmission rate of 10 Mbps, "Base" represents the fact that it uses baseband transmission, and the "2" represents its maximum segment length of 185 m (roughly 200 m). Thinnet is easier to handle and install than Thicknet, but provides less resistance to noise.

❏ Thinnet uses BNC connectors between the network backbone, drop cables, and network nodes.

❏ Both Thicknet and Thinnet coaxial cable rely on the bus topology and must be terminated at both ends with a resistor to prevent signal bounce. Thicknet and Thinnet cable must also be grounded at one end.

❏ Twisted-pair cable consists of color-coded pairs of insulated copper wires, each with a diameter of 0.4 to 0.8 mm, twisted around each other and encased in plastic coating. The twists in the wire help to reduce the effects of crosstalk.

❏ Shielded twisted-pair (STP) cable consists of twisted wire pairs that are not only individually insulated, but also surrounded by a shielding made of a metallic substance such as foil, to reduce the effects of noise on the signal.

❏ Unshielded twisted-pair (UTP) cabling consists of one or more insulated wire pairs encased in a plastic sheath. As its name suggests, UTP does not contain additional shielding for the twisted pairs. As a result, UTP is both less expensive and less resistant to noise than STP.

◻ UTP comes in a variety of specifications, including CAT1 through CAT7, as specified by the TIA/EIA 568 standard. You will probably encounter CAT5 or CAT5e on contemporary LANs.

◻ CAT3 is a form of UTP that contains four wire pairs and can carry data at a rate as high as 10 Mbps, with a possible bandwidth of 16 MHz. CAT3 has typically been used for 10-Mbps Ethernet or 4-Mbps Token Ring networks.

◻ CAT5 and CAT5e are the most popular form of UTP for new network installations and upgrades to Fast Ethernet. CAT5 contains four wire pairs and supports up to 100-Mbps throughput and a 100-MHz signal rate. In addition to 100-Mbps Ethernet, CAT5 wiring can support other fast networking technologies.

◻ 10BaseT is a physical specification for an Ethernet network that is capable of 10-Mbps throughput and uses baseband transmission and twisted-pair media. It has a maximum segment length of 100 meters.

◻ 100BaseT is a physical specification for an Ethernet network that is capable of 100-Mbps throughput and uses baseband transmission and twisted-pair media.

◻ Two types of 100BaseT exist: 100BaseTX, which uses only two wire pairs, and 100BaseT4, which uses all four wire pairs in the cable. 100BaseTX is capable of full duplexing while 100BaseT4 can only achieve half duplexing and also requires different connectivity equipment than 10BaseT or 100BaseTX. 100BaseT may also be called "Fast Ethernet."

◻ Fiber-optic cable contains one or several glass fibers in its core. Data are transmitted via pulsing light sent from a laser or light-emitting diode through the central fiber(s). Outside the fiber(s), a layer of glass called cladding acts as a mirror, reflecting light back to the core in different patterns that vary depending on the transmission mode. Outside the cladding, a plastic buffer and strands of Kevlar protect the inner core. A plastic sheath covers the braiding.

◻ Fiber cable variations fall into two categories: single-mode and multimode. Single-mode fiber uses a small-diameter core, over which light generated by a laser travels mostly down its center, reflecting very few times. Because it reflects little, the light does not disperse as the signal travels along the fiber. This continuity allows single-mode fiber to accommodate high bandwidths and long distances (without requiring repeaters).

◻ Multimode fiber uses a core with a larger diameter, over which many pulses of light generated by a light emitting diode (LED) travel at different angles. Because light is being reflected many different ways in a multimode fiber cable, the waves become less easily distinguishable the longer they travel.

◻ On today's networks, fiber is used primarily as a backbone cable. Fiber-optic cable provides the benefits of very high throughput, very high resistance to noise, and excellent security.

◻ 10BaseF is a Physical layer specification for a network that can achieve 10-Mbps throughput using baseband transmission and running on multimode fiber. Depending on the version, 10BaseF networks may have a maximum segment length of 1000 or 2000 meters.

◻ 100BaseF is a Physical layer specification for a network that can achieve 100-Mbps throughput using baseband transmission running on multimode fiber. Its maximum segment length is 400 meters. It may also be called "Fast Ethernet."

◻ In 1991, TIA/EIA released their joint 568 Commercial Building Wiring Standard, also known as structured cabling, for uniform, enterprise-wide, multivendor cabling systems. Structured cabling is based on a hierarchical design that divides cabling into six subsystems: entrance facility, backbone (vertical) wiring, equipment room, telecommunications closet, horizontal wiring, and work area.

◻ The best practice for installing cable is to follow the TIA/EIA 568 specifications and the manufacturer's recommendations. Be careful not to exceed a cable's bend radius, untwist wire pairs more than one-half inch, or remove more than 1 inch of insulation from copper wire. Install plenum-rated cable in ceilings and floors, and run cabling far from where it might suffer physical damage.

◻ Wireless LANs can use either radiofrequency (RF) or infrared transmission. Wireless transmission is typically used in very specialized applications, often to facilitate mobile computing.

◻ Infrared transmission comes in two main flavors: indirect infrared and direct infrared. Indirect infrared signals bounce off ceilings, walls, and any other obstacles between the sender and receiver. Direct infrared signals require that the sender and receiver establish an unobstructed path through the air.

◻ RF transmission also comes in two flavors: narrowband and spread spectrum. Narrowband RF uses a single frequency and can be easily intercepted and decoded. Spread spectrum RF distributes the signals over several frequencies and is difficult to intercept.

◻ To determine which transmission media are right for a particular networking environment, you must consider the organization's required throughput, cabling distance, noise resistance, security, flexibility, and plans for growth.

KEY TERMS

1 gigabit per second (Gbps) — 1,000,000,000 bits per second.

1 kilobit per second (Kbps) — 1000 bits per second.

1 megabit per second (Mbps) — 1,000,000 bits per second.

1 terabit per second (Tbps) — 1,000,000,000 bits per second.

10Base2 — See *Thinnet*.

10Base5 — See *Thicknet*.

10BaseF — A Physical layer standard for networks that specifies baseband transmission, multimode fiber cabling, and 10-Mbps throughput. 10BaseF networks have a maximum segment length of 1000 or 2000 meters, depending on the version, and employ a star topology.

10BaseT — A Physical layer standard for networks that specifies baseband transmission, twisted pair media, and 10-Mbps throughput. 10BaseT networks have a maximum segment length of 100 meters and rely on a star topology.

100BaseFX — A Physical layer standard for networks that specifies baseband transmission, multimode fiber cabling, and 100-Mbps throughput. 100BaseFX networks have a maximum segment length of 400 meters. 100BaseFX may also be called "Fast Ethernet."

100BaseT — A Physical layer standard for networks that specifies baseband transmission, twisted-pair cabling, and 100-Mbps throughput. 100BaseT networks have a maximum segment length of 100 meters and use the star topology. 100BaseT is also known as Fast Ethernet.

100BaseT4 — A type of 100BaseT network that uses all four wire pairs in a twisted-pair cable to achieve its 100-Mbps throughput. 100BaseT4 is not capable of full-duplex transmission and requires CAT3 or higher media.

100BaseTX — A type of 100BaseT network that uses two wire pairs in a twisted-pair cable, but uses faster signaling to achieve 100-Mbps throughput. It is capable of full-duplex transmission and requires CAT5 or higher media.

100BaseVG (100VG-AnyLAN) — A Physical layer standard for networks that specifies baseband transmission, twisted-pair media, and 100-Mbps throughput. 100BaseVG uses a different and more efficient method than 100BaseT for allowing nodes to transmit data on the media. However, 100BaseVG is rarely used.

alien crosstalk — A type of interference that occurs when signals from an adjacent cable interfere with another cable's transmission.

amplifier — A device that boosts, or strengthens, an analog signal.

amplitude — A measure of a signal's strength.

amplitude modulation (AM) — A modulation technique in which the amplitude of the carrier signal is modified by the application of a data signal.

analog — A signal that uses variable voltage to create continuous waves, resulting in an inexact transmission.

attenuate — To lose signal strength as a transmission travels farther away from its source.

attenuation — The amount of signal loss over a given distance.

AUI (Attachment Unit Interface) — An Ethernet standard for connecting coaxial cables with transceivers and networked nodes.

backbone — A network of networks. Backbone wiring provides interconnection between telecommunications closets, equipment rooms, and entrance facilities.

bandwidth — A measure of the difference between the highest and lowest frequencies that a medium can transmit.

baseband — A form of transmission in which digital signals are sent through direct current pulses applied to the wire. This direct current requires exclusive use of the wire's capacity, so baseband systems can transmit only one signal, or one channel, at a time. Every device on a baseband system shares a single channel.

bend radius — The radius of the maximum arc into which you can loop a cable before you will cause data transmission errors. Generally, a twisted-pair cable's bend radius is equal to or greater than four times the diameter of the cable.

binary — A system founded on using 1s and 0s to encode information.

bit — Short for binary digit. A bit equals a single pulse in the digital encoding system. It may have only one of two values: 0 or 1.

BNC barrel connector — A connector used on Thinnet networks with two open ends used to connect two Thinnet coaxial cables.

BNC T-connector — A connector used on Thinnet networks with three open ends. It attaches to the Ethernet interface card at the base of the "T" and to the Thinnet cable at its two sides so as to allow the signal in and out of the NIC.

braiding — A braided metal shielding used to insulate some types of coaxial cable.

broadband — A form of transmission in which signals are modulated as radiofrequency analog pulses with different frequency ranges. Unlike baseband, broadband technology does not involve binary encoding. The use of multiple frequencies enables a broadband system to operate over several channels and therefore carry much more data than a baseband system.

broadcast — A transmission that involves one transmitter and multiple receivers.

byte — Eight bits of information. In a digital signaling system, broadly speaking, one byte carries one piece of information.

cable plant — The hardware that constitutes the enterprise-wide cabling system.

capacity — See *throughput*.

CAT — Abbreviation for the word "category" when describing a type of twisted-pair cable. For example, Category 3 unsheilded twisted-pair cable may also be called CAT3. See *Category 1, Category 2, Category 3, Category 4, Category 5, Enhanced Category 5, Category 6,* and *Category 7*.

Category 1 (CAT1) — A form of UTP that contains two wire pairs. CAT1 is suitable for voice communications, but not for data. At most, it can carry only 128 Kbps of data.

Category 2 (CAT2) — A form of UTP that contains four wire pairs and can carry up to 4 Mbps of data. CAT2 is rarely found on modern networks, because most require higher throughput.

Category 3 (CAT3) — A form of UTP that contains four wire pairs and can carry up to 10-Mbps, with a possible bandwidth of 16 MHz. CAT3 has typically been used for 10-Mbps Ethernet or 4-Mbps Token Ring networks. Network administrators are gradually replacing CAT3 cabling with CAT5 to accommodate higher throughput. CAT3 is less expensive than CAT5.

Category 4 (CAT4) — A form of UTP that contains four wire pairs and can support up to 16-Mbps throughput. CAT4 may be used for 16-Mbps Token Ring or 10-Mbps Ethernet networks. It is guaranteed for data transmission up to 20 MHz and provides more protection against crosstalk and attenuation than CAT1, CAT2, or CAT3.

Category 5 (CAT5) — The most popular form of UTP for new network installations and upgrades to Fast Ethernet. CAT5 contains four wire pairs and supports up to 100-Mbps throughput and a 100 MHz signal rate. In addition to 100-Mbps Ethernet, CAT5 wiring can support other fast networking technologies, such as Asynchronous Transfer Mode (ATM) and Fiber Distributed Data Interface (FDDI).

Category 6 (CAT6) — A twisted-pair cable that contains four wire pairs, each wrapped in foil insulation. Additional foil insulation covers the bundle of wire pairs, and a fire-resistant plastic sheath covers the second foil layer. The foil insulation provides excellent resistance to crosstalk and enables CAT6 to support at least six times the throughput supported by regular CAT5.

Category 7 (CAT7) — A twisted-pair cable that contains multiple wire pairs, each separately shielded then surrounded by another layer of shielding within the jacket. CAT7 can support up to a 1-GHz signal rate. But because of its extra layers, it is less flexible than other forms of twisted-pair wiring.

channel — A distinct communication path between two or more nodes, much like a lane is a distinct transportation path on a freeway. Channels may be separated either logically (as in multiplexing) or physically (as when they are carried by separate wires).

cladding — The glass shield around the fiber core of a fiber-optic cable. Cladding acts as a mirror, reflecting light back to the core in patterns that vary depending on the transmission mode. This reflection allows fiber to bend around corners without impairing the light-based signal.

coaxial cable — A type of cable that consists of a central copper core surrounded by an insulator, a braided metal shielding, called braiding, and an outer cover, called the sheath or jacket. Coaxial cable, called "coax" for short, was the foundation for Ethernet networks in the 1980s and remained a popular transmission medium for many years.

conduit — Pipeline used to contain and protect the cabling. Conduit is usually made from metal.

connectors — The pieces of hardware that connect the wire to the network device, be it a file server, workstation, switch, or printer.

core — The central component of a fiber-optic cable, consisting of one or several pure glass fibers.

crossover cable — A twisted-pair patch cable in which the termination locations of the transmit and receive wires on one end of the cable are reversed.

crosstalk — A type of interference caused by signals traveling on nearby wire pairs infringing on another pair's signal.

DB-15 — A general term for connectors that use 15 metal pins to complete a connection between devices. "DB" stands for Data bus, while the number "15" indicates how many pins are used to make the connection.

demultiplexer (demux) — A device that separates multiplexed signals once they are received and regenerates them in their original form.

digital — As opposed to analog signals, digital signals are composed of pulses that can have a value of only 1 or 0.

direct infrared transmission — A type of infrared transmission that depends on the transmitter and receiver being within the line of sight of each other.

4

DIX (Digital, Intel, and Xerox) — A type of AUI connector used on Thicknet networks.

drop cable — The cable that connects a device's Ethernet interface to a transceiver in a Thicknet network.

duplex — See *full-duplex*.

electromagnetic interference (EMI) — A type of interference that may be caused by motors, power lines, televisions, copiers, fluorescent lights, or other sources of electrical activity.

enhanced CAT5 (CAT5e) — A higher-grade version of CAT5 wiring that contains high-quality copper, offers a high twist ratio, and uses advanced methods for reducing crosstalk. Enhanced CAT5 can support a signaling rate of up to 200 MHz, double the capability of regular CAT5.

enterprise-wide network — A network that spans an entire organization and often services the needs of many diverse users. It may include many locations (as a WAN), or it may be confined to one location but include many different departments, floors, and network segments.

Fast Ethernet — A type of Ethernet network that is capable of 100-Mbps through-put. 100BaseT and 100BaseFX are both examples of Fast Ethernet.

fiber-optic cable — A form of cable that contains one or several glass fibers in its core. Data are transmitted via pulsing light sent from a laser or light-emitting diode through the central fiber (or fibers). Outside the central fiber, a layer of glass called cladding acts as a mirror, reflecting light back to the core in patterns that vary depending on the transmission mode. Outside the cladding, a plastic buffer protects the core and absorbs any light that might escape. Outside the buffer, strands of Kevlar provide further protection from stretching and damage. A plastic jacket surrounds the Kevlar strands.

fiber-optic modem (FOM) — A demultiplexer used on fiber networks that employ wave division multiplexing. The fiber-optic modem separates the multiplexed signals into individual signals according to their different wavelengths.

frequency — The number of times that a signal's amplitude changes over a fixed period of time, expressed in cycles per second, or hertz (Hz).

frequency modulation (FM) — A method of data modulation in which the frequency of the carrier signal is modified by the application of the data signal.

full-duplex — A type of transmission in which signals may travel in both directions over a medium simultaneously. May also be called, simply, "duplex."

half-duplex — A type of transmission in which signals may travel in both directions over a medium, but in only one direction at a time.

hertz (Hz) — A measure of frequency equivalent to the number of amplitude cycles per second.

indirect infrared transmission — A type of infrared transmission in which signals bounce off walls, ceilings, and any other objects in their path. Because indirect infrared signals are not confined to a specific pathway, they are not very secure.

infrared — A type of data transmission in which infrared light signals are used to transmit data through space, similar to the way a television remote control sends signals across the room. Networks may use two types of infrared transmission: direct or indirect.

latency — The delay between the transmission of a signal and its receipt.

media access unit (MAU) — The type of transceiver used on a Thicknet network to connect network nodes to the backbone.

modem — A device that modulates analog signals into digital signals at the transmitting end for transmission over telephone lines, and demodulates digital signals into analog signals at the receiving end.

modulation — A technique for formatting signals in which one property of a simple, carrier wave is modified by the addition of a data signal during transmission.

multimode fiber — A type of fiber-optic cable that contains a core with a diameter between 50 and 100 microns, over which many pulses of light generated by a light emitting diode (LED) travel at different angles. Because light is being reflected many different ways in a multimode fiber cable, the waves become less easily distinguishable the longer they travel. Thus, multimode fiber is best suited for shorter distances than single-mode fiber.

multiplexer (mux) — A device that separates a medium into multiple channels and issues signals to each of those subchannels.

multiplexing — A form of transmission that allows multiple signals to simultaneously travel over one medium.

n-series connector (n connector) — A type of connector used on Thicknet networks in which a screw-and-barrel arrangement securely connects coaxial cables to devices.

narrowband — A type of radiofrequency transmission in which signals travel over a single frequency. The same method is used by radio and TV broadcasting stations, and signals can be easily intercepted and decoded.

noise — Unwanted signals, or interference, from sources near network cabling, such as electrical motors, power lines and radar.

optical loss — The degradation of a light signal on a fiber-optic network.

overhead — The nondata information that must accompany data in order for a signal to be properly routed and interpreted by the network.

patch cable — A relatively short section (usually between 3 and 50 feet) of twisted-pair cabling, with connectors on both ends, that connects network devices to data outlets.

patch panel — A wall-mounted panel of data receptors into which cross-connect patch cables from the punch-down block are inserted.

phase — A point or stage in a wave's progress over time.

plenum — The area above the ceiling tile or below the subfloor in a building.

point-to-point — A data transmission that involves one transmitter and one receiver.

punch-down block — A panel of data receptors into which horizontal cabling from the workstations is inserted.

radiofrequency (RF) — A type of transmission that relies on signals broadcast over specific frequencies, in the same manner as radio and TV broadcasts. RF may use narrowband or spread spectrum technology.

radiofrequency interference (RFI) — A kind of interference that may be generated by motors, power lines, televisions, copiers, fluorescent lights, or broadcast signals from radio or TV towers.

regeneration — The process of retransmitting a digital signal. Regeneration, unlike amplification, repeats the pure signal, with none of the noise it has accumulated.

repeater — A device used to regenerate a signal.

risers — The backbone cabling that provides vertical connections between floors of a building.

RJ-45 — The standard connector used with shielded twisted-pair and unshielded twisted-pair cabling. "RJ" stands for registered jack.

sheath — The outer cover, or jacket, of a cable.

shielded twisted-pair (STP) — A type of cable containing twisted wire pairs that are not only individually insulated, but also surrounded by a shielding made of a metallic substance such as foil. The shielding acts as an antenna, converting the noise into current (assuming that the wire is properly grounded). This current induces an equal, yet opposite current in the twisted pairs it surrounds. The noise on the shielding mirrors the noise on the twisted pairs, and the two cancel each other out.

signal bounce — A phenomenon caused by improper termination on a bus network in which signals travel endlessly between the two ends of the network, preventing new signals from getting through.

simplex — A type of transmission in which signals may travel in only one direction over a medium.

single-mode fiber — A type of fiber-optic cable with a narrow core that carries light pulses along a single path data from one end of the cable to the other end. Data can be transmitted faster and for longer distances on single-mode fiber than on multimode fiber. Single-mode fiber is extremely expensive.

spread spectrum — A type of radiofrequency transmission in which lower-level signals are distributed over several frequencies simultaneously. Spread spectrum RF is more secure than narrowband RF.

statistical multiplexing — A method of multiplexing in which each node on a network is assigned a separate time slot for transmission, based on the node's priority and need.

straight-through cable — A twisted-pair patch cable in which the wire terminations in both connectors follow the same scheme.

structured cabling — A method for uniform, enterprise-wide, multivendor cabling systems specified by the TIA/EIA 568 Commercial Building Wiring Standard. Structured cabling is based on a hierarchical design using a high-speed backbone.

subchannel — One of many distinct communication paths established when a channel is multiplexed or modulated.

Thicknet — A type of coaxial cable, also known as thickwire Ethernet, that is a rigid cable approximately 1-cm thick. Thicknet was used for the original Ethernet networks. Because it is often covered with a yellow sheath, Thicknet is also called "yellow Ethernet." IEEE has designated Thicknet as 10Base5 Ethernet, with the "10" representing its throughput of 10 Mbps, the "Base" standing for baseband transmission, and the "5" representing the maximum segment length of a Thicknet cable, 500 m.

thickwire Ethernet — See *Thicknet*.

thin Ethernet — See *Thinnet*.

Thinnet — A type of coaxial cable, also known as thin Ethernet, that was the most popular medium for Ethernet LANs in the 1980s. Like Thicknet, Thinnet is rarely used on modern networks. IEEE has designated Thinnet as 10Base2 Ethernet, with the "10" representing its data transmission rate of 10 Mbps, the "Base" representing the fact that it uses baseband transmission, and the "2" roughly representing its maximum segment length of 185 m.

throughput — The amount of data that a medium can transmit during a given period of time. Throughput is usually measured in megabits (1,000,000 bits) per second, or Mbps. The physical nature of every transmission media determines its potential throughput.

time division multiplexing (TDM) — A method of multiplexing that assigns a time slot in the flow of communications to every node on the network and in that time slot, carries data from that node.

transceiver (transmitter/receiver) — A device that both transmits and receives signals. Since a transceiver is concerned with applying signals to the wire, it belongs in the Physical layer of the OSI Model. Many different types of transceivers exist in networking.

transmission — In networking, the application of data signals to a medium or the progress of data signals over a medium from one point to another.

twist ratio — The number of twists per meter or foot in a twisted-pair cable.

twisted-pair (TP) — A type of cable similar to telephone wiring that consists of color-coded pairs of insulated copper wires, each with a diameter of 0.4 to 0.8 mm, twisted around each other and encased in plastic coating.

unshielded twisted-pair (UTP) — A type of cabling that consists of one or more insulated wire pairs encased in a plastic sheath. As its name implies, UTP does not contain additional shielding for the twisted pairs. As a result, UTP is both less expensive and less resistant to noise than STP.

vampire tap — A connector used on Thicknet MAUs that pierces a hole in the coaxial cable, thus completing a connection between the metal tooth in the vampire tap and the copper core of the cable.

volt — Measurement used to describe the degree of pressure an electrical current exerts on a conductor.

voltage — The pressure (sometimes informally referred to as the strength) of an electrical current.

wavelength — The distance between corresponding points on a wave's cycle. Wavelength is inversely proportional to frequency.

4

wavelength division multiplexing (WDM) — A multiplexing technique in which each signal on a fiber-optic cable is assigned a different wavelength, which equates to its own subchannel. Each wavelength is modulated with a data signal. In this manner multiple signals can be simultaneously transmitted in the same direction over a length of fiber.

Webcasting — A broadcast transmission from one Internet-attached node to multiple other Internet-attached nodes.

wireless — Networks that transmit signals through the atmosphere via infrared or RF signaling.

REVIEW QUESTIONS

1. When they become faint, analog signals are regenerated while digital signals are amplified. True or False?

2. Which two of the following technologies cannot achieve full-duplex transmission?

    a. 10BaseT

    b. 100BaseTX

    c. 100BaseFX

    d. 100BaseT4

    e. 100BaseVG

3. What is the origin of the word "modem?"

    a. modifier/demodifier

    b. modulator/demodulator

    c. modulator/decoder

    d. multiplexer/demultiplexer

    e. moderator/demoderator

4. How does noise affect a digital signal?

    a. Noise enhances a digital signal.

    b. Noise weakens a digital signal.

    c. Noise increases the frequency of a digital signal.

    d. Noise distorts the signal.

    e. Noise does not affect digital signals.

5. Which two of the following transmission techniques can increase the potential throughput of a network?

    a. simplexing

    b. multiplexing

    c. full duplexing

    d. broadcasting

    e. amplifying

6. Which of the following would not be a source of EMI?

    a. fluorescent lighting

    b. a microwave

    c. a loud gong

    d. a cord that carries electricity to a printer

    e. a lightning storm

7. When determining the cost of a cabling system, what—besides the cost of the wire—must you bear in mind?

8. What is the term that refers to the outermost covering of a cable?

    a. cladding

    b. insulation

    c. plenum

    d. sheath

    e. braiding

9. What type of coaxial cable would you use to connect network nodes on a Thinnet network?

    a. RG-11

    b. RG-58A/U

    c. RG-59/U

    d. RG-8

    e. RG-62A/U

10. What are two advantages of using twisted-pair cabling over coaxial cabling on a network?

    a. Twisted-pair cable is more reliable.

    b. Twisted-pair cable is less expensive.

    c. Twisted-pair cable is more resistant to noise.

    d. Twisted-pair cable is more resistant to physical damage.

    e. Twisted-pair cable is required for modern transmission standards, such as 100BaseT.

11. In which of the following network types would you use a cable with AUI connectors?

    a. 10Base5

    b. 10Base2

    c. 10BaseT

    d. 10BaseF

    e. 100BaseFX

12. Describe the differences between baseband and broadband transmission.

13. What type of terminator is required at both ends of a Thinnet or Thicknet cable?

    a. 20 ohms

    b. 25 ohms

   c. 50 ohms

   d. 100 ohms

   e. 200 ohms

14. Which two of the following network types require a bus topology?

   a. 10Base5

   b. 10Base2

   c. 10BaseT

   d. 100BaseTX

   e. 100BaseVG

15. Crosstalk does not present a problem for UTP cable. True or False?

16. What is the maximum throughput currently supported by CAT5 wiring?

   a. 10 Mbps

   b. 100 Mbps

   c. 200 Mbps

   d. 1 Gbps

   e. 10 Gbps

17. How many wire pairs are in a typical CAT5 cable?

   a. 2

   b. 3

   c. 4

   d. 5

   e. 8

18. What type of fiber-optic cable is most frequently found on LANs?

   a. multithreaded fiber

   b. twisted fiber

   c. single-mode fiber

   d. braided fiber

   e. multimode fiber

19. Which two of the following are drawbacks to using fiber-optic cable for LANs?

   a. It is expensive.

   b. It cannot handle high bandwidth transmissions.

   c. It can carry transmissions using only the TCP/IP protocol.

   d. It can be difficult to install and repair.

   e. It is not yet an accepted standard for high-speed networking.

20. What is the maximum allowable distance for a horizontal wiring subsystem?

   a. 10 m

   b. 90 m

c. 100 m

d. 200 m

e. 400 m

21. What is the maximum segment length on a 100BaseT network?

    a. 10 m

    b. 100 m

    c. 200 m

    d. 400 m

    e. 1000 m

22. What is the maximum segment length on a Thicknet network?

    a. 50 m

    b. 100 m

    c. 200 m

    d. 500 m

    e. 1000 m

23. In what subsystem of a structured cabling design are patch cables used?

    a. in the horizontal wiring

    b. in the work area

    c. in the backbone wiring

    d. in the entrance facilities

    e. on the backbone

24. What part of the TIA/EIA structured cabling recommendations provides connectivity to a telecommunications service provider?

    a. work area

    b. horizontal wiring

    c. telecommunications closet

    d. entrance facilities

    e. patch panel

25. On what type of network would you use BNC connectors?

    a. 10Base5

    b. 10Base2

    c. 10BaseT

    d. 100BaseTX

    e. 100BaseT4

26. On a 100BaseTX Ethernet network, where will you most likely find the transceivers?

    a. in the modems

    b. in the MAUs

   c. in the NICs

   d. in the horizontal cabling

   e. in the work area cabling

27. In general, what type of cabling can sustain the most bending without impairing transmission?

   a. Thinnet

   b. Thicknet

   c. STP

   d. UTP

   e. fiber-optic

28. What is the *maximum* amount of insulation you should strip from copper wires before inserting them into connectors?

   a. ¼ inch

   b. ½ inch

   c. 1 inch

   d. 2 inches

   e. 4 inches

29. What is the *maximum* amount you should untwist twisted-pair wires before inserting them into connectors?

   a. ¼ inch

   b. ½ inch

   c. 1 inch

   d. 2 inches

   e. 4 inches

30. On a 10BaseT network, which of the following best describes how the wires of a UTP cable are used to transmit and receive information?

   a. One wire pair handles data transmission, while another wire pair handles data reception.

   b. One wire in one pair handles data transmission, while the other wire in that pair handles data reception.

   c. Three wires of two wire pairs handle both data transmission and reception, while the fourth wire acts as a ground.

   d. All four wires of two wire pairs handle both data transmission and reception.

31. If you wanted to allow two workstations to transmit and receive data between their NICs without using a connectivity device, which of the following would you need?

   a. crossover cable

   b. straight-through cable

   c. AUI cable

4

    d. DIX cable

    e. Multimode cable

32. What are the two main types of infrared transmission, and how do they differ?

33. Radiofrequency transmissions can be easily intercepted. True or False?

34. What kind of transmission media is best suited to videoconferencing between two buildings that are across the street from each other?

    a. coaxial cable

    b. fiber-optic cable

    c. STP

    d. CAT5 UTP

    e. infrared

35. Which government agency in the United States allocates radio frequencies?

    a. FTA

    b. FTC

    c. SEC

    d. CCC

    e. FCC

HANDS-ON PROJECTS

Project 4-1

One of the characteristics that you must consider when choosing the right type of cable for your network is its bend radius. Bending a cable may affect its ability to transmit data. When you bend a cable past its maximum bend radius, data errors may occur. In this exercise, you will attempt to impair the transmission of data over a Thinnet coaxial cable by bending it past its maximum bend radius.

For this project, you will need a Windows 98 or 2000 Professional workstation connected to a Windows 2000 or NetWare server via Thinnet coaxial cable. You will also need a compass and a tape measure. In the first five steps of this project, you will create a continuously looping batch file, called "dirtest.bat," that repeatedly lists the contents of one directory on the server. The purpose of this batch file is to generate a steady flow of traffic between the server and your workstation.

1. At the Windows 98 or 2000 workstation, click **Start**, point to **Programs**, point to **Accessories**, and then click **Notepad**. The Notepad window opens.

2. Type the following three lines in the open document:

   :TEST

   dir /s

   goto TEST

3. Click **File** on the menu bar, then click **Save**. The Save As dialog box opens.
4. Save the file as **dirtest.bat** in the root directory of the C: drive.
5. Close Notepad.
6. If you are using a Windows 98 workstation, click **Start**, point to **Programs**, then click **MS-DOS Prompt**. If you are using a Windows 2000 workstation, click **Start**, point to **Programs**, point to **Accessories**, then click the **Command Prompt**.
7. At the DOS prompt type **cd** to make sure you are in the root directory.
8. At the DOS prompt, type **dirtest**. The batch file runs. You should see a directory listing continually scrolling down the screen.
9. While watching the DOS window, take a 4-foot section of the coaxial cable in your hands and slowly bend it as if you were trying to create a circle. At what point does the traffic between the workstation and the server slow down? At what point does it stop, if ever?
10. Using the compass, measure the bend radius of the cable when you notice that the transmission begins to slow down, and again when you notice that it stops.
11. After completing the exercise, close the Command Prompt (or MS-DOS) window.

Project 4-2

You may sometimes need to create your own patch cables or install a new connector on an existing cable. In this exercise, you will practice putting an RJ-45 connector on a twisted-pair cable, and then use the cable to connect a workstation to the network. The process of inserting wires into the connector is called crimping, and it is a skill that requires practice— so don't be discouraged if the first cable you create doesn't reliably transmit and receive data.

For this project, you will need a crimping tool, a wire stripper, a wire cutter, a 5-foot length of CAT5 UTP, two RJ-45 connectors, and a simple client/server network (for example, a Windows 98, 2000, or XP workstation connected to wall jack or hub as part of a Windows 2000 server network) that you have verified works with a reliable twisted-pair cable.

1. Using the wire cutter, make a clean cut at both ends of the UTP cable.
2. Using the wire stripper, remove the sheath off of one end of the UTP cable, beginning at approximately one inch from the end. Be careful to not damage the insulation on the twisted pairs inside.
3. Separate the four wire pairs slightly. Carefully unwind each pair no more than ½ inch.
4. Align all eight wires on a flat surface, one next to the other, ordered according to their colors and positions listed in Table 4-5.
5. Keeping the wires in order and in line, gently slide them all the way into their positions in the RJ-45 plug.
6. After the wires are fully inserted, place the RJ-45 plug in the crimping tool and press firmly to crimp the wires into place. (Be careful to not rotate your hand or the wire as you do this, otherwise only some of the wires will be properly terminated.) Crimping causes the pins to pierce the insulation of the wire, thus creating contact between the two conductors.
7. Now remove the RJ-45 connector from the crimping tool. Examine the end and see whether each wire appears to be in contact with the pin. It may be difficult to tell simply by looking at the connector. The real test is whether your cable will successfully transmit and receive signals.

8. Repeat Steps 2 through 7 for the other end of the cable. After completing Step 7 for the other end, you will have created a CAT5 patch cable

9. Use your newly created patch cable to connect your workstation to the network. Can you log on? Can you open a file?

10. If you cannot communicate reliably with the network, try the process again, beginning at Step 1. (You have to re-cut the wires; otherwise they will not properly connect with the RJ-45 connector.) Continue until you can reliably log on to the network using the patch cable you've made.

4

Project 4-3

As you learned in this chapter, it is sometimes useful to connect two computers directly, rather than go through a traditional network, as you did in the previous exercise. In this exercise you will make a crossover cable and use it to connect two workstations. For this project you will need one workstation running either the Windows 98 or Windows 2000 Professional operating system and one server running the Windows 2000 operating system. Both must contain functioning NICs. You will also need a crimping tool, a wire stripper, a wire cutter, a 5-foot length of CAT5 UTP, and two RJ-45 connectors.

1. On one end of your CAT5 UTP cable, install an RJ-45 connector by following Steps 1–5 of Project 4-2.

2. On the opposite end of the same cable, install an RJ-45 connector in a similar manner, but reverse the locations of the transmit and receive wires. Refer to Figure 4-37 for a visual representation of the crossover cable's RJ-45 terminations.

3. Now that your crossover cable is complete, insert one of the cable's RJ-45 connectors into the workstation's NIC and the other RJ-45 connector into the server's NIC.

4. To test whether your cable works, from the workstation, attempt to view your network connections. To do this from the Windows 98 workstation, double-click the **Network Neighborhood icon**, then double-click the **Entire Network icon** within the Network Neighborhood window. To do this from a Windows 2000 workstation, double-click the **My Network Places icon**, then double-click the **Entire Network icon** in the My Network Places window. Do you see the icon for your server?

5. Now double-click the **server icon** and log on to the server.

6. Once you have logged on, copy a file from your workstation to the server.

Project 4-4

In this exercise, you will have the opportunity to use an atmospheric transmission medium, infrared signaling. Recall that infrared is a line-of-sight medium, meaning that it depends on a direct path between two devices that are trying to communicate.

For this project, you will need a workstation running Windows 98 or Windows 2000 Professional and a printer with an infrared port. Your first step is to make sure that the printer drivers are correctly installed on the workstation.

1. Install and configure drivers for the infrared ports on each device, if they are not already installed.

2. Place the workstation and the printer on the same table, approximately 2 feet apart, with their infrared ports facing each other. Ensure that the workstation recognizes the printer.

3. Print a document using the infrared port.

4. Now turn the printer 180 degrees so that its infrared port faces away from the workstation. Attempt to print the same document. Are you successful?

5. Experiment with moving the devices farther and farther away from each other, while their infrared ports have a direct and clear path between them. At what distance does communication break down?

CASE PROJECTS

1. You have been asked to design the entire cabling system for a medical instrument manufacturer's new central warehouse. The company already has three buildings on two city blocks, and the warehouse will be its fourth building. Currently, the buildings run on separate networks, but the company would like to be able to exchange data among them. In addition, the Marketing Department would like to hold videoconferences with the Sales Department in the next building. In the warehouse, 50 shipping and packing personnel will be riding up and down the aisles on forklifts pulling inventory off the shelves on a daily basis. What kind of transmission media would you recommend for the different departments of the medical instrument company and why?

2. Now the medical instrument company is experiencing data transmission problems in the Quality Control Department, which is located in one corner of the research building. Because only part of a floor is affected, you head for the telecommunications closets in that building. What will you look for?

3. Thanks to your fast thinking, the medical instrument company was able to keep its quality control tasks on track. It has just one more problem: The company has a secret project under way at a warehouse across the street, which is disguised as an antique mall. The project is highly sensitive and its existence cannot be divulged, even to current staff. The medical instrument company executives will not allow any new construction or cabling that might raise suspicion. Nevertheless, they need a way to transmit data to and from the warehouse. What do you suggest?

CHAPTER 5

PHYSICAL AND LOGICAL TOPOLOGIES

After reading this chapter and completing the exercises, you will be able to:

➤ Describe the basic and hybrid LAN physical topologies, their uses, advantages, and disadvantages

➤ Describe a variety of enterprise-wide and WAN physical topologies, their uses, advantages, and disadvantages

➤ Compare the different types of switching used in data transmission

➤ Understand the transmission methods underlying Ethernet, Token Ring, LocalTalk, and FDDI networks

---

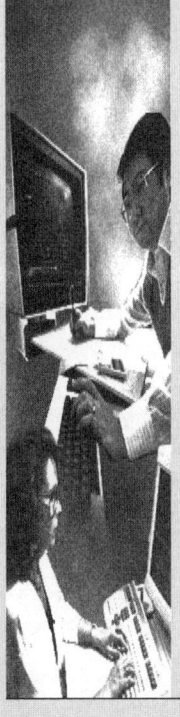

ON THE JOB

I've worked as a senior networking engineer at a large furniture manufacturer for almost a decade. Many years ago, a consultant had nearly convinced us that we should upgrade our old Thinnet LAN to Token Ring. He insisted that Token Ring was much more reliable, scalable, and easier to support. This was true enough, compared to our old network. But replacing the cabling, connectivity devices, and NICs (not to mention retraining our staff to use the new network) would be a huge investment, so our IT department took plenty of time to mull it over. The other senior engineer and I had an ongoing debate about whether Token Ring or Ethernet would win out as the preferred standard of the networking world. He pointed out that Token Ring, although slightly more expensive to implement, was more efficient. Therefore, he projected, it could surpass Ethernet in speed, given the right advances in technology. I had a feeling that Ethernet, because it was less expensive and gaining in popularity, would win out as the transmission of choice.

In the end, we all agreed to replace our Thicknet network with Token Ring. It took almost a full year to complete the transition, and we all quickly learned about the idiosyncrasies of this unfamiliar transmission method. Unfortunately, however, a few years later it became clear that Ethernet technology was quickly advancing and becoming the standard of the networking world. Fast Ethernet was going to be a reality. Meanwhile, our Token Ring equipment was becoming more expensive and seemed too slow for our needs. We recognized that although Token Ring is a solid technology, it might be headed the way of the dinosaurs. We began the process of evaluating our network all over again, and in 1999 decided to make the plunge to Fast Ethernet.

Stan Myzlowski
Hartford Products

Just as an architect of a house must decide where to place walls and doors, where to install electrical and plumbing systems, and how to manage traffic patterns through rooms to make a house more livable, a network architect must consider many factors, both seen and unseen, when designing a network. This chapter details some basic elements of network architecture: physical and logical topologies. These elements are crucial to understanding networking hardware, design, troubleshooting, and management, all of which are discussed later in this book.

In this chapter you will learn the basic layouts of LANs and WANs, the advantages and disadvantages of each layout, and the optimal application for each layout. You will also learn about the most commonly used network transmission methods: Ethernet, Token Ring, LocalTalk, FDDI, and ATM. Once you master the physical and logical fundamentals of network architecture, you will have all the tools necessary to design a network as elegant as the Taj Mahal.

SIMPLE PHYSICAL TOPOLOGIES

A **physical topology** is the physical layout, or pattern, of the nodes on a network. It depicts a network in broad scope; that is, it does not specify device types, connectivity methods, or addresses on the network. Physical topologies are divided in three fundamental geometric shapes: bus, ring, and star. These shapes can be mixed to create hybrid topologies. Before you design a network, you need to understand physical topologies, because they are integral to the type of network (for example, Ethernet or Token Ring), cabling infrastructure, and transmission media you use. You must also understand a network's physical topology to troubleshoot its problems or change its infrastructure. A thorough knowledge of physical topologies is necessary to obtain Network+ certification.

This chapter builds on the terms and concepts discussed in Chapters 2, 3, and 4. If you do not have a clear understanding of the material covered in those chapters, take time to review them now.

Physical topologies and logical topologies (discussed later) are two different networking concepts. You should be aware that when used alone, the word "topology" often refers to a network's *physical* topology.

Bus

A **bus topology** consists of a single cable connecting all nodes on a network without intervening connectivity devices. Figure 5-1 depicts a typical bus topology.

The single cable is called the **bus** and can support only one channel for communication; as a result, every node shares the bus's total capacity. Most bus networks—for example, Thinnet and Thicknet—use coaxial cable as their physical medium. A bus topology can be considered a peer-to-peer topology, because every device on the network shares the responsibility for getting data from one point to another. Each node on a bus network passively listens for data directed to it. When one node wants to transmit data to another node, it broadcasts an alert to the entire network, informing all nodes that a transmission is being sent; the destination node then picks up the transmission. Nodes between the sending and receiving nodes ignore the message.

For example, suppose that you want to send an instant message to your friend Diane, who works across the hall, asking whether she wants to have lunch with you. You click the send button after typing your message, and the data stream that contains your message is sent to your NIC. Your NIC then sends a message across the shared wire that essentially says, "I have a message for Diane's computer." The message passes by every NIC between your computer and Diane's computer until Diane's computer recognizes that the message is meant for it and responds by accepting the data.

Figure 5-1   A bus topology network

At the ends of each bus network are 50-ohm resistors known as terminators. As you learned in Chapter 4, terminators stop signals after they have reached the end of the wire. Without these devices, signals on a bus network would travel endlessly between the two ends of the network—a phenomenon known as signal bounce—and new signals could not get through. To understand this concept, imagine that you and a partner, standing at opposite sides of a canyon, are yelling to each other. When you call out, your words echo; when your partner replies, his words also echo. Now imagine that the echoes never fade. After a short while you could not continue conversing because all of the previously generated sound waves would still be bouncing around, creating too much noise for you to hear anything else. On a network, terminators prevent this problem by halting the transmission of old signals. Figure 5-2 depicts a terminated bus network.

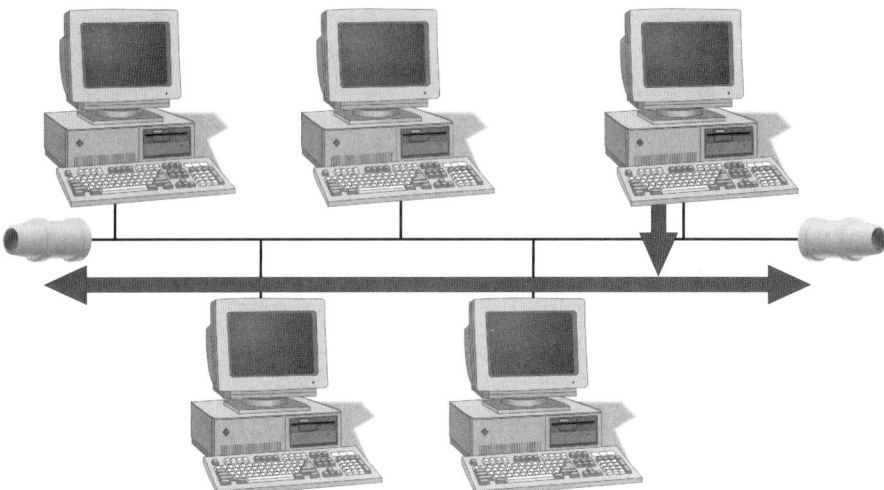

Figure 5-2   A terminated bus network

Although networks based on a bus topology are inexpensive to set up, they do not scale well. As you add more nodes, the network's performance degrades. Because of the single-channel limitation, the more nodes on a bus network, the more slowly the network will transmit and deliver data. For example, suppose a bus network in your small office supports two workstations and a server, and saving a file to the server takes two seconds. During that time, your NIC first checks the communication channel to make sure it is free, then issues data directed to the server. When the data reach the server, the server accepts them. Suppose, however, that your business experiences tremendous growth, and you add five more workstations during one weekend. The following Monday, when you attempt to save a file to the server, the save process might take five seconds, because the new workstations may also be using the communications channel, and your workstation may have to wait for a chance to transmit. As this example illustrates, a bus topology would not be practical for a network of more than 200 workstations. In fact, it is rarely practical for networks with more than a dozen workstations.

Bus networks are also difficult to troubleshoot, because it is a challenge to identify fault locations. To understand why, think of the game called "telephone," in which one person whispers a phrase into the ear of the next person, who whispers the phrase into the ear of another person, and so on, until the final person in line repeats the phrase aloud. The vast majority of the time, the phrase recited by the last person bears little resemblance to the original phrase. When the game ends, it's hard to determine precisely where in the chain the individual errors cropped up. Similarly, errors may occur at any intermediate point on a bus network, but at the receiving end it's possible to tell only that an error occurred. Finding the source of the error can prove very difficult, because you cannot retrace the data's progress from one node to the next; that is, the nodes don't "remember" the data after they pass it on. (In the telephone game analogy, this situation would be similar to every person in the line forgetting the phrase after he or she passed it on—a situation that would make it impossible to trace the evolution of the phrase as it moves from one person to the next.)

A final disadvantage to bus networks is that they are not very fault-tolerant, because a break or a defect in the bus affects the entire network. As a result, and because of the other disadvantages associated with this topology, you will rarely see a network run on a pure bus topology. You may, however, encounter hybrid topologies that include a bus component, as discussed later in this chapter.

Ring

In a **ring topology**, each node is connected to the two nearest nodes so that the entire network forms a circle, as shown in Figure 5-3. Data are transmitted clockwise, in one direction (unidirectionally), around the ring. Each workstation accepts and responds to packets addressed to it, then forwards the other packets to the next workstation in the ring. Because a ring network has no "ends," and because data stop at their destination, ring networks do not require terminators. In most ring networks, twisted-pair or fiber-optic cabling is used as the physical medium.

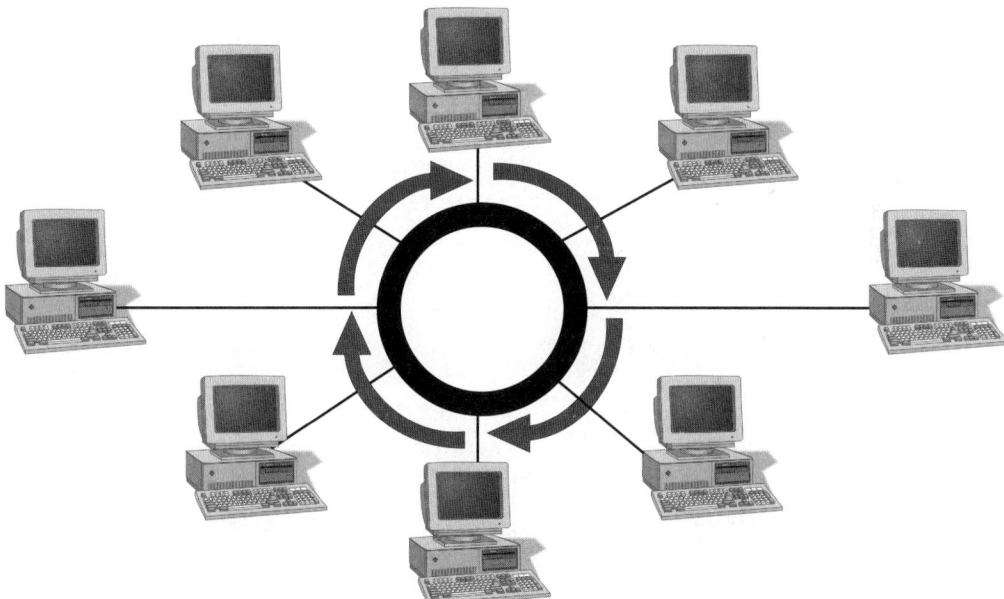

Figure 5-3   A typical ring network

One method for passing data on a ring network is token passing. In **token passing**, a 3-byte packet, called a token, is transmitted from one node to another around the ring. If a computer on the ring has information to transmit, it picks up the token packet, adds control and data information plus the destination node's address to transform the token into a data frame, and then passes the token on to the next node. The transformed token, now in the form of a frame, circulates around the network until it reaches its intended destination. The destination node picks it up and returns an acknowledgment message to the originating node. After the originating node receives the acknowledgment, it releases a new free token and sends it down the ring. This approach ensures that only one workstation transmits data at any given time. Because each workstation participates in sending the token around the ring, this architecture is known as an **active topology**. Each workstation acts as a repeater for the transmission.

The drawback of a simple ring topology is that a single malfunctioning workstation can disable the network. For example, suppose that you and five colleagues share a pure ring topology LAN in your small office. You decide to send an instant message to Thad, who works three offices away, telling him that you accidentally received a package addressed to him. Between your office and Thad's office are two other offices, and two other workstations on the ring. Your instant message must pass through the two intervening workstations' NICs before it reaches Thad's computer. If one of these workstations has a malfunctioning NIC, your message will never reach Thad.

In addition, just as in a bus topology, the more workstations that must participate in token passing, the slower the response time. Consequently, pure ring topologies are not very flexible or scalable.

Contemporary LANs rarely use pure ring topologies. A variation of the ring topology, known as a star-wired ring, is popular for some types of networks, such as Token Ring networks. Star-wired rings and Token Ring technology will be discussed later in this chapter.

Star

In a **star topology**, every node on the network is connected through a central device, such as a hub. Figure 5-4 depicts a typical star topology. Star topologies are usually built with twisted-pair or fiber cabling. Any single cable on a star network connects only two devices (for example, a workstation and a hub), so a cabling problem will affect two nodes at most. Devices such as workstations or printers transmit data to the hub, which then retransmits the signal to the network segment containing the destination node.

Star topologies require more cabling than ring or bus networks. They also require more configuration. However, because each node is separately connected to a central connectivity device, they are more fault-tolerant. A single malfunctioning cable or workstation cannot disable star networks. A failure in the central connectivity device (such as a hub), can take down a LAN segment, though.

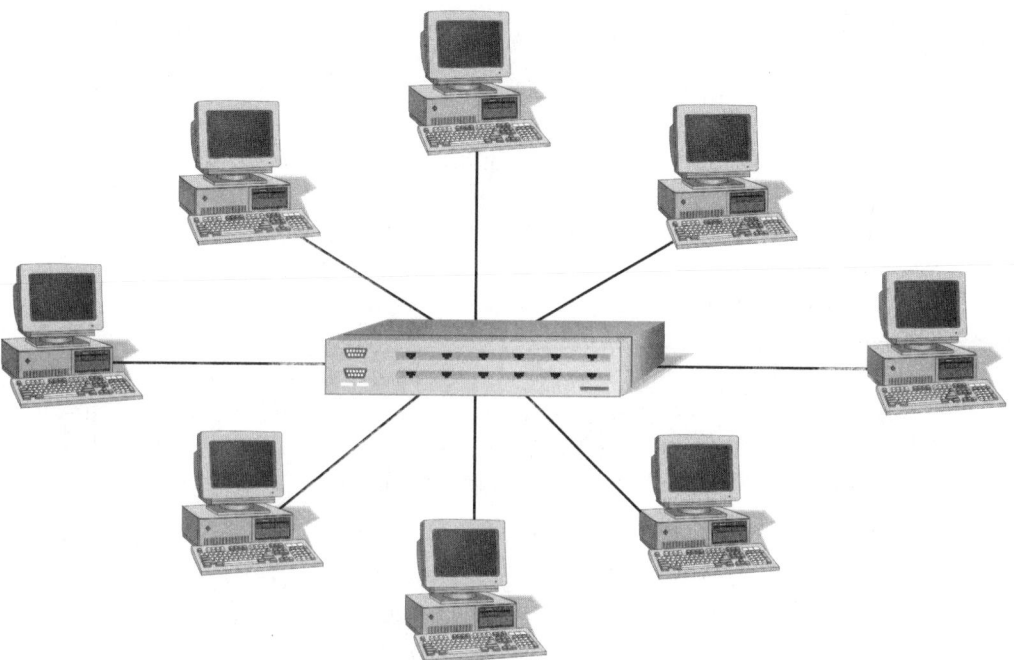

Figure 5-4 A typical star topology network

Because they include a centralized connection point, star topologies can easily be moved, isolated, or interconnected with other networks; they are therefore scalable. For this reason, and because of their fault tolerance, the star topology has become the most popular fundamental layout used in contemporary LANs. Many network administrators have replaced their old bus or ring networks with star networks in recent years. Single star networks are commonly interconnected with other networks through hubs and switches to form more complex topologies.

As you learned in Chapter 4, 10BaseT and 100BaseT Ethernet networks are based on the star topology, as are most LocalTalk networks. These networks can support a maximum of only 1024 addressable nodes on a logical network. Thus, you can say that star networks support a maximum of 1024 nodes. For example, if you have a campus with 3000 users, hundreds of networked printers, and scores of other devices, you must strategically create smaller logical networks. Even if you had 1000 users and *could* put them on the same logical network, you probably wouldn't, because doing so would result in poor performance and impossible management. Instead, you should subdivide the users and their peripherals into workgroups according to their needs or geographic locations. Chapter 16 describes the process of evaluating user and organizational requirements when designing a network.

HYBRID PHYSICAL TOPOLOGIES

Except in very small networks, you will rarely encounter a network that follows a pure bus, ring, or star topology. Simple topologies are too restrictive, particularly if the LAN must accommodate a large number of devices. More likely, you will work with a complex combination of these topologies, known as a **hybrid topology**. Several kinds of hybrid topologies are explained in the following sections.

Star-Wired Ring

The **star-wired ring topology** uses the physical layout of a star in conjunction with the token–passing data transmission method. In Figure 5-5, which depicts this architecture, the solid lines represent a physical connection and the dotted lines represent the flow of data. Data are sent around the star in a circular pattern. This hybrid topology benefits from the fault tolerance of the star topology (data transmission does not depend on each workstation to act as a repeater) and the reliability of token passing. Modern Token Ring networks, as specified in IEEE 802.5, use this hybrid topology.

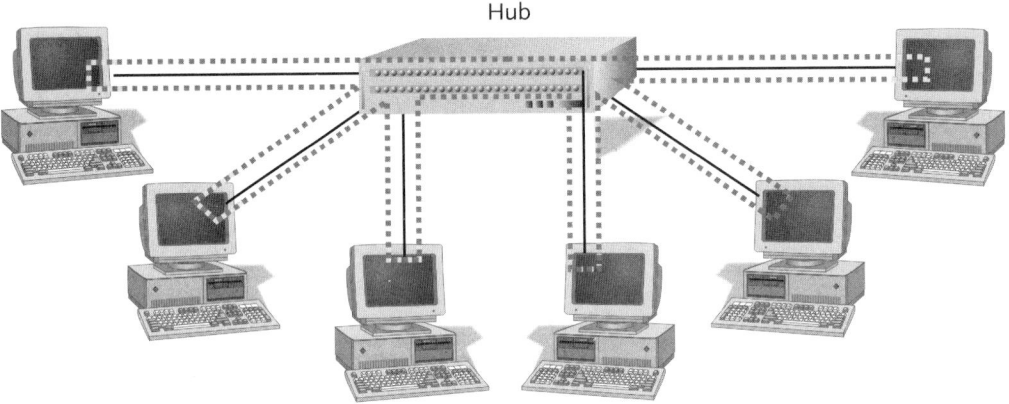

Figure 5-5 A star-wired ring topology network

Star-Wired Bus

Another popular hybrid topology combines the star and bus formations. In a **star-wired bus topology**, groups of workstations are star-connected to hubs and then networked via a single bus, as shown in Figure 5-6. With this design, you can cover longer distances and easily interconnect or isolate different network segments. One drawback is that this option is more expensive than using either the star or, especially, the bus topology alone because it requires more cabling and potentially more connectivity devices. The star-wired bus topology commonly forms the basis for modern Ethernet and Fast Ethernet networks.

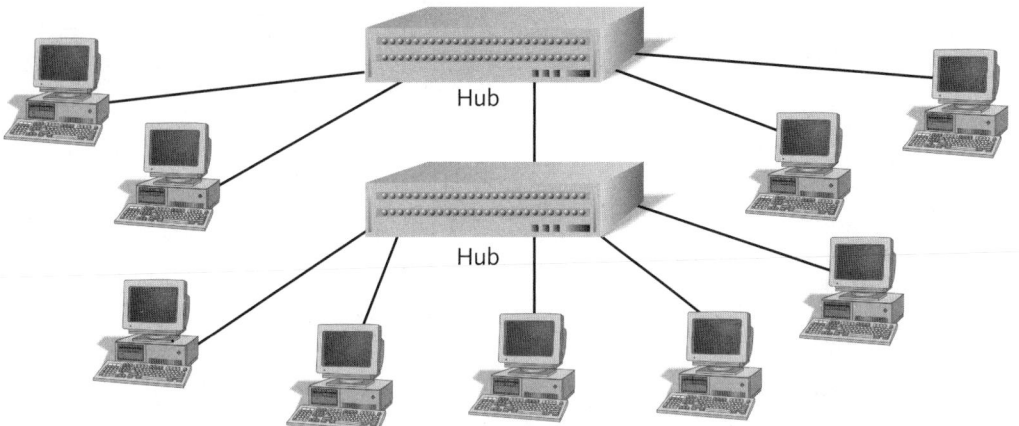

Figure 5-6   A star-wired bus topology network

Daisy-Chained

Even the star-wired ring and bus network topologies are too simplistic to represent a typical medium-sized LAN. Nevertheless, hubs that service star-wired bus or ring topologies can be daisy-chained to form a more complex hybrid topology, as shown in Figure 5-7. A **daisy chain** is a linked series of devices. (As you will learn later in this chapter, in an enterprise network, a daisy-chained network is called a serial backbone network.) Because the star-wired hybrids provide for modular additions, daisy-chaining is a logical solution for growth. Also, because hubs can be easily connected through cables attached to their ports, little additional cost is required to expand a LAN's infrastructure in this way.

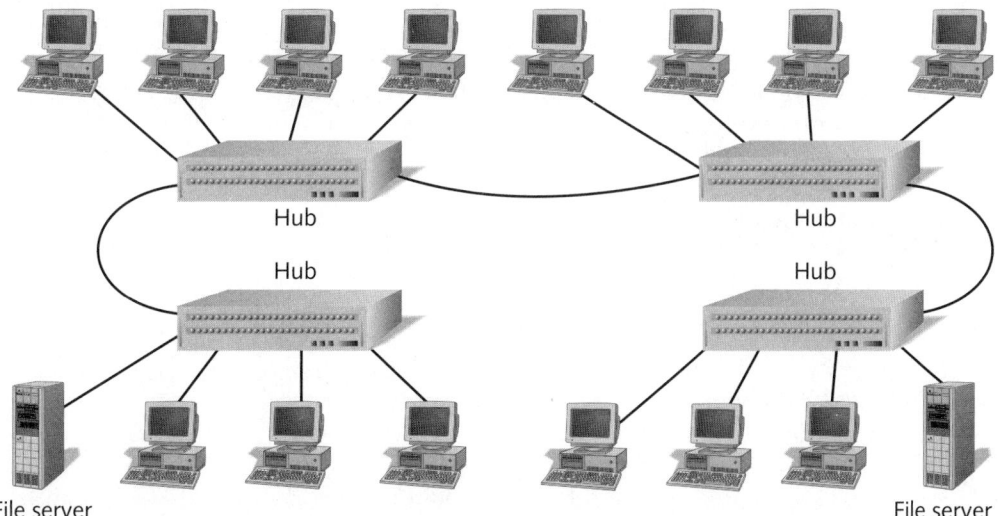

Figure 5-7   Daisy-chained star-wired bus topology

Daisy-chaining simple topologies can present hazards. For example, IEEE specifications such as the Ethernet 802.3 standard dictate the maximum number of hubs that may be connected in sequence to maintain transmission integrity. These standards vary according to the network type. For example, in a 10BaseT network, you may use a maximum of four hubs to connect five network segments. Using more hubs than the standard suggests (in other words, exceeding the maximum network length) will adversely affect the functionality of a LAN. Among other things, if you extend a LAN beyond its recommended size, intermittent and unpredictable data transmission errors will result. Similarly, if you daisy-chain a topology with limited bandwidth, you risk overloading the channel and generating more data errors.

Hierarchical

None of the topologies discussed previously distinguishes between the functions or priorities of the various workgroups. For example, a server that contains a payroll database and serves 50 clients may be attached to the same hub as a workstation that is used only twice each week for data processing. Although both devices are connected to the same hub, they perform vastly different functions. Accordingly, you should assign the payroll server a higher priority for network access. For example, you need to ensure that the payroll server almost never loses network connectivity as a result of a device failure on the network. Thus, you might choose to connect the payroll server directly to the backbone using a more expensive, fault-tolerant hub. The less important, data-processing workstation could be connected to a small, inexpensive hub that is connected to a better hub, which is in turn connected to the backbone. This arrangement minimizes the possibility of the payroll server losing connectivity but increases the possibility of the data-processing workstation losing connectivity.

There are many reasons for separating devices in a hierarchy. You may want to separate hubs, switches, and routers for reasons related to security, cost, scalability, network addressing, bandwidth, or reliability. In addition, there are many ways to separate devices and workgroups, leading to many variations on the hierarchical topology. You can consider the hierarchical topology as similar to an organizational chart in a company, where groups are divided by function, and different personnel belong to different levels in the organizational chart.

One possible way to group devices on a network is to divide them into layers. In the context of topologies, you can think of a layer as a logical division between devices on a network. A hierarchical hybrid topology uses layers to separate devices based on their priority or function. A hierarchical topology may have any number of layers and may connect different types of simple topologies. For example, Figure 5-8 depicts a hierarchical ring topology with three layers. The top layer services the network's backbone, while the second layer provides direct connectivity for the file server ring and intermediate connectivity to the third layer. The third layer then services multiple workgroups, such as Administration, Sales, and IT.

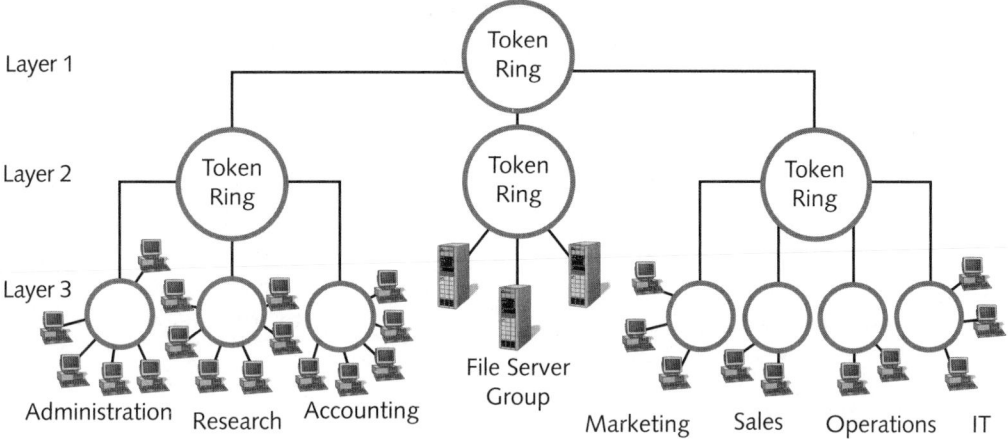

Layer 1

Layer 2

Layer 3

Administration   Research   Accounting   File Server Group   Marketing   Sales   Operations   IT

5

Figure 5-8   Hierarchical ring topology

Arranging topologies in a hierarchy offers several advantages: the ability to segregate bandwidth among different groups, ease in adding or isolating different network groups, and the flexibility to interconnect different network types. For these reasons, hierarchical topologies underlie high-speed LAN and WAN designs.

ENTERPRISE-WIDE TOPOLOGIES

In networking, the term **enterprise** refers to an entire organization, including its local and remote offices, a mixture of computer systems, and a number of departments. Enterprise-wide computing must therefore take into account the breadth and diversity of a large organization's computer needs. Enterprise-wide networks expand on the simple and hybrid LAN topologies. As a result, their topologies require more interconnection devices and more reliable routes than simple LAN topologies can provide. An enterprise-wide network may include or form part of a WAN, but an enterprise-wide network connects only one organization's resources. A WAN (for example, the Internet) may connect resources from many different organizations.

As with LAN topologies, a number of variations on the basic enterprise-wide topologies exist. This section describes some popular methods of arranging these larger networks.

Backbone Networks

As you learned in Chapter 4, a network backbone is the cabling that connects the hubs, switches, and routers on a network. Backbones usually are capable of more throughput than the cabling that connects workstations to hubs. This added capacity is necessary because backbones carry more traffic than any other cabling in the network. For example, an increasing number of businesses are implementing fiber-optic backbone but continue to use CAT5 wiring for the cabling from hubs to workstations. Although even the simplest LAN (including a star or bus topology LAN) technically has a backbone, enterprise-wide back-bones are more complex and more difficult to plan. The backbone is the most significant building block of these networks.

Serial Backbone

A **serial backbone** is the simplest kind of backbone network. It consists of two or more hubs connected to each other by a single cable. Serial backbone networks are identical to the daisy-chained networks discussed in the "Hybrid Physical Topologies" section. As mentioned earlier, they are not suitable for large networks or long distances. Although the serial backbone topology could be used for enterprise-wide networks, it is rarely implemented for that purpose.

Distributed Backbone

A **distributed backbone** consists of a number of hubs connected to a series of central hubs or routers in a hierarchy, as shown in Figure 5-9. In Figure 5-9, the cross-hatched lines represent the backbone. This kind of topology allows for simple expansion and lim-ited capital outlay for growth, because more layers of hubs can be added to existing lay-ers. For example, suppose that you are the network administrator for a small publisher's office. You might begin your network with a distributed backbone consisting of two hubs that supply connectivity to your 20 users, 10 on each hub. When your company hires more staff, you can connect another hub to one of the existing hubs, and use the new hub to connect the new staff to the network.

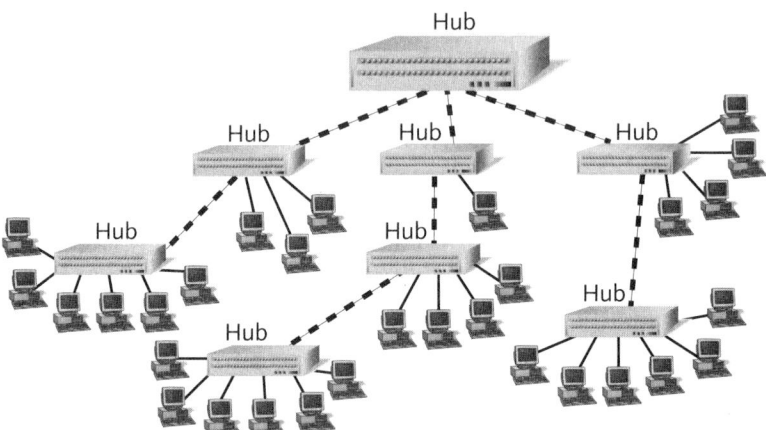

Figure 5-9   A simple distributed backbone network

A more complicated distributed backbone connects multiple LANs or LAN segments using routers, as shown in Figure 5-10. In this example, the routers form the highest layer of the backbone to connect the LANs.

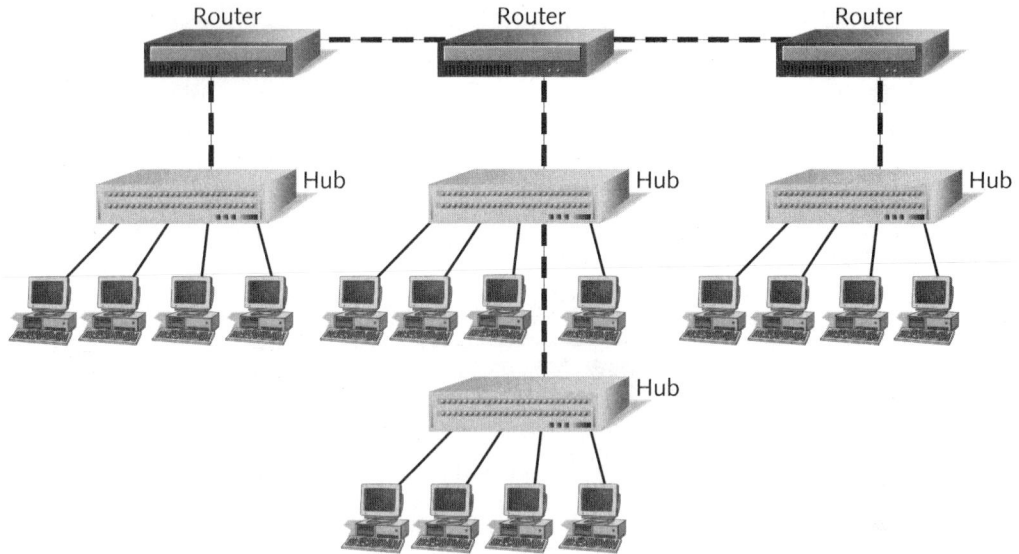

Figure 5-10   A distributed backbone connecting multiple LANs

A distributed backbone also provides network administrators with the ability to segregate workgroups and therefore manage them more easily. It adapts well to an enterprise-wide network confined to a single building, where layers of hubs can be assigned according to the floor or department. When designing a network with a distributed backbone, however, you must consider the maximum allowable distance between nodes and the server dictated by the network media. Another possible problem in this design relates to the central point of failure, the hub at the uppermost layer. Despite these potential drawbacks, implementing a distributed backbone network can be relatively simple, quick, and inexpensive.

Collapsed Backbone

The **collapsed backbone** topology uses a router or switch as the single central connection point for multiple subnetworks, as shown in Figure 5-11. Contrast Figure 5-11 with Figure 5-10, where multiple LANs are connected via a distributed backbone. In a collapsed backbone, a single router or switch is the highest layer of the backbone. The router or switch that makes up the collapsed backbone must contain multiprocessors to handle the heavy traffic going through it. The dangers of using this arrangement relate to the fact that a failure in the central router or switch can bring down the entire network. In addition, because routers cannot move traffic as quickly as hubs, using a router may slow data transmission. (You will learn more about hubs and routers in Chapter 6.)

Nevertheless, a collapsed backbone topology offers substantial advantages. Most significantly, this arrangement allows you to interconnect different types of subnetworks. You can also centrally manage maintenance and troubleshooting chores.

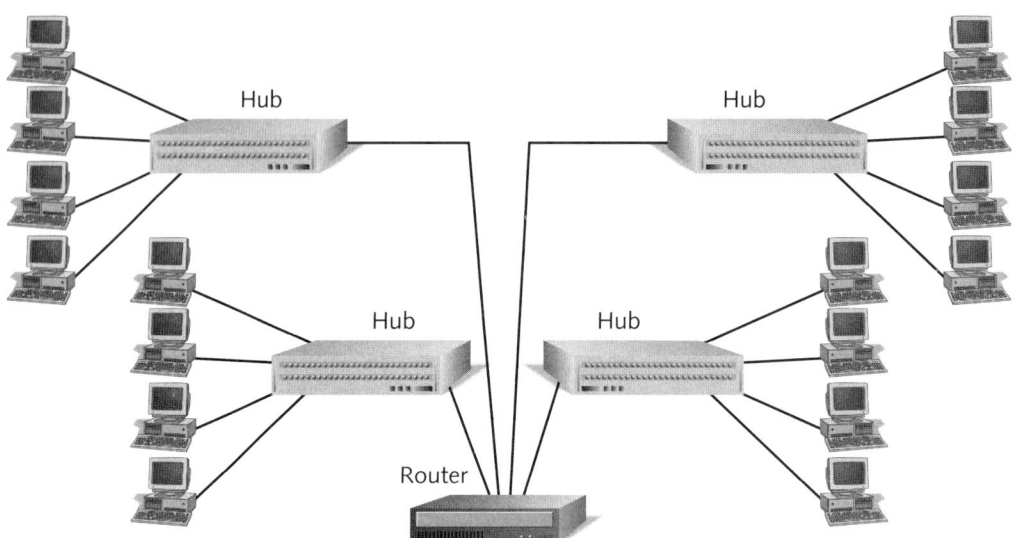

Figure 5-11   A collapsed backbone network

Parallel Backbone

A **parallel backbone** is the most robust enterprise-wide topology. This variation of the collapsed backbone arrangement consists of more than one connection from the central router or switch to each network segment. Figure 5-12 depicts a simple parallel backbone topology. As you can see, each hub is connected to the router or switch by more than one cable. The most significant advantage of using a parallel backbone is that its redundant (duplicate) links ensure network connectivity to any area of the enterprise. Parallel backbones are more expensive than other enterprise-wide topologies because they require much more cabling than the others. However, they make up for the additional cost by offering increased performance.

As a network administrator, you might choose to implement parallel links to only some of the most critical devices on your network. For example, if the first and second hubs in Figure 5-12 connected your Facilities and Payroll departments to the rest of the network, and your organization could never afford to lose connectivity with those departments, you might use a parallel structure for those links. If the third and fourth hubs in Figure 5-12 connected your organization's Recreation and Training departments to the network, you might decide that parallel links were unnecessary for these departments. By selectively implementing the parallel structure, you can lower connectivity costs and leave available additional ports on the connectivity devices.

5

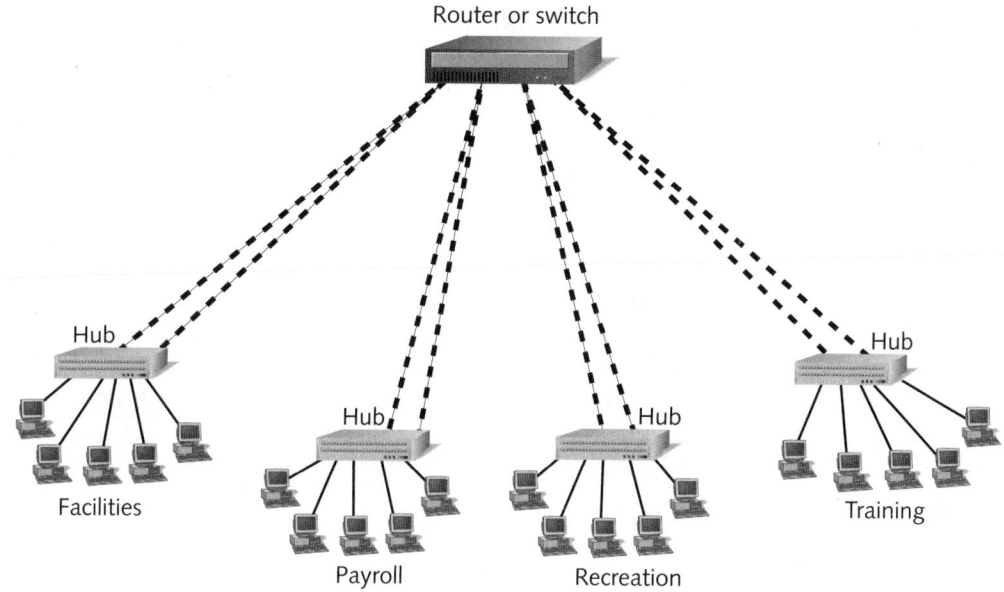

Figure 5-12   A parallel backbone network

Mesh Networks

Of course, backbone networks are not the only type of topology used in enterprise-wide networks. Some organizations use a more intricate topology, known as a mesh network. In a **mesh network**, routers are interconnected with other routers, with at least two pathways connecting each router. (See Figure 5-13.) The mesh network is more complex than the backbone networks. In fact, it typically contains several different backbone networks. Indeed, the term "mesh network" is a general topology term that can apply to many different arrangements of workgroups and interconnection devices.

Although a simple LAN can be a mesh network, most often this topology is employed for enterprise-wide networks and WANs. The Internet is an example of a mesh WAN.

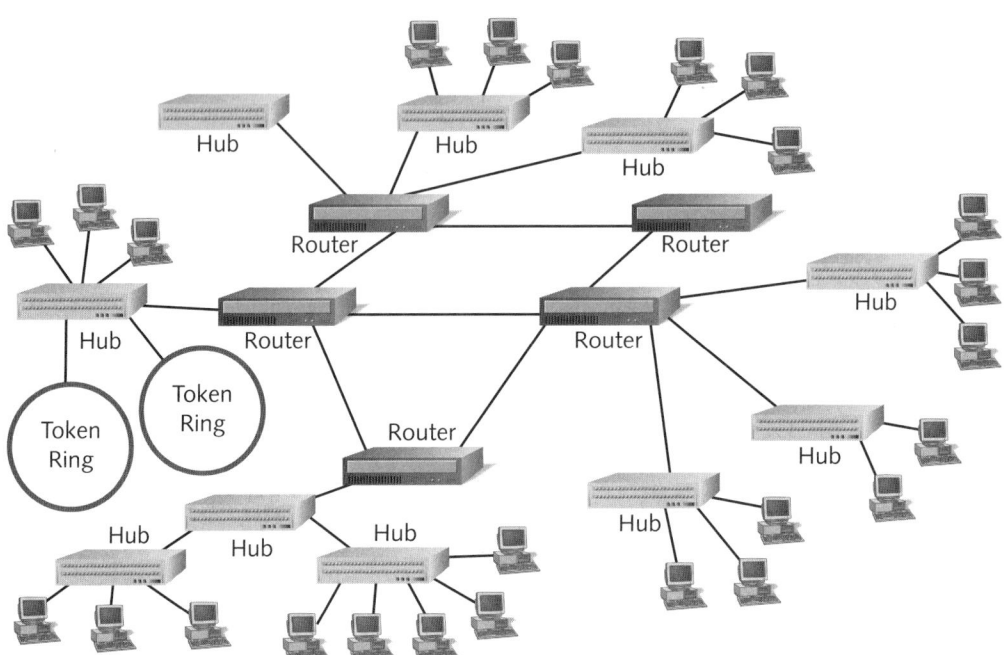

Figure 5-13   An example of a mesh network

WAN TOPOLOGIES

As you learned in Chapter 1, a wide area network (WAN) is a network connecting geographically distinct locations, which may or may not belong to the same organization. WAN topologies use both LAN and enterprise-wide topologies as building blocks, but add more complexity because of the distance they must cover, the larger number of users they serve, and the heavy traffic they often handle. For example, although a simple ring topology may suffice for a small office with 10 users, it does not scale well and therefore cannot serve 1000 users. The particular WAN topology you choose will depend on the number of sites you must connect, the distance between the sites, and any existing infrastructure.

WAN topologies also differ from LAN topologies in the type and extent of interconnectivity devices they use. This difference is directly related to the fact that networking protocols are handled differently on local network segments than they are on segments involving longer distances. For example, a LAN might carry NetBEUI, IPX/SPX, and TCP/IP traffic over a single segment. Because WANs depend on routers to interconnect LANs, and because NetBEUI is not a routable protocol, however, a WAN link will carry only IPX/SPX and/or TCP/IP traffic. WAN networking technologies, such as ISDN, DSL, and SONET, are discussed in detail in Chapter 7.

Peer-to-Peer

A WAN with single interconnection points for each location is arranged in a **peer-to-peer topology**. A WAN peer-to-peer topology is similar to peer-to-peer communications on a LAN in that each site depends on every other site in the network to transmit and receive its traffic. However, the peer-to-peer LANs use computers with shared access to one cable, whereas the WAN peer-to-peer topology uses different locations, each one connected to another one through (usually) dedicated circuits.

The WAN peer-to-peer topology is often the best option for organizations with only a few sites and the capability to use **dedicated circuits**—that is, continuously available communications channels between two access points that are leased from a telecommunications provider, such as an ISP. You will learn more about dedicated circuits, such as T1 or ISDN connections, in Chapter 7. For now, you simply need to know that dedicated circuits make it possible to transmit data regularly and reliably. Figure 5-14 depicts a peer-to-peer WAN using T1 and ISDN connections.

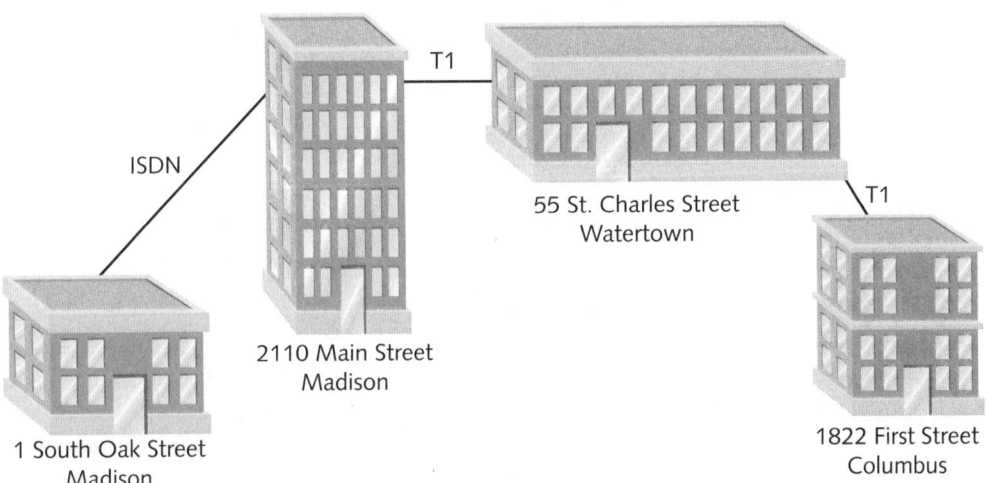

Figure 5-14 A peer-to-peer WAN

Peer-to-peer WAN topologies are suitable for only small WANs. Because all sites must participate in carrying traffic, this model does not scale well. The addition of more sites can cause performance to suffer. Also, a single failure on a peer-to-peer WAN can take down communications between all sites.

Ring

In a **ring WAN topology**, each site is connected to two other sites so that the entire WAN forms a ring pattern, as shown in Figure 5-15. This architecture is similar to the ring LAN topology, except that a ring WAN topology connects locations rather than local nodes. The advantages of a ring WAN over a peer-to-peer WAN are twofold: a single cable problem will not affect the entire network, and routers at any site can redirect data to another route if one route becomes too busy. On the other hand, expanding ring-configured WANs can be difficult, and it is more expensive than expanding a peer-to-peer WAN because it requires at least one additional link. For these reasons, WANs that use the ring topology are only practical for connecting fewer than four or five locations.

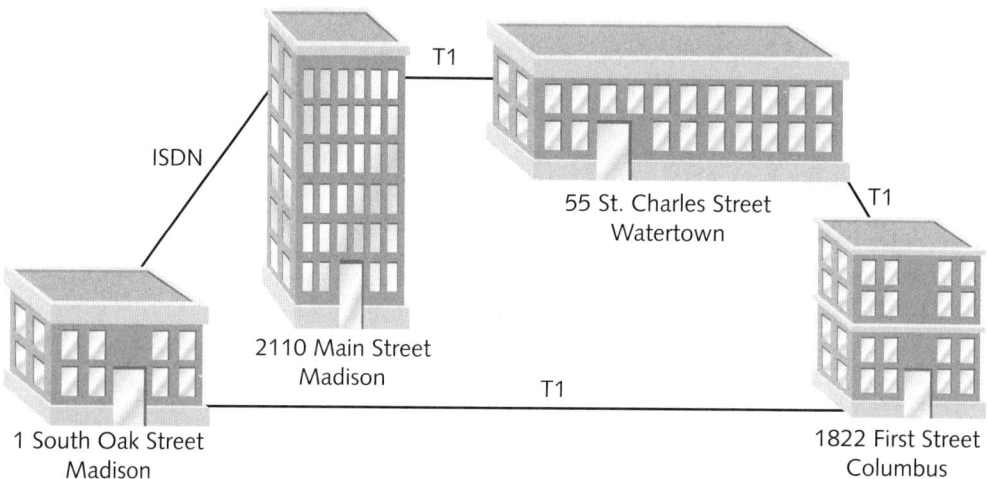

Figure 5-15   A ring-configured WAN

Star

The **star WAN topology** mimics the arrangement of a star LAN. A single site acts as the central connection point for several other points, as shown in Figure 5-16. This arrangement provides separate routes for data between any two sites. As a result, star WANs are more reliable than the peer-to-peer or ring WANs. As a general rule, reliability increases with the number of potential routes data can follow. For example, if the T1 link between the Oak Street and Main Street locations fails, the Watertown and Columbus locations can still communicate with the Main Street location because they use different routes. In a peer-to-peer or ring topology, however, a single failure would halt all traffic between all sites.

Another advantage of a star WAN is that when all of its dedicated circuits are functioning, a star WAN provides shorter data paths between any two sites.

Extending a star WAN is easy, and this expansion costs less than extending a peer-to-peer or ring WAN. For example, if the organization that uses the star WAN pictured in Figure 5-16 wanted to add a Maple Street, Madison, location to its topology, it could simply lease a new dedicated circuit from the Main Street office to its Maple Street office. None of the other offices would be affected by the change. If the organization were using a peer-to-peer or ring WAN topology, however, two separate dedicated connections would be required to incorporate the new location into the network.

As with star LAN topologies, the greatest drawback of a star WAN is that a failure at the central connection point can bring down the entire WAN. In Figure 5-16, for example, if the Main Street office suffered a catastrophic fire, the entire WAN would fail.

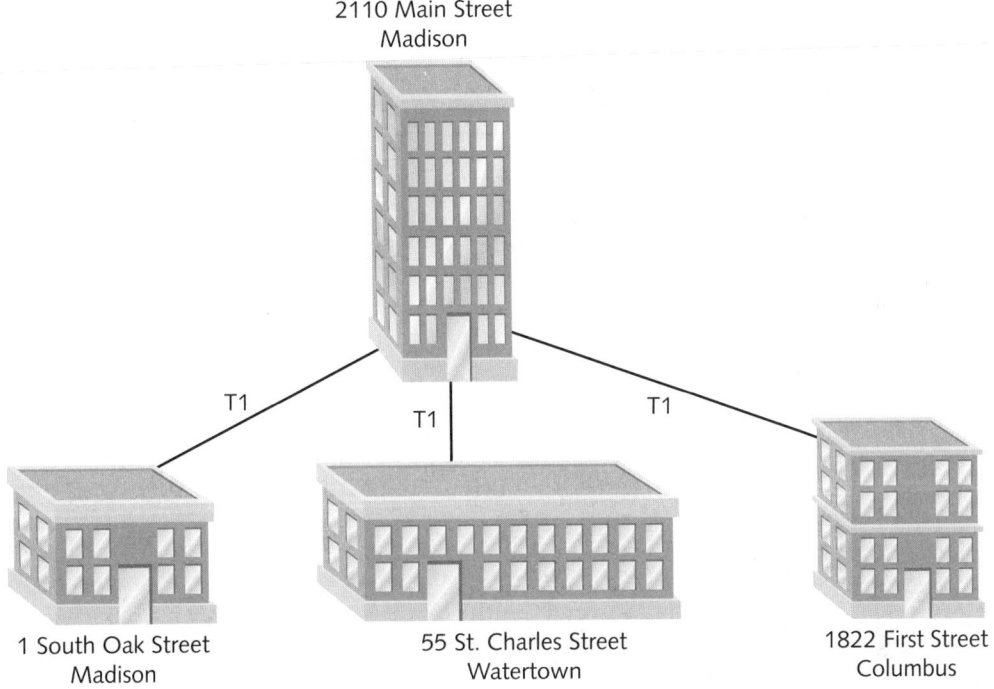

2110 Main Street
Madison

T1   T1   T1

1 South Oak Street   55 St. Charles Street   1822 First Street
Madison   Watertown   Columbus

Figure 5-16   A star-configured WAN

Mesh

Like an enterprise-wide mesh, a **mesh WAN topology** incorporates many directly interconnected nodes—in this case, geographical locations. Because every site is interconnected, data can travel directly from its origin to its destination. If one connection suffers a problem, routers can redirect data easily and quickly. Mesh WANs are the most fault-tolerant type of WAN configuration because they provide multiple routes for data to follow between any two points. For example, if the Madison office in Figure 5-17 suffered a catastrophic fire, the Dubuque office could still send and transmit data to and from the Detroit office by going directly to the Detroit office. If both the Madison and Detroit offices failed, the Dubuque and Indianapolis offices could still communicate.

One drawback to a mesh WAN is the cost; connecting every node on a network to every other entails leasing a large number of dedicated circuits. With larger WANs, the expense can become enormous. To reduce costs, you might choose to implement a partial mesh, in which critical WAN nodes are directly interconnected and secondary nodes are connected through star or ring topologies, as shown in Figure 5-17. Partial-mesh WANs are more practical, and therefore more common in today's business world, than full-mesh WANs.

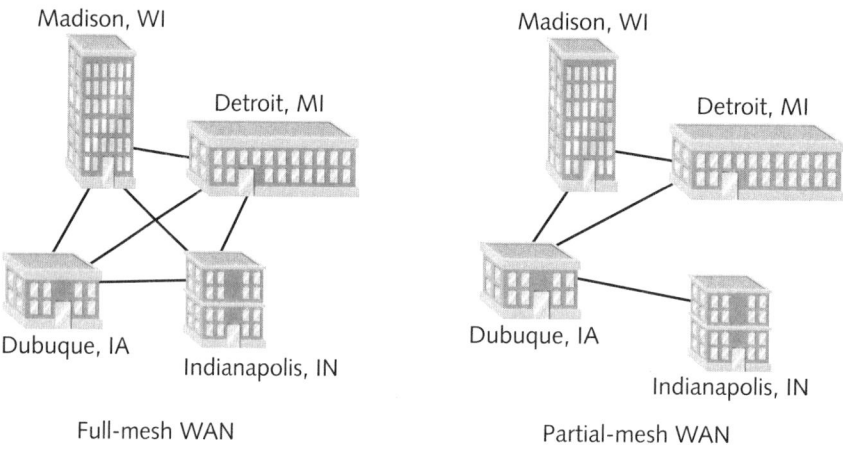

Figure 5-17   Full-mesh and partial-mesh WANs

Tiered

Tiered WAN topologies are similar to the hierarchical hybrid topologies used with LANs. In a **tiered WAN topology**, WAN sites connected in star or ring formations are interconnected at different levels, with the interconnection points being organized into layers. Figure 5-18 depicts a tiered WAN. In this example, the Madison, Detroit, and New York offices form the upper tier, and the Dubuque, Indianapolis, Toronto, Toledo, Washington, and Boston offices form the lower tier. If the Detroit office suffers a failure, the Toronto and Toledo offices cannot communicate with any other nodes on the WAN. Similarly, the Dubuque and Indianapolis offices depend on the Madison office for their WAN connectivity, just as the Washington and Boston offices depend on the New York office for their connectivity.

Variations on this topology abound. Indeed, flexibility makes the tiered approach quite practical. A network architect can determine the best placement of top-level routers based on traffic patterns or critical data paths. In addition, tiered systems allow for easy expansion and inclusion of redundant links to support growth. On the other hand, their enormous flexibility means that creation of tiered WANs requires careful consideration of geography, usage patterns, and growth potential.

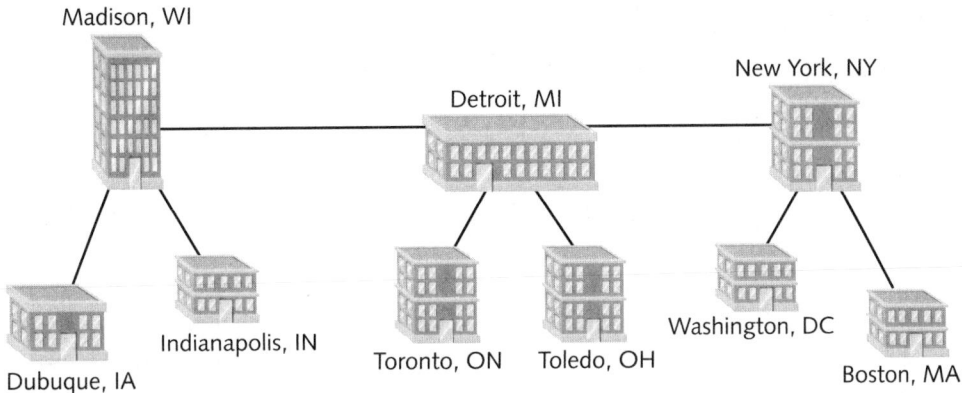

Figure 5-18   A tiered WAN topology

LOGICAL TOPOLOGIES

The term **logical topology** refers to the way in which data are transmitted between nodes, rather than the physical layout of the paths that data take. The most common logical topologies are bus and ring. In a bus logical topology, signals travel from one network device to all other devices on the network (or network segment). They may or may not travel through an intervening connectivity device. As you would expect, a network that uses a bus physical topology also uses a bus logical topology. In addition, networks that use either the star or star-wired bus physical topologies also use a bus logical topology. In contrast, a ring logical topology describes a network in which signals follow a circular path between sender and receiver. Networks that use a pure ring topology use a ring logical topology. The ring logical topology is also used by the star-ring hybrid physical topology, because signals follow a circular path, even as they travel through a connectivity device (as shown by the dashed lines in Figure 5-5). Different types of networks are characterized by different logical topologies. For example, Ethernet networks use the bus logical topology while Token Ring networks use the ring logical topology. You learn more about Ethernet and Token Ring networks later in this chapter.

SWITCHING

Switching is a component of a network's logical topology that determines how connections are created between nodes. You will learn more about switches, the hardware that manages network switching, in Chapter 6. For now, you should be aware of the three methods for switching: circuit switching, message switching, and packet switching. Every network relies on one of these switching mechanisms.

Circuit Switching

In **circuit switching**, a connection is established between two network nodes before they begin transmitting data. Bandwidth is dedicated to this connection and remains available until the users terminate communication between the two nodes. While the nodes remain connected, all data follow the same path initially selected by the switch. When you place a telephone call, for example, your call goes through a circuit-switched connection.

Because circuit switching monopolizes its piece of bandwidth while the two stations remain connected (even when no actual communication is taking place), it is not an economical technology. Some network applications that cannot tolerate the time delay it takes to reorganize data packets, such as live audio or videoconferencing, benefit from such a dedicated path, however. When you connect your home PC via modem to your Internet service provider's access server, that connection uses circuit switching. WAN technologies, such as ISDN and T1 service, which are discussed in Chapter 7, also use circuit switching. Finally, ATM, which is discussed later in this chapter, uses circuit switching as well.

Message Switching

Message switching establishes a connection between two devices, transfers the information to the second device, and then breaks the connection. The information is stored and forwarded from the second device once a connection between that device and a third device on the path is established. This "store and forward" routine continues until the message reaches its destination. All information follows the same physical path; unlike with circuit switching, however, the connection is not continuously maintained. E-mail systems use message switching. Message switching requires that each device in the data's path have sufficient memory and processing power to accept and store the information before passing it to the next node. None of the network transmission technologies discussed in this chapter uses message switching.

Packet Switching

A third method for connecting nodes on a network is packet switching. **Packet switching** breaks data into packets before they are transported. Packets can travel any path on the network to their destinations, because each packet contains the destination address and sequencing information. Consequently, packets can attempt to find the fastest circuit available at any instant. They need not follow each other along the same path, nor must they arrive at their destination in the same sequence as when they left the transmitting node.

To understand this technology, imagine that you organized a field trip for 50 colleagues to the National Air and Space Museum in Washington, DC. You gave the museum's precise address to your colleagues and told them to leave precisely at 7:00 A.M. from your office building across town. You did not tell your coworkers which route to take. Some might choose the subway, others might hail a taxicab, and still others might choose to drive their own cars. All of them will attempt to find the fastest route to the museum. But if a group of six decide to take a taxicab and only four people fit in that taxi, the next two people have to wait for a taxi. Or a taxi might get caught in rush hour traffic and be forced to find an alternate route. Thus, the fastest route might not be evident upon departure. But no matter which transportation method your colleagues choose, you will all arrive at the museum and reassemble as a group. This analogy illustrates how packets travel in a packet-switched network.

5

The destination node on a packet-switched network reassembles the packets based on their control information. Because of the time it takes to reassemble the packets into a message, packet switching is not suited to live audio or video transmission. Nevertheless, it is a fast and efficient mechanism for transporting typical network data, such as word-processing or spreadsheet files. The greatest advantage to packet switching lies in the fact that it does not waste bandwidth by holding a connection open until a message reaches its destination, as circuit switching does. And unlike message switching, it does not require devices in the data's path to process any information. Examples of packet-switched networks include Ethernet and FDDI. The Internet is also an example of a packet-switched network.

Now that you are familiar with the various types of switching, you are ready to investigate specific network technologies that may make use of switching.

ETHERNET

As you learned in Chapter 2, Ethernet is a network technology originally developed by Xerox in the 1970s and later improved by Xerox, Digital Equipment Corporation (DEC), and Intel. This flexible technology can run on a variety of network media and offers excellent throughput at a reasonable cost. Ethernet is, by far, the most popular network technology used on modern LANs.

Ethernet has evolved through many variations, and continues to improve. As a result of this history, it supports many different versions—so many, in fact, that you will probably find the many variations a little confusing. In Chapter 4 you learned how Ethernet networks may differ at the Physical layer. In this section you will learn how Ethernet networks may differ at the Data Link layer. First, however, you will learn about CSMA/CD, the network access method that all Ethernet networks have in common.

Carrier Sense Multiple Access with Collision Detection (CSMA/CD)

The defining characteristic of Ethernet is its **access method**, or its method of controlling how network nodes access the communications channel. The access method used in Ethernet is called **Carrier Sense Multiple Access with Collision Detection (CSMA/CD)**. All Ethernet networks, independent of their speed or frame type, rely on CSMA/CD. To understand Ethernet, you must first understand CSMA/CD.

Take a minute to think about the full name "Carrier Sense Multiple Access with Collision Detection." The term "Carrier Sense" refers to the fact that Ethernet NICs listen on the network and wait until they detect (or sense) that no other nodes are transmitting data over the signal (or carrier) on the communications channel before they begin to transmit. The term "Multiple Access" refers to the fact that several Ethernet nodes can be connected to a network and can monitor traffic, or access the media, simultaneously.

In CSMA/CD, when a node wants to transmit data it must first access the transmission media and determine whether the channel is free. If the channel is not free, it waits and checks again after a random (but very brief) amount of time. If the channel is free, the node transmits its data. Any node can transmit data once it determines that the channel is free. But what if two nodes simultaneously check the channel, determine that it's free, and begin to transmit? When this happens, their two transmissions will interfere with each other; this is known as a **collision**. In this event, the network performs a series of steps known as the collision detection routine. If a station's NIC determines that its data has been involved in a collision, it will immediately stop transmitting. Next, in a process called **jamming**, it will issue a special 32-bit sequence that indicates to the rest of the network nodes that the station's previous transmission was faulty and that they should not accept those data frames as valid. After waiting, the node will determine if the line is again available; if it is available, the line will retransmit its data.

On heavily trafficked networks, collisions are fairly common. Not surprisingly, the more nodes transmitting data on a network, the more collisions will take place (although a collision rate greater than 5% of all traffic is unusual and may point to a problematic NIC or poor cabling on the network). When an Ethernet network grows to include a particularly large number of nodes, you may see performance suffer as a result of collisions. This "critical mass" number depends on the type and volume of data that the network regularly transmits. Collisions can corrupt data or truncate data frames, so it is important that the network detect and compensate for them. Figure 5-19 depicts the way CSMA/CD regulates data flow to avoid and, if necessary, detect collisions.

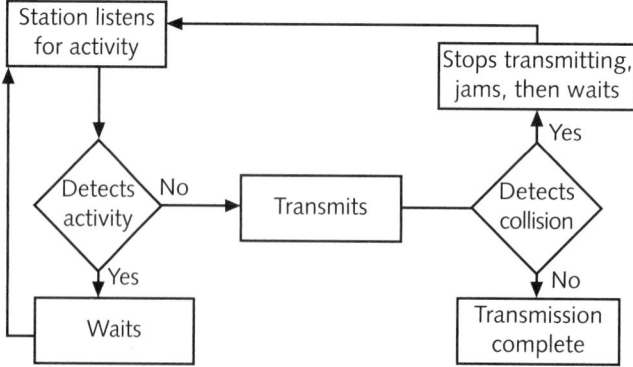

Figure 5-19 CSMA/CD process

On an Ethernet network, an individual segment is known as a **collision domain**, or a portion of a network in which collisions will occur if two nodes transmit data at the same time. When designing an Ethernet network, it's important to note that, since repeaters simply regenerate any signal they receive, they repeat collisions just as they repeat data. Thus, connecting multiple parts of a network with repeaters results in a larger collision domain. Higher-layer connectivity devices, such as switches and routers, however, can separate collision domains.

Collision domains play a role in the Ethernet cabling distance limitations. For example, if the distance between two nodes on a segment connected to the same 100BaseT network bus exceeds 100 meters, data propagation delays will be too long for CSMA/CD to work. A **data propagation delay** is the length of time data take to travel from one point on the segment to another point. When data takes a long time, CSMA/CD's collision detection routine cannot identify collisions accurately. In other words, one node on the segment might begin its CSMA/CD routine and determine that the channel is free even though a second node has begun transmitting, because the second node's data is taking so long to reach the first node.

In Fast Ethernet, data travel so quickly that NICs can't always keep up with the collision detection and retransmission routines. Because of the speed employed on a 100BaseT network, the window of time for the NIC to both detect and compensate for the error is much less than that of a 10BaseT, 10Base2, or 10Base5 network. To minimize undetected collisions, 100BaseT buses can support a maximum of three network segments connected with two hubs, while 10BaseT buses can support a maximum of five network segments connected with four hubs. This shorter path reduces the highest potential propagation delay between nodes.

Demand Priority

In Chapter 4 you learned about multiple Physical layer specifications for Ethernet networks, including 10BaseT and 100BaseT. All these types rely on CSMA/CD for data flow control. You also learned about a networking technology that is similar to Ethernet—100BaseVG (or 100BaseVG-AnyLAN). One significant difference between 100BaseVG and 100BaseT (and the characteristic that makes it not quite "Ethernet") is that 100BaseVG does not use CSMA/CD, but rather an access method called demand priority. In **demand priority**, each device on a star or hierarchical network sends a request to transmit to the central hub. The hub then grants the requests one at a time. It examines incoming data packets, determines the location of the destination node, and forwards the packets to that destination. Because demand priority runs on a star topology, in which each node is linked directly to a connectivity device, no workstations except the source and destination can "see" the data. Data travel from one device to the hub, then to another device. The hub acts as a central transfer point. Figure 5-20 contrasts CSMA/CD with demand priority techniques.

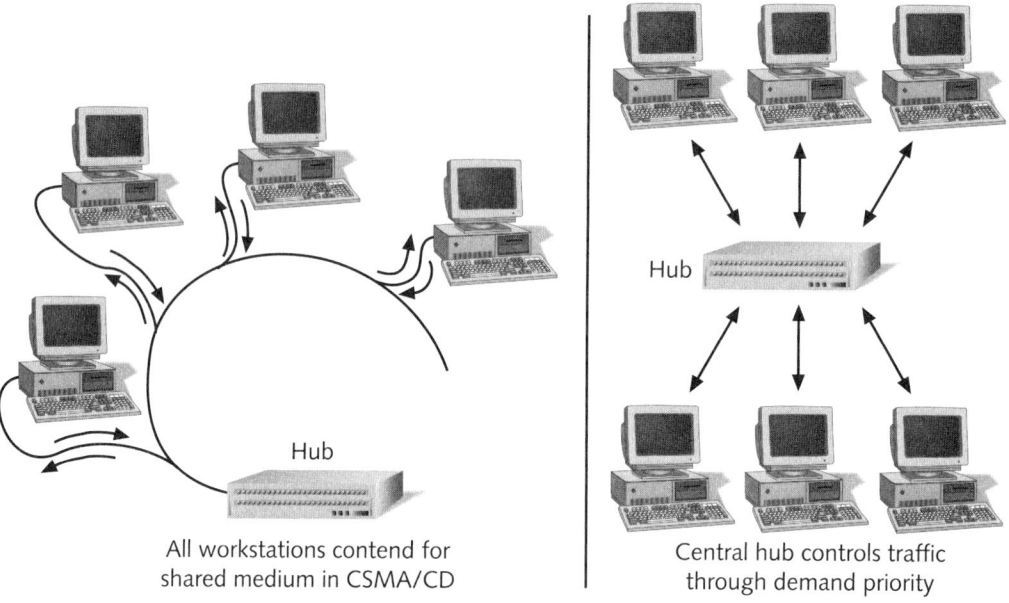

All workstations contend for
shared medium in CSMA/CD

Central hub controls traffic
through demand priority

Figure 5-20   CSMA/CD versus demand priority

Because the hub determines which nodes transmit and when, data collisions do not happen on demand priority networks. Data travel unimpeded, with no need for the collision detection and correction required by CSMA/CD. Another advantage to demand
priority networks is that, because data do not pass by each node on the network, they
remain secure; packets transmitted from one workstation cannot be trapped and decoded
by any workstation on the network except for the destination. In addition, in a demand
priority network, the hub can prioritize transmission requests. If multiple requests arrive
at the hub simultaneously, the hub services the highest-priority request first. This
approach allows 100BaseVG to better serve networks that carry audio, video, or other
time-sensitive data. (The "VG" part of its name stands for voice grade specification.)
Before you can use demand priority on your network, you must ensure that NIC drivers compatible with the 100BaseVG priority assignment scheme have been installed.

Demand priority requires an **intelligent hub**—that is, a hub that can manage transmissions
by dictating which nodes send and receive data at every instant—rather than a hub that
simply regenerates signals. Some Ethernet networks do not have intelligent hubs. Another
disadvantage of a demand priority network is that the time the hub takes to process each
request reduces the network's overall performance, so that a 100BaseVG network usually
cannot match the speed of a 100BaseT (CSMA/CD) network. And as you learned in
Chapter 4, 100BaseVG networks cannot take advantage of full duplexing, which can potentially double a network's bandwidth. For these reasons (and because compatible hardware
is difficult to find), 100BaseVG networks based on demand priority are uncommon.

Switched Ethernet

Traditional Ethernet LANs, called **shared Ethernet**, supply a fixed amount of bandwidth that must be shared by all devices on a segment. Stations cannot send and receive data simultaneously, nor can they transmit a signal when another station on the same segment is sending or receiving data. This is because they share a segment and a hub or repeater, which merely amplifies and retransmits a signal over the segment. In contrast, a **switch** is a device that can separate a network segment into smaller segments, with each segment being independent of the others and supporting its own traffic. **Switched Ethernet** is a newer Ethernet model that enables multiple nodes to simultaneously transmit and receive data over different logical network segments. By doing so, each node can individually take advantage of more bandwidth. Figure 5-21 shows how switches can isolate network segments. You will learn more about switches in Chapter 6.

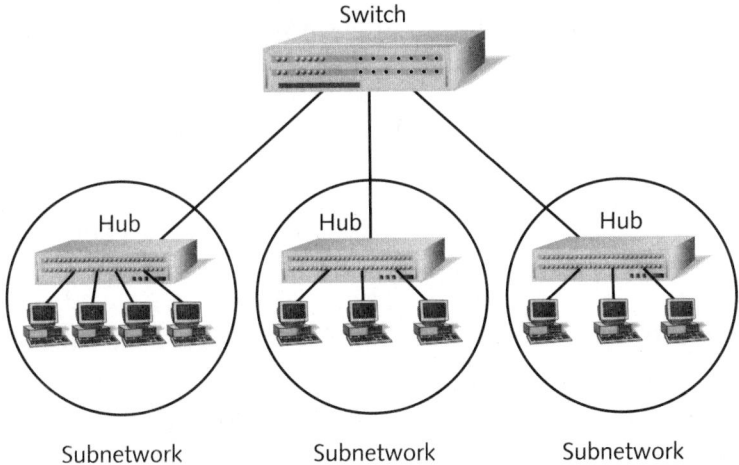

Figure 5-21   A switched Ethernet network

Using switched Ethernet increases the effective bandwidth of a network segment because fewer workstations must vie for the same time on the wire. In fact, applying switches to a 10-Mbps Ethernet LAN can increase its effective data transmission rate to 100 Mbps. For organizations with existing 10BaseT infrastructure, switches offer a relatively simple and inexpensive way to add bandwidth. Switches can be placed strategically on an organization's network to balance traffic loads and reduce congestion.

Note, however, that switches are not always the best answer to heavy traffic and a need for greater speeds. In a case where an enterprise-wise Ethernet LAN is generally overtaxed, you should consider upgrading the network's design or infrastructure.

Gigabit Ethernet

As you would probably guess, the evolution of Ethernet has not stopped with the development of switched Ethernet and the 100-Mbps standard. IEEE established specifications for an Ethernet version that runs at 1000 Mbps, called **1 Gigabit Ethernet**. 1 Gigabit Ethernet can technically run over unshielded twisted-pair (UTP) cable. However, it performs much better over (multimode) fiber, which is specified by the IEEE 802.3z project. A segment of 1 Gigabit Ethernet running on UTP can span a maximum of 100 meters, while a segment running on fiber can span a maximum of 550 meters. Like Fast Ethernet, a fiber-based 1 Gigabit Ethernet network uses CSMA/CD transmission and the IEEE 802.3 frame type (discussed below) and is capable of full duplexing.

You will most likely encounter 1 Gigabit Ethernet as part of a network's backbone. It is well suited to connecting multiple buildings on a single campus, for example. Currently, this scheme would not be appropriate for connecting workstations to hubs, for example, because workstations' NICs and CPUs could not process data fast enough to make the cost worthwhile. In the near future, however, PCs will be equipped with adequate hardware and processing power to take advantage of 1 Gigabit Ethernet.

But the race for greater throughput has not stopped at 1 gigabit. In March 1999 representatives from the networking industry began discussing a **10 Gigabit Ethernet** standard. The standards for 10 gigabits are currently being defined by the IEEE 802.3ae committee and will include full-duplexing and multimode fiber requirements. IEEE is aiming to make the 10 Gigabit standard compatible with the Physical layer standards for 1 Gigabit Ethernet to allow organizations to easily upgrade their networks. The 1- and 10-Gigabit technologies will compete directly with other fast networking solutions such as Asynchronous Transfer Mode (ATM), which is covered later in this chapter.

Ethernet Frame Types

Chapter 2 introduced you to data frames, the packages that carry higher-layer data and control information that enable data to reach their destinations without errors and in the correct sequence. The Ethernet data frame discussed in Chapter 2 is an example of a typical Ethernet data frame. In fact, networks may use one (or a combination) of four kinds of Ethernet data frames: Ethernet IEEE 802.3, Novell Proprietary 802.3, Ethernet II, and IEEE 802.3 SNAP. This variety of Ethernet "types" came about as different organizations released and revised Ethernet standards during the 1980s, changing as LAN technology evolved.

 All Ethernet networks, no matter what their frame type, are standardized by the IEEE 802.3 committee and therefore fall under the "802.3" standards. In other words, even if one company calls one particular Ethernet frame type "802.2," the frame falls under the 802.3 networking standard.

Each frame type differs slightly in the way it codes and decodes packets of data traveling from one device to another. The routines that manage Data Link layer functions on a node must be configured to expect one type of frame. On a workstation or server, you can specify the network's frame type through the operating system, usually within the NIC configuration interface. If a node receives a different type of frame than it expects, it will not be able to decode the data contained in the frame. The result is that a device cannot log onto the network or exchange data. For this reason, it is important for LAN administrators to standardize the type of frame used on their Ethernet networks. This is simple to achieve on networks that use only one type of network operating system and client software, but networks commonly use multiple versions of both.

Ethernet frame types do not depend on the Ethernet's Physical layer specification. In other words, frame types have no relation to the topology or cabling characteristics of the network. Thus, Physical layer standards, such as 10Base2 and 10BaseT, have no effect on the type of framing that occurs in the Data Link layer. At the same time, framing also takes place independent of the higher-level layers. Thus, most types of frames can carry any one of many higher-layer protocols. For example, a single Ethernet IEEE 802.3 data frame may carry either TCP/IP or IPX/SPX traffic (but not both simultaneously).

Ethernet frame sizes vary. However, no matter what its type, each frame contains a 14-byte header and a 4-byte Frame Check Sequence field. These two fields add 18 bytes to the frame size. The data portion of the frame may contain from 46 to 1500 bytes of information. (If less than 46 bytes of data are carried, the network fills out the data portion with extra bytes until it totals 46 bytes. The extra bytes are known as **padding** and have no effect on the data being transmitted.) Thus the minimum Ethernet frame size is 18 + 46, or 64, bytes and the maximum Ethernet frame size is 18 + 1500, or 1518, bytes. Because of the overhead present in each frame and the time required to enact CSMA/CD, the use of larger frame sizes on a network generally results in faster throughput. To some extent, you cannot control frame sizes. You can, however, minimize the number of broadcast frames on your network, which is desirable because broadcast frames tend to be very small and, therefore, inefficient.

Each Ethernet frame also contains a 7-byte preamble. The original Ethernet frame type (which predated the IEEE standard) calls for an 8-byte preamble. The IEEE 802.3 standard changed the last byte of this preamble to a start-of-frame delimiter (SFD), which identifies where the data field begins. Thus, the preamble itself is only 7 bytes, but taken with the SFD, it is equivalent to the original 8-byte preamble. Now that you understand the similarities between different Ethernet frame types, you can learn about what distinguishes each type.

IEEE 802.3 ("Ethernet 802.2," or "LLC")

IEEE 802.3 frame is the default frame type for versions 4.x and higher of the Novell NetWare network operating system. It is the most popular Ethernet frame type for use with IPX/SPX traffic on most contemporary LANs. The defining characteristics of its data portion are the source and destination service access points that belong to the Logical Link Control (LLC) layer, a sublayer of the Data Link layer. Because the IEEE 802.3 Ethernet frame includes this LLC element, it is sometimes called an **LLC frame**. In Novell's lexicon, which was adopted by many other companies, this frame is called an **Ethernet 802.2 frame**. Figure 5-22 depicts an IEEE 802.3 frame.

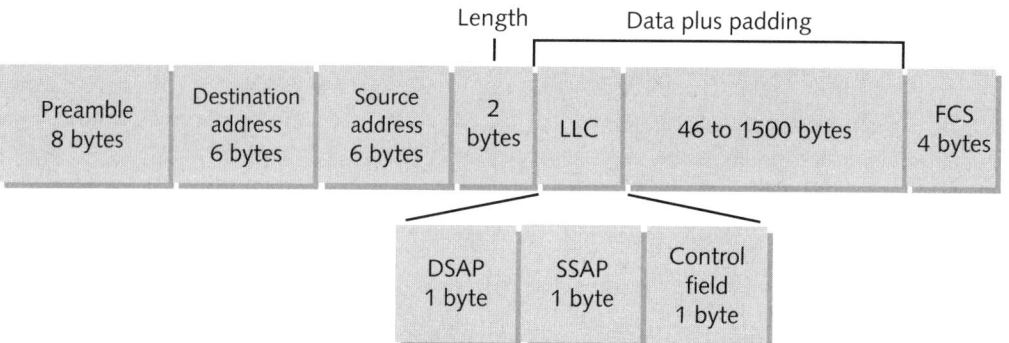

Figure 5-22   An IEEE 802.3 frame

Like other Ethernet frame types, an IEEE 802.3 frame contains an 8-byte preamble. This preamble signals the receiving node that data are incoming and indicates when the data flow is about to begin. Preambles are not included when you calculate a frame's total size.

The destination address and source address fields in an IEEE 802.3 frame are each 6 bytes long. As you might guess, the destination address identifies the recipient of the data frame, and the source address identifies the network node that originally sent the data. Recall from Chapter 3 that any network device can be identified by its logical address (protocol-dependent) or its physical address (hardware-dependent). The physical address is also called the Medium Access Control (MAC) address. Because MAC addresses are hard-coded into the node's NIC, and each manufacturer uses a different identifying code, no two devices should ever have the same address. The source address and destination address fields of an IEEE 802.3 frame use the MAC address to identify where data originated and where it should be delivered. The same is true for all Ethernet frame types.

IEEE 802.3 frames also include a field 2 bytes long that identifies the length of the data field. The data field in an IEEE 802.3 frame contains not only the data transmitted by the source node, but also Logical Link Control (LLC) layer information whose purpose is to distinguish among multiple clients on a network. It may also include padding, if the LLC and data information do not total at least 46 bytes. The length field, however, does account for padding. It will report only the length of LLC plus data information.

The LLC information comprises three fields: Destination Service Access Point (DSAP), Source Service Access Point (SSAP), and a control field. Each of these fields is 1 byte long, making the total LLC field 3 bytes long. A **Service Access Point (SAP)** identifies a node or internal process that uses the LLC protocol. Each process between a source and destination node on the network may have a unique SAP. The control field identifies the kind of LLC connection that must be established, from unacknowledged (connectionless) to fully acknowledged (connection-oriented).

The data field of the IEEE 802.3 frame is the easiest field to understand. It contains the data sent by the originating node, before the packet was passed down from the top layer of the OSI Model.

The **Frame Check Sequence (FCS)** field ensures that the data are received just as they were sent. When the source node transmits the data, it performs an algorithm (a mathematical routine) called a **Cyclical Redundancy Check (CRC)**. CRC takes the values of all of the preceding fields in the frame and generates a unique 4-byte number, the FCS. When the destination node receives the frame, it unscrambles the FCS via CRC and makes sure that the frame's fields match their original form. If this comparison fails, the receiving node assumes that the frame has been damaged in transit and requests that the source node retransmit the data.

Novell Proprietary 802.3 (or "Ethernet 802.3")

The **Novell proprietary 802.3 frame** type is the original NetWare frame type and the default frame type for networks running NetWare versions lower than 3.12. It supports only the IPX/SPX protocol. The Novell proprietary 802.3 frame type is sometimes also called **802.3 Raw** because its data portion contains no control bits. Novell and other companies also call this type of Ethernet frame simply **Ethernet 802.3 frame**. Its fields match those of IEEE 802.3, minus the Logical Link Control layer information. Figure 5-23 depicts a Novell proprietary 802.3 frame.

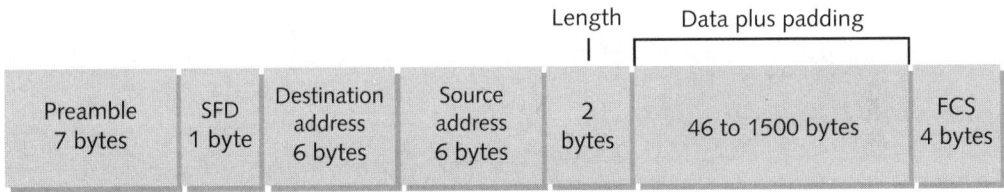

Figure 5-23   A Novell proprietary 802.3 frame

Since the release of later versions of NetWare, most organizations that rely on Novell LANs have migrated their frame types to IEEE 802.3. Thus, the Novell proprietary 802.3 frame type is rarely used on modern networks.

Ethernet II

Ethernet II frame was the original Ethernet frame type developed by DEC, Intel, and Xerox, before the IEEE began to standardize Ethernet. The Ethernet II frame is similar to the Novell proprietary 802.3 frame, in that it lacks LLC information. Ethernet II frames contain a 2-byte type field, however, whereas the IEEE 802.3 and the Novell proprietary 802.3 frames contain a 2-byte length field. This type field identifies the upper-layer protocol contained in the frame. For example, IPX uses a type field of 8137. IP uses a type field of 0800. This field enables Ethernet II to support Novell IPX/SPX, TCP/IP, and AppleTalk protocols, and it compensates for the lack of LLC information. Figure 5-24 depicts an Ethernet II frame.

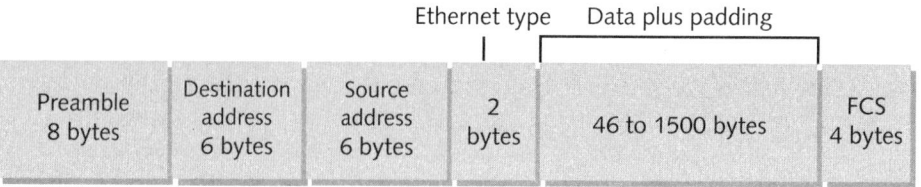

Figure 5-24   An Ethernet II frame

IEEE 802.3 SNAP

IEEE 802.3 SNAP frame is an adaptation of IEEE 802.3 and Ethernet II. "SNAP" stands for Sub-Network Access Protocol. The SNAP portion of the frame is what IEEE 802.3 SNAP borrowed from IEEE 802.3—the three LLC fields (DSAP, SSAP, and the Control field). The IEEE 802.3 SNAP frame, however, contains an additional field: the Organization ID (OUI), a method of identifying the type of network on which the frame is running. In addition, IEEE 802.3 SNAP frames carry Ethernet type information, just as an Ethernet II frame does. IEEE 802.3 SNAP is compatible with IPX/SPX, TCP/IP, and AppleTalk protocols, but it is rarely used on contemporary LANs. Figure 5-25 depicts an IEEE 802.3 SNAP frame.

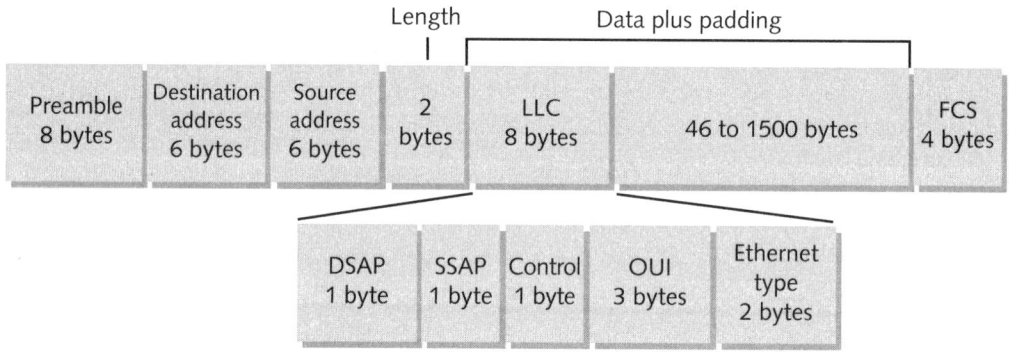

Figure 5-25   An IEEE 802.3 SNAP frame

Understanding Frame Types

You might wonder why you should learn about frame types, which represent the underlying structure of data signals. It's a good question, and the answer relates to problem solving in networks. As a networking professional, you may need to capture data and analyze frames when troubleshooting with a protocol analyzer. When analyzing the frames, you can actually decode the data in every field, if you know what the fields are.

Learning about networks is analogous to learning a foreign language, with the frame type being the language's syntax. Just as you might know the Japanese word for "go," but not know how to use it in a sentence, you may know all about the IPX/SPX protocol, but not how devices handle it. (Chapter 12 covers this kind of troubleshooting in more detail.)

A good knowledge of frame types will help you in many areas of your networking career. For example, to improve a network's performance, you might need to identify the kinds of frames that traverse the network. When working with switches and routers, you might have to configure the device to handle a certain frame type. Or you might decide to configure a switch to accept all types of frames, with the understanding that network performance will suffer as a result of the device having to examine each incoming packet. Probably the most common problem relating to frame types arises from incompatibility between the frame type a workstation expects to receive and the frame type the server actually transmits.

As you learned in Chapter 2, you can use multiple frame types on a network, but you cannot expect interoperability between the frame types. For example, in a mixed environment of NetWare 3.11 and NetWare 4.11 servers, your network will probably support both Ethernet 802.3 and Ethernet 802.2 frames. A workstation connecting to the NetWare 3.11 server might be configured to use the Ethernet 802.3 frame, while a workstation connecting to the NetWare 4.11 server might use Ethernet 802.2.

Modern networks simplify the issue of frame type specification by allowing you to instruct a NIC, through the device driver software, to automatically sense what types of frames are running on a network and adjust themselves to that specification. This feature, called **autosense**, is generally available on all NICs manufactured in the last few years. Workstations, networked printers, and servers added to an existing network can all take advantage of autosense. Even if you use autosense, you should nevertheless know what frame types are running on your network so that you can troubleshoot connectivity problems. As easy as it is to configure, the autosense feature is not infallible.

Design Considerations for Ethernet Networks

In the previous chapter you learned about the Physical layer characteristics of different Ethernet versions. For reference, the following list summarizes essential information from that chapter and from the preceding section about this most important type of network.

- *Cabling*—Ethernet networks can use coaxial cable or unshielded twisted-pair cabling.

- *Connectivity devices*—Ethernet NICs, switches, hubs, routers, and bridges are generally less expensive than comparable Token Ring or LocalTalk equipment.

- *Number of stations*—The number of allowable stations on a 10BaseT or 100BaseTX Ethernet network is limited to 1024.

- *Speed*—Ethernet networks may have a throughput of 10 Mbps, 100 Mbps, 1 Gbps, and soon, 10 Gbps.

- *Scalability*—You can easily expand Ethernet networks by adding connectivity devices on the bus. However, bear in mind each type of network's size limitations.

- *Topology*—10BaseT and 100BaseTX Ethernet networks use a star-wired bus hybrid topology, which is highly fault-tolerant.

LOCALTALK

Now that you have learned about Ethernet, a very common network access method, you will learn about some less common network technologies, including LocalTalk. **LocalTalk** is a network access method designed by Apple Computer, Inc. specifically for networking Macintosh computers. It has been included with the Macintosh operating system since 1984, and it provided a simple, cost-effective way of interconnecting Macintosh devices. However, LocalTalk is only capable of 230 Kbps maximum through-put—much less than the 10-Mbps or 100-Mbps throughput of an Ethernet network. Also, LocalTalk is not easily supported by non-Macintosh devices. And, since Macintosh computers are capable of using Ethernet as a network access method, Ethernet is usually preferred over LocalTalk. An instance in which LocalTalk might still be appropriate is for a home network that requires simple configuration and does not require high through-put. Although you may never need to build a LocalTalk network, the essential details of this network technology are included here in case you must modify or troubleshoot one.

LocalTalk uses a transmission method called **Carrier Sense Multiple Access/Collision Avoidance (CSMA/CA)**. It is similar to the CSMA/CD used in Ethernet networks, except that a node on a LocalTalk network signals its intent to transmit before it actually does so. In this way, collisions and the need for data retransmittals are (mostly) avoided. At the Physical layer, LocalTalk networks require twisted-pair wiring and, in fact, use the same type of cabling used for telephone connections. They may rely on a star or, more often, a bus physical topology. Their maximum segment length is 1000 feet, or approximately 305 meters. Up to 32 nodes may be connected to any single LocalTalk network before data errors begin to occur.

The latest Macintosh computers don't even include a serial port into which a LocalTalk cable could be inserted. But these computers can communicate with LocalTalk devices (such as an older printer) through a special LocalTalk-to-Ethernet adapter.

To connect a Macintosh device to a LocalTalk network, insert one end of a cable into a serial port (for example, the printer or modem port), and then connect this cable to its transceiver (which, in LocalTalk terminology, is called a **teleconnector**). In case the device is being incorporated into a bus topology, this teleconnector contains a resistor to guard against signal bounce. The teleconnector is then connected with a twisted-pair patch cable to the wall jack, which leads to the network's horizontal wiring.

The Macintosh operating system allows devices connected in this manner to share resources in a peer-to-peer fashion without any additional software. A client-server net-work can be established by introducing a server and AppleShare software and configuring workstations as clients. As with other network access methods, such as Ethernet, LocalTalk networks support multiple higher-layer protocols. By default, LocalTalk relies on the AppleTalk protocol (discussed in Chapter 3), but it may also support the Macintosh ver-sion of TCP/IP called **MacTCP**. In order to support other versions of TCP/IP, LocalTalk requires that these TCP/IP packets be encapsulated by AppleTalk packets.

TOKEN RING

Now that you have learned about LocalTalk and the many forms of Ethernet, you are ready to learn about Token Ring, a less common, but still important network access method. As you learned in Chapter 2, Token Ring is a network technology first developed by IBM in the 1980s. In the early 1990s, the Token Ring architecture competed strongly with Ethernet to be the most popular access method. Since that time, the economics, speed, and reliability of Ethernet have improved, leaving Token Ring behind. Because IBM developed Token Ring, some IBM-centric IT departments continue to use it. Many other network managers have changed their former Token Ring networks into Ethernet networks.

Token Ring networks are generally more expensive to implement than Ethernet networks. Proponents of the Token Ring technology argue that, although some of its connectivity hardware is more expensive, its reliability results in less downtime and lower network management costs than Ethernet. On a practical level, Token Ring has probably lost the battle for superiority because its developers were slower to develop a high-speed standard. Token Ring networks can run at either 4, 16, or 100 Mbps. The 100-Mbps Token Ring standard, finalized in 1999, is known as **High-Speed Token Ring (HSTR)**. HSTR can use either twisted-pair or fiber-optic cable as its transmission medium. While it is as reliable and efficient as Fast Ethernet, it is less common because of its more costly implementation.

Token Ring networks use the token-passing routine and a star-ring hybrid physical topology. Recall from the discussion of the ring topology earlier in this chapter that a token designates which station on the ring can transmit information on the wire. On a Token Ring network, one workstation, called the active monitor, acts as the controller for token passing. Specifically, the **active monitor** maintains the timing for ring passing, monitors token and frame transmission, detects lost tokens, and corrects errors when a timing error or other disruption occurs. Only one workstation on the ring can act as the active monitor at any given time.

In token passing, a 3-byte token circulates around the network. When a station has something to send, it picks up the token, changes it to a frame, and then adds the header, information, and trailer fields. The header includes the address of the destination node. All nodes read the frame as it traverses the ring to determine whether they are the intended recipient of the message. If they are, they pick up the data, then retransmit the frame to the next station on the ring. When the frame finally reaches the originating station, the originating workstation reissues a free token that can then be used by another station. The token passing control scheme ensures high data reliability (no collisions) and an efficient use of bandwidth. It also does not impose distance limitations on the length of a LAN segment, unlike CSMA/CD. On the other hand, token ring passing generates extra network traffic.

The Token Ring architecture is often mistakenly described as a pure ring topology. In fact, it uses a star-ring hybrid topology in which data circulate in a ring fashion, but the physical layout of the network is a star.

IEEE standard 802.5 describes the specifications for Token Ring technology. Token Ring networks transmit data at either 4 Mbps, 16, or 100 Mbps over shielded or unshielded twisted-pair wiring. You may have as many as 255 addressable stations on a Token Ring network that uses shielded twisted-pair or as many as 72 addressable stations on one that uses unshielded twisted-pair. All Token Ring connections rely on a NIC that taps into the network through a **Multistation Access Unit (MAU)**, Token Ring's equivalent of a hub. NICs can be designed and configured to run specifically on 4-, 16-, or 100-Mbps networks or they can be designed to accommodate both data transmission rates. In the star-ring hybrid topology, the MAU completes the ring internally with Ring In and Ring Out ports at either end of the unit. In addition, MAUs typically provide eight ports for workstation connections. You can easily expand a Token Ring network by connecting multiple MAUs through by their Ring In and Ring Out ports, as shown in Figure 5-26. Unused ports on a MAU, including Ring In and Ring Out ports, have self-shorting data connectors that internally close the loop.

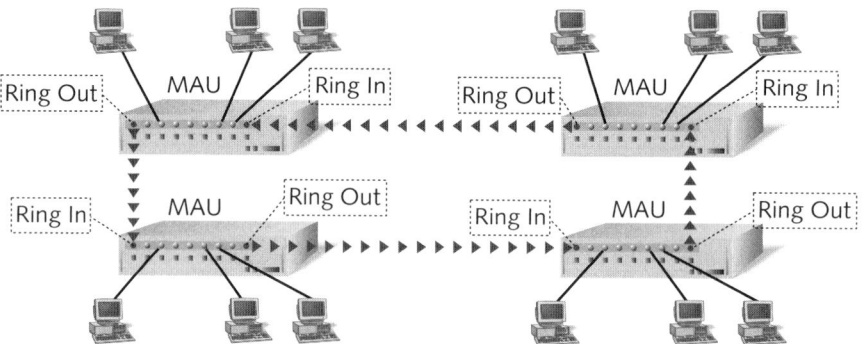

Figure 5-26   Interconnected Token Ring MAUs

The self-shorting feature of Token Ring MAU ports makes Token Ring highly fault-tolerant. For example, if you discover a problematic NIC on the network, you can remove that workstation's cable from the MAU, and the MAU's port will close the ring internally. Similarly, if you discover a faulty MAU, you can remove it from the ring by disconnecting its Ring In and Ring Out cables from its adjacent MAUs and connect the two good MAUs to each other to close the loop.

Now you have learned two definitions for "MAU." Depending on the context, a MAU can refer to a media access unit used as a transceiver in a Thicknet Ethernet network or it can mean a multistation access unit, a hub in a Token Ring network. These are two, unrelated devices. If the term MAU is used on your Network+ certification exam, be certain you understand the context in which it is used before answering the question.

A node on a Token Ring network may also connect to a **Controlled Access Unit (CAU)**. A CAU is a connectivity device similar to a MAU, but in addition to passing data between nodes, a CAU provides more flexibility and easier management of connected nodes. For example, as a network administrator, you could connect to a CAU from your desktop PC and determine what type of traffic is passing through the device or even reconfigure the device. CAUs are more flexible than MAUs because they contain interchangeable modules that you can plug into the Ring In and Ring Out connections. With interchangeable modules, you can use STP for a backbone cable for some time, then upgrade to a fiber-optic backbone by simply inserting the fiber-optic module.

Because of their added functionality, CAUs are more expensive than MAUs. A CAU contains a limited number of receptacles for connected devices. In order to expand the number of nodes you can connect to a CAU, you can plug in a **Lobe Attachment Module (LAM)**. LAMs typically allow up to 20 devices to plug into each CAU receptacle. So, for example, using four LAMs on a single CAU allows 80 devices to be connected to the CAU.

A Token Ring network may use one of three types of connectors on its cables: RJ-45, DB-9, or type 1 IBM. Modern Token Ring networks with UTP cabling use RJ-45 connectors, which are identical to the RJ-45 connector used on 10BaseT or 100BaseT Ethernet networks. Token Ring networks with STP cabling may use a **type 1 IBM connector**, which is depicted in Figure 5-27. Type 1 IBM connectors contain interlocking tabs that snap into an identical connector when one of the connectors is flipped upside-down, making for a secure connection. A **DB-9 connector** (containing 9 pins) is another type of connector found on STP Token Ring networks. This connector is also pictured in Figure 5-27.

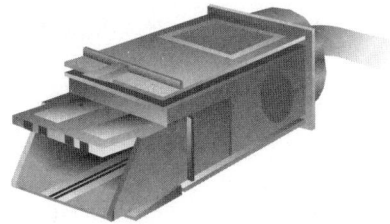
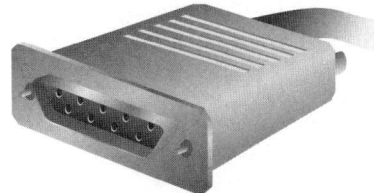

Type 1 IBM connector   DB-9 connector

Figure 5-27   Type 1 IBM and DB-9 Token Ring connectors

Occasionally you may work on a network that incorporates a mix of different connectors. (This is more likely to happen on a Token Ring network, given its many connector types.) In this case, you might consider using a **media filter** to enable these different connectors and receptors to fit together. For example, in order to allow a Token Ring NIC with a DB-9 receptor to connect with a network cable that uses an RJ-45 plug, a **Token Ring media filter** is necessary as pictured in Figure 5-28.

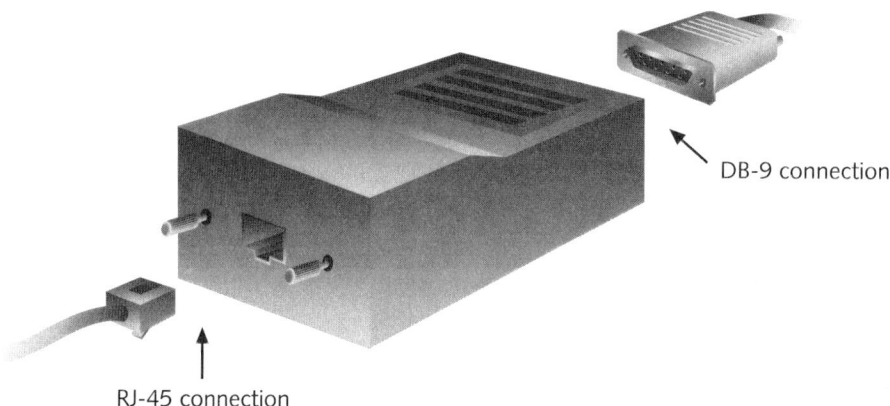

DB-9 connection

RJ-45 connection

Figure 5-28   A Token Ring media filter

Token Ring Switching

Like Ethernet networks, Token Ring networks can take advantage of switching to better utilize limited bandwidth. Token Ring switching products are typically more expensive and more difficult to manage than Ethernet switches, although they perform essentially the same function. A Token Ring switch can subdivide a large network ring into several smaller network rings. For example, if a 16-Mbps Token Ring network supports 40 users, each workstation has access to approximately 0.4 Mbps. Installing a Token Ring switch that is configured to subdivide the network into four logical subnetworks provides each workstation with approximately 1.6 Mbps (under optimal physical conditions). Thus switching effectively quadruples the bandwidth in this example.

Remember, however, that Token Ring technology does not allow collisions. For this reason, the bandwidth available to each user does not quickly degrade as more users are added; contrast this characteristic to the performance hit that Ethernet takes when more users connect to a single segment.

Token Ring Frames

Token Ring networks may use one of two types of frames: the IEEE 802.5 or the IBM Token Ring frame. The only difference between the two types is that the IBM Token Ring frame adds 2 to 16 octets of routing information that only IBM applications use. Figure 5-29 shows an IEEE 802.5 Token Ring frame.

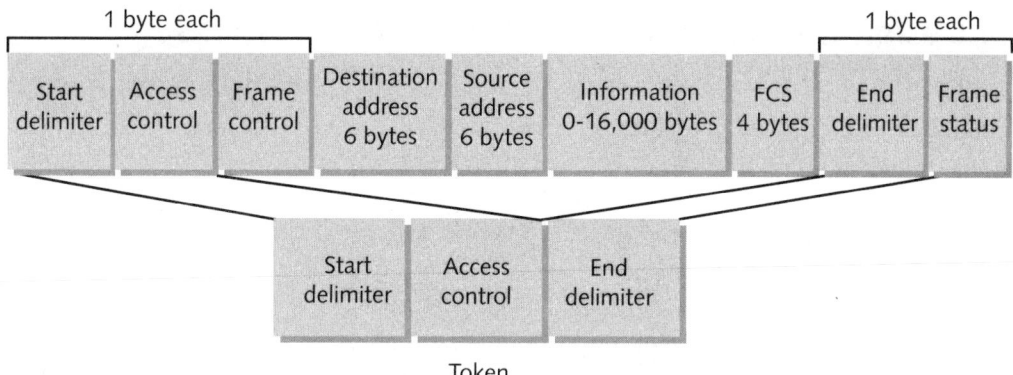

Figure 5-29   An IBM Token Ring frame

Every Token Ring frame includes Starting Delimiter (SD), Access Control (AC), and Ending Delimiter (ED) fields. These three fields of 1 octet each make up the token. Remember that the token is not a frame, but rather is transformed into a frame after a workstation picks it up. The Access Control byte of the token equals 0 bytes if the token is available and 1 if the token is part of a frame currently carrying data, thus signaling that it is not free.

Token Ring frames, just like Ethernet frames, contain destination address and source address fields. As with Ethernet, Token Ring addresses use the MAC address of the device. The destination address is the MAC address of the workstation that will receive the data. The source address is the MAC address of the workstation that transmitted the data. On Token Ring networks, you may also encounter manually administered addresses. Manually assigning network addresses is not a good policy, however. By doing so, you create more work for network administrators and increase the potential for errors.

Both IEEE 802.5 and IBM Token Ring frames contain an information field. Depending on the speed of the Token Ring network, this field can contain from 0 to more than 4000 bytes (for a 4-Mbps network) or from 0 to more than 16,000 bytes (for a 16-Mbps network). Altogether, the maximum frame size for a 4 Mbps network is 4094 bytes; for a 16-Mbps network, it is 17,800 bytes. Notice how much larger the Token Ring frames are than Ethernet frames. As you have learned, larger frame sizes result in more efficient data transmission.

After the data field, each Token Ring frame includes a frame check sequence (FCS). As in Ethernet networks, Token Ring frames use a CRC algorithm to ensure that the data received matches the data sent. The FCS contains the results of this algorithm. In addition, Token Ring frames use a Frame Status (FS) to provide low-level acknowledgment that the frame was received whole.

Design Considerations for Token Ring Networks

If you work on Token Ring networks, you will most likely use a long-established LAN rather than a newly implemented one. In this case, your design considerations will apply to expansion and improvement of an existing infrastructure. Bear in mind these characteristics of Token Ring networks:

- *Cabling*—Token Ring networks can run on shielded or unshielded twisted-pair cabling.

- *Connectivity devices*—Token Ring NICs, switches, hubs, routers, and bridges are generally more expensive than comparable Ethernet equipment.

- *Number of stations*—The number of allowable stations on a Token Ring network is limited, depending on its cabling. You may attach 255 addressable stations on a Token Ring network that runs on shielded twisted-pair, or as many as 72 addressable stations on one that runs on unshielded twisted-pair.

- *Speed*—Token ring networks can run at either 4, 16, or 100 Mbps.

- *Scalability*—You can easily daisy-chain Token Ring MAUs to expand the network. The star layout makes it easy to add nodes to a Token Ring network.

- *Topology*—Token Ring networks are based on a star-wired ring topology, which is highly fault-tolerant.

FIBER DISTRIBUTED DATA INTERFACE (FDDI)

Fiber Distributed Data Interface (FDDI) is a network technology whose standard was originally specified by ANSI in the mid-1980s and later refined by ISO. FDDI (pronounced "fiddy") uses a double ring of multimode or single mode fiber to transmit data at speeds of 100 Mbps. FDDI was developed in response to the throughput limitations of Ethernet and Token Ring technologies used at the time. In fact, FDDI was the first network technology to reach the 100-Mbps threshold. For this reason, you will frequently find it supporting network backbones that were installed in the late 1980s and early 1990s. A popular implementation of FDDI involves connecting LANs located in multiple buildings, such as those on college campuses. FDDI links can span distances as large as 62 miles. Because Ethernet and Token Ring technologies have developed faster transmission speeds, FDDI is no longer the much-coveted technology that it was in the 1980s.

Nevertheless, FDDI is a stable technology that offers numerous benefits. Its reliance on fiber-optic cable ensures that FDDI is more reliable and more secure than transmission methods that depend on copper wiring. Another advantage of FDDI is that it works well with Ethernet 100BaseTX technology.

One drawback to FDDI technology is its high cost relative to Fast Ethernet (costing up to 10 times more per switch port than Fast Ethernet). If an organization has FDDI installed, however, it can use the same cabling to upgrade to Fast Ethernet or Gigabit

Ethernet, with only minor differences to consider, such as Ethernet's lower maximum segment length.

FDDI is based on ring physical logical topologies similar to a Token Ring network, as shown in Figure 5-30. It also relies on the same token-passing routine that Token Ring networks use. However, unlike Token Ring technology, FDDI runs on two complete rings. During normal operation, the primary FDDI ring carries data, while the secondary ring is idle. The secondary ring will assume data transmission responsibilities should the primary ring experience Physical layer problems. This redundancy makes FDDI networks extremely reliable.

5

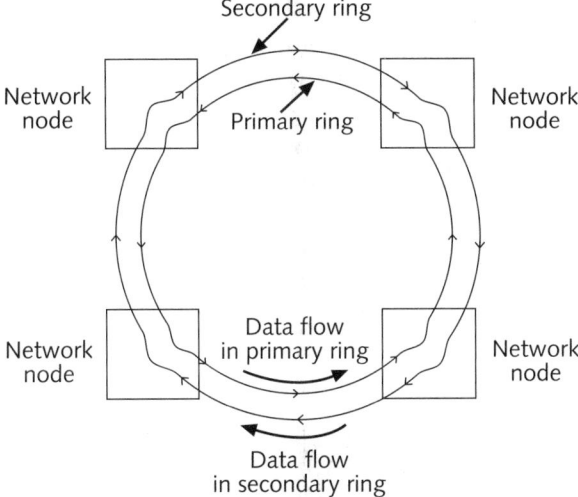

Secondary ring

Network node

Primary ring

Network node

Network node

Data flow in primary ring

Network node

Data flow in secondary ring

Figure 5-30   A FDDI network

ASYNCHRONOUS TRANSFER MODE (ATM)

ATM (Asynchronous Transfer Mode) is a networking standard that describes both a network access method and a multiplexing technique. ATM is unique not only in its broad scope, but also because it relies on a fixed packet size to achieve data transfer rates up to 9953 Mbps. It was first conceived by researchers at Bell Labs in 1983 as a higher-bandwidth alternative to FDDI, but it took a dozen years before standards organizations could reach an agreement on its specifications. ATM may run over specific types of fiber or copper networks, such as SONET or T-carriers (which you will learn about in Chapter 7). It is typically used on WANs, particularly by large data carriers such as telephone companies and Internet service providers.

Like Token Ring and Ethernet, ATM specifies Data Link layer data packaging and Physical layer signaling techniques. But what sets ATM apart from Token Ring and Ethernet is its fixed packet size. The fixed packet in ATM, which is called a **cell**, consists of 48 bytes of data plus a 5-byte header. This fixed packet size allows ATM to provide predictable traffic patterns and better control over bandwidth utilization. However, recall that a smaller packet size requires more overhead. In fact, ATM's smaller packet size does decrease its potential throughput, but the efficiency of using cells compensates for that loss. Compare ATM's maximum throughput of 9953 Mbps with Fast Ethernet's maximum throughput of 100 Mbps. Even though an ATM cell is a fraction of the size of an Ethernet frame, ATM's throughput is significantly faster.

Another unique aspect of ATM technology is that it relies on virtual circuits. **Virtual circuits** are connections between network nodes that, while based on potentially disparate physical links, logically appear to be direct, dedicated links between those nodes. On an ATM network, switches determine the optimal path between the sender and receiver, then establish this path before the network transmits data. One advantage to virtual circuits is their efficient use of limited bandwidth. Several virtual circuits can be assigned to one length of cable or even to one channel on that cable. A virtual circuit uses the channel only when it needs to transmit data. Meanwhile, the channel is available for use by other virtual circuits.

Because ATM packages data into cells before transmission, each of which travels separately to its destination, ATM is typically considered a packet switching technology. At the same time, the use of virtual circuits means that ATM provides the main advantage of circuit switching—that is, a point-to-point connection that remains reliably available to the transmission until it completes. This reliable connection allows ATM to guarantee a specific **Quality of Service (QoS)**. QoS is a standard that specifies that data will be delivered within a certain period of time after their transmission. ATM networks can supply four QoS levels, from a "best effort" attempt for noncritical data to a guaranteed, real-time transmission for time-sensitive data. This is important for organizations using networks for time-sensitive applications such as video and audio transmissions. For example, a company that wants to use its physical connection between two offices located at opposite sides of a state to carry its voice phone calls might choose the ATM network technology with the highest possible QoS to carry that data. Without QoS guarantees, data may arrive in the wrong order or too slowly to be properly interpreted by the receiving node.

Because ATM is a recent technology, its developers have made certain it is compatible with other leading network technologies. Its cells can support multiple types of higher-layer protocols, including TCP/IP, AppleTalk, and IPX/SPX. In addition, the ATM networks can be integrated with Ethernet or Token Ring networks through the use of **LAN Emulation (LANE)**. LANE encapsulates incoming Ethernet or Token Ring frames, then converts them into ATM cells for transmission over an ATM network.

Currently, ATM is very expensive and, because of its cost, it is rarely used on small LANs and almost never used to connect typical workstations to a network. Gigabit Ethernet—a faster, cheaper, and more standard technology—poses a substantial threat to ATM. In addition to having better-established standards, Gigabit Ethernet is less expensive and a more natural upgrade for the multitude of Fast Ethernet users. It overcomes the QoS issue by simply providing a larger pipe for the greater volume of traffic using the network. While ATM caught on among the very largest carriers in the late 1990s, many networking professionals are now following the Gigabit Ethernet standard rather than spending extra dollars on ATM infrastructure.

CHAPTER SUMMARY

- A physical topology is the basic physical layout of a network; it does not specify devices, connectivity methods, or addresses on the network. Physical topologies are categorized into three fundamental geometric shapes: bus, ring, and star.

- A bus topology consists of a single cable connecting all nodes on a network without intervening connectivity devices. At either end of a bus network, 50-ohm resistors (terminators) stop signals after they have reached their destination. Without terminators, signals on a bus network experience signal bounce.

- In a ring topology, each node is connected to the two nearest nodes so that the entire network forms a circle. Data are transmitted in one direction around the ring. Each workstation accepts and responds to packets addressed to it, then forwards the other packets to the next workstation in the ring.

- In a star topology, every node on the network is connected through a central device, such as a hub. Any single physical wire on a star network connects only two devices, so a cabling problem will affect only two nodes. Nodes transmit data to the hub, which then retransmits the information to the rest of the network segment where the destination node can pick it up.

- Except for home office networks, few LANs use the simple physical topologies in their pure form. More often, LANs employ a hybrid of more than one simple physical topology.

- The star-wired ring topology is a network that uses the physical layout of a star and the token-passing data transmission method. Data are sent around the star in a circular pattern. Modern Token Ring networks, as specified in IEEE 802.5, use this hybrid topology.

- In a star-wired bus topology, groups of workstations are connected in a star formation; each of the stars is connected to a hub, with all the hubs then networked via a single bus. This design allows you to cover longer distances and easily interconnect or isolate different network segments, although it is more expensive than using either the star or bus topology alone. The star-wired bus topology commonly forms the basis for Ethernet and Fast Ethernet networks.

- Hubs that service star-wired bus or star-wired ring topologies can be daisy-chained to form a more complex hybrid topology.

- A hierarchical hybrid topology can designate hubs at different layers to perform different functions.

- The cabling that connects each hub, or different level of the hierarchy, is called the backbone. A backbone is sometimes called "a network of networks." Backbones usually transmit data at faster speeds than does the cabling that connects each workstation, because they handle the largest loads.

- A serial backbone is the simplest kind of backbone. It consists of two or more hubs connected to each other by a single cable.

- A distributed backbone consists of a number of hubs connected to a series of central hubs or routers in a hierarchy.

- The collapsed backbone topology uses a router or switch as the single central connection point for multiple subnetworks.

- A parallel backbone is the most robust enterprise-wide topology. It is a variation of the collapsed backbone arrangement that consists of more than one connection from the central router or switch to each network segment.

- In a mesh network, routers are interconnected with other routers so that at least two pathways connect each node.

- WAN topologies use the LAN and enterprise-wide topologies as building blocks, but add more complexity because of the distance they must cover, the higher number of users they serve, and heavier traffic they often handle.

- A WAN with single interconnection points for each location is arranged in a peer-to-peer topology. This topology often represents the best solution for organizations with only a few sites and access to dedicated circuits.

- The star topology in a WAN mimics the arrangement of a star LAN. A single site acts as the central connection point for several other points. This arrangement provides several routes for data to follow between any two sites and is, therefore, more reliable than the peer-to-peer or ring WANs.

- In WAN ring topology, each site is connected to two other sites so that the entire WAN forms a ring pattern. This architecture is similar to the LAN ring topology, except that a WAN ring topology connects locations rather than local nodes.

- As with an enterprise-wide mesh, a mesh WAN topology consists of many directly interconnected nodes—in this case, locations. Mesh WANs are the most fault-tolerant WAN configuration. Connecting every node on a network is very expensive, however.

- Tiered WAN topologies are similar to the hierarchical hybrid topologies used with LANs. In a tiered topology, WAN sites connected in star or ring formations are interconnected at different levels, with the interconnection points being organized into layers.

- Network logical topologies describe how signals travel over a network. The two main types of logical topologies are bus and ring. Ethernet networks use a bus logical topology and Token Ring networks use a ring logical topology.

- Switching manages the filtering and forwarding of packets between nodes on a network. Every network relies on one of three types of switching: circuit switching, message switching, or packet switching.

- Ethernet is a networking technology originally developed by Xerox in the 1970s and improved by Xerox, Digital Equipment Corporation, and Intel. This flexible technology can run on a variety of network media and offers excellent throughput at a reasonable cost. Ethernet is the most common type of modern LAN.

❑ Ethernet follows a network access method called Carrier Sense Multiple Access with Collision Detection (CSMA/CD). All Ethernet networks, independent of their speed or frame type, use CSMA/CD.

❑ On heavily trafficked Ethernet networks, collisions are common. The more nodes that are transmitting data on a network, the more collisions that will take place. When an Ethernet network grows to a particular number of nodes, performance may suffer as a result of collisions.

❑ A switch is a device that can separate a network segment into smaller segments, each independent of the other and supporting its own traffic. The use of switched Ethernet increases the effective bandwidth of a network segment because fewer workstations vie for the same time on the wire.

❑ Networks may use one (or a combination) of four kinds of Ethernet data frames: Ethernet IEEE 802.3, Novell Proprietary 802.3, Ethernet II, and IEEE 802.3 SNAP. Each frame type differs slightly in the way it codes and decodes packets of data from one device to another.

❑ Token Ring networks currently run at either 4 or 16 Mbps, as specified by IEEE 802.5. Token Ring is generally more expensive to implement than Ethernet, but offers high reliability and fault tolerance.

❑ Token Ring networks use the token-passing routine and a star-ring hybrid physical topology. Workstations connect to the network through Multistation Access Units (MAUs). Token Ring networks may use shielded or unshielded twisted-pair cabling.

❑ Fiber Distributed Data Interface (FDDI) is a networking standard originally specified by ANSI in the mid-1980s and later refined by ISO. It uses a dual fiber-optic ring to transmit data at speeds of 100 Mbps.

❑ FDDI's required fiber-optic cable and dual fiber rings offer greater reliability and security than twisted-pair copper wire. It is much more expensive than Fast Ethernet.

❑ Asynchronous Transfer Mode (ATM) relies on a fixed packet size to achieve data transfer rates up to 9953 Mbps. The fixed packet, called a cell, consists of 48 bytes of data plus a 5-byte header. The fixed packet size allows ATM to provide predictable traffic patterns and better control over bandwidth utilization.

❑ ATM relies on virtual circuits, logical point-to-point connections that rely on ATM switches, to determine the optimal path between sender and receiver. The ATM switch establishes this path before the network transmits ATM data; in contrast, Ethernet transmits data first and lets the routers and switches down the wire direct the data.

❑ Applications that benefit from ATM's quality of service guarantees include time-sensitive data, such as video and audio. Currently, ATM is very expensive. It is used on large data carriers' WANs, but rarely on smaller LANs.

KEY TERMS

1 Gigabit Ethernet — An Ethernet standard for networks that achieve 1-Gbps maximum throughput. 1 Gigabit Ethernet runs (preferably) on fiber, but may also run over twisted pair. It is primarily used for network backbones.

10 Gigabit Ethernet — A standard currently being defined by the IEEE 802.3ae committee. 10 Gigabit Ethernet will allow 10-Gbps throughput and will include full-duplexing and multimode fiber requirements.

802.3 Raw — See *Novell proprietary 802.3 frame.*

access method — A network's method of controlling how network nodes access the communications channel. CSMA/CD is the access method used by Ethernet networks.

active monitor — On a Token Ring network, the workstation that maintains timing for token passing, monitors token and frame transmission, detects lost tokens, and corrects problems when a timing error or other disruption occurs. Only one workstation on the ring can act as the active monitor at any given time.

active topology — A topology in which each workstation participates in transmitting data over the network.

Asynchronous Transfer Mode (ATM) — A technology originally conceived in 1983 at Bell Labs, but standardized only in the mid-1990s. It relies on a fixed packet size to achieve data transfer rates up to 9953 Mbps. The fixed packet consists of 48 bytes of data plus a 5-byte header. The fixed packet size allows ATM to provide predictable traffic patterns and better control over bandwidth utilization.

autosense — A feature of modern NICs that enables a NIC to automatically sense what types of frames are running on a network and set itself to that specification.

backbone — The cabling that connects each connectivity device, or the different levels of a hierarchy of connectivity devices.

bus — The single cable connecting all devices in a bus topology.

bus topology — A topology in which a single cable connects all nodes on a network without intervening connectivity devices.

Carrier Sense Multiple Access/Collision Avoidance (CSMA/CA) — A network access method used on LocalTalk networks in which nodes on a shared communication channel signal their intent to transmit data before doing so, thus avoiding collisions.

Carrier Sense Multiple Access/Collision Detection (CSMA/CD) — Rules for communication used by shared Ethernet networks. In CSMA/CD each node waits its turn before transmitting data, to avoid interfering with other nodes' transmissions.

cell — A packet of a fixed size. In ATM technology, a cell consists of 48 bytes of data plus a 5-byte header.

circuit switching — A type of switching in which a connection is established between two network nodes before they begin transmitting data. Bandwidth is dedicated to this connection and remains available until users terminate the communication between the two nodes.

collapsed backbone — A type of enterprise-wide backbone in which a router or switch acts as the single central connection point for multiple subnetworks.

5

collision — In Ethernet networks, the interference of one network node's data transmission with another network node's data transmission.

collision domain — The portion of an Ethernet network in which collisions will occur if two nodes transmit data at the same time.

Controlled Access Unit (CAU) — A connectivity device used on a Token Ring network. In addition to passing data between nodes, a CAU provides more flexibility and easier management of connected nodes than a MAU.

Cyclical Redundancy Check (CRC) — An algorithm used by the FCS field in Ethernet frames. CRC takes the values of all preceding fields in the frame and generates a unique 4-byte number, the FCS. When the destination node receives the frame, it unscrambles the FCS via CRC and makes sure that the frame's fields match their original organization. If this comparison fails, the receiving node assumes that the frame has been damaged in transit and requests that the source node retransmit the data.

daisy chain — A linked series of devices.

data propagation delay — The length of time data take to travel from one point on the segment to another point. On Ethernet networks, CSMA/CD's collision detection routine cannot operate accurately if the data propagation delay is too long.

DB-9 connector — A connector containing nine pins that is used on STP-based Token Ring networks.

dedicated circuits — Continuous physical or logical connections between two access points that are leased from a communications provider, such as an ISP or local phone company.

demand priority — A method for data transmission used by 100BaseVG Ethernet networks. Each device on a star or hierarchical network sends a request to transmit to the central hub, which grants the requests one at a time. The hub examines incoming data packets, determines the destination node, and forwards the packets to that destination. Because demand priority runs on a star topology, no workstations except the source and destination can "see" the data. Data travel from one device to the hub, then to another device.

distributed backbone — A type of enterprise-wide backbone that consists of a number of hubs connected to a series of central hubs or routers in a hierarchy.

enterprise — An entire organization, including local and remote offices, a mixture of computer systems, and a number of departments. Enterprise-wide computing takes into account the breadth and diversity of a large organization's computer needs.

Ethernet 802.2 frame — See *IEEE 802.3 frame.*

Ethernet 802.3 frame — See *Novell proprietary 802.3 frame.*

Ethernet II frame — The original Ethernet frame type developed by Digital, Intel, and Xerox, before the IEEE began to standardize Ethernet. Ethernet II lacks Logical Link Control layer information but contains a 2-byte type field to identify the upper-layer protocol contained in the frame. It supports TCP/IP, AppleTalk, IPX/SPX, and other higher layer protocols.

Fiber Distributed Data Interface (FDDI) — A networking standard originally specified by ANSI in the mid-1980s and later refined by ISO. FDDI uses a dual fiber-optic ring to transmit data at speeds of 100 Mbps. It was commonly used as a backbone technology in the 1980s and early 1990s, but lost favor as fast Ethernet technologies emerged in the mid-1990s. FDDI provides excellent reliability and security.

Frame Check Sequence (FCS) — A field located at the end of an Ethernet frame that ensures data are received just as they were sent.

hierarchical hybrid topology — A network topology in which devices are divided into separate layers according to their priority or function.

High-Speed Token Ring (HSTR) — A standard for Token Ring networks that operate at 100 Mbps.

hybrid topology — A complex combination of the simple physical topologies.

IEEE 802.3 frame — A popular Ethernet frame type used on IPX/SPX networks. The defining characteristics of its data portion are the source and destination service access points that belong to the Logical Link Control layer, a sublayer of the Data Link layer. Also called LLC or, in Novell lingo, Ethernet 802.2.

IEEE 802.3 SNAP frame — A rarely used Ethernet frame type that is an adaptation of IEEE 802.3 and Ethernet II. SNAP stands for Sub-Network Access Protocol. The SNAP portion of the frame contains the three Logical Link Control fields (DSAP, SSAP, and Control). The Organization ID (OUI) field provides a method of identifying the type of network on which the frame is running. In addition, Ethernet SNAP frames carry Ethernet type information, just as an Ethernet II frame does.

intelligent hub — A hub that, rather than simply regenerating signals, can manage transmissions by dictating which nodes can send and receive data at every instant.

jamming — A part of CSMA/CD in which, upon detecting a collision, a station issues a special 32-bit sequence to indicate to all nodes on an Ethernet segment that its previously transmitted frame has suffered a collision and should be considered faulty.

LAN Emulation (LANE) — A method for transporting Token Ring or Ethernet frames over ATM networks. LANE encapsulates incoming Ethernet or Token Ring frames, then converts them into ATM cells for transmission over an ATM network.

LAN topology — The physical layout, or pattern, of nodes on a local area network (LAN).

layer — A logical division between devices on a network.

LLC frame — See *IEEE 802.3 frame*.

Lobe Attachment Module (LAM) — A device that attaches to a CAU to expand the capacity of that device. LAMs typically allow up to 20 devices to plug into each CAU receptacle.

LocalTalk — A logical topology designed by Apple Computer, Inc. especially for networking Macintosh computers. LocalTalk uses the CSMA/CA network access method, and its throughput is limited to a maximum of 230 Kbps. Because of its throughput limitations, LocalTalk has been replaced by Ethernet on most modern Macintosh-based networks.

logical topology — A networking technology defined by its Data Link layer data packaging and Physical layer signaling techniques.

MacTCP – A version of the TCP/IP protocol supplied with LocalTalk.

media filter — A device that enables two types of cables or connectors to be linked.

mesh network — An enterprise-wide topology in which routers are interconnected with other routers so that at least two pathways connect each node.

mesh WAN topology — A WAN topology that consists of many directly interconnected locations forming a complex mesh.

message switching — A type of switching in which a connection is established between two devices in the connection path; one device transfers data to the second device, then breaks the connection. The information is stored and forwarded from the second device once a connection between that device and a third device on the path is established.

Multistation Access Unit (MAU) — A device on a Token Ring network that regenerates signals; equivalent to a hub.

network access method — See *access method*.

Novell proprietary 802.3 frame — The original NetWare Ethernet frame type and the default frame type for networks running NetWare versions lower than 3.12. It supports only the IPX/SPX protocol. Sometimes called 802.3 "raw," because its data portion contains no control bits.

packet switching — A type of switching in which data are broken into packets before they are transported. In packet switching, packets can travel any path on the network to their destination, because each packet contains a destination address and sequencing information.

padding — Bytes added to the data (or information) portion of an Ethernet frame to make sure this field is at least 46 bytes in size. Padding has no effect on the data carried by the frame.

parallel backbone — The most robust enterprise-wide topology. This variation on the collapsed backbone arrangement consists of more than one connection from the central router or switch to each network segment.

peer-to-peer topology — A WAN with single interconnection points for each location.

physical topology — The physical layout of a network. A physical topology depicts a network in broad scope; it does not specify devices, connectivity methods, or addresses on the network. Physical topologies are categorized into three fundamental geometric shapes: bus, ring, and star. These shapes can be mixed to create hybrid topologies.

quality of service (QoS) — The result of standards for delivering data within a certain period of time after their transmission. For example, ATM networks can supply four QoS levels, from a "best effort" attempt for noncritical data to a guaranteed, real-time transmission for time-sensitive data.

ring topology — A network layout in which each node is connected to the two nearest nodes so that the entire network forms a circle. Data are transmitted unidi-

5

rectionally around the ring. Each workstation accepts and responds to packets addressed to it, then forwards the other packets to the next workstation in the ring.

ring WAN topology — A WAN topology in which each site is connected to two other sites so that the entire WAN forms a ring pattern. This architecture is similar to the LAN ring topology, except that a WAN ring topology connects locations rather than local nodes.

serial backbone — The simplest kind of backbone, consisting of two or more hubs connected to each other by a single cable.

Service Access Point (SAP) — A feature of Ethernet networks that identifies a node or internal process that uses the LLC protocol. Each process between a source and destination node on the network may have a unique SAP.

shared Ethernet — A version of Ethernet in which all the nodes share a common channel and a fixed amount of bandwidth.

star topology — A physical topology in which every node on the network is connected through a central device, such as a hub. Any single physical wire on a star network connects only two devices, so a cabling problem will affect only two nodes. Nodes transmit data to the hub, which then retransmits the data to the rest of the network segment where the destination node can pick it up.

star WAN topology — A WAN topology that mimics the arrangement of star LANs. A single site acts as the central connection point for several other locations.

star-wired bus topology — A hybrid topology in which groups of workstations are connected in a star fashion to hubs that are networked via a single bus.

star-wired ring topology — A hybrid topology that uses the physical layout of a star and the token-passing data transmission method.

switch — The hardware that manages network switching; used to separate a network segment into smaller segments, with each segment being independent of the others, and supporting its own traffic.

switched Ethernet — An Ethernet model that enables multiple nodes to simultaneously transmit and receive data and individually take advantage of more bandwidth because they are assigned separate logical network segments through switching.

switching — A component of a network's logical topology that manages how packets are filtered and forwarded between nodes on the network.

teleconnector — A transceiver used on LocalTalk networks. The teleconnector is linked to the node's serial port on one side, and to the wall jack on the other side.

tiered WAN topology — A WAN topology in which sites are connected in star or ring formations and interconnected at different levels with the interconnection points organized into layers.

token passing — A means of data transmission in which a 3-byte packet, called a token, is passed around the network in a round-robin fashion.

Token Ring media filter — A device that enables a DB-9 cable and a type 1 IBM cable to be connected.

type 1 IBM connector — A type of Token Ring connector that uses interlocking tabs that snap into an identical connector when one is flipped upside-down, making for a secure connection. Type 1 IBM connectors are used on STP-based Token Ring networks.

virtual circuits — Connections between network nodes that, while based on potentially disparate physical links, logically appear to be direct, dedicated links between those nodes.

WAN topology — The physical layout, or pattern, of locations on a wide area network (WAN).

wide area network (WAN) — A network connecting geographically distinct locations, which may or may not belong to the same organization.

5

REVIEW QUESTIONS

1. Under what circumstance might you use a simple bus topology?

   a. when you your LAN services many users

   b. when your LAN services multiple locations

   c. when your LAN services few users

   d. when you want to ensure the highest level of security

   e. when you use hubs to separate workstation groups

2. What kind of topology is susceptible to signal bounce?

   a. mesh

   b. bus

   c. ring

   d. hierarchical

   e. star

3. What are the primary advantages of using a star topology over a ring or bus topology?

4. Most modern networks with more than a few nodes use a hybrid topology. True or False?

5. Why might you want to use a hierarchical topology?

   a. to differentiate levels of connectivity devices and workstation groups

   b. to enable multiprotocol routing between LAN segments

   c. to account for signal bounce between two LAN segments

   d. to use multiple frame types on an Ethernet network

   e. to ensure greater reliability for critical network connections

6. What network access method relies most often on a star–wired bus physical topology?

    a. Ethernet

    b. FDDI

    c. ATM

    d. Token Ring

    e. LocalTalk

7. How do workstations in a ring topology negotiate their data transmissions?

    a. by using CSMA/CD

    b. by using RARP

    c. by using demand priority

    d. by using tokens

    e. by using CSMA/CA

8. Which of the following is a potential problem with daisy-chaining hubs?

    a. exceeding the maximum network length

    b. exceeding the maximum number of workstations per hub

    c. exceeding the maximum collision rate

    d. exceeding the maximum transmission rate

    e. exceeding the maximum number of workstations per segment

9. What type of network backbone is the most reliable?

    a. distributed

    b. collapsed

    c. parallel

    d. serial

    e. hierarchical

10. The Internet is an example of what kind of WAN topology?

    a. peer-to-peer

    b. bus

    c. mesh

    d. ring

    e. tiered

11. Why is packet switching more efficient than circuit switching?

    a. In packet switching, two communicating nodes establish a channel first, then begin transmitting, thus ensuring a reliable connection and eliminating the need to retransmit.

    b. In packet switching, packets can take the quickest route between nodes and arrive independently of when other packets in their data stream arrive.

    c. In packet switching, data are sent to an intermediate node and reassembled before being transmitted, en masse, to the destination node.

    d. In packet switching, packets are synchronized according to a timing mechanism in the switch.

5

12. Describe the steps a workstation takes under the rules of CSMA/CD.

13. On a 100BaseT (Fast Ethernet) network, what is the maximum number of hubs that can be connected along the bus of a star-wired bus topology?

    a. 2
    b. 3
    c. 4
    d. 5
    e. 6

14. What is the maximum number of addressable stations on a 10BaseT Ethernet network?

    a. 64
    b. 100
    c. 200
    d. 512
    e. 1024

15. Which two of the following might cause excessive data collisions on an Ethernet network?

    a. The network is attempting to use two incompatible frame types.

    b. The overall network length exceeds IEEE 802.3 standards for that network type.

    c. A router on the network is mistakenly forwarding packets to the wrong segment.

    d. A switch on the network has established multiple virtual circuits for a path between two nodes.

    e. A server on the network contains a faulty NIC.

16. What type of media is best suited to 1 Gigabit Ethernet networks?

    a. fiber-optic

    b. unshielded twisted-pair

    c. thick coaxial

    d. shielded twisted-pair

    e. infrared

17. In order to use demand priority on a network (for example, when running 100BaseVG), what type of hub is necessary?

    a. modular

    b. repeater

    c. stackable

    d. intelligent

    e. managed

18. What fields do all Ethernet frame types have in common?

19. At what layer of the OSI Model does framing occur?

    a. Physical layer

    b. Data Link layer

    c. Network layer

    d. Transport layer

    e. Session layer

20. What is the purpose of padding in an Ethernet frame?

    a. ensuring that the frame and data arrive without error

    b. ensuring that the frame arrives in sequence

    c. indicating the length of the frame

    d. indicating the type of higher-layer protocol supported by the frame

    e. ensuring that the data portion of the frame totals at least 46 bytes

21. What is the purpose of a Frame Check Sequence field in an Ethernet frame?

    a. ensuring that data are received without errors at the destination node

    b. ensuring that the frame's length stays constant through transmission

    c. ensuring that the frame is synchronized with other frames in its data stream

    d. ensuring that the frame arrives at the proper destination address

    e. indicating the frame's source address

22. NIC device drivers come with what feature that reduces the need for you to worry about frame types?

    a. autodetect

    b. autonegotiate

    c. autosense

    d. autorespond

    e. autotranslate

23. What are the minimum and maximum sizes for an Ethernet frame?

    a. 46 and 64 bytes

    b. 46 and 128 bytes

    c. 64 and 1518 bytes

    d. 64 and 1600 bytes

    e. 128 and 1600 bytes

24. What type of TCP/IP protocol does LocalTalk use?

    a. MS TCP/IP

    b. MacTCP

    c. AppleTalk

    d. EtherTCP

    e. Apple TCP/IP

25. What is the name of a hub used on a Token Ring network?

    a. Multistation Access Unit

    b. Multiple Carrier Control Unit

    c. Multinode Access Station

    d. Media Access Control Unit

    e. Media Access Unit

26. Which two of the following are disadvantages to using Token Ring networks rather than Ethernet networks?

    a. Their standards are not as well defined as Ethernet's.

    b. They are slower than Ethernet.

    c. They require more expensive connectivity equipment than Ethernet

    d. They are less reliable than Ethernet.

    e. They can't extend as far as Ethernet.

5

27. Modern Token Ring networks may transmit data at either 4, 16, 32, or 64 Mbps. True or False?

28. If you were working on a Token Ring network that used cables with DB-9 connectors and needed to connect a NIC that contained an RJ-45 receptor, which of the following would help you accomplish your goal?

    a. media access unit

    b. crossover cable

    c. vampire tap

    d. media filter

    e. type 1 IBM connector

29. Which of the following IEEE standards describes Token Ring networks?

    a. IEEE 802.2

    b. IEEE 802.3

    c. IEEE 802.4

    d. IEEE 802.5

    e. IEEE 802.11

30. Which of the following network access methods is capable of the fastest throughput?

    a. LocalTalk

    b. Fast Ethernet

    c. FDDI

    d. Token Ring

    e. ATM

31. What type of Physical layer is required for FDDI?

    a. a single ring of single mode fiber

    b. a dual ring of single mode or multimode fiber

    c. a dual ring of unshielded twisted-pair cabling

    d. a single ring of shielded twisted-pair cabling

    e. a single ring of multimode fiber

32. Besides their ring-based topologies, what else do FDDI and Token Ring networks have in common?

    a. Both require fiber at the Physical layer.

    b. Both require twisted-pair cabling at the Physical layer.

    c. Both use token passing to mediate data transmission.

    d. Both are less expensive and easier to implement than Ethernet.

    e. Both rely on the parallel backbone structure.

33. You have been asked to serve on a technical committee planning an upgrade from your university's FDDI network to a Gigabit Ethernet network. The rest of the committee asserts this will be a relatively simple transition. What concern should you raise that contradicts their assertion?

   a. All of the FDDI fiber will have to be dug up and replaced with single mode fiber.

   b. The maximum allowable distance for a FDDI network is longer than that of an Ethernet network, so the existing FDDI network will need to be divided into smaller subnetworks.

   c. The connectors on the ends of the FDDI cables are SMA connectors, which will not fit into the receptors on Gigabit Ethernet routers.

   d. Since the transmission rate on the Ethernet network will be less than that of the FDDI network, users will notice dramatically slower response times.

34. What type of switching do ATM networks use?

   a. circuit switching

   b. packet switching

   c. multiprotocol switching

   d. message switching

   e. Layer 1 switching

35. Which two of the following might explain why network administrators prefer Gigabit Ethernet over ATM?

   a. Gigabit Ethernet is a more natural upgrade for their existing Ethernet networks.

   b. Gigabit Ethernet is typically less expensive to implement than ATM.

   c. Gigabit Ethernet can carry TCP/IP traffic, while ATM cannot.

   d. Gigabit Ethernet is endorsed by Microsoft and Novell, while ATM is not.

   e. Gigabit Ethernet offers quality of service guarantees, while ATM does not.

HANDS-ON PROJECTS

Project 5-1

In this exercise, you will create a simple star-wired bus network, one of the most typical forms of an Ethernet network. This project requires two Ethernet 10-Mbps hubs, containing at least four ports each, six (straight through) patch cables, three workstations, and one file server, all with 10-Mbps NICs (installed and correctly configured). The server should be running Windows 2000, and the workstations should run either Windows 98 or Windows 2000. All should have TCP/IP properly installed and configured. Make sure that user accounts are established that can be used to log onto the server. Finally, you will also need a paper and pencil.

1. Make sure that all the hubs, workstations, and the server are plugged in.

2. Connect the two hubs to each other by inserting one end of a patch cable in one hub's link port and the other end of the patch cable in the second hub's link port. Turn on both hubs if they are not already on.

3. Using another patch cable, connect one of the workstations to another port in the first hub. In the same manner, connect the server to the first hub, then turn on the workstation and server. Notice what happens to the lights on the hub when the workstation and server start up.

4. Repeat Step 3, but connect two different workstations to the second hub and then turn on the workstations.

5. Log onto the server from one of the four workstations. If you can see the server's resources, you have successfully created a star-wired bus Ethernet network, where the two hubs form the network's backbone. If you cannot log onto the server, check the cable connections from your workstations to the hub, between the hubs, and between the hub and the server.

6. On a separate piece of paper, draw the physical topology you have just created, marking the server, workstations, hubs, and cables on your drawing.

Project 5-2

In this exercise, you will use Windows 2000 Server's Network Monitor. Network Monitor is a tool that comes with the Windows 2000 Server operating system that allows you to view different data frames traveling to and from a server's NIC. You can also use it to determine various characteristics about the frames, including the networking protocols they carry. Network Monitor is especially useful when troubleshooting network connection problems. This project requires a Windows 2000 server that is running IPX/SPX and TCP/IP, with at least two clients attached and logged in. (If a Windows 2000 server is not available, a Windows NT server with the Network Monitor tool installed will also work.) The clients may be Windows 98 or Windows 2000 workstations.

1. Log onto the Windows 2000 server as an administrator.

2. On the Windows 2000 server, click **Start**, point to **Programs**, point to **Administrative Tools**, then click **Network Monitor**. The Network Monitor window opens. (Maximize the Network Monitor screen if it does not maximize automatically.)

3. If your server is connected to more than one network, you may be asked to select the network on which you want to monitor data. Choose the network to which your clients are connected (the local network). In the next step, you will begin the capture process to gather data that can later be analyzed.

4. Click **Capture** on the menu bar, then click **Start** to begin capturing network traffic information. In the next step, you will generate traffic to and from the server by accessing its shared resources.

5. From one of the workstations that is logged into the server, open a file on the server (for example, a spreadsheet or word-processing document).

6. From another workstation that is logged into the server, double-click the **Network Neighborhood** icon (in the case of a Windows 98 workstation) or **My Network Places** icon (in the case of a Windows 2000 workstation). Find the server's icon and double-click that. Then open some shared folders on the server.

7. Now that you have generated traffic to and from the server, return to the server to stop capturing data. In the Network Monitor menu bar, click **Capture**, then click **Stop**.

8. In the Network Monitor menu bar, click **Capture**, then click **Display Captured Data**.

9. As shown in Figure 5-31, at the bottom of the screen, Network Monitor lists the packets it has captured. Double-click one of the packets to view more information about it.

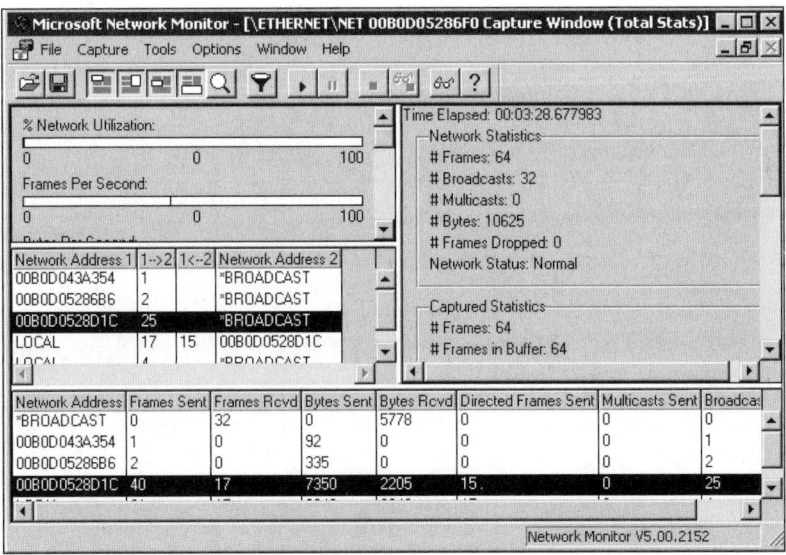

Figure 5-31   The Windows 2000 Network Monitor window

10. The Nework Monitor window displays three panes. The top pane contains a list of captured frames; the middle frame provides header and delivery details; and the bottom pane shows a hexadecimal/ASCII representation of the frame's content.

11. In the top pane, choose to view a frame that has a different kind of protocol listed in its protocol column than the frame you just viewed. Browse through its fields to find its protocol type, length, and source address information.

12. To close Network Monitor, click **File**, then click **Exit**. Do not save the information you have captured.

Project 5-3

In this exercise, you will survey organizations in your area to determine which network transport model, cabling types, and transmission speeds are used on their LANs. From this information, you can determine the most popular networking design approaches. You may also be able to tell what approaches will grow in popularity and which ones will become obsolete.

1. Identify five businesses, schools, or civic organizations in your area that use networking technology—for example, an insurance company, a utility company, a local school district, a chain of retail stores, an architectural firm, or an ISP.

2. For each organization, find contact information for its manager of the Information Technology (IT) department.

3. Call the IT department manager and ask him or her the following questions:

   ❑ Does your network use Ethernet, Token Ring, or both?

   ❑ What transmission speed does your network use?

   ❑ On what type of backbone does your network rely?

   ❑ What type of wiring does your network use? Do you use the same type of wiring for the backbone as you do for connecting workstations?

   ❑ Do you use WAN technologies? If so, in what kind of a topology are your separate locations arranged?

   ❑ If you had all the money you wanted in your budget, what type of upgrades would you make to your network?

   ❑ If you had money enough to make only one of these upgrades, which one would it be?

4. Compile the answers from all five managers. Which network access method is most popular? Which transmission speed? Which type of backbone? How do the economics of each networking approach affect the manager's decisions regarding wiring and logical topology? Compare your results with the results of others in your group.

5. Write and send a thank you note to each of the IT managers you interviewed, thanking them for sharing their valuable time with you.

CASE PROJECTS

1. You have been asked to design a LAN for a very successful CPA firm with five departments in one building and a total of 560 employees. Currently, the firm has no networked computers, and it is open to any suggestions you can offer. The firm does have a few requirements, however. It wants to make sure that it can easily expand its LAN in the future without exorbitant costs and moving a lot of equipment. The firm also wants to make sure that every department has very fast access to the LAN, and, of course, it wants the LAN to remain up at all times. It has already decided to use the NetWare 5.0 network operating system. What kind of LAN will you design for this company?

2. AstroTech Components, a company that manufactures parts for the aeronautics industry, is having trouble with a network segment in one of its plants and has asked you for help. According to the network administrator, the plant was incorporated into the existing Ethernet 10BaseT network two weeks ago. Since then, the users have been complaining of intermittent lockups, software errors, and disconnections. During your visit, she shows you the very organized telecommunications closet. Then, the network administrator escorts you to the production floor, where she points out the 20 Windows 98 machines that the supervisors use to enter numbers into a database from their desks in the production area. The supervisors try to explain their problems in detail, but you and the network administrator can barely hear above the roar of stamping machines. You begin to walk away when you notice that the network cabling is strung along the outside of support posts between stamping machines. When you reach her office, what suggestions do you make to the network administrator to fix the problem?

3. Because you solved AstroTech's plant dilemma so quickly, the network administrator has time to ask you more questions. In particular, she is concerned about the CAD/CAM workgroup. The users in this group fought for months to get new machines. Now that her technicians finally installed the more powerful workstations, however, the users can't access the network. You ask what kind of network they are on, and the network administrator says that this group was upgraded to 100BaseT, along with two other groups, just yesterday, because these users needed the extra speed. When you ask whether all users are affected, she says that everyone—even the department vice president, who has full rights to the network—is prevented from logging on. You suspect that the CAD/CAM users' network access is the problem. What steps do you take next?

5

4. The network administrator understands everything you've explained so far, and although your solution will cost a little more, she's glad to have the company's CAD/CAM workgroup problem resolved. Now she asks about the Finance Department, which is experiencing problems logging on. These personnel are running on Windows 95 workstations connected to a 10BaseT bus Ethernet segment. The problem happens about half the time. Once they're logged on, these users occasionally experience other problems, but they haven't recorded any of the error messages. For a long time, the network administrator thought that Finance staff members were just forgetting their passwords, but her technicians have verified that the connectivity problem is real. She admits that the wiring closet for the Finance area is a mess because the department doubled in size when the company bought out its main competitor, Solstice, Inc., a few months ago. What do you think might be causing the problem?

5. Before you leave, the network administrator asks your opinion about upgrading the rest of the company to 100BaseT from 10BaseT. Although her technicians have told her that this move is necessary, she is concerned about the costs associated with replacing wiring, NICs, switches, and hubs. As it is, she has to purchase 500 new desktop PCs this year. The network administrator has heard about 1 Gigabit Ethernet and wonders whether it would be better to wait for that architecture. What considerations do you point out that might help her with her decision?

CHAPTER 6

NETWORKING HARDWARE

After reading this chapter and completing the exercises, you will be able to:

➤ Identify the functions of LAN connectivity hardware

➤ Install and configure a network adapter (network interface card)

➤ Identify problems associated with connectivity hardware

➤ Describe the factors involved in choosing a network adapter, hub, switch, or router

➤ Understand the functions of repeaters, hubs, bridges, switches, and gateways

➤ Describe the uses and types of routing protocols

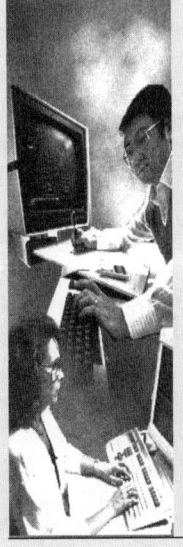

ON THE JOB

As a network architect, I was asked to investigate why a large insurance company was experiencing performance degradation between campus buildings. This company was planning to expand its staff, but felt it needed to solve the network problem before adding any more users. The link between the buildings was fiber-optic cable, which should have provided plenty of capacity for mainframe data from one building to quickly reach the screens of claims processors at another building.

Realizing that wiring wasn't the problem, I looked at the connectivity hardware on the network. This network relied on a single router and 10 hubs for over 200 users. The router was software-based and ran on a Novell server (as opposed to a hardware-based router). Software-based routers are never as efficient as hardware-based routers; that was probably one bottleneck. In addition, having a network comprised of hubs and routers meant that all bandwidth was being shared by the devices. To cut down congestion, I replaced the router with a switch.

That replacement solved the performance problem. Now, instead of waiting three seconds for a screen to be refreshed, the insurance company employees get a new screen instantly after pressing the Enter key.

Carrie McClelland
ARK Consulting

In Chapter 4, you learned how data are transmitted over cable or through the atmosphere. Now you need to know how data arrive at their destination. To understand this process, it's helpful to compare data transmission to the means by which the U.S. Postal Service delivers mail: Mail trucks, airplanes, and delivery staff serve as the transmission media that move information from place to place. Machines and personnel at the post office interpret addresses on the envelopes and either deliver the mail to a transfer point or to your home. Inefficiencies in mail delivery, such as letters being misdirected to the wrong transfer point, frustrate both the sender and the receiver of the mail and increase the overall cost of delivery.

In data networks, the task of directing information to the correct destination in as efficient a manner as possible is handled by hubs, routers, bridges, and switches. In this chapter, you will learn about these devices and their roles in managing data traffic. Whereas earlier chapters focused mainly on the Physical layer of the OSI Model, this chapter delves into the Data Link and Network layers. It introduces the concepts involved in moving data from place to place, including issues related to switching and routing protocols. It also provides pictures of the hardware—repeaters, hubs, switches, bridges, and routers—that make data transfer possible. (It's important for you to have an accurate mental image of this equipment because, in a cluttered telecommunications closet, it may prove difficult to identify the hardware underneath the wiring.) In addition, you will learn all about network interface cards, which serve as the workstation's link to the network and are often the source of many connectivity problems.

NETWORK ADAPTERS

In Chapter 1, you learned that network adapters (also called network interface cards, or NICs) are connectivity devices that enable a workstation, server, printer, or other node to receive and transmit data over the network media. You also learned that in most modern network devices, network adapters contain the data transceiver, the device that transmits and receives data signals. NICs belong to both the Physical layer and Data Link layer of the OSI Model because they apply data signals to the wire and assemble or disassemble data frames. They do not, however, analyze the data from higher layers. For example, they could not determine whether the data they are transmitting and receiving are encoded nor could they decide how to decode them.

Advances in network adapter technology are making this hardware smarter than ever. Not only do all network adapters read addressing information so as to deliver data to their proper destination (and, in the case of Ethernet networks, to detect collisions), but many can also perform prioritization, network management, buffering, and traffic-filtering functions.

Network interface cards come in a variety of types depending on the logical topology (for example, Ethernet versus Token Ring), network transmission speed (for example, 10 Mbps versus 100 Mbps), connector interfaces (for example, BNC versus RJ-45), type of compatible system board or device, and, of course, manufacturer. Popular network adapter manufacturers include 3Com, Adaptec, D-Link, IBM, Intel, Kingston, Linksys, Netgear, SMC, and Western Digital, to name just a few. In fact, during your networking career, you may run into network adapters made by at least a dozen manufacturers.

As you learn about installing, configuring, and troubleshooting network adapters, you should concentrate first on generalities, then move on to special situations. Because network adapters are common to every networking device and every network, knowing all about them may prove to be the most useful tool you have at your disposal.

Types of Network Adapters

Before you order or install a network adapter in a network device, you need to know the type of interface required by the device. For a desktop or tower PC, the network adapter is likely to be a type of expansion board. An **expansion board** is a circuit board used to connect a device to the system board (the main circuit board that controls a computer, also known as a motherboard). Expansion boards connect to the system board through **expansion slots**, which are openings with multiple electrical contacts into which the expansion board can be inserted. Inserting an expansion board into an expansion slot establishes an electrical connection between the expansion board and the system board. Thus, the device connected to the expansion board becomes connected to the computer's main circuit. This connection enables the computer to centrally control its peripheral devices.

 Expansion boards may also be called expansion cards, adapter cards, daughter cards, or daughter boards.

The circuit used by the system board to transmit data to the computer's components is the computer's **bus**. The type of expansion board, and therefore the type of network adapter you choose, must match the computer's bus. Buses differ according to their capacity. The capacity of a bus is defined principally by the width of its data path (expressed in bits) and its speed (expressed in MHz). A data path on a bus equals the number of data bits that it can transmit in parallel at any given time. In the earliest PCs, buses had an 8-bit data path. Later, manufacturers expanded buses to handle 16 bits of data, then 32 bits. Most new Pentium computers use buses capable of exchanging 64 bits of data, and some are even capable of 128 bits. As the number of bits of data that a bus can handle increases, so too does the speed of the devices attached to the bus.

In addition to the amount of data that can travel through their circuits, buses differ by type. The following list describes PC bus types you may encounter. (If you have already completed coursework for CompTIA's A+ certification, this material will look familiar.)

- *Industry Standard Architecture (ISA)*—The original PC bus, developed in the early 1980s to support an 8-bit and later 16-bit data transfer capability. 8-bit ISA (pronounced "ice-uh") bus connectors contain one long row of pins, and 16-bit ISA bus connectors add another, shorter row, for a second 8 bits, as shown in Figure 6-1. ISA buses cannot support 100-Mbps throughput; because of this limitation, they are typically not used for network adapters in new PCs, although they may still be found in "economy" PCs. ISA buses may connect serial devices, such as mice or modems, in new PCs.

- *MicroChannel Architecture (MCA)*—IBM's proprietary 32-bit bus for personal computers, introduced in 1987 and later replaced by the standardized EISA and PCI buses. Unless you are working in an IBM-centric environment with older PS/2 or AIX equipment, you probably won't be concerned with MCA devices. Figure 6-1 shows an MCA network adapter.

- *Extended Industry Standard Architecture (EISA)*—A 32-bit bus that is compatible with older ISA devices because it shares the same length and pin configuration as the ISA bus, but that uses an extra layer of pins (resulting in a deeper, two-layered slot connector) for a second 16 bits to achieve faster throughput. An EISA expansion card is shown in Figure 6-1. The EISA (pronounced "ees-uh") bus was introduced in the late 1980s to compete with IBM's MCA bus.

- *Peripheral Component Interconnect (PCI)*—A 32- or 64-bit bus introduced in the 1990s that has become the network adapter connection type used for nearly all of today's new PCs. It's characterized by a shorter connector length than ISA, MCA, or EISA cards, but offers a much faster data transmission capability. PCI adapters are now standard for both PCs and Macintosh computers, allowing an organization to standardize on one make and model of NIC for use with all of their workstations. Figure 6-1 shows a typical PCI network adapter.

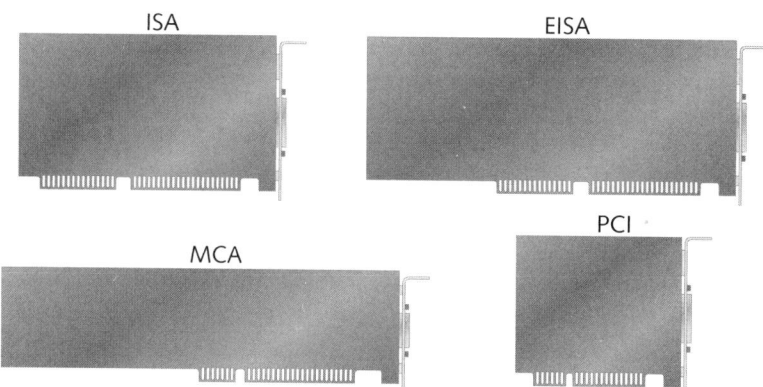

Figure 6-1   The four primary expansion card network adapters

You can easily determine what type of bus your PC uses by reading the documentation that came with the computer. This information should appear either on the purchase order or in the very beginning of the booklet that lists the computer's specifications. Someday, however, you may need to replace a network adapter on a PC whose documentation is missing. To verify what type of bus a PC uses, look inside the PC case. (Later in this chapter, you will learn how to safely open a computer case, check the computer's bus, and install a network adapter.) Most PCs have at least two different types of bus connections on the same board, as illustrated in Figure 6-2.

If a system board supports more than one kind of expansion slot, refer to the network adapter and PC manufacturers' guidelines for information on the preferred type of network adapter to install. If possible, you should choose a network adapter that matches the most modern bus on the system board. For example, if a PC supports both ISA and PCI, attempt to use a PCI network adapter. Although you may be able to use the older bus and network adapter types without any adverse effects, some network adapters (such as 3Com's products) will not work in an older bus if a faster, newer bus is available on the system board.

6

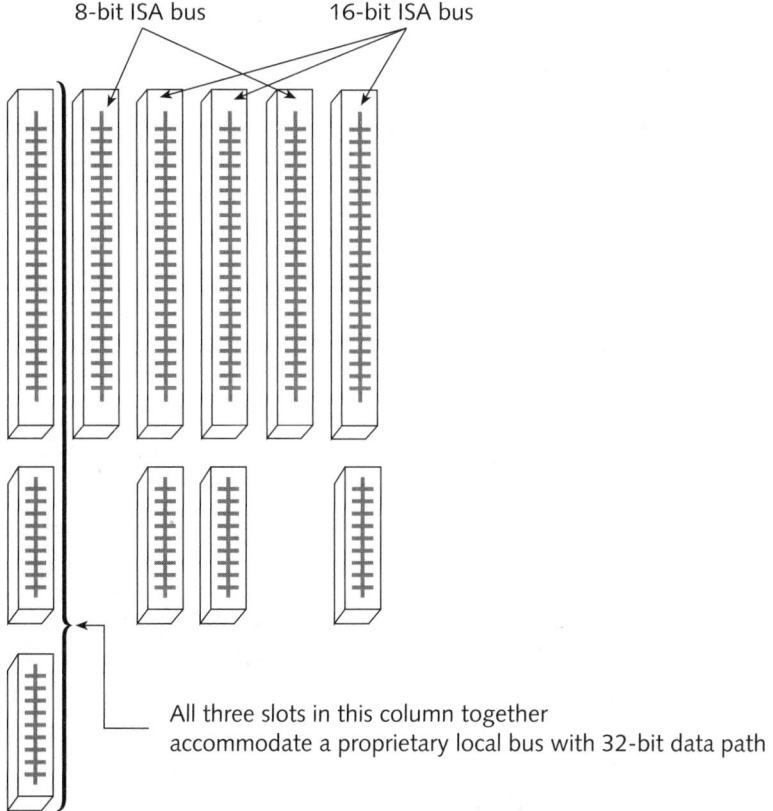

Figure 6-2   A system board with multiple bus types

Network adapters may connect to interfaces other than a PC's bus. For laptop computers, USB (universal serial bus) or Personal Computer Memory Card International Association (PCMCIA) slots may be used to connect network adapters; in older models of laptop computers, parallel ports may serve the same function. **PCMCIA** interfaces were developed in the early 1990s to provide a standard interface for connecting any type of device to a portable computer. PCMCIA devices are now more commonly known as **PC Cards**.

Some professionals also call them "credit card adapters" because they are approximately the same size as a credit card. PC Card slots may hold modem cards, network adapters, external hard disk cards, or CD-ROM cards. Most often, they are used for network adapters or modems; in fact, some PC Cards contain both devices. Figure 6-3 depicts a typical PC Card network adapter.

Figure 6-3   A typical PC Card network adapter

Another type of externally attached network adapter is one that relies on a **USB (universal serial bus) port**. USB is a standard external bus that can be used to connect multiple types of peripherals, including modems, mice, audio players, and network adapters. The original USB standard was developed in 1995 by a group of computer manufacturers working to make a low-cost, simple-to-install method of connecting peripheral devices to any make or model of computer. Since 1998, USB ports have been supplied on most modern laptop and desktop computers. The standard has become so popular that over 100 different types of devices have been designed to interface with the USB port.

One advantage to using a USB network adapter is its simple installation. A USB device needs only to be plugged into the USB port to be physically installed. An expansion board network adapter, on the other hand, requires the user to turn off the computer, remove its cover, insert the board into an expansion slot, fasten the board in place, replace the cover, and turn on the computer. Simple installation makes USB network adapters preferable for mobile users and novice users, such as those setting up a home network. However, the disadvantage of using a USB network adapter is that most USB ports in use today have a maximum data transfer rate of 12 Mbps (a newer high-speed USB standard that will support up to 480-Mbps throughput has been developed, but is not yet widely used). The traditional 12-Mbps limit means that a USB network adapter cannot be used on a network conforming to the 100BaseT standard unless the network's connectivity devices are capable of automatically adjusting between 10 Mbps and 100 Mbps. In any case, the USB port's throughput limitation makes this type of network adapter less desirable for networks on which data transfer speed is a critical variable. Figure 6-4 shows an example of a USB network adapter, which has a USB connector on one end and an RJ-45 receptacle on the other end.

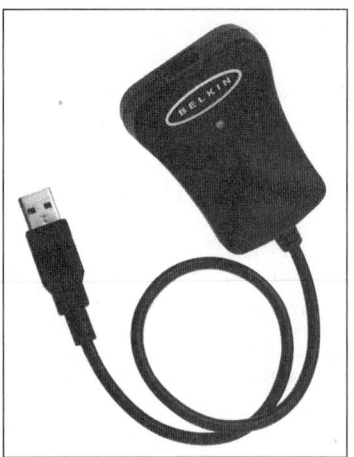

Figure 6-4   A USB network adapter

6

A third type of externally attached network adapter is the parallel port network adapter. As the name implies, a parallel port network adapter attaches to the parallel port of a computer on one side and to the network cable (with a BNC or RJ-45 connector) on the other side. Parallel port network adapters were the first type of externally attached network adapter and were designed primarily for use on laptops. They enjoyed some popularity in the early 1990s. However, since the advent of PC Card and USB port network adapters, parallel port network adapters are rarely used on modern computers. In fact, these specialized devices can be difficult to obtain or support. The most popular parallel port network adapter manufacturer is Xircom. Figure 6-5 depicts a typical parallel port network adapter.

Figure 6-5   A parallel port network adapter

In addition to network adapters that connect with network cabling, you can employ network adapters designed for wireless transmission. Typically, a wireless network adapter uses an antenna (either internal or external) to exchange signals with a base station transceiver or another wireless NIC. Expansion slot network adapters, PC Card network adapters and USB network adapters can all be wireless. However, the most popular type of wireless network adapter available today comes in the form of a PC Card network adapter.

Wireless network adapters are well suited to environments where cabling cannot be installed or in which clients need to move about while staying connected to the network. For example, library assistants can walk through stacks of books and record inventory data in the library's central database using handheld PCs require wireless connectivity. One disadvantage to using wireless network adapters is that they are generally more expensive than wire-dependent network adapters. Wireless connectivity manufacturers include 3Com, AMP, Cisco, ComStar, D-Link, Lucent, Proxim, Raytheon, and Webgear. Figure 6-6 depicts wireless PC Card and ISA network adapters.

Figure 6-6   Wireless network adapters

As mentioned earlier, network adapters also vary by the type of logical topology they support (for example, Ethernet or Token Ring) and their connector types. Figure 6-7 shows a variety of network adapters that might be used on Ethernet networks, and Figure 6-8 shows a variety of network adapters designed for Token Ring networks. Notice that some network adapters provide only one type of cabling connector, while others provide two or even three types of connectors.

6

Figure 6-7   A variety of Ethernet network adapters

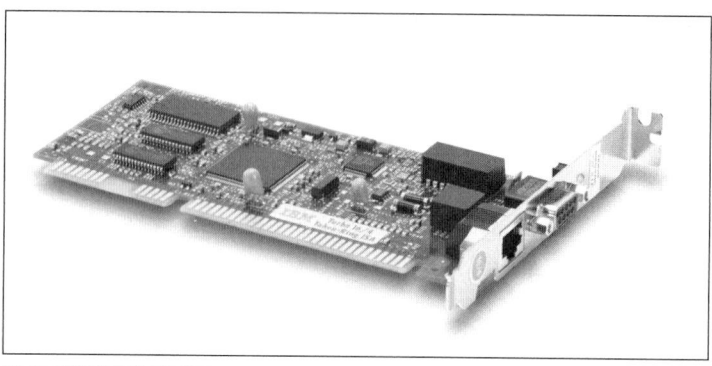

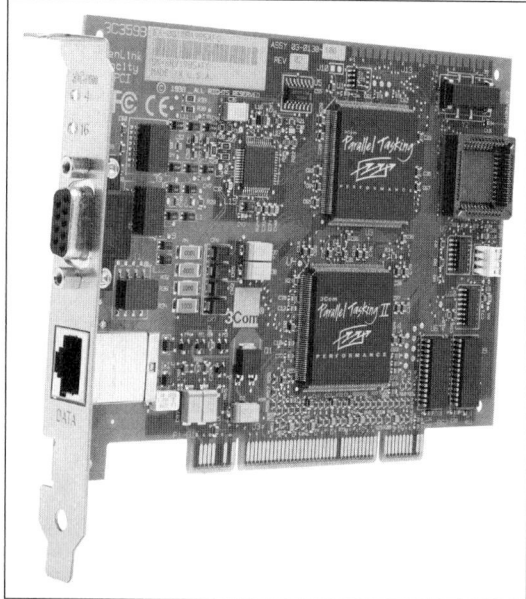

Figure 6-8   Token Ring network adapters

Devices other than PCs require specialized network adapters as well. Printer network adapters, for example, come in a variety of styles suited to different applications. By far, the most popular printer network adapter is Hewlett-Packard's JetDirect card. Printer network adapters often provide processing and support for all seven OSI Model layers (making them even more complex than PC network adapters) so as to handle print server functions. Figure 6-9 depicts typical Ethernet network adapters for networked printers.

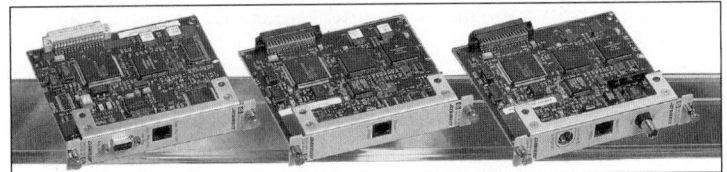

Figure 6-9   Ethernet network adapters for printers

Installing Network Adapters

To install a modern network adapter, you must first install the hardware, and then install the software that shipped with the NIC. In some cases, you may also have to perform a third step: configuring the **firmware**, which is a combination of hardware and software. The hardware component of firmware is a read-only memory (ROM) chip (built into the NIC) that stores data established at the factory. The ROM may be changed by configuration utilities (the software component of firmware) that come with the network adapter. Because its data can be erased or changed by applying electrical charges to the chip (via the software program), this particular type of ROM is called **electrically erasable programmable read-only memory (EEPROM)**.

A network adapter's firmware contains information about its transmission speed capabilities, its preferred IRQ (discussed later in this chapter) and input/output (I/O) port address, and duplexing capabilities, among other things. In many cases, especially if you are using Windows 2000 plug-and-play technology, you will not have to change the network adapter's firmware.

The following sections explain the steps involved in installing an expansion board network adapter, as well as how to install externally attached network adapters.

Installing and Configuring Network Adapter Hardware

As with any hardware installation, you should first read the manufacturer's documentation that accompanies the network adapter hardware. The following steps generally apply to any kind of expansion card network adapter installation (in a desktop computer), but your experience may vary.

To install an expansion card network adapter:

1. Make sure that your toolkit includes a Phillips-head screwdriver, a ground strap, and a ground mat to protect the internal components from electrostatic discharge. Also, make sure that you have ample space in which to work, whether it be on the floor, a desk, or table.

2. Turn off the computer's power switch, and then unplug the computer. In addition to endangering you, opening a PC while it's turned on can damage its internal circuitry.

3. Attach the ground strap to your wrist and make sure that it's connected to the ground mat underneath the computer.

4. Open the computer's case. Desktop computer cases are attached in several different ways. They might use four or six Phillips-head screws to attach the housing to the back panel or they might not use any screws and slide off instead. Remove all necessary screws and slide the computer's case off.

5. Select a slot on the computer's system board where you will insert the network adapter. Make sure that the slot matches the type of expansion card you have. Remove the metal slot cover for that slot from the back of the PC. Some slot covers are attached with Phillips-head screws; others are merely metal parts with perforated edges that you can punch out with your fingers.

6. Insert the network adapter by lining up its slot connector with the slot and pressing it firmly into the slot. Don't be afraid to press down hard, but make sure the expansion card is properly aligned with the slot when you do so. If you have correctly inserted the network adapter, you should not be able to wiggle it from side to side. If you can wiggle it, press it in farther. A loose network adapter will cause connectivity problems. Figure 6-10 depicts a properly inserted network adapter.

Figure 6-10 A properly inserted network adapter

7. The metal bracket at the end of the network adapter should now be positioned where the metal slot cover was located before you removed the slot cover. Attach the bracket with a Phillips-head screw to the back of the computer cover to secure the network adapter in place.

8. Make sure that you have not loosened any cables or cards inside the PC or left any screws or debris inside the computer.

9. Replace the cover on the computer and reinsert the screws that you removed in Step 4, if applicable.

10. Plug in the computer and turn it on. Proceed to configure the network adapter's software, as discussed later in this chapter.

Installing a PC Card network adapter is much easier than installing an expansion card network adapter. In general, you can simply turn off the machine, insert the PC Card into the PC Card slot, as shown in Figure 6-11, then turn on the computer. Most modern operating systems (such as Windows 2000) allow you to insert and remove the PC Card adapter without restarting the machine. Make sure that the PC Card is firmly inserted. If you can wiggle it, you need to push it in farther.

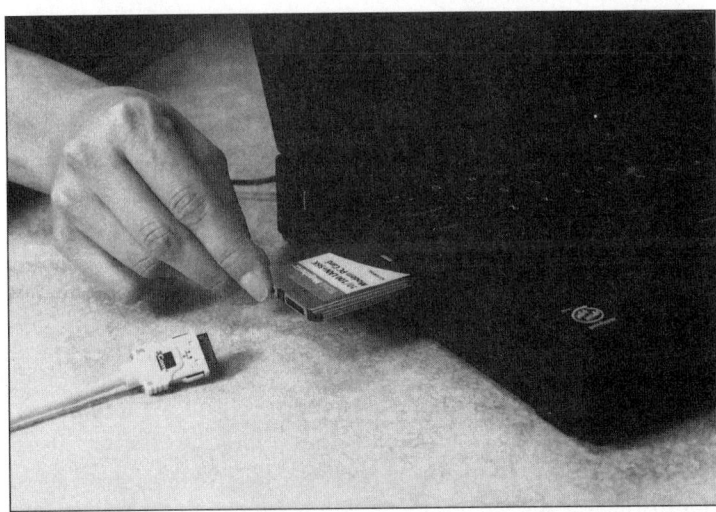

Figure 6-11   Installing a PC Card network adapter

Physically installing other types of external network adapters, such as parallel port or USB port adapters, is similar. All you need to do is insert the device into the computer's port, making sure that it is securely attached.

On servers and other high-powered computers, you may need to install multiple network adapters. For the hardware installation, you can simply repeat the installation process for the first network adapter, choosing a different slot. The trick to using multiple network adapters on one machine lies in correctly configuring the software for each network adapter. Simple network adapter configuration is covered in the following section. The exact steps involved in configuring network adapters on servers will depend on the server's networking operating system. Chapters 8 and 9 will describe the network adapter configuration process for servers running the Windows 2000 Server and NetWare network operating systems.

On older expansion board network adapters, rather than using firmware utilities to modify settings, you may need to use, or set, a jumper. A **jumper** is a small, removable piece of plastic that contains a metal receptacle. This metal receptacle fits over a pair of pins on a circuit board to form a bridge that completes a circuit between those two pins. By moving the jumper from one set of pins to another set of pins, you can modify the board's circuit, thereby giving it different instructions. Jumper settings may be used to indicate an "on/off" situation or in more complex configurations, they may indicate one of multiple options. Figure 6-12 depicts how a jumper and a row of three pins can be used to indicate two different settings.

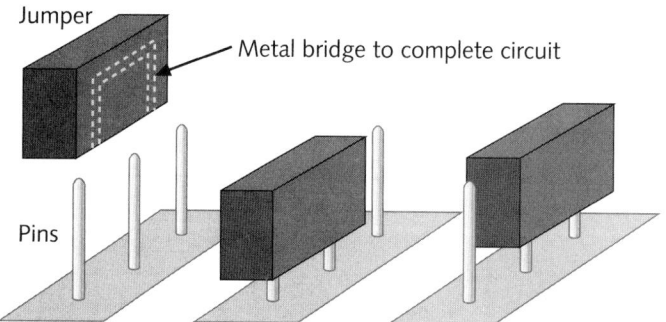

Figure 6-12   A jumper and a row of pins indicating two different settings

Jumpers are still used on hard drive controllers and system boards today, but rarely on modern network adapters. However, older NICs (such as those manufactured up to the mid-1990s) may use jumpers to modify their settings, including their transmission rate and duplexing capabilities. If you work on a network adapter that uses jumpers in its configuration, you must have the adapter's documentation in order to know which jumper settings correspond to which parameter setting. Jumper settings on one type of NIC will likely be different from those on another type of NIC.

Another method of changing parameters on a network adapter is by modifying the position of a DIP (dual inline package) switch. A **DIP switch** is a small, plastic toggle switch that can represent an "on" or "off" status. This status indicates a parameter setting. Just as with jumpers, DIP switches may be used to modify system resource settings such as the NIC's IRQ or other settings such as its maximum transmission speed. And as with jumpers, DIP switches are rarely used on modern NICs. You must have the documentation for the adapter in order to know which DIP switch settings represent a particular configuration. Figure 6-13 depicts a row of DIP switches on a NIC.

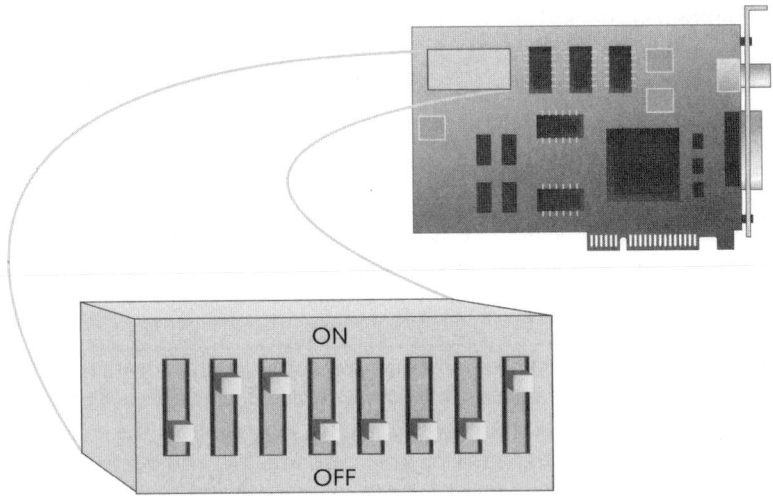

Figure 6-13 DIP switches on a NIC

 Jumpers and DIP switches are both small and somewhat fragile components of a circuit board and as such, require care when handling. Jumpers can be easily dropped and are so small that they may get lost. One way to avoid this is to handle them with tweezers. DIP switches can be broken if they are handled roughly. To change the position of a DIP switch, you can use the tip of a paperclip or a small screwdriver.

Installing and Configuring Network Adapter Software

Even if your computer runs Windows 2000, Windows 9x, or an older Windows operating system with plug-and-play technology, you must ensure that the correct device driver is installed for the network adapter and that it is configured properly. A **device driver** is software that enables an attached device to communicate with the computer's operating system. When you purchase a computer that already contains an attached peripheral (such as a sound card), the device drivers should already be installed. However, when you add hardware, you must install the device drivers too. Some operating systems, such as Windows 2000, come with a multitude of built-in device drivers. In that case, after you physically install new hardware and reboot, the operating system will automatically recognize the hardware and install the device's drivers. Each time a computer boots up, the device drivers for all its connected peripherals are loaded into RAM so that the computer can communicate with those devices at any time.

In other cases, the operating system might not contain appropriate device drivers for the hardware you've added. This section describes how to install and configure network adapter software on a Windows 2000 Professional desktop operating system that does not contain the correct device drivers. For other operating systems, the process will be similar. Regardless of which operating system you use, you should first refer to the network adapter's documentation, because your situation may vary. Read the network adapter documentation carefully before installing the relevant drivers, and make sure you are installing the appropriate drivers. Performing a Windows 95 installation on a Windows 2000 computer, for example, may cause problems.

The following steps describe a typical network adapter software installation from a Windows 2000 interface. For this process, you will need access to the Windows 2000 software (via either a Windows 2000 CD or hard disk) and the floppy disk that came with the network adapter. This floppy disk should contain device drivers specific to your network adapter.

 If you do not have the floppy disk that shipped with the network adapter and the Windows 2000 software does not supply device drivers for your network adapter, you can download the network adapter software from the manufacturer's Web site. If you choose this option, make sure that you get the appropriate drivers for your operating system and network adapter type. Also, make sure that the drivers you download are the most current version (sometimes called "shipping drivers") and not beta-level (unsupported) drivers.

To install and configure NIC software:

1. Physically install the network adapter, and then restart the PC.

2. As long as you haven't disabled the plug-and-play technology in the computer's CMOS settings, Windows 2000 should automatically detect the new hardware. Upon detecting the network adapter, it should also install the NIC's driver. In many cases, you need not install any other software or adjust the configuration in order for the NIC to operate properly.

3. There are certain situations in which you might want to change or update the device driver that the operating system has chosen, however. To do this, right-click the **My Computer** icon and click **Properties**. The System Properties dialog box appears. (You may also reach the System Properties dialog box as follows: click Start, point to Settings, click Control Panel, and then double-click the System icon.)

4. Click the **Hardware** tab.

5. Click the **Device Manager** button.

6. The Device Manager window opens, with a list of installed devices. Double-click the **Network adapters** icon. A list of installed network adapters appears.

7. Double-click the adapter for which you want to install new device drivers. The network adapter's Properties dialog box appears.

8. Select the **Driver** tab. Details about your network adapter's current driver appear.

9. Click **Update Driver**. A Windows 2000 wizard appears to walk you through the device driver update process.

10. Click **Next** to continue. You are asked to choose whether you want Windows to select the most appropriate driver or whether you want to be prompted for suitable drivers.

11. Click the "Display a list of the known drivers for this device so that I can choose a specific driver" radio button, then click **Next** to continue. You are asked to choose the network adapter for which you want to install a new driver, as shown in Figure 6-14.

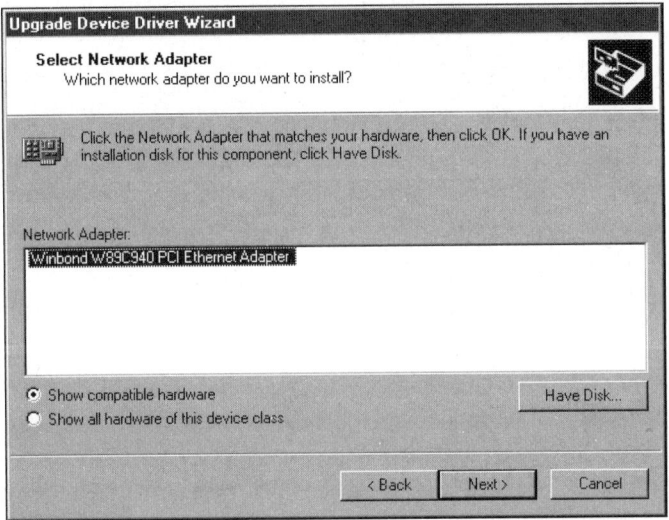

Figure 6-14   Windows 2000 Upgrade Device Driver Wizard

12. If your computer has more than one NIC, click the one whose drivers you want to upgrade, then click **Have Disk**. The Install from Disk dialog box appears.

13. Insert the disk that came with the network adapter into your floppy drive.

14. You will be prompted to enter the path for the appropriate driver or click **Browse** to find the driver's directory on your disk. The drivers will probably appear in a subdirectory on the disk, because most network adapters ship with a single disk that contains drivers for multiple platforms. Once you select the correct path, click **OK**.

15. If the disk sent with the network adapter contains drivers for more than one type of network adapter, you will be asked to select the precise model you are using. After making your choice, click **OK**.

16. The driver files for the network adapter will be installed onto your hard disk and their specifications written to the Registry. In the process, you may be asked for the location of the Windows 2000 system files. If so, insert the Windows 2000 installation CD. When prompted, direct the installation program to that drive (usually D:, E:, or F:), then click **OK**.

17. Once the network adapter drivers have been successfully installed, you will be prompted to restart your PC. Confirm that you want to restart it by clicking **Yes**.

The preceding steps will work in most situations. Because every situation is different, however, you should always read the manufacturer's documentation and follow its installation instructions. Some manufacturers supply setup programs that automatically install and register network adapter software once you run them, thereby eliminating the need to follow the steps outlined above.

The next sections describe the variable settings you should understand when configuring network adapters. Depending on your computer's use of resources, network adapter configuration may or may not be necessary after installation. For troubleshooting purposes, however, you need to understand how to view and adjust these variables. If you completed coursework for the A+ certification or have worked with PCs in the past, you should already be familiar with these variables.

IRQ (Interrupt Request)   When a device attached to a computer's bus, such as a keyboard or floppy disk drive, requires attention from the computer's processor, it uses an interrupt request. An **interrupt request (IRQ)**, as its name implies, is a message to the computer that instructs it to stop what it is doing and pay attention to something else. An **interrupt** is the wire on which a device issues voltage to signal this request. Each interrupt must have a unique **IRQ number**, a number that uniquely identifies that component to the main bus. An IRQ number is the means by which the bus understands which device to acknowledge. The term "IRQ" is frequently substituted for "IRQ number" in casual conversation, even though they are technically two different things.

IRQ numbers range from 0 to 15. Many computer devices reserve the same IRQ number by default no matter what type of system. For example, on every type of computer, a floppy disk controller claims IRQ 6 and a keyboard controller takes IRQ 1. On the other hand, some IRQ numbers are not reserved by default, but are available to additional devices such as sound cards, graphics cards, modems, and network adapters. Most often, network adapters will use IRQ 9, 10, or 11. In order to obtain Network+ certification, you should be familiar with the IRQ numbers reserved by common computer devices as well as those most apt to be used by network adapters. Table 6-1 lists all of the IRQ numbers and their default device assignments, if they have any.

Table 6-1   IRQ assignments

IRQ Number	Typical Device Assignment
0	System timer (only)
1	Keyboard controller (only)
2	Access to IRQs 8–15
3	COM2 (second serial port) or COM4 (fourth serial port)
4	COM1 (first serial port) or COM3 (third serial port)
5	Sound card or LPT2 (second parallel port)
6	Floppy disk drive controller
7	LPT1 (parallel port 1)
8	Real-time clock (only)
9	No default assignment
10	No default assignment
11	No default assignment
12	PS/2 mouse
13	Math coprocessor (only)
14	IDE channel (for example, an IDE hard disk drive)
15	Secondary IDE channel

Generally, if two devices attempt to use the same interrupt, resource conflicts and performance problems will result. For example, if a keyboard uses IRQ number 1 and you configure the network adapter to use IRQ number 1 as well (if the operating system allows you do this), the computer's CPU will not know whether the request received through interrupt number 1 comes from the computer or the network adapter; thus the CPU will be unable to follow the instructions of either device.

 Some plug-and-play devices are designed to coexist with other devices on the same IRQ. In such a situation, having two or more devices assigned to the same IRQ may not present a problem.

If IRQ conflicts occur, you must manually reassign a device's IRQ. Keep in mind that the BIOS or the operating system will attempt to assign free IRQs. Typically, it will assign IRQs 9, 10, or 11 to network adapters, because other devices do usually not take these numbers. The BIOS or the operating system can be wrong, however.

When two devices attempt to use the same IRQ, any of the following problems may occur:

- The computer may lock up or "hang" either upon starting or when the operating system is loading.

- The computer may run much more slowly than usual.

- Although the computer's network adapter may work properly, other devices—such as serial or parallel ports—may stop working.

- Video or sound card problems may occur. For example, after the operating system loads, you may see an error message indicating that the video settings are incorrect, or your sound card may stop working.

- The computer may fail to connect to the network (as evidenced by an error message after you attempt to log onto a server).

- The computer may experience intermittent data errors during transmission.

To view IRQ settings on computers running Windows 2000 Professional:

1. Right-click the **My Computer** icon. A shortcut menu opens.

2. Click **Properties**. The System Properties dialog box opens.

3. Click the **Hardware** tab.

4. Click the **Device Manager** button. The Device Manager window appears.

5. In the Device Manager menu bar, click **View**, and then click **Resources by connection**. A list of the system resources appears

6. Double-click the **Interrupt request (IRQ)** option to view your computer's IRQ assignments, as shown in Figure 6-15.

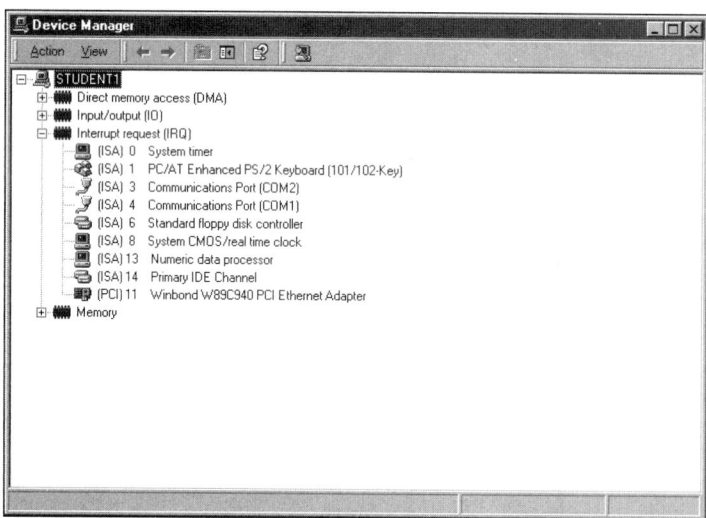

Figure 6-15   Computer resource settings in Windows 2000

You can also view IRQ settings in the computer's CMOS utility. **CMOS (complementary metal oxide semiconductor)** is a type of microchip that requires very little energy to operate. In a PC, the CMOS holds settings pertaining to the configuration of a computer's devices, among other things. These settings are saved even after you turn off a PC because the CMOS is powered by a small battery in your computer. Information saved in CMOS is used by the computer's **BIOS (basic input/output system)**. The BIOS is a simple set of instructions that enables a computer to initially recognize its hardware. When you turn on a computer, the BIOS performs its start-up tasks. Once a computer is up and running, the BIOS provides an interface between the computer's software and hardware, allowing it to recognize which device is associated with each IRQ.

Although you can usually modify IRQ settings in the CMOS utility, whether you can change them from the operating system software depends on the type of network adapter involved. For example, on a PCI network adapter, which requires a PCI bus controller, the PCI controller's settings will dictate whether this type of modification is possible. The default setting prevents you from changing the network adapter's IRQ from the operating system; if you attempt to make this change on a Windows 2000 computer, for example, in the Resources tab in the PCI network adapter's Properties dialog, a box titled "No modifications allowed" will display the following message: "This resource setting cannot be modified."

Thus, if you need to alter the IRQ for a PCI network adapter, you should make the change in the CMOS. Different system board manufacturers use different keystrokes to invoke the CMOS setup program when the computer starts. You may need to press Del, Shift-F1, F10, Ctrl-Shift-Enter, or another key (or set of keys) to access the CMOS setup utility. The required keystroke or combination of keystrokes should appear on the screen shortly after the computer starts. Once you are in the CMOS setup utility, follow the menu selections until you find the network adapter IRQ setting, change it, then save your changes and restart the computer.

Sometimes you cannot access a computer's CMOS setup utility. In this case, you *may* be able to resolve an IRQ conflict by physically moving the network adapter from its present slot to another slot, by physically resetting dip switches on the network adapter, or by using a special setup program that is shipped with the network adapter. You could also try temporarily disabling or removing conflicting devices such as infrared ports or modems. Alternately, you may need to update the BIOS on the workstation. If nothing else works, you may need to install a different type or model of network adapter.

Memory Range The **memory range** indicates, in hexadecimal notation, the area of memory that the network adapter and CPU will use for exchanging, or buffering, data. As with IRQs, some memory ranges are reserved for specific devices—most notably, the system board. Reserved address ranges should never be selected for new devices.

Network adapters typically use a memory range in the high memory area, which in hexadecimal notation equates to the A0000–FFFFF range. As you work with network adapters, you will notice that some manufacturers prefer certain ranges. For example, a 3Com PC Card adapter might, by default, choose a range of C8000–C9FFF. An IBM Token Ring adapter might choose a range of D8000–D9FFF.

Memory range settings are less likely to cause resource conflicts than IRQ settings, mainly because there are more available memory ranges than IRQs. Nevertheless, you may run into situations in which you need to change a network adapter's memory address. In such an instance, you may or may not be able to change the memory range from the operating system. Refer to the manufacturer's guidelines for instructions.

Base I/O Port   The **base I/O port** setting specifies, in hexadecimal notation, which area of memory will act as a channel for moving data between the network adapter and the CPU. Like its IRQ, a device's base I/O port cannot be used by any other device. Most network adapters use two memory ranges for this channel, and the base I/O port settings identify the beginning of each range. Although a network adapter's base I/O port will vary depending on the manufacturer, some popular addresses (in hexadecimal notation) are 300 (which means that the range is 300–30F), 310, 280, or 2F8.

You will probably not need to change a network adapter's base I/O port. If you do, bear in mind that, as with IRQ settings, base I/O port settings for PCI cards can be changed in the computer's CMOS setup utility or sometimes through the operating system.

Firmware Settings   Once you have adjusted the network adapter's system resources, you may need to modify its transmission characteristics—for example, whether it uses full duplexing or whether it can detect a network's speed. These settings are held in the adapter's firmware. As mentioned earlier, firmware comprises the combination of an EEPROM chip on the network adapter and the data it holds. When you change the firmware, you are actually writing to the EEPROM chip on the network adapter. You are not writing to the computer's hard disk. Although most configurable settings can be changed in the operating system or network adapter setup software, you may encounter complex networking problems that require a change to firmware settings.

To change a network adapter's firmware, you will need a bootable floppy disk (DOS version 6.0 or higher) containing the configuration or DOS install utility that shipped with the network adapter. If you don't have the utility, you can usually download it from the manufacturer's Web site. To run the utility, you must start the computer with this floppy disk inserted. The network adapter configuration utility may not run if an operating system or memory management program is already running.

Each configuration utility will differ slightly, but all should allow you to view the IRQ, I/O port, base memory, and node address. Some may allow you to change settings such as the network adapter's CPU utilization, its ability to handle full duplexing, or its capability to be used with only 10BaseT or 100BaseT media, for example (although many of these can also be changed through the network adapter's properties from the operating system interface). The changeable settings will vary depending on the manufacturer. Again, read the manufacturer's documentation to find out the details for your hardware.

Network adapter configuration utilities also allow you to perform diagnostics—tests of the network adapter's physical components and connectivity. Most of the tests can be performed without additional hardware. However, in order to perform the entire group of the diagnostic tests on the NIC's utility disk, you must have a loopback plug. A **loopback plug** is a connector that plugs into a port, such as a serial or parallel or an RJ-45 port, and crosses over the transmit line to the receive line so that outgoing signals can be redirected back into the computer for testing. One connectivity test, called a loopback test, requires you to install a loopback plug into the network adapter's media connector. Note that none of the connectivity tests should be performed on a live network. If a network adapter fails its connectivity tests, it is probably configured incorrectly. If a network adapter fails a physical component test, it may need to be replaced.

The word loopback implies that signals are routed back toward their source, rather than toward an external destination. When used in the context of network adapters, the loopback test refers to a check of the adapter's ability to transmit and receive signals. Recall that the term "loopback" is also used in the context of TCP/IP protocol testing. In that context, pinging the loopback address provides you with information on TCP/IP functionality.

Choosing the Right Network Adapter

You should consider several factors when choosing a network adapter for your workstation or server. Of course, the most critical factor is compatibility with your existing system. You will need to determine whether your workstation requires an ISA, EISA, MCA or PCI card in addition to choosing a network adapter that matches your network's media, connector types, transmission speed, and network model. You also need to ensure that drivers available for that network adapter will work with your operating system.

Beyond these considerations, however, you should examine more subtle differences, such as those that affect network performance. Table 6-2 lists some features available on network adapters that specifically influence performance and ease of use. As you review this table, keep in mind that performance is especially important if the network adapter will be installed in a server.

Table 6-2   Network adapter characteristics

NIC Feature	Function	Benefit
Automatic speed selection	Enables NICs to automatically sense and adapt to a network's speed and mode (half- or full-duplex)	Aids configuration and performance
One or more on-board NIC CPU	Allows the card to perform some data processing independently of the PC's CPU	Improves performance
Direct Memory Access (DMA)	Enables the card to directly transfer data to the computer's memory	Improves performance
Diagnostic LEDs (lights on the NIC)	Indicate traffic, connectivity, and, sometimes, speed	Aid in troubleshooting (for more information, see Chapter 12)
Dual channels	Effectively creates two NICs in one slot	Improves performance; suited to servers
Load balancing	Allows the NIC's processor to determine when to switch traffic between internal cards	Improves performance for heavily-trafficked networks; suited to servers
"Look Ahead" transmit and receive	Allows the NIC's processor to begin processing data before it has received the entire packet	Improves performance
Management capabilities (SNMP)	Allows the NIC to perform its own monitoring and troubleshooting, usually through installed application software	Aids in troubleshooting, can find a problem before it becomes dire
Power management capabilities	Allows a NIC to participate in the computer's power saving measures; found on PC Card	Increases the life of the battery for laptop computers
RAM buffering	Provides additional memory on the NIC, which in turn provides more space for data buffering	Improves performance
Upgradeable (flash) ROM	Allows on-board chip memory to be upgraded	May improve ease of use and performance

The quality of the printed documentation that you receive from a manufacturer about its network adapters may vary. What's more, this documentation may not apply to the kinds of computers or networking environments you are using. To find out more about the type of network adapter you are installing or troubleshooting, visit the manufacturer's Web site.

REPEATERS

Now that you have learned about the many types of network adapters and how to install and configure them, you are ready to learn about connectivity devices. As you'll recall from Chapter 4, the telecommunications closet is the area containing the connectivity equipment (usually for a whole floor of a building). Within the telecommunications closet, horizontal cabling from the workstations attaches to punch-down blocks, patch panels, hubs, switches, routers, and bridges. In addition, telecommunications closets may house repeaters. As you learned in Chapter 4, repeaters are the connectivity devices that regenerate a digital signal.

Repeaters operate in the Physical layer of the OSI Model and, therefore, have no means to interpret the data they retransmit. For example, they cannot improve or correct a bad or erroneous signal; they merely repeat it. In this sense, they are not "intelligent" devices. Since they cannot read higher-layer information in the data packets, repeaters cannot direct data to their destination. Instead, repeaters simply regenerate a signal over an entire segment. It is up to the receiver to recognize and accept its data.

A repeater is limited not only in function, but also in scope. A repeater contains one input port and one output port, as shown in Figure 6-16, so it is capable of receiving and repeating only the data stream. Furthermore, repeaters are suited only to bus topology networks. The advantage to using a repeater is that it allows you to extend a network inexpensively.

For example, suppose that you need to connect a single PC located in a school's gymnasium to the rest of the network, that the nearest data jack is 220 meters away, and that you are using 10Base2 Ethernet, which limits the maximum cable length to 185 meters. In this instance, you could use a repeater to add 185 meters to the existing 185-meter limitation and connect the gymnasium workstation to the network. Bear in mind that the overall network distance limitations still apply. Because the entire network cannot exceed 1000 meters, you cannot use more than five repeaters in sequence to extend the cabling's reach.

Figure 6-16   Repeaters

Hubs

At its most primitive, a **hub** is a multiport repeater. A simple hub may contain multiple ports that can connect a group of computers in a peer-to-peer fashion, accepting and repeating signals from each node. A slightly more sophisticated hub may contain multiple ports for devices and one port that connects to a network's backbone. On Ethernet networks, hubs typically serve as the central connection point for branches of a star or star-based hybrid topology. On Token Ring networks, hubs are called Multistation Access Units (MAUs) and are used to connect nodes in a star-based ring topology. As you learned in Chapter 5, MAUs internally complete the ring topology using their Ring In and Ring Out ports.

In addition to connecting Macintosh and PC workstations, hubs can connect print servers, switches, file servers, or other devices to a network. They can support a variety of different media and data transmission speeds. Some hubs also allow for multiple media connector types or multiple data transmission speeds. As you can imagine, you can choose from a huge number of different hubs. By classifying hubs into categories according to their uses and features, however, you will quickly get the lay of the land and soon learn to understand any hub. Figure 6-17 details the various elements of a hub, some of which are optional. The elements shared by most hubs are described next.

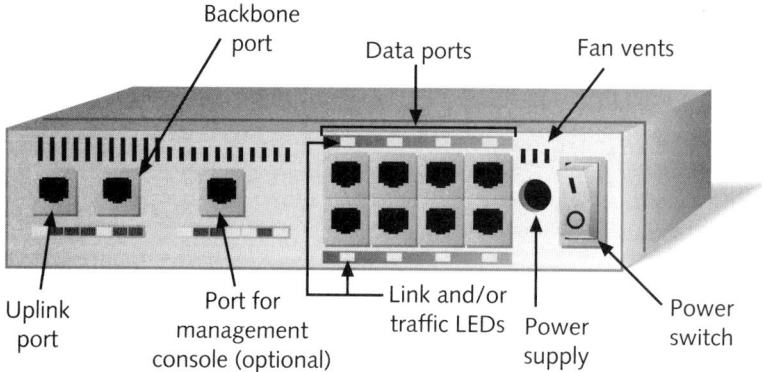

Figure 6-17   Detailed diagram of a hub

- *Ports*—Receptacles where patch cables connect workstations or other devices to the hub. The type of receptacle (RJ-45 versus BNC, for example) will depend on your network technology. The number of ports on a hub generally ranges from 4 to 24, but can be higher. This number does not include the uplink port, described below.

- *Uplink port*—The receptacle used to connect one hub to another hub in a daisy-chain or hierarchical fashion. An uplink port may look like any other port, but it should be used only to interconnect hubs.

- *Port for management console*—A receptacle used to connect some type of display, or console (such as a laptop PC), that enables you to view the hub's management information, such as the traffic load or number of collisions. Not all hubs provide management information, so not all have a management console port.

- *Backbone port*—The receptacle used to connect a hub to the network's backbone.

- *Link LED*—The light on a port that indicates whether it is in use. If a connection is live, this light should be solid green. If no connection exists, the light will be off. If you think that the connection is live but the light is not on, you need to check connections, transmission speed settings, and power supplies for both the network adapter and the hub.

- *Traffic (transmit or receive) LED*—The light on a port that indicates that traffic is passing through the port. Under normal data traffic situations, this light should blink green. Some hubs include separate LEDs for the transmission and receipt of data; others do not even have traffic LEDs for their ports. If they exist, traffic LEDs are normally found adjacent to link LEDs beside each data port.

- *Collision LED (Ethernet hubs only)*—The light that roughly indicates collisions by blinking. The faster the light blinks, the more collisions that are occurring on the network. The hub may include one collision LED for the entire hub or individual lights for each port. If this light is continuously lit, a node is experiencing dire connectivity or traffic problems and may need to be disconnected. Because only Ethernet hubs have collision LEDs, Figure 6-17 does not show one.

6

- *Power supply*—The device that provides power to the hub. Every hub has its own power supply (for this reason, you will want to connect critical hubs to a UPS, as explained in Chapter 14). Every hub also has its own power-on light. If the power-on light is not lit, the hub has lost power. The power light is normally found on the front of a hub, and so is not shown in Figure 6-17.

- *Ventilation fan*—A device used to cool a device's internal electronics. Hubs, like other electronic devices, generate heat. To function properly, most hubs must cool their processors, components, and circuitry with a ventilation fan (although very small hubs may not require a ventilation fan). When installing, you should be careful not to block or cover the air-intake vents.

Placement of hubs in a network design can vary. The simplest structure would employ a standalone workgroup hub that is connected to another connectivity device such as a switch or router. Most networks use several hubs to serve different workgroups, thereby benefiting from not having a single point of failure and possibly having switching and data management abilities. Figure 6-18 indicates how hubs may fit into the overall design of a network.

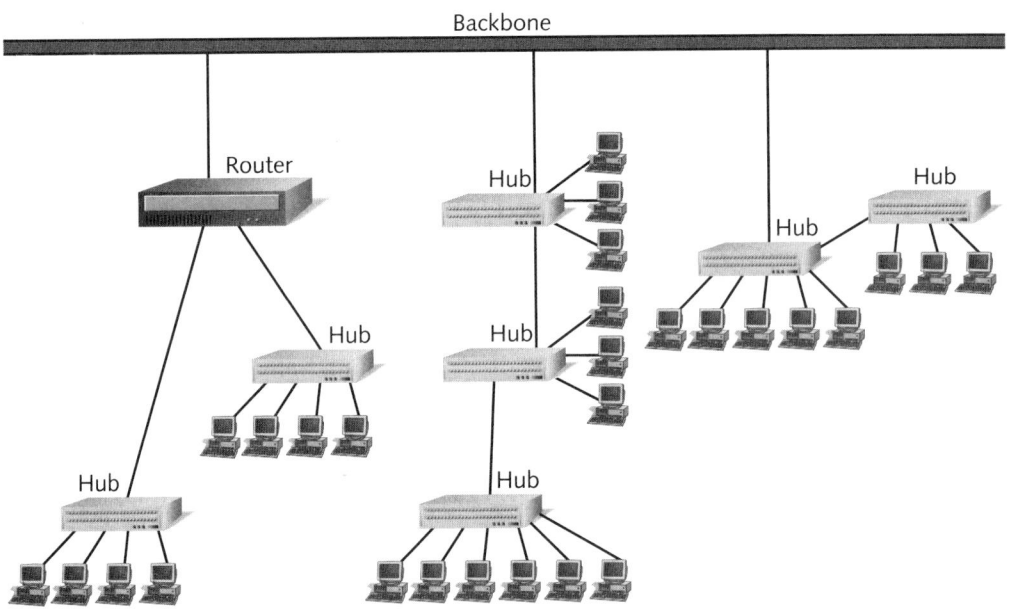

Figure 6-18   Hubs in a network design

Many hubs—known as **passive hubs**—do nothing but repeat signals. Like network adapters, however, some hubs possess internal processing capabilities. For example, they may permit remote management, filter data, or provide diagnostic information about the network. Hubs that can perform any of these functions are known as **intelligent hubs**.

Technological advances are making hubs more capable and more vital in network management. The following sections introduce the different types of hubs, their functions, advantages, and disadvantages. Hubs represent a significant element in network design, configuration, and troubleshooting. To prepare for the Net+ certification exam, you should pay close attention to the material in the following sections.

Standalone Hubs

Standalone hubs, as their name implies, are hubs that serve a group of computers that are isolated from the rest of the network. A standalone hub may be connected to another hub by a coaxial, fiber-optic, or twisted-pair cable; however, they are typically not connected in a hierarchical or daisy-chain fashion. Standalone hubs are best suited to small, independent departments, home offices, or test lab environments. They can be passive or intelligent, and they are simple to install and connect for a small group of users.

Standalone hubs do not follow one design, nor do they contain a standard number of ports (though they usually contain 4, 8, 12, or 24 ports). A small, standalone hub that contains only four ports (primarily used for a small or home office) may be called a "hubby," "hublet," or a "minihub." On the other hand, standalone hubs can provide as many as 200 connection ports. The disadvantage to using a single hub for so many connections is that you introduce a single point of failure on the network. A **single point of failure** is a device or connection on a network that, were it to fail, could cause the entire network to stop functioning. In general, a large network would include multiple hubs (or other connectivity devices). Figure 6-19 depicts some standalone hubs.

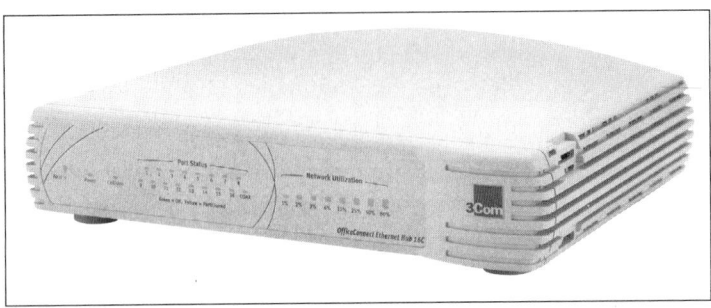

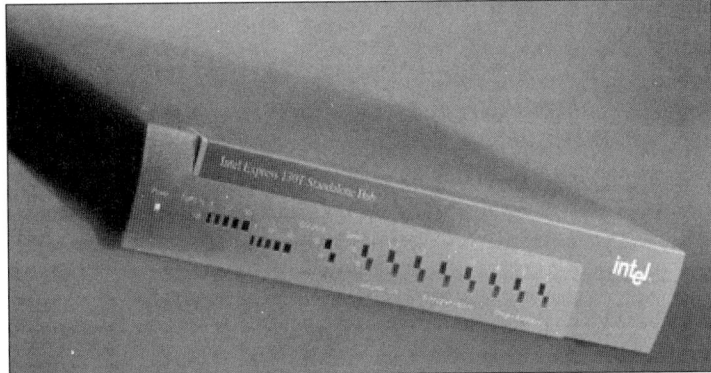

Figure 6-19   Standalone hubs

Stackable Hubs

Stackable hubs resemble standalone hubs, but they are physically designed to be linked with other hubs in a single telecommunications closet. Stackable hubs linked together logically represent one large hub to the network. A great benefit to using stackable hubs is that your network or workgroup does not depend on a single hub, which could present a single point of failure.

Models vary in the maximum number that can be stacked. For instance, some hub manufacturers restrict the number of their stacked hubs to five; others can be stacked eight units high.

Although many stackable hubs include Ethernet uplink ports, some use a proprietary high-speed cabling system to link the hubs together for better interhub performance. This setup often creates incompatibilities between the bus cabling of different product lines, even when those products come from the same manufacturer. Hubs that use standard Ethernet uplink ports can usually be interconnected with components of other product lines. As a general rule, although stacked hubs do not have to be made by the same manufacturer to work together properly, it is always preferable to interconnect hardware that is known to be compatible right out of the box.

Like standalone hubs, stackable hubs may support a number of different media connectors and transmission speeds and may come with or without special processing features. The number of ports they provide also varies, although you will most often see

6, 12, or 24 ports on a stackable hub. Figure 6-20 depicts a variety of stackable hubs, and Figure 6-21 shows a rack-mounted stackable hub system, such as you might find in a telecommunications closet.

Figure 6-20   Stackable hubs

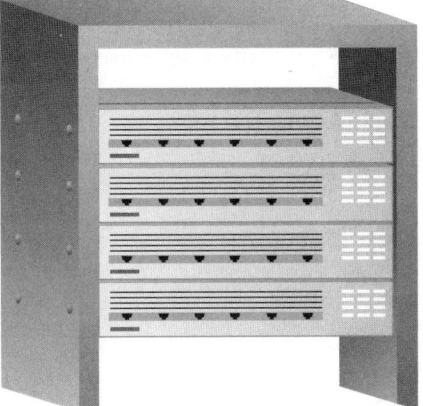

Figure 6-21   Rack-mounted stackable hubs

Modular Hubs

Modular hubs provide a number of interface options within one chassis, making them more flexible than either stackable or standalone hubs. Similar to a PC, a modular hub contains a system board and slots into which you can insert different adapters. These adapters may connect the modular hub to other types of hubs, routers, WAN links, or Token Ring or Ethernet network backbones. They may also connect the modular hub to management workstations or redundant (extra) components, such as a second power supply. Because you can attach redundant components to modular hubs, they offer the highest reliability of any type of hub. Another benefit to modular hubs is that they allow for a network's future growth by providing expansion slots for additional devices. In addition, they can accommodate many types of devices. In other words, you can customize a modular hub to your network's needs. On the downside, modular hubs are the most expensive type of hub, and for a small network they may be overkill. Modular hubs are nearly always intelligent hubs.

Intelligent Hubs

Earlier in this chapter, you learned that an intelligent hub can process data, monitor traffic, and provide troubleshooting information, among other things. Intelligent hubs are also called **managed hubs**, because they can be managed from anywhere on the network. Remember that standalone, stackable, or modular hubs may all have processing capabilities and, therefore, be considered intelligent.

The advantage of intelligent hubs derives from their ability to analyze data. A network administrator can store the information generated by intelligent hubs in a MIB. A **MIB (management information base)** is a collection of data used by management programs (which may be part of the network operating system or third-party programs) to analyze network performance and problems. MIBs are typically used by programs that generate data via the SNMP protocol. Novell's ManageWise is one example of a program that relies on MIBs. From such a program, the network administrator can view the network layout in graphical form, disconnect problem nodes, set alarms to go off when certain events occur, identify nodes that may be generating unnecessary traffic, or find out information (such as IP addresses) about remote nodes. Using this tool, the network administrator can also track historical data about network traffic patterns—for example, to determine where greater bandwidth is needed.

Although you might be tempted to assume that intelligent hubs are your best solution in every situation, they have their disadvantages. For example, an intelligent hub will report every time a port detects a lost connection. In fact, lost connections happen hundreds of times each day—when a formerly connected workstation is restarted, for example. This event, its trivial nature notwithstanding, is recorded in the MIB, along with hundreds of other inconsequential events. When the MIB includes so many inconsequential events, network administrators may find it difficult to determine which errors are critical and which can be ignored. In addition, intelligent hubs are significantly more expensive than passive hubs. For a routine networking environment with limited staff, intelligent hubs might be more trouble than they are worth.

Installing a Hub

As with network adapters, the best way to ensure that you install a hub properly is to follow the manufacturer's guidelines. Most of the time, hubs are simple to install—arguably even simpler than connecting workstations to the network, because they require very little configuration.

First, plug the hub in and turn it on. Make sure that the hub's power light goes on. Most hubs will perform self-tests when turned on, and blinking lights will indicate that these tests are in progress. When the tests are completed (as indicated by a steady, lit power light on most hubs), attach the hub to the network by connecting a patch cable from it to the backbone or to an intermediate switch or router. Next, connect patch cables from the patch panel or workstations to the hub's receptacles, as shown in Figure 6-22. Once the workstation connects to the network through the newly installed hub, check to verify that the link and traffic lights act as they should, according to the hub's documentation.

6

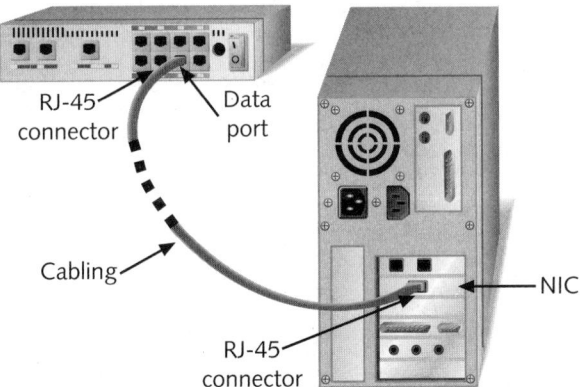

Figure 6-22   Connecting a workstation to a hub

Unless you are using a small, inexpensive hub, you will probably need to configure the hub's firmware and, in the case of intelligent hubs, its software as well. For example, you will need to assign an IP address to the hub. Refer to the instructions that came with your hub to find out how to configure its firmware and software.

If you are installing a stackable hub or a rack-mounted hub, you will need to use the screws and clamps that came with the hub to secure it to the rack or connect it to the other hubs. In the case of a stackable hub, you may need to connect it with its proprietary cabling or through its uplink port. Again, the best approach is to read the instructions that came with the hub.

Choosing the Right Hub

Any one of thousands of hubs might work on your network. So how do you decide which is right for you? First, narrow your list of options to hubs that match your network's logical topology, transmission speed, and media type. Then examine the following list of variables and decide which enhancements are necessary for your network and how much you can afford.

- *Performance*—If performance is your concern, you may want to use switches, rather than hubs, to subdivide a current LAN segment into several, smaller segments. You may also want to upgrade part of your network to a faster transmission technology (for example, from 10BaseT to 100BaseTX). To support this transition, you may need a hub that can handle traffic at *either* 10 Mbps or 100 Mbps. Because of the way in which hubs work, you should avoid mixing hubs that can handle only speeds of 10 Mbps with hubs that can handle speeds of 100 Mbps, because all 100 Mbps devices will be slowed down by the presence of even a single 10-Mbps device. Switches (discussed later in this chapter) do support the mixing of speeds.

- *Cost*—If your budget is tight and your environment does not demand the flexibility, reliability, or security of more sophisticated hubs, a passive stand-alone hub or a few passive stackable hubs might be your answer. If you have unlimited dollars to spend and need a hub with more features, you might consider an intelligent hub.

- *Size and growth*—You need to determine how many devices will connect to each hub in each telecommunications closet. If one segment consists of only 10 connections now but you know its size will double in six months, purchase a hub with at least 24 ports. (You must balance the number of hubs with the number of points of failure you are willing to risk on the network.)

- *Security*—If your network carries sensitive data, you should probably consider using more sophisticated connectivity equipment such as switches, routers, or firewalls.

- *Management benefits*—If you manage a huge enterprise-wide network containing many different types of devices and potential problems, you will want to purchase an intelligent hub, which is capable of providing management information to your network management program. This purchase will require more planning and technical expertise than other types of hubs.

- *Reliability*—If your network cannot tolerate any downtime, consider purchasing a modular hub with redundant power supplies and possibly redundant connections to the backbone as well.

As with network adapters, the hub manufacturer's documentation can vary.

BRIDGES

Bridges are devices that look like repeaters, in that they have a single input and a single output port, as shown in Figure 6-23. They differ from repeaters in that they can interpret the data they retransmit. Bridging occurs at the Data Link layer of the OSI Model; as you will recall from Chapter 3, this layer encompasses flow control, error handling, and physical addressing. Bridges analyze incoming frames and make decisions about how to direct them to their destination. Specifically, they read the destination (MAC) address information and decide whether to forward (retransmit) the packet to another segment on the network or, if the destination address belongs to the same segment as the source address, filter (discard) it. As nodes transmit data through the bridge, the bridge establishes a **filtering database** (also known as a **forwarding table**) of known MAC addresses and their locations on the network. The bridge uses its filtering database to determine whether a packet should be forwarded or filtered, as illustrated in Figure 6-24.

6

Figure 6-23   A bridge

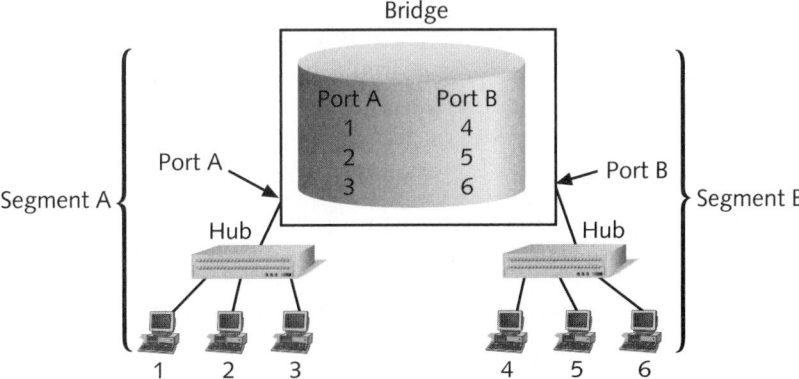

Figure 6-24   A bridge's use of a filtering database

Using Figure 6-24 as an example, imagine that you sit at workstation 1 on segment A of the LAN, and your colleague Abby sits at workstation 2 on segment A. When you attempt to send data to Abby's computer, your transmission will go through your segment's hub and then to the bridge. The bridge will read the MAC address of Abby's computer. It will then search its filtering database to determine whether that MAC address belongs to the same segment you're on or whether it belongs on a different segment. The bridge can determine only that the MAC address of Abby's workstation is associated with its port A. If the MAC address belongs to a different segment, the bridge forwards the data to that segment, whose corresponding port identity is also in the filtering database. In this case, however, your workstation and Abby's workstation reside on the same LAN segment, so the data would be filtered (that is ignored) and your message would be delivered to Abby's workstation through segment A's hub.

Conversely, if you wanted to send data to your supervisor's computer, which is workstation 5 in Figure 6-24, your transmission would first pass through segment A's hub and then on to the bridge. The bridge would read the MAC address for your supervisor's machine (the destination address in your data stream) and search for the port associated with that machine. In this case, the bridge would recognize workstation 5 as being connected to port B, and it would forward the data to that port. Subsequently, the segment B hub would ensure delivery of the data to your supervisor's computer.

After you install a new bridge, it will use one of several methods to learn about the network and discover where the destination address for each packet it handles resides. Once it discovers this information, it will record the destination node's MAC address and its associated port in its filtering database. Over time, it will discover all nodes on the network and construct database entries for each.

Because bridges cannot interpret higher-level data, such as Network layer information, they do not distinguish between different protocols. They can forward frames from AppleTalk, TCP/IP, IPX/SPX, and NetBIOS with equal speed and accuracy. This flexibility is a great advantage. Because they are protocol-ignorant, bridges can move data more rapidly than traditional routers, for example, which do care about protocol information (as you will learn later in this chapter). On the other hand, bridges take longer to transmit data than either repeaters or hubs, because bridges actually analyze each packet, while hubs do not.

Bridges may follow one of several types of methods for forwarding or filtering packets. A discussion of each of these methods is beyond the scope of this book, but you should at least be aware of the most popular options. The method used on many Ethernet networks is called **transparent bridging**. In transparent bridging a bridge begins polling a network to learn about its physical topology as soon as it is installed. When a bridge receives a packet from an unknown source, it adds the location of that source to its filtering database. Over time, it compiles database entries for each network node, and forwards packets according to the examples discussed earlier in this section. The disadvantage of transparent bridging is that, on large LANs containing multiple bridges, each bridge may recognize a different path to a particular network node. When this is the case, data that must traverse more than one bridge to get to its destination may get bounced back and forth among the bridges. This causes packets to travel endlessly over the network, never reaching their destination. To avoid this problem, networks may use the spanning tree algorithm. The **spanning tree algorithm** is a routine that can detect circular traffic patterns and modify the way multiple bridges work together, in order to avoid such patterns.

The bridging method used on most Token Ring networks is called **source-route bridging**. In source-route bridging, a bridge polls the network to determine what path is the best way for a packet to get from point A to point B. The bridge then adds this information to the data packet. Because forwarding information becomes part of the data, source-route bridging is not susceptible to the circular traffic problems that transparent bridging may suffer. This makes source-route bridging especially well suited to WANs, where multiple bridges and long routes are common.

When bridges were first introduced in the early 1980s, they were designed to forward packets between homogenous networks. Since then, however, bridges have evolved to handle data transfer between different types of networks. A method of bridging that can connect networks that use different logical topologies is called **translational bridging**. In translational bridging, the bridge not only forwards packets, but also translates packets between one logical topology and another. Translational bridging may be used, for example, to connect a Token Ring network to an Ethernet network, or a FDDI network to an Ethernet network.

Bridges have also enjoyed advances in their filtering techniques and transmission speed. Even though sophisticated routers and switches have replaced many network bridges, bridges may still be adequate and appropriate in some situations. The inclusion of a bridge on a network enhances the network performance by filtering traffic directed to the various nodes; the nodes therefore spend less time and resources listening for data that may or may not be destined for them. Also, a bridge can detect and discard flawed packets that may create congestion on the network. Perhaps most importantly, bridges extend the maximum distance of a network beyond its previous limits.

 Standalone bridges became popular in the 1980s and early 1990s, but they have largely been made obsolete by advanced switching and routing technology. In general, you will rarely work with bridges as standalone devices. Nevertheless, understanding the concept of bridging is essential to understanding how switches work. You will learn more about switches in the next section.

SWITCHES

In recent years, advances in connectivity hardware have blurred the strict distinctions between hubs, switches, routers, and bridges. **Switches** subdivide a network into smaller logical pieces. Unlike hubs, which operate at Layer 1 of the OSI Model, they operate at the Data Link layer (Layer 2) of the OSI Model and can interpret MAC address information. In this sense, switches resemble bridges. In fact, they can be described as multiport bridges. Figure 6-25 illustrates several switches.

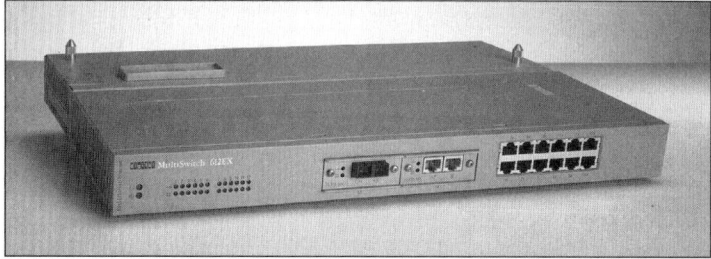

Figure 6-25   Examples of LAN switches

Because they have multiple ports, switches can make better use of limited bandwidth and prove more cost-efficient than bridges. Each port on the switch acts like a bridge, and each device connected to a switch effectively receives its own dedicated channel. In other words, a switch can turn a shared channel into several channels.

From the Ethernet perspective, each dedicated channel represents a collision domain. Recall from Chapter 5 that a collision domain is a logically or physically distinct Ethernet network segment on which all participating devices must detect and accommodate data collisions. Because a switch limits the number of devices in a collision domain, it limits the potential for collisions.

Switches have historically been used to replace hubs and ease traffic congestion in LAN workgroups. Introducing a switch on a congested segment is only a temporary solution, however, and arguably not the best use of such a device. More recently, network managers have replaced backbone routers with switches, and switch sales are, therefore, booming.

The inclusion of switches on a network backbone provides at least two advantages. First, switches are generally very secure because they isolate one device's traffic from other devices' traffic. Second, switches provide separate channels for (potentially) every device. As a result, applications that transfer a large amount of traffic and are sensitive to time delays, such as videoconferencing applications, can make full use of the network's capacity.

Switches have their disadvantages, too. Although they contain buffers to hold incoming data and accommodate bursts of traffic, they can become overwhelmed by continuous, heavy traffic. In that event, the switch cannot prevent data loss. On a shared environment, where many nodes share the same data channel, devices can compensate for collisions; on a fully switched network, where every node uses its own port on the switch and therefore has a separate data channel, devices cannot detect collisions. Also, although higher-layer protocols, such as TCP, will detect the loss and respond with a timeout, others, such as UDP, will not. For packets using such protocols, the number of collisions will mount up, and eventually all network traffic will grind to a halt. For this reason, you should plan placement of switches carefully to match backbone capacity and traffic patterns.

Switches can be classified into a few different categories. One type, a LAN switch, functions on a local area network. LAN switches can be designed for Ethernet or Token Ring networks, although Ethernet LAN switches are more common. LAN switches also differ in the method of switching they use—namely, cut-through mode or store and forward mode. These methods of switching on a LAN are discussed in the next two sections.

 Keep in mind that the term *switch* is also sometimes applied to WAN and access server devices. You will learn more about WAN and remote connectivity in Chapter 7.

Cut-Through Mode

A switch running in **cut-through mode** will read a frame's header and decide where to forward the data before it receives the entire packet. Recall from Chapter 5 that the first 14 bytes of a frame constitute its header, which contains the destination MAC address. This information is sufficient for the switch to determine which port should get the frame and begin transmitting the frame (without bothering to hold the data and check its accuracy).

What if the frame becomes corrupt? Because the cut-through mode does not allow the switch to read the frame check sequence before it begins transmitting, it can't verify data integrity in that way. On the other hand, cut-through switches can detect **runts**, or packet fragments. Upon detecting a runt, the switch will wait to transmit that packet until it determines its integrity. It's important to remember, however, that runts are only one type of data flaw. Cut-through switches *cannot* detect corrupt packets; indeed, they may increase the number of errors found on the network by propagating flawed packets.

The most significant advantage of the cut-through mode is its speed. Because it does not stop to read the entire data packet, a cut-through switch can forward information much more rapidly than a store and forward switch can (as described in the next section). The time-saving advantages to cut-through switching become insignificant, however, if the switch is flooded with traffic. In this case, the cut-through switch must buffer (or temporarily hold) data, just like a store and forward switch. Cut-through switches are best suited to small workgroups where speed is important and the relatively low number of devices minimizes the potential for errors.

Store and Forward Mode

In **store and forward mode**, a switch reads the entire data frame into its memory and checks it for accuracy before transmitting the information. Although this method is more time-consuming than the cut-through method, it allows store and forward switches to transmit data more accurately. Store and forward mode switches are more appropriate for larger LAN environments because they do not propagate data errors. In contrast, cut-through mode switches do forward errors, so they may contribute to network congestion if a particular segment is experiencing a number of collisions. In large environments, a failure to check for errors can result in problematic traffic congestion.

Store and forward switches can also transfer data between segments running different transmission speeds. For example, a high-speed network printer that serves 50 students could be attached to a 100-Mbps port on the switch, thereby allowing all of the student workstations to connect to 10-Mbps ports on the same switch. With this scheme, the printer can quickly service multiple jobs. This characteristic makes store and forward mode switches preferable in mixed-speed environments.

Using Switches to Create VLANs

In addition to improving bandwidth usage, switches can create **virtual local area networks (VLANs)**, a logically separate network within a network, by grouping a number of ports into a broadcast domain. A **broadcast domain** is a combination of ports that make up a Layer 2 segment and must be connected by a Layer 3 device, such as a router or Layer 3 switch. The ports do not have to reside on the same switch or even on the same network segment. A VLAN can include servers, workstations, printers, routers, or any other network device you can connect to a switch. Figure 6-26 illustrates a simple VLAN design. Note, however, that one great advantage of VLANs is their ability to link geographically distant users and create small workgroups from large LANs.

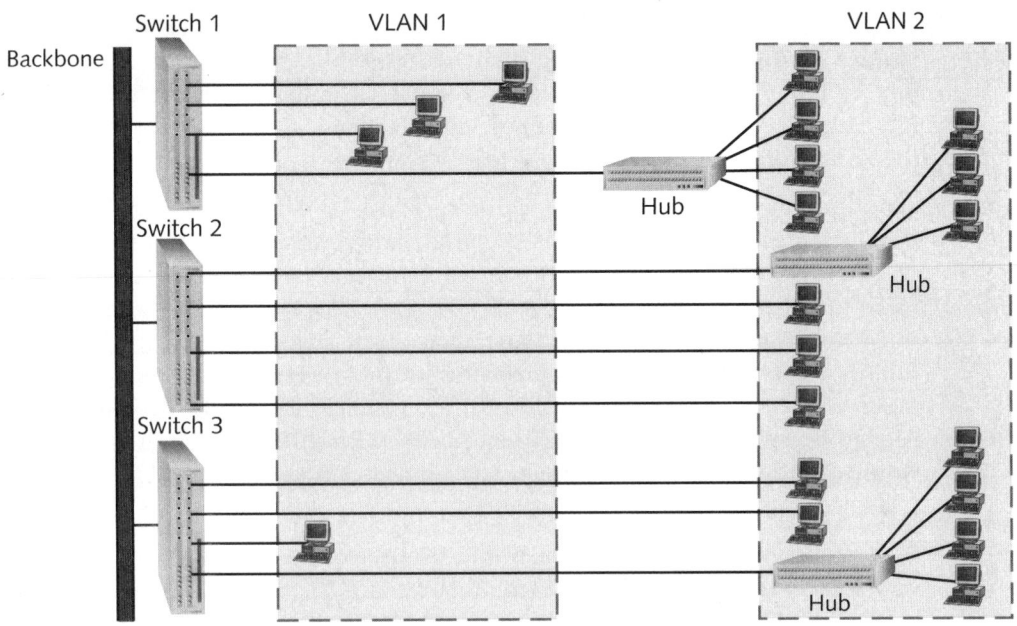

Figure 6-26   A simple VLAN design

To create a VLAN, you must configure the switch properly. In addition to identifying the ports that belong to each logical network, you can specify security parameters, filtering instructions (if the switch should not forward any frames from a certain segment, for example), performance requirements for certain users, and network management options. Clearly, switches are very flexible devices.

Describing the variety of ways in which VLANs may be implemented is beyond the scope of this book. If you are charged with designing a network or installing switches, however, you should research VLANs further. Some trade publications (and many switch manufacturers) have touted VLANs as the most advanced approach to networking and the wave of the future.

In setting up a VLAN, you are not merely including a certain group of nodes—you are also excluding another group. As a result, you can potentially cut a group off from the rest of the network. VLAN implementation requires careful planning to ensure that all the groups of users who need to communicate can do so after the VLAN is in operation.

Higher-Layer Switches

Earlier in this chapter, you learned that switches operate in Layer 2 (Data Link layer) of the OSI Model, routers operate in Layer 3, and hubs operate in Layer 1. You also learned that the distinctions between hubs, bridges, switches, and routers are blurring. This melding of categories will become more pronounced as switch technology advances. Indeed, manufacturers are already producing switches that can operate at Layer 3 (Network layer) and Layer 4 (Transport layer), making them act more like routers. A switch capable of interpreting Layer 3 data is called a **Layer 3 switch**. Similarly, a switch capable of interpreting Layer 4 data is called a **Layer 4 switch**. These higher-layer switches may also be called **routing switches** or **application switches**.

Among other things, the ability to interpret higher-layer data enables switches to perform advanced filtering, statistics keeping, and security functions. Layer 3 and Layer 4 switches may also transmit data more rapidly than a router and will probably remain easier to install and configure than routers. In general, these switches aren't as fully featured as routers. For example, they typically cannot translate between Token Ring and Ethernet networks, encapsulate protocols, or prioritize traffic. These critical differences make switches inappropriate for specific connectivity needs. In other words, if you needed to connect a 10BaseT Ethernet LAN with a 100BaseT Ethernet LAN, a switch would be adequate. If you wanted to connect a Token Ring LAN with an Ethernet LAN, you would want to use a router.

As with other connectivity devices, the features of these Layer 3 and Layer 4 switches vary widely depending on the manufacturer and the price. (This variability is exacerbated by the fact that key players in the networking trade have not agreed on standards for these switches.) Higher-layer switches can cost three times more than Layer 2 switches, and network administrators are only beginning to try them. In general, higher-layer switches are yet another technology you will need to watch closely.

ROUTERS

A **router** is a multiport connectivity device that can integrate LANs and WANs running at different transmission speeds and using a variety of protocols. Routers operate at the Network layer (Layer 3) of the OSI Model. Recall from Chapter 2 that the Network layer directs data from one segment or type of network to another. Historically, routers have been slower than switches or bridges because they pay attention to information in Layers 3 and higher, such as protocols and logical addresses. Consequently, unlike bridges and Layer 2 switches, routers are protocol-dependent. They must be designed or configured to recognize a certain protocol before they can forward data transmitted using that protocol.

As is the case with bridges, traditional standalone LAN routers are being replaced by Layer 3 switches that support the routing functions. The concept of routing remains extremely important, however, and everything described in the remainder of this section also applies to Layer 3 switches. Standalone routers are still the technology of choice for connecting remote offices using WAN technology.

Router Features and Functions

A router's strength lies in its intelligence. Not only can routers only keep track of the locations of certain nodes on the network, as switches can, but they can also determine the shortest, fastest path between two nodes. For this reason, and because they can connect dissimilar network types, routers are powerful, indispensable devices on large LANs and WANs. The Internet, for example, relies on a multitude of routers across the world.

 As noted in Chapter 3, some protocols are not routable. Routable protocols include TCP/IP, IPX/SPX, and AppleTalk. Because NetBEUI and SNA are not routable, for example, networks that run these protocols cannot use routers. On the other hand, some routers provide advanced support for Layer 2 bridging that far exceeds what a bridge or switch can accomplish. These bridge-routers (or brouters) are discussed later in this chapter.

A typical router has an internal processor, its own memory and power supply, input and output jacks for different types of network connectors (depending on the network type), and, usually, a management console interface, as shown in Figure 6-27. High-powered, multiprotocol routers may have several slot bays to accommodate multiple network interfaces (RJ-45, BNC, FDDI, and so on). A router with multiple slots that can hold different interface cards or other devices is called a **modular router**.

Figure 6-27   Routers

A router is a very flexible device. Although any one can be specialized for a variety of tasks, all routers can do the following: connect dissimilar networks, interpret Layer 3 information, determine the best path for data to follow from point A to point B, and reroute traffic if a primary path is down but another path is available. In addition to performing these basic functions, routers may perform any of the following optional functions:

- Filter out broadcast transmissions to alleviate network congestion

- Prevent certain types of traffic from getting to a network, enabling customized segregation and security

- Support simultaneous local and remote connectivity

- Provide high network fault tolerance through redundant components such as power supplies or network interfaces

- Monitor network traffic and report statistics to a MIB

- Diagnose internal or other connectivity problems and trigger alarms

In addition, routers may use one of two methods for directing data on the network: static or dynamic routing. **Static routing** is a technique in which a network administrator programs a router to use specific paths between nodes. Since it does not account for occasional network congestion, failed connections, or device moves, static routing is not optimal. If a router or a segment connected to a router is moved, the network administrator must reprogram the static router's tables. The fact that static routing requires human intervention makes it less efficient and accurate than dynamic routing. **Dynamic routing**, on the other hand, automatically calculates the best path between two nodes and accumulates this information in a routing table. If congestion or failures affect the network, a router using dynamic routing can detect the problems and reroute data through a different path. Most modern networks primarily use dynamic routing, but may include some static routing to indicate a router of last resort, the router that accepts all unroutable packets.

Because of their customizability, routers are not simple devices to install. Typically, a technician or engineer must be very familiar with routing technology to figure out how to place and configure a router to best advantage. Figure 6-28 gives you some idea of how routers fit into a LAN environment, although this example is oversimplified. If you plan to specialize in network design or router configuration, you should research router technology further. You might begin with Cisco System's online documentation at *www.cisco.com/univercd/home/home.htm*. Cisco Systems currently provides the majority of networking routers installed in the world.

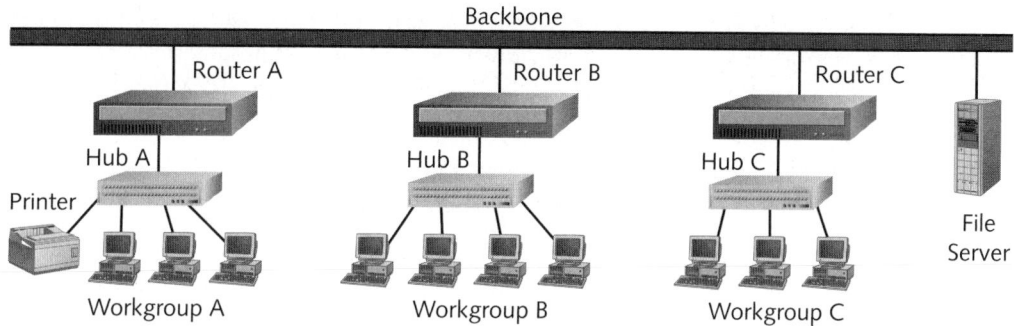

Figure 6-28   The placement of routers on a LAN

In the setup depicted in Figure 6-28, if a workstation in workgroup C wanted to print to a networked printer in workgroup A, it would create a transmission containing the address of the workgroup A printer. Then it would send its packets to hub C. Hub C would simply retransmit the signal to router C. When router C received the transmission, it would temporarily store the packets as it read the Layer 3 information. Upon determining that the packets were destined for a printer in workgroup A, router C would then decide the best way to get the data to the workgroup A printer. In this example, it might send the data directly to router A. Before it forwards the packet, however, router C would increment (increase) the number of hops tallied in the packet. A **hop** is the term used in networking to describe each trip data take from one connectivity device to another. (Usually, the term is used in the context of routing.) For example, a trip from a workstation in Workgroup A to Hub A would constitute one hop, and a trip from Hub A to Router A would constitute another hop. Each time a packet passes through a router, it has made a hop. Packets can only take a certain number of hops before they are discarded. (Recall the network distance limitations you learned about in Chapter 4.)

After it incremented the number of hops tallied in the packet, router C would forward the data to router A. Router A would increment the packet's hop count, read the packet's destination address and forward it to hub A, which would then broadcast the transmission to workgroup A until the printer picked it up.

Routing Protocols: RIP, OSPF, EIGRP, and BGP

Finding the best route for data to take across the network is one of the most valued and sophisticated functions performed by a router. The term **best path** refers to the most efficient route from one node on a network to another. The best path in a particular situation depends on the number of hops between nodes, the current network activity, the unavailable links, the network transmission speed, and the topology. To determine the best path, routers communicate with each other through **routing protocols**. Keep in mind that routing protocols are *not* the same as routable protocols, such as TCP/IP or IPX/SPX, although routing protocols may piggyback on top of routable protocols. Routing protocols are used only to collect data about current network status and contribute to the selection of the best paths. From these data, routers create routing tables for use with future packet forwarding.

In addition to its ability to find the best path, a routing protocol can be characterized according to its **convergence time**, the time it takes for a router to recognize a best path in the event of a change or network outage. Its **bandwidth overhead**, the burden placed on the underlying network to support the routing protocol, is also a distinguishing feature.

Although you do not need to know precisely how routing protocols work in order to qualify for the Network+ certification, you should be familiar with the most common routing protocols: RIP, OSPF, EIGRP, and BGP. (Several more routing protocols exist, but are not widely used.) These four common routing protocols are described below.

- *RIP (Routing Information Protocol) for IP and IPX*—The oldest routing protocol, RIP, which is still widely used, factors in only the number of hops between nodes when determining a path from one point to another. It does not consider network congestion or link speed, for example. Routers using RIP broadcast their routing tables every 30 seconds to other routers, whether or not the tables have changed. This broadcasting creates excessive network traffic, especially if a large number of routes exist. If the routing tables change, it may take several minutes before the new information propagates to routers at the far reaches of the network; thus the convergence time for RIP is poor. However, one advantage to RIP is its stability. For example, RIP prevents routing loops from continuing indefinitely by limiting the number of hops a packet can take between its source and its destination to 15. If the number of hops in a path exceeds 15, the network destination is considered unreachable. Thus, RIP does not work well in very large network environments where data may have to travel through more than 15 routers to reach their destination (for example, on the Internet). Also, compared with other routing protocols, RIP is slower and less secure.

- *OSPF (Open Shortest Path First) for IP*—This routing protocol makes up for some of the limitations of RIP and can coexist with RIP on a network. OSPF uses a more complex algorithm for determining best paths. Under optimal network conditions, the best path is the most direct path between two points. If excessive traffic levels or an outage preclude data from following the most direct path, a router may determine that the most efficient path actually goes through additional routers. Each router maintains a database of the other routers' links, and if notice is received indicating the failure of a given link, the router can rapidly compute an alternate path. This approach requires more memory and CPU power on the routers, but it keeps network bandwidth to a minimum and provides a very fast convergence time, often invisible to the users. OSPF is the second most frequently supported protocol, after RIP.

- *EIGRP (Enhanced Interior Gateway Routing Protocol) for IP, IPX, and AppleTalk*—This routing protocol was developed in the mid-1980s by Cisco Systems. It has a fast convergence time and a low network overhead, and is easier to configure and less CPU-intensive than OSPF. EIGRP also offers the benefits of supporting multiple protocols and limiting unnecessary network traffic between routers. It accommodates very large and heterogeneous networks, but is only supported by Cisco routers.

- *BGP (Border Gateway Protocol) for IP*—BGP is the routing protocol of Internet backbones. The demands on routers created by Internet growth have driven the development of BGP, the most complex of the routing protocols. The developers of BGP had to contend with not only the prospect of 100,000 routes, but also the question of how to route traffic efficiently and fairly through the hundreds of Internet backbones.

Brouters and Routing Switches

By now it should not surprise you that routers, too, can act like other devices. The networking industry has adopted the term **bridge router**, or **brouter**, to describe routers that take on some characteristics of bridges. The advantage of crossing a router with a bridge is that you can forward nonroutable protocols, such as NetBEUI, plus connect multiple network types through one device. A bridge router offers support at both Layers 2 and 3 of the OSI Model. It intelligently handles any packets that contain Layer 3 addressing information and simply forwards the rest.

Another router hybrid, a **routing switch**, combines a router and a switch. It can also interpret data from both Layers 2 and 3 of the OSI Model. (*Routing switch* is another term for the higher-layer switches covered earlier in this chapter.) A routing switch is not as fully featured as a true router, and therefore routing switches have not gained wide acceptance from networking professionals.

GATEWAYS

Gateways do not fall neatly into the networking hardware category. In broad terms, they are combinations of networking hardware and software that connect two dissimilar kinds of networks. Specifically, they may connect two systems that use different formatting, communications protocols, or architecture. Unlike the connectivity hardware discussed earlier in this chapter, gateways actually repackage information so that it can be read by another system. To accomplish this task, gateways must operate at multiple layers of the OSI Model. They must communicate with an application, establish and manage sessions, translate encoded data, and interpret logical and physical addressing data.

Gateways can reside on servers, microcomputers, or mainframes. They are more expensive than routers because of their vast capabilities and almost always application-specific. In addition, they transmit data much more slowly than bridges or routers because of the complex translations they conduct. Because they are slow, gateways have the potential to cause extreme network congestion. In certain situations, however, only a gateway will suffice.

During your networking career, you will most likely hear gateways discussed in the context of e-mail systems. Popular types of gateways, including e-mail gateways, are described below.

6

- *E-mail gateway*—A gateway that translates messages from one type of e-mail system to another. For example, an e-mail gateway would allow people who use Eudora e-mail to correspond with people who use GroupWise e-mail.

- *IBM host gateway*—A gateway that establishes and manages communication between a PC and an IBM mainframe computer.

- *Internet gateway*—A gateway that allows and manages access between LANs and the Internet. An Internet gateway can restrict the kind of access LAN users have to the Internet, and vice versa.

- *LAN gateway*—A gateway that allows segments of a LAN running different protocols or different network models to communicate with each other. A router, a single port on a router, or even a server may act as a LAN gateway. The LAN gateway category might also include remote access servers that allow dial-up connectivity to a LAN.

CHAPTER SUMMARY

❐ Network interface cards (NICs) come in a variety of types depending on logical topology (Ethernet versus Token Ring), network transmission speed (for example, 10 Mbps versus 100 Mbps), connector interfaces (for example, BNC versus RJ-45), type of compatible system board or device, and manufacturer.

❐ For a desktop or tower PC, an expansion card network adapter is used. It must match the system's bus. A bus is the type of circuit used by the system board to transmit data to components. Network adapters may fit ISA, EISA, MCA, or PCI buses. New computers almost always use PCI buses.

❐ Network adapters may also be externally attached, through the PCMCIA, USB, or parallel port.

❐ In addition to network adapters that interface with network cabling, network adapters can be designed for wireless transmission. A wireless network adapter uses an antenna to exchange signals with the network. This type of connectivity suits environments where cabling cannot be installed or where roaming clients must be supported.

❐ Devices other than PCs, such as networked printers, use specialized network adapters. Printer network adapters also come in a variety of styles suited to different applications. By far, the most popular printer network adapter is Hewlett-Packard's JetDirect card.

❐ To install a NIC, you must physically attach it to the bus (or port), install the NIC device drivers, and configure its settings.

❐ On servers, you may need to install multiple network adapters. For the hardware installation, you can repeat the same installation process used for the first network adapter, choosing a different slot. The trick to using multiple network adapters lies in correctly configuring the software for each.

- Some older NICs require hardware adjustments to indicate different variables, such as IRQ or I/O address settings. They may use jumpers, small plastic pieces containing a metal bridge that closes a circuit between two pins on the expansion card, or DIP switches, small plastic toggle switches that can indicate an "on" or "off" position.

- Firmware combines hardware and software. The hardware component of firmware is an electrically erasable programmable read-only memory (EEPROM) chip that stores data established at the factory. This data can be changed by configuration software.

- An IRQ is the means by which a device can request attention from the CPU. IRQ numbers range from 0 to 15. The BIOS will attempt to assign free IRQ numbers to new devices. Typically, it will assign IRQ numbers 9,10, or 11, to network adapters. If conflicts occur, you must manually assign a device's IRQ number rather than accept the default suggested by the BIOS.

- Many IRQ numbers are preassigned to system devices. For example, a keyboard uses IRQ 1, COM1 and COM3 use IRQ 4, a floppy disk drive uses IRQ 6, LPT1 uses IRQ 7, the clock uses IRQ 8, and the math coprocessor uses IRQ 13.

- To change a network adapter's firmware, you will need a bootable floppy disk (DOS version 6.0 or higher) containing the configuration or the DOS install utility that shipped with the network adapter. To run the utility, you must start the computer with this floppy disk inserted.

- Repeaters are the connectivity devices that perform the regeneration of a digital signal. They belong to the Physical layer of the OSI Model; therefore, they do not have any means to interpret the data they are retransmitting.

- At its most primitive, a hub is a multiport repeater. A simple hub may contain multiple ports that can connect a group of computers in a peer-to-peer fashion, accepting and repeating signals from each node. A slightly more sophisticated hub may contain multiple ports for devices and one port that connects to a network's backbone. Hubs typically support a star or hybrid topology on an Ethernet network. On Token Ring networks, hubs are called Multistation Access Units (MAUs).

- Hubs that merely repeat signals are called passive hubs.

- Intelligent hubs are also called managed hubs, because they can be managed from anywhere on the network. A standalone, stackable, or modular hub may include processing capabilities and, therefore, be considered intelligent.

- A MIB (management information base) is a collection of data used by management programs (which may be part of the network operating system or a third-party program) to analyze network performance and problems.

- Bridges resemble repeaters in that they have a single input and a single output port, but they can interpret the data they retransmit. Bridging occurs at the Data Link layer of the OSI Model. Bridges read the destination (MAC) address information and decide whether to forward (retransmit) a packet to another segment on the network or, if the destination address belongs to the same segment as the source address, filter (discard) it.

◻ As nodes transmit data through the bridge, the bridge establishes a filtering database of known MAC addresses and their locations on the network. The bridge uses its filtering database to determine whether a packet should be forwarded or filtered.

◻ Switches subdivide a network into smaller logical pieces. They operate at the Data Link layer (Layer 2) of the OSI Model and can interpret MAC address information. In this respect, switches resemble bridges.

◻ Switches are generally secure because they isolate one device's traffic from other devices' traffic. Because switches provide separate channels for (potentially) every device, they allow applications that transfer a large amount of traffic and that are sensitive to time delays, such as videoconferencing, to make full use of the network's capacity.

◻ A switch running in cut-through mode will read a frame's header and decide where to forward the data before it receives the entire packet.

◻ In store and forward mode, switches read the entire data frame into their memory and check it for accuracy before transmitting it. Although this method is more time-consuming than the cut-through method, it allows store and forward switches to transmit data more accurately.

◻ In addition to improving bandwidth usage, switches can create virtual local area networks (VLANs) by logically grouping several ports into a broadcast domain. The ports do not have to reside on the same switch or even on the same network segment.

◻ Manufacturers are producing switches that can operate at Layer 3 (Network layer) and Layer 4 (Transport layer) of the OSI Model, making them act more like routers. The ability to interpret higher-layer data enables switches to perform advanced filtering, statistics keeping, and security functions.

◻ A router is a multiport device that can connect dissimilar LANs and WANs running at different transmission speeds and using a variety of protocols. Routers operate at the Network layer (Layer 3) or higher of the OSI Model. Historically, routers have transmitted data more slowly than switches or bridges because they pay attention to Layer 3 information, such as protocols and logical addresses.

◻ Unlike bridges and traditional switches, routers are protocol-dependent. They must be designed or configured to recognize a certain protocol before they can forward data transmitted using that protocol.

◻ A typical router has an internal processor, its own memory and power supply, input and output jacks for different types of network connectors (depending on the network type), and, usually, a management console interface.

◻ Finding the best route for data to take across the network is an important router function. The best path will depend on the number of hops between nodes, the current network activity, the unavailable links, the network transmission speed, and the topology. To determine the best path, routers communicate with each other through routing protocols.

❏ Static routing is a technique in which a network administrator programs a router to use specific paths between nodes.

❏ Dynamic routing automatically calculates the best path between two nodes and accumulates this information in a routing table. If congestion or failures affect the network, a router using dynamic routing can detect the problems and reroute data through a different path. Most modern networks primarily use dynamic routing.

❏ The networking industry has adopted the term "brouter" to describe routers that take on some of the characteristics of bridges. Crossing a router with a bridge allows you to forward data using nonroutable protocols, such as NetBEUI, and to connect multiple network types through one device. A brouter offers support at both Layers 2 and 3 of the OSI Model.

❏ Gateways are combinations of networking hardware and software that connect two dissimilar kinds of networks. Specifically, they may connect two systems that use different formatting, communications protocols, or architecture. To accomplish this task, they must operate at multiple layers of the OSI Model.

❏ Typically, gateways are used for one of four purposes: as an e-mail gateway, as an IBM host gateway, as an Internet gateway, or as a LAN gateway.

KEY TERMS

adapter card — See *expansion board*.

application switch — Another term for a Layer 3 or Layer 4 switch.

bandwidth overhead — The burden placed on the underlying network to support a routing protocol.

base I/O port — A setting that specifies, in hexadecimal notation, which area of memory will act as a channel for moving data between the network adapter and the CPU. Like its IRQ, a device's base I/O port cannot be used by any other device.

best path — The most efficient route from one node on a network to another. Under optimal network conditions, the best path is the most direct path between two points.

BIOS (basic input/output system) — Firmware attached to the system board that controls the computer's communication with its devices, among other things.

Border Gateway Protocol (BGP) — The routing protocol of Internet backbones. The router stress created by Internet growth has driven the development of BGP, the most complex of the routing protocols. The developers of BGP had to contend with the prospect of 100,000 routes as well as the goal of routing traffic efficiently and fairly through the hundreds of Internet backbones.

bridge — A connectivity device that operates at the Data Link layer of the OSI Model and reads header information to forward packets according to their MAC addresses. Bridges use a filtering database to determine which packets to discard and which to forward. Bridges contain one input and one output port and separate network segments.

bridge router (brouter) — A router capable of providing Layer 2 bridging functions.

broadcast domain — In a virtual local area network (VLAN), a combination of ports that make up a Layer 2 segment and must be connected by a Layer 3 device, such as a router or Layer 3 switch.

brouter — See *bridge router.*

bus — The type of circuit used by the system board to transmit data to components. Most new Pentium computers use buses capable of exchanging 32 or 64 bits of data. As the number of bits of data a bus handles increases, so too does the speed of the device attached to the bus.

CMOS (complementary metal oxide semiconductor) — Firmware on a PC's system board that enables you to change its devices' configurations.

collision domain — A portion of a LAN encompassing devices that may cause and detect collisions among their group. Bridges and switches can logically create multiple collision domains.

convergence time — The time it takes for a router to recognize a best path in the event of a change or network outage.

cut-through mode — A switching mode in which a switch reads a frame's header and decides where to forward the data before it receives the entire packet. Cut-through mode is faster, but less accurate, than the other switching method, store and forward mode.

daughter board — See *expansion board.*

daughter card — See *expansion board.*

device driver — Software that enables an attached device to communicate with the computer's operating system.

DIP (dual inline package) switch — A small plastic toggle switch on a circuit board that can be flipped to indicate either an "on" or "off" status, which translates into a parameter setting.

dynamic routing — A method of routing that automatically calculates the best path between two nodes and accumulates this information in a routing table. If congestion or failures affect the network, a router using dynamic routing can detect the problems and reroute data through a different path. Most modern networks primarily use dynamic routing.

electrically erasable programmable read-only memory (EEPROM) — A type of ROM that is found on a circuit board and whose configuration information can be erased and rewritten through electrical pulses.

Enhanced Interior Gateway Routing Protocol (EIGRP) — A routing protocol developed in the mid-1980s by Cisco Systems that has a fast convergence time and a low network overhead, but is easier to configure and less CPU-intensive than OSPF. EIGRP also offers the benefits of supporting multiple protocols and limiting unnecessary network traffic between routers.

expansion board — A circuit board used to connect a device to a computer's system board.

expansion card — See *expansion board*.

expansion slots — Openings on a computer's system board that contain multiple electrical contacts into which the expansion board can be inserted.

Extended Industry Standard Architecture (EISA) — A 32-bit bus that is compatible with older ISA devices (because it shares the same length and pin configuration as the ISA bus), but that uses an extra layer of pins (resulting in a deeper, two-layered slot connector) for a second 16 bits to achieve faster throughput. The EISA bus was introduced in the late 1980s to compete with IBM's MCA bus.

filtering database — A collection of data created and used by a bridge that correlates the MAC addresses of connected workstations with their locations. A filtering database is also known as a forwarding table.

firmware — A combination of hardware and software. The hardware component of firmware is a read-only memory (ROM) chip that stores data established at the factory and possibly changed by configuration programs that can write to ROM.

forwarding table — See *filtering database*.

gateway — A combination of networking hardware and software that connects two dissimilar kinds of networks. Gateways perform connectivity, session management, and data translation, so they must operate at multiple layers of the OSI Model.

hop — A term used in networking to describe each trip data take from one connectivity device to another.

hub — A multiport repeater containing multiple ports to interconnect multiple devices. Unless they are used on a peer-to-peer network, hubs also contain an uplink port, one port that connects to a network's backbone. Hubs regenerate digital signals.

Industry Standard Architecture (ISA) — The original PC bus, developed in the early 1980s to support an 8-bit and later 16-bit data transfer capability. Although an older technology, ISA buses are still used to connect serial devices, such as mice or modems, in new PCs.

intelligent hub — A hub that possesses processing capabilities and can therefore monitor network traffic, detect packet errors and collisions, poll connected devices for information, and send the data gathered to a management information base (MIB).

interrupt — A wire through which a device issues voltage, thereby signaling a request for the processor's attention.

interrupt request (IRQ) — A message sent to the computer that instructs it to stop what it is doing and pay attention to something else. IRQ is often used (informally) to refer to the interrupt request number.

interrupt request number (IRQ number) — The unique number assigned to each interrupt in a computer. Interrupt request numbers range from 0 to 15, and many PC devices reserve specific numbers for their use alone.

jumper — A small, removable piece of plastic that contains a metal receptacle that fits over a pair of pins on a circuit board to complete a circuit between those two pins.

By moving the jumper from one set of pins to another set of pins, you can modify the board's circuit, thereby giving it different instructions on how to operate.

Layer 3 switch — A switch capable of interpreting data at Layer 3 (Network layer) of the OSI Model.

Layer 4 switch — A switch capable of interpreting data at Layer 4 (Transport layer) of the OSI Model.

loopback plug — A connector used for troubleshooting that plugs into a port (for example, a serial, parallel, or RJ-45 port) and crosses over the transmit line to the receive line, allowing outgoing signals to be redirected back into the computer for testing.

managed hub — See *intelligent hub*.

memory range — A hexadecimal number that indicates the area of memory that the network adapter and CPU will use for exchanging, or buffering, data. As with IRQs, some memory ranges are reserved for specific devices—most notably, the system board.

MIB (management information base) — A collection of data used by management programs (which may be part of the network operating system or a third-party program) to analyze network performance and problems.

MicroChannel Architecture (MCA) — IBM's proprietary 32-bit bus for personal computers, introduced in 1987 and later replaced by the more standard EISA and PCI buses.

modular hub — A type of hub that provides a number of interface options within one chassis. Similar to a PC, a modular hub contains a system board and slots accommodating different adapters. These adapters may connect to other types of hubs, routers, WAN links, or to both Token Ring and Ethernet network backbones. They may also connect the modular hub to management workstations or redundant components, such as an extra power supply.

modular router — A router with multiple slots that can hold different interface cards or other devices so as to provide flexible, customizable network interoperability.

network adapter — A synonym for NIC (network interface card). The device that enables a workstation, server, printer, or other node to connect to the network. Network adapters belong to the Physical layer of the OSI Model.

open shortest path first (OSPF) — A routing protocol that makes up for some of the limitations of RIP and can coexist with RIP on a network.

passive hub — A hub that simply amplifies and retransmits signals over the network.

PC Card — See *PCMCIA*.

PCMCIA — An interface developed in the early 1990s by the Personal Computer Memory Card International Association to provide a standard interface for connecting any type of device to a portable computer. PCMCIA slots may hold modem cards, network interface cards, external hard disk cards, or CD-ROM cards. PCMCIA cards are also known as PC Cards or credit card adapters.

Peripheral Component Interconnect (PCI) — A 32-, 64-, or 128-bit bus introduced in its original form in the 1990s. The PCI bus is the network adapter connection type used for nearly all new PCs. It's characterized by a shorter length than ISA, MCA, or EISA cards, but a much faster data transmission capability.

router — A multiport device that can connect dissimilar LANs and WANs running at different transmission speeds and using a variety of protocols. In addition, a router can determine the best path for data transmission and perform advanced management functions. Routers operate at the Network layer (Layer 3) or higher of the OSI Model. They are intelligent, protocol-dependent devices.

routing information protocol (RIP) — The oldest routing protocol that is still widely used. RIP does not work in very large network environments where data may have to travel through more than 16 routers to reach their destination (for example, on the Internet). And, compared to other routing protocols, RIP is slower and less secure.

routing protocols — The means by which routers communicate with each other about network status. Routing protocols determine the best path for data to take between nodes. They are not identical to routable protocols such as TCP/IP or IPX/SPX, although they may piggyback on top of routable protocols.

routing switch — Another term for a Layer 3 or Layer 4 switch. A routing switch is a hybrid between a router and a switch and can therefore interpret data from Layer 2 and either Layer 3 or Layer 4.

runts — Packet fragments.

single point of failure — A device or connection on a network that, were it to fail, could cause the entire network to stop functioning.

source-route bridging — A type of bridging in which the bridge polls the network to determine the best path for data between two points. Source-route bridging is not susceptible to circular routing and, for this reason, is particularly well suited to WANs.

spanning tree algorithm — A technique used in bridging that can detect circular traffic patterns and modify the way multiple bridges work together in order to avoid such patterns.

stackable hub — A type of hub designed to be linked with other hubs in a single telecommunications closet. Stackable hubs linked together logically represent one large hub to the network.

standalone hub — A type of hub that serves a workgroup of computers that are separate from the rest of the network. A standalone hub may be connected to another hub by a coaxial, fiber-optic, or twisted-pair cable. Such hubs are not typically connected in a hierarchical or daisy-chain fashion.

static routing — A technique in which a network administrator programs a router to use specific paths between nodes. Since it does not account for occasional network congestion, failed connections, or device moves, static routing is not optimal.

store and forward mode — A method of switching in which a switch reads the entire data frame into its memory and checks it for accuracy before transmitting it. While this method is more time-consuming than the cut-through method, it allows store and forward switches to transmit data more accurately.

switch — A connectivity device that logically subdivides a network into smaller, individual collision domains. A switch operates at the Data Link layer of the OSI

Model and can interpret MAC address information to determine whether to filter (discard) or forward packets it receives.

translational bridging — A type of bridging in which bridges can not only forward packets, but also translate packets between one logical topology and another. For instance, translational bridging can connect Token Ring and Ethernet networks.

transparent bridging — The method of bridging used on most Ethernet networks.

USB (universal serial bus) port — A standard external bus that can be used to connect multiple types of peripherals, including modems, mice, and network adapters, to a computer. The original USB standard was capable of transmitting only 12 Mbps of data; a new standard is capable of transmitting 480 Mbps of data.

virtual local area network (VLAN) — A network within a network that is logically defined by grouping its devices' switch ports in the same broadcast domain. A VLAN can consist of servers, workstations, printers, routers, or any other network device you can connect to a switch.

REVIEW QUESTIONS

1. If you purchase a new desktop computer today, what kind of network adapter is it likely to require?
    a. PCI
    b. ISA
    c. EISA
    d. MCA
    e. Parallel port

2. What does "ISA" stand for?
    a. International Standard Attachment
    b. Industry Standard Architecture
    c. Industry Selected Apparatus
    d. International Standard Architecture
    e. Institutional Standard Apparatus

3. Describe the process for installing a PCMCIA network adapter.

4. In which of the following instances is a wireless network adapter most appropriate?
    a. A salesperson needs to access data on her company's server while traveling.
    b. An administrative assistant needs to share files with his supervisor in the office across the hall.
    c. A warehouse employee needs to record inventory levels in the company's database for products stored throughout the warehouse.
    d. A professor needs to distribute homework assignments to her many classes of students.

e. A marketing manager needs to run digital video product demonstrations at a trade show.

5. You have just installed a new NIC on your desktop computer, which runs Windows 2000 Professional. When you reboot the machine, you can tell that neither the sound card nor the NIC is working. You suspect that they have chosen the same IRQ. How can you confirm your suspicion?

   a. Right-click the My Computer icon, click Properties, click the Hardware tab, click Device Manager, click Network Adapter, select your adapter, and select the Resources tab.

   b. Click Start, point to Settings, click Control Panel, click Network and Dial-up Connections, then double-click the Local Area Connection icon and choose Properties.

   c. Double-click My Network Places, right-click the Entire Network icon, then click Properties.

   d. Click Start, point to Settings, click Control Panel, right-click Network and Dial-up Connections, and then click Properties.

6. Which two of the following IRQs could you probably assign to a network adapter without causing a conflict with preassigned devices?

   a. 6

   b. 8

   c. 9

   d. 11

   e. 13

7. Which IRQ is typically reserved by COM1?

   a. 1

   b. 4

   c. 6

   d. 9

   e. 11

8. You can install only one network adapter in a computer. True or False?

9. On older NICs, what type of switches enable you to change the adapter's configuration?

   a. single inline pin

   b. dual inline package

   c. dual pin set

   d. single integrated pin set

   e. single pin adapter

10. Which of the following could be a symptom of a resource conflict involving the network adapter?

    a. The computer won't power on.

    b. The computer beeps three times when it starts up.

    c. The computer presents you with an error message about a video display driver.

    d. The computer alerts you that your device is conflicting with another device on the network.

    e. The computer alerts you that the NIC device drivers have not been properly installed.

11. Which two of the following methods could allow you to change the rate at which a NIC can transmit and receive data?

    a. modifying the CMOS settings

    b. modifying the NIC's IRQ

    c. modifying the operating system's network adapter resource settings

    d. modifying the NIC's settings through the network adapter's configuration utility that manages its EEPROM

    e. modifying the network adapter's jumper settings

12. Name three enhancements or features that manufacturers might add to network adapters to improve these devices' performance.

13. To which layer of the OSI Model do repeaters belong?

    a. Physical

    b. Data Link

    c. Network

    d. Transport

    e. Session

14. What is the function of a hub's uplink port?

    a. to connect it to the server on a network

    b. to connect it to the nearest workstation

    c. to connect it to another hub

    d. to connect it to a router

    e. to connect it to a management console

15. You are a network technician working on a 10BaseT network. A coworker has been having trouble logging on to the server and asks whether you can quickly tell her if her workstation's NIC is operating properly. You do not have the NIC's utility disk on hand, but you look at the back of her workstation and learn that although the

NIC is properly installed and connected to the network, something's wrong with it. What might you have seen that causes you to come to this conclusion?

a. Its LED is blinking green.

b. Its loopback plug is improperly terminated.

c. It has two types of receptacles—BNC and RJ-45—and the wrong one is in use.

d. Its LED is not lit.

e. Its jumper is improperly set.

16. Intelligent hubs differ from passive hubs in part because they can perform which of the following functions?

a. regenerate attenuated signals

b. provide expansion ports

c. connect with other hubs in a daisy-chain fashion

d. allow more than 24 nodes on one segment

e. provide network management information

17. What kind of hub introduces a single point of failure into a network design?

a. standalone hub

b. intelligent hub

c. switching hub

d. routing hub

e. modular hub

18. What is a MIB?

a. management information base

b. multimode information basis

c. multimode integration base

d. media integration base

e. managing indicator baseline

19. At what layer of the OSI Model do bridges function?

a. Physical layer

b. Data Link layer

c. Network layer

d. Transport layer

e. Session layer

20. Before they will forward packets, bridges must be configured to accept the type of protocol (for example, TCP/IP or IPX/SPX) in use by the network. True or False?

6

21. How do bridges keep track of whether they should forward or filter packets?

    a. From each packet they carry, they extract source node addresses; all source node addresses that don't belong to the bridge's broadcast domain are filtered.

    b. They maintain a filtering database that identifies which packets can be filtered and which should be forwarded, based on their destination address.

    c. They hold each packet until it is requested by the destination node, at which time the bridge forwards the data.

    d. They compare the incoming data's protocol with the previous data's protocol and filter those incoming packets that don't match.

22. Which of the following is an advantage of using switches rather than hubs?

    a. Switches can provide network management information.

    b. Switches can assign dedicated channels to certain nodes, making their transmissions more secure.

    c. Switches can more accurately transmit data from one segment to another.

    d. Switches can alert the network administrator to high data collision rates.

    e. Switches do not examine Network layer protocol information, which makes them faster than hubs.

23. In cut-through switching, which frame field does the switch never read?

    a. start frame delimiter

    b. source address

    c. destination address

    d. frame check sequence

24. Which type of switching is more appropriate for heavily trafficked networks?

    a. QoS switching

    b. circuit switching

    c. store and forward switching

    d. cut-through switching

    e. message switching

25. A VLAN can be created using only one switch. True or False?

26. Which two of the following are important functions performed by a router?

    a. determine the best path for forwarding data to its destination

    b. regenerate attenuated signals

    c. separate groups of network devices into broadcast domains

    d. send broadcast signals to all network segments

    e. integrate LANs using different Network-layer protocols

27. How do routing protocols and routable protocols differ?
    a. Routable protocols contain addressing information, and routing protocols do not.
    b. Routable protocols are generated by routers, and routing protocols are interpreted by routers.
    c. Routable protocols can be interpreted by routers, and routing protocols assist routers in communicating with other routers.
    d. Routable protocols enable communication between routers, and routing protocols enable communication between all nodes on a network.

28. OSPF is a more efficient routing protocol than RIP. True or False?

29. A brouter contains characteristics of which two of the following devices?
    a. hub
    b. bridge
    c. switch
    d. repeater
    e. router

30. Why can't routers forward packets as quickly as bridges can?
    a. Routers operate at Layer 3 of the OSI Model and, therefore, take more time to interpret logical addressing information.
    b. Routers have smaller data buffers than bridges and, therefore, can store less traffic at any given time.
    c. Routers wait for acknowledgment from destination devices before sending more packets to those devices.
    d. Routers operate at Layer 4 of the OSI Model and, therefore, act as the traffic cops for all data, making them slower than bridges, which operate at Layer 3.
    e. Routers are susceptible to broadcast storms; therefore, they must periodically clear their cache and request retransmission of data that have already been transmitted.

31. Describe the difference between static and dynamic routing.

32. At which layers of the OSI Model do gateways function?
    a. Layers 1 and 2
    b. Layers 2 and 3
    c. Layers 1, 2, and 3
    d. Layers 6 and 7
    e. at all layers

6

33. EIGRP is a routing protocol that was developed by which company?

    a. Intel

    b. Nortel

    c. Cisco

    d. IBM

    e. 3Com

34. Which of the following routing protocols is used on the Internet's backbone?

    a. EIGRP

    b. OSPF

    c. GRP

    d. BGP

    e. RIP

35. What is the function of an e-mail gateway?

    a. It translates e-mail messages from one type of e-mail software package to another.

    b. It translates e-mail messages from one type of operating system to another.

    c. It translates e-mail messages from one type of network transport model to another.

    d. It translates e-mail messages between two or more collision domains.

    e. It translates e-mail messages between different languages.

HANDS-ON PROJECTS

Project 6-1

In this exercise, you will have the opportunity to install a PCI network adapter in a workstation, then properly configure it to connect to the network. For this project and Project 6-2, you will need a new Ethernet PCI network adapter, the floppy disk and documentation that came with it, and a desktop computer with Windows 2000 Professional installed. You will also need a Windows 2000 Professional installation CD, a Phillips-head screwdriver, and a wrist strap and mat to guard against electrostatic discharge.

1. Before installing the network adapter, turn on the PC and note the icons present on the Windows 2000 Professional desktop. Do you see a My Network Places icon?

2. Click Start, point to Settings, then click Network and Dial-up Connections. The Network and Dial-up Connections window opens.

3. Right-click the **Local Area Connection** icon and choose **Properties** in the shortcut menu. The Local Area Connection Properties dialog box opens.

4. Click the **General** tab, if necessary. Which components are listed as installed?

5. To make certain that you are peforming a fresh installation, you will now remove any existing network adapter drivers. Right-click **My Computer**, then choose **Properties** from the shortcut menu. The System Properties dialog box appears.

6. Click the **Hardware tab,** then click the **Device Manager** button. The Device Manager window opens.

7. In the list of installed components, double-click on **Network Adapters**. A list of your installed network adapters should appear.

8. For each installed adapter, right-click on the adapter name and choose **Uninstall** from the shortcut menu. The Confirm Device Removal window will appear, warning you that you are about to uninstall the device from your system. Click **OK** to confirm that you want to uninstall the network adapter.

9. Close the Device Manager window, then close the System Properties dialog box.

10. Click **Start**, then click **Shut Down**. The Shut Down Windows dialog box opens, prompting you to indicate your choice. Make sure the Shut Down option is selected, then click **Yes** to confirm that you want to shut down the computer. You must always shut down a workstation before installing an expansion card NIC.

11. Now physically install the network adapter in the PC as described earlier in this chapter, making sure to turn off the power before opening the case. Be sure that the network adapter is securely inserted before replacing the computer's cover. If you are unsure about whether the network adapter is pushed into the slot far enough, ask your instructor for assistance.

12. Replace the computer's cover, insert the power cable, and turn the computer on.

13. Watch the NIC's LED as the computer reboots. What does it do?

14. Does your computer start up without locking up or presenting you with error messages? Either way, proceed to Project 6-2, in which you will have the opportunity to change the network adapter's settings in the CMOS utility.

Project 6-2

In this exercise, you will view and, if necessary, change the CMOS settings for the network adapter you installed in Project 6-1. Note that each computer may require a different keystroke (for example, Del or Shift+F1) to invoke the CMOS setup utility while it starts up. Pay attention to the instructions that appear on your screen to find out the correct keystroke or combination of keystrokes.

1. Turn off the computer. Wait at least eight seconds to allow the hard disk to stop spinning, then turn on the computer again.

2. Watch the screen to find out which key or keys you need to press to enter the setup program, then press those keys.

3. You should now be in the CMOS setup utility. Because each CMOS setup utility looks different, you will have to search through the menus to find where the IRQs of PCI devices are listed.

4. Which IRQ has been assigned to your network adapter? Do you see any error messages about conflicting devices?

5. Try changing the IRQ assigned to your network adapter. Usually, you will want to highlight the current value, then press either the Page Up key, the + key, or Enter to change the value. The key you press will depend on the type of BIOS used by your computer. Read the screen to determine which key or combination of keys you should press.

6. Try changing the network adapter's IRQ to 6. Does the BIOS utility prevent you from choosing IRQ 6? If so, what message does it display?

7. Change the IRQ to a number that, according to the BIOS, does not conflict with any other devices.

8. Exit the CMOS setup utility, making sure to save your changes. (Because each CMOS utility uses different keystrokes or combinations of keystrokes, read the screen to find out how to save changed settings.)

9. Upon restarting, does the computer freeze up or display any error messages? If so, try reinstalling the network adapter from the beginning. (You may want to enlist your instructor's help with this.) Otherwise, continue to Project 6-3.

Project 6-3

Now that you have installed the network adapter (in Projects 6-1 and 6-2), you need to install the appropriate software so that you can connect to the network. In this exercise, you will allow the operating system to choose and install its drivers for the NIC, then you will update those with the drivers on the disk that came with your network adapter.

At the end of Project 6-2, you restarted your computer after installing the network adapter. Providing that you have not disabled the plug-and-play technology on your workstation, Windows 2000 should recognize the new hardware and install the device drivers automatically. The first step in this project begins at this point.

1. Once Windows 2000 reboots, the operating system will install device drivers for your new NIC.

2. Follow the steps described under the "Installing and Configuring Network Adapter Software" section of this chapter for updating NIC drivers. (*Note*: if the Update Driver Wizard informs you that the driver you are installing is older than the driver already present for the adapter, continue installing the device driver from the disk anyway.)

3. At the end of these steps your NIC should be functioning using the new device driver. Upon rebooting, verify this by viewing the NIC's LED.

Project 6-4

In this exercise, you will verify that the network adapter you installed and configured in Projects 6-1, 6-2, and 6-3 works, by viewing the device's properties through the operating system and attempting to connect to the network. (Obviously, if Windows 2000 displayed error messages pertaining to the network adapter after rebooting, it is not installed correctly. You may want to remove it, using the Add/Remove Hardware Wizard. To open this dialog box, click Start, point to Settings, click Control Panel, double-click Add/Remove Hardware, and follow the instructions. After you have removed the network adapter, change its device driver back to the one originally chosen by the operating system, or change its CMOS settings. Usually, if you can get to the point where Windows recognizes the network adapter, but still presents errors pertaining to its use of resources such as its IRQ, you can at least be certain that it is physically installed correctly.)

1. Right-click the **My Computer** icon. A shortcut menu opens.

2. Click **Properties**. The System Properties dialog box opens.

3. Select the **Hardware** tab.

4. Click the **Device Manager** button. The Device Manager window appears.

5. In the list of devices, double-click **Network adapters**.

6. Double-click the name of the adapter for which you are verifying system resources. The network adapter's Property dialog box appears.

7. Click the **Resources** tab.

8. Note the IRQ number in use by this device. Does it match the number you set through the CMOS utility in Project 6-2?

9. Close the network adapter's Property dialog box by clicking **Cancel**.

10. Close the Device Manager window.

11. Click **OK** or **Cancel** to close the System Properties dialog box.

Project 6-5

In this exercise, you will use the workstation whose network adapter you configured in the previous projects to connect to a server as part of a LAN. You will use a hub to connect the workstation and server to the LAN. If you are working in a classroom setting, your classmates will use the same hub to connect to the network, thus forming a small LAN. This project uses a Windows 2000 server and, as part of configuring your workstation to connect to this server, you will install Client for Microsoft Networks. You will configure this client so that you and your classmates belong to a Windows 2000 workgroup (that is, a group of devices).

6

For this project, you will need a working Windows 2000 server with valid logon IDs and a workgroup called CLASS, plus a folder called C:\TEMP established, a standalone hub, the instruction manual that came with the hub, two or more patch cables compatible with your network adapter and the hub's ports, and the Windows 2000 workstation whose network adapter you configured in the preceding Hands-on Projects.

1. Set up the hub according to the instruction manual's directions. Usually, summarized directions for installing the hub will appear at the beginning of such a manual. For a small standalone hub, setup should involve little more than connecting it to the wall outlet, making sure it lights up correctly, then connecting it to the server.

2. Connect a patch cable from one of the hub's ports (but not the uplink port) to your workstation's network adapter.

3. Connect another patch cable from the hub into the network adapter of the server.

4. On your workstation, right-click **My Network Places**, then click **Properties**. The Network and Dial-up Connections window opens. (Another way to open this window is as follows: Click **Start**, point to **Settings**, click **Network and Dial-up Connections**.)

5. Right-click the network connection that corresponds to the small network you have established with your hub, server, and workstation, then choose **Properties**.

6. The Local Area Connection Properties dialog box appears. Note the list of installed components. Click **Install** to begin installing a new component.

7. The Select Network Component Type dialog box opens. In the list of components, double-click **Client**. The Select Network Client dialog box opens.

8. In the list of network clients, click **Client for Microsoft Networks**. (If the Microsoft Client for Networks is already installed on the workstation, click **Cancel**, then **Cancel** again, and proceed to Step 11.)

9. Click **OK** to begin installing the Client for Microsoft Networks.

10. Once the Client for Microsoft Networks has been installed, you are ready to configure its properties.

11. Close the Local Area Connection Properties dialog box by clicking **OK**. Next you will identify the workstation and assign it to a workgroup.

12. Right-click the **My Computer** icon, click **Properties**, and then click the **Network Identification** tab. The computer's default name and workgroup should be visible.

13. To change these settings, click **Properties**.

14. For the Computer name, type: **StudentX**, where X is a unique number (if you are in a classroom; if you are not in a classroom, you can replace X with any number). Make sure the Workgroup radio button is selected, and underneath the Workgroup prompt type: **CLASS**.

15. Click **OK**, and then click **OK** again at the System Properties dialog box to save your changes. Click **Yes** to confirm that you want to restart the computer.

16. When Windows 2000 starts up again, type the student login ID and password that your instructor has created for you on the server.

17. After some of your classmates have completed Steps 1 through 11, double-click the **My Network Places** icon. What do you see?

18. Double-click the server's icon in the My Network Places window (You may need to navigate through the network to find your server.)

19. Open the **C:\TEMP** directory on the server and view its contents. You are now generating more traffic between the workstation and the server. Watch what happens to the lights next to the hub's port that connects your workstation.

20. Disconnect your workstation from its port in the hub while the data are being copied. What kind of error messages, if any, appear on your workstation and on the server?

21. Wait a few minutes, then reinsert the patch cable. What happens?

6

CASE PROJECTS

1. Evco Insurance, a multimillion-dollar life insurance firm, has asked you to help troubleshoot the network at its corporate headquarters. The network manager admits that he has not kept very close tabs on the network's growth over the last year, and he thinks this omission has something to do with the congestion problems. The Marketing Department, which is experiencing the worst network response, has added 40 people in the last six months to make a total of 146 people. At some times during the day, the marketing director has complained of waiting 10 minutes before one small e-mail message can get across the wire. He shows you to the telecommunications closet that serves the troubled department. Inside, you find a stack of eight expensive new hubs, blinking away. What are your first thoughts about why these users might be getting such poor response?

2. While you are in the telecommunications closet at Evco Insurance, you notice that one hub has two ports whose collision lights are blinking almost constantly. Being a conscientious network professional, you point out this problem to the network manager. What do you suggest you and he do next?

3. The network manager at Evco Insurance likes the fact that you have helped figure out some of his hub problems. He is especially pleased to know that he does have switching hubs and can reconfigure them to give certain users or groups of users a dedicated channel to the LAN. He thinks he might want to take this approach. The network manager understands the performance benefits that users would gain, but he still isn't sure who should get the benefit of switching. What can you tell him about switching and security that might help him decide which users' nodes should be switched?

4. The network manager at Evco Insurance understands that switches are becoming increasingly more advanced. Evco currently uses routers to connect most of its network segments to the backbone, and it uses routers to connect its 12 satellite offices around town to the corporate headquarters. The network manager asks whether you think he would be wise to replace these routers with switches in the future. What is your response?

CHAPTER 7

WANs and Remote Connectivity

After reading this chapter and completing the exercises, you will be able to:

➤ Identify network applications that require WAN technology

➤ Describe a variety of WAN transmission and connection methods

➤ Identify criteria for selecting an appropriate WAN topology, transmission method, and operating system

➤ Understand the hardware and software requirements for connecting to a network via modem

➤ Install and configure remote connectivity for a telecommuting client

ON THE JOB

As a consultant for a small networking firm, I was thrilled to have the chance to work on the implementation of a WAN for a large West Coast city. The city wanted to connect more than 40 locations, including a sports arena, seniors' center, bus terminal, and maintenance plant, plus its business offices, so as to centrally control all file sharing, messaging, and printing occurring within the city government. It also wanted to provide Internet access for its employees. Some of the locations were situated 20 miles from the city center.

Our team of consultants recommended a combination of T1 and ISDN technology. For some locations, such as the city transportation office, we used both a T1 and an ISDN backup to the central connecting point, the city government's headquarters. Although the city didn't want to pay for a full-mesh topology, we did create a partial-mesh WAN by providing alternate routes around critical links. For example, we implemented a 56-KB dial-up link from one government building to another that would carry traffic between the buildings in case one of the T1s failed. We placed all servers at the headquarters, which allowed the city's IT staff to centrally control security and account administration. Finally, we connected the city to an ISP using a fractional T1. As a result, the city government is completely and reliably networked.

James Furness
CSI Networks

Now that you understand the basic transmission media, network models, and networking hardware associated with local area networks (LANs), you need to expand that knowledge to encompass wide area networks (WANs). As you learned in Chapter 1, a WAN is a network that connects two or more geographically distinct LANs. You might assume that WANs are the same as LANs, only bigger. Although a WAN is based on the same principles as a LAN, including reliance on the OSI Model, its distance requirements affect its entire infrastructure. As a result, nearly all characteristics of a WAN differ from the characteristics of a LAN.

To understand the difference between a LAN and WAN, think of the hallways and stairs of your house as LAN pathways. These interior passages allow you to go from room to room. To reach destinations outside of your house, however, you need to use sidewalks and streets. These public thoroughfares are analogous to WAN pathways—except that WAN pathways are not necessarily public.

This chapter discusses the technical differences between LANs and WANs and describes in detail WAN transmission media and methods. It also notes the potential pitfalls in establishing and maintaining WANs. In addition, it introduces you to remote connectivity for LANs—a technology that, in some cases, can be used to extend a LAN into a WAN. Remote connectivity and WANs are significant concerns for organizations attempting to meet the needs of telecommuting workers, global business partners, and Internet-based commerce. To pass the Net+ certification exam, you must be familiar with the variety of WAN and remote connectivity options. You also need to understand the hardware and software requirements for dial-up networking.

WAN ESSENTIALS

As you know, a WAN traverses a large geographical area—connecting LANs across the city or across the nation. For example, a WAN might connect the headquarters of an insurance company in New York with its satellite insurance offices in Hartford, Dallas, and San Francisco. The individual geographic locations (Hartford, Dallas, San Francisco) are known as WAN sites. A **WAN link** is a connection between one WAN site (or point) and another site (or point). A WAN link is typically described as point-to-point—because it connects one site to only one other site. That is, it does not typically connect one site to several other sites, in the way that LAN hubs or switches connect multiple segments or workstations. Nevertheless, one location may be connected to more than one location by multiple WAN links. Figure 7-1 illustrates the difference between WAN and LAN connectivity.

On the one hand, WANs and LANs are similar in some fundamental ways. In general, both can use any of the protocols mentioned in Chapter 3. Also, both primarily carry digital data. Finally, WANs and LANs have a similar function: to enable communications between clients and hosts that are not directly attached to each other.

On the other hand, WANs use different transmission systems, topologies, and sometimes, media, than LANs do. LANs typically use internal cabling, such as coaxial or twisted-pair. In contrast, WANs typically send data over public communications links, such as the telecommunications backbone provided by local and long-distance telephone companies. For better throughput, an organization might lease a continuously available link through another carrier, such as an Internet service provider (ISP). This kind of connection is called a **dedicated** line. Unlike a dial-up connection, dedicated lines do not require a user to connect and disconnect for a specified period of usage. They come in a variety of types that are distinguished by their capacity and transmission characteristics. You will learn about technology that relies on dedicated WAN connections, such as DSL and T1, later in this chapter.

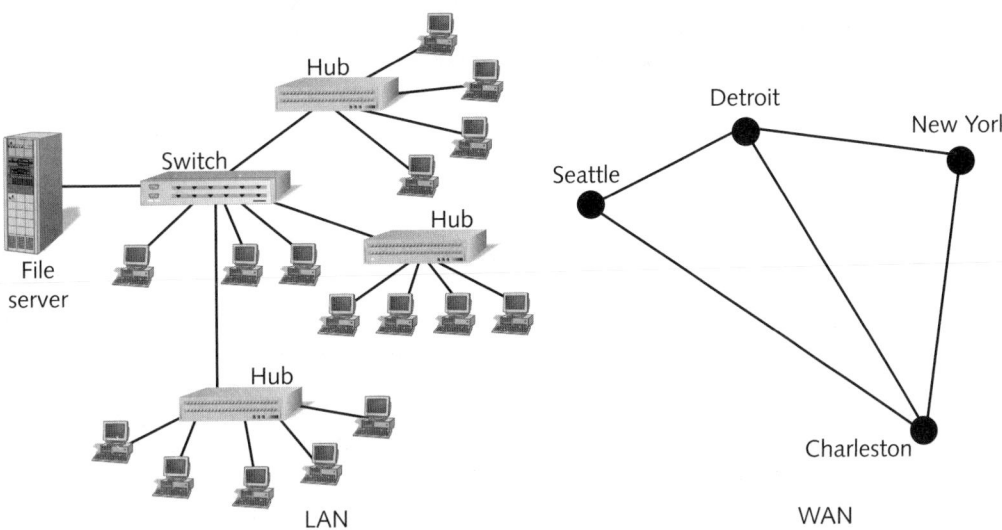

Figure 7-1   Differences in LAN and WAN connectivity

Chapter 5 introduced the various WAN topologies: star, ring, mesh, partial mesh, and hybrid. In that chapter, you learned that most WANs do not take the form of simple star or ring networks, but more likely employ mesh or partial-mesh configurations. As you know, the Internet is the largest WAN in existence today. Typically, the enterprise-wide WANs of individual organizations are conceived on a much smaller scale. For example, a WAN might begin by connecting only two offices (such as two branches of a bookstore chain that are located at either end of a city). As the organization grows, the WAN might grow to connect more and more sites, located across the city or around the world. Only an organization's information technology budget and aspirations limit the dimensions of its WAN.

Why might an organization need a WAN? Any organization that has multiple sites scattered over a wide geographical area needs a way to exchange data between those sites. Each of the following scenarios demonstrates a need for a WAN:

- A bank with offices around the state needs to connect those offices to gather transaction and account information into a central database.

- Regional sales representatives for a national pharmaceutical company need to dial in their sales figures and receive e-mail from headquarters.

- An insurance company allows parents on family leave to work from home by dialing into the company's network.

- An automobile manufacturer in Detroit contracts its plastic parts manufacturing out to a Delaware-based company. Through WAN links, the auto manufacturer can videoconference with the plastics manufacturer, exchange specification data, and even examine the parts for quality online.

- A support technician for the remote pharmaceutical salesperson may need to show the salesperson how to create a macro in an Excel spreadsheet. A remote control program, such as pcAnywhere, enables the support technician to "take over" the salesperson's PC (over a WAN link) and demonstrate how to create the macro.

- A clothing manufacturer sells its products over the Internet to customers throughout the world.

Although all of these businesses need WANs, they may not need the same kinds of WANs. Depending on the traffic load, budget, and geographical breadth, each might implement a different transmission method. For every business need, only a few (or possibly only one) appropriate WAN connection types may exist. However, many WAN technologies can coexist on the same network. As you learn about each technology, pay attention to its characteristics and think about its possible applications. To qualify for Net+ certification, you must be familiar with the variety of WAN connection types and be able to identify the types of networking environments that each suits best. You will learn about the various WAN transmission methods and connection types in the next section.

The WAN technologies discussed in the following section differ in terms of speed, reliability, cost, distance covered, and security. Also, some are defined by specifications at the Data Link layer, while others are defined by specifications at the Physical layer of the OSI Model. Both types of technology are included in this chapter because both types are used on WANs.

PSTN

PSTN, which stands for **Public Switched Telephone Network**, refers to the network of typical telephone lines and carrier equipment that service most homes. PSTN may also be called **plain old telephone service (POTS)**. It was originally composed of analog lines and developed to handle voice-based traffic. Now, however, most of the PSTN uses digital transmission through fiber-optic and copper twisted-pair cable, microwave, and satellite connections. This system is currently used for most dial-up connections to LANs. Indeed, for individuals simply picking up their e-mail or surfing the Web, PSTN is usually adequate. For example, a salesperson traveling to a conference might dial into her office's LAN from her hotel each night to pick up e-mail. So long as she doesn't have to download a significant amount of data, the throughput of her hotel room phone line connection would suffice.

A **dial-up** connection uses a PSTN or other line to access a remote server via modems at both the source (for example, the salesperson's computer) and destination (for example, the office LAN's server). As you have learned, a modem converts a computer's digital pulses into analog signals for the PSTN (because not all of the PSTN is necessarily capable of handling digital transmission), then converts the analog signals back into digital pulses at the receiving computer's end. Unlike other types of WAN connections, dial-up connections provide a fixed period of access to the network, just as the phone call you make to a friend has a fixed length, determined by when you initiate and terminate the call. Ways to configure dial-up connections and establish remote connectivity are discussed in detail later in this chapter.

The advantages to using the PSTN are its ubiquity, ease of use, and low cost. A person can travel virtually anywhere in the world and have access to a phone line and, therefore, remote access to a network. Within the United States, the dial-up configuration for one location differs little from the dial-up configuration in another location. And nearly all mobile personal computers contain a modem, the only hardware a computer requires to establish this type of connection.

The disadvantage of the PSTN comes from its inability to ensure the quality or throughput required by many WAN applications. The quality of a WAN connection is largely determined by how many data packets that it loses or that become corrupt during transmission, how quickly it can transmit and receive data, and whether it drops the connection altogether. To improve this quality, most data transmission methods employ error-checking techniques. For example, TCP/IP depends on acknowledgments of the data it receives. In addition, many (though not all) PSTN links are now digital, and digital lines are more reliable than the older analog lines. Such digital lines reduce the quality problems that once plagued purely analog PSTN connections.

The more significant limiting factor of the PSTN is its capacity, or throughput. Currently, the most advanced PSTN modems advertise a connection speed of 56 Kbps. The 56-Kbps maximum is actually a *theoretical* threshold that assumes that the connection between the initiator and the receiver is pristine. Splitters, fax machines, or other devices that a modem connection traverses between the sender and receiver will all reduce the actual throughput. The number of points through which your phone call travels will also affect throughput. In addition, the **Federal Communications Commission (FCC)**, the regulatory agency that sets standards and policy for telecommunications transmission and equipment in the United States, limits the use of PSTN lines to 53 Kbps in order to reduce the effects of crosstalk. Thus, you will never actually achieve full 56-Kbps throughput using a modem over the PSTN.

To demonstrate how throughput diminishes over a PSTN connection, it's useful to follow a typical dial-up call from modem to modem, as pictured in Figure 7-2. Imagine you dial into your ISP to surf the Web through a 56-Kbps modem. You first initiate a call through your computer's modem. Your modem converts the digital signal from your computer into an analog signal that travels over the phone line to the local telephone company's **point of presence (POP)**. A POP is the place where the two telephone systems meet—either a long-distance carrier with a local telephone company, or a local carrier with an ISP's data center. At the POP, your signal is converted back to digital pulses and transmitted to your ISP's POP through a digital backbone (usually made of fiber-optic cable). The ISP's POP connects to its Internet service provider (the "larger ISP" in the figure) through a digital link, perhaps a T1 or T3 (discussed later in this chapter). Your request for information enters the Internet, and the transmission process is then reversed to bring you the desired Web page. Each time your transmission travels through a POP, or is converted from analog to digital or digital to analog, it loses a little through-put. By the time the Web page returns to you, the connection may have lost from 5 to 30 Kbps, and your effective throughput might have been reduced to 30 Kbps or less.

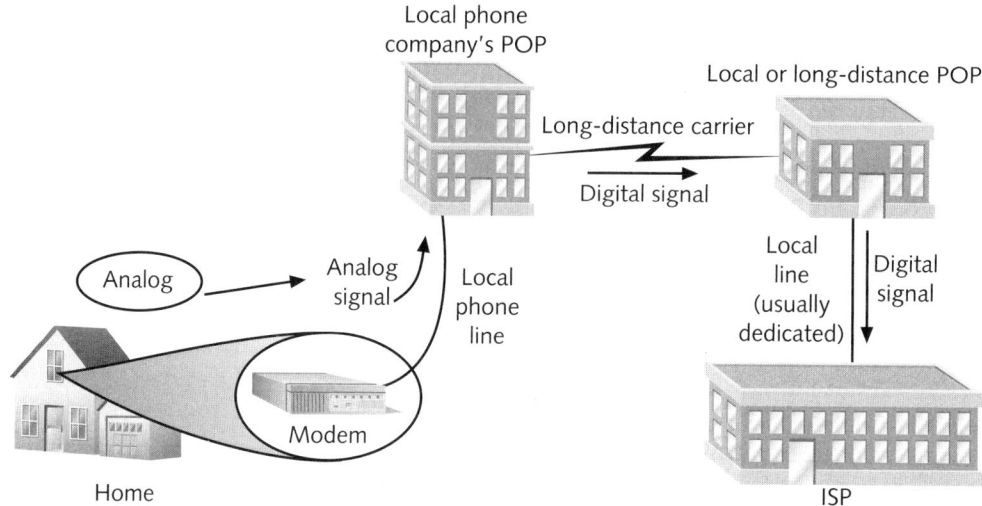

Figure 7-2   A typical PSTN connection to the Internet

 "POP" is another network-related acronym that can have two completely dif-ferent meanings, depending on its context. In this discussion of WAN and remote connectivity, a POP refers to a telecommunications service carrier's point of presence. In Chapter 11's in-depth discussion of TCP/IP protocols, POP will refer to the Post Office Protocol, used in e-mail transmission.

The PSTN uses circuit switching. (Recall from Chapter 5 that circuit switching is a means of transmitting data between two nodes with a dedicated point–to–point con-nection.) You might think that circuit switching makes the PSTN more secure than other types of WAN connections; in fact, the PSTN offers only marginal security. Granted, the PSTN is more secure than some forms of communication, such as cellular communications. Because it is a public network, however, PSTN presents many points at which communications can be intercepted and interpreted on their way from sender to receiver. For example, an eavesdropper could easily tap into the connection where your local telephone company's line enters your house. To make PSTN transmissions more secure, you must encrypt the data before it is sent. Chapter 15 describes data encryption techniques.

X.25 AND FRAME RELAY

X.25 is an analog, packet-switched technology designed for long-distance data transmission and standardized by the ITU in the mid-1970s. The original standard for X.25 specified a maximum of 64-Kbps throughput, but by 1992 the standard was updated to include maximum throughput of 2.048 Mbps. It was originally developed as a more reliable alternative to the voice telephone system for connecting mainframe computers and remote terminals. X.25 ensures data reliability over long distances by verifying the transmission at every node. Unfortunately, this verification also renders X.25 comparatively slow and unsuitable for time-sensitive applications such as audio or video. X.25 was never widely adopted in the United States, but was accepted by other countries and was for a long time the dominant packet-switching technology used on WANs around the world.

 Recall from Chapter 5 that, in packet switching, packets belonging to the same data stream may follow different, optimal paths to their destination. As a result, packet switching uses bandwidth more efficiently and allows for faster transmission than if each packet in the data stream had to follow the same path, as in circuit switching. Packet switching is also more flexible than circuit switching, because packet sizes may vary.

Frame relay is an updated, digital version of X.25 that also relies on packet switching. The name is derived from the fact that data is separated into frames, which are then relayed from one node to another without any verification or processing. Partially because it doesn't perform the same level of error detection that X.25 performs, frame relay supports higher bandwidth than X.25. It offers a maximum of either 1.544-Mbps or 45-Mbps throughput. It was standardized in 1984 and became popular in the United States and Canada for reliable long-distance WAN connections. However, frame relay is being replaced by newer, faster technologies. On networking diagrams, packet-switched networks such as X.25 and frame relay are depicted as clouds, as shown in Figure 7-3, because of the indeterminate nature of their traffic patterns.

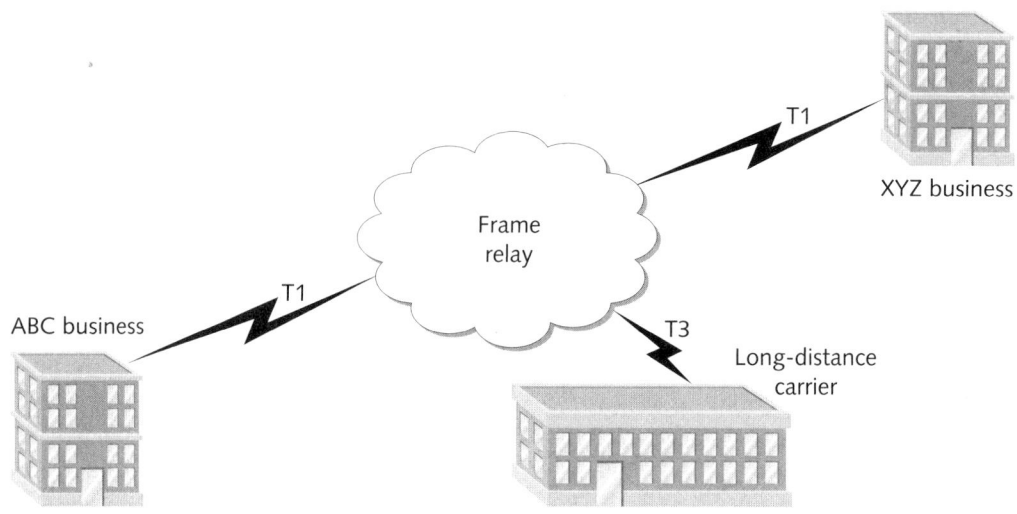

Figure 7-3   A WAN using frame relay

 You may have seen the Internet depicted as a cloud on networking diagrams, similar to the frame relay cloud in Figure 7-3. In its early days, the Internet relied largely on X.25 or frame relay transmission—hence the similar illustration.

Both X.25 and frame relay may be configured as switched virtual circuits (SVCs) or more often, as permanent virtual circuits (PVCs). **SVCs** are connections that are established when parties need to transmit, then dismantled once the transmission is complete. **PVCs** are connections that are established before data needs to be transmitted and maintained after the transmission is complete. Note that in a PVC, the connection is established only between the two points (the sender and receiver); the connection does not specify the exact route the data will travel. Thus, in a PVC, data may follow any number of different paths to move from point A to point B. For example, a transmission traveling over a PVC from Baltimore to Phoenix might go from Baltimore to Washington, D.C., to Chicago, then to Phoenix; the next transmission over that PVC, however, might go from Baltimore to Boston to Chicago to Kansas City to Phoenix.

PVCs are *not* dedicated like T-carrier services. When you lease an X.25 or frame relay circuit from your local carrier, your contract reflects the endpoints you specify and the amount of bandwidth you require between those endpoints. The service provider guarantees a minimum amount of bandwidth, called the **committed information rate (CIR)**. Provisions usually account for bursts of traffic that occasionally exceed the CIR. When you lease a PVC, you share bandwidth with the other X.25 and frame relay users on the backbone. Most X.25 and frame relay circuits travel over T-carriers.

The advantage to leasing a frame relay circuit over leasing a dedicated service (such as a T1) is that you pay for only the amount of bandwidth required. Another advantage is that frame relay is much less expensive than the newer WAN technologies offered today, such as ATM. Also, frame relay follows an established worldwide standard.

On the other hand, because frame relay and X.25 use shared lines, their throughput remains at the mercy of variable traffic patterns. In the middle of the night, data over your frame relay network may zip along at 1.544 Mbps; during midday, when everyone is surfing the Web, it may slow down to less than your CIR. In addition, frame relay circuits are not as private as dedicated circuits. Nevertheless, because they use the same connectivity equipment as T-carriers, they can easily be upgraded to T-carrier dedicated lines.

ISDN

ISDN (Integrated Services Digital Network) is an international standard, established by the International Telecommunications Union (ITU), for transmitting data over digital lines. ISDN uses the telephone carrier's lines and either a dial-up or dedicated connection. It is distinguished from PSTN by the fact that it relies exclusively on digital connections and by the fact that it can carry data and voice simultaneously. ISDN lines may carry as many as two voice calls and one data connection simultaneously. To achieve this feat, however, the ISDN user must have the correct devices to accept all three connections, as described later in this section. Through their ability to transmit voice and data simultaneously, ISDN lines can eliminate the need to pay for separate phone lines to support faxes, modems, and voice calls at one location. Local phone companies began offering ISDN in the mid-1980s, anticipating that the United States would convert to this all-digital system by the turn of the century. ISDN hasn't caught on as quickly as predicted, and other types of digital transmission methods now compete with it to serve customers who require moderate to fast throughput over phone lines.

All ISDN connections are based on two types of channels: B channels and D channels. The **B channel** is the "bearer" channel, employing circuit-switching techniques to carry voice, video, audio, and other types of data over the ISDN connection. A single B channel has a maximum throughput of 64 Kbps, although it is sometimes limited to 56 Kbps by the ISDN provider. As you will learn, the number of B channels in a single ISDN connection may vary. The **D channel** is the "data" channel, employing packet switching techniques to carry information about the call, such as session initiation and termination signals, caller identity, call forwarding, and conference calling signals. A single D channel has a maximum throughput of 16 or 64 Kbps, depending on the type of ISDN connection. Each ISDN connection uses only one D channel.

In North America, two types of ISDN connections are commonly used: Basic Rate Interface (BRI) and Primary Rate Interface (PRI). A third type of ISDN connection, called Broadband ISDN (B-ISDN), was developed by the ITU in the late 1980s to provide more capacity than BRI or PRI. Today, organizations in need of the capacity offered by B-ISDN tend to choose newer, high-capacity lines, such as those using xDSL or T1 technology (both described later in this chapter).

7

BRI (Basic Rate Interface) uses two B channels and one D channel, as indicated by the following notation: 2B+D. The two B channels are treated as separate connections by the network and can carry voice and data or two data streams simultaneously and separate from each other. In a process called **bonding**, these two 64-Kbps B channels can be combined to achieve an effective throughput of 128 Kbps—the maximum amount of data traffic that a BRI connection can accommodate. Most consumers who subscribe to ISDN from home use BRI, which is the most economical type of ISDN connection.

Figure 7-4 illustrates how a typical BRI link supplies a home consumer with an ISDN link. (Note that the configuration depicted in Figure 7-4 applies to installations in North America only. Because transmission standards differ in Europe and Asia, different numbers of B channels are used in the standard ISDN connections in those regions.) From the telephone company's lines, the ISDN channels connect to a Network Termination 1 device at the customer's site. The **Network Termination 1 (NT1)** device connects the twisted-pair wiring at the customer's building with the ISDN terminal equipment via RJ-11 (standard telephone) or RJ-45 data jacks. The ISDN **terminal equipment (TE)** may include cards or standalone devices used to connect computers to the ISDN line (similar to a network adapter used on Ethernet or Token Ring networks).

So that the ISDN line can connect to analog equipment, the signal must first pass through a terminal adapter. A **terminal adapter (TA)** converts digital signals into analog signals for use with ISDN phones and other analog devices. (Terminal adapters are sometimes called ISDN modems, though they are not, technically, modems.) Typically, telecommuters who want more throughput than their analog phone line will afford choose BRI as their ISDN connection. For a home user, the terminal adapter would most likely be an ISDN router, such as the 800 series router from Cisco Systems, while the terminal equipment would be an Ethernet card in the user's workstation plus, perhaps, a phone.

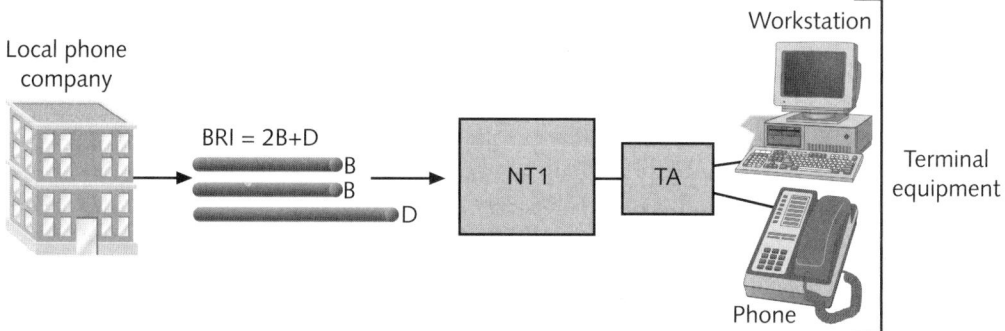

Figure 7-4   A BRI link

PRI (Primary Rate Interface) uses 23 B channels and one 64-Kbps D channel, as represented by the following notation: 23B+D. PRI is less commonly used by individual subscribers than BRI is, but it may be selected by businesses and other organizations that need more throughput. As with BRI, the separate B channels in a PRI link can carry voice and data, independently of each other or bonded together. The maximum potential throughput for a PRI connection is 1.544 Mbps, the same as that for T1; in fact, PRI channels can be carried by T1 trunks.

PRI and BRI connections may be interconnected on a single network. PRI links use the same kind of equipment as BRI links, but require the services of an extra network termination device, called a **Network Termination 2 (NT2)**, to handle the multiple ISDN lines. Figure 7-5 depicts a typical PRI link as it would be installed in North America.

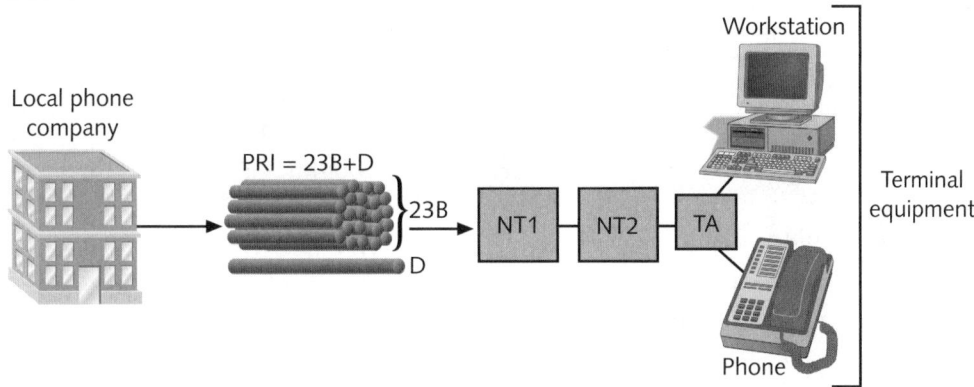

Figure 7-5 A PRI link

Individual customers who need to transmit more data than a typical modem can handle or who want to use a single line for both data and voice commonly use ISDN lines. ISDN, although not available in every location of the United States, can be purchased from most local telephone companies. The cost of using BRI averages $100 to $250 per month, depending on the customer's location. PRI and B-ISDN are significantly more expensive. In some areas, ISDN providers may charge customers additional usage fees based on the total length of time they remain connected.

One disadvantage of ISDN is that it can span a distance of only 18,000 linear feet before repeater equipment is needed to boost the signal. For this reason, it is only feasible to use for the **local loop** portion of the WAN link—that is, the part of a phone system that connects a customer site with a public carrier's POP.

T-CARRIERS

So far you have learned about WAN connections capable of relatively low throughput. Now you will learn about connections and transmission methods capable of 1.544-Mbps and higher throughput. Together, these transmission methods are known as **broadband** technologies. Note that this definition of broadband is different from the definition you learned in Chapter 4. Examples of this type of broadband technology are cable modem services, DSL, and the group of connections that include T1s, fractional T1s, and T3s—collectively known as **T-carriers**. This section focuses on T-carrier technology. Subsequent sections cover DSL and cable modem technology.

T-carrier transmission uses time division multiplexing over two wire pairs (one for transmitting and one for receiving) to divide a single channel into multiple channels. For example, multiplexing enables a single T1 circuit to carry 24 channels, each capable of 64-Kbps throughput; thus a T1 has a maximum capacity of 24 × 64 Kbps, or 1.544 Mbps. Each channel may contain data, voice, or video signals.

AT&T developed T-carrier technology in 1957 in an effort to digitize voice signals, thereby enabling such signals to travel long distances. Before that time, voice signals, which were purely analog, were expensive to transmit over long distances because of the number of connectivity devices needed to keep the signal intelligible. In the 1970s, many businesses installed T1s to obtain more voice throughput per line. With increased data communication needs, such as Internet access and geographically dispersed offices, T1s have become common WAN links for use in medium to large businesses.

The next section describes the various types of T-carriers, then the chapter moves on to T-carrier connectivity devices.

Types of T-carriers

A number of T-carrier varieties are available to businesses today, as shown in Table 7-1. The most common T-carrier implementations are T1 and, for higher bandwidth needs, T3. A **T1** circuit can carry the equivalent of 24 voice or data channels, giving a maximum data throughput of 1.544 Mbps. A **T3** circuit can carry the equivalent of 672 voice or data channels, giving a maximum data throughput of 44.736 Mbps (its throughput is typically rounded up to 45 Mbps for the purposes of discussion).

The speed of a T-carrier depends on its signal level. The **signal level** refers to the T-carrier's Physical layer electrical signaling characteristics as defined by ANSI standards in the early 1980s. **DS0 (digital signal, level 0)** is the equivalent of one data or voice channel. All other signal levels are multiples of DS0.

You may hear signal level and carrier terms used interchangeably—for example, DS1 and T1. Technically, T1 is the North American implementation of the international DS1 standard. In Europe, the DS1 standard is implemented as E1 and offers a slightly higher throughput than T1.

Table 7-1 Carrier specifications

Signal Level	Carrier	Number of T1s	Number of Channels	Throughput (Mbps)
DS0	—	1/24	1	.064
DS1	T1	1	24	1.544
DS1C	T1C	2	24	3.152
DS2	T2	4	96	6.312
DS3	T3	28	672	44.736
DS4	T4	168	4032	274.176

As a networking professional, you are most likely to work with T1 or T3 lines. In addition to knowing their capacity, you should be familiar with their costs and uses. T1s are commonly used by businesses to connect branch offices or to connect to a carrier, such as an ISP. Telephone companies also use T1s to connect their smaller central offices. ISPs may use one or more T1s or T3s, depending on the provider's size, to connect to their Internet carriers.

Because a T3 provides 28 times more throughput than a T1, many organizations may find that a few T1s—rather than a single T3—can accommodate their throughput needs. For example, suppose a university research laboratory needed to transmit molecular images over the Internet to another university, and its peak throughput need (at any given time) was 10 Mbps. The laboratory would require seven T1s (10 Mbps divided by 1.544 Mbps equals 6.48 T1s). Leasing seven T1s would prove much less expensive for the university than leasing a single T3.

The cost of T1s varies from region to region. On average, a T1 might cost between $500 and $2000 to install, plus an additional $500 to $2000 per month in access fees. The longer the distance between the provider (such as an ISP or a telephone company) and the subscriber, the higher a T1's monthly charge. Charges for local T1s may be based on mileage, whereas costs for long distance T1s vary on a city-to-city basis. For example, a T1 between Houston and New York will cost more than a T1 between Washington, D.C., and New York. Similarly, a T1 from the western suburbs of Detroit to the city center will cost more than a T1 from the city center to a business three blocks away.

For organizations that do not need constant bandwidth, a dial-up ISDN solution may prove more cost-effective than a T1. For businesses that *do* need a dedicated circuit, but don't always need as much as 1.544-Mbps throughput, a fractional T1 is a better option. A **fractional T1** lease allows organizations to use only some of the channels on a T1 line and be charged according to the number of channels they use. Thus fractional T1 bandwidth can be leased in multiples of 64 Kbps. A fractional T1 is best suited to businesses that expect their traffic to grow and that may require a full T1 eventually, but can't currently justify leasing a full T1.

T3s are very expensive and are used by the most data-intensive businesses—for example, computer consulting firms that provide online data backups and warehousing for a number of other businesses or large long-distance carriers. A T3 is much more expensive than even multiple T1s. It may cost as much as $3000 to install, plus monthly service fees based on usage. If a customer uses the full T3 bandwidth of 45 Mbps, for example, the monthly charges might be as high as $18,000. Of course, T3 costs will vary depending on the carrier, your location, and the distance covered by the T3. In any event, however, this type of connection is significantly more expensive than a T1. Therefore, only businesses with extraordinary bandwidth requirements should consider using T3s.

T-carrier Connectivity

The approximate costs mentioned previously include monthly access and installation, but not connectivity hardware. Every T-carrier line requires connectivity hardware at both the customer site and the local carrier's POP. Connectivity hardware may be purchased or leased. If your organization uses an ISP to establish and service your T-carrier line, you will most likely lease the connectivity equipment. If you lease the line directly from the local carrier and you anticipate little change in your connectivity requirements over time, however, you may want to purchase the hardware.

T-carrier lines require specialized connectivity hardware that cannot be used with other WAN transmission methods. In addition, T-carrier lines require different media, depending on their throughput. In this section, you will learn about the physical components of a T-carrier connection between a customer site and a local carrier.

Wiring

As mentioned earlier, the T-carrier system is based on AT&T's original attempt to digitize existing long-distance telephone lines. As a result, T1 technology can use unshielded or shielded twisted-pair copper wiring—in other words, plain telephone wire. Because the digital signals require a cleaner connection (that is, one less susceptible to noise and attenuation), however, shielded twisted-pair is preferable. For T1s using shielded twisted-pair, repeaters must regenerate the signal approximately every 6000 feet. Twisted-pair wiring cannot adequately carry the high throughput of multiple T1s or T3 transmissions. Thus, for multiple T1s, coaxial cable, microwave, or fiber-optic cabling may be used. For T3s, microwave or fiber-optic cabling is necessary.

CSU/DSU (Channel Service Unit/Data Service Unit)

Although CSUs (channel service units) and DSUs (data service units) are actually two separate devices, they are typically combined into a single box called a **CSU/DSU**. The CSU/DSU is the connection point for a T1 line at the customer's site. The **CSU** provides termination for the digital signal and ensures connection integrity through error correction and line monitoring. The **DSU** converts the digital signal used by bridges, routers, and multiplexers into the digital signal sent via the cabling. The CSU/DSU box connects the incoming T1 with the multiplexer, as shown in Figure 7-6.

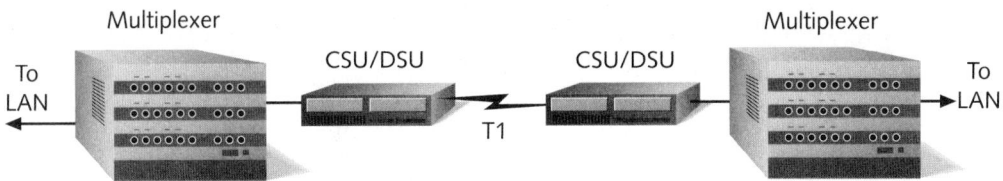

Figure 7-6   A CSU/DSU connecting a T1

Multiplexer

As you learned earlier, a multiplexer is a device that combines multiple voice or data channels on one line. The devices that connect to the multiplexer are collectively known as terminal equipment. Multiplexers can take input from a variety of terminal equipment, such as bridges, routers, or telephone exchange devices that accept only voice transmissions (such as a PBX system). Figure 7-7 depicts a typical use of a multiplexer with a T1-connected data network. In some network configurations, the multiplexer is integrated with the CSU/DSU. In the following sections, you will learn how routers and bridges integrate with CSU/DSUs and multiplexers to connect T-carriers to a LAN.

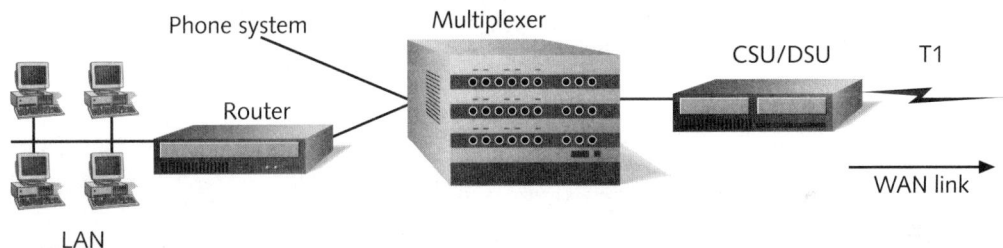

Figure 7-7   Typical use of a multiplexer on a T1-connected data network

Routers and Bridges

On a typical T1-connected data network, the terminal equipment will consist of bridges, routers, or a combination of the two. The bridges and routers used in this situation are identical to the bridges and routers you learned about in Chapter 6. With the T1 connection, the bridge or router would typically integrate two types of networks: the Internet and an Ethernet or Token Ring LAN at the customer's site. A router, which can convert TCP/IP to other protocols, is necessary if the internal LAN does not run TCP/IP. Figure 7-8 depicts the use of a router with a T1-connected network.

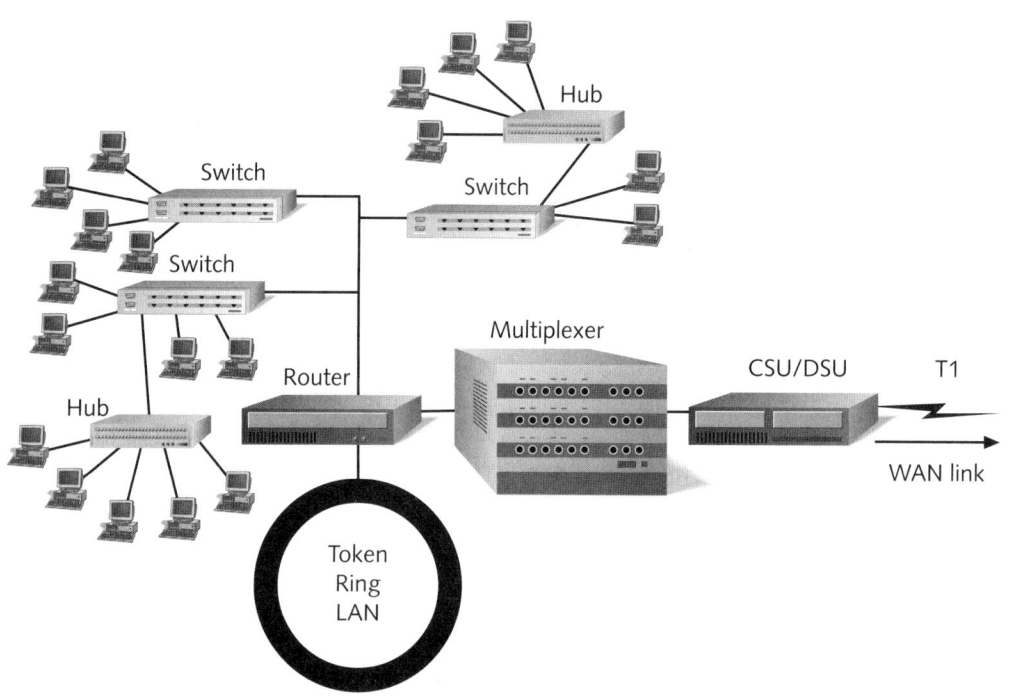

Figure 7-8   A router on a T1-connected network

DSL

Digital subscriber line (DSL) is a type of WAN connection introduced in the late 1990s that competes directly with ISDN and T1 services. Like ISDN, DSL can span only limited distances without the help of repeaters and is therefore best suited to the local loop portion of a WAN link. Also, like ISDN, DSL can support multiple data and voice channels over a single line.

DSL uses advanced data modulation techniques to achieve extraordinary throughput over regular phone lines. Recall from Chapter 4 that in data modulation, one signal alters the frequency, phase, or amplitude of another signal to enable multiple signals to traverse the same wire without interfering with each other. Depending on the type, DSL may use any one of these three types of modulation.

Many individuals and businesses are choosing DSL for its low cost, ease of installation, and high throughput. In most areas of the United States, a DSL connection that can supply nearly as much throughput as a T-1 costs less than $100 per month. Consumer-grade DSL, with approximately half as much bandwidth, can cost as low as $20 per month. Because it runs over existing telephone lines, DSL installation is relatively simple, requiring only a special modem and some configuration at the user end. Also, DSL is a dedicated service, which means a connection is always available for use. In the next section you will learn about the many varieties of DSL in use today.

Types of DSL

The term **xDSL** refers to all DSL varieties, of which at least eight currently exist. The better-known DSL varieties include Asymmetric DSL (ADSL), G.Lite (a version of ADSL), High Bit-Rate DSL (HDSL), Symmetric or Single-Line DSL (SDSL), and Very High Bit-Rate DSL (VDSL)—the "x" in "xDSL" is replaced by the variety name. DSL types can be divided into two categories: asymmetrical and symmetrical.

To understand the difference between these two categories, you must understand the concept of downstream and upstream data transmission. The term **downstream** refers to data traveling from the carrier's POP to the customer. The term **upstream** refers to data traveling from the customer to the carrier's POP. In some types of DSL, the throughput rates for downstream and upstream traffic differ. That is, if you were connected to the Internet via a DSL link, you might be able to pick up your e-mail messages more rapidly than you could send them because the downstream throughput is usually greater. A technology that offers more throughput in one direction than in the other is considered **asymmetrical**. In asymmetrical communications, downstream throughput is usually much higher than upstream throughput. Asymmetrical communication is well suited to users who pull more information off the network than they send to it—for example, people watching videoconferences or people surfing the Web.

Conversely, **symmetrical** technology provides equal capacity for data traveling both upstream and downstream. Symmetrical transmission is suited to users who both upload and download significant amounts of data—for example, a bank's branch office, which sends large volumes of account information to the central server at the bank's headquarters and in turn, receives large amounts of account information from the central server at the bank's headquarters. ADSL and VDSL are examples of asymmetrical DSL; HDSL and SDSL are examples of symmetrical DSL.

The types of DSL also vary in terms of their capacity and maximum line length. A VDSL line that carries as much as 52 Mbps in one direction and as much as 6.4 Mbps in the opposite direction can extend a maximum of 1000 feet between the customer's premises and the carrier's POP. This limitation might suit businesses located close to a telephone company's data center (for example, in the middle of a metropolitan area), but it won't work for most individuals. The most popular form of DSL, ADSL, provides a maximum of 8 Mbps in one direction and a maximum of 1.544 Mbps in the other direction; at its highest speeds, it is limited to a distance of 12,000 feet between the customer's premises and the carrier's POP. This distance (more than two miles) renders it suitable for most telecommuters. Table 7-2 compares current specifications for five DSL types.

7

Table 7-2 Comparison of DSL types

DSL Type	Maximum Upstream Capacity (Mbps)	Maximum Downstream Capacity (Mbps)	Distance Limitation (feet)
ADSL ("full rate")	1	8	18,000
G.Lite (a type of ADSL)	0.512	1.544	25,000
HDSL	1.544 or 2.048	1.544 or 2.048	12,000
SDSL	1.544	1.544	9,000
VDSL	1.6, 3.2, or 6.4	13, 25.9, or 51.8	1000 – 5000

In addition to their data modulation techniques, capacity, and distance limitations, DSL types vary according to how they use the PSTN. Following you will learn about how DSL connects to a business or residence over the PSTN.

DSL Connectivity

DSL connectivity, like ISDN, depends on the PSTN. To understand how DSL uses the PSTN, it is helpful to first understand that voice signals use a very small range of frequencies, between 0 and 35 KHz. This leaves higher, inaudible frequencies unused and available for carrying data. Some versions of DSL, such as the popular full-rate ADSL, G.Lite, and VDSL, use the same pair of wires that carry voice signals, but modulate data on the higher frequencies. In the case of full-rate ADSL, a splitter must be installed at the carrier and at the customer's premises to separate the data signal from the voice signal before it reaches the terminal equipment (for example, the phone or the computer). G.Lite, a slower and less expensive version of ADSL, eliminates the splitter but requires the use of a filter to prevent high-frequency DSL signals from reaching the telephone. This makes G.Lite easier to install. Other types of DSL, such as HDSL and SDSL, cannot use the same wire pair that is used for voice signals. Instead, these types of DSL use the extra pair of wires contained in a telephone cable (that are typically unused).

Once inside the customer's office or home, the DSL line must pass through a **DSL modem**, a device that demodulates the signal, extracting the information and passing it on to the computer. The DSL modem may also contain a splitter (for example, in the case of ADSL) to separate the line into multiple channels for voice and data signals. The DSL modem may be external to the computer and connect to a computer's Ethernet NIC via UTP cable or to the computer's USB port. Newer DSL modems come in the form of internal, PCI expansion boards. If the DSL bandwidth is to be shared on a LAN, the DSL modem could connect to a connectivity device, such as a hub or router, rather than to just one computer. Figure 7-9 represents a typical DSL connection, including its termination inside an office. Figure 7-10 depicts a DSL modem.

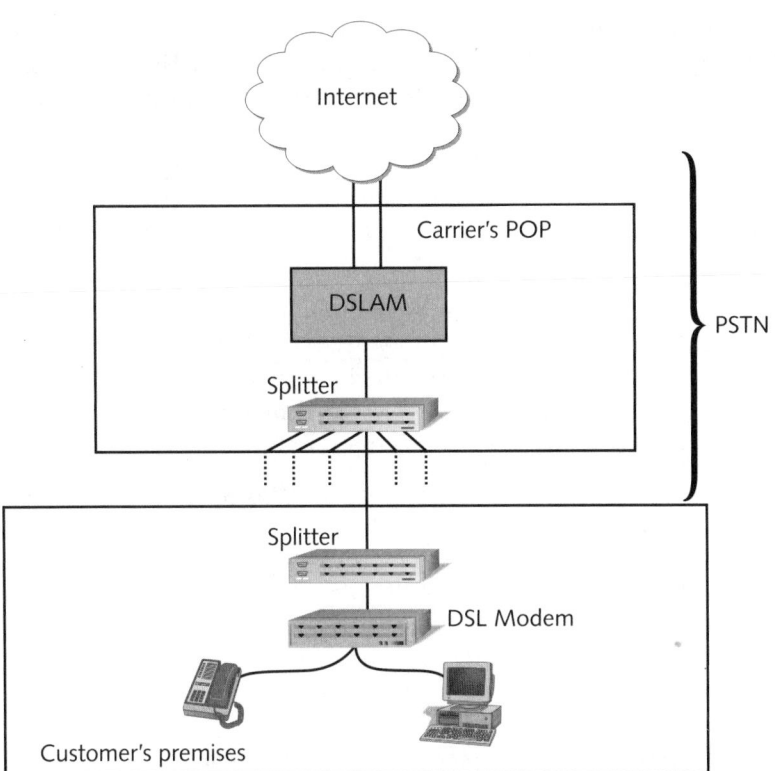

Figure 7-9   A DSL connection

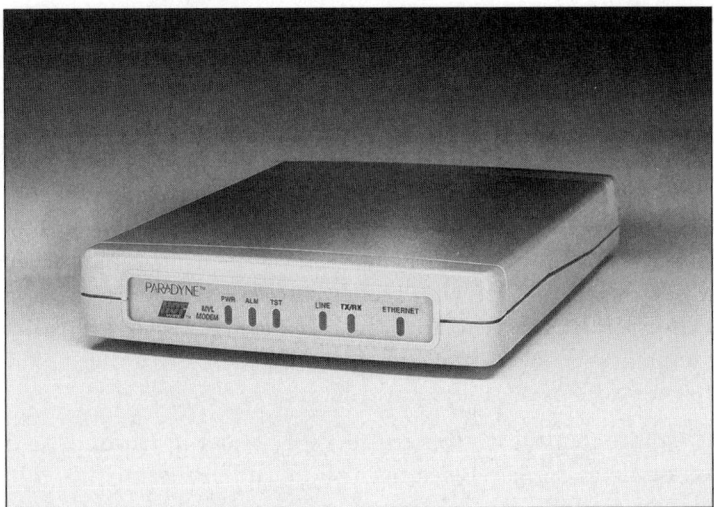

Figure 7-10   A DSL modem

On the other end of the line, the DSL connection terminates at a carrier's POP. If necessary, a splitter is placed between the incoming line and the telephone and data switches. In order to accept the DSL signals, the carrier must have newer digital switching equipment. In areas of the country where carriers have not updated their switching equipment, DSL service is not available. Inside the carrier's POP, a device called a **DSL access multiplexer (DSLAM)** aggregates multiple DSL subscriber lines and connects them to a larger carrier or to the Internet backbone, as pictured in Figure 7-9.

As mentioned earlier, standards for DSL continue to evolve. Service providers and manufacturers have positioned DSL as a competitor for T1, ISDN, and cable modem services. The installation, hardware, and monthly access costs for DSL are similar to those for ISDN lines but are significantly less than the cost for T1s. Considering that DSL technology can provide faster throughput than T1s, it presents a formidable challenge to the T1 industry, especially given that T1s are typically too expensive for home users.

One drawback to DSL is that it is not available in all areas, and even where it is available, it may be subject to severe distance limitations. Another drawback is that DSL's relative newness (compared with ISDN and T1 technology, for example) has led to a backlog in DSL installations. Subscribers may wait a few months after ordering their DSL service before it can be installed. Add to that the fluctuating state of DSL standards and providers, and DSL appears to be a technology that will require some time to stabilize. Nevertheless, DSL has won over many consumers and small businesses who want more bandwidth than ISDN or PSTN can afford. As of 2000 over 2 million DSL lines were installed in the United States, and by some estimates that number is predicted to grow to over 23 million by 2004.

CABLE

While local and long-distance phone companies race to make DSL the preferred method of Internet access for consumers, cable companies are pushing their own connectivity option, based on the coaxial cable wiring used for TV signals. Such wiring could theoretically transmit as much as 36 Mbps downstream and as much as 10 Mbps upstream. Thus cable is an asymmetrical technology. Realistically, however, cable will allow approximately 3 to 10 Mbps downstream and 2 Mbps upstream due to its shared nature (described later in this section) as well as bottlenecks that occur either at the Internet carrier's data facilities or on the Internet itself. The asymmetry of cable technology makes it a logical choice for users who want to surf the Web or download data from a network. Some companies are also developing services to deliver music, videoconferencing, and Internet services over cable infrastructure.

Cable connections require that the customer use a special **cable modem**, a device that modulates and demodulates signals for transmission and reception via cable wiring. Figure 7-11 provides an example of a cable modem. The cable modem then connects to a customer's PC via its USB port or through a UTP cable to a (typically Ethernet) NIC. Alternately, the cable modem could connect to a connectivity device, such as a hub or router, to supply bandwidth to a LAN rather than to just one computer. Before customers can subscribe to cable modem service, however, their local cable company must have the necessary infrastructure.

 Although the device that connects a subscriber's home computer to the cable infrastructure is called a cable modem, it is not a true modem. Rather it is a connectivity device containing network interfaces, similar to a hub or router.

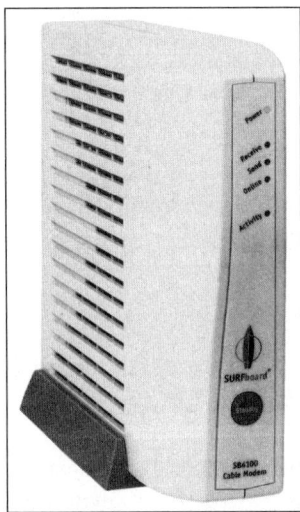

Figure 7-11   A cable modem

Traditional cable TV supplies the infrastructure for downstream communication (the TV programming), but not for upstream communication. To provide Internet access through its network, the cable company must upgrade its existing equipment to support bidirectional, digital communications. For starters, the cable company's network wiring must be replaced with **hybrid fiber-coax (HFC)**, a very expensive fiber-optic link that can support high frequencies. The HFC connects the cable company's offices to a node location near the customer. Then, either fiber-optic or coaxial cable may connect the node to the customer's business or residence via a connection known as a **cable drop**. All cable drops for the cable subscribers in the same neighborhood connect to the local node. These nodes then connect to the cable company's central office, which is known as its **head-end**. At the head-end, the cable company can connect to the Internet through a variety of means (often via fiber-optic cable) or it can pick up digital satellite or microwave transmissions. The head-end can transmit data to as many as 1000 subscribers, in a one-to-many communication system. Figure 7-12 illustrates the infrastructure of a cable system.

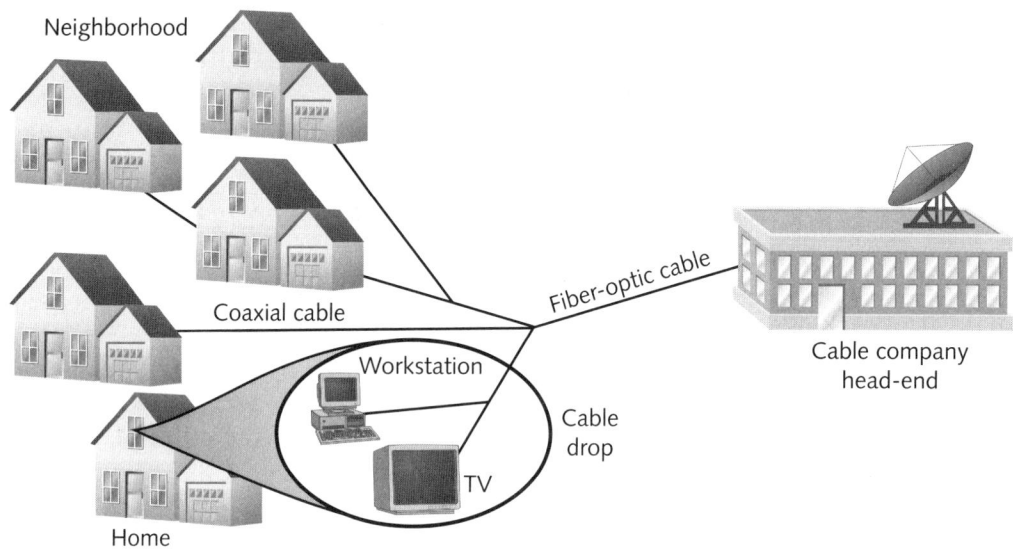

Figure 7-12   Cable infrastructure

One advantage of cable is that, like DSL, it provides a dedicated, or continuous, connection that does not require dialing up a service provider. On the other hand, cable technology requires many subscribers to share the same line, thus raising concerns about security and actual (versus theoretical) throughput. For example, if your cable company supplied you and five of your neighbors with cable access to the Internet, your neighbors could capture the data that you transmit to the Internet. Thus cable users must consider methods of securing their data, such as encryption. Moreover, the throughput of a cable line is fixed. As with any fixed resource, the more one claims, the less that is left for others. In other words, the greater the number of users sharing a single line, the less throughput available to each individual user.

Although cable competes with DSL for servicing consumers who demand higher bandwidth than that offered by PSTN or ISDN, it may not be able to keep up with the pace of DSL evolution. Instead, DSL may have the edge because its infrastructure (the PSTN) is already in place, while cable is not quite ubiquitous. Also, the prices of consumer DSL service have come down to nearly the same level as cable. Cable modems are less often used in businesses than DSL, partly because of security and bandwidth concerns that arise from its shared nature. More importantly, this service is less common in businesses because most office buildings do not contain a coaxial cable infrastructure.

SONET (SYNCHRONOUS OPTICAL NETWORK)

SONET (Synchronous Optical Network) can provide data transfer rates from 64 Kbps to 39.8 Gbps using the same TDM technique used by T-carriers. Bell Communications Research developed SONET technology in the 1980s to link different phone systems around the world. SONET has since emerged as the best choice for linking WANs between North America, Europe, and Asia, because it can work directly with the different standards used in different countries. Internationally, SONET is known as **SDH (Synchronous Digital Hierarchy)**. SONET integrates well with T-carriers, making it a good choice for connecting WANs and LANs over long distances (even within the same country). In fact SONET is often used to aggregate multiple T1s or T3s. SONET is also used as the underlying technology for ATM transmission.

SONET depends on fiber-optic transmission media to achieve its extraordinary quality of service and throughput. Like T-carriers, it also uses multiplexers and terminal equipment to connect at the customer's end. A typical SONET network takes the form of a ring topology, similar to FDDI, in which one ring acts as the primary route for data and a second ring acts as a backup. If, for example, a backhoe operator severs one of the rings, SONET technology would automatically reroute traffic along the backup ring. This characteristic, known as **self-healing**, makes SONET very reliable. Companies can lease an entire SONET ring from their local or long-distance carrier or they can lease part of a SONET, a circuit that offers T1 throughput, to take advantage of SONET's reliability. Figure 7-13 illustrates a SONET ring and its dual-fiber connections.

7

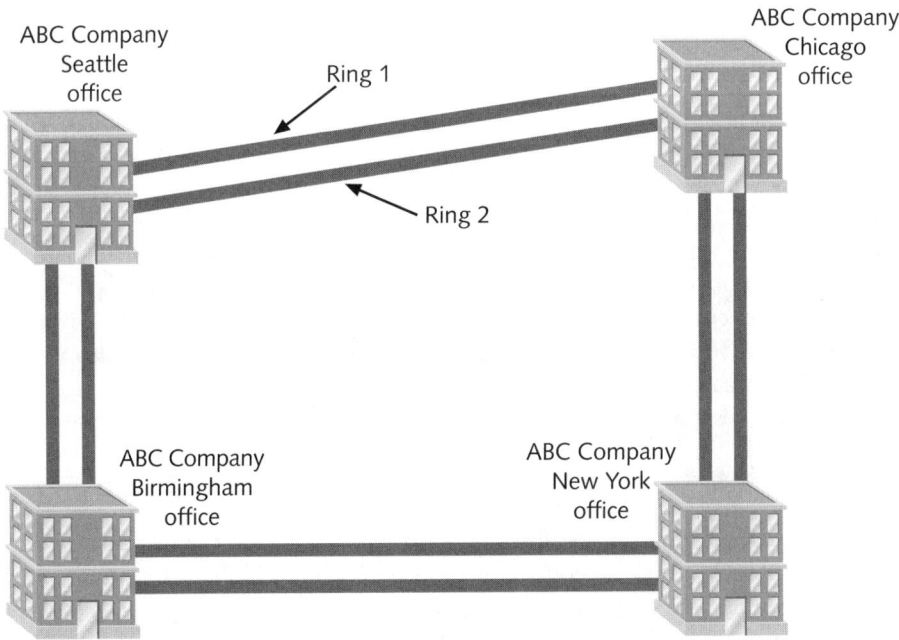

Figure 7-13   SONET technology on a long-distance WAN

The data rate of a particular SONET ring is indicated by its Optical Carrier (OC) level, a rating that is internationally recognized by networking professionals and standards organizations. OC levels in SONET are analogous to the digital signal levels of T1s. Table 7-3 lists the OC levels and their maximum throughput.

Table 7-3   SONET OC levels

OC Level	Throughput (Mbps)
OC1	51.84
OC3	155.52
OC12	622
OC24	1244
OC48	2480
OC96	4976
OC192	9953
OC768	39813

SONET technology is typically not implemented by small or medium-sized businesses, because of its high cost. It is more commonly used by large global companies, long-distance companies linking metropolitan areas and countries, or ISPs that want to guarantee fast, reliable access to the Internet. SONET is particularly suited to audio, video, and imaging data transmission. As you can imagine, given its reliance on fiber-optic cable and its redundancy requirements, SONET technology is very expensive to implement.

WAN Implementation

You need to weigh many factors when choosing a WAN for your organization. Among other things, you need to consider how well a new WAN will integrate with your existing LAN or WAN equipment, the transmission speed that is required by your users and applications, the kind of security you need, the geographical distance spanned by your WAN, the extent to which the WAN might grow over time and, of course, your budget. This section compares the WAN technologies mentioned previously on the basis of the most significant and predictable factors: speed, reliability, and security. Although cost is, of course, an important factor, it will vary dramatically depending on your circumstances. For cost estimates, you should contact an ISP or a local or long-distance service provider.

Speed

You have learned that WAN links offer a wide range of transmission speeds, from 56 Kbps for a PSTN dial-up connection to potentially 39.8 Gbps for a full-speed SONET connection. Table 7-4 summarizes the speeds offered by each technology discussed in this chapter. Bear in mind that each technology's transmission techniques (for example, switching for frame relay versus point-to-point for T1) will affect real throughput, so the maximum transmission speed is a theoretical limit. Actual transmission speeds will vary.

Table 7-4   A comparison of WAN technology transmission speeds

WAN Technology	Typical Media	Maximum Transmission Speed
Dial-up over PSTN	UTP or STP	56 Kbps
X.25	UTP/STP (DS1 or DS3)	64 Kbps or 2.048 Mbps
frame relay	UTP/STP (DS1 or DS3)	45 Mbps
BRI (ISDN)	UTP/STP (PSTN)	64–128 Kbps
PRI (ISDN)	UTP/STP (PSTN)	1.544 Mbps
T1	UTP/STP (PSTN), microwave, or fiber-optic cable	1.544 Mbps
Fractional T1	UTP/STP (PSTN), microwave, or fiber-optic cable	n times 64 Kbps (where n = number of channels leased)
T3	Microwave or fiber-optic cable	45 Mbps
DSL	UTP/STP (PSTN)	1.544 Mbps–52 Mbps (depends on the type)
Cable	Hybrid fiber-coaxial cable	36 Mbps downstream, 10 Mbps upstream
SONET	Fiber-optic cable	51, 155, 622, 1244, 2480, 4976, 9952, or 39813 Mbps (depending on the OC level)

Reliability

WAN technologies vary in their reliability. A WAN's reliability depends partly on the transmission medium it uses (for example, fiber-optic cable is more reliable than copper wire) and partly on its topology and transmission methods (for example, a fully meshed WAN provides better reliability than a partially meshed WAN, because more potential data paths are available should one link fail). WAN technologies can be roughly divided as follows:

- *Not very reliable, suited to individual or unimportant transmissions:* PSTN dial-up

- *Sufficiently reliable, suited for day-to-day transmissions:* ISDN, T1, fractional T1, T3, DSL, cable, X.25, and frame relay

- *Very reliable, suited to mission-critical applications:* SONET

Although PSTN lines are the least reliable of all WAN technologies, they are adequate for most telecommuting purposes. Their reliability depends on the quality of the local phone connection to a user's residence, which will vary from city to city and from neighborhood to neighborhood. Some connections may be entirely digital; others (particularly in rural areas) may be analog. Some may be subject to more noise than others are. The quality of PSTN dial-up lines also depends on the quality of a user's modem, which will undoubtedly vary from user to user.

For employees picking up e-mail and data files from a business's branch offices across the state, ISDN or T1 lines will usually suffice. Some applications, however, require the highest reliability. For example, if you were transmitting a videoconference of a United Nations meeting in New York to diplomats in Switzerland, you would want to use a very reliable technology such as SONET.

Security

Wise network managers will inspect security at every juncture in their WAN. Although fiber-optic media are the most secure transmission media (as you learned in Chapter 4), it's important to keep in mind that security is affected by more than simply the type of transmission media used. Among other things, you should consider the following issues:

- WAN security depends in part on the encryption measures each carrier provides for its lines. When leasing T1s, frame relay circuits, or SONET rings, you should ask a number of providers how they secure information in transit. In addition, you should verify that secure connectivity devices, such as firewalls, are employed at both ends of the connection. (You will learn about firewalls in detail in Chapter 15.)

- Enforce password-based authorization for LAN and WAN access and teach users how to choose difficult-to-decrypt passwords.

- Take the time to develop, publish, and enforce a security policy for users in your organization.

- Maintain restricted access to network equipment rooms and data centers.

All of these factors contribute to the security of your network. In other words, the type of WAN you choose does not affect security as much as the security considerations that apply to all networks. Network security is discussed further in Chapter 15.

Virtual Private Networks (VPNs)

Virtual private networks (VPNs) are wide area networks logically defined over public transmission systems that serve an organization's users, but isolate that organization's traffic from other users of the same public lines. They provide a way of constructing a WAN from existing public transmission systems. For example, an organization can carve out a private WAN on the Internet to serve only its offices across the country, while keeping the data secure and isolated from other (public) traffic.

Because VPNs do not require leasing a full T1 circuit, for example, or paying for a frame relay system, they provide inexpensive solutions for creating long-distance WANs. VPNs employ specific protocols and security techniques to ensure that data can be interpreted only at the WAN's nodes. The security techniques used may be purely software-based or they may include hardware such as a firewall. You will learn more about VPN security techniques in Chapter 15.

The software required to establish VPNs is usually inexpensive, in some cases being included with other widely used software. For example, Windows 2000 Server comes with a remote access utility called RAS that allows you to create a simple VPN. For

Novell-based networks, you can use BorderManager, a NetWare add-on product, to construct VPNs. In addition, many other companies offer software that will work with either of these network operating systems to create VPNs. Figure 7-14 depicts one possible implementation of a VPN. The beauty of VPNs is that they are tailored to a customer's distance and bandwidth needs, so, of course, every one is different.

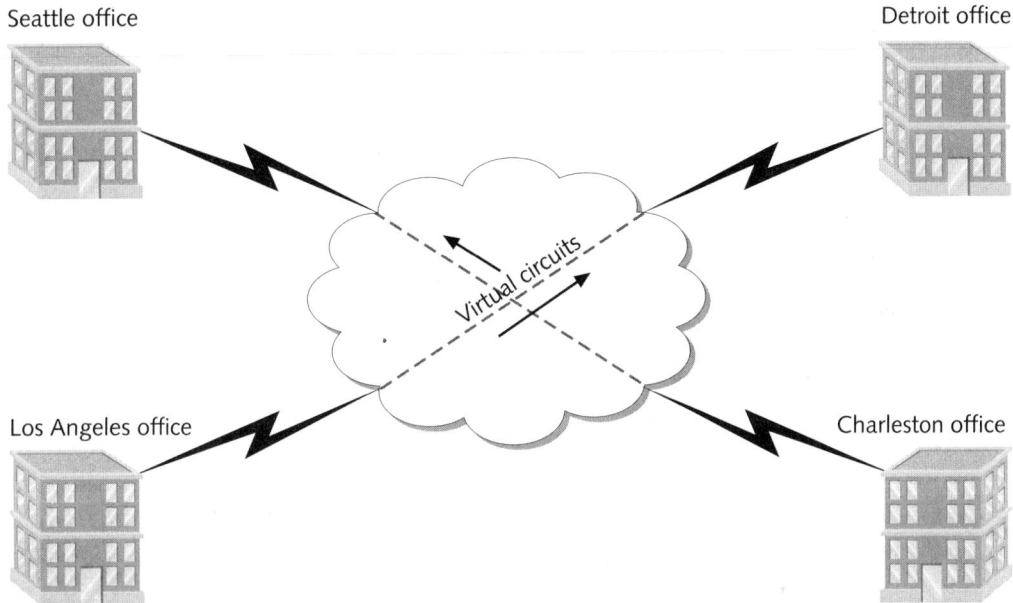

Figure 7-14   An example of a VPN

 Do not confuse virtual private networks (VPNs) with the virtual LANs (VLANs) discussed in Chapter 6. VLANs are logically defined LANs created from an organization's existing LAN or WAN infrastructure, usually to serve a particular group of users.

REMOTE CONNECTIVITY

You have learned about almost every type of connection available for long-distance networking, but you may not know how the average user connects to a WAN. In a large organization with an enterprise-wide network, using a WAN is no different from using a LAN. You might log onto your company's network in Dallas, open Windows Explorer, and choose to view a PowerPoint presentation on a server in Phoenix. Your computer doesn't care about the location of the presentation file, because the WAN link makes it appear to be part of one big network (assuming that the network manager has done his or her job!). If you are at home or on the road, however, connecting to a WAN or LAN is somewhat different.

As a remote user, you must connect to a LAN via **remote access**, which can be accomplished in one of three ways: use a modem to dial directly into the LAN, use a modem to dial directly to a workstation, or use an Internet connection with a Web interface. Each of these methods offers different advantages and disadvantages, as described in the following material. Bear in mind that the true limiting factor in a remote connection is typically the speed of the modem, PSTN, or other access method that you're using.

- *Direct dial to the LAN*—The client uses dial-in software supplied with its operating system to connect to a remote access server on the LAN. As you learned in Chapter 1, a remote access server (also called a dial-in server) is a combination of software and hardware that provides a central access point for multiple users to dial into a LAN or WAN. The LAN treats the direct-dial remote client like any other client on the LAN; that is, the remote user can perform the same functions he or she could perform while in the office. The computer dialing into the LAN becomes a **remote node** on the network. Although this remote access method is the most complex to configure, especially on the server side, it can provide the best security. Also, the transmission speed of a direct-dial connection does not suffer when the Internet becomes congested. With the proper server hardware and software, this kind of connection can offer multiple users simultaneous remote access to the LAN.

- *Direct dial to a workstation*—The remote client uses dial-in software supplied with its operating system to connect to a workstation that is directly attached to the LAN. Software (such as Symantec's pcAnywhere) running on both the remote user's computer and the LAN computer allows the remote user to "take over" the LAN workstation, a solution known as **remote control**. Remote control is not as difficult to configure and confers the same security and throughput benefits as directly dialing into a remote access server. In addition, this method provides the best performance for processing-intensive applications such as databases, because the data processing can occur on the LAN-attached workstation without having to traverse the slower modem connection to the remote workstation. One disadvantage to this solution is that it allows only one connection to the LAN at any given time.

- *Internet/Web interface*—Through a browser such as Netscape Communicator or Microsoft's Internet Explorer, a user at home or on the road connects to a LAN whose files are made visible to the Web through Web server software. This method requires some setup steps on both the client and the server, but it is not usually as complex as a direct-dial configuration. Its security and throughput cannot be controlled as thoroughly as those of the direct-dial solutions, however, because the remote user's connection is not dedicated. Nevertheless, a Web interface is very simple to use and widely available. Also, a nearly unlimited number of remote users can simultaneously access the LAN resources using this method.

Remote connectivity can be established between almost any combination of workstation and operating system, given the appropriate software and hardware configuration. A popular method for gaining remote access to LANs is by using Citrix System, Inc.'s **ICA (Independent Computing Architecture) client** to connect with a remote access server. Once installed on a remote user's workstation, the ICA client enables the workstation to communicate with the LAN from anywhere over any type of connection, public or private. Because the ICA client exchanges only keystrokes, mouse clicks, and screen updates with the server, this type of remote access is particularly well suited to slower connections, such as dial-up PSTN connections. Citrix's ICA client can work with virtually any operating system or application. Its ease of use and broad compatibility has made the ICA client one of the most popular methods for supplying widespread remote access across an organization. In order to function properly, the ICA requires Citrix's remote access software running on the access server. Potential drawbacks to this method include cost of Citrix's products and the complex nature of its server software configuration.

Perhaps the simplest dial-in server is the **Remote Access Service** (**RAS**, pronounced "razz"), which comes with Windows 2000 Server. Because it is a good example of a remote access server, you should investigate RAS when you work with Windows 2000 servers. Knowing RAS will help you understand more complex access server technologies.

In addition to Microsoft's remote access methods, networking hardware manufacturers such as Bay Networks, Cisco Systems, and 3Com market their own remote access technologies. In addition, a number of specialized software companies provide programs that run on Windows 2000, NetWare, or UNIX servers. The method you choose will depend on your requirements for security, throughput, number of connections, and cost, and the technical expertise of your users and support staff. If you enable remote access for your network, you will need to be familiar with the process of configuring clients for connection and be able to support those clients. The next section describes how to configure a dial-up networking client.

Dial-Up Networking

Dial-up networking refers to the process of dialing into a LAN's (private) access server or to an ISP's (public) access server to log onto a network. Most telecommuters use some form of dial-up networking to connect to their LAN. This section describes how to configure a workstation to dial into a remote access server. For discussion purposes, the example of a Windows 2000 Professional client logging onto a private access server is used. Later, in the projects at the end of this chapter, you will have the opportunity to create a dial-up networking connection that enables you to log onto an ISP's access server.

First make sure that your modem is installed and working properly. To create a new dial-up connection:

1. Click **Start**, point to **Settings**, and then click **Network and Dial-up Connections**. The Network and Dial-up Connections window appears.

2. Double-click the **Make New Connection** icon. The Network Connection Wizard opens.

3. If you have not previously configured a dial-up connection on your computer, you will be asked to provide your area code in the Location Information dialog, and then click **OK**. Then you will be asked to provide your location in the Phone and Modem Options dialog and click **OK**. Click **Next** to continue.

4. You are prompted to identify the type of dial-up connection you want to create, as shown in Figure 7-15. For this exercise, select **Dial-up to private network**, then click **Next** to continue.

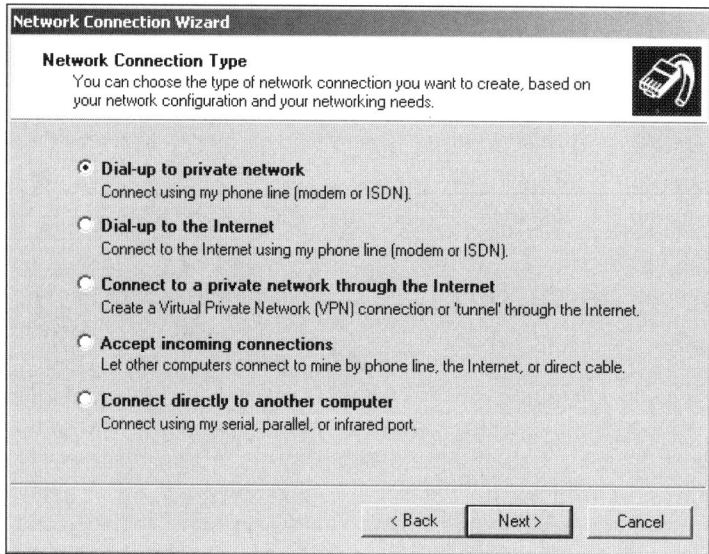

Figure 7-15   Choosing a network connection type

5. At the next screen you are prompted to enter the number of the RAS server. Type the server's dial-up number and click **Next** to continue.

6. You are prompted to select the availability of the connection—whether you want the connection available to all users or only to the user under whose ID you are currently logged in. For this exercise, keep the default selection of **For all users**, then click **Next** to continue.

7. You are asked to name the connection. Type a word or phrase that will help you identify this connection when it appears as an icon in your Network and Dial-up Connections window.

8. Click **Finish** to complete the task of creating a new dial-up connection.

After creating a new Dial-up Networking profile, you may need to configure its connectivity options. Unless you configure it precisely according to the server's parameters, your connection will not work properly. In some cases, if you enter incomplete or incorrect information, you may be able to establish a session between your client and the server, but be unable to send or receive data. If you are dialing into an ISP's server, the ISP will provide the information used for this configuration.

The following steps provide an example of how to configure a dial-up connection:

1. In the Network and Dial-up Connections window, right-click the connection you want to configure. A shortcut menu opens.

2. Click **Properties**. A Properties window (whose title begins with the name of your profile) opens.

3. Click the **Networking** tab to display the network properties, including the type of dial-up server and network components that are available to this connection. The Type of dial-up server option provides a choice between PPP or SLIP connections. (PPP and SLIP connections are discussed in the next section.) Your RAS server will probably use PPP, which is selected as the default. However, you should check to make sure the proper type of server is selected. If you select the wrong type, you will not be able to connect to the ISP's server.

4. In the list of components used by this connection, make sure that the "Client for Microsoft Networks" and the "Internet Protocol (TCP/IP)" check boxes are checked. If other components (for example, the NWLink IPX/SPX/NetBIOS Compatible Transport Protocol) are selected, deselect them.

5. Double-click the **Internet Protocol (TCP/IP)** component to view its properties. The default options of "Obtain an IP address automatically" and "Obtain DNS server address automatically" are probably the options your server will require. However, if your RAS server does not assign IP addresses automatically, you will need to obtain an IP address and DNS server address from your network administrator and enter them here.

6. Click **OK** to close the Internet Protocol (TCP/IP) Properties dialog box.

If you have both a modem and a NIC on your PC, changing the TCP/IP properties for the dial-up connection will not affect the TCP/IP properties you have set for your NIC. In Network properties, you will see that TCP/IP is bound to both your NIC and your Dial-up Adapter and that the properties differ for each TCP/IP binding.

7. Click the **Security** tab. Here you can choose the level of security you want for your connection. The default level is to accept an unsecured password, which means that the password you use to log onto the RAS server does not need to meet strict password guidelines (for example, a length of at least eight characters). For this exercise, click the down arrow next to this default option and choose **Require secured password** from the drop-down list.

8. Notice that the options below the drop-down box become available. Select the **Automatically use my Windows logon name and password (and domain if any)** option.

9. Click the **Options** tab to view and modify some general properties of this dial-up connection.

10. Here you can change the nature of how your connection is dialed, including how many times the computer will redial if it fails to connect the first time. Choose the **Redial if line is dropped** option.

11. Click **OK** to close the Dial-up Connection properties dialog box and save your changes.

12. Test your connection to the remote server.

Now that you have become familiar with remote connectivity methods and know how to create and configure a dial-up networking profile, you will learn about the two most common dial-up networking protocols, PPP and SLIP. In order to qualify for Net+ certification, you should understand how to assign these protocols to a dial-in connection; you should also understand the differences between the two protocols.

Serial Line Internet Protocol (SLIP) and Point-to-Point Protocol (PPP)

Serial Line Internet Protocol (SLIP) and **Point-to-Point Protocol (PPP)** are two communications protocols that enable a workstation to connect to a server using a serial connection (in the case of dial-up networking, *serial connection* refers to a modem). Such protocols are necessary to transport Network layer traffic over serial interfaces, which belong to the Data Link layer of the OSI Model. Both SLIP and PPP encapsulate higher-layer networking protocols in their lower-layer data frames. SLIP is a version of the protocol that can carry only IP packets, however, and PPP can carry many different types of Network layer packets, such as IPX or AppleTalk. Another difference between SLIP and PPP is that SLIP supports only asynchronous data transmission and PPP supports both asynchronous and synchronous transmission.

Asynchronous refers to a communications method in which data being transmitted and received by nodes do not have to conform to any predetermined schemes that specify when they can transmit data. In asynchronous communications, a node can transmit at any time, and the destination node must accept the transmission as it comes. To ensure that the receiving node knows when it has received a complete frame, asynchronous communications provide start and stop bits for each character transmitted. When the receiving node recognizes a start bit, it begins to accept a new character. When it receives the stop bit for that character, it ceases to look for the end of that character's transmission. Asynchronous data transmission therefore occurs in random stops and starts.

Conversely, **synchronous** refers to a communications method in which data being transmitted and received by nodes must conform to a timing scheme. A clock maintains time for all nodes on a network. A receiving node in synchronous communications recognizes that it should be receiving data by looking at the time on the clock. In synchronous communications, start and stop bits are not necessary, because the clocking indicates where transmission should begin and where it should end. As an analogy, imagine a marathon with 1000 participants, in which each runner starts the race precisely five minutes after the previous runner started. The race's official timekeeper keeps track of when each runner begins, so that when a runner arrives at the finish line, his or her total time can be calculated. Runner B, who starts ten minutes after Runner A, will not be expected to arrive at the finish line at the same time as Runner A. In this analogy, the race official is like the clocking mechanism in synchronous communications.

PPP is the more popular communications protocol for dial-up connections to the Internet, primarily because it does not require as much configuration on the client as SLIP does. When using SLIP, you typically have to specify the IP addresses for both your client and for your server in your dial-up networking profile. PPP, on the other hand, can automatically obtain this information as it connects to the server. Because it is more difficult to configure, SLIP is rarely used.

7

CHAPTER SUMMARY

- ❐ WANs are distinguished from LANs by the fact that WANs traverse a wider geographical area. They usually employ point-to-point communications rather than point-to-many communications (where LAN hubs or switches connect multiple segments or workstations). WANs also provide better and faster transmission than LANs.

- ❐ WAN transmission methods differ in terms of their speed, reliability, cost, distance covered, and security. For every business need, only one or a handful of appropriate WAN transmission methods may exist. Several WAN technologies may be used together on the same network.

- ❐ One WAN transmission method, PSTN (Public Switched Telephone Network), relies on the network of telephone lines that typically services homes. The PSTN was originally composed of analog lines but now uses digital transmission over fiber-optic and copper twisted-pair cable, microwave, and satellite connections. PSTN is usually adequate for at-home dial-up LAN or Internet users.

- ❐ A remote user can use the PSTN to access a remote server via a dial-up connection. In a dial-up connection, the user's modem converts the computer's digital pulses into analog signals. These signals travel through PSTN to the receiving computer's modem, which then converts the analog signals back into digital pulses. Unlike other types of WAN connections, dial-up connections provide a fixed period of access to the network.

- ❐ X.25 is an analog, packet-switched technology optimized for long-distance data transmission and standardized by the ITU in the mid-1970s. It can support 2-Mbps throughput. X.25 was originally developed and used for communications between mainframe computers and remote terminals. Though rare in North America, it remains a WAN standard around the world.

◻ Frame relay also relies on packet switching. Because it is digital, and because it does not analyze frames, but simply relays them from node to node, frame relay supports higher bandwidth than X.25, offering a maximum of 45-Mbps throughput.

◻ Both X.25 and frame relay are configured as permanent virtual circuits (PVCs). PVCs are point-to-point connections over which data may follow any number of different paths. When you lease an X.25 or frame relay circuit from your local carrier, your contract reflects the endpoints you specify and the amount of bandwidth required between those endpoints.

◻ Another WAN transmission method, ISDN (Integrated Services Digital Network), is an international standard established by the ITU for transmitting data over digital lines. ISDN uses the telephone carrier's lines and dial-up connections, like PSTN. It differs from PSTN in that it travels exclusively over digital lines and switches.

◻ ISDN lines may carry voice and data signals simultaneously, but require an ISDN phone to carry voice traffic and an ISDN router and ISDN terminal adapter to carry data. ISDN lines circumvent the need to pay for separate phone lines to support faxes, modems, and voice calls at one location.

◻ Two types of ISDN connections are commonly used by consumers in North America: Basic Rate Interface (BRI) and Primary Rate Interface (PRI).

◻ BRI uses two 64-Kbps circuit-switched bearer channels (or B channels) to transmit and receive data or voice. These two channels carry the traffic from point to point. An additional 16-Kbps channel called a D channel, for "data" channel, carries information about the call, such as session initiation and termination signals, caller identity, call forwarding, and conference calling signals.

◻ B channels in ISDN lines are treated as separate connections by the network and can carry voice and data or two data streams simultaneously and separate from each other. A process called bonding can combine the throughput of the B channels into a larger effective throughput.

◻ PRI uses 23 B channels and one 64-Kbps D channel. Individual subscribers rarely use PRI, preferring BRI instead, but PRI may be used by business and other organizations needing more throughput. The maximum potential throughput for a PRI connection is 1.544 Mbps, the same as that for a T1 circuit.

◻ Another WAN transmission method is digital subscriber line (DSL). DSL uses advanced data modulation techniques to achieve extraordinary throughput over regular phone lines. Data modulation uses one signal to alter the frequency, phase, or amplitude of another signal. In the case of DSL, multiple high-frequency carrier signals are modulated by modems' data signals, enabling DSL connections to support high throughput over copper wire.

◻ DSL comes in seven different varieties, each of which is either asymmetrical or symmetrical. In asymmetrical transmission, more data can be sent in one direction than in the other direction. In symmetrical transmission, equal amounts of data can be sent in either direction. The most popular form of DSL is ADSL.

◻ DSL technology creates a dedicated circuit. At the consumer end, a DSL modem connects computers and telephones to the DSL line. At the carrier end, a DSL access multiplexer (DSLAM) aggregates multiple incoming DSL lines before connecting them to the Internet or to larger carriers.

◻ Cable is another option for high bandwidth local loop WAN transmission. Cable relies on the cable wiring used for TV signals. Such wiring could realistically transmit approximately 3 to 10 Mbps downstream and 2 Mbps upstream. The asymmetry of cable technology makes it a logical choice for users who want to surf the Web or download data from a network.

◻ Cable connections require that the customer use a special cable modem to transmit and receive signals over cable wiring. In addition, most cable companies will have to replace part of their coaxial cable plant with fiber-optic cable to support bidirectional, digital communications.

◻ Like DSL, cable provides a dedicated, or continuous, connection that does not require dialing up a service provider.

◻ T-carrier technology uses time division multiplexing (TDM) to divide a single channel into multiple channels for carrying voice, data, video, or other signals. Devices at the sending end arrange the data streams (multiplex), then devices at the receiving end filter them back into separate signals (demultiplex).

◻ A number of T-carrier varieties are currently available. The most common T-carrier implementations are T1 and, for higher bandwidth needs, T3. A T1 circuit can carry the equivalent of 24 voice channels, giving a maximum data throughput of 1.544 Mbps. A T3 can carry the equivalent of 672 voice channels, giving a maximum data throughput of 44.736 Mbps.

◻ The signal level of a T-carrier refers to its Physical layer electrical signaling characteristics, as defined by ANSI standards in the early 1980s. DS0 is the equivalent of one data or voice channel. All other signal levels are multiples of DS0.

◻ A fractional T1 lease allows organizations to use only some channels on a T1 line and pay for only those channels actually used. Thus fractional T1 bandwidth can be leased in multiples of 64 Kbps. A fractional T1 is suited to businesses that expect their traffic to grow and that can't currently justify leasing a full T1.

◻ T1 technology can use unshielded or shielded twisted-pair copper wiring. Because the digital signals require a cleaner connection, shielded twisted-pair is considered preferable. Twisted-pair wiring cannot adequately carry the high throughput of multiple T1s or T3 transmissions. For multiple T1s, coaxial cable may be used or either of the T3 transmission media—either microwave or fiber-optic cabling.

◻ The CSU/DSU is the connection point for a T1 line at the customer's site. The CSU provides termination for the digital signal and ensures connection integrity through error correction and line monitoring. The DSU converts the digital signal used by bridges, routers, and multiplexers into the digital signal carried via cabling.

7

❐ The devices that connect to the multiplexer are collectively known as terminal equipment. On a typical T1-connected data network, this equipment consists of bridges and/or routers. A bridge or router would typically integrate two types of networks: the incoming T1 (Internet) and an Ethernet or Token Ring LAN at the customer's site.

❐ SONET can provide data transfer rates from 64 Kbps to 39.8 Gbps using the same TDM technique employed by T-carriers. It is the best choice for linking WANs between North America, Europe, and Asia, because it can link directly with the different standards used in different countries.

❐ Internationally, SONET is known as SDH (Synchronous Digital Hierarchy). SONET integrates well with T-carriers, ISDN, and ATM technology.

❐ SONET depends on fiber-optic transmission media and uses multiplexers and terminal equipment to connect at the customer's end. A typical SONET network takes the form of a ring topology. If one ring breaks, SONET technology automatically reroutes traffic along a backup ring. This characteristic, known as self-healing, makes SONET very reliable.

❐ SONET technology is typically implemented by large global companies, long-distance companies linking metropolitan areas and countries, or ISPs that want to guarantee fast, reliable access to the Internet. SONET is particularly suited to audio, video, and imaging data transmissions but is very expensive.

❐ When implementing a new WAN installation or upgrade, you should consider the following factors: the WAN's ability to integrate with your existing LAN or WAN equipment, the kind of transmission speed required by your users and applications, the kind of security needed, the geographical distance the WAN must span, the extent to which the WAN might grow over time, and, of course, the expense.

❐ Virtual private networks (VPNs) represent one way to construct a WAN from existing public transmission systems. An organization can carve out a private WAN on the Internet (or over leased lines) to serve only its offices, while keeping the data secure and isolated from other (public) traffic.

❐ As a remote user, you can connect to a LAN in one of three ways: direct dial to the LAN, direct dial to a workstation, or an Internet connection with a Web interface. Each method has different advantages and disadvantages pertaining to its throughput, security, complexity, and number of simultaneous users allowed.

❐ Serial Line Internet Protocol (SLIP) and Point-to-Point Protocol (PPP) are communications protocols that enable a workstation to connect to a server using a serial connection (in the case of dial-up networking, "serial connection" refers to a modem). Such protocols are necessary to transport Network layer traffic over serial interfaces, which belong to the Data Link layer of the OSI Model. Because it is easier to configure and supports more than one type of Network layer protocol, PPP is preferred over SLIP.

KEY TERMS

asymmetrical — The characteristic of a transmission technology that affords greater bandwidth in one direction (either from the customer to the carrier, or vice versa) than in the other direction.

asymmetrical DSL — A variation of DSL that offers more throughput when data travels downstream—downloading from a local carrier's POP to the customer—than when it travels upstream—uploading from the customer to the local carrier's POP.

asynchronous — A transmission method in which data being transmitted and received by nodes do not have to conform to any timing scheme. In asynchronous communications, a node can transmit at any time and the destination node must accept the transmission as it comes.

B channel — In ISDN, the "bearer" channel, so named because it bears traffic from point to point.

bonding — The process of combining more than one bearer channel of an ISDN line to increase throughput. For example, BRI's two 64-Kbps B channels are bonded to create an effective throughput of 128 Kbps.

BRI (Basic Rate Interface) — A variety of ISDN that uses two 64-Kbps bearer channels and one 16-Kbps data channel, as summarized by the following notation: 2B + D. BRI is the most common form of ISDN employed by home users.

broadband — A group of network connection types or transmission technologies that are generally capable of exceeding 1.544 Mbps throughput. Examples of broadband include DSL and SONET.

cable drop — Fiber-optic or coaxial cable that connects a neighborhood cable node to a customer's house.

cable modem — A device that modulates and demodulates signals for transmission and reception via cable wiring.

CIR (committed information rate) — The guaranteed minimum amount of bandwidth selected when leasing a frame relay circuit. Frame relay costs are partially based on CIR.

CSU (channel service unit) — A device used with T-carrier technology that provides termination for the digital signal and ensures connection integrity through error correction and line monitoring.

CSU/DSU — A combination of a CSU (channel service unit) and a DSU (data service unit) that serves as the connection point for a T1 line at the customer's site.

D channel — In ISDN, the "data" channel used to carry information about the call, such as session initiation and termination signals, caller identity, call forwarding, and conference calling signals.

dedicated — A continuously available link or service that is leased through another carrier. Examples of dedicated lines include ADSL, T1, and T3.

dial-up — A type of connection that uses modems at the transmitting and receiving ends and PSTN or other lines to access a network.

7

dial-up networking — The process of dialing into a LAN's access server or into an ISP. Dial-up Networking is also the name of the utility that Microsoft provides with its operating systems to achieve this type of connectivity.

downstream — A term used to describe data traffic that flows from a local carrier's POP to the customer. In asymmetrical communications, downstream throughput is usually much higher than upstream throughput. In symmetrical communications, downstream and upstream throughputs are equal.

DS0 (digital signal, level 0) — The equivalent of one data or voice channel in T-carrier technology, as defined by ANSI physical layer standards. All other signal levels are multiples of DS0.

DSL (digital subscriber line) — A dedicated remote connectivity or WAN technology that uses advanced data modulation techniques to achieve extraordinary throughput over regular phone lines. DSL currently comes in seven different varieties, the most common of which is Asymmetric DSL (ADSL).

DSL access multiplexer (DSLAM) — A connectivity device located at a carrier's office that aggregates multiple DSL subscriber lines and connects them to a larger carrier or to the Internet backbone.

DSL modem — A device that demodulates an incoming DSL signal, extracting the information and passing it on to the data equipment (such as telephones and computers) and modulates an outgoing DSL signal.

DSU (data service unit) — A device used in T-carrier technology that converts the digital signal used by bridges, routers, and multiplexers into the digital signal used on cabling. Typically, a DSU is combined with a CSU in a single box, a CSU/DSU.

Federal Communications Commission (FCC) — The regulatory agency that sets standards and policy for telecommunications transmission and equipment in the United States.

fractional T1 — An arrangement that allows organizations to use only some channels on a T1 line and pay for only the channels actually used.

frame relay — An updated, digital version of X.25 that relies on packet switching. Because it is digital, frame relay supports higher bandwidth than X.25, offering a maximum of 45-Mbps throughput. It provides the basis for much of the world's Internet connections. On network diagrams, the frame relay system is often depicted as a cloud.

head-end — A cable company's central office, which connects cable wiring to many nodes before it reaches customers' sites.

hybrid fiber-coax (HFC) — A link that consists of fiber cable connecting the cable company's offices to a node location near the customer and coaxial cable connecting the node to the customer's house. HFC upgrades to existing cable wiring are required before current TV cable systems can serve as WAN links.

ICA (Independent Computing Architecture) client — A remote access client developed by Citrix Systems, Inc. that enables remote users to use virtually any LAN application over any type of connection, public or private. The ICA client is especially well suited to slower connections, as it exchanges only keystrokes, mouse clicks, and screen updates with the server. The ICA client requires that Citrix's server software run on the access server.

ISDN (Integrated Services Digital Network) — An international standard, established by the ITU, for transmitting data over digital lines. Like PSTN, ISDN uses the telephone carrier's lines and dial-up connections, but it differs from PSTN in that it exclusively uses digital lines and switches.

leased lines — Permanent dedicated connections established through a public telecommunications carrier and billed to customers on a monthly basis.

local loop — The part of a phone system that connects a customer site with a public carrier's POP. Some WAN transmission methods, such as ISDN, are suitable for only the local loop portion of the network link.

multiplexer — In the context of T-carrier technology, a device that provides the means of combining multiple voice and/or data channels on one line. Multiplexers can take input from a variety of terminal equipment, such as bridges, routers, or telephone exchange devices, for use with voice traffic.

Network Termination 1 (NT1) — A device used on ISDN networks that connects the incoming twisted-pair wiring with the customer's ISDN terminal equipment.

Network Termination 2 (NT2) — An additional connection device required on PRI to handle the multiple ISDN lines between the customer's network termination connection and the local phone company's wires.

plain old telephone service (POTS) — See *PSTN*.

point of presence (POP) — The place where the two telephone systems meet—either a long-distance carrier with a local telephone company or a local carrier with an ISP's facility.

Point-to-Point Protocol (PPP) — A communications protocol that enables a workstation to connect to a server using a serial connection. PPP can support multiple Network layer protocols, can use both asynchronous and synchronous communications, and does not require much (if any) configuration on the client workstation.

PRI (Primary Rate Interface) — A type of ISDN that uses 23 bearer channels and one 64-Kbps data channel as represented by the following notation: 23B + D. PRI is less commonly used by individual subscribers than BRI, but it may be used by businesses and other organizations needing more throughput.

PSTN (Public Switched Telephone Network) — The network of typical telephone lines that has been evolving for 100 years and still services most homes.

PVC (permanent virtual circuit) — A point-to-point connection over which data may follow any number of different paths, as opposed to a dedicated line that follows a predefined path. X.25, frame relay, and some forms of ATM use PVCs.

remote access — A method for connecting and logging onto a LAN from a workstation that is remote, or not physically connected, to the LAN. Remote access can be accomplished one of three ways: by using a modem to dial directly into the LAN; by using a modem to dial directly to a workstation; or by using an Internet connection with a Web interface. Remote access may complete a connection via public or private lines.

remote access server — A combination of software and hardware that provides a central access point for multiple users to dial into a LAN or WAN.

7

Remote Access Service (RAS) — One of the simplest dial-in servers. This software is included with Windows 2000 Server. Note that RAS is pronounced *"razz"*.

remote control — A remote access method in which the remote user dials into a workstation that is directly attached to a LAN. Software running on both the remote user's computer and the LAN computer allows the remote user to "take over" the LAN workstation.

remote node — A client that has dialed directly into a LAN's remote access server. The LAN treats a remote node like any other client on the LAN, allowing the remote user to perform the same functions he or she could perform while in the office.

SDH (Synchronous Digital Hierarchy) — The international equivalent of SONET.

self-healing — A characteristic of dual-ring topologies that allows them to automatically reroute traffic along the backup ring if the primary ring becomes severed.

Serial Line Internet Protocol (SLIP) — A communications protocol that enables a workstation to connect to a server using a serial connection. SLIP can support only asynchronous communications and IP traffic, and requires some configuration on the client workstation.

signal level — An ANSI standard for T-carrier technology that refers to its Physical layer electrical signaling characteristics. DS0 is the equivalent of one data or voice channel. All other signal levels are multiples of DS0.

SONET (Synchronous Optical Network) — A WAN technology that provides data transfer rates ranging from 64 Kbps to 39.8 Gbps, using the same time division multiplexing technique used by T-carriers. SONET is the best choice for linking WANs between North America, Europe, and Asia, because it can link directly using the different standards used in different countries.

SVC (switched virtual circuit) — Logical, point-to-point connections that rely on switches to determine the optimal path between sender and receiver. ATM technology uses SVCs.

symmetrical — A characteristic of transmission technology that provides equal throughput for data traveling both upstream and downstream and is suited to users who both upload and download significant amounts of data.

symmetrical DSL — A variation of DSL that provides equal throughput both upstream and downstream between the customer and the carrier.

synchronous — A transmission method in which data being transmitted and received by nodes must conform to a timing scheme.

T1 — A T-carrier technology that provides 1.544-Mbps throughput and 24 channels for voice, data, video, or audio signals. T1s may use shielded or unshielded twisted-pair, coaxial cable, fiber-optic, or microwave links. Businesses commonly use T1s to connect to their ISP, and phone companies typically use at least one T1 to connect their central offices.

T3 — A T-carrier technology that can carry the equivalent of 672 channels for voice, data, video, or audio, with a maximum data throughput of 44.736 Mbps (typically rounded up to 45 Mbps for purposes of discussion). T3s require either fiber-optic or microwave transmission media.

T-carriers — The term for any kind of leased line that follows the standards for T1s, fractional T1s, T1Cs, T2s, T3s, or T4s.

terminal adapter (TA) — Devices used to convert digital signals into analog signals for use with ISDN phones and other analog devices. Terminal adapters are sometimes called ISDN modems.

terminal equipment (TE) — Devices that connect computers to the ISDN line. Terminal equipment may include standalone devices or cards (similar to the network adapters used on Ethernet and Token Ring networks) or ISDN routers.

upstream — A term used to describe data traffic that flows from a customer's site to the local carrier's POP. In asymmetrical communications, upstream throughput is usually much lower than downstream throughput. In symmetrical communications, upstream and downstream throughputs are equal.

virtual private network (VPN) — A logically constructed WAN that uses existing public transmission systems. VPNs can be created through the use of software or combined software and hardware solutions. This type of network allows an organization to carve out a private WAN on the Internet (or, less commonly over leased lines) that serves only its offices, while keeping the data secure and isolated from other (public) traffic.

WAN link — The line that connects one location on a WAN with another location.

X.25 — An analog packet switched WAN technology optimized for long-distance data transmission and standardized by the ITU in the mid-1970s. X.25 can support 2-Mbps throughput. It was originally developed and used for communications between mainframe computers and remote terminals.

xDSL — Term used to refer to all varieties of DSL.

REVIEW QUESTIONS

1. Name three networking scenarios that would require a WAN.
2. What kind of public lines do most telecommuters use for dial-up connections?
   a. DSL
   b. cable
   c. PSTN
   d. T1s
   e. SONET
3. What is the maximum throughput of a BRI ISDN line?
   a. 56 Kbps
   b. 128 Kbps
   c. 256 Kbps
   d. 56 Mbps
   e. 128 Mbps

4. What is the purpose of ISDN's D channel?

    a. to carry call session information

    b. to carry error-checking information

    c. to enable symmetrical transmission

    d. to enable time division multiplexing

    e. to carry the data "payload"

5. Which of the following WAN technologies is represented in network diagrams by a cloud?

    a. frame relay

    b. ISDN

    c. DSL

    d. cable

    e. T-carrier

6. Which of the following WAN links is the most reliable?

    a. frame relay

    b. DSL

    c. T1

    d. T3

    e. SONET

7. Which of the following customers would symmetrical DSL best suit?

    a. a home office user who researches technology on the Web

    b. a convention center that provides multiple businesses with videoconferencing facilities

    c. a car manufacturer that obtains specifications from its quality control team across town

    d. a radiology clinic that uploads and downloads real-time images to and from a hospital across town

    e. a home user who watches movies on the Web

8. What technique enables DSL to achieve high bandwidth over PSTN lines?

    a. full duplexing

    b. message switching

    c. packet switching

    d. data modulation

    e. framing

9. A home user of DSL is likely to connect to his external DSL modem through either of what two methods?

   a. IR port

   b. Parallel port

   c. Ethernet NIC

   d. USB port

   e. AUI port

10. DS1 is equivalent to T1 throughout the world. True or False?

11. Which two of the following are symmetrical versions of DSL?

   a. ADSL

   b. G.Lite

   c. HDSL

   d. SDSL

   e. VDSL

12. What technique does T1 technology use to transmit multiple signals over a single telephone line?

   a. wave division multiplexing

   b. time division multiplexing

   c. amplitude modulation

   d. frequency modulation

   e. phase modulation

13. One T3 is equivalent to how many T1s?

   a. 3

   b. 9

   c. 18

   d. 28

   e. 42

14. How many 64-Kbps channels does a single T1 circuit carry?

   a. 4

   b. 12

   c. 16

   d. 24

   e. 32

15. Why are SONET networks considered "self-healing"?

16. Which of the following is a drawback of cable modem technology, compared to DSL?

    a. Its standards are less developed.

    b. Its installation is more difficult.

    c. Multiple subscribers must share a fixed amount of bandwidth.

    d. It does not interface easily with Ethernet LANs.

    e. It is an asymmetrical technology, while DSL is symmetrical.

17. What is the maximum throughput supported by X.25 technology?

    a. 24 Kbps

    b. 128 Kbps

    c. 384 Kbps

    d. 1.455 Mbps

    e. 2.048 Mbps

18. What do frame relay and ATM connections have in common?

    a. Both rely on the Internet.

    b. Both utilize existing PSTN lines.

    c. Both rely on virtual circuits.

    d. Both are affordable technologies for small businesses.

    e. Both are capable of over 1-Gbps throughput.

19. Which of the following may limit a DSL connection's capacity?

    a. the number of different customers who share the connection

    b. the distance from the customer to the carrier's POP

    c. the existence of more than one copper-wire phone line at the customer's location

    d. the distance from the carrier's POP to the ISP

    e. the lack of a splitter between the DSL modem and the carrier's POP

20. What does "CSU/DSU" stand for?

    a. channel service unit/data service unit

    b. communications server unit/digital server unit

    c. communications serial unit/data serial unit

    d. clean serial unit/dirty serial unit

    e. connected server unit/disconnected server unit

21. Which two of the following transmission media could a T3 use?

    a. UTP

    b. STP

    c. fiber-optic cable

    d. coaxial cable

    e. microwave

22. Outside of the United States, SONET is known as which of the following?

    a. SNS

    b. SDH

    c. STT

    d. SON

    e. STS

23. Name five factors that you should consider when planning a WAN implementation.

24. What type of equipment is used to convert incoming digital signals from an ISDN line into analog signals for use by an attached telephone?

    a. cable modem

    b. terminal adapter

    c. CSU/DSU

    d. Network Termination 1 (NT1)

    e. Network Termination 2 (NT2)

25. Which transmission medium does SONET use?

    a. coaxial cable

    b. microwave

    c. fiber-optic cable

    d. UTP

    e. STP

26. Why might a company choose to implement a VPN?

    a. to lower its WAN transmission costs

    b. to avoid using an ISP

    c. to increase its WAN security

    d. to increase the reliability of its WAN

    e. to allow remote access for its WAN

7

27. If you are configuring a Windows 2000 dial-up connection to an ISP, how would you begin to create this connection?

   a. Right-click on the My Network Places icon, choose Properties, choose the Connections tab, then click Make New Connection.

   b. Double-click the My Network Places icon, then double-click the Add Network Place icon.

   c. Click Start, point to Settings, click Network and Dial-up Connections, then double-click the Make New Connection icon.

   d. Right-click the My Computer icon, choose Properties, choose the Network Identification tab, then click Make New Connection.

28. Dial-up connections from a Windows 2000 Professional client will work only with Windows 2000 Remote Access Service (RAS). True or False?

29. For a user running queries on her office LAN's database server from home, which of the following access types makes the most sense?

   a. RAS connection to an ISP

   b. remote control of the database server

   c. Web interface to a domain controller

   d. dial-in VLAN

30. Which of the following is the most popular communications protocol for dial-up networking connections?

   a. SLIP

   b. NCP

   c. LDAP

   d. PPP

   e. RAS

HANDS-ON PROJECTS

For these projects, you will need a Windows 2000 Professional workstation with a working, configured modem, access to a phone line, and a valid ISP account. You will also need a Web browser, such as Internet Explorer or Netscape Communicator, installed on your workstation.

Project 7-1

Because you will probably be both a user of and technical support person for dial-up connections, it is important that you know how to both create and configure them. In this exercise, you will create and configure a dial-up connection to an ISP. Later, you will change some of its parameters to see what happens.

1. Make sure that you have the dial-in parameters (for example, the dial-in number, the name or address of the name server, and what types of protocols the network accepts) specified by your ISP. Usually, these are supplied when you sign up for a dial-in account. They may also be listed in the technical support section of your ISP's Web site. Also make sure that your phone line is plugged into your modem.

2. Click **Start**, point to **Settings**, and then click **Network and Dial-up Connections**. The Network and Dial-up Connections window appears.

3. Double-click the **Make New Connection** icon. The Network Connection Wizard welcome screen appears.

4. If you have not previously configured a dial-up connection on your computer, you will be asked to provide your area code in the Location Information dialog, and then click **OK**. Then you will be asked to provide your location in the Phone and Modem Options dialog and click **OK**. Click **Next** to continue.

5. Choose the second option, **Dial-up to the Internet**, and click **Next** to continue. The Internet Connection Wizard appears with a welcome message, as shown in Figure 7-16.

6. Choose the last option, **I want to set up my Internet connection manually, or I want to connect through a local area network (LAN)**, then click **Next** to continue. You are prompted to indicate how you will connect to the Internet.

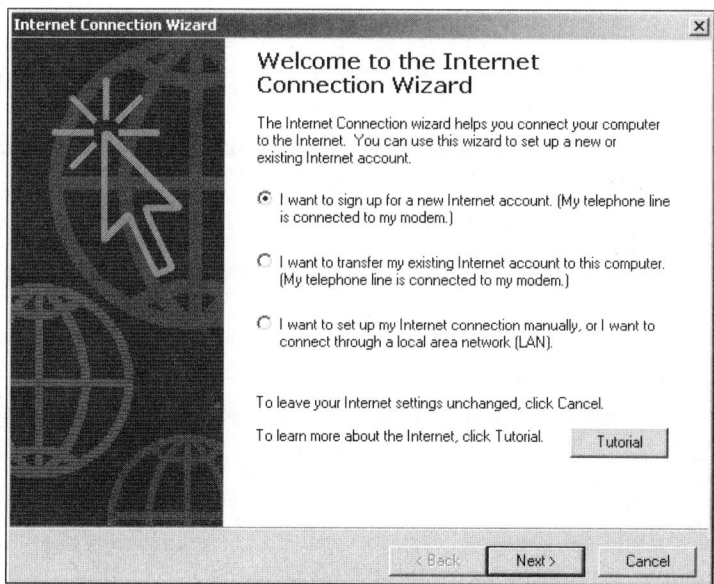

Figure 7-16   The Internet Connection Wizard

7. Choose **I connect through a phone line and modem** (the default), then click **Next** to continue. You are prompted to provide the phone number for your ISP.

8. Type the correct area code and telephone number, and verify that the correct country is selected. For this exercise, you will not need to configure advanced settings. Click **Next** to continue.

9. Provide the user name and password you will use to log into your ISP. This information should have been supplied to you by the ISP. Often the password is case-sensitive, so make sure you type it in correctly and that you don't have the Caps Lock key on. Click **Next** to continue. You are asked to supply a name for this connection.

10. Call this connection TEST, then click **Next** to continue. You are prompted to indicate whether you want to set up an Internet mail account.

11. Choose **No**, then click **Next** to continue. The final screen of the Internet Connection Wizard appears.

12. Click **Finish** to close the wizard and connect to the Internet using your new connection. (Note: if your ISP specifies an unusual configuration for your connection, you may need to adjust the connection's properties before the dial-up connection will work. Do so before continuing to Project 7-2.)

13. If Internet Explorer opens automatically, close it. Disconnect from your ISP.

Project 7-2

Now that you have successfully created an Internet dial-up connection, you will modify some of its parameters to see how configuration changes can affect the connection. This exercise will familiarize you with some of the error messages you might encounter while troubleshooting dial-up networking.

1. Choose **Start**, point to **Settings**, and then click **Control Panel**. The Control Panel window appears.

2. Double-click **Network and Dial-up Connections**. The Network and Dial-up Connections window appears.

3. Right-click the dial-up connection called **TEST**, then choose **Properties** from the drop-down menu. The connection's properties dialog box appears.

4. Select the **Networking** tab.

5. Under "Type of dial-up server I am calling:" choose **SLIP: Unix Connection**.

6. Click **OK** to save your changes and close the properties dialog box.

7. Now try connecting to your ISP using the TEST connection. What happens?

8. Next, you will change another property in the TEST connection configuration. Right-click the dial-up connection called **TEST** in the Network and Dial-up Connections window, then choose **Properties** from the drop-down menu. The connection's properties dialog box appears.

9. Select the **Networking** tab and change the "Type of dial-up server I am calling:" option to **PPP: Windows 95/98/NT 4/2000, Internet**.

10. Under the list of components used by this connection, deselect **Internet Protocol (TCP/IP)**.

11. If NWLink is not already installed, click **Install**. (If NWLink is already installed, skip to Step 13.) The Select Network Component Type dialog box appears.

12. Choose **Protocol**, then click **Add** to continue. The Select Network Protocol dialog box appears.

13. Highlight **NWLink IPX/SPX/NetBIOS Compatible Transport Protocol**, then click **OK**. The NWLink protocol is installed. You will then be returned to the connection's properties dialog box.

14. Click the box next to the **NWLink IPX/SPX/NetBIOS Compatible Transport Protocol** to select it.

15. Click **Close** to save your changes. You return to the Network and Dial-up Connections window.

16. Now double-click the **TEST** icon to make a connection to your ISP. What happens?

Project 7-3

In Chapter 8, you will learn more about Internet networking and, in particular, TCP/IP troubleshooting. One TCP/IP utility, called tracert, allows you to view each node that an Internet connection passes through between your station and the destination you are trying to reach. Even if you aren't troubleshooting a TCP/IP connection, using tracert will help you understand the extent of the Internet's WAN links. For example, you can see how many routers and gateways packets travel through (in other words, how many hops they take) between your workstation and a host far away. For this exercise, you will need a workstation connected to the Internet (either via a dial-up or LAN connection).

1. While connected to the Internet, click **Start**, point to **Programs**, point to **Accessories**, click **Command Prompt**. The Command Prompt window opens.

2. Type **tracert novell.com** at the C:\> prompt, then press **Enter**.

3. Watch the route that your packets take between your computer and the host you have identified. How many nodes do they pass? Can you see the names of long-distance carriers in any of the host names that appear in the route—for example, *mci.net* or *att.net*? Do any of the host names contain acronyms that might give you an idea of what kind of WAN technology the node uses—for example, FDDI or ATM?

4. Try the same exercise with different host names, such as microsoft.com, amazon.com, cisco.com, and npr.org. Do any of your tracert attempts time out? If so, after how many hops?

Project 7-4

If you are asked to recommend software, hardware, or an architecture for WAN links, you will definitely need to know the technologies in greater depth than that provided by this chapter. Even if you are not in that position, however, you will benefit from staying current on WAN technology developments. One of the most interesting evolving fields in WAN technology is the competition between DSL and cable modems for the home user market. In this project, you will find out more about the current state of this contest.

1. Connect to your ISP and open a new browser window.

2. Point your browser to **www.zdnet.com**.

3. In the Search for field, type **DSL** and press **Enter**.

4. Scroll to the bottom of the page until you reach the "Top News and Opinion Items" heading. Click the **See Expanded Results** link to view more titles related to DSL.

5. Choose one article that appears to pertain to DSL technology today and read it. Write a paragraph summarizing its main points.

6. Point your browser to **www.techweb.com**.

7. In the SEARCH field, type **cable modem** and press **Enter**.

8. Choose one article that appears to pertain to the current status of cable modem technology and read it. Write a paragraph summarizing its main points.

CASE PROJECTS

1. A national, nonprofit organization of small business owners called PERKS is holding two simultaneous conferences: one in an Atlanta convention center and one in a Seattle hotel. Both conferences will include speakers, workshops, and exhibit booths showing off new products. The technical manager for PERKS asks for your help in making sure that everything is in order for the conferences. One requirement is having a small LAN established on the exhibit hall floor that will allow visitors to register their names, addresses, and comments. This registration information from attendees at both the Atlanta and Seattle conferences needs to be instantly combined in a single database. What kind of system do you recommend, and why? What additional information might you want to get from the technical manager before you implement anything?

2. A month before the conferences, the technical manager at PERKS decides to add two more hosting locations: Boston and Chicago. The technical manager also wants the keynote speech, which will be delivered at the Boston conference, to be available at the other locations as a live video feed on computers in the exhibit areas. The technical manager wants each of the 15 computers in each location to play the video. How does this new development change your recommendation? What kind of cautionary advice might you give the technical manager about what he is attempting to achieve?

3. You have made the PERKS technical manager a little concerned. Because it is a nonprofit organization, PERKS doesn't have the money to implement the nation-wide videoconference solution you proposed. He had no idea how much it would cost. He suggests simply playing the audio portion of the keynote speech on just two computers in each location. From listening to radio broadcasts on the Web, you know that audio files require at least a 56-Kbps connection—but the more throughput, the better. What kind of solution do you recommend now?

4. While the technical manager is out of town at the PERKS conference, he needs to dial from his hotel room to his office's server to pick up his e-mail each night. When he discovers that he can't connect to the server, he calls you for help. The error message he receives says something about not being able to establish a dial-up connection. He uses the Windows 2000 Professional operating system. List the steps you will use to troubleshoot his connection.

7

NETWORK OPERATING SYSTEMS AND WINDOWS 2000-BASED NETWORKING

After reading this chapter and completing the exercises, you will be able to:

➤ Discuss the functions and features of a network operating system

➤ Define the requirements for a Windows 2000 network environment

➤ Describe how a Windows 2000 server fits into an enterprise-wide network

➤ Perform a simple Windows 2000 Server installation

➤ Manage simple user, group, and rights parameters in Windows 2000 Server

➤ Understand how Windows 2000 Server integrates with other popular network operating systems

ON THE JOB

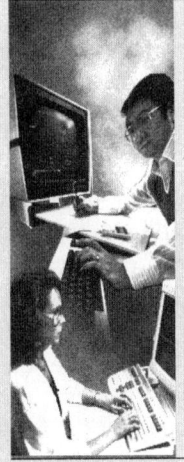

A few years ago I started working for a large consumer goods distributor that relied on Windows NT Server to run its truck distribution software. This software performed route mapping, allowed drivers to scan their bills of lading and receipts, and also kept our company's inventory. More than 100 users used it heavily, day and night. We found that Windows NT was sometimes unstable. We added extra servers to take over in case one of the servers froze up during the night, but we still had problems to resolve in the morning.

Because of our problems, we were eager to try Windows 2000 Server when it was released. We waited until it had been out a few months and the magazine reviews looked positive. We tried it on a test server. Right away we noticed how much more reliable this operating system was compared to Windows NT. We decided to upgrade all of our servers to Windows 2000, and we haven't looked back.

Bob Steigel
Mercury Foods

Network operating systems enable servers to share resources with clients. They also facilitate other services such as communications, security, and user management. Network operating systems do not fit neatly into one layer of the OSI Model. Some of their functions—those that facilitate communication between computers on a network—belong in the Application layer. However, many of their functions—those that interact with users—take place above the Application layer (that is, above the top layer) of the OSI Model. Consequently, the OSI Model does not usefully describe all aspects of network operating systems.

During your career as a networking professional, you will probably work with more than one network operating system (NOS). At the same time, you may work with several versions of the same network operating system. To qualify for Net+ certification, you must understand the inner workings of network operating systems in general. In addition, you must be familiar with the three major network operating systems (Windows 2000 Server, NetWare, and UNIX) and be able to discuss their similarities and differences. Finally, you must be able to integrate the major operating systems, when necessary.

This chapter introduces the basic concepts related to network operating systems and discusses in detail one of the most popular network operating systems, Windows 2000 Server. The following two chapters focus on NetWare and UNIX.

INTRODUCTION TO NETWORK OPERATING SYSTEMS

So far you have focused on the foundations of networking—that is, the lower layers of the OSI Model. Specifically, you've learned about the Physical layer up through the middle layers, where protocol addressing, error checking, and session negotiation occur. Now you will tackle the upper layers of the OSI Model, without which you could not control the lower layers.

Some pieces of network operating systems belong to the seventh layer of the OSI Model, the Application layer. This layer allows you to control the transmission of data by taking your requests and translating them into instructions to the lower-layer processes. The pieces of a network operating system that provide the user interface (such as the dialog boxes in Windows 2000 Server with which you can add users or create groups of users) actually belong *above* the Application layer. Strictly speaking, then, a network operating system does not belong entirely to the Application layer, but rather straddles the Application layer and an imaginary eighth layer (which the OSI Model does not address) above the Application layer.

Recall from Chapter 1 that most modern networks are based on a client/server architecture, in which a server enables multiple clients to share resources. Once installed on a server, a network operating system can oversee user and group management, central data storage, file and print sharing, communications, security, and messaging. It may also support many other functions, such as Internet and remote connectivity, network management, and data backup and recovery. Network operating systems are entirely software-based and can run on a number of different hardware platforms and network topologies.

When installing a network operating system, you may accept the default settings or customize your configuration to more closely meet your needs. You may also take advantage of special services or enhancements that come with a basic network operating system. For example, if you install Windows 2000 Server with only its minimum components, you may later choose to install a clustering solution so that multiple servers can share the network's processing burden. The components included in each different network operating system and every version of a particular network operating system vary. This variability is just one reason that you should plan your network operating system installation very carefully before beginning the implementation. The myriad ways to install and configure network operating systems are beyond the scope of this book.

In this chapter, the word "server" refers to the hardware on which a network operating system runs. In the field of networking, the word "server" may also refer to an application that runs on this hardware to provide a dedicated service. For example, although you may use a Compaq server as your hardware, you may run Novell's BorderManager application as your proxy server on that hardware.

Although each network operating system discussed in this book supports file and print sharing, plus a host of other services, network operating systems differ in how they achieve those functions, what type of environment they suit, and how they are administered. In the next section, you will learn how to select a network operating system for your network.

Selecting a Network Operating System

Realistically, when designing a local area network, you can select from only a handful of network operating systems—specifically, Windows NT Server, Windows 2000 Server, NetWare, and some version of UNIX or Linux. The only reason not to choose one of these options is if your network is outdated or runs a proprietary, specialized application (for example, a quality control system that measures performance of catalytic converters in a test laboratory) that requires a less familiar network operating system (such as Banyan VINES). Many LAN environments include a mix of all three major network operating systems, making interoperability a significant concern.

When choosing a network operating system, you should certainly weigh the strengths and weaknesses of the available options before making a choice. Nevertheless, your decision will probably depend largely on the operating systems and applications already running on the LAN. In other words, your choice may be limited by the existing infrastructure. (Infrastructure includes other network operating systems, and also LAN topology, protocols, transmission methods, and connectivity hardware.)

For example, suppose that you are the network manager for a community college that uses 150 NetWare 4.11 servers to manage all IDs, security, and file and print sharing for 4000 users. In addition, you oversee five Windows 2000 servers that provide Web development and backup services. You have been asked to select a network operating system for a new server for the college's Theater Department. You probably wouldn't choose Windows 2000 Server, because a NetWare server would integrate more seamlessly with your existing network and facilitate administrative tasks, such as adding new users or resources. At another organization, the opposite situation may prevail.

8

The following list summarizes the questions you should ask when deciding to invest in a network operating system. You need to weigh the importance of each factor in your organization's environment separately.

- Is it compatible with my existing infrastructure?

- Will it provide the security required by my resources?

- Can my technical staff manage it effectively?

- Will my applications run smoothly on it?

- Will it accommodate future growth (that is, is it scalable)?

- Does it support the additional services my users require (for example, remote access, Web site hosting, and messaging)?

- Does it fit my budget?

- Can I count on competent and consistent support from its manufacturer?

The importance of these concerns will vary from one network administrator to the next. For example, imagine that you are the network administrator for a multinational chemical company with locations across the globe. Your company's plants and profitability may depend on your network always being available, and your IT budget may be large. In this case, the cost of a network operating system may be less important than its ability to accommodate future growth and the availability of the vendor's technical support. In contrast, if you were the network administrator for a local nonprofit food pantry, your greatest concern may be the cost of the network operating system. In this case, you probably won't care whether the system can easily grow to support hundreds of servers.

In addition to assessing each NOS according to your needs, you should test your network operating system choice in your environment before making a purchase. You can perform such testing on an extra server, using a test group of typical users and applications with specific test criteria in mind. Chapter 16 discusses the implementation of test (or "pilot") networking systems. Bear in mind that you cannot rely on trade magazine articles or a vendor's marketing information to accurately predict which network operating system will best suit your circumstances.

Network Operating Systems and Servers

Most networks include servers that exceed the minimum hardware requirements suggested by the software vendor. Every situation will vary, but to determine the optimal hardware for your servers, you should consider the following issues:

- How many clients will connect to the server?

- What kinds of applications will run on the server?

- How much storage space will each user need?

- How much downtime is acceptable?
- What can the organization afford?

Perhaps the most important question in this list involves the types of applications to be run by the server. You can purchase an inexpensive, low-end server that runs Windows 2000 Server adequately, but that will suffice only for file and print sharing. To perform more functions with your network, you would need to invest in a server that has sufficient processing and memory resources to run applications as well. The particular type of server you choose will depend on the applications you want to run. As you can imagine, every application comes with different processor, RAM, and storage requirements. (Consult the application's installation guide for specifics.) In general, you can assume that a database program (such as MS SQL Server) will require more processor and RAM resources than a word-processing application (such as MS Word).

Keep in mind that the particular way an application uses resources may influence your choice of software and hardware. Applications may or may not provide the option of sharing the processing burden between the client and server. For example, you might install a group scheduling and messaging package that requires every client to run executable files from a network drive, thereby almost exclusively using the server's processing resources. Alternately, you may install the program files on each client workstation and use the server only to distribute messages. The latter solution puts the processing burden on the client.

If your server assumes most of the application-processing burden, or if you have a large number of services and clients to support, you will need to add more hardware than the minimum network operating system requirements. For example, you might add multiple processors, as discussed in the next section. You might also install more RAM, multiple NICs, fault-tolerant hard disks, a backup drive, and an uninterruptible power supply (UPS). Each of these components will enhance network reliability or performance. (You will learn more about performance and reliability in Chapters 13 and 14.) For now, it suffices to know that you must carefully analyze your current situation and plans for growth before making a hardware purchasing decision. Whereas high-end servers with massive processing and storage resources plus fault-tolerant components can cost as much as $100,000, your department may need only a $2000 server. No matter what your needs, you should ensure that your hardware vendor has a reputation for high quality, dependability, and excellent technical support. Although you may be able to trim your costs on workstation hardware by using generic models, you should spare no expense in purchasing your server. A component failure in a server can cause problems for many people, whereas a workstation problem will probably affect only one person.

8

Network Operating System Services and Features

By now you are familiar with the basic functions that network operating systems provide, including resource sharing, security, and network management. In this section you will learn more about fundamental NOS functions and the meaning of terms used when comparing NOSs. You will also learn about some advanced features that enable NOSs to service clients more quickly and reliably. These features are available in all of the popular NOSs. However, the degree to which each NOS can support these features may differ. As you read about Windows 2000 Server in this chapter, and NetWare and UNIX in later chapters, you will learn more about their differences.

Client Support

The primary reason for using networks is to enable clients to communicate and share resources efficiently. Therefore, client support is one of the most important functions provided by an NOS. For purposes of this discussion, client support includes the following tasks:

- Creating client accounts and enabling them to connect to the network
- Managing client accounts
- Enabling clients to share resources
- Managing client access to shared resources
- Enabling clients to communicate with other clients

In Chapter 3 you learned how clients and servers communicate through the layers of the OSI Model (recall the example of sending an e-mail message). The following discussion provides a more general view of client/server communication.

Client/server Communication

Both the client software and the network operating system participate in logging a client onto the server. Although client software differs according to the NOS and desktop operating system, the process of logging on is similar no matter what software is used. First, the user launches the client software from his desktop. Then he enters his user name and password and presses the Enter key. At this point a service on the client workstation (called the **redirector**) intercepts the request to determine whether it should be handled by the client or by the server. A redirector, which belongs to the Presentation layer of the OSI Model, is a service of both the network operating system and the client operating system. Once the client's redirector decides that the request is meant for the server, the client transmits this data over the network to the server. (If the redirector had determined that the request was meant for the client, rather than the server, it would have issued the request to the client's CPU.) For security's sake, most modern clients will encrypt user name and password information before transmitting it to the network media. Recall from Chapter 2 that encryption is another Presentation layer function.

At the server, the network operating system receives the client's request for service and unencrypts it, if necessary. It attempts to match the user name to a name in its user database. If it is successful, it then compares the password associated with that user name to the password supplied by the user. If the passwords match, the NOS responds to the client by granting it access to resources on the network, according to limitations it has specified for this client. This process is known as **authentication**. Figure 8-1 depicts the process of a client connecting to a network operating system.

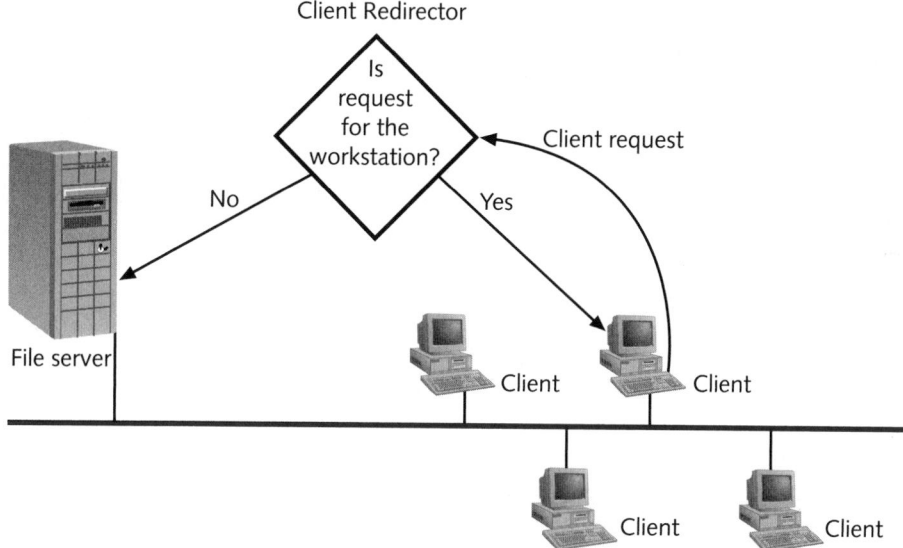

Figure 8-1 A client connecting to a network operating system

 You should understand the login process for troubleshooting purposes. For example, if after entering her name and password, a user receives an error message indicating that the server was not found, you can conclude that the request never made it to the server's NOS. In this case a physical connection problem may be at fault. However, if after entering her name and password, a user receives an error message indicating that the user name or password is invalid, you know that at least the physical connection is working because the request reached the NOS and the NOS attempted to verify the user name. In this case, the password or user name may have been typed incorrectly.

Once the client has successfully logged on, the client software communicates with the network operating system each time the client requests services from the server. For example, if you wished to open a file on the server's hard disk, you would interact with your workstation's operating system to make the file request; the file request would then be intercepted by the redirector and passed to the server via the client software.

In some instances a piece of software called **middleware** is necessary to translate requests and responses between the client and server. Middleware may be used as a messaging service between clients and servers, as a universal query language for databases, or as means of coordinating processes between multiple servers that need to work together in servicing clients. For example, a library's database of materials is contained on a UNIX server, and multiple workstations using different client OSs need to access that single database. In this case, middleware can enable the multiple types of clients to access the database in one standard format. This prevents the library from having to install multiple instances of their database, one for each different client platform. It also allows the clients to have little responsibility for processing requests and therefore, use little of the client's resources. A client/server environment that uses middleware in this fashion is also known as a **3-tier architecture**, because of its three layers: client, middleware, and server. To take advantage of a 3-tier architecture a client workstation requires a special type of software known as a **thin client**. Middleware typically runs on the server, but may run on both the server and the client. Figure 8-2 illustrates the concept of middleware.

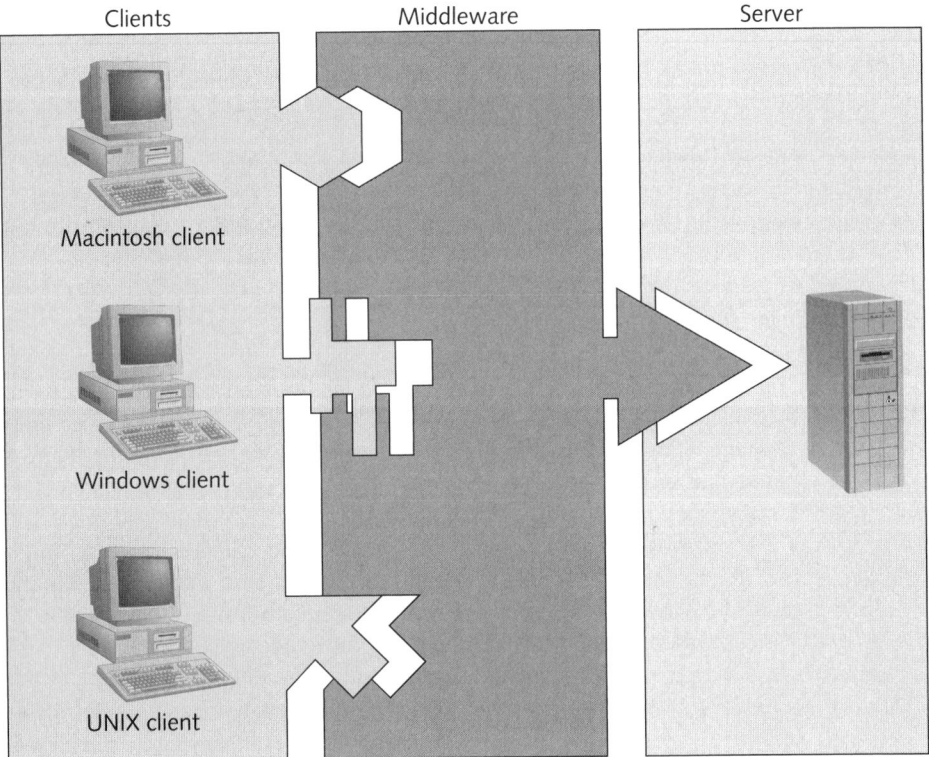

Figure 8-2   Middleware between clients and a server

In the early days of networking, client software from one manufacturer could not always communicate with network software from another manufacturer. Now, however, most every type of client can log onto most every type of network operating system. In some cases this communication may require a special utility or third-party software. But usually, the NOS manufacturer supplies a preferred client software package for each popular type of client. For example, Novell recommends installing its "Novell Client for Windows 95/98" on Windows 95 or Windows 98 workstations and its "Novell Client for Windows 2000" on Windows 2000 workstations. Microsoft requires the "Client for Microsoft Networks" for Windows workstations connecting to its Windows 2000 Server NOS. Client software other than that recommended by the NOS manufacturer may work, but it is wise to follow the NOS manufacturer's guidelines.

Users and Groups

After a client is authenticated by the NOS, it is granted access to services and resources managed by the NOS. The type of access a client (or user) has depends on her user account and what groups she belongs in. In this section, you will learn about users and groups of users. Later in this chapter (and in Chapters 9 and 10), you will learn how to create users and groups and give them rights to resources in each of the three common NOSs. You will also learn which tools each NOS provides for managing users and groups.

You have probably worked with enough computers and networks to know why user names are necessary: to grant each user on a network access to files and other shared resources. Imagine that you are the network administrator for a large college campus with 20,000 user names. Assigning directory, file, printer, and other resource rights for each user name would consume all of your time, especially if the user population changed regularly. To more easily manage network access, you can combine users with similar needs and restrictions into **groups**.

Groups form the basis for resource and account management for every type of network operating system. Many network administrators create groups according to department or, even more specifically, according to job function within a department. They then assign different file or directory access rights to each group. For example, on a high school's network, the administrator may create a group called "students" for the students and a group called "teachers" for teachers. The administrator could then easily grant the teachers group rights to view all attendance and grade records on the server, but deny the same access to the students group.

To better understand the role of groups in resource sharing, first consider their use on a relatively small scale. Suppose you are the network administrator for a public elementary school. You might want to give all teachers and students access to run instructional programs from a network directory called PROGRAMS. In addition, you might want to allow teachers to install their own instructional programs in this same directory. Meanwhile, you need to allow teachers and administrators to record grade information in a central database called GRADES. Of course, you don't want to allow students to read information from this database. Finally, you might want administrators to use a shared drive called STAFF to store performance review information, which should not be accessible to instructors or students. Table 8-1 illustrates how you can provide this security by dividing separate users into three groups: instructors, students, and administrators.

Table 8-1   Providing security through groups

Group	Rights to PROGRAMS	Rights to GRADES	Rights to STAFF
Instructors	Read, modify	Full control	No access
Students	Read	No access	No access
Administrators	No access	Read, modify	Full control

Plan your groups carefully. Creating many groups (for example, a separate group for every job classification in your organization) may impose as much of an administrative burden as not using any groups.

As you learned earlier, once an NOS authenticates a user, it checks the user name against a list of resources and their access restrictions list. If the user name is part of a group with specific access permissions or restrictions, the system will apply those same permissions and restrictions to the user's account.

For simpler management, groups can be nested (one within another) or arranged hierarchically (multiple levels of nested groups) according to the type of access required by different types of users. The way groups are arranged will affect the permissions granted to each group's members. For example, if you created a group called Temps within the Administrators group for temporary office assistants, the Temps group would be nested within the Administrators group and would, by default, share the same permissions as the Administrators group. If you wanted to restrict the Temps users from seeing the staff performance reviews, you would have to separately assign restrictions to the Temps group for that purpose. Once you assign different rights to the Temps group, you have begun creating a hierarchical structure of groups. NOSs differ slightly in how they treat nested and hierarchical groups, and enumerating these differences is beyond the scope of this book. However, if you are a network administrator, you must thoroughly understand the implications of complex group arrangements. For the Network+ exam, you should at least understand how groups can be used to efficiently manage permissions and restrict or allow access to resources.

Once the user and group restrictions are applied, the client is allowed to share resources on the network, including data, data storage space, applications, and peripherals. You will learn more about resource sharing later in this chapter. To understand how NOSs enable resource sharing, though, it is useful to first understand their fundamental design, beginning with their directories.

Directories

A **directory** is a list that organizes resources and associates them with their properties, or characteristics. For example, the table of contents of this book is an example of a directory. In this analogy, each chapter is a resource; the page numbers associated with each heading in a chapter are properties of the chapter. To determine where the book discusses network operating systems, you would find "network operating systems" in the table of contents, then note what pages were listed for this topic. On a personal computer, a directory provides information about the way in which files are organized, plus information about those files, such as their size and creation date.

In the context of the Windows 2000 Server and NetWare 5.x network operating systems, a directory is a method for organizing and managing objects. An **object** is a representation of a thing or person associated with the network. Objects commonly managed by NOS directories include users, printers, groups, computers, data files, and applications. Each object may have a multitude of **attributes**, or properties, associated with it. For example, a user's attributes may include a first and last name, location, mail address, group membership, access restrictions, and so on. A printer's attributes may include an administrator, location, model number, printing preferences (for example, double-sided printing), and so on.

To better organize and manage objects, a network administrator places objects in containers. **Containers** are logically defined receptacles that serve only to assemble similar objects. Returning to the example of a school network, suppose each student, teacher, and administrator were assigned a user name and password for the network. Each of these users would be considered an object, and each would require an account. (An **account** is the record of a user that contains all of his or her properties, including rights to resources, password, name, and so on.) One way of organizing these objects would be to put all the user objects in one container called "Users." But suppose the school provided a server and a room of workstations strictly for student use. The use of these computers would be restricted to applications and Internet access during only certain hours of the day. As the network administrator, you could gather the student user names (or the "Students" group), the student server, the student printers, and the student applications in a container called "Students." You could associate the restricted network access (an attribute) with this container so that these students could access the school's applications and the Internet only during certain hours of the day. Unlike an object, a container can hold multiple objects. Also, a container is a logical construct—that is, a means of organizing other things; it does not represent something real. A container is different from a group because it can hold and apply parameters for many different types of objects, not only users.

Another concept you should understand when working with NOS directories is the idea of a tree. A **tree** is a logical representation of multiple, hierarchical levels in a directory. The term "tree" is drawn from the fact that the whole structure shares a common starting point (the root) and from that point extends branches (or containers), which may

8

extend additional branches, and so on. Objects are the last items in the hierarchy connected to the branches (and in fact, are sometimes called "leaf objects"). Figure 8-3 depicts a simple directory tree.

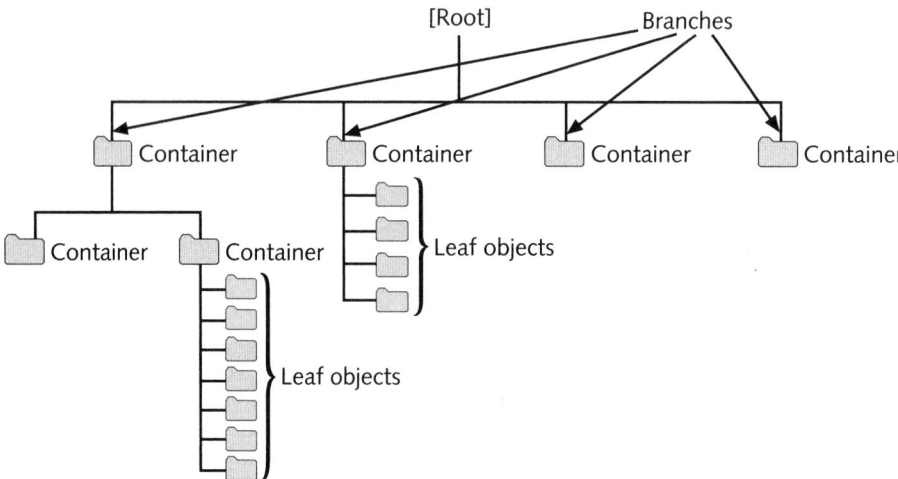

Figure 8-3   A directory tree

Before you install a network operating system, be sure to plan the directory tree with current and future needs in mind. For example, suppose you work at a new manufacturing firm called Circuits Now that produces high-quality, inexpensive circuit boards. You might decide to create a simple tree that branches into three containers: users, printers, and computers. But if Circuits Now plans to open new manufacturing facilities sometime in the future (for instance, one devoted to making memory chips and another for transistors), you might want to call the first container in the tree "circuit boards." This would separate the existing circuit board business from the new businesses, which would employ different people and require different resources. Figure 8-4 shows both possible trees.

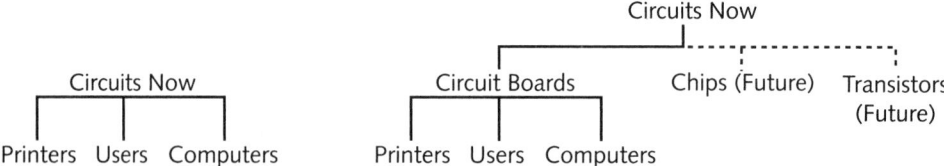

Figure 8-4   Two possible trees for the same organization

Directory trees are very flexible, and as a result, may seem complicated. Chances are that you will enter an organization that has already established its tree, and you will need to understand the logic of that tree to perform your tasks. Later in this chapter and in the two following chapters you will learn more about each NOS's directory and the differences between them.

File Systems

The term **file system** refers to an operating system's method of organizing, managing, and accessing its files through logical structures and software routines. Be careful not to confuse file systems with directories. A file system is different from a directory of files (such as you would view on a PC) because a file system interacts with the operating system. Its purpose is to ensure that the operating system can find requested files on the hard disk. A directory, on the other hand, logically organizes files so that a user can find them on a hard disk. In fact, two files located in the same directory on a computer may be in two different places in the file system.

To administer a network, you should understand the file system (or files systems) used by your NOS. Different file systems not only organize files differently, but also have different file access, speed, compression, defragmentation, and security characteristics. You will need to know which file system your NOS can use and, also, which file systems are compatible with each other. If you completed coursework for the A+ certification, you should already be familiar with the general file systems discussed in the following sections. File systems specific to Windows 2000 Server, NetWare 5.x, and UNIX are discussed elsewhere in this chapter and in Chapters 9 and 10.

8

FAT (File Allocation Table)

FAT (File Allocation Table) is the original PC file system that was designed in the 1970s to support floppy disks and, later, hard disks. To understand FAT, you must first understand the distribution of data on a disk. Disks are divided into allocation units (also known as clusters). Each allocation unit represents a small portion of the disk's space; depending on your operating system, the allocation unit's size may or may not be customizable. A number of allocation units combine to form a partition. The FAT, a hidden file positioned at the beginning of a partition, keeps track of used and unused allocation units on that partition. The FAT also contains information about the files within each directory, as well as the size of files, their names, and the times that they were created and updated.

 When part of a disk uses the FAT method of tracking files, that portion of the disk is called a "FAT partition."

FAT16

The original version of the FAT file system, designed for floppy disks, allows for allocation units that are 12 bits in size. Another version of FAT, designed for computer hard disks, uses 16-bit allocation units. This version of the FAT file system is known as **FAT16**. FAT16 was the standard file system for early DOS- and Windows-based computers. But FAT16 has proved inadequate for most modern operating systems because of its partition size limitations, naming limitations, fragmentation, security, and speed issues. Some significant FAT16 characteristics are listed below. (Note the differences between Microsoft's version of FAT16 and the standard FAT16.)

- A FAT16 partition or file cannot exceed 2 GB (when FAT16 is used with the Windows 2000 file system, its maximum size is 4 GB).

- FAT16 uses 16-bit fields to store file size information.

- FAT16 (without additional utilities) supports only filenames with a maximum of eight characters in the name and three characters in the extension.

- FAT16 categorizes files on a disk as Read (a user can read the file), Write (a user can modify or create the file), System (only the operating system can read or write the file), Hidden (a user cannot see the file on the drive without explicitly searching for hidden files), or Archive (used to indicate whether the file has recently been backed up). The term "file attributes" refers to these settings. For example, one file might have a Read file attribute, while another might have a Write file attribute.

- A FAT16 drive stores data in noncontiguous blocks and uses links between fragments to ensure that data belonging to the same file, for example, can be pieced together when the file is requested by the operating system. This approach is unreliable and inefficient, and it may cause corruption.

- Because of FAT16's low overhead, it can write data to a hard disk very quickly.

FAT32

The FAT16 file system was enhanced in the mid-1990s to accommodate longer filenames and permit faster data access via 32-bit addressing. This version of FAT, called **FAT32**, retains some features of the original FAT, such as the Read, Write, System, Hidden, and Archive file attributes. But in contrast to FAT16, FAT32 reduces the maximum size limit file clusters so that space on a disk is used more efficiently. In some cases, FAT32 can conserve as much as 15% of the space that would be required for the same number of files on a FAT16 partition. These and other FAT32 characteristics are listed below:

- FAT32 uses 28-bit fields to store file size information (4 of the 32 bits are reserved).

- FAT32 supports long filenames.

- FAT32 theoretically supports partitions up to 2 Terabytes in size (in Windows 2000, however, the maximum FAT32 partition size is 32 Megabytes).

- Unlike FAT16 partitions, FAT32 partitions can be easily resized without damaging data.

- FAT32 provides greater security than FAT16. For these reasons, FAT32 is preferred over FAT16 for modern operating systems.

- FAT32 is supported by Windows 9x, Windows Me, and Windows 2000.

HPFS (High-Performance File System)

HPFS (High-Performance File System) is a file system originally designed for IBM's OS/2 operating system that offers greater efficiency and reliability than FAT. HPFS organizes data in contiguous blocks, allows data to wait in memory if the processor is too busy to accept it, and assigns information about other data on the disk to each block of data. Collectively, all of these measures enhance HPFS's speed. HPFS also supports extended attributes. In this context, the term **extended attributes** refers to the attributes beyond the basic Read, Write, System, Hidden, and Archive attributes supported by FAT. For example, HPFS provides information about file history, the application to which the file belongs, executable code, icons, and files that depend on other files to function properly. Because it uses 32-bit fields to store file size information, HPFS can handle larger disk sizes than FAT can. HPFS also supports long filenames.

Sharing Applications

As you have learned, one of the significant advantages of the client/server architecture is the ability to share resources, thereby reducing costs and the time required to manage the resources. Along with data storage, applications are an important shared resource. In this section you will learn how a network operating system enables clients to share applications.

Shared applications are often installed on a file server that is specifically designed to run applications. In a smaller organization, however, they may be installed on the same server that provides other functions, such as Internet, security, and remote access services. As a network administrator, you must be sure to purchase a license for the application that allows it to be shared among clients. In other words, you cannot legally purchase one licensed copy of Microsoft Office, install it on a server, and allow all of your 1000 users to share it. Most software vendors sell client licenses for multiple users, which are still much less expensive than purchasing a separate software package for each user. For some applications, you can purchase a **site license**, which (for a fixed price) allows any number of users in one location to legally access that application.

 Before selecting an application to run on your network, make sure it is supported by your NOS. You can determine which applications an NOS supports by reading the NOS's documentation or consulting the vendor's Web site. Microsoft, for example, allows you to check whether your applications are Windows 2000 Server-compliant using a search form at *www.microsoft.com/windows2000/ professional/howtobuy/upgrading/compat/search/software.asp*.

Once you have purchased the appropriate type and number of licenses, you are ready to install the application on a server. Before doing so, however, you should make sure your server has enough hard disk, memory, and processing power to run the application. Then follow the software manufacturer's guidelines for a server installation. Depending on the application, this process may be the same as installing the application on a workstation or much different.

8

Once you have installed the software on a server, you are ready to make it available to clients. Through the network operating system, you must assign users rights to the directories where the application's files are installed. Users will at least need rights to access and read files in those directories. For some applications, you may also need to give users rights to create, erase, or modify files associated with the application. For example, a database program may create a small temporary file on the server when a user launches the program to indicate to other potential users that the database is open. If this is the case, users must have rights to create files in the directory where this temporary file is kept. An application's installation guidelines will indicate the rights you need to assign users for each of the application's directories.

Next you will need to provide users a way of accessing the application. On Windows-based or Macintosh clients, you can create an icon on the user's desktop that is associated with the application file. When the user double-clicks the icon, her client software will issue the request to the server to open the application. In response, the network operating system will send a part of the program to her workstation, where it will be held in RAM. This allows the user to interact with the program quickly, without having to relay every command over the network to the server. As the user works with the application, the amount of processing that occurs on her workstation versus the amount of processing that the server handles will vary according to the network architecture. In the preceding example, where a client launches the application directly from a file on the server, the client performs nearly all of the processing. In the case of 3-tier applications, the processing burden is shared between the client and server. And in the case of remote access application sharing, the server performs all of the processing and sends only screen images over the network to the client.

You may wonder how an application can operate efficiently or accurately when multiple users are simultaneously accessing its files. After all, an application's program file is a single resource. If two or more network users double-click their application icon simultaneously, how does the application know which client to respond to? In fact, the network operating system is responsible for arbitrating access to these files. In the case of multiple users simultaneously launching a network application from their desktop icons, the network operating system will respond to one request, then the next, then the next, each time issuing a copy of the program to the client's RAM. In this way, each client is technically working with a separate instance of the application.

Shared access becomes more problematic when multiple users are simultaneously accessing the same data files as well as the same program files. For example, an online auction site accepts bids on many items from many Internet users. Imagine that an auction is nearing a close with three users simultaneously bidding on the same stereo. How does the auction site's database accept bid data for that stereo from multiple sources? One solution to this problem is middleware. The three Internet bidders cannot directly modify the database, located on the auction site's server. Instead, a middleware program runs on the server to accept data from the clients. If the database is not busy, the middleware passes a bid to the database. If the database is busy (or open), the middleware queues the bids (forces them to wait) until the database is ready to rewrite its existing data, then passes one bid, then another, and another, to the database until its queue is empty. In this way, only one client's data can be written to the database at any point in time.

Sharing Printers

You have learned that sharing peripherals, such as printers, can increase the efficiency of managing resources and reduce costs for an organization. In this section you will learn how networks enable clients to share printers. Sharing other peripheral devices, such as fax machines, works in a similar manner.

In most cases an organization will designate a server as the print server—that is, as the server in charge of managing print services. A printer may be directly attached to the print server or more likely, be attached to the network in a location convenient for the users. In other cases, shared printers may be attached to networked workstations. In order for these printers to be accessible, the workstation must be turned on and functioning properly. Figure 8-5 depicts multiple ways to share printers on a network.

8

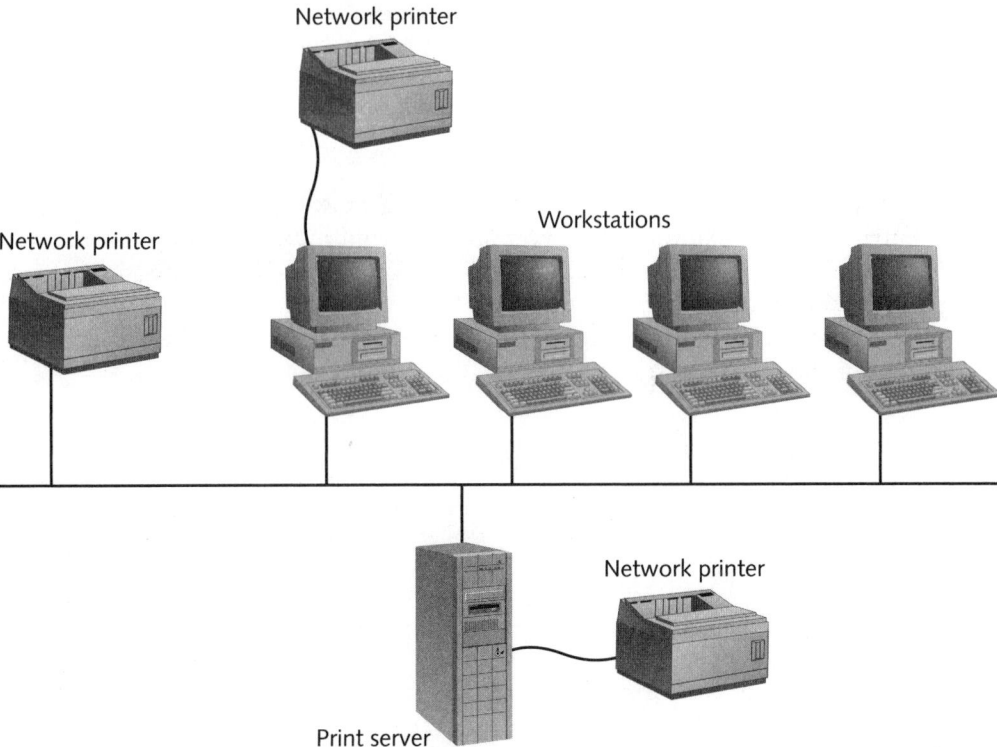

Figure 8-5   Shared printers on a network

Once the printer is physically connected to the network, it needs to be recognized and managed by the NOS before users can access it. Different NOSs have different interfaces for managing printers, but all NOSs can:

- Create an object that identifies the printer to the rest of the network
- Assign the printer a unique name
- Install drivers associated with the printer
- Modify printer attributes, such as location and printing preferences
- Establish or limit access to the printer
- Remotely test and monitor printer functionality
- Update and maintain printer drivers

 As a network administrator, you should establish a plan for naming printers before you install them. Since the names you assign the printers will appear in lists of printers available to clients, you should choose names that users can easily decipher. For example, an HP LaserJet 5M in the Engineering Department may be called "ENG_HP5M," or an HP LaserJet 6P in the southwest corner of the building may be called "HP6P_SOUTHWEST." Whatever convention you choose, remain consistent to avoid user confusion and to make your own job easier.

NOSs provide special interfaces for creating new printer objects and assigning them attributes. In Windows 2000 Server, an Add Printer Wizard takes you through the printer creation process step by step. In NetWare 5.x you begin by choosing to create a new object; then a series of menu options leads you through the process, beginning with a printer identification screen, as shown in Figure 8-6. Note the type of attributes this screen allows you to specify.

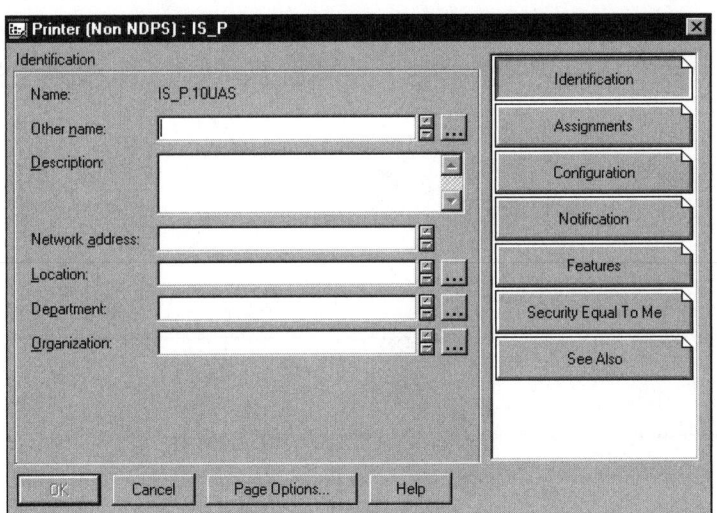

Figure 8-6   NetWare printer identification screen

As you create the new printer, the NOS will require you to install a printer driver, unless one is already installed on the server. This makes the printer's device driver files accessible to users who wish to send jobs to that printer. Before users can access the printer, however, you must ensure that they have proper rights to the printer's queue. The **printer queue** (or share, as it is known in Microsoft terminology) is a logical representation of the printer's input and output. That is, a queue does not physically exist, but rather acts as a sort of "virtual in box and out box" for the printer. When a user wants to print a document, he sends it to the printer queue. To send it to the printer queue, he must have rights to access that queue. As with shared data, the rights to shared printers can vary. Users may have minimal privileges, which allow them to simply send jobs to the printer, or they may have advanced privileges, which allow them to change the priority of print jobs in the queue, or even (in the case of an administrator) change the name of the queue.

Networked printers appear as icons in the Printers folder on Windows and Macintosh workstations, just as local printers would appear. Once they have found a networked printer, users can send documents to that printer just as they would send documents to a local printer. When a user chooses to print, the client redirector determines whether the request should be transmitted to the network or remain at the workstation. On the network, the user's request gets passed to the print server, which puts the job into the appropriate printer queue for transmission to the printer. Figure 8-7 depicts this process.

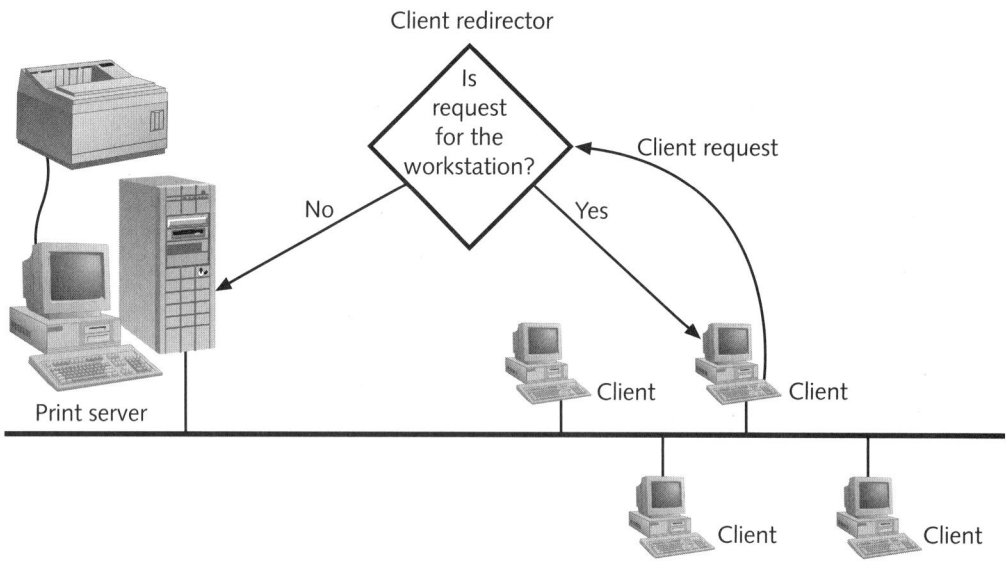

Figure 8-7 Client issuing a job to a networked printer

Managing System Resources

Because a server's system resources (for example, memory and CPU) are limited and are required by multiple users, it is important to make the best use of them. Modern network operating systems have capabilities that maximize the use of a server's memory, CPU, bus, and hard disk. The result is that a server can accommodate more client requests faster—thus improving overall network performance. In the following sections, you will learn about some NOS techniques for managing a server's resources.

Memory

From working with PCs, you may be familiar with the technique of using virtual memory to boost the total memory available to a system. Servers can use both physical and virtual memory, too, as this section describes.

Before learning about virtual memory, you should understand physical memory. The term **physical memory** refers to the (RAM) chips installed on the computer's system board that provide dedicated memory to that machine. The amount of physical memory required by your server varies depending on the tasks that it performs. For example, the minimum amount of physical memory required to run a Windows 2000 Server is 256 MB. However, if you intend to run file and print sharing, Internet, and remote access services on one server, you will need additional physical memory. (When deciding on the appropriate amount of physical memory for your server, remember that the ability to process instructions also depends on processing speed.)

Another type of memory may be logically carved out of space on the hard disk for temporary use. In this arrangement, both the space on the hard disk and the RAM together form **virtual memory**. Virtual memory is stored on the hard disk as a **page file** (or **swap file**), the use of which is managed by the operating system. Each time the system exceeds its available RAM, blocks of information, called pages, are moved out of RAM and into virtual memory on disk. This technique is called **paging**. When the processor requires the information moved to the page file, the blocks are moved back from virtual memory into RAM.

Virtual memory is both a blessing and a curse. On the one hand, if your server has plenty of hard disk space, you can use virtual memory to easily expand the memory available to server applications. This is a great advantage when a process temporarily needs more memory than the physical memory can provide. Virtual memory is typically engaged by default; it requires no user or administrator intervention and is accessed without the clients' knowledge. (However, as a network administrator, you can modify the amount of hard disk space available for virtual memory). On the other hand, using virtual memory slows operations, because accessing a hard disk takes longer than accessing physical memory. Therefore, an excessive reliance on virtual memory will cost you in terms of performance.

Multitasking

Another technique that helps servers use their system resources more efficiently is multitasking. **Multitasking** is the ability of a processor to perform many different operations in a brief period of time. If you have opened multiple programs simultaneously on a desktop computer, you have taken advantage of your operating system's multitasking capability.

All of the major NOSs can perform multiple tasks at one time. If they couldn't, network performance would be considerably slower, since busy servers are continually receiving and responding to multiple requests. However, NOSs differ in their multitasking abilities.

In NetWare, UNIX, and Windows 2000 Server, the server actually performs one task at a time, allowing one program to use the processor for a certain period of time, and then suspending that program to allow another program to use the processor. Thus, each program has to take turns loading and running. Because no two tasks are ever actually performed at one time, this capability is not considered true multitasking; instead, it is referred to as **preemptive multitasking**. Preemptive multitasking happens so quickly, however, that the average user could probably not distinguish between it and true multitasking.

Multiprocessing

Before you learn about the next method of managing system resources, you need to understand the terms used when discussing data processing. A **process** is a routine of sequential instructions that runs until it has achieved its goal. A word-processing program's executable file is an example of a process. A **thread** is a self-contained, well-defined task within a process. A process may contain many threads, each of which may run independently of the

8

others. All processes have at least one—the main thread. For example, to eliminate the waiting time when you save a file in your word processor, the programmer who wrote the word-processor program might have chosen to implement the file save operation as a separate thread. That is, the part of the program that implements the file save operation executes in a thread that is independent of the main thread. This independent execution allows you to continue typing while the document is being written to the disk.

On systems with only one processor, only one thread can be handled at any time. Thus, if a number of programs are running simultaneously, no matter how fast the processor, a number of processes and threads will be left to await execution. Using multiple processors allows different threads to run on different processors. The support and use of multiple processors to handle multiple threads is known as **multiprocessing**. Multiprocessing is often used on servers as a technique to improve response time. To take advantage of more than one processor on a computer, its operating system must be capable of multiprocessing. For example, Windows 2000 Server supports the use of four processors.

Multiprocessing splits tasks among more than one processor to expedite the completion of any single instruction. To understand this concept, think of a busy metropolitan freeway during rush hour. If five lanes are available for traffic, drivers can pick any lane—preferably the fastest lane—to get home as soon as possible. If traffic in one lane slows, drivers may choose another, less congested lane. This ability to move from lane to lane allows all traffic to move faster. If the same amount of traffic had to pass through only one lane, everyone would go slower and get home later. In the same way, multiple processors can handle more instructions more rapidly than a single processor could.

NetWare 5.x and Windows 2000 Server support a special type of multiprocessing called **symmetric multiprocessing**, which splits all operations equally among two or more processors. Another type of multiprocessing, **asymmetric multiprocessing**, assigns each subtask to a specific processor. Continuing the freeway analogy, asymmetric multiprocessing would decree that all semi trucks must use the far right lane, all pickup trucks must use the second to the right lane, all compact cars must use the far left lane, and so on. The efficiency of each multiprocessing model is open to debate, but, in general, symmetric processing completes operations more quickly because the processing load is more evenly distributed.

Multiprocessing offers a great advantage to servers with high CPU usage—that is, servers that perform numerous tasks simultaneously. If an organization uses its server merely for file and print sharing, however, multiple processors may not be necessary. You should carefully assess your processing needs before purchasing a server with multiple processors. Some processing bottlenecks are not actually caused by the processor—but rather by the time it takes to access the server's hard disks or by problems related to cabling or connectivity devices. Determining the source of network performance degradation can be an art, and you will learn more about this practice in Chapter 12.

INTRODUCTION TO WINDOWS 2000 SERVER

Windows 2000 Server is the latest version of Microsoft's network operating system. It was released in 1999 but was under development for five years before that. Windows 2000 Server serves as a redesign and enhancement of its predecessor, Windows NT Server. Windows NT Server was a popular network operating system known for its intuitive graphical user interface, multitasking capabilities, and compatibility with a huge array of applications. A **graphical user interface** (**GUI**; pronounced "gooey") is a pictorial representation of computer functions that, in the case of network operating systems, enables administrators to manage files, users, groups, security, printers, and so on. When Windows NT Server was commercially released in 1993, it was the first network operating system based entirely on a GUI, making network administration easier than ever before. Prior to Windows NT, the only option Microsoft provided for sharing resources between Windows-based workstations was Windows for Workgroups, which employed a peer-to-peer network model.

Windows 2000 Server carries on many of the advantages of Windows NT Server, plus provides additional features and capabilities. Some benefits of the Windows 2000 Server NOS include:

- An advanced system of organizing and managing network objects, called Active Directory
- Multiple, integrated Web services with an easy to use administrator interface
- Support for a great deal of RAM and multiple processors
- Support for multiple, modern protocols and security standards
- Excellent integration with other network operating systems
- Simple centralized management of multiple clients
- Flexible, customizable network management interface

With Windows 2000, Microsoft in fact released three different, but related NOSs: Windows 2000 Server, Windows 2000 Advanced Server, and Windows 2000 Datacenter Server. Windows 2000 Advanced Server offers the same benefits and includes the same features as Windows 2000 Server, but adds support for **clustering**, a method of connecting multiple servers to enable resource sharing and load balancing between them. You will learn more about clustering in Chapter 14. Windows 2000 Advanced Server also supports servers with up to eight processors and up to 8 GB of RAM, while Windows 2000 Server supports up to four processors and up to 4 GB of RAM. In short, Windows 2000 Advanced Server is generally suitable for a larger enterprise. Windows 2000 Datacenter Server is designed for environments that make heavy use of databases and data manipulation. Windows 2000 Datacenter Server supports up to 32 processors and 64 GB of RAM.

8

In addition to these options, Microsoft also offers Windows 2000 Professional, a desktop operating system that can also accept some client connections. You may wonder how Windows 2000 Server differs from Windows 2000 Professional. In general, Windows 2000 Server provides more services specifically targeted to networks. While Windows 2000 Professional can accept up to 10 client connections, Windows 2000 Server can accept nearly unlimited client connections. Windows 2000 Server also provides network security, storage, Web, and management features that are not included in Windows 2000 Professional.

This chapter gives a broad overview of how Windows 2000 Server (the basic version) fits into a network environment. It also provides other information necessary to qualify for Net+ certification. It does not attempt to give exhaustive details of the process of installing, maintaining, or optimizing Windows 2000 networks. For this in-depth knowledge (particularly if you plan to pursue MCSE certification), you should invest in books devoted to Windows 2000 Server, such as Course Technology's *MCSE Guide to Microsoft Windows 2000 Server*, ISBN 0-619-01517-9.

WHY CHOOSE WINDOWS 2000 SERVER?

Windows 2000 Server is a popular network operating system because it addresses most of a network administrator's needs very well. Microsoft is, of course, a well-established vendor that wields its size and influence to ensure that other programs will be compatible with its systems. Its large market share also guarantees that technical support—whether through Microsoft, private developer groups, or third-party newsgroups—are readily available. If you become MCSE-certified, you will be eligible to receive enhanced support directly from Microsoft. This enhanced support (including a series of CDs) will help you solve problems more quickly and accurately. Because Windows 2000 is so widely used, you can also search newsgroups on the Web and will probably find someone who has encountered and solved a problem like yours.

Windows 2000 supports any type of topology or protocol that you are likely to run on a LAN. This efficient network operating system takes advantage of multiple processors. Its multitasking capabilities allow server-based processes (for example, retrieving a file, sending a command to a networked printer, or authorizing a user to log on) to share CPU resources. Also, its customizable, graphical administrative interface called the **Microsoft Management Console (MMC)** makes Windows 2000 Server a simple operating system to manage. Thus, technical staff members who are unfamiliar with the system can quickly learn how to perform routine maintenance and operation activities. Windows 2000 Server also provides excellent security features, which are highly customizable and easily managed from the server console.

One potential drawback to using Windows 2000 Server is its performance. In independent benchmark tests, Windows 2000 Server has been found to read and write data somewhat slower than NetWare 5.x and certain versions of UNIX. On the other hand, performance greatly depends on the type of routines and commands tested. Windows 2000 Server's broad range of features overshadows any perceived performance disadvantage for most environments. Its ease of centralized management, Web integration, storage management, and built-in system monitoring tools are unique advantages over the other major NOSs.

Since its release in 1999, Windows 2000 Server has become the NOS of choice for a wide variety of environments. If you have used the Web to research a topic, conduct online banking transactions, reserve a hotel, or purchase gifts, chances are you have connected to Windows 2000 Server. Windows 2000 Server is also used in hospitals, schools, government offices, warehouses, manufacturing plants, utilities, stores, and media outlets. Because of Windows 2000's cross-industry acceptance, understanding this NOS will likely provide you with a valuable career skill.

WINDOWS 2000 SERVER HARDWARE

You have learned that servers generally require more processing power, more memory, and more hard disk space than workstation machines do. In addition, servers may contain redundant components for fault tolerance, self-monitoring firmware, multiple processors and NICs, or peripherals other than the common CD-ROM and floppy disk drives. The type of servers you choose for your network will depend partly on your network operating system. As you learned earlier, each network operating system demands specific requirements in terms of server hardware.

An important resource for determining what kind of Windows 2000 hardware to purchase is Microsoft's Hardware Compatibility List. The **Hardware Compatibility List (HCL)** lists all computer components proven to be compatible with Windows 2000 Server. The HCL appears on the same CD-ROM as your Windows 2000 Server software. If you don't find a hardware component on the HCL that shipped with your software, you can look it up on Microsoft's Web site. At the time of this writing, Microsoft's searchable hardware compatibility list could be accessed from the following Web site: *www.microsoft.com/windows2000/server/howtobuy/upgrading/compat/default.asp*. You should always consult this list before buying new hardware. Although hardware that is *not* listed on the HCL may work with Windows 2000 Server, Microsoft's technical support won't help you solve problems related to such hardware.

Table 8-2 lists Microsoft's minimum server requirements for Windows 2000 Server.

Table 8-2   Minimum hardware requirements for Windows 2000 Server

Component	Requirement
Processor	133 MHz or higher Pentium or Pentium-compatible processor. Windows 2000 Server supports up to four CPUs in one server; however, Windows 2000 Advanced Server can support up to eight CPUs and Windows 2000 Datacenter Server can support up to 32 CPUs
Memory	256 megabytes (MB) of RAM is the recommended minimum (but a 128 MB minimum is supported). A computer running Windows 2000 Server may hold a maximum of 4 gigabytes (GB) of memory
Hard disk drive	A hard drive supported by Windows 2000 (as specified in the HCL) with a minimum of 1 GB of free space available for system files (2 GB recommended)
NIC	Although a NIC is not required to install the Windows 2000 Server NOS, it is required to connect to a network. Use a NIC found on the HCL. More than one NIC can be supported
CD-ROM	A CD-ROM drive found on the HCL is required unless the installation will take place over the network
Pointing device	A mouse or other pointing device found on the HCL
Floppy disk drive	Not required

Minimum requirements specify the *least* amount of RAM, hard disk space, and processing power you must have to run the network operating system. Your applications and performance demands, however, may require more resources. Some of the minimum requirements listed in Table 8-2 (for example, the 133 MHz Pentium processor) may apply to the smallest test system—not a realistic networking environment. Be sure to calculate the optimal configuration for your network's server based on your environment's needs before you purchase new hardware. For instance, you should make a list of every application and utility you expect the server to run in addition to the NOS. Then look up the processor, memory, and hard disk requirements for each of those programs and estimate how significantly their requirements will affect your server's overall hardware requirements. It is easier and more efficient to perform an analysis before you install the server than to add hardware after your server is up and running.

A CLOSER LOOK AT THE WINDOWS 2000 SERVER NETWORK OPERATING SYSTEM

By now you should understand some of the features that are important to all network operating systems. You should also have a sense of the type of organization that might choose Windows 2000 Server as its preferred NOS. In the next sections, you will learn specifically how Windows 2000 Server manages its system resources, data files, and network objects.

Windows 2000 Server Memory Model

Earlier you learned that Windows 2000 Server can make use of up to 4 processors and, further, that it employs a type of multiprocessing called symmetric multiprocessing. You also learned that Windows 2000 Server can make use of virtual memory. This section provides more information on how Windows 2000 optimizes its use of a server's memory to perform many complex tasks simultaneously.

The Windows 2000 Server memory model uses a 32-bit addressing scheme. To appreciate the advantages of this feature, you may want to review the material on addressing in Chapter 6 (in the discussion of bus-adapter NICs). Essentially, the larger the addressing size, the more efficiently instructions can be processed. Microsoft's original network operating system used a 16-bit addressing scheme, half the size of that supported by Windows 2000 Server.

The Windows 2000 Server memory model also assigns each application (or process) its own 32-bit memory area. This memory area is a logical subdivision of the entire amount of memory available to the server. Assigning separate areas to processes helps prevent one process from interfering with another's operations, even though the processes are running simultaneously. The technique is analogous to a company giving each employee a car to commute to work. You can imagine the disadvantage of this approach: It is less efficient than supplying employees with a few commuter vans that can transport 10 people to work at the same time. The risk of losing employees to injuries suffered in an accident is lower, however, because a commuter van accident affects more employees than an accident involving an individual car driver. Similarly, if each application uses the same memory area, one misbehaving process can take down all applications running in that memory area. On the other hand, if each application uses a separate memory area, each one can harm only itself. As in the car-van scenario, using separate memory spaces for each application is, however, less efficient.

Another important feature of the Windows 2000 Server memory model is that it allows you to install more physical memory on the server than previous versions of Windows did, which in turn means that the server can process more instructions faster.

Finally, as you have learned, Windows 2000 Server can make use of virtual memory. To find out how much virtual memory your Windows 2000 server uses, open the Control Panel, double-click the System icon, click Advanced, click Performance Options, and then click the Change button. If multiple drives are listed in the Drive box, choose the drive that contains your page file. The Paging file size indicates how much hard disk space is available for virtual memory, as pictured in Figure 8-8. If you suspect that your server's processing is being degraded because it relies on virtual memory too often, you should invest in additional physical memory (RAM).

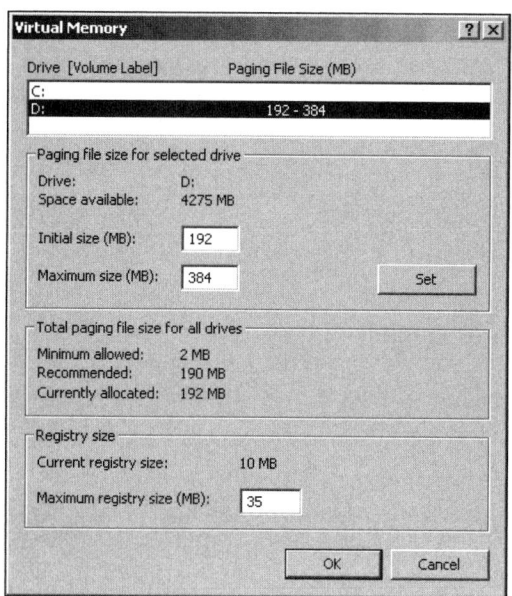

Figure 8-8   Viewing virtual memory

Windows 2000 File Systems

In addition to the FAT, FAT32, and HPFS file systems you learned about earlier, Windows 2000 Server supports other types of file systems, including CDFS and NTFS. You will learn about both in the following sections. You will also learn when it is most appropriate to use NTFS and FAT32 on your Windows 2000 server.

CDFS (CD-ROM File System) and UDF (Universal Disk Format)

The **CDFS (CD-ROM File System)** is the file system used to read from and write to a CD-ROM disk. Windows 2000 Server supports CDFS so as to allow program installations and CD-ROM file sharing over the network. No intervention is necessary to install or configure the CDFS—it is installed automatically when you install Windows 2000 Server. In addition to CDFS, Windows 2000 Server supports the **Universal Disk Format (UDF),** which is another file system used on CD-ROMs and digital video disc (DVD) media. DVDs and CD-ROMs can be used to store large quantities of data in a networking environment. However, they are more commonly used to store digital audio and video data, such as movies.

NTFS (New Technology File System)

Microsoft developed **NTFS (New Technology File System)** expressly for its Windows NT platform. With the release of Windows 2000, Microsoft updated NTFS to version 5. Among other things, this upgrade provided NTFS with better support for other file systems and for newer security techniques. NTFS is reliable and makes it possible to compress files so they take up less space. At the same time, NTFS can handle massive files, and allow fast access to data, programs, and other shared resources. It is used only on Windows NT or Windows 2000 servers (in other words, UNIX and NetWare servers cannot, by default, make use of NTFS). If you are working with Windows 2000 Server, choose NTFS for your server's file system (for reasons discussed later in this section). Therefore, you should familiarize yourself with the following NTFS features:

- NTFS filenames can be a maximum of 255 characters long.

- NTFS stores file size information in 64-bit fields.

- NTFS files or partitions can theoretically be as large as 16 exabytes, (2^{64} bytes).

- NTFS is required for Macintosh connectivity.

- NTFS incorporates sophisticated, customizable compression routines. These compression routines reduce the space taken by files by as much as 40%. A 10 GB database file, for example, could be squeezed into 6 GB of disk space.

- NTFS keeps a log of file system activity to facilitate recovery if a system crash occurs.

- NTFS is required for encryption and advanced access security for files, user accounts, and processes.

- NTFS improves fault tolerance through RAID and system file redundancy.

8

Before installing Windows 2000 Server, you should decide which file system (or systems) you will use. In general, you need to worry about only the FAT32 and NTFS file systems, because HPFS is not native to Windows 2000 and CDFS and UDF are installed automatically. Although FAT32 improves upon the FAT16 file system and typically appears on Windows 9x workstations, it is not optimal for Windows 2000 servers. Instead, the NTFS file system is preferred because it enables a network administrator to take advantage of the Windows 2000 security and file compression enhancements.

One drawback to using an NTFS partition is that it cannot be read by FAT16, FAT32, or HPFS partitions (unless you employ a third-party utility). However, NTFS partitions can read FAT partitions. You should also be aware that you can convert a FAT drive into an NTFS drive on a Windows 2000 server, but you cannot convert an NTFS drive into a FAT drive.

Typically, due to all the benefits listed above, you will select NTFS whenever you install Windows 2000 Server. (Later in this chapter, you will have the opportunity to plan and execute a Windows 2000 Server installation.) The only instance in which you should not use NTFS is if one of your server's applications is incompatible with this file system.

Microsoft Management Console (MMC)

If you have worked with Windows NT servers, you understand that for each administrative function, the NOS provides a separate tool. Also, each tool has a unique, but similar graphical interface. In Windows 2000 Server, Microsoft has integrated all of the
NOS's administrative tools into a single interface called the Microsoft Management
Console (MMC). This section provides an overview of MMC, its capabilities, and how
you can customize it for your network environment.

An MMC is simply an interface. Its purpose is to gather multiple administrative tools
into a convenient console for your network environment. If an MMC doesn't contain
the tools you want, you can add or remove administrative tools to suit your situation.
The tools you add to the interface are known as **snap-ins**. For example, you may be the
network administrator for two servers, one that performs data backup services and
another dedicated to Web services, on the same network. On the backup server, your
MMC should definitely include the disk management snap-in, which allows you to easily manage the hard disk's volumes and the event viewer snap-in, which allows you to
view what processes have run on the server and whether they generated any errors. On
the Web server, you might want to install the FrontPage Server Extensions, Internet
Information Services, and the Internet Authentication Service (IAS) snap-ins. However,
if the first server is only used for data backup, there is no need to add these three
Internet-related snap-ins to its MMC. You can create multiple MMCs on multiple
servers, or even multiple MMCs on one server.

 You can find snap-ins either through an MMC or as separate selections from
the Administrative Tools menu.

Before using MMCs for the first time, you must create a custom console by running it
for the first time and adding your selections. To do so, click Start, click Run, type **mmc**
in the text box in the Run dialog box, and then click OK. The Console1 (MMC) window opens as a window separated into two panes, as shown in Figure 8-9. The left pane
lists the administrative tools. The right pane lists specific details for a selected tool.

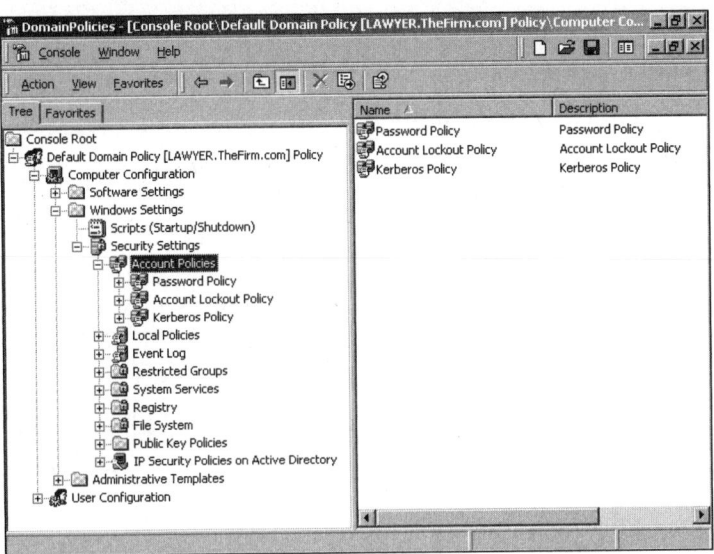

Figure 8-9   MMC window

When you first open the MMC, it does not contain any snap-ins; the panes of its window are empty. You can customize the MMC by adding administrative tools.

To add administrative tools to your MMC interface:

1. Click **Console** in the MMC main menu bar and then click **Add/Remove Snap-in**. The Add/Remove Snap-in dialog box appears, listing the currently installed snap-ins.

2. Click the **Add** button. The Add Standalone Snap-in dialog box appears with a list of available snap-ins.

3. In the Add Standalone Snap-in dialog box, click the tool you want to add to your console and then click **Add**. Continue adding snap-ins until you have chosen all that you want to include in your MMC. (When you add some snap-ins, such as Event Viewer and Device Manager, you will be asked to select the computer that you want the snap-in to manage, and to indicate whether the snap-in should manage the local computer or another computer on the network.)

4. Once you have added all the snap-ins you want, click **Close**. The Add Standalone Snap-in dialog box closes.

5. Click **OK**. The Add/Remove Snap-in dialog box closes and the new tools are added to the MMC. Notice that the left pane of your MMC window now includes the snap-ins you've added.

After you have customized your MMC, you need to save your settings. When you save your settings, you assign a name to the specific console (or administrative interface) that you have just created. Assign the MMC a name that indicates its function. For example, you might create an MMC specifically for managing users and groups and then name that MMC "My User Tool." Later, you can access this same MMC by choosing Start/Programs/Administrative Tools/My User Tool.

MMC can operate in two modes—author mode and user mode. Network administrators who have full permissions on the server typically use author mode, which allows full access for adding, deleting, and modifying snap-ins. However, sometimes an administrator may want to delegate certain network management functions to colleagues, without giving them full permissions on the servers. In such a situation, the administrator can create an MMC that runs in user mode—in other words, that provides limited user privileges. For example, the user might be allowed to view administrative information, but not to modify the snap-ins.

Active Directory

Early in this chapter you learned about NOS directories, the methods for organizing and managing objects on the network. Windows 2000 Server uses a directory service called Active Directory, which was designed especially for Windows 2000 networks. This section provides an overview of how Active Directory is structured and how it uses standard naming conventions to better integrate with other networks. You'll also learn how Active Directory stores information for Windows domains.

Schema

Before installing a NOS, you must have a thorough understanding of how its servers, users, groups, and resources are logically and physically organized and related. This is especially significant if you are planning a new Windows 2000 network.

To begin with, you should understand the foundation of Active Directory's structure. Active Directory is a database that contains records of objects and information about those objects. To be logically organized and easily accessible by multiple types of programs, a database must have definitions for its components. For example, if you design a payroll database for your company's human resources department, you would probably want to include "employee" as a component, and "first name," "last name," "phone number," "address," "salary," and other information associated with an employee. Once you decide how to organize the database and what to include, you must make note of the components and information fields you have created. That way, when a programmer creates a user interface to the database, he will know that he should call the "employee" component when retrieving an employee's record. The same principle applies to Active Directory's objects. A **schema** is the set of definitions of the kinds of objects and information associated with those objects that the database can contain. For example, one type of object is a printer, and one type of information associated with that object is the location of the printer. Thus, "printer," and "location of printer" would be definitions contained within the schema.

Figure 8-10 shows the relationship between Active Directory and a simple user account schema.

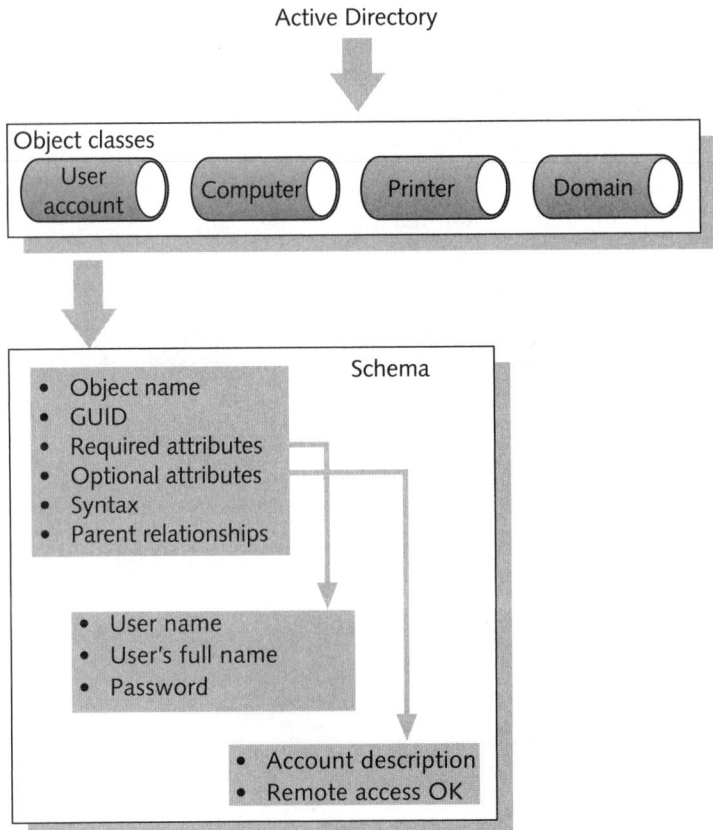

Figure 8-10   Active Directory and a simple user schema

Active Directory's schema may contain two types of definitions: classes and attributes. **Classes** (also known as **object classes**) identify what type of objects can be specified in Active Directory. User account is an example of an object class. Another object class is Printer. An attribute, as you learned before, is a property associated with an object. For example, Home Directory is the name of an attribute associated with the User object, while Location is an attribute associated with the Printer object. Classes are composed of many attributes. When you create an object, you also create a number of attributes that store information about that object. The object class and its attributes are then saved in Active Directory's database.

Workgroups

A Windows 2000 network can be set up in a workgroup model or a domain model. This section describes the workgroup model. In the next section you will learn about the more popular domain model.

A **workgroup** is a group of interconnected computers that share each other's resources without relying on a central server. In other words, a workgroup is a type of peer-to-peer network. Computers in a Windows 2000 workgroup may run either the Windows 2000 Professional or the Windows 2000 Server operating system. Each computer in the workgroup has its own database of user accounts and security privileges, as shown in Figure 8-11.

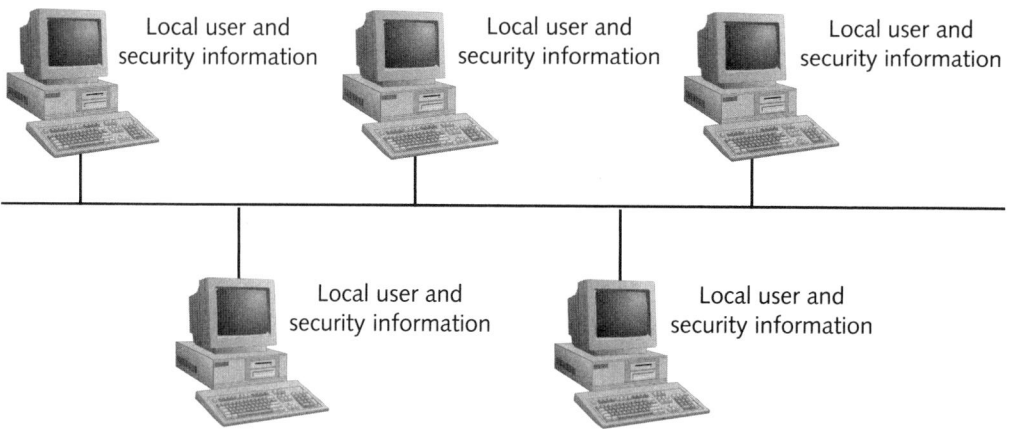

Figure 8-11   A Windows 2000 workgroup network

Because each computer maintains its own database, each user must have a separate account on each computer he wants to access. This decentralized management results in significantly more administration effort than a client/server Windows 2000 network would require. In addition, workgroups are not practical for groups of more than 10 computers. On the other hand, peer-to-peer networks such as a Windows 2000 workgroup are simple to design and implement and may be the best solution for small groups of users who have few security concerns.

Domains

The type of Windows 2000 network that follows the client/server architecture is known as a domain model (meaning that it relies on domains). A **domain** is a group of users, servers, and other resources that share a database of account and security information. The database that domains use to record their objects and attributes is contained within Active Directory (as you will learn, Active Directory contains still more information). Domains are established on a network to make it easier to organize and manage resources and security. For example, a university might create separate domains for each of the following colleges: Life Sciences, Humanities, Business, Communications, and Engineering. Within the Engineering domain, additional domains such as "Chemical Engineering," "Industrial Engineering," "Electrical Engineering," and "Mechanical Engineering" may be created, as shown in Figure 8-12. In this example, all users, workstations, servers, printers, and other resources within the Engineering domain would share a distinct portion of the Active Directory database.

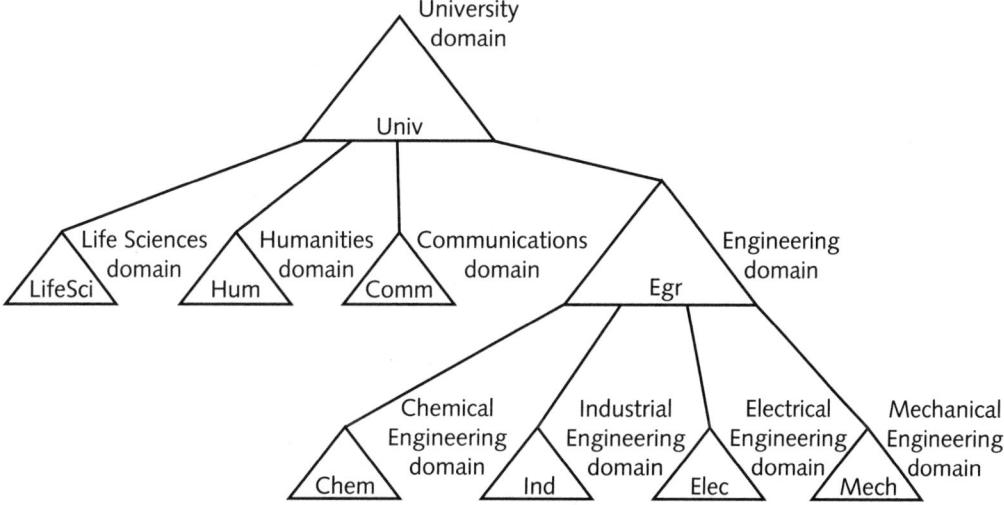

Figure 8-12   Multiple domains in one organization

Keep in mind that a domain is not confined by geographical boundaries. Computers and users belonging to the university's Engineering domain may be located at five different campuses across a state, or even across the globe. No matter where they are located, they obtain their object, resource, and security information from the same database and the same portion of Active Directory.

Depending on the network environment, an administrator can define domains according to function, location, or security requirements. For example, if you worked at a large hospital whose WAN connected the city's central healthcare facility with several satellite clinics, you could create separate domains for each WAN location or you could create separate domains for each clinical department, no matter where they are located. Alternately, you might choose to use only one domain and assign the different locations and specialties to different containers within the domain.

The directory containing information about objects in a domain resides on computers called **domain controllers**. A Windows 2000 network may use multiple domain controllers. In fact, you should use at least two domain controllers on each network so that if one domain controller fails, the other will continue to retain your domains' databases.

Servers on a Windows 2000 network that do not store directory information are known as **member servers**. Because member servers do not contain a database of users and their associated attributes (such as password or permissions to files), member servers cannot authenticate users. Only domain controllers can do that. Every server on a Windows 2000 network is either a domain controller or a member server, as shown in Figure 8-13.

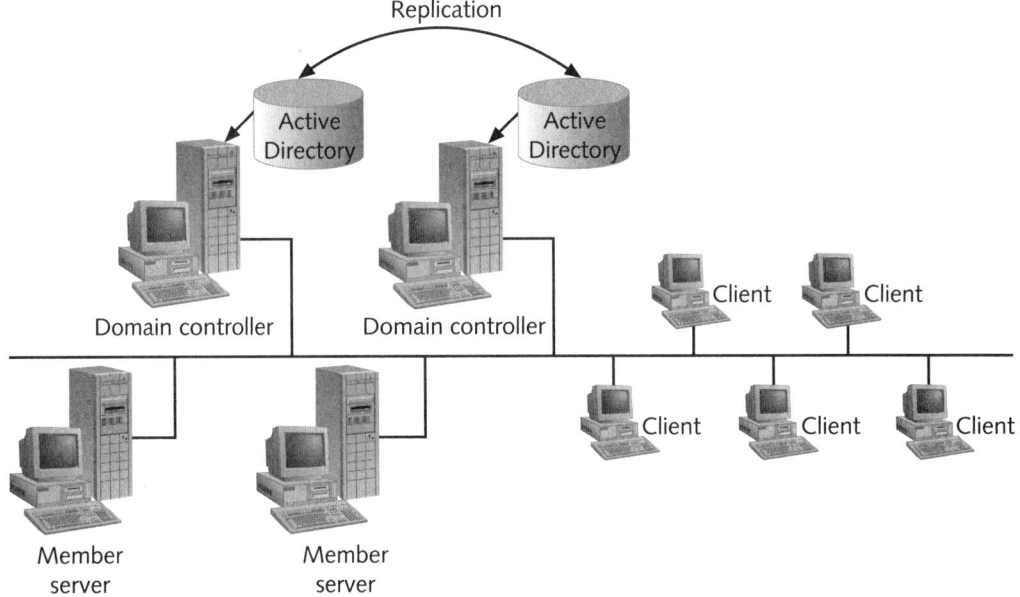

Figure 8-13   A Windows 2000 domain model network

When a network uses multiple domain controllers, a change to the database contained on one domain controller is copied to the databases on other domain controllers so that their databases are always identical. The process of copying directory data to multiple domain controllers is known as **replication**. Replication ensures redundancy so that in case one of the domain controllers fails, another can step in to allow clients to log onto the network, be authenticated, and access resources.

Organizational Units

Earlier you learned that NOSs use the concept of containers to hold multiple objects that have similar characteristics. In Windows 2000, such containers are also known as **organizational units (OUs)**. An OU can contain over 10 million objects. And each OU can contain multiple OUs. For example, suppose you were the network administrator for the university described previously, which has the following domains: Life Sciences, Humanities, Business, Communications, and Engineering. Further, suppose you decided that rather than making additional domains beneath each college, you would group objects according to containers. For the Life Sciences domain, you might create the following organizational units that correspond to the Life Sciences departments: Biology, Geology, Zoology, and Botany. In addition, you might want to create organizational units for each building that the departments use. For example, "Schroeder" and "Randall" for Biology, "Morehead" and "Kaiser" for Geology, "Randall" and "Arthur" for Zoology, and "Thorne" and "Grieg" for Botany. Figure 8-14 depicts a tree based on this example.

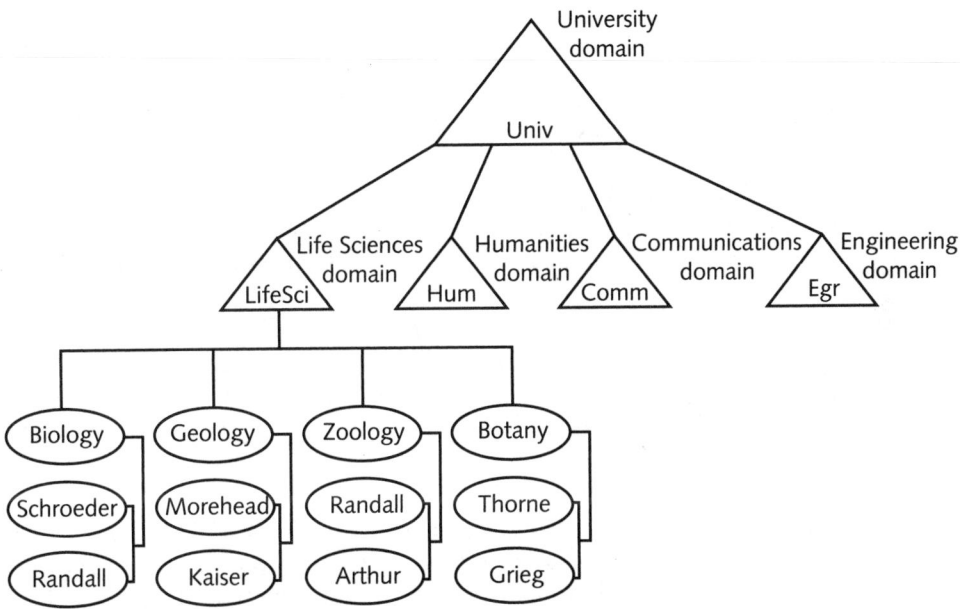

Figure 8-14   A tree with multiple domains and OUs

Trees and Forests

Now that you understand how an NOS directory can contain multiple levels of domains and organizational units, you are ready to learn the structure of the directory that exists above domains. It is common for large organizations to use multiple domains in their Windows 2000 networks. Active Directory organizes multiple domains hierarchically in a **domain tree** (or simply, tree). (Recall that NOS trees were introduced earlier in the chapter. Active Directory's domain tree is an example of a typical NOS tree.) At the base of the Active Directory tree is the **root domain**. From the root domain, **child domains** branch out to separate objects with the same policies, as you saw in Figure 8-12. Underneath the child domains, multiple organizational units branch out to further subdivide the network's systems and objects.

A collection of one or more domain trees is known as a **forest**. All trees in a forest share a common schema. Domains within a forest can communicate, but only domains within the same tree share a common Active Directory database. In addition, objects belonging to different domain trees are named separately, even if they are in the same forest. You will learn more about naming later in this chapter.

Trust Relationships

In order for your network to work efficiently, you must give some thought to the relationships between the domains in a domain tree. The relationship between two domains in which one domain allows another domain to authenticate its users is known as a **trust relationship**. Active Directory supports two types of trust relationships: two-way transitive trusts and explicit one-way trusts. Each child and parent domain within a domain tree and each top-level domain in a forest share a **two-way transitive trust** relationship. This means that a user in domain A is recognized by and can be authenticated by domain B, and vice versa. In addition, a user in domain A may be granted rights to any of the resources managed by domain B, and vice versa.

When a new domain is added to a tree, it immediately shares a two-way trust with the other domains in the tree. These trust relationships allow a user to log onto and be authenticated by a server in any domain within the domain tree. However, this does not necessarily mean that the user has privileges to access any resources in the tree. A user's permissions must be assigned separately for the resources in each different domain. For example, suppose Betty is a research scientist in the Mechanical Engineering Department. Her user account belongs to the Engineering domain at the University. One day, due to construction in her building, she has to temporarily work in an office in the Zoology Department's building across the street. The Zoology Department OU, and all its users and workstations, belong to the Life Sciences domain. When Betty sits down at the computer in her temporary office, she can log onto the network from the Life Sciences domain, which happens to be the default selection on her logon screen. She can do this because the Life Sciences and Engineering domains have a two-way trust. Once she is logged on, she can access all her usual data, programs, and other resources in the Engineering domain. But even though the Life Sciences domain authenticated Betty, she will not automatically have privileges for the resources in the Life Sciences domain. For example, she can retrieve her research reports from the Mechanical Engineering Department's server, but unless a network administrator grants her rights to access the Zoology Department's printer, she cannot print the document to the networked printer outside her temporary office.

Figure 8-15 depicts the concept of a two-way trust between domains in a tree.

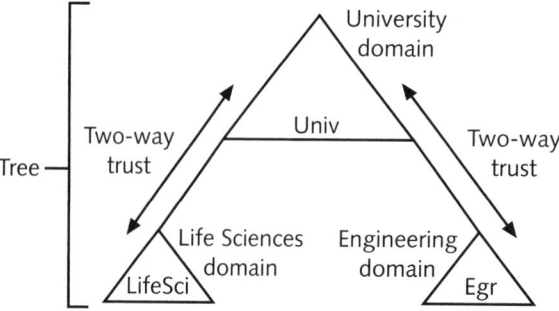

Figure 8-15   Two-way trusts between domains in a tree

The second type of trust relationship supported by Active Directory is an **explicit one-way trust**. In this scenario, two domains that are not part of the same tree are assigned a trust relationship. The explicit one-way trust does not apply to other domains in the tree, however. Figure 8-16 shows how an explicit one-way trust can enable domains from different trees to share resources. In this figure, notice that the Engineering domain in the University tree and the Research domain in the Science Corporation tree share a one-way trust. However, this trust does not apply to parent or child domains associated with the Engineering or Research domains. In other words, the Research domain could not have access to the entire University domain (including its child domains such as Life Sciences).

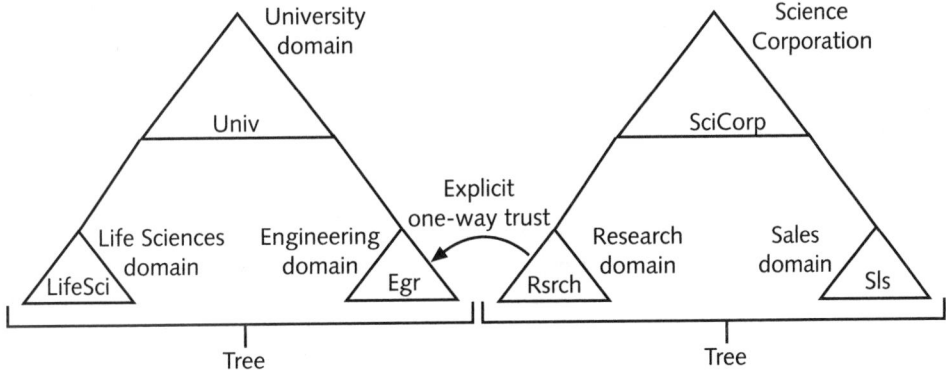

Figure 8-16   Explicit one-way trust between domains in different trees

This section introduced you to the basic concepts of a Windows 2000 network structure. If you are charged with establishing a new Windows 2000 network, you will need to learn a lot more about Active Directory. In that case, you'll want to buy a book on the topic, and perhaps take a class exclusively devoted to Active Directory.

Naming Conventions

In the preceding section you learned to think about domains in terms of their hierarchical relationships. Getting to know the structure of a network by studying its domain tree is similar to understanding your ancestry by studying a genealogical chart. Another way to look at ancestors is to consider their names and their relationship to you. For example, suppose that John Smith is your grandfather. Depending on the speaker and his relationship to this man, one might recognize him as "John Smith," "My paternal grandfather, John Smith," or simply, "John." In the same way, different types of names, depending on where in the domain they are located, may identify objects in a domain.

Naming (or addressing) conventions in Active Directory are based on the conventions used in the Internet. In Internet terminology, the term **namespace** refers to the complete database of hierarchical names used to map IP addresses to their hosts' names. The Internet namespace is not contained on just one computer. Instead, it is divided into many smaller pieces on computers at different locations on the Internet. In the genealogy analogy, this would be similar to having part of your family records in your home file cabinet, part of them in the state historical archives, part of them in the Ellis Island immigrant files, and part of them in the municipal records of another country. Somewhere in the Internet's vast, decentralized database of names and IP addresses (its namespace), your office workstation's IP address indicates that it can be located at your organization and, further, that it is associated with your computer. In Active Directory, the term namespace refers to a collection of object names and their associated places in the Windows 2000 network. In a genealogy analogy, this would be similar to having one relative (the Active Directory) who knows the names of each family member and how everyone is related. If this relative recorded the information about every relative in a database (for instance, Mary Smith is the wife of John Smith and the mother of Steve and Jessica Smith), this would be similar to what Active Directory does via its namespace.

Because Active Directory namespace follows the conventions of the Internet's namespace, when you connect your Windows 2000 network to the Internet, these two namespaces are compatible. For example, suppose you work for a company called Trinket Makers, and a few years back you contracted with a Web development firm to create a Web site. Further, suppose that the firm chose the Internet domain name "trinketmakers.com" to uniquely identify your company's location on the Internet. When you plan your Windows 2000 network, you will want to call your root domain "trinketmakers" to match its existing Internet domain name (the ".com" part is assumed to be a domain). That way, objects within the Active Directory namespace can be assigned names related to the :trinketmakers.com" domain name, and they will match the object's name in the Internet namespace, should that be necessary.

Each object on a Windows 2000 network can have three different names, as described in the following list:

- **Distinguished name (DN)**—A long form of the object name that explicitly indicates its location within a tree's containers and domains. A distinguished name includes a domain component (DC) name, the names of the domains to which the object belong, an organizational unit (OU) name, the names of the organizational units to which the object belongs, and a common name (CN), or the name of the object. A common name must be unique within a container. In other words, you could have a user called "Msmith" in the Legal container and a user called "Msmith" in the Accounting container, but you could not have two users called "Msmith" in the Legal container. Distinguished names are expressed with the following notation: DC=domain name, OU=organizational unit name, CN=object class, CN=object name. For example, the user Mary Smith in the Legal OU of the trinketmakers domain would have the following distinguished name: DC=Com, DC=trinketmakers, OU=Legal, CN=Msmith. Another way of expressing this distinguished name would be trinketmakers.com/legal/msmith.

- **Relative distinguished name (RDN)**—A name that uniquely identifies an object within a container. For most objects, the relative distinguished name is the same as its common name (CN) in the distinguished name convention. A relative distinguished name is an attribute that belongs to the object. This attribute is assigned to the object when the administrator creates the object (as you will learn to do later in this chapter). Figure 8-17 provides an example of an object, its distinguished name, and its relative distinguished name.

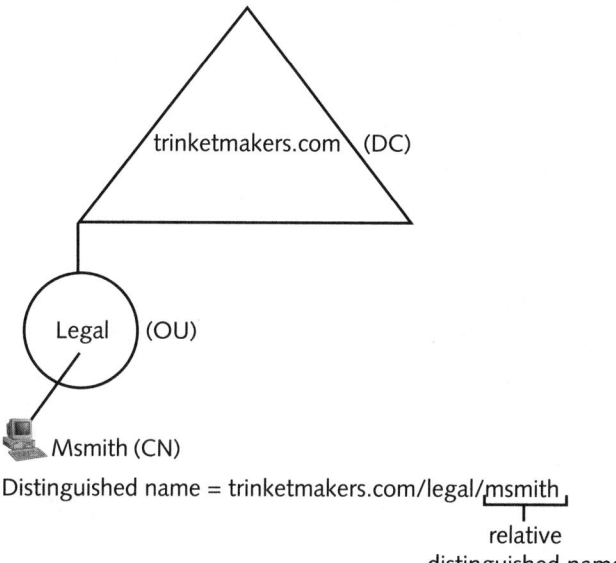

Distinguished name = trinketmakers.com/legal/msmith

relative
distinguished name

Figure 8-17   Distinguished name and relative distinguished name

- **User principal name (UPN)**—The preferred naming convention for users in e-mail and related Internet services. A user's UPN looks like a familiar Internet address, including the positioning of the domain name after the @ sign. When you create a user account, the user's login name is added to a **UPN suffix**, the portion of the user's UPN that follows the @ sign. A user's default UPN suffix is the domain name of his or her root domain. For example, if Mary Smith's user name is msmith and her root domain is trinketmakers.com, her UPN suffix is trinketmakers.com, and her UPN is *msmith@trinketmakers.com*.

The naming conventions used by Windows 2000 follow those specified in the **Lightweight Directory Access Protocol (LDAP)**, a protocol for accessing network directories. LDAP relies on TCP/IP and can be used by any modern NOS. Because it is a standard, LDAP allows any application to access the directory of any system according to a single naming convention.

In addition to these names, each object has a **globally unique identifier (GUID)**, a 128-bit number that ensures that no two objects have duplicate names. The GUID is generated and assigned to an object upon its creation. Rather than use any of the alphabetical names, network applications and services communicate with an object via the object's GUID.

Now that you have been introduced to the Windows 2000 Server Active Directory structure and naming conventions, you are ready to learn about installing the NOS.

PLANNING FOR INSTALLATION

When installing and configuring a network operating system, before you insert the installation CD, you must create a plan for your server and its place in your network. You need to consider many factors, including organizational structure, server function, applications, number of users, LAN architecture, and optional services (such as remote access) when developing this plan. Once you have installed and configured the network operating system, changing its configuration may prove difficult and cause service disruptions for users.

The value of planning for installation cannot be overemphasized. Any seasoned network administrator can probably tell a story about a server operating system installation for which he or she should have prepared better. Poor planning results in more work for the installer, potential downtime for users, and headaches for whoever supports the server after installation. To prepare for installation you must first ensure that your server hardware meets the Windows 2000 Server requirements (see Table 8-2). Next, you must prepare answers to the following list of critical preinstallation decisions.

- *How many, how large, and what kind of partitions will the server require?* Windows 2000 must be installed on a single partition. When you install it, you will have a choice of:
  - Creating a new partition on a nonpartitioned portion of a hard disk
  - Creating a new partition on a partitioned hard disk
  - Installing Windows 2000 on an existing partition
  - Removing an existing partition and creating a new one for installation

The option you choose will depend on how your server is currently partitioned, whether you wish to keep data on existing partitions, and how you want to subdivide your server's hard disk. If you know the number and size of the partitions you need (for example, on a 16-GB hard disk you might want to create a 6-GB system partition and a 10-GB data partition), it is best to create them during installation.

- *What type of file system will the server use?* Recall from the discussion about Windows 2000 file systems that the optimal file system for a Windows 2000 server is NTFS. Choose NTFS unless your applications require a different file system. NTFS must be used if you intend to use Active Directory and the domain model for centralized resource and client management.

- *What will the server's name be?* You may use any name that includes a maximum of 15 characters, but you cannot use the following characters: > < [ ] : ; | = , + * " ? Choose a practical, descriptive name that distinguishes the server from others and that is easy for you and your users to remember. For example, you might use geographical server names, such as Boston or Chicago. Alternately, you might name servers according to their function, such as Marketing or Research. If the server is a member of a large domain, you might identify it in relationship to its domain name. For example, the Marketing server in the Pittsburgh domain might be called Pitts-Mktg.

- *Which protocols and network services should the server use?* Before you begin installing Windows 2000 Server, you need to know which protocol (or protocols) your network requires. Recall from Chapter 3 that most organizations are moving toward TCP/IP-based transmission because it is flexible, reliable, and widely supported. On Windows 2000 Server, TCP/IP is the default protocol, and depending on your circumstances, you should probably leave it as such. If your server runs Web services or requires connectivity with UNIX systems, you *must* run TCP/IP. Install NetBEUI on your Windows 2000 server only if you need to communicate with computers running Windows for Workgroups. If your Windows 2000 server must communicate with a NetWare server that does not rely on TCP/IP (for example, a server running NetWare version 3.11), you should also install the NWLink IPX/SPX Compatible Protocol and Gateway Services for NetWare.

- *What will the Administrator password be?* Use a strong password—in other words, one that is difficult to crack. It should consist of at least eight characters, include both letters and numbers, and not resemble any known English words, particularly words that have some association to you or your company. For example, the password "GIANTS" is not secure, while the password "GZ477OPS1" is more secure.

- *Should the network use domains or workgroups, and, if so, what will they be called?* First, you must decide whether your Windows 2000 network will use workgroups or domains. During installation you will be asked whether the server should join an existing workgroup, be a new workgroup server, or join an existing domain. As you learned, in a workgroup situation, computers share network access in a peer-to-peer fashion. It is more likely that your environment will require domains, in which the security for clients and resources is centralized. If the server will be joining an existing domain, you must know the domain name, domain controller name, and the DNS server name. Domain names should describe the logical group of servers and users they support. You may use any name that includes a maximum of 15 alphanumeric characters, but not the following characters into the names: > < [ ] : ; | = , + * " ? Popular schemes for naming domains incorporate geography and function into the names. For example, in a domain model for a WAN spanning several cities, you might want to name your domains Boston,

8

Chicago, Detroit, Pittsburgh, and so on. In a very large organization, you may want to use a less limiting convention. For example, if your company's business is chemical production, you might want to name your domains Hydrocarbons, Resins, Fertilizers, and so on.

- *Will the server support additional services?* During installation, you will be asked to choose which services your server will support. Of course, you must install certain protocols and network services in order for clients to access the server. You may also want to install optional services, such as: Internet Information Services (applications for creating and hosting Web sites), Terminal Services (to enable remote networking via "thin" clients), Windows Media Services, Message Queuing, and Management and Monitoring Tools. Although it's easiest to include additional services during the original installation, they can be added later as well.

- *Which licensing mode should I choose?* You may choose one of two licensing modes: per seat or per server. The **per server** licensing mode allows a limited number of clients to access the server simultaneously. (The actual number is determined by your Windows 2000 Server purchase.) In per server mode, any of your organization's clients may be capable of connecting to the server. The number of concurrent connections is restricted. Per server mode is a popular choice in organizations that have a limited number of servers and many users, or where multiple users share workstations (for example, a mail-order catalog's call center). The **per seat** mode requires a license for every client capable of connecting to the Windows 2000 server. In environments that include multiple Windows 2000 servers and in which each user has his own workstation, this choice is probably more economical than per server licensing.

 If you are running a Windows 2000 server as a Web or FTP server for anonymous clients (for example, Internet users from anywhere in the world), you do not need separate Windows 2000 Server client licenses for these types of clients.

- *How can I remember all of this information?* As you make these preinstallation decisions, you should note your choices on a server installation form and keep the form with you during installation. Appendix D offers an example of such a form.

The preceding list describes only the most significant installation options. You should also be prepared to:

- Read and accept the license agreement
- Identify your organization
- Provide your registration key
- Select the appropriate time and date

- Specify display settings
- Identify and supply drivers for hardware components such as video cards, network adapters, printers, and so on

If you are upgrading from Windows NT Server to Windows 2000 Server, your preparation will include the additional considerations discussed in the following list. (If you are not familiar with Windows NT, this list may include some concepts that are unfamiliar to you.):

- Back up the existing Windows NT server, including its Registry, so that you can return to a working state in case the Windows 2000 Server installation fails.

- On a Windows NT network that includes multiple servers and domain controllers, you should upgrade your Windows NT primary domain controller (PDC) to a Windows 2000 domain controller first. Servers upgraded after the Windows NT PDC has been upgraded can become either domain controllers or member servers.

- Be certain to select the "Upgrade to Windows 2000 (Recommended)" option on the first setup screen.

- If you are upgrading the Windows NT PDC to a Windows 2000 domain controller, indicate that you want to start a new domain or forest during the Active Directory Setup Wizard. On subsequent server upgrades you can choose to join this existing domain.

- After all Windows NT servers on your network are upgraded to Windows 2000 Server, you should convert the domains to native mode. This will indicate to the network that no more Windows NT primary domain controllers (PDCs) or backup domain controllers (BDCs) remain on the network. You can do this by clicking Start/Programs/Administrative Tools/Active Directory Domains and Trusts. Right-click the domain you want to convert and click Properties. Select the General tab and click the Change Mode button.

- Carefully follow the upgrade instructions that come with your Windows 2000 Server software or consult the Microsoft Windows 2000 Server Web site for complete information.

 If you are installing Windows 2000 Server on a computer currently running Windows 9x, you must choose the "Clean Install" option, which will overwrite the current operating system. In this instance, you cannot choose the "Upgrade to Windows 2000" option. Therefore, it is very important to create a full backup of your system in case the Windows 2000 Server installation fails and you need to revert to Windows 9x.

INSTALLING AND CONFIGURING A WINDOWS 2000 SERVER

Once you have devised a plan for your Windows 2000 server installation, you can begin the actual installation process. In this section, you will learn about the available options and the decisions you must make when installing and initially configuring your Windows 2000 server.

The Installation Process

When you begin installing Windows 2000 Server, you can install the server from a CD-ROM or remotely over the network. The most popular method of installing Windows 2000 is from a CD-ROM drive. If you must use the network method, be aware that this type of installation generates a high volume of network traffic and shouldn't be performed while clients are attempting to use the network.

The following summary of the Windows 2000 Server installation process assumes, for simplicity, that you are using a CD-ROM. This installation also assumes your computer has a single partition and that you will convert this partition from FAT32 to NTFS. It represents a typical, simple installation. It does not take into consideration any anomalies you might encounter with your server or network environment. As a result, your installation may not proceed effortlessly. The first part of the installation presents GUI interface, then it reverts to a text-based interface, and later a GUI interface once again takes over.

To install Windows 2000 Server from a CD-ROM on a server or workstation already running a Windows 9.x operating system:

1. Make sure there is no disk in the floppy disk drive and then boot the server or workstation.

2. Insert the Windows 2000 Server installation CD into the server's CD-ROM drive. The Microsoft Windows 2000 CD window appears.

3. If your CD-ROM drive is configured to automatically run the program on the CD, you will be asked whether you want to upgrade to Windows 2000. To install Windows 2000 Server, click **Yes**.

   If your CD-ROM drive is not configured to automatically run the program on the CD, the Microsoft Windows 2000 CD window offers you four options: Install Windows 2000, Install Add-on Components, Browse this CD, or Exit. Click the **Install Windows 2000** option to continue.

4. If you are attempting to install Windows 2000 Server on a machine that is already running Windows 9x, a Windows 2000 Setup message appears instructing that you cannot upgrade from this version of the operating system. This means you must perform a clean install (in other words, one that creates an entirely new copy of the operating system on the computer). Click **OK** to continue.

Otherwise, the Windows 2000 Setup window asks whether you want to upgrade to Windows 2000 or install a new copy of Windows 2000. Click the **Install a new copy of Windows 2000 (Clean Install)** option button, and then click **Next** to continue.

5. The Windows 2000 Setup - License Agreement window appears. Read the complete agreement, click the **I accept this agreement** option button, and then click **Next** to continue.

6. The Windows 2000 Setup – Your Product Key window appears. On the Windows 2000 Server package, find your product key, which uniquely identifies your copy of Windows 2000 Server. Enter your product key and click **Next** to continue.

7. The Windows 2000 Setup – Select Special Options window appears. Use this window to choose special options, such as languages and accessibility options, for your Windows 2000 Server install. Click the **Language Options** button.

8. The Language Options dialog box opens, where you can select your default language. Verify that your preferred language (probably English) is selected. If it is, click **OK**. Otherwise, click the list arrow, click your preferred language, and then click **OK**. You return to the Windows 2000 Setup – Select Special Options screen. Click **Next** to continue.

9. The Windows 2000 Setup – Upgrading to the Windows 2000 NTFS File System window appears, urging you to upgrade your drive to the NTFS file system, if it does not already use this file system. Make sure the **Yes, upgrade my drive** option is selected, and then click **Next** to continue.

10. The Microsoft Windows 2000 Server Setup – Directory of Applications for Windows 2000 window appears. You can use this window to connect to Microsoft's Web site to view the Directory of Applications for Windows 2000. This directory lists applications and describes to what extent they have been tested with the Windows 2000 Server operating system. Click **Next** to continue.

11. The Microsoft Windows 2000 Server Setup – Copying Installation Files window appears, and Setup begins loading an information file that contains data you have entered about your installation, and then starts copying installation files to your computer's hard drive. Once those files have been copied, Setup restarts your computer and continues the installation process. You should not need to interfere with this process.

12. After rebooting, the text-based Windows 2000 Server Setup – Welcome to Setup window appears, as shown in Figure 8-18.

8

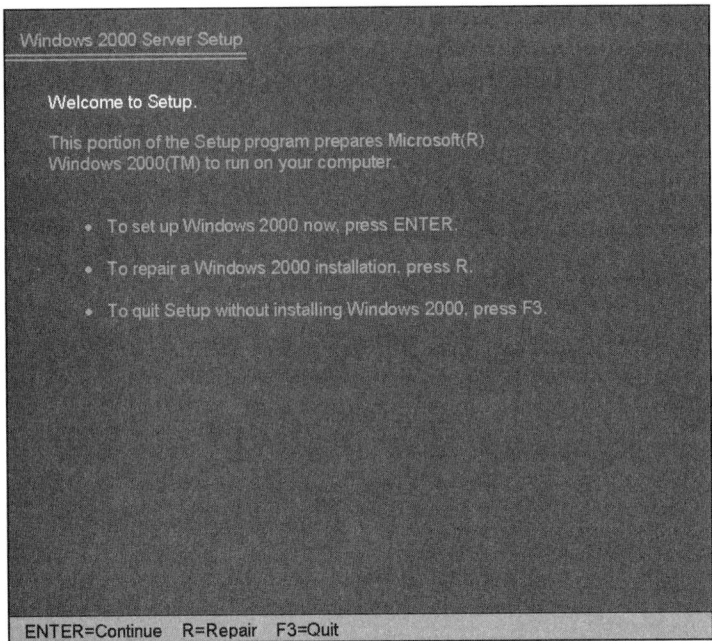

Figure 8-18   Beginning setup options

Press **Enter** to continue with the Windows 2000 Setup process.

13. If you are installing Windows 2000 Server on a computer that already contains a version of this operating system, you can choose to attempt to repair the existing installation or install a new copy of Windows 2000 over the current version. Press **Esc** to install a new copy of the software.

14. Setup identifies the partitions on your computer's hard disk. You can install Windows 2000 Server in an existing partition, create a new partition for this installation, or delete an existing partition. These steps show you how to create an NTFS partition. To begin creating this partition, use the **Up** or **Down Arrow** key to select the partition on which you want to install Windows 2000 Server, and then press **Enter**.

15. If you receive a warning message about installing Windows 2000 on a partition that contains another operating system, continue by pressing **C**.

16. If the partition you selected in Step 14 was not already using the NTFS file system, a warning message informs you that you should not convert the drive to NTFS if you must access the drive via an older operating system. Press **C** to confirm that you want to convert the drive.

17. If you selected an unformatted partition in Step 14, a warning message informs you that existing files on the selected partition will be deleted. Press **F** to format the partition.

18. After the disk is formatted, Setup examines the space on your server's hard disk, and then copies files to the Windows 2000 installation folders. Wait until the process is completed and Setup restarts the computer.

19. After restarting, if the partition you chose in Step 14 was using the FAT32 file system, Setup now converts the partition to NTFS, and then restarts the computer.

20. After restarting, the Windows 2000 Setup program begins again, this time displaying a graphical interface. Eventually, the Windows 2000 Server Setup Wizard screen appears, and then the Windows 2000 Server Setup – Installing Devices window appears. Setup attempts to identify your server's basic hardware and install the device drivers necessary to use that hardware (your screen may momentarily turn black at some point in this process). Although Setup may choose the wrong devices on occasion, it is usually correct. If you have a special NIC, mouse, keyboard, monitor, or other hardware device for which you want to install specific drivers, you can choose to change the components after the program detects them.

21. Once Setup has detected your hardware devices, it prompts you to choose regional settings. Make sure the system locale and keyboard layout are correct, and then click **Next** to continue.

22. In some cases, the Windows 2000 Server Setup – Regional Settings window appears. If you see this window, you can use it to customize the system locale (the identification of your geographic location, which determines the format of numbers, currency, and dates) and your keyboard layout. If you don't see this window, skip to Step 23. Click **Next** to continue.

23. The Windows 2000 Server Setup – Personalize Your Software window appears. To personalize Windows 2000, type your name in the Name text box and then the name of your organization in the Organization text box. Note that these names do not affect your workgroup or domain names for the network.

24. The Windows 2000 Server Setup – Licensing Modes window appears. Setup asks you to select the licensing mode you want to use, either per server or per seat. Choose **per server** licensing if you are planning a network in which only a certain number of clients can be connected to that server at one time. Choose **per seat** licensing if you are guaranteeing that every registered client can connect to the server at any time. Then click **Next** to continue.

25. The Windows 2000 Server Setup – Computer Name and Administrator Password window appears. Enter a computer name and administrator password for your Windows 2000 Server. Use a computer name that reflects the server's purpose. For example, if the server will provide resource sharing to employees in the Marketing Department, you might want to call it "MARKETING-01."

8

If the server will supply Web pages to the Internet, you might want to call it "WEB_SERVER-01." Standard computer names may contain letters, numbers, and hyphens (-), but no spaces. (If you use a nonstandard computer name, other computers on the network may not be able to easily find the server on the network.) Choose a strong password as described in the installation planning process section. Then click **Next** to continue.

26. The Windows 2000 Server Setup – Windows 2000 Components window appears, where you can add or remove Windows 2000 Server components. (See Figure 8-19.) Scroll down the list of components and click the check boxes next to the following options to add them: **Management and Monitoring Tools**, **Networking Services**, and **Other Network File and Print Services**. Click **Next** to continue.

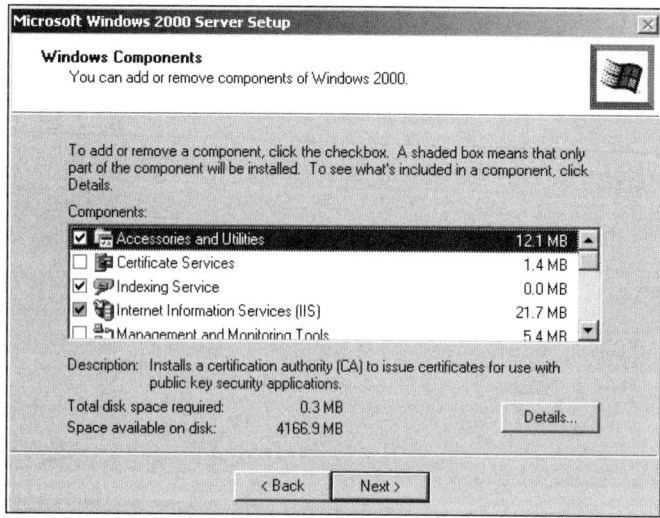

Figure 8-19   Selecting Windows 2000 components

27. If your server has a modem and communication services are installed, the Windows 2000 Server Setup – Modem Dialing Information window appears. Enter modem dialing information by selecting your country and typing your area code. Then click **Next** to continue.

28. The Windows 2000 Server Setup – Date and Time Settings window appears. Select the correct date, time, and time zone, and then **Next** to continue.

29. The Windows 2000 Server Setup – Networking Settings window appears, and Setup installs the networking software that enables your server to connect with other devices on the network. Once this software has been installed, you can choose typical or custom settings for your networking preferences (for example, clients and protocols). Because the typical settings option includes

the most commonly used protocol (TCP/IP), client software (Client for Microsoft Networks), and service (File and Print Sharing for Microsoft Networks), you can accept the default selections. Click **Next** to continue.

30. The Windows 2000 Server Setup – Workgroup or Computer Domain window appears, where you specify whether this server belongs to a domain and, if so, the name of the domain to which it belongs. For the purposes of this installation (considering your server may not be connected to a real network), accept the default option of not belonging to a workgroup or domain and click **Next** to continue.

31. Setup begins installing Windows 2000 components, displaying the Windows 2000 Server Setup – Installing Components window shown in Figure 8-20.

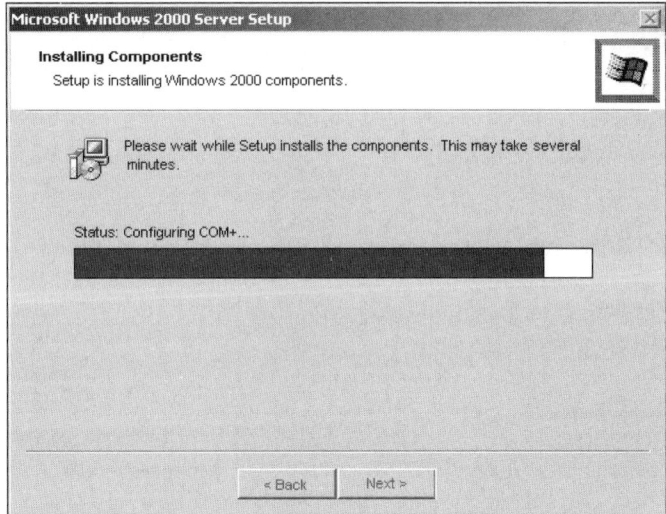

Figure 8-20   Installing Components window

32. Near the end of the process you may see a message window informing you that you should use only statically assigned IP addresses for this server (if it is to be used as a WINS server), and that you will have the option to change the existing, dynamically assigned IP address. Click **OK** to continue. If you do not see this message window, you can skip to Step 36.

33. The Local Area Connection Properties dialog box appears. Click the **Internet Protocol** component to highlight it, and then click **Properties**.

34. The Internet Protocol (TCP/IP) Properties dialog box appears. Click the **Use the following IP address** option button to begin assigning the server a static IP address. For this installation (assuming you are not going to use this server to connect to external LANs or WANs), enter the IP address **100.100.100.100** and the default gateway **100.100.100.1**. The subnet mask is automatically assigned a default value of 255.0.0.0. Click **OK** to save your changes.

35. You return to the Local Area Connection Properties dialog box. Click **OK** again to save your changes and continue.

36. The Windows 2000 Server Setup – Completing the Windows 2000 Setup Wizard appears. Click **Finish** to complete the setup process.

Your computer restarts, signaling that the Windows 2000 Server installation is complete. A Welcome to Windows window appears. In the next section you will learn how to log on for the first time, and then configure your newly installed NOS.

This sample installation uses the default selections and simplest methods of configuring the server. In reality, your server installations may not be as straightforward.

Initial Configuration

Although you have completed the Windows 2000 Server installation, the server isn't yet ready to support clients on a network. First you must configure the software (for instance, assign it a place in the domain).

To configure Windows 2000 Server:

1. After installing Windows 2000 Server, press **Ctrl+Alt+Del** when prompted, to access a login screen. Enter the default user name **Administrator** (if it has not been entered for you), and the password you chose in Step 25 of the preceding section.

To enhance security, at some point you should create a new user ID with administrative privileges to perform network administration, and disable the Administrator user ID. If you keep the Administrator ID active with full privileges, hackers have half the information they need to break into your system.

2. The Windows 2000 Configure Your Server wizard starts, preparing to guide you through configuring the server. First, you specify whether this server is the only server on the network or is one of many servers on the network. For the purposes of this exercise, click the **This is the only server in my network** option button, and then click **Next**.

3. The next window in the wizard informs you that Windows will configure the server as a domain controller and set up Active Directory, DNS, and DHCP on your network. For the purposes of this exercise, click **Next** to accept these conditions.

4. In the next window in the wizard, enter a domain name to create a domain. Type the name of the domain that this server will control. For example, if this server will control all resources for the executives in the organization, you might want to call it "EXECUTIVES."

5. Type **local** in the registered domain name text box. This option assumes that your server will not connect to the Internet. Click **Next** to continue.

6. You see a message indicating that the computer must be restarted so your settings can take effect. Click **Next** to restart your server.

7. The c:\WINNT\System32\netsh.exe window appears, and the Windows Components Wizard begins configuring components according to the information you specified. Then the Configuring Active Directory window appears, indicating that the wizard is configuring Active Directory and that the process may take a while.

8. Eventually, your computer restarts and Windows 2000 Server presents the Log On to Windows window. In the next section, you will learn how to configure users, groups, and other objects on your Windows 2000 Server.

Establishing Users, Groups, and Rights

Earlier in this chapter you learned how networks manipulate user and group accounts to restrict or allow access to specific resources. Now you are ready to learn how to establish users and groups through the Windows 2000 Server interface.

After installation, your Windows 2000 Server will already have two predefined accounts: Guest and Administrator. The **Guest** account is a predefined user account with limited privileges that allows a user to log onto the computer. The **Administrator** account is a predefined user account that has the most extensive privileges for resources both on the computer and on the domain that it controls (if it is a domain controller). These two predefined user accounts are designed primarily to allow you to log onto a computer after installation and before you have created any additional user accounts. The Guest and administrator accounts cannot be deleted; however, they may be disabled. Additional accounts that you create may be **local accounts**, or those that only have rights on the server they are logged onto and **domain accounts**, those that have rights throughout the domain. To create domain accounts, you must have Active Directory installed and your domains properly configured. This exercise assumes that Active Directory is installed on your Windows 2000 server and that domains are in use.

To create a domain user account:

1. Make sure you are logged on as Administrator.

2. Click **Start**, point to **Programs**, point to **Administrative Tools**, and then click **Active Directory Users and Computers**. The Active Directory Users and Computers snap-in opens.

3. Double-click the Active Directory container in which you want to create the new user. This may be a domain or an OU.

4. Right-click the **Users** folder, point to **New** on the shortcut menu, and then click **User**. The New Object – User dialog box appears.

8

5. Type the user's last and first name in the appropriate text boxes. You then see the user's full name in the Full name text box.

6. Enter a user name in the User logon name text box. This name uniquely identifies the user in a domain or forest. The domain name is provided automatically. Click **Next** to continue.

7. In the New Object – User dialog box, enter a password for the user, as shown in Figure 8-21. Enter a strong password (one that consists of at least eight characters, cannot be found in the dictionary, and contains both numbers and letters). Retype the password in the Confirm password text box. You may also select from four additional options: User must change password at next logon, User cannot change password, Password never expires, or Account is disabled. It's a good policy to force the user to pick a new password the first time they log in, so that they have a password that is meaningful to them and so that you, as the network administrator, don't know their password. It is also a good policy to allow the password to periodically expire. With this in mind, check the first option, **User must change password at next logon**, and then click **Next**.

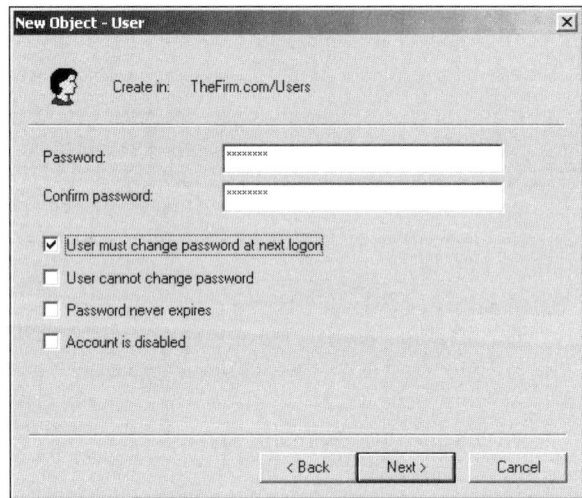

Figure 8-21   User account password properties

8. The next New Object – User window displays the information you have entered. Click **Finish** to complete the creation of a new domain user account.

Once you have created a new user, configure the properties for that user, including their address, telephone number, and e-mail address, their rights to use remote access, their position in the organization, their group memberships, what hours of the day they may log onto the network, and so on. To modify user account properties, you can use the Active Directory Users and Computers snap-in. In the snap-in window, double-click the user account in the right-hand pane. The User Account Properties dialog box opens, with multiple tabs that represent different categories of attributes you may change.

Before you add many users, you will probably want to establish groups into which you can collect user accounts. But before creating a group, you must know what type of scope the group will have: domain local, global, or universal. The group's scope identifies how broadly across the Windows 2000 network its privileges can reach. A **domain local group** is one that allows its members access to resources within a single domain. Domain local groups are used to control access to certain folders, directories, or other resources. They may also contain global groups. A **global group** allows its members access to resources within a single domain also. However, a global group usually contains user accounts and can be inserted (or nested) into a domain local group to gain access to resources in other domains. A **universal group** is one that allows its members access to resources across multiple domains and forests.

To create a group in Windows 2000 Server:

1. First make sure you are logged on as Administrator.

2. Click **Start**, point to **Programs**, point to **Administrative Tools**, and then click **Active Directory Users and Computers**. The Active Directory Users and Computers snap-in starts.

3. Double-click the Active Directory container in which you want to create the new user. This may be a domain or an OU.

4. Click the **New Group** button (which looks like two faces in profile) on the toolbar. The New Object – Group dialog box appears, as shown in Figure 8-22.

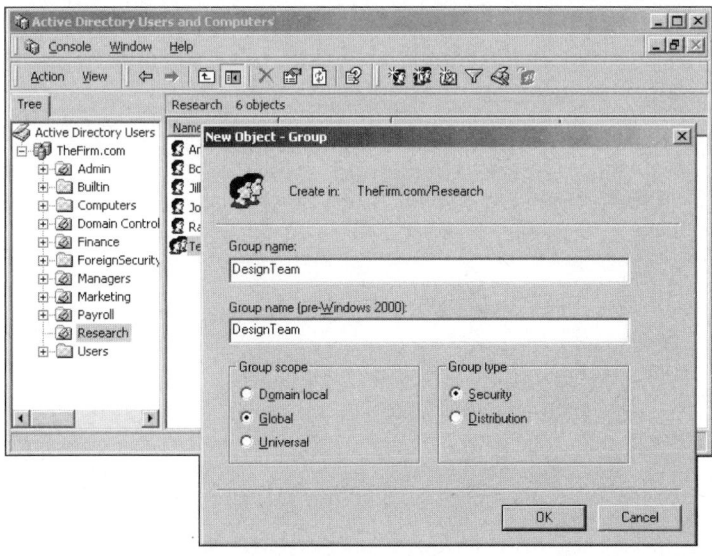

Figure 8-22   Creating a group

5. In the New Object – Group dialog box, enter the name of the group in the Group name text box. In case you are using both Windows 2000 and Windows NT servers on your network, the Group name (pre-Windows 2000) text box is automatically completed.

6. Choose the group scope: Domain local, Global, or Universal. Select the type of group you want to create.

7. Select the type of group you want to create: Security or Distribution. A security group can be assigned access to resources, while distribution groups are used solely for e-mail distribution. Once you have made your selection, click **OK** to complete creating the new group.

Modifying the properties of a group account is similar to modifying the properties of a user account. To do so, double-click the group in the right pane of the Active Directory Users and Computers snap-in window. This opens the group's Properties dialog box, which contains four tabs: General, Members, Member Of, and Managed By. Through this dialog box you can add user accounts to the group, make the group a member of another group, and identify a user account to manage the group.

As mentioned earlier, users and groups are virtually useless unless they have some rights to the server's data and system directories. As an example, the following steps describe how to assign a group called "Instructors" permission to access and modify data in the server's Program Files directory. These steps assume that your server's disk uses the NTFS file system.

To modify the permissions for a directory:

1. Double-click the **My Computer** icon on the Windows 2000 Server desktop. The My Computer window opens.

2. Double-click the **Local Disk (C:)** icon. The Local Disk (C: drive) window opens.

3. Right-click the **Program Files** folder, and then click **Properties** on the shortcut menu. The Program Files Properties dialog box opens, with four tabs: General, Web Sharing, Sharing, and Security, as shown in Figure 8-23.

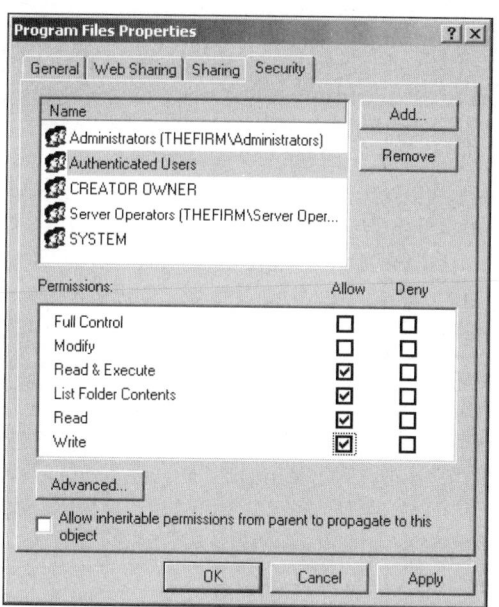

Figure 8-23   The Program Files Properties dialog box

4. Click the **Security** tab.

5. To add a group, click **Add**. The Select Users, Computers, or Groups dialog box opens.

6. Select the **Users** group from the list of users, computers, and groups. Click **Add**, and then click **OK**. The Select Users, Computers, or Groups dialog box closes and you are returned to the Program Files Properties dialog box.

7. Now you need to select the permissions you want to grant to the group. The permissions options are Full Control (allows users to read, add, delete, execute, and modify files and subfolders, and decide who else has permissions in the folder), Modify (allows users to read, add, delete, execute, and modify files), Read & Execute (allows users to view and execute files but not change them in any way), List Folder Contents (allows users to view the directory and subdirectory listings, but not their files), Read (allows users to view files but not execute them or change them in any way), and Write (allows users to create new files, add to existing files, delete files, modify files, and create folders within the folder). In this example, click the check box under "Allow" for the **Modify** permission, and then click **OK**.

8. The group Properties dialog box closes and you return to the Local Disk (C:) window.

INTERNETWORKING WITH OTHER NETWORK OPERATING SYSTEMS

Windows 2000 Server can communicate with almost any kind of client and, given the proper software and configuration, with the other major NOSs. Interoperability is a major concern, as more organizations face the challenge of dealing with mixed networks. In the interest of the consumer, Microsoft and other network operating system vendors have made efforts to close the gap. You will encounter situations in which Windows 2000 must coexist on the same network with NetWare or UNIX or both. This section focuses on Microsoft's solution to the interoperability question. The next chapter discusses the Novell approach.

You might think that establishing communications between two network operating systems is simply a matter of installing the same protocol on both systems. For example, you might think that because both NetWare and Windows 2000 can run versions of the IPX/SPX protocol, the two should be able to communicate directly. (Recall from Chapter 3 that the NWLink IPX/SPX-compatible is required by NetWare versions 3.x and lower and supported by higher versions of NetWare.) In fact, a protocol match is merely one part of the interoperability equation.

To be fully compatible—in other words, to integrate both print and file services, directories, accounts, and other objects—operating systems must also run compatible redirectors. Windows 2000 and NetWare use different client redirector languages that are incompatible. To bridge this gap on a Windows 2000 server, you have two options: either the Windows 2000 Server can run Microsoft's **Gateway Services for NetWare (GSNW)** or the clients that depend on the Windows 2000 Server can run Microsoft's **Client Services for NetWare (CSNW)**. GSNW is a service that runs on the Windows 2000 Server and acts as a translator, or gateway, between its redirector services and those on the NetWare server. With GSNW and NWLink installed, a Windows 2000 server and its clients can access files and other shared resources on any NetWare server on the network through the NetWare Directory Service (NDS). CSNW is a service that runs on a Windows 2000 client and in conjunction with NWLink enables the client to log on directly to the NetWare server to access its printers, files, and other resources. The advantage to using the gateway service over the client service is that the former requires only one setup. The client services require separate setup for each client. However, the gateway service cannot apply different security levels to each different user and, therefore, may be less secure.

 Keep in mind, however, that installing the NWLink IPX/SPX-compatible protocol and GSNW or CSNW may not suffice to allow your two kinds of servers to communicate. You must be careful to configure the NWLink parameters exactly right. If the two network operating systems still do not communicate, you may need to reconfigure NWLink, paying special attention to the Frame Type option.

If you are in an environment that contains both Windows 2000 and NetWare servers, and both use TCP/IP as their preferred protocol, you do not necessarily have to install

GSNW or CSNW (nor do you need to install NWLink). Instead, on each workstation you could install Novell's recommended client software (as described in the next chapter) to access NetWare servers in addition to Microsoft's Client for Networks to access Windows 2000 servers. If for some reason you did not want to install Novell's client on your workstations, you could use the Windows 2000 Server with GSNW installed (and use the TCP/IP protocol rather than the NWLink protocol) as a means for those clients to access NetWare resources.

Even though you may enable clients to access a NetWare server through either gateway or client services for NetWare, you still have to create the user accounts and provide them permissions in the NetWare NOS. You will learn how to do this in the next chapter.

Windows 2000 Server also comes with a migration utility, called the **Directory Services Migration Tool (DSMIGRATE)** that enables you to migrate accounts, groups, files, and permissions from a NetWare NDS directory to the Windows 2000 Server Active Directory.

Interconnecting UNIX and Windows 2000 networks is somewhat easier, because you can assume that both rely on the TCP/IP protocol. In order for clients on Windows 2000 networks to access UNIX servers and make use of their files and account privileges, you would install Microsoft's Services for UNIX on each client. The Services for UNIX include the ability for the client to be recognized by UNIX's file system and utilities for manipulating UNIX files and directories. You will learn more about UNIX client connections in Chapter 10.

8

CHAPTER SUMMARY

- ❐ Network operating systems are entirely software-based and can run on a number of different hardware platforms and network topologies.

- ❐ Network administrators choose an appropriate NOS according to what's compatible with the existing infrastructure; whether it supports the applications, services, and security required by the environment; whether it will grow with the organization; whether the vendor will provide reliable technical support; and whether it fits in the budget.

- ❐ A redirector, which belongs to the Presentation layer of the OSI Model, is inherent in both the network operating system and the client operating system. On the client side, it intercepts client communications and decides whether the request is meant for the server or for the client.

- ❐ When a client attempts to log on, the network operating system receives the client's request for service and tries to match the user name and password with the name and password in its user database. If the passwords match, the NOS grants the client access to resources on the network, according to limitations. This process is known as authentication.

- ❐ Users with similar needs and restrictions are collected in groups to more easily manage their access and privileges.

❐ A directory is an NOS's method of organizing and managing objects, such as users, printers, server volumes, and applications. It is sometimes compared to a tree, because it has one common starting point and branches into multiple containers, which may branch into additional containers.

❐ A file system is an operating system's method of organizing, managing, and accessing its files through logical structures and software routines. In general, when installing a Windows 2000 server, you will want to choose the NTFS file system.

❐ In order for clients to share a server application, the network administrator must assign users rights to the directories where the application's files are installed. Users will at least need rights to access and read files in those directories. For some applications, you may also need to give users rights to create, erase, or modify files associated with the application.

❐ In order for clients to share a network printer, the printer must be created as an object, assigned a name and properties, and then shared among clients. Users or groups may be assigned different levels of privileges to operate printers.

❐ The type of multitasking supported by NetWare, UNIX, and Windows 2000 Server performs one task at a time, allowing one program to use the processor for a certain period of time, and then suspending that program to allow another program to use the processor. This is called preemptive multitasking.

❐ Multiprocessing splits tasks among multiple processors to expedite the completion of any single instruction. It's a great advantage for servers with high CPU utilization, because it improves performance. Windows 2000 Server and Netware support symmetric multiprocessing, which splits all operations equally among two or more processors.

❐ Windows 2000 supports any type of topology or protocol you are likely to run on a LAN. This efficient network operating system uses multiple processors and employs multitasking to allow processes on the server to share CPU resources. It's also easy to manage and well supported.

❐ Windows 2000 Server requires the following minimum hardware: Pentium processor with a minimum clock speed of 133 MHz, 128 MB RAM, at least 1 GB free hard disk space for system files (but 2 GB is recommended), and a pointing device. A CD-ROM and a NIC that are included on Microsoft's Hardware Compatibility List (HCL) are optional. By default, it supports a maximum of four processors on one server.

❐ Windows 2000 Server's memory model assigns each process its own 32-bit memory area. This memory area is a logical subdivision of the entire amount of memory available to the server. Assigning processes separate areas makes the processes less prone to interfering with each other when they run simultaneously.

❐ The description of object types, or classes, and their required and optional attributes that are stored in Active Directory is known as a schema.

❐ Domains define a group of systems and resources that share common security and management policies. The database that domains use to record their objects and attributes is contained within Active Directory. Domains are established on a network to make it easier to organize and manage resources and security.

❏ When multiple domain controllers are used, a change to the database contained on one domain controller is copied to the databases on other domain controllers so that their databases are always identical. The process of copying directory data to multiple domain controllers is known as replication.

❏ To collect domains into logical groups, Windows 2000 Server uses a domain tree (or simply, tree). At the base of the tree is the root domain. From the root domain, child domains branch out to separate objects with the same policies. Underneath the child domains, multiple organizational units branch out to further logically subdivide the network's systems and objects. A collection of domain trees is known as a forest.

❏ Each tree, domain, container, and object has a unique name that becomes part of the namespace. The names of these elements may be used in one of three different ways to uniquely identify an object in a Windows 2000 tree: as a distinguished name, as a relative distinguished name, and as a user principal name.

❏ Prior to installation, you need to make a number of decisions regarding your server and network pertaining to the domain characteristics, the file system, the disk partitioning, the optional services to be installed, the administrator password, the protocols to be installed, and the server's name.

❏ If you are integrating Windows 2000 network with a NetWare network running IPX/SPX, you need to install the NWLink protocol on both clients and servers and either Gateway Services for NetWare (GSNW) on the Windows 2000 server or Client Services for NetWare (CSNW) on its clients.

8

KEY TERMS

3-tier architecture — A client/server environment that uses middleware to translate requests between the client and server.

account — A record of a user that contains all of his or her properties, including rights to resources, password, username, and so on.

Active Directory — Windows 2000 Server's method for organizing and managing objects associated with the network.

Administrator — A user account that has unlimited privileges to resources and objects managed by a server or domain. The administrator account is created during NOS installation.

asymmetric multiprocessing — A multiprocessing method that assigns each subtask to a specific processor.

attribute — A variable property associated with a network object. For example, a restriction on the time of day a user can log on is an attribute associated with that user object.

authentication — The process whereby a network operating system verifies that a client's user name and password are valid and allows the client to log onto the network.

CD-ROM File System (CDFS) — The read-only file system used to access resources on a CD. Windows 2000 supports this file system to allow CD-ROM file sharing.

child domain — A domain found beneath another domain in a Windows 2000 domain tree.

class — A type of object recognized by an NOS directory and defined in an NOS schema. Printers and users are examples of object classes.

Client Services for NetWare (CSNW) — A Microsoft program that can be installed on Windows 2000 clients to enable them to access NetWare servers and make full use of the NetWare Directory System (NDS), its objects, files, directories, and permissions.

clustering — A method for connecting multiple servers to enable resource sharing and load balancing between them.

container — A logical receptacle for holding like objects in an NOS directory. Containers form the branches of the directory tree.

directory — In general, a listing that organizes resources and correlates them with their properties. In the context of network operating systems, a method for organizing and managing objects.

Directory Services Migration Tool (DSMIGRATE) — A tool provided with Windows 2000 Server that enables network administrators to migrate accounts, files, and permissions from a NetWare NDS directory to the Windows 2000 Active Server Directory.

distinguished name (DN) — A long form of an object's name in Active Directory that explicitly indicates the object name, plus the names of its containers and domains. A distinguished name includes a domain component (DC), organizational unit (OU), and common name (CN). A client uses the distinguished name to access a particular object, such as a printer.

domain — A group of users, servers, and other resources that share account and security policies through a Windows 2000 network operating system.

domain account — A type of user account on a Windows 2000 network that has privileges to resources across the domain onto which it is logged.

domain controller — A Windows 2000 server that contains a replica of the Active Directory database.

domain local group — A group on a Windows 2000 network that allows members of one domain to access resources within that domain only.

domain tree — A group of hierarchically arranged domains that share a common namespace in the Windows 2000 Active Directory.

explicit one-way trust — A type of trust relationship in which two domains that belong to different NOS directory trees are configured to trust each other.

extended attributes — Attributes beyond the basic Read, Write, System Hidden, and Archive attrevutes supported by FAT. HPFS supports extended attributes.

FAT16 (16-bit File Allocation Table) — A file system designed for use with early DOS- and Windows-based computers that allocates file system space in 16-bit units. Compared to FAT32, FAT16 is less desirable because of its partition size, file naming, fragmentation, speed, and security limitations.

File Allocation Table (FAT) — The original PC file system designed in the 1970s to support floppy disks and, later, hard disks. FAT is inadequate for most server operating systems because of its partition size limitations, naming limitations, and fragmentation and speed issues.

FAT (File Allocation Table) — An enhanced version of FAT that accommodates the use of long filenames and smaller allocation units on a disk. FAT32 makes more efficient use of disk space than the original FAT.

file system — An operating system's method of organizing, managing, and accessing its files through logical structures and software routines.

forest — In the context of Windows 2000 Server, a collection of domain trees that use different namespaces. A forest allows for trust relationships to be established between trees.

Gateway Services for NetWare (GSNW) — A Windows 2000 service that acts as a translator between the Windows 2000 and NetWare client redirector services. With GSNW installed, a Windows 2000 server can access files and other shared resources on any NetWare server on a network.

global group — A group on a Windows 2000 network that allows members of one domain to access resources within that domain as well as resources from other domains in the same forest.

globally unique identifier (GUID) — A 128-bit number generated and assigned to an object upon its creation in the Windows 2000 Active Directory. Network applications and services use an object's GUID to communicate with it.

graphical user interface (GUI) — A pictorial representation of computer functions and elements that, in the case of network operating systems, enables administrators to more easily manage files, users, groups, security, printers, and other issues.

group — A means of collectively managing users' permissions and restrictions applied to shared resources. Groups form the basis for resource and account management for every type of network operating system, not just Windows 2000 Server. Many network administrators create groups according to department or, even more specifically, according to job function within a department.

Guest — A user account with very limited privileges that is created during the installation of a network operating system.

Hardware Compatibility List (HCL) — A list of computer components proven to be compatible with Windows 2000 Server. The HCL appears on the same CD as your Windows 2000 Server software and on Microsoft's Web site.

High-Performance File System (HPFS) — A file system designed for IBM's OS/2 operating system that offers greater efficiency and reliability than does FAT. HPFS is rarely used but can be supported by Windows 2000 servers.

8

Lightweight Directory Access Protocol (LDAP) — A standard protocol for accessing network directories.

local account — A type of user account on a Windows 2000 network that has rights to the resources managed by the server the user has logged onto.

member server — A type of server on a Windows 2000 network that does not hold directory information and therefore cannot authenticate users.

Microsoft Management Console (MMC) — A graphical network management interface used with Windows 2000 Server.

middleware — Software that sits between the client and server in a 3-tier architecture. Middleware may be used as a messaging service between clients and servers, as a universal query language for databases, or as means of coordinating processes between multiple servers that need to work together in servicing clients.

multi-master replication — The technique of replicating an Active Directory database to multiple domain controllers so they each have the same data and the same privileges to modify that data. Multi-master replication is used within a domain tree.

multiprocessing — The technique of splitting tasks among multiple processors to expedite the completion of any single instruction.

multitasking — The ability of a processor to perform multiple activities in a brief period of time (often seeming simultaneous to the user).

namespace — The complete database of hierarchical names (including host and domain names) used to resolve IP addresses with their hosts.

New Technology File System (NTFS) — A file system developed by Microsoft for use with its Windows NT and Windows 2000 operating systems. NTFS integrates reliability, compression, the ability to handle massive files, system security, and fast access. Most Windows 2000 Server partitions employ either FAT32 or NTFS.

NWConv — A utility provided with Windows 2000 that converts (migrates) an existing NetWare server's user account, file, and other information to a Windows 2000 server.

object — A representation of a thing or person associated with the network that belongs in the NOS directory. Objects include users, printers, groups, computers, data files, and applications.

object class — See *Class.*

organizational unit (OU) — A container within an NOS directory used to group objects with similar characteristics or privileges.

page file — A file on the hard disk that is used for virtual memory.

paging — The process of moving blocks of information, called pages, between RAM and into a page file on disk.

per seat — A Windows 2000 Server licensing mode that requires a license for every client capable of connecting to the Windows 2000 server.

per server — A Windows 2000 Server licensing mode that allows a limited number of clients to access the server simultaneously. (The number is determined by your Windows 2000 Server purchase agreement.) The restriction applies to the number of concurrent connections, rather than specific clients. Per server mode is the most popular choice for installing Windows 2000 Server.

physical memory — The RAM chips installed on the computer's system board that provide dedicated memory to that computer.

preemptive multitasking — The type of multitasking supported by NetWare, UNIX, and Windows 2000 Server that actually performs one task at a time, allowing one program to use the processor for a certain period of time, then suspending that program to allow another program to use the processor.

printer queue — A logical representation of a networked printer's functionality. To use a printer, clients must have access to the printer queue.

process — A routine of sequential instructions that runs until it has achieved its goal. For example, a spreadsheet program is a process.

redirector — A service that runs on a client workstation and determines whether the client's request should be handled by the client or the server.

relative distinguished name (RDN) — An attribute of the object that identifies an object separately from its related container(s) and domain. For most objects, the relative distinguished name is the same as its common name (CN) in the distinguished name convention.

replication — The process of copying Active Directory data to multiple domain controllers. This ensures redundancy so that in case one of the domain controllers fails, clients can still log onto the network, be authenticated, and access resources.

root domain — In Windows 2000 networking, the single domain from which child domains branch out in a domain tree.

schema — The description of object types, or classes, and their required and optional attributes that are stored in an NOS's directory.

site license — A type of software license that, for a fixed price, allows any number of users in one location to legally access an application.

snap-in — An administrative tool, such as Computer Management, that can be added to the Microsoft Management Console (MMC).

swap file — See *Page file*.

symmetric multiprocessing — A method of multiprocessing that splits all operations equally among two or more processors. Windows 2000 Server supports this type of multiprocessing.

thin client — A type of software that enables a client to accomplish functions over a network while utilizing little of the client workstation's resources and, instead, relying on the server to carry the processing burden.

thread — A well-defined, self-contained subset of a process. Using threads within a process enables a program to efficiently perform related, multiple, simultaneous activities. Threads are also used to enable processes to use multiple processors on SMP systems.

8

tree — A logical representation of multiple, hierarchical levels in a directory. It is called a tree because the whole structure shares a common starting point (the root) and from that point extends branches (or containers), which may extend additional branches, and so on.

trust relationship — The relationship between two domains on a Windows 2000 or Windows NT network that allows a domain controller from one domain to authenticate users from the other domain.

two-way transitive trust — The security relationship between domains in the same domain tree in which one domain grants every other domain in the tree access to its resources and, in turn, that domain can access other domains' resources. When a new domain is added to a tree, it immediately shares a two-way trust with the other domains in the tree.

Universal Disk Format (UDF) — A file system used on CD-ROMs and digital video disc (DVD) media.

universal group — A group on a Windows 2000 network that allows members from one domain to access resources in multiple domains and forests.

user principal name (UPN) — The preferred Active Directory naming convention for objects when used in informal situations. This name looks like a familiar Internet address, including the positioning of the domain name after the @ sign. UPNs are typically used for e-mail and related Internet services.

user principal name (UPN) suffix — The portion of a universal principal name (in Windows 2000 Active Directory's naming conventions) that follows the @ sign.

virtual memory — Memory that is logically carved out of space on the hard disk and added to physical memory (RAM).

wizard — A simple graphical program that assists the user in performing complex tasks, such as configuring a NIC on a server.

workgroup — A group of interconnected computers that share each others' resources without relying on a central file server.

REVIEW QUESTIONS

1. List four factors that you should consider before purchasing a network operating system.

2. What is the function of a redirector?

    a. to route CPU requests to the appropriate IRQ on the client

    b. to enable multiple processes to be handled by the same CPU on the server

    c. to determine whether a request is meant for the client CPU or the server

    d. to balance the processing load between the client and the server

    e. to store unfinished processes in a cache until the server can accept them

3. Which of the following must be installed on a Windows 2000 Professional client workstation in order for it to be able to log onto a Windows 2000 server?

   a. Client Services for Windows 2000

   b. Client Gateway to Windows 2000

   c. Services for TCP/IP networks

   d. Client for Microsoft Networks

   e. Windows-compatible client services

4. What are the 3 tiers in a 3-tier architecture?

   a. client, server, network

   b. client, hub, server

   c. client, middleware, server

   d. client, server, client agent

   e. client, server, router

5. If a user has Modify rights to a folder on a Windows 2000 server, what is he or she able to do?

   a. List, read, add, delete, execute, and modify files in the folder

   b. Add, delete, and modify files in the folder

   c. List, read, add, and delete files in the folder

   d. Add, delete, execute, and modify files in the folder

   e. List, read, add, delete, execute, and modify files in the folder, plus set permissions for the folder

6. Groups can contain other groups. True or False?

7. You have created a printer object for a new HP LaserJet in your Windows 2000 server Active Directory. Before users can print to this printer, what else must you create in Active Directory?

   a. a print queue (or share)

   b. a printer folder

   c. a Printers group

   d. a printer administrator

   e. a logical printer port

8. Name at least five attributes that may be associated with a user account.

9. What is the purpose of a container in an NOS directory?

   a. to represent a person or device on the network

   b. to limit the amount of hard disk space each user can use for data files

   c. to indicate in which domain objects belong

    d. to organize similar objects for easier management

    e. to separate partitions with different file systems

10. What is the maximum amount of memory that a Windows 2000 server can utilize?

    a. 2 GB

    b. 4 GB

    c. 8 GB

    d. 10 GB

    e. 12 GB

11. What primary advantage does Windows 2000 gain by assigning each operation its own 32-bit address space?

12. What is the common name in the following distinguished name: widgets.com/charleston/marketing/jkessel?

    a. widgets.com

    b. com

    c. charleston

    d. marketing

    e. jkessel

13. What do threads have to do with multiprocessing?

    a. Threads are made of processes; as processes are split among multiple processors, threads keep track of how they were separated in order for them to be rejoined.

    b. Threads are made of processes; in order for a multithreaded application to perform instructions faster, each process should use a separate processor.

    c. Processes are made of threads; threads within a process can be handled by different processors to improve server performance.

    d. Processes are made of threads; threads within each separate process must use the same processor, but different processes can use different processors.

14. In comparing an NOS directory to a tree, what are analogous to leaves?

    a. properties

    b. containers

    c. OUs

    d. objects

    e. branches

15. In case RAM runs out of space, where can it store unused information blocks?

    a. ROM

    b. a swap file on the hard disk

    c. a cache on the client workstation

    d. EEPROM

    e. BIOS

16. What kind of trust relationship do multiple domains within the same domain tree on a Windows 2000 network use?

    a. master domain trust

    b. one-way trust

    c. two-way trust

    d. global trust

    e. multi-master domain trust

17. On a Windows 2000 server, two domains, named Marketing and Engineering, are within the same domain tree. Thus, a user from the Engineering domain has access to run any of the programs on a server in the Marketing domain. True or False?

18. When talking about a Windows 2000 domain tree, what would you call the one domain from which all other domains and their containers emanate?

    a. branch domain

    b. child domain

    c. leaf domain

    d. root domain

    e. grandfather domain

19. You are a user on a Windows 2000 network who wants to print a memo to a printer across the hall. What kind of name would your client software use to direct your memo to this printer?

    a. distinguished name

    b. attribute name

    c. relative distinguished name

    d. user principal name

    e. global name

20. Which file system must a Windows 2000 server use to accept Macintosh clients?

    a. FAT

    b. FAT32

    c. CDFS

    d. NTFS

    e. MFS

21. What kind of multiprocessing does Windows 2000 support?

    a. symmetric

    b. synchronous

    c. preemptive

    d. asymmetric

    e. asynchronous

22. Name six things you need to know before you begin installing the Windows 2000 Server operating system.

23. After you install Windows 2000 Server, you want to use the Microsoft Management Console (MMC) to manage users and groups. What is the first thing you must do?

    a. add the Local Users and Groups snap-in to the MMC

    b. run the MMC command from the Run dialog box to initiate a new MMC

    c. install the MMC as an optional service from the Windows 2000 Server CD-ROM

    d. choose MMC from the Control Panel, then modify its properties to assign your console a name

    e. convert the Active Directory schema into an MMC-compliant format

24. What is the purpose of replication on a Windows 2000 network?

    a. to create multiple instances of the Active Directory database in case one server fails

    b. to create multiple instances of groups to enable access across all the domains in a domain tree

    c. to copy one domain tree's Active Directory database to another domain tree

    d. to copy all the user objects from one domain within a tree to another domain within a tree

    e. to create a system backup for the domain controller so that in case it fails, all of its files can be restored

25. What is the maximum length for an NTFS file name?

    a. 8 characters

    b. 16 characters

    c. 64 characters

    d. 128 characters

    e. 255 characters

26. You work at an organization with 12 servers and 1000 employees, each of whom works full-time and has his or her own workstation. Which Windows 2000 licensing mode should you purchase?

27. You are the network administrator for a school district. During August, you create a number of new student user accounts, but you do not want them to be functional at that time. What option should you choose when you create the user accounts?

    a. User must change password at next login

    b. User cannot change password

    c. User requires no password

    d. Password never expires

    e. Account is disabled

28. What utility allows you to transform NetWare directory objects to a Windows 2000 Server's Active Directory?

    a. NWConv

    b. NW-Migrate

    c. DSMIGRATE

    d. OSTranslate

    e. Win2KConv

29. Which of the following is not a valid name for a Windows 2000 domain?

    a. MKTG+SALES

    b. MKTG_SALES

    c. MKTGandSALES

    d. MKTG-SALES

    e. MarketingandSales

30. What two methods can you use for installing Windows 2000 Server?

    a. remote installation over the network

    b. installation from multiple floppy disks

    c. installation from a locally attached DAT tape drive

    d. installation from a CD-ROM

    e. installation via FTP over the Internet

8

HANDS-ON PROJECTS

Project 8-1

Every network operating system vendor likes to boast about how organizations are using their software to its fullest potential. In this project you will mine the Microsoft Web site to discover how various organizations use networks and their NOS software. You will need a computer with Internet access that has installed on it a modern Web browser program such as Internet Explorer version 4 or higher or Netscape Navigator version 4.5 or higher.

1. If you are not already connected, connect to the Internet and then launch your browser software.

2. Point your browser to the following URL: *www.microsoft.com/windows2000/ server/evaluation/casestudies/default.asp*

3. This page lists case studies and success stories of companies that used Windows 2000 Server on their networks. Scroll through the page to get an idea of what type of companies are using this NOS. How many of them look familiar to you? Can you make any generalizations about what industries are most likely to use Microsoft products?

4. Click one of the case studies to read more about it. What services does Windows 2000 Server provide for the company in question (for example, file sharing, printing, communications, network management, Internet services, and so on)? What features does Microsoft seem to emphasize the most? What does that emphasis tell you about their competition with NetWare or UNIX?

5. As you read through the success story, on a separate piece of paper make a note of any terms you do not understand. Which of these terms do you think are Microsoft trademarks and which do you think are general networking terms?

6. Read the entire case study or success story and note the Microsoft products that this customer uses. Besides Windows 2000 Server, what other Microsoft products do they use? Why might it make sense for the customer to use Web server and application programming language software, for example, from the same company that made its NOS?

7. Close your browser window and terminate your Internet connection.

Project 8-2

In this project you will install Windows 2000 Server. You must have a computer that meets the system requirements for Windows 2000 Server, plus the Windows 2000 Server installation CD-ROM and a valid registration key. You will also need the disk that came with the computer's NIC.

1. First, create an installation checklist that identifies the choices you will need to make during installation of this server. (Appendix D provides an example of an installation checklist.) Plan to make your server act as domain controller.

2. Make sure that your server is not networked with any other computers.

3. Install Windows 2000 Server according to the steps provided earlier in this chapter, with the following exceptions:

- Rather than creating one large partition, create two equal-sized NTFS partitions: one called **SYS** and one called **DATA**.

- Use the domain name **CLASSX** and call your server **STUDENTY**, where *X* is your pair number (assuming the class can divide into pairs) and *Y* is your seat number.

- Instead of letting the setup program detect your NIC, when prompted, choose **Select From List** and **Have Disk**. Install the drivers from your NIC configuration disk.

4. When asked for the Administrator password, choose a password you believe to be secure.

5. After the installation is complete, restart the computer and log on as the Administrator.

Project 8-3

In this project you will create a customized MMC console on the Windows 2000 server that you just created.

1. Log onto the Windows 2000 server as Administrator or as a user with equivalent privileges.

2. Click **Start**, and then click **Run**. The Run dialog box appears.

3. In the text box, type **mmc**, then click **OK**.

4. The Console window appears, with a space for the administrative tools listing in the left pane and the details listing for each administrative tool in the right pane. Next you will add snap-in tools that allow you to manage Active Directory.

5. Click **Console** on the menu bar, and then click **Add/Remove Snap-in**. The Add/Remove Snap-in dialog box appears.

6. Click **Add**. The Add Standalone Snap-in dialog box appears.

7. Select the **Active Directory Users and Computers** tool, and then click **Add**.

8. Click **Close** to close the Add Standalone Snap-in dialog box.

9. Click **OK** to save your changes. You return to the MMC console window. Next you will save the console you have created.

10. Click **Console** on the menu bar and then click **Save As**. The Save As dialog box appears. In the File name text box, type a name for your console, such as MyMgr.

11. Click **Save**. Notice that the name of your MMC console window changes to "MyMgr."

12. Close the MyMgr console window.

13. Click **Start** on the menu bar, point to **Programs**, and then point to **Administrative Tools**. Notice that your console appears as a new menu option.

Project 8-4

In this project you will practice creating and configuring a user account on a Windows 2000 server. You should use the server that you installed in Project 8-2 or another properly installed and configured Windows 2000 server.

1. Log onto the Windows 2000 server as Administrator.

2. Follow the steps described earlier in this chapter for creating a domain user account.

3. After creating the account, while in the Active Directory Users and Computers snap-in window, double-click the user account you just created. The user's property dialog box should appear.

4. Note the tabs that appear, and that the **General** tab is selected by default. In the Description text box, enter the job title **Consultant** for this user.

5. Next you will limit the hours that this user can access the network. Select the **Account** tab. Notice the default parameters for this option.

6. Click **Logon Hours**. The Logon Hours dialog box appears, as shown in Figure 8-24.

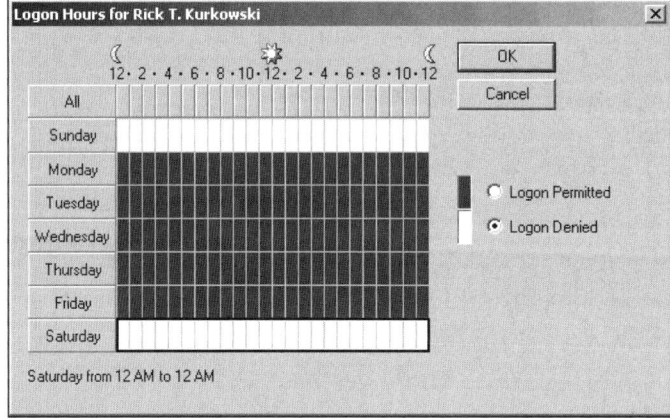

Figure 8-24   Logon Hours dialog box

7. Point to the cell in the last row, first column—the cell that corresponds to 12 A.M. on Saturday. Click and drag the pointer to the far column to select the entire day. Click **Logon Denied**, and then click **OK** to save your changes.

8. Click the **Dial-in** tab of the user's property dialog box. Note the variety of properties that can be associated with a user's dial-in connection to the server.

9. Select the following options in the Dial-in tab: **Allow access**, **No Callback**, and check the **Assign a Static IP address** option. After you select the last option, enter a made-up IP address in the Assign Static IP address text box. What would be the advantage of assigning an employee a static IP address that applies only when she remotely dials in to the server?

10. Click the other tabs in the user's property dialog box to find out what else you can configure.

11. When you have finished, click **Apply** to save the changes you have made to this user account.

Project 8-5

In this project you will have the opportunity to view and modify the virtual memory settings for a Windows 2000 server. This project requires a properly installed and configured Windows 2000 server.

1. Log onto the Windows 2000 server as Administrator or as a user with equivalent privileges.

2. Click **Start**, point to **Settings**, and then click **Control Panel**. The Control Panel window opens.

3. Double-click the **System** icon, click the **Advanced** tab, click **Performance Options**, and then click the **Change** button. The Virtual Memory dialog box appears.

4. If multiple drives are listed in the Drive box, choose the drive that contains your page file. The Paging file size indicates how much hard disk space is available for virtual memory. In the Initial Size text box, enter a number that is double the default number of MB initially available for virtual memory.

5. In the Maximum Size text box, also enter a number that is double the default. What effect do you suppose this change will have on your server's performance? What effect would it have if your server had a low volume of traffic and sufficient RAM to handle its processing needs?

6. Click **OK** to save your change.

CASE PROJECTS

1. A statewide healthcare insurance provider, Evergreen Health, has asked you to help plan a new Windows 2000 network. The organization has been using Windows NT servers until now, but because the organization is now under new management and because Evergreen has just acquired a few smaller health insurance providers, the IT Department wants to rethink the network design from scratch. You meet with a team of employees that includes the IT Director, network administrator, and several network technicians. Unfortunately, none of Evergreen's professionals has had time to learn anything about Windows 2000 Server. Describe what could make Windows 2000 Server particularly well suited to Evergreen's environment.

8

2. One of Evergreen's network technicians says she doesn't believe the servers are capable of handling Windows 2000 Server. She adds that Evergreen has 12 servers that each contain two 333 MHz Pentium processors, 64 MB RAM, dual NICs, dual power supplies, and 6 GB hard disks. The IT Director, worrying about her budget, indicates that it would be most cost effective to upgrade the existing server hardware, rather than purchase new servers. They ask you to research the total cost of upgrading all of their servers to the minimal Windows 2000 Server requirements. Search the Web for the parts necessary to do this and provide an estimate of how much the upgrades will cost.

3. Even though you were able to provide the IT Director with a cost for the upgrades, you tell the team that you don't recommend leaving all the servers at the minimum hardware requirements. Write down four questions you will ask them about their network environment to help determine which servers might need more system resources.

4. Months later, Evergreen Health has upgraded its hardware and is ready to plan for the installation. The IT department would like your help designing the directory's logical structure. Evergreen contains the departments, locations, and users shown in Table 8–3, below. Users in each department need to share files with users in every other department. Except for the sales offices, users in each location are self-sufficient; that is, they use their location's servers and printers and do not regularly rely on resources in other locations.

Table 8-3   Evergreen Health departments, locations and users

Department	Location	Users
Information Technology	Boston	32
Customer Service	Boise	240 (over three shifts)
Accounting	Boston	20
Claims	New York	38
Operations	Boston	10
Sales	Cincinnati	5
Sales	Boston	10
Sales	Phoenix	8
Sales	San Diego	5
Sales	Chicago	6
Sales	New York	10
Sales	Seattle	7
Marketing	New York	24
Human Resources	Boston	6
Legal	Boston	18

- What type of licensing options should Evergreen purchase?

- Sketch two different domain hierarchies that may work for Evergreen. Include multiple domains and organizational units as you see fit.

- Assign names to the domains and OUs you've created. List the advantages to each of the two models.

- Upon reflection, which domain model would you recommend?

- Insert the following user objects into the San Diego Sales office of your recommended domain model: Sue Anderson, Del Boudreau, Ann Nicastro, Everett Schultz, and Clay Velacruz and assign them user names. Now list the distinguished names for each user, including their OUs and domains.

8

NETWARE-BASED
NETWORKING

After reading this chapter and completing the exercises, you will be able to:

➤ Identify the advantages of using the NetWare network operating system

➤ Describe NetWare's server hardware requirements

➤ Describe NetWare's memory, directory structure, and file system architectures

➤ Plan for and perform a simple NetWare server installation

➤ Explain how NetWare integrates with other network operating systems

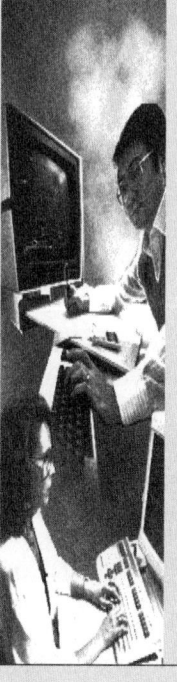

ON THE JOB

A few years ago, I switched from a programming position to a network administrator position. I didn't know much about networks before making the change, but I realized that I wanted to do something other than type code for the rest of my life. One of my first projects was to install a NetWare 4.11 server for a school district. The new server would provide a centralized backup point for all files on the network. I figured the NetWare installation process would be painless, and I worried only about getting the backup software working.

I should have given more thought to the installation! My boss had provided me with an old, but powerful workstation to use for my new server. This workstation still had Windows 95 and a number of applications installed on its hard drive. I knew that I had to reformat the hard disk before installing NetWare. After doing so, I began the installation. Just as I chose the "install in English" option from the installation program, however, the screen went black. I could go no further. I reformatted the hard disk twice, but the same thing happened each time.

Finally I sought the help of a colleague who had many years of experience with NetWare. After I explained my problem, she smiled and confessed that she had once made the same mistake. NetWare's operating system, she told me, cannot be installed over the version of DOS used by Windows. Even though I had erased Windows and the applications from the hard disk, I hadn't erased enough. Instead, I had to install DOS 6.22, format the hard disk, and begin all over. Once I took these steps, the installation worked perfectly.

Rose Suyemoto
Brighton School District

As you learned in Chapter 8, a network operating system is software that resides at the highest layer of the OSI Model and manages resources on a server. In this chapter, you will learn about NetWare, another popular type of LAN and WAN network operating system. Windows 2000 Server and NetWare share many characteristics, such as their use of a centralized directory, graphical interfaces for management, and processor optimization techniques. Both provide file and print sharing in a client/server networking environment, and both enable you to use additional services such as remote access, Internet connectivity, and network management. As you will see, however, NetWare and Windows 2000 Server also differ in significant ways.

This chapter will not attempt to cover all of the details of installing, managing, and optimizing a NetWare networking environment. For that type of knowledge, and especially if you intend to pursue CNE certification, you should invest in a book devoted to Novell's NetWare. This chapter merely provides an overview of the requirements, characteristics, and basic structure of Novell's popular network operating system.

INTRODUCTION TO NETWARE

In 1983, Novell introduced its NetWare network operating system. At that time, Windows NT Server (the precursor to Windows 2000 Server) had not yet been developed and UNIX was used primarily to make applications available to clients, rather than share resources among clients. NetWare quickly became the operating system of choice for LANs and WANs, providing reliable file and print sharing services to millions of users. In subsequent years, Novell has refined NetWare so that it now includes support for TCP/IP, intranet services, a graphical user interface, and better integration with other operating systems.

Currently, several different versions of NetWare exist. Although versions 3.1 through 3.2 (collectively referred to as **NetWare 3.x**) were introduced in the early 1990s, some network administrators have not replaced their NetWare 3.x installations with newer versions because of the 3.x version's high reliability. You may find NetWare 3.x still running in cost-conscious organizations such as schools or nonprofit agencies, because these organizations cannot justify upgrading their network operation systems to a newer version.

Novell introduced NetWare 4.0, 4.1, and 4.11 (collectively known as **NetWare 4.x**) in the mid-1990s. NetWare 4.11 is sometimes referred to as **IntraNetware** because it was the first version of NetWare to support intranet services such as Web server software, IP address management, and FTP hosting. Novell changed the look of its network operating system with NetWare 4.x in an attempt to make this software more user-friendly, replacing most of the old DOS-based commands with a graphical user interface. In fact, many 3.x commands were replaced with new commands in version 4.x. NetWare 4.x also provided much better support for enterprise-wide networks containing multiple servers.

In 1998, Novell released version 5.0 of NetWare, and since then has released versions 5.1 and 5.11; collectively, they are known as **NetWare 5.x**. NetWare 5.x not only increases the extent and ease of network management, but also provides a network operating system wholly based on the IP protocol. As you know, the IP protocol is the de facto protocol of the Internet. In addition to being compatible with Windows 2000 and UNIX operating systems, NetWare 5.x offers flexibility and easy integration thanks to its use of IP. Another difference between NetWare 5.x and previous versions of NetWare is that many of its interfaces and services rely on the Java programming language. In addition, NetWare 5.x offers better printer and file system administration than version 4.x.

You do not need to know the specific differences between versions of NetWare to achieve Net+ certification. As a network administrator or technician, however, you will likely encounter environments that use one or several NetWare versions. This chapter focuses on the most significant features of NetWare 4.x and 5.x, which are similar in use and design. Both use Novell Directory Services (NDS) to organize users, groups, servers, and other network resources. (You will learn more about NDS later in this chapter.) Both provide a graphical interface for managing network resources. In addition, both support integration with other network operating systems, Web services, multiple protocols, asset management, migration utilities, and software distribution. You can therefore use this chapter as a starting point in your exploration of NetWare.

WHY CHOOSE NETWARE?

As you learned in Chapter 8, you need to answer some basic questions when choosing a network operating system.

- Can it be integrated with my existing infrastructure? (The infrastructure includes other network operating systems, and LAN topology, protocols, transmission methods, and connectivity hardware.)

- Will it provide the security required by my resources?

- Is my technical staff capable of managing it?

- Will my applications run smoothly on it?

- Will it accommodate future growth (that is, is it scalable)?

- Does it support the additional services required by my users (for example, remote access, Web site hosting, and messaging)?

- How much does it cost?

- What kind of support does the vendor offer?

Like Windows 2000 Server, NetWare offers excellent answers to these questions. In their fierce competition for the network operating system market, NetWare and Windows 2000 Server have both been forced to address the issues that cause the greatest concern for network administrators: performance, cost, flexibility, interoperability, and support. NetWare has been around for a long time and has a faithful following among network administrators. This popularity arises partly because some veteran networking professionals are more comfortable with NetWare, which was the first network operating system designed for file and print sharing. It also reflects NetWare's efficient processing, reliable services, and strong vendor support.

Like Microsoft, Novell can leverage its size to ensure that network applications are compatible and that support is easily accessible. Novell provides extensive online support from its support Web site, *www.support.novell.com*. From that Web page, you can search Novell's Knowledgebase, a database of technical information documents (TIDs), or join a forum in which networking professionals from around the world share their experiences with Novell products. You can also learn about known bugs in different versions of NetWare and find explanations of common problems at the Novell support site. In addition, the company provides enhanced technical support to Certified NetWare Engineers (CNEs) through CDs and discounted calls to Novell's help desk. As with Microsoft products, you can find a number of third-party discussion groups on the Web as well as technical manuals and books that focus on NetWare products.

As noted earlier, NetWare is flexible, efficient, and secure. One feature contributing to its flexibility is the ability to natively support many different protocols. NetWare 4.x supports IP encapsulated by Novell's native IPX, and NetWare 5.x supports the use of pure (not encapsulated) IP. Both versions support the AppleTalk, IPX/SPX, and TCP/IP protocols, and both can handle Ethernet or Token Ring networks. Another advantage of NetWare is its ability to run multiple services simultaneously and use as many as 32 internal processors. Its modularity allows the network administrator to isolate some processes from others or change the priority of critical applications. For instance, if your NetWare server runs mail services, file services, and printer services for just one printer, you can make the print service have a lower priority than the mail and file services.

In addition to supporting a number of protocols and permitting quick configuration changes, NetWare offers native interoperability solutions for Macintosh-, Windows-, DOS-, OS/2-, and UNIX-based systems. To improve security, it provides encryption and other security measures to prevent intruders from hacking into the server or its resources.

In addition, both NetWare 4.x and 5.x supply graphical interfaces for managing network resources, including users, printers, groups, profiles, and shared drives. You can use NetWare's graphical interface from any workstation on the network. NetWare 5.x also provides a graphical server console based on the Java programming language, called ConsoleOne. In addition, version 5.x provides graphical wizards for part of the server installation. In versions lower than 5.x, you must install and configure NetWare servers entirely through DOS-based commands and menus. This requirement could be considered a drawback for less experienced network administrators.

Like Windows 2000 Server, however, NetWare does not necessarily suit all organizations. For example, if your organization depends heavily on enterprise-wide Microsoft solutions, such as SQL Server or Internet Information Server, you may want to forego a NetWare purchase. Although NetWare offers graphical interfaces for both management and console functions, one could argue that they are less intuitive than the Microsoft graphical interfaces since the Windows GUI is generally better recognized. If members of your technical staff prefer a simple, familiar graphical interface, Windows 2000 Server may therefore be a better choice.

Another difference between NetWare 4.x and Windows 2000 Server is that NetWare 4.x (and lower versions) cannot support virtual memory. Instead, it can use only the physical memory installed in the machine. Although this feature means that the operating system accesses memory more quickly, it does not allow the operating system to draw on extra hard disk space when physical memory becomes limited. Note, however, that you can use virtual memory with NetWare 5.x.

Ideally, you should test your critical applications (including network management functions such as backup and restore services) on all types of operating systems (NetWare, Windows 2000, and UNIX) to determine which will work most efficiently in your environment. Nevertheless, you probably will not have the luxury of designing a network from scratch and being the person who picks the network operating system. As mentioned in Chapter 8, the network operating systems that run on your servers will likely depend on political and technical issues in your environment or current business trends.

NetWare Server Hardware

You have learned that servers generally require more hard disk space, memory, and processing power than do client workstations on the network. Servers may also boast redundant disk drives, NICs, or power supplies or multiple processors. The more components you install on a server, the more expensive the machine. At the same time, however, the machine will likely operate more reliably and quickly with the added components.

Table 9-1 lists the minimum hardware requirements for versions 4.1 and 5.0 of NetWare, as outlined by Novell. If you plan to run applications or certain services on NetWare, such as a Web server or software distribution service (a network management function that was introduced in Chapter 1), your server will need more than these minimum requirements.

9

Table 9-1   Minimum hardware requirements for NetWare 4.x and 5.0 servers

Component	NetWare 4.x Requirement	NetWare 5.0 Requirement
Processor	An IBM or IBM-compatible PC with a 386sx, 486, or better processor. Out of the box, NetWare 4.x can support as many as 32 processors.	An IBM or IBM-compatible PC with Pentium processor. Out of the box, NetWare 5.0 can support as many as 32 processors.
Memory	20 MB RAM (the number should be increased for better performance; 64 MB is recommended).	64 MB RAM (the number should be increased for better performance; 128 MB is recommended).
Hard Disk	IDE or SCSI hard disk with at least 15 MB DOS partition and at least 75 MB NetWare partition.	IDE or SCSI hard disk with at least 50 MB DOS partition and at least 550 MB NetWare partition.
NIC	A NIC that supports your network type and for which you have drivers available.	A NIC that supports your network type and for which you have drivers available
CD-ROM	A model that can read ISO 9660 formatted CDs is recommended.	A model that can read ISO 9660 formatted CDs is recommended.
Pointing device	Optional.	Optional, but necessary if you want to use the GUI console.
Floppy disk	Optional, but a 3.5" floppy disk drive is useful for installing the NetWare operating system license.	Optional, but a 3.5" floppy disk drive is useful for installing the NetWare operating system license.

As you learned in Chapter 8, most networking environments actually require servers that far exceed the minimum hardware requirements suggested by the software vendor. Every situation will vary, but to determine the optimal hardware for your server, you should consider the following:

- How many clients will connect to the server?

- What kinds of applications will run on the server?

- How much storage space will each user need?

- How much down time is acceptable?

- What can your organization afford?

Perhaps the most important question on this list refers to the types of applications that the server will run. As is the case with Windows 2000 Server hardware, you can purchase an inexpensive server that runs NetWare 5.x, but suffices only for file and print sharing. To accomplish more with your network, you will want to run applications on the server; you will therefore need a more powerful machine. Every application has its own processor, RAM, and storage requirements. Consult the application's installation guide to find out its specific requirements.

When considering the NetWare operating system requirements, you need to keep in mind the number of **NetWare loadable modules (NLMs)** used by each service. NLMs are routines that enable the server to run a range of programs and offer a variety of services, such as protocol support and Web publishing. Each NLM consumes some of the server's memory and processor resources (at least temporarily). For example, when you install NetWare out of the box, your server will run many critical NLMs. If you install Novell's GroupWise e-mail and scheduler software, the server may require another five NLMs. If you install Novell's BorderManager software, the server may require still another five or so NLMs, and so on. The amount of resources consumed by each NLM depends on the NLM's size and complexity.

Novell provides a worksheet to determine how much memory your NetWare server will require. This worksheet, which contains blanks in which you can enter your network's specifications (such as the number of users), can be found in your NetWare documentation or at Novell's Web site. Before you recommend buying or actually purchase memory for your NetWare server, you should consult this worksheet.

As with Windows 2000, you can add components to your NetWare server to enhance its fault tolerance and performance. The most popular additional components include multiple processors, extra RAM, multiple NICs, fault-tolerant hard disks, a backup drive, and an uninterruptible power supply. You will learn more about how such components enhance network performance and reliability in Chapters 13 and 14. For now, it suffices to know that you must carefully analyze your current situation and plans for growth before making a hardware purchasing decision. Remember—paying more for a dependable server can be economical if it prevents down time.

A Closer Look at the NetWare Operating System

By now, you have probably noticed many similarities between the major features of NetWare and those of Windows 2000. You'll discover even more similarities, as well as some differences, in their operating system details. This section compares and contrasts the various details of the NetWare, Windows 2000, and UNIX operating systems.

 If you have forgotten any of the concepts discussed in Chapter 8, refer to the Key Terms list in that chapter to refresh your memory.

Multiprocessing

In versions 4.x and higher, NetWare supports the use of as many as 32 processors on one server. Like Windows 2000, it takes advantage of symmetric multiprocessing, in which tasks are equally distributed among the processors. As you learned in Chapter 8, multiprocessing increases a server's performance when the server runs several operations simultaneously. For servers performing many processor-intensive activities, having multiple processors is usually worth the investment in the extra hardware. You will learn more about analyzing and optimizing network performance in Chapter 13.

To use NetWare 5.x's multiprocessing capabilities, you simply install multiple processors in the server. The operating system will automatically detect and make use of these processors, whether 1 or 32 are present, without additional configuration. In lower versions of NetWare, you must load a symmetric multiprocessing (SMP) module to take advantage of multiple processors.

NetWare's Memory Model

Whereas NetWare 4.x can use only physical memory, NetWare 5.x can work with both virtual memory and physical memory. Remember that virtual memory is actually composed of RAM and hard disk space that can provide temporary memory. NetWare 5.x benefits from virtual memory because many of its services use the Java programming language, which has high memory requirements.

Like Windows 2000, NetWare 5.x dynamically (in other words, without intervention and only as necessary) manages its use of both physical and virtual memory. For example, if a printing service currently resides in physical memory but hasn't been accessed for two hours, NetWare 5.x can push it into virtual memory so that a critical Java application (such as one needed immediately for file backup services) can use the physical memory. When the contents of virtual memory are required again, NetWare moves the printing service back into physical memory; at the same time, it sends another process from physical memory to virtual memory to open up the desired space.

Since the United States lifted tariffs that had been imposed on memory imported from other countries in the mid-1990s, good-quality memory chips have become very inexpensive. Therefore, you should never force your server to rely on the slower virtual memory to handle its typical processing loads. If the server suffers from too little physical memory and must spend all of its time swapping data to virtual memory, it will have no time to accomplish useful work.

NetWare, like Windows 2000, uses 32-bit addressing to provide quick access to the physical memory. It also allows you to run services in a separate memory area from the operating system, which prevents one rogue routine from taking the server down. Assigning a separate memory area to a service is known as running the service in **protected mode**. Protected mode prevents the service and its supporting routines from harming critical server processes.

In NetWare, you can generally customize the extent to which applications are isolated from one another in memory. Many of the core components of the NetWare operating system run in protected mode by default. The only services that cannot run in protected mode are those that must directly access the server hardware. In fact, Novell allows network administrators to adjust the server's use of memory in a number of ways. This flexibility can be both a blessing and a curse, however. If you change a setting in the wrong direction, for example, you may restrict the server's ability to process requests efficiently. Nevertheless, every environment will require some fine-tuning to maximize the use of memory, and every organization's memory needs will vary.

Although you can customize memory on a Novell network, both NetWare 4.x and 5.x manage physical memory very efficiently right out of the box. One important technique for managing memory is caching. **Caching** is the process of saving frequently used data to an area of the physical memory where it will be readily available for future requests. Caching accelerates the process of accessing the server because the operating system does not have to search for the requested data on the disk.

Conceptually, caching is similar to what goes on at a help desk. If 90% of the time a company's users call the help desk to ask questions about e-mail, the help desk manager might decide to publish a Web site giving answers to frequently asked e-mail questions. This Web site resembles a cache in that it provides commonly required information in an easy-to-access form.

The more physical memory that is present in your server, the more space the server can use for caching. On the other hand, the more services and applications run by your server, the less space the server will have for caching. As with most other memory settings in NetWare, you can change Cache Read and Write parameters to suit your environment.

The Kernel and Console Operations

At the heart of NetWare lies the **kernel**, or the core of the operating system. NetWare's 32-bit kernel is responsible for overseeing all critical server processes. The program SERVER.EXE runs the kernel from a server's DOS partition. Typically, a server will start by activating an AUTOEXEC.BAT file that launches SERVER.EXE; from that point forward, NetWare controls the machine's operations. SERVER.EXE loads the critical NLMs that the kernel needs to run the NetWare operating system. In fact, once an NLM loads into memory, it is considered part of the kernel.

You can envision the kernel as a train with multiple cars. A train may leave Duluth with an engine, two tank cars, and five freight cars. These eight pieces, collectively, make up the train. In St. Paul, the train may pick up four more tank cars and six more freight cars. Now the train contains 18 pieces. If the train stops in Dubuque to deliver (or unload) five cars of iron ore, it does not fundamentally change. It will always need an engine, and no matter how many cars it carries, it remains a train. Much in the same way, NLMs can be loaded and unloaded (either automatically, by a program that requires them, or manually, by a network administrator) based on whether the kernel needs them. Loading and unloading NLMs does not change the kernel, however. The ability to dynamically load and unload NLMs makes the kernel modular and efficient. It also affords network administrators comprehensive control over their network operations.

The network administrator's primary interface to a NetWare server is the **server console**. Unlike in Windows 2000, this interface is not entirely graphical. NetWare 4.x employs only text-based server menus at the console. In NetWare 5.x, however, commands can be accessed through either a text-based or graphical menu system. The graphical interface in NetWare 5.x is called ConsoleOne.

Figure 9-1 illustrates a typical text-based console screen on a NetWare 5.x server. This console is launched from an NLM called Monitor. **Monitor** enables the system administrator to view server parameters such as protocols, bindings, system resources, and loaded modules. In many cases, it also allows the system administrator to modify these parameters. If you plan to specialize in NetWare administration (no matter which version of NetWare is involved), you should become very familiar with the Monitor NLM.

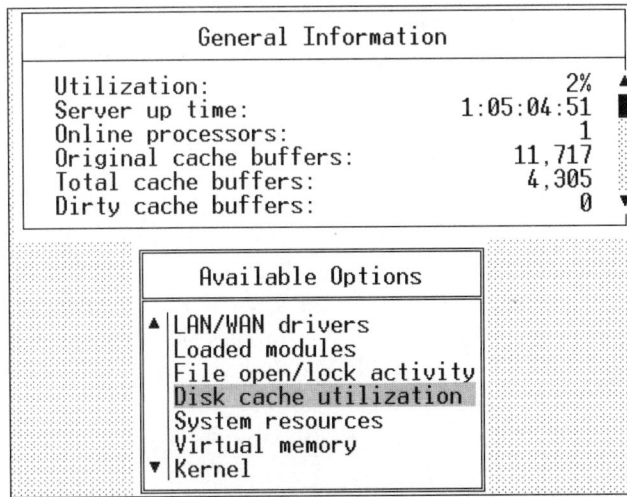

Figure 9-1   A NetWare console screen at the Monitor menu

Hundreds of NLMs are available for the NetWare operating system. In fact, developers can write their own NLMs for special purposes because Novell shares its operating system code. Nevertheless, you probably won't write your own, because most of the NLMs you'll ever need will come with your server software or the additional utilities you install.

You can view the NLMs currently running on your NetWare server by typing **mod-ules** at the NetWare server console. To find out more about a single NLM, type **help** *XXX,* where *XXX* is the name of the NLM. For example, to find out more about the Monitor command, type **help monitor** at the console prompt. The server will respond with an explanation of the purpose of the command, its syntax, and its switches.

The NetWare server console prompt is not the same as a DOS prompt (which, among other things, allows you to view, copy, or delete files and directories on a computer). The purpose of the console is not to manage the file system, but rather to manage the server parameters. To manage the file system, you should log on to the server as an administrator from a workstation connected to the network. The next section discusses the NetWare file system in more detail.

The NetWare File System

As you learned in Chapter 8, a file system is an operating system's method of organizing, managing, and accessing its files through logical structures and software routines. NetWare does not allow you to specify the file system types in the same way that Windows 2000 does, but it offers its own high-performance file system that supports DOS, Macintosh, UNIX, OS/2, and Windows. Whereas the operating system supports DOS filenames by default, achieving support for other filenames (from other OSs) requires loading the proper NLMs on the server. Once you have installed the necessary modules, Macintosh, Windows, UNIX, or OS/2 clients can read from the server as if the server were running the Macintosh, Windows, UNIX, or OS/2 operating system, respectively. Because NetWare uses modules rather than file systems to support access by other operating systems, file/directory size limitations and performance do not vary between NetWare volumes or servers.

Like Windows 2000, NetWare uses volumes as the basis for organizing files and directories on the server. When you install NetWare, a volume called SYS is automatically created. At the time of installation, you may choose to create additional volumes such as DATA (for user data) or APPS (for shared applications), as well. (You should make additional volume names short, simple, and descriptive.) You should design the file system so that it meets your performance, security, growth, and data sharing goals. For example, by assigning all user data to its own volume called DATA, separate from the SYS volume that contains system files, you can protect your system files from accidental deletion. Creating a separate DATA volume for data files therefore provides more security than putting all data and system files on one volume.

Plan carefully before establishing a server's volume and directory structure—once established, they are very difficult to change. When installing a NetWare network from scratch, you should consult resources that can guide you through the process of planning the volume and directory structure for your network.

After planning and creating your server's volumes, you must determine whether the network should take advantage of NetWare's file compression capabilities.

Compression

NetWare 4.x and 5.x both support file compression, which is performed on a file-by-file basis. In other words, each file is compressed separately; an entire directory or volume is not compressed at the same time. Another feature of NetWare's file compression is that the processes of compression and decompression are transparent to the user. For example, if a directory containing e-mail has been compressed, a user who requests data from that directory will never know that, during the few seconds she waits to pick up the e-mail message, it is being decompressed.

In both NetWare 4.x and NetWare 5.x, unless the network administrator specifically chooses to prevent compression, compression on the server is enabled automatically. The average overall degree of compression attained by a NetWare 5.x server is 63%. Thus a 4 GB volume with 1 GB of uncompressed data and 3 GB of free space could gain 630 MB of extra free space (for a total of 3.63 GB free space) with normal compression. The compression ratio will vary for each file.

Compression does increase file access time slightly; for this reason, it is not recommended for extremely large files. NetWare will not compress files that exceed 256 MB in size. If you choose to use compression on your server, you'll find that NetWare provides numerous options for optimizing disk compression. Among other things, you can instruct the server to wait a specific period of days before first compressing new files, and you can disable compression altogether for some types of files or directories. You can also set a threshold of compression below which the operating system will not compress files. For example, if you specify that a very large database can be compressed by only 10%, it may not be worthwhile to compress it, because it would increase file access time and provide little space savings.

 Some applications, such as older DOS-based databases, may not work when compressed on a NetWare server. Although the NetWare operating system can determine which of its own files can be compressed safely, you should verify that other system files and applications will work when compressed.

Block Suballocation

Block suballocation is a technique for using hard disk space more efficiently. To understand block suballocation, you must understand how data are stored on the hard disk. As you learned in Chapter 8's discussion of FAT32, each file on a computer is placed into one or more allocation units, or **blocks**, on the hard disk. (You can configure the standard block size on your server.) Normally, if an entire file does not fit into one block, it will consume as many blocks as required to meet its storage requirements, even if it doesn't use all of the space in every block. For example, suppose your block size is 4 KB. A 17 KB file would require five blocks, or 20 KB of hard disk space, as pictured in the left-hand side of Figure 9-2. This arrangement wastes 3 KB of space.

Suballocation allows you to break blocks into smaller pieces, or suballocation blocks, of 512 bytes. If a file exceeds a whole number of blocks, it will use parts of additional blocks in increments of 512 bytes. The 17 KB file in the previous example would therefore use only 4.25 blocks, as shown in the right side of Figure 9-2. Other files can then occupy the remaining 3 KB piece of the fifth block. In this way, block suballocation permits you to use much more of the available space on the server's hard disk.

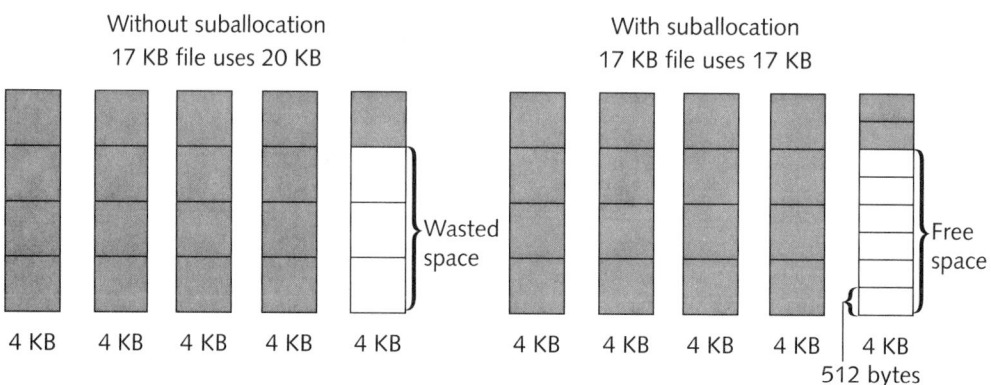

Figure 9-2   Block suballocation

Block suballocation is enabled by default when you install NetWare. To prevent block suballocation, you must deselect this option during a custom installation. Once block suballocation is activated on a volume, you can deactivate it only by reinstalling the server software (that is, NetWare).

NDS

NetWare Directory Services is a major development that Novell introduced with version 4.0. **NetWare Directory Services (NDS)** provides a system for managing multiple servers and their resources, including users, volumes, groups, profiles, printers, and so on. (In NetWare versions below 4.0, the Bindery contained this information.) The NDS model is similar to Active Directory in Windows 2000 Server. NDS treats every networked resource as a separate object with distinct properties. Each object can then be centrally managed from a single interface.

To understand how NetWare 4.x and 5.x work, you must first understand NDS. This section introduces the principles of NDS. Although it sounds like a simple concept, NDS can have a very complex implementation in large organizations. For more details on designing and managing NDS structures, you should consult the NetWare documentation or purchase a book devoted to the topic of NetWare administration.

The NetWare installation process for the first server in a network generates the network's initial NDS. When adding servers or other resources to the network, you build upon this original NDS in a hierarchical fashion. Novell uses the analogy of a tree to describe this hierarchical layout. The **NDS tree** is the logical representation of resources in a NetWare enterprise. As with Active Directory's domain tree, the NDS tree is upside-down, with a single root at the top and multiple branches at the bottom, as shown Figure 9-3.

The NDS tree can have only one root, which is created during the first NetWare (4.x or higher) server installation on the network. Once created, the root cannot be moved, deleted, or renamed. Consequently, before you begin a NetWare 4.x or 5.x installation, you should meticulously plan your NDS structure and make sure that all decision makers in your Information Technology department agree on its naming convention.

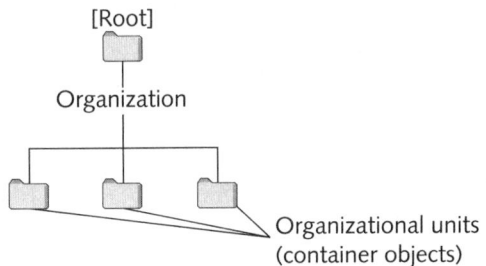

Figure 9-3 A simple NDS tree

The root leads to a hierarchical arrangement of branches. As in the Windows 2000 Server's Active Directory, these branches are called **container objects** (or **organizational units**) because their purpose is to logically subdivide the NDS tree and hold other objects that belong together.

Container objects may organize users and resources by geographical location, department, professional function, security authorization, or other criteria significant to the particular network. For example, if the root of the Sutkin Manufacturing Company's NDS tree is called "Sutkin," the container objects may be called "Maintenance," "Inventory," "Packing," "Shipping," "Information Services," "Accounting," and so on. On the other hand, if Sutkin Manufacturing is a small company with only a handful of users and other resources in the Maintenance, Inventory, Packing, and Shipping departments, these users and resources may be grouped in a larger branch called "Operations" and departments within the "Operations" container may be distinguished through the use of groups.

Figure 9-4 compares the various ways of grouping objects. For any organization, no single correct way to arrange an NDS tree usually exists. Instead, the organization of resources and container objects is a decision that network administrators must plan carefully.

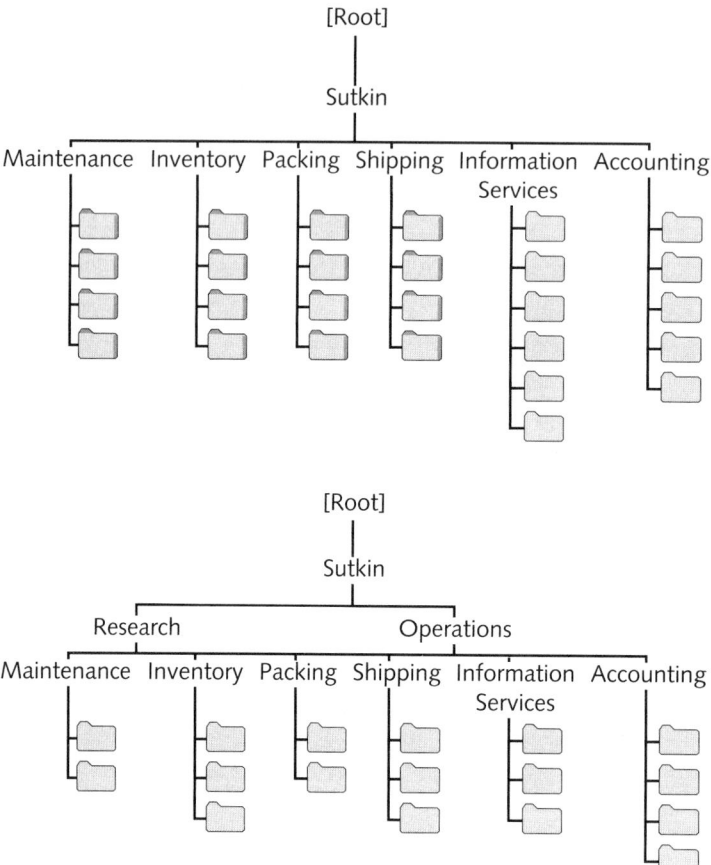

Figure 9-4   Two ways of grouping objects in an NDS tree

Moving away from the root of the tree, branch objects lead to either more branch objects or leaf objects. As you learned in Chapter 8, a leaf object is an object in the directory tree that does not contain other objects. For example, a print queue is a leaf object because it handles only the printer queue. A user is a leaf object because it does not contain or manage any objects other than the network user it represents. Several kinds of leaf objects exist. You will typically deal with user-related leaf objects such as users, groups, profiles, templates, and aliases or printer-related objects such as printers, queues, and print servers. Some Novell packages, such as ManageWise or ZenWorks, introduce other kinds of leaf objects into the tree. Nevertheless, all Novell products integrate with the NDS structure to allow easy, centralized administration. Figure 9-5 depicts a more complex NDS tree with several branch and leaf objects. (Compared to a real-world NDS tree, this example is still greatly simplified.)

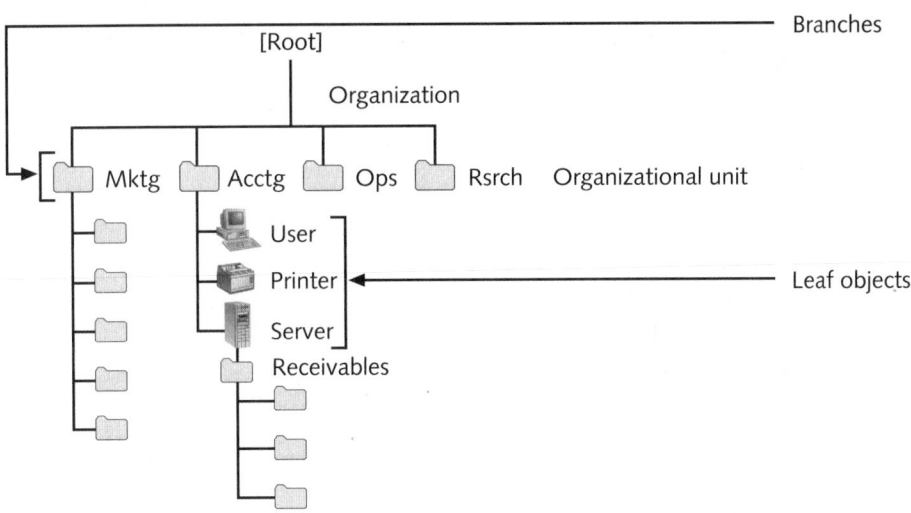

Figure 9-5   A more complex NDS tree

Each object in an NDS tree has a **context** that indicates where that object belongs in the tree. A context consists of an object's organizational unit names, arranged from most specific to most general, plus the organization name. Periods separate the organizational unit names within the context. You can envision the context as a kind of roadmap for locating an object.

Contexts may be expressed in two ways: typeful and typeless. The **typeful** notation is a relatively lengthy way of expressing context that includes identifiers for the organization and organizational units. For example, a user named Phil who works in the Receivables area of the Accounting ("Acctg") department of Sutkin Manufacturing in Figure 9-5 would have a typeful context of OU=Receivables.OU=Acctg.O=Sutkin. In this typeful context "OU" stands for "organizational unit" (another name for a container) and "O" stands for "organization" (which is associated with the root of your tree). A **typeless** notation eliminates the "OU" and "O" designations. In the preceding example, Phil's typeless context would be Receivables.Acctg.Sutkin. Both the typeful and the typeless contexts indicate that Phil is a member of the Receivables organizational unit, which is located in the Acctg organizational unit, which is part of the Sutkin organization.

In a large corporation with a complex NDS tree, a user's context can quickly become very long. Users do not always have to know or provide their context, however. Instead, the workstation support group or network administrator can configure users' client software to assume by default the context and the organization to which each user belongs. Users can then log on to their organizations with only a user name. In the preceding example, a user named Phil with the typeful context of OU=Receivables.OU=Acctg.O=Sutkin would simply type "phil" when prompted for his user ID.

Another significant similarity between Active Directory and NDS is the use of the word schema to refer to the set of objects (such as user or printer) and their attributes in an NDS tree. The simplest schema is the one that ships with NDS. A network administrator can extend the schema to include additional object classes and attributes. For example, you may want to add a user's fax number as an optional attribute. Think of the word *schematic* as it applies to a building design. An architect's schematic drawing might guide him in choosing which materials should be used for walls and doors, how a building should be positioned on a site, where gas and electrical conduits may be installed, and how old structures can be integrated with new additions. Similarly, the NDS schema serves as a reference for the logical design of your network.

 Do not confuse NDS with the NetWare file system. The two are completely different entities. The file system pertains to the physical servers and the arrangement and maintenance of the data. NDS refers to the logical organization of servers and resources across an enterprise-wide network.

The NetWare operating system stores NDS information in a database format and distributes the information over several volumes. In larger organizations, NDS information may be distributed over several servers for two reasons: to accommodate its size and ensure its integrity. Conceptually, NDS does not appear to be tied to the server's hard disk. For example, the server does not have a big database file called "NDS.DB" that holds all of the tree and object information. In fact, NetWare keeps NDS information in hidden storage areas across (usually multiple) servers.

Typically, only network administrators have rights that allow them to modify the NDS tree. NDS management can be performed only through NetWare resource management tools, such as the NetWare Administrator utility. The **NetWare Administrator utility (NWAdmin)** is a graphical NDS management interface that can be launched from a Windows 9x or Windows 2000 workstation. Figure 9-6 shows an example of an NWAdmin screen with NDS objects. You will learn more about managing objects through NWAdmin later in this chapter.

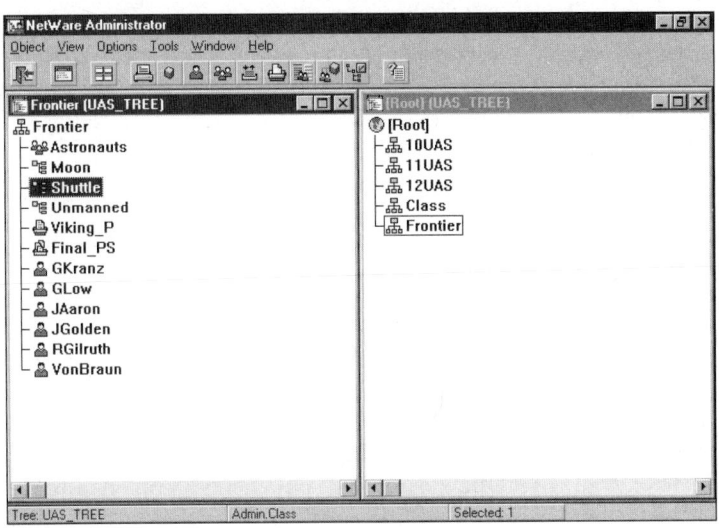

Figure 9-6   An NWAdmin interface

9

INSTALLING AND CONFIGURING A NETWARE SERVER

As with any major installation, you should first draw up a plan before beginning to install NetWare. Before you insert the NetWare CD into your CD-ROM drive, you should consider many factors, including the organization's structure, function of the server, server hardware, applications, number of users, LAN architecture, and optional services (such as Web hosting). As you learned in the discussion of Windows 2000 Server in Chapter 8, once you have installed and configured the network operating system, changing its configuration may prove difficult and perhaps cause service disruptions for users. This section provides an overview of the decisions you need to make when installing and configuring your NetWare server.

Planning for Installation

The importance of planning for installation cannot be overemphasized. Poor planning results in more work for the installer, potential down time for users, and headaches for whomever supports the server after installation. The following list summarizes the critical preinstallation decisions you should make. As you will see, the list is very similar to the decisions that you must make before installing Windows 2000 Server; where Windows 2000 deals in Active Directory, NetWare focuses on the NDS tree.

- *Where does the server fit in the NDS tree?* The place occupied by the server in your network's NDS tree (its context) will depend largely on its function. If this function is merely to allow a group of students to print to a classroom printer, then the server might belong to a small organizational unit for that classroom. If the server will provide network access for all of the math instructors, it may belong in the Math container of your tree. If the server will provide mail services to the entire company, it may have its own organizational unit off the root of the tree called Mail. Clearly, you should develop your organization's tree and its policies for container and leaf objects before you begin installation. The server's place in the NDS tree will affect how easily it can be accessed and managed. Once you have established the server's context, you cannot change it.

- *What name will the server have?* Choose a practical, descriptive name that distinguishes the server from all other servers. You might use geographical server names, such as Boston or Buffalo. Alternatively, you might name servers according to their function, such as Marketing or Research. Bear in mind that the server name can (and usually will) differ from its NDS container's name. For example, the high school Math department server in a school system's NDS structure might be called "MATH_DEPT," but it might belong to the "Math" organizational unit, which might in turn belong to a larger organizational unit called "HS" under the school system's root.

- *How many and what kinds of network adapter cards will the server use?* Before you begin installing NetWare, you should have driver and diagnostics disks on hand for the server's NICs. The NetWare installation process will attempt to find your NIC's driver in its own collection of software, but it may not always be successful in this quest. You should therefore be prepared to supply the NIC software, and the NIC's IRQ, shared memory address, and I/O base address before beginning the server installation.

- *What protocols and network services should the server use?* You need to know which protocols your network requires. As you will recall from Chapter 3, more networks are moving toward TCP/IP-based transmission because this family of protocols is flexible, reliable, and widely supported. If your NetWare server will run Web services or connect to UNIX systems, for example, you must install IP. NetWare 4.x provides support for TCP/IP, whereas NetWare 5.x runs TCP/IP natively. By default, the NetWare 5.x installation process selects IP as a protocol that the server will support.

- *What kind of disk controllers does my server have?* NetWare's installation program will attempt to detect what kind of hard disk and CD-ROM drive your server possesses. If the program can correctly identify the hardware, it will install the drivers. Otherwise, it will prompt you to choose drivers from a list or install a driver from a disk. Either way, you should know what kind of disk controllers your server has (you can find this information in the server's hardware specifications). Note that the NetWare installation process does not always choose the right controller by default. NetWare can support SCSI, IDE, and ESDI hard disk controllers.

- *How many, how large, and what kind of volumes will the server require?* NetWare's installation program will ask you to identify the size, number, and names of the server volumes. Initially, the program assigns all free space on the hard disk to its default volume, SYS. To add volumes, you must modify the size of SYS (by subtracting the size of the other volumes you intend to create from SYS's current size).

- *What additional services will the server support?* You may choose to perform a custom or simple installation of NetWare, depending on the services and applications that your server will run. In a **simple installation**, the most popular installation options are chosen for you. This type of installation takes place more rapidly than a **custom installation**, which allows you to determine which services and programs should be installed, among other things. The first time you install a NetWare server (ideally, in a test environment), you will probably want to choose a simple setup to see how the installation process works. If you know the exact requirements for your environment and you feel comfortable with the NetWare installation process, you may choose to perform a custom installation. In that case, a list of additional services to install will appear near the end of the installation process. These services include support for Web and FTP hosting, backup utilities, OS/2 utilities, and TCP/IP address management. If you neglect to install a service during this process, you can always install it later.

- *What kind of license do I have?* When you purchased the NetWare operating system, you chose a licensing option for your organization. During the installation of the operating system, you will be prompted for the license diskette (or file, if you've copied it to the server's hard disk) that came with your NetWare software. NetWare licenses vary chiefly in terms of how many concurrent (simultaneously connected) users are supported by the server.

- *How can I remember all of this information?* Once you have made these decisions, you should create a server installation form and keep it with you during installation. Appendix C offers an example of such a form.

The preceding list highlights only the most significant installation options. You should also be prepared to read and accept the license agreement, identify your time zone, and specify an administrator account ID and password.

The Installation Process

After you have planned your installation, you can actually perform it. NetWare can be installed from a CD (the most popular method), floppy disks (not recommended), or another server on the network; the latter process is called an "over-the-wire" installation because the files are copied over the network's wiring. In this section, you can follow the steps to carry out a simple standalone NetWare 5.1 server installation performed from a CD-ROM. For simplicity's sake, this example uses the default installation options. You should perform a NetWare installation on a server that has a new installation of DOS version 6.22 or higher (do not attempt this installation from a DOS prompt on a server running a Windows operating system or from the DOS version that comes with Windows).

To perform a simple NetWare 5.1 installation:

1. Boot your server with a DOS system floppy diskette.

2. At the command prompt type **FDISK** to start the disk formatting utility. Follow the FDISK instructions to create a DOS partition that is at least 100 MB in size. Be sure to mark the partition Active (in other words, designate the partition as the one from which the server will boot).

3. After creating the DOS partition and making it active, exit the FDISK utility and restart the server (leaving the DOS system diskette in the floppy disk drive).

4. At the command prompt, type **FORMAT C:/S** to format the DOS partition with system files.

5. Install the necessary CD-ROM drivers to the DOS partition you have just created. Remove the DOS floppy diskette from the floppy disk drive and restart your computer.

6. Insert the NetWare 5.1 CD-ROM and change your working directory to the CD-ROM drive letter (typically, this is D: or E:).

7. At the CD-ROM command prompt, type **INSTALL**.

8. The NetWare Installation program starts, displaying a license agreement screen. Read the license agreement, then press **F10** to continue.

9. Press **Enter** to continue.

10. The next NetWare Installation screen prompts you to select a type of installation: upgrade or new server. For the purposes of this exercise, use the Enter key to select **New server** (if it is not already selected), accept the default installation of **\NWSERVER**, and then press **Tab** to move to the text menu window. Make sure the **Continue** option is highlighted in the text menu and press **Enter** to continue. The Server Settings screen appears.

11. The Server Settings screen contains NDS, Server ID, and Server boot options. Verify that NDS 8 is selected in the NDS version field. NDS 8 enables NetWare 5.1 to take advantage of new Web product support. The Server ID is a randomly generated 8-digit hexadecimal number unique to the server. Leave the Server ID as is. The Load server at reboot option allows you to choose whether the NetWare 5.1 software will load automatically when the server is restarted. Leave this option at its default, also.

12. Select **Continue** and press **Enter**. The Regional Settings screen appears.

13. Select **Continue** and press **Enter** to accept the default Country, Keyboard, and Code options in the Regional Settings screen. The Display and Mouse settings screen appears.

14. At the Display and Mouse settings screen, modify display or mouse settings as necessary, make sure the **Continue** option is highlighted, then press **Enter** to continue.

15. The NetWare installation program copies initial files to your server's hard disk. Next it attempts to identify the server's storage adapters, and present you with a screen that identifies drivers for the Platform Support Module, HotPlug Support Module, and Storage adapters. Make sure the device driver identified for the storage adapter matches your computer's storage adapter type. If it does not, modify the storage adapter device driver. When you have identified the correct storage adapter device driver, select **Continue** and press **Enter**.

16. The NetWare installation program attempts to identify the network adapter driver and displays the updated list of device drivers that it has selected for storage devices, network boards, and NetWare loadable modules. Make sure the drivers listed match your server's device types, then highlight **Continue** and press **Enter** to proceed to the next installation step.

17. After checking for free space on your server's hard disk, the NetWare installation program displays the Create a NetWare partition and volume SYS screen. By default, all free space on the NetWare partition is assigned to the SYS volume. For the purposes of this exercise, highlight **Continue** and press **Enter** to accept this default and continue. (In a more realistic situation you would reduce the default size of the SYS volume and allow free space to later create additional volumes on your server.)

18. The NetWare installation program begins copying files to the SYS volume. When it finishes copying, it launches a GUI interface that replaces the text-based menu screens for the remainder of the NetWare 5.1 installation process. The first GUI screen that appears is the Server Properties dialog box.

19. Enter the server name CLASS_TEST in the Server Name text box, then click **Next** to continue. The Configure File System dialog box appears.

20. Click **Advanced** to view the File System dialog box. Click **Mount Volumes** to make the volumes accessible to the server at this time, and then click **Next** to return to the Configure File System dialog box.

21. For the purposes of this exercise, click **Next** to accept the default of a single SYS volume on the server. The Protocols dialog box appears.

22. The Protocols dialog box allows you to specify and configure protocols for each network adapter in your server. Select the network adapter in the Network Boards list, then click in the **IP** check box to run the IP protocol on this network adapter.

23. Type an IP address of **198.76.54.21** in the IP Address text boxes. If necessary, type **255.255.255.0** in the Subnet Mask text boxes. Click **Next** to continue. The Domain Name Service dialog box appears.

9

24. The Domain Name Service dialog box contains text boxes to identify this server's host and domain name, as well as the IP address of the DNS server it will use to resolve its name to its IP address. Since this is a standalone server, leave the text boxes on this screen blank, then click **Next** to continue.

25. A message warning you that no host name or domain name has been specified appears. Click **OK** to respond to the warning message and continue.

26. The Time Zone dialog box appears. Choose your time zone and click **Next** to continue.

27. The NDS Install dialog box appears, asking whether you want to upgrade an existing NDS tree or create a new NDS tree. Click on the **New NDS Tree** option and click **Next**. The NDS Install dialog box appears.

28. Type **Global_Corp** in the Tree Name text box. Type **Class** in the Context for Server Object text box. If necessary, type **Admin** in the Admin Name text box. If it isn't automatically filled in, type **O=Class** in the Admin Context text box. Finally, type **myglo889** in the Password text box and retype the password in the Retype Password text box.

29. Click **Next** to install NDS and display a summary window containing the NDS context information. Record the information for later reference, then click **Next** to continue. The Licenses dialog box appears.

30. Insert the NetWare 5.1 license diskette that came with your NetWare 5.1 software into your server's floppy disk drive. Use the **Browse** button to locate the NLF license file in the floppy diskette's \license folder. Click **OK** to accept and install this license file.

31. After the license file is installed, click **Next** to display the Installation Options dialog box.

32. In the Installation Options dialog box, click the **Custom** option, then click **Next** to continue. The Components dialog box appears.

33. In the Components dialog box, click the check boxes next to **NetWare Enterprise Web Server** and **NetWare FTP Server** options to deselect these components. Verify that only **Novell Distributed Print Services (NDPS)** is selected, then click **Next** to continue.

34. The Novell Certificate Server 2.0 Objects dialog box appears. The purpose of the Novell Certificate Server is to enable support for secure data transmission by NetWare Internet services components (you will learn more about digital certificates in Chapter 15). Click **Next** to accept the default certificate server settings, then click **OK** to accept the Organizational Certificate of Authority warning message.

35. A Summary dialog box appears, listing the selected NetWare 5.1 products that will be installed, along with the amount of hard disk space each requires.

Verify that the listed information is correct, and then click **Finish** to initiate the main NetWare 5.1 file copy process.

36. Once the NetWare 5.1 software has been copied to the server, a Completion window appears. Click **Yes** to complete the installation and restart the server.

> In actual practice, your NetWare installation will probably involve more decisions (particularly with regard to volume sizes and names, NDS context, and NetWare services to install) than indicated in this example. You may want to experiment with a simple installation such as this one, however, before you perform installations on your working servers.

After performing a NetWare 5.x installation and restarting the machine, your server should be functional. If you chose the simple installation, the TCP/IP protocol will be installed and bound to your NIC. To install other protocols at a later date, you must run a configuration utility from the console called inetcfg. Modifying the server's network properties through these commands is beyond the scope of this chapter. If you plan to become a NetWare expert, however, you should study the capabilities of the nwconfig utility.

After you have installed a NetWare server, verify that you can log on to that server as administrator from a Windows 2000 or Windows 9x workstation using the Novell Client for NetWare. If this effort fails, you may need to use the configuration commands to verify that the server has network connectivity.

By default, the NetWare installation process creates the NDS tree (if one didn't previously exist), a SYS volume, an administrator user called Admin who has supervisory rights to all objects in the NDS tree and all files in the file system, and a group called [Public] that has Browse rights to view all objects in the NDS tree.

Using the NetWare Administrator Utility (NWAdmin)

To make your server functional, you will need to add users and other objects to the NDS tree. After adding objects, you may want to modify their properties or even delete them. This section introduces an important tool in NetWare server management, the NetWare Administrator utility (NWAdmin). As explained earlier in this chapter, NWAdmin is a graphical interface that runs from a Windows workstation and enables network administrators to manage NDS objects. Through the use of drop-down menus and toolbars, it simplifies the process of viewing, creating, changing, and deleting objects.

The best way to learn about NWAdmin is to experiment with it on a test server. You will have such an opportunity in the following exercise and in a Hands-on Project at the end of this chapter.

To create objects in the NDS tree:

1. To manage the NDS tree through NWAdmin, you must have administrator rights. Log on to your NetWare 4.x or 5.x server from a Windows workstation as an administrator.

2. Launch the following executable file from your server's SYS volume:
PUBLIC\WIN32\NWADMN32.EXE. The NetWare Administrator
(NWAdmin) window opens, as shown in Figure 9-7.

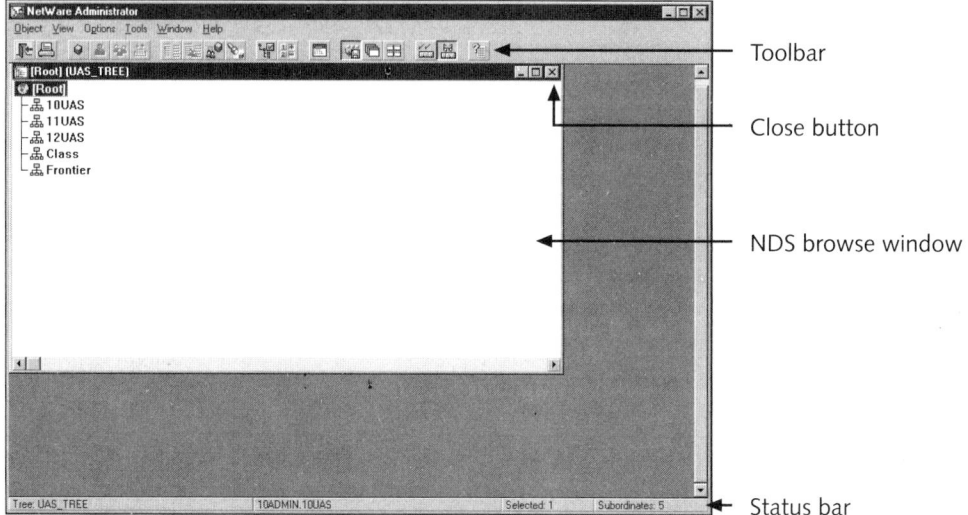

Figure 9-7   NetWare Administrator window

3. If the NWAdmin screen does not display your NDS tree by default, you can
specify the tree by choosing **View** on the menu bar, and then choosing **Set
Context**. Enter **[Root]** in the context field, and then click **OK**.

4. Double-click the root object, if necessary, to reveal your server's NDS tree,
with organizational objects underneath the root and leaf objects (if they exist)
underneath the organizational (container) objects. Proceed through the following steps to add objects to your NDS tree.

5. To create an organization, right-click the root object, then choose **Create**.

6. A list of objects appears. Scroll down the list, highlight **Organization**, and
then click **OK**.

7. The Organization dialog box opens. Enter your Organization name, and then
click **Create**. The newly created Organization appears in the NDS tree.

8. To create an object inside the Organization, right-click the Organization,
then choose **Create** from the menu that appears.

9. The program displays a list of objects that you can choose to create within
the Organization. Notice how many more options appear in this list than
were shown in the list of objects you could create from the Root.

10. To create an Organizational Unit beneath your Organization, select the Organizational Unit object, then click **OK**. The Create Organizational Unit dialog box opens.

11. Enter the name of the Organizational Unit, and then click **Create**. To see the name of the newly created Organizational Unit in the NDS tree, double-click the Organization object.

12. To create a user belonging to your Organizational Unit, right-click the Organizational Unit, then choose **Create** from the menu. The program displays a list of objects you can choose to create within the Organizational Unit.

13. Press **U** to select the User object in the list of objects you can create.

14. Press **Enter** to create a User object.

15. The Create User dialog box appears, as shown in Figure 9-8. You are prompted to enter the user's ID and last name. These two fields are the only fields you must complete to create a user. Often, you will want to choose additional options, such as granting a home directory to the user or assigning a template to the user. Click **create** after entering the user's ID and last name.

9

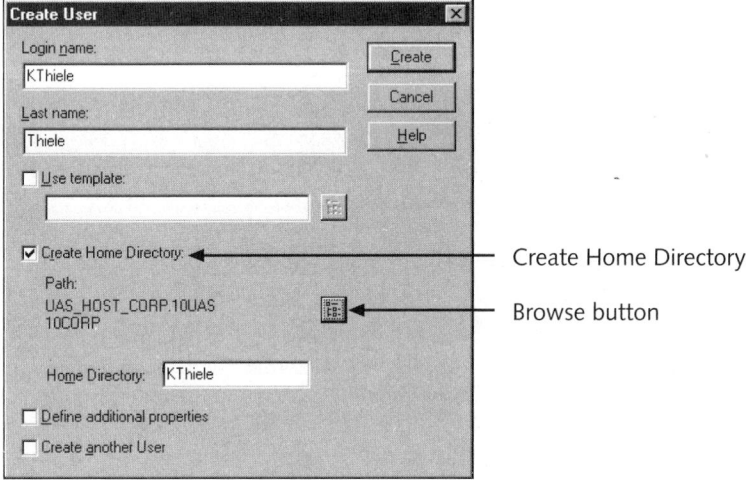

Figure 9-8   Create User dialog box

If you choose to establish a user's home directory when you create the user ID, that user will have all rights to his or her home directory by default. As a result, you do not have to assign Read, Write, Erase, or other rights for the user's home directory later. If you do not create a user's home directory when you create the user ID, and you later decide to grant a home directory to the user, you must manually assign rights before the user can save, change, or delete files in his or her home directory.

After you have created NDS objects, you may want to change their properties. For example, if one of your staff members changes her last name, you will want to change the last name property within her User object. To view or change the properties of any leaf object (such as a printer, user, template, or group), you can right-click the object in the tree, then choose Details from the menu that appears.

To modify the properties of a User object through NWAdmin:

1. Right-click the User object whose properties you want to modify, then choose **Details** from the menu that appears. Alternatively, you can double-click the User object to view its Properties dialog box.

2. The object's Properties dialog box appears. The right side of the properties dialog box contains a number of properties buttons. Click the button whose properties you want to change. For example, if you want to modify the user's password, click the **Password Restrictions** button. The Password Restrictions window appears, as shown in Figure 9-9.

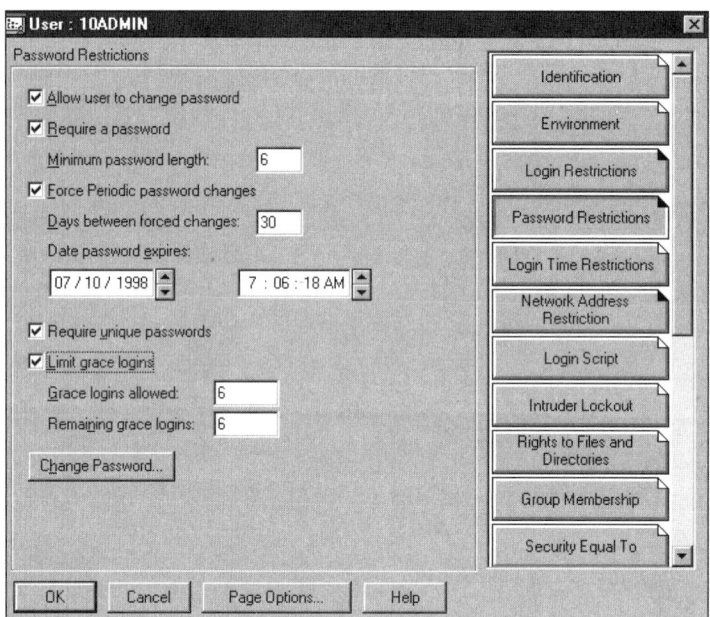

Figure 9-9   Password Restrictions dialog box

3. Change the properties as instructed by the Properties dialog box. For example, in the Password Restrictions window, you may choose to force users to change their passwords upon logging in, enforce a minimum length for passwords, or change a user's password.

To delete an NDS object through NWAdmin:

1 Right-click the object, then click **Delete** on the shortcut menu.

2. NWAdmin asks whether you really want to delete the object. Click **Yes** to confirm the deletion.

NWAdmin will not allow you to delete an object that contains leaf objects. If you want to delete a container object, you must delete its subordinate objects first. To do so, highlight the first object in the container to be deleted, hold down the Shift key, and then click the last object to be deleted. You should see the objects between the first and the last object highlighted. Press the Delete key. NWAdmin will ask you to confirm that you want to delete the group of objects.

The operations described in this section cover only a small fraction of NWAdmin's capabilities. In real-world day-to-day network operations, you will find that your most frequent use of NWAdmin will consist of viewing, modifying, and creating objects. In addition to carrying out these operations, you may manage other Novell programs, such as NetWare Distributed Printing Services, GroupWise, or ZenWorks from NWAdmin. You may also manage Windows 2000 resources if Windows 2000 servers are integrated into your NDS tree. Using NWAdmin, you can search for objects, move objects from one container to another, or assign templates or profiles to objects. In short, NWAdmin is your link to managing your NDS tree.

INTERNETWORKING WITH OTHER OPERATING SYSTEMS

In Chapter 8, you learned that both Novell and Microsoft have made great strides in enabling their network operating systems to interact. Microsoft has devised one solution (Gateway Services for NetWare), and Novell has created another, called **NDS eDirectory** for Windows NT/2000. The NDS eDirectory works with the NetWare 5.x operating systems and Windows NT or 2000 servers to enable Windows domains to appear as container objects in NWAdmin. In Novell's terminology, NDS eDirectory extends the schema to include Windows NT or 2000 resources. Windows NT and 2000 servers appear as server objects, and groups and users from Windows domains appear as NDS group and user objects, respectively. With NDS eDirectory enabled, users who require services from both Windows 2000 and NetWare servers can simply log on to the NDS tree, rather than logging on to both types of servers.

NDS eDirectory provides a simple solution to a network administrator's challenge of integrating Windows 2000 and NetWare. On Windows 2000 servers, an NDS eDirectory client and service must be installed and bound to the network cards. Once this tool is installed, the Windows 2000 server appears as a container object in the NetWare NDS tree when it connects to the network. Once the Windows 2000 server is an NDS object, it can be managed centrally through the NetWare Administrator utility. This ability makes the network administrator's job of managing mixed server environments much easier.

Realistically, you would probably use NDS eDirectory in a networking environment dominated by NetWare products or in an environment in which the complex structure of servers, users, locations, and so on demands the comprehensive management capabilities of NWAdmin. If most of your servers run Windows 2000 Server, using Microsoft's Gateway Services for NetWare, as described in Chapter 8, may make more sense.

On the client side, Novell provides client software specifically designed for Windows 2000, Windows NT, Windows 9x, OS/2, Macintosh, and UNIX clients. These packages come at no extra cost with the NetWare 4.x and 5.0 operating systems, or they can be downloaded from Novell's Web site.

CHAPTER SUMMARY

❑ Currently, several versions of NetWare are available. NetWare 3.x includes versions 3.1 through 3.2. Although these versions were introduced in the early 1990s, many have not been replaced with newer versions—a testament to their high reliability. Novell introduced NetWare 4.x in the mid-1990s. NetWare 4.x is more user-friendly and provides much better support for enterprise-wide networks containing multiple servers than NetWare 3.x.

❑ In 1998, Novell released version 5.0 of NetWare, which not only increases the extent and ease of network management, but also provides a network operating system based on the IP protocol. It uses the programming language Java for many of its interfaces and services. NetWare 5.x also offers better printer and file system administration than version 4.x does.

❑ Both NetWare 4.1 and 5.x use Novell Directory Services (NDS) to organize users, groups, servers, and other network resources. Both versions provide a graphical interface for managing network resources. In addition, both support integration with other network operating systems, Web services, multiple protocols, asset management, migration utilities, and software distribution.

❑ Novell provides extensive online support from its support Web site. The company also provides enhanced technical support to Certified NetWare Engineers (CNEs) through CDs and discounted calls to its help desk. In addition, a number of third-party discussion groups on the Web focus on NetWare products.

❑ NetWare is optimal for file and print sharing. It can run multiple services simultaneously and use multiple processors. Its modularity allows the network administrator to isolate some processes from others or change the priority of critical applications. NetWare does not require you to restart the server when you change its configurations, keeping service interruptions brief.

❑ NetWare offers native interoperability solutions for Macintosh-, DOS-, Windows-, OS/2-, and UNIX-based systems.

❑ NetWare may not suit every organization. If your organization depends heavily on enterprise-wide Microsoft solutions you may want to forego a NetWare purchase. If your technical staff prefers or demands a simple graphical interface, Windows 2000 Server may be a better choice. Although NetWare offers graphical interfaces for both management and console functions, its interfaces are less responsive or intuitive than Microsoft's graphical interfaces.

❑ At a minimum, your NetWare 5.x server should contain a Pentium processor, at least 64 MB RAM, a CD-ROM drive, a floppy disk drive, a hard disk with a DOS partition larger than 50 MB and a NetWare partition larger than 300 MB, a pointing device, and a NIC. In reality, your server will probably require more RAM and hard disk space than the minimum configuration suggested.

❑ To determine your NetWare server's requirements, you will want to consider the number of NetWare loadable modules (NLMs) used by each service. NLMs are routines that enable the server to run programs and services ranging from protocol support to Web publishing. Each NLM consumes some of the server's memory and processor resources (at least temporarily).

❑ You can add components to your NetWare server to enhance its fault tolerance and performance. The most popular additional components include multiple processors, more RAM, multiple NICs, fault-tolerant hard disks, a backup drive, and an uninterruptible power supply.

❑ In versions 5.x and higher, NetWare supports the use of as many as 32 processors on one server and uses symmetric multiprocessing, in which tasks are equally distributed among the processors.

❑ Whereas NetWare 4.x can use only physical memory, NetWare 5.x can use both virtual memory and physical memory.

❑ Like Windows 2000, NetWare uses 32-bit addressing to provide quick access to the physical memory. NetWare also allows you to run services in a separate memory area from the operating system, which prevents one rogue routine from taking the server down. Assigning a separate memory area to a service is known as running the service in protected mode. In this mode, the service and its supporting routines cannot harm critical server processes.

❑ Novell allows network administrators to adjust the server's use of memory in a number of ways. This flexibility can be both a blessing and a curse. If you change a setting in the wrong direction you can restrict the server's ability to send or transmit data efficiently. On the other hand, every environment will require some fine-tuning to maximize the use of memory and every organization will have its own memory needs.

❑ At the heart of NetWare lies the kernel, or the core of the operating system. NetWare's 32-bit kernel is responsible for overseeing all critical server processes. The program SERVER.EXE runs the kernel from a server's DOS partition. Typically, a server will start from an AUTOEXEC.BAT file that launches SERVER.EXE; from that point forward, NetWare controls the machine's operations.

❑ The network administrator's primary interface to a NetWare server is the server console. Unlike Windows 2000, the NetWare server interface is not entirely graphical. NetWare 4.x uses only text-based server menus at the console. NetWare 5.x, allows you to access commands through either a text-based or graphical menu system. The graphical interface in NetWare 5.x is called ConsoleOne.

❑ Hundreds of NLMs are available for the NetWare operating system. In fact, developers can write their own NLMs for special purposes because Novell shares its operating system code. Most of the NLMs you'll ever need, however, will come with your server software or the additional utilities you install.

❑ NetWare's high-performance file system supports DOS, Macintosh, UNIX, OS/2, and Windows. Although DOS filenames are supported by default, you must load the proper NLMs on the server to gain support for other filenames. Once you have installed the necessary modules, Macintosh, Windows, UNIX, or OS/2 clients can read from the server as if the server were speaking their language. Because NetWare uses modules—rather than file systems—to support this type of access, file/directory size limitations and performance do not vary between NetWare volumes or servers.

❑ Like Windows 2000, NetWare uses volumes as the basis for organizing files and directories on the server. When you install NetWare, a volume called SYS is created automatically. At the time of installation, you may also choose to create additional volumes, such as DATA (for user data) or APPS (for shared applications).

❑ You should design a file system hierarchy that meets your performance, security, growth, and data sharing goals. Keep volume names short, simple, and descriptive. Plan carefully before establishing a server's volume and directory structure—once established, this structure is very difficult to change. If you are installing a NetWare network from scratch, you should consult resources for guidance on planning the volume and directory structure for your network.

❑ NetWare 4.x and 5.x both support file compression. Novell's compression is performed on a file-by-file basis, and the compression and decompression operations are transparent to the user. In both NetWare 4.x and NetWare 5.x, file compression is enabled by default during installation of the operating system.

❑ Block suballocation is a technique employed by NetWare for using hard disk space more efficiently. It enables files that don't fit neatly into a whole number of blocks to take up fractions of blocks, leaving the remaining fractions free for use by other data.

❑ A major development that Novell introduced with version 4.0 is NetWare Directory Services (NDS). NDS is a system of managing multiple servers and their resources, including users, volumes, groups, profiles, and printers. The NDS model is similar to Active Directory Windows 2000. In NDS, every resource is treated as a separate object with distinct properties. All objects can be centrally managed from a single interface.

❏ The NetWare installation process for the first server in a network generates the network's initial NDS. When adding subsequent servers or other resources to the network, you build upon this original NDS in a hierarchical fashion.

❏ Novell uses the analogy of a tree when describing this hierarchical layout. The NDS tree is upside-down, with a single root at the top and the leaves at the bottom. The root is created during the first NetWare (4.x or higher) server installation on the network. Once created, the root cannot be moved, deleted, or renamed.

❏ In the hierarchical NDS structure, the root leads to branches. These branches are called container objects (or organizational units) because their primary purpose is to logically subdivide and hold other objects that belong together, thus simplifying rights assignments, group login scripts, and so on. Container objects may organize resources by geographical location, department, professional function, security authorization, or other criteria significant to the particular network.

❏ Moving away from the root of the tree, branch objects lead to either more branch objects or leaf objects. A leaf object is an object in the NDS tree that does not contain other objects. Several kinds of leaf objects exist. You will typically deal with user-related leaf objects such as users, groups, profiles, templates, and aliases or printer-related objects such as printers, queues, and print servers. The place where an object belongs in an NDS tree is called its context.

❏ Novell uses the term schema to refer to the set of objects (such as user or printer) and their attributes in an NDS tree. The NDS schema serves as a reference for the logical design of your network, just as an architect's schematic drawing serves as the guiding reference for a building project.

❏ Before you insert the NetWare CD to begin installation of the operating system, you should consider many factors, including the organization's structure, function of the server, server hardware, applications, number of users, LAN architecture, and optional services (such as Web hosting). Once you have installed and configured the network operating system, changing its configuration may prove difficult and perhaps cause service disruptions for users.

❏ NWAdmin is a graphical interface that runs from a Windows workstation and enables network administrators to manage NDS objects. Through the use of drop-down menus and toolbars, NWAdmin simplifies the process of viewing, creating, changing, and deleting objects.

❏ The NDS eDirectory tool enables Windows 2000 domains to appear as container objects in NWAdmin. In Novell's terminology, NDS eDirectory extends the schema to include Windows 2000 resources. Windows 2000 servers appear as server objects, and groups and users from Windows 2000 domains appear as NDS group and user objects, respectively. With NDS eDirectory enabled, users who require services from both Windows 2000 and NetWare servers need to log in to only the NDS tree, rather than logging on to both types of servers.

9

KEY TERMS

block — A unit of disk space and the smallest unit of disk space that can be controlled by the NetWare system. Smaller blocks require more server memory.

block suballocation — A NetWare technique for using hard disk space more efficiently. Files that don't fit neatly into a whole number of blocks can take up fractions of blocks, leaving the remaining fractions free for use by other data.

caching — The process of saving frequently used data to an area of the physical memory so that it becomes more readily available for future requests. Caching accelerates the process of accessing the server because the operating system no longer needs to search for the requested data on the disk.

container objects — Logical subdivisions (or "branches") in NetWare's NDS tree that organize resources by geographical location, department, professional function, security authorization, or other criteria significant to the particular network.

context — A kind of road map for finding an object in an NDS tree. A context is made up of an object's organizational unit names, arranged from most specific to most general, plus the organization name. Periods separate the organizational unit names in context.

custom installation — A NetWare installation option that allows you to determine which services and programs are installed, among other things.

IntraNetWare — Another term for NetWare version 4.11, the version in which support for Internet services was first introduced.

kernel — The core of the NetWare operating system. NetWare's 32-bit kernel is responsible for overseeing all critical server processes. The program SERVER.EXE runs the kernel from a server's DOS partition.

Monitor — An NLM that enables the system administrator to view server parameters such as protocols, bindings, system resources, and loaded modules. In many cases, it also allows the system administrator to modify these parameters.

NDS eDirectory — Novell's integration tool for Windows 2000 networks. It works with the NetWare 5.x operating systems and Windows 2000 servers to enable the Windows 2000 domains to appear as container objects in NWAdmin.

NDS tree — A logical representation of how resources are grouped by NetWare in the enterprise.

NetWare 3.x — The group of NetWare versions that includes versions 3.0, 3.1, and 3.2.

NetWare 4.x — The group of NetWare versions that includes versions 4.0, 4.1, and 4.11.

NetWare 5.x—The group of NetWare versions that includes versions 5.0, 5.1, and 5.11.

NetWare Administrator utility (NWAdmin) — The graphical NetWare utility that allows administrators to manage objects in the NDS tree from a Windows workstation.

NetWare Directory Services (NDS) — A system of managing multiple servers and their resources, including users, volumes, groups, profiles, and printers. The NDS model is similar to Active Directory in Windows 2000. In NDS, every networked resource is treated as a separate object with distinct properties.

NetWare loadable modules (NLMs) — Routines that enable the server to run programs and services. Each NLM consumes some of the server's memory and processor resources (at least temporarily). The kernel requires many NLMs to run NetWare's core operating system.

object — A resource in NetWare's NDS tree. An object may represent a user, group, print queue, server volume, user template, mailbox, and so on. It may or may not contain other objects. All objects can be centrally managed in NDS.

organizational unit — See *container objects*.

protected mode — A manner in which NetWare runs services in a separate memory area from the operating system. Running services in protected mode prevents one rogue routine from taking the server down. As a result, the service and its supporting routines cannot harm critical server processes.

server console — The network administrator's primary interface to a NetWare server. Unlike Windows NT, the NetWare server interface is not entirely graphical. NetWare 4.x offers only text-based server menus at the console. NetWare 5.0 allows you to access commands through either a text-based or graphical menu system.

simple installation — A NetWare installation option in which the most popular installation options are chosen for you, and the installation takes less time than if you had chosen a custom installation.

typeful — A way of denoting an object's context in which the Organization and Organizational Unit designators ("O" and "OU," respectively) are included. For example, OU=Inv.OU=Ops.OU=Corp.O=Sutkin.

typeless — A way of denoting an object's context in which the Organization and Organizational Unit designators ("O" and "OU," respectively) are omitted. For example, Inv.Ops.Corp.Sutkin.

REVIEW QUESTIONS

1. Which versions of NetWare support TCP/IP services such as Web site hosting?
   a. 3.x and 4.x
   b. 4.0 and 4.1
   c. 4.x and 5.0
   d. 5.x and 6.x

2. Which version of NetWare contains many services coded in the Java programming language?
   a. 3.11
   b. 3.12
   c. 4.11
   d. 5.0

3. How many processors can a NetWare 5.0 server support?

   a. 4

   b. 16

   c. 32

   d. 64

4. What is the minimum amount of RAM required for a NetWare 5.0 server?

   a. 8 MB

   b. 16 MB

   c. 32 MB

   d. 64 MB

5. Why might you want to install more than the minimum RAM required by NetWare 5.x?

6. Where can you go to find out about known bugs in NetWare?

   a. *www.help.novell.com*

   b. *www.support.novell.com*

   c. *www.novell.com/bugs*

   d. *www.novell.com/help*

7. How might NLMs provide better stability on your NetWare server?

   a. They can be loaded and unloaded without taking down the server.

   b. They can use multiple processors.

   c. They can prevent users from tampering with system files.

   d. They can be integrated with intrusion detection devices to recognize security breaches.

8. Which version of NetWare supports the use of virtual memory?

   a. 2.x

   b. 3.x

   c. 4.x

   d. 5.x

9. What stands at the very top of the NDS tree?

   a. root

   b. branch

   c. leaf

   d. trunk

10. If you decide to change the name of your NDS tree after you've installed NetWare, you can rename it through a server console command. True or False?

11. What is the name of the graphical server manager utility in NetWare 5.x?

    a. ServMan

    b. ConsoleOne

    c. NetManager

    d. NetMon

12. Which DOS command loads the NetWare operating system kernel?

    a. INSTALL

    b. LOAD KERNEL

    c. KERNEL.EXE

    d. SERVER.EXE

13. Which of the following file systems does NetWare not support?

    a. DOS

    b. NTFS

    c. UNIX

    d. Macintosh

14. What is the name of the volume created automatically when you install NetWare 5.x?

    a. DATA

    b. VOL1

    c. VOL2

    d. SYS

15. File compression is enabled by default during a NetWare 5.x installation. True or False?

16. Which server resource does block suballocation conserve?

    a. memory

    b. CPU

    c. hard disk space

    d. power draw

17. What is the purpose of a container object in an NDS tree?

    a. to logically subdivide objects in the tree

    b. to integrate a Windows 2000 domain

    c. to logically separate users according to usage patterns

    d. to logically group subnets

9

18. A user is an example of what kind of NDS object?

    a. tree

    b. root

    c. leaf

    d. branch

19. If a user's login ID is "james" and the user belongs to the "marketing" organizational unit, which is in turn part of the "Corporate" organizational unit within the "ABC" Organization, what is this user's context?

    a. james.marketing.corporate.ABC

    b. ABC.corporate.marketing

    c. O_ABC_OU_marketing_OU_corporate_U_james

    d. marketing.corporate.ABC

20. Which utility allows you to manage NDS objects?

    a. NDSCON

    b. NDSadmin

    c. NWAdmin

    d. NWManager

21. List five questions that you should answer before beginning a NetWare server installation.

22. After right-clicking an object within NWAdmin, which option should you choose to modify that object's properties?

    a. Details

    b. Properties

    c. More

    d. Tools

23. In a typeful context notation, how is a user object's container designated?

    a. CXT

    b. CN

    c. OU

    d. O

24. Why might you want to create an administrator-equivalent ID that isn't called "Admin"?

    a. for easier management

    b. for security purposes

    c. to share administrative rights among many users

    d. to enable remote administration

25. After a simple NetWare 5.x installation, what rights does the default group called PUBLIC have to the NDS tree?

    a. Supervisory

    b. Browse, Modify, Erase

    c. Browse, Modify

    d. Browse

26. In NWAdmin, you can grant users rights to save files in a directory. True or False?

27. In NetWare version 5.x, which command should you use to access the protocol and NIC configuration utility?

    a. inetcfg

    b. ipconfig

    c. netconfig

    d. nwconfig

28. What must the network administrator do in NWAdmin before he or she can delete a container object?

    a. delete all objects within the container

    b. rename the container

    c. move the container to the trash

    d. ensure that the container is not part of another container

29. Which Novell utility enables Windows 2000 servers to appear as objects in the NDS tree?

    a. NetWare Windows Gateway Services

    b. Windows 2000–NDS Gateway

    c. NDS eDirectory

    d. NetWare for Windows 2000

30. If you use NetWare's Windows 2000 integration tool, what type of an object will a Windows 2000 domain appear as in an NDS tree?

    a. container

    b. group

    c. server

    d. organizational unit

9

HANDS-ON PROJECTS

Project 9-1

For this project you will need only a pencil and paper.

Before you install your first NetWare server, or even work with objects in an NDS tree, you should have a good understanding of the organization of the NDS tree. This exercise will help you to conceptualize an NDS tree.

1. A city school district has five elementary schools, two middle schools, and one high school running a NetWare 5.1 network. Give the schools and the organization (root of the NDS tree) names.

2. Draw an NDS tree in which each type of school (elementary, middle, and high school) belongs to a separate container object.

3. Add two teacher IDs to one of the containers you created. Based on the names you gave to your containers and tree, write the users' names in typeful context under the user ID you assigned them underneath the users you added (you may want to refer to the examples of typeful context names given in this chapter).

Project 9-2

In this exercise, you will experiment with using commands from the NetWare prompt. With such commands, you can check which modules are running on your server, load new modules, and unload already running modules. For this project you will need a working NetWare 5.x server installed with no more than the basic operating system.

1. At the NetWare server console prompt, type **modules**. (If your server's screen does not show the prompt, press the **Alt+Esc** key combination until the screen with the prompt appears.) How many modules are loaded on your NetWare server?

2. Sometimes you will want to know whether a module is running, but with hundreds of modules on your server, you may not remember the module's name. In this case, you can simply look for all modules beginning with the same letter. To demonstrate, type **modules c*** at the NetWare system prompt. On a piece of paper, write the names of the NLMs running on your server that begin with the letter "c."

3. To view information about how the server is running, type **monitor** at the console prompt. Write down your server's CPU utilization data.

4. Press the **Alt+Esc** key sequence. What happens?

5. At the console prompt, type **nwconfig**. Look at the menu options. Which one will allow you to install an additional NetWare service? Which one will let you manage the protocols bound to the server's NIC(s)?

6. Press the **Alt+Esc** key sequence. What happens?

7. Display the monitor screen again.

8. Highlight **Connections** in the Available Options window, then press **Enter**.

9. How many users are connected to the server?

10. Press **Esc** to return to the main menu.

11. Press **Esc** again, highlight **Yes**, then press **Enter** to confirm that you want to exit the monitor screen.

12. Use the **Alt+Esc** key sequence to return to the nwconfig screen.

13. Press **Esc**. When prompted, confirm that you want to exit the nwconfig screen.

14. At the console prompt, type **volumes**, then press **Enter**. How many volumes are installed on your server? What are their names? What kind of file systems does each volume support?

15. As a network administrator, you will sometimes need to take the server down (for example, to repair a faulty memory module or to install a new NIC). This process can be accomplished by one simple command. To demonstrate, type **down**, then press **Enter**. What kind of message appears? Click **Yes** to confirm that you want to down the server. What happens?

16. After all of the processes have stopped running, type **exit**, then press **Enter**. At the DOS prompt, type **dir**. Which directory do you suppose contains the NetWare operating system?

17. Look at the machine's AUTOEXEC.BAT file by typing **type c:\autoexec.bat** at the DOS prompt. What commands are in the server's AUTOEXEC.BAT?

18. To start the NetWare server again, type **server**. Alternatively, you can restart the machine.

Project 9-3

In this exercise, you will experiment with using NetWare Administrator to create users and modify their object properties. For this project, you will need a Windows 2000 Professional workstation connected to a NetWare 5.x network. Your workstation should have (at least) the IPX/SPX protocol and the NetWare client (version 2.2 or higher) installed. You will also need to know the network's administrator-equivalent user ID and password.

1. From your Windows 2000 workstation, log on to the server as your administrator-equivalent user.

2. Double-click the **My Network Places** icon.

3. Find your server in the My Network Places window and double-click it. (You may need to navigate through the Novell Connections to find the server.)

4. Double-click your server's SYS volume.

5. Open the **PUBLIC** folder on the SYS volume.

6. Open the **Win32** folder.

7. Double-click the **NWADMN32.EXE** file. The NetWare Administrator utility (NWAdmin) loads.

8. Using the steps provided in the chapter as a guide, add two organizational units in the organization of your NDS tree, one called **ACCT** and another called **MKTG**.

9. Add two users to the ACCT container: **Arnold Thomas** and **Faye Bernstein**, making their user IDs be a combination of the first letter of the first name plus the last name. Give the users home directories as you create them.

10. Add two users to the MKTG container: **Debby Chang** and **Matt Winzer**, following the same naming convention you used for the ACCT users. Do not assign these users home directories.

11. Double-click the **AThomas** user icon. The user's Properties dialog box should appear.

12. Make sure that the **Identification** button on the right side of the user's Properties dialog box is selected. Enter the user's first and last name, plus his department, phone number, and location.

13. Click the **Password Restrictions** button from the right side of the user's Properties dialog box. The user's password restrictions properties appear.

14. Click **Change Password**, then type **nw5user** in the new password text box. Type the password again to confirm it.

15. Click **OK** to save your changes. You will return to the user's Properties dialog box.

16. Click **OK** to accept your changes. The user's Properties dialog box will close.

17. In the NWAdmin menu, click **Object**, and then click **Exit**.

18. Click **Start**, click **Shut Down**, click **Log off administrator** from the drop-down list, then click **OK**.

19. Log on to the NetWare 5.x server as **AThomas**, using the password you specified in Step 14.

20. Follow steps 2 through 7 to launch NWAdmin.

21. Double-click the **MKTG** container to see its contents.

22. Right-click the user **DChang**, then choose **Delete** from the menu that appears. Click **Yes** to confirm that you want to delete this account.

23. What happens? Why?

24. Exit NWAdmin, then log on as your administrator ID again.

25. Try deleting the user called **DChang**.

26. What happens? Why?

27. Close NWAdmin, then log on as **FBernstein**.

28. What kind of password prompt do you receive? Why?

29. Using Network Neighborhood, open the SYS volume of your NetWare server.

30. Double-click the **Users** folder.

31. What do you see? Why?

CASE PROJECTS

1. An office furniture manufacturer called Advanced Ergonomics Solutions (AES) asks you to help the company design a new network. The network managers plan to throw out the obsolete ARCNet system they have used for eight years and install new NetWare 5.1 servers. They do not know how many servers they need or how to organize the servers, users, and groups. AES has two offices in town. The corporate headquarters houses 100 users, including 20 users in Marketing, 20 users in Operations, 40 users in Research, and 20 users in Customer Service. The users in Research save confidential data that no one else in the company is allowed to see. You've been informed that the company plans to increase the headcount at headquarters fourfold within the next 18 months. AES's other office in town is located at a warehouse and includes only 10 shift workers. What recommendations can you provide to the network managers at AES about organizing their network? How many servers will they need? (More than one solution is possible.) Sketch your proposed NDS solution in tree form, beginning with the root object.

2. The network managers at AES have implemented the system that you recommended and they are very pleased. The only problem is that the performance on the Research server seems sluggish compared with the performance of the other servers. The researchers use database files that are nearly 200 MB large to hold their test results, and these files load excruciatingly slowly. The network managers wonder whether they should buy faster servers or change the system somehow. Realizing that you accepted all of the defaults when you installed the NetWare 5.1 operating system, what kinds of things would you check to ensure that performance is at its peak on their servers? What other recommendations can you give?

3. Now the network managers at AES have called you regarding an unrelated problem. One of the company's vendors has developed a chair stress simulation program that can be accessed from a network. AES researchers and customer service personnel are eager to start using it, but the vendor insists that the simulation program can run only on a Windows 2000 server. AES let the vendor bring in a Windows 2000 server on a test basis, but now users who want to access the program must log on to the network twice: once for NetWare servers, and once for the Windows 2000 server. What can you tell the network managers about integration between these two systems that might make sense in their organization?

9

CHAPTER 10

NETWORKING WITH UNIX

After reading this chapter and completing the exercises, you will be able to:

➤ Describe the origins and history of the UNIX operating system

➤ Identify similarities and differences between popular implementations of UNIX

➤ Understand why you might choose a UNIX server for a corporate network

➤ Explain and execute basic UNIX commands

➤ Install Linux on an Intel-based PC

➤ Use Linux to add groups and users and to change file access permissions

➤ Explain how UNIX can be internetworked with other network operating systems

ON THE JOB

I started working with UNIX systems in the early 1980s. I learned UNIX (and the C programming language) at the same time I learned CP/M and MS-DOS, but I tended to prefer the UNIX systems. The most attractive part of UNIX was the incredible power of the command interpreter (or shell). With the UNIX shell, I could create complex new commands out of a few existing commands. I could accomplish things that the programmers of the original commands never imagined. The community of UNIX programmers enjoys thinking about and tinkering with the system, aiming to continually improve it.

The other significant facet of the UNIX community is the support that people offer to each other. It's nearly guaranteed that someone else has experienced the problem you're facing at any given time. A simple query posted to the Internet often receives an answer within a few hours. The low number of UNIX-based computer viruses illustrates this community's supportive attitude.

Networking with UNIX is simple and straightforward. The UNIX shell is a great place to experiment with networking ideas because it's easy to test those ideas by typing simple commands in the shell and watching the results. With the advent of Linux and other open UNIX-like operating systems, the opportunity to tinker with networking is now readily available to many more people. It's easy for me to understand why UNIX in general and Linux in particular have experienced such explosive growth in the past few years.

David Klann
Berbee Information Networks, Inc.

Along with Windows 2000 and Novell NetWare, UNIX is one of the most popular network operating systems. Although all three operating systems enable servers to provide resource sharing, UNIX differs in fundamental ways from NetWare and Windows 2000. Researchers at AT&T Bell Laboratories developed UNIX in 1969; thus it is much older than NetWare and Windows 2000. In fact, UNIX preceded and led to the development of the TCP/IP protocol suite in the early 1970s. For this reason, it is considered the parent of TCP/IP networking. Today, most Internet servers are computers running UNIX. Reflecting this operating system's efficiency and flexibility, the number of UNIX systems continues to grow.

Many local and wide area networks include servers that run UNIX. You should be familiar with UNIX so you can set up and maintain these networks. Mastering UNIX can be complicated because it is not controlled and distributed by a single software manufacturer. Instead, numerous vendors sell a number of varieties, such as Solaris from Sun Microsystems, AIX from IBM, and HP-UX from Hewlett-Packard. Each of these varieties is known as a proprietary implementation, or, more casually, as a "flavor." Although the various flavors of UNIX follow some accepted standards, each has unique characteristics. In addition, nonproprietary, freely distributed UNIX-like implementations such as Linux, the GNU Hurd, and FreeBSD are available. Fortunately, the differences between implementations are relatively minor, and with a little effort you can understand them and move from one implementation to another with ease. This chapter introduces the UNIX operating system in general and describes Linux in more detail.

 UNIX and Linux share many characteristics, but are subtly and often confusingly different. UNIX is the trademarked name given to the operating system originally developed at Bell Labs. A nonprofit industry association named The Open Group owns the trademark. An operating system must pass The Open Group's qualification tests to be called UNIX. Linux grew out of an independent effort to create an operating system that behaves like the trademarked UNIX operating system. This would be equivalent, in the Windows world, to a large group of people getting together and writing a version of Windows 2000 based on the public specifications. (UNIX, however, has been publicly available for much longer than Windows 2000, and Microsoft keeps the specifications to many parts of Windows 2000 a closely guarded secret.)

A Brief History of UNIX

The UNIX operating system is characterized by a rich tradition and a culture of personal friendships in an era of impersonal disconnectedness that, some would say, the computer itself has fostered.

In the late 1960s, a few programmers grew dissatisfied with the existing programming environments. In particular, they didn't like the cumbersome nature of the existing systems that required a programmer to write a set of instructions, submit them all at once, and then wait for the results. Instead, programmers desired a more interactive operating environment that allowed them to build and test their programs piece by piece. In addition, the programmers sought a system that imposed as few predetermined structures as possible on the users. Structures that they chose to leave up to users and application programmers include the format of data within data files and the notion of assigning significance to filenames. For example Windows assigns meaning to the period (".") and the last three characters of filenames. UNIX imposes no file-naming constraints. Two employees at Bell Labs in Murray Hill, New Jersey, Ken Thompson and Dennis Ritchie, decided to overcome the limitations of existing operating systems by creating an entirely new programming environment. To properly design this new environment, they decided to start at the lowest level—at the operating system. This environment ultimately evolved into the UNIX operating system.

Antitrust law prohibited AT&T from profiting from the sale of computers and software during the 1970s. Thus, for a nominal licensing fee, anyone could purchase the source code to the work produced at Bell Labs. The word spread rapidly, and researchers in educational institutions and large corporations all over the world soon had this curious new software running on their lab computers. Versions of UNIX that come from the Bell Labs are known as **System V**. Researchers at the University of California at Berkeley were among the first enthusiastic supporters of early versions of UNIX. They added many useful features to the system, including the TCP/IP network subsystem. Berkeley versions of UNIX are known as **BSD (Berkeley Software Distribution)**.

The 1980s saw the breakup of AT&T. This event enabled the company to begin actively marketing the UNIX system to other computer manufacturers. After a number of fits and starts, AT&T eventually sold its rights to the UNIX system. These rights changed hands a number of times during the early 1990s. Today, ownership of the UNIX system is shared by three organizations—Caldera International, Inc., Tarantella, Inc., and The Open Group.

Caldera International and Tarantella (formerly The Santa Cruz Operation), jointly own the rights to the UNIX source code. They therefore have the right to distribute copies of the **source code**—the raw materials for creating a UNIX system. Anyone could write a UNIX operating system, but the effort required to do so is prohibitive. Most organizations choose to start with the existing source code by obtaining it from Caldera International and Tarantella and then make modifications for their specific computer hardware.

The Open Group, as mentioned earlier, owns the UNIX trademark. After a vendor changes the code licensed from Caldera International and Tarantella, its modified system must pass The Open Group's verification tests before the operating system may be called UNIX. Compaq, for example, pays source code licensing fees to Caldera International or Tarantella and verification and trademark use fees to The Open Group so that it can call its operating system Tru64 UNIX.

Although many versions of UNIX may be used as network operating systems, all UNIX versions share the following features:

- The ability to support multiple, simultaneously logged in users
- Hierarchical file systems that incorporate demountable volumes
- Consistent interfaces for input of data to and output of data from hardware devices, files, and running programs
- The ability to start processes in the background
- Hundreds of subsystems, including dozens of programming languages

10

- Program source code portability

- Window interfaces that the user can configure, the most popular of which is the X Window system

You will learn more about the UNIX memory model, file system, processing capabilities, and network integration later in this chapter.

THE CURRENT STATE OF THE MARKET

The UNIX market is huge and highly segmented. As a result, stating its size with precision is difficult. People use UNIX-based systems for everything from running general-purpose workstations to controlling industrial robots and telecommunications equipment. In fact, even some **real-time** implementations of the UNIX system exist, in which the operating system must respond to input immediately. One such implementation, QNX, is used to run a computer vision system for the NASA space shuttle and the international space station.

Proprietary implementations and open source implementations are two of the most significant UNIX market segments, as explained in the following sections.

Proprietary UNIX

Many companies market both hardware and software based on the UNIX operating system. An implementation of UNIX for which the source code is either unavailable or available only by purchasing a licensed copy from Caldera International and Tarantella (costing as much as millions of dollars) is known as **proprietary UNIX**. By most counts, the three most popular vendors of proprietary UNIX are Sun Microsystems, IBM, and Hewlett-Packard. Sun's proprietary version of UNIX, called **Solaris**, runs on the company's proprietary SPARC-based workstations and servers, as well as Intel-based Pentium-class workstations and servers. IBM's proprietary version, **AIX**, runs on its PowerPC-based RS-6000 computers. HP's proprietary version, **HP-UX**, runs on its PA-RISC–based systems. Many other organizations have licensed the UNIX source code and created proprietary UNIX versions that run on highly customized computers (that is, computers that are appropriate for very specific tasks).

Choosing a proprietary UNIX system has several advantages:

- *Accountability and support*—An organization might choose a proprietary UNIX system so that when something doesn't work as expected, it has a resource on which to call for assistance.

- *Optimization of hardware and software*—Workstation vendors who ship proprietary UNIX invest a great deal of time in ensuring that their software runs as well and as fast as possible on their hardware.

- *Predictability and compatibility*—Purveyors of proprietary UNIX systems strive to maintain backward-compatibility with new releases. They schedule new releases at somewhat regular, predictable intervals. Customers usually know when and how things will change with proprietary UNIX systems.

One drawback of choosing a proprietary UNIX system, however, relates to the fact that the customer has no access to the system's source code and, thus, cannot customize the operating system. Open source UNIX solves this problem.

Open Source UNIX

An interesting factor in the UNIX marketplace over the past few years has been the emergence of UNIX-like systems that are not owned by any one company. This software is developed and packaged by a few individuals and made available to anyone, without licensing fees. Often referred to as **open source software**, or **freely distributable software**, this category includes UNIX-like systems such as the **GNU** (whose kernal is known as Hurd), **FreeBSD**, and **Linux**. Each of these systems, in turn, comes in a variety of implementations with slightly different features and capabilities. As mentioned, these packages are often referred to as the different **flavors** of the open source software. For example, the different flavors of Linux include RedHat, Caldera, Mandrake, and a host of others. While these packages are free of licensing fees and are available at no cost to users, you can purchase the software. In the case of purchasing Red Hat Linux, for example, you are paying for the convenience of a package that includes the software on CD-ROM, documentation, and access to Red Hat's customer support. Choosing to obtain Red Hat Linux for free means a (potentially) long download (more than 650 megabytes), writing the software to a CD-ROM, and learning how to install it without the aid of printed documentation. Many people find the convenience worth the nominal purchase price of software with a licensing fee.

The key difference between freely distributable UNIX and proprietary implementations of UNIX relates to the copyright specification. Freely distributable versions of UNIX include a copyright (called the **General Public License**) that *requires* the source code to be made available to anyone receiving the system. What's more, this license requires programmers to publish source code changes so that others can make use of them. This ensures that programmers have access to the original source code and each change made to it. The General Public License further ensures that no one person or entity can claim ownership of the source code. Although Linus Torvalds holds the copyright to the Linux operating system, even he cannot prevent others from obtaining and sharing the source code. A primary advantage of open source UNIX is that users can add functionality not provided by a vendor of proprietary UNIX. A manufacturing company that uses computer-controlled robotic spot welders, for example, might combine open source UNIX with custom software to control its robots. In contrast, it might be very difficult or costly to integrate the robotic control software with a proprietary UNIX system.

10

Versions of freely distributable UNIX run not only on Intel-based processors, but also on other processor brands such as PowerPC (used in Apple Macintoshes), SPARC (used in Sun Microsystems workstations), and Alpha (used in Compaq workstations). Although this range of choices is wider than with proprietary UNIX systems, it can also complicate the decision-making process when choosing a network server.

The discussion of UNIX in the remainder of this chapter will focus on one popular open source version, Linux. Linux follows standard UNIX conventions, is highly stable, and is free. Linus Torvalds, then a second-year Finnish computer science student, developed it in 1991. After developing Linux, Torvalds posted it on the Internet and recruited a number of other UNIX aficionados and programmers to help enhance it. Today, Linux is used for file, print, and Web servers across the globe. Its popularity has even convinced large corporations that own proprietary UNIX versions, such as IBM, Silicon Graphics and Sun Microsystems to publicly embrace and support Linux.

WHY CHOOSE UNIX?

Let's say that your supervisor assigns you the task of choosing and installing a new server on your organization's LAN. To make your network as compatible as possible with other networks, you limit your operating system options to the big three: NetWare, Windows 2000, and UNIX. Given these options, what considerations might lead you to choose UNIX? The same set of questions asked in Chapters 8 and 9 apply to your consideration of this operating system:

- Can it be integrated with my existing infrastructure?

- Will it provide the security required by my resources?

- Is my technical staff capable of managing it?

- Will my applications run smoothly on it?

- Will it accommodate future growth (that is, is it scalable)?

- Does it support the additional services required by my users (for example, remote access, Web site hosting, and messaging)?

- How much does it cost?

- What kind of support does the vendor offer?

UNIX systems offer a host of features, including the TCP/IP protocol suite and all applications necessary to support the networking infrastructure as a part of the basic operating system. You get the programs necessary to perform operations such as routing, firewalling, domain name service, and automatic IP address assignment when you install the system on your computer. UNIX supports non-IP protocols such as Novell's IPX/SPX and AppleTalk. Like Windows 2000 and NetWare, UNIX also supports many different network topologies and physical media, including Ethernet, Token Ring, FDDI, and wireless LANs.

UNIX systems can act as file servers to Windows, NetWare, and Macintosh clients. The open source software package called **Samba**, for example, is a complete Windows 2000–style file and printer sharing facility. Other proprietary and open source software packages are available that implement the NetWare file and print server facilities as well as Macintosh file and print facilities.

UNIX efficiently and securely handles the growth, change, and stability requirements of today's diverse networks. The source code on which UNIX systems are based is mature, as it has been used and thoroughly debugged for nearly 30 years. Like NetWare, UNIX allows you to change the server's configuration—for example, assigning a different IP address to an interface—without restarting the server. Similarly, you can easily modify a UNIX system while it is running. When you need to access a tape drive, for example, you can enable the tape driver, access the tape, and disable the tape driver without restarting the server. This functionality allows you to use memory on your server very efficiently.

A key difference between UNIX and other network operating systems such as NetWare relates to resource sharing. UNIX was originally developed as a **time-sharing system**— that is, a computing system to which each user must attach directly (usually with a "dumb terminal") to share the resources of that computer. You must log onto a UNIX system and run applications on the system to share its resources.

To understand how this model differs from other client/server resource-sharing methods, consider your company's office environment. You share certain resources: file cabinet space, conference rooms, printers, copiers, and so on. When you are working in your office, you share office resources in the same way that a UNIX system shares its resources. For example, you might walk over to the file cabinet, remove a file, and then replace it when you're done with it.

In the NetWare model, in contrast, a workstation is attached to the network. When you want to use the server's resources, you simply map a drive to your local computer or send a print job to the server's printer queue. This approach is analogous to a telecommuting situation in which you work at home, but still have access to many of the office's resources. To share your office resources, you can simply call someone at the office and ask to have a paper file sent to your home by courier. Later, the courier can shuttle the file back to the office and replace it in the file cabinet. The disadvantage of this model is that you cannot use some of the office's resources, such as the conference rooms, when you telecommute. Similarly, you can't perform some tasks on a NetWare server because you don't attach directly to the system; instead, you simply use its resources over the LAN.

A real advantage of UNIX is that people have added applications and services that enable sharing of resources in the telecommuter model without eliminating the "drive-to-the-office" model. With UNIX systems, you get the best of both worlds.

UNIX systems also include a robust and mature security model. Some proprietary UNIX systems have even received **Orange Book** certification, which is a rigorous operating system security specification that the U.S. Department of Defense first published in 1985. These characteristics of the UNIX system contribute to its ability to handle networks' growth and changes, and provide stability.

10

UNIX SERVER HARDWARE

UNIX systems may be implemented as workstations or as servers. Unlike Windows 2000, in which the server and workstation versions vary considerably, a UNIX server and a UNIX workstation differ only by the set of optional packages included during installation. A UNIX system configured as a server has the necessary software to enable sharing of resources such as print queues, file systems, and processor time. Hardware requirements are very similar to those for NetWare and Windows 2000 servers.

In UNIX, the use of a graphical user interface (GUI) remains optional—that is, you choose to use the GUI, a command-line interface, or a combination of the two. By contrast, in all versions of NetWare except 5.0 and later, you must use a character-based console (one which uses textual menus and submenus). In Windows 2000, on the other hand, you *must* use the GUI for many operations. Many people see the flexibility of UNIX as an advantage. For example, you might choose to use the GUI for operations that require a great deal of user interaction such as adding new users or configuring services. However, for server operations that run unattended, it often makes sense to use the command-line interface (which uses up less of the computer's memory and other resources).

The hardware for a UNIX server consists of a base system unit, which must include the following equipment:

- A motherboard with CPU, memory, and I/O control
- A network interface card (NIC)
- A floppy disk drive
- A CD-ROM drive
- One or more fixed disks

High-performance video cards, sound cards, and other I/O devices are optional. Your major decisions in choosing the hardware for a general-purpose UNIX server can be summarized as follows:

- Which applications and services will run on the server?
- How many users will this system serve?
- How much random access memory (RAM) will the server need?
- How much secondary storage (hard disk) will the server need?

Table 10-1 shows the minimum hardware requirements for the various components of a Linux server. You may find more current lists of supported hardware on the hardware compatibility list (HCL) at *www.linuxdoc.org/HOWTO/Hardware-HOWTO/*.

Table 10-1   Typical hardware requirements for a Linux server

Component	Requirement	Notes
Processor	Intel-compatible x86	Recent versions of Linux (2.0 and later) include support for as many as 16 Intel processors.
Memory	32 MB RAM	You should consider more RAM than this minimum for better performance; most network administrators opt for 64 MB or 128 MB of RAM for servers.
Hard disk	A hard drive supported by Linux (as specified in the HCL), such as an IDE or SCSI, with a minimum of 500 MB free space	Most server implementations require additional hard drive space.
NIC	A NIC supported by Linux (as specified in the HCL)	
CD-ROM	Choose a drive listed on the HCL.	Recent versions of Linux support SCSI, IDE, and ATAPI CD-ROM drives.
Floppy disk	Without a bootable CD-ROM drive, Linux installation (and most other UNIX systems) requires one or two 3.5-inch floppy disks to get started. You may create emergency repair disks during installation.	
Pointing device	Optional	Only necessary if you install the GUI component.

10

The Linux HCL resembles the NetWare and Windows 2000 hardware guides in that it recommends *minimum* requirements for simply starting the server. You'll need to add more memory and more disk space according to your applications' requirements. Unfortunately, you sometimes cannot learn the memory requirements of an application until you actually run it on the server. In these instances, it is always better to overestimate your needs than to underestimate them.

No one "right" UNIX server configuration exists. To determine the hardware requirements of your UNIX server, you need to take into account the nature of the work to be performed by the system, the type of software to be run, and the number of users.

A CLOSER LOOK AT LINUX

Linux is the third major network operating system discussed in this book. As you probably realize, both similarities and differences exist among Linux, NetWare, and Windows 2000. This section compares Linux with those other network operating systems.

Linux Multiprocessing

Any modern network operating system must use the resources of multiple processors in an efficient manner. Linux is truly a modern operating system in this respect. Like NetWare and Windows 2000, Linux supports symmetric multiprocessing (SMP). This support for SMP was experimental in version 2.0. However, Linux experts consider SMP to be stable in versions 2.2 and later. SMP support and performance improved with the release of Linux version 2.4. The operating system supports SMP using a maximum of 16 processors per server. The guidelines outlined in the previous chapters for NetWare and Windows 2000 apply to Linux as well. You must know how your servers will be used and plan for multiprocessing servers according to your estimated application processing loads.

Default Linux installations prior to version 2.2 leave SMP disabled. You must configure your system so as to enable SMP if you're using version 2.0. Consult the Linux SMP guide at *www.linux.org.uk/SMP/title.html* for details.

The Linux Memory Model

From its inception, Linux was created to use both physical and virtual memory efficiently. (See the "Windows 2000 Server's Memory Model" section in Chapter 8 for details.) Like Windows 2000, Linux allocates a memory area for each application. It attempts to decrease the inefficiency of this practice, however, by sharing memory between programs wherever it can. For example, if five people are using FTP on your Linux server, five instances of the FTP program will run. In reality, only a small part of each FTP program (called the private data region—the part that stores the user name, for example) will receive its own memory space; most of the program will remain in a region of memory shared by all five instances of the program. In this case, rather than using five times the memory required by one instance of the program, Linux sets aside only a little more memory for five FTP users than it does for one FTP user.

Most current versions of Linux use a 32-bit addressing scheme that enables programs to access 4 GB of memory. Linux also runs on CPUs that employ 64-bit addresses, enabling programs to access more than 18 exabytes (2^{64} bytes) of memory. That's more than 18 billion billion bytes of data; three times the total number of words ever spoken by human beings, by one estimate! Virtual memory in a Linux server can take the form of a disk partition (created with the Windows fdisk command), or it can be in a file (much like the virtual memory file pagefile.sys in Windows 2000).

The Linux Kernel

Linux is similar to NetWare in that the core of the system consists of the **kernel**. The Linux kernel is loaded into memory from disk and runs when you turn on your computer. Also, as with NetWare, you can add or remove functionality by loading and unloading Linux **kernel modules**, which are analogous to NetWare NLMs. Unlike NetWare, however, Linux does not use loadable modules exclusively to extend the functionality of the system. Rather, you start and stop Linux services and applications by typing commands (much like running commands in a Windows 2000 command window). Linux offers the best of both worlds: loadable kernel modules to extend the functionality of the Linux kernel (like NetWare), and services and applications that run to perform most of the work of the server (like Windows 2000).

 When vendors speak of Linux version numbers, such as 2.2 or 2.4, they are referring to the kernel version. Although vendors (such as Red Hat) may also use their own version-numbering scheme (such as Red Hat 7.0), all purveyors of Linux distributions use the same Linux kernel version scheme to identify which kernel is included in the package.

Linux File and Directory Structure

The UNIX system was one of the first operating systems to implement a **hierarchical file system**. This hierarchy somewhat resembles the structure of the NDS inverted tree discussed in Chapter 9. The notion of a file system organized in this way was considered revolutionary at the time of UNIX's inception. Today, most operating systems, including all Microsoft operating systems, NetWare, and even the Apple Macintosh's MacOS, use hierarchical file systems. Figure 10-1 shows a typical UNIX and Linux file system hierarchy.

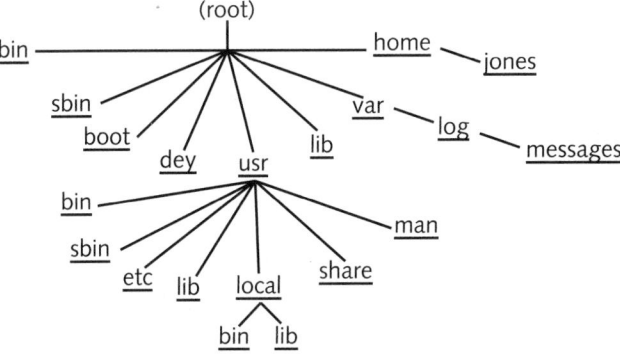

Figure 10-1   Linux file system hierarchy

The */boot* directory contains the Linux kernel and other system initialization files. Linux keeps applications and services in */bin and /sbin* (applications and services in */sbin* support the system initialization process; you'll rarely use these programs). The */var* directory holds variable data (such as log files and print jobs waiting to be printed). The file */var/log/messages*, for example, stores system log messages. Users' login directories appear in */home*. When you create a new user account, the system assigns a directory in */home* to that user. The login (or home) directory matches the account's user name. Thus */home/jones* is the login (or home) directory for the user *jones*.

Linux File Services

In Chapter 8, you learned about the file systems supported by Windows 2000. As you will recall, the file system constitutes the operating system's method for organizing, managing, and accessing its files through logical structures and software routines. Linux includes support for multiple types of file systems, including local and remote file systems. The native file system type, called *ext2*, is the "second extended" file system for Linux. Rather than trying to fix some of the problems with the "first extended" file system, the programmers decided to create a new file system from scratch, and named it (creatively) the second extended file system.

Linux allows you to access partitions formatted with the DOS FAT file system as well as the Windows 2000 NTFS file system (in read-only mode) and the OS/2 HPFS file system. It also supports remote file systems, which are analogous to Windows shares or NetWare network volumes. With Linux, you can both map shared file systems (drives) from Windows or NetWare servers and share local partitions with other users. Sun Microsystems' **Network File System (NFS)** is the other significant remote file system type supported by Linux. Given how many file system types are accommodated, it's easy to see why Linux has become such a popular server platform in large, diverse networks.

Linux Internet Services

As you learned earlier, UNIX has deep roots in Internet services. For instance, the leading Internet Web server is an open source software application called **Apache** that originally ran only on UNIX systems. What's more, the original Web tools—including the first browsers and servers—were developed on UNIX-based systems. UNIX-based systems acted as the development platforms for the original ARPAnet and Internet services such as FTP, Telnet, gopher, HTTP, and POP. It should, therefore, come as no great surprise that current implementations of UNIX include the full range of Internet services as standard components.

Linux Processes

Another UNIX innovation is the notion of separate, numbered processes. Each process represents an instance of a running program in memory (RAM). The UNIX kernel allocates separate resources (such as memory space) to each process as it is created. It also manages all programs' access to these resources. This novel approach enables partitioning of processes in memory, thereby preventing one program from disrupting the operation of the entire system. When one program ends unexpectedly on a UNIX system, it doesn't cause the whole computer to crash. In addition to processes, Linux also supports threads, discussed in Chapter 8.

A LINUX COMMAND SAMPLER

The command line is the primary method of interacting with a Linux system. Even when you're running a GUI, the GUI actually executes commands on your behalf in response to your manipulation of the graphical elements on the screen. This section discusses some of the basics of the Linux user interface, interaction with the Linux command line, and some fundamental Linux commands.

The program that accepts your typing and runs the commands for you is called a **command interpreter**. Also known as a **shell**, a command interpreter translates your typed commands into machine instructions that the operating system can understand. Thus, the command interpreter is a program that runs other programs. UNIX command interpreters also perform file globbing (described later) and keep track of the command history (much like the **doskey** command in DOS and Windows 2000). The primary UNIX command interpreter is */bin/sh*. It has a similar function to the primary Windows 2000 command interpreter, *cmd.exe*. To use the shell effectively, you should be familiar with at least some basic commands.

One especially useful feature of UNIX (including Linux) is its online documentation. UNIX systems include documentation, known as the **manual pages**, for all commands. You can review the instructions for any command by reading its manual page entry. Although their organization differs slightly in various flavors of UNIX, manual pages are typically arranged in nine sections:

- *Section 1* covers the commands that you most typically enter while typing in a command window.

- *Sections 2 through 5* document the programmer's interface to the UNIX system.

- *Section 6* documents some of the amusements and games that are included in the UNIX system.

- *Section 7* describes the device drivers for the system.

- *Section 8* covers the commands used by administrators to manage the system.

- *Section 9* documents the UNIX kernel functions programmers use when writing device drivers.

You can access manual pages by entering the **man** command in a Linux command window. For example, to read the manual page entry for the **telnet** command, you would type **man telnet** in a command window, and then press Enter.

Although the Linux manual pages are accurate and complete, Linux newcomers often complain that they can't find the appropriate manual page if they don't know the name of the command they want to use. That's why the **apropos** command exists. It enables you to find possible manual page entries for the command you want to use. For example, you might type **apropos list** to search for a command that lists files. The **apropos** command would then display all commands and programming functions that include the keyword *list* in their manual page entries. Type `man  <command>` (where `<command>` is a command name displayed by apropos) when you find a command name that looks like it might do what you want.

Commands function in much the same way as sentences in ordinary language. Some sentences are one-word directives to the system requesting that it perform a simple task on your behalf (such as *date* for "tell me the current date and time"). Other sentences are detailed instructions to the system containing the equivalent of nouns, adjectives, and adverbs and creating a precise description of the task you wish the system to perform. For example, to instruct the system to "print the names of all files in the current directory that have been accessed in the past five days," you would type: `find. —type f —atime +5 —print`.

A few rules exist to guide your use of Linux commands and, as you might expect, exceptions to most of the rules also exist. Most commands (though not all) are lowercase alphabetic characters. Using the analogy of a sentence, the command itself would be the verb—that is, the action you want the system to take (for example, *ls* to list information about files). The things on which you want the system to operate (often files) would be the nouns. (So for example, you would type `ls  accounts.xls` to list a file named account.xls.) Options to the commands are analogous to adjectives and the adverbs—that is, modifiers that give more specifics about the command. To specify an option, you usually type a dash (-) followed by a letter (such as *ls -a* to list all files, even the "invisible" files in the current directory). You can make commands even more specific by using file **globbing**—the equivalent to using wildcards in Windows and DOS. On a Linux system, this operation is also called filename substitution (for example, `ls —l a*` would produce a detailed listing of all files beginning with the letter "a").

A significant (and perhaps initially confusing) difference between the Linux and Windows 2000 command-line interfaces relates to the character you use to separate directory names when you type in a command window. The Windows 2000 separator character is "\" (backslash). The equivalent Linux directory separator character is "/" (forward slash). For example, in a Windows 2000 command window, you type the *telnet* command as `\windows\system32\telnet.exe`. The `telnet` command in Linux is `/usr/bin/telnet`.

Windows 2000 and UNIX share the powerful concept of directing output from one command to the input of another command. A **pipe** (entered as a vertical bar " | ") serves as the connection between two commands. Think of data "flowing" from one command to another. Most commands that display output on the monitor allow you to direct the output to another command. Most commands that accept typing from your keyboard also accept input from other commands. Two or more commands connected by a pipe are called a **pipeline**. UNIX pipes make it easy to create sequences of commands that might require custom programming on other systems.

Table 10-2 lists some common Linux commands and provides a brief description of each.

Note
The developers of the original UNIX system worked at AT&T, then the largest public corporation in the world. Two features of communication within large corporations are the tendency to abbreviate words and the reliance on acronyms. The command names in the Linux system reflect this culture in that they drop vowels and syllables (*cp* for *copy*, *cat* for *concatenate*, and so on), and name commands with the "initials" of their intended use (`grep` for *general regular expression parser*, `ftp` for *File Transfer Protocol*). Refer to the relevant manual pages when you encounter command names that you don't understand. The *synopsis* section usually indicates the origin of the command name.

10

Table 10-2   Commonly used Linux commands

Command	Function
date	Display the current date and time.
ls -la	Display with details all the files in the current directory.
ps -ef	Display details of the current running programs.
find *dir* *filename* -print	Search for *filename* in the directory *dir* and display the path to the name on finding the file.
cat *file*	Display the contents of *file*.
cd /d1/d2/d3	Change the current directory to *d3*, located in */d1/d2*.
cp *file1 file2*	Make a copy of *file1*, named *file2*.
rm *file*	Remove (delete) *file* (Note that this is a permanent deletion, there is no trash can or recycle bin from which to recover the deleted file.)
mv *file1 file2*	Move (or rename) *file1* to *file2*.
mkdir *dir*	Make a new directory named *dir*.
rmdir *dir*	Remove the directory named *dir*.
who	Display a list of users currently logged in.
vi file	Use the "visual" editor named *vi* to edit *file*.
grep *"string" file*	Search for the string of characters in *string* in the file named *file*.
ifconfig	Display the network interface configuration, including the IP address, MAC address, and usage statistics for all network interface cards in the system.
netstat -r	Display the system's TCP/IP network routing table.
sort *filename*	Sort alphabetically the contents of *filename*.
man *"command"*	Display the manual page entry for *"command."*
chmod *rights file*	Change the access rights (the mode) of *file* to *rights*.
telnet *host*	Start a virtual terminal connection to *host* (where *host* may be an IP address or a host name).
ftp *host*	Start an interactive file transfer to (or from) *host* using the FTP protocol (where *host* may be an IP address or a host name).

Table 10-2   Commonly used Linux commands (continued)

Command	Function
startx	Start the X Window system.
kill *process*	Attempt to stop a running program with the process ID *process*.
tail *file*	Display the last 10 lines of *file*.
exit	Stop the current running command interpreter. Log off the system if this is the initial command interpreter started on logging in.

The most frequently used Linux command is *ls*. By entering *ls* (and specifying *-l*, the detailed listing option), you learn everything about a file except its contents. Linux systems keep quite a bit of information about each file including:

- The filename
- The file size (in bytes)
- The date and time that the file's i-node (file information node, discussed below) was created
- The date and time that the file was last accessed (viewed or printed)
- The date and time that the file contents were last modified (created, edited, or changed in any way)
- The number of "aliases" or links to the file
- The numeric identifier of the user who owns the file
- The numeric identifier of the group to which the file belongs
- The access rights for the owner, the group, and all others

The system stores this information for each file (except the filename) in a file information node (abbreviated **i-node**). The beginning of each disk partition contains reserved space for all i-nodes on that partition. I-nodes also contain pointers to the actual file contents on the disk. The file's name is stored in the directory that contains the file. To learn about the i-node information, you use the *ls* command. Figure 10-2 shows a sample list generated by *ls*.

```
% ls -l
total 1278
drwxr-xr-x    2 root     bin          2048 Dec 11 17:05 bin
drwxr-xr-x    2 root     root         1024 Sep 24 01:38 boot
drwxr-xr-x    2 root     root         1024 Feb 26  1998 cdrom
drwxr-xr-x    3 root     root        19456 Jan 16 02:52 dev
drwxr-xr-x    9 root     root         3072 Feb  2 07:27 etc
drwxr-xr-x    2 root     root         1024 May 27  1997 floppy
drwxr-xr-x   78 root     root         2048 Jan 30 11:55 home
drwxrwxr-x    4 root     root         1024 Dec 15 13:12 home2
drwxr-xr-x    3 root     root         1024 Sep 28 13:18 lib
drwxr-xr-x    2 root     root        12288 May 27  1997 lost+found
drwxr-xr-x    2 root     root         1024 Jun 21  1996 mnt
drwxrwxr-x    9 root     root         1024 Jan 16 05:42 nfs
dr-xr-xr-x    5 root     root            0 Jan 15 20:52 proc
drwxr-x--x    6 root     root         1024 Dec 22 05:56 root
drwxr-xr-x    2 root     bin          2048 Jul  7  1998 sbin
drwxr-xr-x    2 root     root         1024 May 27  1997 shlib
drwxrwxrwt   45 root     root        12288 Feb  2 07:56 tmp
drwxrwxr-x   24 root     root         1024 Jan 16 03:54 usr
drwxr-xr-x   17 root     root         1024 Dec 14 08:10 var
-r--------    1 root     root       359327 May 27  1997 vmlinuz-2.0.29
-r--------    1 root     root       468684 May 27  1997 vmlinuz-2.0.29-1
-r--------    1 root     root       404117 Apr  8  1998 vmlinuz-2.0.33
drwxrwxr-x    5 root     binc         1024 Jan 16 05:56 www
%
```

Figure 10-2   Example of output from `ls`

The strings of r's, w's, x's, and so on, in the left column, represent the access permissions for the files. The first character in the access permissions field (on the far left) indicates the file type. Files with a type of "d" are directories. Files whose type is shown with a "-" are regular files such as word-processing files or spread sheet files—that is, they simply contain unstructured (to the operating system) data. Other valid file types are as follows:

- "l" for symbolic link files (much like Windows 2000 shortcuts)
- "b" for block device files (such as disk partitions)
- "c" for character device files (such as serial ports)

Figure 10-3 shows how to interpret the rest of the output of `ls`.

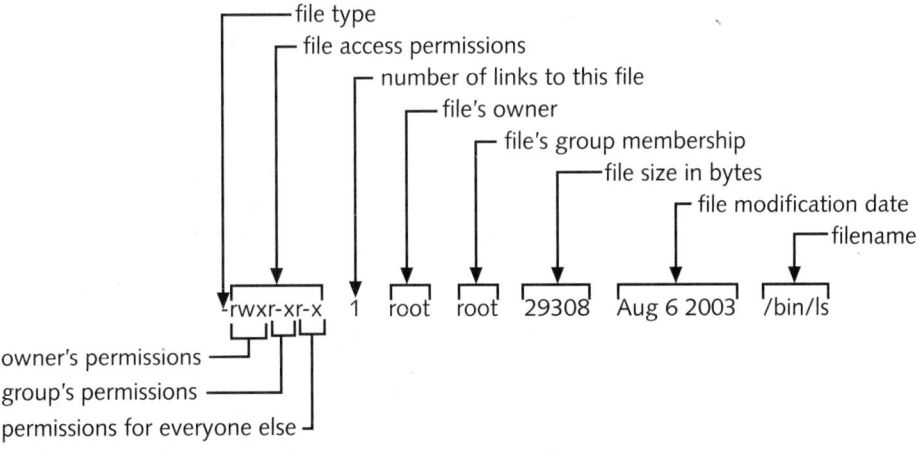

Figure 10-3   Anatomy of `ls` output

INSTALLING AND CONFIGURING A LINUX SERVER

You've had a taste of the Linux system. Now it's time to build one. This section will walk you through the installation process for the Intel-based Red Hat Linux. Although you can install Red Hat Linux over a network using FTP or NFS, this section describes the quickest way—using a CD-ROM.

Preinstallation Requirements

In previous chapters, you learned about the importance of thorough planning in the installation of a new server. These considerations apply to Linux as well as to Windows 2000 and NetWare. Although making changes to the server setup after you install a Linux system is easier and less disruptive than with Windows 2000, you should nevertheless plan as carefully as possible to avoid service unavailability after a Linux server is running.

Before installing Linux, you should be prepared to answer the following questions:

- *What is the new server's name?* This name is a less important issue for Linux systems than for Windows 2000 or NetWare systems, but it's still a good idea to choose it before beginning installation. You can add the server's name to your network name service (DNS, for example) as soon as you choose it. (See Chapter 11 for details about TCP/IP domain names.) You may use any name containing a maximum of 32 alphanumeric characters, not including the following:

  >< [ ]._:; | = , + * " ?

- *What is the server's IP address?* You'll need this address to enable the network on the new server. Network administrators usually configure workstations to obtain an IP address automatically when they start up, but they often configure servers with reserved or static IP addresses because some client applications require configuration with a server's IP address rather than a server's name. You'll also need the network mask (see Chapters 3 and 11 for details about TCP/IP addressing), the IP address of the server's primary gateway (in other words, the default gateway), and the IP address of the new server's TCP/IP domain name server.

- *What kind of video card is installed in the server?* The Linux setup process attempts to detect the video card and will install the correct driver if possible. Otherwise, it will prompt you to choose the type of video card from a list. Either way, you should know what kind of video card your server contains.

- *What kind of monitor is attached to the new server?* As yet, an operating system cannot automatically learn this information. You'll need to supply the monitor manufacturer and model number to the Linux setup program.

- *What is the administrative user's password?* Choose a difficult-to-guess password for the Linux administrator account. Chapter 15 provides advice on choosing good passwords.

- *How can I remember all of this information?* Once you have answered these questions, you should create a server installation form and keep the form with you during installation. Appendix C offers an example of such a form.

This list highlights only the most significant installation options. In addition, you should be prepared to identify your keyboard and mouse type, choose a time zone, and specify an administrator account ID.

Although this example involves a standalone Linux system, Linux very peacefully coexists with other operating systems on your primary hard drive. (Read more about multi-boot systems at the Linux installation **HOWTO** site:

www.linuxhq.com/ldp/howto/Installation-HOWTO/index.html.

For this installation, you'll need the following:

- A clean PC (one without any operating system installed) that satisfies the Linux hardware requirements detailed previously

- The distribution media for Red Hat Professional Server version 7.0 (CD-ROM and floppy disk)

- Two hours of available time, most of it for the installation process to copy files from the installation CD-ROM to your computer's hard drive

10

The Installation Process

The package containing Red Hat Professional Server version 7.0 includes a manual, 10 CD-ROMs, and a bootable floppy disk labeled "Boot Diskette." Place the first Red Hat CD-ROM near your computer. You won't need the floppy disk if your computer's BIOS configuration allows you to boot from the CD-ROM. Turn off your computer before beginning the installation. As you work your way through the installation screens, keep in mind that you can use the mouse to click the desired button. Use the Tab key to select actions, and press Enter to proceed from one screen to the next.

To install Red Hat Linux version 7.0:

1. Turn on your computer and insert the first CD-ROM disk into your computer's CD-ROM drive.

2. After reading the CD-ROM, the computer displays the Welcome to Red Hat screen, as shown in Figure 10-4.

```
                  Welcome to Red Hat Linux 7.0!

    o  To install or upgrade a system running Red Hat Linux 3.0.3
       or later in graphical mode, press the <ENTER> key.

    o  To install or upgrade a system running Red Hat Linux 3.0.3
       or later in text mode, type: text <ENTER>.

    o  To enable expert mode, type: expert <ENTER>.  Press <F3> for
       more information about expert mode.

    o  To enable rescue mode, type: linux rescue <ENTER>.  Press <F5>
       for more information about rescue mode.

    o  If you have a driver disk, type: linux dd <ENTER>.

    o  Use the function keys listed below for more information.




[F1-Main] [F2-General] [F3-Expert] [F4-Kernel] [F5-Rescue]
boot: _
```

Figure 10-4   Welcome to Red Hat Linux screen

3. Press **Enter**. The Language Selection screen appears. Choose the language you'll use by clicking your choice with the left mouse button. Click **Next**.

4. The Keyboard Configuration screen appears. Use the scroll bars at the right of each section to locate your keyboard model and layout. Click your choice of keyboard model and layout. The highlighted selections should be fine for most English-speaking users with standard keyboards. Unless you know you need to disable "dead keys" do nothing in the "Dead Keys" section of this screen. Click in the Test your selection here text box and type a few characters. Click **Next**.

5. The Mouse Configuration screen appears. Red Hat Linux attempts to identify your mouse and highlights its choice for you. Choose your mouse by clicking the appropriate selection if you know your mouse is different from the choice highlighted. Expand and collapse mouse groups by clicking the **+/−** symbol at the left of the mouse list box. Serial port mouse users must also choose the COM port to which the mouse is connected. Click the appropriate selection to choose your mouse port. Click the **Emulate 3 buttons** check box if your mouse has only two buttons. Click **Next**.

6. The Welcome to Red Hat Linux screen appears. Read the instructions in the left panel, using the scroll bar to read all of the text. Click **Next**.

7. The Install Options screen appears. Click the **Server System** icon. Click **Next**.

8. The Initialize dialog box appears. Click **Initialize** to continue.

9. The Automatic Partitioning screen appears. Select automatic partitioning by clicking the **Automatically partition and remove data** diamond. Click **Next**.

Automatic partitioning will destroy *all* the data on your hard drive. Ensure that this is what you want to do before continuing.

10. The Network Configuration screen appears as shown in Figure 10-5. Click in the IP Address text box and type the IP address you chose for this server. Press **Tab** to continue to the Netmask text box and enter the correct network mask for this server. Press **Tab** to move to the Network text box; the network address in the Network text box should be correct. If it is not correct, change it now, and then press **Tab** to continue to the Broadcast text box, which should contain the correct broadcast IP address for this server. (If it is not correct, change it now.) Click in the Hostname text box and type the name of this server. Press **Tab** to continue to the Gateway text box and enter the IP address of this server's primary gateway. Press **Tab** to continue to the Primary DNS text box and type the IP address of this server's primary domain name server. Enter the IP addresses of the secondary and ternary (third) domain name servers if you know them. Click **Next**.

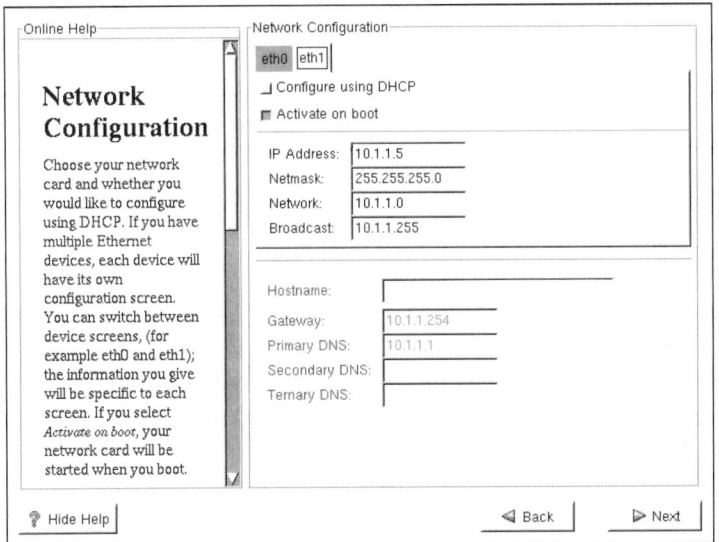

Figure 10-5   Network Configuration screen

11. The Time Zone Selection screen appears. You may select the appropriate time zone for this server in one of two ways: click the visual map of the world, or locate in the list below the map the country and city closest to the server's location and select it by clicking it. Using either method of choosing the time zone, a red "x" will appear on the map indicating the geographical location of the city you chose. Click the **System clock uses UTC** check box if your server's hardware clock is not set to the local time. Click the **UTC Offset** tab at the top of the Time Zone Selection box. Locate your time zone in the list and then click the appropriate selection. Click **Next**.

12. The Account Configuration screen appears. Click in the Root Password text box and type a password for the server's administrator (or root user). Press **Tab** and retype the root password in the Confirm text box. Note that the Next button remains gray (that is, inactive) until a valid root password and confirmation are entered. Do not enter a new account name. Click **Next**.

13. The Selecting Package Groups screen appears. The Web Server check box is selected by default. Make sure the Select individual packages check box is not selected. Click **Next**.

14. The About to Install screen appears. Click **Next**.

 This is your last chance to stop before the installation process erases *all* the data on your hard drive.

15. The Installing Packages screen appears with a status table and progress bars, indicating the installation progress of individual packages and the overall installation. This is the most time-consuming step in the installation and will take more than an hour. The Next button will change from gray to black and will become active when package installation is complete. Click **Next**.

16. The Boot Disk Creation screen appears. Insert a blank, formatted floppy disk in the server floppy disk drive, and click **Next**.

17. Log in to your new Linux server using the user name **root**. The system presents you with the login prompt. Use the password you entered in Step 12.

Configuring Linux for Network Administration

A Linux server is little more than a powerful workstation when it has no user accounts. This section introduces you to the setup process for Linux system administration. You'll learn:

- The basics of adding users and groups
- The basics of modifying file access permissions

This section introduces two commands: `groupadd` and `useradd`. Both are documented with their own manual pages. Their names imply their function: `groupadd` enables you to add a new group to the system, and `useradd` enables you to add a new user to the system.

Like Windows 2000 and NetWare, Linux requires the use of user names and passwords to connect clients to the network. Also like these operating systems, it assigns access rights to groups, and allows users to be members of multiple groups. For example, the Linux group named *mail* can access the electronic mail programs and electronic mail files. This section assumes that you are logged in to a Linux system as the administrative user ("*root*") and that your system has presented you with a command prompt. You'll press Enter after typing each command to allow Linux to carry out the operation. You may want to reread Table 8-2, which covers security for groups, because that information is relevant here.

Adding Groups and Users

You use the `groupadd` command to add a new group ID to a Linux system. It does not assign users to the new group, but rather makes a new group name available for use. Linux assigns a unique identification number to each group. Note that creating a new group does not automatically assign access rights to that group; you'll learn how to accomplish that task later in this section. You'll use the same school groups and access rights given in Table 8-2 for this section. Creating a new Linux group for instructors is simply a matter of typing the necessary commands. Note that the commands display no information if they successfully complete the operation.

To add group IDs to your Linux system:

1. Type **groupadd instructors**, and then press **Enter** at the command prompt. The group *instructors* is added.

2. Type **groupadd students**, and then press **Enter**. The group *students* is added.

3. Type **groupadd administrators**, and then press **Enter**. The group *administrators* is added.

You use the `useradd` command to add a new user ID to a Linux system. It creates a new user ID and assigns that user ID to one or more groups. In this example, you'll create a new user, Thomas, and assign that user to the group *instructors*. The new user should be a member of the general users group as well as the group *instructors*. You must use two options when typing the `useradd` command: the −g option specifies the initial (or primary) group for the user, and the −G option specifies the additional groups to which the new user will belong (*instructors,* in this case). Note that `useradd` does not assign a password for the new user ID, so you'll use the `passwd` command to assign a password for *thomas*.

 Linux passwords are case-sensitive. You may use any of the characters on the keyboard in your password.

You can use the `passwd` command in one of two ways: while logged onto the system as the administrative user, root, to change another user's password, or while logged onto the system as a normal user to change your own password. As you type the password, notice that the characters do not appear on the screen. This security precaution prevents people from peering over your shoulder and seeing your password as you type it. Read the `passwd` manual page (`man passwd`) to learn more about this command.

10

To add a new user and assign the user a password:

1. Type **useradd -g users -G instructors thomas**, and then press **Enter** to add a new user account named *thomas*.

2. Type **passwd thomas**, and then press **Enter**. Linux prompts you to type the new password. After you type the password and press **Enter**, Linux prompts you to retype your password. Enter the same password again; this confirmation helps ensure that you type your new password accurately.

Now that you've added a new group and a new user to the system, you may restrict access to resources owned by the user *thomas* or the group *instructors*.

Changing File Access Permissions

Linux restricts access to resources by comparing user and group IDs with the owner and group membership of files. Every file and directory on a Linux system is owned by exactly one user and is a member of exactly one group. You may assign access permissions for the file's owner, the file's group, and everyone else. Linux assigns new files and directories to the creator's primary group (*users*, in this example). The example from Table 8-1 shows that the directory *PROGRAMS* contains instructional programs. You want to allow teachers to place new programs in *PROGRAMS*. Students should be able to run the programs, but not to add new ones or to delete them.

To create a directory and assign it to a group:

1. To log off your Linux system, type **exit**, and then press **Enter**.

2. To log back onto your system as user *thomas*, enter **thomas** at the login prompt.

3. Enter the password you assigned for *thomas*.

4. You see a command window and a command prompt. To create the new directory, type the command **mkdir PROGRAMS**, and then press **Enter**.

5. List the file with **ls -l**. Notice that the directory belongs to the group *users*.

6. Type the command **chgrp instructors PROGRAMS** (remember to press **Enter**) to assign *PROGRAMS* to the group *instructors*.

7. List the files again with **ls -l** and notice that the file is now assigned to the group *instructors*.

Now that you've created the directory *PROGRAMS* and assigned it to the group *instructors*, you must limit access to the files. You use the **chmod** command to change the access permissions of files and directories. Read about **chmod** in its manual page (using the command **man chmod**). Your goal is to enable members of the group *instructors* to create new files in and delete files from *PROGRAMS*, and to limit access to all others (specifically, members of the group *students*). To accomplish this task, you must add write permission to PROGRAMS for the group (in this case "instructors") and remove write permission for all others.

To change the access permissions for the PROGRAMS directory:

1. Type **chmod g+w PROGRAMS** to add write access for the *instructors* group to *PROGRAMS*, and then press **Enter**.

2. Type **chmod o-rw PROGRAMS** to remove read and write access by others to *PROGRAMS*, and then press **Enter**.

3. Type **ls -l** to view the access permissions assigned to *PROGRAMS*. You should see a line for *PROGRAMS* that includes permissions of *drwxrwxr-x*.

INTERNETWORKING WITH OTHER NETWORK OPERATING SYSTEMS

People have modified the UNIX system over the years to work with other network operating systems and protocols besides TCP/IP. Programmers and network administrators alike have added functionality to the system because they find it so productive. Their changes include the addition of Windows networking, NetWare networking, IBM mainframe terminal emulation, and Windows programming tools. Examples of these tools are described below.

10

- *Samba*—The UNIX-based server message block (SMB) and common Internet file system (CIFS) package. This application provides everything needed to make your UNIX system a fully featured Windows file and printer-sharing server.

- *IPX/SPX*—The original Novell networking protocol. It is implemented as a native UNIX protocol in many UNIX versions. Proprietary and open source software solutions, such as Caldera's NetWare for Linux, exist to turn your UNIX server into a NetWare server by including full NDS support.

- *AppleTalk*—The Apple Macintosh network protocol. Many UNIX system vendors support this protocol and all application programs needed to implement Macintosh file and print servers.

- *X3270*—An X Window–based 3270 terminal emulator for accessing your mainframe over a TCP/IP connection. This standard application is included with the X Window system for UNIX.

- *WINE*—An open source application that implements a Win32 programming subsystem for UNIX including support for running Windows programs (such as Word). This ongoing project is slowly improving with age as more people begin to use it and contribute changes to the source code.

- *VMWare*—A commercial application that emulates a complete Intel-based computer. VMWare uses special Intel CPU instructions to perform its emulation. This hardware support for emulation enables VMWare virtual computers to run almost as fast as the actual computers themselves. Unlike WINE, VMWare emulates the computer hardware (rather than the programming environment) and can run any Intel-based operating system.

- Dozens and dozens of command-line utilities that enable you to access the contents of files generated on other systems

CHAPTER SUMMARY

❑ The UNIX system is a stable, robust network operating system. It forms the basis of much of the Internet. You must be familiar with the operation of UNIX so as to set up and maintain most local and wide area networks. Despite the preponderance of proprietary implementations of UNIX systems, the differences between the various versions are relatively minor.

❑ UNIX was born at AT&T's Bell Laboratories, when a few programmers grew dissatisfied with the programming environments available in the late 1960s. Ken Thompson and Dennis Ritchie were the original authors of the system.

❑ Currently, Caldera International and Tarantella, Inc. own the rights to the UNIX source code. The Open Group, a nonprofit trade association, owns the UNIX trademark.

❑ Sun Microsystems, IBM, and Hewlett-Packard sell the three most popular UNIX-based workstations. These products are based on these companies' proprietary implementations of UNIX, which conform to most UNIX standards.

❑ Recently, nonproprietary implementations of UNIX-like systems have become popular. Often referred to as open source software or freely distributable software, this category includes the UNIX-like systems FreeBSD, GNU, and Linux.

❑ The key difference between freely distributable UNIX and proprietary implementations is that the copyright on freely distributable implementations requires that anyone purchasing an open source version of UNIX receive access to the source code.

❑ UNIX systems make great Internet servers. In fact, the leading Internet Web server is an open source software project called Apache. The original Web tools—including browsers and servers—were developed on UNIX-based systems. UNIX systems underlay the original ARPAnet and Internet services such as FTP, Telnet, gopher, HTTP, and POP. These services are standard with current implementations of UNIX.

❑ One characteristic of all UNIX systems is a user-definable command interpreter. Its development arose in part because the command line was the primary interface with the system.

❑ Other characteristics of UNIX systems are as follows: the ability to support multiple, simultaneous users; hierarchical file systems with demountable volumes; a consistent interface for files, devices, and interprocess input/output; hundreds of subsystems and dozens of programming languages; program source code portability between different implementations of the system; and user-definable windowing systems.

❑ Minimum hardware requirements for a Linux server include an Intel-compatible x86 processor, 32 MB RAM, 500 MB of hard disk space, a network interface card compatible with the rest of your network, a CD-ROM drive, and a floppy disk drive.

❑ The UNIX system was among the first operating systems to include a hierarchical file system. This approach led to better-organized data and subsystems.

❑ Each UNIX process represents an instance of a running executable program in core memory (RAM). The UNIX kernel allocates separate resources (such as buffer space, stack space, and open file pointers) to each process as it is created. The kernel manages access to these resources.

❑ You can liken UNIX commands to ordinary sentences. The things you want the system to operate on are the nouns—often files. Options to the commands are the adjectives and the adverbs.

❑ Most UNIX commands are lowercase alphabetic characters. To specify an option, you usually type a dash ("−") followed by a letter. The letter is often (but not always) a mnemonic abbreviation for the option (such as *−l* for a long file listing).

❑ Command names are usually acronyms or abbreviations. Consult the command's manual (man) page when you encounter a command name that makes no sense to you. The synopsis usually indicates the origin of the command name.

❑ The UNIX *ls* command is the most frequently used. When you use *ls* with the *−l* option, it allows you to learn everything about a file except its contents. *ls −l* reports the filename, the file size, the date and time that the file was created, the date and time that it was last accessed, the date and time that it was last modified, the number of "aliases" or links to the file, the user who owns the file, the group to which the file belongs, and the access rights for the owner, the group, and all others.

❑ The system uses information nodes (i-nodes) to store everything other than the actual contents of files. I-nodes also contain pointers to file contents on the disk.

❑ Linux distributions are binary compatible. They differ mainly in the methods they use for installing additional software packages. The Red Hat Linux distribution is one of the most popular.

❑ Use the **useradd** command to add new users to your Linux system.

❑ Use the **groupadd** command to add new groups to your Linux system.

❑ The **chgrp** command assigns a file to a group.

❑ The **chmod** command changes file access permissions.

❑ UNIX systems quite competently interoperate with other network operating systems. You can use them to share files with Windows-based computers and NetWare-based computers, for example. In addition, you can use a UNIX-based computer to access mainframe sessions. You can even run Windows software on UNIX systems with the proper emulation package installed.

10

KEY TERMS

AIX — IBM's proprietary implementation of the UNIX system.

Apache — A popular open source software Web server application often used on Linux Internet servers.

BSD (Berkeley Software Distribution) — A UNIX distribution that originated at the University of California at Berkeley. The BSD suffix differentiates these distributions from AT&T distributions. No longer being developed at Berkeley, the last public release of BSD UNIX was version 4.4.

command interpreter — A (usually text-based) program that accepts and executes system programs and applications on behalf of users. Often it includes the ability to execute a series of instructions that are stored in a file.

doskey — A command used on MS-DOS and Windows systems that enables the user to recall (using the keyboard's arrow keys) and edit previously entered commands.

flavor — Term used to refer to the different implementations of a particular UNIX-like system. For example, the different flavors of Linux include Red Hat, Caldera, and Mandrake.

FreeBSD — An open source software implementation of the Berkeley Software Distribution version of the UNIX system.

freely distributable software — A term used to describe software with a very liberal copyright. Often associated with open source software.

General Public License — The copyright that applies to freely distributable versions of UNIX and specifies that the source code must be made available to anyone receiving the system.

globbing — A form of filename substitution, similar to the use of wildcards in Windows and DOS.

GNU — The name given to the free software project to implement a complete source code implementation of UNIX, the collection of UNIX-inspired utilities and tools that are included with Linux distributions and other free software UNIX systems. The acronym within an acronym stands for "GNUs Not UNIX."

hierarchical file system — The organization of files and directories (or folders) on a disk partition in which directories may contain files and other directories. When displayed graphically, this organization resembles a tree-like structure.

HOWTO — A series of brief, highly focused documents giving Linux system details. The people responsible for the Linux Documentation Project centrally coordinate the HOWTO papers (see *www.linuxhq.com/ldp/howto/HOWTO-INDEX/howtos.html*).

HP-UX — Hewlett-Packard's proprietary implementation of the UNIX system.

Hurd — The kernel in the GNU operating system. While many UNIX and Linux systems include GNU utilities such as the EMACS editor or the GNU C compiler, the Hurd is the only operating system kernel that can currently be called a GNU kernel.

i-node — A UNIX file system information storage area that holds all details about a file. This information includes the size, access rights, date and time of creation, and a pointer to the actual contents of the file.

kernel — The core of a UNIX system. This part of the operating system is loaded and run when you turn on your computer. It mediates between user programs and the computer hardware.

kernel modules — Portions of the Linux kernel that you can load and unload to add or remove functionality on a running Linux system.

Linux — A freely distributable implementation of the UNIX system. Finnish computer scientist Linus Torvalds originally developed it.

manual pages — UNIX online documentation. This documentation describes the use of the commands and the programming interface to the UNIX system.

NFS — Network File System. A client/server application that allows you to view, store and update files on a remote computer as though they were on your own computer. Can be used to install Linux.

open source software — Term used to describe software that is distributed without any restriction and whose source code is freely available. See also *freely distributable*.

Orange Book — A rigorous security specification for computer operating systems published in 1985 by the U.S. Department of Defense.

pipe — The facility in a UNIX system that enables you to combine commands to form new commands. It is one of the most powerful facilities of the UNIX system.

pipeline — A series of two or more UNIX commands connected together with pipe symbols.

proprietary UNIX — Any implementation of UNIX for which the source code is either unavailable or available only by purchasing a licensed copy from Caldera International and Tarantella, Inc. (costing as much as millions of dollars).

real-time — The term used to describe an operating system that includes at least one of the following two characteristics: the ability to respond to external events (for example, a change in temperature), and an ability to respond to those events deterministically—with predictable response time (for example, turning on a heating element within three microseconds).

Samba — An open source software package that provides complete Windows 2000-style file and printer sharing facility.

shell — Another term for command interpreter.

Solaris — Sun Microsystems' proprietary implementation of the UNIX system.

source code — Computer instructions written in a programming language that is readable by humans. Source code must be translated into a form that is executable by the machine, typically called binary code (for the sequence of zeros and ones) or target code.

System V — The proprietary version of UNIX, originally developed at AT&T Bell Labs, currently distributed by Caldera International and Tarantella, Inc.

time-sharing system — A computing system to which users must attach directly so as to use the shared resources of the computer.

10

REVIEW QUESTIONS

1. In what year did work begin on the UNIX system?

   a. 1990

   b. 1987

   c. 1975

   d. 1969

2. Which two of the following are open source software implementations of UNIX-like systems?

   a. Solaris

   b. IRIX

   c. Linux

   d. FreeBSD

   e. HP-UX

3. Which of the following services might not be appropriate for a UNIX server?

   a. Internet services

   b. file and print services

   c. image database services

   d. music on hold service

   e. DHCP service

4. It is appropriate to use UNIX systems for network firewalls. True or False?

5. What is the primary method for interacting with the UNIX system?

   a. speaking to it through a microphone

   b. moving a mouse and clicking icons

   c. typing commands at a command prompt

   d. typing commands in a dialog box

6. Which of the following is a characteristic common to all UNIX systems?

   a. the same font for all windows

   b. availability in multiple foreign languages

   c. the ability to start processes in the background

   d. file systems in which directories cannot contain other directories

   e. the availability of Windows emulation programs

7. Which character is used to separate directory names on UNIX systems?

a. backslash

b. colon

c. comma

d. period

e. forward slash

8. Hardware requirements for UNIX servers are roughly equivalent to those of Windows 2000 or NetWare servers. True or False?

9. Which of the following are stored in a file's i-node?

a. access rights

b. the filename

c. the first 16 bytes of the file

d. the time and date that the file was last printed

10. Which letter does the `ls` command use to identify a UNIX symbolic link (much like a Windows 2000 shortcut) in a detailed file listing?

a. L

b. S

c. l

d. y

e. s

11. Which two of the following items are you required to know when installing a Red Hat Linux server?

a. your Internet service provider's name

b. your printer brand and model

c. the number of buttons on your mouse

d. the server's IP address

12. The administrative user "root" is subject to which of the following access restrictions, just like any other UNIX system user?

a. read access

b. create access

c. write access

d. execute access

e. none of the above

13. Which open source software application enables UNIX systems to participate in SMB file sharing on a network?

    a. Tango

    b. Samba

    c. Jitterbug

    d. Waltz

14. Which three of the following tools might enable you to run Windows programs from your Linux system?

    a. Samba

    b. X3270

    c. WINE

    d. Windows 2000

15. Which command would you use to create a new directory on a UNIX system?

    a. `make`

    b. `makedir`

    c. `mkdir`

    d. `md`

16. Which command would you use to remove a directory on a UNIX system?

    a. `mkdir`

    b. `rmdir`

    c. `deldir`

    d. `rd`

    e. `removedir`

17. Which option would you use to tell the `ls` command to display all files in the current directory?

    a. `—all`

    b. `-listall`

    c. `/a`

    d. `—a`

    e. `/all`

18. What does `grep` stand for?

    a. globbing relocation expert processor

    b. general replication executable pointer

    c. generic regular expression pointer

    d. general regular expression parser

    e. none of the above

19. Which UNIX command might you use to display the last 10 lines of a file?

    a. `grep`

    b. `exit`

    c. `tail`

    d. `who`

    e. `list`

20. Under what circumstances would file globbing be useful?

21. If a UNIX command is like a sentence, which part of the command is like the sentence's verb?

    a. the command name

    b. the command options

    c. the Enter key

    d. the filename associated with the command

22. Which part of a UNIX command is like the noun in a sentence?

    a. the command name

    b. the command options

    c. the Enter key

    d. the filename associated with the command

23. How would you learn about a command for which you know the name, but not the purpose?

    a. Use the `help` command.

    b. Use the `manual` command.

    c. Use the `man` command.

    d. Use the `apropos` command.

24. How would you learn about a command for which you know the purpose, but not the exact name?

    a. Use the `help` command.

    b. Use the `manual` command.

    c. Use the `man` command.

    d. Use the `apropos` command.

25. What is the full command you would use to revoke write permission for everyone other than yourself for the file named *sent-mail?*

    a. `chown root sent-mail`

    b. `chmod —write sent-mail`

    c. `chmod og-w sent-mail`

    d. `chgrp system sent-mail`

26. What is the full command you would use to create the directory named *GRADES*?

    a. `cp new GRADES`

    b. `makedir GRADES`

    c. `mkdir GRADES`

    d. `make dir GRADES`

27. What is a Linux kernel module?

    a. a shared Linux library

    b. the same thing as a Linux process

    c. a small part of the Linux source code

    d. part of the Linux kernel that you can load and unload to add or remove functionality on a running Linux system

28. A UNIX thread is:

    a. the same thing as a UNIX process

    b. sometimes called a lightweight process

    c. what holds the UNIX kernel together

    d. the portion of RAM that holds the process information

29. Which two of the following choices describes how the open source application WINE differs from the commercial application VMWare?

    a. They are not different, they do the same thing.

    b. WINE implements the Win32 programming interface, and VMWare emulates a complete personal computer.

    c. WINE emulates a complete personal computer, and VMWare implements the Win32 programming interface.

    d. VMWare enables you to run any Intel-based operating system, but WINE runs only Windows programs.

    e. VMWare runs only Windows programs, but WINE enables you to run any Intel-based operating system.

30. What is the UNIX `telnet` command used for?

    a. to start the networking system

    b. to stop the networking system

    c. to access the Ethernet interface

    d. to begin a virtual terminal connection to a remote server

    e. to initiate a network broadcast

HANDS-ON PROJECTS

Project 10-1

In this exercise, you'll learn about some of the basic differences between the Windows (or DOS) command line and the UNIX command line. To complete this project, you'll need a computer system running Red Hat Linux Version 7.0. If you have not already done so, install Linux by following the steps in this chapter, using a computer that meets at least the minimum hardware requirements, also described in this chapter.

1. Turn on your computer and wait for it to start Linux.

2. Type your user name and password at the login and password prompts.

3. The system presents you with a command-line window (usually called a terminal window) and a command prompt. Type a slash character (/), then press **Enter**. What happened? The command interpreter was awaiting a command, and you typed a directory name (/).

4. Type a backslash character (\), then press **Enter**. What happened? The backslash character tells the system not to process the command, but to wait for the rest of the command. You can use this feature to enter very long commands on multiple lines and still maintain the readability when you print a copy of the command.

5. Press **Enter** again. What happened this time? The backslash you typed in Step 4 instructed the system to wait for more input, but the rest of your input was empty. The system did nothing and displayed the command prompt, awaiting your next command.

6. Press **Ctrl+D**. What happened? Ctrl+D is a special control sequence, signaling to the command interpreter that it should end current processing. As it was sent to your login command interpreter, you signaled to the system that you were logging out.

Project 10-2

In this exercise, you'll get more exposure to the UNIX `ls` command. Keep the "verbs," "nouns," and rules in mind when trying this exercise, and remember to press Enter after each command. You'll need a running Linux system for this exercise—that is, a computer that meets the minimum hardware requirements with a copy of Linux installed.

1. Turn on your computer and wait for it to start Linux.

2. Log on with your user name and password.

3. Type `ls` at the command-line prompt. What do you see? Don't be alarmed. UNIX designers subscribe to the notion that "no news is good news." The fact that running `ls` generated no output simply means that it found no files to list. This response is quite normal for brand new user accounts.

10

4. Add the adjective "all" to the verb as follows: **ls —a**. In what way is this command different from that given in Step 3? Linux "hides" filenames beginning with a period, much as Windows Explorer can hide files with certain extensions.

5. Read the manual page for *ls* (**man ls**). How does **ls** sort the output by default? How can you instruct **ls** to sort the output by the files' timestamps instead?

6. Tell the system you want to see the details of all files in the current directory (**ls —la**). How is this command different from the listing performed in Step 4?

7. Produce a detailed listing of all files in the directory /usr/bin, sorting the listing by file timestamp in reverse date order (**ls -alrt /usr/bin**). Is there a different way to specify the options in this command? Many UNIX commands accept both short and long options. You invoke **ls** with long options by typing two hyphen characters followed by the descriptive option name. The **ls** manual page documents the long and the short options.

Project 10-3

This project introduces the notion of connected commands. The connection method you'll use is a pipe, the mechanism that directs the output and input of commands. UNIX pipes are used to combine the output of one command with the input of another command; they represent one of the most powerful features of the UNIX system, and a feature that has been mimicked by many other computing systems, including Windows 2000. As explained in this chapter, the symbol used for a pipe in the UNIX shell is " | ", the vertical bar, usually located on computer keyboards above the backslash. You type a pipe symbol by pressing SHIFT and backslash. A UNIX pipeline is simply two or more commands on one command line with a " | " between them. You'll use two commands in this project: **who** and **grep**. The **who** command displays the users who are currently logged onto the system. Running **who** on a busy server might show as many as 100 users logged on. The UNIX command **grep** is used to search for strings of characters in files. As in the previous projects, you'll need a running Linux system to complete this exercise. You must be logged into your lab system at a shell prompt.

1. Type **who**, then press **Enter**. You should see a list of all logged-on users (possibly just one).

2. Press **Alt+F2** to switch to a new terminal window. At the login prompt, type **thomas** and press **Enter**. At the password prompt, type the password you chose in the exercise in "Adding Users and Groups." Press **Alt+F1** to switch back to the first terminal window.

Red Hat Linux systems are configured with seven "virtual" terminal windows, all of which are active at the same time. You access them by pressing **Alt+F1**, **Alt+F2**, **Alt+F3**, and so on. This feature offers you the possibility of starting up to seven simultaneous login sessions without using a graphical user interface.

3. Type **who | grep root**. You should see just one line displayed: the line representing the login information for the user *root*.

Project 10-4

Linux supports many different network services One of the most basic network services is remote host command-line access. Telnet is the Internet remote command-line service. In this exercise, you'll access a Linux server with a Windows telnet client. For this exercise, make sure that the server you built is running Linux. You also need to be logged into a Windows 2000 workstation.

1. To start the Windows Telnet client click **Start** and click **Run**. The Run dialog box opens.

2. Type **Telnet** in the text box and click **OK**. The Telnet window opens.

3. Type **open** followed by the IP address of the Linux server (**10.1.1.5** in this example) and press **Enter**. Figure 10-6 shows an example Windows Telnet session. The Telnet session starts, and you are presented with a login prompt.

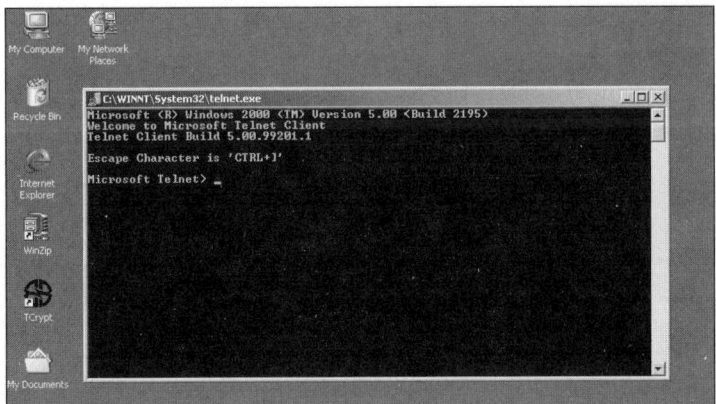

Figure 10-6   Windows Telnet Session

4. Type the user name **thomas** at the login prompt and press **Enter**. A password prompt appears.

5. Enter the password you chose when you added the user *thomas* above. You see a shell prompt. You are now logged into the remote Linux server via Telnet. The Telnet window on the Windows workstation is connected to the Linux server just as if you were using the keyboard and monitor directly attached to the Linux server. Type **ls −l /** and then press **Enter**. Figure 10-7 shows the output of the *ls −l /* command.

10

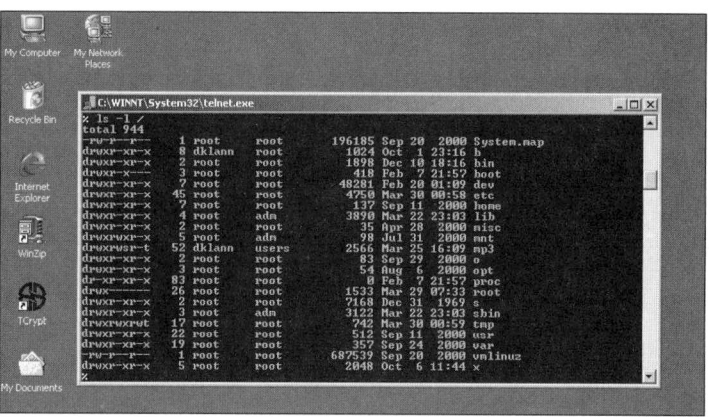

Figure 10-7   Output of IS-1/command in a Telnet session

6. Type **exit**, and press **Enter** to end your Telnet session.

CASE PROJECTS

1. Rick Gomez, the director of product development for EarTech, has asked you to investigate setting up a test network for the company's product development team. The network will support the company's new "EarRadio 2010" FM radio cochlear implant. The network should be connected to the company LAN, but only through one system and only for purposes of Internet access. All of the usual services (such as file sharing, printing, and backup) will be handled on the local LAN. Rick suggests that you plan for a maximum of 30 users, 12 of whom might use the network at any given time. After investigating the situation, you learn that the test network will include several kinds of workstations: Windows PCs, Hewlett-Packard UNIX workstations, and Silicon Graphics UNIX workstations, plus two networked read-only memory (ROM) programming devices (these look to the users very much like network printers). Draw a network diagram that includes the following items:

   ❒ The connection to the existing company LAN

   ❒ The gateway between the test network and the company LAN

   ❒ Eight workstations

   ❒ The file server

   ❒ The print server

   ❒ The printer

   ❒ The ROM programming devices

You also learn that the company has an unused Intel-based PC that has two network interface cards installed, and you have received permission to use this computer as the gateway between the test network and the company LAN. Why might you choose to run Linux on the gateway? How would you learn whether the NICs in the gateway are supported by the Linux operating system?

2. After mapping the network, you learn that the users of both workstation types need to share some common files. Describe how you might set up a single file server that could handle the requirements of both Windows and UNIX network file systems. Which facilities of a UNIX server might help to share files with workstations running both of these operating systems?

3. Knowing that UNIX systems provide superior print spooling service as well as file sharing, you decide to streamline the network even more. Describe how you might eliminate a separate print server from the network. Do you think the UNIX file server could be used as a print server as well? Why or why not?

4. After you install Linux on the gateway you want to ensure that IP packets will pass from the workstations on the test network to the Internet. How would you determine whether the gateway was properly set up to route packets between the two networks?

10

NETWORKING WITH TCP/IP
AND THE INTERNET

After reading this chapter and completing the exercises, you will be able to:

➤ Discuss additional details of TCP/IP addressing and subprotocols

➤ Comprehend the purpose and procedure for subnetting

➤ Understand the history and uses of BOOTP, DHCP, WINS, DNS, and host files

➤ Employ multiple TCP/IP utilities for network troubleshooting

➤ Understand TCP/IP applications, such as Internet browsers, e-mail, and voice over IP

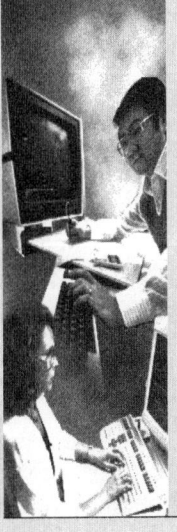

ON THE JOB

My company, which designs custom-made bicycle frames, was one of the first companies on the block to use the Internet for e-mail. It allowed us to economically exchange information with our parts manufacturers and our distributors around the nation. As our company grew, and we opened a second office, we decided it would be great if we could use an intranet on our internal LAN to share information about orders, schedules, and budgets and to hold forums between staff. This turned out to be a great way to bring staff together.

Still, we felt we could do more with TCP/IP technology. Just last year, with the help of a local consulting company, we made our foray into e-commerce and opened up shop on the Internet. Our Internet sales were slow to begin with, but as word of our site traveled, we began receiving orders from around the world. Now our monthly revenue from Internet sales surpasses sales from all other means (including sales from our storefront).

Because of our success with e-commerce, I plan to steer most of my expenditures in the next fiscal year toward developing and supporting our Web site.

Terry Voss
ZAST, Inc.

The Internet is fast becoming not only a means of communication, but also a means of global commerce, development, and distribution. Industries such as banking, manufacturing, and healthcare depend on the Internet for daily transactions, recordkeeping, and sales. Individuals, too, are increasingly relying on the Internet for purchasing and data-gathering operations.

In previous chapters, you learned that the Internet depends on the TCP/IP suite of protocols, as do a number of network operating systems. Because of the increasing popularity of the Internet, having TCP/IP expertise can pave the way to a lucrative, challenging, and rewarding career. Even if your organization doesn't connect to the Internet, you will probably need to master TCP/IP to manage your network competently. In Chapter 3, you learned about the basic uses of TCP/IP, as well as TCP/IP subprotocols, routing capabilities, and addressing schemes. You also learned that TCP/IP is a complex and highly customizable protocol. This chapter builds on these basic concepts, examining how TCP/IP networks are managed, maintained, secured, and analyzed. You will start by learning more about TCP/IP addressing.

ADDRESSING AND NAME RESOLUTION

As you learned in Chapter 2, nodes on a network have both logical and physical addresses. (To refresh your memory about addressing and the OSI Model, it may be helpful to review Chapter 2 now.) The physical, or MAC, address is a unique number assigned to a device's NIC by the manufacturer at the factory. It belongs to the Data Link layer of the OSI Model. In contrast, the logical address belongs to the Network layer of the OSI Model and depends on the networking protocol used for data transmission in the Network layer (IP versus IPX, for example). A network administrator must manage logical addresses to ensure that every node on a network can communicate with other nodes, a process known as IP addressing. This section briefly reviews (logical) IP addressing before turning to ways to manage IP addressing that can make data transmission more reliable and your job easier.

IP Addressing

Just as you have a unique street address so as to ensure reliable delivery of your bills, letters, and magazines, every device on a TCP/IP-based network has a unique IP address to ensure accurate delivery of data. Without the existence of IP addresses, data could not be routed between networks and devices. Like street addresses, IP addresses must adhere to certain conventions. The following IP addressing characteristics should look familiar:

- An IP address is 32 bits in size.

- Every IP address is grouped into four 8-bit octets.

- Octets are separated by decimal points.

- Valid octet numbers range from 0 to 255 and represent a binary address. For example, an octet with the value of 68 equals 01 00 01 00 in an 8-bit binary pattern.

- Each address consists of two parts: network and host. The network portion is common to all nodes on one network, whereas the host portion is unique to each device. For example, two devices on the same Class C network might have the following IP addresses: 208.133.78.11 and 208.133.78.17. In this example, the network portion of the address for both devices is "208.133.78"; the host portion is ".11" for the first device and ".17" for the second device.

- The network portion of an address indicates whether the device belongs to a Class A, B, C, D, or E network.

- Some octet numbers are reserved for special functions. For example, an address whose numeric value is the highest value in that network (host bits all equal to one) is a broadcast address—that is, an address used to communicate simultaneously with all nodes on a network. Other reserved addresses include those with a first octet of 127; these addresses are used exclusively for loopback testing.

Given these conventions, an example of a valid IP address for a networked workstation, printer, or other device might be 123.45.67.89.

IP addresses can be assigned manually on each device or automatically for a group of devices by a service called Dynamic Host Configuration Protocol (DHCP). (You will learn more about DHCP later in this chapter.) Typically, a network that supports DHCP uses this protocol for all of its devices, except those such as Web servers, which must have the same IP address at all times so that clients can reliably connect to them. An address that is assigned manually is called a **static address**, because it does not change unless a network technician reconfigures the device. An address that is assigned automatically by a service such as DHCP is called a **dynamic address**, because it can change over time.

Regardless of whether IP addresses are assigned manually or automatically, the network administrator must ensure that IP addresses are assigned consistently according to a plan and within the boundaries of an organization's valid IP address range. Recall from Chapter 3 that ICANN and IANA are the global authorities for Internet addressing. In order to communicate over the Internet, you must first obtain a group of valid IP addresses from your ISP or another authority authorized by ICANN to distribute addresses.

Suppose that you are the network administrator for a company of 100 employees located in three separate offices (Downtown, East, and West) and that your ISP has assigned the range of IP addresses from 166.22.120.1 to 166.22.120.254 to your company. In total, you have 255 addresses to manage. If you have fewer than 10 servers, you might choose to assign the numbers 166.22.120.2 through 166.22.120.9 to your servers (as you'll learn later in this chapter, IP addresses ending in .1 are typically reserved for gateways). If you later analyze your network for performance or errors, you will know that a single digit in the last octet identifies a server node. You might then use DHCP to automatically assign addresses 166.22.120.10 through 166.22.120.99 to devices at the Downtown office, 166.22.120.100 through 166.22.120.199 to devices at the East office, and 166.22.120.200 through 166.22.120.254 to devices at the West office. Now, whenever you discover errors with a workstation whose last octet begins with a 2, you know that

11

you must examine the West office's network. This example illustrates merely one way that IP addresses can be managed to ease configuration and troubleshooting. Your assignment method will depend largely on the size of your network, its geographic scope, and the preferences of your technical staff.

The IP addresses given in the previous example (for example, 166.22.120.100) were expressed in dotted decimal notation. **Dotted decimal notation**, the most common way of expressing IP addresses, refers to the "shorthand" convention used to represent IP addresses and make them more easily readable by people. In dotted decimal notation, a decimal number between 1 and 255 represents each binary octet (a total of 256 possibilities). A period, or dot, separates each decimal. An example of a dotted decimal IP address is 10.65.10.18. Each number in the address has a binary equivalent, which is readable by the devices on the network. The binary value for 10.65.10.18, for example, is 00001010 01000001 00001010 00010010. You can easily calculate the binary value for a dotted decimal IP number by using the binary conversion feature on the calculator that comes with any Windows-based operating system (as described in Chapter 3).

Although you will most often use the dotted decimal notation in configuring and troubleshooting networks, to understand TCP/IP design issues such as subnetting (discussed later in this chapter), you must understand the binary foundation of IP addressing. Part of that binary foundation includes the network class to which each IP address belongs.

Network Classes

In Chapter 3, you learned that most IP addresses belong to one of three network classes—A, B, or C—and that the network class octets identify the network segment to which a device is attached. For example, your organization might have 20 workstations connected to one hub. All of these workstations would belong to the same network class.

A portion of each IP address contains clues about the network class. For example, an IP address whose first octet is in the range of 1–126 belongs to a Class A network. All IP addresses for devices on a Class A segment share the same first octet, or bits 0 through 7, as shown in Figure 11-1. The second through fourth octets (bits 8 through 31) in a Class A address identify the host.

An IP whose first octet is in the range of 128–191 belongs to a Class B network. All IP addresses for devices on a Class B segment share the first two octets, or bits 0 through 15. The third and fourth octets (bits 16 through 31) on a Class B network identify the host, as shown in Figure 11-1.

An IP address whose first octet is in the range of 192–223 belongs to a Class C network. All IP addresses for devices on a Class C segment share the first three octets, or bits 0 through 23. The fourth octet (bits 24 through 31) on a Class C network identifies the host, as shown in Figure 11-1.

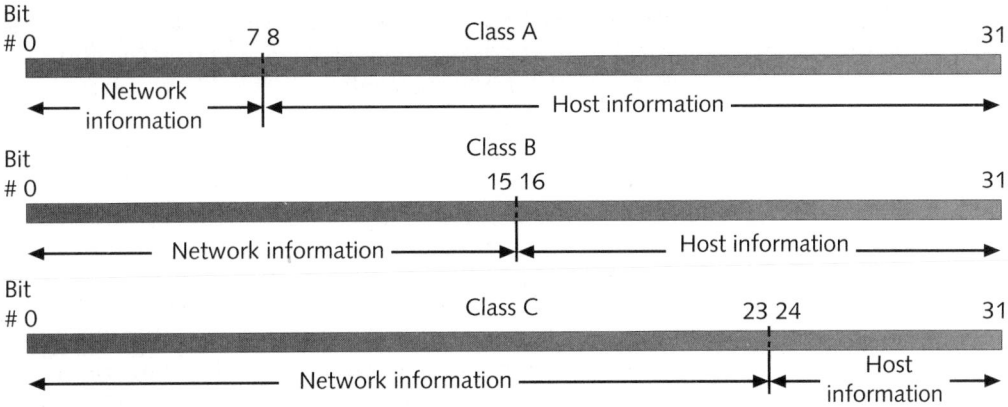

Figure 11-1   IP addresses and their classes

Chapter 3 also explained that each network class has a different number of networks and IP addresses available. For example, because Class A networks must begin with a number between 1 and 126, only 126 Class A networks exist in the world. More host names can be assigned to Class A networks, however, giving a total of more than 16 million possible addresses per network. Table 11-1 reviews what you have learned about the number of networks and addresses that belong to each class of network.

Table 11-1   The three commonly used classes of TCP/IP networks

Network Class	Beginning Octet	Number of Networks	Host Addresses per Network
A	1–126	126	16,777,214
B	128–191	> 16,000	65,534
C	192–223	> 2,000,000	254

In addition to Class A, B, and C networks, Class D and Class E networks also exist, but consumers and companies do not use them. Class D addresses, which begin with an octet whose value is between 224 and 239, are reserved for a special type of transmission called multicasting. **Multicasting** allows one device to send data to a specific group of devices (not the entire network segment). Whereas most data transmission is on a point-to-point basis, multicasting is a point-to-multipoint method. It can be used for teleconferencing or videoconferencing over the Internet, for example. The Internet Engineering Task Force (IETF) reserves Class E addresses, which begin with an octet whose value is between 240 and 254, for experimental use. You should never use Class D or Class E addresses when configuring your network.

You may think that the use of network classes automatically provides easy organization and a sufficient quantity of IP addresses on the Internet. Although this goal is what the Internet's founders intended, it hasn't necessarily come to pass. In the early days of the Internet, Class A addresses were distributed liberally, with some organizations receiving more reserved addresses than they had devices. Today, many addresses on the Internet go unused, but cannot be reassigned. In addition, although potentially more than 4.3 billion Internet addresses are available, the demand for such addresses grows exponentially every year. The early designers of Internet addressing did not anticipate this kind of growth. To respond to this demand, a new addressing scheme is being developed that can supply the world with enough addresses to last well into the twenty-first century. **IP version 6 (IPv6)**, also known as the next-generation IP, will incorporate this new addressing scheme.

The Web contains a wealth of information about the Internet, including statistics on the number of currently used IP addresses. One example of such a repository is found at Internet Software Consortium's site at *www.isc.org/ds/*. The Internet Software Consortium estimates the number of hosts on the Internet by querying machines worldwide and compiling records of Internet address assignments. It also offers links to graphs that depict the Web's growth over the last decade. Another good site for information on Internet usage, developments, and standards information is hosted by the Internet Sciences Institute at the University of Southern California and can be found at *info.internet.isi.edu/1/in-notes/*.

Subnetting

Subnetting is the process of subdividing a single class of network into multiple, smaller networks. Because it results in a more efficient use of IP addresses, subnetting was implemented throughout the Internet in the mid-1980s. Before subnetting, each segment on a network required its own Class A, B, or C network number. With this scheme, if you used a 10Base2 network with a 30-node limitation, once you exceeded 30 devices on your network, you would have needed to request another class of addresses from your ISP or another addressing authority. As you can imagine, this approach was not an efficient use of IP addresses or network managers' time. Not only did a network manager have to apply (and pay) for a new class of addresses, but he or she also needed to change the network's routing tables to accommodate each new network class.

With subnetting, however, a network manager can use one class of addresses for several network segments. This approach becomes possible because one of the address's octets is used to indicate how the network is subdivided, or subnetted. Rather than consisting simply of network and host information, a subnetted address includes network, subnet, and host information, as shown in Figure 11-2. For example, under normal circumstances, if an ISP granted your organization all of the IP addresses that shared the Class B network ID of 166.144, the last two octets would be available for host information. To better organize your addresses and allow for growth, however, you would be wise to devote the third octet to subnet information. By using the third octet to subdivide the network, you create the functional equivalent of 254 Class C networks (166.144.0.0 through 166.144.254.0) from your single Class B network. As far as the Internet addressing authorities are concerned, you continue to use a Class B network; within your organization, on the other hand, your LAN is fooled into recognizing several Class C networks.

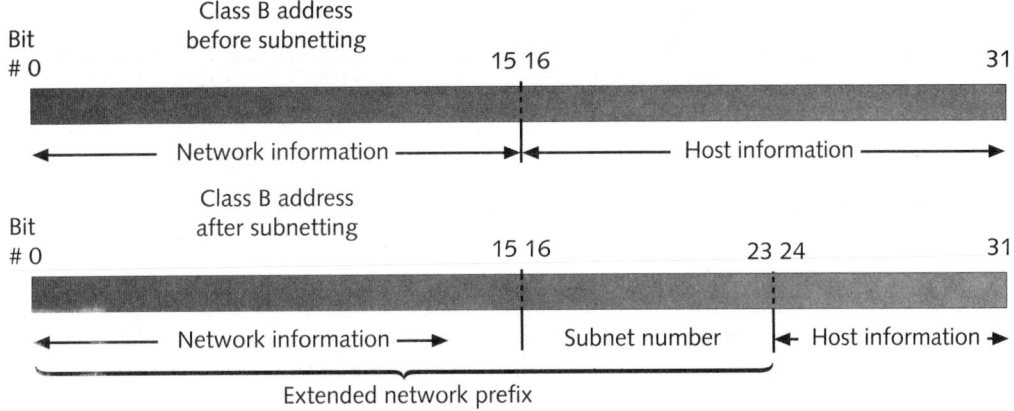

Figure 11-2   IP addresses before and after subnets

The combination of an address's network and subnet information constitutes its extended network prefix. By interpreting an address's **extended network prefix,** a device can determine the subnet to which an address belongs. But how does the device know whether an address is part of a subnet in the first place? After all, the third octet in an IP address could be either a Class B address's subnet number or a part of a Class B address's network information. For example, how can a device tell whether the address 166.144.40.33 belongs to a Class B subnetted network or a Class B network that has not been subnetted?

To make this determination, the device interprets a subnet mask. A **subnet mask** is a special 32-bit number that, when combined with a device's IP address, informs the rest of the network about the network class to which the device is attached. Subnet masks are specified in the same way that IP addresses are specified—either manually, within a device's TCP/IP configuration, or automatically, through a service such as DHCP.

Subnet masks, like IP addresses, are composed of four octets and can be expressed in either binary or dotted decimal notation. An octet of all 1s (using binary notation) in a subnet mask represents part of the extended network prefix in a subnetted IP address that uses that subnet mask. Otherwise, the subnet mask bits are all 0s, and the corresponding octets in the subnetted IP address that uses that subnet mask are assumed to represent host information. Thus, for the subnetted IP address 166.144.40.33, the subnet mask would be 11111111 11111111 11111111 00000000 in binary notation or 255.255.255.0 in dotted decimal notation. In this example, the first three octets make up the extended network prefix. Figure 11-3 shows the correlation between an IP address and its subnet mask.

11

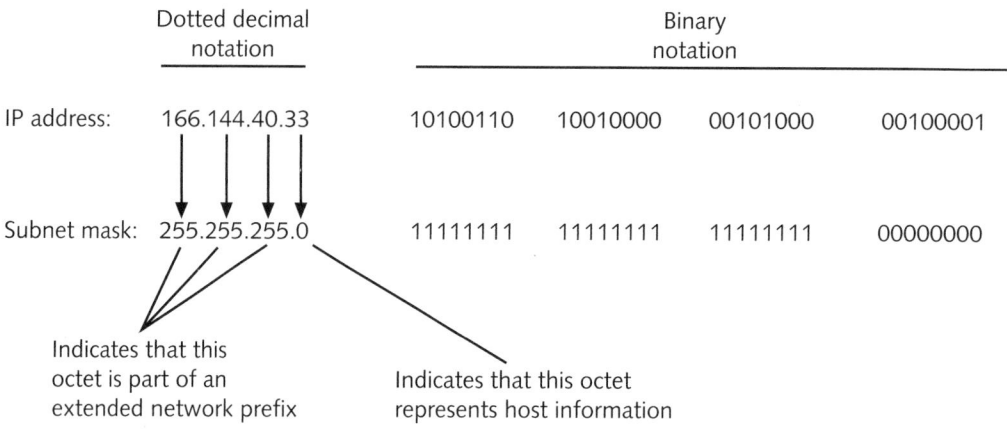

Figure 11-3   A subnetted IP address and its subnet mask

If you do not use subnetting, the extended network prefix will simply equal the network portion of the IP address. You might not want to use subnetting in only three situations: (1) if you have a very small network (as in your home office), (2) if you never want to connect to the Internet and so do not have to follow IP addressing standards, or (3) if your organization has more IP addresses than it can ever conceivably use. If you don't specify a subnet mask, the default subnet mask is 255.0.0.0 for a Class A network, 255.255.0.0 for a Class B network, and 255.255.255.0 for a Class C network. To qualify for Net+ certification, you should be familiar with the default subnet masks associated with each network class.

If you use subnetting on your LAN, only your LAN's devices need to interpret your devices' subnetting information. Routers external to your LAN, such as those on the Internet, pay attention to only the network portion of your devices' IP addresses when transmitting data to them. Recall that the network portions of an organization's addresses are not affected by subnetting and that subnetting modifies only octets that would otherwise be used for host information. As a result, devices external to a subnetted LAN (such as routers on the Internet) can direct data to those LAN devices without interpreting the LAN's subnetting information.

Figure 11-4 illustrates a situation in which a LAN has been granted the Class B range of addresses that begin with 166.144. The network administrator has subnetted this Class B network into at least six smaller networks that begin with the following Class C network prefixes: 166.144.40, 166.144.42, 166.144.56, 166.144.59, 166.144.60, and 166.144.63. When a router on the internal LAN needs to direct data from a machine with the IP address of 166.144.40.12 to a machine with the IP address of 166.144.60.12, its interpretation of the workstations' subnet masks (255.255.255.0) tells the router that they are on different subnets. When a server on the Internet attempts to deliver a Web page to the machine with IP address 166.144.40.12, however, the Internet router does not use the subnet mask information but rather assumes that the machine is on a Class B network. That's all the information it needs to know to reach the organization's router. Once the data enter the organization's LAN, the LAN's router then interprets the subnet mask information as if it were transmitting data internally to deliver data to the machine with IP address 166.144.40.12. Because subnetting does not affect how a device is addressed by external networks, a network administrator does not need to inform Internet authorities about new networks created via subnets.

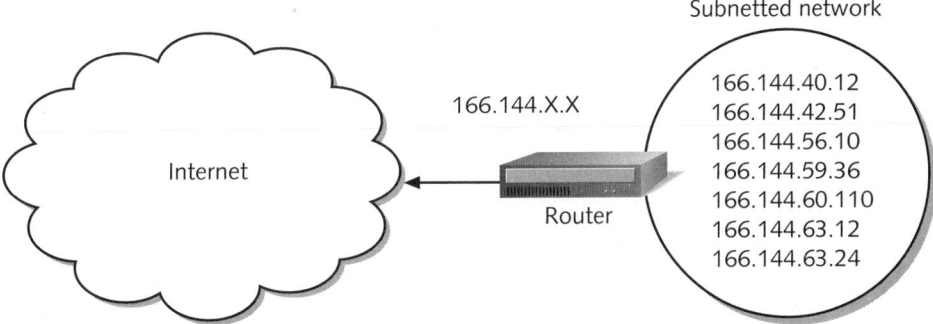

Figure 11-4 A subnetted network connected to the Internet

As you know, routers connect different network segments via their physical interfaces. In the case of subnetting, a router must interpret IP addresses from different subnets and direct data from one subnet to another. Each subnet corresponds to a different interface on the router, and each interface is associated with a default gateway address (described later in this chapter) that ends with "1". Figure 11-5 depicts a network with several subnets connected through a router.

11

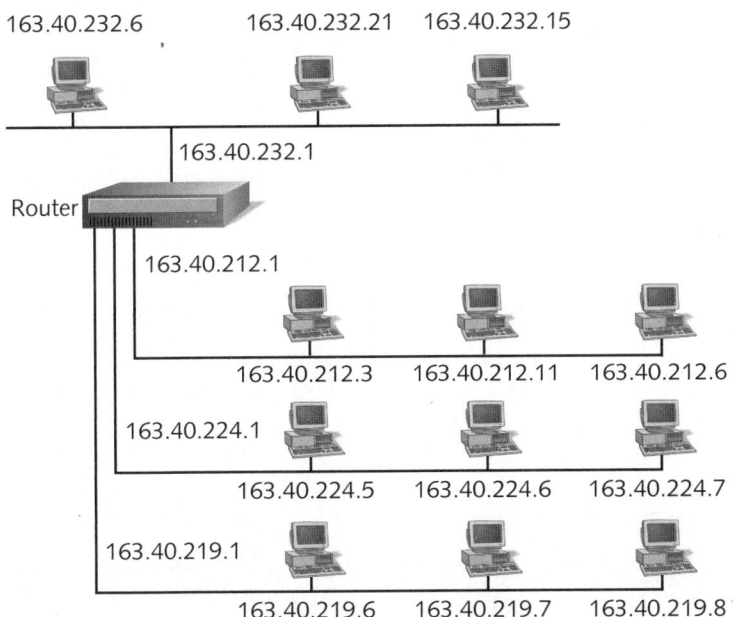

Figure 11-5 A network with several subnets

To understand how subnets and IP addresses work on a network, it's helpful to follow the (simplified) path of data between nodes on different subnets. Imagine you are sitting at the Marketing PC in Figure 11-6. Your colleague has asked you to retrieve a research report from the Internet and then print it for her. The closest printer is located in the IT department, which resides on a different subnet.

First, you connect to the Internet and request the report from the marketing research Web site. Your network's router processes your request, determining that the IP address of the Web site is on the Internet, and passes your request to the Internet routers. The Internet routers forward your request to the marketing research Web site by reading the network information in the destination IP address. The marketing research Web site's server interprets your request for data and sends the report back to the Internet routers, with your IP address in the destination portion of the header. The routers on the Internet read only the network portion of your IP address and forward the data to your router. Your router analyzes the extended network prefix in the destination address to discover your subnet, then uses the host information to send the data to your machine.

When you choose to print the report, your network router interprets your request. It reads the printer's IP address, recognizes that it is a subnetted address, and looks at its extended network prefix to find out the subnet to which it belongs. Then your router forwards the request to the router interface that services the printer's subnet (it may be on the same router or another router). The request proceeds to the printer.

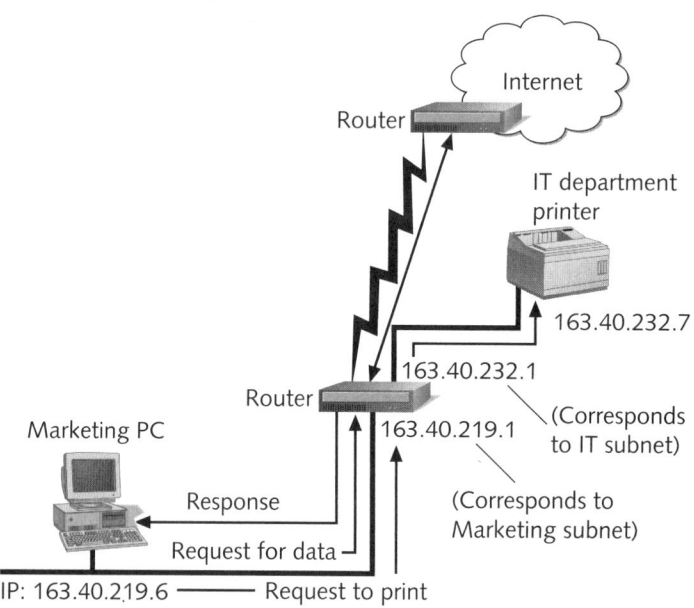

Figure 11-6   Data traveling over subnets

Gateways

In Chapter 6, you learned that **gateways** are a combination of software and hardware that enable two different network segments to exchange data. In the context of IP addressing, a gateway facilitates communication between different subnets. Because one device on the network cannot send data directly to a device on another subnet, a gateway must intercede and hand off the information. Every device on a TCP/IP-based network has a **default gateway**—that is, the gateway that first interprets its outbound requests to other subnets, and then interprets its inbound requests from other subnets.

A gateway is analogous to your local post office. Your post office gathers your outbound mail and decides where to forward it. It also handles your inbound mail just before it heads for your mailbox. Just as a large city has several local post offices, a large organization will have several gateways to route traffic for different groups of devices. Each node on the network can have only one default gateway; that gateway is assigned either manually or automatically (in the latter case, through a service such as DHCP). Of course, if your network includes only one segment and you do not connect to the Internet, your devices would not need a default gateway because traffic would not need to cross the network's boundary.

In many cases a default gateway is not a separate device, but rather a network interface on a router. In this way, one router can supply multiple gateways. Each default gateway is assigned its own IP address. In Figure 11-7, workstation 10.3.105.23 (workstation A) uses the 10.3.105.1 gateway to process its requests, and workstation 10.3.102.75 (workstation B) uses the 10.3.102.1 gateway for the same purpose.

11

 An IP gateway is usually assigned an IP address that ends with an octet of .1.

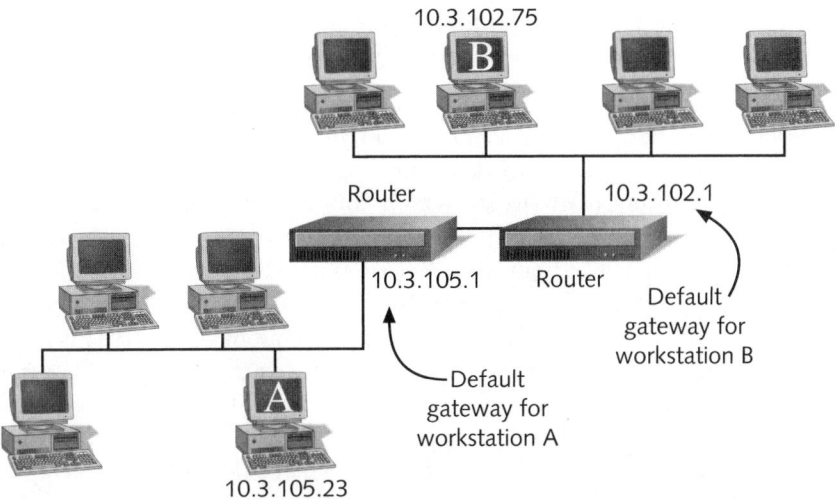

Figure 11-7 The use of default gateways

Default gateways may connect multiple internal networks, or they may connect an internal network with external networks such as WANs or the Internet. As you learned in Chapter 6, routers that connect multiple networks must maintain a routing table to determine where to forward information. When a router is used as a gateway, it must maintain routing tables as well.

The Internet contains a vast number of routers and gateways. If each gateway had to track addressing information for every other gateway on the Internet, it would be overtaxed. Instead, each handles only a relatively small amount of addressing information, which it uses to forward data to another gateway that knows more about the data's destination. Like routers on an internal network, Internet gateways maintain default routes to known addresses to expedite data transfer. The gateways that make up the Internet backbone, called **core gateways**, are managed by the Internet Network Operations Center (INOC).

Network Address Translation (NAT)

IP gateways can also be used to "hide" the IP numbers assigned within an organization and keep its devices' IP addresses secret from any public network (such as the Internet). Not only can hiding the IP addresses protect their identity, but it can also allow network managers more flexibility in assigning addresses. Clients behind the gateway may use any IP addressing scheme, whether or not it is legitimately recognized by the Internet authorities. But once those clients need to connect to the Internet, they must have a legitimate IP address in order to exchange data. When the client's transmission reaches the IP gateway, the gateway assigns the client's transmission a valid IP address. This process is known as **network address translation (NAT)**.

One reason for hiding IP addresses is to add a marginal amount of security to a private network when it is connected to a public network (such as the Internet). Because your transmission is assigned a new IP address when it reaches the public sphere, others outside your organization cannot trace the origin of your transmission.

Another reason for using NAT is to enable a network administrator to develop her own network addressing scheme that does not conform to a scheme dictated by ICANN. For example, suppose you are the network administrator for a private elementary school. You maintain the school's entire network, which, among other things, includes 200 client workstations. Suppose half of these clients are used by students in the classrooms or library and half are used expressly by staff. In order to make your network management easier, you might decide to assign each student workstation an IP address whose first octet begins with the number 10 and whose second octet is the number of the classroom where the computer is located. (For example, a student workstation in room 235 might have an IP address of 10.235.1.12.) You might then assign each staff workstation an IP address whose first octet is the number 50 and whose second octet is the number of the employee's office or classroom. (For example, the principal's workstation, which is located in his office in Room 110, might have an IP address of 50.110.1.10.) These IP addresses would be used strictly for communication between devices on the school's network. When staff or students wanted to access the Internet, however, you would need to have at least some IP addresses that would be legitimate for use on the Internet. Now suppose that, because the school has limited funds and does not require that all clients be connected to the Internet at all times, you decide to purchase a block of only 20 IP numbers and set up an IP gateway to translate your internal addresses to addresses that can be used on the Internet. Each time a client attempts to reach the Internet, the IP gateway would replace its source address field in the data packets with one of the 20 legitimate IP addresses. Figure 11-8 depicts how the process of NAT works.

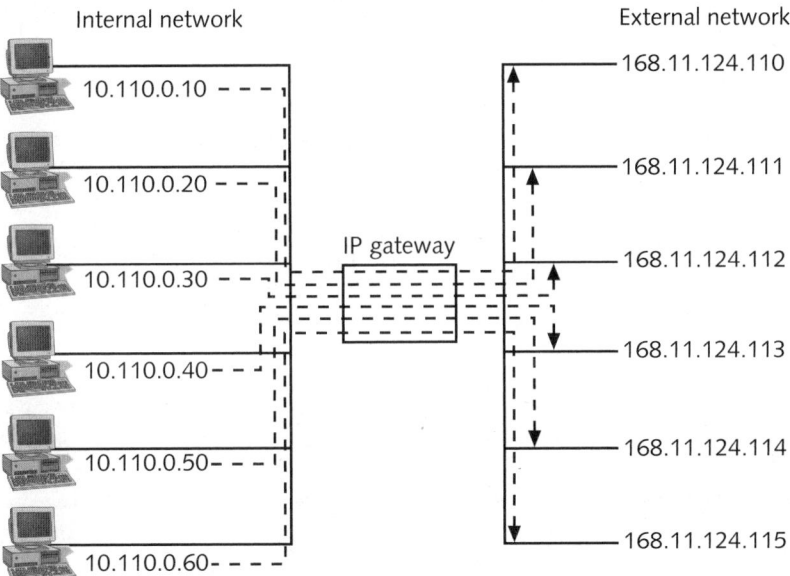

Figure 11-8   NAT through an IP gateway

Sockets and Ports

In Chapter 3, you learned that a **socket** is a logical address assigned to a specific process running on a host computer. It forms a virtual connection between the host and client. The socket's address combines the host computer's IP address with the **port number** associated with a process. For example, the Telnet service on a Web server with an IP address of 10.43.3.87 might have a socket address of 10.43.3.87:23, where 23 is the standard port number for the Telnet service. In other words, after installation, the Web server software assumes that any requests coming into port number 23 are Telnet requests, unless you configure the software differently. Note that a port number is expressed as a number following a colon after an IP address. The 23 is not considered an additional octet in the socket number, but simply a pointer to that port.

Port numbers can have any value. Some software programs that use TCP/IP (for example, Novell's GroupWise and Hewlett–Packard's Performance Data Alarm Manager) choose their own port numbers by default. The default port numbers for commonly used TCP/IP services generally have values lower than 255, as shown in Table 11-2. Port numbers in the range of 0 to 1023 are also called **well-known ports**, because they were long ago assigned by Internet authorities to popular services (for example, FTP and Telnet), and are therefore well known and frequently used.

Although you do not need to memorize every port number for the Net+ Certification exam, you may be asked about the port numbers associated with common services, such as Telnet, FTP, SNMP, and HTTP. Knowing them will also help you in configuring and troubleshooting TCP/IP networks.

Table 11-2   Commonly used TCP/IP port numbers

Port Number	Process Name	Protocol Used	Description
1	TCPMUX	TCP	TCP Port Multiplexer Service
5	RJE	TCP	Remote job entry
7	ECHO	TCP and UDP	Echo
11	USERS	TCP and UDP	Active users
13	DAYTIME	TCP and UDP	Daytime
17	QUOTE	TCP and UDP	Quote of the Day
20	FTP-DATA	TCP	File transfer - data
21	FTP	TCP	File transfer - control
23	TELNET	TCP	Telnet
25	SMTP	TCP	Simple Mail Transfer Protocol
35	Printer	TCP and UDP	Any private printer service
37	TIME	TCP and UDP	Time
41	GRAPHICS	TCP and UDP	Graphics
42	NAMESERV	UDP	Host name server
43	NICNAME	TCP	Who is
49	LOGIN	TCP	Login Host Protocol
53	DNS	TCP and UDP	Domain name server
67	BOOTPS	UDP	Bootstrap Protocol server
68	BOOTPC	UDP	Bootstrap Protocol client
69	TFTP	UDP	Trivial File Transfer Protocol
79	FINGER	TCP	Finger
80	HTTP	TCP and UDP	World Wide Web HTTP
101	HOSTNAME	TCP and UDP	NIC host name server
105	CSNET-NS	TCP and UDP	Mailbox name server
110	POP3	TCP	Post Office Protocol 3

Table 11-2   Commonly used TCP/IP port numbers (continued)

Port Number	Process Name	Protocol Used	Description
119	NNTP	TCP and UDP	Network News Transport Protocol
137	NETBIOS-NS	TCP and UDP	NETBIOS Name Service
138	NETBIOS-DG	TCP and UDP	NETBIOS Datagram Service
139	NETBIOS-SS	TCP and UDP	NETBIOS Session Service
161	SNMP	UDP	Simple Network Management Protocol
162	SNMPTRAP	UDP	SNMPTRAP
179	BGP	TCP	Border Gateway Protocol

The use of port numbers simplifies TCP/IP communications and ensures that data are transmitted to the correct application. When a client requests communications with a server and specifies port 23, for example, the server knows immediately that the client wants a Telnet session. No extra data exchange is necessary to define the session type, and the server can initiate the Telnet service without delay. The server will connect to the client's Telnet port—by default, port 23—and establish a virtual circuit. Figure 11-9 depicts this process.

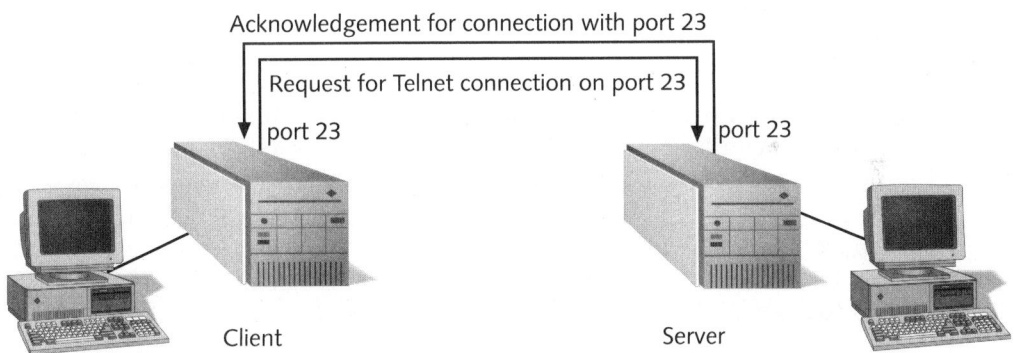

Figure 11-9   A virtual circuit for the Telnet service

As mentioned earlier, you can configure port numbers through software. Most servers maintain an editable, text-based file of port numbers and their associated services. If necessary, you could change the default port number for the Telnet service on your server from 23 to 2330. Changing a default port number is rarely a good idea, however, because it violates the standard. Nevertheless, some network administrators who are preoccupied with security may change their servers' port numbers in an attempt to confuse potential hackers.

Host Names and Domain Name System (DNS)

As you have seen, much of TCP/IP addressing involves numbers—often long, complicated numbers. Computers can manage numbers easily. However, most people can remember words better than numbers. Imagine if you had to identify your friends' and families' Social Security numbers whenever you wanted to write a note or talk to them. Communication would be frustrating at the very least, and perhaps even impossible—especially if you're the kind of person who has trouble remembering even your own Social Security number. Similarly, people prefer to associate names with networked devices rather than remember IP addresses. For this reason, the Internet authorities established a naming system for all nodes on the Internet.

As you learned in Chapter 3, every device on the Internet is technically known as a host. Every host can take a **host name**, a name that describes the device. For example, someone named Peggy Sue McDonald might name her workstation "PeggySue." If the computer is reserved for a specific purpose, you may want to name it accordingly. For example, a company that offers free software downloads through the FTP service might call its host machine "ftpserver." Often, when networking professionals refer to a machine's host name, they mean its local host name plus its domain name—in other words, its fully qualified host name. The following sections discuss host names and domain names.

Domain Names

Every host is a member of a domain, or a group of computers that belong to the same organization and have part of their IP addresses in common. A domain is identified by its domain name. Usually, a **domain name** is associated with a company or other type of organization, such as a university or military unit. For example, IBM's domain name is ibm.com, and the U.S. Library of Congress's domain name is loc.gov. If you worked at the Library of Congress and had named your workstation "PeggySue," your full host name (also known as your fully qualified host name) might be "PeggySue.loc.gov."

 Although an individual user can name his or her workstation, organizations cannot arbitrarily choose their own domain names. Domain names must be registered with an Internet naming authority that works on behalf of ICANN and IANA. If you use an ISP, your ISP can obtain a domain name for you, providing someone else hasn't already reserved your desired name.

ICANN has established conventions for domain naming in which certain suffixes apply to every type of organization that uses the Internet. These suffixes are also known as **top-level domains (TLDs)**. Table 11-3 lists common TLDs. The first eight TLDs listed in this table were established in the mid 1980s. In the past few years, organizations have appealed to ICANN to add the remaining seven TLDs, some of which have been approved, and some of which are still pending approval. In addition, each country has its own domain suffix. For example, Canadian domains end with .ca and Japanese domains end in .jp.

Although domain names may use the international domain suffix, such as .ca for Canada and .jp for Japan, organizations do not necessarily have to use these suffixes. For example, although IBM's headquarters are located in the United States, the company's domain name is *www.ibm.com*. On the other hand, some U.S. organizations do use the .us suffix. For example, the domain name for the Garden City, New York, public school district is *www.gardencity.k12.ny.us*.

Table 11-3   Domain naming conventions

Domain Suffix	Type of Organization
ARPA	Reverse lookup domain (special Internet function)
COM	Commercial
EDU	Educational
GOV	Government
ORG	Non-commercial organization (such as a nonprofit agency)
NET	Network (such as an ISP)
INT	International Treaty Organization
MIL	U.S. military organization
BIZ	Businesses
INFO	Unrestricted use
AERO	Air-transport industry
COOP	Cooperatives
MUSEUM	Museums
NAME	Individuals
PRO	Professionals (such as doctors, lawyers, and engineers)

Once an organization reserves a domain name, the rest of the world's computers know to associate that domain name with that particular organization, and no other organization can legally use it (as long as the reserving organization pays the required annual registration fee to ICANN). For example, you might apply for the domain name called "YourName.com"; not only would the rest of the Internet associate that name with your machine, but also no other parties in the world could use "YourName.com" for their machines.

Host names come with some naming restrictions. You can use any alphanumeric combination with a maximum of 63 characters, and you can include hyphens, underscores, or periods in the name, but no other special characters. The interesting part of host and domain naming relates to how all Internet-connected machines in the world know which names belong to which machines. Before tackling the entire world, however, you can start by thinking about how one company might deal with its local host names.

11

Host Files

The first incarnation of the Internet (called ARPAnet) was used by fewer than 1000 hosts. The entire Internet relied on one text file called HOSTS.TXT to associate names with IP addresses. This file was generically known as a **host file**. The explosive growth of the Internet soon made this simple arrangement impossible to maintain—the host file would require constant changes, searching through one file from all over the nation would strain the Internet's bandwidth capacity, and the entire Internet would fail if the file were accidentally deleted.

Within a company or university, you may still encounter this older system of straightforward ASCII text files that associate internal host names with their IP addresses. Figure 11-10 provides an example of such a file. Notice that each host is matched by one line identifying the host's name and IP address. In addition, a third field, called an **alias**, provides a nickname for the host. An alias allows a user within an organization to address a host by a shorter name than the full host name. Typically, the first line of a host file begins with a pound sign and contains comments about the file's columns. A pound sign may precede comments anywhere in the host file.

# IP address	host name	aliases
132.55.78.109	bingo.games.com	bingo
132.55.78.110	parcheesi.games.com	parcheesi
132.55.78.111	checkers.games.com	checkers
132.55.78.112	darts.games.com	darts

Figure 11-10   An example of a host file

On a UNIX-based computer, a host file is called **hosts** and is located in the /etc directory. On a Windows 9x computer, it is called **lmhosts** and must be located in the c:\windows directory in order to be recognized by the operating system. On a Windows NT or Windows 2000 computer, the file may be called hosts or lmhosts, and must be located in the %systemroot%\system32\drivers\etc folder (where %systemroot% is the directory in which the operating system is installed). Each Windows operating system includes a sample lmhosts file called lmhosts.sam, which is a plain text file you can view in the Notepad program. If you are using hosts or lmhosts files, you should not only master the syntax of this file, but you should also research the implications of using a static host file on your network.

Domain Name System (DNS)

A simple host file can satisfy the needs of one organization, and it can even allow one organization's network to contact hosts on another network. A single host file is no longer sufficient for the Internet, however. Instead, a more automated solution has become mandatory. In the mid-1980s, the Network Information Center (NIC) at Stanford Research Institute devised a hierarchical way of tracking domain names and their addresses, called the **Domain Name System (DNS)**. The DNS database does not rely on one file or even one server, but rather is distributed over several key computers across the Internet to prevent catastrophic failure if one or a few computers go down. DNS is a TCP/IP service that belongs to the Application layer of the TCP/IP Model.

In a simple world, the responsibility for resolving addresses to names might be broken down into national, regional, local, and organizational levels, as depicted in Figure 11-11. In this example, if you worked in the Atlanta office and wanted to exchange data with a machine at another company located in Fairbanks, your organizational DNS server would take your request and pass it off to the local server, which would then pass it off to the regional server, which would in turn pass it off to the national DNS server. The reverse process would occur as the national DNS server passed the request down to the regional, local, and finally organizational servers that know about Fairbanks. This address resolution process assumes that your local DNS server and the Fairbanks local DNS server do not know where to find each other.

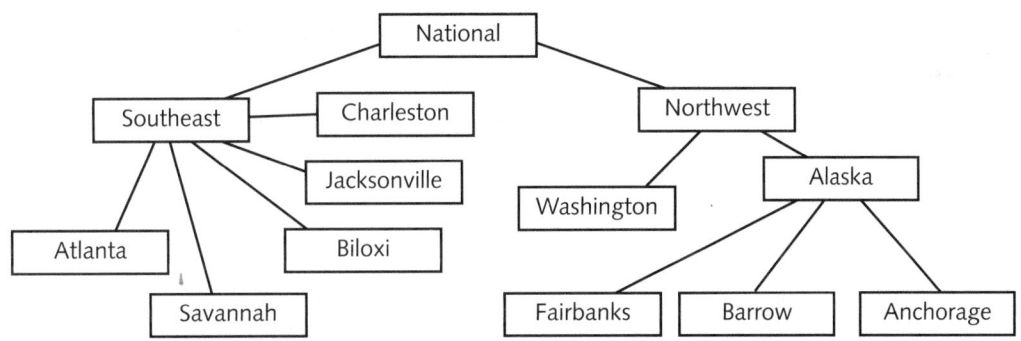

Figure 11-11   Simplified DNS server hierarchy by geography

The actual DNS is somewhat more sophisticated than the previous example implies. To route traffic more efficiently, it is divided into three components: resolvers, name servers, and name space. **Resolvers** are any hosts on the Internet that need to look up domain name information. In the example given in the previous paragraph, your machine in Atlanta is a resolver. The resolver client is built into TCP/IP applications such as Telnet, HTTP, and FTP. If you type the command telnet support.novell.com, your Telnet client software will kick off the resolver service to find the IP address for support.novell.com. If you have Telnetted to the site before, the information may exist in temporary memory and may be retrieved very quickly. Otherwise, the resolver service queries your machine's name server to find the IP address for support.novell.com.

Name servers are servers that contain databases of names and their associated IP addresses. A name server supplies a resolver with the information it requires. If the name server cannot resolve the IP address, the query passes to a higher-level name server. In Figure 11-11, the local, regional, and national servers are all name servers. Each name server manages a group of devices, collectively known as a **zone**; these devices, in turn, distribute naming information. In the example in Figure 11-11, the Southeast name server's zone would include the Atlanta, Savannah, Jacksonville, Biloxi, and Charleston name servers. If the Atlanta server doesn't know the address of a machine in the Savannah area, it can rely on the Southeast name server to supply that information. In a small company, the primary DNS server's zone would include all the computers at the company.

Configuring DNS

Any host that must communicate with other hosts on the Internet needs to know how to find its name server. Although some organizations use only one name server, large organizations often maintain two name servers—a primary and a secondary name server—to help ensure Internet connectivity. If the primary name server experiences a failure, all devices on the network will attempt to use the secondary name server. Each device on the network relies on the name server and therefore must know how to find it. When configuring the TCP/IP properties of a workstation, you need to specify a name server IP address so that the workstation will know which machine to query when it needs to look up a name.

To view or change the name server information on a Windows 2000 workstation:

1. Click **Start**, point to **Settings**, point to **Control Panel**, and then click **Network and Dial-up Connections**. The Network and Dial-up Connections window opens.

2. Right-click the **Local Area Connection** icon and click **Properties** in the shortcut menu. The Local Area Connection Properties dialog box appears.

3. Click **Internet Protocol (TCP/IP)** in the list of network components, and then click **Properties**. The Internet Protocol (TCP/IP) Properties dialog box opens, as shown in Figure 11-12.

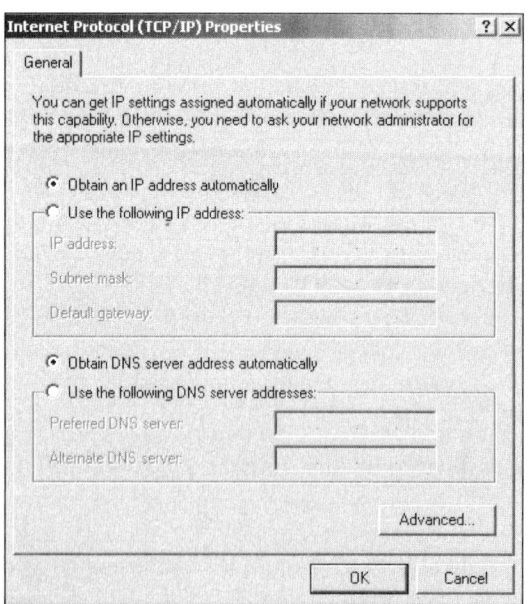

Figure 11-12   Internet Protocol (TCP/IP) Properties dialog box in Windows 2000

4. If necessary, click the **Use the following DNS server addresses** option button to select it.

5. Enter the IP address of your primary DNS server in the Preferred DNS server text box.

6. Enter the IP address of your secondary DNS server, if you have one, in the Alternate DNS server text box.

7. Click **OK** to close the Internet Protocol (TCP/IP) Properties dialog box and save your changes.

8. Click **OK** to close the Local Area Connection Properties dialog box.

To view or change the name server information on a Windows 9x machine:

1. Right-click the **Network Neighborhood** icon, and then click **Properties** in the shortcut menu. The Network Properties dialog box opens.

2. In the list of installed network components, double-click the TCP/IP protocol that is bound to your network adapter. The TCP/IP Properties dialog box opens.

3. Click the **DNS Configuration** tab. The DNS Configuration tab appears, as shown in Figure 11-13.

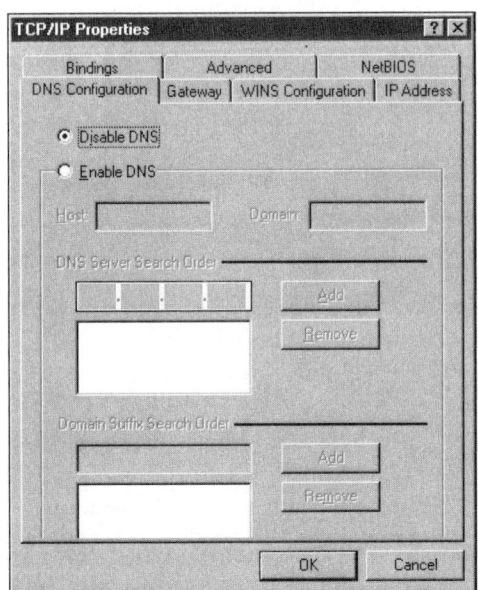

Figure 11-13   DNS Configuration properties tab

4. Click the **Enable DNS** option button to select it (unless you are using DHCP or, in some cases, dial-up networking).

5. Type your computer's host name in the Host text box.

6. Type your organization's domain name in the Domain text box.

7. Type your organization's DNS server IP address in the space provided under the heading "DNS Server Search Order."

8. Click **Add** to save the DNS server's IP address.

9. Add as many as two more DNS server IP addresses in the same manner.

10. Click **OK** to save your changes.

11. Click **OK** to close the Network Properties dialog box.

12. Click **Yes** to confirm that you want to restart your computer.

DNS Name Space

As you learned previously, many name servers across the globe cooperate to keep track of IP addresses and their associated domain names. **Name space** refers to the actual database of Internet IP addresses and their associated names. Every name server holds a piece of the DNS name space. At the highest level in the hierarchy sit the root servers. A **root server** is a name server that is maintained by ICANN and that acts as the ultimate authority on how to contact the top-level domains, such as those ending with .com, .edu, .net, .us, and so on. ICANN maintains 13 root servers around the world. In Figure 11-11, the national-level name server would actually be a root server for the United States.

Name space is not a database that you can open and view like a store's inventory database. Rather, this abstract concept describes how the name servers of the world share DNS information. Pieces of it are tangible, however, and are stored on a name server in a **resource record**, which is a single record that describes one piece of information in the DNS database. For example, an **address resource record** is a type of resource record that maps the IP address of an Internet-connected device to its domain name.

Resource records come in many different types, depending on their function. Each resource record contains a name field to identify the domain name of the machine to which the record refers, a type field to identify the type of resource record involved, a class field to identify the class to which the record belongs (usually "IN" or "Internet"), a time to live field to identify how long the record should be saved in temporary memory, a data length field to identify how much data the record contains, and the actual record data. Approximately 20 types of resource records are currently used.

Each resource record type adheres to specific data field requirements, thus ensuring that any name server across the world can interpret it. For example, the data field of a simple network address record would include only the network address, whereas the data field of a mailbox information record would include the name of the mailbox responsible for error messages and the name of the mailbox responsible for mailing lists. In the following fictitious address resource record, knight.chess.games.com is the host domain name, IN stands for the Internet record class, A identifies the record type as "address," and 203.99.120.76 is the host's IP address:

```
knight.chess.games.com    IN    A    203.99.120.76
```

This book does not provide in-depth coverage of DNS domains, hierarchy, zones, and databases. If you are interested in Internet server administration, you should investigate host files and DNS in more detail. For Net+ certification, you should know the purpose of DNS and host files, understand the hierarchical nature of DNS, and be able to specify name servers on a client workstation.

BOOTP

To communicate with other devices through TCP/IP, every workstation, printer, or other node on a network requires a unique IP address. On the earliest TCP/IP networks, each device was manually assigned its own number through a local configuration file; that number never changed until someone edited the configuration file. As networks grew larger, however, local configuration files became more difficult to implement. Imagine the arduous task faced by a network administrator who must visit each of 8000 workstations, printers, and hosts on a company's LAN to assign IP addresses and ensure that no single IP address is used twice. Now imagine how much extra work would be required to restructure the company's IP address management system (for example, to implement subnetting) or to move a department's machine to a different network segment.

To facilitate IP address management, a service called the Bootstrap Protocol was developed in the mid-1980s. The **Bootstrap Protocol (BOOTP)** uses a central list of IP addresses and their associated devices' MAC addresses to dynamically assign IP addresses to clients. When a client that relies on BOOTP first connects to the network, it sends a broadcast message to the network asking to be assigned an IP address. This broadcast message includes the MAC address of the client's NIC. The BOOTP server recognizes a BOOTP client's request, looks up the client's MAC address in its BOOTP table, and responds to the client with the following information: the client's IP address, the IP address of the server, the host name of the server, and the IP address of a default router. Figure 11-14 outlines this process.

11

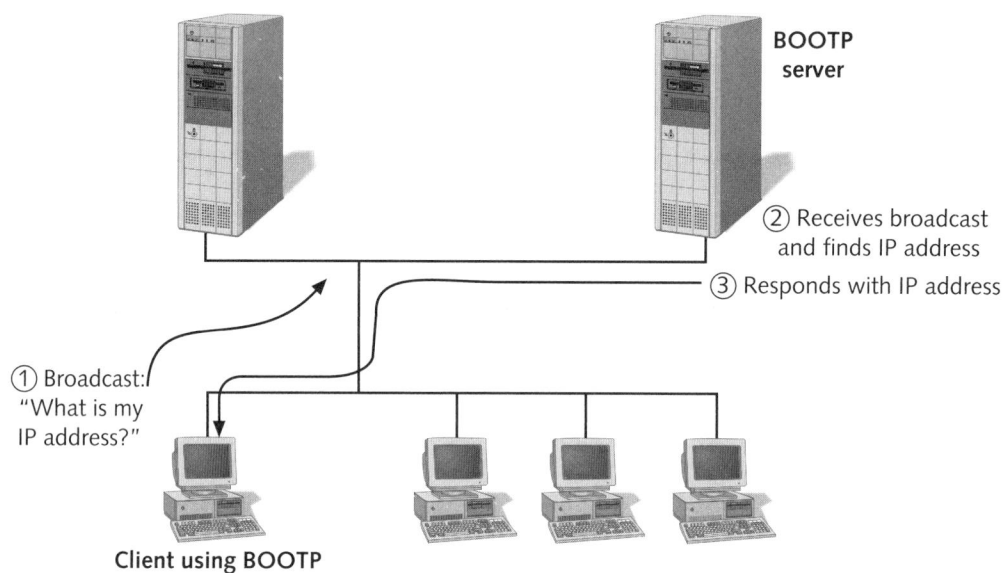

Figure 11-14 The BOOTP process

Thanks to BOOTP, a client does not have to remember its own IP address, and therefore network administrators do not have to go to each workstation on a network in order to manually assign its IP address. This situation is ideal for **diskless workstations** (that is, workstations that do not contain hard disks, but rely on a small amount of read-only memory to connect to a network and to pick up their system files).

For other kinds of clients, BOOTP has been surpassed by the more sophisticated IP address management tool, Dynamic Host Configuration Protocol (DHCP). As you will learn in the next section, DHCP requires little intervention, whereas BOOTP requires network administrators to enter every IP and MAC address manually into the BOOTP table. As you can imagine, the BOOTP table can be difficult to maintain on large networks. You may still encounter BOOTP in existing networks, but most likely it will support only diskless workstations (which are sometimes called network computers).

Dynamic Host Configuration Protocol (DHCP)

By now, you have seen several references to DHCP. **Dynamic Host Configuration Protocol (DHCP)** is an automated means of assigning a unique IP address to every device on a network. Reasons for implementing DHCP include the following:

- *To reduce the time and planning spent on IP address management.* Central management of IP addresses eliminates the need for network administrators to edit the TCP/IP configuration on every network workstation, printer, or other device.

- *To reduce the potential for errors in assigning IP addresses.* With DHCP, no possibility exists that a workstation will be assigned an invalid address, and almost no possibility exists that two workstations will attempt to use the same IP address and thereby cause network errors (occasionally the DHCP server software may make a mistake). On the other hand, when manually assigning IP addresses on each workstation, or even manually editing a BOOTP table, it is easy to type in the wrong address or use the same address twice.

- *To enable users to move their workstations and printers without having to change their TCP/IP configuration.* As long as a workstation is configured to obtain its IP address from a central server, the workstation can be attached anywhere on the network and receive a valid address.

- *To make IP addressing transparent for mobile users.* For example, if a salesperson brought her Windows 2000 laptop to your conference room to make an online presentation about Internet commerce, she could attach to your network and receive an IP address without having to change her laptop's configuration.

DHCP was developed by the Internet Engineering Task Force as a replacement for BOOTP. Unlike BOOTP, DHCP does not require the network administrator to maintain a table of IP and MAC addresses on the server. It does, however, require the network administrator in charge of IP address management to install and configure the DHCP service on a server (such as Windows NT, Windows 2000, NetWare 4.11 or higher, or UNIX) that can run DHCP.

DHCP Leasing Process

With DHCP, a device borrows, or **leases**, an IP address while it is attached to the network. In other words, it uses the IP address on a temporary basis. When, for example, a client logs off the network, it relinquishes the IP address, and the DHCP server can assign it to another device.

Configuring DHCP involves specifying a range of addresses that can be leased to any network device on a particular segment. As a network administrator, you configure the duration of the lease (in the configuration of the DHCP server) to be as short or long as necessary, from a matter of minutes to forever. Once the DHCP server is running, clients can attach to it and receive their unique IP addresses. More specifically, the client and server take the following steps to negotiate the client's first lease (this example applies to a workstation, but devices such as networked printers may also take advantage of DHCP):

1. When the client workstation starts (assuming it has the TCP/IP protocol installed and bound to the NIC), it sends out a DHCP discover packet in broadcast fashion via the UDP protocol to the DHCP/BOOTP server port (by default, port number 67).

2. Every DHCP server that is connected to the same subnet as the client receives the broadcast request. Each DHCP server responds with an available IP address, while simultaneously withholding that address from other clients.

The response message includes the available IP address, subnet mask, IP address of the DHCP server, and the lease duration. This message goes out through the DHCP/BOOTP port 68 in broadcast fashion. Because the client doesn't have an IP address, the DHCP server cannot send the information directly to the client.

In some instances, BOOTP and DHCP may appear lumped together under the same category or service. For example, if you are configuring a Hewlett-Packard LaserJet that uses a JetDirect print server card, you can select "BOOTP/DHCP" from the printer's TCP/IP Configuration menu. BOOTP and DHCP are not always distinguished as separate services because they appear the same to the client and use the same server ports to handle their communications to and from the server. The main difference between the two services lies in how the server software distributes IP addresses.

3. The client accepts the first IP address that it receives, responding with a broadcast message that essentially confirms to the DHCP that it wants to accept the address. Because this message is broadcast, all other DHCP servers that might have responded to the client's original query see this confirmation and hence return the IP addresses they had reserved for the client to their pool of available addresses.

4. When the selected DHCP server receives the confirmation, it replies—in a broadcast fashion—with an acknowledgment message. It also provides more information, such as DNS or gateway addresses that the client might have requested.

The preceding steps involve the exchange of only four packets and therefore do not usually increase the time it takes for a client to log onto the network. Figure 11-15 depicts the DHCP leasing process. The client and server do not have to repeat this exchange until the lease is terminated. The IP address will remain in the client's TCP/IP settings even after the device restarts.

DHCP Server
② Broadcast:
"Hi Client A; please use
IP address 123.45.67.89."

④ Broadcast:
"Client A has now been
assigned the IP address"
123.45.67.89."

Client A
① Broadcast:
"This is Client A; What
IP address can I use?"

③ Broadcast:
"This is Client A; I'll take it."

Figure 11-15   The DHCP leasing process

11

Terminating a DHCP Lease

A DHCP lease may expire based on the period established for it in the server configuration or it may be manually terminated at any time from either the client's TCP/IP configuration or the server's DHCP configuration. In some instances, a user must terminate a lease. Consider what might happen to the previously mentioned salesperson after she presents her online demonstration in your conference room. She returns to her office, plugs her laptop network cable into the outlet under her desk, and turns on her machine. Her TCP/IP settings will still contain the IP address and other information (such as DNS server and gateway address) she received from your DHCP server in the conference room. In addition, because the DHCP lease period lasts 30 days, her TCP/IP service will not attempt to pick up a new IP address from her own company's DHCP server. What will happen when the salesperson tries to pick up her e-mail? She will receive an error message, because her IP address will no longer be valid. Unfortunately, the error message will say only that it cannot establish a TCP/IP connection (not that a new IP address is needed). In this situation, the user needs to terminate her lease. In Windows terms, this event is called a **release** of the TCP/IP settings.

To release TCP/IP settings on a computer running the Windows 2000 operating system:

1. Click **Start**, point to **Programs**, point to **Accessories**, and then click **Command Prompt**. The Command Prompt window opens.

2. At the command prompt, type `ipconfig /release`.

3. Press **Enter**. The values for your IP Address, Subnet Mask, and Default Gateway in the IP Configuration dialog box revert to all zeros.

To release TCP/IP settings on a computer running the Windows 9x operating system:

1. Click **Start**, and then click **Run**. The Run dialog box opens.

2. Type **winipcfg**, and then click **OK**. The IP Configuration dialog box opens, displaying the workstation's TCP/IP settings.

3. To release the DHCP lease, click **Release All**.

4. The values for IP Address, Subnet Mask, and Default Gateway in the IP Configuration dialog box revert to all zeros. Click **OK** to close the IP Configuration dialog box.

Releasing old DHCP information is the first step in the process of obtaining a new IP address. In the preceding example, the salesperson would also have to instruct her TCP/IP service to request a new IP address. This task is easily accomplished from most workstations or laptops.

To obtain a new IP address on a Windows 2000 workstation:

1. Click **Start**, point to **Programs**, point to **Accessories**, and then click **Command Prompt**. The Command Prompt window opens.

2. At the command prompt, type `ipconfig /renew`.

3. Press **Enter**. The values for your IP Address and Subnet Mask will be appropriate for the subnet to which you are now attached.

To obtain a new IP address on a Windows 9x workstation:

1. Click **Start**, and then click **Run**. The Run dialog box opens.

2. Type **winipcfg**, and then click **OK**. The IP Configuration dialog box opens, displaying the workstation's TCP/IP settings.

3. Click **Renew All** to obtain new TCP/IP settings from the DHCP server.

   The values for your IP Address and Subnet Mask in the IP Configuration dialog box will be appropriate for the subnet to which you are now attached.

4. Click **OK** to close the IP Configuration dialog box.

With TCP/IP becoming the protocol of choice on most networks, you will most certainly have to work with DHCP—either from the client, the server side, or both—at some point in your networking career. As mentioned earlier, DHCP services run on several types of servers. The installation and configurations for each type of server vary; for specifics, you must refer to the DHCP server software's manual. To qualify for Net+ certification, you need not know the intricacies of installing and configuring DHCP server software. You do, however, need to know what DHCP does and how it accomplishes it. You also need to understand the advantages of using DHCP rather than other means of assigning IP addresses.

Windows Internet Naming Service (WINS)

The **Windows Internet Naming Service (WINS)** provides a means of resolving NetBIOS names to IP addresses. Recall from Chapter 3 that NetBIOS is used primarily with Windows-based systems, and that a NetBIOS name is a unique alphanumeric name assigned to each Windows-based workstation on a network. WINS is used exclusively with systems that use NetBIOS—therefore, it usually appears on Windows-based systems. With fewer and fewer networks relying on NetBIOS, WINS is quickly becoming scarce.

A computer's NetBIOS name and its TCP/IP host name are different entities, though you can choose to use the same name for the NetBIOS name as you use for the TCP/IP name. Earlier, you learned that DNS provides resolutions of TCP/IP host names and IP addresses. WINS, on the other hand, provides resolution of NetBIOS names and IP addresses. Essentially, WINS has the same relationship to NetBIOS as DNS has to TCP/IP. That is, both WINS and DNS associate names with IP addresses.

Unlike DNS, however, WINS is an automated service that runs on a server. In this sense, it resembles DHCP. WINS may be implemented on servers running Windows NT Server version 3.5 or higher or on servers running Windows 2000 Server. It maintains a database on the server that accepts requests from Windows or DOS clients to register with a particular NetBIOS name. Note that WINS does not assign names or IP addresses, but merely keeps track of which NetBIOS names are linked to which IP addresses.

WINS offers several advantages:

- Guarantees that a unique NetBIOS name is used for each computer on a network. WINS manages which NetBIOS name is associated with each IP address, and it will not allow two machines with the same name to register.

- Support for DHCP. WINS can be integrated with the dynamic IP addressing method used by DHCP.

- Better network performance. As long as WINS manages the mappings between IP addresses and NetBIOS names, clients do not have to broadcast their NetBIOS names to the rest of the network. The elimination of this broadcast traffic improves network performance.

Every client workstation that needs to register with the WINS server must know how to find the server. Thus the WINS server cannot use a dynamic IP address (such as one assigned by a DHCP server). Instead, a specific IP address must be assigned to it manually.

11

To configure a Windows 2000 workstation to use the WINS service:

1. Click **Start**, point to **Settings**, and then click **Control Panel**.

2. Double-click **Network and Dial-up Connections**. The Network and Dial-up Connections window opens.

3. Right-click the **Local Area Connection** icon, and then click **Properties** in the shortcut menu. The Local Area Connection Properties dialog box appears.

4. Highlight **Internet Protocol (TCP/IP)** in the list of network components, and then click **Properties**. The Internet Protocol (TCP/IP) Properties dialog box opens.

5. Click the **Advanced** button. The Advanced TCP/IP Settings dialog box opens, as shown in Figure 11-16.

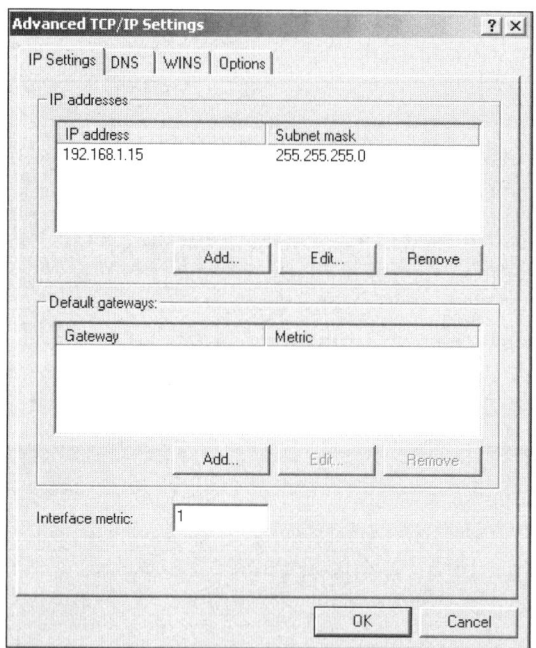

Figure 11-16   Advanced TCP/IP Settings dialog box in Windows 2000

6. Click the **WINS** tab.

7. To add a WINS server address, click **Add**. The TCP/IP WINS Server dialog box appears.

8. Enter the IP address of your WINS server in the WINS server search order text box. Click **Add** to add this server's address to your list of WINS servers.

9. If you have a secondary WINS server, you can add that by repeating Steps 7 and 8.

10. Click **OK** to close the Advanced TCP/IP Settings dialog box and save your changes.

11. Click **OK** to close the Internet Protocol (TCP/IP) Properties dialog box.

12. Click **OK** to close the Local Area Connection Properties dialog box.

To configure a Windows 9x workstation to use the WINS service:

1. Right-click the **Network Neighborhood** icon, and then click **Properties** in the shortcut menu. The Network dialog box opens.

2. Click the **Configuration** tab.

3. Select the TCP/IP protocol that is bound to your network adapter in the list of installed networking components, and then click **Properties**. The TCP/IP Properties dialog box opens.

4. Click the **WINS Configuration** tab.

5. To establish the identity of your WINS server, click **Enable WINS Resolution**.

6. Type the IP address of your WINS server in the spaces provided under "WINS Server Search Order" and then click **Add**.

7. If you have a secondary WINS server, repeat Step 6 to add its IP address number.

8. Click **OK** to save your changes.

9. Click **OK** to exit the Network dialog box.

10. You will be asked whether you want to restart your computer to save your changes. Click **Yes** to confirm that you want to restart it.

As with DNS, a complete discussion of WINS could fill at least an entire chapter. If you plan to specialize in Windows NT or Windows 2000 networking and clients running NetBIOS, you should investigate this topic further. For Net+ certification, you should be familiar with the purpose and advantages of WINS.

Addressing in IPv6

Up to this point, you have learned about IP addressing according to the IPv4 scheme. This section introduces you to addressing in IPv6 and the differences between addressing in IPv4 and addressing in IPv6.

As you have learned, IP version 6 (IPv6) (also known as **IP next generation**, or **IPng**) is slated to replace the current IP protocol, IPv4. Some applications, operating systems, and servers already provide support for IPv6, but many organizations have not made the switch due to the anticipated difficulty of changing their addressing scheme. In the coming years, however, switching to IPv6 will become not only desirable, but imperative. IPv6 offers several advantages over IPv4, including a more efficient header, the inclusion of the IPSec security technique, better support for QoS, and automatic IP address configuration.

11

But perhaps the most valuable advantage IPv6 offers is its promise of billions and billions of additional IP addresses through its new addressing scheme. As you have learned, the explosive growth of the Internet has meant that nearly all the traditional IP addresses are now in use. Scientists who developed the Internet over 20 years ago did not foresee this growth and therefore, did not make allowances for the volume of IP addresses the global network would require. IPv6 has been designed to correct this problem.

The most notable difference between IP addresses in IPv4 and IPv6 is their size. While IPv4 addresses are composed of four 8-bit fields (or octets), for a total of 32 bits, IPv6 addresses are composed of eight 16-bit fields and total 128 bits. The added fields and the larger address size result in an increase of 2^{96} (or 4 billion times 4 billion times 4 billion) available IP addresses in the IPv6 addressing scheme. The addition of more IP addresses not only allows every interface on every Internet-connected device to have a unique number, but also eliminates the need for IP address conservation. For example, organizations that use NAT through IP gateways in order to share limited IP addresses among several workstations will no longer need to do so after they adopt IPv6 addressing.

A second difference between IPv4 and IPv6 addresses is the way they are represented. While each octet in an IPv4 address contains binary numbers separated by a period (for example, 123.45.67.89), each field in an IPv6 address contains hexadecimal numbers separated by a colon. An example of a valid IPv6 address is F:F:0:0:0:0:3012:0CE3. Because many IPv6 addresses will contain multiple fields that have values of 0, a shorthand for representing these fields has been established. This shorthand substitutes "::" for any number of multiple, zero-value fields. Thus, the IPv6 address example above could be also be written as FF::3012:0CE3. An interesting, easily shortened address is the IPv6 loopback address. Recall that in IPv4 the loopback address has a value of 127.0.0.1. In IPv6, however, the loopback address has a value of 0:0:0:0:0:0:0:1. Abbreviated, the IPv6 loopback address becomes ::1. The substitution of multiple zero value fields can only be performed once within an address; otherwise, you would not be able to tell how many fields the "::" symbol represented.

A third difference between the two types of IP addresses is that in IPv6, each interface on a device is assigned its own IP address, rather than each node having its own IP address. Thus, if you were the network administrator for a network containing two VLANs, each associated with a different port on a switch, you could issue data transmissions to all interfaces on one VLAN by simply directing your transmission to the switch port associated with that VLAN. In addition to allowing different interfaces to have different IP addresses, IPv6 addressing distinguishes between different types of interfaces. One type of IPv6 address is a **unicast address**, or an address that represents a single interface on a device. A unicast address is the type of address that would be assigned, for example, to a workstation's NIC or a hub port. A **multicast address** represents multiple interfaces (often on multiple devices). Multicast addresses are useful for transmitting the same data to many different devices simultaneously. In IPv6, multicast addressing prevents the need for a broadcast address. Thus, there is no such thing as a broadcast address in IPv6. An **anycast address** represents any one interface from a group of interfaces (often on multiple nodes), any one of which (usually the first available) can accept a transmission.

Anycast addresses could be useful for identifying all of the routers that belong to one ISP, for example. In this instance, an Internet transmission destined for one of that ISP's servers could be accepted by the first available router in the anycast group. The result is that the transmission finishes faster than if it had to wait for one specific router interface to become available. At this time, anycast addresses are not designed to be assigned to hosts, such as servers or workstations.

A fourth significant difference between IPv4 and IPv6 addressing is that in IPv6, each address contains a **Format Prefix**, or a variable-length field at the beginning of the address that indicates what type of address it is. The Format Prefix also establishes the arrangement of the rest of the address's fields. In the IPv4 addressing scheme, no distinction is made between an address that represents one device or interface and an address that represents multiple devices or interfaces. For example, if you used the `netstat` command and noticed that your workstation was connected to a device with the IP address of 161.45.03.88, you could not conclude anything about the device or its transmission from that number. However, in IPv6, the first field of the IP address would provide a clue as to what type of interface the address represented. A unicast or anycast address begins with one of the two following hexadecimal strings: FEC0 or FE80. A multicast address begins with the following hexadecimal string: FF0x, where x is a character that corresponds to a group scope ID (for example, a group of addresses that belongs to an entire organization or a group of addresses that belongs to one site on a WAN).

Although IPv6 has been defined since the mid-1990s, organizations have been slow to adopt it. However, the use of IPv6 is predicted to grow rapidly as more and more devices (particularly wireless electronics) are connected to the Internet. During this transition phase, IPv4 and IPv6 will need to coexist. To do so, modern connectivity devices will most likely translate IPv4 addresses into IPv6 addresses for transmission over the Internet by padding the extra fields with zeros to fill the 128-bit address space.

11

TCP/IP SUBPROTOCOLS

In Chapter 3, you learned that TCP/IP is not a single protocol, but rather a suite of protocols, commonly called subprotocols, each of which performs a distinct function. That chapter introduced the core subprotocols, including IP, TCP, UDP, ICMP, and ARP, as well as Application layer protocols such as Telnet, FTP, SMTP, and SNMP. This section briefly reviews these subprotocols and introduces several new subprotocols. In addition, it describes in more depth the subprotocols with finite purposes such as SMTP and POP, as opposed to the more general-purpose subprotocols such as TCP and UDP.

In your networking career, you will need to be familiar with all of the subprotocols covered in this book, even if you do not choose to master the fine points of TCP/IP networking. Suppose, for instance, that you are troubleshooting a problem with the e-mail package at your organization. Before you can talk to the vendor's technical support personnel, you must know whether your e-mail software uses POP or IMAP. In troubleshooting and managing a network, you will encounter many situations such as this one that require you to know which TCP/IP subprotocols your network uses and how those subprotocols are implemented.

A Review of TCP/IP Subprotocols

The following list of subprotocols and their functions should look familiar to you. If you do not remember how they fit into the OSI Model or what some of the terms (such as "connectionless") mean, you should review the summary at the end of Chapter 3.

- *Internet Protocol (IP)*—A core protocol in the TCP/IP suite that belongs to the Internet layer of the TCP/IP model and provides information about how and where data should be delivered. IP is the subprotocol that enables TCP/IP to internetwork.

- *Transmission Control Protocol (TCP)*—A core protocol of the TCP/IP suite. TCP belongs to the Transport layer and provides reliable data delivery services because it is connection-oriented.

- *User Datagram Protocol (UDP)*—A core protocol in the TCP/IP suite that sits in the Transport layer, between the Internet layer and the Application layer of the TCP/IP model. Unlike TCP, UDP is a connectionless transport service.

- *Internet Control Message Protocol (ICMP)*—A core protocol in the TCP/IP suite that notifies the sender that something has gone wrong in the transmission process and that packets were not delivered.

- *Address Resolution Protocol (ARP)*—A core protocol in the TCP/IP suite that belongs in the Internet layer and obtains the MAC (physical) address of a host, or node, and then creates a local database that maps the MAC address to the host's IP (logical) address.

- *Telnet*—An Application layer terminal emulation protocol used to log onto remote hosts using TCP/IP.

- *File Transfer Protocol (FTP)*—An Application layer protocol used to send and receive files via TCP/IP.

- *Simple Network Management Protocol (SNMP)*—A communication protocol used to manage devices on a TCP/IP network.

Additional and Highlighted Subprotocols

In addition to the subprotocols introduced in Chapter 3, you should understand the subprotocols described in the following sections. Some of these will be new to you, while others (such as POP) will be familiar. Note that many of these protocols belong to the Application layer of the TCP/IP Model, which translates to the Application, Presentation, and Session layers of the OSI Model.

Reverse Address Resolution Protocol (RARP)

The Address Resolution Protocol (ARP) is a means of obtaining the MAC address of a local host and keeping that information in a local cache. If a device doesn't know its own IP address, however, it can't use ARP, because it cannot issue ARP requests or receive ARP replies. One solution to this problem is to allow the client to send a broadcast message with the MAC address of a device and receive the device's IP address in reply. This process, which is the reverse of ARP, is made possible by the **Reverse Address Resolution Protocol (RARP)**. A RARP server maintains a table of MAC addresses and their associated IP addresses (similar to a BOOTP table). By consulting this table, a RARP server can respond to a client's request for an IP address associated with a particular MAC address. Only a RARP server can provide this service. A network may use more than one RARP server to balance the load caused by RARP requests and responses.

RARP was originally developed as a means for diskless workstations to obtain IP addresses from a server before BOOTP emerged. Figure 11-17 illustrates how RARP can provide an IP address to a diskless workstation.

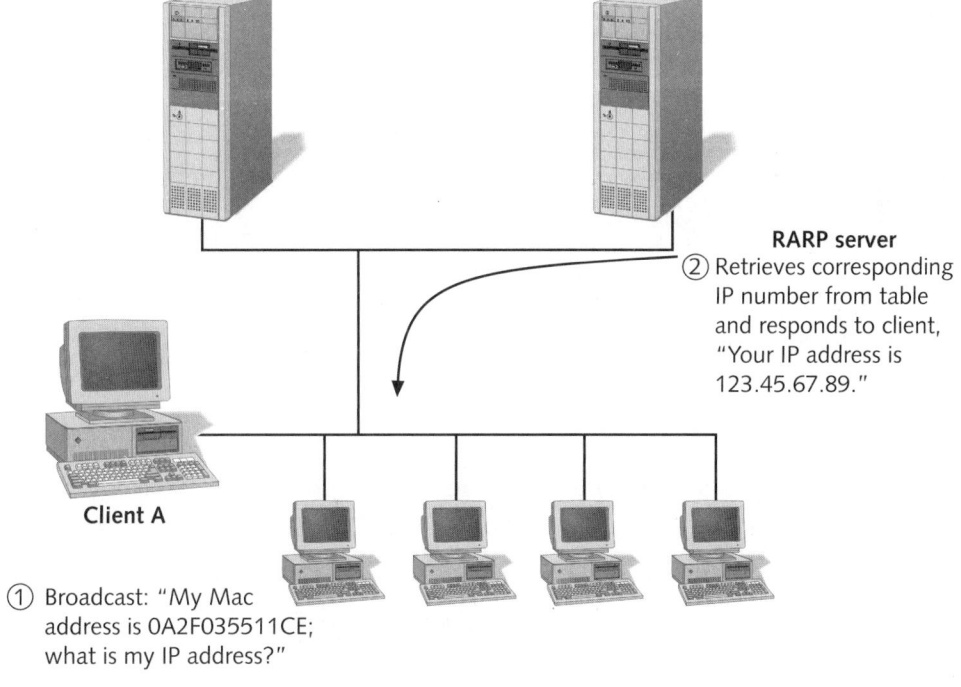

RARP server
② Retrieves corresponding
IP number from table
and responds to client,
"Your IP address is
123.45.67.89."

Client A

① Broadcast: "My Mac
address is 0A2F035511CE;
what is my IP address?"

Figure 11-17   How RARP works

Simple Mail Transfer Protocol (SMTP)

In Chapter 3, you learned that the **Simple Mail Transfer Protocol (SMTP)** is responsible for moving messages from one e-mail server to another over TCP/IP-based networks. SMTP belongs to the Application layer of the TCP/IP Model and relies on TCP at the Transport layer. It operates from port 25. (That is, requests to receive mail and send mail go through port 25 on the SMTP server.) SMTP, which provides the basis for Internet e-mail service, relies on higher-level programs for its instructions. Although SMTP comes with a set of human-readable commands that you could conceivably use to transport mail from machine to machine, this method would be laborious, slow, and error-prone. Instead, other services, such as the UNIX sendmail software, provide more friendly and sophisticated mail interfaces that rely on SMTP as their means of transport.

SMTP is a simple subprotocol, incapable of doing anything more than transporting mail or holding it in a queue. In the post office analogy of data communications, SMTP is like the mail carrier who picks up his day's mail load at the post office and delivers it to the homes on his route. The mail carrier does not worry about where the mail is stored overnight or how it gets from another city's Post Office to his Post Office. If a piece of mail is undeliverable, he simply holds onto it; the mail carrier does not attempt to figure out what went wrong. In Internet e-mail transmission, higher-level mail protocols such as POP and IMAP, which are discussed in the next two sections, take care of these functions.

When you configure clients to use Internet e-mail, you need to identify the user's SMTP server. (Sometimes this server is called the mail server.) Each e-mail program will specify this setting in a different place, though most commonly in the Mail Preferences section. Assuming that your client uses DNS, you do not have to identify the IP address of the SMTP server-only the name. For example, if a user's e-mail address is jdoe@usmail.com, his SMTP server is probably called "usmail.com." You do not have to specify the TCP/IP port number used by SMTP, because both the client workstation and the server will assume that SMTP requests and responses flow through port 25.

Post Office Protocol (POP)

The **Post Office Protocol (POP)** is a protocol that provides centralized storage for e-mail messages. It belongs to the Application layer of the TCP/IP Model and relies on SMTP. In the Postal Service analogy, POP is like the Post Office that holds mail until its delivery to customers. A storage mechanism such as POP is necessary because users are not always logged onto the network and available for receiving messages. Both SMTP and a service such as POP are necessary for a mail server to receive, store, and forward messages. These two protocols cannot work without each other.

Users need an SMTP-compliant mail program to connect to their POP server and download mail from storage. POP does not allow users to keep the mail on the server after they retrieve it, which can create a problem for users who move from machine to machine. For example, if three receptionists share a company's front desk PC, each will need a separate area on the hard disk to save mail if the network uses POP. But what happens if someone from the Accounting Department needs to fill in at the reception desk one afternoon, but also wants to read mail while stationed there. With POP, he would have to create yet another area for his mail on the front desk PC. When he returns to his desk in Accounting, however, the mail will not be accessible because it would have been saved on a different PC. A few options exist for circumventing this problem (such as keeping users' mail on a LAN server), but a more thorough solution has been provided by a new, more sophisticated e-mail protocol called IMAP, described in the next section.

The "POP" acronym has multiple meanings in the world of networking. In Chapter 7's discussion of remote connectivity, POP stood for a carrier's point of presence. In this chapter's discussion of Internet e-mail, POP stands for Post Office Protocol. Other acronyms also have double meanings in the computer world, so when reading or talking about data communications, you need to understand the particular context. Often the Post Office Protocol will be identified with its version number as well—for example, POP2 or POP3. To make matters more confusing, some networking professionals use POP as a verb, as in the following sentence: "I always pop for mail before I go to lunch."

Internet Mail Access Protocol (IMAP)

The **Internet Mail Access Protocol (IMAP)** is a mail storage and manipulation protocol that also depends on SMTP's transport system. IMAP was developed as a more sophisticated alternative to POP. The most current version of IMAP is version 4 (IMAP4). IMAP4 can (and eventually will) replace POP without the user having to change e-mail programs. The single biggest advantage IMAP4 has over POP is that users can store messages on the mail server, rather than always having to download them to a local machine. This feature benefits users who move from workstation to workstation. In addition, IMAP4 provides the following features:

- *Users can retrieve all or only a portion of any mail message.* The remainder can be left on the mail server. This feature benefits users who move from machine to machine and users who have slow connections to the network or minimal free hard disk space.

- *Users can review their messages and delete them while the messages remain on the server.* This feature preserves network bandwidth, especially when the messages are long or contain attached files, because the data need not travel over the wire from the server to the client's workstation. For users with a slow modem connection, deleting messages without having to download them represents a major advantage over POP.

- *Users can create sophisticated methods of organizing messages on the server.* A user might, for example, build a system of folders to contain messages with similar content. Also, a user might search through all of the messages for only those that contain one particular keyword or subject line.

11

- *Users can share a mailbox in a central location.* For example, if several mainte-nance personnel who use different PCs need to receive the same messages from the Facilities Department head but do not need e-mail for any other purpose, they can all log on with the same ID and share the same mailbox on the server. If POP were used in this situation, only one maintenance staff member could read the message; she would then have to forward or copy it to her colleagues.

- *IMAP4 can provide better security than POP because it supports authentication.* Security is an increasing concern for network managers as more organiza-tions connect to the public Internet.

Although IMAP provides significant advantages over POP, it also comes with a few dis-advantages. For instance, IMAP servers require more storage space and usually more pro-cessing resources than POP servers do. By extension, network managers must keep a closer watch on IMAP servers to ensure that users are not consuming more than their fair share of space on the server. In addition, if the IMAP server fails, users cannot access the mail left there. (IMAP does allow users to download messages to their own PCs, however.)

Until recently, another consideration was that most popular e-mail programs were designed for use with POP servers only. This standard is changing, however, and you should have no difficulty obtaining mail programs that use IMAP4. For example, Eudora Pro, GroupWise, Lotus Notes, Netscape, and Microsoft Outlook all support IMAP4.

Hypertext Transport Protocol (HTTP)

Hypertext Transport Protocol (HTTP) is a protocol that operates in the Application layer of the TCP/IP model. You can think of it as the language that Web clients and servers use to communicate. HTTP therefore forms the backbone of the Web. When you type the address of a Web page in your Web browser's address field, HTTP transports the information about your request to the Web server on port 80. It interprets your request and returns the Web server's information to you in **Hypertext Markup Language (HTML)**, the Web document formatting language. If you access a Web page that con-tains links to other Web pages, HTTP allows you to connect those links after you click on them. Figure 11-18 outlines this process.

HTTP/0.9, the original version of HTTP, was released in 1990. This version provided only the simplest means of transferring data over the Internet. Since then, HTTP has been greatly improved to make Web client/server connections more efficient, reliable, and secure. For example, HTTP/1.1, the current version of HTTP, allows servers to transmit multiple objects, such as text and graphics, over a single TCP connection using longer packets. It also allows a client to save Web pages via caching and to compare the saved pages with requested pages. If the two are identical, the Web browser will use the cached copy of the page to save bandwidth and time.

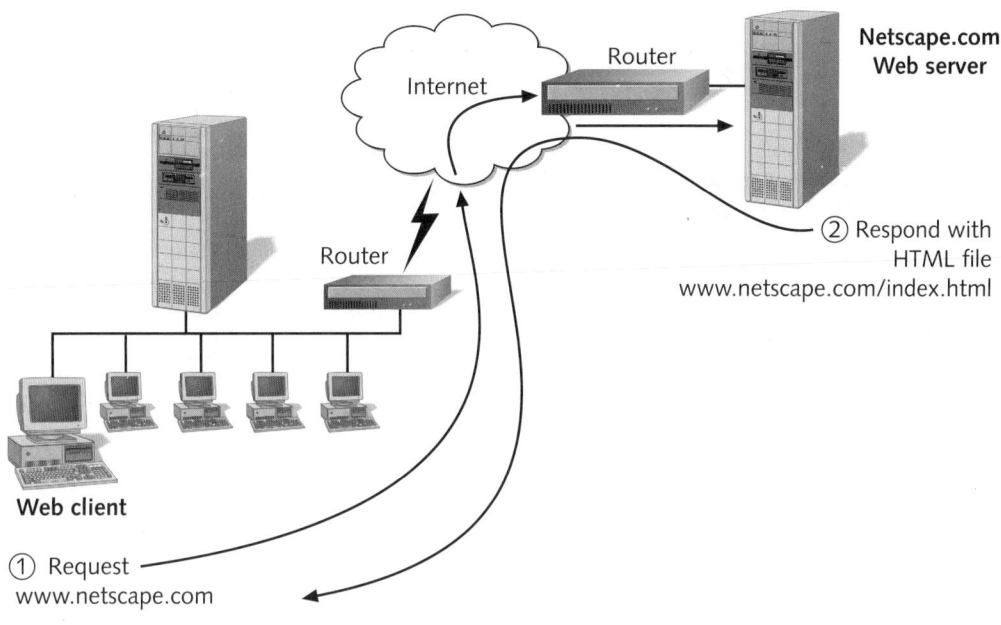

Figure 11-18   Web client/server transmission using HTTP

Network Time Protocol (NTP)

NTP, the **Network Time Protocol**, is used to synchronize the clocks of computers on a network. It is a very simple protocol that belongs to the Application layer of the TCP/IP Model and depends on UDP. Although it is simple, it is also important. Since many packets have a predefined period of time to reach their destination (after which they will be discarded), it is critical that all computer clocks on a network be synchronized. Otherwise, packets might expire prematurely, resulting in sporadic data loss. Time is also used in routing to determine the most efficient path for data over a network. NTP is a protocol that benefits from UDP's quick, connectionless nature at the Transport layer. NTP is time-sensitive and cannot wait for the error checking that TCP would require.

TCP/IP TROUBLESHOOTING

Of all network protocols, TCP/IP is the most likely to cause problems because it requires the most planning and post-installation configuration. As with any type of communication, many potential points of failure exist in the TCP/IP transmission process. Fortunately, TCP/IP comes with a complete set of troubleshooting tools that can help you to track down most TCP/IP-related problems without using expensive software or hardware to analyze network traffic. You should be familiar with the use of the following tools and their **switches** (the letters or words added to a command that allow you to customize the utility's output), not only because the Network+ certification exam covers them, but also because you will regularly need these diagnostics in your work with TCP/IP networks. Each of these utilities can be accessed from the command prompt on a server or client running TCP/IP.

Each TCP/IP utility can be used by nearly any client that runs TCP/IP. However, the syntax of these commands may differ, depending on your client's operating system. For example, the command that traces the path of packets from one host to another is known as `traceroute` in the UNIX operating system, but as `tracert` in the Windows operating systems. Similarly, the options used with each command may differ according to the operating system. When working on a UNIX system, you can limit the maximum number of router hops the `traceroute` command allows by typing the —m switch. On a Windows system, the —h switch accomplishes the same thing. The following sections focus on the proper command syntax for Windows-based computers, but also refer to UNIX-specific commands when relevant.

ARP

You have learned that ARP is a protocol that obtains the MAC address of a host and then creates a local database that maps the MAC address to the host's IP address. The database that lists the associated MAC and IP addresses is called an **ARP table**. An ARP table contains two types of entries: dynamic and static. **Dynamic ARP table entries** are created when a client makes an ARP request that cannot be satisfied by data already in the ARP table. **Static ARP table entries** are those that a networking professional has entered using the ARP utility. The ARP utility provides a way of obtaining information from and manipulating a device's ARP table. It can be a valuable troubleshooting tool for discovering the identity of a machine whose IP address you know, or for solving the problem of two machines trying to use the same IP address.

Typing the **arp** command only from a Windows system will display the proper syntax and list of switches available for this command. To return useful data, the **arp** command requires at least one switch. For example, typing **arp** —a provides the entire ARP table for your host. Following is a list of the most popular ARP switches.

- —a—Displays the ARP table for the host at which you issue the command

- —g—Does the same thing as the —a switch

- —d—Removes an entry from the ARP table; this switch must be followed by the hostname corresponding to the ARP entry that you wish to remove

- —s—Adds an entry to the ARP table—in other words, creates a static ARP table entry. This switch must be followed by the host name and MAC address of the device you wish to add. On a server, using the **arp** command with this switch will only work if you are logged in as an administrator.

- *hostname*—You must replace "hostname" with a network host name. The command then lists the ARP table entry for the device with that host name.

Packet Internet Groper (PING)

The **Packet Internet Groper (PING)** is a utility that can verify that TCP/IP is installed, bound to the NIC, configured correctly, and communicating with the network. It is often employed simply to determine whether a host is responding (or "up"). PING uses ICMP to send echo request and echo reply messages that determine the validity of an IP address. These two types of messages work much in the same way that sonar operates. First, a signal, called an **echo request**, is sent out to another computer. The other computer then rebroadcasts the signal, in the form of an **echo reply**, to the sender. The process of sending this signal back and forth is known as **pinging**.

You can ping either an IP address or a host name. For example, to determine whether the ftp.netscape.com site is responding, you could type: `ping ftp.netscape.com` and press Enter. Alternately, you could type: `ping 205.188.212.121` (the IP address of this site) and press Enter. If the site is operating correctly, you would receive a response that includes multiple replies from that host. If the site is not operating correctly, you will receive a response indicating that the request timed out or that the host was not found. Figure 11-19 gives examples of a successful and an unsuccessful ping.

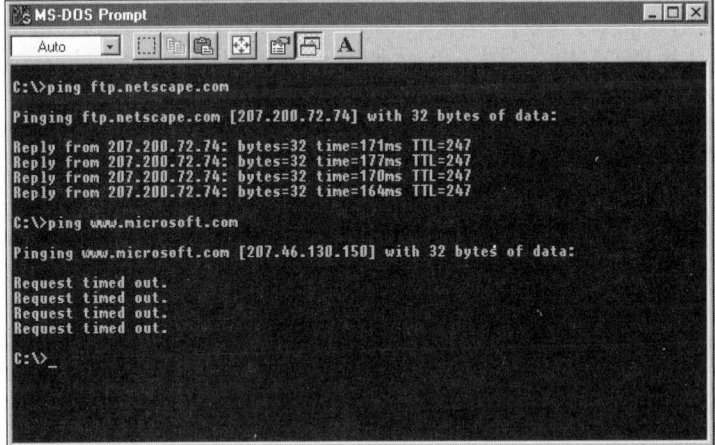

Figure 11-19   Example of a successful and an unsuccessful PING test

By pinging the loopback address, 127.0.0.1, you can determine whether your workstation's TCP/IP services are running. The loopback address automatically transmits a message back to the sending computer—that is, the message "loops back" to the sender. By pinging a host on another subnet, you can determine whether the problem lies with your gateway or DNS server.

For example, suppose that you have recently moved from the Accounting Department to the Advertising Department, and now you cannot access the Web. The first test you should perform is pinging the loopback address. If that test is successful, then you know that your workstation's TCP/IP services are running correctly. Next, you might try pinging your neighbor's machine. If you receive a positive response, you know that your network connection is working. You should then try pinging a machine on another subnet that you know is connected to the network—for example, a computer in the IT department. If this test is unsuccessful, you can safely conclude that you do not have the correct gateway or DNS settings in your TCP/IP configuration or that your organization's gateway is malfunctioning.

As with other TCP/IP commands, PING can be used with a number of different options, or switches. A ping command begins with the word "ping" followed by a hyphen (-) and a switch, followed by a variable pertaining to that switch. For example, if you wanted to ping Netscape's FTP site with only two echo requests (rather than the standard four), you could type the following command: `ping -n 2 ftp.netscape.com`. The following list describes some of the most common switches used with the PING utility:

- `-?`—Displays the help text for the PING command, including its syntax and a full list of switches

- `-a`—When used with an IP address, resolves the address to a host name

- `-n`—Allows you to specify a number of echo requests to send

- `-r`—When used with a number from 1 to 9, displays the route taken during ping hops

- `-w`—Limits the time to wait for each echo response to a specific number of milliseconds (requires the specification of the number of milliseconds to wait)

Netstat

The **netstat** utility displays TCP/IP statistics and details about TCP/IP components and connections on a host. Information that can be obtained from the `netstat` command include: the port on which a particular TCP/IP service is running, whether or not a remote node is logged into a host, which network connections are currently established for a client, how many packets have been handled by a network interface since it was activated, and how many data errors have occurred on a particular network interface. As you can imagine, with so much information available, the netstat utility makes a powerful diagnostic tool.

For example, suppose you are a network administrator in charge of maintaining file, print, Web, and Internet servers for an organization. You discover that your Web server, which has multiple processors, sufficient hard disk space, and multiple NICs, is suddenly taking twice as long to respond to HTTP requests. Of course, you would want to check the server's memory resources as well as its Web server software to determine that nothing is wrong with either of those. In addition, you can use the netstat utility to determine the characteristics of the traffic going in and out of each network interface card. You may discover that one network card is consistently handling 80 percent of the traffic, even though you had configured the server to share traffic equally among the two. This fact may lead you to run hardware diagnostics on the NIC, and perhaps discover that its onboard processor has failed, making it much slower than the other NIC. Netstat provides a quick way to view traffic statistics, without having to run a more complex program such as Windows 2000 Network Monitor.

If you use the `netstat` command without any switches, it will display a list of all the active TCP/IP connections on your machine, including the Transport layer protocol used (UDP or TCP), packets sent and received, IP address, and state of those connections, as shown in Figure 11-20.

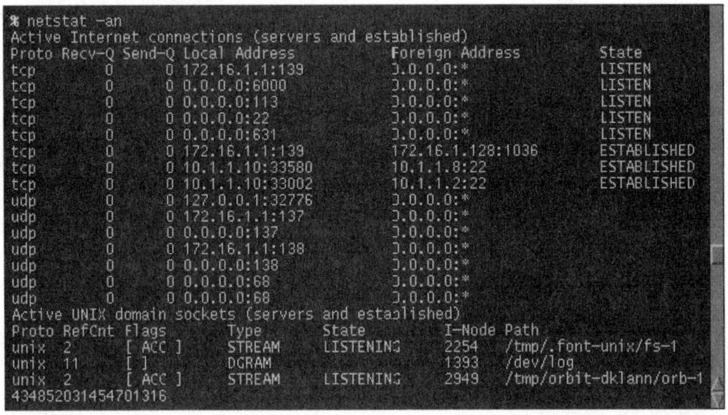

```
% netstat -an
Active Internet connections (servers and established)
Proto Recv-Q Send-Q Local Address          Foreign Address        State
tcp        0      0 172.16.1.1:139         0.0.0.0:*              LISTEN
tcp        0      0 0.0.0.0:6000           0.0.0.0:*              LISTEN
tcp        0      0 0.0.0.0:113            0.0.0.0:*              LISTEN
tcp        0      0 0.0.0.0:22             0.0.0.0:*              LISTEN
tcp        0      0 0.0.0.0:631            0.0.0.0:*              LISTEN
tcp        0      0 172.16.1.1:139         172.16.1.128:1036     ESTABLISHED
tcp        0      0 10.1.1.10:33580        10.1.1.8:22           ESTABLISHED
tcp        0      0 10.1.1.10:33002        10.1.1.2:22           ESTABLISHED
udp        0      0 127.0.0.1:32776        0.0.0.0:*
udp        0      0 172.16.1.1:137         0.0.0.0:*
udp        0      0 0.0.0.0:137            0.0.0.0:*
udp        0      0 172.16.1.1:138         0.0.0.0:*
udp        0      0 0.0.0.0:138            0.0.0.0:*
udp        0      0 0.0.0.0:68             0.0.0.0:*
udp        0      0 0.0.0.0:68             0.0.0.0:*
Active UNIX domain sockets (servers and established)
Proto RefCnt Flags       Type       State         I-Node Path
unix  2      [ ACC ]     STREAM     LISTENING     2254   /tmp/.font-unix/fs-1
unix  11     [ ]         DGRAM                    1393   /dev/log
unix  2      [ ACC ]     STREAM     LISTENING     2949   /tmp/orbit-dklann/orb-1
434852031454701316
```

Figure 11-20   Output of a simple `netstat` command

However, as with other TCP/IP commands, netstat can be used with a number of different switches. A `netstat` command begins with the word `netstat` followed by a hyphen and a switch, followed by a variable pertaining to that switch, if required. For example, `netstat -a` displays all current TCP and UDP connections from the issuing device to other devices on the network, as well as the source and destination service ports. The `netstat -r` command allows you to post a listing of the routing table on a given machine. The following list describes some of the most common switches used with the netstat utility:

- `-a`—Provides a listing of all available TCP and UDP connections, even if they are simply listening and not currently exchanging data

- `-e`—Displays details about all the packets that have been sent over a network interface

- `-n`—Lists currently connected hosts according to their port and IP address (in numerical form)

- `-p`—Allows you to specify what type of protocol statistics to list; this switch must be followed by a protocol specification (TCP or UDP)

- `-R`—Provides a list of routing table information

- `-s`—Provides statistics about each packet transmitted by a host, separated according to protocol type (for example, IP, TCP, UDP, or ICMP)

11

Nbtstat

Recall from Chapter 3 that NetBIOS is a protocol that runs in the Session and Transport layers of the OSI Model and associates NetBIOS names with workstations. NetBIOS alone is not routable because it does not contain Network layer information. However, when encapsulated in another protocol such as TCP/IP, it can be routed. On networks that run NetBIOS over TCP/IP, the **nbtstat** utility can provide information about NetBIOS statistics and resolve NetBIOS names to their IP addresses. In other words, if you know the NetBIOS name of a workstation, you can use nbtstat to determine its IP address.

Nbtstat is useful on networks that run Windows-based operating systems and NetBIOS (because Novell and UNIX operating systems do not use NetBIOS, nbtstat is not useful on these types of networks). For example, suppose you are a network technician sitting at the help desk and troubleshooting a connectivity problem with a user's workstation. Suppose also that your network uses NetBIOS over TCP/IP. The user tells you she cannot view her files on the server. Although this may be a symptom of a permissions problem or a client software problem, you decide to check the obvious first. You quickly type the **nbtstat -all** and you discover that no other computer names appear. You conclude that her NetBIOS protocol is probably not functioning properly, is not installed, or is incorrectly configured, so you begin your troubleshooting by examining her workstation's network protocol properties.

As more and more networks run pure TCP/IP (and not NetBIOS over TCP/IP), nbtstat is becoming a less popular TCP/IP diagnostic utility.

As with netstat, nbtstat offers a variety of switches to tailor the output of the command. For example, you can type **nbtstat -A ip_address** to determine what machine is registered to a given IP address. Popular switches used with the nbtstat command are listed below. Notice that they are case-sensitive; the —a switch has a different meaning than the —A switch.

- —a—Displays a machine's name table given its NetBIOS name; the name of the machine must be supplied after the —a switch

- —A—Displays a machine's name table given its IP address; the IP address of the machine must be supplied after the —A switch

- —n—Displays the local machine's name table; it does not require a variable after the switch since it operates on the local machine

- —r—Lists statistics about names that have been resolved to IP addresses by broadcast and by WINS. This switch is useful to determine whether a workstation is resolving names properly or to see whether WINS is operating correctly.

- —s—Displays a list of all the current NetBIOS sessions for a machine. When the small letter **s** is used, the **nbtstat** command attempts to resolve IP addresses to NetBIOS names in the listing. If the machine has no current NetBIOS connections, the result of this command will indicate that fact.

- ■ –S—Displays a list of all the current NetBIOS sessions for a machine according to their IP address. If the machine has no current NetBIOS connections, the result of this command will indicate that fact.

Nslookup

The **nslookup** utility allows you to query the DNS database from any computer on the network. Using nslookup, you can find the DNS host name of a device by specifying its IP address, or vice versa. This ability is useful for verifying that a host is configured correctly or for troubleshooting DNS resolution problems. For example, if you wanted to find out whether the host whose name is ftp.netscape.com is operational, you could type: `nslookup ftp.netscape.com` and press Enter. The response would look something like the output in Figure 11-21.

```
% nslookup ftp.netscape.com
Server:  proxy1.mdsn1.wi.home.com
Address:  24.6.204.15

Non-authoritative answer:
Name:    ftp.netscape.com
Address: 64.12.168.249

% 
```

Figure 11-21   Output of a simple `nslookup` command

Notice that the command provides not only the host's IP address, but also provides the primary DNS server name and address that holds the record for this name. To find the host name of a device whose IP address you knew, you would type: `nslookup ip_address` and press Enter. The response would include not only the host name for that device, but also its IP address and the IP address and host name of its primary DNS server.

> Nslookup is available on all UNIX systems as well as on Windows 2000 systems. The `nslookup` command does not come with the Windows 9x operating systems, however.

`Nslookup` can reveal much more than just the IP address or host name of a device. If you type the command by itself and press Enter, you will enter the nslookup utility, and your command prompt will change to a >. You can then use a number of UNIX-based commands to find out more about the contents of the DNS database. For example, you could view a list of all the host name and IP address correlations on a particular DNS server by typing `ls`. Or you could set the period to wait for a response to five seconds by typing `timeout=5` (the default is 10 seconds). Many other nslookup options exist, and as with other UNIX-based commands, you can find the complete list of them in the nslookup man pages. (You learned about man pages, a reference system built into UNIX, in Ch. 10.) To exit the nslookup utility and return to the normal command prompt, type `exit`.

Tracert (Traceroute)

The **traceroute** command (also known as **tracert** on Windows systems) uses ICMP to trace the path from one networked node to another, identifying all intermediate hops between the two nodes. This utility is useful for determining router or subnet connectivity problems.

To find the route, the traceroute utility transmits a series of UDP datagrams to a specified destination, using either the IP address or the host name to identify the destination. The first three datagrams that traceroute transmits have their TTL (time to live) set to 1. Because the TTL determines how many more network hops a datagram can make, datagrams with a TTL of 1 expire as they hit the first router. When they expire, they are returned to the source—in this case, the node that began the traceroute. In this way, traceroute obtains the identity of the first router. After it learns about the first router in the path, traceroute transmits a series of datagrams with a TTL of 2. The process continues for the next router in the path, and then the third, fourth, and so on, until the destination node is reached. Traceroute also returns the amount of time it took for the datagrams to reach each router in the path.

You can infer from traceroute's method and output that this utility can help diagnose network congestion or network failures. Traceroute is not foolproof, however. In fact, its results can be misleading, because traceroute cannot detect router configuration problems or detect whether a router uses different send and receive interfaces. In addition, routers may not decrement the TTL value correctly at each stop in the path. Therefore, traceroute is best used on a network with which you are already familiar. You can then use your judgment and experience to compare the actual test results with what you anticipate the results should be.

The simplest form of the **traceroute** command is `traceroute ip_address`. On computers that use the Windows-based operating system, the proper syntax is `tracert ip_address`. This command will return a list as shown in Figure 11-22.

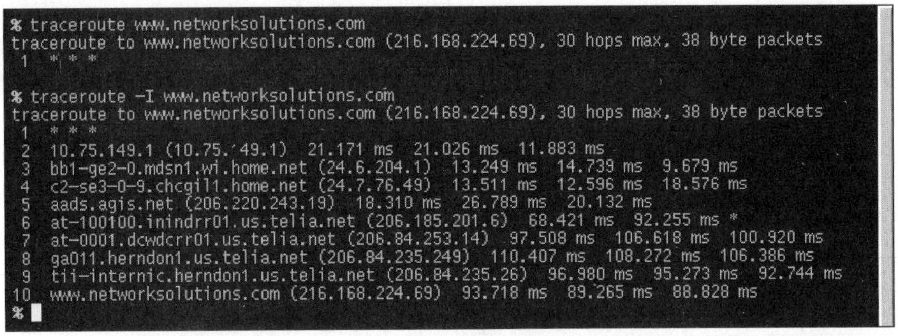

```
% traceroute www.networksolutions.com
traceroute to www.networksolutions.com (216.168.224.69), 30 hops max, 38 byte packets
 1  * * *

% traceroute -I www.networksolutions.com
traceroute to www.networksolutions.com (216.168.224.69), 30 hops max, 38 byte packets
 1  * * *
 2  10.75.149.1 (10.75.149.1)  21.171 ms  21.026 ms  11.883 ms
 3  bb1-ge2-0.mdsn1.wi.home.net (24.6.204.1)  13.249 ms  14.739 ms  9.679 ms
 4  c2-se3-0-9.chcgil1.home.net (24.7.76.49)  13.511 ms  12.596 ms  18.576 ms
 5  aads.agis.net (206.220.243.19)  18.310 ms  26.789 ms  20.132 ms
 6  at-100100.inindrr01.us.telia.net (206.185.201.6)  68.421 ms  92.255 ms *
 7  at-0001.dcwdcrr01.us.telia.net (206.84.253.14)  97.508 ms  106.618 ms  100.920 ms
 8  ga011.herndon1.us.telia.net (206.84.235.249)  110.407 ms  108.272 ms  106.386 ms
 9  tii-internic.herndon1.us.telia.net (206.84.235.26)  96.980 ms  95.273 ms  92.744 ms
10  www.networksolutions.com (216.168.224.69)  93.718 ms  89.265 ms  88.828 ms
%
```

Figure 11-22   Output of a `traceroute` command

As with other TCP/IP commands, `traceroute` has a number of switches that may be used with the command. A `traceroute` command begins with either "`traceroute`" or "`tracert`" (depending on the operating system your computer uses), followed by a hyphen, a switch, followed by a variable pertaining to a particular switch, if required. For example, `tracert -a` displays all current TCP and UDP connections from the issuing device to other devices on the network, as well as the source and destination service ports. The following list describes some of the popular traceroute switches:

- `-d`—Instructs the `tracert` command not to resolve IP addresses to host names

- `-h`—Specifies the maximum number of hops the packets should take when attempting to reach a host (the default is 30); this switch must be followed by a variable

- `-w`—Identifies a timeout period for responses; this switch must be followed by a variable to indicate the number of milliseconds the utility should wait for a response

Ipconfig

Ipconfig is the TCP/IP administration utility for use with Windows NT, 2000, and XP operating systems. If you work with these operating systems, you will frequently use this tool to check a computer's TCP/IP configuration. It is a command-line based utility that provides information about a network adapter's IP address, subnet mask, and default gateway.

To use the ipconfig utility from a Windows 2000 computer, for example, click Start, point to Programs, point to Accessories, and then click Command Prompt to open the Command Prompt window. At the command prompt, type `ipconfig`. You should see TCP/IP information for your computer, similar to the output shown in Figure 11-23.

11

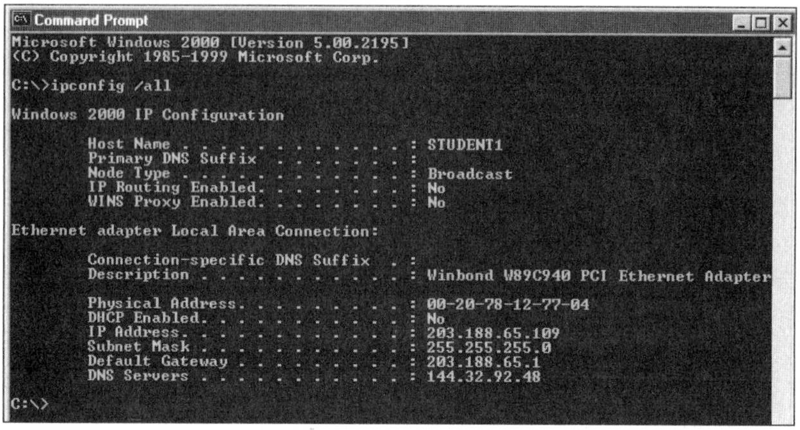

Figure 11-23   Output of an `ipconfig` command on a Windows 2000 workstation

In addition to being used alone to list information about the TCP/IP configuration, the ipconfig utility can be used with switches to manage a computer's TCP/IP settings. For example, if you wanted to view complete information about your TCP/IP settings, including your MAC address, when your DHCP lease expires, the address of your WINS server, and so on, you could type: `ipconfig /all`. Note that the syntax of this command differs slightly from other TCP/IP utilities. With `ipconfig`, a forward slash (/) precedes the command switches, rather than a hyphen. The following list describes some popular switches that can be used with the `ipconfig` command.

- `/?`—Displays a list of switches available for use with the `ipconfig` command

- `/all`—Displays complete TCP/IP configuration information for each network interface on that device

- `/release`—Releases DHCP-assigned addresses for all of the device's network interfaces

- `/renew`—Renews DHCP-assigned addresses for all of the device's network interfaces

Winipcfg

The **winipcfg** utility performs the same TCP/IP configuration and management as the ipconfig utility, but applies to Windows 9x and Me operating systems. It differs also in that it supplies the user with a graphical interface. As with ipconfig, networking technicians frequently use the `winipcfg` command when diagnosing TCP/IP problems.

To launch the winipcfg utility from a Windows 9x workstation, click Start, and then click Run to open the Run dialog box. In the Open text box, type `winipcfg`, and then click OK. The Winipcfg dialog box appears, displaying your network adapter's MAC and IP addresses, as well as your subnet mask and default gateway, as shown in Figure 11-24.

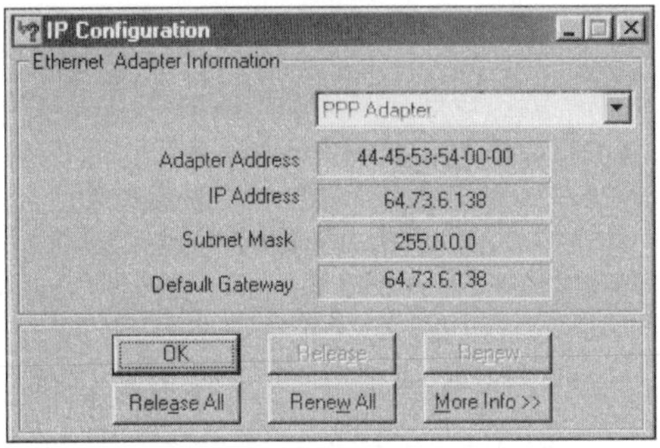

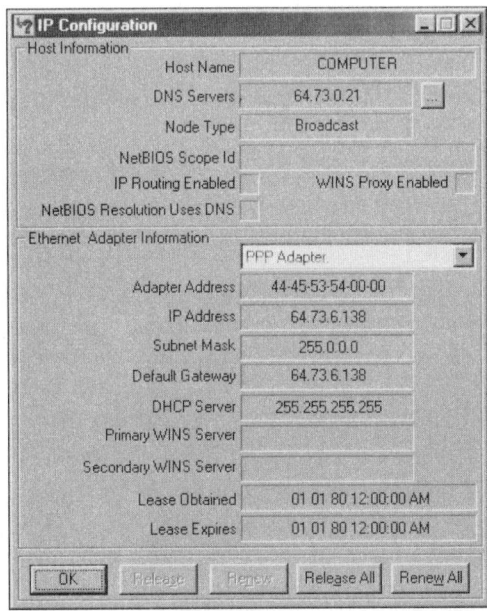

Figure 11-24   Winipcfg dialog box

As with the ipconfig utility, you can release or renew DHCP-assigned addresses through the Winipcfg dialog box. To renew all DHCP-assigned addresses, simply click the Renew All button. To release all DHCP-assigned addresses, simply click the Release All button. You also have the option to view more information about a machine's TCP/IP configuration. By clicking the More Info button, you can also view host name, node type, WINS server, when your DHCP lease was obtained, when it expires, and other information, as shown in Figure 11-25.

11

Figure 11-25   Detailed information available through winipcfg

Ifconfig

Ifconfig is the TCP/IP configuration and management utility used on UNIX systems. As with ipconfig on Windows 2000 systems and winipcfg on Windows 9x systems, ifconfig enables you to modify TCP/IP settings for a network interface, release and renew DHCP-assigned addresses, or simply check the status of your machine's TCP/IP settings. Ifconfig is also a utility that runs when a UNIX system starts, to establish the TCP/IP configuration for that system.

As with the other operating systems' TCP/IP configuration utilities, ifconfig can be used alone, or it can be used with switches to reveal more customized information. For example, if you wanted to view the TCP/IP information associated with every interface on a device, you could type: `ifconfig -a`. The output would resemble the output shown in Figure 11-26. Notice that the syntax of the `ifconfig` command uses a hyphen (-) before some of the switches and no preceding character for other switches. The following list describes some of the popular switches you may use with ifconfig. To view a complete list of options, you can read the ifconfig man pages. (You learned about man pages, a reference system built into UNIX, in Chapter 10.)

- `-a`—Applies the command to all interfaces on a device; can be used with other switches

- `down`—Marks the interface as unavailable to the network

- `up`—Reinitializes the interface after it has been taken "down," so that it is once again available to the network

 Other ifconfig switches, such as those that apply to DHCP settings, vary according to the type and version of the UNIX operating system you use. Refer to your operating system's help manual (or man pages) for more information.

```
% ifconfig -a
eth0      Link encap:Ethernet  HWaddr 00:10:A4:B6:24:82
          inet addr:10.1.1.10  Bcast:10.1.1.255  Mask:255.255.255.0
          UP BROADCAST RUNNING MULTICAST  MTU:1500  Metric:1
          RX packets:38130 errors:1 dropped:0 overruns:0 frame:0
          TX packets:36103 errors:0 dropped:0 overruns:0 carrier:0
          collisions:0 txqueuelen:100
          RX bytes:32055118 (30.5 Mb)  TX bytes:3424759 (3.2 Mb)
          Interrupt:11 Base address:0x200

lo        Link encap:Local Loopback
          inet addr:127.0.0.1  Mask:255.0.0.0
          UP LOOPBACK RUNNING  MTU:16436  Metric:1
          RX packets:374 errors:0 dropped:0 overruns:0 frame:0
          TX packets:374 errors:0 dropped:0 overruns:0 carrier:0
          collisions:0 txqueuelen:0
          RX bytes:29705 (29.0 Kb)  TX bytes:29705 (29.0 Kb)
%
```

Figure 11-26   Detailed information available through ifconfig

APPLICATIONS AND SERVICES

By now, you should be familiar with some Internet services such as e-mail and FTP. The following sections discuss how TCP/IP networks provide these and other services, what protocols each service relies upon, and how these services benefit the network administrators who manage and support them. With the growth of Internet commerce and VPNs, chances are good that you will install, configure, or support at least one of the services described in the following sections.

World Wide Web (WWW)

In the most general sense, the **World Wide Web (WWW, or Web)** is a collection of internetworked servers that share resources and exchange information according to specific protocols and formats. On the client side, access to the Web requires the TCP/IP protocol, a unique IP address, a connection to the Internet, and a local interface to the Web called a **browser**. The two most popular browsers in use today are Netscape Navigator (or Communicator) and Microsoft's Internet Explorer. On the server side, a Web site requires the TCP/IP protocol, a connection to DNS servers, routers, Web server software, and remote connections to the Internet.

You have learned that Web servers and clients transmit content through HTTP and HTML. In addition, every Web page is identified by a **Uniform Resource Locator (URL)** that specifies the service it uses, its server's host name, and its HTML page or script name. For example, a valid URL is *http://www.gao.gov/fedrules.html*, where *"http"* is the service used by the page, *"www.gao.gov"* is the server's host name, and *"fedrules.html"* is the content page. If a URL does not specify the page name, the Web server displays a default page, called index.html (or index.htm) on most systems. On most new versions of browsers, you can type an unqualified host name instead of a fully qualified host name in the browser's URL field. An **unqualified host name** is a host name minus its prefix and suffix. For example, some browsers allow you to type simply "weather" in the URL field to retrieve the *www.weather.com* Web site. The browser would automatically add the prefix *"www"* and the suffix *"com"* to find the site. Not all URLs specify the HTTP protocol. They can also specify Telnet, file, or FTP, as in the following URL: *ftp://ftp.netscape.com/pub*.

As a network administrator, you may be charged with installing and configuring Web server software. You may have to choose from more than 100 Web server software types, and your decision must take into account your operating system, hardware, performance requirements, security requirements, budget, and existing software. Popular Web server software includes Apache, AOLServer, Lotus Domino, Microsoft's Internet Information Service, and Netscape's FastTrack. Although each program requires a different method of installation and configuration, all contain features for user account management, access (security) management, and content management.

11

As you can imagine, references for Web protocols, programming, and customization abound on the World Wide Web. If you're searching for more information about the topics covered in this chapter, you might want to start at a site that lists many different Web-related links, such as *www.webreference.com* or *www.internet.com*.

E-Mail

Through this chapter's discussion of SMTP, POP, and IMAP4, you have learned a great deal about how TCP/IP-based e-mail systems work. Currently, e-mail is the most frequently used and, therefore, the most relied-upon Internet service you will manage. Thus, you need to know how to support and troubleshoot your organization's e-mail package.

Although e-mail packages vary in how they look and, to some degree, how they act, they all work on the same principles. If a user cannot retrieve her e-mail messages from the server, you must verify her TCP/IP settings. If an entire department cannot retrieve or send e-mail, you should investigate possible problems with the department's gateway. Finally, if your entire organization's e-mail system fails, you must troubleshoot your mail server (or servers) and connection to the Internet.

Supporting and troubleshooting e-mail are no different than supporting and troubleshooting any other networked application. Because so many people depend on this service for their daily business, however, it's critical that you understand how it works.

File Transfer Protocol (FTP)

In Chapter 3, you learned that the **File Transfer Protocol (FTP)** manages file transfers between TCP/IP hosts. The FTP service depends on an FTP server that is always waiting for requests. Once a client connects to the FTP server, FTP data are exchanged via TCP using port 20. FTP commands are sent and received through TCP port 21. FTP belongs to the Application layer of the TCP/IP Model.

FTP is a simple, yet important part of the TCP/IP suite. Before the Web provided an easier means of transferring files, FTP commands were regularly used to exchange data between machines. FTP commands will still work without using browser software or special client software—that is, from the operating system's command prompt. As a network professional, you may need to use these commands to download software (such as NOS patches or client updates) from hosts. For example, if you need to pick up the latest version of the Novell Windows 2000 client, you can use FTP from your workstation's command prompt to download the compressed software from the ftp.novell.com server to your hard disk.

In order to do so, you must first start the FTP utility by typing **FTP** from the OS command prompt. The result is an FTP command prompt that appears as follows: **FTP>**. Once you have invoked the FTP utility, you can use the open command to connect to an FTP host. For example, to connect to Novell's FTP server, you would type **open ftp.novell.com** at the FTP prompt. However, these two operations—starting FTP and connecting to a host—can be accomplished more simply through a single FTP command. For example, to FTP to Novell's FTP server from an OS prompt, you could type **FTP ftp.novell.com**, then press Enter to make the connection.

If the host is running, it will respond with a greeting and a request for you to log on, as shown in Figure 11-27. Many FTP hosts, especially those whose purpose is to provide software updates, accept anonymous logins. This means that when prompted for a user name, you need only type the word **anonymous** (in all small letters). When prompted for a password on an anonymous FTP site, you can usually use your e-mail address. The host's login screen should indicate whether this is acceptable. On the other hand, if you are logging onto a private FTP site, you must obtain a valid user name and password from the site's network administrator in order to make a successful connection.

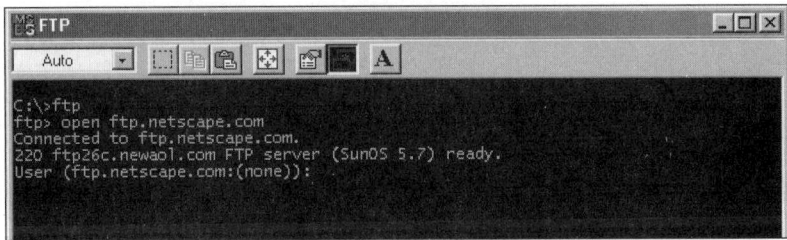

Figure 11-27   FTP login screen

Once you have successfully connected to a host, additional commands allow you to manage the connection and manipulate files. For example, after you have connected to Novell's FTP site, you could type: **cd public** to change your working directory to the "public" directory. Once in that directory, you could download a file by typing: **get *XXX***, where "*XXX*" is the name of the file you want to download. To terminate the connection, simply type **quit**.

The following list summarizes a handful of useful FTP commands and their syntax. To learn more about these and other FTP commands, type **help** after starting the FTP utility.

- **ascii**—Sets the file transfer mode to "ASCII." Most FTP hosts store two types of files: ASCII and binary. Text files are typically ASCII-based and contain formatting characters, such as carriage returns. Binary files (for example, executable programs) typically contain no formatting characters. Before downloading files from an FTP host, you must understand what type of file you are downloading. If you download a file while in the wrong mode (ASCII if the file is binary or vice versa), your file will appear as gibberish when you open it. If the file you want to download is an ASCII file, type **ascii** at the FTP prompt and press Enter before starting your file transfer.

- **binary**—Sets the file transfer mode to "binary." If the file you want to download from an FTP site is binary (for example, an executable program or a compressed software patch) type **binary** at the FTP prompt and press Enter before starting your file transfer.

- **cd**—Changes your working directory on the host machine

- **delete**—Deletes a file on the host machine (provided you have permissions to do so)

- **get**—Transfers a file from the host machine to the client. For example, to transfer the file called update.exe from the host to your workstation, you can type: **get update.exe**. Unless you specify a target directory and filename, the file will be saved to your hard disk in the directory from where you started the FTP utility. Therefore, if you wanted to save the update.exe file to your C:\download\patches directory, you would type:

  get update.exe "c:\download\patches"

  (Make sure to include the quotation marks.)

- **help**—Provides a list of commands when issued from the FTP prompt. When used in conjunction with a command, it provides information on the purpose of that command. For example, after typing **help ls** you would learn that the **ls** command lists the contents of a remote directory.

You can substitute a "?" for the help command in order to learn more about FTP commands. For example, instead of typing: **help get**, you could type **? get** to learn more about the get command.

- **ls**—Lists the contents of the directory on the host where you are currently located.

- **mget**—Transfers multiple files from the FTP site to your workstation simultaneously. For example, to transfer all the text files within one directory, you could type: **mget *.txt** at the FTP> prompt.

- **mkdir**—Creates a new directory on the FTP host (provided you have permission to do so)

- **mput**—Transfers multiple files from your workstation to the FTP host

- **open**—Creates a connection with an FTP host

- **put**—Transfers a file from your workstation to the FTP host

- **quit**—Terminates your FTP connection and closes the FTP utility

As mentioned earlier, the advent of browsers and FTP client software have rendered this command-line method of FTPing files less common. What's more, modern FTP programs provide graphical interfaces for transferring files from a server to a client. Examples of popular, inexpensive (if not free) FTP clients include MacFTP, WS_FTP, CuteFTP, and SmartFTP. You can also accomplish FTP file transfers directly from a modern Web browser such as Internet Explorer or Netscape Communicator. In order to do this, you need only connect to the FTP host. From there, you can move through directories and exchange files just as you would on your desktop OS.

 FTP and Telnet share some similarities, including their reliance on TCP and their ability to log onto a remote host and perform commands on that host. However, they differ in that, when you use Telnet, the commands you type require a syntax that is relative to your local workstation. When you use FTP, the commands you type require a syntax that is relative to the remote host that you have logged into. Also, Telnet has no built-in commands for transferring files between the remote host and your workstation.

Trivial File Transfer Protocol (TFTP)

The **Trivial File Transfer Protocol (TFTP)** is similar to FTP, in that it is a TCP/IP Application layer protocol that enables file transfers between computers. But TFTP relies on UDP at the Transport layer. Its use of UDP means that TFTP is connectionless and does not guarantee reliable delivery of data. Also, TFTP differs from FTP in that it does not actually log onto the remote host before enabling file transfers. Instead, when using TFTP, your computer issues a read request or a write request to the remote host. The remote host responds with an acknowledgement, then the two computers begin transferring data. Each time a packet of data is transmitted to the host, the local workstation waits for an acknowledgement from the host before issuing another packet. In this way, TFTP overcomes some of the limitations of relying on a connectionless Transport layer protocol.

TFTP is useful when you need to load programs on a diskless workstation. For example, suppose you ran a computer lab for a daycare facility that could only afford old computers with no hard disks but with 64 MB of memory. You could configure a server to hold multiple programs and respond to TFTP requests to transfer those programs into the diskless workstations' memory only when they are needed. In this situation, the fact that TFTP does not require a user to log onto a host is an advantage. It makes the transfer of program files quick and easy. (As you can imagine, however, in other cases, not requiring a login presents a security risk.)

In order for a file to be transferred via TFTP, it must be a file with full read and write privileges for all remote users. In other words, if you stored budget spreadsheets on your server and wanted to allow only the executives at your organization to download them, then TFTP could not be used as the means for accomplishing the downloads. Thus, before relying on TFTP you should make sure that the files to be transferred are not sensitive and are available to everyone connected to the network.

Gopher

Another Internet service that predates the WWW is **gopher**. A text-based utility, gopher allows you to navigate through a series of menus to find and read specific files. (The program is called "gopher" because it was developed at the University of Minnesota, whose mascot is the gopher.) Gopher is not sophisticated enough to interpret document formatting commands, such as HTML, but it does allow you to transfer files from one host to another by connecting with FTP. In addition, gopher was the first Internet interface to provide links from one host to another that are transparent to the user.

This utility requires a local gopher client and a gopher server. In the early 1990s, thousands of gopher servers provided information over the Internet. Gopher is rarely used today, however, because Web servers and browsers have made it obsolete.

Newsgroups

Newsgroups are similar to e-mail, in that they provide a means of conveying messages; they differ from e-mail in that they are distributed to a wide group of users at once rather than from one user to another. Newsgroups have been formed to discuss every conceivable topic, such as political issues, professional affiliations, entertainment interests, and sports. To belong to a newsgroup, a user subscribes to the server that hosts the newsgroup. From that point forward, the user receives all messages that other newsgroup members post with the newsgroup list as their mail-to address.

Newsgroups require news servers and, on the client side, e-mail programs capable of reading newsgroups or special newsgroup reading software. Rather than using SMTP, as e-mail does, newsgroup messages are transported by the **Network News Transport Protocol (NNTP)**. NNTP supports the process of reading newsgroup messages, posting new messages, and transferring news files between news servers. News servers are organized hierarchically, similarly to DNS servers. Your Internet service provider, for example, has a news server that uses a larger carrier's news server to communicate with other large carrier news servers.

E-commerce

One of the fastest growing sectors of the Internet is electronic commerce, or e-commerce. The term **e-commerce** refers to a means of conducting business over the Web—be it in retailing, banking, stock trading, consulting, or training. Any buying and selling of products or services that occurs over the Internet belongs in the e-commerce category. The first industries to take advantage of e-commerce were retailing and finance. In the past five years, more businesses have realized that e-commerce is critical to their success. Indeed, the number of online purchases has grown exponentially each year since 1996. You have probably used the Web to purchase books, music, clothes, or even furniture.

If you have an interest in Internet technologies, you may want to consider specializing in e-commerce. E-commerce involves customized HTML scripting, software programming, multimedia, graphics, networking, and security skills. Because it often relies on credit card purchases or money transfers over the Internet, security is a significant concern. Web security is becoming more sophisticated to counter hackers, who continually find new ways to break into systems. Personal identification numbers and file encryption, for example, can no longer guarantee that information cannot be picked up by others in transit. Some day, we may use retinal patterns or fingerprints to provide secure access to Web sites. Chapter 15 discusses network security in more detail.

Voice over IP (VoIP)

Another growing service is **Voice over IP** (**VoIP**—pronounced "voyp"), the provision of telephone service over a TCP/IP network. When VoIP is carried over by Internet, it is often called **Internet telephony**. But not all VoIP calls are carried over the Internet. In fact, VoIP over private lines is a very effective and economical method of completing calls between two locations within an organization. And because the line is private, its congestion can be easily controlled, thus resulting in better sound quality than the Internet can provide. But given the Internet's breadth and low cost, it is appealing to consider the Internet for carrying conversations that we currently transmit over the PSTN.

Voice can be carried over TCP/IP networks in a variety of configurations. The following list describes three categories of VoIP technology:

- *Phone-to-phone*—In this configuration, two traditional telephones are connected through a TCP/IP network. On one end, a user picks up his telephone to make a call. His telephone is connected to a local telephone switch, which handles call routing for his business. The telephone switch accepts his voice signals, then passes them on to a gateway. Recall that a gateway is a combination of software and hardware that connects two dissimilar networks. In this case, the gateway connects the PSTN with a TCP/IP network (such as the Internet). The gateway may be located at a client's office or at a telephone carrier's facility. The gateway digitizes the analog voice signals, compresses the data, then assembles them into packets. As you have learned, packets contain routing and error-checking information, as well as data. The packets traverse the network and are accepted by another gateway at the receiving end. The receiving gateway reverses what the transmitting gateway did; that is, it disassembles the packets, decompresses the data, and converts it into an analog signal. The result is the original voice signal, which is passed to another telephone switch, to which the other telephone is connected. Both gateways perform their functions simultaneously. This enables the VoIP call to be full-duplex, just as a phone call over the PSTN, which means that both parties can speak and listen at the same time. Figure 11-28 depicts the configuration required for this type of VoIP call.

11

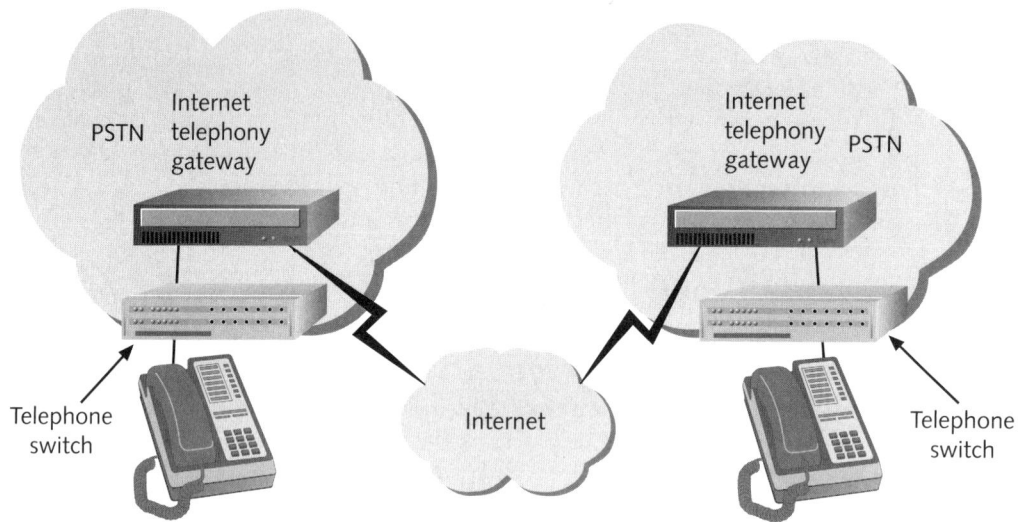

Figure 11-28   A phone-to-phone VoIP call

- *PC-to-phone*—In this scheme, one end of the call uses a PC, while the other end relies on a traditional telephone. On one end, a PC equipped with a microphone, speaker, and the appropriate software initiates calls over its network connection. Voice signals are converted to digital data by the PC's software, then transmitted through the PC's NIC and over the network just as any other data are transmitted. At the receiving end, a gateway accepts the data and translates them into voice signals (just as the receiving gateway does in the phone-to-phone VoIP call). These voice signals are then transmitted to a telephone switch, to which a traditional telephone is connected. (The process is reversed in a phone-to-PC configuration, when the traditional telephone user responds to the PC caller.) Figure 11-29 depicts this type of VoIP call.

- *PC-to-PC*—In this configuration, two PCs connect through a TCP/IP network to complete calls. The call is initiated just as a PC-to-phone call. On one end, a PC equipped with a microphone, speaker, and the appropriate software transforms voice signals into digital data. These data are transmitted over the network. On the other end, another PC with the same basic setup accepts the call from the network. During the call, users speak into the PC's microphone and listen via the PC's speakers. In this scheme, an IP address essentially becomes a telephone number, and the computer acts as a telephone. Figure 11-30 depicts this type of VoIP call.

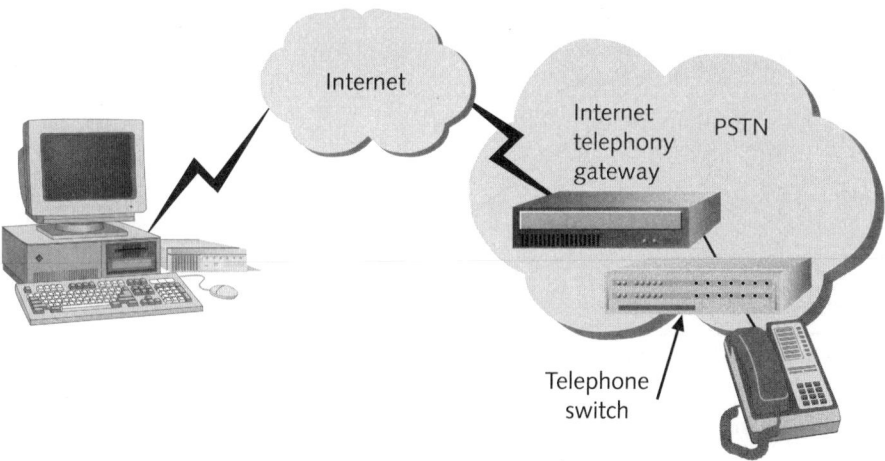

Figure 11-29   A PC-to-phone VoIP call

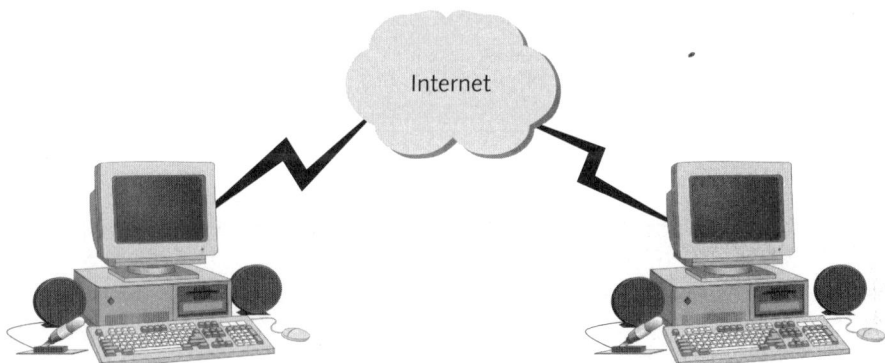

Figure 11-30   A PC-to-PC VoIP call

A tremendous benefit of VoIP, and Internet telephony in particular, is its low cost. For example, the cost of a call from New York to Tokyo would be the same as a call across town. Nevertheless, significant technical obstacles have prevented Internet telephony from becoming a widespread reality to date. First, more so than data transmissions, voice conversations can easily be distorted by the wire's quality of service. When you talk with your mother, you need to hear her syllables in the order in which she mouthed them, and preferably, without delay. (In contrast, data do not necessarily need to be received in the same order in which they were transmitted, because the destination node will sort the information out when it arrives.) Also, voice transmissions are subject to distortion if the connection becomes too noisy. In general, to prevent delays, disorder, and distortion, a voice connection requires more dedicated bandwidth than a data connection.

Another challenge to VoIP is the difficulty in billing for network-based calls, because their costs depend on so many factors. In addition, multiple carriers are typically involved in any Internet-based call. Also, while standardization of Internet telephony and VoIP has begun, it is not even close to completion. The U.S. government is taking a hands-off approach in its regulation, letting the vendors and professional organizations sort out VoIP implementation. Therefore, VoIP is a rapidly changing area of networking. You can count on it to undergo significant modifications and continually improve in the coming years.

 The use of networks to carry data, plus video and voice signals is known as **convergence**.

Chapter Summary

- ❏ Every device on a TCP/IP-based network must have a unique IP address to ensure reliable data delivery. Without the correct IP address, data cannot be routed between networks and devices.

- ❏ Each IP address is a unique 32-bit number, divided into four groups of octets that are themselves separated by periods. An example of a valid IP address is 144.92.43.178. An IP address is typically represented in dotted decimal notation. It contains two types of information: network and host. It may also include subnet information.

- ❏ All nodes on a Class A network share the first octet of their IP numbers, a number between 1 and 126. Nodes on a Class B network share the first two octets, and all of their IP addresses begin with a number between 128 and 191. Class C network IP numbers share the first three octets, with their first octet being a number between 192 and 223.

- ❏ In addition to Class A, B, and C networks, Class D and Class E networks exist, although consumers and companies do not use them. Class D addresses begin with an octet whose value is between 224 and 239 and are reserved for a special type of transmission called multicasting. Class E addresses begin with an octet whose value is between 240 and 254, and are reserved for experimental use by IETF. Multicasting allows one device to send data to a specific group of devices (not the entire network segment) in a point-to-multipoint fashion.

- ❏ To use IP addresses more efficiently, the concept of subnetting was applied to the Internet in the mid-1980s. Subnetting is the process of subdividing a single class of network into multiple, smaller networks.

- ❏ Subnetting adds a third type of octet to the standard IP address. Rather than consisting of simply network and host information, a subnetted address includes network, subnet, and host information.

- ❏ The combination of an address's network and subnet information is called its extended network prefix. By interpreting an address's extended network prefix, a device can determine the subnet to which an address belongs.

❒ To determine whether an address is part of a subnet in the first place, a device interprets a subnet mask. A subnet mask is a special 32-bit number that, combined with a device's IP address, tells the rest of the network which kind of subnet the device is on. The bits of the subnet mask are set to 1 if the IP address information in the corresponding octets belongs to the extended network prefix. Otherwise, the subnet mask bits are 0, and the corresponding octets are assumed to represent host information.

❒ Routers external to an organization use only the network portion of the IP address to direct data to devices within that organization. External routers (such as those on the Internet) do not recognize subnets on specific LANs.

❒ Gateways are a combination of software and hardware that enable two different network segments to exchange data. In the context of IP addressing, a gateway facilitates communication between different subnets. Because one device on the network cannot send data directly to a device on another subnet, a gateway must intercede and hand off the information.

❒ Internet gateways maintain default routes to known addresses to expedite data transfer. The gateways that make up the Internet backbone are called core gateways. The Internet Network Operations Center (INOC) operates core gateways.

❒ A socket is a logical address assigned to a specific process running on a host computer. It forms a virtual connection between the host and client. The socket's address represents a combination of the host computer's IP address and the port number associated with a process.

❒ The use of port numbers simplifies TCP/IP communications and ensures that data are transmitted to the correct application. When a client requests communication with a server and specifies port 23, the server knows immediately that the client wants a Telnet session. No extra data exchange is necessary to define the session type, and the server can initiate the Telnet service without delay.

❒ Every host belongs to a domain; every domain is identified by its domain name. Usually, a domain name is associated with a company or other type of organization, such as a university or military unit.

❒ In the mid-1980s, the Network Information Center (NIC) at Stanford Research Institute devised a hierarchical way of tracking domain names and their addresses, called the Domain Name System (DNS). The DNS database does not rely on one file or even one server, but rather is distributed over several key computers across the Internet to prevent catastrophic failure if one or a few computers go down.

❒ Resolvers are any hosts on the Internet that need to look up domain name information. The resolver client is built into TCP/IP applications such as Telnet, HTTP, and FTP.

❒ Name servers are servers that contain databases of names and their associated IP addresses. A name server supplies a resolver with the requested information. If the name server cannot resolve the IP address, the query passes to a higher-level name server. Each name server manages a group of machines called a zone. DNS relies on the hierarchical zones to distribute naming information.

❐ When a host needs to communicate with other hosts on the Internet, that host must first find its name server. Large organizations often maintain more than one name server—a primary and a secondary name server—to help ensure Internet connectivity. When configuring the TCP/IP properties of a workstation, you need to specify a name server's IP address so that the workstation will know which machine to query when it must look up a name.

❐ A root server is a name server maintained by ICANN and IANA that is an authority on how to contact top-level domains, such as those ending with .com, .edu, .net, .us, and so on.

❐ To communicate with other devices through TCP/IP, every workstation, printer, or other node on a network requires a unique IP address. On the earliest TCP/IP networks, each device was manually assigned its own number through a local configuration file, and the number did not change until someone edited the configuration file.

❐ To ease IP address management, a service called the Bootstrap Protocol (BOOTP) was developed in the mid-1980s. BOOTP uses a central list of IP addresses and their associated devices' MAC addresses to assign IP addresses to clients.

❐ With BOOTP, a client does not have to remember its own IP address, and therefore network administrators do not have to manage each workstation on a network separately. This situation is ideal for diskless workstations.

❐ DHCP is an automated means of assigning a unique IP address to every device on a network. Reasons for implementing DHCP include the following: to reduce the time and planning spent on IP address management; to reduce the potential for human errors in assigning IP addresses; to enable users to move their workstations and printers without changing their TCP/IP configuration; and to make IP addressing transparent for mobile users.

❐ DHCP was developed by the IETF as a replacement for BOOTP. Unlike BOOTP, DHCP does not require the network administrator to maintain a table of IP and MAC addresses on the server. It does, however, require the network administrator in charge of IP address management to install and configure the DHCP service on a server.

❐ DHCP configuration involves specifying a range of addresses that can be leased to any network device on a particular segment. The term lease identifies how a client borrows a DHCP-assigned IP address.

❐ The Windows Internet Naming Service (WINS) provides a means of resolving NetBIOS names with IP addresses. WINS is used exclusively with systems that rely on NetBIOS—therefore, it is usually used on Windows-based systems.

❐ A computer's NetBIOS name and its TCP/IP host name are different entities, which may or may not be equivalent. DNS provides resolutions of host names and IP addresses, so you can think of WINS being to NetBIOS what DNS is to TCP/IP.

❐ The Address Resolution Protocol (ARP) is a means of obtaining the MAC address of a local host and keeping that information in a local cache. If a device doesn't know its own IP address, however, it can't use ARP. A solution to this problem is to allow the client to send a broadcast message with the MAC address of a device and then receive the device's IP address in reply. This process, which is the reverse of ARP, is called the Reverse Address Resolution Protocol (RARP).

❑ Simple Mail Transfer Protocol (SMTP) is responsible for moving messages from one e-mail server to another over TCP/IP-based networks. SMTP operates through port 25, with requests to receive mail and send mail going through that port on the SMTP server.

❑ The Post Office Protocol (POP) runs on top of SMTP and provides centralized storage for e-mail messages. A storage mechanism such as POP is necessary because users are not always logged onto the network and available for receiving messages. Both SMTP and a service such as POP are required before a mail server can receive, store, and forward messages.

❑ The Internet Mail Access Protocol (IMAP), a mail storage and manipulation protocol that depends on SMTP's transport system, is a more sophisticated alternative to POP. The single biggest advantage IMAP4 has relative to POP is that it allows users to store messages on the mail server, rather than always having to download them to the local machine.

❑ Hypertext Transport Protocol (HTTP) is the language used by Web clients and servers to communicate with each other. When you type the address of a Web page in your Web browser's address field, HTTP transports the information about your request to the Web server and returns the Web server's information to you in the Hypertext Markup Language (HTML), the Web document formatting language.

❑ The Packet Internet Groper (PING) can verify that TCP/IP is installed, bound to the NIC, configured correctly, and communicating with the network. PING uses ICMP to send echo request and echo reply messages that determine the validity of an IP address.

❑ The netstat utility displays TCP/IP statistics and the state of current TCP/IP components and connections. It also displays ports, which can signal whether services are using the correct ports.

❑ The nbtstat utility provides information about NetBIOS names and their addresses. If you know the NetBIOS name of a workstation, you can use nbtstat to determine the workstation's IP address.

❑ The nslookup utility allows you to look up the DNS host name of a network node by specifying it's the node's IP address, or vice versa. This allows you to verify that a host is configured correctly. Nslookup is also useful for troubleshooting DNS resolution problems.

❑ The traceroute utility, also known as tracert on Windows systems, uses ICMP to trace the path from one networked node to another, identifying all intermediate hops between the two nodes. This utility is useful for determining router or subnet connectivity problems.

11

❐ The World Wide Web (WWW, or Web) is a collection of internetworked servers that share resources and exchange information according to specific protocols and formats. On the client side, access to the Web requires the TCP/IP protocol, a unique IP address, a connection to the Internet, and a local interface to the Web called a browser.

❐ A Uniform Resource Locator (URL) that specifies the service used, its server's host name, and its HTML page or script name, identifies every Web page.

❐ Currently, e-mail is the most frequently used Internet service you will manage. Although e-mail packages vary in how they look and, to some degree, how they act, they all work on the same principles.

❐ The File Transfer Protocol (FTP) manages file transfers between TCP/IP hosts. FTP is a simple, yet important part of the TCP/IP suite. Before the WWW provided an easier means of transferring files, FTP commands were regularly used to exchange data between machines.

❐ Gopher is a text-based utility that allows you to navigate through a series of menus to find and read specific files. It is not sophisticated enough to interpret document formatting commands, such as HTML, but it does allow you to transfer files from one host to another by connecting with FTP.

❐ Newsgroups are similar to e-mail, in that they provide a means of conveying messages; they differ from e-mail, in that messages are distributed to a wide group of users at once rather than from one user to another.

❐ Rather than using SMTP (as e-mail does), newsgroup messages are transported by the Network News Transport Protocol (NNTP). NNTP supports the process of reading newsgroup messages, posting new messages, and transferring news files between news servers.

❐ The term "e-commerce" refers to a means of conducting business over the Web—be it in retailing, banking, stock trading, consulting, or training. Any buying and selling of products or services that occurs over the Internet belongs in the e-commerce category.

❐ An emerging Web-based service is Internet telephony, the provision of telephone service over the Internet. Given the Internet's breadth and economy, it seems logical that we would look to the Internet to carry the conversations that we currently transmit over PSTN. With a basic desktop computer equipped with a microphone, speaker, and the appropriate software, you could call anyone else with the same setup, essentially using your IP address as a telephone number.

❐ Today, significant technical obstacles prevent Internet telephony from becoming a widespread reality. First, voice conversations depend on the wire's quality of service. Also, voice transmissions are subject to distortion if the connection becomes too noisy. To compensate for delays, disorder, and distortion, a voice connection requires more dedicated bandwidth.

KEY TERMS

address resource record — A type of DNS data record that maps the IP address of an Internet-connected device to its domain name.

alias — A nickname for a node's host name. Aliases can be specified in a local host file.

anycast address — A type of address specified in IPv6 that represents a group of interfaces, any one of which (and usually the first available of which) can accept a transmission. At this time, anycast addresses are not designed to be assigned to hosts, such as servers or workstations, but rather to routers.

ARP table — The database that lists MAC addresses and their associated IP addresses used for ARP queries.

Bootstrap Protocol (BOOTP) — A service that simplifies IP address management. BOOTP maintains a central list of IP addresses and their associated devices' MAC addresses, and assigns IP addresses to clients when they request it.

browser — Software that provides clients with a simple, graphical interface to the Web.

convergence — The use of networks to carry data, plus video and voice signals.

core gateways — Gateways that make up the Internet backbone. The Internet Network Operations Center (INOC) operates core gateways.

default gateway — The gateway that first interprets a device's outbound requests, and then interprets its inbound requests to and from other subnets. In the postal service analogy, the default gateway is similar to a local post office.

11

diskless workstations — Workstations that do not contain hard disks, but instead rely on a small amount of read-only memory to connect to a network and to pick up their system files.

domain name — The symbolic name that identifies a domain. Usually, a domain name is associated with a company or other type of organization, such as a university or military unit.

Domain Name System (DNS) — A hierarchical way of tracking domain names and their addresses, devised in the mid-1980s. The DNS database does not rely on one file or even one server, but rather is distributed over several key computers across the Internet to prevent catastrophic failure if one or a few computers go down. DNS is a TCP/IP service that belongs to the Application layer of the OSI Model.

dotted decimal notation — The shorthand convention used to represent IP addresses and make them more easily readable by humans. In dotted decimal notation, a decimal number between 1 and 254 represents each binary octet. A period, or dot, separates each decimal.

dynamic address — An IP address that is assigned to a device through DHCP and may change when the DHCP lease expires or is terminated.

dynamic ARP table entry — A record (of an IP address and its associated MAC address) created in an ARP table when a client makes an ARP request that cannot be satisfied by data already in the ARP table.

Dynamic Host Configuration Protocol (DHCP) — An automated means of assigning a unique IP address to every device on a network.

echo reply — The response signal sent by a device after another device pings it.

echo request — The request for a response generated when one device pings another device on the network.

e-commerce — A means of conducting business over the Web — be it in retailing, banking, stock trading, consulting, or training. Any buying and selling of products or services that occurs over the Internet belongs in the e-commerce category.

extended network prefix — The combination of an address's network and subnet information. By interpreting an address's extended network prefix, a device can determine the subnet to which an address belongs.

File Transfer Protocol (FTP) — An Application layer TCP/IP protocol that manages file transfers between TCP/IP hosts.

Format Prefix — A variable-length field at the beginning of an IPv6 address that indicates what type of address it is (for example, unicast, anycast, or multicast).

gateway — A combination of hardware and software that enables one type of system to communicate with another type of system.

gopher — A text-based utility that allows you to navigate through a series of menus to find and read specific files.

host file — A text file that associates TCP/IP host names with IP addresses. On Windows 9x, NT, and 2000 platforms, the host file is called "lmhosts." On UNIX platforms the file is called "hosts" and is located in the /etc directory.

host name — A symbolic name that describes a TCP/IP device.

hosts — Name of the DNS host file found on a UNIX computer. The hosts file is usually found in the /etc directory.

Hypertext Markup Language (HTML) — The language that defines formatting standards for Web documents.

Hypertext Transport Protocol (HTTP) — The language that Web clients and servers use to communicate. HTTP forms the backbone of the Web.

ifconfig — A TCP/IP configuration and management utility used with UNIX systems (similar to the ipconfig utility used on Windows NT and 2000 systems).

Internet Mail Access Protocol (IMAP) — A mail storage and manipulation protocol that depends on SMTP's transport system and improves upon the shortcomings of POP. The most current version of IMAP is version 4 (IMAP4). IMAP4 can (and eventually will) replace POP without the user having to change e-mail programs. The single biggest advantage IMAP4 has relative to POP is that it allows users to store messages on the mail server, rather than always having to download them to the local machine.

Internet telephony — The provision of telephone service over the Internet.

ipconfig — The TCP/IP configuration and management utility for use with Windows NT or Windows 2000 systems.

IP next generation (IPng) — See *IP Version 6.*

IP version 6 (IPv6) — A new standard for IP addressing that will replace the current IP version 4 (IPv4). Most notably, IPv6 uses a newer, more efficient header in its packets and allows for 128-bit source and destination IP addresses. The use of longer addresses will allow for more total IP addresses to be in circulation.

lease — The agreement between a DHCP server and client on how long the client will borrow a DHCP-assigned IP address. As network administrator, you configure the duration of the lease (in the DHCP service) to be as short or long as necessary, from a matter of minutes to forever.

lmhosts — A host file on a Windows-based computer that maps IP addresses to host names and aliases.

multicast address — A type of address in the IPv6 that represents multiple interfaces, often on multiple nodes. An IPv6 multicast address begins with the following hexadecimal field: FF0x, where x is a character that identifies the address's group scope.

multicasting — A means of transmission in which one device sends data to a specific group of devices (not the entire network segment) in a point-to-multipoint fashion. Multicasting can be used for teleconferencing or videoconferencing over the Internet, for example.

name server — A server that contains a database of TCP/IP host names and their associated IP addresses. A name server supplies a resolver with the requested information. If it cannot resolve the IP address, the query passes to a higher-level name server.

name space — The database of Internet IP addresses and their associated names distributed over DNS name servers worldwide.

nbtstat — A TCP/IP troubleshooting utility that provides information about NetBIOS names and their addresses. If you know the NetBIOS name of a workstation, you can use nbtstat to determine its IP address.

netstat — A TCP/IP troubleshooting utility that displays statistics and the state of current TCP/IP connections. It also displays ports, which can signal whether services are using the correct ports.

network address translation (NAT) — A technique in which private (or hidden) IP addresses are assigned a public IP address by an IP gateway, thus masking their true origin.

Network News Transfer Protocol (NNTP) — The protocol that supports the process of reading newsgroup messages, posting new messages, and transferring news files between news servers.

Network Time Protocol (NTP) — A simple TCP/IP protocol that is used to synchronize the clocks of computers on a network. NTP belongs to the Application layer of the TCP/IP Model and depends on UDP.

newsgroups — An Internet service similar to e-mail that provides a means of conveying messages, but in which information is distributed to a wide group of users at once rather than from one user to another.

nslookup — A TCP/IP utility on Windows NT, Windows 2000, and UNIX systems that allows you to look up the DNS host name of a network node by specifying its IP address, or vice versa. This ability is useful for verifying that a host is configured correctly and for troubleshooting DNS resolution problems.

11

Packet Internet Groper (PING) — A TCP/IP troubleshooting utility that can verify that TCP/IP is installed, bound to the NIC, configured correctly, and communicating with the network. PING uses ICMP to send echo request and echo reply messages that determine the validity of an IP address.

pinging — The process of sending an echo request signal from one node on a TCP/IP network to another, using the PING utility.

port number — A unique number associated with a process running on a computer. For example, 23 is the standard port number associated with the Telnet utility.

Post Office Protocol (POP) — A TCP/IP subprotocol that provides centralized storage for e-mail messages. In the postal service analogy, POP is like the post office that holds mail until it can be delivered.

release — The act of terminating a DHCP lease.

resolver — Any host on the Internet that needs to look up domain name information.

resource record — The element of a DNS database stored on a name server that contains information about TCP/IP host names and their addresses.

Reverse Address Resolution Protocol (RARP) — The reverse of ARP. RARP allows the client to send a broadcast message with the MAC address of a device and receive the device's IP address in reply.

root server — A DNS server maintained by ICANN and IANA that is an authority on how to contact the top-level domains, such as those ending with .com, .edu, .net, .us, and so on. ICANN oversees the operation of 13 root servers around the world.

Simple Mail Transfer Protocol (SMTP) — The TCP/IP subprotocol responsible for moving messages from one e-mail server to another.

socket — A logical address assigned to a specific process running on a host computer. It forms a virtual connection between the host and client.

static address — An IP address that is manually assigned to a device and remains constant until it is manually changed.

static ARP table entry — A record (of an IP address and its associated MAC address) that is manually entered in the ARP table using the ARP utility.

subnet mask — A special 32-bit number that, when combined with a device's IP address, informs the rest of the network as to what kind of subnet the device is on.

subnetting — The process of subdividing a single class of network into multiple, smaller networks.

switch — The letters or words added to a command that allow you to customize a utility's output. Switches are usually preceded by a hyphen or forward slash character.

top-level domain (TLD) — The highest-level category used to distinguish domain names—for example, .org, .com, .net. A TLD is also known as the domain suffix.

traceroute (or tracert) — A TCP/IP troubleshooting utility that uses ICMP to trace the path from one networked node to another, identifying all intermediate hops between the two nodes. Traceroute is useful for determining router or subnet connectivity problems.

Trivial File Transfer Protocol (TFTP) — A TCP/IP Application layer protocol that enables file transfers between computers. Unlike FTP, TFTP relies on UDP at the Transport layer and does not require a user to log onto the remote host.

unicast address — A type of IPv6 address that represents a single interface on a device. An IPv6 unicast address begins with either FFC0 or FF80.

Uniform Resource Locator (URL) — A standard means of identifying every Web page, which specifies the service used, its server's host name, and its HTML page or script name.

unqualified host name — A TCP/IP host name minus its prefix and suffix.

Voice over IP (VoIP) — The provision of telephone service over a TCP/IP network. (Pronounced "voyp".) One form of VoIP is Internet telephony.

well-known ports — TCP/IP port numbers 0 to 1023, so called because they were long ago assigned by Internet authorities to popular services (for example, FTP and Telnet), and are therefore well known and frequently used.

Windows Internet Naming Service (WINS) — A service that resolves NetBIOS names with IP addresses. WINS is used exclusively with systems that use NetBIOS—therefore, it is usually found on Windows-based systems.

winipcfg — The TCP/IP configuration and management utility for use with Windows 9x systems. Winipcfg differs from ipconfig in that it supplies a graphical user interface.

World Wide Web (WWW or Web) — A collection of internetworked servers that share resources and exchange information according to specific protocols and formats.

zone — The group of machines managed by a DNS server.

REVIEW QUESTIONS

1. How many octets are used for the network portion of a Class B IP address?
   a. 4
   b. 3
   c. 2
   d. 1
   e. 0

2. Which of the following dotted decimal addresses corresponds to the binary IP address 11111111 11111111 11111111 11111111?
   a. 10.10.10.10
   b. 100.100.100.100
   c. 127.0.0.1
   d. 255.255.255.255
   e. 1.1.1.1

3. What is another term for the address represented by 11111111 11111111 11111111 11111111?

   a. multicast address

   b. broadcast address

   c. loopback address

   d. qualified address

   e. RARP address

4. Why would a network manager choose to divide his or her TCP/IP networks into subnets?

   a. to conserve router interfaces

   b. to minimize traffic between segments on the network

   c. to use a limited number of IP addresses more efficiently

   d. to reduce the potential for IP addressing conflicts

   e. to enable a hierarchical addressing scheme for servers and workstations

5. What is the default subnet mask for a Class A network?

   a. 0.0.0.0

   b. 255.0.0.0

   c. 255.255.0.0

   d. 255.255.255.0

   e. 255.255.255.255

6. If a client workstation's IP address equals 119.55.60.122, and the network administrator is using subnetting, which of the following is probably the workstation's subnet mask?

   a. 0.0.0.0

   b. 255.0.0.0

   c. 255.255.0.0

   d. 255.255.255.0

   e. 255.255.255.255

7. Each node on a TCP/IP network has only one default gateway. True or False?

8. What is the primary advantage to using sockets?

   a. They enable clients and servers to communicate more expeditiously.

   b. They enable servers to keep a service available at all times.

   c. They eliminate the possibility that service requests might become corrupted.

   d. They ensure that error-correction is used during transmission.

   e. They ensure that a connection-oriented protocol is used when requesting services.

9. Which two ports are commonly used in FTP transmission?

   a. 23 and 24

   b. 21 and 22

   c. 20 and 21

   d. 22 and 23

   e. 24 and 25

10. Which top-level domain would the U.S. Congressional offices use?

    a. .loc

    b. .info

    c. .com

    d. .gov

    e. .mil

11. You are the network manager for a realtor with 50 workstations in its TCP/IP-based LAN. One day your supervisor tells you that the company is doubling in size in the next month and that you will have to add 50 new workstations to the network in the next two weeks, making sure they can use both internal and external resources. However, you realize that you only have enough Internet-authorized IP addresses for the existing 50 workstations and cannot get new IP addresses in time for setting up the new workstations. Which of the following is the best solution to this problem?

    a. Create new lmhosts files for each Windows-based system that map the IP address of each other system to its MAC address.

    b. Assign each of the 50 IP addresses to two workstations and configure the border router to allow only one of those workstations to access a public network at any time.

    c. Call a local ISP and ask to lease another 50 IP addresses until you can reserve your own through ICANN.

    d. Establish a peer-to-peer network that enables the 100 workstations to share the 50 legitimate IP addresses.

    e. Set up an IP gateway that can perform network address translation and assign the new workstations addresses that can only be used within the organization.

12. What three columns of information would you find in a file called "lmhosts" on a Windows 2000 workstation?

    a. IP address, domain name, and NetBIOS address

    b. IP address, NetBIOS address, and alias

    c. IP address, domain name, and alias

    d. IP address, host name, and alias

    e. IP address, MAC address, and host name

11

13. How can a resolver quickly find addresses for previously visited sites?

14. Which of the following symbols indicates a comment in an lmhosts file?

    a. $

    b. &

    c. ^

    d. /

    e. #

15. An organization may use only one name server. True or False?

16. What is the significant disadvantage to using BOOTP?

    a. It requires two servers to hold the information for a single subnet.

    b. Its tables must be manually updated.

    c. It does not conform to the hierarchical DNS model.

    d. It is unreliable.

    e. It is not supported by newer operating systems.

17. Although DHCP enables users to move their machines from one location on the net-work to another without reconfiguring TCP/IP settings, what might a user have to do once she has moved to a new part of the network so as to use TCP/IP applications?

    a. change her primary DNS setting

    b. change her default protocol setting

    c. release and renew her IP address

    d. adjust the time on her DHCP lease

    e. change her SNMP server name

18. When a client needs to obtain an IP address from a DHCP server, what kind of transmission does it send?

    a. broadcast UDP

    b. multicast TCP

    c. broadcast RARP

    d. multicast RARP

    e. unicast UDP

19. In total, how many packets are exchanged in the process of a client requesting and obtaining an IP address from a DHCP server?

    a. 2

    b. 4

    c. 6

    d. 8

    e. 10

20. Which of the following is a benefit of using WINS?

   a. It ensures that every device on the network has a unique IP address.

   b. It ensures that every device on the network has a unique host name.

   c. It ensures that every device on the network has a unique NetBIOS name.

   d. It ensures that every device on the network has a unique socket address.

   e. It ensures that every device on the network has a unique port address.

21. What is the primary difference between UDP and TCP?

   a. UDP is a Data Link layer protocol and TCP is a Network layer protocol.

   b. UDP is connectionless and TCP is connection-oriented.

   c. UDP relies on IPX/SPX and TCP relies on TCP/IP.

   d. UDP is more secure than TCP.

   e. UDP does not require IP while TCP does.

22. How could RARP benefit diskless workstations?

23. What is SMTP's primary function?

   a. to provide management information about network devices

   b. to monitor security breaches at the router interface level

   c. to transport mail from one host to another

   d. to supply port usage information

   e. to automatically issue network alerts when the nameserver goes down

24. Where does mail go after it is retrieved by an e-mail program that uses POP?

   a. to the user's mail directory on the mail server

   b. to the user's mail directory on the client workstation

   c. to the root directory on the client workstation

   d. to the recycle bin on the mail server

   e. to an archive disk on the mail server

25. Which two of the following are benefits of using IMAP4 relative to POP?

   a. It provides mail delivery guarantees.

   b. It allows users to review and delete mail without downloading it.

   c. It allows users to create mail messages on the server.

   d. It provides better encryption for message attachments.

   e. It enables multiple users to easily share a central mailbox.

26. IMAP4 can work without SMTP, but POP3 cannot. True or False?

11

27. Why is it critical that the clocks of all computers on a network are synchronized?

    a. so that multiple servers on a network can manage shared, external storage devices without, for example, overwriting the most recent version of a file with an older version of the file

    b. so that DHCP servers do not inadvertently assign the same IP address to two different devices

    c. so that packets are not prematurely discarded due to a difference in time between the source node and the devices between the source and target nodes

    d. so that data backups will not begin while users are still connected to the network, potentially opening files and making them vulnerable to corruption

    e. so that the DHCP server can accurately track which devices have leased IP addresses that will soon expire

28. What can you learn by pinging the loopback address?

29. If you know that your boss's TCP/IP host name is JSMITH, and you need to find out what her IP address is, what command (with correct syntax) should you type at your DOS prompt?

    a. `nslookup jsmith`

    b. `netstat jsmith`

    c. `tracert jsmith`

    d. `whois jsmith`

    e. `nbtstat jsmith`

30. What command might you use to find out whether your ISP's router is especially slow on a particular afternoon?

    a. `traceroute`

    b. `nbtstat`

    c. `netstat`

    d. `nslookup`

    e. `ipconfig`

31. How can you view a list of FTP commands once you have connected to an FTP server?

    a. type: `commands`

    b. type: `show`

    c. type: `quit`

    d. type: `help`

    e. type: `Q`

32. What command would you use to list the TCP/IP configuration for all three of the NICs in your Linux server?

    a. `nslookup —all`

    b. `ipconfig —all`

    c. `ipconfig /all`

    d. `ifconfig —a`

    e. `nslookup -a`

33. Which protocol is used to transmit and receive messages to and from newsgroups?

    a. NNTP

    b. SNMP

    c. NCP

    d. SMTP

    e. NSFT

34. Why is security a concern for Web sites that offer e-commerce?

35. What type of device digitizes, compresses, and assembles into packets a voice phone call, which it receives from a telephone switch?

    a. TCP/IP switch

    b. NIC

    c. IP telephone

    d. name server

    e. gateway

11

HANDS-ON PROJECTS

Project 11-1

In this exercise, you will set up a Windows 2000 workstation with everything it needs to access the Internet. For this project, you will need a Windows 2000 workstation that currently has TCP/IP installed and bound to the NIC, but doesn't have any settings specified. You will need to obtain the correct settings for your network from your instructor. In this project, it's important to type the numbers exactly as they are given to you; otherwise, the TCP/IP connection will not work. Each student should use a unique IP address and host name.

1. Obtain the following numbers from your instructor: IP address, subnet mask, DNS primary name server, DNS secondary name server, default gateway, and domain name.

2. Click **Start**, point to **Settings**, and then click **Control Panel**.

3. Double-click **Network and Dial-up Connections**. The Network and Dial-up Connections window opens.

4. Right-click the **Local Area Connection** icon, then click **Properties** in the shortcut menu. The Local Area Connection Properties dialog box appears.

5. Select **Internet Protocol (TCP/IP)** in the list of installed network components, then click **Properties**. The Internet Protocol (TCP/IP) Properties dialog box opens.

6. Make sure the **Use the following IP address** option is selected.

7. Type your network's IP address in the space provided.

8. Type your network's subnet mask in the space provided.

9. Type your network's default gateway in the space provided.

10. Make sure the **Use the following DNS server addresses** option is selected.

11. Enter the IP address of your primary DNS server in the **Preferred DNS server** text box.

12. Enter the IP address of your secondary DNS server, if you have one, in the **Alternate DNS server** text box.

13. Click **OK** to save your changes to the TCP/IP properties. The dialog box closes.

14. Click **OK** to save the changes to the Network properties. The dialog box closes and you are prompted to restart your computer to save your changes.

15. Click **Yes** to confirm that you want to restart your computer. When your workstation restarts, it will be properly configured for TCP/IP to browse the Web and to use TCP/IP applications such as FTP and Telnet.

16. To test whether your change worked, click **Start**, point to **Programs**, point to **Accessories** point to, and then click **Command Prompt**. The Command Prompt window opens.

17. At the command prompt, type **telnet locis.loc.gov** and press **Enter**.

18. If you see a text screen entitled "LOCIS: Library of Congress Information System," you have successfully modified your TCP/IP properties. If you see a window titled Connect Failed!, you either typed the host name incorrectly or need to retrace your steps from the beginning of this exercise to ensure that your TCP/IP properties are correct.

19. Following the instructions on the screen, logout from the Library of Congress system, then close the Command Prompt window.

Project 11-2

Computer scientists around the world collaborate to devise Internet protocols and standards. These standards, along with comments and Internet-related meeting notes, are then transformed into Requests for Comments (RFCs). When you want to find the source of an Internet standard, you can look in its RFCs. Some RFCs were written at the genesis of the Internet and have since been revised several times. New RFCs are continually being written. In this exercise, you will use an FTP client to find RFCs at different Internet host sites and explore their content.

For this and subsequent exercises, you will need a PC workstation with access to the World Wide Web (a standard TCP/IP installation and an Internet connection such as the one you configured in Project 11-1). Your workstation should also have a Web browser, such as Internet Explorer or Netscape Communicator, installed.

1. Verify that your workstation is connected to the Internet.

2. At the command prompt, type **ftp** and press **Enter** to begin an FTP session.

3. At the ftp prompt, type **help** and press **Enter**. How many FTP commands does your FTP client provide? Do any of the commands look familiar?

4. Type **open ftp.isi.edu** and press **Enter** to connect to the University of Southern California Information Sciences Institute FTP site, where an official record of RFC documents is kept.

5. Now you need to enter your user name. Because this site allows guests to log in with the user name "anonymous," type **anonymous** and press **Enter**. (Because the user name is case-sensitive, make sure you don't type any capital letters.)

6. Now you need to enter a password. Type your e-mail address as your password, and then press **Enter**. If you do not have a valid e-mail address, ask your instructor to provide an address you can use for this purpose.

7. To confirm that you have logged in, the ISI FTP server greets you with a long message that begins: "Guest login ok, …."

8. To change directories to the folder that contains the RFC documents, type **cd in-notes** at the ftp prompt, and then press **Enter**. This command is case-sensitive, so be sure not to use any capital letters.

9. To show a listing of all RFCs in this directory, type **ls** and press **Enter**. Because there are so many RFC documents, this listing will take a while to complete.

10. To copy RFC number 1816 to your hard disk, type **get rfc1816.txt "c:\rfc.txt"** and press **Enter**. Note that "get" is the FTP command for retrieving a file. The name of the file on the FTP server is "rfc1816.txt" and "c:\rfc.txt" is the filename you will save it under on your computer. Also note that the default file transfer mode is ASCII, which is appropriate because the RFC is a text file.

11. Open the file c:\rfc.txt using a text editor program (if you are working on a Windows workstation, you can use WordPad).

12. Read the header and at least a few paragraphs from this RFC. What is the topic of this RFC? What previously written RFC does it replace? On what date was it published?

13. Repeat Step 10, but rather than retrieving RFC 1816, retrieve RFC 2146, saving it to a file named c:\rfc2.txt. Open the file in a text editor program and note how it pertains to RFC 1816.

11

14. Now repeat Step 10 to retrieve another RFC, this time RFC 2151, saving it to a file named c:\rfc3.txt. Review this file in a text editor program. How much of it looks familiar? What new information can you learn from this document?

15. To close the FTP session, type **quit** and press **Enter**. Close the Command Prompt window.

Project 11-3

In this exercise, you will use a Web browser to locate an RFC. In addition, you will perform Web searches and use services other than HTTP. To complete this project, you need a workstation with Internet access.

1. Verify that your workstation is connected to the Internet.

2. Go to the following Web site: *www.rfc-editor.org/rfcsearch.html*.

3. Under the Search text box, type **1816**, and then click the **SEARCH** button.

4. A list of matching RFC documents appears in the bottom half of the screen. Click the number **RFC1816** to open this document in your browser window.

5. According to this RFC, which domain suffix should local and state agencies use? (*Hint*: If you are reading the document in a browser window, you can use your browser's search function to look for any instance of the phrase "local and state.")

6. Go to the Internet Engineering Task Force's home page: *www.ietf.org*.

7. To view a list of the IETF's working groups, click the **IETF Working Groups** link.

8. Scroll through the page to get an idea of how many emerging Internet technologies need to be standardized or refined. Under the Operations and Management Area, choose to view more information about the Remote Network Monitoring group. What is the purpose of this group? What RFCs have resulted from its work?

9. Go to the following Web site: *ftp://ftp.isi.edu/in-notes/*. Look at the list of text files and directories that appear. It is the same list that you viewed through the FTP command **ls** in Project 11-2.

10. Type **altavista** in your Web browser's address box, press **Enter**, and see whether your browser adds the prefix and suffix to the unqualified host name and finds the appropriate site. If it doesn't, point your browser to the fully qualified host name, *www.altavista.com*.

11. At the AltaVista search engine site, type the following question in the search field: **What is SMTP**? Click **Search**.

12. What kind of response do you get from the search engine?

Project 11-4

In this project, you will gain more experience with simple TCP/IP troubleshooting commands. To complete this project you will need a Windows 2000 Professional workstation that can connect to the Internet.

1. Connect to the Internet, click **Start**, point to **Programs**, point to **Accessories**, and then click **Command Prompt**. The Command Prompt window appears.

2. At the command prompt, type **netstat —a** and press **Enter**. Recall that **netstat** is the command that reveals all TCP/IP port connections, even if they are not actively exchanging data. How many connections are listed on your computer? Of those connections, how many rely on the TCP protocol and how many rely on UDP?596

3. Now look at the "State" column of your connection listing. How does the value in this column differ for TCP and UDP connections? Why do you suppose this is the case?

4. Now type **netstat —s** and press **Enter**. How many different TCP/IP core protocols are currently in use on your machine? Of those, which one has sent and received the most packets?

5. Now you will experiment with another TCP/IP utility, the traceroute function. At the command prompt, type **tracert www.course.com** and press **Enter**. How many hops does it take to go from your computer to the Course Technology home page's computer? How many hops are listed as the maximum for the tracert command?

6. Now use the traceroute utility but allow it to omit the host names of every hop between your workstation and the destination by typing **tracert —d www.course.com** and pressing **Enter**. Notice how the output differs from the output you received in Step 5. Close the Command Prompt window.

Project 11-5

In this exercise, you will configure an e-mail program with the correct mail server settings. In a typical LAN environment, users will not know how to specify their mail servers or whether their software uses POP or IMAP4. In addition to knowing this basic information, you should be familiar with any special mail program settings required by your organization, such as whether users are allowed to leave messages on the server and, if so, how long they are allowed to maintain them there.

For this exercise, you will need a Windows 9x or Windows 2000 Professional workstation with one of the popular e-mail programs, such as Eudora Light, installed. If you do not have the disks to install Eudora Light, you can download the software from Qualcomm's Web site at *www.eudora.com/products/eudora/download/* at no cost. Your instructor can provide the configuration information for your network, such as the mail server name, if you do not already know it.

11

Although this exercise focuses on the configuration process for the Eudora e-mail package, all Internet e-mail packages will require you to enter the same information, if not more. Many e-mail programs share similar menu structures, too. Once you have experience configuring a few popular programs, therefore, you can easily figure out how to configure other e-mail programs.

1. To run the Eudora Light mail program, click **Start**, point to **Programs**, point to **Eudora**, and then click **Eudora**. The Eudora window opens.

2. Click **Tools** on the menu bar, and then click **Options**. The Options dialog box opens, as shown in Figure 11-31.

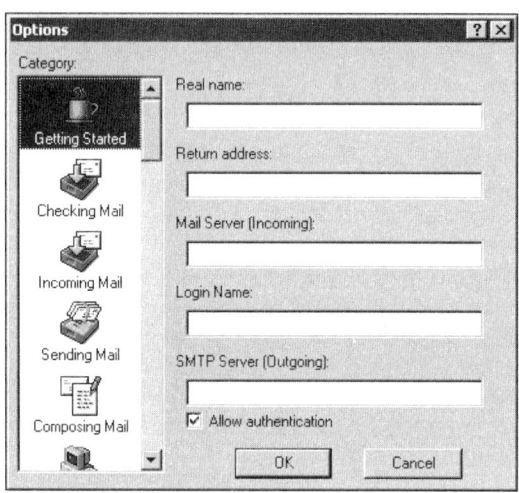

Figure 11-31   Eudora Options dialog box

3. Scroll to the top of the Category list box, and then click the **Getting Started** icon.

4. In the Real name text box, type your first and last name.

5. In the Return address text box, type your full e-mail address.

6. In the Mail Server (Incoming) text box, type your mail server name. In the Login Name text box, type your e-mail account name. In the SMTP Server (Outgoing) text box, type your SMTP server name (which may be the same as your mail server name).

7. In the Category list box, click the **Sending Mail** icon.

8. In the Domain to add to unqualified addresses text box enter your mail server's domain name. For example, if your e-mail address is jdoe@usa.com, enter usa.com. This choice enables you to send mail to your friend usam@usa.com by typing simply usam in the To: field of your e-mail message.

9. In the SMTP server text box, enter your SMTP server name.

10. Save your settings by clicking **OK**. You return to the main Eudora Light window.

11. To test your mail client, click **File** on the menu bar, and then click **Check Mail**. Why didn't you have to restart your workstation for these changes to take effect?

12. In the next steps, you will see what happens when a mail server name is spelled incorrectly. To start, click **Tools** on the menu bar, and then click **Options**.

13. Click the **Sending Mail** icon. The sending mail options appear.

14. Change one letter in the name of your SMTP server, and then click **OK** to save your changes.

15. To create a test message to send to yourself, click **Message** on the menu bar, and then click **New Message**. A new message window appears, prompting you to enter the recipient's e-mail address.

16. Type your own e-mail address (correctly) in the To text box.

17. In the Subject: text box, type **test**.

18. Click the **Send** button. What happens? What kind of error message do you receive when you attempt to retrieve your mail?

19. Follow Steps 13 through 17 again, this time typing in your correct SMTP server name to restore your ability to send e-mail from the Eudora Light client.

CASE PROJECTS

1. Katie Stark, who owns a local greenhouse called Katydid Nursery, knows you from college. She has heard you're a networking expert and calls to ask how she can sell bulbs, seeds, garden tools, and houseplants on the Web. To date, Katie has used computers only to keep her inventories, but she's heard that e-commerce is an easy way to make more money. Her greenhouse employees use five computers, all Pentium IIIs. She doesn't think that they are even connected to the Internet. Katie has a limited budget and frankly isn't sure whether having a Web site is something she can afford. If she had a Web site, she tells you, she would call it www.katydids.com. Based on what you know about Internet connections, Web sites, and e-commerce, what kind of connection do you recommend? What advice can you provide about establishing a Web site and preparing her computers to use the Web?

11

2. Katie told her friend Andy about your skills with computers. Andy knows a bit about computers himself, as he is the sole network technician at a chain of six hardware stores in the Pacific Northwest. His network is connected to the Internet through a dedicated T1 link, and he has registered the address range from 205.38.123.1 through 205.38.123.100 with his ISP. For the most part, the clients Andy supports use the Internet for e-mail, Web surfing, and exchanging files. The problem with his network is that he's the only employee who knows anything about TCP/IP, and the network is growing faster than he can handle. Andy is constantly visiting one or another of his users' machines to check their IP address in their TCP/IP properties window, or finding that they've accidentally deleted their gateway setting. How can you help him?

3. Andy's surprised that you know so much about TCP/IP. On a day when his connection to the Internet is extremely slow, he challenges you to find out why the performance is so bad. Andy jokes that it might have something to do with the earthquake that just took place in San Jose. What do you do?

TROUBLESHOOTING NETWORK PROBLEMS

After reading this chapter and completing the exercises, you will be able to:

➤ Describe the elements of an effective troubleshooting methodology

➤ Follow a systematic troubleshooting process to solve networking problems

➤ Use a variety of software and hardware tools to diagnose problems

➤ Discuss practical issues related to troubleshooting

ON THE JOB

Our ISP division hosts Web sites for a number of corporate clients. Each site requires a separate Web server, but multiple Web servers can run on the same machine. Once, at about 3:00 A.M. on a Sunday morning, one of our engineers began upgrading the hardware that supported about 100 of these corporate Web servers. The engineer finished the work on schedule, and everything appeared to be fine. We expected the sites to perform much better with the new hardware installed.

At roughly 6:00 A.M. that morning, I was with a customer working on a network topology conversion project, when the engineer called with bad news. Contrary to our expectations, the Web sites were performing dismally on the new hardware. The exact problem wasn't clear. I made my apologies to the customer (a down condition always takes precedence) and headed back to the office to do some troubleshooting.

Indeed, the performance of the Web sites on the new hardware was awful. I plugged in a Network General Sniffer to our core Ethernet switch and then set the sniffer port to spanning mode so that the sniffer could examine all traffic on the Web server VLAN. I set the sniffer filters such that I was monitoring only packets to the Web server in question. Almost immediately, a problem became apparent. The packets destined for the Web server were plainly seen on the network, but no replies came from the Web server. For some reason, the Web server was not "seeing" the traffic directed to it. A number of causes seemed possible: For example, the wiring to the new Web server might be bad, the Web server might have a defective network interface card (NIC), or, less likely, the switch might have a bad Ethernet port.

I tried the easiest option first, replacing the Category 5 Ethernet cable to the Web server. Sure enough, the problem went away, and the Web pages were quickly served. The sniffer showed normal network protocol behavior.

The company had engaged in discussions about getting a cable tester several times, but never quite got around to making a purchase. After this incident, we ordered a cable tester immediately. We also implemented a policy requiring engineers to test each cable before installing it on the network.

James G. Berbee
Berbee Information Networks, Inc.

By now, you know how networks should work. Like other complex systems, however, they don't always work as planned. Many things can go wrong on a network, just as many things can go wrong with your car, house, or a project at work. In fact, a network professional probably spends more time fixing network problems than designing or upgrading a network. Some breakdowns (such as an overtaxed processor) come with plenty of warning, but others (such as a hard disk controller failure) can strike instantly.

As with your car, the best defense against problems is prevention. Just as you should have your car serviced regularly, so you should monitor the health of your network regularly. Of course, even the most well-monitored network will sometimes experience unexpected problems. For example, a utility company could dig a new hole for its cable and accidentally cut your dedicated line to the Internet. In such a situation, your network can go from perfect to disastrous performance in an instant. In this chapter, you learn how to diagnose and solve network problems in a logical, step-by-step fashion, using a variety of tools.

TROUBLESHOOTING METHODOLOGY

Successful troubleshooters proceed logically and methodically. This section introduces a basic troubleshooting methodology, leading you through a series of general problem-solving steps. Bear in mind that experience in your network environment may prompt you to follow the steps in a different order or to skip certain steps entirely. For example, if you know that one segment of your network is poorly cabled, you may try replacing a section of cable in that area to solve a connectivity problem before attempting to verify the physical and logical integrity of the workstation's NIC. In general, however, it is best to follow each step in the order shown. Such a logical approach can save you from undertaking wasteful, time-consuming efforts such as unnecessary software or hardware replacements.

Steps for troubleshooting network problems are as follows:

1. Identify the symptoms. Carefully document what you learn from people or systems that alerted you to the problem and keep that documentation handy.

2. Identify the scope of the problem. Is it universal—that is, are all users on the network experiencing the problem at all times? Or is the problem limited to a specific geographic area of the network, to a specific demographic group of users, or to a particular period of time? In other words, is the problem subject to geographic, demographic, or chronological constraints?

3. Establish what has changed on the network. Recent hardware or software changes may be causing the symptoms.

4. Determine the most probable cause of the problem. This determination may include the following techniques:

   a. Verify user competency.
   b. Re-create the problem, and ensure that you can reproduce it reliably.
   c. Verify the physical integrity of the network connection (such as cable connections, NIC installations, and power to devices), starting at the affected nodes and moving outward toward the backbone.
   d. Verify the logical integrity of the network connection (such as addressing, protocol bindings, software installations, and so on).

5. Implement a solution.

6. Test the solution.

7. Recognize the potential effects of the solution. For example, if you have to reassign IP addresses, how will the change of an IP address on a server affect its clients? Or, in another case, if you upgrade the type of client software used on a workstation, how will that affect a user's daily routine?

8. Document the solution. Make sure that both you and your colleagues understand the cause of the problem and how you solved it. This information should be kept in a centrally available repository, such as an online database.

Depending on your findings, you may skip from one step to another step further down in the list, eliminating the need to carry out the intervening steps. For example, if you determine that a NIC has been improperly seated in a workstation's system board, you may skip directly to Step 5 (in this case, reinstall the NIC) without analyzing recent changes to the network. Above all, use common sense in your troubleshooting efforts. As you read through the following sections, you will understand how the suggested troubleshooting steps are interrelated and how answering a question under one step might prompt you to skip to another step.

The flowchart in Figure 12-1 illustrates how these steps are related. Each decision step in the flowchart is discussed in more detail in the following sections, and in some sections the flowchart is expanded to reflect different outcomes based on different findings. The following sections also explain how to narrow down the possible causes of a problem by answering specific questions. In particular, you can question users to get clues about the problem. Finally, the chapter describes ways to test your attempted resolution of a network problem.

 In addition to the organized method of troubleshooting described in this section, a good, general rule for troubleshooting can be stated as follows: Pay attention to the obvious! Although some questions may seem too simple to bother asking, don't discount them. You can often save much time by checking cable connections first. Every networking professional can tell a story about spending half a day trying to figure out why a computer wouldn't connect to the network, only to discover that the network cable was not plugged into the wall jack or the device's NIC.

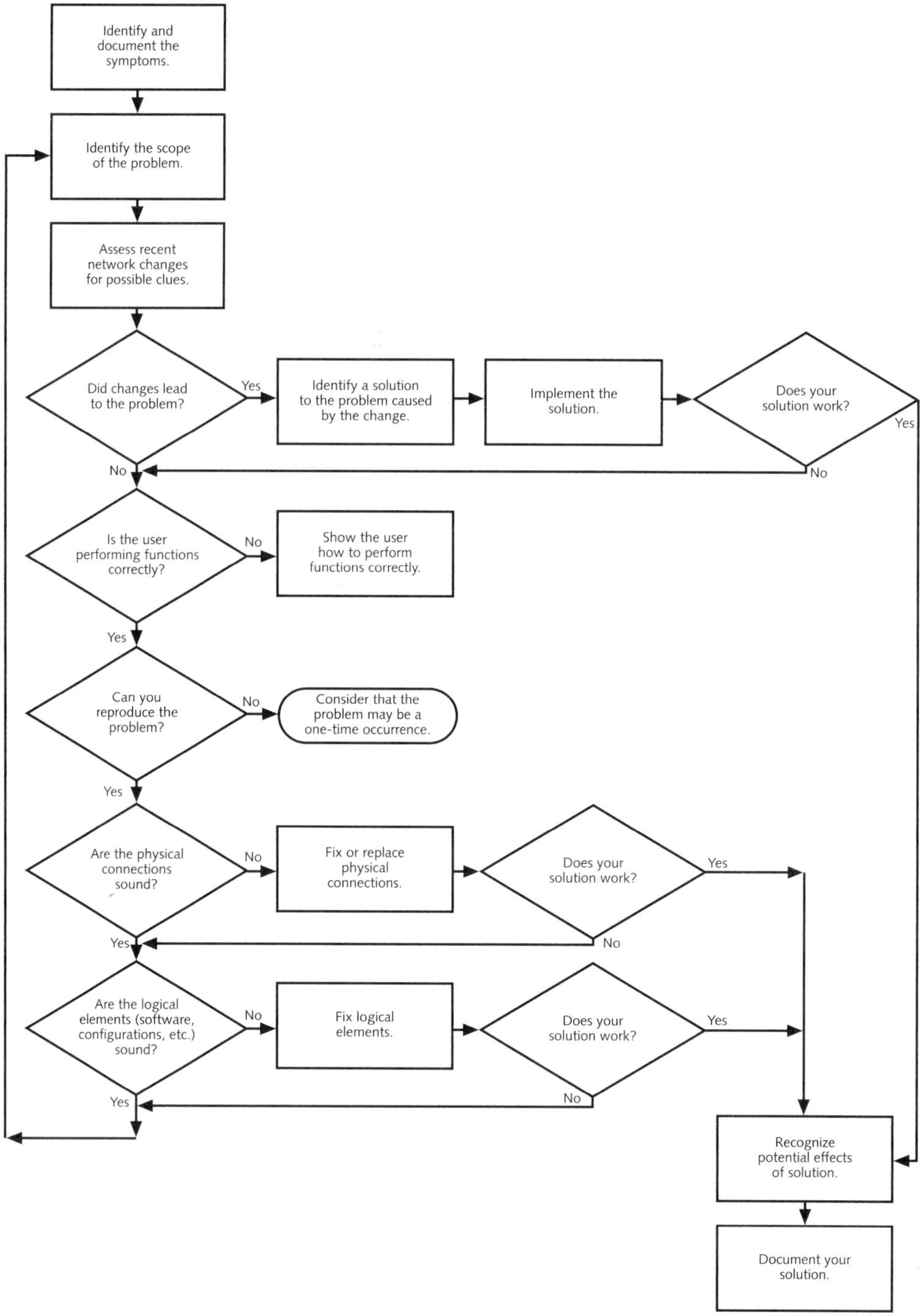

Figure 12-1   A simple flowchart of troubleshooting steps

Identify the Symptoms

When troubleshooting a network problem, act like a doctor diagnosing a patient's illness. Your first step should be to identify the specific symptoms of the problem. In a broad sense, this step brings you closer to pinpointing the cause of the problem. For example, identifying a patient's sore throat and headache as symptoms, rules out carpal tunnel syndrome and a host of other ailments. Nevertheless, the problem may still be anything from mononucleosis to allergies.

In a network, symptoms of a single problem might include a user's inability to access a network drive, send e-mail, or print to a specific printer. The problem may be caused by a number of things, including a faulty NIC, a faulty cable, a faulty hub, a faulty router, an incorrect client software configuration, a server failure, or a user error. On the other hand, you can probably rule out a power failure, a printer failure, an Internet connectivity failure, an e-mail server failure, and a host of other problems.

Answering the following questions may help you identify the symptoms of a network problem:

- Is access to the network affected?
- Is network performance affected?
- Are data or programs affected? Or are both affected?
- Are only certain network services (such as printing) affected?
- If programs are affected, does the problem include one local application, one networked application, or multiple networked applications?
- What specific error messages do users report?
- Is one user or are multiple users affected?
- Do the symptoms manifest themselves consistently?

One danger in troubleshooting technical problems lies in jumping to conclusions about the symptoms. For example, you might field 12 questions from users one morning about a problem printing to the network printer in the Facilities Department. You might have already determined that the problem is an addressing conflict with the printer and be in the last stages of resolving the problem. Minutes later, when a 13th caller says, "I'm having problems printing," you might immediately conclude that she is another Facilities staff member and that her inability to print results from the same printer addressing problem. In fact, this user may be in the Administration Department, and her inability to print could represent a symptom of a larger network problem.

Take time to pay attention to the users, system and network behaviors, and any error messages. Treat each symptom as unique (but potentially related to others). In this way, you will avoid the risk of ignoring problems or—even worse—causing more problems.

12

Take note of the error messages reported by users. If you aren't near the users, ask them to read the messages to you directly off their screens or, better yet, print the screens that contain the error messages. (On some computers, pressing the Print Screen button—which is sometimes labeled "Print Scrn" or "Prt Sc"—will perform the Print Screen function. On other computers, you can use the Shift-Print Screen or Alt-Print Screen keystroke combinations.) Keep a record of these error messages along with your other troubleshooting notes for that problem.

Identify the Scope of the Problem

After you have identified the problem's symptoms and ruled out user error, you should determine the scope of the problem—whether the problem appears only with a certain group of users, with certain areas of the organization, or at certain times. For example, if a problem affects only users on one network segment, you may deduce that the problem lies with that network segment's cabling, configuration, router port, or gateway. On the other hand, if symptoms are limited to one user, you can typically narrow the cause of the problem down to a single cable, workstation (hardware or software) configuration, or user.

In the doctor/patient analogy, this scope identification process is similar to that of the doctor who asks a patient how long his sore throat has lasted and whether anyone else in his family is affected. If the patient answers that the sore throat started yesterday and his twin toddlers both have colds, the doctor might suspect a cold virus. Conversely, if the patient indicates that no one he knows is ill and that his sore throat has lingered for 10 days, the doctor might suspect something other than a simple cold.

Answering the following questions may help you ascertain the scope of a network problem:

- How many users or network segments are affected?

   One user or workstation?

   A workgroup?

   A department?

   One location within an organization?

   An entire organization?

- When did the problem begin?

   Has the network, server, or workstation ever worked properly?

   Did the symptoms appear in the last hour or day?

   Have the symptoms appeared intermittently for a long time?

   Do the symptoms appear only at certain times of the day, week, month, or year?

Like identifying symptoms, narrowing down a problem's scope can eliminate some causes and point to others. In particular, narrowing down the affected groups of users or areas of your organization can help to distinguish workstation (or user) problems from network problems. If the problem affects only a department or floor of your organization, for example, you will probably need to examine that network segment, its router interface, its cabling, or a server that provides services to those users. If a problem affects users at a remote location, you should examine the WAN link or its router interfaces. If a problem affects all users in all departments and locations, a catastrophic failure has occurred, and you should assess critical devices such as central switches and backbone connections.

 If a problem is universal—that is, if it affects the entire LAN or WAN—you will naturally want to answer these questions very quickly. In the doctor/patient analogy, this situation would be similar to performing triage in an emergency room.

Usually, network problems are not catastrophic, and you can take a little time to troubleshoot them correctly, by asking specific questions designed to identify their scope. For example, suppose a user complains that his mail program isn't picking up e-mail. You should begin by asking when the problem began, whether it affects only that user or everyone in his department, and what error message (or messages) the user receives when he attempts to pick up mail. In answering your questions, he might say, "The problem began about 10 minutes ago. Both my neighbors are having problems with e-mail, too. And as a matter of fact, a network technician was working on my machine this morning and installed a new graphics program."

As you listen to the user's response, you may need to politely filter out information that is unlikely to be related to the problem. In this situation, the user relayed two significant pieces of information: (1) the scope of the problem includes a group of users, and (2) the problem began 10 minutes ago. With this knowledge, you can then delve further in your troubleshooting. In this example, you would proceed by focusing on the network segment rather than on one workstation.

Discovering the time or frequency with which a problem occurs can reveal more subtle network problems. For example, if multiple users throughout the organization cannot log onto the server at 8:05 A.M., you may deduce that the server needs additional resources to handle the processing burden of accepting so many logins. If a network fails at noon every Tuesday, you may be able to correlate this problem with a test of your building's power system, which causes a power dip that affects the servers, routers, hubs, and other devices.

Identifying the scope of the problem will lead you to your next troubleshooting steps. The path may not always be clear-cut, but as the flowcharts in Figures 12-2 and 12-3 illustrate, some direction can be gained from narrowing both the demographic (or geographic) and chronological scope of a problem. Notice that these flowcharts end with the process of further troubleshooting. In the following sections, you will learn more about these subsequent troubleshooting steps.

The processes of identifying a problem's scope by demographics and by chronology are not mutually exclusive, but rather can be followed simultaneously. For example, you might quickly determine that users in the Software Department experience frequent network

12

disconnections, but only during the hours between midnight and 2:00 A.M. Knowing that the only staff members working at that time are software engineers, you might choose not to continue through the process of narrowing the problem's demographic scope. Instead, you would want to focus on the network activity during those two hours.

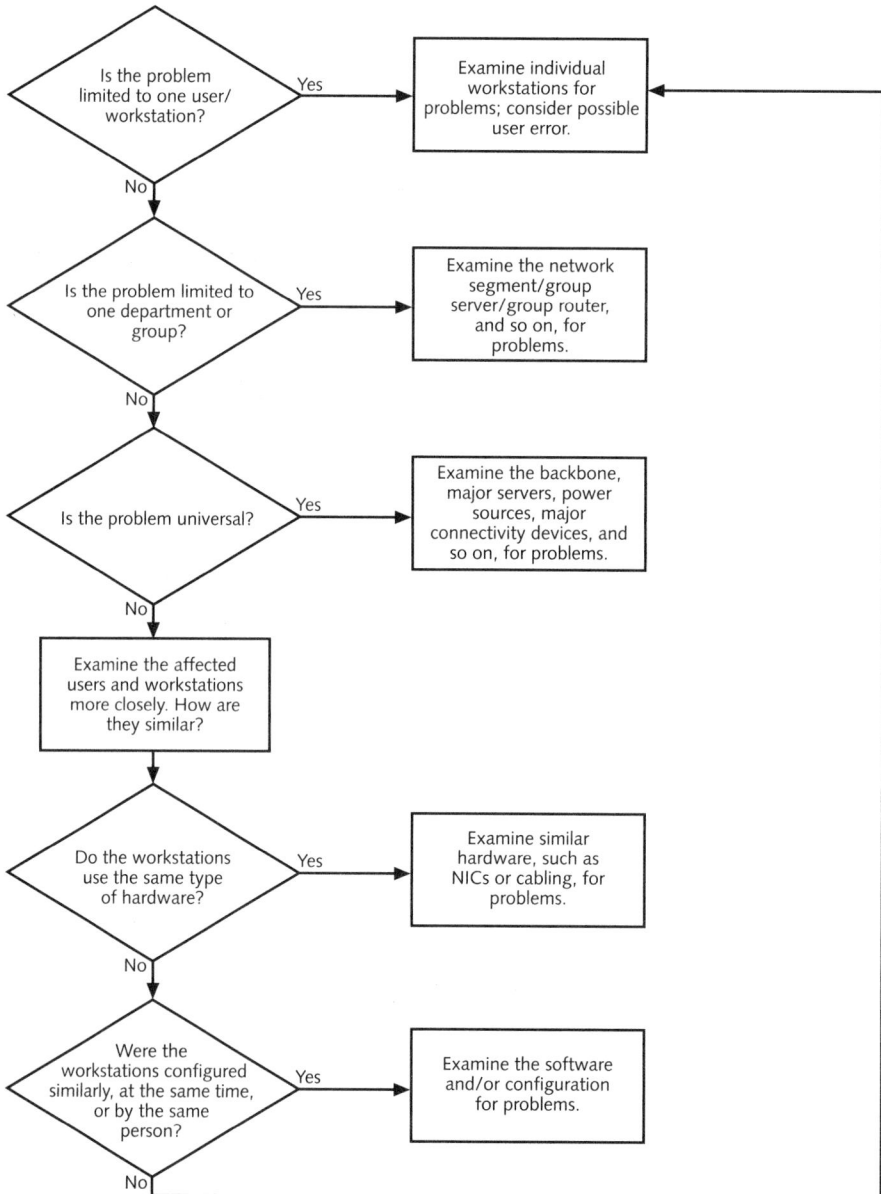

Figure 12-2 Troubleshooting while identifying the demographic scope of a problem

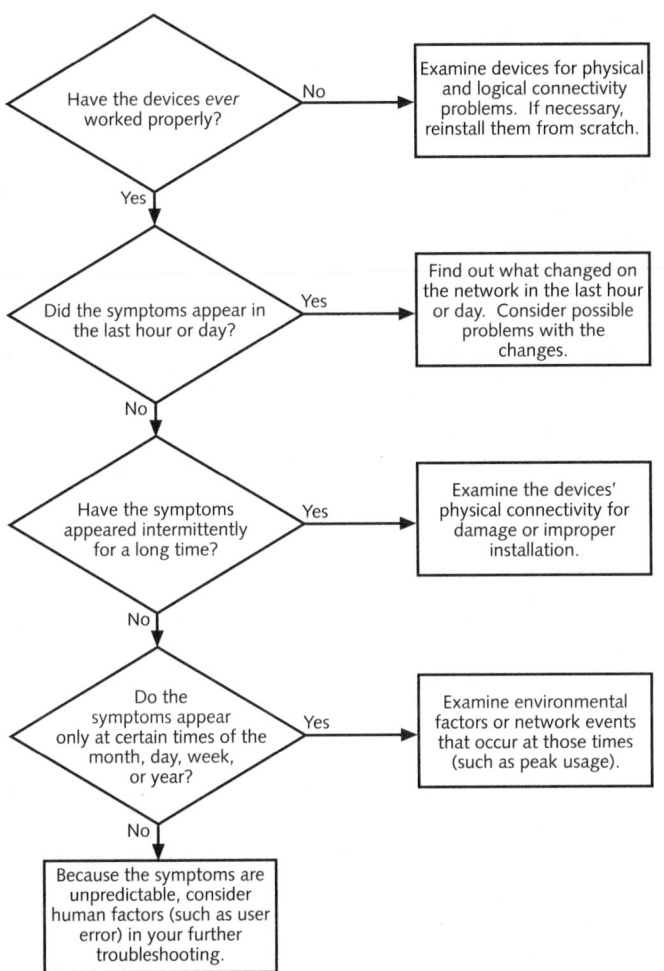

Figure 12-3   Troubleshooting while identifying the chronological scope of a problem

One fascinating example of scope-based (or chronological) troubleshooting was experienced by a wireless networking engineer working on a small metropolitan area network. His spread-spectrum RF network links, which connected businesses to a carrier's POP via a transmitter and receiver on a hospital's roof, worked perfectly all day, but failed when the sun went down each day. When the sun came up the next morning, the wireless links worked again. The engineer confirmed that the equipment was fully operational (as he suspected), then talked with the hospital personnel. The hospital's director informed him that the hospital had installed security cameras on the outside of the building. The cameras used the same RF frequency as the network's wireless links. When the security cameras were activated at sunset, their signals interfered with the wireless network's signals, preventing data from reaching their destination.

12

Establish What Has Changed

One could argue that considering recent network changes is not a separate step, but rather a continual and integral part of the troubleshooting process. As you begin troubleshooting, you should be aware of any recent changes to your network. These changes may include—among other things—the introduction of new equipment (cabling, connectivity devices, servers, and so on); repair of existing equipment; removal of equipment; installation of new components on existing equipment; installation of new services or applications on the network; equipment moves; addressing or protocol changes; software configuration changes on servers, connectivity devices, or workstations; and modifications to rights, groups, or users. As you can imagine, such changes can create problems if not planned and implemented carefully.

To determine what has changed on a network, you and your colleagues in the IT department should keep complete network change records. You will learn more about maintaining change records in Chapter 13. The more precisely you describe a change, its purpose, and the time and date when it occurred, in your records, the easier your troubleshooting will be if the change subsequently causes problems.

In addition to keeping thorough records, you must make them available to staff members who might need to reference them. For example, you might want to keep a record of changes in a spreadsheet file on a file server, and then use a Web-based form to retrieve and submit information from and to the spreadsheet. That way, no matter where a network technician was working in the organization, she could retrieve the information from any Web-enabled workstation. A simpler alternative is to keep a clipboard in the computer room with notes about changes.

Often, network changes cause unforeseen problems. For example, if you have narrowed a connectivity problem to a group of six users in the Marketing Department, you might refer to your network's change log and find that a hub in the Marketing Department's telecommunications closet was recently moved from one end of the closet to another. Reviewing the record of this change can help you more quickly pinpoint the hub as a possible cause of the problem. Perhaps the hub was incorrectly reconnected to the backbone after the move, or perhaps it became damaged in the move or lost its configuration.

The following questions may help you pinpoint a problem that results from a network change:

- Did the operating system or configuration on a server, workstation, or connectivity device change?

- Were new components added to a server, workstation, or connectivity device?

- Were old components removed from a server, workstation, or connectivity device?

- Was a server, workstation, or connectivity device moved from its previous location to a new location?

- Was a server, workstation, or connectivity device replaced?

- Was new software installed on a server, workstation, or connectivity device?

- Was old software removed from a server, workstation, or connectivity device?

If you suspect that a network change has generated a problem, you can react in two ways: you can attempt to correct the problem that resulted from the change, or you can attempt to reverse the change and restore the hardware or software to its previous state. Both options come with hazards. Of the two, reverting to a previous state is probably less risky and less time-consuming.

However, correcting the problem is sometimes the best solution. For example, if you immediately suspect that a change-related problem can be fixed easily, try correcting the problem first. If it is impossible to restore a software or hardware configuration to its previous state, you must solve the problem with the change in place. You will learn more about modifying a network and then reversing the change in Chapter 13.

 Before changing a network device or configuration, develop a plan and gather the proper resources for reversing the change in case things go wrong. For example, if you replace the memory module in a server, you should keep the old memory module handy in case the new one has flaws. In another situation, you might keep a backup of device or application configurations—perhaps by making a copy of the directory that stores the target configuration.

Select the Most Probable Cause

12

Once you have identified the scope of the problem and analyzed recent changes to the network, you are close to determining the problem's cause. The following sections provide techniques on how to zero in on the most likely cause among several plausible scenarios.

Verify User Competency

You have probably experienced a moment in your dealings with computers in which you were certain you were doing everything correctly, but still couldn't access the network, save a file, or pick up your e-mail. For example, you may have typed your case-sensitive network password without realizing that the Caps Lock function was turned on. Even though you were certain that you typed the right password, you received a "password incorrect" error message each time you tried to enter your password. All users experience such problems from time to time.

It's natural for human beings to make mistakes. Thus, as a troubleshooter, one of your first steps should be to ensure that human error is not the source of the problem. This approach will save you time and worry. In fact, a problem caused by human error is usually simple to solve. It's much quicker and easier to assist a user in remapping a network drive, for example, than to perform diagnostics on the file server.

Often, an inability to log onto the network results from a user error. Users become so accustomed to typing their passwords every morning and logging onto the network that, if something changes in the logon process, they don't know what to do. In fact, some users might never log out, so they don't know how to log on properly. Although these kinds of problems may seem simple to solve, unless a user receives training in the proper procedures and understands what might go wrong, he or she will never know how to solve a logon problem without assistance. Even if the user took a computer class that covered logging on, he or she may not remember what to do in unfamiliar situations.

When diagnosing user errors, your most powerful tool may be patience. The best way to verify that a user is performing network tasks correctly is by watching the user. If this tactic isn't practical, the next best way is to talk with the user by phone while he or she tries to replicate the error. At every step, calmly ask the user to explain what appears on the screen and what, exactly, he or she is doing. After every keystroke or command, ask the user again what appears on the screen. With this methodical approach, you will be certain to catch any user-generated mistakes. At the same time, if the problem does not result from human error, you will gain important clues for further troubleshooting.

Re-create the Problem

An excellent way to learn more about the causes of a problem is to try to re-create the symptoms yourself. If you cannot reproduce the symptoms, you may suspect that a problem was a one-time occurrence or that a user performed an operation incorrectly.

You should try to reproduce symptoms both while logged on as the user who reported the problem and while logged on under a privileged account (such as an administrator-equivalent ID). If the symptoms appear only when you're logged on under the user's ID, you may suspect that the problem relates to the user's limited rights on the network. For example, a user may complain that he was able to edit a particular spreadsheet in the Accounting directory on the file server on Friday, but was unable to open the file on Monday. When you visit his workstation, you can verify this sequence of events while logged on with his user name. When you then log on as Administrator, however, you may be able to open and edit the file. The difference in your experiences points to a user rights problem. At that point, you should check the user's privileges—especially whether they have changed since he could last retrieve the file. Perhaps someone removed him from a group that had Read and Modify rights to the Accounting directory.

Answering the following questions may help you determine whether a problem's symptoms are truly reproducible and, if so, to what extent:

- Can you make the symptoms recur every time?
- Can you make the symptoms recur some of the time?

- Do the symptoms happen only under certain circumstances? For instance, if you log on under a different ID or try the operation from a different machine, do the symptoms still appear?

- Do the symptoms ever happen when you try to repeat them?

When attempting to reproduce the symptoms of a problem, you should follow the same steps that the person reporting the symptoms followed. As you know, many computer functions can be achieved through different means. For example, in a word-processing program, you might save a file by using the menu bar, using a keystroke combination, or clicking a button on a toolbar. All three methods result in the same outcome. Similarly, you might log onto the network from a command prompt, from a predefined script inside a batch file, or from a window presented by the client software. If you attempt to reproduce a problem by performing different functions than those employed by the user, you may not be able to reproduce a legitimate problem and thus might assume that the symptoms resulted from user error. In fact, you may be missing a crucial clue to solving the problem.

To reproduce a symptom reliably, ask the user precisely what she did before the error appeared. For example, if a user complains that her network connection mysteriously drops when she's in the middle of surfing the Web, you should try to replicate the problem at her workstation; also, find out what else was running on the user's workstation or what kind of Web sites she was surfing.

 Use good judgment when attempting to reproduce problems. In some cases, reproducing a problem could wreak havoc on the network, its data, and its devices; you should not attempt to reproduce such a problem. An obvious example involves a power outage in which your backup power source failed to supply power. After your network equipment comes back online, you would not want to try cutting the power again simply to verify that the problem derived from a faulty backup power source.

Verify Physical Connectivity

After you have reproduced the problem's symptoms, you should examine the most straightforward potential flaw in network communications—the physical connectivity. Physical connectivity may include the cabling from workstation or server to data jack, from data jack to punch-down block, from punch-down block to patch panel, or from patch panel to hub or switch. It may also include the proper physical installation of devices such as NICs, hubs, routers, servers, and switches. As noted earlier, you can save much time by checking the obvious first. Physical connectivity problems can be easy to spot and easy to fix.

12

Answering the following questions may help you identify a problem pertaining to physical connectivity:

- Is the device turned on?

- Is the NIC properly inserted?

- Is a device's network cable properly (that is, not loosely) connected to both its NIC and the wall jack?

- Do patch cables properly connect punch-down blocks to patch panels and patch panels to hubs or switches?

- Is the hub, router, or switch properly connected to the backbone?

- Are all cables in good condition (without signs of wear or damage)?

- Are all connectors (for example, RJ-45) in good condition and properly seated?

- Do network (maximum and segment) lengths conform to the IEEE 802 specifications?

A first step in verifying the physical integrity of a connection is to follow that connection from one endpoint on the network to the other. For example, if a workstation user cannot log onto the network, and you have verified that he is typing his password correctly, check the physical connectivity from his workstation's NIC and patch cable. Follow his connection all the way through the network to the server that he cannot reach.

Often, physical connectivity problems will manifest as a continuous or intermittent inability to connect to the network and perform network-related functions. Physical connectivity problems do not typically (but occasionally can) result in application anomalies, the inability to use a single application, poor network performance, protocol errors, software licensing errors, or software usage errors. Some software errors, however, can point to a physical connectivity problem. For example, a user might be able to log onto his file server without problems. When he chooses to run a query on a database, however, his report software might produce an error message indicating that the database is unavailable or not found. If the database resides on a separate server, this symptom could point to a physical connectivity problem with the database server.

In addition to verifying the connections between devices, you must verify the soundness of the hardware used in those connections. A sound connection means that cables are inserted firmly in ports, NICs, and wall jacks; NICs are seated firmly in the system board; connectors are not broken; and cables are not damaged. Damaged or improperly inserted connectivity elements may result in only occasional (and therefore difficult-to-troubleshoot) errors.

For example, you might receive a call from a user who cannot log onto the network in two out of every five attempts. The user might say that she could previously log onto the network without errors and that she thinks the errors have recently become more frequent. Because the error doesn't occur every time, it is probably caused by damaged or improperly installed connectivity hardware or by a segment length that exceeds IEEE 802 specifications. Because the errors are increasing in frequency, they are probably caused by hardware that is sustaining progressively more damage and will eventually fail. Assuming that no one else in this user's department is receiving similar errors, you might examine the cable connecting the user's workstation to the wall jack. Quite possibly, a chair rolling over it could damage this cable.

Even if a cable does not show obvious physical damage, it may still have flaws. For example, it might have been poorly manufactured or damaged internally from age or misuse. If you suspect a flawed cable, the quickest way to test your theory may be to replace the cable and note whether the errors disappear. Alternately, you could use a cable tester to verify the quality of a cable. You will learn more about cable testers later in this chapter.

Other physical components (such as NICs, hubs, or ports on any device) may also have flaws. Often, you can perform diagnostics on the device to determine whether it works correctly. For example, in Chapter 6, you learned that most NIC manufacturers ship a diagnostics program on a floppy disk with the NIC. In some cases, you may need to replace (or "swap out") a part. Later in this chapter, you will learn about the techniques and potential hazards of swapping equipment.

Finally, if symptoms seem to point to a physical connectivity problem, but you cannot find any loose or missing connections or flawed cables, the problem may relate to a network segment whose length exceeds IEEE 802 standards. Recall from Chapter 4 that the different types of networks must adhere to maximum segment lengths. For example, a 10BaseT network segment (the total amount of cabling between the connectivity device and a node) cannot exceed 100 meters. If your segment spans a greater distance, the devices at the end of the segment will experience intermittent connectivity errors or excessive transmission delays. If you have exceeded the maximum segment length, you must rearrange that segment to bring devices closer to the connectivity equipment.

The flowchart in Figure 12-4 illustrates how a logical approach to checking physical connectivity can help you solve a network problem. The steps in this flowchart apply to a typical problem: a user's inability to log onto the network. They assume that you have already ruled out user error and that you have successfully reproduced the problem under both your and the user's login IDs.

12

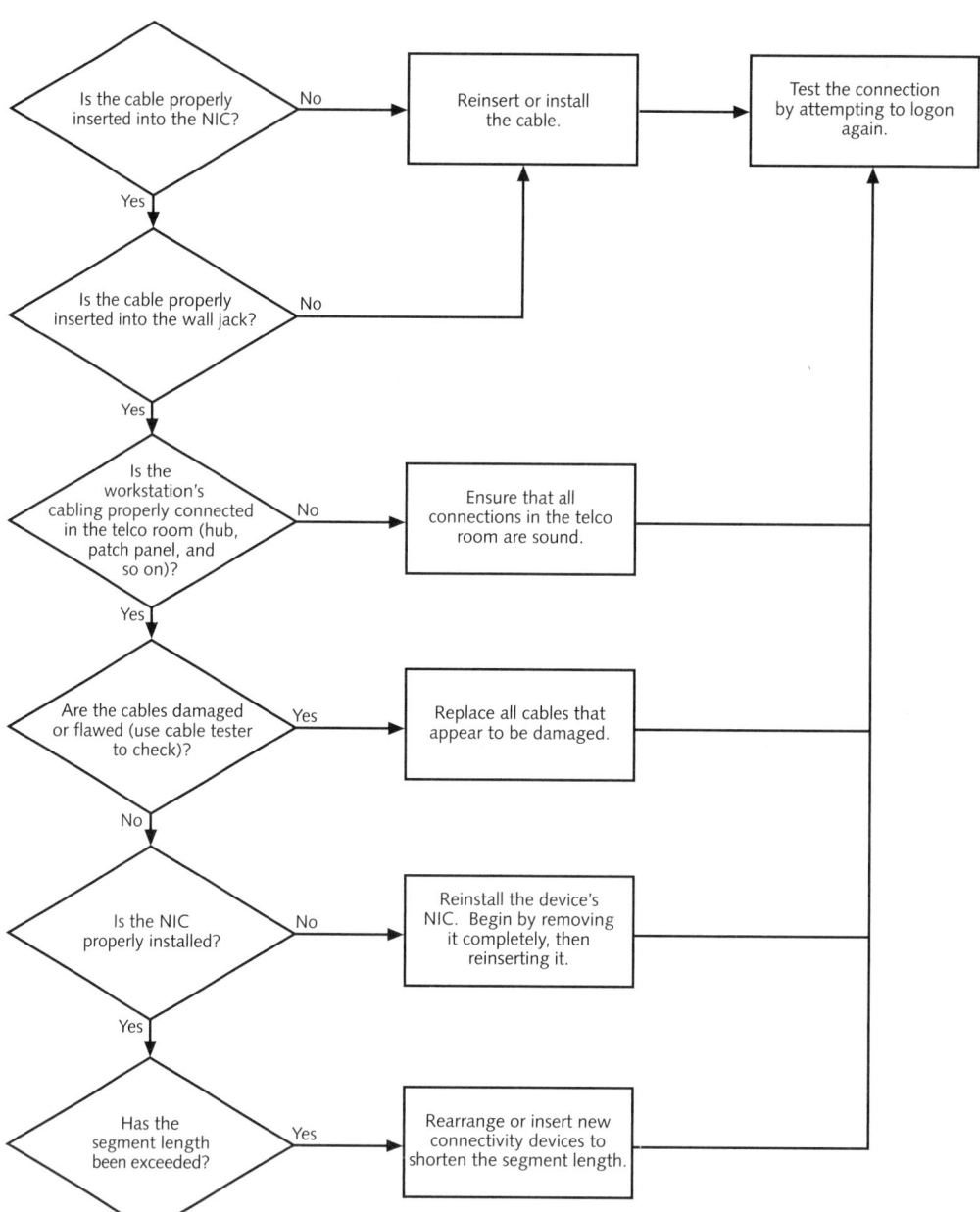

Figure 12-4   Troubleshooting while verifying physical connectivity

As noted in Figure 12-4, physical connectivity errors can frequently be traced to recent changes in the network, such as a replaced hub or a moved server. If you suspect a physical connectivity problem, you should find out whether anything on the network has changed recently. The potential effect of changes on network integrity is covered in detail later in this section. Most modern NICs have at least one LED that flashes green or amber, indicating the NIC's status. Although the meaning and number of these lights may vary according to the NIC model, typically a steady green light indicates that the NIC has successfully connected to the network. The LED will usually blink as the NIC searches for and finds a network connection. A steady blinking amber light generally means that the NIC can't make a network connection. For specific information on your NIC's LEDs, read the NIC's user manual.

Verify Logical Connectivity

Once you have verified the physical connections, you must examine the firmware and software configurations, settings, installations, and privileges. Depending on the type of symptoms, you may need to investigate networked applications, the network operating system, or hardware configurations, such as NIC IRQ settings. All of these elements belong in the category of "logical connectivity."

Answering the following questions may help you identify a problem with logical connectivity:

- Do error messages reference damaged or missing files or device drivers?
- Do error messages reference malfunctioning or insufficient resources (such as memory)?
- Has an operating system, configuration, or application been recently changed, introduced, or deleted?
- Does the problem occur with only one application or a few, similar applications?
- Does the problem happen consistently?
- Does the problem affect a single user or one group of users?

Logical connectivity problems often prove more difficult to isolate and resolve than physical connectivity problems because they can be more complex. For example, a user might complain that she has been unable to connect to the network for the last two hours. After you go to her workstation and find that you can reproduce the symptoms both under her login ID and your own ID, you check the physical connections. Everything seems to be in order. Next, you may ask the user whether anything changed on her machine approximately two hours ago. She tells you that she didn't do a thing to the machine—it just stopped working.

12

At this point, you may investigate the workstation's logical connectivity. Some possible software-based causes for a failure to connect to the network include (but are not limited to) the following: resource conflicts with the NIC's configuration, an improperly configured NIC (for example, it may be set to the wrong data rate), improperly installed or configured client software, and improperly installed or configured network protocols or services. In this example, you may take another look at the client login screen and notice that the wrong server is selected as the default. Once you change the default server setting in the user's client software, she will likely be able to log onto the network.

Like many physical connectivity problems, many logical connectivity problems are created by changes to network elements. In the next section, you will learn how to trace the symptoms of a problem to a recent change in the network.

Implement a Solution

At last, after you have found the problem, you can implement a solution. This step may be very brief (such as correcting the default server designation in a user's client login screen) or it may take a long time (such as replacing the hard disk of a server). In either event, record your solution in a central location, such as a call-tracking database. You will learn more about documenting problems and solutions later in this chapter.

Implementing a solution requires foresight and patience, whether it consists of talking a user through changing a setting in his e-mail program or reconfiguring a router. As with finding the problem, the more methodically and logically you can approach the solution, the more efficient the correction process will be. If a problem is causing catastrophic outages, however, you should solve the problem as quickly as possible.

The following steps will help you implement a safe and reliable solution:

1. Collect all the documentation you have about a problem's symptoms from your investigation and keep it handy while solving the problem.

2. If you are reinstalling software on a device, make a backup of the device's existing software installation. If you are changing hardware on a device, keep the old parts handy in case the solution doesn't work. If you are changing the configuration of a program or device, take the time to print out the program or device's current configuration. Even if the change seems minor, jot down notes about the original state. For example, if you intend to add a user to a privileged group to allow her to access the Accounting spreadsheets, first write down the groups to which she currently belongs.

3. Perform the change, replacement, move, or addition that you believe will solve the problem. Record your actions in detail so that you can later enter the information into a database.

4. Test your solution (see the following section).

5. Before leaving the area in which you were working, clean it up. For instance, if you created a new patch cable for a telco room, remove the debris from splicing the cable.

6. If the solution fixes the problem, record the details you have collected about the symptoms, the problem, and the solution in your organization's call tracking database.

7. If your solution involved a significant change or addressed a significant problem (one that affected more than a few users), revisit the solution a day or two later to verify that the problem has, indeed, been solved and that it hasn't created additional problems.

Test the Solution

After implementing your solution, you must test it to verify that it works properly. Obviously, the type of testing you perform depends on your solution. For example, if you replaced a patch cable between a hub port and a patch panel, a quick test of your solution would be to determine whether you could connect to the network from the device that relies on that patch cable. If the device does not successfully connect to the network, you may have to try another cable or reconsider whether the problem stems from physical or logical connectivity or some other cause.

Suppose you replaced a switch that served four different departments in an organization. To test your solution, you might not only test connectivity from each department's workstations, but also use a network analysis tool (such as those discussed later in this chapter) to verify that the switch is handling data correctly.

It's often a good idea to enlist the user who reported the problem in testing your solution, too. That strategy ensures that you will get an objective assessment of the results. You may have been working on the solution so long that you've forgotten the original problem. You might also have enough technical knowledge to circumvent small problems that might flummox the average user. In addition, having the user test your solution will prevent you from leaving a device in a state that is familiar to you, but unfamiliar to the user.

For example, in the process of diagnosing a problem with a user's access to a mail directory, you may have reconfigured his mail settings to log on with your own ID and rule out the possibility of a physical connectivity error. After discovering that the problem was actually due to an IP addressing conflict, you may fix the IP addressing problem but forget that you changed the user's e-mail configuration. Having the user test your solution would reveal this oversight—and prevent you from having to return to the workstation to solve another problem.

12

You may not be able to test your solution immediately after implementing it. In some cases, you may have to wait days or weeks before you know for certain whether it worked. For example, you may have discovered that a server was sometimes running out of processor capacity when handling clients' database queries, causing users to experience unacceptably slow response times. To solve this problem, you might add two processors and reconfigure the server to use symmetric multiprocessing. The timing of the database usage may be unpredictable, however. As a result, you may not find out whether the added processors eliminated the problem until a certain number of users attempt the operations that will push the server to its peak processor usage.

A copy of all questions included in the preceding sections appears on a form in Appendix D, "Examples of Standard Networking Forms." You might want to create your own form based on these questions but tailored to your particular networking environment. Take your form along whenever you set out on a troubleshooting mission. It will help remind you of possibilities that you might otherwise forget to investigate.

Recognize the Potential Effects of a Solution

Even before fixing a problem on your network, you should consider how the change might affect users and network functionality. Consider the scope, tradeoffs, security, scalability, and cost when implementing a solution. These factors are discussed further in the following section.

One of the most important aspects to consider is the breadth, or scope, of your change. For example, replacing a cable that connects a workstation to a hub may affect only one user, but replacing a cable that connects a server to a hub will affect all users who access that server. Assess the scope of your solution—whether it is a single workstation, a workgroup, a location, or the entire network—before implementing that solution. If the problem does not pose an emergency, wait until no one is on the network before implementing solutions that will affect many users. That way, you will have time to assess the solution's effects systematically and fix any new problems that might arise.

Along with the scope, another factor to consider is the tradeoff your solution might impose. In other words, your solution may restore functionality for one group of users, but remove it for others. For example, let's say you are a network technician at a stationery company that uses specialized software to program custom logos and control its embossing machines. When you add a group of new Windows 2000 workstations to your network, you discover that the embossing control software doesn't work properly with them. The software vendor tells you that to be compatible with Windows 2000, you must install a new version of the software on your file server. You may be thrilled to hear of such a simple solution and begin to install the software immediately. In the next half hour, you receive numerous phone calls from employees using Windows 98 workstations who cannot properly use the embossing control software. Now you have solved one problem, but created another. In this situation, it would have been wise to ask the software vendor about their upgrade's compatibility with all the other operating systems your company uses. If the vendor told you about a problem with Windows 98 workstations, you could have kept the old installation on the server for these users, then installed the new version of the software in another directory for use by Windows 2000 users.

Be aware of the security implications of your solution, because it may inadvertently result in the addition or removal of network privileges for a user or group of users. The consequence may be simply that a user can no longer access a data file or application he is used to accessing. But a worse consequence is that you could create a security opening that allows unauthorized people to access your network.

You should also consider the scalability of the solution you intend to implement. Does it position the network for additions and enhancements later on, or is it merely a temporary fix that the organization will outgrow in a year? Ideally, your solution would be perfectly suited to your network and allow for future growth. But a temporary fix is not necessarily wrong, depending on the scenario. For example, you might walk into the office one day to find that none of your users can access the network. You may track down the problem as an internal hardware problem with your IP gateway. Since the gateway is under warranty, you quickly call the manufacturer to either get the gateway replaced or fixed immediately. The manufacturer may tell you that while they don't have the identical gateway available in their local office, they can substitute a different, smaller model to get your users reconnected today and meanwhile order the identical gateway that you can install when you have more time. In this situation, it is preferable to take the temporary gateway and restore functionality than to wait for the ideal solution.

12

Another factor to consider when implementing your solution is cost. Obviously, replacing one patch cable or faulty network adapter is a fairly inexpensive proposition, and you don't need to analyze cost in these cases. But if the solution you have proposed requires significant dollars for either software or hardware, you should spend time carefully considering your options. For example, you may discover a problem with performance on your network. After some investigation you may determine that the best solution is to replace all of your 400 workstations' network adapters with newer, faster network adapters. If you purchase quality NICs, this solution could cost over $10,000 for the hardware alone, not to mention the time it will take technicians to replace the devices, which may cost more. Also you should consider when these workstations will be replaced and if you will have to either discard or remove the network adapters you just installed. It may be more prudent to identify where the network's performance is poor and address those areas separately—for example, by adding a switch to a busy segment or adding a more powerful server for a heavily used application.

Last, if you are uncertain about whether your proposed solution is the *best* solution, even after your thorough diagnosis and research, you should consult with others, either within or outside of your organization. Colleagues or consultants may share an experience that leads you to prefer one solution to another.

After your solution is in place, communicate your solution to your colleagues, thus adding to the store of knowledge about your network. Next you will learn about how best to document your troubleshooting efforts.

Document Problems and Solutions

Whether you are a one-person network support team or one of a hundred network technicians at your organization, you should always write down the symptoms of a problem and your solution for it. Given the volume of problems you and other analysts will troubleshoot, it will be impossible to remember the circumstances of each incident. In addition, networking personnel frequently change jobs, and everyone will appreciate clear, thorough documentation. An effective way to document problems and solutions is in a centrally located database to which all networking personnel have online access.

Some organizations use a software program for documenting problems, known as a **call tracking system** (also informally known as help desk software). Examples of popular call tracking systems include Clientele, Expert Advisor, ServiceIT, and Track-It! These programs provide user-friendly graphical interfaces that prompt the user for every piece of information associated with the problem. They assign unique identifying numbers to each problem, in addition to identifying the caller, the nature of the problem, the time necessary to resolve it, and the nature of the resolution.

Most call tracking systems are highly customizable, so you can tailor the form fields to your particular computing environment. For example, if you work for an oil refinery, you might add fields for identifying problems with the plant's flow-control software. In addition, most call tracking systems allow you to enter free-form text explanations of problems and solutions. Some also offer Web-based interfaces.

If your organization does not have a call tracking system, you should at least keep records in a simple electronic form. You can find an example of a network problem record in Appendix D, "Examples of Standard Networking Forms." A typical problem record form should include at least the following fields:

- The name, department, and phone number of the problem originator (the person who first noticed the problem)

- Information regarding whether the problem is software- or hardware-related

- If the problem is software-related, the package to which it pertains; if the problem is hardware-related, the device or component to which it pertains

- Symptoms of the problem, including when it was first noticed
- The name and telephone number of the network support contact
- The amount of time spent troubleshooting the problem
- The resolution of the problem

As discussed earlier in this chapter, many organizations operate a help desk staffed with personnel who have only basic troubleshooting expertise and who record problems called in by users. To effectively field network questions, an organization's help desk staff must maintain current and accurate records for network support personnel. Your department should take responsibility for managing a supported services list that help desk personnel can use as a reference. A **supported services list** is a document (preferably online) that lists every service and software package supported within an organization, plus the names of first- and second-level support contacts for those services or software packages. Anything else you or your department can do to increase communication and availability of support information will expedite troubleshooting.

In addition to communicating problems and solutions to your peers whenever you work on a network problem, you should follow up with the user who reported the problem. Make sure that the client understands how or why the problem occurred, what you did to resolve the problem, and who to contact should the problem recur. This type of education will not only help your clients make better decisions about the type of support or training they need, but will also improve their understanding of and respect for your department.

12

TROUBLESHOOTING TOOLS

So far, this chapter has focused on using a systematic method of trial and error to diagnose network problems. In the real world, however, this technique may lead nowhere or take too much time. In some cases, the most efficient approach is to use a tool specifically designed to analyze and isolate network problems. Several tools are available, ranging from simple cable testers that indicate whether a cable is faulty, to sophisticated protocol analyzers that capture and interpret all types of data traveling over the network. The tool you choose will depend on the particular problem you need to investigate and the characteristics of your network.

The following sections describe a variety of network troubleshooting tools, their functions, and their relative costs. In the Hands-on Projects at the end of this chapter, you will have the opportunity to try some of these network troubleshooting tools.

Hardware Troubleshooting Tools

This section describes tools that can assist you in identifying a problem with a cable, connector, or network adapter.

Crossover Cable

As you learned in Chapter 4, a crossover cable is one in which the transmit and receive wire pairs in one of the connectors are reversed. This reversal enables you to use a crossover cable to directly interconnect two nodes without using an intervening connectivity device such as a hub. A crossover cable is useful in troubleshooting to quickly and easily verify that a node's network adapter is transmitting and receiving signals properly. For example, suppose you are a network technician on your way to fix urgent network problems. A user flags you down and says that over the last week he has occasionally had problems connecting to the network and as of this morning, he hasn't been able to connect at all. He's very frustrated, so you kindly say that if you can help him in 10 minutes, you will; otherwise, he'll have to call the help desk. You follow him to his workstation and, by asking around, you determine that he is the only one suffering this problem. Thus, you can probably narrow the problem down to his workstation (either hardware or software) or his cabling (or less likely, his port on the hub in the telecommunications closet). Because you have your laptop and troubleshooting gear in your bag, you quickly connect one plug of the crossover cable to his workstation's network adapter and the other plug to your laptop's network adapter. You then try logging onto your laptop from his workstation. Because this process is successful, you suggest that the problem lies with his network cable, and not with his workstation's software or hardware. As you rush off, you hand him a new patch cable to replace his old one.

Tone Generator and Tone Locator

Ideally, you and your networking colleagues would label each port and wire termination in a telecommunications closet so that problems and changes can be easily managed. However, because of personnel changes and time constraints, a telecommunications closet often winds up being disorganized and poorly documented. If this is the case where you work, you may need a tone generator and a tone locator to determine where one pair of wires (out of possibly hundreds) terminates.

A **tone generator** is a small electronic device that issues a signal on a wire pair. A **tone locator** is a device that emits a tone when it detects electrical activity on a wire pair. By placing the tone generator at one end of a wire and attaching a tone locator to the other end, you can verify the location of the wire's termination. Figure 12-5 depicts the use of a tone generator and a tone locator. Of course, you must work by trial and error, guessing which termination corresponds to the wire over which you've generated a signal until the tone locator indicates the correct choice. This combination of devices is also known as a **fox and hound**, because the locator (the hound) chases the generator (the fox).

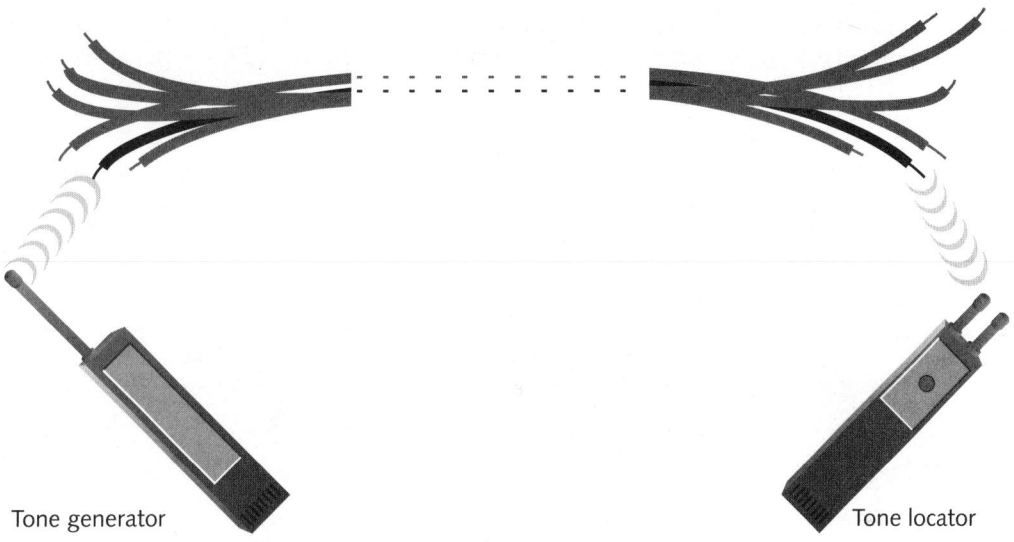

Figure 12-5   Use of a tone generator and tone locator

Tone generators and tone locators cannot be used to determine any characteristics about a cable, such as whether it has defects or whether its length exceeds IEEE standards for a certain type of network. They are only used to determine where a wire pair terminates. In fact, because of their limited functionality, tone generators and tone locators are rarely used on modern networks. (However, they are still widely used by telephone technicians.)

 A tone generator should never be used on a wire that may connect to a device's port or network adapter. Because a tone generator transmits electricity over the wire, it may damage the device or network adapter.

Multimeter

Cable testing tools are essential for both cable installers and network troubleshooters, as cables are often at fault when a network problem arises. Symptoms of cabling problems can be as elusive as occasional lost packets or as obvious as a break in network connectivity. You can easily test cables for faults with specialized tools. In this section and in the ones following, you will learn about different tools that can help isolate problems with network cables. The first device you will learn about is a **multimeter**, a simple instrument that can measure many characteristics of an electric circuit, including its resistance and voltage.

If you have taken any introductory electronics classes, you are probably familiar with a **voltmeter**, the instrument that measures the pressure, or voltage, of an electric current. Recall that voltage is used to create signals over a network wire. Thus, every time data travel over a wire, the wire carries a small voltage. In addition, each wire has a certain amount of **resistance**, or opposition to electric current. Resistance is a fundamental

12

property of wires that depends on the wire's molecular structure and size. Every type of wire has different resistance characteristics (for example, each type of coaxial cable listed in Table 4-2 has a different amount of resistance). Resistance is measured in ohms, and the device used to measure resistance is called an **ohmmeter**.

Although electricians and network professionals could use separate instruments for measuring resistance and voltage on a wire, it is more convenient to have one instrument that accomplishes both of these functions. The multimeter is such an instrument. Figure 12-6 shows a multimeter.

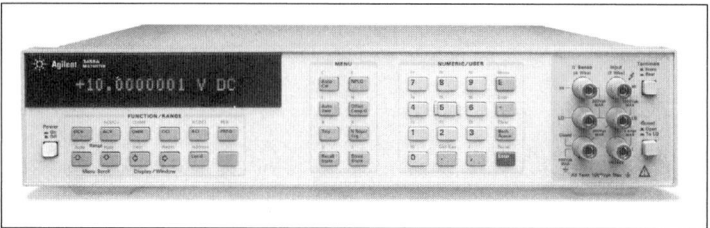

Figure 12-6   A multimeter

As a network professional, you might use a multimeter to:

- Verify that a cable is properly conducting electricity—that is, whether its signal can travel unimpeded from one node on the network to another

- Check for the presence of noise on a wire (by detecting extraneous voltage)

- Verify that the amount of resistance generated by terminators on coaxial cable networks (such as 10Base5 Ethernet) is appropriate or whether terminators are actually present and functional

- Test for short or open circuits in the wire (by detecting unexpected resistance or loss of voltage)

You should be aware that multimeters are at the low end of the cable testing tool spectrum because of their limited capabilities. More sophisticated tools, such as cable testers, can perform the same tests that multimeters perform, in addition to other, more network-specific, functions.

Cable Checkers

Basic **cable checkers** simply determine whether your cabling can provide connectivity. To accomplish this task, they apply a small voltage to each conductor at one end of the cable, and then check whether that voltage is detectable at the other end. They may also check whether voltage cannot be detected on other conductors in the cable. Figure 12-7 depicts a typical simple cable checker.

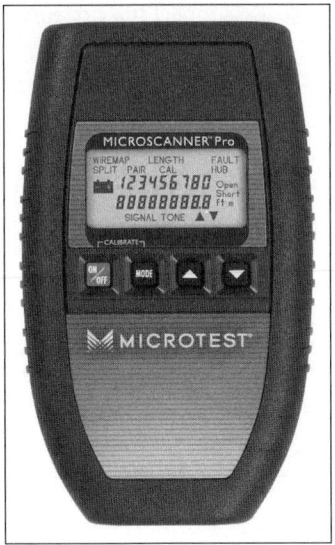

Figure 12-7   A basic cable checker

Most cable checkers provide a series of lights that signal pass/fail. Some also indicate a cable pass/fail with an audible tone. A pass/fail test provides a simple indicator of whether a component can perform its stated function.

In addition to checking cable continuity, a good cable checker will verify that the wires are paired correctly and that they are not shorted, exposed, or crossed. Recall from Chapter 4 that different network models use specific wire pairings and follow cabling standards set forth in EIA/TIA 568. Make sure that the cable checker you purchase can test the type of network you use—for example, 10BaseT Ethernet, 100BaseTX Ethernet, or Token Ring.

When you make your own cables, be sure to verify their integrity with at least a cable checker (better yet, a cable tester). Even if you purchase cabling from a reputable vendor, you should make sure that it meets your network's required standards. Just because a cable is labeled "CAT5" does not necessarily mean that it will live up to that standard. Testing cabling before installing it may save many hours of troubleshooting after the network is in place.

Cable checkers cannot test the continuity of fiber-optic cabling, because fiber cable uses light rather than voltage to transmit data. To test fiber-optic cabling, you need a specialized fiber cable tester.

12

Do not use a cable checker on a live network cable. Disconnect the cable from the network, and then test its continuity.

For convenience, most cable checkers are portable and lightweight and typically use one 9-volt battery. A basic cable checker costs between $100 and $300, but it may save many hours of work. Popular cable checker manufacturers include Belkin, Fluke, Microtest, and Paladin.

Cable Testers

The difference between cable checkers and cable testers lies in their sophistication and price. A **cable tester** performs the same continuity and fault tests as a cable checker, but also provides the following functions:

- Ensures that the cable is not too long
- Measures the distance to a cable fault
- Measures attenuation along a cable
- Measures near-end crosstalk between wires
- Measures termination resistance and impedance for Thinnet cabling
- Issues pass/fail ratings for CAT3, CAT5, CAT6, or even CAT7 standards
- Stores and prints cable testing results

Some cable testers may provide even more features—for example, a graphical output depicting a cable's attenuation and crosstalk characteristics over the length of the cable. Because of their sophistication, cable testers cost significantly more than cable checkers. A high-end unit may cost from $5000 to $8000, and a low-end unit may cost between $1000 and $4000. Popular cable tester manufacturers include Fluke and Microtest. Figure 12-8 shows an example of a high-end cable tester.

When choosing a cable tester for twisted-pair networks, make sure to purchase one that performs attenuation and crosstalk testing for the frequency range used by your network. For example, if you want to test a 100BaseT Ethernet network, purchase a cable tester capable of testing up to 100 MHz.

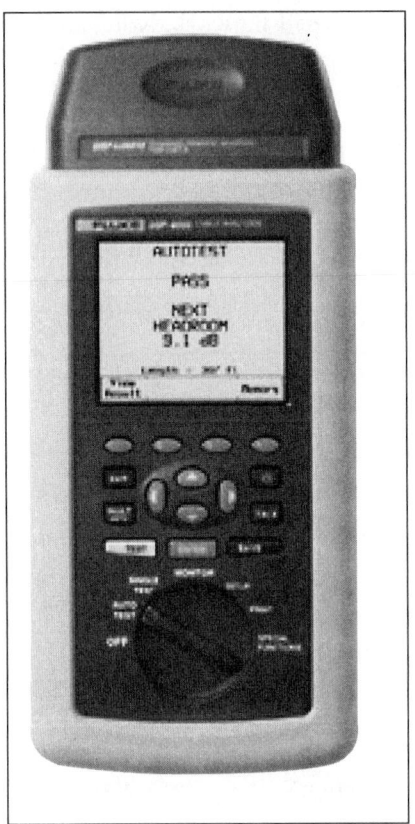

AUTOTEST

PASS

NEXT
HEADROOM
3.1 dB

Length = 302 ft

View
Result   Rerun

Figure 12-8   A high-end cable tester

To better appreciate how many problems a good cable tester can diagnose, recall from Chapter 4 that network segments must adhere to strict length limits to ensure that data reach their destinations on time and error-free. If one room of workstations continually experiences intermittent problems logging onto the network or very slow connections, you could use a cable tester to discover whether those workstations are situated beyond their maximum distance from the network hub. If another group of workstations frequently experiences slow responses from the network, a cable tester might reveal the presence of too many stations between the sending and receiving nodes, which causes excessive signal attenuation.

Another significant factor in wire-based data transmission is crosstalk. Recall from Chapter 4 that crosstalk occurs when the signals on one wire interfere with signals on an adjacent wire. The result is interference, much in the same way that the voices from two conversations in a loud room interfere with each other and prevent listeners from understanding the words. Crosstalk often arises when wires are crushed or crossed at the connector end of a cable. For this reason, you can accurately test for crosstalk only after installation of a cable, and you should perform the test at both ends of the wire.

12

In addition to cable testers for coaxial and twisted-pair networks, you can also find cable testers for fiber-optic networks. Rather than issue an electrical signal over the cable as twisted-pair cable testers do, a fiber-optic cable tester transmits light-based signals of different wavelengths over the fiber. These tests can indicate the amount of attenuation on the cable, and the continuity and the length of the cable. Note that since crosstalk does not apply to light-based signals, a fiber tester cannot (and need not) test for crosstalk. Because of the relatively high cost of installing fiber-optic cable, you should use a fiber tester on your cable before you install it, as well as after you install it.

Time Domain Reflectometers (TDRs)

A **time domain reflectometer (TDR)** is a high-end instrument for testing the qualities of a cable. It works by issuing a signal on a cable and measuring the way the signal bounces back (or reflects) to the TDR. Connectors, crimps, bends, short circuits, cable mismatches, or other defects modify the signal's amplitude before it returns to the TDR, thus changing the way it reflects. The TDR then accepts and analyzes the return signal, and based on its condition and the amount of time the signal took to return, determines cable imperfections. In the case of a coaxial cable network, a TDR can indicate whether terminators are properly installed and functional. A TDR can also indicate the distance between nodes and segments.

As with cable testers, time domain reflectometers are also made for fiber-optic networks. Such instruments are called **optical time domain reflectometers (OTDRs)**. Rather than issuing an electrical signal, OTDRs issue a light-based signal over the fiber. Based on the type of return light signal, the OTDR can accurately measure the length of the fiber, determine the location of faulty splices, breaks, connectors, or bends, and measure attenuation over the cable.

Because some loss of a signal is expected with the addition of nodes and connectors, TDRs are a good way of taking a baseline measurement for your network cabling. A **baseline** is a record of how well the network operates under normal conditions (including its performance, collision rate, utilization rate, and so on). Baselines are used for comparison when conditions change. A TDR can provide a baseline for the characteristics and performance of a network's cable infrastructure. Then later, if you suspect cabling problems, you can use the TDR and compare your new results with your baseline measurement to ascertain whether signaling characteristics have changed.

Software Troubleshooting Tools

As noted earlier, once you have ruled out user error and physical connectivity problems (including faulty cabling) in your troubleshooting, a more in-depth analysis of the network may be necessary. Software-based tools that enable you to analyze network traffic include NOS log files, network monitors, and network analyzers. While log files can reveal what has happened on a server, network monitors and analyzers can capture and interpret data traveling across the network.

Network Monitors

A **network monitor** is usually a software-based tool that continually monitors traffic on the network from a server or workstation attached to the network. Network monitors typically can interpret up to Layer 3 of the OSI Model. They can determine the protocols passed by each packet, but can't interpret the data inside the packet. By capturing data they can provide either a snapshot of network activity at one point in time or a historical record of network activity over a period of time.

Network monitoring tools are generally less expensive than network analyzers (discussed next) and may be included in your network operating system software. In the following sections, you will learn about two tools that can be part of your network operating system: Microsoft's Network Monitor (which ships with Windows NT Server version 4.0 or Windows 2000) and Novell's LANalyzer agent (which is bundled with Novell's ManageWise software package). These packages actually blur the distinction between network monitors and network analyzers, because they provide some of the same functionality as high-end protocol analyzers. In addition, you will learn about network analyzers, such as Network Associates' Sniffer Portable software, and sniffer hardware. Once you have worked with one network monitoring or analyzing tool, you will find that other products work in much the same way. Most even use very similar graphical interfaces.

To take advantage of software-based network monitoring and analyzing tools, the network adapter installed in your machine must support promiscuous mode. In **promiscuous mode**, a device driver directs the network adapter card to pick up all frames that pass over the network—not just those destined for the node served by the card. You can determine whether your network adapter supports promiscuous mode by reading its manual or checking with the manufacturer. Some network monitoring software vendors may even suggest which network adapters to use with their software.

12

Before adopting a network monitor or analyzer, you should be familiar with some of the data errors that these tools can distinguish. The following list defines some commonly used terms for abnormal data patterns and packets, along with their characteristics:

- **Local collisions**—Collisions that occur when two or more stations are transmitting simultaneously. A small number of collisions are normal on an Ethernet network. Excessively high collision rates within the network usually result from cable or routing problems.

- **Late collisions**—Collisions that take place outside the window of time in which they would normally be detected by the network and redressed. Late collisions are usually caused by one of two problems: (1) a defective station (for example, a card or transceiver) that is transmitting without first verifying line status, or (2) failure to observe the configuration guidelines for cable length, which results in collisions being recognized too late.

- **Runts**—Packets that are smaller than the medium's minimum packet size. For instance, any Ethernet packet that is smaller than 64 bytes is considered a runt. Runts are often the result of collisions.

- **Giants**—Packets that exceed the medium's maximum packet size. For example, any Ethernet packet that is larger than 1518 bytes is considered a giant.

- **Jabber**—A device that handles electrical signals improperly, usually affecting the rest of the network. A network analyzer will detect a jabber as a device that is always retransmitting, effectively bringing the network to a halt. A jabber usually results from a bad NIC. Occasionally, it can be caused by outside electrical interference.

- **Negative frame sequence checks**—The result of the cyclic redundancy checksum (CRC) generated by the originating node not matching the checksum calculated from the data received. It usually indicates noise or transmission problems on the LAN interface or cabling. A high number of negative CRCs usually result from excessive collisions or a station transmitting bad data.

- **Ghosts**—Frames that are not actually data frames, but aberrations caused by a repeater misinterpreting stray voltage on the wire. Unlike true data frames, ghosts have no starting delimiter.

Microsoft's Network Monitor (NetMon)   Microsoft's **Network Monitor (NetMon)** is a software-based network monitoring tool that comes with Windows NT Server 4.0 and Windows 2000. It offers the following capabilities:

- Capturing network data traveling from one or many segments

- Capturing frames sent by or to a specified node

- Reproducing network conditions by transmitting a selected amount and type of data

- Detecting any other running copies of NetMon on the network (depending on the placement and configuration of routers)

- Generating statistics about network activity

Probably NetMon's most useful capability is capturing data as it travels across the network. As with hardware-based network analyzers, you can instruct NetMon to pay attention to the network for a period of time and to capture all data that travel across the particular segment. (Because NetMon takes advantage of promiscuous mode, it captures all data—not just data to or from the NetMon console.)

 If you completed the Hands-on Projects in Chapter 5, you had an opportunity to experiment with Network Monitor. See Figure 5-31 for a view of Network Monitor's interface as it captures network traffic.

How can capturing data help you solve a problem? Imagine that traffic on a segment of the network you administer suddenly grinds to a halt one morning at about 8:00. You no sooner step in the door than everyone from the help desk calls to tell you how slowly the network is running. Nothing has changed on the network since last night, when it ran normally, so you can think of no obvious reasons for problems. You suspect a faulty NIC on one workstation is using network bandwidth by continually transmitting bad packets.

At the workstation where you have previously installed NetMon, you capture all data transmissions for approximately five minutes. You can then sort out the erroneous frames in NetMon, arranging the nodes in order based on how many bad packets each has generated. If your suspicion is correct, the workstation at the top of the list will be the culprit, generating significantly more bad data transmissions than any other node.

Novell's LANalyzer   Novell provides a network monitoring tool that is similar to Microsoft's Network Monitor, called the **LANalyzer** agent. It can act as a standalone program on a Windows 9x or 2000 workstation or as part of the ManageWise suite of network management tools on a NetWare server. LANalyzer performs the following functions:

- Initially discovering all network nodes on a segment
- Continuously monitoring network traffic
- Tripping alarms when traffic conditions meet preconfigured thresholds (for example, if usage exceeds 50% of capacity)
- Capturing traffic to and from all or selected nodes

Like Network Monitor, LANalyzer enables you to capture traffic, identify data errors by node, and generate traffic statistics by segment. In addition, as part of the ManageWise suite, the LANalyzer agent can poll the network to find all nodes on a particular segment. It can use this data to build a network management system that can gather more than simple traffic information—for example, discovering how many times a user has logged on at a certain workstation or noting what kind of programs a workstation typically requests from the server.

12

LANalyzer can also provide real-time network statistics and send alert messages and/or sound alarms when network thresholds are reached. For example, to make sure that average network traffic never exceeds 50% of your network's capacity, you could configure LANalyzer to warn you when the average reaches 49%. If this warning occurs frequently on one segment of your network, you can take steps to redistribute the traffic or reinforce your network's capacity. Note that an average utilization means that LANalyzer would have to measure a 49% reading more than a single time; a single reading represents a **spike**. You can also customize the sensitivity of the triggers.

Network Analyzers

A **network analyzer** (also known as a **protocol analyzer**) is a tool that can capture traffic and analyze packets, typically all the way to Layer 7 of the OSI Model. For example, it can identify that a packet uses TCP/IP and, more specifically, that it is an ARP request from one particular workstation to a server. Analyzers can also interpret the payload portion of packets, translating from binary or hexadecimal code to human-readable form. As a result, network analyzers can capture passwords going over the network, if their transmission is not encrypted. Some network analyzer software packages can run on a standard PC, but others require PCs equipped with special network adapters and operating system software.

In addition to using the software that comes with the network operating system, you can purchase network analyzing software from vendors that specialize in products for network management. One popular example is Network Associates' **Sniffer Portable**, network analyzer software that provides data capture and analysis, node discovery, traffic trending, history, alarm tripping, and utilization prediction. Essentially, Sniffer Portable has the same features as Network Monitor and LANalyzer, plus a few extras. It can also generate traffic in an attempt to reproduce a network problem and monitor multiple network segments simultaneously. Its graphical interface makes this product very easy to use, readily revealing the traffic flow across the network. In addition, Sniffer Portable supports a multitude of protocols and network topologies.

One advantage to using a network monitor or analyzer that is not part of the network operating system relates to mobility. With Sniffer Portable software installed on your laptop, for instance, you can roam from one network segment to another, analyzing traffic without having to install multiple network monitoring consoles. Hardware-based network analyzers, such as the sniffers discussed below, also offer the advantage of mobility.

Network Associates has also led the way in developing hardware-based network analyzers, known as sniffers. **Sniffers** usually resemble regular laptops, but are equipped with a special network adapter and network analysis software. The sole job of a sniffer is to analyze network problems. Unlike laptops that have a network monitoring tool installed, sniffers typically cannot be used for other purposes, because they don't depend on a familiar desktop operating system such as Windows. They have their own, proprietary operating system (developed by Network Associates, for example). Because they do not rely on a desktop operating system such as Windows, hardware-based network analyzers have an advantage over network monitoring software. Because they do not rely on Windows device drivers (for the NIC), for example, they can capture information that the NIC would automatically discard, such as runt packets.

Sniffers offer a great deal of versatility in the type and depth of information they can reveal. The danger in using this type of tool is that it may collect more information than you or the machine can reasonably process, thus rendering your exercise futile. To avoid this problem, you should set filters on the data gathered. For example, if you suspect that a certain workstation is causing a traffic problem, you should filter the data collection to accept only packets to or from that workstation's MAC address. If you suspect that you have a gateway-related TCP/IP problem, you would set a filter to capture only TCP/IP packets and to ignore other protocols from the gateway's MAC address.

Sniffers are tailored to a particular type of network. For example, one sniffer may be able to analyze both Ethernet and Token Ring networks, but another sniffer may be necessary to analyze fiber or ATM networks. A sniffer represents a significant investment, with costs ranging from $10,000 to $30,000.

Recall from Chapter 6 that using a switch logically separates a network into several segments. If a network is fully switched (that is, if every node is connected to its own switch port), your network analyzer can capture only broadcast packets and packets destined for the node on which you're running the software, because those packets are the only ones that will travel through a switched environment. The increasing use of switches has made network monitoring more difficult, but not impossible. One solution to this problem is to reconfigure the switch to reroute the traffic so that your network analyzer can pick up all traffic. Obviously, you would want to weigh the disruptive effects of this reconfiguration against the potential benefits from being able to analyze the network traffic and solve a problem.

12

PRACTICAL TROUBLESHOOTING

You have learned about following a troubleshooting methodology and using specialized tools to diagnose network problems. You will acquire much of your troubleshooting expertise through experience. But if you don't yet have experience, you can get a head start by learning some practical tips and strategies for troubleshooting based on the experience of others. The following sections provide real-world techniques for network troubleshooting that do not neatly fit into a troubleshooting methodology.

Physical Layer Problems and Symptoms

By now you have probably realized that one symptom, such as a user not being able to log onto the network, could result from a number of possible problems. In addition to systematically following a troubleshooting methodology, you may discover a symptom's cause by identifying the OSI Model layer where it is occurring. That way, you can analyze connections, settings, or traffic within that layer and move closer to a solution. Figure 12-9 summarizes the services and devices that you have already learned about according to their OSI Model layer.

User Programs

Application layer:	Program-to-(N)OS interaction
Presentation layer:	Text formatting, encryption, code conversion
Session layer:	Establishing, maintaining, coordinating connections
Transport layer:	Flow control, sequencing, acknowledgment
Network layer:	Logical addressing, routing (routers, layer 3 switches)
Data Link layer:	Framing and physical addressing (bridges, switches)
Physical layer:	Voltage detection, signaling (NICs, hubs, repeaters, cabling)

Topology

Figure 12-9 Services and devices in the OSI Model

By some estimates, more than half of all network problems occur at the Physical layer of the OSI Model, which includes cabling, network adapters, repeaters, and hubs. The Physical layer also controls signaling and the voltage levels used in signaling. Thus, RFI and EMI noise can cause network problems at the Physical layer. Because Physical layer faults are so common (and often easily fixed), you should be thoroughly familiar with the symptoms of such problems. The following list details some common Physical layer problems and their symptoms on an Ethernet network. It also suggests troubleshooting steps that you can follow to verify whether the problem indeed exists. Finally, it provides some possible solutions to consider once you have verified the problem.

- Segment Problems

  Problem: Segment or network lengths that exceed the IEEE maximum standards (for example, an Ethernet 100BaseT segment that exceeds 100 meters)

  Symptoms: An excessive number of late collisions. Users recognize this problem as intermittent difficulty connecting to the network or exchanging data over the network.

  Troubleshooting hints: A scope limited to a geographical area or workgroup within the LAN could point to this problem. A protocol analyzer can help determine specifically which segments or nodes are experiencing late collisions. Observation (or relying on network documentation) can help determine which network lengths may exceed IEEE standard maximums.

  Solution: Reconfigure the topology of the network to avoid excessive segment or network lengths.

- Signal noise

  Problem: Noise affecting a signal (from EMI or RFI sources, improper grounding, or crosstalk)

  Symptoms: Excessive number of packet errors such as runts, giants (in the case of improper grounding), and damaged frame check sequence fields, but no evidence of excessive collisions. Users recognize this problem as intermittent difficulty connecting to the network or exchanging data over the network.

  Troubleshooting hints: The nodes or segments affected by the errors can be identified with the help of a protocol analyzer. A simple AM radio may be used to detect EMI near cables. Examine the cables' environment for noise sources. See if network problems disappear when those sources (for example, fluorescent lights or microwaves) are turned off.

  Solution: Remove sources of EMI or RFI from cabling areas, encase cables in conduit, or reroute cabling. If this is not possible, consider changing the cable type to one with better resistance to noise. Ensure proper grounding on coaxial cable networks. Reduce crosstalk on twisted-pair networks by using wires with a higher twist ratio and making sure cables are not bundled too tightly.

12

- Cable damage

  Problem: Damaged cables (for example, crimped, bent, nicked, or partially - severed)

  Symptoms: Excessive number of normal collisions or packet errors (such as giants and runts), but few late collisions. Users recognize this problem as frequent difficulty connecting to or exchanging data with the network, very poor network response time, or a complete inability to connect to the network (depending on the severity of the cable damage).

  Troubleshooting hints: The scope of this problem may be a single user (in the case of a workstation patch cable) or a whole segment or network of users. Once you have identified a suspicious cable, a cable tester or cable checker can help determine the integrity and reliability of that cable. A protocol analyzer can indicate which nodes are experiencing excessive numbers of packet errors. A network monitor can indicate where traffic bottlenecks are occurring, in the case of a severely damaged cable.

  Solution: Replace the faulty cable with a good cable.

- Connector flaws

  Problem: Improper terminations, faulty connectors, loose connectors, or poorly crimped connections

  Symptoms: Excessive number of normal collisions and packet errors (such as giants and runts), but few late collisions. Users will recognize this as frequent problems connecting to or exchanging data with the network, very poor network response time, or a complete inability to connect to the network (depending on the severity of the connector fault).

  Troubleshooting hints: As with a faulty cable, the scope of this problem may be a single user or a whole segment or network of users. A simple PING test may help determine the location of the fault. A protocol analyzer can indicate which nodes are experiencing excessive numbers of packet errors. A network monitor can indicate where traffic bottlenecks are occurring, in the case of a very loose or completely faulty connector.

  Solution: Replace the connector with a good connector, reseat the loose connector, or correct the termination error.

- Adapter flaws

  Problem: Faulty network adapter

  Symptoms: Some types of NIC faults result in an excessive number of packet errors (for example, giants, runts, or damaged frame check sequence fields), but no apparent increase in collisions; other types of NIC faults result in an excessive number of late collisions (when the NIC's carrier sense mechanism is not operating properly). Users will recognize either of these situations as intermittent problems connecting to the network or exchanging data over the network.

  Troubleshooting hints: The scope of this problem is limited to the nodes that rely on the network adapter (for example, if it is a workstation NIC, only the workstation user should notice the problem; if it is a switch NIC, all switched connections will share the problem). A protocol analyzer can indicate which nodes are experiencing excessive numbers of late collisions. A network monitor can indicate which node is issuing bad packets (and therefore, which NIC is to blame).

  Solution: Replace the faulty network adapter with a good network adapter (making sure they are identical or compatible models).

Staff Involved in Troubleshooting

Many staff members may contribute to troubleshooting a network problem. Often the division of duties is formalized, with a help desk acting as the first, single point of contact for users to call in regarding errors. A help desk is typically staffed with help desk analysts—people proficient in basic (but not usually advanced) workstation and network troubleshooting. Larger organizations may group their help desk analysts into teams based on their expertise. For example, a company that provides users with word-processing, spreadsheet, project planning, scheduling, and graphics software might assign different technical support personnel at the help desk to answer questions pertaining to each application.

The help desk analysts are often considered first-level support, because they provide the first level of troubleshooting. When a user calls with a problem, a help desk analyst typically creates a record for the incident and attempts to diagnose the problem. The help desk analyst may be able to solve a common problem over the phone within minutes by explaining something to the user. On other occasions, the problem may be rare or complex. In such cases, the first-level support analyst will refer the problem to a second-level support analyst. A second-level support analyst is someone who has specialized knowledge in one or more aspects of a network. For example, if a user complains that she can't connect to a server, and the first-level support person narrows the problem down to a failed file server, that first-level support analyst would then refer the problem to the second-level support person. Typically, first-level support analysts stay at the help desk while second-level support analysts are mobile.

12

In addition to having first- and second-level support analysts, most help desks include a help desk coordinator. The help desk coordinator ensures that analysts are divided into the correct teams, schedules shifts at the help desk, and maintains the infrastructure to enable analysts to better perform their jobs.

Most organizations also have an operations manager, who supervises the help desk coordinator. This person knows less about the day-to-day activities of the help desk, but works with the help desk coordinator to determine how to improve customer service and supply analysts with the needed infrastructure. For example, the operations manager may control the budget that provides help desk analysts with office space, call tracking software, a call distribution system, and any additional resources necessary to perform their jobs.

Examples of How to Investigate Problems

The following scenarios illustrate how to narrow down the cause of a network problem. Notice that all questions do not apply in all situations. You should use common sense to decide which questions apply to a particular situation and to interpret the answers you receive. In addition to reviewing the scenarios given here, you will have more opportunities to exercise your investigative and troubleshooting skills in the Case Projects at the end of this chapter.

Scenario 1: Unable to Access the Network

Perhaps one of the most common problems you'll address as a network troubleshooter is an inability to access the network. This problem can be caused by a variety of failures (either hardware or software) and situations (for example, user error or changes in the network infrastructure). If you receive notice of the problem from a user, rather than from your automated network monitoring system or a fellow computer professional, the initial information you receive may not be very helpful. Your conversation with the user might go something like this:

USER: I can't log onto the network.

YOU: When did the problem begin?

USER: Just this morning. I came into work and I couldn't log on. I really have to get my invoices done now, because they're due to my boss by 10:00 A.M.

YOU: As far as you know, are you the only person in your area who's having this problem?

USER: I think so.

YOU: And what kind of error message do you receive when you try to log on?

USER: It says something about the network being unavailable.

YOU: Let's check to make sure your network cable hasn't accidentally been pulled out or loosened.

USER: I checked it already, and I'm sure it's all right.

YOU: Well, humor me a little. I just want to rule out any possibility of a connection problem. Sometimes the janitors accidentally jar a connection loose when they clean the floors.

USER: OK. (Checks the connections according to your guidance.) Nope, they seem to be plugged in just fine.

YOU: All right, thanks for checking. Has anything changed on your computer in the last day? For example, did you have to add any programs, or did a PC technician work on your machine?

USER: Yeah, someone was in here last night trying to get my sound card working.

YOU: Let's take a look at the configuration for the sound card . . .

By following this set of questions, you have narrowed the scope of the problem to only one workstation, verified that the physical connections work correctly, and discovered that a configuration change on the workstation might have caused the problem. At this point, you can probably assume that whoever worked on the user's sound card created a resource conflict between the sound card and the NIC, preventing the NIC from making a connection to the network. If you feel comfortable talking the user through checking the device settings, you could proceed with that approach. If not, you could visit the workstation yourself and fix the problem.

Scenario 2: A Misbehaving Network Printer

Network printers cause as many problems as network workstations (although they are usually less critical than servers). Typically, a malfunctioning network printer affects everyone who tries to use it. Although user input may prove helpful in solving network printer problems, you will probably get more information faster by checking the printer yourself. Following are some logical steps you might take to assess a network printer problem:

1. Try to narrow the scope of the problem by determining whether everyone or only a few of those who normally use the printer are having problems printing.

2. Try to replicate the error yourself. First, try to print to the printer from your machine (which is properly connected to the network and has the printer device drivers properly installed) to discover whether the problem might derive from workstation configurations. If you receive an error, note the exact wording of the error. If you do not receive an error, the symptoms are not network-wide, and the problem may be caused by either a user error or an incorrect printer device configuration on one workstation.

3. If you cannot replicate the problem from your computer, go to the workstations that have problems and try to replicate the error from them.

12

4. If the error occurs on only one workstation, the problem may be caused by physical connectivity problems or logical connectivity problems with that workstation. Check that workstation's network cable and NIC, and then check its printer device drivers and settings. Reinstall the device drivers if necessary.

5. If the error occurs on multiple workstations, the problem probably has to do with the printer itself. Visit the printer and verify its physical and logical connectivity. Make sure that the printer is turned on. Verify that the printer is properly connected to the network. Also, verify that the printer is ready to print—that is, it is online and has no internal errors.

6. If the printer is connected and ready to print, print a test page to view the printer's configuration. From this test page, you can determine whether the printer is connecting to the correct server, is receiving protocols correctly, and has a properly setup network configuration (for example, if it's on an Ethernet network and using IPX/SPX, make sure it has the correct frame type setting).

This logical sequence of steps allows you to zero in on the possible causes of the problem. Once you have determined that multiple workstations are experiencing the problem, that the problem is repeatable, that the device drivers are installed correctly on every workstation, and that the printer is properly physically connected to the network, you can turn your attention to the printer's network configuration. By process of elimination, this configuration is probably the source of the fault.

Scenario 3: Unable to Connect to the Internet

If your organization depends on e-mail and other Internet-related services, such as Web databases or e-commerce, an inability to connect to the Internet can quickly hamper productivity and perhaps affect the organization's profitability. At the least, being disconnected from the Internet is an inconvenience. An inability to connect to the Internet, like many network problems, may be caused by errors at a number of different points in the system. In the following scenario, a large group of users is affected by an Internet-related problem. The following steps suggest a way to troubleshoot the problem:

1. A user calls and complains that he can't pick up his e-mail. At the same time, the other two network administrators in your department are fielding similar calls. When you finish your phone calls and compare notes, you realize that the users who called are all located in your company's Finance Department.

2. You call your company's help desk and tell the first-level support analysts that the Finance Department has lost Internet access. You ask the analysts to let you know whether any other departments report the same problem.

3. You attempt to reproduce the problem by trying to access the Internet from your workstation.

4. If you fail to connect to the Internet, you would use the PING utility to see whether you could contact your TCP/IP gateway.

5. In this example, let's assume that you can reach the Internet. You, therefore, know that the problem must be isolated to other areas of the company, which include the Finance Department.

6. Still at your desk, you try pinging the Finance department's default gateway address. A positive response indicates that physical connectivity to that gateway is sound. A negative response tells you that the gateway may be physically disconnected or otherwise incapacitated.

7. If you receive a positive response from the default gateway PING, your next step is to go to a Finance Department workstation and attempt to ping a host on another subnet (perhaps your own workstation, as you know that its TCP/IP resources are functional). A positive response from this test indicates that the workstation can communicate with and through the Finance Department's gateway. Thus the Finance gateway may not be incapacitated, but rather something else in the network (such as cabling from the router to the backbone) may not be working.

8. In this example, let's assume that you receive a negative response from the default gateway PING, which suggests either workstation or subnet connectivity problems from that node. Your next step is to try pinging the loopback address. A positive response to the loopback PING indicates that the workstation's TCP/IP services are installed and operating properly. Thus, you have narrowed the problem down to the subnet that includes the Finance Department.

9. A help desk analyst pages you with a message that the Accounting and Human Resources Departments are experiencing the same problems. You know that these departments are on the same subnet as Finance.

With the information you have gathered, you can conclude that the TCP/IP connectivity fault lies somewhere on the subnet that serves those three departments. You leave the Finance department and begin analyzing the network to find out whether the problem lies in the subnet's router or cabling.

Swapping Equipment

If you suspect a problem lies with a network component, one of the easiest ways to test your theory is to exchange that component for a functional one. In many cases, such a swap will resolve the problem very quickly, so you should consider trying this tactic early in your troubleshooting process. It won't always work, of course, but with experience you will learn what types of problems are most likely due to component failure.

For example, if a user cannot connect to the network, as in Scenario 1 in the "Examples of How to Investigate Problems" section, and even after entering the correct user ID and password still can't log on, you might consider swapping the user's network cable with a functional one. As you learned in Chapter 4, network cables must meet specific standards to operate properly. If one becomes damaged (for example, by a chair repeatedly rolling over it), it will prevent a user from connecting to the network. Swapping an old network cable with a new one is a quick test that may save you further troubleshooting.

In addition to swapping network cables, you might need to change a patch cable from one port in a hub or switch to another, or from one data jack to another. Ports and data jacks can be operational one day and faulty the next. You might also swap a network adapter from one machine to another or try installing a new network adapter, making sure it's precisely the same make and model as the original. It's more difficult to swap a switch or router because of the number of nodes serviced by these components and the potentially significant configuration they require; if network connectivity has failed, however, this approach may provide a quicker answer than attempting to troubleshoot the faulty device.

A better alternative to swapping parts is to have redundancy built into your network. For example, you might have a server that contains two network adapters, allowing one network adapter to take over for the other if one adapter should fail. If properly installed and configured, this arrangement results in no downtime; in contrast, swapping parts requires at least a few minutes of service disruption. In the case of swapping a router, the downtime might last for several hours.

Before swapping any network component, make sure that the replacement has exactly the same specifications as the original part. By installing a component that doesn't match the original device, you risk thwarting your troubleshooting efforts, because the new component might not work in the environment. In the worst case, you may damage existing equipment by installing a component that isn't rated for it.

Using Vendor Information

Some networking professionals pride themselves in being able to install, configure, and troubleshoot devices without reading the instructions—or at least exhausting all possibilities before they submit to reading a manual. Although some manufacturers clearly write better documentation than others, you have nothing to lose by referring to the manual, except a little time. Chances are you will find exactly what you need—jumper settings for a NIC, configuration commands and their arguments for a router, and troubleshooting tips for a network operating system function.

In addition to the booklets that ship with the networking component (which are often lost in a network manager's pile of documentation and miscellaneous equipment), most network software and hardware vendors provide free online troubleshooting information. For example, both Microsoft and Novell offer searchable databases in which you can type your error message or a description of your problem and receive lists of possible solutions. Reputable equipment manufacturers, such as 3Com, Cisco, IBM, Intel, and Hewlett-Packard also offer sophisticated Web interfaces for troubleshooting their equipment. If you cannot find the documentation for a networking component, you should try looking for information on the Web.

Bear in mind that some vendors require you to register for online support, and occasionally you may have to pay for this service. Nevertheless, most vendors provide a significant amount of information (including entire manuals) free of charge from their Web sites. Table 12-1 lists links to technical support Web sites for popular networking vendors. (Note that these URLs were verified at the time of this writing, but may change without notice.)

Table 12-1   Links for troubleshooting resources on the Web

Vendor	Technical Support Web Site Address
3Com	www.3com.com/support/en_US/index3.html
Cisco	www.cisco.com/univercd/home/home.htm
Compaq	www.compaq.com/support/
Dell	www.dell.com/support/index.htm
Hewlett Packard	welcome.hp.com/country/us/eng/support.htm
IBM	www-1.ibm.com/support/
Intel	www-cs.intel.com/
Lucent	www.lucent.com/support/
Microsoft	support.microsoft.com/
Nortel/Bay	www12.nortelnetworks.com/cgi-bin/cnss/cs/main.jsp
Novell	support.novell.com/
Oracle	www.oracle.com/support/
SMC	www.smc.com/smc/pages_html/support.html
Sun	www.sun.com/service/online/

12

Call the vendor's technical support phone number only after you have read the manual and searched the vendor's Web page. In some cases, you may wait a long time before getting an answer when you call. With some manufacturers, you can talk to a technical support agent only if you have established and paid for a support agreement. With others, you must pay per phone call. Each vendor has a different pricing structure for technical support, so before you agree to pay for technical support, you should find out whether the vendor charges on a per hour or per problem basis.

Keep a list handy (preferably online, either on a Web page or in a shared file on the network) of the hardware and software vendors for your networking equipment; the list should include not only the company's name, but also its technical support phone number, a contact name (if available), its technical support Web site address, policies for technical support, and the type of agreement you currently have with the vendor. You can find an example of such a form in Appendix D, "Examples of Standard Networking Forms." Make sure the list is updated regularly and available to all Information Services personnel who might need it.

Notify Others of Changes

After solving a particularly thorny network problem, you should not only record its resolution in your call tracking system, but also notify others of your solution and what, if anything, you needed to change to fix the problem. This communication serves two purposes: (1) it alerts others about the problem and its solution, and (2) it notifies others of network changes you made, in case they affect other services.

The importance of recording changes cannot be overemphasized. Imagine that you are the network manager for a group of five network technicians who support a WAN consisting of three different offices and 150 users. One day the company's CEO travels from headquarters to a branch office for a meeting with an important client. At the branch office, she needs to print out a financial statement, but encounters a printing problem. Your network technician discovers that her login ID does not have rights to that office's printer, because users on your WAN do not have rights to printers outside the office to which they belong. The network technician quickly takes care of the problem by granting all users rights to all printers across the WAN. What are the implications of this change? If your technician tells no one about this change, at best users may incorrectly print to a printer in Duluth from the St. Paul office. In a worst-case scenario, a "guest" user account may gain rights to a networked printer, potentially creating a security hole in your network.

Large organizations often implement change management systems to methodically track changes on the network. A **change management system** is a process or program that provides support personnel with a centralized means of documenting changes to the network. In smaller organizations, a change management system may be as simple as one document on the network to which networking personnel continually add entries to mark their changes. In larger organizations, it may consist of a database package complete with graphical interfaces and customizable fields tailored to the computing environment. Whatever form your change management system takes, the most important element is participation. If networking personnel do not record their changes, even the most sophisticated software is useless.

The types of changes that network personnel should record in a change management system include the following:

- Adding or upgrading software on network servers or other devices

- Adding or upgrading hardware components on network servers or other devices

- Adding new hardware on the network (for example, a new server)

- Changing the network properties of a network device (for example, changing the IP address or NetBIOS name of a server)

- Increasing or decreasing rights for a group of users

- Physically moving networked devices

- Moving user IDs and their files/directories from one server to another

- Making changes in processes (for example, a new backup schedule or a new contact for DNS support)

- Making changes in vendor policies or relationships (for example, a new hard disk supplier)

It is not necessary to record minor modifications, such as changing a user's password, creating a new group for users, creating new directories, or changing a network drive mapping for a user. Each organization will have unique requirements for its change management system, and analysts who record change information should clearly understand these requirements.

Preventing Future Problems

If you review the list of questions and the troubleshooting scenarios given at the beginning of this chapter, you can predict how some network problems can be averted by network maintenance, documentation, security, or upgrades. Although not all network problems are preventable, many can be avoided. Just as with your body's health, the best prescription for network health is prevention.

For example, to avoid problems with users' access levels for network resources, you can comprehensively assess users' needs, set policies for groups, use a variety of groups, and communicate to others who support the network why those groups exist. To prevent overusing network segments, you should perform regular network health checks—perhaps even continual network monitoring—and ensure that you have the means to either redesign the network to distribute traffic or purchase additional bandwidth well before utilization reaches critical levels. With experience, you will be able to add more suggestions for network problem prevention. When planning or upgrading a network, you should consciously think about how good network designs and policies can prevent later problems—not to mention, make your job easier and more fun.

CHAPTER SUMMARY

❒ Before you can resolve a network problem, you need to determine its cause. The key to solving network problems is to approach them methodically and logically, using your experience to inform your decisions, and knowing when to ask for someone else's help.

❒ When assessing a network problem, act like a doctor diagnosing a patient. First, ask the user a series of standard questions in a logical order to learn about the problem's symptoms. Never ignore the obvious! Although some questions may sound too simple to bother asking, don't discount them.

❒ Next identify the scope of the problem. In general, a network problem may be limited by the number of users, departments, or areas it affects or by what times of day or week it occurs.

❒ At each point in the troubleshooting process, stop to consider what kind of changes have occurred on the network that might have created a problem. Changes pertaining to hardware may include the addition of a new device, the removal of an old device, a component upgrade, a cabling upgrade, or an equipment move. Changes pertaining to software may include an operating system upgrade, device driver upgrade, a new application, or a changed configuration.

❒ Early in the troubleshooting process, you should ensure that the user is performing all functions correctly. It's easy for a user to make mistakes and assume that something is wrong with the network.

❒ Attempt to reproduce the problem's symptoms. If possible, go to the location where the problem is occurring and try to repeat the steps precisely. Note also whether a problem is repeatable only under specific circumstances.

❒ Check whether the affected device (or devices) have sound connections to the network, from workstation to backbone. Physical connectivity may be impaired by poorly or incorrectly installed cabling, NICs, or connectivity devices; flawed or damaged components; or excessive segment length.

❒ If you find no physical connectivity problems, determine whether the affected device(s) have properly configured software, including applications, hardware configurations, operating system software, and client software.

❒ After implementing your solution, you must test it to ensure that it works correctly. The type of testing you perform will depend on your solution. Enlist the help of users to test the solution. If the solution required significant network changes, revisit the solution a day or two after you implement it to verify that it has truly worked and not caused additional problems.

❏ A tone generator and tone locator are used to identify the terminating location of a wire pair. Telephone technicians use these tools more often than network technicians, and this combination of devices may also be known as a fox and hound.

❏ A multimeter is a simple device that can measure the voltage, resistance, and other characteristics of an electrical circuit.

❏ Basic cable checkers determine whether your cabling can provide connectivity. To accomplish this task, they apply a small voltage to each conductor at one end of the cable, and then check whether that voltage is detectable at the other end. They may also verify that voltage cannot be detected on other conductors in the cable. A good cable checker will also verify that the wires are paired correctly and that they are not shorted, exposed, or crossed.

❏ A cable tester performs the same continuity and fault tests as a cable checker, but also ensures that the cable length is not too long, measures the distance to a cable fault, measures attenuation along a cable, measures near-end crosstalk between wires, measures termination resistance and impedance for Thinnet cabling, issues pass/fail ratings for CAT3, CAT5, CAT6, or even CAT7 standards, and stores and prints cable testing results.

❏ Because of their sophistication, cable testers cost significantly more than cable checkers.

❏ A network monitor is usually a software-based tool that continually monitors traffic on the network from a server or workstation attached to the network. Network monitors typically can interpret up to Layer 3 of the OSI Model. They can determine the protocols passed by each packet, but can't interpret the data inside the packet.

❏ Network analyzers can typically interpret data up to Layer 7 of the OSI Model. They can also interpret the payload portion of packets, translating from binary or hexadecimal code to human-readable form.

❏ Before adopting a network monitor or analyzer, you should be familiar with some of the data errors that these tools can distinguish, such as runts, late collisions, jabber, and negative frame sequence checks.

❏ To take advantage of software-based network monitoring and analyzing tools, the network adapter installed in your machine must support promiscuous mode. Promiscuous mode means that a device driver directs the network adapter card to pick up all frames that pass over the network—not just those destined for the node served by the card.

❏ Microsoft's Network Monitor (NetMon) is a software-based network monitoring tool that comes with Windows NT Server 4.0 and Windows 2000.

12

❒ Novell provides a network monitoring tool called the LANalyzer agent. It can act as a standalone program on a Windows 9x or 2000 workstation or as part of the ManageWise suite of network management tools on a NetWare server. Like Network Monitor, LANalyzer can capture traffic, identify data errors by node, and generate traffic statistics by segment.

❒ You may choose to purchase network analyzing software from vendors that specialize in products for network management. One popular example is Network Associates' Sniffer Portable, network analyzer software that provides data capture and analysis, node discovery, traffic trending, history, alarm tripping, and utilization prediction.

❒ Network Associates has also led the way in hardware-based network analyzers, known as sniffers. Sniffers are usually regular laptops equipped with a special network adapter and software dedicated to network analysis.

❒ Sniffers are tailored to a particular type of network. For example, one sniffer may be able to analyze both Ethernet and Token Ring networks, but another sniffer may be necessary to analyze fiber or ATM networks. The cost of sniffers can range from $10,000 to $30,000.

❒ Most organizations operate a help desk staffed with first-level support personnel who field user questions, perform initial problem diagnosis, and record problems in a call tracking database. Help desks also use second-level support personnel, who are experts in some aspect in a specific area of computing. In addition, help desk coordinators maintain help desk schedules and ensure that help desk staff members have the resources necessary to perform their jobs. An operations manager typically supervises the help desk coordinator and approves the help desk's budget.

❒ If you suspect that a problem lies with a network component, one of the easiest ways to test your theory is to exchange that component for a functional one. In many cases, this tactic will resolve the problem very quickly, so you should consider trying it early in your troubleshooting process.

❒ Although some manufacturers clearly write better documentation than others, you have nothing to lose by referring to a product's manual. Most network software and hardware vendors also provide free online troubleshooting information.

❒ Keep a list of the hardware and software vendors for your networking equipment. This list should include not only the company's name, but also its technical support phone number, a contact name, technical support Web site address, policies for technical support, and the type of agreement that you currently have with the vendor.

❒ Some organizations use a software program for documenting problems, known as a call tracking system (or help desk software). These programs provide a user-friendly graphical interface that prompts the user for every piece of information associated with the problem.

❏ Whether you use a formal call tracking system or a simple form, you should record the following details about a problem: the originator's name, department, and phone number; whether the problem is software- or hardware-related; if the problem is software-related, the package to which it pertains; if the problem is hardware-related, the device or component to which it pertains; the symptoms of the problem, including when it was first noticed; the name and telephone number of the network support contact; the amount of time spent troubleshooting the problem; and the resolution of the problem.

❏ In addition to communicating problems and solutions to your peers whenever you work on a network problem, you should follow up with the person who reported the problem. Make sure that the client understands how or why the problem occurred, what you did to resolve the problem, and who to contact should it recur.

❏ Organizations often implement change management systems to methodically track changes on the network. A change management system is a process or program that provides support personnel with a centralized means of documenting changes to the network.

❏ Network personnel should record the following types of changes in a change management system: adding or upgrading software, adding or upgrading hardware, changing the network properties of a network device, increasing or decreasing rights for a group of users, physically moving networked devices, moving user IDs and their files/directories from one server to another, making changes in processes, and making changes in vendor policies or relationships.

12

KEY TERMS

baseline — A record of how well the network operates under normal conditions (including its performance, collision rate, utilization rate, and so on). Baselines are used for comparison when conditions change.

cable checker — A simple handheld device that determines whether cabling can provide connectivity. To accomplish this task, a cable checker applies a small voltage to each conductor at one end of the cable, then checks whether that voltage is detectable at the other end. It may also verify that voltage cannot be detected on other conductors in the cable.

cable tester — A handheld device that not only checks for cable continuity, but also ensures that the cable length is not excessive, measures the distance to a cable fault, measures attenuation along a cable, measures near-end crosstalk between wires, measures termination resistance and impedance for Thinnet cabling, issues pass/fail ratings for wiring standards, and stores and prints cable testing results.

call tracking system — A software program used to document problems (also known as help desk software). Examples of popular call tracking systems include Clientele, Expert Advisor, Professional Help Desk, Remedy, and Vantive.

change management system — A process or program that provides support personnel with a centralized means of documenting changes made to the network. In smaller organizations, a change management system may be as simple as one document on the network to which networking personnel continually add entries to mark their changes. In larger organizations, it may consist of a database package complete with graphical interfaces and customizable fields tailored to the particular computing environment.

fox and hound — Another term for the combination of devices known as a tone generator and a tone locator. The tone locator is considered the hound because it follows the tone generator (the fox).

ghosts — Frames that are not actually data frames, but rather aberrations caused by a repeater misinterpreting stray voltage on the wire. Unlike true data frames, ghosts have no starting delimiter.

giants — Packets that exceed the medium's maximum packet size. For example, any Ethernet packet that is larger than 1518 bytes is considered a giant.

jabber — A device that handles electrical signals improperly, usually affecting the rest of the network. A network analyzer will detect a jabber as a device that is always retransmitting, effectively bringing the network to a halt. A jabber usually results from a bad NIC. Occasionally, it can be caused by outside electrical interference.

LANalyzer — Novell's network monitoring software package. LANalyzer can act as a standalone program on a Windows 9x or 2000 workstation or as part of the ManageWise suite of network management tools on a NetWare server. LANalyzer offers the following capabilities: discovery of all network nodes on a segment, continuous monitoring of network traffic, alarms that are tripped when traffic conditions meet preconfigured thresholds (for example, if usage exceeds 70%), and the capturing of traffic to and from all or selected nodes.

late collisions — Collisions that take place outside the normal window in which collisions are detected and redressed. Late collisions are usually caused by a defective station (such as a card, or transceiver) that is transmitting without first verifying line status or by failure to observe the configuration guidelines for cable length, which results in collisions being recognized too late.

local collisions — Collisions that occur when two or more stations are transmitting simultaneously. Excessively high collision rates within the network can usually be traced to cable or routing problems.

multimeter — A simple instrument that can measure multiple characteristics of an electric circuit, including its resistance and voltage.

negative frame sequence checks — The result of the cyclic redundancy checksum (CRC) generated by the originating node not matching the checksum calculated from the data received. It usually indicates noise or transmission problems on the LAN interface or cabling. A high number of (nonmatching) CRCs usually results from excessive collisions or a station transmitting bad data.

network analyzer — A portable, hardware-based tool that a network manager connects to the network expressly to determine the nature of network problems. Network analyzers can typically interpret data up to Layer 7 of the OSI Model.

network monitor — A software-based tool that continually monitors traffic on the network from a server or workstation attached to the network. Network monitors typically can interpret up to Layer 3 of the OSI Model.

Network Monitor (NetMon) — A software-based network monitoring tool that comes with Windows NT Server 4.0 or Windows 2000. Its capabilities include capturing network data traveling from one or many segments, capturing frames sent by or to a specified node, reproducing network conditions by transmitting a selected amount and type of data, detecting any other running copies of NetMon, and generating statistics about network activity.

ohmmeter — A device used to measure resistance in an electrical circuit.

optical time domain reflectometer (OTDR) — A time domain reflector specifically made for use with fiber-optic networks. It works by issuing a light-based signal on a fiber-optic cable and measuring the way in which the signal bounces back (or reflects) to the OTDR.

promiscuous mode — The feature of a network adapter card that allows a device driver to direct it to pick up all frames that pass over the network — not just those destined for the node served by the card.

protocol analyzer — See *network analyzer.*

resistance — The opposition to an electric current. Resistance of a wire is a factor of its size and molecular structure.

runts — Packets that are smaller than the medium's minimum packet size. For instance, any Ethernet packet that is smaller than 64 bytes is considered a runt.

sniffer — A laptop equipped with a special network adapter and software that performs network analysis. Unlike laptops that may have a network monitoring tool installed, sniffers typically cannot be used for other purposes, because they don't depend on a desktop operating system such as Windows.

Sniffer Portable — Network analyzer software from Network Associates that provides data capture and analysis, node discovery, traffic trending, history, alarm tripping, and utilization prediction.

spike — A single (or short-lived) jump in a measure of network performance, such as utilization.

supported services list — A document (preferably online) that lists every service and software package supported within an organization, plus the names of first- and second-level support contacts for those services or software packages.

time domain reflector (TDR) — A high-end instrument for testing the qualities of a cable. It works by issuing a signal on a cable and measuring the way in which the signal bounces back (or reflects) to the TDR.

tone generator — A small electronic device that issues a signal on a wire pair. When used in conjunction with a tone locator, it can help locate the termination of a wire pair.

12

tone locator — A small electronic device that emits a tone when it detects electrical activity on a wire pair. When used in conjunction with a tone generator, it can help locate the termination of a wire pair.

voltmeter — A device used to measure voltage (or electrical pressure) on an electri-cal circuit.

REVIEW QUESTIONS

1. If, after several tries, you cannot reproduce symptoms of a problem, what might you suspect as the cause of the problem?

   a. user error

   b. faulty cabling

   c. incorrect software configuration

   d. incompatible protocols

   e. an improperly installed NIC

2. Which of the following symptoms probably points to a physical connectivity problem?

   a. a group of users consistently experiences delays on the network

   b. a user always loses his drive mappings to file server directories

   c. a group of users complain that they cannot log onto the network

   d. a user can send e-mail but can't pick it up

   e. a user is receiving instant network messages intended for someone else

3. Which part of the network should you examine if a network problem affects a single workstation?

   a. the segment's router interface

   b. the cabling between the switch and the backbone

   c. the workgroup's hub

   d. the entrance facility connections

   e. the workstation's NIC and cabling

4. You are troubleshooting a problem in which a dial-in remote user claims he cannot make a connection to your organization's access server. Of the following steps, which should you take first and second as you diagnose this problem?

   a. Ask the user his password so you can replicate the problem from a workstation at your desk.

   b. Ask the user how long the problem has been occurring.

   c. Ask the user to try pinging the organization's Web server and read the results to you.

   d. Ask the user what type of error message he sees when he tries to connect.

   e. Ask the user whether he has changed any of his software configurations lately.

5. You have recently resolved a problem in which a user could not print to a particular shared printer, by upgrading her workstation's client software. Which of the following might be an unintended consequence of your solution?

   a. The user is no longer able to use her e-mail application from her hard disk.

   b. The user complains that her login screen looks different.

   c. The shared printer no longer allows users to print double-sided documents.

   d. The shared printer no longer responds to form feed commands from the print server.

   e. The workgroup to which the user belongs cannot see the printer on the network.

6. Answering which two of the following questions may help you identify the demographic scope of a problem?

   a. When did the problem first occur?

   b. How frequently does the problem occur?

   c. How many users have similar symptoms?

   d. Do the symptoms appear on all workstations in one department?

   e. Are the cables properly inserted into the hub, wall jack, and device NIC?

7. Which of the following is a characteristic symptom of a gateway failure?

   a. All workstations on a segment are unable to perform networked functions at all times.

   b. All workstations on a segment are intermittently prevented from connecting to the network.

   c. All workstations on a segment lose their IP addresses.

   d. Only one workstation is unable to log onto the network.

   e. Some workstations on a segment cannot run the same application from the server.

8. Under what circumstances should you try swapping equipment?

9. You have just discovered that your backup device is not properly writing files to your backup media. Which of the following would be the *last* two steps you take in troubleshooting this problem?

   a. Determine when the last good backup was made.

   b. Document your solution and share your notes with colleagues.

   c. Call the backup software vendor's technical support line.

   d. Check the backup software log for errors.

   e. Upgrade the backup software according to the vendor's recommendation.

12

10. Which of the following is an example of a network change that could cause a group of workstations to lose connectivity to one local file server?

    a. The server is renamed.

    b. The dedicated line to the Internet fails.

    c. One of the server's two NICs fails.

    d. The server's backup device fails.

    e. The server's external storage device fails.

11. Which of the following tools could you use to determine whether a user's workstation is transmitting packets in the proper Ethernet frame type for your network?

    a. multimeter

    b. cable checker

    c. time domain reflectometer

    d. cable tester

    e. network analyzer

12. Which of the following symptoms would definitely be present if your Ethernet network length exceeds the maximum specified by IEEE standards?

    a. excessive normal collisions

    b. excessive late collisions

    c. giants

    d. ghosts

    e. crosstalk

13. Which member of the IT department staff is usually the first to receive notice of a network problem?

    a. help desk analyst

    b. IT director

    c. network administrator

    d. help desk supervisor

    e. chief information officer

14. If you don't have the manual for your 3Com NIC, how can you find out whether it supports promiscuous mode?

    a. Read its label.

    b. Look up the information on 3Com's Web site.

    c. Attach it to a network protocol analyzer.

    d. Attempt to flood it with traffic and gauge its response.

    e. Read the manual of another type of 3Com NIC.

15. What kind of tool would you use to verify that your new cable meets CAT5 standards?

    a. cable tester

    b. cable checker

    c. cable monitor

    d. tone generator and tone locator

    e. multimeter

16. Which TCP/IP command can you use to find out whether a workstation's TCP/IP stack is operating properly?

    a. netstat

    b. nbtstat

    c. ftp

    d. ping

    e. nslookup

17. Where is crosstalk most likely to occur?

18. Which two of the following tools can help you determine whether your Thinnet connection has the proper amount of impedance at each end?

    a. protocol analyzer

    b. cable tester

    c. cable gauge

    d. time domain reflectometer

    e. multimeter

19. Which of the following frequently results in negative frame sequence checks?

    a. improper flow control

    b. excessive nodes on a segment

    c. excessive segment length

    d. incorrect protocol configuration

    e. noise

20. Which of the following frequently causes a jabber?

    a. near-end crosstalk

    b. faulty cabling

    c. faulty NIC

    d. excessive segment length

    e. noise

12

21. With what operating system does NetMon work?

    a. UNIX

    b. NetWare

    c. Linux

    d. Windows 98

    e. Windows 2000

22. The LANalyzer agent can help you determine when network traffic exceeds 50%. True or False?

23. If you wanted to determine the average daily traffic on your network's backbone, what type of tool would you use?

    a. network analyzer

    b. cable tester

    c. time domain reflectometer

    d. network monitor

    e. multimeter

24. Name two advantages of using a sniffer over using NetMon or LANalyzer.

25. Which two of the following functions can both network monitors and network analyzers perform?

    a. capture and analyze data traveling from one node to another

    b. identify a faulty cable

    c. provide trend information on data traffic from a switch port

    d. capture and interpret unencrypted passwords on the network

    e. discover nodes on the network

26. How do switches affect network analyzers?

    a. They prevent network analyzers from working.

    b. They limit the amount of the traffic that a network analyzer can capture.

    c. They cause interference that can skew the data captured by a network analyzer.

    d. They generate excessive numbers of bad packets, thereby flooding the network analyzer with data.

    e. They initiate frequent broadcasts that require filtering before an analyzer can capture useful data.

27. You can typically use the same sniffer for your Token Ring and ATM networks. True or False?

28. You have just purchased a new network adapter to replace the faulty network adapter in your file server. The adapter is so new that your Windows 2000 Server software does not provide a device driver for it. As you install the network adapter, where should you obtain the device driver from?

    a. the Windows 2000 Server technical support Web site

    b. the network adapter manufacturer's Web site

    c. the floppy disk that came with the network adapter

    d. a server directory containing device drivers for other network adapters used on your network

    e. a client on the network that uses the same network adapter

29. You work in a small office with only six employees and a small, peer-to-peer network that uses a single hub to connect all the workstations. One day you glance at the hub and notice that one of the port's LEDs has gone from blinking green to blinking amber. What can you conclude about the workstation connected to that port?

    a. It has been shut down.

    b. Its NIC has a problem.

    c. Its NIC has switched speeds from 10 Mbps to 100 Mbps.

    d. Its file-sharing capability has been turned off.

    e. Its TCP/IP settings have been changed to use DHCP rather than static addressing.

30. Which of the following is a network change that does not need to be recorded in the change management system?

    a. adding a new disk drive to a server

    b. moving a hub from one closet to another

    c. replacing the NIC in a router

    d. changing a user's password

    e. upgrading the network operating system

HANDS-ON PROJECTS

Until you use a network troubleshooting tool, such as Network Monitor, it's difficult to understand how these programs work. The following Hands-on Projects offer you a chance to try out cable testers and network monitors. In a real networking environment, you will probably use a number of different tools, depending on your network environment. They are similar enough, however, so that if you master one you can easily master another.

For the following exercises, you will need the cable you created during the Hands-on Projects in Chapter 4, a cable tester (such as the Fluke DSP-4000 CableAnalyzer), a penknife (or scissors), and a Windows 2000 server with several clients connected to it.

Project 12-1

In this project, you will find out how a cable tester detects and reports a damaged cable.

1. In the Hands-on Projects in Chapter 4, you created a CAT5 cable with two RJ-45 connectors. Retrieve that cable (or make a new one), and use the cable tester to find out whether it meets CAT5 standards.

2. If your cable does not meet CAT5 standards, cut off both connectors and recrimp it according to the standard. Test it again.

3. If your cable does meet CAT5 standards, use a penknife to slice about one-fourth of the way through the cable, making sure to pass the housing and at least nick one of the twisted pairs.

4. Try testing the cable again with your cable tester. What kind of message (or messages) do you receive?

Project 12-2

In this exercise, you will use Network Monitor from a Windows 2000 server to capture data on the network.

1. With at least five clients connected to your Windows 2000 server, open Network Monitor as follows: Click **Start**, point to **Programs**, point to **Administrative Tools**, and then click **Network Monitor**.

2. Maximize one or both Network Monitor screens, if necessary.

3. Click **Capture** on the menu bar, and then click **Start**. Network Monitor begins capturing frames.

4. Go to (or have one of your classmates go to) one of the clients connected to the Windows 2000 server and start an application from the server. Exit to a DOS prompt, and then ping the server's IP address. Have someone log onto the server from a different client on the network.

5. After you have generated a few minutes of network traffic, click **Capture** on the menu bar, and then click **Stop**.

6. To view more detail on the captured data, click **Capture** on the menu bar, and then click **Display Captured Data**. Close the Capture Summary after viewing it.

7. Use the scroll bars on each pane within the Microsoft Network Monitor window to view the captured data, including network utilization, statistics, and address information.

8. In the bottom window, click a network address to view its data frames in more detail. What kind of protocols do the frames use? If the network is based on Ethernet, what version are you using? What is your server's MAC address?

9. Find the frames that pertain to the logon process mentioned in Step 4. Can you read the person's password in ASCII form?

10. Close the Network Monitor program without saving the data you have captured.

Project 12-3

In this project, you will use the troubleshooting methodology discussed in this chapter to solve a network problem of your own creation. (If you are in a classroom setting and can work in pairs, it may be more fun to have a partner create a connectivity problem with your workstation, and then troubleshoot the problem.) For this exercise, you will use one of the clients from Hands-on Project 12-2, in addition to the Windows 2000 server.

1. Turn off your workstation and remove the cover, as you learned to do when installing network adapters in Chapter 6.

2. Find the network adapter and loosen it from its slot until approximately half of the pins are above the slot connector. (Depending on how far you remove the NIC, you may experience different types of symptoms.)

3. Close your workstation's cover and turn on the workstation, making sure that the network cable is properly connected to the network adapter and data jack.

4. Follow the steps in the troubleshooting methodology described at the beginning of this chapter, answering all questions under each step. Keep your answers on a separate sheet of paper.

5. Once you have followed the troubleshooting steps, summarize how the problem manifested itself. At Step 3 of the troubleshooting process, to how many different types of problems could your symptoms have applied? How many at Step 5?

6. Resolve the problem.

7. After you have resolved the problem, create a method for testing the problem to verify that your solution worked. Did it work? How can you be sure?

12

Project 12-4

In this project you will have the opportunity to act as if you are either experiencing a network problem or troubleshooting a network problem.

1. First, pair up with another student.

2. Designate one person in your pair as the user and the other person as the troubleshooter.

3. The user should pick one of the network problems listed below and take a few moments to consider the likely symptoms of those problems. The user should also anticipate which questions the troubleshooter will ask and prepare answers to those questions (which the user will deliver acting as if he or she does not know the cause of the problem). The user should not reveal which problem that has been selected to the troubleshooter.

   ❏ Interference from nearby machinery is influencing a group of users' workstations.

   ❏ A mouse has chewed through the cable that connects a print server to the network backbone.

❑ A network manager has used your workstation to log on as administrator and left the client software configured with his settings.

❑ The infrared port on your laptop is covered with grime and preventing the laptop's wireless network adapter from working.

❑ The RJ-45 connector for your workgroup's hub has been knocked out of its switch port.

❑ The same address assigned to an organization's Web server has been assigned to your workstation.

❑ You have inadvertently uninstalled the client software for your workstation.

❑ The carrier that supplies your organization's Internet connection has suffered a construction accident that severed its fiber-optic cables.

❑ A technician mistakenly replaced your workstation's patch cable with a crossover cable.

❑ You are typing in the wrong logon password.

❑ On a network you use IPX/SPX for local file and print services, but TCP/IP for Internet connectivity, and you have inadvertently deleted your DNS settings from the TCP/IP configuration.

❑ A smoldering fire has broken out in the plenum above the server room where the network's backbone cables lie.

❑ Someone has replaced your CAT5 connection between the patch panel and the hub with a CAT3 cable.

❑ You are new to the organization, and your workstation has been added to the end of a 100BaseTX segment whose length is 180 meters.

4. While the user is thinking about how to characterize the problem, the troubleshooter should write down four questions he or she will ask sometime early in their conversation.

5. Next, the user should initiate the conversation with a vague complaint that pertains to the problem. The troubleshooter should ask as many of his or her four questions as are applicable and write down the answers. If the troubleshooter can guess which problem the user has, that's great. If not, he or she should write down four more questions that will lead to the answer.

6. Now that the troubleshooter knows which problem was selected, the user and the troubleshooter should discuss a possible solution and agree on the best course of action.

7. After user and troubleshooter have determined a good solution, reverse roles and begin the project again at Step 3.

CASE PROJECTS

1. You are a network support technician for a college with 4,000 users scattered over five locations. A group of users from the downtown location has called your help desk, complaining that they cannot send or receive messages from the Internet, although they can receive messages on the college's internal GroupWise system. List the steps you will take to troubleshoot this problem and describe why each step is necessary.

2. While you're downtown fixing the first problem, a fellow network technician asks you to look at the library's server. She informs you that it's "flaky." Sometimes it doesn't allow users to log on; other times, it works perfectly. Sometimes it responds so slowly to requests for programs or files that users think it's frozen, but after several minutes it does finally respond. How would you troubleshoot this problem in the most efficient manner? Explain why you chose the steps you propose and how each might save you time.

3. You're in high demand because the word has gotten around the college that you can fix problems quickly. A small satellite campus requests that you visit it and examine a group of workstations in a computer lab that often—but not always—has problems connecting to a server. Your contact is a new instructor who teaches Interior Design in the lab. The workstations worked perfectly until the beginning of the semester, and no hardware or software changes have been made to the machines. Explain how you would troubleshoot this problem and why you chose the steps you propose.

4. Suggest ways that the problems in Case Projects 12-1, 12-2, and 12-3 might have been prevented.

5. Your friend Joseph, who works as a network technician for a global long-distance firm with 300 networked locations along the Eastern seaboard, calls you for help. Usually, five other technicians are on duty to help him handle technical problems. Today, two of his co-workers are out sick, one is away on jury duty, and another has not shown up for work yet. That leaves Joseph and one other technician to solve all of the problems that have occurred on this particular morning, including the following:

   ❐ A WAN link is down between the Washington and New York locations, causing traffic to be rerouted from Washington to Boston, then to New York. As a result, customers are complaining about slow performance.

   ❐ The Albany, New York, location's network appears to have suffered a catastrophic failure. This failure has caused outages for thousands of customers in the upstate New York region.

   ❐ Three executive users at Joseph's corporate headquarters in Baltimore cannot pick up their e-mail, and they are calling every five minutes to ask when the problem will be fixed.

12

❐ A networked printer that provides services to the Accounting group at the Baltimore headquarters is not accepting any print jobs. The users have asked Joseph to troubleshoot the printer. They need to send invoices out to customers by noon.

❐ Half of the workstations in the Advertising Department seem to be infected with a virus, and Joseph is worried that these users will copy the virus to the network, thus risking widespread data damage.

❐ Joseph asks for advice about the order in which he and his other colleague should address the problems (or which ones to address simultaneously). What do you tell him, and why would you place them in that order?

6. Joseph is very grateful for your assistance and calls you at the end of the day to tell you how things turned out. One problem was particularly difficult to diagnose, because he didn't get all of the details until well into the troubleshooting process. As it turned out, the three executives—Sal, Martha, and Gabe—who couldn't pick up their e-mail messages were all sitting in a conference room with another two executives, Barb and Darrel. Barb and Darrel are vice presidents in the Operations group and had scheduled the meeting in a conference room down the hall from their offices. Sal, Martha, and Gabe, on the other hand, are vice presidents of Marketing, Engineering, and Research. They had to travel from other buildings on the headquarters' grounds to reach the conference room. Although Barb and Darrel could pick up their e-mail before the meeting started, the other three executives couldn't. He asks you to guess what the problem was. What do you tell him?

7. Joseph tells you that he first received the call for help from Sal at 7:54 A.M. and finally solved the executives' problem by 10:00 A.M. Write a sample tracking record for the incident described in Case Project 12-6. Include all pertinent details that will help future troubleshooters more quickly diagnose the same kind of problem and that will enable you to give the executives thorough, clear answers in case they call to ask why the problem took so long to fix.

MAINTAINING AND UPGRADING A NETWORK

After reading this chapter and completing the exercises, you will be able to:

➤ Perform a baseline analysis to determine the state of your network

➤ Plan and follow regular hardware and software maintenance routines

➤ Describe the steps involved in upgrading network operating system software

➤ Describe the steps involved in adding or upgrading network hardware

➤ Address the potential pitfalls of making changes to the network

➤ Research networking trends to plan future network upgrades

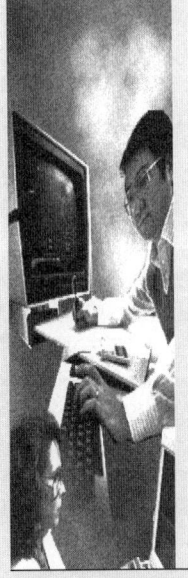

ON THE JOB

I once worked in the computer services department of a world-class opera house and theater. Two years ago it became clear that our needs had outgrown our network. Users experienced slow responses and frequent down time, and the networking professionals found it difficult to support the outdated equipment. It was time for an upgrade.

We found the financing to completely overhaul our network, from backbone to desktop. We enlisted a consulting firm to help us plan this undertaking. Because the project was so large (affecting every bit of our operation, from Marketing to Payroll), the consultants recommended dividing the conversion into phases that would be less disruptive: backbone upgrade, LAN cabling, network device migration, desktop migration, and documentation and maintenance. One of the most difficult tasks was recabling our facility—a building that didn't resemble your average office building. Nevertheless, over a period of six months, and with help from several contractors, we completed the entire project.

The new network allows the theater's staff to work more efficiently. The network handles data more quickly and almost never suffers down time. And I now work for the consulting company that performed the upgrade!

Sophie Harris
Sage Systems

A network, like any other complex system, is in a constant state of flux. Whether the changes are due to internal factors, such as increased demand on the server's processor, or external factors, such as the obsolescence of a certain model of hub, you should count on spending a significant amount of time investigating, performing, and troubleshooting changes to your network. In Chapter 12, you learned how to find and resolve problems on a network. Some of the solutions discussed there required changes to software or hardware. In this chapter, you will build on this knowledge to learn about changes dictated by immediate needs as well as those required to enhance the network's functionality, growth, performance, or security.

Ideally, you will plan and budget for all changes to your network. In reality, however, many network changes result from sudden, unexpected requirements. For example, a security breach at your organization might prompt the Vice President of IT to declare that all firewall operating systems must be upgraded and that all system access permissions must be scrutinized. To accomplish these quick changes, you must possess excellent technical skills, understand your network thoroughly, and think fast. Upgrading firewalls is one small example of a network enhancement that you need to properly plan and test. In this chapter, you will learn about a variety of ways to maintain and upgrade your network so as to make it more secure, reliable, and responsive.

Keeping Track

As you learned in Chapter 12, keeping accurate and updated documentation on every aspect of your network will facilitate troubleshooting and help you manage your network more effectively. With network maintenance tasks, you should track all changes and upgrades you perform. You should also note the state of the network before and after you implement any modifications. The first topic in this section, baselining, suggests how to begin this process of documentation.

Baselining

The first step in properly maintaining your network is to identify its current state. You cannot predict how a network will perform in the future until you have analyzed its past performance. The practice of measuring and recording a network's current state of operation is called **baselining**. Baselining measurements may include the utilization rate for your network backbone, number of users logged on per day or per hour, number of protocols that run on your network, statistics about errors (such as runts, collisions, jabbers, or giants, described in Chapter 12), frequency with which networked applications are used, or information regarding which users take up the most bandwidth. Figure 13-1 shows a graph that provides a baseline for daily network traffic over a six-week period.

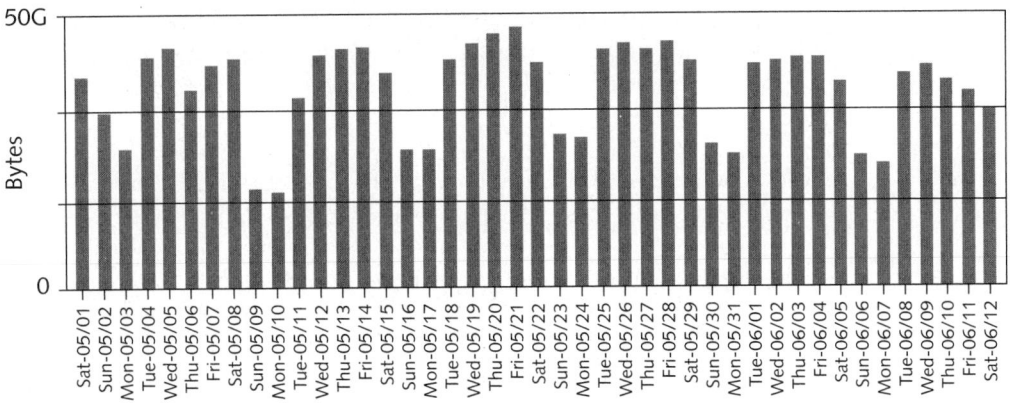

Figure 13-1   Baseline of daily network traffic

Each network will require its own baselining approach. The elements you measure will depend on which functions are most critical to your network and its users. If your staff members run the Lotus Notes application from their local hard disks, for example, but need to post the data they generate through queries to the Internet, you will probably be most concerned about the utilization rate of your gateway, rather than that of your server.

Baseline measurements allow you to compare future performance increases or decreases caused by network changes with past network performance. Baselining is the only way to know for certain whether your upgrades or changes help or harm your level of service.

For example, imagine that you have just added a new switch for the shared workstations in your organization's Customer Service department. Your manager wants you to prove that the switch is really worth the money she paid for it. If you have previously baselined the Customer Service department's network segment in terms of utilization and response time, you can measure the same characteristics after you install the switch and demonstrate how much more rapidly the users receive their data off the network. If the response time becomes worse, you will know that you probably configured or installed the switch improperly.

In another example, suppose that a group of users from the corporate headquarters complains about slow response time over the WAN. If you have baselined the characteristics of that WAN link, you can determine whether their slow response reflects higher-than-normal traffic or whether traffic is excessive and possibly caused by a network error.

In addition, baselining can help you predict the impact of a significant network change. When you are planning system upgrades, it provides the best way to predict your needs. For instance, suppose that your network currently serves 500 users and that your backbone traffic exceeds 50% at 10:00 A.M. and 2:00 P.M. each business day. That pattern constitutes your baseline. Now suppose that your company decides to add 200 users who

13

perform the same types of functions on the network. The added number of users equals 40% of the current number of users (200/500). Therefore, you can predict that your backbone's capacity should increase by approximately 40% to maintain your current service levels.

 Network traffic patterns are notoriously difficult to forecast, because you cannot predict users' habits, the effects of new technology, or changes in demand for resources over a given period of time. For instance, the preceding example assumed that all new users would share the same network usage habits as the current users. In fact, however, the new users may generate a great deal more, or a great deal less, network traffic.

Baselining may help you decide how to accommodate capacity increases. For example, determining which, if any, groups of users generate the most network traffic can help you decide whether to upgrade the network from 10-Mbps to 100-Mbps Ethernet, whether to upgrade only certain segments of the network, or whether to manage the increase by adding switches and further subnetting the network.

How do you gather baseline data on your network? Although you could theoretically use a network monitor or network analyzer and record its output at regular intervals, several programs can perform the baselining for you. These programs range from freeware available on the Internet to expensive, customizable hardware and software combination products.

Before choosing a network baselining tool, you should determine how you will use it. If you manage a small network that provides only one critical application to users, an inexpensive tool may suffice. If you work on a WAN with several critical links, however, you should investigate purchasing a more comprehensive program. Look for a program with a familiar and easy-to-use interface, preferably one that provides templates and wizards to enable you to set your measurement parameters quickly. Make sure that the tool can be integrated with your operating system environment and that it supports the networking hardware used by your organization.

The baselining tool should also be capable of measuring the statistics needed. For example, only a sophisticated baselining tool can measure traffic generated by each node on a network, filter traffic according to types of protocols and errors, and simultaneously measure statistics from several different network segments.

In most cases, baselining tools record the information they collect in common database formats that enable you to generate reports and graphs depicting the health of your network. Examples of popular baselining tools include Concord Communications' Network Health, NetScout Systems' NetScout Manager Plus, and Wandel and Goltermann's WG Wizard.

Once you have identified the network statistics critical for your organization, chosen a baselining tool, and completed the initial baselining, you should set a regular schedule for reevaluating your network. You may want to perform baselining after any major network change or according to dates on the calendar. Regardless of which option you choose, regularly repeating the baseline measurements is the only way to establish a history of your network's performance. By creating such a history, you can identify trends and predict future needs.

Asset Management

Another key component in the evaluation of your network is identifying and tracking the hardware and software on your network, a process called **asset management**. The first step in asset management is to take an inventory of each node on the network. This inventory should include not only the total number of components on the network, but also each device's configuration files, model number, serial number, location on the network, and a technical contact for support. In addition, you will want to keep records of every piece of software purchased by your organization, its version number, vendor, and technical support contact.

As with a baselining tool, the asset management tool you choose will depend on your organization's needs. You may purchase a program that can automatically discover all devices on the network and then save that information in a database, or you may use a simple spreadsheet to save the data. In either case, your asset management records should be comprehensive and accessible to all personnel who may become involved in maintaining or troubleshooting the network. In addition, you should ensure that the asset management database is regularly updated, either manually or automatically, as changes to network hardware and software occur. The information you retain is useful only while it is current.

Asset management simplifies maintaining and upgrading the network chiefly because you know what the system includes. For example, if you discover that a router purchased two years ago requires an upgrade to its operating system software to fix a security flaw, you need to know how many routers are installed, where they are installed, and whether any have already received the software upgrade. An up-to-date asset management system allows you to avoid searching through old invoices and troubleshooting records to answer these questions.

In addition, asset management provides network administrators with information about the costs and benefits of certain types of hardware or software. For example, if you conclude that 50% of your staff's troubleshooting time is spent on one flawed brand of NIC, an asset management system can reveal how many NICs you would need to replace if you chose to replace those cards, and whether it would make sense to replace the entire installed base. In addition, some asset management programs can track the length of equipment leases and alert network managers when leases will expire.

13

The term "asset management" originally referred to an organization's system for keeping tabs on every piece of equipment it owned. This function was usually handled through the Accounting department. Some of the accounting-related tasks included under the original definition for asset management, such as managing the depreciation on network equipment or tracking the expiration of leases, apply to asset management in networking as well.

Change Management

In Chapter 12, you learned about using a change management system to track every modification you make while troubleshooting a network problem. You should also use your change management system to record any changes resulting from network maintenance or upgrades. In general, updating your change management system regularly will alert your colleagues of changes you've made and help you remember when you instituted them. This type of system will also enable you to correlate additions, removals, or changes in network components with differences in the network's performance. This benefit may simplify the process of taking baseline and network performance measurements.

Like asset management systems, change management systems are useful only if they are kept current. Unlike asset management records, however, change management records cannot be created by a program that automatically discovers hardware and software on the network. Instead, you (or your fellow network administrators) must supply information regarding when, why, and how changes occur.

SOFTWARE CHANGES

If you have ever supported desktop computers professionally or even maintained your own computer at home, you know that an important part of keeping a system running optimally is upgrading its software.

You are most likely to implement the following types of software changes on your network: patches (improvements or enhancements to a particular piece of a software program), upgrades (major changes to the existing code), or revisions (a general term for minor or major changes to the existing code). Although the specifics vary for each type of software change, the general steps involved can be summarized as follows:

1. Determine whether the change (whether it be a patch, revision, or upgrade) is necessary.

2. Research the purpose of the change and its potential effects on other programs.

3. Determine whether the change should apply to some or all users and whether it will be distributed centrally or machine-by-machine.

4. If you decide to implement the change, notify system administrators, help desk personnel, and users. Schedule the change for completion during off-hours (unless it is an emergency).

5. Back up the current system or software before making any modifications.

6. Prevent users from accessing the system or part of the system being altered (for example, disable logins).

7. Keep the upgrade instructions handy and follow them during installation of the patch or revision.

8. Make the change.

9. Test the system fully after the change, preferably exercising the software as a typical user would. Note any unintended or unanticipated consequences of the modification.

10. If the change was successful, reenable access to the system. If it was unsuccessful, revert to the previous version of the software.

11. Inform system administrators, help desk personnel, and users when the change is complete. If you had to reverse it, explain why.

12. Record your change in the change management system.

As a general rule, upgrading or patching software according to a vendor's recommendations is a good idea and can often prevent network problems. For example, a vendor may issue an alert to its customers regarding a security flaw in its Web browser product. To fix this flaw, it may supply a patch. At other times, you may have to search for product upgrades on your own. Whatever your means of finding patches and upgrades, you should take responsibility for this task and make the necessary changes to your network's software. Bear in mind, however, that such changes can sometimes create even more trouble on your system. You should therefore be prepared to reverse software upgrades or patches, just in case.

In the following sections, you will learn about the types of software changes associated with sensible network maintenance. You will also see the best way to approach these changes.

Patches

As mentioned earlier, a **patch** is a correction, improvement, or enhancement to a particular piece of a software program. It differs from a revision or software upgrade in that it changes only part of a software program, leaving most of the code untouched. Patches are often distributed at no charge by software vendors in an attempt to fix a bug in their code or to add slightly more functionality.

You'll encounter patches in all areas of routine networking maintenance. Among other things, network maintenance sometimes requires patching the server's network operating system. For example, if your server runs NetWare 5.x, you may need to patch it to enable it to act as a reliable NAT router. A Windows 2000 server might require similar patches or perhaps something quite different.

 Microsoft calls its significant patches for Windows 2000 Server "**service packs**." You may see them abbreviated as "SP1" and "SP2" for Service Pack 1 and Service Pack 2, respectively.

Keep in mind that a patch is not a replacement for an entire software package; instead, a patch is installed on top of the existing software. Patches apply to more than just network operating system software. For example, you might have to patch the software on your Cisco switch to allow it to handle IP multicasts over a Token Ring network. Alternatively, you might patch the program that allows you to centrally control your printers across the network.

 If you install new hardware on a Windows 2000 server after installing a service pack, you will be prompted to insert your original Windows 2000 installation CD to obtain the device driver and support files for that hardware. By doing so, however, you may overwrite some of the files that were updated by the service pack. Therefore, it is a good idea to upgrade your server's hardware *before* applying service packs. If you do upgrade the server's hardware after installing a service pack, you may have to implement the service pack a second time.

Patch installations are no more difficult than installations of new software programs. The patch itself should come with installation instructions and a description of its purpose, at the very least, in the form of a text file. As with any significant system change, you should back up the system before installing a patch. Although patches ought to be fully tested by the vendor before release, you cannot assume that they will work flawlessly on your system. This consideration is especially important when you are patching network operating system software. Although some patch programs will automatically make a backup of the system before installation begins, you should not rely on this method. Always make sure you have a way to reverse a software change if it does more harm than good.

In addition, try to perform software patches during a time when users cannot and will not attempt to access the network. Even if you suspect that a patch can be implemented quickly and without adverse effects on current users, don't take a chance by applying it during normal business hours. If the patch does create problems, you will need extra time to reverse the process. Depending on how complicated or comprehensive the patch is, you may want to alert users to stay off the system for only a few hours or perhaps overnight.

After applying the patch, test the system to verify that its desired enhancements have taken effect. At this time, you should review the vendor's documentation to ensure that you have correctly understood the patch's purpose and installed it correctly. For some patches to take effect, you will have to change system configuration files and restart the system. Test the software to verify that the patch hasn't caused any unintentional, undesired effects. Once you are certain that the patch worked successfully, you can allow users to access the system again.

To stay apprised of patches released by your vendors, you should regularly check the vendor's technical support Web site or subscribe to its mailing list. Manufacturers will usually attempt to bundle a number of bug fixes into one large patch; if you're a registered user, they will alert you about the release of significant patches. News about patches from vendors as large as Novell and Microsoft will also probably appear in trade magazines. Smaller vendors may need to release a patch that fixes a single problem with their program only occasionally.

Make it a policy to keep informed about patches to your network software, whether it involves the operating system, an application, or a client program. If you work in a large organization with several servers, routers, and other devices, you may want to assign one network administrator to manage patches for the servers, one to manage patches for the printers, and so on.

Client Upgrades

As you are probably aware, a software **upgrade** is a major change to a software package's existing code. An upgrade may or may not be offered free from a vendor and may or may not be comprehensive enough to substitute for the original program. An upgrade to the client program replaces the existing client program. In general, upgrades are designed to add functionality and fix bugs in the previous version of the client. For example, Microsoft's technical support site offers an upgrade for the Windows 2000 operating system that improves its level of encryption to provide better security. On a Novell client, you might perform an upgrade that enables clients to take advantage of the new features in NetWare 5.1. The scope and purpose of client upgrades vary widely, depending on whether the upgrade is a redesign or simply a bug fix.

 The term **bug** is frequently used to describe a flaw in a software program that causes some part of the program to malfunction. Less frequently, this term may also be used to describe a hardware defect. Legend has it that the term originated when a moth became trapped inside the electrical workings of the first digital computer.

Before upgrading client software, carefully read the instructions accompanying the upgrade. It should reveal how to best install the software, whether the upgrade requires you to first install any previous upgrades, whether the upgrade requires any special preparation, and how its changes will affect users.

A client upgrade may be transparent to users, or it may completely change the appearance of the network login interface. Client upgrades typically overwrite some system files (such as .dll files) on the workstation, so their installation may affect other programs adversely. They may even prevent other programs from working as they did in the past. For example, a user who receives an upgrade to his or her Windows 98 Dial-up Networking client may later experience problems with an older version of AOL software that worked perfectly for the last two years. In this case, the best solution may be to upgrade the AOL software as well.

As with all upgrades, you should test a client upgrade on a single workstation before distributing it to all users. Also, you should prepare a way to reverse the process. Because most client upgrades do not back up the previous version automatically, you should keep the old client software close at hand, either on the network or on disk, in case you need to reinstall it.

You may either perform client upgrades on a workstation-by-workstation basis or use a software distribution program such as Microsoft's Systems Management Server to upgrade multiple workstations simultaneously from the network. Although the latter approach is more efficient, it may not be appropriate in all situations. Consider a network of 500 users who have different software, hardware, and usage requirements. Can you be certain that the client upgrade will be compatible with each workstation's hardware and software? Can you be certain that the client upgrade will not adversely affect any user's current software setup? Can you be certain that every user will log in to the network to receive his or her upgrade? (For instance, what happens if many users are mobile?)

In general, you need to plan carefully and become familiar with your client characteristics before allowing a software distribution program to upgrade client software. In addition, you should notify clients about the upgrade and explain how their workstation might change as a result. If you don't, users may become alarmed at the changes and flood the help desk with questions.

Application Upgrades

Like client upgrades, application upgrades represent modifications to all or part of a program that are designed to enhance functionality or fix problems related to software. Application upgrades, however, apply to software shared by clients on the network. Bear in mind that changes to shared applications will affect all users at once. You should therefore take extra precautions to ensure that the application upgrade does not cause unanticipated problems. It's essential to test it fully before allowing users to access the new version.

The principles underlying the modification of shared applications on the network are the same as those for the modification of client software. Before applying the change, you should determine the need for it and its potential effects. You should also back up the current software before upgrading it, prevent users from accessing the software during the implementation process, and keep users and system administrators informed of all changes.

Unlike client or system software upgrades, application upgrades are not usually designed to fix problems in the software, but rather to enhance the program's functionality. For this reason, an application upgrade may be more a matter of convenience than necessity. Therefore, the time, cost, and effort involved in application upgrades should be weighed against the necessity of performing operating system or client upgrades. This consideration is especially important if a networking professional's time is limited (as it usually is). For example, users may urge a network administrator to upgrade the company's version of WordPerfect. If the only advantage in doing so is to allow users to print watermarks on their labels, the upgrade may be a waste of time and money. On the other hand, if the application upgrade will add a necessary feature, such as integration with the company's messaging system, it may be well worth the effort.

For a significant application upgrade, you may also need to provide (or suggest classes for) user training. If you choose to refer your users to an outside training facility, make sure they will learn about the particulars of the application in your networking environment. For instance, if you make it a policy never to install the sample spreadsheets for a Lotus 1-2-3 program, make sure your users know about this constraint. Likewise, if you have limited the functionality of a program (for example, preventing users from posting the Web pages they create in Microsoft FrontPage to the server), you should publicize this policy. The better you prepare and inform your users, the fewer support calls your help desk will have to field.

Network Operating System Upgrades

Perhaps the most critical type of software upgrade you'll perform is an upgrade to your network operating system. It usually involves significant, potentially drastic, changes to the way your servers and clients operate. As such, it requires plenty of forethought, product research, and rigorous testing before you implement it. In fact, for any network with more than a few users, you should create and follow a project plan for this undertaking. This plan should include all of the precautions typically associated with other software upgrades. In addition, you should consider the following in your project plan:

- How will the upgrade affect user IDs, groups, rights, and policies?

- How will the upgrade affect file, printer, and directory access on the server?

- How will the upgrade affect applications or client interactions on the server?

- How will the upgrade affect configuration files, protocols, and services running on the server?

- How will the upgrade affect the server's interaction with other devices on the network?

- How accurately can you test the upgrade software in a simulated environment?

- How can you take advantage of the new operating system to make your system more efficient?

13

- What is your technical support arrangement with the operating system's manufacturer if you need help in the midst of the upgrade?

- Have you allotted enough time to perform the upgrade (for example, would it be more appropriate to do it over a weekend rather than overnight?)?

- Have you ensured that the users, help desk personnel, and system administrators understand how the upgrade will affect their daily operations and support burdens?

The preceding items are only some of the critical questions you need to ask before embarking on a network operating system upgrade. Your networking environment may warrant additional considerations. For example, suppose that you are the network administrator for a company that is merging with a second company. Your two companies may use dissimilar network operating systems, and the IT Director may ask you to upgrade your network's operating system to match the other company's version. In this situation, you would have not only the previous list of questions to consider, but also a list of questions pertaining to the other company's operating system. For instance, how are its NOS directories organized? By addressing these questions before you upgrade your own network operating system, you will ensure that the merger of the two networks goes more smoothly.

A network operating system upgrade is a complex and far-reaching change. It should not be undertaken with severe budgetary, resource, or time constraints. The following scenario illustrates how careful planning and a methodical process can help you accomplish a network operating system upgrade. In this scenario, a network administrator performs an exemplary network operating system upgrade.

Tom is the network administrator for an accounting firm that employs 400 full-time staff members and uses three NetWare 4.11 servers. Tom is considering upgrading the servers to NetWare 5.1. He has read about the benefits of NetWare 5.1 and thinks his organization may be outgrowing its NetWare 4.11 servers. In addition, his colleagues and a few of his knowledgeable users have been asking when the servers will be upgraded. Tom decides to make the upgrade one of his priorities. He delegates some of his other tasks to co-workers and gets to work.

1. Research—Tom gathers the trade magazine articles he's seen about NetWare 5.1. Because he knows that trade magazine articles can be inaccurate or biased, he also searches Novell newsgroups on the Internet to find out what network administrators who have performed a similar upgrade report about their experiences. He calls a trusted local consultant to ask her advice. In addition, Tom searches through Novell's Web site to see if the features provided by NetWare 5.1 are needed for his network and users. Finally, he finds out how much the software will cost. Once he has collected this information, Tom summarizes it in an outline form, just as if he were writing a term paper. In his outline, he lists the benefits and risks involved in embarking on this network operating system upgrade.

2. Proposal—Tom's initial research indicates that installing NetWare 5.1 would solve a number of technical problems, not to mention simplifying the centralized management of the company's 400 computers. Based on his research outline, Tom writes a proposal to evaluate the product, including a plan to purchase and implement NetWare 5.1 if his proposal is accepted. His proposal includes the following elements:

   - Questions to answer during evaluation (for example, "Can NetWare 5.1 work with my current network monitoring software?")

   - Names of personnel who will assist with evaluation and final approval

   - A rough timeline and plan for implementing the change if it is approved

   - A rough project plan for implementing the change if it is approved

   - Cost considerations

   - A review of the short- and long-term benefits of the upgrade

   - A review of the risks involved in the upgrade

   - A recommendation for or against performing the operating system upgrade

   - A plan for purchasing the software and implementing the change

3. Evaluation—Assuming that Tom's proposal concluded that his firm should proceed with an upgrade and that his superiors approved his recommendation, Tom is ready to begin the evaluation phase. He orders an evaluation copy of NetWare 5.1 from his Novell sales representative. He installs the software on an old server that is currently unused, but whose hardware is similar to the hardware of his three production servers (making sure that his servers meet Novell's recommended hardware requirements). On this system, he creates several mock user IDs and groups to simulate the real network environment. Tom also installs all of the applications and services that the server will support if it goes into production.

   Tom distributes updated client software to his team of engineers and asks them to use the mock IDs and groups to test the system. Over a given time period, they test the system and keep notes on how the system meets the requirements specified in Tom's proposal. The engineers pay particular attention to the new user interface for clients, the way in which their company's critical applications operate, the system's response time, and any new features provided by the upgrade. Tom and the engineers meet regularly during the evaluation period to discuss and compare their experiences. In addition, Tom asks the engineers (or a consultant, if the engineers don't have the appropriate knowledge) to double-check his work in installing NetWare 5.1. This approach ensures that the test provides a fair trial of the software.

13

4. Training—Judging by the results of the initial stages of evaluation, Tom predicts that his company will purchase the upgrade. To prepare for this event, he sends the networking engineers to NetWare 5.1 training. He also recommends training for the help desk personnel. In addition, Tom discusses possibilities for user training with the company's computer training manager. Most importantly, he signs up for NetWare 5.1 training himself, because he will actually perform the upgrade. He schedules his training to take place only a few weeks before the anticipated implementation date so that his new skills will be fresh when he begins the conversion.

5. Pre-implementation—As the first step of implementation, Tom expands on the rough timeline and plan that he created in his proposal. The result is a full-fledged project plan for the upgrade. He plans the transfer of the IDs, groups, and their rights to the new system. He decides how he would like to reorganize the NetWare NDS tree and what types of volumes to create. In addition, Tom reviews the existing servers to determine which applications, files, and directories should be transferred and which can be archived. He plans to upgrade the operating system on only one server at a time.

Two weeks before upgrading the first server, Tom informs users, help desk personnel, and other networking staff of the timeline and explains what changes to expect. He recommends to users that they clean up their data directories on the server and discard any unnecessary files. Similarly, he asks networking staff to remove any unnecessary applications or services they have installed on the server. If necessary, he and his staff arrange to upgrade the client software on all workstations that will be affected by the operating system upgrade. A few days before the upgrade, he issues a final warning to staff specifying how long he will have the server down to accomplish the upgrade.

6. Implementation—Tom decides to implement the upgrade over a weekend. Before beginning the process, he gathers the software documentation and his plan, along with the software CDs and a bootable disk for the server (making certain that the CD-ROM device driver is on the bootable disk). At 7:00 P.M. on Saturday, he sends a broadcast warning to all users on the network that the server will be going down in five minutes. Five minutes later, he disables all logins to the network. He then backs up the entire server to a tape drive. When the backup is complete, he uses his backup software to verify that critical files were successfully copied.

Once he's certain that the backup worked, Tom starts the server with DOS and follows Novell's instructions for upgrading from NetWare version 4.11 to version 5.1. This process may take an hour or more. After the upgrade finishes, Tom configures the server according to Novell's instructions and his network's specifications (for example, setting the TCP/IP parameters). Once he has added all services and configured the server properly, he enables himself (but no other users) to log in and test the server's functionality. Tom also tests the critical applications on the server as well as the server's connectivity with the rest of the systems and devices on the network. Not only does he test the network using his (privileged) ID, but Tom also tests it using an average client's ID.

7. Post-implementation—After he is satisfied that the network operating system upgrade was successful, Tom reenables logins to the network and informs all staff that the system is running again. He and his staff review the upgrade process to see if they learned any lessons that could make the other server upgrades more efficient and less troublesome. They work with the help desk personnel to understand the kinds of support calls generated by the upgrade. They also continue testing the new operating system, fine-tuning when necessary, to fix problems or find errors before they become problems for users.

Unfortunately, the careful process of evaluation, planning, and implementation described in these steps rarely reflects reality. Most network administrators are too busy to perform all of these functions themselves. With some foresight, however, they can strive to perform most of these steps and save themselves the consequences of poor planning during or after the operating system is upgraded.

Reversing a Software Upgrade

If the software upgrade you perform creates problems in your existing system, you should be prepared to reverse the process. The process of reverting to a previous version of software after attempting to upgrade it is known as **backleveling**. Every network professional has been forced to backlevel at some point in his or her career. The steps that constitute this process differ depending on the complexity of the upgrade and the network environment involved.

Although no hard and fast rules for backleveling exist, Table 13-1 summarizes some basic suggestions. Bear in mind that you must always refer to the software vendor's documentation to reverse an upgrade. If you must backlevel a network operating system upgrade, you should also consult with experienced professionals about the best approach for your network environment.

Table 13-1   Reversing a software upgrade

Type of Upgrade	Options for Reversing
Operating system patch	Use the patch's automatic uninstall utility
Client software upgrade	Use the upgrade's automatic uninstall utility or reinstall previous version of the client on top of the upgrade
Application upgrade	Use the application's automatic uninstall utility or maintain complete copy of the previous installation of the application and reinstall it over the upgrade
Operating system upgrade	Prior to the upgrade, make a complete backup of the system; to backlevel, restore entire system from the backup; uninstall an operating system upgrade only as a last resort

Hardware and Physical Plant Changes

Hardware and physical plant changes may be required when a network component fails or malfunctions, but more often they are performed as part of an upgrade to increase capacity, improve performance, or add functionality to the network. In this section, you will learn about the simplest and most popular form of hardware change—adding more of what you already use, such as adding four more switches to the backbone or adding 10 new networked printers. You will also learn about more complex hardware changes, such as replacing the entire network backbone with a more robust system.

Many of the same issues apply to hardware changes as apply to software changes. In particular, proper planning is the key to a successful upgrade. When considering a change to your network hardware, use the following steps as a guide:

1. Determine whether the change is necessary.

2. Research the upgrade's potential effects on other devices, functions, and users.

3. If you decide to implement the change, notify system administrators, help desk personnel, and users and schedule it during off-hours (unless it is an emergency).

4. If possible, back up the current hardware's configuration. Most hardware (for example, routers, switches, and servers) has a configuration that you can easily copy to a disk. In other cases (for example, networked printers), you may have to print out the hardware's configuration.

5. Prevent users from accessing the system or the part of the system that you are changing.

6. Keep the installation instructions and hardware documentation handy.

7. Implement the change.

8. Test the hardware fully after the change, preferably putting a higher load on the device than it would incur during normal use in your organization. Note any unintended or unanticipated consequences of the change.

9. If the change was successful, reenable access to the device. If it was unsuccessful, isolate the device or reinsert the old device, if possible.

10. Inform system administrators, help desk personnel, and users when the change is complete. If it was not successful, explain why.

11. Record your change in the change management system.

Adding or Upgrading Equipment

The difficulty involved in adding or upgrading hardware on your network will depend largely on whether or not you have used the hardware in the past. For instance, if your organization always uses Intel hubs, adding one more Intel hub to your second-floor telecommunications closet may take only a few minutes and cause absolutely no disruption of service to your users. On the other hand, even if your company uses Intel hubs, adding an Intel router to your network may be an entirely new experience. You should research, evaluate, and test any unfamiliar piece of equipment that you intend to add or upgrade on your network, even if it is manufactured by a vendor that supplies much of your other hardware.

With the rapid changes in the hardware industry, you may not be able to purchase identical hardware even from one quarter to the next. If consistency is a concern—for example, if your technical staff is familiar with only one brand and model of printer, and you do not have the time or money to retrain personnel—you would be wise to purchase as much hardware as possible in a single order. If this approach is not feasible, purchase equipment from vendors with familiar products and solid reputations.

Each type of device that you add or upgrade on the network will have different preparation and implementation requirements. Knowing exactly how to handle the changes will require not only a close reading of the manufacturer's instructions, but also some experience with the type of networking equipment at hand. The following list provides a very general overview of how you might approach adding or upgrading devices on the network, from the least disruptive to the most complex types of equipment. The devices at the bottom of the list are not only the most disruptive and complex to add or upgrade, but also the most difficult to remove or backlevel.

- *Networked workstation*—A networked workstation is perhaps the simplest device to add. It directly affects only a few users but does not alter network access for anyone else. If your organization has a standard networked workstation configuration (for example, a disk image—a compressed snapshot of the workstation's contents—on the server), adding a networked workstation will be a quick operation as well. You can successfully add a networked workstation without notifying users or support staff and without worrying about down time.

- *Networked printer*—A networked printer is easy to add to your network, too. Adding this equipment is slightly more complex than adding a networked workstation, however, because of its unique configuration process and because it is shared. Although it affects multiple users, a networked printer does not typically perform a mission-critical function in an organization, so the length of time required to install one does not usually affect productivity. Thus, although you should notify the affected users of a networked printer addition, you do not need to notify all users and support staff. Likewise, you do not need to restrict access to the network or worry about down time in this instance.

- *Hub*—As you learned in Chapter 6, a single hub may service as few as 4 or as many as 64 users. You do not have to worry about down time or notifying users when adding a new hub, however, because it cannot affect anyone until it is actually in use. If you are upgrading or swapping out an existing hub, you must notify the affected users. The upgrade or swap will create down time;

13

you may have to perform the operation during off-hours. In addition, you must consider the traffic and addressing implications of adding or upgrading a hub. For example, if you need to expand the capacity of a TCP/IP-based network segment from 24 users to 60 users, you can easily enough swap your 24-port hub with a 64-port hub. Before doing so, make sure that the segment has enough free IP addresses to service 60 users; otherwise, these users will not be able to access the network.

- *Server*—A server addition or upgrade can be tricky. Typically, this type of change (unless it is the replacement of a minor component) requires a great deal of foresight and planning. Before installing a new server, you need to consider the hardware and connectivity implications of the change, as well as issues relating to the network operating system. Even if you are adding a server that will not be used immediately, you still need to plan for its installation. Preferably, you should add the server while network traffic is low or non-existent. You should also restrict access to the servers; otherwise, one of your users could find the server while browsing the network and try to save files to it or run an application from it.

  Upgrading the hardware (such as a NIC or memory) on an existing server requires almost the same amount of planning as adding an entirely new server. You should schedule upgrades to an existing server for off-hours, so that you can shut down the server without inconveniencing any users who rely on it.

- *Switches and routers*—Switches and routers are the most complex type of additions or changes to a network design for several reasons. First, they can be physically disruptive—that is, they often require the installation of new racks or other support frames in your telecommunications room. Second, they affect many users—perhaps all users—on the network. For instance, if you must replace the Internet gateway for your organization's headquarters, you will cut every user's access to the Internet in the process (unless you have redundant gateways, which is the optimal setup if you rely on the Internet for mission-critical services). You should notify all users on the network about the impending change, even if you don't think that they will be affected—sometimes a router or switch may have unintended effects on segments of the network other than the one it services. In addition, you should plan at least weeks in advance for switch or router changes and expect at least several hours of down time. Because routers and switches are expensive, you should take extraordinary care when handling and configuring the equipment. Also, because switches and routers serve different purposes, rely on the manufacturer's documentation to guide you through the installation process.

The best way to safely gain experience with adding, upgrading, or repairing devices is to experiment with devices that are not currently used on a network. If you are taking a networking class, ask your instructor whether you can spend extra time in the computer lab polishing your skills with the equipment. Work with a partner, if possible, so you can question each other about what you are doing and why.

Bear in mind that adding a new processor to a server, a new NIC to a router, or more memory to a printer may affect your service or warranty agreement with the manufacturer. Before purchasing any components to add or replace in your network devices, check your agreement for stipulations that might apply. You may be allowed to add only components made by the same manufacturer or risk losing all support from that manufacturer.

Above all, keep safety in mind when you upgrade or install hardware on a network. Never tinker with the insides of a device that is turned on. Make sure that all cords and devices are stowed safely out of the way and cannot cause trips or falls. Avoid wearing jewelry, scarves, or very loose clothing when you work on equipment; if you have long hair, tie it back. Not only will you prevent injury this way, but you will also be less distracted. By removing metal jewelry, you may prevent damage to the equipment caused by a short if the metal touches a circuit. If the equipment is heavy (such as a large switch or server), do not try to lift it by yourself. Finally, to protect the equipment from damage, follow the manufacturer's temperature, ventilation, antistatic, and moisture guidelines.

Cabling Upgrades

Cabling upgrades (unless they involve the replacement of a single faulty patch cable) may require significant planning and time to implement, depending on the size of your network. Remember from Chapter 12 that troubleshooting cabling problems may be difficult because the cable layout may be undocumented and poorly planned, particularly if it was installed years before and survived intact despite building changes and network growth. For the same reason, cabling is rarely simple to upgrade. The best way to ensure that future upgrades go smoothly is to carefully document the existing cable *before* making any upgrades. If this assessment is not possible, you may have to compile your documentation as you upgrade the existing cabling.

Because a change of this magnitude will affect all users on the network, you should upgrade the network cabling in phases. Perhaps you can schedule an upgrade of the first-floor east wing of your building one weekend, then the first-floor west wing of your building the next, and so on. Weigh the importance of the upgrade against its potential for disruption. For example, if the Payroll department is processing end-of-month checks and having no difficulties other than somewhat slow response time, it is not critical to take away its access to install CAT5 wiring. On the other hand, if the building maintenance staff needs a 100-Mbps connection to run a new HVAC controls system, you will probably make it a priority to take down this access temporarily and replace the wiring. In this case, not only will you have to replace the wiring, but you may also need to replace hubs and NICs.

For the most part, only organizations that run very small networks upgrade or install their own network cabling. Most other organizations rely on contractors who specialize in this service. Nevertheless, as a networking professional you should know how to run a cable across a room, either under a raised floor or through a ceiling, in order to connect a device to the network.

13

Backbone Upgrades

The most comprehensive and complex upgrade involving network hardware is a backbone upgrade. Recall from Chapter 5 that the network backbone represents the main conduit for data on LANs and WANs, connecting major routers, servers, and switches. A backbone upgrade requires not only a great deal of planning, but also the efforts of several personnel (and possibly contractors) and a significant investment. You may upgrade parts of the backbone—a NIC in a router or a section of cabling, for example—at any time, but upgrading the entire backbone changes the whole network.

Examples of backbone upgrades include migrating from Token Ring to Ethernet, migrating from Ethernet to ATM, migrating from a slower technology to a faster one, and replacing all routers with switches (to make use of VLANs, for example). Such upgrades may satisfy a variety of needs: a need for faster throughput, a physical move or renovation, a more reliable network, greater security, more consistent standards, support of a new application, or greater cost-effectiveness. For example, switching from Token Ring to Ethernet may make a LAN less expensive to maintain because Ethernet's components are more economical and technical support may be easier to find. The need for faster throughput may prompt an upgrade from an older Ethernet technology to Gigabit Ethernet. Likewise, the need to support videoconferencing may require a backbone upgrade from CAT5 to fiber and from Ethernet to ATM.

If you recall from Chapters 4 and 6 the cabling and hardware required for the different networking technologies, you will get an idea of how far-reaching a backbone upgrade can be. For example, to convert from Token Ring to Ethernet, you must replace or upgrade connectivity equipment such as hubs and routers. In addition, you must replace the NIC in every workstation and printer on the network and change the configuration for each device so that it works with Ethernet rather than Token Ring. For a small network, this effort may not be more than a weekend's work. For a network of thousands of users, such an upgrade requires the services of a dedicated team.

Because backbone upgrades are expensive and time-consuming, the first step in approaching such a project is to justify it. Will the benefits outweigh the costs? Can the upgrade wait a year or more? If so, you might be wise to wait and find out whether a cheaper or better technical solution will become available later. Don't try to wait until the technology "settles down," because networking progress never stands still. On the other hand, do wait to implement brand-new technology until you can find out how it has worked on other networks similar to your own or until the manufacturer eliminates most of the bugs.

The second step is to determine which kind of backbone design to implement. To make this decision, you must analyze the future capacity needs of your network, decide whether you want a distributed or collapsed backbone, discover whether you want to rely on switches or routers, decide whether to use subnetting and to what extent, and so on. Although some of these predictions will be guesswork, you can minimize the variables by examining the history of your organization's growth and needs. This effort is where your baselining proves valuable.

For example, if you work with a retailer that opened 15 new stores across the country this year and predicts a growth rate of 30% over the next 5 years, you can predict that your WAN will grow by approximately 20 nodes next year and approximately 27 nodes the following year. You should plan a network upgrade that can accommodate that growth: one that uses a reliable service provider, an addressing scheme that can be expanded, and connectivity devices that can be upgraded easily.

After designing your backbone upgrade, you should develop a project plan to accomplish the upgrade. Given that you don't upgrade your backbone every day, you might want to contract this work to a firm that specializes in network design and upgrades. In that case, you will draft a request for proposal (RFP) to specify what that contractor should do. (Drafting an RFP is just one step in managing a large networking project. You will learn more about this process in Chapter 16, "Managing Network Design and Implementation.")

Regardless of whether you employ specialists, your project plan should include a logical process for upgrading the backbone one section at a time (if possible). Because this process will cause network outages, determine how best to proceed based on users' needs. If you are lucky, you will choose a time when usage is low (such as over a holiday) to perform your upgrade.

Reversing Hardware Changes

As with software changes, you should provide a way to reverse the hardware upgrade and reinstall the old hardware if necessary. If you are replacing a faulty component or device, this restoration will, of course, not be possible. If you are upgrading a component in a device, on the other hand, you should keep the old component safe (for example, keep network interface cards in static-resistant containers) and nearby. Not only might you need to put it back in the device, but you might also need to refer to it for information. For example, if you have not documented the necessary jumper settings for an interface card in a switch, the old card might indicate the jumper settings needed on your new card. Even if the device seems to be operating well with the new component, keep the old component for a while, especially if it is the only one of its kind at your organization.

13

MANAGING GROWTH AND CHANGE

One of the most challenging and exciting aspects of being a networking professional is keeping up with the myriad changes in the industry. Technology trends come and go, as do software and hardware suppliers. Because no one can predict the future, you must learn to do the next best thing—prepare for the future. You will not always make the right decisions, but understanding the history of networking trends and researching possibilities for the future ensure that you can make well-reasoned decisions. The following sections will help you decide how to manage your organization's networking needs.

Trends in Networking Technology

You have probably recognized trends in networking technology while reading this book (for example, the debate over cable modem versus DSL technology for low-cost, high-bandwidth WAN connections mentioned in Chapter 7) or while working in an IT department. Switches are becoming more like routers. Older transmission media such as Thicknet and Thinnet Ethernet have been replaced by twisted-pair cabling. TCP/IP is becoming the protocol of choice on many networks. These trends have been developing for a long time, however. The more interesting question is, What can we learn from these trends that will help us predict new trends over the next decade?

Each of the networking trends evident today provides users with at least one of the following advantages: faster data processing and transmission, more comprehensive integration, open standards, greater accessibility for a more diverse population, or smarter devices (which facilitates more automation of tasks, usually saving time and money). Consider how each of these factors might influence currently developing trends:

- Faster data processing and transmission will bring network access to more people in less time. If you apply this trend to the Internet, you can imagine how commerce, education, and entertainment can be easily carried worldwide over the Web. Will it replace your TV or phone? Or will your TV rely on the Web?

- More comprehensive integration means that more products sold by different vendors will work well together. This compatibility not only makes your job as a networking professional easier (because you have fewer systems to master), but also merges industries. Think of how the roles of telephone companies and Internet service providers are converging. ISPs are now selling voice over IP services, whereas telephone companies are providing Internet access over their networks.

- Open standards (as described in Chapter 10) will make networking careers less specialized and probably more interesting. With TCP/IP networking skills, for example, you could just as easily get a job with a large aerospace firm as you could with an organic food coop.

- Greater accessibility will bring technology to more users. In the 1950s, computers were used only by elite computer scientists and a single computer didn't even fit into one room. Today, the majority of U.S. households own a computer, and millions of users are connected around the world through the Internet. How might this trend affect the global economy? How might it affect cultures and political systems around the world?

- Smarter devices will contribute to each of the trends mentioned above, enabling the development of faster, more open standards and providing greater accessibility. For example, advanced wireless devices now enable users to pick up their e-mail from handheld devices while sipping coffee at an outdoor café.

Note

Notice that lower cost is not necessarily a driving factor in networking technology trends. It doesn't have to be, because the trend toward smarter, faster, and more standardized devices also implies lower costs. Because networking equipment develops so rapidly, today's expensive and powerful devices become tomorrow's inexpensive commodities.

Some of the current trends will bring a greater concern for security. As systems adopt the same (open) standards, they become more vulnerable to hackers who can easily figure out the code after mastering similar systems. As accessibility increases, security threats also increase, because the network offers more entry opportunities for hackers. In Chapter 15, you will learn about protecting data from the unintended consequences of business's increasing reliance on the networking trends discussed above.

Researching Networking Trends

If you are charged with purchasing or planning decisions in your IT department, you will need to research networking technology trends before making any choices. Often you will hear about new technologies from colleagues, classmates, or trade magazine articles, but you cannot rely on the accuracy of everything you hear. The best way to evaluate networking technology is to test it in your organization. That way you can find out how it operates in your networking environment—with your equipment, applications, and users. During the testing, you can note what you like or don't like and decide whether you even need the technology.

On the other hand, many networking trends require such drastic or expensive upgrades that you cannot afford to test them first. In this case, you must rely on someone else who has experience with the technology. A good option is to discuss your needs with a reputable consulting firm that has implemented the same technology at other organizations. Discuss the project not only with the consultants who performed the upgrade work, but also with the customer that is currently using the new technology. If possible, visit facilities that have already adopted the technology.

Newsgroups on the Web can provide valuable information, too. After a new technology has been marketed for a month or more, you should be able to find comments from other networking professionals regarding their experience with the technology. Post a message to the newsgroup inquiring about the technology's pros and cons. Most technicians will happily share their experiences. If the technology works as promised, they will undoubtedly want to spread the good news. If it causes more problems than it solves, they will want to warn others. As you read the postings on a newsgroup, one message will come through loud and clear: Don't rely on the manufacturer's claims regarding the merits of a particular product or service. Instead, test the technology yourself, or at least discuss it with someone who has tested it.

13

CHAPTER SUMMARY

❏ In every aspect of networking, keeping accurate and updated documentation will reduce troubleshooting time and help you manage the network more effectively. When maintaining the network, you should track all changes and upgrades that you perform, as well as the state of the network before and after the changes were implemented.

❏ The practice of measuring and recording your network's current state of operation is called baselining. Baselining measurements may include the utilization rate on your network backbone, the number of users per day or per hour, the number of protocols run on your network, statistics about errors (such as runts, collisions, jabbers, or giants), the frequency with which networked applications are used, or the identification of those users who take up the most bandwidth.

❏ Baseline measurements allow you to compare future performance increases or decreases due to network changes with past network performance. Baselining offers the only way to discern whether your upgrades or changes really helped or harmed the level of service.

❏ Baselining can also help you predict the effect of a significant network change. When you are planning system upgrades, baselining provides the best way to predict your needs.

❏ Baselining differs from network monitoring. A baselined characteristic can be used as a gauge for future reference, whereas network monitoring provides a continual check for problems on the network. These tools work well together, but they are not identical.

❏ An asset management system includes an inventory of the total number of components on the network as well as each device's configuration files, model number, serial number, location on the network, and a technical contact for support. In addition, it records every piece of software purchased by your organization, its version number, vendor, and technical support contact.

❏ You should document any changes to a network as the result of maintenance or upgrades in a change management system. This information will alert your colleagues to changes made and help you remember when you implemented them. It will also assist in baselining and network performance measurement, because you will know exactly when a network component was added, removed, or changed, and can correlate this information with performance data.

❏ No matter what type of software upgrade you perform, you should generally follow the same process. First, determine whether the change (whether it be a patch, revision, or upgrade) is necessary. Next, research the upgrade's purpose and potential effects on other programs. Determine whether the change should apply to all or only some users and whether it will be distributed centrally or machine-by-machine. If you decide to implement the change, notify system administrators, help desk personnel, and users and schedule the upgrade during off-hours (unless it is an emergency). Back up the current system or software before making any changes. Prevent users from accessing the system or part of the system affected (for example, disable logins). Keep the upgrade instructions handy and follow them during installation of the patch or revision. Make the change. Test the system fully after the change, noting any unintended or unanticipated consequences. If the change was successful, reenable access to the system. If it was unsuccessful, revert to the previous version of the software. Inform system administrators, help desk personnel, and users when the change is complete, or if you had to reverse it, explain why. Record your change in the change management system.

❑ A patch is an enhancement or improvement to a part of a software program, often distributed at no charge by software vendors to fix a bug in their code or to add slightly more functionality. Patches differ from revisions and software upgrades because they change only part of the software program, leaving most of the code untouched.

❑ Make it a policy to keep informed about patches to your network software, whether they involve the operating system, an application, or a client program. If you work in a large organization with several servers, routers, and other devices, you may want to assign one network administrator to manage patches for the servers, another to manage patches for the printers, and so on.

❑ A software upgrade represents a major change to the existing code, which may or may not be offered free from a vendor and may or may not be comprehensive enough to substitute for the original program. An upgrade to the client program replaces the existing client program so as to add functionality and fix bugs found in the previous version.

13

❑ Before upgrading client software, carefully read the instructions that accompany the upgrade to find out how best to apply it, whether it depends on any previous upgrades, whether it requires any special preparation, and how its changes will affect users. Client upgrades typically overwrite some system files (such as .dll files) on the workstation, so their installation may affect other programs adversely.

❑ Like client upgrades, application upgrades consist of modifications to all or part of a program that are designed to enhance functionality or fix problems with the software. Application upgrades, however, affect software programs shared by clients on the network.

❑ Perhaps the most critical type of software upgrade you'll perform comprises an upgrade to your network operating system. This effort usually involves significant, potentially drastic, changes to the operation of your servers and clients. As such, it requires plenty of forethought, product research, and rigorous testing before you implement it. In fact, for any network with more than a few users, you should create and follow a project plan for this undertaking.

❑ The process of upgrading a network operating system should include research, proposal, evaluation, training, pre-implementation, implementation, and post-implementation phases.

❑ If the software upgrade you perform causes problems to your existing system(s), you should know how to reverse the process. The restoration of a previous version of software after an attempted upgrade is known as backleveling.

❑ Hardware and physical plant changes may be required when your network has problems. More often, however, they are performed as part of a move to increase capacity, improve performance, or add functionality to the network.

❑ Research, evaluate, and test any unfamiliar piece of equipment you intend to add or upgrade on your network, even if it is manufactured by a vendor that supplies much of your other hardware. The process of implementing a hardware upgrade is very similar to that of carrying out a software upgrade, including notifying users and preparing to bring the system down during the change.

❑ Each type of device you add or upgrade on the network will have its own preparation and implementation requirements. Knowing exactly how to handle the changes will require a close read of the manufacturer's instructions as well as some experience with the type of networking equipment to be installed.

❑ A networked workstation is perhaps the simplest device to add. It directly affects only one or a few users but does not alter network access for anyone else.

❑ A networked printer is easily added to your network. Adding one is slightly more complex than adding a networked workstation because of its unique configuration process and because it is shared. Although it affects multiple users, a networked printer does not typically perform a mission-critical function in an organization, so the length of time required for its installation does not affect productivity.

❑ If you are adding a new hub, you do not have to worry about down time or notification of users. If you are upgrading or swapping out an existing hub, you must notify the affected users. The upgrade or swap will cause down time and may require that you perform it during off-hours. In addition, you must consider the traffic and addressing implications of adding or upgrading a hub.

❑ Installing a new server will require that you consider not only the hardware and connectivity but also the network operating system implications of the new server. Even if you are adding a server that will not be used immediately, you need to plan for its addition and preferably install it while the network has little traffic. Typically, a server addition or upgrade (unless it is the replacement of a minor component) requires a great deal of foresight and planning.

❑ Switches and routers are complex additions or changes to a network design for several reasons. First, they can be physically disruptive, often requiring the installation of new racks or other support frames in your telecommunications room. Second, they affect many users—perhaps all users—on a network. You should notify all users on the network about the impending change, even if you don't think that they will be affected. A router or switch can have unintended effects on segments of the network other than the one it services. In addition, you should plan at least weeks in advance for switch or router changes and expect at least several hours of down time.

◻ Cabling upgrades (unless they involve the replacement of a single faulty patch cable) may require significant planning and time to implement, depending on the size of your network. Because an upgrade of this magnitude will affect all users on the network, you should upgrade the network in phases.

◻ The most comprehensive and complex upgrade involving network hardware is a backbone upgrade. The network backbone serves as the main conduit for data on LANs and WANs, connecting major routers, servers, and/or switches. A backbone upgrade not only requires a great deal of time to plan, but also the efforts of several staff members (and possibly contractors) and a significant investment.

◻ A variety of needs may drive backbone upgrades: for faster throughput, a physical move or renovation, a more reliable network, greater security, more consistent standards, support of a new application, or greater cost-effectiveness.

◻ Because backbone upgrades are expensive and time-consuming, the first step in approaching such a project is to justify it. The next step is to determine what kind of backbone design to implement. To make this decision, you must analyze the future capacity needs of your network, determine whether you want a distributed or collapsed backbone, decide whether you need to rely on switches or routers, decide whether to use subnetting and to what extent, and so on. After you have designed your backbone upgrade, you should develop a project plan to accomplish it.

◻ You should provide a way to reverse the hardware upgrade and replace it with the old hardware. If you are upgrading a component in a device, keep the old component safe (for example, keep NICs in static-resistant containers) and nearby. Not only might you need to put it back in the device, but you might also need to refer to it for information.

◻ Each of the networking trends observed today provides users at least one of the following advantages: faster data processing and transmission, more comprehensive integration, open standards, greater accessibility for a more diverse population, or smarter devices (which increases the automation of tasks, usually saving time and money).

◻ Some of the current trends will raise greater concerns for security. As systems adopt the same (open) standards, they become more vulnerable to hackers who can easily figure out the code after mastering similar systems. As accessibility increases, security threats also increase, because the network offers more entry opportunities for hackers.

◻ The best way to evaluate networking technology is to test it in your organization. That way you can find out how it operates in your networking environment—with your equipment, applications, and users. Another good option is to discuss your needs with a reputable consulting firm that has implemented the same technology at other organizations. Discuss the project not only with the consultants who performed the upgrade work, but also with the customer that is currently using the new technology. If possible, visit facilities that have already adopted the technology.

KEY TERMS

asset management — A system for identifying and tracking the hardware and software on a network.

backleveling — The process of reverting to a previous version of a software program after attempting to upgrade it.

baselining — The practice of measuring and recording a network's current state of operation.

bug — A flaw in software or hardware that causes it to malfunction.

patch — A correction, improvement, or enhancement to part of a software program, often distributed at no charge by software vendors to fix a bug in their code or to add slightly more functionality.

service pack — A significant patch to Windows NT or 2000 Server software.

upgrade — A major change to the existing code in a software program, which may or may not be offered free from a vendor and may or may not be comprehensive enough to substitute for the original program.

REVIEW QUESTIONS

1. Which of the following is *not* a benefit of a baselining tool?

   a. It helps predict the impact of future device additions.

   b. It helps predict bandwidth needs.

   c. It helps determine how much traffic currently travels over the network.

   d. It helps determine where additional WAN nodes ought to be located.

2. Name three network characteristics that might belong in a baseline measurement.

3. If you were planning to purchase a baselining tool for your network, which of the following is one factor you would *not* use to evaluate your options?

   a. interoperability with word-processing applications

   b. compatibility with network hardware and software

   c. measurement of data critical to your network's performance

   d. ease of use

4. What hardware-related data might you record in an asset management system and why?

5. Some asset management programs can automatically discover all devices on a network. True or False?

6. Which of the following times would be the best time to install a patch to your network operating system?

    a. 7:00 A.M. on Monday

    b. 6:00 P.M. on Wednesday

    c. 1:00 A.M. on Sunday

    d. 2:00 P.M. on Friday

7. How does a software patch differ from an upgrade?

    a. A patch is more comprehensive than an upgrade.

    b. A patch is more current than an upgrade.

    c. A patch only fixes bugs, while an upgrade fixes bugs and upgrades old files.

    d. A patch usually changes fewer files than an upgrade.

8. Under what circumstances should network administrators inform users of software changes?

    a. always

    b. when the change might affect applications or utilities relied on by the users

    c. when the change might result in the addition of an application

    d. when the change might affect how users are added to the system

9. Name five considerations that you should address before undertaking a network operating system upgrade.

10. When considering a major upgrade, such as a network operating system or backbone upgrade, you should depend on a manufacturer's Web site materials to determine whether the upgrade is necessary and useful. True or False?

11. What is another name for reversing a software upgrade?

    a. uninstalling

    b. backleveling

    c. reverting

    d. undoing

12. Which of the following is the best way to reverse a network operating system upgrade?

    a. Reinstall the previous version of the operating system.

    b. Uninstall the upgrade.

    c. Remove the upgrade software folder from the server.

    d. Restore the server's software and configuration from a backup.

13

13. Name three reasons to perform a hardware upgrade on a network.

14. Which of the following changes probably requires the most planning?

    a. modifying a router's access list

    b. upgrading the network client on a department's workstations

    c. replacing a router with a switch

    d. applying a patch to a networked application

15. You can assume that installing a switch from one manufacturer is similar to installing a hub from the same manufacturer. True or False?

16. Why are cabling and backbone upgrades often implemented in phases?

17. What is the first step in a backbone upgrade?

    a. Justify it.

    b. Create a project plan.

    c. Determine its effect on users.

    d. Determine its effect on routing traffic.

18. Name two good reasons to perform a backbone upgrade.

19. Which of the following networking trends makes security a greater concern for network managers?

    a. greater network accessibility

    b. faster devices

    c. smarter devices

    d. increased use of wireless technology

20. Which of the following is the best way to research a new networking technology you are considering adapting?

    a. Ask friends about it.

    b. Read articles about it.

    c. Test it in your organization.

    d. Based on what you read, create a hypothetical scenario for the technology in your environment.

HANDS-ON PROJECTS

Even though you may not be in a position to upgrade your company's entire network backbone, you will probably have to upgrade software and hardware components on a regular basis. From these smaller upgrades and the troubles you encounter in their implementation, you can learn about more complex types of upgrades. In the next three Projects, you will perform minor software and hardware upgrades and use the information you learn to prepare for a hypothetical major network upgrade. For these exercises, you will need a Windows 98 or Windows 2000 Professional computer with Web access that is connected to a Windows 2000 server. You will need administrator-equivalent rights on the server. The server should have at least 710 MB of hard disk space free. It should not have Service Pack 2 installed, but you should have CDs containing this patch. You should also have a Windows 2000 Server CD and a blank floppy disk. For the hardware upgrade exercise (Project 13-2), you should have a memory chip compatible with your server's hardware and space in your server to accept additional memory.

Project 13-1

In this exercise, you will install Service Pack 2 (SP2) to a working Windows 2000 server, paying attention to the patch's effects on users and applications.

1. Before you install SP2 on your Windows 2000 server, you need to find out what it does and how it will change your system. Search Microsoft's Web site to find the features of SP2 (you will find the link at **www.microsoft.com/windows2000/ downloads/default.asp**). On a separate piece of paper, list five changes made by this patch. What types of improvements do the changes entail?

2. Now that you know what SP2 is supposed to achieve, research it a little more to find out whether it will be truly beneficial to your network. You can do this by searching through technical trade magazine articles to find out what others have said about SP4. Point your browser to these URLs: **www.techweb.com/search/advancedsearch** and **www.zdnet.com**. Perform searches on the term **service pack 2** at both sites. If you have the option, search the magazine sites for the term according to its relevance in the article, rather than according to the date of the article (for example, at the Techweb site, deselect the **Sort results by date** option). Note that you may have to sift through the articles to find one that concentrates on Windows 2000 SP2 (as opposed to Windows NT SP2). Does anything in the articles you find make you skeptical about performing the upgrade? Why?

3. Log on to your Windows 2000 server as an administrator equivalent and insert the SP2 CD.

4. Find the instructions for installing the service pack on the CD (in the readmesp.htm file) and study them before beginning the installation.

5. Close all applications currently running on the server.

6. To disable all logins to the Windows 2000 server, click **Start**, point to **Settings**, click **Control Panel**. The Control Panel window opens. Double-click **Administrative Tools**, then double-click **Services**. In the list of Services, right-click **Server** and choose **Stop** from the shortcut menu. Click **Yes** to confirm that you want to disable logins, then close the Service console and Control Panel.

7. In this step you will create an emergency repair disk to ensure that you have a good copy of the server's configuration in case the software installation (or later backleveling) causes problems. To create an emergency repair disk, click **Start**, point to **Programs**, point to **Accessories**, point to **System Tools**, then click **Backup**.

13

8. The Backup window opens. Click **Emergency Repair Disk**.

9. The Emergency Repair Diskette dialog box appears. Check the check box that indicates you also want to back up the Windows registry to the hard disk. Insert a blank, formatted, floppy diskette into your floppy disk drive, then click **OK** to continue.

10. Wait while the system data is copied to your disk.

11. Once the configuration files are copied to your floppy disk, click **OK** to close the Repair Disk Utility, then close the Backup utility. Now that you have a good copy of your server's configuration, you can install SP2 by following the instructions that came with it.

12. Start the SP2 installation, following the prompts on your screen. At the Begin Installation screen, choose the **Backup files necessary to uninstall this Service Pack at a later time** option. You should always create an uninstall folder when you install service packs. In the case of SP2, you need 270 MB of space to create the uninstall folder.

13. After the service pack has finished installing, restart the Windows 2000 server and remove the service pack CD from the CD-ROM drive. The Windows 2000 Server service will restart to enable users to log in.

14. Log on to the server as the administrator. Do you receive any messages notifying you that the service pack was installed or that certain features have changed?

Project 13-2

In this exercise, you will add memory to your Windows 2000 server. If you are familiar with PC technology, you know that each machine has its own physical memory requirements. Figure 13-2 shows some popular types of memory modules (or chips).

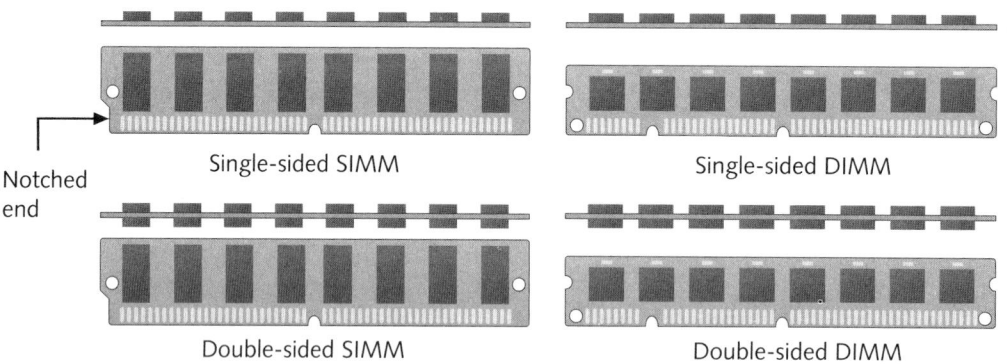

Figure 13-2   Popular memory chips

1. Log on to the Windows 2000 server as the administrator.

2. Click **Start**, point to **Programs**, point to **Administrative Tools**, then click **Computer Management**. The Computer Management window opens.

3. Double-click the **System Information** icon. Click the **System Summary** folder.

4. The system information appears in the right-hand pane of the Computer Management window. Note the amount of Total Physical Memory installed in your server.

5. Before taking down the server to perform a memory upgrade, you must ensure that no users are currently connected. At the Computer Management console, double-click the **Shared Folders** folder. Then double-click the **Sessions** folder. Assuming that no users are connected, you can shut down the server. Otherwise, you could use the **Action – Disconnect All Sessions** option from the main menu to terminate these users' connections. Close the Computer Management console.

6. Click **Start**, then click **Shut down** to shut down the server. Make certain that the Shut down option is selected in the drop-down dialog box, then click **OK**.

7. Turn off the server and unplug it. Detach all cables, including the monitor, network, mouse, and keyboard connectors.

8. Wear a static-dissipating wristband and use a static guard mat while you open the server's casing. Because each computer is different, you should consult with your instructor to find out how to remove the casing.

9. Once you have opened the computer, insert the new memory chip by following your instructor's instructions.

10. When you have successfully installed the chip, reattach the server's cover and reconnect the power, keyboard, network, mouse, and monitor cables.

11. Turn the server on.

12. When prompted, log on to Windows 2000 as the administrator.

13. Repeat steps 2 through 4 to find out how much memory the server now has.

13

Project 13-3

In this exercise, you will reverse, or uninstall, the service pack that you installed in Project 13-1. Because it is not uncommon to have to uninstall a service pack, you should always create an uninstall folder. An uninstall folder contains files that can be used to reverse (or uninstall) a patch installation or upgrade. Creating an uninstall folder is an option during the installation of a service pack. Note that you should never attempt to uninstall software (especially on a Windows-based system) by deleting the new software from the system (for example, by dragging the software's folder to the Recycle Bin). Instead, you must follow proper uninstall procedures to ensure that the software's removal will not cause harm.

1. Log on to your Windows NT 2000 Server as an administrator (if you aren't already).

2. Click **Start**, point to **Settings**, click **Control Panel**, then double-click the **Add/Remove Programs** icon.

3. Select **Windows 2000 Service Pack 2**, then click **Change/Remove**. Click **Yes** to confirm the uninstall.

4. After the removal is complete, you will be prompted to restart the server to make the changes effective. Choose **Yes**.

After removing the service pack, you will have returned all applications and services to their previous state, for better or for worse. Note that the uninstall process will not remove the newer security files installed by SP2. If you want to reinstall SP2 in the future, you will need to create another uninstall folder.

Project 13-4

In this project, you will investigate one of the most popular network baselining tools—Concord Communications' Network Health. Rather than installing the program (which is expensive), you can view Concord Communications' online demo for its product. This demo includes graphs of network performance for an imaginary LAN/WAN environment. This exercise requires a workstation with Internet access and a Web browser.

1. Point your browser to the following URL:
   www.concord.com/products/demos/demos.htm

2. Select the Service Providers Scenario by clicking the arrow to the right of this product's description. The Service Providers Demo opens in a new browser window.

3. The Concord Communications' Network Health demo page opens. Read about the scenarios and follow the instructions in the yellow balloons to view different types of network data that this product tracks.

4. Once you reach the "At-a-Glance" report for a WAN link, examine the different data graphs that describe network activity over a link. When is the total bandwidth utilization highest? What is the relationship between bandwidth coming in (to the service provider's site) over the link and the bandwidth going out? What is the relationship between the number of bytes per second and the bandwidth graphs?

5. Continue with the demonstration and examine the page of graphs pertaining to the Web server. Is there any correlation between the database's use of the Web system's resources and the bandwidth levels on the link? Why might this be so?

6. Continue to investigate the Network Health demos. While doing so, consider the advantages and disadvantages of having so much information available to network administrators. Also, consider what types of reports would be important to a company that uses its network for e-commerce versus a company that uses a WAN to perform videoconferencing.

CASE PROJECTS

1. You work as one of five networking engineers in a large insurance company with 500 small offices located across the United States. The headquarters, where you work, relies on 10 Windows NT 4.0 servers with 128 MB RAM, Pentium II 333 processors, and redundant disk arrays; roughly half of these disk arrays provide remote access for field users, and the other half provide applications to headquarters. You have been migrating most of your routers to switches this year, and you run an Ethernet 100 Mbps LAN at headquarters. All of the 500 field offices have their own Windows NT servers, but the remote users often complain of poor support and slow or unreliable access to headquarters. Managers are also concerned about security and a need to update the company's intranet. Your manager is currently developing next year's budget. She tells you that she has more than $500,000 to spend on networking upgrades, both hardware and software. She asks your opinion about which items to include in the budget. How would you research your recommendations? What factors would influence you? What additional information should you gather? What kinds of immediate upgrades would you suggest, and which ones are optional or could wait another year?

2. Because one of your suggestions was to upgrade the server hardware, you have been asked to work with a database programmer to develop a customized asset management tool. This tool should track not only the basic facts about your hardware, but also the lease periods and the maintenance needs. Write a one-page request for proposal that will enable a developer to understand your needs. Explain the project's goals and indicate why you included the requirements, time frames, and necessary tasks that you did. Also, describe how the developer and you can make this tool easy to use and adaptable to future needs.

3. You have worked with a friend to upgrade the network operating system on a NetWare 4.11 server to NetWare 5.1 at his small auto repair office. His LAN consists of 1 server and 15 users who rely on the server for billing, customer service, word processing, and Internet access. You helped your friend follow the correct procedure of researching the upgrade, informing the users, creating a backup, and implementing the upgrade. You and he work from 6:00 P.M. to midnight performing the upgrade. When you start your testing at midnight, it looks as though the billing system doesn't work with the new operating system. The staff will begin coming to work at 5:00 A.M. What do you do, how do you do it, and why?

13

ENSURING INTEGRITY AND AVAILABILITY

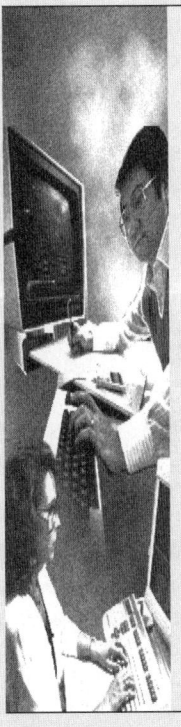

ON THE JOB

I work at a weekly local newspaper with a circulation of about 50,000. Although I'm not an IT professional, I usually end up taking care of our computers, answering technical questions, and picking consultants to help with our network. Our internal network is small, with about 30 workstations connected over Ethernet. But our connection to the outside world—the Web, e-mail, printers, and other news agencies—is really our lifeblood. Without our WAN connections, we could not produce a paper.

A few years ago I hired a consultant to make sure our WAN connections were optimized. He decided we needed a DSL link to a regional DSL provider. The DSL provider also supplied Web hosting and e-mail services for us, all for an attractive price. This worked well for a long time, which means that I didn't even have to think about the WAN. But one day, without notice, our DSL provider went out of business. Suddenly we lost all contact with the outside world. We could not retrieve stories from our freelance writers, nor could we issue files to our printer. In fact, the staff couldn't even communicate electronically with each other. And we had a paper to get out in two days.

Needless to say, I did not call the same consultant who arranged for our original WAN installation. Instead, I called a larger network consulting firm in town that had experience with high availability and fault-tolerant networking. They quickly provided our newspaper with an emergency WAN link, in order to meet our immediate deadlines. Then they taught us how to keep data and connections always available. Among other things, we now have two connections to the Internet, each of which uses a different ISP.

Paige DeYoung
Cormier Consolidated News

As networks take on more of the burden of transporting and storing a day's work, you need to pay increasing attention to the risks involved. You can never assume that data are safe on the network until you have taken explicit measures to protect the information. In this book, you have learned about the architecture of a robust enterprise-wide network as well as hardware, network operating systems, and network troubleshooting. But all the best equipment and software cannot ensure that server hard drives will never fail or that a malicious employee won't sabotage your network.

The topic of protecting data covers a lot of ground, from fault-tolerant servers to security cameras in the computer room. This chapter provides a broad overview of measures that you can take to ensure that your data remain safe. Undoubtedly, these issues will continue to evolve quickly as networks become more open and ubiquitous. If you are interested in specializing in fault tolerance, for example, you can read entire books on the topic. The far-reaching topic of network security is covered in the next chapter.

WHAT ARE INTEGRITY AND AVAILABILITY?

Before learning how to ensure integrity and availability, you should fully understand what these terms mean. **Integrity** refers to the soundness of a network's programs, data, services, devices, and connections. To ensure a network's integrity, you must protect it from anything that might render it unusable. Closely related to the concept of integrity is availability. **Availability** of a file or system refers to how consistently and reliably it can be accessed by authorized personnel. For example, a server that allows staff to log on and use its programs and data 99.99% of the time is considered to be highly available. To ensure availability, you need not only a well-planned and well-configured network, but also data backups, redundant devices, and protection from malicious intruders who could potentially immobilize the network.

A number of phenomena may compromise both integrity and availability, including security breaches, natural disasters (such as tornadoes, floods, hurricanes, and ice storms), malicious intruders, power flaws, and human error. Every network administrator should consider these possibilities when designing a sound network. You can readily imagine the importance of integrity and availability of data in a hospital, for example, where the network not only stores patient records but also provides quick medical reference material, video displays for surgical cameras, and perhaps even control of critical care monitors.

Even if you don't have sophisticated hardware and software to address availability and integrity, as network administrator you can and should take several precautions. This section will remind you of common-sense approaches to data integrity and availability, such as properly restricting file access and developing an enterprise-wide security policy. Later in this chapter, you will learn about more specific or formal (and potentially more expensive) approaches to data protection.

If you have ever supported computer users, you know that they sometimes unintentionally harm their own data, applications, software configurations, or even hardware. Networks may also be intentionally harmed by users unless network administrators take precautionary measures and pay regular, close attention to systems and networks so as to protect them. Although you can't predict every type of vulnerability, you can take measures to guard against most damaging events. Following are some general guidelines for protecting your network:

- *Prevent anyone other than a network administrator from opening or changing the system files.* Pay attention to the rights assigned to regular users (including the groups "users" or "everyone"). The use of rights to restrict network access to servers will be discussed in depth in Chapter 15. For now, bear in mind that the worst consequence of applying overly stringent file restrictions is a temporary inconvenience to a few users. In contrast, the worst consequence of applying overly lenient file restrictions could be a network disaster.

- *Monitor the network for unauthorized access or changes.* You can install programs that routinely check whether and when the files you've specified (for example, autoexec.ncf on a NetWare server) have changed. Such monitoring programs are typically inexpensive and easy to customize. They may even enable the system to page or e-mail you when a system file changes. In addition, you can monitor the network for unauthorized access to devices such as routers or switches. This practice, called **intrusion detection**, is described in more detail later in this chapter.

- *Record authorized system changes in a change management system.* In Chapters 12 and 13, you learned about the importance of change management. Recording system changes in a change management system will enable you and your colleagues to understand what's happening to your network and protect it from harm. For example, suppose that a Windows 2000 server hangs up when you attempt to restart it. Before launching into troubleshooting techniques that may create more problems and reduce the availability of the system, you could review the change management log. It might indicate that a colleague recently installed a new service pack. With this information in hand, you could focus on the service pack as the probable source of the problem.

- *Install redundant components.* The term **redundancy** refers to a situation in which more than one component is installed and ready to use for storing, processing, or transporting data. To maintain high availability, you should ensure that critical network elements, such as your WAN connection to the Internet or your single file server's hard disk, are redundant. Some types of redundancy require large investments, so your organization should weigh the risks of losing connectivity or data against the cost of adding expensive duplicate components such as data links or high-end servers.

- *Perform regular health checks on the network.* Prevention is the best weapon against network down time. By implementing a network monitoring program such as those discussed in Chapter 13, you can anticipate problems before they affect availability or integrity. For example, if your network monitor alerts you to rapidly rising utilization on a critical network segment, you can analyze the network to discover where the problem lies and perhaps fix it before it takes down the segment.

14

- *Monitor system performance, error logs, and the system log book regularly.* By keeping track of system errors and trends in performance, you have a better chance of correcting problems before they cause a hard disk failure and potentially damage your system files. By default, all network operating systems keep error logs. It's important that you know where these error logs reside on your server and understand how to interpret them.

- *Keep backups, boot disks, and emergency repair disks current and available.* If your file system or critical boot files become corrupted by a system crash, you can use the emergency or boot disks to recover the system. Otherwise, you may need to reinstall the software before you will be able to start the system. If you ever face the prospect of recovering from a system loss or disaster, you will need to recover in the quickest manner possible. For this effort, you will need not only backup devices, but also a backup strategy tailored to your environment.

- *Implement and enforce security and disaster recovery policies.* Everyone in your organization should know what he or she is allowed to do on the network. For example, if you decide that it's too risky for employees to download games off the Internet because of the potential for virus infection, you may inform them of a ban on downloading games. You might enforce this policy by restricting users' ability to create or change files (such as executable files) that are copied to the workstation during the downloading of games. Making such decisions and communicating them to staff should be part of your security policy. Likewise, everyone in your organization should be familiar with your disaster recovery plan, which should detail your strategy for bringing the network back to functionality in case of an unexpected failure. Although such policies take time to develop and may be difficult to enforce, they can directly affect your network's availability and integrity.

These measures are merely first steps to ensuring network integrity and availability, but they are essential. The following sections describe what types of policies, hardware, and software you can implement to achieve availability and integrity, beginning with virus detection and prevention.

VIRUSES

Strictly speaking, a **virus** is a program that replicates itself so as to infect more computers, either through network connections or through floppy disks passed among users. A virus may damage files or systems, or it may simply annoy users by flashing messages or pictures on the screen or by causing the computer to beep. In fact, some viruses cause no harm and can remain unnoticed on a system forever.

Many other unwanted and potentially destructive programs are mistakenly called viruses. For example, a program that disguises itself as something useful but actually harms your system is called a **Trojan horse**, after the famous wooden horse in which soldiers were hidden.

Because Trojan horses do not replicate themselves, they are not technically viruses. An example of a Trojan horse is an executable file that someone sends you over the Internet, promising that the executable will install a great new game, when in fact it reformats your hard disk.

In this section, you will learn about the different types of viruses and other malicious programs that may infect your network, their methods of distribution, and, most importantly, protection against them. Viruses can infect computers running any type of operating system—Macintosh, NetWare, Windows, or UNIX—at any time. As a network administrator, you must take measures to guard against them.

Types of Viruses

Many thousands of viruses exist, although only a relatively small number cause the majority of virus-related damage. Viruses can be classified into different categories based on where they reside on a computer and how they propagate themselves. Often, creators of viruses apply slight variations to their original viruses to make them undetectable by antivirus programs. The result is a host of related, albeit different viruses. The makers of antivirus software must then update their checking programs to recognize the new variations, and the virus creators may again alter their viruses to render them undetectable. This cycle continues, ad infinitum. No matter what their variation, all viruses belong to one of the categories described below:

- *Boot sector viruses*—The most common types of viruses, **boot sector viruses** reside on the boot sector of a floppy disk and become transferred to the partition sector or the DOS boot sector on a hard disk. The only way to infect a computer with a boot sector virus is to attempt to start the computer from an infected floppy disk. This event may happen unintentionally if a floppy disk is left in the drive when a machine starts.

  For example, one afternoon a colleague may give you a floppy disk with a spreadsheet that you need to edit and return to him. You put the floppy into your disk drive and open the spreadsheet file. So far, the virus in the floppy disk's boot sector has gone unnoticed. You begin to edit the spreadsheet, but get sidetracked by a critical file server problem. It's six o'clock by the time you have fixed the file server, and you're late for your evening cooking class, so you close all programs, turn off your machine, and rush out the door. The next morning, you switch on your machine and walk away to refill your coffee cup. Because you left the floppy disk in your disk drive, your computer attempts to start from the floppy disk drive. It loads the first sector into memory and executes it (normally, this sector contains a program written by Microsoft to load DOS or, if it can't find DOS on the disk, to tell you so). Because the floppy drive is infected with a boot sector virus, however, it executes the virus program instead. The virus installs itself on your computer's hard disk, replacing the hard disk's boot sector record. Until you disinfect your computer, the virus will propagate to every floppy disk to which you write information.

14

Boot sector viruses are very common in part because most users don't understand how they work, and because floppy disks are frequently passed from user to user without any virus checking. Examples of boot sector viruses include "Stoned," "Boot-437," "Goldbug," "Lilith," "Jerusalem," and "Cascade." The Stoned virus, for example, originated in New Zealand in 1988; since then, a multitude of variations on it have been distributed under different names. Its main symptom of infection is a message that appears upon starting the computer, announcing that "This PC is now stoned." In addition, boot sector viruses often make it impossible for the file system to access at least some of the workstation's files.

- *Macro viruses*—**Macro viruses** are newer types of viruses that take the form of a word-processing or spreadsheet program macro, which may be executed as the user works with a word-processing or spreadsheet program. Macro viruses were the first type of virus to infect data files rather than executable files. Because data files are more apt to be shared among users, and because macro viruses are typically easier to write than executable viruses, macro viruses have quickly become prevalent. Although the earliest versions of macro viruses proved annoying but not harmful, currently circulating macro viruses may threaten data files.

Because macro viruses work under different applications, they can travel between computers that use different operating systems. For example, you might send a Microsoft Word document as an attachment to an e-mail message, or give it to someone on a floppy disk. If that document contains a macro virus, when the recipient opens the document, the macro runs, and all future documents created or saved by that program will be infected. Examples of macro viruses include "W97M/Ethan.A," "Laroux," "Trasher," "Caligula," and "Jedi." Symptoms of macro virus infection vary widely but may include missing options from application menus; damaged, changed, or missing data files; or strange pop-up messages that appear when you use an application such as Microsoft's Word or Excel.

- *File-infected viruses*—**File-infected viruses** attach themselves to executable files. When the infected executable file runs, the virus copies itself to memory. Later, the virus will attach itself to other executable files. Some file-infected viruses can attach themselves to other programs even while their "host" executable runs a process in the background, such as a printer service or screen saver program. Because they stay in memory while you continue to work on your computer, these viruses can have devastating consequences, infecting numerous programs and requiring you to not only disinfect your computer, but also reinstall virtually all software. Examples of file-infected viruses include "Tequila," "Concept," "Anxiety," "Tentacle," and "Cabanas." Symptoms of a virus infection may include damaged program files, inexplicable file size increases, changed icons for programs, strange messages that appear when you attempt to run a program, or the inability to run a program.

- *Network viruses*—**Network viruses** propagate themselves via network protocols, commands, messaging programs, and data links. Although all viruses could theoretically travel across network connections, network viruses are specially designed to take advantage of network vulnerabilities. For example, a network virus may attach itself to FTP transactions to and from your Web server. Another type of network virus may spread through Microsoft Exchange messages only.

  Because network access has become more sophisticated over the last decade, few network viruses have had the opportunity to thrive. Examples of network viruses include "Homer," "WDEF," and "Remote Explorer." Because network viruses are characterized by their transmission method, their symptoms may include almost any type of anomaly, ranging from strange pop-up messages to file damage.

- *Worms*—**Worms** are not technically viruses, but rather programs that run independently and travel between computers and across networks. They may be transmitted by any type of file transfer, including e-mail. Worms do not alter other programs in the same way that viruses do, but they may carry viruses. Because they can transport (and hide) viruses, you should be concerned about picking up worms when you exchange files from the Internet or through floppy disks. Examples of worms include "W32/Roach@MM," "SunOS/BoxPoison," and "W32/Mona." Symptoms of worm infection may include almost any type of anomaly, ranging from strange pop-up messages to file damage.

- *Trojan horse*—As mentioned earlier, a Trojan horse (sometimes simply called a "Trojan") is not actually a virus, but rather a program that claims to do something useful but instead harms the computer or system. Trojan horses range from being nuisances to causing significant system destruction. Most virus-checking programs will recognize known Trojan horses and eradicate them. The best way to guard against Trojan horses, however, is to refrain from downloading an executable file whose origins you can't confirm.

  Suppose, for example, that you needed to download a new driver for a NIC on your network. Rather than going to a generic "network support site" on the Internet, you should download the file from the NIC manufacturer's Web site. Most importantly, never run an executable file that has been sent to you over the Internet as an attachment to a mail message whose sender or origins you cannot verify.

  Examples of Trojan horses include "BackDoor-G2.svr," "*VBS/FreeLink@MM*," "Sadcase," "Perl-WSFT-Exploit," and "DOS/Blitz." One Trojan horse program, "Antigen," disguises itself as an antivirus program; when executed, it scans the computer's hard disk for personal information such as network IDs, passwords, and telephone numbers. It then compiles this information and mails it to a specific e-mail address.

14

Virus Characteristics

Viruses that belong to any of the preceding categories may have additional characteristics that make them harder to detect and eliminate. Some of these characteristics are discussed below:

- **Encryption**—Some viruses are encrypted to prevent detection. As you will learn in the following section, most virus-scanning software searches files for a recognizable string of characters that identify the virus. If the virus is encrypted, it may thwart the antivirus program's attempts to detect it.

- **Stealth**—Some viruses hide themselves to prevent detection. Typically, stealth viruses disguise themselves as legitimate programs or replace part of a legitimate program's code with their destructive code.

- **Polymorphism**—Polymorphic viruses change their characteristics (such as the arrangement of their bytes, size, and internal instructions) every time they are transferred to a new system, making them harder to identify. Some polymorphic viruses use complicated algorithms and incorporate nonsensical commands to achieve their changes. Polymorphic viruses are considered to be the most sophisticated and potentially dangerous type of virus.

- **Time-dependence**—Time-dependent viruses are programmed to activate on a particular date. These types of viruses, also known as "time bombs," can remain dormant and harmless until their activation date arrives. Like any other type of virus, time-dependent viruses may have destructive effects or may cause some innocuous event periodically. For example, viruses in the "Time" family cause a PC's speaker to beep approximately once per hour.

Hundreds of new viruses are unleashed on the world's computers each month. Although it is impossible to keep abreast of every virus in circulation, you should at least know where you can find out more information about viruses. An excellent resource for learning about new viruses, their characteristics, and ways to get rid of them is McAfee's Virus Information Library at *vil.mcafee.com/default.asp*.

Virus Protection

Now that you know about the different types of viruses, you may think that you can simply install a virus-scanning program on your network and move on to the next issue. In fact, virus protection involves more than just installing antivirus software. It requires choosing the most appropriate antivirus program for your environment, monitoring the network, continually updating the antivirus program, and educating users. In addition, you should draft and enforce an antivirus policy for your organization.

Antivirus Software

Even if a user doesn't immediately notice a virus on his or her system, the virus will generally leave evidence of itself, whether by changing the operation of the machine or by announcing its signature characteristics in the virus code. Although the latter can be detected only via antivirus software, users can typically detect the former changes without any special software. For example, you may suspect a virus on your system if any of the following symptoms appear:

- Unexplained increases in file sizes

- Programs (such as Microsoft Word) launching, running, or exiting more slowly than usual

- Unusual error messages appearing without probable cause

- Significant, unexpected loss of system memory

- Fluctuations in display quality

Often, however, you will not notice a virus until it has already damaged your files.

Although virus programmers have become more sophisticated in disguising their viruses (for example, using encryption and polymorphism), antivirus software programmers have kept pace with them. The antivirus software you choose for your network should at least perform the following functions:

- It should detect viruses through **signature scanning**, a comparison of a file's content with known virus signatures (that is, the unique identifying characteristics in the code) in a signature database. This signature database must be frequently updated so that the software can detect new viruses as they emerge. Updates can usually be downloaded from the antivirus software vendor's Web site.

- It should detect viruses through **integrity checking**, a method of comparing current characteristics of files and disks against an archived version of these characteristics to discover any changes. The most common example of integrity checking involves the use of a checksum, though this tactic may not prove effective against viruses with stealth capabilities.

- It should detect viruses by monitoring unexpected file changes or virus-like behaviors.

- It should receive regular updates and modifications from a centralized network console. The vendor should provide free upgrades on a regular (at least monthly) basis, plus technical support.

- It should consistently report only valid viruses, rather than reporting "false alarms." Scanning techniques that attempt to identify viruses by discovering "virus-like" behavior, also known as **heuristic scanning**, are the most fallible and most likely to emit false alarms. As you might imagine, using an antivirus package that detects more viruses than are actually present can be not only annoying, but also a waste of time.

14

Occasionally, shrink-wrapped, off-the-shelf software will ship with viruses on its disks. Therefore, it is always a good idea to scan authorized software from known sources just as you would scan software from unknown sources.

Your implementation of antivirus software will depend on your computing environment's needs. For example, you may use a desktop security program on every computer on the network that prevents users from copying executable files to their hard disks or to network drives. In this case, it may be unnecessary to implement a program that continually scans each machine; in fact, this approach may be undesirable because the continual scanning may adversely impact performance. On the other hand, if you are the network administrator for a student computer lab where potentially thousands of different users will bring their own disks for use on the computers, you will want to scan the machines thoroughly at least once a day and perhaps more often.

When installing antivirus software on a network, one of your most important decisions is where to put it. If you install antivirus software only on every desktop, you have addressed the most likely point of entry, but ignored the most important files that might be infected—those on the server. If the antivirus software resides on the server and checks every file and transaction, you will protect important files but slow your network performance considerably. Likewise, if you put antivirus software on firewalls and routers, your network will experience performance problems, bringing all network communication to a crawl. How can you find a balance between sufficient protection and minimal impact on performance? Depending on your network infrastructure, you may want to implement antivirus software that scans each desktop once daily, as well as scans new files on the e-mail server, as those locations are the most likely places for viruses to enter. You should also ensure that file servers are scanned regularly, although continual may be unnecessary.

Obviously, the antivirus package you choose should be compatible with your network and desktop operating systems. Popular antivirus packages include Network Associate's (McAfee's) VirusScan, Computer Associates' Innoculan AntiVirus, Norman Virus Control, and Symantec's (Norton's) AntiVirus.

In addition to using specialized antivirus software to guard against virus infection, you may find that your applications can help identify viruses. Microsoft's Word and Excel programs, for example, will warn you when you attempt to open a file that contains macros. You then have the option of disabling the macros (thereby preventing any macro viruses from working when you open the file) or allowing the macros to remain usable. In general, it's a good idea to disable the macros in a file that you have received from someone else, at least until after you have checked the file for viruses with your virus scanning software.

Antivirus Policies

Antivirus software alone will not keep your network safe from viruses. You also need to implement policies that limit the potential for users to introduce viruses to their workstations and to the network. The importance of these policies will increase as a network grows larger and more accessible and therefore becomes more susceptible to viruses.

To understand why, think of a day-care center attended by only two children with one adult supervising. These three people will bring and share whatever germs they have encountered outside the day-care center; any one person could catch the germs of the other two. If the day-care center houses 20 children and seven adults, however, the number of germs that people may pass to each other multiplies. Now any single person could catch the germs of 26 others. Similarly, a network with 1,000 users, each of whom might bring floppy disks from home and download files off the Web, inherently carries a greater risk of virus infection than a network serving only 10 users.

Because most computer viruses can be prevented by the application of a little technology and a little intelligence, it's important that all network users understand how to prevent viruses. An antivirus policy should provide rules for using antivirus software and policies for installing programs, sharing files, and using floppy disks. Furthermore, it should be authorized and supported by the organization's management, and sanctions should by outlined for disobeying the policy. Some good, general guidelines for an antivirus policy are as follows:

- Every computer in an organization should be equipped with virus detection and cleaning software that regularly scans for viruses. This software should be centrally distributed and updated to stay current with newly released viruses.

- Users should not be allowed to alter or disable the antivirus software.

- Users should know what to do in case their antivirus program detects a virus. For example, you might recommend that the user not continue working on his or her computer, but instead call the help desk and receive assistance in disinfecting the system.

- Every organization should have an antivirus team that focuses on maintaining the antivirus measures in place. This team would be responsible for choosing antivirus software, keeping the software updated, educating users, and responding in case of a significant virus outbreak.

- Users should be prohibited from installing any unauthorized software on their systems. This edict may seem extreme, but in fact users bringing programs (especially games) on disk from home are the most common source of viruses. If your organization permits game playing, you might institute a policy in which every game must be first checked for viruses and then installed on a user's system by a technician.

- Organizations should impose penalties on users who do not follow the antivirus policy.

14

When drafting an antivirus policy, bear in mind that these measures are not meant to restrict users' freedom, but rather to protect the network from serious damage and expensive down time. Explain to users that the antivirus policy protects their own data as well as critical system files. If possible, automate the antivirus software installation and operation so that users barely notice its presence. Do not rely on users to run their antivirus software each time they insert a disk or download a new program, because they will quickly forget to do so.

Virus Hoaxes

As in any other community, rumors sometimes spread through the Internet user community. One type of rumor consists of a false alert about a dangerous, new virus that could cause serious damage to your workstation. Such an alert is known as a **virus hoax**. Virus hoaxes usually have no realistic basis and should be ignored, as they merely attempt to create panic. Sometimes the origins of virus hoaxes can be traced (for example, the famous virus hoax, "GoodTimes," was traced to students at Swarthmore College), but often their sources remain anonymous.

A typical example of a virus hoax is one called "It Takes Guts to Say 'Jesus'," in which the body of the message says the following:

> VIRUS WARNING !!!!!!!
> If you receive an e-mail titled "It Takes Guts to Say 'Jesus'," DO NOT open it. It will erase everything on your hard drive. Forward this letter to as many people as you can. This is a new, very malicious virus and not many people know about it. This information was announced yesterday morning from IBM; please share it with people who might access the Internet.

Notice that the hoax warns that the virus will erase everything on your hard drive. In fact, no current virus can erase your hard drive when you merely open an infected e-mail message. Only an executable file, such as a Trojan horse, can accomplish this damage. Virus hoaxes also typically demand that you pass the alert to everyone in your Internet address book, thus propagating the rumor.

Virtually the only way to decide whether a message that warns about a virus is a hoax is to look it up on a Web page that lists virus hoaxes. A good resource for verifying virus hoaxes is *www.icsalabs.com/html/communities/antivirus/hoaxes.stml*. This Web site also allows you to learn more about the phenomenon of virus hoaxes.

If you or your colleagues receive a virus hoax, simply ignore it. Educate your colleagues to do the same, explaining why virus hoaxes should not cause alarm. Remember, however, that even a virus hoax message could potentially contain an *attached* file that does cause damage if executed. Once again, the best policy is to refrain from running any program whose origins you cannot verify.

FAULT TOLERANCE

Besides guarding against viruses, another key factor in maintaining the availability and integrity of data is fault tolerance. **Fault tolerance** is the capacity for a system to continue performing despite an unexpected hardware or software malfunction. Before you can understand the issues related to fault tolerance, you must recognize the difference between failures and faults as they apply to networks. In broad terms, a **failure** is a deviation from a specified level of system performance for a given period of time. In other words, a failure occurs when something doesn't work as promised or as planned. For example, if your car breaks down on the highway, you can consider the breakdown to be a failure. A **fault**, on the other hand, involves the malfunction of one component of a system. A fault can result in a failure. For example, the fault that caused your car to break down might be a leaking water pump. The goal of fault-tolerant systems is to prevent faults from progressing to failures.

Fault tolerance can be achieved in varying degrees, with the optimal level of fault tolerance for a system depending on how critical its services and files are to productivity. At the highest level of fault tolerance, a system would remain unaffected by a drastic problem, such as a power failure. For example, an uninterruptible power supply (UPS) or a gas-powered generator that supplies electricity to a server despite a city-wide power failure provides high fault tolerance.

In addition to using alternative power sources, fault tolerance can be achieved through mirroring. When two servers mirror each other, they can quickly take over for their partner if it should fail. The process of one component immediately assuming the duties of an identical component is known as automatic **fail-over**. Even if one server's NIC fails, for example, fail-over ensures that the other server can automatically handle the first server's responsibilities. In highly fault-tolerant schemes, network users will not even recognize that a problem has occurred. In a moderately fault-tolerant system, on the other hand, users may have to endure brief service outages. An example of a moderately fault-tolerant system is one in which two servers mirror each other's data, but require a network administrator to intervene and switch users from one server to the other.

An excellent way to achieve fault tolerance is to provide duplicate, or redundant, elements to compensate for faults in critical components. You can implement redundancy for servers, cabling, routers, hubs, gateways, NICs, hard disks, power supplies, and other components. The most common type of network redundancy is data backup. **Hard disk redundancy**, called **RAID (Redundant Array of Inexpensive Disks)**, represents a sophisticated means for dynamically replicating data over several physical hard drives. These and other fault-tolerant techniques are discussed in more depth in later sections, which are ordered according to the layer of the OSI Model to which they correspond, from the Physical layer to the Application layer.

To assess the fault tolerance of your network, you must identify any single point of failure—that is, a point on the network where, if a fault occurs, the transfer of data may break down without possibility of an automatic recovery. For instance, if a LAN in your home consists of three PCs, each of which is connected to a hub and a file server in the basement, your

14

LAN has several single points of failure: the connection between the hub and the file server; the hub itself; each of the hub's ports; the electrical connection that powers the hub; the electrical connection that powers the file server; the file server's NIC, fan, hard disk, memory, and processor; and—depending on the criticality of each PC—potentially all of their connections and components.

Redundancy is intended to eliminate single points of failure. If your network cannot tolerate any down time, you must consider redundancy for power, cabling, hard disks, NICs, data links, and any other components that might halt operations if they suffer a fault. As you can imagine, complete redundancy is expensive. Therefore, you must understand not only where your network's single points of failure exist, but also how their malfunctioning might affect the network.

Environment

As you consider sophisticated fault-tolerance techniques for servers, routers, and WAN links, remember to analyze the physical environment in which your devices operate. Part of your data protection plan involves protecting your network from excessive heat or moisture, break-ins, and natural disasters. In the case of natural disasters, the best approach is to store data backups in a location other than where your servers reside.

In addition, you should make sure that your telecommunications closets and equipment rooms are air-conditioned and maintained at a constant humidity, according to the hardware manufacturer's recommendations. You can purchase temperature and humidity monitors that trip alarms if specified limits are exceeded. These monitors can prove very useful because the temperature can rise rapidly in a room full of equipment, causing overheated equipment to fail.

Power

No matter where you live, you have probably experienced a complete loss of power (a blackout) or a temporary dimming of lights (a brownout). Such fluctuations in power are frequently caused by forces of nature such as hurricanes, tornadoes, or ice storms. They may also occur when a utility company performs maintenance or construction tasks. The following section describes the types of power fluctuations for which network administrators should prepare. The next two sections describe alternative power sources, such as a UPS (uninterruptible power supply) or electrical generator, that can compensate for these flaws.

Power Flaws

Whatever the cause, networks cannot tolerate power loss or less than optimal power. The following list describes power flaws that can damage your equipment:

- **Surge**—A momentary increase in voltage due to distant lightning strikes or electrical problems. Surges may last only a few thousandths of a second, but several surges can degrade a computer's power supply. Surges are common. Indeed, without a surge protector, systems will be subjected to multiple surges each year.

- **Line noise**—A fluctuation in voltage levels caused by other devices on the network or electromagnetic interference. Some line noise is unavoidable, but excessive line noise may cause a power supply to malfunction, immediately corrupting program or data files and gradually damaging motherboards and other computer circuits. When you turn on fluorescent lights or a laser printer and the lights dim, you have probably introduced noise into the electrical system. If you continue working on your computer during a lightning storm, your computer will be subject to line noise. Some UPSs guard against line noise, and any critical system should have this type of protection.

- **Brownout**—A momentary decrease in voltage; also known as a **sag**. An overtaxed electrical system may cause brownouts, which you may recognize in your home as a dimming of the lights. Such decreases in voltage can cause significant problems for computer devices. Most UPSs guard against brownouts.

- **Blackout**—A complete power loss. A blackout may or may not cause significant damage to your network. If you are performing a network operating system upgrade when a blackout occurs and you have not protected the server, its network operating system may be damaged so completely that the server will not restart and its operating system must be reinstalled from scratch. If the file server is idle when a blackout occurs, however, it may recover very easily. All UPSs are designed to compensate for blackouts, but how quickly and completely and for how long will depend on the particular unit. To handle extended blackouts or to support a building full of computers, you will need something more powerful than a UPS, such as a gas- or diesel-powered electrical generator.

Each of these power problems can adversely affect network devices and their availability. Not surprisingly then, network administrators must spend a great deal of money and time ensuring that power remains available and problem-free. The following sections describe devices and ways of dealing with unstable power.

Uninterruptible Power Supply (UPS)

A popular way to ensure that a network device does not lose power is to install an **uninterruptible power supply (UPS)**. A UPS is a battery-operated power source directly attached to one or more devices and to a power supply (such as a wall outlet), which prevents undesired features of the wall outlet's A/C power from harming the device or interrupting its services.

UPSs vary widely in the type of power aberrations they can rectify, the length of time for which they can provide power, and the number of devices they can support. Of course, they also vary widely in price. Some UPSs are intended for home use, designed to merely keep your PC running long enough for you to properly shut it down in case of a blackout. Other UPSs perform sophisticated operations such as line conditioning, power supply monitoring, and error notification. The type of UPS you choose will depend on your budget, the number and size of your systems, and the critical nature of those systems.

14

UPSs are classified into two general categories: standby and online. A **standby UPS** provides continuous voltage to a device by switching virtually instantaneously to the battery when it detects a loss of power from the wall outlet. Upon restoration of the power, the standby UPS switches the device back to using A/C power again. One problem exists with standby UPSs: in the brief amount of time that it takes the UPS to discover that power from the wall outlet has faltered, a sensitive device (such as a server) may have already detected the power loss and shut down or restarted. Technically, a standby UPS doesn't provide continuous power; for this reason, it is sometimes called an "offline" UPS. Nevertheless, standby UPSs may prove adequate even for critical network devices such as servers, routers, and gateways. They cost significantly less than online UPSs. Figure 14-1 depicts a standby UPS.

Figure 14-1   Standby UPSs

An **online UPS** uses the A/C power from the wall outlet to continuously charge its battery, while providing power to a network device through its battery. In other words, a server connected to an online UPS always relies on the UPS battery for its electricity. An online UPS offers the best kind of power redundancy available. Because the server never needs to switch from the wall outlet's power to the UPS's power, there is no risk of momentarily losing service. Also, because the UPS always provides the power, it can deal with noise, surges, and sags before the power reaches the attached device. As you can imagine, online UPSs are much more expensive than standby UPSs. Figure 14-2 shows an online UPS.

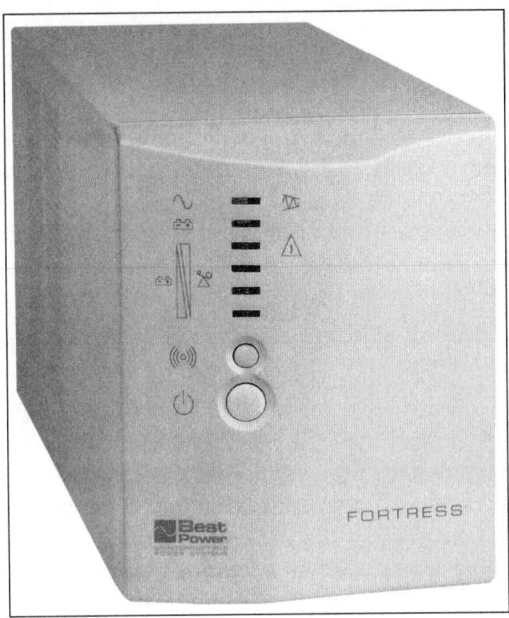

Figure 14-2   An online UPS

How do you decide which UPS is right for your network? You must consider a number of factors:

- *Amount of power needed*—The more power required by your device, the more powerful the UPS needed. Suppose that your organization decides to cut costs and purchase a UPS that cannot supply the amount of power required by a device. If the power to your building ever fails, this UPS will not support your device—you might as well have not installed any UPS.

  Electrical power is measured in volt-amps. A **volt-amp (VA)** is the product of the voltage and current (measured in amps) of the electricity on a line. To determine approximately how many VAs your device requires, you can use the following conversion: 1.4 volt-amps = 1 watt (W). A desktop computer, for example, may use a 200 W power supply and therefore require a UPS capable of at least 280 VA to keep the CPU running in case of a blackout. If you want backup power for your entire home office, however, you must account for the power needs for your monitor and any peripherals, such as printers, when purchasing a UPS. A medium-sized server with a monitor and external tape drive may use 402 W, thus requiring a UPS capable of providing at least 562 VA power. Determining your power needs can prove a challenge. Not only do you have to account for your existing equipment, but you should also consider how you might upgrade the supported device over the next several years. For example, you may purchase a server with only 4 GB of hard disk space, but plan to add 24 GB next year. When you upgrade the hard disk, you may also need to

14

upgrade the UPS. Before you spend thousands of dollars on a UPS, consult with your equipment manufacturer to obtain its recommendations on power needs.

- *Period of time to keep a device running*—Most UPSs are rated to support a device for 15 to 20 minutes. The longer you anticipate needing a UPS to power your device, the more powerful your UPS must be. For example, the medium-sized server that could rely on a 574 VA UPS to remain functional for 20 minutes would need a 1100 VA server to remain functional for 90 minutes. To determine how long your device might require power from a UPS, consider the length of your typical power outages. If you live in an area that frequently suffers severe thunderstorms, you might want to purchase a higher-capacity UPS to cover longer outages.

- *Line conditioning*—Any UPS used on a network device should also offer surge suppression to protect against surges and line conditioning, or filtering, to guard against line noise. Line conditioners and UPS units include special noise filters that remove line noise. The manufacturer's technical specifications should indicate the amount of filtration required for each UPS. Noise suppression is expressed in decibel levels (dB) at a specific frequency (KHz or MHz). The higher the decibel level, the greater the protection.

- *Cost*—Prices for good UPSs vary widely, depending on the unit's size and extra features. A relatively small UPS that can power one server for 5 to 10 minutes might cost between $50 and $300. A large UPS that can power a sophisticated router for 10 to 20 minutes might cost between $200 and $3,000. On a critical system, however, you should not try to cut costs by buying an off-brand, potentially unreliable, or weak UPS.

As with other large purchases, you should research several UPS manufacturers and their products before reaching a decision. Also ensure that the manufacturer provides a warranty and lets you test the UPS with your equipment. It's important to try out the UPS with your equipment to ensure that it will satisfy your needs. Popular UPS manufacturers are APC, Best, Deltec, MGE, and Tripp Lite.

Generators

If your organization cannot withstand a power loss of any duration, either because of its computer services or other electrical needs, you might consider investing in an electrical generator for your building. Generators can be powered by diesel, liquid propane gas, natural gas, or steam. Although they do not provide surge protection, generators do provide clean (free from noise) electricity.

As when choosing a UPS, you should calculate your organization's crucial electrical demands to determine what size of generator you need. You should also estimate how long the generator may be required to power your building. Gas or diesel generators may cost between $10,000 and $3,000,000 (for the largest industrial types). Alternatively, you can rent electrical generators. To find out more about options for renting or purchasing generators in your area, contact your local electrical utility.

Topology

You have read about topology and architecture fault tolerance in previous chapters of this book. In Chapter 5, you learned about a variety of physical network topologies: star, ring, bus, mesh, and hybrid. Recall that each of these topologies inherently assumes certain advantages and disadvantages, and you need to assess your network's needs before designing your data links.

A mesh topology offers the best fault tolerance. To refresh your memory, a mesh network is one in which nodes are connected either directly or indirectly by multiple pathways. Figure 14-3 depicts a fully meshed network.

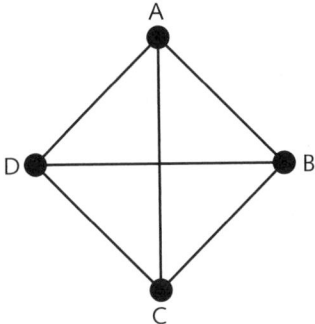

Figure 14-3   A fully meshed network

In a mesh topology, data can travel over multiple paths from any one point to another. For example, if the direct link between point A and point B in Figure 14-3 becomes severed, data can be rerouted automatically from point A to point C and then to point B. Alternatively, it may be rerouted from point A to point D to point B, and so on. You can see that a fully meshed network provides multiple redundancies and therefore greater fault tolerance than a network with a single redundancy.

Figure 14-4 illustrates a network that contains single redundancy. In this example, if one link between point A and point B becomes severed, data can automatically be rerouted over the second link. If the link between point A and point B and the link between point A and point C are both severed, however, the network will suffer a failure.

14

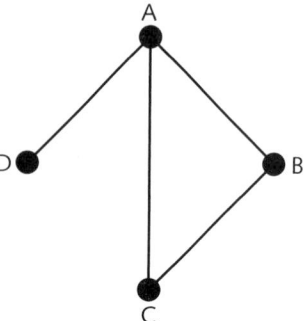

Figure 14-4   A network with one redundant connection

The physical media you use may also offer redundancy. Recall from Chapter 7 that a SONET ring can easily recover from a fault in one of its links because it forms a ring, as pictured in Figure 14-5. In this example, if the outer SONET link between point A and point B becomes severed, data can circumvent the fault to move between the two points.

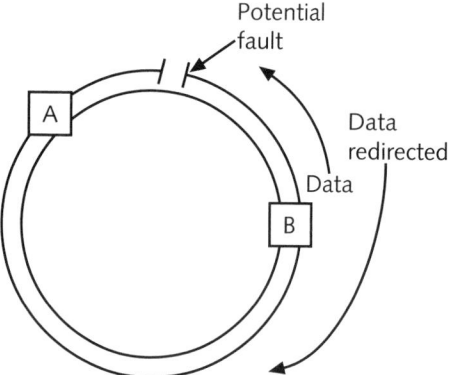

Figure 14-5   A self-healing SONET ring

Mesh topologies and SONET rings are good choices for highly available LANs and WANs. But what about connections to the Internet? Or data backup connections? You may need to establish more than one of these types of links.

As an example, imagine that you work for a data services firm called PayNTime that processes payroll checks for a large oil company in the Houston area. Every day you receive updated payroll information over a T1 link from your client, and every Thursday PayNTime compiles this information and then cuts 2,000 checks that you ship overnight to the client's headquarters. What would happen if the T1 link between PayNTime and the oil company suffered damage in a flood and became unusable on a Thursday morning? How would you ensure that the employees received their pay? If no redundant link to the oil company existed, you would probably need to gather and input the data into your system at least partially by hand. Even then, chances are that you wouldn't process the payroll checks in time to be shipped overnight.

In this type of situation, you would want a duplicate connection between PayNTime and the oil company's site. You might contract with two different service carriers to ensure the redundancy. Alternatively, you might arrange with one service carrier to provide two redundant routes. However you provide redundancy in your network topology, you should make sure that the critical data transactions can follow more than one possible path from source to target.

Redundancy in your network offers the advantage of reducing the risk of losing functionality, and potentially profits, from a network fault. As you might guess, however, the disadvantage of redundancy is its cost. If you subscribed to two different service providers for two T1 links in the PayNTime example, you would probably double your monthly leasing costs of approximately \$1,000. Multiply that amount times 12 months, and then times the number of clients for which you need to provide redundancy—and the extra layers of protection quickly become expensive. Redundancy is like a homeowner's insurance policy: you may never need to use it, but if you don't get it, the cost can be much higher than your premiums. As a general rule, you should invest in connection redundancies where they are absolutely necessary.

Now suppose that PayNTime provides services not only to the oil company, but also to a temporary agency in the Houston area. Both links are critical because both companies need their payroll checks cut each week. With links to two customers, you may be able to take advantage of a T1 connection between the customers' sites to create a partially meshed network, as pictured in Figure 14-6. Now if the link between PayNTime and the oil firm suffers a fault, data can theoretically be rerouted through the temporary agency's connection.

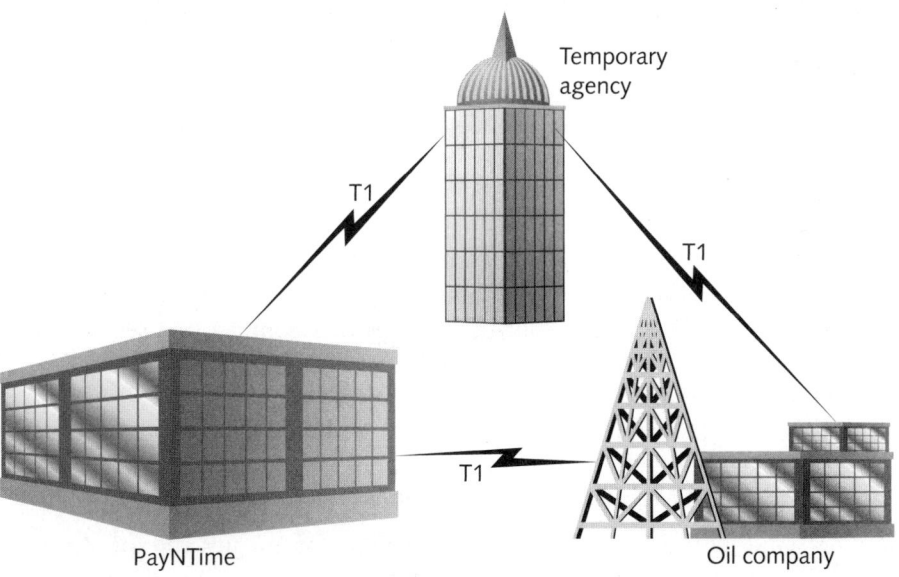

Figure 14-6   Redundancy between a firm and two customers

You may notice a problem with this scenario, however. What if the temporary agency doesn't want the oil company's transactions using its bandwidth, even in case of emergency? And what happens when the third and fourth customers are added to the network? To address concerns of capacity and scalability, you may want to consider partnering with an ISP and establishing secure VPNs with your clients. With a VPN, PayNTime could shift the costs of redundancy and network design to the service provider and concentrate on the task it does best—processing payroll. Figure 14-7 illustrates this type of arrangement.

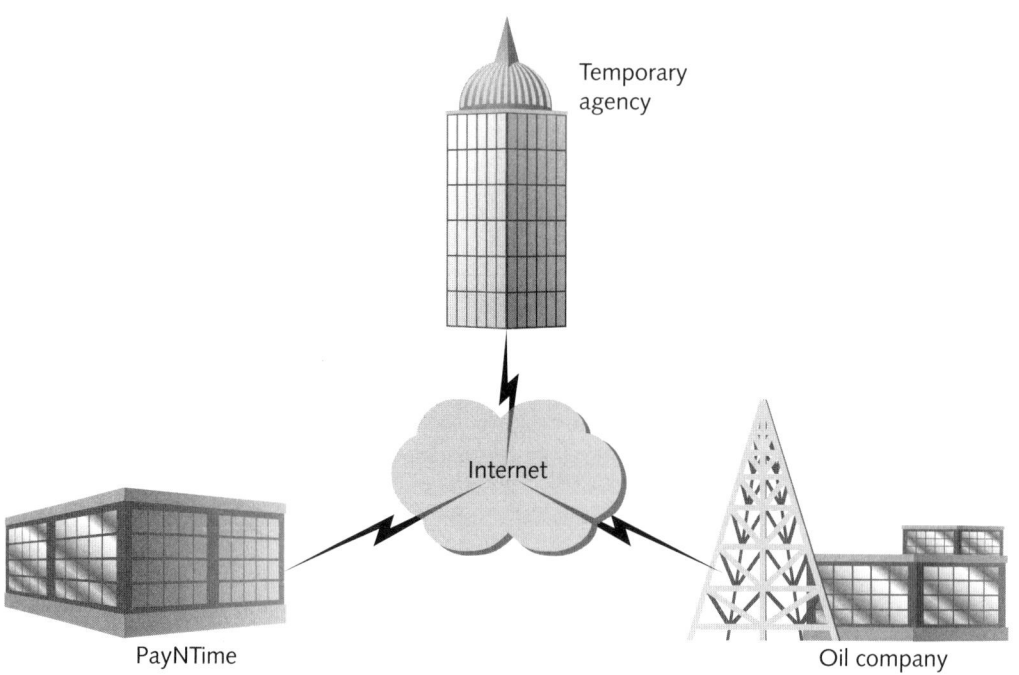

Figure 14-7   VPNs linking multiple customers

Connectivity

In the previous section, you learned the basics about providing fault tolerance in a LAN or WAN topology. But what about the devices that connect one segment of a LAN or WAN to another? What happens when they experience a fault? In Chapter 6, you learned how routers, bridges, hubs, and switches work. In Chapter 7, you saw how dedicated lines terminate at a customer's premises and in a service provider's data center. In this section, you will consider how to fundamentally increase the fault tolerance of connectivity devices and a LAN's or WAN's connecting links.

To understand how to increase the fault tolerance of not just the topology, but also the network's connectivity, let's return to the example of PayNTime. Suppose that the company's network administrator decides to establish a VPN agreement with a national ISP.

PayNTime's bandwidth analysis indicates that a T1 link will be sufficient to transport the data of five customers from the ISP's office to PayNTime's data room. Figure 14-8 provides a detailed representation of this arrangement.

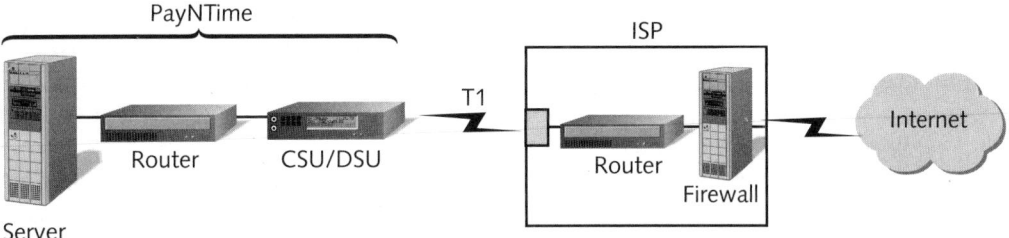

Figure 14-8 ISP connectivity

Notice the single points of failure in the arrangement depicted in Figure 14-8. As mentioned earlier, the T1 connection could incur a fault. In addition, any one of the routers, CSU/DSUs, or firewalls might suffer faults in their power supplies, NICs, or circuit boards. In a critical component such as a router or switch, high fault tolerance necessitates the use of redundant power supplies, cooling fans, interfaces, and I/O modules, all of which should ideally be hot swappable. The term **hot swappable** refers to identical components that automatically assume the functions of their counterpart if one suffers a fault. They are called hot swappable because they can be changed (or swapped) while a machine is still running (hot). In a sense, hot swappable components work like your kidneys. If one fails, the other will automatically assume all responsibility for filtering waste from the blood. In much the same way, if a router's processor fails, the redundant processor will automatically take over all data-processing functions. When you purchase switches or routers to support critical links, look for those that contain hot swappable components. As with other redundancy provisions, these features will add to the cost of your device purchase.

Purchasing connectivity devices does not address all faults that may occur on a WAN. In fact, faults may also affect the connecting links. For example, if you connect two offices with a dedicated T1 connection and the T1 fails, it doesn't matter whether your router has redundant NICs. The connection will still be down. Because a fault in the T1 link has the same effect as a bad T1 interface in a router, a fully redundant system might be a better option. Such a system is depicted in Figure 14-9.

14

Figure 14-9 A fully redundant system

The preceding scenario utilizes the most expensive and reliable option for providing network redundancy for PayNTime. In addition, this solution allows for **load balancing**, or an automatic distribution of traffic over multiple links or processors to optimize response. Load balancing would maximize the throughput between PayNTime and its ISP because the aggregate traffic flowing between the two points could move over either T1 link, avoiding potential bottlenecks on a single T1 connection. Although one company might be willing to pay for such complete redundancy, another might prefer a less expensive solution. A less expensive redundancy option might be to use a dial-back WAN link. For example, a company that depends on a Frame Relay WAN might have an access server with an ISDN or 56 KB modem link that automatically dials the remote site when it detects a failure of the primary link.

Servers

As with other devices, you can make servers more fault-tolerant by supplying them with redundant components. Critical servers (such as those that perform user authentication for an entire LAN, or those that run important, enterprise-wide applications such as an electronic catalog in a library) often contain redundant NICs, processors, and hard disks. These redundant components provide assurance that if one item fails, the entire system won't fail; at the same time, they enable load balancing.

For example, a server with two 100-Mbps NICs, such as the one pictured in Figure 14-10, may be receiving and transmitting traffic at a rate of 46 Mbps during a busy time of the day. With additional software provided by either the NIC manufacturer or a third party, the redundant NICs can work in tandem to distribute the load, ensuring that approximately half the data travels through the first NIC and half through the second. This approach improves response time for users accessing the server. If one NIC fails, the other NIC will automatically assume full responsibility for receiving and transmitting all data to and from the server. Although load balancing does not technically fall under the category of fault tolerance, it helps to justify the purchase of redundant components that do contribute to fault tolerance.

The following sections describe more sophisticated ways of providing server fault tolerance, beginning with server mirroring.

Server Mirroring

Server mirroring is a fault-tolerance technique in which one server duplicates the transactions and data storage of another. The servers involved must be identical machines using identical components. As you would expect, mirroring requires a link between the servers. It also entails software running on both servers that allows them to synchronize their actions continually and, in case of a failure, that permits one server to take over for the other.

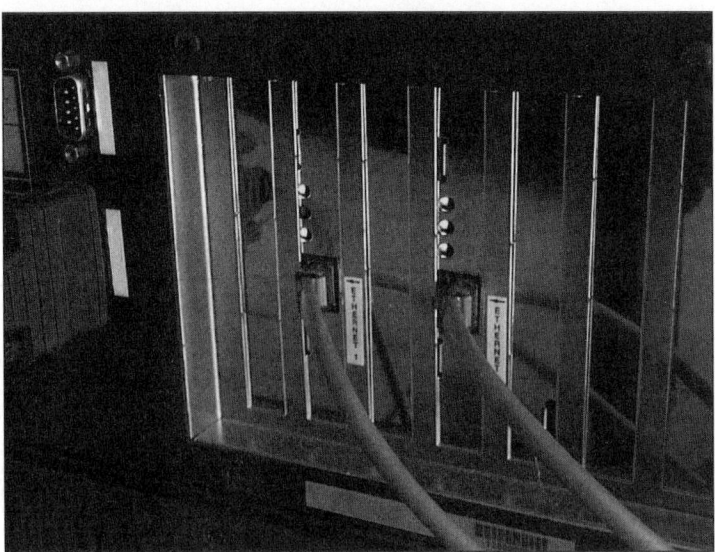

Figure 14-10   A server with redundant NICs

To illustrate the concept of mirroring, suppose that you give a presentation to a large group of people, with the audience being allowed to interrupt you to ask questions at any time. You might talk for two minutes, then wait while someone asked a question, then answer the question, then begin lecturing again, take another question, and so on. In this sense, you act like a primary server, busily transmitting and receiving information. Now imagine that your identical twin is standing in the next room and can hear you over a loudspeaker. Your twin was instructed to say exactly what you were saying as quickly as possible after you speak, but to an empty room containing only a tape recorder. Of course, your twin must listen to you before imitating you. It takes time for the twin to digest all that you're saying and repeat it, so you must slow down your lecture and your room's question-and-answer process. A mirrored server acts in much the same way. The time it takes to duplicate the incoming and outgoing data will detrimentally affect network performance if the network handles a heavy traffic load. But if you should faint during your lecture, for example, your twin can step into your room and take over for you in very short order. The mirrored server also stands ready to assume the responsibilities of its counterpart.

One advantage to mirroring is that the servers involved can stand side by side or be positioned in geographically side-by-side locations—perhaps in two different buildings of a company's headquarters, or possibly even on opposites sides of a continent. One potential disadvantage to mirroring, however, is the time it takes for a mirrored server to assume the functionality of the failed server. This delay may last 15 to 90 seconds. Obviously, this down time makes mirroring imperfect; when a server fails, users lose network service and any data in transit at the moment of the failure will be susceptible to corruption. Another disadvantage to mirroring is its toll on the network as data are copied between sites.

14

Examples of mirroring software include Legato System's StandbyServer and NSI Software's Double-Take. Although such software can be expensive, the hardware costs of mirroring are even more significant because one server is devoted to simply acting as a "tape recorder" for all data in case the other server fails. Depending on the potential cost of losing a server's functionality for any period of time, however, the expense involved may be justifiable.

 You may be familiar with the term "mirroring" as it refers to Web sites on the Internet. Mirrored Web sites are locations on the Internet that dynamically duplicate other locations on the Internet, to ensure their continual availability. They are similar to, but not necessarily the same as, mirrored servers.

Server Clustering

Server clustering is a fault-tolerance technique that links multiple servers together to act as a single server. In this configuration, clustered servers share processing duties and appear as a single server to users. If one server in the cluster fails, the other servers in the cluster will automatically take over its data transaction and storage responsibilities. Because multiple servers can perform services independently of other servers, as well as ensure fault tolerance, clustering is more cost-effective than mirroring.

To understand the concept of clustering, imagine that you and several colleagues (who are not exactly like you) are giving separate talks in different rooms in the same conference center simultaneously. All of your colleagues are constantly aware of your lecture, and vice versa. If you should faint during your lecture, one of your colleagues can immediately jump into your spot and pick up where you left off, without the audience ever noticing. (At the same time, your colleague must continue to present his own lecture, which means that he will have to split his time between these two tasks.)

To detect failures, clustered servers regularly poll each other on the network, essentially asking, "Are you still there?" They then wait a specified period of time before again asking, "Are you still there?" If they don't receive a response from one of their counterparts, the clustering software initiates the fail-over. This process may take anywhere from a few seconds to a minute, because all information about a failed server's shared resources must be gathered by the cluster. Unlike with mirroring, users will not notice the switch. Later, when the other servers in the cluster detect that the missing server has been replaced, they will automatically relinquish that server's responsibilities. The fail-over and recovery processes are transparent to network users.

One disadvantage to clustering is that the clustered servers must be geographically close—although the exact distance depends on the clustering software employed. Typically, clustering is implemented among servers located in the same data room. Some clusters can contain servers as far as a mile apart, but clustering software manufacturers recommend a closer proximity. Before implementing a server cluster, you should determine your organization's fault-tolerance needs and fully research the options available on your servers' platforms.

Despite its geographic limitations, clustering offers many advantages over mirroring. Each server in the cluster can perform its own data processing; at the same time, it is always ready to take over for a failed server if necessary. Not only does this ability to perform multiple functions reduce the cost of ownership for a cluster of servers, but it also improves performance.

Like mirroring, clustering is implemented through a combination of software and hardware. Novell's NetWare 5.x and Microsoft's Windows 2000 DataCenter Server and Advanced Server NOSs now incorporate options for server clustering. Clustering has been part of the UNIX operating system since the early 1990s.

Storage

Related to the availability and fault tolerance of servers is the availability and fault tolerance of data storage. In the following sections you will learn about different methods for making sure shared data and applications are never lost or irretrievable.

Redundant Array of Inexpensive Disks (RAID)

A Redundant Array of Inexpensive Disks (RAID) is a collection of disks that provide fault tolerance for shared data and applications. A group of hard disks is called a disk **array** (or a drive). The collection of disks that work together in a RAID configuration is often referred to as the "RAID drive." To the system, the multiple disks in a RAID drive appear as a single logical drive. The advantage of using RAID is that a single disk failure will not cause a catastrophic loss of data.

Although RAID comes in many different forms (or levels), all types use shared, multiple physical or logical hard disks to ensure data integrity and availability. Some RAID designs also increase storage capacity and improve performance. RAID is typically used on servers, but not on workstations because of its cost. It's important to keep in mind that RAID relies on a combination of software and hardware. The software may be a third-party package, or it may exist as part of the network operating system. On a Windows 2000 server, for example, RAID drives are configured through the Disk Management tool.

RAID Level 0 – Disk Striping.   **RAID Level 0** (otherwise known as **disk striping**) is a very simple implementation of RAID in which data are written in 64 KB blocks equally across all disks in the array. Disk striping is not a fault-tolerant method because if one disk fails, the data contained in it will be inaccessible. Thus RAID Level 0 does not provide true redundancy. Nevertheless, it does use multiple disk partitions effectively, and it improves performance by utilizing multiple disk controllers. The multiple disk controllers allow several instructions to be sent to the disks simultaneously.

Figure 14-11 illustrates how data are written to multiple disks in RAID Level 0. Notice how each 64 KB piece of data is written to one discreet area of the disk array. For example, if you were saving a 128 KB file, the file would be separated into two pieces and saved in different areas of the drive. Although RAID Level 0 is easy to implement, it should not be used on mission-critical servers because of its lack of fault tolerance.

14

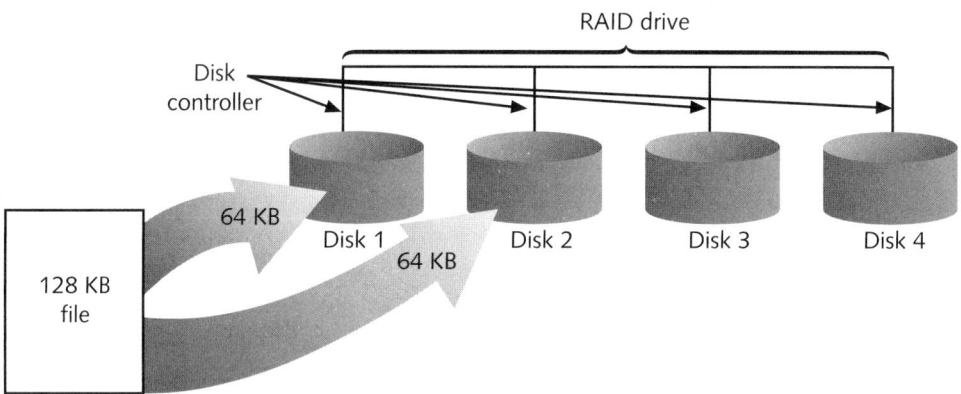

Figure 14-11   RAID Level 0 — disk striping

RAID Level 1 – Disk Mirroring. RAID Level 1 provides redundancy through a process called **disk mirroring**, in which data from one disk are copied to another disk automatically as the information is written. Because data are continually saved to multiple locations, disk mirroring provides a dynamic data backup. If one disk in the array fails, the disk array controller will automatically switch to the disk that was mirroring the failed disk. Users will not even notice the failure. After repairing the failed disk, the network administrator must perform a resynchronization to return it to the array. As the disk's twin has been saving all of its data while it was out of service, this task is rarely difficult.

The advantages of RAID Level 1 derive from its simplicity and its automatic and complete data redundancy. On the other hand, because it requires two identical disks instead of just one, RAID Level 1 is somewhat costly. In addition, it is not the most efficient means of protecting data, as it usually relies on system software to perform the mirroring, which taxes CPU resources. Figure 14-12 depicts a 128 KB file being written to a disk array using RAID Level 1.

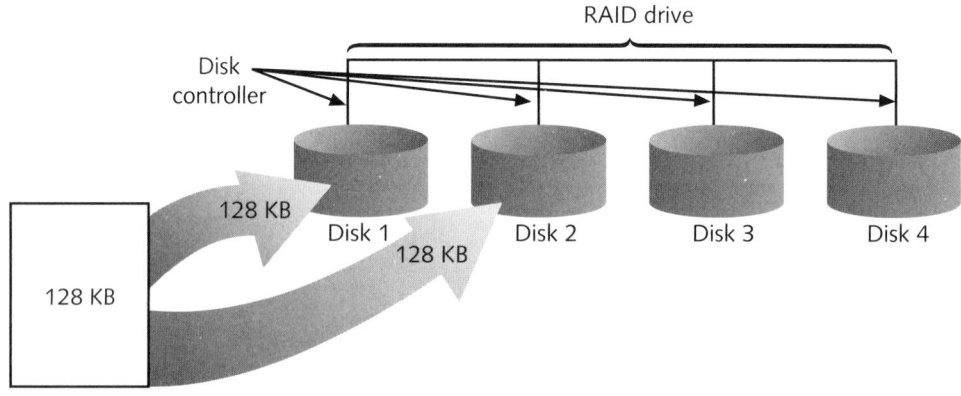

Figure 14-12   RAID Level 1 — disk mirroring

Although they are not covered in this chapter, RAID levels 2 and 4 also exist. These versions of RAID are rarely used, however, because they are less reliable or less efficient than Levels 1, 3, and 5.

RAID Level 3 – Disk Striping with Parity ECC.

RAID Level 3 involves disk striping with a special type of error correction code (ECC) known as parity error correction code. The term **parity** refers to the mechanism used to verify the integrity of data by making the number of bits in a byte sum to either an odd or even number. To accomplish parity, a parity bit (equal to either 0 or 1) is added to the bits' sum. Table 14-1 expresses how the sums of many bits achieve even parity through a parity bit. Notice that the numbers in the fourth column are all even. If the summed numbers in the fourth column were odd, an odd parity would be used. A system may use either even parity or odd parity, but not both.

Table 14-1   The use of parity bits to achieve parity

Original Data	Sum of Data Bits	Parity Bit	Sum of Data Plus Parity Bits
01110010	4	0	4
00100010	2	0	2
00111101	5	1	6
10010100	3	1	4

Parity tracks the integrity of data on a disk. It does not reflect the data type, protocol, transmission method, or file size. A parity bit is assigned to each data byte when it is transmitted or written to a disk. When data are later read from the disk, the data's bits plus the parity bit are summed again. If the parity does not match (for example, if the end sum is odd but the system uses even parity), then the system assumes that the data have suffered some type of damage. The process of comparing the parity of data read from disk with the type of parity used by the system is known as **parity error checking**.

In RAID Level 3, parity error checking takes place when data are written across the disk array. If the parity error checking indicates an error, the RAID Level 3 system can automatically correct it. The advantage of using RAID 3 is that it provides a high data transfer rate when reading from or writing to the disks. This quality makes RAID 3 particularly well suited to applications that require high speed in data transfers, such as video editing. A disadvantage of RAID 3 is that the parity information appears on a single disk, which represents a potential single point of failure in the system. Figure 14-13 illustrates how RAID Level 3 works.

14

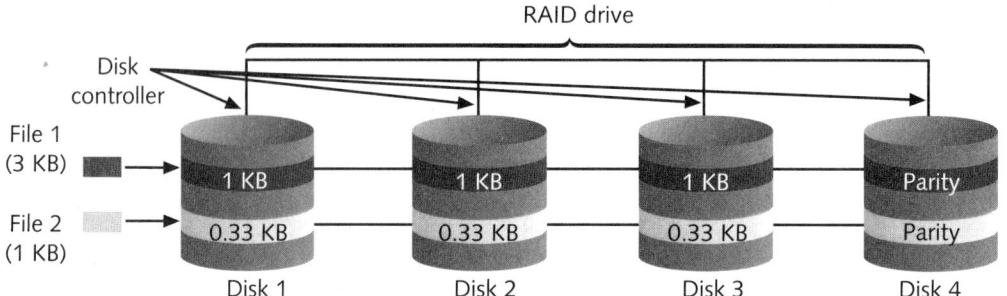

Figure 14-13 RAID Level 3 — disk striping with parity ECC

RAID Level 5 – Disk Striping with Distributed Parity. **RAID Level 5** is the most popular, highly fault-tolerant, data storage technique in use today. In RAID Level 5, data are written in small blocks across several disks. At the same time, parity error checking information is distributed among the disks, as pictured in Figure 14-14.

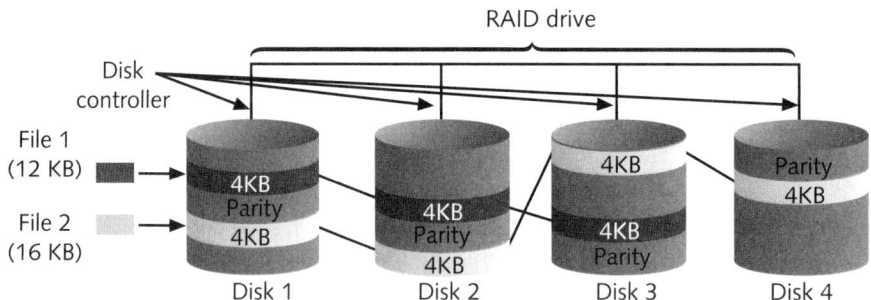

Figure 14-14 RAID Level 5 — disk striping with distributed parity

RAID Level 5 is similar to, but has several advantages over, RAID Level 3. First, it can write data more rapidly because the parity information can be written by any one of the several disk controllers in the array. Unlike RAID Level 3, RAID Level 5 uses several disks for parity information, making it more fault-tolerant. Also, RAID Level 5 allows you to replace failed disks with good ones without any interruption of service.

Network Attached Storage

Network attached storage (NAS) is a specialized storage device or group of storage devices that provides centralized fault-tolerant data storage for a network. NAS differs from RAID in that it maintains its own interface to the LAN rather than relying on a separate server to connect it to the network and control its functions. In fact, you can think of NAS as a unique type of server dedicated to data sharing. The advantage to using NAS over a typical file server is that a NAS device contains its own file system that is optimized to save and serve files (as opposed to also managing printing, authenticating login IDs, and so on). Because of this optimization, NAS reads and writes from its disk significantly faster than other types of servers could.

Another advantage to using NAS is that it can be easily expanded without interrupting service. For instance, if you purchased a NAS device with 40 GB of disk space, then six months later realized you need three times as much storage space, you could add the new 80 GB to the NAS device without requiring users to log off the network or taking down the NAS device. After physically installing the new disk space, the NAS device would recognize the added storage and add it to its pool of available reading and writing space. Compare this process to adding hard disk space to a typical server, for which you would have to take the server down, install the hardware, reformat the drive, integrate it with your NOS, then add directories, files, and permissions as necessary.

Although NAS is a separate device with its own file system, it still cannot communicate directly with clients on the network. When using NAS, the client requests a file from its usual file server (such as a Windows 2000, Linux, or NetWare 5.1 server) over the LAN. The server then requests the file from the NAS device on the network. In response, the NAS device retrieves the file and transmits it to the server, which transmits it to the client. Figure 14-15 depicts how NAS operates on a LAN.

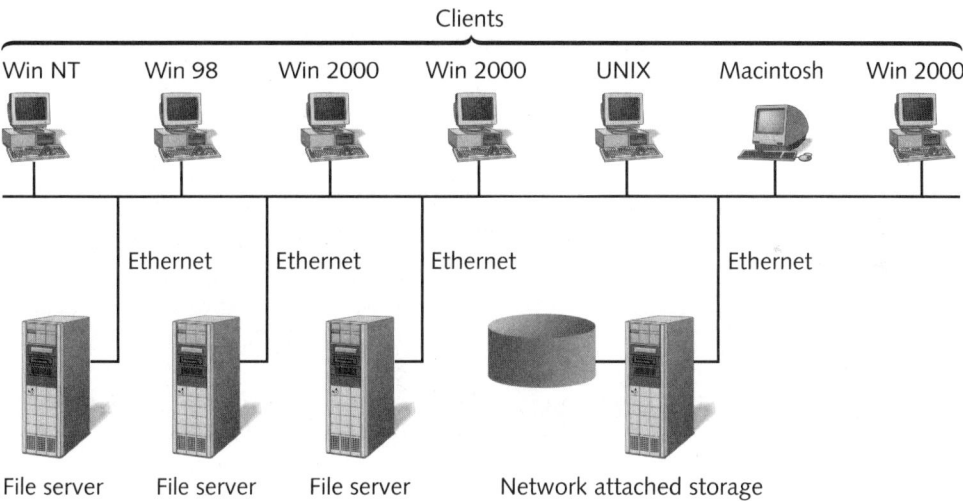

Figure 14-15   Network attached storage on a LAN

NAS is appropriate for small- or medium-sized enterprises that require not only fault tolerance, but also fast access for their data. For example, a local ISP might use NAS for hosting its customers' Web pages. Since NAS devices can store and retrieve data for any type of client (providing it can run TCP/IP), NAS is also appropriate for organizations that use a mix of different operating systems on their desktops.

The two major vendors of network attached storage are Network Appliance, Inc. and EMC Corporation. In addition, computer manufacturers such as Hewlett-Packard, Compaq and Dell now offer their own NAS solutions.

Larger enterprises that require even faster access to data and larger amounts of storage, might prefer storage area networks over NAS. You will learn about storage area networks in the following section.

Storage Area Networks

As you have learned, NAS devices are separate storage devices, but they still require a file server to interact with other devices on the network. In contrast, **storage area networks (SANs)** are distinct networks of storage devices that communicate directly with each other and with other networks. In a typical SAN, multiple storage devices are connected to multiple, identical servers. This type of architecture is similar to the mesh topology in WANs, the most fault-tolerant type of topology possible. If one storage device within a SAN suffers a fault, data is automatically retrieved from elsewhere in the SAN. If one server in a SAN suffers a fault, another server steps in to perform its functions.

Not only are SANs extremely fault tolerant, but they are also extremely fast. Much of their speed can be attributed to **Fibre Channel**, a distinct network transmission method that relies on fiber-optic media and its own, proprietary protocol. Fibre Channel connects devices within the SAN and also connects the SAN to other networks. Fibre Channel is capable of 1-Gbps (and soon, 2-Gbps) throughput. Because it depends on Fibre Channel, and not on a traditional network transmission method (for example, 10BaseT or 100BaseT), a SAN is not limited to the speed of the client/server network for which it provides data storage. In addition, since the SAN does not belong to the client/server network, it does not have to contend with the normal overhead of that network, such as broadcasts and acknowledgments. Likewise, a SAN frees the client/server network from the traffic-intensive duties of backing up and restoring data.

Figure 14-16 shows a SAN connected to a traditional Ethernet network.

Like NAS, SANs provide the benefit of being highly scalable. Once you establish a SAN, you can easily add not only further storage, but also new devices to the SAN without disrupting client/server activity on the network. Finally, SANs use a more efficient method of writing data than both NAS devices and typical client/server networks use, making them even faster.

SANs are not without drawbacks, however. One noteworthy disadvantage to implementing SANs is their high cost. A small storage area network can cost $500,000 (as much as the most expensive type of NAS) while a large SAN costs several millions of dollars. In addition, since SANs are appreciably more complex than NAS or RAID systems, investing in a SAN means also investing in long hours of training for technical staff before installation, plus significant administration efforts to keep the SAN functional.

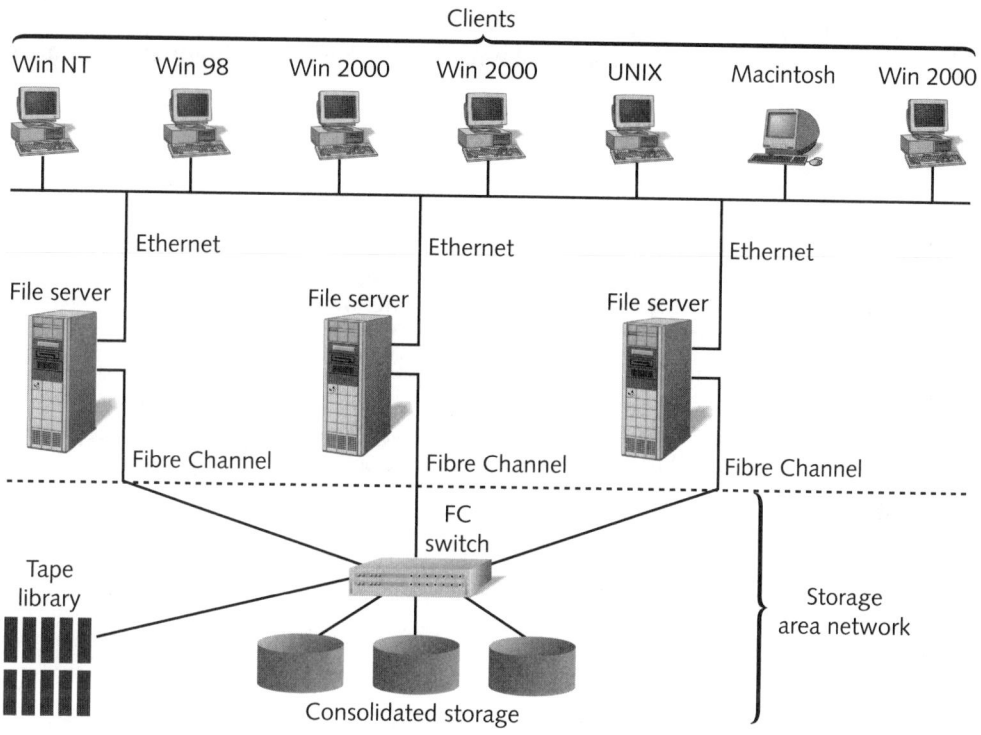

Figure 14-16   A storage area network

Because of their very high fault tolerance, massive storage capabilities and speedy data access, SANs are best suited to environments with huge quantities of data that must always be quickly available. Usually, such an environment belongs to a very large enterprise. A SAN is typically used to house multiple databases—for example, inventory, sales, safety specifications, payroll, and employee records for an international manufacturing company.

DATA BACKUP

You have probably heard or even spoken the axiom, "Make regular backups!" A **backup** is a copy of data or program files created for archiving or safekeeping purposes. Without backing up your data, you risk losing everything through a hard disk fault, fire, flood, or malicious or accidental erasure or corruption. No matter how reliable and fault-tolerant you believe your server's hard disk (or disks) to be, you still risk losing everything unless you make backups on separate media and store them off-site.

To fully appreciate the importance of backups, imagine coming to work one morning to find that everything disappeared from the server: programs, configurations, data files, user IDs, passwords, and the network operating system. It doesn't matter how it happened.

14

What matters at this point is how long it will take to reinstall the network operating systems; how long it will take to duplicate the previous configuration; and how long it will take to figure out which IDs should reside on the server, which groups they should belong in, and which rights each group should have. What will you say to your colleagues when they learn that all of the data that they have worked on for the last year is irretrievably lost? When you think about this scenario, you will quickly realize that you can't afford *not* to perform regular backups.

Some network administrators don't pay enough attention to backups because they find the process confusing or difficult to track. True, many different options exist for making backups. They can be performed by different types of software and hardware combinations, including via network operating system utilities. In this section, you will learn about the most common methods of performing data backup, ways to schedule them, and methods for determining what you need to back up. Backup methods unsuitable for large systems, such as floppy disks or other removable storage media, are not covered in this section. Note that backing up workstations and backing up servers and other host systems are different operations. To qualify for Net+ certification, you should focus on making server backups.

Tape Backups

Currently, the most popular method for backing up networked systems is tape backup, because this method is simple and relatively economical. Tape backups require the use of a tape drive connected to the network (via a system such as a file server or dedicated, networked workstation), software to manage and perform backups, and, of course, backup media. The tapes used for tape backups resemble small cassette tapes, but they are of a higher quality, specially made to reliably store data. Figure 14-17 depicts two types of backup tape media: 4 mm and 8 mm.

On a relatively small network, standalone tape drives may be attached to each server. On a large network, one large, centralized tape backup device may manage all of the subsystems' backups. This tape backup device will usually be connected to a computer other than a busy file server to reduce the possibility that backups might cause traffic bottlenecks. Extremely large environments (for example, global manufacturers with several terabytes of inventory and product information to safeguard) may require robots to retrieve and circulate tapes from a tape storage library (or **vault**) that may be as large as a warehouse. Figure 14-18 illustrates how tape drives typically fit into a medium or large network.

Figure 14-17   Examples of backup tape media

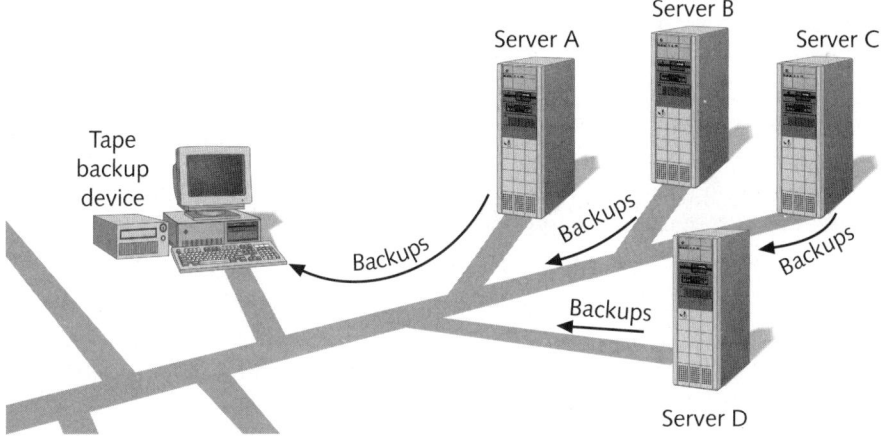

Figure 14-18   A tape drive on a medium or large network

To select the appropriate tape backup solution for your network, you should consider the following questions:

- Does the backup drive or media provide sufficient storage capacity?
- Are the backup software and hardware proven to be reliable?

- Does the backup software use data error checking techniques?
- Is the system quick enough to complete the backup process before daily operations resume?
- How much do the tape drive, software, and media cost?
- Will the backup hardware and software be compatible with existing network hardware and software?
- Does the backup system require frequent manual intervention? (For example, will staff members need to become involved in tape rotation?)
- Will the backup hardware, software, and media accommodate your network's growth?

Examples of tape backup software include Computer Associates' ARCserve, Dantz Development Corporation's Retrospect, Hewlett-Packard's Colorado and OmniBack, IBM's ADSTAR Distributed Storage Manager (ADSM), NovaStor Corporation's NovaNET, and Veritas Software Corporation's Backup Exec. Popular tape drive manufacturers include Exabyte, Hewlett-Packard, IBM, Quantum, Seagate, and Sony. You will need to consult the software and hardware specifications to determine whether a particular backup system is compatible with your network.

Online Backups

Many companies on the Internet now offer to back up data over the Internet—that is, to perform **online backups**. Usually, online backup providers require you to install their client software. You also need a connection to the Internet. Online backups implement strict security measures to protect the data in transit, as the information must traverse public carrier links. Most online backup providers allow you to retrieve your data at any time of day or night, without calling a technical support number. Both the backup and restoration processes are entirely automated. In case of a disaster, the online backup company may offer to create CD-ROMs containing your servers' data.

A potential drawback to online backups is that the cost of this service can vary widely. In addition, despite strict security controls, it may be difficult to verify that your data has been backed up successfully. Online backup providers include @Backup, Atrieva, Connected, HotWired, and Safeguard.

When evaluating an online backup provider, you should test its speed, accuracy, security, and, of course, the ease with which you can recover the backed up data. Be certain to test the service before you commit to a long-term contract for online backups.

Backup Strategy

After selecting the appropriate tool for performing your servers' data backups, you should devise a backup strategy to guide you and your colleagues in performing reliable backups that provide maximum data protection. This strategy should be documented in a common area (for example, on a Web site accessible to all IT staff) and should address at least the following questions:

- What kind of rotation schedule will backups follow?
- At what time of day or night will the backups occur?
- How will you verify the accuracy of the backups?
- Where will backup media be stored?
- Who will take responsibility for ensuring that backups occurred?
- How long will you save backups?
- Where will backup and recovery documentation be stored?

Different backup methods provide varying levels of certainty and corresponding labor and cost. The various methods are described below:

- **Full backup**—All data on all servers are copied to a storage medium, regardless of whether the data are new or changed.
- **Incremental backup**—Only data that have changed since the last backup are copied to a storage medium.
- **Differential backup**—Only data that have changed since the last backup are copied to a storage medium, and that information is then marked for subsequent backup, regardless of whether it has changed.

When managing network backups, you need to determine the best possible **backup rotation scheme**—that is, you need to create a plan that specifies when and how often backups will occur. The aim of a good backup rotation scheme is to provide excellent data reliability without overtaxing your network or requiring a lot of intervention. For example, you might think that backing up your entire network's data every night is the best policy because it ensures that everything is completely safe. But what if your network contains 50 GB of data and is growing by 10 GB per month? Would the backups even finish by morning? How many tapes would you have to purchase? Also, why should you bother backing up files that haven't changed in three weeks? How much time will you and your staff need to devote to managing the tapes? How would the transfer of all of the data affect your network's performance? All of these considerations point to a better alternative than the "tape-a-day" solution—that is, an option that promises to maximize data protection but reduce the time and cost associated with backups.

14

When planning your backup strategy, you can choose from several standard backup rotation schemes. The most popular of these schemes, called **grandfather-father-son**, uses daily (son), weekly (father), and monthly (grandfather) backup sets. As depicted in Figure 14-19, in the grandfather-father-son scheme, three types of backups are performed each month: daily incremental (every Monday through Thursday), weekly full (every Friday), and monthly full backups (last day of the month).

In this scheme, backup tapes are reused regularly. For example, week 1's Monday tape would also serve as week 2's and week 3's Monday tape. One day each week, a full backup, called "father," is recorded in place of an incremental one and labeled for the week to which it corresponds—for example, "week 1," "week 2," and so on. This "father" tape is reused monthly—for example, October's week 1 tape would be reused for November's week 1 tape. The final set of media is labeled "month 1," "month 2," and so on, according to which month of the quarter the tapes will be used. This "grandfather" medium records full backups on the last business day of each month and is reused quarterly. Each of these media may consist of a single tape or a set of tapes, depending on the amount of data involved. A total of 12 media sets are required for this basic rotation scheme, allowing for a history of two to three months.

	Monday	Tuesday	Wednesday	Thursday	Friday	
Week 1	A	A	A	A	B	
Week 2	A	A	A	A	B	
Week 3	A	A	A	A	B	One month of backups
Week 4	A	A	A	A	B	
Week 5	A	A	C			

A = Incremental "son" backup (daily)
B = Full "father" backup (weekly)
C = Full "grandfather" backup (monthly)

Figure 14-19   The grandfather-father-son backup rotation scheme

Once you have determined your backup rotation scheme, you should ensure that backup activity is recorded in a backup log. Information that belongs in a backup log include the backup date, tape identification (day of week or type), type of data backed up (for example, Accounting Department spreadsheets or a day's worth of catalog orders), type of the backup (full, incremental, or differential), files that were backed up, and site at which the tape is stored. Having this information available in case of a server failure will greatly simplify data recovery.

Finally, once you begin to back up network data, you should establish a regular schedule of verification. In other words, from time to time (depending on how often your data change and how critical the information is), you should attempt to recover some critical files from your backup media. Many network administrators can attest that the darkest hour of their career was when they were asked to retrieve critical files from a backup tape and found that no backup data existed because their backup system never worked in the first place!

DISASTER RECOVERY

Disaster recovery is the process of restoring your critical functionality and data after an enterprise-wide outage that affects more than a single system or a limited group of users. Disaster recovery must take into account the possible extremes, rather than relatively minor outages, failures, security breaches, or data corruption. In a disaster recovery plan, you should consider the worst-case scenarios, from a far-reaching hurricane to a military attack. You should also consider what might happen if your typical networking staff isn't available. The plan should outline multiple contingencies, in case your best options don't pan out. Although you must attend to all of the protection methods discussed in this chapter, disaster recovery also requires a comprehensive strategy for restoring functionality and data after things go terribly awry.

Every organization should have a disaster recovery team (with an appointed coordinator) and a disaster recovery plan. This plan should address not only computer systems, but also power, telephony, and paper-based files. When writing the sections of the plan related to computer systems, your team should specifically address the following issues:

- Contact names for emergency coordinators who will execute the disaster recovery response in case of disaster, as well as roles and responsibilities of other staff.

- Details on which data and servers are being backed up, how frequently backups occur, where backups are kept (off-site), and, most importantly, how backed up data can be recovered in full.

- Details on network topology, redundancy, and agreements with national service carriers, in case local or regional vendors fall prey to the same disaster.

- Regular strategies for testing the disaster recovery plan.

- A plan for managing the crisis, including regular communications with employees and customers. Consider the possibility that regular communications modes (such as phone lines) might be unavailable.

Having a comprehensive disaster recovery plan not only lessens the risk of losing critical data in case of extreme situations, but also makes potential customers and your insurance providers look more favorably on your organization.

14

CHAPTER SUMMARY

❏ Integrity refers to the soundness of your network's files, systems, and connections. To ensure their integrity, you must protect them from anything that might render them unusable, such as corruption, tampering, natural disasters, and viruses. Availability of a file or system refers to how consistently and reliably it can be accessed by authorized personnel.

❏ Several basic measures can be employed to protect data and systems on a network: (1) prevent anyone other than a network administrator from opening or changing the system files; (2) monitor the network for unauthorized access or changes; (3) record authorized system changes in a change management system; (4) install redundant components; (5) perform regular health checks on the network; (6) monitor system performance, error logs, and the system log book regularly; (7) keep backups, boot disks, and emergency repair disks current and available; and (8) implement and enforce security and disaster recovery policies.

❏ A virus is a program that replicates itself so as to infect more computers, either through network connections or through floppy disks passed among users. Viruses may damage files or systems or simply annoy users by flashing messages or pictures on the screen or by causing the computer to beep.

❏ Many other unwanted and potentially destructive programs are mistakenly called viruses. For example, a program that disguises itself as something useful but actually harms your system is called a Trojan horse. An example of a Trojan horse is an executable file sent to you over the Internet that purportedly installs a new game, but actually reformats your hard disk.

❏ Boot sector viruses are the most common types of viruses. They reside on the boot sector of a floppy disk and become transferred to the partition sector or the DOS boot sector on a hard disk. The only way a boot sector virus can move from a floppy to a hard disk is if the floppy disk is left in the drive when the machine starts up.

❏ Macro viruses take the form of a word-processing or spreadsheet program macro, which may be executed when you use the word-processing or spreadsheet program. Macro viruses were the first type of virus to infect data files rather than executable files. Because data files are more apt to be shared among users and because macro viruses are typically easier to write than executable viruses, these viruses have quickly become widespread.

❏ File-infected viruses attach themselves to executable files. When the infected executable file runs, the virus copies itself to memory. Later, the virus will attach itself to other executable files.

❏ Network viruses take advantage of network protocols, commands, messaging programs, and data links to propagate themselves. Although all viruses could theoretically travel across network connections, network viruses are specially designed to take advantage of network vulnerabilities.

❑ Worms are not technically viruses, but rather programs that run independently and travel between computers and across networks. Although they do not alter other programs as viruses do, worms may carry viruses.

❑ Any type of virus may have additional characteristics that make it harder to detect and eliminate. These characteristics may be encrypted, stealth, polymorphic, or time-dependent.

❑ Although a well-written virus attempts to avoid detection, you may suspect the presence of a virus on your system if you notice any of the following symptoms: unexplained increases in file sizes; programs (such as Microsoft Word) launching, running, or exiting more slowly than usual; unusual error messages appearing without probable cause; significant, unexpected loss of system memory; or fluctuations in display quality.

❑ A good antivirus program should be able to detect viruses through signature scanning, integrity checking, and heuristic checking. It should also be compatible with your network environment, centrally manageable, easy to use (transparent to users), and not prone to false alarms.

❑ Antivirus software is merely one piece of the puzzle in protecting your network from viruses. An antivirus policy is another essential component. It should provide rules for using antivirus software and policies for installing programs, sharing files, and using floppy disks. Furthermore, it should be authorized and supported by the organization's management and should include sanctions for disobeying the policy.

❑ A virus hoax is a false alert about a dangerous, new virus that could seriously damage your workstation. Virus hoaxes usually have no realistic basis and should be ignored.

❑ In broad terms, a failure is a deviation from a specified level of system performance for a given period of time. A fault, on the other hand, is the malfunction of one component of a system. A fault can result in a failure. The goal of fault-tolerant systems is to prevent faults from progressing to failures.

❑ Fault tolerance is a system's capacity to continue performing despite an unexpected hardware or software malfunction. It can be achieved in varying degrees, with the optimal level of fault tolerance for a system depending on how critical its services and files are to productivity. At the highest level of fault tolerance, a system will be unaffected by a drastic problem, such as a power failure.

❑ An excellent way to achieve fault tolerance is to provide duplicate elements to compensate for faults in critical components, a practice known as redundancy. You can implement redundancy for servers, cabling, routers, hubs, gateways, NICs, hard disks, power supplies, and other components.

❑ To assess the fault tolerance of your network you must look for single points of failure—places on the network where, if a fault occurs, the transfer of data may break down without possibility of an automatic recovery.

❑ As you consider sophisticated fault-tolerance techniques for servers, routers, and WAN links, remember to address the environment in which your devices operate. Protecting your data also involves protecting your network from excessive heat or moisture, break-ins, and natural disasters.

14

❐ Networks cannot tolerate power loss or less than optimal power. You will have to guard against the following power flaws: blackouts, brownouts (sags), surges, and line noise.

❐ A UPS is a battery-operated power source directly attached to one or more devices and to a power supply (such as a wall outlet), which prevents undesired features of the power source from harming the device or interrupting its services. UPSs vary widely in the type of power aberrations they can rectify, the length of time they can provide power, and the number of devices they can support.

❐ A standby UPS provides continuous voltage to a device by switching virtually instantaneously to the battery when it detects a loss of power from the wall outlet. Upon restoration of the power, the standby UPS switches the device to use A/C power again. A standby UPS requires a brief service outage when it detects that A/C power has stopped; in this time, a sensitive device (such as a server) may have already detected the power loss and shut down or restarted.

❐ An online UPS uses the A/C power from the wall outlet to continuously charge its battery, while providing power to a network device through its battery. In other words, a server connected to an online UPS always relies on the UPS battery for its electricity. An online UPS provides the best kind of power redundancy available. Because the server never needs to switch from the wall outlet's power to the UPS's power, no risk of momentarily losing service exists.

❐ To choose the best UPS for your network, you must consider a number of factors: the amount of power needed, the period of time in which you must keep a device running, line conditioning, and cost.

❐ If your organization cannot withstand a power loss, either because of its computer services or other electrical needs, you might consider investing in an electrical generator for your building. Generators can be powered by diesel, liquid propane gas, natural gas, or steam. They do not provide surge protection, but they do provide clean (free from noise) electricity.

❐ The type of network topology that offers the best fault tolerance is a mesh topology. In a mesh network, nodes are connected either directly or indirectly by multiple pathways. In a mesh topology, data can travel over these multiple paths from any one point to another.

❐ The physical media you use may also offer redundancy. A SONET ring, for example, can easily recover from a fault in one of its links because it forms a self-healing ring.

❐ When components are hot swappable, they have identical functions and can automatically assume the functions of their counterpart if it suffers a fault. They are called hot swappable because they can be changed (or swapped) while a machine is still running (hot).

❐ The use of multiple components enables load balancing, or an automatic distribution of traffic or processing to optimize response.

❐ As with other devices, you can make servers more fault-tolerant by supplying them with redundant components. Critical servers often contain redundant NICs, processors, and/or hard disks. These redundant components provide assurance that if one fails, the whole system won't fail, and they enable load balancing.

❏ A fault-tolerance technique that involves utilizing a second, identical server to duplicate the transactions and data storage of one server is called server mirroring. Mirroring can take place between servers that are either geographically side by side or distant. Mirroring requires not only a link between the servers, but also software running on both servers to enable the servers to continually synchronize their actions and to permit one to take over in case the other fails.

❏ Server clustering is a fault-tolerance technique that links multiple servers together to act as a single server. In this configuration, clustered servers share processing duties and appear as a single server to users. If one server in the cluster fails, the other servers in the cluster will automatically take over its data transaction and storage responsibilities.

❏ An important server redundancy feature is a Redundant Array of Inexpensive Disks (RAID). All types of RAID use shared, multiple physical or logical hard disks to ensure data integrity and availability; some designs also increase storage capacity and improve performance. RAID is typically used on servers, but not on workstations because of its added cost. RAID is accomplished through a combination of both software and hardware.

❏ RAID Level 0 is a very simple implementation of RAID in which data are written in 64 KB blocks equally across all of the disks in the array, a technique known as disk striping. Disk striping is not a fault-tolerant method because if one disk fails, the data contained in it will be inaccessible. Thus RAID Level 0 does not provide true redundancy.

❏ RAID Level 1 provides redundancy through a process called disk mirroring, in which data from one disk are automatically copied to another disk as the information is written. This option can be considered a dynamic data backup. If one disk in the array fails, the disk array controller will automatically switch to the disk that was mirroring the failed disk.

❏ RAID Level 3 involves disk striping with parity error correction code. Parity refers to the integrity of the data as expressed in the number of 1s contained in each group of correctly transmitted bits. In RAID Level 3, parity error checking takes place when the data are written across the disk array.

❏ RAID Level 5 is the most popular, highly fault-tolerant, data storage technique in use today. In RAID Level 5, data are written in small blocks across several disks; parity error checking information is also distributed among the disks.

❏ Network attached storage (NAS) is a device or group of devices attached to a client/server network dedicated to data storage. It uses its own file system but relies on a traditional network transmission method such as Ethernet to interact with the rest of the client/server network.

❏ A storage area network (SAN) is a distinct network of multiple storage devices and servers that provides fast, highly available, and highly fault-tolerant access to large quantities of data for a client/server network. SAN uses a proprietary network transmission method (such as Fibre Channel) rather than a traditional network transmission method such as Ethernet.

14

◻ A backup is a copy of data or program files created for archiving or safekeeping purposes. If you do not back up your data, you risk losing everything through a hard disk fault, fire, flood, or malicious or accidental erasure or corruption. No matter how reliable and fault-tolerant you believe your server's hard disk (or disks) to be, you still risk losing everything unless you make backups on separate media and store them off-site.

◻ Currently, the most popular method for backing up networked systems is tape backup, because it is simple and relatively economical. Tape backups require a tape drive connected to the network (via a system such as a file server or dedicated, networked workstation), software to manage and perform backups, and backup media.

◻ To select the appropriate tape backup solution for your network, you should consider the following issues: storage capacity; proven reliability; data error checking techniques; speed; cost of the tape drive, software, and media; compatibility with existing network hardware and software; and extent of automation.

◻ Many companies on the Internet now offer to back up data over the Internet—that is, to perform online backups. Usually, online backup providers require that you have their client software in addition to a connection to the Internet. They implement strict security measures to protect the data in transit, because the information must traverse public carrier links. Both the backup and restore processes are entirely automated.

◻ A good backup strategy should be well documented and should address at least the following questions: What kind of rotation schedule will backups follow? At what time of day or night will the backups occur? How will you verify the accuracy of backups? Where will backup media be stored? Who will take responsibility for ensuring that backups occurred? How long will you save backups? Where will backup and recovery documentation be stored?

◻ Different backup methods provide varying levels of certainty and corresponding labor and cost. A full backup copies all data on all servers to a storage medium, regardless of whether the data are new or changed. An incremental backup copies only data that have changed since the last backup A differential backup copies only data that have changed since the last backup, and that information is marked for subsequent backup, regardless of whether it has changed.

◻ If you are responsible for the network's backups, your most important decision will relate to the backup rotation scheme. The aim of a good backup rotation scheme is to provide excellent data reliability but not to overtax your network or require much intervention.

◻ The most popular backup rotation scheme is called "grandfather-father-son." This scheme uses daily (son), weekly (father), and monthly (grandfather) backup sets.

◻ Once you have determined your backup rotation scheme, you should ensure that backup activity is recorded in a backup log. Information that belongs in a backup log include the following: when the backup took place; which tape was used (day of week or type); which data were backed up; whether the backup was full, incremental, or differential; which files were backed up; and where the tape is stored. Having this information available in case of a server failure will greatly simplify data recovery.

◻ Disaster recovery is the process of restoring your critical functionality and data after an enterprise-wide outage that affects more than a single system or a limited group of users. It must account for the possible extremes, rather than relatively minor outages, failures, security breaches, or data corruption. In a disaster recovery plan, you should consider the worst-case scenarios, from a hurricane to a military attack.

◻ Every organization should have a disaster recovery team (with an appointed coordinator) and a disaster recovery plan. The plan should address not only computer systems, but also power, telephony, and paper-based files.

KEY TERMS

array — A group of hard disks.

availability — How consistently and reliably a file, device, or connection can be accessed by authorized personnel.

backup — A copy of data or program files created for archiving or safekeeping purposes.

backup rotation scheme — A plan for when and how often backups occur, and which backups are full, incremental, or differential.

blackout — A complete power loss.

boot sector virus — A virus that resides on the boot sector of a floppy disk and is transferred to the partition sector or the DOS boot sector on a hard disk. A boot sector virus can move from a floppy to a hard disk only if the floppy disk is left in the drive when the machine starts up.

brownout — A momentary decrease in voltage, also known as a *sag*. An overtaxed electrical system may cause brownouts, recognizable as a dimming of the lights.

differential backup — A backup method in which only data that have changed since the last backup are copied to a storage medium, and that information is marked for subsequent backup, regardless of whether it has changed.

disaster recovery — The process of restoring critical functionality and data to a network after an enterprise-wide outage that affects more than a single system or a limited group of users.

disk mirroring — A RAID technique in which data from one disk are automatically copied to another disk as the information is written.

disk striping — A simple implementation of RAID in which data are written in 64 KB blocks equally across all disks in the array.

encrypted virus — A virus that is encrypted to prevent detection.

fail-over — The capability for one component (such as a NIC or server) to assume another component's responsibilities without manual intervention.

failure — A deviation from a specified level of system performance for a given period of time. A failure occurs when something doesn't work as promised or as planned.

fault — The malfunction of one component of a system. A fault can result in a failure.

fault tolerance — The capacity for a system to continue performing despite an unexpected hardware or software malfunction.

14

Fibre Channel — A distinct network transmission method that relies on fiber-optic media and its own, proprietary protocol. Fibre Channel is capable of 1-Gbps (and soon, 2-Gbps) throughput.

file-infected virus — A virus that attaches itself to executable files. When the infected executable file runs, the virus copies itself to memory. Later, the virus will attach itself to other executable files.

full backup — A backup in which all data on all servers are copied to a storage medium, regardless of whether the data are new or changed.

grandfather-father-son — A backup rotation scheme that uses daily (son), weekly (father), and monthly (grandfather) backup sets.

hard disk redundancy — See *Redundant Array of Inexpensive Disks (RAID).*

heuristic scanning — A type of virus scanning that attempts to identify viruses by discovering "virus-like" behavior.

hot swappable — A characteristic that enables identical components to be inter-changed (or swapped) while a machine is still running (hot). Once installed, hot swappable components automatically assume the functions of their counterpart if it suffers a fault.

incremental backup — A backup in which only data that have changed since the last backup are copied to a storage medium.

integrity — The soundness of a network's files, systems, and connections. To ensure integrity, you must protect your network from anything that might render it unusable, such as corruption, tampering, natural disasters, and viruses.

integrity checking — A method of comparing the current characteristics of files and disks against an archived version of these characteristics to discover any changes. The most common example of integrity checking involves a checksum.

intrusion detection — The process of monitoring the network for unauthorized access to its devices.

line noise — Fluctuations in voltage levels caused by other devices on the network or by electromagnetic interference.

load balancing — An automatic distribution of traffic over multiple links, hard disks, or processors intended to optimize responses.

macro viruses — A newer type of virus that takes the form of a word-processing or spreadsheet program macro, which may execute when a word-processing or spread-sheet program is in use.

network attached storage (NAS) — A device or set of devices attached to a client/server network that is dedicated to providing highly fault-tolerant access to large quantities of data. NAS depends on traditional network transmission methods such as Ethernet.

network virus — A type of virus that takes advantage of network protocols, com-mands, messaging programs, and data links to propagate itself. Although all viruses could theoretically travel across network connections, network viruses are specially designed to attack network vulnerabilities.

online backup — A technique in which data are backed up to a central location over the Internet.

online UPS — A power supply that uses the A/C power from the wall outlet to continuously charge its battery, while providing power to a network device through its battery.

parity — The mechanism used to verify the integrity of data by making the number of bits in a byte sum to either an odd or even number.

parity error checking — The process of comparing the parity of data read from a disk with the type of parity used by the system.

polymorphic virus — A type of virus that changes its characteristics (such as the arrangement of its bytes, size, and internal instructions) every time it is transferred to a new system, making it harder to identify.

RAID Level 0 — An implementation of RAID in which data are written in 64 KB blocks equally across all disks in the array.

RAID Level 1 — An implementation of RAID that provides redundancy through disk mirroring, in which data from one disk are automatically copied to another disk as the information is written.

RAID Level 3 — An implementation of RAID that uses disk striping for data and parity error correction code on a separate parity disk.

RAID Level 5 — The most popular, highly fault-tolerant, data storage technique in use today, RAID Level 5 writes data in small blocks across several disks. At the same time, it writes parity error checking information among several disks.

redundancy — The use of more than one identical component for storing, processing, or transporting data.

Redundant Array of Inexpensive Disks (RAID) — A server redundancy measure that uses shared, multiple physical or logical hard disks to ensure data integrity and availability. Some RAID designs also increase storage capacity and improve performance. See also *disk striping,* and *disk mirroring.*

sag — See *brownout.*

server clustering — A fault-tolerance technique that links multiple servers together to act as a single server. In this configuration, clustered servers share processing duties and appear as a single server to users. If one server in the cluster fails, the other servers in the cluster will automatically take over its data transaction and storage responsibilities.

server mirroring — A fault-tolerance technique in which one server duplicates the transactions and data storage of another, identical server. Server mirroring requires a link between the servers and software running on both servers so that the servers can continually synchronize their actions and take over in case the other fails.

signature scanning — The comparison of a file's content with known virus signatures (unique identifying characteristics in the code) in a signature database to determine whether the file is a virus.

standby UPS — A power supply that provides continuous voltage to a device by switching virtually instantaneously to the battery when it detects a loss of power from the wall outlet. Upon restoration of the power, the standby UPS switches the device to use A/C power again.

14

stealth virus — A type of virus that hides itself to prevent detection. Typically, stealth viruses disguise themselves as legitimate programs or replace part of a legitimate program's code with their destructive code.

storage area network (SAN) — A distinct network of multiple storage devices and servers that provides fast, highly available, and highly fault-tolerant access to large quantities of data for a client/server network. SAN uses a proprietary network transmission method (such as Fibre Channel) rather than a traditional network transmission method such as Ethernet.

surge — A momentary increase in voltage due to distant lightning strikes or electrical problems.

time-dependent virus — A virus programmed to activate on a particular date. This type of virus, also known as a "time bomb," can remain dormant and harmless until its activation date arrives.

Trojan horse — A program that disguises itself as something useful but actually harms your system.

uninterruptible power supply (UPS) — A battery-operated power source directly attached to one or more devices and to a power supply (such as a wall outlet), which prevents undesired features of the power source from harming the device or interrupting its services.

vault — A large tape storage library.

virus — A program that replicates itself so as to infect more computers, either through network connections or through floppy disks passed among users. Viruses may damage files or systems or simply annoy users by flashing messages or pictures on the screen or by causing the keyboard to beep.

virus hoax — A rumor, or false alert, about a dangerous, new virus that could supposedly cause serious damage to your workstation.

volt-amp (VA) — A measure of electrical power. A volt-amp is the product of the voltage and current (measured in amps) of the electricity on a line.

worm — An unwanted program that travels between computers and across networks. Although worms do not alter other programs as viruses do, they may carry viruses.

Review Questions

1. Describe five scenarios that might detrimentally affect the integrity or availability of your network's data.

2. Which of the following percentages represents the highest availability for a network?

   a. 0.10%

   b. 0.01%

   c. 99%

   d. 99.99%

3. To ensure that a system change does not detrimentally affect integrity and availability, what information should you record about the change?

   a. who performed the change and why it was necessary

   b. when the change occurred, why it was necessary, who performed the change, and what the change involved

   c. what the change involved and when it occurred

   d. when the change occurred and how to reverse it

4. Which of the following symptoms might make you suspect that your workstation is infected with a macro virus?

   a. Your computer takes a long time to start up.

   b. While in Microsoft Word, you receive a message that says, "WXYC rules the roost."

   c. While navigating through folders, your icons suddenly switch from pictures of folders to pictures of pineapples.

   d. You can no longer save word-processing files to your hard disk.

5. Why are stealth viruses difficult to detect?

   a. They attach themselves to legitimate programs.

   b. They frequently change their file size characteristics.

   c. They disguise themselves as legitimate programs.

   d. They destroy the file allocation table to prevent directory scanning.

6. Name three key components of an enterprise-wide antivirus policy.

7. Which of the following is a popular antivirus program?

   a. Norton VirusPro

   b. Scandisk

   c. Norton AntiVirus

   d. McAfee Virex

8. A worm is a type of polymorphic virus. True or False?

9. How does a Trojan horse disguise itself?

   a. It frequently changes its code characteristics.

   b. It disguises itself as a useful program.

   c. It prevents the user from performing directory scans.

   d. It does not appear in a directory listing.

10. Which of the following techniques does a polymorphic virus employ to make itself more difficult to detect?

    a. It frequently changes its code characteristics.

    b. It disguises itself as a useful program.

14

    c. It damages the file allocation table to prevent directory scanning.

    d. It moves from one location to another on the hard disk.

11. If your antivirus software uses signature scanning, what must you do to keep its virus-fighting capabilities current?

    a. Purchase new virus signature scanning software every three months.

    b. Reinstall the virus scanning software each month.

    c. Manually edit the signature scanning file.

    d. Regularly update the antivirus software's signature database.

12. What might you tell a user who receives what seems to be a virus hoax message?

    a. Ignore and delete the message.

    b. Open the message to verify that it is indeed a hoax.

    c. Send the message to the help desk.

    d. Save the message for you to review.

13. Describe the main difference between a fault and a failure.

14. Fail-over is a technique used in highly fault-tolerant systems. True or False?

15. What makes two components hot swappable?

    a. Both are similar and installed in the same device.

    b. Both are similar and one can be quickly swapped in for the other in case of a fault.

    c. Both are identical, both are installed in the same device, and one can instantly take over from the other in case of a fault.

    d. Both are identical and one can be quickly swapped in for the other in case of a fault.

16. Over time, what might electrical line noise do to your system?

    a. wear down the power switch

    b. damage the internal circuit boards

    c. increase the system board's response time

    d. cause more frequent outages

17. How long will an online UPS take to switch its attached devices to battery power?

    a. 15 seconds

    b. 10 seconds

    c. 5 seconds

    d. no time

18. Which of the following is the most highly fault-tolerant network topology?

    a. bus

    b. ring

    c. partial mesh

    d. full mesh

19. Which characteristic of SONET rings makes them highly fault-tolerant?

    a. They are self-healing.

    b. They are geographically diverse.

    c. They are made of fiber-optic cable.

    d. They share traffic over many lines.

20. Describe how load balancing between redundant NICs works.

21. Why is simple disk striping not fault-tolerant?

    a. It can be performed only on a single disk drive.

    b. If one disk fails, data contained on that disk are unavailable.

    c. It does not keep a dynamic record of where data are striped.

    d. It relies on a single disk controller.

22. Why is RAID Level 5 superior to RAID Level 3?

23. Which of the following can be considered an advantage of server clustering over server mirroring?

    a. Clustering does not affect network performance.

    b. Clustering fail-over takes place more rapidly.

    c. Clustering has no geographical distance limitations.

    d. Clustering keeps a more complete copy of a disk's data.

24. What is currently the greatest disadvantage to using server clustering?

    a. It's expensive.

    b. It detrimentally affects performance.

    c. It requires that servers in a cluster be geographically close.

    d. It is difficult to maintain.

25. List four considerations that you should weigh when deciding on a data backup solution.

14

26. Which factor must you consider when using online backups that you don't typically have to consider when backing up to a LAN tape drive?

    a. reliability

    b. geographical distance

    c. security

    d. time to recover

27. In a grandfather-father-son backup scheme, the October–week 1–Thursday backup tape would contain what types of files?

    a. files changed since last Thursday

    b. files changed since a month ago Thursday

    c. files changed since Wednesday

    d. files changed since a week ago Wednesday

28. Which of the following is a major disadvantage to performing full system backups on a daily basis?

    a. They would take too long to perform.

    b. They would take too long to restore.

    c. They would be less reliable than incremental backups.

    d. They would require manual intervention.

29. How can you verify the accuracy of tape backups?

30. Name four components of a smart disaster recovery plan.

HANDS-ON PROJECTS

In the following Hands-on Projects, you will have a chance to experiment with some fault-tolerance measures. Bear in mind that solutions will vary with each network environment.

Project 14-1

For this project, you will need a NetWare 5.x server with a Windows 2000 Professional client workstation attached. The server should contain at least a Pentium processor, 70 MB of RAM, 100 MB of free disk space, in addition to the NetWare operating system (with all the latest patches) and its connection to the network. The client workstation should contain at least a Pentium processor, 64 MB of RAM, 200 MB of free disk space, a CD-ROM drive, and the Novell Client for NetWare. You should be able to connect to not only the NetWare server, but also the Internet from that workstation. You will also need a copy of the Norton AntiVirus Corporate Edition for NetWare Servers software on CDs.

To install Norton AntiVirus on a NetWare server:

1. Log onto the server as an administrator from the Windows 2000 Professional workstation attached to your NetWare server.

2. Map a drive to the server's **SYS** volume.

3. Insert the Norton AntiVirus CD number 2 into your workstation's CD-ROM drive. If the CD menu does not automatically open, open **My Computer**, double-click the CD-ROM drive, then double-click on the **setup.exe** file to begin the installation process.

4. Select the **Install Norton AntiVirus to Servers** option, then click **Next**. The License Agreement dialog box appears.

5. After reading the license agreement, check **I agree**, then click **Next** to continue. The Select Items dialog box appears.

6. Check the **Server Program** option, then click **Next** to continue.

7. Double-click **NetWare Services**. The Select Computers dialog box appears.

8. Double-click **NetWare Directory Services**, then select the SYS volume object where you want to install the AntiVirus software. (To navigate through the NDS tree, double-click the tree object, then select organizational units until you find the one that contains the SYS volume object you want.) Click **Add**.

9. Enter the appropriate container name, and the user name and password for this container, as prompted, then click **Next** to continue.

10. You will be prompted for a location to install the Norton AntiVirus program. Keep the default install path and click **Next** to continue. The Select Server Group dialog box appears.

11. Type the name **CLASS** for the new server group and click **Next** to continue. You will be asked to confirm that you want to create this server group. Click **Yes** to confirm.

12. Select **Manual Startup** and click **Next** to continue. The Using The Symantec System Center Program dialog box appears.

13. Click **Next** until you reach the final Setup screen, reading each screen of instructions carefully, then click **Close**. The AntiVirus installation commences.

14. Now that you have installed the software on the server, you will need to initialize it. At the server console, type **load sys:nav\vpstart.nlm /install** to initialize the Norton AntiVirus program. After the NLM has loaded, you can use Norton AntiVirus on your NetWare server to detect viruses.

15. At the Windows 2000 Professional workstation, experiment with the NAV program to immediately scan servers, change configuration options, and set a regularly scheduled server scan.

Project 14-2

Because the Norton AntiVirus software uses signature scanning as one of its antivirus measures, you will have to update the signature database on a regular schedule. In this exercise, you will update the software you installed on your NetWare server in Project 14-1.

1. Open your Web browser and go to **www.sarc.com/avcenter/download.html**, the Symantec Security Updates page.

14

2. Click **Download Virus Definitions Updates** in the center of the page. The Download Virus Definitions page opens.

3. Use the list arrow to select **English, US** (if it is not already selected).

4. From the list of Symantec products, click **Norton AntiVirus for NetWare**.

5. Click **Download Updates** to continue. The Download English Updates page appears.

6. Click on the name of the update file that is appropriate for Norton AntiVirus Corporate Edition (the version you installed in Project 14-1). The File Download dialog box opens.

7. Click **OK** to choose to save the file to disk.

8. The Save As dialog box opens. Save the file to your **C:\TEMP** (or a similar temporary) directory. Click **Save** to begin the download.

9. If you aren't already logged in as Administrator, log onto the network from your workstation as an Administrator. Run the file you just downloaded, supplying the location of your NAV NLM.

10. Follow instructions on the screen to ensure that your antivirus signature database was updated.

Project 14-3

In this exercise, you will use an online UPS capacity tool to determine the UPS needed for an imaginary network server. UPS vendors such as APC supply these online tools so that you do not have to calculate by hand the VA necessary for your network. To complete this project, you will need a workstation with access to the Internet.

1. From the networked workstation, launch the Web browser and go to **www.apcc.com/template/size/apc/**. This Size UPS Web site provides a UPS sizing utility that you can use to determine your UPS capacity needs. In this case, you want to determine the needs of your server.

2. Click the **Server** link in the middle of the screen. The UPS Selector page opens. In the middle of the screen, a drop-down list of server types appears.

3. Click the list arrow, click **Compaq ProLiant 850R**, then click **Submit**. A configuration page for this server opens, allowing you to specify a number of options that characterize your server.

4. To the default specifications, add a 22-inch LCD monitor, one attached tape drive, and four external hard drives.

5. Click **Add to Configuration**. A new page opens, allowing you to set more parameters for your server.

6. Click **Continue to User Preferences**.

7. Note the defaults, including a 20-minute run time.

8. Choose your region from the drop-down list to make sure the correct voltage is used in the UPS power requirements calculation.

9. Click **Show Solution**. A new page opens, containing the recommendations for the type of server that you specified.

10. Scroll to the bottom of the page to view your configuration. How many volts did the utility estimate your configuration would require? How many watts and VA would the UPS have to supply to keep the server, monitor, tape drive, and external hard disks running for 20 minutes?

11. Click the **Back** button on your browser to return to the last set of parameters you specified.

12. Click the **Delete Device** button near the bottom of the page to erase the configuration you have just generated.

13. Click **OK** to confirm that you want to delete this device from your list of UPS configurations.

14. The UPS Selector Web page appears. Click **Add Another Device**.

15. Repeat Steps 2 through 8, this time selecting an EMC Celera SE server. How many volts would this configuration require? How many watts and VA would the UPS have to supply to keep the Celera SE server running for 20 minutes?

CASE PROJECTS

1. You have been asked to help a local hospital improve its network's fault tolerance. The hospital's network carries critical patient care data in real time from both a mainframe host and several servers to PCs in operating rooms, doctors' offices, the billing office, teaching labs, and remote clinics located across the region. Of course, all of the data transferred is highly confidential and must not be lost or accessed by unauthorized personnel. Specifically, the network consists of the following:

   ❑ Six hundred PCs are connected to five shared servers that run Novell NetWare 5.0. Fifty of these PCs serve as training PCs in medical school classrooms. Two hundred PCs sit in doctors' offices and are used to view and update patient records, submit accounting information, and so on. Twenty PCs are used in operating rooms to perform imaging and for accessing data in real time. The remaining PCs are used by administrative staff.

   ❑ The PCs are connected in a mostly switched, star-wired bus network using Ethernet 100BaseTX technology. Where switches are not used, some hubs serve smaller workgroups of administrative and physician staff.

   ❑ An Internet gateway supports e-mail, online medical searches, and VPN communications with four remote clinics. The Internet connection is a single T1 link to a local Internet service provider.

14

❑ A firewall prevents unauthorized access from the T1 connection into the hospital's network.

The hospital's IT director has asked you to identify the critical points of failure in her network and to suggest how she might eliminate them. On a sheet of paper, draw a logical diagram of the network and identify the single points of failure, then recommend which points of failure should be addressed to increase availability and how to achieve this goal. For each fault-tolerant component or method you recommend, find manufacturers' data available on the Web to identify its cost.

2. Unfortunately, the solution you provided for the hospital was rejected by the board of directors because it was too expensive. How would you determine where to cut costs in the proposal? What questions should you ask the IT director? What points of failure do you suggest absolutely must be addressed with redundancy?

3. Your second proposal, with its reduced cost, was accepted by the board of directors. Now the hospital's IT director has asked you to outline a disaster recovery plan. Based on what you have learned about the hospital's topology, usage patterns, and current fault-tolerance measures, develop a disaster recovery plan for the hospital that specifically addresses how functionality and data will be restored.

4. After you submitted your outline of the hospital's disaster recovery plan, the IT director takes you aside and confesses that she isn't sure whether her network administrator is doing the right thing with the hospital's antivirus software and policy. Currently, the antivirus software is installed on each workstation in the hospital and scans each workstation's memory and hard disk once per week. She asks whether you have a solution for a better antivirus implementation and whether she should ask users to scan their hard disks more frequently than once per week. How do you respond?

NETWORK SECURITY

After reading this chapter and completing the exercises, you will be able to:

➤ Identify security risks in LANs and WANs

➤ Explain how physical security contributes to network security

➤ Discuss hardware- and design-based security techniques

➤ Use network operating system techniques to provide basic security

➤ Implement enhanced security through specialized software

➤ Describe the elements of an effective security policy

ON THE JOB

With few exceptions, today's commercial computer networks are vulnerable to break-ins. As a network security assessor, I've seen even the most secure commercial networks breached within a few days' time.

Commercial state-of-the-art network security includes such technical solutions as public key encryption, one-time passwords, over 1024-bit strong encryption, fingerprint verification, and even retinal scanning. But the reality remains that an intruder can access secured systems by finding "convenient short cuts" installed by system and network administrators.

During network security assessments, for example, we often find a trusted relationship between two or more hosts. One of the hosts is usually less secure than the others. When we gain access to one system, the others dutifully allow us right in.

In one instance, a firewall-protected network appeared very secure. However, when we scanned the TCP port ranges, we found the signature of a popular commercial mail server. We ran a mail client, attached to the server, and tried a couple of generic user IDs. Incredibly, we were able to gain access to the network manager's mailbox without a password! Even worse, sensitive mail was not encrypted. One message included the complete set of configuration statements for some remote office network routers. Without firewalls, these routers were connected to the Internet and had trusted relationships with the home office. On gaining access to one of the remote office routers, we immediately logged in to the organization's home office router. From there, it was a short time before we found and gained access to a number of UNIX and Windows NT servers—the backbone of the organization's network.

Two small "conveniences" enabled us to circumvent the highly secured firewall and breach the organization's network within a couple of hours!

David Klann
Berbee Information Networks, Inc.

In the early days of computing, when secured mainframes acted as central hosts and data repositories that were accessed only by dumb terminals with limited rights, network security was all but unassailable. As networks have become more geographically distributed and heterogeneous, however, the risk of their misuse has also increased. Consider the largest, most heterogeneous network in existence: the Internet. Because it contains millions of points of entry, millions of servers, and millions of miles of cabling, it is vulnerable to millions of break-ins. Because so many networks connect to the Internet, the threat of an outsider accessing an organization's network via the Internet, and then stealing or destroying data, is very real. In this chapter, you will learn how to assess your network's risks, how to manage those risks, and, perhaps most importantly, how to convey the importance of network security to the rest of your organization through an effective security policy.

TERMINOLOGY

Before delving into network security issues, you should have a clear understanding of terminology frequently used in this field. First, you should understand the difference between a hacker and a cracker. A **hacker** is someone who masters the inner workings of operating systems and utilities in an effort to better understand them. A **cracker** is someone who uses his or her knowledge of operating systems and utilities to intentionally damage or destroy data or systems. The primary difference between hackers and crackers is that hackers do not conduct their experimentation with malicious intent. In fact, hackers may be commissioned to break into networks as part of security audits, in an effort to test whether a cracker could do the same. This chapter will focus on network security in terms of how it protects against crackers.

Another frequently used term related to network security is root. In general, **root** refers to a highly privileged user ID that has all rights to create, delete, modify, move, read, write, or execute files on a system. Specifically, it may mean the administrator on a UNIX-based network. Getting the root ID and password on one system often allows crackers to gain access to attached systems, which is typically their goal. For this reason, information about root accounts should be carefully guarded.

Every network operating system requires that users provide authentication. As you learned in Chapter 8, authentication is the process of verifying a user's validity and authority on a system; it generally takes place during the login process. Different systems use different credentials to authenticate users as they log on. You are probably most familiar with the user ID and password combination. Some systems, however, may also base authentication on digital signatures, IP addresses, session IDs, or a combination of these methods. Generally, the more information required for authentication, the stronger the authentication, and the more secure the system. If a protocol or system uses little information to verify an attempt to access its data, the protocol or system is considered to have weak authentication.

One more term you should understand is "firewall". A **firewall** is a specialized device (usually a router, but possibly only a PC running special software) that selectively filters or blocks traffic between networks. A firewall typically involves a combination of hardware and software (for example, the router's operating system and configuration). The term "firewall" is derived from the physical "wall" installed between rooms in a building or in automobiles between the passenger area and the engine to help prevent fires from spreading from one space to another.

SECURITY AUDITS

Before spending time and money on network security, you should examine your network's security risks. As you learn about each risk facing your network, you should consider the effect that a loss of data, programs, or access would have on your network. The more serious the potential consequences, the more attention you will want to pay to the security of your network. In general, deciding how much to invest in network security is similar to buying life insurance. If you are unmarried with no dependents, no debts, and very few assets, you might not care much about life insurance coverage; you might therefore choose not to invest in monthly premiums. If you have six children and you run a business that employs 200 people, however, you will want to ensure that your loved ones and your business will be protected in case of your death.

In much the same way, different types of organizations have variable levels of network security risk. For example, if you work for a large savings and loan institution that allows its clients to view their current loan status online, you must consider a number of risks associated with data and access. If someone obtained unauthorized access to your network, all of your customers' personal financial data would be vulnerable. On the other hand, if you work for a local greenhouse that is not connected to the Internet and uses its internal LAN only to track plant inventory and sales, you may not be concerned if someone gains access to your network, because you have little to lose and nothing is very confidential. Just as you learned in Chapter 14, the key question is, "What will I lose if my system goes down?" In addition, when considering security risks, you should ask, "How much of the information that I store, transmit, and receive is confidential?"

Every organization should assess its security risks by conducting a **security audit** (a thorough examination of each aspect of the network to determine how it might be compromised). You should perform regular security audits at least annually and preferably quarterly; in addition, you should conduct a security audit after making any significant changes to your network. For each threat listed in the following sections, your security audit should rate the severity of its potential effects, as well as its likelihood. A threat's consequences may be severe, potentially resulting in a network outage or the dispersal of top-secret information, or it may be mild, potentially resulting in a lack of access for one user or the dispersal of a relatively insignificant piece of corporate data. The more devastating a threat's effects and the more likely it is to happen, the more rigorously your security measures should address it. Appendix D, "Examples of Standard Networking Forms," provides an example of a checklist you can use to perform a fundamental security audit.

15

A qualified consulting company can also conduct security audits for your network. The advantage of having an objective third party, such as a consultant, analyze your network is that he or she might find risks that you overlooked because of your familiarity with your environment. Third-party audits may seem expensive, but if your network hosts confidential and critical data, they will be well worth their cost.

After identifying your network's vulnerabilities, you should examine how each security risk might detrimentally affect your data and systems. In the next section, you will learn about risks associated with people, hardware, software, and Internet access.

SECURITY RISKS

Now that you understand the basic terms associated with network security, you are ready to learn about the types of risks facing most networks. The following sections describe these risks. Later in this chapter, you will learn how to protect against each type of threat.

As you learned in Chapter 14, natural disasters, viruses, and power faults can damage a network's data, programs, and hardware. A security breach, however, can harm a network just as easily and quickly. To understand how to manage network security, you should first recognize the types of threats that your network may suffer. Not all security breaches result from a manipulation of network technology. Instead, some occur when staff members purposely or inadvertently reveal their passwords; others result from undeveloped security policies.

As you read about each security threat, think about how it could be prevented, whether it applies to your network (and if so, how damaging it might be), and how it relates to other security threats. Keep in mind that malicious and determined intruders may use one technique which then allows them to use a second technique, which then allows them to use a third technique, and so on. For example, a cracker might discover a user's ID by watching her log onto the network; the cracker might then use a password-cracking program to access the network, where he might plant a program to generate an extraordinary volume of traffic that essentially disables the network's connectivity devices.

Risks Associated with People

By some estimates, human errors, ignorance, and omissions cause more than half of all security breaches sustained by networks. One of the most common methods by which an intruder gains access to a network is to simply ask a user for his or her password. For example, the intruder might pose as a technical support analyst who needs to know the password to troubleshoot a problem, or the password might be learned through a casual conversation about passwords. This strategy is commonly called **social engineering**, because it involves manipulating social relationships to gain access. This and other risks associated with people are listed below. Many people-related risks can be addressed through a clear, simple, and strictly enforced enterprise-wide security policy. You will learn how to develop an effective security policy later in this chapter.

Risks associated with people include the following:

- Intruders or attackers using social engineering or snooping to obtain user passwords

- An administrator incorrectly creating or configuring user IDs, groups, and their associated rights on a file server, resulting in file and login access vulnerabilities

- Network administrators overlooking security flaws in topology or hardware configuration

- Network administrators overlooking security flaws in the operating system or application configuration

- Lack of proper documentation and communication of security policies, leading to deliberate or inadvertent misuse of files or network access

- Dishonest or disgruntled employees abusing their file and access rights

- An unused computer or terminal being left logged onto the network, thereby providing an entry point for an intruder

- Users or administrators choosing easy-to-guess passwords

- Authorized staff leaving computer room doors open or unlocked, allowing unauthorized individuals to enter

- Staff discarding disks or backup tapes in public waste containers

- Administrators neglecting to remove access and file rights for employees who have left the organization

- Users writing their passwords on paper, then placing the paper in an easily accessible place (for example, taping it to their monitor or keyboard)

Human errors account for so many security breaches because taking advantage of them is the easiest way to circumvent network security. Imagine a man named Kyle, who was recently fired from his job at a local bank. Because Kyle felt he was unfairly treated, he wants to take revenge on his employer. He still has a few friends at the bank. Even though the bank's network administrator was wise enough to deactivate Kyle's network logon ID and rights upon his termination, and even though the bank has a policy prohibiting employees from sharing their passwords, Kyle knows his friends' IDs and passwords. Nevertheless, the bank's policy prevents former employees from walking into its offices.

How might Kyle attain his goal of deleting a month's worth of client account activity statements? Although the bank has a network security policy, employees such as Kyle's friends probably don't pay much attention to it. Kyle could most likely walk into the bank's offices, ostensibly to meet one of his friends for lunch. While in the offices, Kyle could either sit down at a machine where his friend was still logged on or log on as his friend because he knows his friend's password. Once in the system, he could locate the account activity statements and delete them. Although this example may be an over-simplification of the process, it isn't far from reality.

Risks Associated with Hardware and Network Design

This section describes security risks inherent in (roughly) Layers 1 and 2 of the OSI Model—the Physical and Data Link layers. Recall that the transmission media, NICs, hubs, and network transmission methods (for example, Ethernet) reside at these layers. This section will also discuss security risks in higher-level hardware, such as routers. At these levels, security breaches require more technical sophistication than those that take advantage of human errors. For instance, to eavesdrop on transmissions passing over

15

CAT5 cabling, an intruder must use a device such as a sniffer. In the middle layers of the OSI Model, it becomes somewhat difficult to distinguish between hardware and software techniques. For example, because a router acts to connect one type of network to another, an intruder might take advantage of the router's security flaws by sending a flood of TCP/IP transmissions to the box, thereby disabling it from carrying legitimate traffic. You will learn about software-related risks in the following section.

The following risks are inherent in network hardware and design:

- Wireless and wire-based transmissions can often be intercepted (whereas spread-spectrum wireless and fiber-based transmissions cannot).

- Networks that use leased public lines, such as T1s or ISDN connections to the Internet, are vulnerable to eavesdropping.

- Network hubs broadcast traffic over the entire segment, thus making transmissions more widely vulnerable to sniffing. (By contrast, switches provide logical point-to-point communications, which limit the availability of data transmissions to the sending and receiving nodes.)

- Unused hub, router, or server ports can be exploited and accessed by crackers if they are not disabled. A router's configuration port, accessible by Telnet, may not be adequately secured.

- If routers are not properly configured to mask internal subnets, users on outside networks (such as the Internet) can read the private addresses.

- Modems attached to network devices may be configured to accept incoming calls, thus opening security holes if they are not properly protected.

- Dial-in access servers used by telecommuting or remote staff may not be carefully secured and monitored.

- Computers hosting very sensitive data may coexist on the same subnet with computers open to the general public.

While security breaches occur less frequently at the lower layers of the OSI Model, they can prove equally, if not more, damaging than security breaches at the higher layers of the OSI Model. Imagine that a cracker wants to bring a library's database and mail servers to a halt. Suppose also that the library's database is public and can be searched by anyone on the Web. The cracker might begin by scanning ports on the database server to determine which have no protection. If she found an open port on the database server, the cracker might connect to the system and deposit a program that would, a few days later, damage operating system files. Or she may launch a heavy stream of traffic that overwhelms the machine and prevents it from functioning. She might also use her newly discovered access to determine the root password on the system, gain access to other systems, and launch a similar attack on the library's mail server, which is attached to the database server. In this way, even a single mistake (not protecting an open port) on one server can lead to failures of multiple systems.

Risks Associated with Protocols and Software

Like hardware, networked software is only as secure as you configure it to be. This section describes risks inherent in the higher layers of the OSI Model, such as the Transport, Session, Presentation, and Application layers. As noted earlier, the distinctions between hardware and software risks are somewhat blurry because protocols and hardware operate in tandem. For example, if a router has not been properly configured, a cracker may exploit the openness of TCP/IP to gain access to a network. Network operating systems and application software present different risks. In most cases, their security is compromised by a poor understanding of file access rights or simple negligence in configuring the software. Remember—even the best encryption, computer room door locks, security policies, and password rules make no difference if you grant the wrong users access to critical data and programs.

The following are some risks pertaining to networking protocols and software:

- TCP/IP contains several security flaws. For example, IP addresses can be falsified easily, checksums can be thwarted, UDP requires no authentication, and TCP requires only weak authentication.

- Trust relationships between one server and another may allow a cracker to access the entire network because of a single flaw.

- Network operating system software typically contains "backdoors" or security flaws. Unless the network administrator performs regular updates, a cracker may exploit these flaws.

- If the network operating system allows server operators to exit to a command prompt, intruders could run destructive command-line programs.

- Administrators might accept the default security options after installing an operating system or application. Often, defaults are not optimal. For example, the default user ID that enables someone to modify anything in Windows 2000 Server is called "Administrator." This default is well known, so if you leave the default ID as "Administrator," you have given a cracker half the information he or she needs to access your system and obtain full rights.

- Transactions that take place between applications, such as databases and Web-based forms, may be open to interception.

To understand the risks that arise when an administrator accepts the default settings associated with a software program, consider the following scenario. Imagine that you have invited a large group of computer science students to tour your IT department. While you're in the computer room talking about subnetting, a bored student standing next to a Windows 2000 Professional workstation that is logged onto the network decides to find out which programs are installed on the workstation. He discovers that this workstation has the SQL Server administrator software installed. Your organization uses a SQL database to hold all of your employees' salaries, addresses, and other confidential information. The student knows a little about SQL, including the facts that the default administrator user ID is called "sa," and that, by default, no password is created for this ID when some-one installs SQL Server. He tries connecting to your SQL database with the "sa" user ID and no password. Because you accepted the defaults for the program during its installation, within seconds the student is able to gain access to your employees' information. He could then change, delete, or steal any of the data.

Risks Associated with Internet Access

Although the Internet has brought computer crime, such as cracking, to the public's attention, network security is more often compromised "from the inside" than from external sources. Nevertheless, the threat of outside intruders is very real, and it will only grow as more people gain access to the Internet.

At the same time, users need to be careful when they connect to the Internet. Even the most popular Web browsers sometimes contain bugs in their most recent releases that permit scripts to access your system while you're connected to the Internet, potentially for the purpose of causing damage. And be careful what information you provide while browsing the Web. Some sites will capture that information to use when attempting to break into systems. Bear in mind that crackers are creative and typically revel in devising new ways of breaking into systems. As a result, new Internet-related security threats arise frequently. By keeping your software current, staying abreast of emerging security threats, and designing your Internet access wisely, you can prevent most of these threats. Common Internet-related security breaches include the following:

- A firewall may not be adequate protection, if it is configured improperly. For example, it may allow outsiders to obtain internal IP addresses, then use those addresses to pretend that they have authority to access your internal network from the Internet—a process called **IP spoofing**. Alternately, a firewall may not be configured correctly to perform even its simplest function—preventing unauthorized packets from entering the LAN from outside. (You will learn more about firewalls later in this chapter.) Correctly configuring a firewall is one of the best means to protect your internal LAN from Internet-based attacks.

- When a user Telnets or FTPs to your site over the Internet, his or her user ID and password will be transmitted in plain text—that is, unencrypted. Anyone monitoring the network can pick up the user ID and password and use it to gain access to the system.

- Crackers may obtain information about your user ID from newsgroups, mailing lists, or forms you have filled out on the Web (for example, to register to win a new car on a promotional site).

- While users remain logged onto Internet chat sessions, they may be vulnerable to other Internet users who might send commands to their machines that cause the screen to fill with garbage characters and require them to terminate their chat sessions. This type of attack is called **flashing**.

- After gaining access to your system through the Internet, a cracker may launch denial-of-service attacks. A **denial-of-service attack** occurs when a system becomes unable to function because it has been deluged with data transmissions or otherwise disrupted. This incursion is a relatively simple attack to launch (for example, a cracker could create a looping program that sent thousands of e-mail messages to your system per minute). The easiest resolution of this problem is to bring down the attacked server, then reconfigure the firewall to deny service (in return) to the attacking machine. Denial-of-service attacks may also result from malfunctioning software. In Chapter 13, you learned how to apply patches to your server's operating system and utilities and research vendors' update alerts. Regularly performing these upgrades is essential to maintaining network security.

ADDRESSING RISKS ASSOCIATED WITH PEOPLE

As you have learned, most network security breaches occur from within an organization, and many take advantage of human errors. This section describes how to minimize the risk of break-ins by communicating with and managing the users in your organization via a thoroughly planned security policy. Before any hardware or software measures can offer effective protection, a security policy must be implemented that tells users how to set secure passwords and that makes critical data accessible only to authorized personnel.

An Effective Security Policy

The first step in securing your network is devising and implementing a security policy. This document identifies your security goals, risks, levels of authority, designated security coordinator and team members, the responsibilities for each team member, and the responsibilities for each employee. In addition, it specifies how to address security breaches. It should not state exactly which hardware, software, architecture, or protocols will be used to ensure security, nor how hardware or software will be installed and configured. These details will change from time to time and should be shared only with authorized network administrators or managers.

15

Security Policy Goals

Before drafting a security policy, you should understand why the security policy is necessary and how it will serve your organization. Typical goals for security policies are as follows:

- Ensuring that authorized users have appropriate access to the resources they need

- Preventing unauthorized users from gaining access to the network, systems, programs, or data

- Protecting sensitive data from unauthorized access, both from within and from outside the organization

- Preventing accidental damage to hardware or software

- Preventing intentional damage to hardware or software

- Creating an environment where the network and systems can withstand and, if necessary, quickly respond to and recover from any type of threat

- Communicating each employee's responsibilities with respect to maintaining data integrity and system security

A company's security policy may also include content that does not pertain to computers or networks. For example, it might state that each employee must shred paper files that contain sensitive data or that each employee is responsible for signing in his or her visitors at the front desk and obtaining a temporary badge for them. Non-computer-related aspects of security policies are beyond the scope of this chapter, however.

After defining the goals of your security policy, you can devise a strategy to attain them. First, you might form a committee composed of managers and interested parties from a variety of departments, in addition to your network administrators. The more decision-making people you can involve, the more supported and effective your policy will be. This committee can assign a security coordinator, who will then drive the creation of a security policy.

To increase the acceptance of your security policy in your organization, tie security measures to business needs and clearly communicate the potential effects of security breaches. For example, if your company sells clothes over the Internet and a two-hour outage (as could be caused by a cracker who uses IP spoofing to gain control of your systems) could cost the company $1 million in lost sales, make certain that users and managers understand this fact. If they do, they will be more likely to embrace the security policy.

A security policy must address an organization's specific risks. To understand your risks, you should conduct a security audit that identifies vulnerabilities and rates both the severity of each threat and its likelihood of occurring, as described earlier in this chapter. Once risks are identified, the security coordinator should assign one person the responsibility for addressing that threat.

For example, imagine that you are the network administrator for a nonprofit organization that collects blood donations from the public and arranges to ship them to victims of disasters across the country. Your LAN contains not only your organization's financial and personnel data, but also databases listing all blood donors in your area and the last date that they gave blood. In addition, your network contains records of the people whom your organization has assisted during the last five years. Your network is connected through the Internet to other, similar organizations, so that you can share your resources with them and they can help you with your needs. What security risks exist in this system, and how should you manage them?

First, your servers hold a great deal of potentially sensitive information—not only financial information, but also health and community data. To prevent unauthorized access to this information, one person should be assigned the task of protecting it. Second, your network presumably has a number of workstations attached to it. At least one person should be given the responsibility of making sure that PCs do not hold sensitive data on their hard disks and that PC users understand and adhere to security policies. Third, your network has a link to the Internet. One person should therefore be assigned the task of verifying that the Internet connection does not permit crackers to access your internal network.

Security Policy Content

After your risks are identified and responsibilities for managing them are assigned, the policy's outline should be generated with those risks in mind. Some subheadings for the policy might include the following: Password policy; Software installation policy; Confidential and sensitive data policy; Network access policy; E-mail use policy; Internet use policy; Modem use policy; Remote access policy; Policies for connecting to remote locations, the Internet, and customers' and vendors' networks; Policies for use of laptops and loaner machines; and Computer room access policy. Although compiling all of this information might seem like a daunting task, the process will ensure that everyone understands the organization's stance on security and the reasons why it is so important.

The security policy should clearly explain to users what they can and cannot do and how these measures protect the network's security. Clear and regular communication about security policies will make them more acceptable and better understood. One idea for making security policies more sustainable is to distribute a "security newsletter" that keeps security issues fresh in everyone's mind. Perhaps the newsletter could highlight industry statistics about significant security breaches and their effect on the victimized organizations. You might also hold a contest for guessing a password, thereby demonstrating how unsafe passwords threaten security.

Another tactic is to create a separate section of the policy that applies only to users. Within the users' section, divide security rules according to the particular function or part of the network to which they apply. This approach will make the policy easier for users to read and understand; it will also prevent them from having to read through the entire document. The following abridged example shows a section organized in this way:

15

3.2.1   Passwords

Users may not share passwords with friends or relatives.

Users must choose passwords that exceed six characters and are composed of both letters and numbers.

Users should choose passwords that bear no resemblance to a spouse's name, pet's name, birth date, anniversary, or other widely available information.

Users must change their passwords every 90 days.

Users may not use the same password until one year after its expiration.

Users may not write down their passwords or send them in e-mail correspondence.

3.2.2   Networks

Users must ensure that confidential data transmitted over the network are encrypted.

Users should be aware that most e-mail programs allow administrators to read any messages that are sent from or received by the system.

Users may not have modems attached to their machines unless they have received authorization from their supervisor.

Users may not install software obtained from the Internet or other outside sources.

Notice that this sample policy asks users to encrypt confidential data when transmitting such information over the network. But how will users know what type of information is confidential? Your security policy should define what "confidential" means to your organization. In general, information is confidential if it could be used by other parties to impair your organization's functioning, decrease your customers' confidence, cause a financial loss, damage your organization's status, or give a significant advantage to a competitor. If you work in an environment such as a hospital, where most data are sensitive or confidential, however, your security policy should classify information in degrees of sensitivity that correspond to how strictly its access is regulated. For example, "top-secret" data may be accessible only by the organization's CEO and vice presidents, whereas "confidential" data may be accessible only to those who must modify or create it (for example, doctors or hospital accountants).

Response Policy

Finally, a security policy should provide for a planned response in the event of a security breach. The response policy should identify the members of a response team, all of whom should clearly understand the security policy, risks, and measures in place. Each team member should be assigned a role and responsibilities. Like a disaster recovery response team, the security response team should regularly rehearse their defense by participating in a security threat drill. Some suggestions for team roles are listed below:

- *Dispatcher*— This team member is the person on call who first notices or is alerted to the problem. The dispatcher notifies the lead technical support specialist and then the manager. He or she opens a record on the incident, detailing the time it began, its symptoms, and any other pertinent information about the situation. The dispatcher remains available to answer calls from clients or employees or to assist the manager.

- *Manager*—This team member coordinates the resources necessary to solve the problem. If in-house technicians cannot handle the break-in, the manager should find outside assistance. The manager also ensures that the security policy is followed and that everyone within the organization is aware of the situation. As the response ensues, the manager continues to monitor events and communicate with the public relations specialist. After the incident has been resolved, the manager should hold a postmortem meeting to discuss how the breach happened, how the problem was resolved, and what measures are being taken to prevent a recurrence.

- *Technical support specialist*—This team member focuses on only one thing: solving the problem as quickly as possible. After the situation has been resolved, the technical support specialist describes in detail what happened and assists the manager in finding ways to avert such an incident in the future. Depending on the size of the organization and the severity of the incident, this role may be filled by more than one person.

- *Public relations specialist*—If necessary, this team member learns about the situation and the response, then acts as official spokesperson for the organization to the public.

After resolving a problem, you need to review what happened, determine how it might have been prevented, then implement those measures to prevent future problems. Better than having to learn from your own mistakes, though, is learning from others' mistakes. By searching the Web, you can find many examples of security breaches that cost businesses millions of dollars in lost revenue either because their systems failed or because they lost valuable trade secrets.

Passwords

Choosing a secure password is one of the easiest and least expensive ways to guard against unauthorized access. Unfortunately, too many people prefer to use an easy-to-remember password. If your password is obvious to you, however, it may also be easy for a cracker to figure out. The following guidelines for selecting passwords should be part of your organization's security policy. It is especially important for network administrators to choose difficult passwords, and also to keep passwords confidential and to change them frequently.

Tips for making and keeping passwords secure include the following:

- Do not use familiar information, such as your birth date, anniversary, pet's name, child's name, spouse's name, own name or nickname, user ID, phone number, address, or any other words or numbers that others might associate with you.

15

- Do not use any word that might appear in a dictionary. Crackers can use programs that try a combination of your user ID and every word in a dictionary to gain access to the network.

- Make the password longer than six characters—the longer, the better.

- Choose a combination of letters and numbers; add special characters, such as exclamation marks or hyphens, if allowed.

- Do not write down your password or share it with others.

- Change your password at least every 90 days, or more frequently, if desired. If you are a network administrator, establish controls through the network operating system to force users to change their passwords at least every 90 days. If you have access to sensitive data, change your password even more frequently.

Password guidelines should be clearly communicated to everyone in your organization through your security policy. Although users may grumble about having to choose a combination of letters and numbers and change their passwords frequently, you can assure them that the company's financial and personnel data will be safer as a result. No matter how much your colleagues protest, do not back down from your password requirements. Many companies mistakenly require employees only to use a password, without helping them choose a good one. This oversight increases the risk of security breaches.

PHYSICAL SECURITY

Another important element in network security is the restriction of physical access to its components. At the very least, only authorized networking personnel should have access to computer rooms. If computer rooms are not locked, intruders may easily steal equipment or sabotage software and hardware. For example, a malicious visitor could slip into an unsecured computer room and take control of a NetWare server console where an administrator is logged in, then shut down the machine—or worse, reformat its hard disk. Although a security policy may define who has access to the computer room, locking the computer room is necessary to keep unauthorized individuals out.

It isn't only the computer room that must be secured. Think of all the points at which your systems or data could be compromised: hubs or switches in a wiring closet, an unattended workstation at someone's desk, a telecommunications closet where your leased line to the Internet terminates, a storage room for archived data and backup tapes. If a wiring closet is left unlocked, for example, a prankster could enter, grab a handful of wires, and pull them out of the patch panels.

Locks may be either physical or electronic. Many large organizations require authorized employees to wear electronic access badges. These badges can be programmed to allow their owner access to some, but not all, rooms in a building. Figure 15-1 depicts a typical badge access security system.

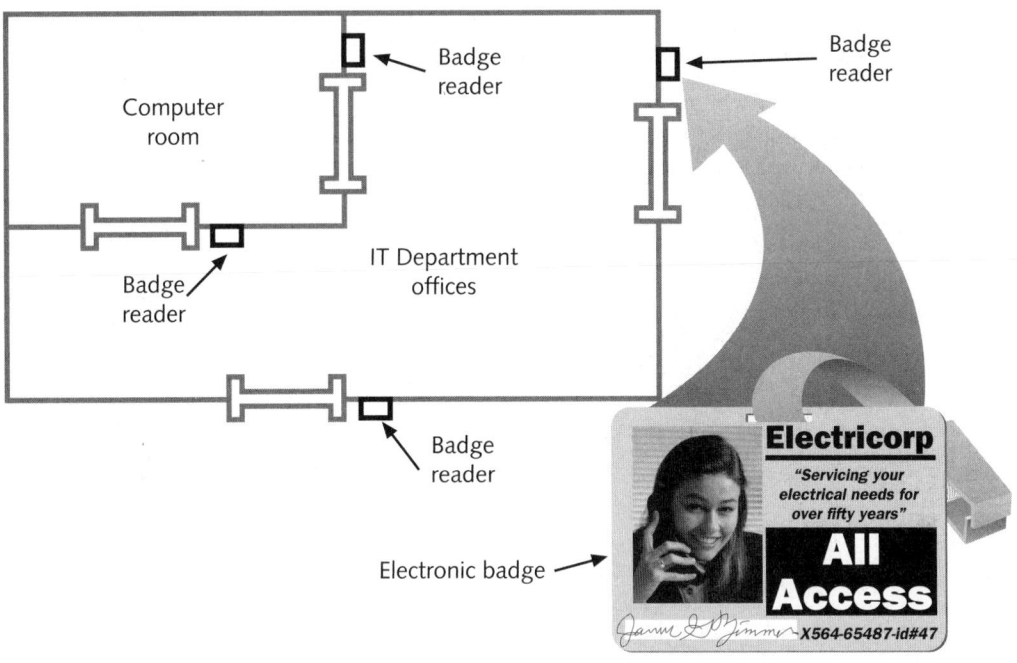

Figure 15-1   A badge access security system

A less-expensive alternative to the electronic badge access system consists of locks that require entrants to punch a numeric code to gain access. For added security, these electronic locks can be combined with key locks. A more expensive solution involves **bio-recognition access**, in which a device scans an individual's unique physical characteristics, such as the color patterns in her eye's iris or the geometry of her hand, to verify her identity. On a larger scale, organizations may regulate entrance through physical barriers to their campuses, such as gates, fences, walls, or landscaping.

Many IT departments also use closed-circuit TV systems to monitor activity in secured rooms. Surveillance cameras may be placed in computer rooms, telco rooms, supply rooms, and data storage areas, as well as facility entrances. A central security office may display several camera views at once, or it may switch from camera to camera. The footage generated from these cameras is usually saved for a time in case it's needed in a security breach investigation or prosecution.

As with other security measures, the most important way to ensure physical security is to plan for it. You can begin your planning by asking questions related to physical security checks in your security audit. Relevant questions include the following:

- Which rooms contain critical systems or data and need to be secured?

- Through what means might intruders gain access to the facility, computer room, telecommunications room, wiring closet, or data storage areas (includ-

15

ing not only doors, but also windows, adjacent rooms, ceilings, temporary walls, hallways, and so on)?

- How and to what extent are authorized personnel granted entry? (Do they undergo background or reference checks? Is their need for access clearly justified? Are their hours of access restricted? Who ensures that lost keys are reported?)

- Are employees instructed to ensure security after entering or leaving secured areas (for example, by not propping open doors)?

- Are authentication methods (such as ID badges) difficult to forge or circumvent?

- Do supervisors or security personnel make periodic physical security checks?

- Are all combinations, codes, or other access means to computer facilities protected at all times, and are these combinations changed frequently?

- Do you have a plan for documenting and responding to physical security breaches?

ADDRESSING RISKS ASSOCIATED WITH HARDWARE AND DESIGN

Addressing the risks associated with people is just one part of a comprehensive security approach. Even if you restrict access to computer rooms, teach employees how to select secure passwords, and enforce a security policy, breaches may still occur due to poor LAN or WAN design. In this section, you will learn how to address some security risks via intelligent networking hardware and design.

Of course, the optimal way to prevent external security breaches from affecting your LAN is to not connect your LAN to the outside world at all. This option is impractical in today's business environment, however. The next best protection is to restrict access at every point where your LAN connects to the rest of the world. This principle forms the basis of hardware- and design-based security.

Much of the information covered in this section builds upon material discussed in Chapter 7, such as WAN design, VPNs, and remote connectivity. It may be helpful to review Chapter 7 before reading this section.

Firewalls

As you learned early in this chapter, a firewall is a specialized device that selectively filters or blocks traffic between networks. A firewall typically involves a combination of hardware and software and may reside between two interconnected private networks or, more typically, between a private network and a public network (such as the Internet), as shown in Figure 15-2. Many types of firewalls exist, and a detailed discussion of each is beyond the scope of this book. To understand secure network design and to qualify for

Net+ certification, however, you should recognize which functions firewalls can provide, where they can appear on a network, and how to decide what you need in a firewall.

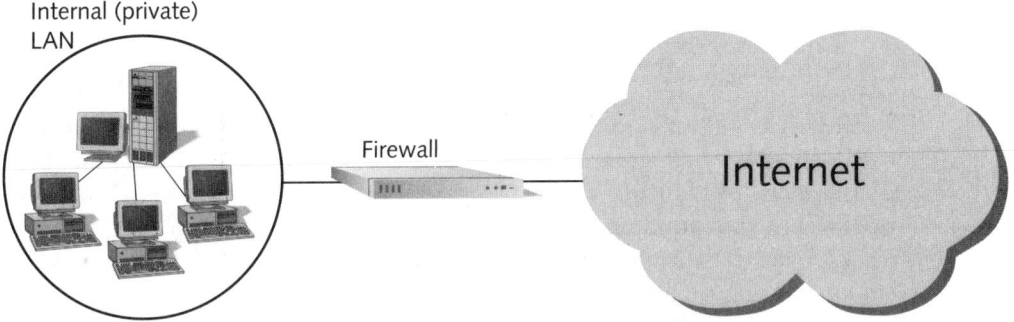

Figure 15-2   Placement of a firewall between a private network and the Internet

The simplest and most common form of a firewall is a **packet-filtering firewall**, which is a router that operates at the Data Link and Transport layers of the OSI Model. It examines the header of every packet of data that it receives to determine whether that type of packet is authorized to continue to its destination. Packet-filtering firewalls are also called **screening firewalls**. An example of a popular packet-filtering firewall is the Cisco PIX 525, pictured in Figure 15-3.

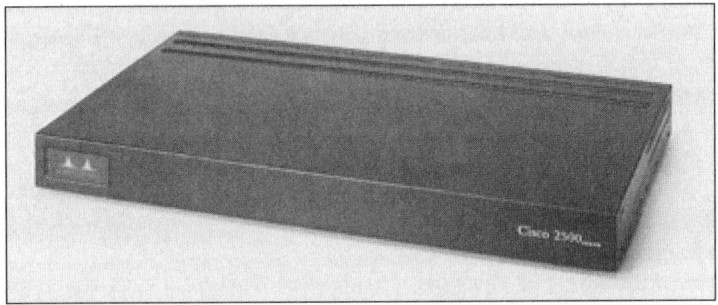

Figure 15-3   A packet-filtering firewall

These types of firewalls require a great deal of custom configuration to be effective; that is, the network administrator must configure the firewall to accept or deny certain types of traffic. Some of the criteria that a firewall might use to accept or deny data include the following:

- Source and destination IP addresses
- Source and destination ports (for example, ports that supply TCP/UDP connections, FTP, Telnet, SNMP, RealAudio, and so on)
- The TCP, UDP, or ICMP protocols

15

- A packet's status as the first packet in a new data stream or a subsequent packet

- A packet's status as inbound to or outbound from your private network

- A packet's status as originating from or being destined for an application on your private network

Based on these options, a network administrator could configure her firewall, for example, to prevent any IP address that does not begin with "196.57," the first two octets of the addresses on her network, from accessing the network's router and servers. Furthermore, she could disable—or block—certain well-known ports, such as the FTP ports (20 and 21) through the router's configuration. Blocking ports prevents *any* user from connecting to and completing a transmission through those ports. This technique is useful to further guard against unauthorized access to the network. In other words, even if a cracker were able to spoof an IP address that began with "196.57," he could not access the FTP ports (which are notoriously insecure) on the firewall. Ports can be blocked not only on firewalls, but also on routers, servers, or any device that uses ports. For example, if you established a Web server for testing but did not want anyone in your organization to connect to your Web pages through his or her browsers, you could block port 80 on that server.

You will recognize examples of firewall placement in most VPN architectures. For example, you might design a VPN that uses the Internet to connect your Milwaukee office with your Denver office. To ensure that only traffic from Milwaukee can access your Denver LAN, you could install a packet-filtering firewall between the Denver LAN and the Internet that accepts incoming traffic only from IP addresses that match the IP addresses on your Milwaukee LAN. In a way, the firewall acts like a bouncer at a private club who checks everyone's ID and ensures that only club members enter through the door. In the case of the Milwaukee-Denver VPN, the firewall will discard any data packets that arrive at the Denver firewall and do not contain source IP addresses that match those of Milwaukee's LAN.

In another example, suppose your network in Denver hosts a server that stores confidential employee information, such as payroll and health benefits, which only the Denver-based human resources manager should be able to access. In this situation, you could add a filter in the firewall to block all external traffic (from the Internet as well as from the Milwaukee LAN) from reaching the destination address of that server.

Because you must tailor a firewall to your network's needs, you cannot simply purchase one, install it between your private LAN and the Internet, and expect it to offer much security. Instead, you must first consider what type of traffic you want to filter, then configure the firewall accordingly. It may take weeks to achieve the best configuration—not so strict that it prevents authorized users from transmitting and receiving necessary data, and not so lenient that you risk security breaches. Further complicating the matter is that you may need to create exceptions to the rules. For example, suppose that your human resources manager is working out of the Milwaukee office while recruiting new employees and needs to access the Denver server that stores payroll information. In this instance, the Denver network administrator might create an exception to allow transmissions from the human resources manager's workstation's IP address to reach that server. In the networking profession, creating an exception to the filtering rules is called "punching a hole" in the firewall.

Because packet-filtering routers operate at the Network and Transport layers of the OSI Model and examine only network addresses, they cannot distinguish between a user who is trying to breach the firewall and a user who is authorized to do so. To ensure that an unauthorized user does not simply sit down at the workstation belonging to an authorized user and try to circumvent the firewall, a more sophisticated technique—such as user authentication—is necessary.

One approach to enhancing the security of the Network and Transport layers provided by firewalls is to combine a packet-filtering firewall (hardware device) with a proxy service. A **proxy service** is a software application on a network host that acts as an intermediary between the external and internal networks, screening all incoming and outgoing traffic. The network host that runs the proxy service is known as a **proxy server**, or gateway. Proxy servers manage security at the Application layer of the OSI Model. To understand how they work, think of the secure data on a server as the president of a country and the proxy server as the secretary of state. Rather than having the president risk his or her safety by leaving the country, the representative travels abroad, speaking for the president and bringing information back to the president. In fact, foreign leaders may never actually meet the dignitary. Instead, the representative acts as his or her proxy.

Although a proxy server appears to the outside world as an internal network server, in reality it is merely another filtering device for the internal LAN. Among other things, it prevents the outside world from discovering the addresses of the internal network. For example, suppose your LAN uses a proxy server, and you want to send an e-mail message from your workstation to your mother via the Internet. Your message would first go to the proxy server (depending on the configuration of your network, you may or may not have to log on separately to the proxy server first). The proxy server would repackage the data frames that make up the message so that, rather than your workstation's IP address being the source, the proxy server would insert its own IP address as the source. Next, the proxy server would pass your repackaged data to the packet-filtering firewall. The firewall would verify that the source IP address in your packets is valid (that it came from the proxy server) and then send your message to the Internet. Examples of proxy server software include Novell's BorderManager and Microsoft's Internet Security and Acceleration (ISA) Server 2000, an optional service for Windows 2000 servers. Figure 15-4 depicts how a proxy server might fit into a WAN design.

15

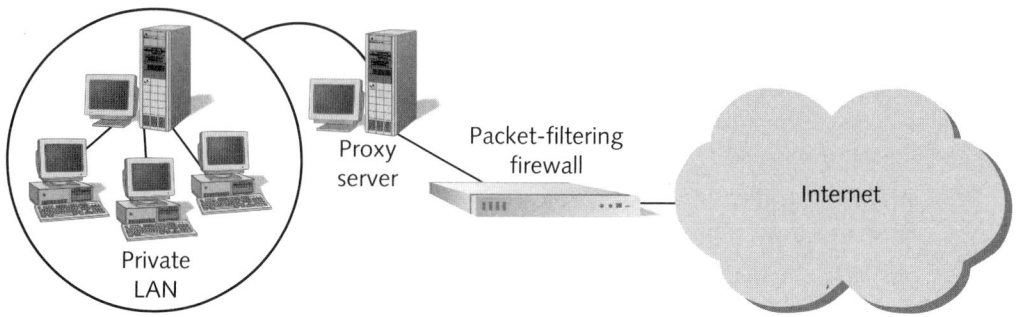

Figure 15-4   A proxy server used on a WAN

Many more sophisticated firewalls—both hardware- and software-based—exist. Choosing the appropriate firewall for your network can be a difficult task. Among the factors you will want to consider when making your decision are the following:

- Does the firewall support encryption? (You will learn more about encryption later in this chapter.)

- Does the firewall support user authentication?

- Does the firewall allow you to manage it centrally and through a standard interface (such as one that uses SNMP)?

- How easily can you establish rules for access to and from the firewall?

- Does the firewall support filtering at the highest layers of the OSI Model, not just at the Data Link and Transport layers?

- Does the firewall provide logging and auditing capabilities, or alert you to possible intrusions?

- Does the firewall protect the identity of your internal LAN's addresses from the outside world?

Remote Access

As you learned in Chapter 7, many companies supply traveling employees, telecommuters, or distant vendors with access to their private LANs or WANs. This type of access is often referred to as remote access. When working with remote access, you must remember that any entry point to a LAN or WAN creates a potential security risk. In other words, if an employee can get to your network in New York from his hotel room in Rome, a smart cracker can likely do the same. You can, however, take advantage of techniques designed to minimize the possibility of such unauthorized remote access. For example, firewalls can prevent certain addresses and users from gaining access to your LAN from the outside. In this section, you will learn about other security measures tailored to remote access solutions, such as remote control and dial-up networking.

Remote Control

Recall from Chapter 7 that remote control systems enable a user to connect to a host system on a network from a distance and use that system's resources as if the user were sitting in front of it. This type of access can have benefits for employees who work at home or who travel frequently. Although such remote control systems can be convenient, they can also present serious security risks. Most remote control software programs (for example, Symantec Corporation's pcAnywhere or Computer Associates International, Inc.'s Control*IT*) offer features that increase the security of remote control systems. If you intend to allow remote control access to a host on your LAN, you should investigate these security features and know how to implement them correctly. Important security features that you should seek in a remote control program include the following:

- A logon ID and password requirement for gaining access to the host system.

- The ability of the host system to call back. This feature enables a remote user to dial into the network, enter a user ID, and hang up. The host system then calls the user back at a predetermined number (the authorized user's modem number), thus preventing a cracker from taking over a system even if he or she obtains the correct user ID and password for the host system.

- Support for data encryption on transmissions between the remote user and the system.

- The ability to leave the host system's screen blank while a remote user works on it. This feature prevents people walking by from seeing (potentially confidential) data that the remote user is accessing.

- The ability to disable the host system's keyboard and mouse. Essentially, this feature turns the host system into a terminal that responds to only remote users.

- The ability to restart the host system when a remote user disconnects from the system. This feature prevents anyone from reviewing what happened during the remote user's session or gaining access if the session was accidentally terminated before the remote user could properly log off.

15

Dial-up Networking

In Chapter 7, you learned about different ways for remote users to log onto a network. One method involved having users dial into a remote access server attached to the network, also known as dial-up networking. Like other remote access solutions, this approach presents security risks. In this section, you will learn how to make dial-up networking more secure.

Dial-up networking differs from remote control in that it effectively turns a remote workstation into a node on the network, through a remote access server. When choosing a remote access software package, you should evaluate its security. A secure remote access server package will include at least the following features:

- Logon ID and password authentication
- The ability to log all dial-up connections, their sources, and their connection times
- The ability to perform callbacks to users who initiate connections
- Centralized management of dial-up users and their rights on the network

In environments where more than a few dozen simultaneous dial-up connections must be supported and their user IDs and passwords managed, a special kind of server known as a **Remote Authentication Dial-In User Service (RADIUS)** may be implemented to offer authentication services to the network's access server (which may run Windows 2000's RAS or Novell's NAS, for example). RADIUS provides a single, centralized point of authentication for dial-in users. It is highly scalable, as it can attach to pools containing hundreds of modems. In addition, RADIUS is also more secure than using a simple remote access solution because its method of authentication prevents users' IDs and passwords from traveling across the phone line in clear text format.

Many Internet service providers use a RADIUS server to allow their subscribers access to the Internet through their modem pools. Other organizations employ it as a central authentication point for mobile or remote users. Figure 15-5 illustrates these two methods for allowing remote users to connect using RADIUS authentication.

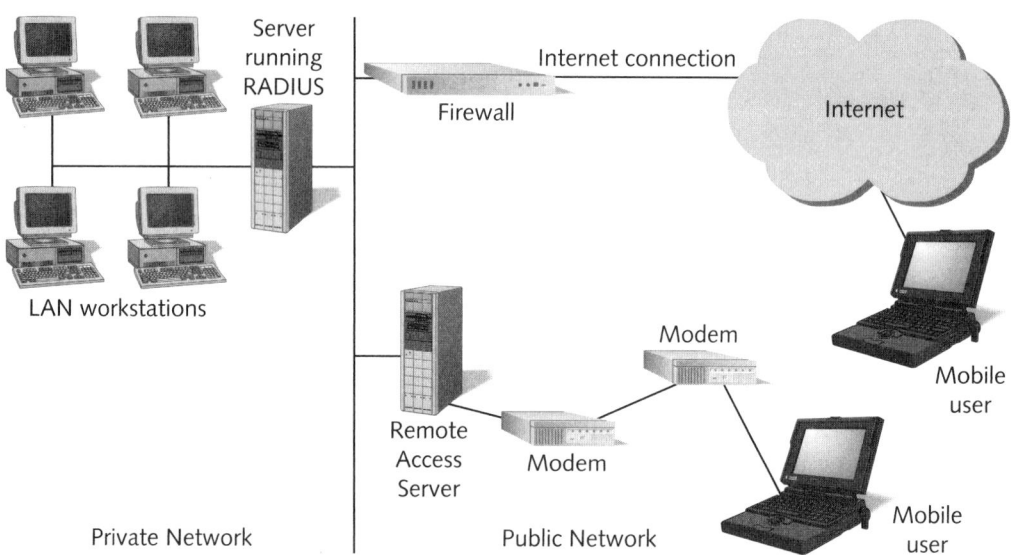

Figure 15-5 A RADIUS server providing central authentication

RADIUS may run on UNIX, Windows 2000, or NetWare networks. A similar, but earlier version of a centralized authentication system is **Terminal Access Controller Access Control System (TACACS)**.

As you learned in Chapter 7, dial-up networking depends on special protocols—for example, PPP or SLIP. Later in this chapter, you will learn about additional protocols that make dial-up networking part of a secure virtual private network.

ADDRESSING RISKS ASSOCIATED WITH PROTOCOLS AND SOFTWARE

Now that you have learned how to design a more secure network, it's time to examine the software tools that can help you protect your network against unauthorized access. Be sure to remember that all of these security techniques complement one another. No single technique is more important than any other, and if you neglect a technique, you may put your network at risk.

The foundation for protecting your organization's data, programs, and access is to master and implement the tools that come with your network operating system. In this section, you will learn the basics of restricting access through this software. You will also learn about a more advanced software-level security technique—encryption.

Network Operating System Authentication

Regardless of whether you run your network on a Novell, Microsoft, or UNIX network operating system, you can implement basic security by restricting what users are authorized to do on a network. This section reiterates what you learned in Chapters 8, 9, and 10 about establishing rights to files and directories on the server.

Every network administrator should understand which resources on the server all users need to access. The rights conferred to all users are called public rights, because anyone can have them and exercising them presents no security threat to the network. In most cases, public rights are very limited. They may include privileges to view and execute programs from the server and to read, create, modify, delete, and execute files in a shared data directory.

In addition, network administrators need to group users according to their security levels and assign additional rights that meet the needs of those groups. As you know, creating groups simplifies the process of granting rights to users. For example, if you work in the IT department at a large college, you will most likely need more than one person to create new user IDs and passwords for students and faculty. Naturally, the staff in charge of creating new user IDs and passwords need the rights to perform this task. You could assign the appropriate rights to each staff member individually, but a more efficient approach is to put all of the personnel in a group, and then assign the appropriate rights to the group as a whole.

15

In addition to restricting users' access to files and directories on the server, a network administrator can constrain the ways in which users can access the server and its resources. The following is a list of additional restrictions that network administrators can use to strengthen the security of their networks:

- *Time of day*—Some user IDs may be valid only during specific hours—for example, between 8:00 A.M. and 5:00 P.M. Specifying valid hours for an ID can increase security by preventing any ID from being used by unauthorized personnel after hours.

- *Total time logged on*—Some user IDs may be restricted to a specific number of hours per day of logged-on time. Restricting total hours in this way can increase security in the case of temporary IDs. For example, suppose that your organization offers a WordPerfect training class to a group of high-school students one afternoon, and the WordPerfect program and training files reside on your staff server. You might create IDs that could log on for only four hours on that day.

- *Source address*—You can specify that user IDs can log on only from certain workstations or certain areas of the network (that is, domains or segments). This restriction can prevent unauthorized use of logon IDs from workstations outside the network.

- *Unsuccessful logon attempts*—Crackers may repeatedly attempt to log on under a valid ID for which they do not know the password. As the network administrator, you can set a limit on how many subsequent unsuccessful logon attempts from a single user ID the server will accept before blocking that ID from even attempting to log on.

Encryption

Encryption is the use of an algorithm to scramble data into a format that can be read only by reversing the algorithm—that is, by decrypting the data. The purpose of encryption is to keep information private. Many forms of encryption exist, with some being more secure than others. Even as new forms of encryption are developed, new ways of cracking their codes emerge, too.

Encryption is the last means of defense against data theft. In other words, if an intruder has bypassed all other methods of access, including physical security (for instance, he has broken into the telecommunications room) and hardware security (for instance, he has logged onto the router), data may still be safe if they are encrypted. Encryption can protect data when they are stored on a medium, such as a hard disk, or while they are in transit over a communications channel. In order to protect data, encryption provides the following assurances:

- Data were not modified after the sender transmitted them and before the receiver picked them up.

- Data can only be viewed by their intended recipient (or at their intended destination).

- All of the data received at the intended destination were truly issued by the stated sender and not forged by an intruder.

The most popular kind of encryption algorithm weaves a **key** (a random string of characters) into the original data's bits—sometimes several times in different sequences—to generate a unique data block. The scrambled data block is known as **cipher text**. The longer the key, the less easily the cipher text can be decrypted by an unauthorized system. For example, a 512-bit key is considered secure, whereas cipher text generated with a 16-bit key could be cracked in no time.

The process of key encryption is similar to what happens when you finish a card game and place your five-card hand into the deck, then shuffle the deck numerous times. After shuffling, it might take you a while to retrieve your hand. As you can imagine, if you shuffled your five cards into four decks of cards at once, it would be even more difficult to find your original hand. In encryption, theoretically only the computer that is authorized to retrieve the data knows how to unshuffle it and compile the original sequence of data. Figure 15-6 provides a considerably simplified view of key encryption and decryption. Note that actual key encryption does not simply weave a key into the data once, but rather inserts the key, shuffles the data, shuffles the key, inserts another copy of the shuffled key into the shuffled data, shuffles the data again, and so on for several iterations.

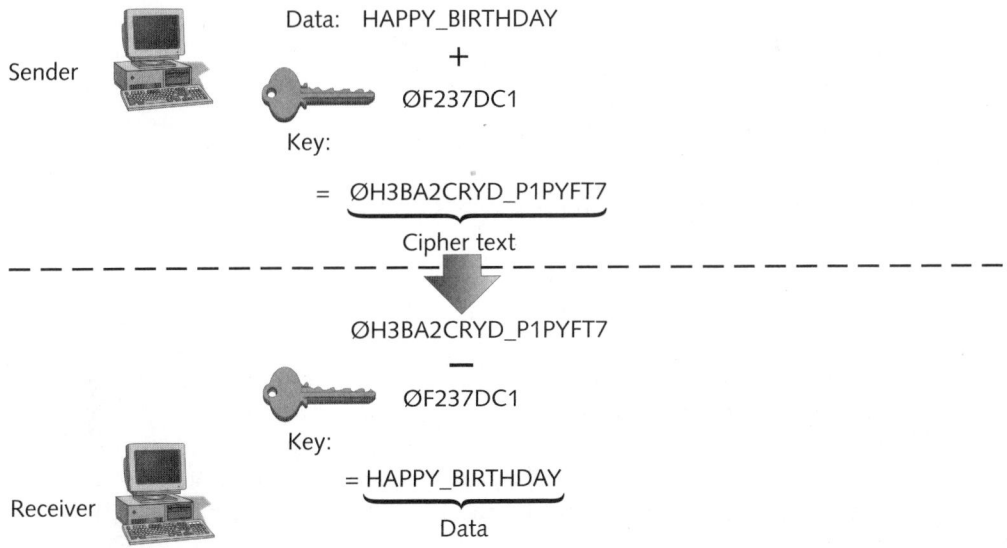

Figure 15-6   Key encryption and decryption

Keys are randomly generated, as needed, by the software that manages the encryption. For example, an e-mail program or a Web browser program may be capable of generating its own keys to encrypt data. In other cases, special encryption software is used to generate keys. This encryption software works with other types of software, such as word-processing or spreadsheet programs, to encrypt data files before they are saved or transmitted.

Key encryption can be separated into two categories: private key and public key encryption. In **private key encryption** data are encrypted using a single key that only the sender and the receiver know, as depicted in Figure 15-7. This method of key encryption is also known as **symmetric encryption**, because the same key is used during both the transmission and reception of the data. The most popular private key encryption is the **data encryption standard (DES)**, which was developed by IBM in the 1970s.

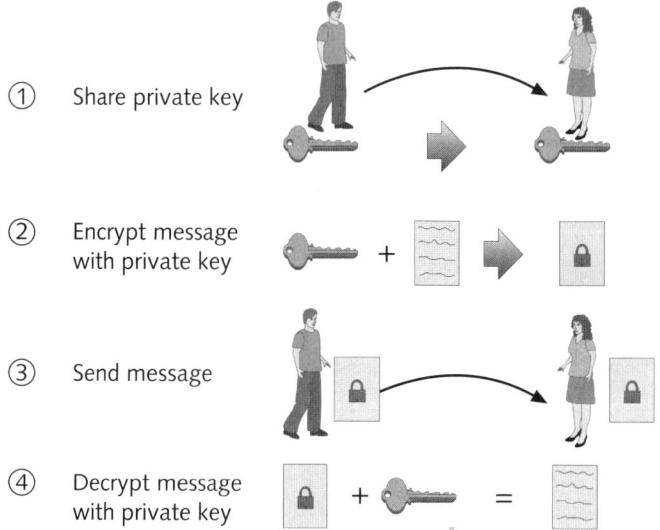

Figure 15-7   Private key encryption

In private key encryption, for example, before Mary can decrypt a message that John sends, he must share his private key with her. Once Mary receives John's encrypted message, she uses a decryption program plus John's private key to decipher the message. The problem with private key encryption is that the sender must somehow share his key with the recipient. For example, John could call Mary and tell her his key, or he could send it to her in an e-mail message. But neither of these methods is very secure. In order to overcome this potential vulnerability, a method of associating publicly available keys with private keys was developed. This method is called public key encryption.

In **public key encryption**, data are encrypted using two keys: one is a key known only to a user (that is, a private key), and the other is a public key associated with the user. A user's public key can be obtained the old-fashioned way—by asking that user—or it can be obtained from a third-party source, such as a public-key server. A **public-key server** is a publicly accessible host (such as an Internet host) that freely provides a list of users' public keys, much as a telephone book provides a list of peoples' phone numbers. When a user receives a message encrypted with his public key, the recipient's software (for example, his e-mail program) prompts to enter his private key in order to decrypt the message. In other words, the public key has an association with the private key, and a message that has been encrypted with a user's public key can only be decrypted with his private key. The combination of the public key and private key is known as a **key pair**. In this arrangement, every user has a key pair, but one key is known only to the user while the other key is known to those with whom she exchanges data. Because the two users use a different combination of keys, public key encryption is also known as **asymmetric encryption**. Figure 15-8 illustrates the process of public key encryption.

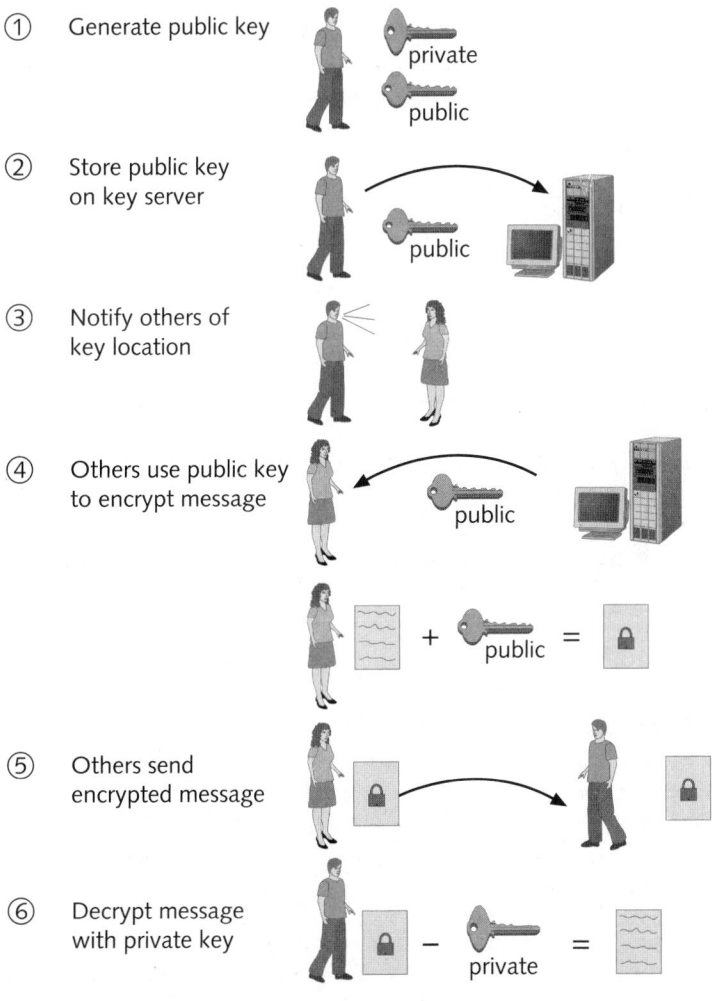

① Generate public key

② Store public key on key server

③ Notify others of key location

④ Others use public key to encrypt message

⑤ Others send encrypted message

⑥ Decrypt message with private key

15

Figure 15-8   Public key encryption

For example, suppose that Mary and John wish to use public key encryption to exchange messages over the Internet. Before sending a message to John, Mary would look up John's public key on a public key server. She would then use her encryption software to scramble her message with John's public key. When John receives the message, his software would recognize that the message has been encoded. Furthermore, the software would recognize that the encryption used John's public key. Based on the public key, it would then prompt John for his private key in order to decrypt the message. Some examples of public key algorithms include RSA (named after its creators, Rivest, Shamir, and Adleman), Diffie-Hellman, and Elliptic-curve cryptography.

With the abundance of private and public keys, not to mention the number of places where each may be kept, users have found a need for easier key management. One answer to this problem is using digital certificates. A **digital certificate** is a password-protected and encrypted file that holds an individual's identification information, including a public key. In the context of digital certificates, the individual's public key is used to verify the sender's digital signature. For example, on the Internet, certificate authorities such as VeriSign, will, for a fee, keep your digital certificate on their server and ensure to all who want to send encrypted messages to you (for example, an order via your e-commerce site) that the certificate is indeed yours. Digital certificates are used in some of the encryption methods discussed below, such as PGP and SSL.

The following sections detail specific public and private key methods of encrypting data as they are transmitted over a network.

Kerberos

Kerberos is a cross-platform authentication protocol that uses key encryption to verify the identity of clients and to securely exchange information once a client logs onto a system. It is an example of a private key encryption service. Kerberos provides significant security advantages over simple network operating system authentication. Whereas an NOS client/server logon process assumes that clients are who they say they are and only verifies a user's name against the password in the NOS database, Kerberos does not automatically trust clients. Instead, it requires a client to prove its identity through a third party. This is similar to what happens when you apply for a passport. The government does not simply believe that you are "Mary Smith," but instead requires you to present proof, such as your birth certificate. In addition to checking the validity of a client, Kerberos communications are encrypted and unlikely to be deciphered by any device on the network other than the client. Contrast this type of transmission to the normally unencrypted and vulnerable communication between an NOS and a client.

In order to understand specifically how a client uses Kerberos, you need to understand some of the terms used when discussing this protocol. In Kerberos terminology, the server that issues keys to clients during initial client authentication is known as the **key distribution center (KDC)**. In order to authenticate a client, the KDC runs an **authentication service (AS)**. An AS issues a **ticket**, which is a temporary set of credentials that a client uses to prove that its identity has been validated (note that a ticket is not the same as a key, which is used to initially validate its identity). A Kerberos client, or user, is known as a **principal**.

Now that you have learned the terms used by Kerberos, you can follow the process it requires for client/server communication. Bear in mind that the purpose of Kerberos is to connect a valid user with the service that that user wishes to access. In order to accomplish this, both the user and the service must have keys registered with the authentication service. When a user, or principal, wants to access that service, he first logs onto the KDC over the network (on a Windows 2000 network, the KDC is the user's domain controller). Suppose the principal is John Smith, and the service is called "inventory." After logging on, John Smith attempts to log onto the inventory service, thereby, in effect, issuing a message to the authentication service on the KDC that says, "User John Smith wishes to access "inventory." The KDC confirms that John Smith is in its database. Then the AS running on the KDC randomly generates two copies of a new key, called the **session key**. The AS then issues one copy to John Smith and the other copy to the inventory service. Further, it creates a ticket that will allow John Smith to use the inventory service. This ticket contains the inventory service key and can only be decrypted by John Smith's key. The AS sends the ticket to John Smith. John Smith's computer decrypts the session key with John Smith's personal key. It then creates a timestamp associated with his request, and encrypts this timestamp with the session key. The encrypted timestamp is known as the **authenticator**. This timestamp will help the service verify that the ticket is indeed associated with John Smith's request to use the inventory service. Next, John Smith's computer sends his ticket and authenticator to the service. The service decrypts the ticket using its own key and decrypts the authenticator using its session key. Finally, the service has verified that the principal requesting its use is truly John Smith, as the KDC indicated.

The events described above illustrate the original version of the Kerberos authentication process. The problem with the original version was that a user would have to request a separate ticket each time he wished to use a different service. To alleviate this inconvenience, Kerberos developers created the **ticket granting service (TGS)**, an application separate from the AS that also runs on the KDC. So that the client does not need to request a new ticket from the TGS each time it wants to use a different service on the network, the TGS issues the client a **ticket granting ticket (TGT)**. After receiving the TGT, any time that the user wishes to contact a service, he requests a ticket not from the AS, but from the TGS. Furthermore, the reply is encrypted not with the user's personal key, but with the session key that the AS provided for use with the TGS. Inside that reply is the new session key for use with the regular service. The rest of the exchange continues as described above.

Kerberos, which is named after the three-headed dog in Greek mythology who guarded the gates of Hades, was designed at Massachusetts Institute of Technology (MIT). MIT still provides free copies of the Kerberos code. In addition, many software vendors have developed their own versions of Kerberos.

15

Pretty Good Privacy (PGP)

You have probably exchanged e-mail messages over the Internet without much concern for what happens with your message between the time you send it and when your intended recipient picks it up. In addition, you have probably picked up e-mails from friends without thinking that they might not be from your friends, but rather from other users who are impersonating your friends over the Internet. In fact, typical e-mail communication is a highly insecure form of data exchange. The contents of a message are usually sent in clear (that is, unencrypted) text, which makes it readable by anyone who can capture the message on its way from you to your recipient. In addition, a person with malicious intentions can easily pretend they are someone else. For example, if your e-mail address is joe@trinketmakers.com, someone else could assume your address and send messages that appear to be sent by joe@trinketmakers.com. In order to secure e-mail transmissions, a computer scientist named Phil Zimmerman developed PGP in the early 1990s. **Pretty Good Privacy (PGP)** is a public key encryption system that can verify the authenticity of an e-mail sender and encrypt e-mail data in transmission. PGP is freely available as both an open source and a proprietary software package. Since its release, it has become the most popular tool for encrypting e-mail.

Secure Sockets Layer (SSL)

Secure Sockets Layer (SSL) is a method of encrypting TCP/IP transmissions—including Web pages and data entered into Web forms—en route between the client and server using public key encryption technology. If you trade stocks or purchase goods on the Web, for example, you are most likely using SSL to transmit your order information. SSL is popular in part because it is widely accepted. The most recent versions of Web browsers such as Netscape Communicator and Internet Explorer include SSL client support in their software.

If you have used the Web, you have probably noticed that URLs for most Web pages begin with the HTTP prefix, which indicates that the request will be handled by TCP/IP port 80 using the HTTP protocol. When Web page URLs begin with the prefix **HTTPS** they are requiring that their data be transferred from server to client and vice versa using SSL encryption. HTTPS uses the TCP port number 443, rather than port 80. Once an SSL connection has been established between a Web server and client, the client's browser indicates this by showing a padlock in the lower-right corner of the screen (this applies to Internet Explorer and Netscape Communicator versions 4.0 and higher).

Each time a client and server establish an SSL connection, they also establish a unique **SSL session**, or an association between the client and server that is defined by an agreement on a specific set of encryption techniques. An SSL session allows the client and server to continue to exchange data securely as long as the client is still connected to the server. An SSL session is created by the SSL handshake protocol, one of several protocols within SSL, and perhaps the most significant. As its name implies, the **handshake protocol** allows the client and server to authenticate (or introduce) each other and establishes terms for how they will securely exchange data. For example, when you are connected to the Web and you decide to open your bank's account access URL, your browser initiates an SSL connection with the handshake protocol. The handshake protocol sends a special message to the server, called a **client_hello** message, which contains information about what level of security your browser is capable of accepting and what type of encryption your browser can decipher (for example, RSA or Diffie-Hellman). The client_hello message also establishes a randomly generated number that uniquely identifies your client and another number that identifies your SSL session. The server responds with a **server_hello** message that confirms the information it received from your client and agrees to certain terms of encryption based on the options your client supplied. Depending on the Web server's preferred encryption method, the server may choose to issue your browser a public key or a digital certificate at this time. Once the client and server have agreed on the terms of encryption, they will begin exchanging data.

SSL was originally developed by Netscape. Since that time, the Internet Engineering Task Force (IETF) has attempted to standardize SSL in a protocol called **Transport Layer Security (TLS)**. Besides standardizing SSL for use with software from multiple vendors, IETF also aims to create a version of SSL that will encrypt UDP as well as TCP transmissions. TLS, which will likely be supported by new Web browsers, uses slightly different encryption algorithms than SSL, but otherwise is very similar to the most recent version of SSL.

Internet Protocol Security (IPSec)

The **Internet Protocol Security (IPSec)** protocol defines encryption, authentication, and key management for TCP/IP transmissions. It is an enhancement to IPv4 and is native to the newer, IPv6 standard. IPSec is somewhat different from other methods of securing data in transit. Rather than applying encryption to a stream of data, IPSec actually encrypts data by adding security information to the header of all IP packets. In effect, IPSec transforms the data packets. To do so, IPSec operates at the Network layer (Layer 3) of the OSI Model.

IPSec accomplishes authentication in two phases. The first phase is key management and the second phase is encryption. **Key management** refers to the way in which two nodes agree on common parameters for the keys they will use. IPSec relies on **Internet Key Exchange (IKE)** for its key management. IKE is a service that runs on UDP port 500. Once IKE has established the rules for the type of keys two nodes will use, IPSec invokes its second phase, encryption. In this phase, two types of encryption may be used: **authentication header (AH)** and **encapsulation security payload (ESP)**. It is not important to know the inner workings of these services in order to qualify for Network+ certification, but you should be aware that both types of encryption provide authentication of the IP packet's data payload through public key techniques. In addition, EPS encrypts the entire IP packet for added security.

IPSec can be used with any type of TCP/IP transmission. However, it most commonly runs on routers or other connectivity devices in the context of VPNs. Because VPNs are

15

used to transmit private data over public networks, they require strict encryption and authentication to ensure that data are not compromised. The next section focuses on traditional VPN security measures.

Virtual Private Network (VPN) Security

As you learned in Chapter 7, virtual private networks (VPNs) are private networks that use public channels to connect clients and servers. Often VPNs integrate a wide variety of clients, from dial-up users at home to networked workstations in offices to Web servers at an ISP. The mix of client types, transmission methods, and services used by VPNs adds to their design complexity, as well as to the complexity of their security needs. Security considerations must be woven into both hardware/design and software for VPNs. These types of networks are so varied and potentially complicated that fully describing their nuances is beyond the scope of this book. In this section, however, you will learn about the significant security techniques particular to VPNs.

VPNs typically use the Internet to connect multiple sites; because the Internet is the largest public network in the world, its use presents obvious security hazards. VPNs often take advantage of firewalls and special protocols that encrypt the data transmitted over public connections. The following sections describe some of the special protocols used in VPN connectivity.

As described in Chapter 7, PPP is a dial-in protocol that belongs in the Data Link layer (Layer 2) of the OSI Model and provides datagram transport services over serial and digital communications lines for the TCP/IP, NetBEUI, and IPX/SPX protocols. PPP originated for use with direct dial-in connections to Windows NT RAS servers. The **Point-to-Point Tunneling Protocol (PPTP)** expands on PPP by encapsulating it so that any type of PPP data can traverse the Internet masked as a pure IP transmission. PPTP supports the encryption, authentication, and LAN access services provided by RAS. Instead of users having to dial directly into an access server, however, they can dial into their ISP using PPTP and thereby gain access to their corporate LAN over the Internet.

The process of encapsulating one protocol to make it appear as another type of protocol is known as **tunneling**. Essentially, tunneling makes a protocol fit a type of network that it wouldn't normally match. PPTP is easy to install, is available at no extra cost with Microsoft networking services, and supports multiple kinds of protocols. For these reasons, it is the most popular VPN tunneling protocol in use today.

PPTP is available with both the server and workstation versions of Windows NT and Windows 2000 as part of RAS. You can purchase an upgrade from Microsoft to enable PPTP to work with the Windows 95 Dial-up Networking client. PPTP support is included automatically in the Windows 98 operating system.

Layer 2 Forwarding (L2F) is similar to PPTP in that it is a Layer 2 protocol that provides tunneling for other protocols and can work with the authentication methods used by PPP. The difference between PPTP and L2F lies in the type of encryption that each supports, and the fact that PPTP was developed by Microsoft, and L2F was developed by Cisco Systems. One disadvantage of L2F as compared to PPTP is that the former protocol requires special hardware on the host system end, whereas PPTP will work with any Windows NT or 2000 server. On the other hand, L2F can encapsulate protocols to fit more than just the IP format, unlike PPTP.

Both PPTP and L2F, however, will gradually be replaced by a third type of tunneling protocol called **Layer 2 Tunneling Protocol (L2TP)**. This Layer 2 tunneling protocol was developed by a number of industry consortia. L2TP is an enhanced version of L2F that, like L2F, supports multiple protocols. Unlike L2F, however, L2TP does not require costly hardware upgrades to implement. It is also optimized to work with the next generation of IP (IPv6) and IPSec.

CHAPTER SUMMARY

- ❏ A hacker is someone who masters the inner workings of operating systems and utilities in an effort to better understand them. A cracker is someone who uses his or her knowledge of operating systems and utilities to intentionally damage or destroy data or systems.

- ❏ The root is a highly privileged user ID that has all rights to create, delete, modify, move, read, write, or execute files on a system. This term may specifically refer to the administrator on a UNIX-based network. Getting the root ID and password on one system often allows crackers to gain access to attached systems.

- ❏ Authentication is the process of verifying a user's validity and authority to use a system. You are familiar with the user ID and password combination. Systems may also base authentication on digital signatures, IP addresses, session IDs, or a combination of these methods. Generally, the more information required for authentication, the more secure the system.

- ❏ Every organization should assess its security risks by conducting a security audit, at least annually and preferably quarterly. For each threat, your security audit should rate the severity of its potential consequences, as well as its likelihood.

- ❏ One of the most common methods by which an intruder gains access to a network is to simply ask a user for his or her password. This strategy is commonly called social engineering, because it involves manipulating social relationships to gain access.

- ❏ Security risks associated with people include the following: intruders or attackers using social engineering to obtain user passwords; an administrator incorrectly creating or configuring user IDs, groups, and their associated rights on a file server; network administrators overlooking security flaws in topology or hardware configu-

15

ration; network administrators overlooking security flaws in operating system or application configuration; lack of proper documentation and communication of security policies; dishonest or disgruntled employees abusing their file and access rights; a computer or terminal being left logged onto the network while its operator is away; users, or even administrators, choosing easy-to-guess passwords; authorized staff leaving computer room doors propped open or unlocked, thereby allowing unauthorized individuals to enter; and administrators neglecting to remove access and file rights for employees who have left the organization.

❐ Risks inherent in network hardware and design include the following: twisted-pair cabling that emits electromagnetic radiation; wireless and wire-based transmissions, which can typically be intercepted (transmissions over fiber-based networks cannot); networks that use leased public lines, which are subject to eavesdropping; network hubs that broadcast traffic over the entire segment, thus making transmissions more widely vulnerable to sniffing; unused hub, router, or server ports that can be exploited and accessed by crackers if not disabled; a router's configuration port, accessible by Telnet, that may not be adequately secured; routers that may not be properly configured to mask internal subnets; modems attached to network devices that may be configured to accept incoming calls; dial-in access servers used by telecommuting or remote staff that may not be carefully secured and monitored; and computers hosting very sensitive data that may coexist on the same subnet with computers open to the general public.

❐ Some risks pertaining to networking protocols and software include the following: TCP/IP security flaws; trust relationships between one server and another; network operating system software "backdoors" or security flaws; a network operating system that allows server operators to exit to a command prompt; administrators who accept default operating system security; and transactions that take place between applications left open to interception.

❐ A denial-of-service attack occurs when a system becomes dysfunctional because it is deluged with traffic. It is a relatively simple attack to launch, and the easiest resolution is to turn off the attacked server.

❐ The first step in securing your network should be to devise and implement an enterprise-wide security policy. This document identifies your security goals, risks, levels of authority, designated security coordinator and team members, responsibilities for each team member, responsibilities for each employee, and strategies for addressing security breaches. It should not include specific information on what hardware, software, architecture, or protocols will be used to ensure security, nor should it indicate how hardware or software will be installed and configured.

❐ Goals for an effective security policy should include the following: ensuring that authorized users have appropriate access to the resources they need, preventing unauthorized users from gaining access to the network and its resources, protecting sensitive data from unauthorized access, preventing accidental damage to hardware or software, preventing intentional damage to hardware or software, creating an environment where the network and systems can withstand and quickly recover from any type of threat, and communicating each employee's responsibilities with respect to maintaining data integrity.

❑ Choosing secure passwords is one of the easiest and least expensive ways to guard against unauthorized access. The following guidelines for selecting passwords should be part of your organization's security policy: do not use the familiar types of passwords; do not use any word that can be found in a dictionary; make the password longer than six characters; choose a combination of letters and numbers; add special characters, such as exclamation marks or hyphens, if allowed; do not write down your password or share it with others; change your password at least every 90 days; and, if you are a network administrator, establish controls through the network operating system to force users to change their passwords at least every 90 days.

❑ One way to help keep a network secure is to restrict access to its physical components. At the very least, computer rooms should allow access only to authorized networking personnel. If computer rooms or wiring closets remain unlocked, intruders may easily enter and steal equipment, or sabotage software and hardware.

❑ A firewall is a specialized device (typically a router, but possibly only a PC running special software) that selectively filters or blocks traffic between networks. It may be placed between two interconnected private networks or, more typically, between a private network and a public network (such as the Internet).

❑ The simplest and most common form of firewall is a packet-filtering firewall. This router operates at the Data Link and Transport layers of the OSI Model, examining the header of every packet of data that it receives to determine whether that type of packet is authorized to continue to its destination. Packet-filtering firewalls are also called screening firewalls.

❑ A more sophisticated security technique is necessary to perform user authentication. One approach is to combine a packet-filtering firewall with a proxy service— a software application on a network host that acts as an intermediary between the external and internal networks, screening all incoming and outgoing traffic.

❑ The network host that runs the proxy service is known as a proxy server or gateway. Although a proxy server appears to the outside world as an internal network server, in reality it is merely another filtering device for the internal LAN. Among other things, it prevents the outside world from discovering the addresses of the internal network.

❑ Important security features that you should seek in a remote control program include the following: a login ID and password requirement to gain access to the host system, the ability for the host system to call back, support for data encryption on transmissions between the remote user and the system, the ability to leave the host system's screen blank while a remote user works on it, the ability to disable the host system's keyboard and mouse, and the ability to restart the host system when a remote user disconnects from the system.

15

❏ A secure remote access server package will include at least the following features: login ID and password authentication; the ability to log all dial-up connections, their sources, and their connection times; the ability to perform callbacks to users who initiate connections; and centralized management of dial-up users and their rights on the network.

❏ In environments where more than a few dozen simultaneous dial-up connections must be supported and their user IDs and passwords managed, a special kind of server, known as a Remote Authentication Dial-In User Service (RADIUS), may be implemented to offer authentication services to the network's access server. RADIUS provides a single, centralized point of authentication for dial-in users. It is highly scalable because it can attach to pools containing hundreds of modems.

❏ Every network operating system provides at least some security by allowing you to limit users' access to files and directories on the network. In addition, network administrators can constrain how those with different types of user IDs can use the network by setting restrictions on, for example, time of day, total time logged on, source address, and number of unsuccessful logon attempts.

❏ Encryption is the use of an algorithm to scramble data into a format that can be read only by reversing the algorithm—or decrypting the data—to keep the information private. Many forms of encryption exist, with some being more secure than others.

❏ The most popular kind of encryption algorithm weaves a key (a random string of characters) into the original data's bits, sometimes several times in different sequences, to generate a unique data block. The longer the key, the less easily the encrypted data can be decrypted by an unauthorized system.

❏ Key encryption comes in two forms: public and private key encryption. You should be familiar with at least the following types of encryption: Kerberos, Pretty Good Privacy (PGP), Secure Sockets Layer (SSL), and Internet Protocol Security (IPSec).

❏ The Point-to-Point Tunneling Protocol (PPTP) expands on PPP by encapsulating it so that any type of PPP data can traverse the Internet masked as a pure IP transmission. PPTP supports the encryption, authentication, and LAN access services provided by RAS. Instead of users having to dial directly into an access server, they can dial into their ISP using PPTP and gain access to their corporate LAN over the Internet.

❏ PPTP and L2F differ in the type of encryption supported by each and the fact that PPTP was developed by Microsoft and L2F was developed by Cisco Systems. One disadvantage to L2F as compared to PPTP is that the former protocol requires special hardware on the host system end, whereas PPTP will work with any Windows NT or 2000 server. On the other hand, L2F can encapsulate protocols to fit more than just the IP format, unlike PPTP.

❏ Layer 2 Tunneling Protocol (L2TP) is an enhanced version of L2F that supports multiple protocols, like L2F; unlike L2F, however, L2TP does not require costly hardware upgrades to implement. L2TP is also optimized to work with the next generation of IP (IPv6) and IPSec.

KEY TERMS

asymmetric encryption — A type of encryption (such as public key encryption) that uses a different key for encoding data than is used for decoding the cipher text.

authentication header (AH) — In the context of IPSec, a type of encryption that provides authentication of the IP packet's data payload through public key techniques.

authentication service (AS) — In Kerberos terminology, the process that runs on a key distribution center (KDC) to initially validate a client who's logging on. The authentication service issues session keys to the client and the service the client wants to access.

authenticator — In Kerberos authentication, the user's timestamp encrypted with the session key. The authenticator is used to help the service verify that a user's ticket is valid.

bio-recognition access — A method of authentication in which a device scans an individual's unique physical characteristics (such as the color patterns in his or her eye's iris or the geometry of his or her hand) to verify the user's identity.

cipher text — The unique data block that results when an original piece of data (such as text) is encrypted (for example, by using a key).

client_hello — In the context of SSL encryption, a message issued from the client to the server that contains information about what level of security the client's browser is capable of accepting and what type of encryption the client's browser can decipher (for example, RSA or Diffie-Hellman). The client_hello message also establishes a randomly generated number that uniquely identifies the client plus another number that identifies the SSL session.

cracker — A person who uses his or her knowledge of operating systems and utilities to intentionally damage or destroy data or systems.

data encryption standard (DES) — A popular private key encryption technique that was developed by IBM in the 1970s.

denial-of-service attack — A security attack caused by a deluge of traffic that disables the victimized system.

digital certificate — A password-protected and encrypted file that holds an individual's identification information, including a public key and a private key. The individual's public key is used to verify the sender's digital signature, and the private key allows the individual to log onto a third-party authority who administers digital certificates.

encapsulation security payload (ESP) — In the context of IPSec, a type of encryption that provides authentication of the IP packet's data payload through public key techniques. In addition, ESP also encrypts the entire IP packet for added security.

encryption — The use of an algorithm to scramble data into a format that can be read only by reversing the algorithm—decrypting the data—to keep the information private. The most popular kind of encryption algorithm weaves a key into the original data's bits, sometimes several times in different sequences, to generate a unique data block.

15

firewall — A specialized device (typically a router, but possibly only a PC running special software) that selectively filters or blocks traffic between networks.

flashing — A security attack in which an Internet user sends commands to another Internet user's machine that cause the screen to fill with garbage characters. A flashing attack will cause the user to terminate his or her session.

hacker — A person who masters the inner workings of operating systems and utilities in an effort to better understand them. A hacker is distinguished from a cracker in that a cracker will attempt to exploit a network's vulnerabilities for malicious purposes.

handshake protocol — One of several protocols within SSL, and perhaps the most significant. As its name implies, the handshake protocol allows the client and server to authenticate (or introduce) each other and establishes terms for how they will securely exchange data during an SSL session.

HTTPS — The URL prefix that indicates that a Web page requires its data to be exchanged between client and server using SSL encryption. HTTPS uses the TCP port number 443, rather than port 80 (the port that normal HTTP uses).

Internet Key Exchange (IKE) — The first phase of IPSec authentication, which accomplishes key management. IKE is a service that runs on UDP port 500. Once IKE has established the rules for the type of keys two nodes will use, IPSec invokes its second phase, encryption.

Internet Protocol Security (IPSec) — A Layer 3 protocol that defines encryption, authentication, and key management for TCP/IP transmissions. IPSec is an enhancement to IPv4 and native to IPv6. IPSec is unique among authentication methods in that it adds security information to the header of all IP packets.

IP spoofing — A security attack in which an outsider obtains internal IP addresses, then uses those addresses to pretend that he or she has authority to access a private network from the Internet.

Kerberos — A cross-platform authentication protocol that uses key encryption to verify the identity of clients and to securely exchange information once a client logs onto a system. It is an example of a private key encryption service.

key — A series of characters that is combined with a block of data during that data's encryption. In order to decrypt the resulting data, the recipient must also possess the key.

key distribution center (KDC) — In Kerberos terminology, the server that runs the authentication service and the ticket granting service in order to issue keys and tickets to clients. On a Windows 2000 network, a user's domain controller serves as his or her KDC.

key management — The method whereby two nodes using key encryption agree on common parameters for the keys they will use in order to encrypt data.

key pair — The combination of a public and private key used to decipher data that has been encrypted using public key encryption.

Layer 2 Forwarding (L2F) — A Layer 2 protocol similar to PPTP that provides tunneling for other protocols and can work with the authentication methods used by PPP. L2F was developed by Cisco Systems and requires special hardware on the host system end. It can encapsulate protocols to fit more than just the IP format, unlike PPTP.

Layer 2 Tunneling Protocol (L2TP) — A Layer 2 tunneling protocol developed by a number of industry consortia. L2TP is an enhanced version of L2F. Like L2F, it supports multiple protocols; unlike L2F, it does not require costly hardware upgrades to implement. L2TP is optimized to work with the next generation of IP (IPv6) and IPSec (the Layer 3 IP encryption protocol).

packet-filtering firewall — A router that operates at the Data Link and Transport layers of the OSI Model, examining the header of every packet of data that it receives to determine whether that type of packet is authorized to continue to its destination. Packet-filtering firewalls are also called screening firewalls.

Point-to-Point Tunneling Protocol (PPTP) — A Layer 2 protocol developed by Microsoft that encapsulates PPP so that any type of data can traverse the Internet masked as pure IP transmissions. PPTP supports the encryption, authentication, and LAN access services provided by RAS. Instead of users having to dial directly into an access server, they can dial into their ISP using PPTP and gain access to their corporate LAN over the Internet.

Pretty Good Privacy (PGP) — A key-based encryption system for e-mail that uses a two-step verification process.

principal — In Kerberos terminology, a user.

private key encryption — A type of key encryption in which the sender and receiver have private keys, which only they know. Data encryption standard (DES), which was developed by IBM in the 1970s, is a popular example of a private key encryption technique. Private key encryption is also known as symmetric encryption.

proxy server — A network host that runs a proxy service. Proxy servers may also be called gateways.

proxy service — A software application on a network host that acts as an intermediary between the external and internal networks, screening all incoming and outgoing traffic and providing one address to the outside world, instead of revealing the addresses of internal LAN devices.

public key encryption — A form of key encryption in which data are encrypted using two keys: one is a key known only to a user, and the other is a key associated with the user and can be obtained from a public source, such as a public key server. Some examples of public key algorithms include RSA (named after its creators, Rivest, Shamir, and Adleman), Diffie-Hellman, and Elliptic-curve cryptography. Public key encryption is also known as asymmetric encryption.

public-key server — A publicly available host (such as an Internet host) that provides free access to a list of users' public keys (for use in public key encryption).

Remote Authentication Dial-In User Service (RADIUS) — A server that offers authentication services to the network's access server (which may run the Windows NT or 2000 RAS or Novell's NAS, for example). RADIUS provides a single, centralized point of authentication for dial-in users and is often used by ISPs.

15

root — A highly privileged user ID that has all rights to create, delete, modify, move, read, write, or execute files on a system. This term may specifically refer to the administrator on a UNIX-based network.

screening firewall — See *packet-filtering firewall*.

Secure Sockets Layer (SSL) — A method of encrypting TCP/IP transmissions—including Web pages and data entered into Web forms—en route between the client and server using public key encryption technology.

security audit — An assessment of an organization's security vulnerabilities. A security audit should be performed at least annually and preferably quarterly or sooner if the network has undergone significant changes. For each risk found, it should rate the severity of a potential breach, as well as its likelihood.

server_hello — In the context of SSL encryption, a message issued from the server to the client that confirms the information the server received in the client_hello message and agrees to certain terms of encryption based on the options the client supplied. Depending on the Web server's preferred encryption method, the server may choose to issue your browser a public key or a digital certificate at this time.

session key — In the context of Kerberos authentication, a key issued to both the client and service by the authentication service that uniquely identifies their session.

social engineering — Manipulating relationships to circumvent network security measures and gain access to a system.

SSL session — In the context of SSL encryption, an association between the client and server that is defined by an agreement on a specific set of encryption techniques. An SSL session allows the client and server to continue to exchange data securely as long as the client is still connected to the server. SSL sessions are established by the SSL handshake protocol.

symmetric encryption — A method of encryption that requires the same key to encode the data as is used to decode the cipher text.

Terminal Access Controller Access Control System (TACACS) — A centralized authentication system for remote access servers that is similar to RADIUS.

ticket — In Kerberos terminology, a temporary set of credentials that a client uses to prove that its identity has been validated by the authentication service.

ticket granting service (TGS) — In Kerberos terminology, an application that runs on the key distribution center that issues ticket granting tickets to clients so that they need not request a new ticket for each new service they want to access.

ticket granting ticket (TGT) — In Kerberos terminology, a ticket that enables a user to be accepted as a validated principal by multiple services.

Transport Layer Security (TLS) — A version of SSL being standardized by the Internet Engineering Task Force (IETF). With TLS, IETF aims to create a version of SSL that will encrypt UDP as well as TCP transmissions. TLS, which will likely be supported by new Web browsers, uses slightly different encryption algorithms than SSL, but otherwise is very similar to the most recent version of SSL.

tunneling — The process of encapsulating one protocol to make it appear as another type of protocol.

REVIEW QUESTIONS

1. If you have root privileges on a system, you could delete user IDs from that system. True or False?

2. What do you call manipulating people to get them to reveal confidential information, such as their passwords?

    a. social engineering

    b. social manipulation

    c. social coercion

    d. social affectation

    e. social posturing

3. Which of the following is the most secure password?

    a. 123

    b. dolphins

    c. !tz0g557x

    d. tchotchke

    e. 1040506

4. Which two of the following would not typically be used for authenticating via a network operating system?

    a. IP address

    b. user name

    c. password

    d. last name

    e. date of last logon

5. Name three different security risks associated with people.

6. What is the most likely way that a network's security will be compromised?

    a. from within the organization

    b. from a cracker on the Internet

    c. from a cracker posing as a contractor

    d. from a cracker using IP spoofing over a modem connection

    e. from a cracker using a remote control program

7. Which device could a cracker use to intercept and interpret transmissions between one router and another router on a WAN?

    a. router

    b. hub

15

    c. switch

    d. sniffer

    e. multimeter

8. Accepting the default options for security on a server-based application is usually a good policy. True or False?

9. If someone obtains one of your LAN's internal IP addresses and uses it to gain access through your firewall from the Internet, what method of security attack is he or she using?

    a. flashing

    b. SSL

    c. denial of service

    d. framing

    e. IP spoofing

10. The UDP protocol is more secure than the TCP protocol. True or False?

11. If someone floods your LAN's router with excessive traffic so that your legitimate traffic cannot go out or come in, what method of security attack is he or she using?

    a. flashing

    b. SSL

    c. denial-of-service

    d. framing

    e. IP spoofing

12. Which of the following is not typically addressed in a security policy?

    a. preventing accidental damage to network software and hardware

    b. specifying what model and make of firewall is appropriate for the network

    c. ensuring that authorized users have appropriate access to the resources they need

    d. communicating each employee's responsibilities with respect to maintaining data integrity

    e. identifying a response to suspected security breaches

13. What is the primary purpose for establishing a security response team?

    a. to demonstrate to users the security risks they face

    b. to train users to respond to security threats as they happen

    c. to devise a coordinated response to security breaches while or after they occur

    d. to comprehensively audit the security of the network

    e. to publicize the sanctions that will befall users who do not follow the security policy

14. What should an organization do to assess its potential security risks?

    a. perform a security audit

    b. freeze any new user ID creation

    c. question users about odd behavior on their workstations

    d. train users to watch for suspicious activity

    e. hire a number of different consultants to provide multiple perspectives on the best approach to network security

15. Name four questions that should be addressed in a security audit.

16. What's the simplest way to stop a denial-of-service attack on a server?

    a. shut down the victimized server

    b. shut down the firewall between your server and the Internet

    c. turn on TCP and UDP filtering

    d. restart your central switch to clear traffic from the server's segment

    e. install a sniffer on the server to filter out traffic issued from the denial-of-service attacker

17. Which of the following transmission media is the most secure?

    a. UTP

    b. STP

    c. coaxial cable

    d. infrared

    e. fiber-optic cable

18. Which of the following encryption methods is most commonly used on VPNs?

    a. SSL

    b. Kerberos

    c. IPSec

    d. PGP

    e. private key encryption

15

19. Which two of the following do not contribute to a network's physical security?

    a. closed-circuit TV

    b. public keys

    c. badge access systems

    d. door locks

    e. digital certificates

20. Which of the following network operating system restrictions is most likely to stop a cracker who is attempting to discover someone's password?

    a. number of unsuccessful logon attempts

    b. time of day

    c. total time logged on

    d. source address

    e. username and password

21. Name four criteria that a packet-filtering firewall might use for filtering traffic.

22. At which two layers of the OSI Model does a packet-filtering firewall operate?

    a. Transport and Network layers

    b. Network and Data Link layers

    c. Data Link and Transport layers

    d. Session and Transport layers

    e. Physical and Data Link layers

23. Before a firewall can effectively filter unwanted traffic, it must be:

    a. placed between a private and public network

    b. configured according to an organization's security needs

    c. combined with a proxy server

    d. attached to a switch on the internal LAN

    e. installed with Kerberos server software

24. Which of the following best describes the function of a proxy server?

    a. to deny LAN access to specific IP addresses

    b. to filter inappropriate content traveling from the Internet to an internal LAN

    c. to encapsulate protocols in the IP format

    d. to act as a gateway between an internal LAN and the outside world, masking the IP addresses of private LAN devices

    e. to issue and retain public keys for users requiring PGP e-mail security

25. Which of the following security risks does using the callback feature on a remote control application address?

    a. the possibility that passersby can take over the host system that is being controlled remotely

    b. the possibility that unauthorized users can take over the host system after they have discovered its phone number and logon ID

    c. the possibility that unauthorized users can scan a host system's ports and discover its phone number

   d. the possibility that passersby can shut down the system in mid-session

   e. the possibility that a cracker can gain access to the system through an intermediate host, such as the file server

26. If a company wants to save office leasing costs and allow 50 of its employees to work at home, what type of arrangement would be the most secure, practical, and economical for granting home workers access to the LAN?

   a. create exceptions in the firewall filtering rules to accept incoming traffic from each home worker's workstation according to their IP addresses

   b. set up a VPN that uses a RADIUS server to centrally authenticate and grant LAN access to dial-in users

   c. establish a Windows 2000 RAS server with direct PPP dial-in capability

   d. program Web front ends for the applications used by home workers and employ SSL to transmit their work over the Internet

27. What service does PPTP provide?

   a. It encapsulates protocols so they can run on IP-based networks such as the Internet.

   b. It authenticates dial-up users according to their source address.

   c. It ensures that remote control callback mechanisms are secure.

   d. It encrypts data using the IPv6 protocol.

   e. It tracks suspicious IP activity on a packet-filtering firewall.

28. If you are entering your account number in a Web page to gain access to your stock portfolio online, which of the following encryption methods are you most likely using?

   a. PGP

   b. Kerberos

   c. L2F

   d. IPSec

   e. SSL

29. In general, the longer the key, the more secure the encryption. True or False?

30. PGP is frequently used for what type of network communication?

   a. e-mail

   b. FTP

   c. HTTP

   d. Telnet

   e. HTTPS

15

HANDS-ON PROJECTS

Project 15-1

For a networking professional, it's important to stay abreast of new security threats and learn how to address them. In fact, in a large organization, a team of professionals might be devoted to network security, with one team member responsible for researching new security threats. In this project, you will look at some Web resources that can help you find out about vulnerabilities on your network. For this project, you will need a workstation with Internet connectivity and a Web browser.

1. Connect to the Internet and point your browser to the following URL: **www.microsoft.com/security/bulletins/current.asp**. The Security Bulletin Search page appears. Scroll down the page until you find the list of security risks associated with Microsoft software according to the date they were discovered.

2. Scroll through the list and click **MS01–024, "Malformed Request to Domain Controller can Cause Memory Exhaustion."**

3. Read the description of the problem and how Microsoft has addressed it. How was this problem discovered and reported to Microsoft? How could Windows 2000 Server allow someone to exploit this vulnerability?

4. Click the **Back** button on your browser and browse more Microsoft security bulletins.

5. Now point your browser to this URL: **developer.novell.com/research/ appnotes/2000/june/03/a0006037.htm**. Read about Novell's recommendations for NDS security.

6. According to what you read in the NetWare security document, how does the concept of "inherited rights" affect users within an organizational unit? Under what circumstances does this document suggest that using network address restrictions on a user account would be helpful? Why does this document recommend that the network administrator have at least two separate accounts: one with Administrator privileges and one with normal user privileges?

7. One organization that provides an updated list of many types of security risks is CERT, a clearinghouse for security risks established by the Carnegie Mellon Software Engineering Institute. To view its current alerts, point your browser to the following URL: **www.cert.org/advisories/**. Notice that the alerts are organized by the date they were released.

8. View information about a denial of service alert by clicking one of the most recent bulletins.

9. Read the advisory. What type of action does CERT recommend network administrators take to defend against or prevent this threat?

10. Click the **Back** button on your browser to return to the list of advisories. Browse through the most recent alerts. To what types of software or systems do most of the alerts pertain?

Project 15-2

As you have learned, password restrictions play a significant role in network security. In Chapter 8 you learned how to impose password restrictions on a user account as you created it. In this project, you will learn how to impose security restrictions on all user accounts within a domain at once. For this exercise, you will need a Windows 2000 server and the capability to log on as Administrator to that server. To test your changes, you will need a Windows 2000 Professional or Windows 9x client and a valid user ID (other than the Administrator) that can log onto the Windows 2000 server.

1. Log onto the server as Administrator.

2. Click **Start**, point to **Programs**, point to **Administrative Tools**, then click **Domain Security Policy**. The Domain Security Policy window appears.

3. In the left-hand pane of the Domain Security Policy window, double-click **Security Settings**, if necessary, to expand the container.

4. Double-click **Account Policies**, if necessary, to expand this option.

5. Click the **Password Policy** option. A list of password policies and their settings appears in the right-hand pane of the Domain Security Policy window, as shown in Figure 15-9.

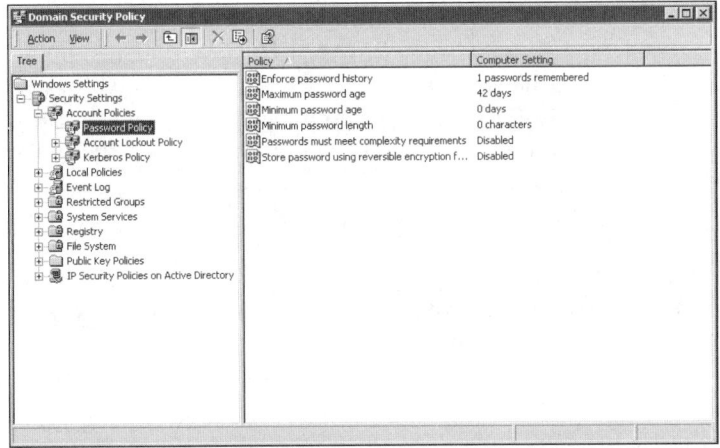

Figure 15-9   Windows 2000 Domain Security Policy window

6. What is the maximum password age set at? Right-click on the **Maximum password age** policy, then click **Security** from the shortcut menu. The Security Policy Setting dialog box appears.

7. Change the number of days after which passwords will expire to 60 days.

8. Click **OK** to close the Security Policy Setting dialog box.

9. What is the minimum password length setting? Right-click the **Minimum password length** policy, then click **Security** in the shortcut menu. The Security Policy Setting dialog box appears.

10. Change the minimum number of characters in the password to 8.

11. Click **OK** to close the Security Policy Setting dialog box.

12. Right-click on the **Passwords must meet complexity requirements** policy, then click **Security** in the shortcut menu. The Security Policy Setting dialog box appears.

13. Make sure the Define this policy setting option is checked, then click the **Enabled** radio button to enable the complexity requirements. Click **OK** to close the Security Policy Setting dialog box.

14. In the left-hand pane of the Domain Security Policy window, click the **Account Lockout Policy** option. Account lockout policies appear in the right-hand pane of the Domain Security Policy window.

15. Right-click the **Account lockout duration** policy, then click **Security** in the shortcut menu. The Security Policy Setting dialog box appears.

16. Check the box next to **Define this policy setting**, then change the number of minutes an account will be locked out to 5.

17. Click **OK** to close the Security Policy Setting dialog box. A Suggested Value Changes window may appear, informing you that because the account lockout duration is now 5 minutes, the settings for the "Account lockout threshold" and "Reset account lockout counter" will also be changed. Why do you think the number of invalid logon attempts was raised when you lowered the lockout duration?

18. Click **OK** to accept the changes and close the Suggested Value Changes window.

19. Close the Domain Security Policy window.

20. From your Windows workstation, attempt to log onto the Windows 2000 server with an ordinary user ID. Are you prompted with any messages about your password?

21. Now attempt to change your password, using each of the following character strings: dog, 12345, and TJ01xxN73. How does the server respond to each?

22. Log off from the server, then attempt to log on again, but deliberately enter the wrong password five times in a row. Then try the correct password on your sixth logon attempt. What happens?

23. Wait six minutes and try logging onto the server with the correct password. What happens?

Project 15-3

Another important principle of protecting network data from security breaches is assigning the proper rights to each individual or group that has access to your network's servers. In this project, you will assign appropriate rights for five groups of users on a Windows 2000 server. You will need a Windows 2000 server with a Windows 2000 Professional client workstation attached and the capability to log onto the server. You should have Administrator rights on the server. The Windows 2000 server should contain the following user IDs: Bob, Patrick, Mary, Errol, Sally, Chris, Inez, Richard, Dave, and Cory. Each ID should be associated with the same password, "3netch15309", and users should have no modifications to their default file access rights. The server should also contain the following directories:

C:\DATA\BUDGET

C:\DATA\SAMPLES

C:\DATA\CONTRACTS

C:\DATA\PAYABLES

C:\DATA\RECEIVABLES

The users should belong to the groups specified in Table 15-1:

Table 15-1   Users and groups for Project 15-3

Users	Group
Bob, Patrick, Mary, Errol, Sally, Chris, Inez, Richard, Dave, Cory	Accounting
Mary, Patrick, Sally	Accounts Payable
Bob, Chris, Cory	Accounts Receivable
Inez, Richard, Chris	Finance
Errol, Patrick, Dave, Inez	Managers

1. Log onto the server from the client workstation as Patrick, using the password 3netch15309.

2. Attempt to open the directory C:\DATA\CONTRACTS on the server. What message do you see?

3. Now you will give group rights to each directory. Begin by logging onto the Windows 2000 server as Administrator.

4. Double-click the **My Computer** icon to see a list of drives on the server.

5. Double-click the **Local Disk (C:)** drive icon to view its contents.

6. Double-click the **DATA** directory to view its subdirectories.

7. Right-click the **BUDGET** folder, then click **Properties**. The BUDGET Properties dialog box opens.

8. Click the **Security** tab.

15

9. Click **Add**. The Select Users, Computers, or Groups dialog box opens.

10. Double-click the **Accounting** group, then click **OK**. You return to the BUDGET Properties dialog box.

11. With the Accounting group highlighted, check the **Write** box in the Allow column. This setting gives the Accounting group permission to create (or add) new files, but not to modify existing files.

12. Click **OK** in the BUDGET Properties dialog box.

13. Repeat Steps 7 through 12 using the directory names and their respective privileges as shown in Table 15-2:

Table 15-2 Directories and group permissions for Project 15-3

Directory	Group	Permissions
C:\DATA\SAMPLES	All groups	Modify
C:\DATA\CONTRACTS	Managers	Full control
C:\DATA\CONTRACTS	Accounts Receivable	Read (only)
C:\DATA\CONTRACTS	Accounts Payable	Read (only)
C:\DATA\PAYABLES	Accounts Payable	Modify
C:\DATA\RECEIVABLES	Accounts Receivable	Modify

CASE PROJECTS

1. As an experienced networking professional, you have been asked to conduct a security audit on a local credit union's network. The union currently has two locations, a headquarters office downtown and a branch office on the east side of town. The headquarters has the following equipment:

   ❏ 20 Windows 2000 Professional workstations, connected to a Windows 2000 server

   ❏ 1 Windows 2000 RAS server accessed by home workers after hours

   ❏ 1 Windows 2000 server for recordkeeping

   ❏ 1 UNIX database server

   ❏ 1 UNIX Web server for members to check their account balances online

   ❏ 1 firewall where the network connects to the credit union's ISP via a T1 dedicated link

   The east-side office has five Windows 2000 Professional workstations, connected to the headquarters office Windows 2000 server through a dedicated ISDN link.

All tape backups are housed in a secure room in the headquarters office, with copies being kept in a file cabinet at the east-side office. At the headquarters, the servers reside in a locked room that admits authorized users with an electronic badge access system. Both locations have numerous security cameras, including cameras in the computer room and backup tape storage vault at the headquarters. The manager also tells you that the credit union has a security policy that all employees are required to read and sign when they become employees. He believes that the network is very secure and asks you if he could do anything else to ensure that the network is safe from security breaches. In response, create a checklist of items on this network that should be evaluated for security. Describe any access points or situations that constitute potential security risks. In addition, explain how the credit union manager could better train his employees to understand network security.

2. As part of your security audit, you have recommended that credit union employees change their passwords so they are more secure and that the IT department enforce password changes every 60 days, because of the confidential nature of the data on the workstations and servers. The credit union employees are not enthusiastic about this change, and they complain that they already have too many things to remember. How might you convince them that choosing secure passwords and changing their passwords frequently are in their own best interest and for the good of their employer?

3. The credit union is experiencing tremendous growth and needs to either open another branch office on the west side of town or allow their auditors and loan-processing staff to work from home. It asks you to compare the security requirements of opening a new branch office versus implementing a dial-VPN solution (using the Internet) for work-at-home employees. As part of your comparison, list the costs associated with these security requirements. For an expansion of 10 users, which solution do you recommend?

15

CHAPTER 16

MANAGING NETWORK DESIGN AND IMPLEMENTATION

After reading this chapter and completing the exercises, you will be able to:

➤ Describe the elements and benefits of project management

➤ Analyze the current status of a network

➤ Perform a needs assessment and recommend changes based on your findings

➤ Manage a network implementation project

➤ Design and test a pilot network

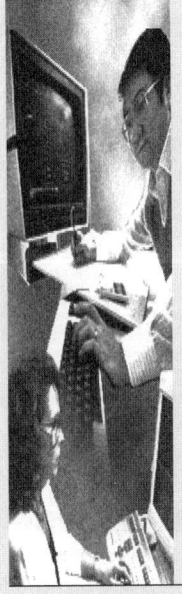

ON THE JOB

I'm a network manager at a packaging company. A year ago we decided to change our network from Token Ring to Ethernet (partly because Token Ring devices are so much more expensive than their Ethernet counterparts). That project began a year ago and it's still going on. We ran into numerous obstacles that we just didn't expect.

One significant problem was staffing the project. Many of my staff are highly skilled engineers who are happy designing networks but aren't enthused about installing new NICs in PCs. We found some temporary staff to help us, but then we spent a lot of time training the staff. The time spent training them caused our project timelines to slip.

Another problem was explaining the change to the rest of our company, who didn't know what Token Ring or Ethernet meant. They only knew that we would be taking down the network and taking over their machines from time to time. Halfway into the project we decided to hold user meetings, in which we would describe the changes and their consequences and field questions from users. These meetings helped users understand what was going on and bolstered our staff's reputation.

While we couldn't have foreseen everything, better planning would have made this project easier and maybe less costly from the start. For my next large project, I'm hiring a professional project manager to help.

Joe Witkowski
M-Star Industries

In preceding chapters, you learned about the various elements that make up networks. In this chapter, you will learn how to put those elements together to improve an existing network or plan a network from start to finish. One of the first steps in implementing a network is devising a plan. Before you can create such a plan, however, you must learn some project management fundamentals. Project management is a broad term that refers to the process of managing timelines, resources, budgets, and personnel so as to reach a specific goal. Each of us regularly embarks on projects—whether the project involves writing a term paper or fixing a car's engine. Rarely do we devise project plans for our own projects. For projects that affect many people, require significant capital outlay, or influence a company's profitability, project management is essential to ensure the project's success. This chapter will discuss not only project management, but also techniques for approaching typical network implementation projects.

INTRODUCTION TO PROJECT MANAGEMENT

Project Management is the practice of managing resources, staff, budget, timelines, and other variables so as to achieve a specific goal within given bounds. For example, if you were a Web site development consultant, you might use project management techniques to establish an online store for a national furniture retailer. The project might be constrained by time (for example, you might aim to establish the e-commerce site before November 1 so as to cater to holiday shoppers), money, or the number of developers who can help you with the project. In the networking field, you might employ the basic principles of project management in the process of replacing the CAT3 wiring in your organization's building with CAT5e wiring.

Every project begins with identifying a need (although, of course, identifying a need may not result in a project). As you will learn later in this chapter, you can conduct a feasibility study to determine whether a particular need warrants a full-fledged project. If the feasibility study confirms that a project is necessary, you must appoint a project manager and begin planning the project. As discussed in the following section, the project manager's first step is to conduct a needs assessment and establish the project goals. Only then can the project manager create a project plan.

The other elements of a full-scale project include participants, funding, a specific means of communication, definitive processes, contingency plans, and a testing and evaluation phase. The following sections describe these elements in more detail.

The Web offers many valuable resources for project managers. A good place to start is at the Project Management Institute's Web site for project managers at www.pmi.org.

The Project Plan

A **project plan** is the way in which details of a managed project (for example, the timeline and the significant tasks) are organized. Plans for small projects may take the form of a simple text or spreadsheet document (in fact, they may begin as notes scribbled on a piece of paper). For larger projects, however, you will typically take advantage of project management software (such as Microsoft Project, PlanView, or PrimaVera Project Planner). Project management software facilitates project planning by providing a framework for inputting tasks, timelines, resource assignments, completion dates, and so on. Such software is also highly customizable, so you can use only a small portion or all of its features, depending on the scope of your project and your project management skills. Figure 16-1 shows a list of tasks as they might appear in Microsoft Project.

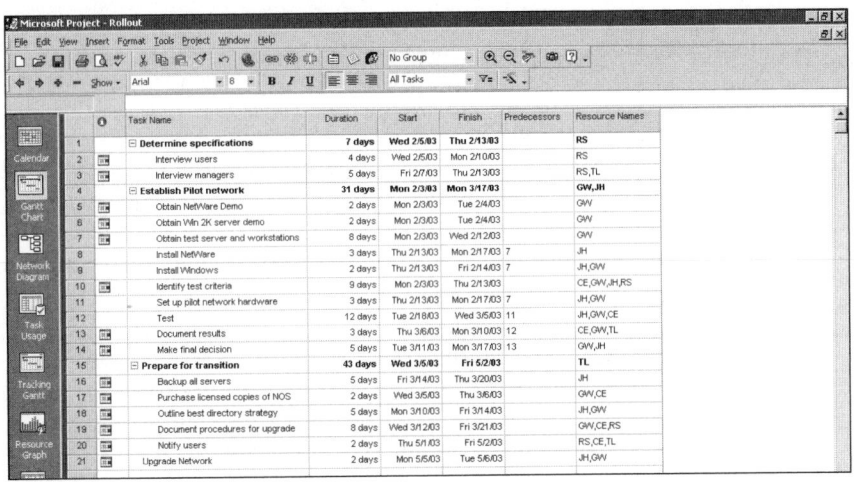

Figure 16-1 View of a project in Microsoft Project

No matter how large or small the project, its project plan will contain some common elements, as described below:

- *Task breakdown*—A project should be divided into specific tasks. Larger tasks are then broken into even smaller subtasks. For example, establishing an e-commerce Web site and server at an Internet service provider's data center represents a large task with numerous subtasks: obtaining racks for the equipment, ensuring backup and bandwidth capacity, obtaining software and hardware, installing equipment and software, configuring the hardware, testing the software, and so on.

You may find it tricky to separate a project into meaningful, discrete tasks that are specific enough to measure progress and guide participants, but not so narrow that they lose meaning. As you gain project planning experience, you will better be able to gauge how to best separate tasks into smaller but significant subtasks.

16

- *Dependencies*—The project plan specifies which tasks depend on the completion of previous tasks before you can begin them. In some project management software, the tasks that must be completed before other tasks can begin are called **predecessors**. In the example of establishing an e-commerce server, you would have to determine which type of server you want to purchase before ordering the equipment racks. This ordering of tasks is necessary because racks come in different widths and depths. Thus the task of determining the type of server needed is a predecessor of the task of obtaining the racks. It's critical to examine potential dependencies in a project plan, because a dependency means that part of the project depends on another part. If you neglect to consider a dependency at the beginning of a project, stopping to address it during the project may delay the schedule and impose unnecessary stress on team members, who must later rush to complete their tasks. Careful planning will reveal any dependencies that might affect the project's timeline and success.

■ *Timeline*—The project plan should identify how long each task will take (with start and finish dates), which tasks take priority (due to dependencies), and how the timeline might change depending on resource availability or dependencies. Timelines are not always easy to predict. Seasoned professionals may be able to gauge how long a particular task might take based on their previous experience with similar tasks. Every project may entail conditions that affect a timeline differently, however. When creating a timeline, you should allow extra time for any especially significant tasks. For instance, in the e-commerce server example, the manufacturer might tell you that obtaining the equipment racks will take one week. If you plan for delivery in a week, and the installation of the Web site depends on this task, your entire project will be delayed if the racks don't arrive for two weeks. A **Gantt chart** is a popular method for depicting when projects begin and end along a horizontal timeline. Figure 16-2 illustrates a simple Gantt chart.

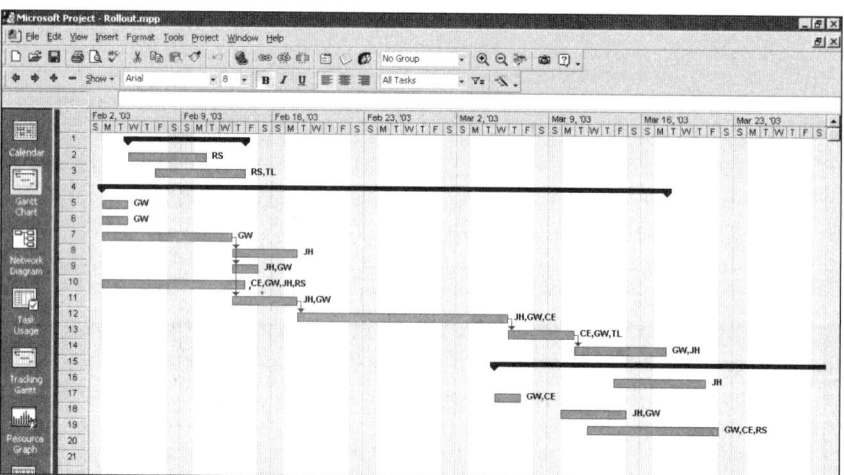

Figure 16-2   A simple Gantt chart

You may be asked to plan a project with seemingly impossible deadlines. One technique for making the project fit into a tight time frame is to work backward to create the timeline. In other words, begin at the project's predetermined endpoint and move toward the beginning of the project, allowing the normal time requirements for tasks. This method will highlight which tasks may delay the project and therefore need to be dropped or modified, at least temporarily.

- *Resources*—All projects require the staffing, materials, and money that are collectively known as **resources**. A project plan can specify all resources needed for each task or group of tasks. At the very least, it should identify who is responsible for tasks, whether it is a committee, consultant, manager, or technical person. This person is the **owner** of the task. The owner does not necessarily have to perform the work himself or herself, but nevertheless must ensure that it is completed on time and within budgetary guidelines.

- *Milestones*—Every project has significant accomplishments that mark specific steps in their progress. In project planning, a **milestone** is a reference point that marks the completion of a major task or group of tasks in the project and contributes to measuring the project's progress. For example, if you were in charge of the e-commerce server project, you might designate the completion of the software installation on your server as being a milestone. Milestones are particularly useful in large projects that have high visibility within the organization. They provide a quick indication of a project's relative success or failure.

In addition to these elements, project plans may provide information on task priority, the amount of flexibility in the timeline, task successors, links to other project plans, and so on. With most project planning software, you can add your own columns to the plan and insert any type of information you deem appropriate. For example, if you are managing a very large network design project, you might create a Web site with links to documentation for each phase of the project. In the project plan, you might include a column to list the URLs of the documents for each task or group of tasks.

During the course of a project, the project plan will likely undergo several changes. Some changes may result from unforeseen circumstances; others may reflect milestone evaluations and adjustments. Later in this section, you will learn more about these contingencies and how to plan for them.

16

Project Participants

As mentioned previously, each project depends on many resources. The human resources involved in a project may be employees from your department or other departments within the organization, outside consultants, vendor representatives, or employees from other organizations. Usually, human resources from various factions work together in teams. Although a single person may handle some project tasks (such as ordering a server, updating a document, or configuring a router), larger tasks should be accomplished by teams. For example, as the project manager for a network redesign, you might assign the task of determining how to upgrade the backbone to a team consisting of a cabling vendor, a network technician, a facilities architect, and an IT manager. In an organization with limited staff members, some project participants may belong to more than one team.

As a project manager, you probably won't supervise everyone involved in the project. Therefore, you need managers who agree with the project's goals and will strive to help you achieve them. These authority figures are called project **sponsors**. Although sponsors rarely participate in project tasks and do not necessarily supervise the project manager, they can lobby for budget increases necessary to complete the project, appeal to a group of managers to extend a project's deadline, assist with negotiating vendor contracts, and so on.

A sponsor may be the person who originated the idea for the project. For example, suppose users in your organization complain about slow network response time, particularly when they try to pick up their e-mail. As a network administrator, you respond to these complaints by finding out the source of the poor network performance. You determine that the problem lies in the fact that the network uses routers and a 10-Mbps transmission rate. To solve the problem, you would like to upgrade the network to be fully switched and to run at 100-Mbps. You write a proposal for the change and bring it to the director of IT. She agrees with your research and your proposal, so she offers to become the project's sponsor. She will take your proposal to your company's executive board and attempt to obtain approval for the resources necessary to complete the project.

Another important group of project participants comprises the stakeholders. A **stakeholder** is any person who may be affected by the project, for better or for worse. In the example of upgrading a network to a fully switched, 100-Mbps environment, the stakeholders will include users (who will benefit from faster network access), executives (not only because they are network users, but also because they have responsibility for the budget), IT managers (who will ultimately determine the success or failure of the project), and project team members. Typically, the stakeholders are the people to whom the project teams must answer. At the beginning of a project, it is wise to communicate the project's goals, timelines, affects, and contingencies to project stakeholders. As you'll learn in the next section, it is also advisable to maintain regular communication with stakeholders about the project's progress.

Funding

Every project—whether it entails a simple hardware upgrade or an entire network redesign—requires funding. A project budget is usually set at the beginning of a project and approved by a hierarchy of managers whose staff participate in the project. Of course, a project's budget will depend on its breadth and complexity. As a project manager, you may have little control over the project's budget after it is established. For this reason, you should estimate your costs generously in the initial proposal for the project. It is always preferable to complete a project under budget than to continually appeal for more funding.

In some cases, the amount of funding available to your project can help to make other resources available. Naturally, if managers allocated $200,000 to your project rather than $20,000, you will have 10 times more money to spend on staffing, tools that might make your teams more efficient, or state-of-the-art hardware and software. Sometimes, however, no matter how much funding is available to your project, other constraints may block your progress. For example, your project of upgrading the company's customer service database may depend on the highly specialized knowledge of just two programmers who originally developed the system. Even a budget allocation of $2,000,000 for contractors or new staff wouldn't help you obtain qualified staff, because only these two programmers truly understand how the application works. In addition, the software they're creating might be constrained by functional limits on how many people can change the code at any given time. Thus your project is forced to rely on the efficiency of those two programmers.

Communications

Even if a project has sufficient funding, technical staff, and support from sponsors, it will falter if communication methods are not well defined and carefully followed. Communications are critical for several purposes:

- To ensure that a project's goals are understood by participants, stakeholders, and sponsors
- To keep a project's timeline and budget on track
- To encourage teamwork among participants
- To allow you to learn from previous mistakes
- To prevent fingerpointing if a task is not completed correctly or on time
- To avoid duplication of efforts
- To prepare stakeholders for the effects of the change

At the beginning of a project, the project manager should take responsibility for establishing the methods of communication. Suggested methods include weekly status meetings, daily status briefings for each team, weekly messages to stakeholders about the project's progress, monthly reports that compare a project's *anticipated* spending and timeline with its *actual* spending and timeline, distribution lists for each project team to share e-mail correspondence, and a Web page containing an archive of meeting minutes and other important documents pertaining to the project. Be creative—you might find other effective ways to communicate within your team. Whatever methods you choose, keep in mind that carefully fostered teamwork will contribute to the success of your project.

16

Processes

In almost everything you do, you follow a process: buying groceries, reading a book, building a deck. When you perform these tasks alone, you can do them whichever way you prefer. When a team of individuals must perform tasks together, however, agreeing on a process beforehand will help to ensure that the task is completed efficiently and that the team's efforts result in a desirable, high-quality outcome.

Process management consists of planning for and handling the steps needed to accomplish a goal in a systematic way. The processes you might manage during a project's implementation include change, support, training, transitioning, delegation, and problem resolution. If you've never managed processes before, it may be difficult to envision this endeavor without concrete examples. Consider how process management can help in the following scenarios:

- You and your colleagues decide to upgrade the network operating system on one of your file servers. You are responsible for ensuring that the change works correctly. Before performing the upgrade, you may want to define a change process. The change process could include notifying potentially affected users at least five business days before you make the modification, documenting exactly what the change will involve and who will make it, backing up the server prior to making the change, and providing a plan for reversing the operation should it cause problems on the server.

- A new network administrator is hired to shoulder some of the responsibilities previously assigned to an existing network administrator. The current network administrator plans to go on a two-week vacation on a remote island only seven days after the new network administrator starts. Before the new employee arrives, you may want to establish a training process. Part of this process could include asking the existing network administrator to identify recently completed tasks, outlining a training plan for the new employee, and identifying other employees who can act as resources for the new employee in different subject areas.

- You manage the 7 days a week, 24 hours a day support team for a corporate LAN. If serious problems arise during the night or on weekends, you may need to help with problem resolution. Having a problem management process in place will make your job and the jobs of the support analysts easier. Part of your problem management process may include notification of all affected customers if the problem hasn't been resolved within 30 minutes, maintenance of a list of second-level support contacts, instructions for how to record the problem in a call-tracking system, and procedures for contacting vendors required to troubleshoot hardware or software.

For any endeavor that requires the cooperation of several team members, process management is a wise investment of time. Creating a process will not be sufficient, however, unless everyone understands the process. You must ensure that the process is communicated to all participants. Begin by proposing the need for a process at a meeting and ask for participants' input. After drafting the process, distribute it as a memo or post it on a Web page where everyone can find it. During the course of a project, urge colleagues to follow the agreed-upon processes.

Processes help you manage unusual or troublesome situations. In the next section, you will learn about another element of project management that can guide participants when things go seriously awry.

Contingency Planning

Even the most meticulously planned project may be derailed by unforeseen circumstances. For instance, a key team participant may quit, your budget may be unexpectedly cut, or a software package may not work as promised. Each of these conditions may threaten to delay your project's completion. To prepare for such circumstances, you must create a contingency plan at the beginning of the project. **Contingency planning** is the process of identifying steps that will minimize the risk of unforeseen events that endanger the quality or timeliness of the project's goals.

Although you cannot predict all possible pitfalls in a project, you should at least plan for the most likely hazards. To identify potential threats to the success of your project, you should analyze your organization's history. For instance, you may work for a company that is notorious for taking team participants who have committed to one project and switching them to new projects. In that case, you may want to increase the number of people working on the project initially, so that losing one or two participants will not detrimentally affect your project's success. Alternately, you may want to budget for subcontractors to step in when or if your organization's staff members become unavailable. In another organization, you may have experience with programmers who chronically underestimate the time needed to customize programs for your users. In this case, you should add time to the customization tasks to plan for the possibility that the programming will take longer than the programmers suggest.

In a networking project, taking some of the following measures in the beginning can prevent you from having to scramble during the project's implementation:

- Order more hardware components than you think you need.
- Ensure that your hardware and software vendors have extra components on hand and that they will respond to your requests.
- Document each piece of hardware and software that you order for the project. Also, keep a tally of supplies as they are received.
- Rely on a pilot network to test your project's goals (for example, to determine whether choosing switches over routers will improve your network's performance), in addition to testing the hardware and software components (for example, each switch that you purchase) that you will use.

16

■ If the technology required to implement the project is new to project participants, ask a local consulting company with expertise in that technology to
be available for questions in case you need help.

The amount of preparation you perform for each contingency should be commensurate
with the potential effects of that possibility. For example, if you were planning a demonstration of your application to a very high-profile client who was considering purchasing
the application for $5,000,000, you would want to plan a backup for everything that could
possibly go wrong with your presentation. On the other hand, if you were planning a
demonstration of the same program to your colleagues, you may not spend much time won-
dering what to do in case the splash screen containing your company logo doesn't appear.

Another way to help ensure your project's success is to perform regular testing and evaluation, as discussed in the following section.

Testing and Evaluation

Once you have reached a project milestone, you will want to verify that you are on the
right path. One way of accomplishing this goal is through testing. For instance, if you
were managing a project to upgrade a building's LAN from 10 Mbps to 100 Mbps, you
might want to tackle one small segment of the network first. Before moving to the next
segment, you should ensure that all workstation and switch or router configurations on
the first segment work correctly. By confirming this fact, you can potentially prevent
future down time or troubleshooting.

To successfully test your implementation, you must establish a testing plan that includes
relevant methods and criteria. For example, your method of testing the network performance may be to use the Windows 2000 Server Network Monitor program from a
server. For each performance test you perform, you will want to replicate this arrangement, so that you can compare your results across the various tests. In this case, the criteria you use to measure network performance may be the number of bytes that travel
from one particular workstation to the server every five minutes.

Once you have devised a testing plan, emphasize to all project participants how vital it
is to adhere to the plan. If participants ignore the testing plan for a backbone upgrade,
for example, they might be tempted to quickly set up a workstation on a new network
segment and assume that if they reach the network login prompt, the change is a success. Unfortunately, this approach may overlook protocol or transmission speed issues
that can cause problems later. To provide an accurate assessment, a test plan should
address at least the following questions:

■ Was the change nominally successful? (For example, if the change comprised a
backbone upgrade, can a client on the new backbone connect to the server?)

■ Did the change fully accomplish its purpose? (For example, if the change
comprised a backbone upgrade, did it result in a performance improvement?)

■ If the change did not fully accomplish its purpose, did it partially accomplish
its goal?

- Did the change result in unexpected consequences?

- Did the change point to a need for additional changes? (For example, if the change comprised a backbone upgrade, did testing reveal that new cabling was required for a segment whose cabling was initially thought to be adequate?)

For testing to be useful, project participants should clearly define the change's purpose before testing commences. For example, network technicians may suggest that a backbone upgrade will result in at least a 25% increase in performance for users on their company's WAN. This figure should be based on technical calculations of expected performance increases (rather than assumptions).

Accurately measuring such increases in performance depends on keeping a baseline of the network's performance before the change occurred. Performance baselines will aggregate network response data from different times of day and different places on the network. After the change is instituted, performance measurement should likewise be conducted at different nodes on the WAN and at different times of day (preferably using a network management software package). The testing team should then compare the new measurements to the baseline to determine whether the change accomplished its goal of increasing network performance by at least 25%.

In addition to developing test criteria, testing large-scale changes will require defining a test period, testing methods, and evaluation methods. In some cases, the testing may be straightforward. For example, if you installed a database software package on the server, you might ask users to attempt to log on and perform a simple query one afternoon to verify that the software works correctly. If all users perform their tasks successfully, then you can assume that the change was successful. Otherwise, you should consider the installation unsuccessful.

In other cases, test results may be more subjective. For example, you may have upgraded a database software package to improve the security of the database. In this case, testing may involve asking skilled security engineers or programmers to attempt to break into the database after implementation of the change. If they quickly break into the entire database, your testing reveals that the change was unsuccessful. If it takes a week for them to obtain only insignificant database information, however, your testing may reveal that the change worked as planned.

16

No matter whether your testing will be straightforward or subjective, the project manager should assign a leader to take charge of the testing team. This team leader will develop testing criteria, recruit testing volunteers, identify ways of gathering test data, compile test data, and, based on the testing results, pass conclusions to the project manager about the success of the change.

 In addition to testing the project's changes and processes, you should test every piece of equipment required by the project as soon as it arrives. By verifying basic hardware functionality immediately, you will avoid later project delays caused by faulty components.

Now that you have been introduced to project management techniques, you are ready to learn about aspects of project management of particular interest to networking professionals.

MANAGING NETWORK IMPLEMENTATION

Although numerous professions perform project management, information technology presents some unique challenges to successfully deploying changes. For example, although a caterer has to consider issues such as the number of dinner guests and the timing of the main meal, a network administrator needs to consider much more complicated issues, such as the compatibility of protocols and connectivity devices. In the previous section, you learned about project management elements that apply to any project. This section describes some project management techniques that apply specifically to network and other technology implementations.

Implementation Steps

This section presents a list of typical steps involved in implementing a network change after stakeholders and participants have identified some kind of unmet need. This outline is meant to be a guide to planning, not an actual project plan. You may find that not every step applies to your network or situation. In that case, you can move to the next step or modify the step to be more appropriate. The most significant steps in this process are described in more detail in the following sections.

1. Determine whether the proposed change is feasible, given your time, resource, and budgetary constraints. Compare proposed costs to proposed benefits.

2. If a change is deemed feasible and desirable, identify specific goals for a project. Break larger, vague goals into smaller, concrete goals.

3. Assess the current state of the network, including physical and logical topology, protocols, applications, operating systems, and number, type, and location of devices. Keep this documentation in a centrally accessible location.

4. Assess the requirements as expressed by stakeholders, including users, technical staff, and managers.

5. Create a project plan that includes tasks and subtasks, dependencies, resource allocation, timelines, and milestones. Specify necessary hardware and software purchases, in addition to desired contributions from contractors or vendors.

6. If possible, build a pilot network—a small-scale replica of your changed network—based on your recommendations. Define testing criteria for the small-scale network and evaluate your results against your needs.

7. If the pilot network shows promise, begin to implement the changes on a larger scale. At this stage, you may have to purchase hardware or software, coordinate with vendors, install or remove wiring, hardware, or software, or reconfigure hardware or software. Before you begin, make sure that you have all of the necessary tools and components.

8. If possible (if the changes are not on a global scale and can be effected in stages), release the changes to a hand-picked group of users who will evaluate the success of your network changes, using predefined criteria.

9. If the evaluation indicates that the changes were successful, release the changes to all users.

10. Update your network baseline documentation to reflect the changes.

Determining Project Feasibility

The first decision to make about any proposed project is whether spending time and resources on this project makes sense—that is, whether it's feasible. Often, and especially in technology-based companies, staff become so enamored with gadgetry and the desire for faster network access that they are willing to push a project through without realistically assessing its costs and benefits. For example, a network manager may attend a week-long conference on IP telephony, then return and announce to his staff that they should replace the entire phone system with a voice-over-data system. This project may be completed, despite the fact that the existing phone system works perfectly well, and despite the fact that spending money on a voice-over-data scheme may be less of a priority than purchasing redundant file servers.

To formalize the process of determining whether a proposed project makes sense, you can conduct a feasibility study. A **feasibility study** outlines the costs and benefits of the project and attempts to predict whether it will result in a favorable outcome (for example, whether it will achieve its goals without imposing excessive cost or time requirements on the organization). You can think of a feasibility study as a "pre-project plan." A feasibility study should be performed for any large-scale project before resources are committed to that project.

Often, organizations hire business consultants to help them develop a feasibility study. The advantage to outsourcing this work is that consultants will not make the same assumptions that internal staff might make when weighing the costs and benefits of a proposed project.

Setting Project Goals

Once a project is deemed feasible, you and the project team should define the project's goals. One technique for setting project goals is to begin with a broad goal, then narrow it down into specific goals that will contribute to the larger goal. For example, if your organization's board of directors has accepted a consultant's recommendation to

16

redesign your WAN so as to improve communications between offices and enable better Internet access, these two goals may equate to the overarching project goals. Beneath those goals, you may insert several smaller goals, such as partnering with a nationwide ISP, increasing WAN performance by 40% between the Chicago and San Diego offices, building an infrastructure that will enable growth into the East Asian market, and so on.

In addition to being specific, project goals should be attainable. The feasibility study should help determine whether you can achieve the project goals within the given time, budgetary, and resource constraints. If project goals are not attainable from the outset, you risk losing backing from both project sponsors and participants. And if you lose backing, chances are good that the project will fail.

Projects without clear goals will suffer from inefficiencies. A lack of well-defined goals can result in misunderstandings between project participants, sponsors, and stakeholders; lack of focus among team members; lack of proper resource allocation; and an uncertainty about whether the project's outcomes constituted success. Before developing the project plan, work with project participants and sponsors to clearly define the project's goals.

Baselining

In Chapter 13, you learned that baselining is the practice of measuring and recording a network's current state of operation. As described in that chapter, baselining includes keeping a history of performance measurements, such as response times and number of collisions. It also involves tracking the physical topology, logical topology, number of devices on the network, operating systems and protocols in use, and number and type of applications in use. In other words, this effort provides a complete picture of the network's current state. Baselining is critical to network implementations because it provides the basis not only for determining which changes may improve the network, but also for later evaluating how successful those improvements were.

The following list details the questions you need to answer as part of a baseline assessment. Bear in mind that your network may use several types of topologies, operating systems, devices, transmission speeds, applications, and so on.

- *Physical topology*—Which types of LAN and WAN topologies does your network use: bus, star, ring, hybrid, mesh, or a combination of these? Which type of backbone does your network use—collapsed, distributed, parallel, serial, or a combination of these? Which type and grade of cabling does your network use?

- *Logical topology*—Which transmission method does your network use—Ethernet or Token Ring? What transmission speed does it provide? Which switching methods does it apply?

- *Protocols*—Which protocols are used by servers, nodes, and connectivity devices?

- *Devices*—How many of the following devices are connected to your network—switches, routers, hubs, gateways, firewalls, servers, UPSs, printers, backup devices, and clients? Where are they (physically) located? What are their model numbers and vendors?

- *Operating systems*—Which network and desktop operating systems appear on the network? Which versions of these operating systems are used by each device? Which type and version of operating systems are used by connectivity devices such as routers?

- *Applications*—Which applications are used by clients and servers? Where do you store the applications? From where do they run?

If you have not already collected and centrally stored this information, it may take the efforts of several people and several weeks to compile it, depending on the size and complexity of your network. This evaluation will involve visits to the telecommunications and equipment rooms, an examination of servers and desktops, a review of receipts for software and hardware purchases, and potentially use of a sniffer or network monitoring software package. A baseline assessment may take a great deal of time and effort to complete, but it promises to save work in the future. Once you have compiled the information, organize it into a format (such as a database) that can be easily updated, allowing your staff to keep the baseline current.

Assessing Needs and Requirements

Everyone in your department might agree that your current e-mail system is too slow and needs to be replaced, or numerous users might complain that the connection between their office and the headquarters' LAN is unreliable. Often a network change project begins with a group of people (or one person in a position of authority) identifying a need. Before you concur with popular opinion about what must be changed and how the change must occur, as a responsible network administrator you should perform a thorough, objective needs assessment. A **needs assessment** is the process of clarifying the reasons and objectives underlying a proposed change. It involves interviewing users and other stakeholders and comparing perceptions to factual data. It may also involve analyzing network baseline data. Your goal in performing a needs assessment is to decide whether the change is worthwhile and necessary; you should also determine the appropriate scope and nature of the change.

A needs assessment may address the following questions:

- Is the expressed need valid, or does it mask a different need?

- Can the need be resolved?

- Is the need important enough to allocate resources to its resolution?

- If fulfilled, will the need result in additional needs? Will fulfilling the need satisfy other needs?

16

- Do users affected by the need agree that change is a good answer? What kind of resolution will satisfy them?

In the following sections, you will learn how to investigate a network's needs and requirements as they relate to users, network performance, availability, scalability, integration, and security. Although only one or a few of these needs may constitute driving forces for your project, you should consider each aspect before drafting a project plan. A project based solely on user requirements may result in unforeseen, negative consequences on network performance, if performance needs are not considered as well.

User Requirements

If you have worked as a computer support technician, you know that customers express their needs in a variety of ways. They may regularly call the help desk and ask why they can't access the company's accounting system, they may appeal to their supervisors for access, or they may simply complain to their friends about their unmet need. Each of these methods makes public a need. Unfortunately, none of these methods clearly details the need. To clarify user requirements, you must undertake a more rigorous investigation.

A good technique for beginning to clarify user requirements is user interviews. Just as if you were a reporter, you should ask pointed questions. If the answer is not complete or sufficiently specific, you should follow up your original question with additional questions. The more narrowly focused the answers, the easier it will be to suggest how a project might address those needs. The questions you ask will depend on the type of need involved as well as the user's knowledge and attitude. You may begin your questioning with the following queries:

- What do you need?
- What makes you think this need should be addressed?
- How quickly do you think this need must be addressed?
- Can you suggest at least three ways we can meet this need?
- What kind of priority would you place on this need?
- Are you willing to ignore other needs to have this need met?

Your aim in interviewing users should not be to interrogate them, but rather to guide them to a better articulation of their need. Users often aren't sure about what they want. You can help by drawing out answers and then restating those answers to verify that you have heard and understood them correctly.

 During the interview process, be certain not to impose your own opinions on what the user is saying. By doing so, you might miss the point entirely or make the user feel as if you don't truly want to understand his or her needs. Like a reporter, be as objective as you possibly can.

In the process of interviewing users, you may recognize that not all users have the same needs. In fact, the needs of one group of users may conflict with the needs of another group. In such cases, you will have to sort out which needs have a greater priority, which needs were expressed by the majority of users, whether the expressed needs have anything in common, and how to address needs that do not fall into the majority.

After you have interviewed users and collected the results of those interviews, you should be better able to articulate the nature and scope of their needs. The next step is to return to the users (perhaps in a group meeting) and reiterate what you think they were saying. Give users an opportunity to dispute or refine your conclusions. The more time you spend clarifying users' needs, the less time you will have to spend later explaining the project to users and attempting to win their approval for your efforts.

Performance Requirements

Another reason for changing a network may be to improve performance. In an ideal world, the IT department would recognize these impending needs before customers even notice them. For example, if the network administrator is tracking the network's performance and notices that it has been degrading very slightly for the last six months, he may initiate a discussion about how to improve the network performance before users experience noticeable slowdowns.

Although you might think that performance needs are easily quantifiable and therefore easily agreed upon, in fact several engineers and technicians will likely have differing opinions about the nature of the needs and the best tactics for addressing them. Having technical staff answer the following questions will help you identify performance requirements:

- Where do current performance bottlenecks exist? Why do they exist there?

- What kind of performance is optimal?

- Compared with other projects, what priority would you assign to improving performance?

- What measures can bring current performance levels to your recommended level?

- How will performance improvements affect access, availability, customer needs, security, and scalability?

- How will you ensure that measures taken to improve performance are successful?

Take the same approach in interviewing technical staff about performance as you would when interviewing users about their needs: be objective, ask follow-up questions to ensure that you understand the needs they express, and try to guide the staff into defining the needs as specifically as possible. After conducting these interviews, draw conclusions based on the opinions of the majority of participants. Reiterate your conclusions to technical staff to verify that you correctly understood the needs they articulated.

16

Availability Requirements

Recall from Chapter 14 that "availability" describes how consistently and reliably a file, device, or connection can be accessed by authorized personnel. A number of factors can affect a network's or system's availability, including policies, security, use of redundant components (such as dual power supplies in a critical router), use of redundancy techniques (such as RAID on a server), and connectivity bottlenecks. The need for higher availability may represent the impetus for a network change.

To best determine availability requirements, you should interview both technical and management staff. Technical staff will provide insight about how availability can best be achieved and where the network currently falls short of availability goals. Management staff will provide insight into what types of availability are most important and why.

For example, you may be asked to identify the availability requirements of your organization's new online catalog, which is hosted on a Windows 2000 server in your equipment room. You interview technical staff to determine what type of availability is currently in place and how it might be improved. You also interview management staff to determine how much down time is acceptable, based on their educated guesses regarding how down time will affect sales. If that prediction points to millions of dollars of lost sales for every hour that the server fails, management may be willing to invest hundreds of thousands of dollars to provide entirely redundant server systems to ensure that the online catalog remains continuously available.

Asking the following questions of technical staff will help you clarify their availability requirements:

- Where do current availability flaws or vulnerabilities exist? Where are the network's single points of failure?

- What kind of availability is acceptable (for example, is 99.5% satisfactory, or must the network be available 99.999% of the time)?

- Compared with other projects, what priority would you assign to improving availability?

- What measures can boost current availability to your recommended percentage?

- How will availability improvements affect access, performance, customer needs, security, and scalability?

Asking the following questions of management staff will help you clarify their availability requirements:

- What is the cost of one hour of down time during business hours?

- What is the cost of one hour of down time during off-hours?

- What is your ideal availability percentage?

- What part of the application or access is most important to keep available?

- Compared with other projects, what priority would you assign to improving availability?

- How much are you willing to spend to ensure that the network or system remains available for your ideal percentage of time?

If managers do not have a networking or systems background, they may not realize the costs associated with high availability. Although achieving 99.5% availability may be feasible given their budgetary constraints, increasing the availability to 99.999% may bring exorbitant costs (for example, rather than simply purchasing one switch with dual NICs and dual power supplies, you may need to purchase two identical switches; this component alone could cost more than $50,000). Use your interview as an opportunity to educate members of management, as well as determining their requirements. It's important to emphasize that 100% availability is not possible and that accomplishing 99.999% availability is very expensive.

Integration and Scalability Requirements

With each network change project, you must consider how the proposed change might affect the network's integration and ability to grow and adapt to future changes. In fact, integration and scalability needs may drive network changes, although they are less likely to represent the primary reason for changes than are customer, performance, or security needs.

Because integration and scalability require input from both technical and management staff (perhaps in the form of interviews focused on availability), you should conduct interviews emphasizing these issues with both groups. Asking technical staff to answer the following questions will help you clarify scalability and integration needs:

- How and where is the network's growth currently limited?

- What needs to change to accommodate growth or new hardware/software?

- In what ways (for example, number of users, number of applications, geographical breadth, speed) do you expect the network to grow over the next two years?

- How will improving scalability and integration affect customers, performance, security, and availability?

- How would you prioritize your suggested measures for accommodating growth?

16

To learn more about scalability and integration needs, you should ask management staff to answer the following questions:

- In what ways do you expect the network (and the organization) to grow over the next one to five years (for example, number of users, number of applications, geographical breadth, speed)?

- Which of these growth directions is your top priority?

- What type of hardware and software do you expect to adopt in coming months and years?

- How much are you willing to spend to optimally position the network and systems for growth?

- Would you place a higher priority on positioning the network and systems for growth or on improving network security, availability, usability, or performance?

- Would you place a higher priority on facilitating better network and systems integration or on improving network security, availability, usability, or performance?

The priorities that technical and management staff place on integration and scalability concerns are particularly important. In most cases, positioning the network for growth and better integration will not be as important to either group as more immediate concerns, such as security (discussed in the following section).

Security Requirements

Some projects result from a need to improve network security rather than an attempt to address user or performance needs. Security needs are typically identified by the technical staff—either network administrators or managers. Examples of projects driven by security needs include installation of firewalls at WAN locations, modifications to firewall or router configurations or operating systems, implementation of intrusion detection systems, or a company-wide effort to enforce security policies, such as good password selection. As you can imagine, the scope and cost of security-related projects can vary dramatically.

No matter what their nature, security needs—like user or performance needs—must be clearly defined before a project commences. Ask management staff how they would prioritize security improvements and how much they would be willing to pay to improve network or systems security. In addition, ask technical staff to answer the following questions to help you identify which needs should be addressed so as to improve your network's security:

- What type of security must be improved (hardware, software, user, facilities)?

- Why does security need to be improved?

- Based on the reasons underlying the need for improved security, to what extent does security need to be improved?

- Will the improvement require extra staff, hardware, software, or consulting services?

- Compared with other needs, what is the priority of security improvements?

- How will security improvements affect network access, performance, or scalability?

As with analyzing user requirements, assessing security requirements may reveal conflicting needs. For example, one faction of network technicians may believe that simply upgrading the version of a server's operating system will address a security flaw, whereas another group of technicians may insist that the security flaw can be resolved only by installing an expensive firewall upgrade. You may find it helpful to gather technical personnel to debate their points of view and reach a consensus. Alternatively, based on the priority assigned to security improvements, you may conclude that a stronger security measure—such as intrusion detection—is warranted at any cost.

For example, suppose you are the network manager for a growing investment firm that currently uses firewalls at each of its WAN locations and has an effective security policy. Even with these firewalls in place, you may experience an IP spoofing attack that brings down your network. Quantifying the cost of this outage may prove difficult, but you might recognize that you lost potentially hundreds of customers and perhaps millions of dollars in sales. As a result of this breach, you may identify a few critical security needs—for example, the need for better firewall configuration and the need for a mechanism (such as intrusion detection) to stop attacks as they begin. You can assume that if you do nothing, another security breach will occur; the next attack might even be worse (perhaps resulting in stolen or damaged data). Therefore, implementing an expensive intrusion detection system may be well worth its cost.

Using a Pilot Network

As you learned in Chapter 13, one of the best ways to evaluate new technology is to test it in your environment. Similarly, the best way of evaluating a large-scale network or systems implementation is to first test it on a small scale. A small-scale network that stands in for the larger network is sometimes called a **pilot network**. Although a pilot network will be much smaller than the enterprise-wide network, it should be similar enough to closely mimic the larger network's hardware, software, connectivity, unique configurations, and load. If possible, you should establish the pilot network in the same location or environment in which the final network will exist.

The following tips will help you create a more realistic and useful pilot network:

- Include at least one of each type of device (whether a critical router or a client workstation) that might be affected by the change.

- Use the same transmission methods and speeds as employed on your network.

- Try to emulate the number of segments, protocols, and addressing schemes in your network.

- Always implement the same server and client software and configurations on your pilot network as found in your current network.

- Once you have established the pilot network, test it for at least two weeks to verify that its performance, security, availability, or other characteristics meet your criteria.

 As the pilot network is intended for testing only, do not connect the pilot network to your live network. By keeping the two networks separate, you will ensure that experimental changes do not inadvertently harm your functioning network.

16

The pilot network offers you opportunities to both educate yourself and test your implementation goals. Use your time with the pilot network to become familiar with any new features in the hardware or software. Be certain to document what you learn about the new technology's features and idiosyncrasies. As you evaluate your results against your predefined test criteria, note where your results show success or failure. All of this documentation will provide valuable information for your final implementation and for future baselining.

Preparing Users

No matter how small and insignificant your network change appears, if it could potentially affect the way that users accomplish their daily work, you must prepare users for the change. In some cases, the likelihood of a change affecting users will be plainly evident. For example, if you upgrade the version of NetWare used by your file servers and therefore must upgrade the Novell networking client version used by clients, every user will see a slightly different screen when he or she starts up the computer and logs onto the network. If you replace a segment of CAT3 cabling with CAT5 cabling, however, users may never notice the difference.

In almost every instance, you are well advised to notify users of impending changes. That way, if something goes wrong with a change that shouldn't have affected users, creating problems when users try to access the network, these employees will not be caught off guard. For example, you and your staff may install additional RAM in all of your servers over the weekend. Normally, no reason exists to notify users of such an upgrade, assuming it is not performed during business hours. If one of the new memory chips causes problems for a server, however, the change will affect users. In this situation, you might prepare users by announcing that the servers will receive memory upgrades over the weekend and that this change should not cause any changes or problems for client access. Inform users that any type of change represents a possibility for problems to arise, however.

For a major network change, you definitely must inform users. As soon as you have firm details about the nature and timeline of the change, let everyone know about it. Among other things, you should explain to users:

- How their access to the network will be affected

- How their data will be protected during the change. (Even if you are confident that the data will remain unaffected by the change, you should explain how the protection works.)

- Whether you will provide any means for users to access the network during the change

- Whether the change will require users to learn new skills

Although providing all of this information may seem burdensome, it will lessen the possibility that your project might be stymied by negative public reaction. To minimize the amount of time spent communicating with users, you might convene company-wide meetings or send mass e-mail distributions. If a network implementation has the potential to drastically change the way that users perform their work, you might want to form a committee of user representatives who can attend project meetings and provide input from the users' point of view.

CHAPTER SUMMARY

- ❏ Project management is the practice of managing resources, staff, budget, timelines, and other variables so as to complete a specific goal within given bounds. The person who designs the project plan and oversees the project is the project manager. A project needs not only a plan, but also participants, funding, a specific means of communication, definitive processes, contingency plans, and a testing and evaluation phase.

- ❏ A project plan describes how the details of a managed project (for example, the timeline and the significant tasks) are organized. Project plans may take the form of a simple text or spreadsheet document for small projects. Larger projects, however, often require the use of project management software (such as Microsoft Project, PlanView, or PrimaVera Project Planner).

- ❏ No matter how large or small the project, its project plan will contain some common elements—tasks and subtasks, timelines, dependencies, resources, and milestones. In addition, project plans may provide information on task priority, flexibility provided in the timeline, task successors, links to other project plans, and so on.

- ❏ Every project depends on many resources. The human resources involved in a project may include employees from your department or other departments within the organization, outside consultants, vendor representatives, or employees from other organizations.

- ❏ People involved in a project may include project participants, task owners, stakeholders, and sponsors. Stakeholders are people affected by a proposed implementation and the ones to whom the project teams must answer. Sponsors are typically managers or executives who believe in the concept of the project and agree to help obtain support and resources for it.

- ❏ Every project, whether it entails a simple hardware upgrade or an entire network redesign, requires funding. A project budget is usually determined as a project begins and approved by a hierarchy of managers whose staff are involved in the project. A project's budget will depend on its breadth and complexity.

- ❏ Communications among project participants, stakeholders, and sponsors are critical for several reasons: to ensure that a project's goals are understood by participants, stakeholders, and sponsors; to keep a project's timeline and budget on track; to encourage teamwork among participants; to learn from previous mistakes; to prevent fingerpointing if a task is not completed correctly or on time; to prevent duplication of efforts; and to ensure that stakeholders are prepared for the effects of change.

16

❐ Process management involves planning for and handling the steps required to accomplish a goal in a systematic way. The processes you might manage during a project's implementation include change, support, training, transitioning, delegation, and problem resolution.

❐ For any endeavor that requires the cooperation of several team members, process management is a wise investment of time. Creating a process is not sufficient, however, unless everyone understands the process. You must ensure that the process is communicated to all participants.

❐ Contingency planning involves identifying steps that will minimize the risk of unforeseen circumstances endangering the quality or timeliness of the project's goals. In other words, it provides a plan for recovering after things go wrong. It's important to spend time planning for contingencies that have a reasonable chance of occurring during the project.

❐ Once you have reached a project milestone, you will want to verify that you are on the right path. You can accomplish this goal through testing. For testing to be useful, project participants should clearly define the change's purpose before the testing phase commences. To successfully test your implementation, you must establish a testing plan that includes methods and criteria.

❐ The first decision to make about any proposed project is whether spending the time and resources on this project makes sense—that is, whether it's feasible. To formalize the process of determining whether a proposed project makes sense, you can conduct a feasibility study. A feasibility study outlines the costs and benefits of the project and attempts to predict whether it will produce a favorable outcome (for example, whether it will achieve its goals without imposing excessive cost or time requirements on the organization).

❐ Once a project is deemed feasible, you and the project team should define the project's goals. One technique for setting project goals is to begin with a broad goal, then create narrower, more specific goals that will contribute to the larger goal.

❐ In addition to being specific, project goals should be attainable. If project goals are not feasible from the outset, you risk losing backing from both project sponsors and participants. If you lose their support, the project will most likely fail.

❐ Baselining includes keeping a history of network performance, the physical topology, logical topology, number of devices on the network, operating systems and protocols in use, and number and type of applications in use. In other words, it provides a complete picture of the network's current state. Baselining is critical to network implementations because it provides the basis not only for determining what types of changes might improve the network, but also for later evaluating how successful the improvements were.

❐ If you have not already collected and centrally stored baseline information, it may take the work of several people and several weeks to compile it, depending on the size and complexity of your network. This evaluation will involve visits to the telecommunications and equipment rooms, an examination of servers and desktops, a review of receipts for software and hardware purchases, and potentially the use of a sniffer or network monitoring software package.

◻ Needs assessment is the process of clarifying the reasons and objectives for proposed change. It involves interviewing users and other stakeholders and comparing their perceptions to factual data. In addition, it may involve analyzing network baseline data. Your goal in performing a needs assessment is to decide whether the change is worthwhile and necessary and to determine the appropriate scope and nature of the change.

◻ A good technique for beginning to clarify user requirements involves user interviews. Just as if you were a reporter, you should ask pointed questions. The more specific the answers provided, the easier it will be to suggest how a project might address those needs. Users often are unsure about what they want. You can help by drawing out answers and then restating those responses to verify that you have heard and understood the users correctly.

◻ In the process of interviewing users, you may recognize that not all share the same needs. In fact, the needs of one group of users may conflict with the needs of another group. In such cases, you must sort out which needs have a higher priority, which needs were expressed by the majority of users, whether the expressed needs have any common suggestions, and how to address needs that do not fall into the majority.

◻ Although you might think that performance needs are easily quantifiable and therefore readily agreed upon, several engineers and technicians will more likely have differing opinions about the nature of the needs and ways to satisfy them. Have technical staff answer a number of questions to clarify performance requirements.

◻ To best determine availability requirements, you should interview both technical and management staff. Technical staff will provide insight about how availability can best be accomplished and where the network currently falls short of availability goals. Management staff will provide insight into what types of availability are most important and why.

◻ If managers do not have a networking or systems background, they may not realize the costs associated with high availability. Although achieving 99.5% availability may be feasible given their budgetary constraints, increasing the availability to 99.999% may bring exorbitant costs. Use your interview as an opportunity to educate managers, as well as to determine their requirements.

◻ Integration and scalability needs may drive network changes, although they are less likely to be the primary reason for changes than are customer, performance, or security needs. Asking both technical and management staff to outline their priorities is particularly important in assessing integration and scalability needs. In most cases, positioning the network for growth and better integration will not be as important to either group as satisfying other requirements.

16

❑ Some projects result from a need to improve network security rather than addressing user or performance needs. Security needs are typically identified by the technical staff—either network administrators or managers.

❑ Like user or performance needs, security needs must be clearly defined before a project commences. Ask management staff how they would prioritize security improvements and how much they would be willing to pay to improve network or system security. In addition, have technical staff answer a number of questions about how best to improve security.

❑ The best way of evaluating a large-scale network or systems implementation is to first test it on a small scale. A small-scale network that stands in for the larger network is sometimes called a pilot network. Although a pilot network will differ from the enterprise-wide network, it should mimic it closely enough to represent the larger network's hardware, software, connectivity, unique configurations, and load.

❑ In almost every instance, it is advisable to notify users of changes. You should share at least the following information: how users' access to the network will be affected; for how long their access to the network will be affected; how their data will be protected during the change; whether you will provide any means for users to access the network during the change; and whether the change will require them to learn new skills.

KEY TERMS

contingency planning — The process of identifying steps that will minimize the risk of unforeseen circumstances endangering the quality or timeliness of the project's goals.

feasibility study — A study that determines the costs and benefits of a project and attempts to predict whether the project will result in a favorable outcome (for example, whether it will achieve its goal without imposing excessive cost or time burdens on the organization).

Gantt chart — A popular method of depicting when projects begin and end along a horizontal timeline.

milestone — A reference point that marks the completion of a major task or group of tasks in a project and contributes to measuring the project's progress.

needs assessment — The process of clarifying the reasons and objectives for a proposed change so as to determine whether the change is worthwhile and necessary and to elucidate the scope and nature of the proposed change.

owner — The person who takes responsibility for ensuring that project tasks are completed on time and within budgetary guidelines.

pilot network — A small-scale network that stands in for the larger network. A pilot network may be used to evaluate the effects of network changes or additions.

predecessors — Tasks in a project that must be completed before other tasks can begin.

process management — Planning for and handling the steps involved in accomplishing a goal in a systematic way. Processes that might be managed during a project's implementation include change, support, training, transitioning, delegation, and problem resolution.

project management — The practice of managing resources, staff, budget, timelines, and other variables so as to complete a specific goal within given bounds.

project plan — The way in which details of a managed project (for example, the timeline and the significant tasks) are organized. Some project plans are created via special project planning software, such as Microsoft Project.

resources — In project management, a term used to refer to staffing, materials, and money.

sponsors — People in positions of authority who support a project and who can lobby for budget increases necessary to complete the project, appeal to a group of managers to extend a project's deadline, assist with negotiating vendor contracts, and so on.

stakeholder — Any person who may be affected by a project, for better or for worse. A stakeholder may be a project participant, user, manager, or vendor.

REVIEW QUESTIONS

1. What type of chart is used in project management to express how tasks will occur over a horizontal timeline?

   a. Pert

   b. Gantt

   c. Stuelt

   d. Ager

2. What do you call a task that must be completed before another task can begin?

   a. decessor

   b. successor

   c. predecessor

   d. subsessor

16

3. What is the purpose of a milestone?

   a. to mark the beginning of a major task

   b. to mark the completion of a subtask within a major task

   c. to mark the completion of a major task or group of tasks

   d. to mark the completion of the project

4. Who would be a likely sponsor for a network backbone upgrade?

   a. help desk technician

   b. network technician

   c. Vice President of Operations

   d. IT director

5. In a project to upgrade the version of Microsoft Exchange on the network, a receptionist who uses Exchange is an example of a project stakeholder. True or False?

6. In what type of situation might additional funding have no effect on an enterprise's ability to complete a project more quickly?

   a. when the project depends on a limited number of highly specialized staff members

   b. when the IT department's budget is fixed

   c. when customers' needs aren't clearly defined

   d. when resource costs exceed the initial estimate

7. Name four benefits of effective communication among project participants.

8. What type of process can be managed to improve the efficiency of how modifications to a project plan are handled?

   a. problem

   b. change

   c. support

   d. training

9. Which predefined process can help you recover when a project suffers a setback?

   a. contingency planning

   b. transition planning

   c. budget reevaluation

   d. feasibility study

10. Which of the following implementation steps should come first?

    a. find vendors for necessary hardware additions

    b. determine the feasibility of the proposed project

    c. evaluate how users' needs might conflict

    d. identify the need for a project

11. Which step in the implementation of network projects should precede the final release of changes to all users?

    a. update the documentation to reflect changes on the network

    b. reinstall client software on older workstations

    c. release the change to a group of test users who will evaluate it

    d. suggest ways to improve the network's availability after the change

12. What is the last step in a network implementation project?

13. Why is it sometimes advisable to hire external consultants to perform a feasibility study?

14. Which of the following is a good example of test criteria that can be used to evaluate the success of a network backbone upgrade?

    a. Did the change improve network performance?

    b. Are 50% of the customers more satisfied with the network's performance?

    c. As a result of the change, are customers receiving e-mail more quickly?

    d. Did the change result in a 30% reduction in the time that it takes for data to travel from the router in building A to the router in building B?

15. Baselining will help you determine how long a project should take. True or False?

16. What can you do if your needs assessment interviews indicate that two groups of customers have conflicting needs?

    a. reinterview customers with the aim of reaching consensus

    b. gather customers with conflicting views in one room and ask them to debate the merits of their positions

    c. determine the costs of addressing each conflicting need and make a decision based on the lowest-cost solution

    d. compile the results of your interviews and determine which needs are better justified and expressed by the majority of users

17. Why does it cost significantly more to achieve 99.999% availability than it does to achieve 99.5% availability?

18. Which of the following questions should you ask your organization's management staff so as to better determine scalability needs?

    a. How much are you willing to spend to optimally position the network and systems for growth?

    b. Where is the network currently inhibited from accommodating new devices?

    c. In what ways can the WAN be expanded to integrate new locations easily?

    d. How will increasing the network's capacity for growth affect its performance?

16

19. Give two examples of projects that might be driven by security concerns.

20. If you were planning to replace all 25 routers in your enterprise-wide network with switches, what kind of pilot network might you design to test whether the switches will work as planned?

HANDS-ON PROJECTS

Project 16-1

To familiarize yourself with project management, you should take some time to experiment with project management software. This exercise introduces you to the most popular project management package, Microsoft Project 2000. You will use Microsoft Project to demonstrate the creation of a project plan. You will identify tasks, subtasks, timelines, and resources for a sample networking project. For this exercise, you will need a computer with Microsoft Project 2000 installed.

1. To launch Microsoft Project, click **Start**, point to **Programs**, then click **Microsoft Project**.

2. Unless you have disabled it, the Microsoft Project Help - Welcome! window opens on the right side of your screen. Close this window to begin adding tasks to the project plan.

3. The main Microsoft Project window expands, with a frame for task listings on the left side of the screen and a blank timeline on the right side of the screen. Click and drag the vertical bar that separates the task list from the timeline to the right so that you can view all columns to the right of the task list. By default, you should see the columns Task Name, Duration, Start, Finish, Predecessors, and Resource Names, as shown in Figure 16-3.

4. Click on the first row of the Task Name column. To add the first task, type **Upgrade Network**.

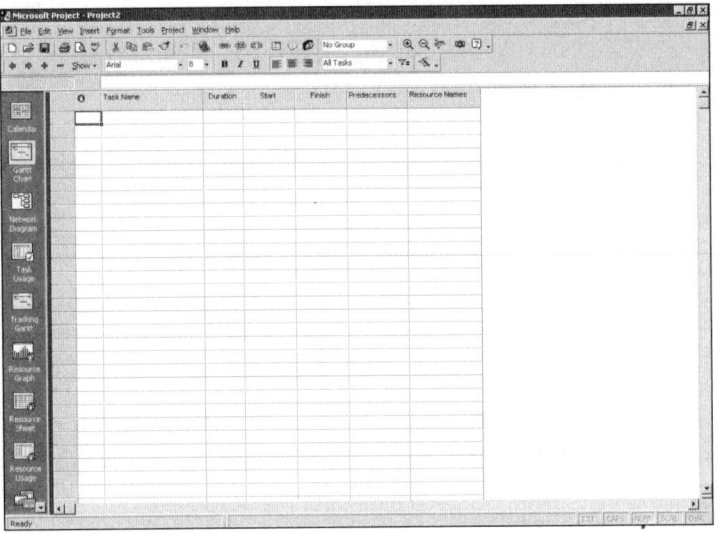

Figure 16-3   Default columns in Microsoft Project

5. Now you will enter some subtasks that make up the larger task you just created. Insert the following tasks in the five rows below the first task: **Perform Network Baseline, Assess Users' Needs, Purchase Hardware and Software, Implement Pilot Network, Implement Backbone Changes**.

6. To identify these five tasks as subtasks belonging to the "Upgrade Network" task, select and highlight each of them (by clicking on the task name), then click the right arrow button on the formatting toolbar to indent the task. Notice that the "Upgrade Network" task becomes bolded.

7. Click the Duration cell next to the task name "Perform Network Baseline," then enter a duration of **10** (days).

8. Enter durations for the remaining four subtasks, based on how long you guess they might take. As you add these durations, the duration for the "Upgrade Network" task changes to reflect the length of its subtasks' durations.

9. By default, the project's Start date for the subtasks will be set to today's date. Change the Start date for "Perform Network Baseline" to a date two weeks from now. Notice that the Finish date changes, based on the durations that you entered in Steps 7 and 8.

10. In the Predecessors column for "Purchase Hardware and Software," enter **2** to indicate that this task is dependent on the second task, "Perform Network Baseline." What happens to this task's Start and Finish dates? Why?

11. Change the Start date for "Assess Users' Needs" to tomorrow's date.

16

12. Now you can insert predecessors for the remaining tasks. Make "Purchase Hardware and Software" also dependent on task 3 (in addition to task 2), "Implement Pilot Network" dependent on task 4, and "Implement Backbone Changes" dependent on task 5.

13. To save the project plan you have created, click **File** on the main menu, and then click Save. The Save As dialog box appears. In the File name text box, type **rollout**. Click **Save** to save the project plan.

14. The Planning Wizard dialog box appears, asking whether you want to save your project plan with a baseline. Click **OK** to save the project plan without a baseline (the default selection).

15. Click **File** on the main menu, and then click **Exit**. Microsoft Project closes.

Now you have created the skeletal beginnings of a project plan, with start and finish dates and predecessors. In the following exercises, you will expand on this simple plan.

Project 16-2

Earlier in this chapter, you were introduced to the concept of a Gantt chart, which offers a way to depict project timelines. In this exercise, you will view and modify a Gantt chart that is based on the simple project plan that you created in Project 16-1. For this project, you will require the computer with Microsoft Project 2000 installed that you used in the previous project.

1. View the project plan that you began in Hands-on Project 16-1.

2. Click **Format** on the menu bar, then click **GanttChartWizard**. The GanttChartWizard - Step 1 dialog box appears.

3. Click **Next** to continue.

4. The GanttChartWizard - Step 2 dialog box opens, prompting you to identify the kind of information you want to include in your Gantt chart. The default selection is **Standard**. Keep this selection, and click **Next** to continue.

5. The GanttChartWizard - Step 9 dialog box opens. (Because you accepted the standard settings in the previous step, the wizard skipped from Step 2 to Step 9.) Here you can identify what kind of task information should appear in your Gantt chart. Select **Dates**, then click **Next** to continue.

6. The GanttChartWizard - Step 13 dialog box opens. (Again, based on your selection in the previous step, the wizard skips ahead to Step 13.) Here you can specify whether the chart should show link lines between dependent tasks. Keep the default selection of **Yes, please**, then click **Next** to continue.

7. The GanttChartWizard - Step 14 dialog box opens, announcing that the wizard is ready to format your Gantt chart. Click **Format It** to continue.

8. Click **Exit Wizard** to close the wizard and return to the project plan.

9. To view the Gantt chart, click and drag the vertical bar that separates your task list from the timeline all the way to the left. The Gantt chart will appear in the center of the screen. Use the scroll bar at the bottom of the screen to view the entire chart.

10. Click File on the main menu, and then click **Exit**. Microsoft Project closes.

Project 16-3

In this project, you will elaborate on the plan that you began in Project 16-1 by assigning resources and adding milestones. This exercise requires the same computer and Microsoft Project file that you used in the two previous exercises.

1. Drag the vertical separator bar to the right to hide the Gantt chart and reveal the list of tasks on the left side of the Microsoft Project screen.

2. Click on the Resource Names cell for the "Perform Network Baseline" task. Enter **RG, BT** to indicate that Reggie Gibson and Brett Turrel will handle this task.

3. Assign resources to the remaining subtasks. In the Resource Names cell for "Assess Users' Needs," enter **KR, SN**. In the Resource Names cell for "Purchase Hardware and Software," enter **SS**. In the Resource Names cell for "Implement Pilot Network," enter **RG, BT, MM, MG**. In the Resource Names cell for "Implement Backbone Changes," enter **BT, MM, SS, AV**.

4. As the task of implementing a pilot network is a significant part of the project, its completion should mark a milestone. To identify this task as a milestone, double-click the task name. The Task Information dialog box appears. The General tab is selected by default, as shown in Figure 16-4.

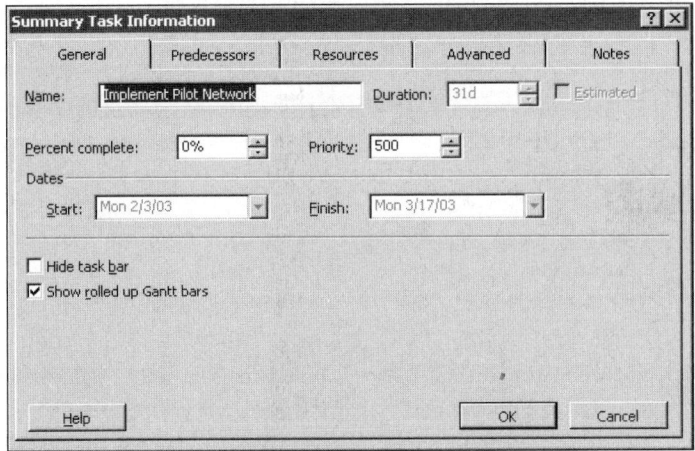

Figure 16-4   Summary Task Information dialog box

16

5. Click the **Advanced** tab to view additional information about the task. On that tab, check the box next to **Mark task as milestone**.

6. Click **OK** to save your changes.

7. Drag the vertical separator bar to the left and notice how the task appears now (as a milestone).

8. Click **File** on the main menu, and then click **Exit**. Click **Yes** to save the changes you have made to your project plan. Microsoft Project closes.

CASE PROJECTS

1. Your colleagues in the IT department are considering migrating your organization's network from 4-Mbps Token Ring to 100-Mbps Ethernet. They posit that the change will provide users with better performance and position your network for easier growth in the future. Your organization's network consists of the following items:

   ◻ 5 file- and print-sharing servers running Novell NetWare 5.0

   ◻ 1 backup server

   ◻ 1 Internet gateway and mail server

   ◻ 350 users in two buildings located across the street from each other and connected via a T1 link

   Each user in your organization depends on the network for e-mail, file storage, printing, and office applications (including word-processing, spreadsheet, and database programs).

   The IT Director has asked you to list the ways in which this change could improve network performance. In addition, list ways that this change could affect users, support, maintenance, profitability, scalability, integration, and security.

2. Your company's project to migrate from Token Ring to Ethernet has been deemed feasible by an independent consultant. As this change represents a major network overhaul, the IT Director decides it might also be time to make smaller changes to accommodate users' needs. He assigns you the task of determining the needs of the 350 users. Draft a questionnaire that you will follow during your user interviews. When writing the questionnaire, consider how you will measure and tally the responses and what you might do if users' needs conflict with one another.

3. As a result of your thorough user needs assessment, the IT management staff has decided that, although the migration from Token Ring to Ethernet is important, a more pressing need is to upgrade the version of the NetWare client on each desktop. The IT Director assigns you to manage the project. Draft a project plan outline that will serve as a roadmap for accomplishing this wholesale client upgrade. Include estimated timelines, dependencies, and milestones.

4. Because the company-wide client upgrade will change the way that every user accesses the network, you want to apprise every user of the change and explain how it might affect him or her. Write a memo to users that communicates this information.

5. While you are conducting the client upgrades across the network, one of your colleagues is planning for the larger project of changing the network from Token Ring to Ethernet. She asks your help in setting up a test lab to use for the pilot network. List every item that should be in the test lab so as to adequately test the change plan.

NETWORK+ EXAMINATION OBJECTIVES

This book covers all of the Network+ examination objectives, which were released by CompTIA (the Computing Technology Industry Association) in January, 2002. The official list of objectives is available at CompTIA's web site, at *www.comptia.org*. For your reference, the following table lists each exam objective and the chapter of this book that explains the objective, plus the amount of the exam that will cover each topic. Each objective belongs to one of four domains (or main topics) of networking expertise. For example, the objective of recognizing an RJ-45 connector belongs to the "Media and Topologies" domain, which accounts for 20 percent of the exam's content.

Domain 1.0 Media and Topologies – 20% of Examination

Table A-1   Network+ Examination Objectives—Media and Topologies

Objective	Chapter	Percentage of Exam Questions Devoted to this Topic
1.1 Recognize the following logical or physical network topologies given a schematic diagram or description:		3
Star/hierarchical	1, 5	
Bus	1, 5	
Mesh	5	
Ring	1, 5	
Wireless	4	
1.2 Specify the main features of 802.2 (LLC), 802.3 (Ethernet), 802.5 (token ring), 802.11b (wireless), and FDDI networking technologies, including:		3
Speed	4, 5	
Access	4, 5	
Method	5	
Topology	5	
Media	4, 5	
1.3 Specify the characteristics (e.g., speed, length, topology, cable type, etc.) of the following technologies:		3
802.3 (Ethernet) standards	4, 5	
10BaseT	4, 5	
100BaseT	4, 5	
100BaseTX	4, 5	
10Base2	4, 5	
10Base5	4, 5	
100BaseFX	4, 5	
Gigabit Ethernet	4, 5	
1.4 Recognize the following media connectors and/or describe their uses:		3
RJ-11	4, Appendix C	
RJ-45	4, Appendix C	
AUI	4, Appendix C	
BNC	4, Appendix C	
ST	4, Appendix C	
SC	4, Appendix C	

Table A-1   Network+ Examination Objectives—Media and Topologies (continued)

Objective	Chapter	Percentage of Exam Questions Devoted to this Topic
1.5 Choose the appropriate media type and connectors to add a client to an existing network.	4	3
1.6 Identify the purpose, features, and functions of the following network components:		5
Hubs	4, 6	
Switches	6	
Bridges	6	
Routers	6, 15	
Gateways	6, 11	
CSU/DSU	7	
Network Interface Cards/ISDN adapters/system area network cards	6, 7	
Wireless access points	4, 7	
Modems	4, 7	

Domain 2.0 Protocols and Standards – 25% of Examination

Table A-2   Network+ Examination Objectives—Protocols and Standards

Objective	Chapter	Percentage of Exam Questions Devoted to this Topic
2.1 Given an example, identify a MAC address.	3, 6	1
2.2 Identify the seven layers of the OSI Model and their functions.	2, 6, 11, 12	2
2.3 Differentiate between the following network protocols in terms of routing, addressing schemes, interoperability, and naming conventions:		2
TCP/IP	3, 11	
IPX/SPX	3, 9	
NetBEUI	3	
AppleTalk	3	

Table A-2 Network+ Examination Objectives—Protocols and Standards (continued)

Objective	Chapter	Percentage of Exam Questions Devoted to this Topic
2.4 Identify the OSI layers at which the following network components operate:		2
Hubs	2, 6	
Switches	6	
Bridges	6	
Routers	2, 6	
Network Interface Cards	2, 6	
2.5 Define the purpose, function and/or use of the following protocols within TCP/IP:		2
IP	3, 11	
TCP	3, 11	
UDP	3, 11	
FTP	3, 11	
TFTP	11	
SMTP	11	
HTTP	11	
HTTPS	11	
POP3/IMAP4	11	
Telnet	3, 11	
ICMP	3, 11	
ARP	3, 11	
NTP	11	
2.6 Define the function of TCP/UDP ports. Identify well-known ports.	11	2
2.7 Identify the purpose of the following network services:		2
DHCP	11	
BOOTP	11	
DNS	11	
NAT/ICS	11	
WINS	11	
SNMP	11	
2.8 Identify IP addresses (IPv4 and IPv6) and their default subnet masks.	3, 11	2
2.9 Identify the purpose of subnetting and default gateways.	11	2

Table A-2   Network+ Examination Objectives—Protocols and Standards (continued)

Objective	Chapter	Percentage of Exam Questions Devoted to this Topic
2.10 Identify the differences between public vs. private networks.	7, 11, 15	2
2.11 Identify the basic characteristics (e.g., speed, capacity, media) of the following WAN technologies:		2
Packet switching vs. circuit switching	4, 7	
ISDN	7	
FDDI	5	
ATM	5	
Frame Relay	7	
SONET/SDH	7	
T1/E1	7	
T3/E3	7	
OCx	7	
2.12 Define the function of the following remote access protocols and services:		2
RAS	7	
PPP	7	
PPTP	7	
ICA	7	
2.13 Identify the following security protocols and describe their purpose and function:		2
IPSec	15	
L2TP	15	
SSL	15	
Kerberos	15	

Domain 3.0 Network Implementation – 23% of Examination

Table A-3   Network+ Examination Objectives—Network Implementation

Objective	Chapter	Percentage of Exam Questions Devoted to this Topic
3.1 Identify the basic capabilities (i.e., client support, interoperability, authentication, file and print services, application support, and security) of the following server operating systems:		4
UNIX/Linux	10	
NetWare	9	
Windows	8	
Macintosh	8	
3.2 Identify the basic capabilities (i.e., client connectivity, local security mechanisms, and authentication) of the following clients:		2
UNIX/Linux	10	
Windows	2, 3, 9	
Macintosh	2, 3, 9	
3.3 Identify the main characteristics of VLANs.	6, 7	2
3.4 Identify the main characteristics of network attached storage.	14	2
3.5 Identify the purpose and characteristics of fault tolerance.	14	2
3.6 Identify the purpose and characteristics of disaster recovery.	14	2
3.7 Given a remote connectivity scenario (e.g., IP, IPX, dial-up, PPPoE, authentication, physical connectivity, etc.), configure the connection.	7	2
3.8 Identify the purpose, benefits, and characteristics of using a firewall.	15	2
3.9 Identify the purpose, benefits, and characteristics of using a proxy.	15	2
3.10 Given a scenario, predict the impact of a particular security implementation on network functionality (e.g., blocking port numbers, encryption, etc.).	15	2
3.11 Given a network configuration, select the appropriate NIC and network configuration settings (DHCP, DNS, WINS, protocols, NetBIOS/host name, etc.).	3, 6, 11	2

Domain 4.0 Network Support – 32% of Examination

Table A-4   Network+ Examination Objectives—Network Support

Objective	Chapter	Percentage of Exam Questions Devoted to this Topic
4.1 Given a troubleshooting scenario, select the appropriate TCP/IP utility from among the following:		3
Tracert	11, 12	
Ping	3, 11, 12	
Arp	3, 11, 12	
Netstat	11	
Nbtstat	11	
Ipconfig	11, 12	
Ifconfig	11, 12	
Winipcfg	11, 12	
Nslookup	11	
4.2 Given a troubleshooting scenario involving a small office/home office network failure (e.g., xDSL, cable, home satellite, wireless, POTS), identify the cause of the failure.	4, 6, 7, 12	2
4.3 Given a troubleshooting scenario involving a remote connectivity problem (e.g., authentication failure, protocol configuration, physical connectivity), identify the cause of the problem.	7, 12	2
4.4 Given specific parameters, configure a client to connect to the following servers:		2
UNIX/Linux	3, 6, 10	
NetWare	3, 6, 9	
Windows	3, 6, 8	
Macintosh	3, 5, 6, 8	
4.5 Given a wiring task, select the appropriate tool (e.g., wire crimper, media tester/certifier, punch down tool, tone generator, optical tester, etc.).	4, 12, Appendix E	2
4.6 Given a network scenario, interpret visual indicators (e.g., link lights, collision lights, etc.) to determine the nature of the problem.	6, 12	2
4.7 Given output from a diagnostic utility (e.g., tracert, ping, ipconfig, etc.), identify the utility and interpret the output.	11	2

Table A-4   Network+ Examination Objectives—Network Support (continued)

Objective	Chapter	Percentage of Exam Questions Devoted to this Topic
4.8 Given a scenario, predict the impact of modifying, adding, or removing network services (e.g., DHCP, DNS, WINS, etc.) on network resources and users.	11, 12	2
4.9 Given a network problem scenario, select an appropriate course of action based on a general troubleshooting strategy. This strategy includes the following steps:		4
1. Establish the symptoms	12	
2. Identify the affected area	12	
3. Establish what has changed	12	
4. Select the most probable cause	12	
5. Implement a solution	12	
6. Test the result	12	
7. Recognize the potential effects of the solution	12, 13	
8. Document the solution	12, 13	
4.10 Given a troubleshooting scenario involving a network with a particular physical topology (i.e., bus, star/hierarchical, mesh, ring, or wireless) and including a network diagram, identify the network area affected and the cause of the problem.	1, 4, 5, 7, 12	3
4.11 Given a network troubleshooting scenario involving a client connectivity problem (e.g., incorrect protocol/client software/authentication configuration, or insufficient rights/permissions), identify the cause of the problem.	2, 3, 8, 9, 10, 11, 12	5
4.12 Given a network troubleshooting scenario involving a wiring/infrastructure problem, identify the cause of the problem (e.g., bad media, interference, network hardware).	4, 12	3

NETWORK+ PRACTICE EXAM

The following exam contains questions similar in content and format to what you will encounter on CompTIA's Network+ certification exam. The exam consists of 65 questions, all of which are multiple choice. Some questions have more than one answer, and some questions require that you study a figure in order to determine the right answer. The questions are in no particular order. The number of questions on each topic reflects the weighting that CompTIA assigned to these topics in their January, 2002 exam objectives. If you want to simulate taking the CompTIA Network+ certification exam, you should allow yourself 90 minutes to answer all of the questions.

1. What TCP/IP utility would you use to determine the number of hops between two routers?

   a. FTP

   b. Nslookup

   c. NBTSTAT

   d. Tracert

   e. Telnet

2. You are the network administrator for a NetWare 5.0 network that runs the TCP/IP protocol. A new user in your organization can log onto the network, but cannot retrieve her spreadsheet files from the network. Which two of the following situations could be the cause of her problem?

   a. She has entered the wrong login ID or password.

   b. She does not have permission to read files in the directory where the spreadsheets are stored.

   c. Her network cable is not inserted into her workstation's NIC.

   d. She does not have permission to view files on the volume where the spreadsheets are stored.

   e. The DHCP settings in her workstation's TCP/IP configuration are incorrect.

3. Which of the following figures reflects the type of physical topology commonly used on a 100BaseTX network?

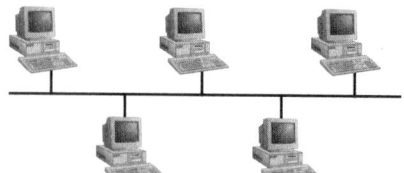

a.

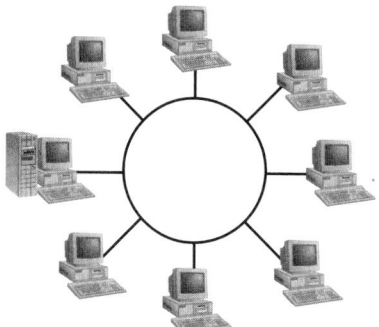

b.

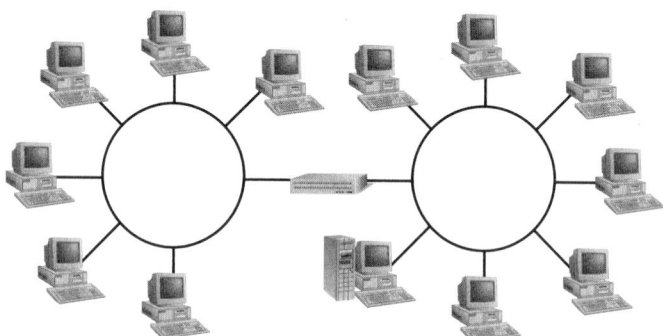

c.

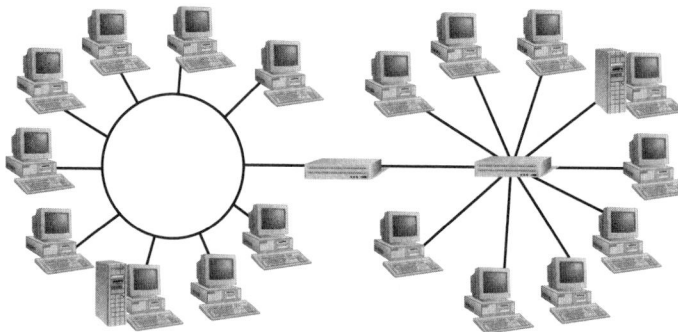

d.

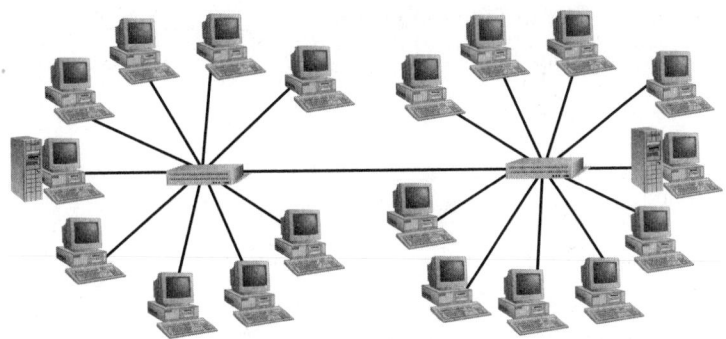

e.

4. When the URL of a Web page begins with "https://," what type of security can you assume the Web page employs for receiving and transmitting data to and from the Web server?

    a. Kerberos

    b. SSL

    c. IPSec

    d. L2TP

    e. Packet filtering firewall

5. You are a support technician for an Internet service provider (ISP) called Alpha Enterprises. A brand new customer calls to ask why his dial-up connection to your company's RADIUS access server won't work. After the user double-clicks the ISP dial-up networking connection icon on his Windows 98 desktop, you can hear his modem dialing. And even though another machine seems to answer, his connection never gets established. You verify that his phone line is connected properly and that he has entered the correct phone number. You also make sure he is using the correct, case-sensitive user name and password that he just received from your Customer Service Department. What do you ask him to check next in order to get closer to solving his problem?

    a. the type of server specified in his Alpha Enterprises Properties dialog box

    b. the version of Windows 98 his system uses

    c. whether the "Save Password" box is checked in his Connect to Alpha Enterprises dialog box

    d. whether he has disabled the call waiting feature in his Alpha Enterprises Properties dialog box

    e. the maximum baud rate his modem can handle

6. Which of the following protocols is not routable?

   a. NetBIOS

   b. NetBEUI

   c. TCP/IP

   d. IPX/SPX

   e. AppleTalk

7. Which layer of the OSI Model contains the Logical Link and MAC sublayers?

   a. Physical layer

   b. Data Link layer

   c. Network layer

   d. Transport layer

   e. Session layer

8. You are a networking technician in a radiology clinic, where physicians use the network to transmit and store patients' diagnostic results. Shortly after a new wing, which contains X-ray and magnetic resonance imaging (MRI) machines, is added to the building, computers in that area begin having intermittent problems saving data to the file server. Once you have identified the symptoms, what are your second and third steps in troubleshooting this problem?

   a. Determine the number of workstations affected, which segment the affected workstations belong to, and which area of workstations is affected.

   b. Verify the soundness of both the physical connections and client software configurations for each workstation having a problem.

   c. Research the problem on your NOS vendor's technical support Web site.

   d. Identify recent changes to the network in order to determine whether a hardware or software change may be responsible for the problem.

   e. Identify the potential effects of the solution you are about to apply, to make sure that you do not inadvertently create new problems.

9. Which two of the following media are capable of providing the foundation for a Fast Ethernet network?

   a. RG-8 coaxial cable

   b. RG-58A/U coaxial cable

   c. CAT5 UTP

   d. CAT1 UTP

   e. fiber-optic cable

B

10. In which of the following situations would a crossover cable be useful for troubleshooting a network connectivity problem with a workstation?

    a. to connect the workstation to a hub

    b. to connect the workstation's hub port to a punch down block

    c. to connect the workstation to another workstation

    d. to connect the workstation's switch port to its hub port

    e. to connect between the workstation's wall plate and its hub port

11. Which of the following WAN topologies is the most fault-tolerant?

    a. full mesh

    b. mesh

    c. peer-to-peer

    d. ring

    e. hierarchical

12. Which of the following is a valid MAC address?

    a. C3000000FFFF

    b. 111.111.111.111

    c. ::9F53

    d. AEFFG0930110

    e. D0000000

13. What type of network uses the type of connector shown below?

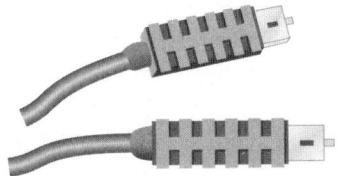

    a. 100BaseFX

    b. 100BaseTX

    c. 100BaseVG-AnyLAN

    d. 10BaseT

    e. 10Base2

14. Your organization has just ordered its first T-1 connection to the Internet. Prior to that, your organization was relying on a DSL connection. Which of the following devices must you now have that your DSL connection didn't require?

    a. modem

    b. CSU/DSU

    c. switch

    d. hub

    e. MAU

15. What type of addresses do bridges read, and to what layer of the OSI Model do bridges belong?

    a. IP addresses; the Network layer

    b. IP addresses; the Transport layer

    c. MAC addresses; the Network layer

    d. MAC addresses; the Data Link layer

    e. IP addresses; the Data Link layer

16. You have been asked to provide a connectivity solution for a small, locally owned franchise of a national restaurant chain. The owners of the franchise would like to send their confidential sales figures, personnel information, and inventory updates to the national office, which is 1200 miles away, once per week. Their total monthly data transfer will amount to almost 50 megabytes. The franchise owners do not plan to use the connection for any other purposes, and they do not have any IT staff to support the connection. Also, they do not want to spend more than $75 per month nor more than $500 to install their connection. Considering cost, speed, reliability, technical expertise, distance, security, and the nature of their environment, what is the best solution for this client?

    a. a T1 that connects to the national office via a router at the local franchise and a router at the national office and uses IPSec to ensure the security of the data en route

    b. a PSTN connection to a local Internet service provider that uses PPP to dial into an access server, then sends data via e-mail to the national office

    c. a DSL connection to a local telephone and Internet service provider that uses IPSec to encrypt the data before it is sent to the national office's file server over the Internet

    d. a private SONET ring to connect with two local telephone and Internet service providers that connects to the national office's T3 and sends data via TCP/IP over ATM

    e. an ISDN connection to a local Internet service provider that allows you to copy files to the national office's anonymous FTP site

B

17. IEEE's Physical layer standards for wireless networking are established by which IEEE committee?

    a. 802.3

    b. 802.5

    c. 802.11

    d. 802.3au

    e. 802.5w

18. You are a software programmer using a development Web server at your office to test your programs. Although your Web server is connected to the Internet for test purposes, you want to ensure that no one on the Internet can access your Web files. In order to make it more difficult for someone to connect to your Web server from the Internet, which TCP/IP default port number would you change in your Web server software configuration?

    a. 21

    b. 22

    c. 65

    d. 80

    e. 90

19. What is the maximum segment length on a 10BaseT network?

    a. 85 meters

    b. 100 meters

    c. 185 meters

    d. 200 meters

    e. 1000 meters

20. You are the network administrator for a large college whose network contains nearly 10,000 workstations, over 200 routers, 80 switches, and 2000 printers. You are researching a proposal to both upgrade the routers and switches on your network and at the same time improve the management of your network. What type of protocol should you ensure that the new routers and switches can accept in order to more easily automate your network management?

    a. TFTP

    b. SMTP

    c. NNTP

    d. ICMP

    e. SNMP

21. Frame Relay is a WAN technology that relies on which one of the following media?

    a. twisted pair

    b. coaxial cable

    c. fiber-optic cable

    d. infrared

    e. radio frequency

22. What is the most likely logical address of the IP gateway in the drawing shown below?

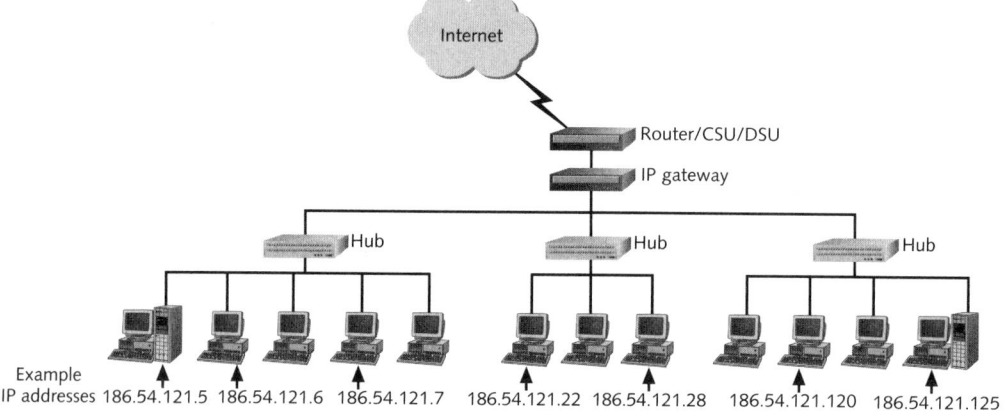

    a. 186.54.121.0

    b. 186.54.121.1

    c. 186.54.121.121

    d. 186.54.121.123

    e. 186.54.121.255

23. Which two of the following is critical to a successful disaster recovery plan?

    a. records detailing network topology and equipment, vendor support numbers, and key networking personnel

    b. regular backups of the file server data and configurations

    c. a third-party assessment of disaster recovery readiness

    d. multiple connections to an Internet service provider

    e. insurance for the physical plant and building structure

24. What type of device is typically used to create a VLAN?

    a. hub

    b. bridge

    c. switch

    d. router

    e. firewall

25. You are a support technician for a 10/100BaseT Ethernet network. A user has complained that she can only log on to the network about 25% of the times she tries. A few months ago, this problem was only happening once a week. You look at the hub port to which her workstation is connected, and you can tell that her workstation's NIC is experiencing a high number of collisions. What led you to this conclusion?

    a. The workstation's hub port's LED was solid green.

    b. The workstation's hub port's LED was blinking green.

    c. The workstation's hub port's LED was solid amber.

    d. The workstation's hub port's LED was blinking amber.

    e. The workstation's hub port's LED was not lit.

26. What is one of the main purposes of a proxy server?

    a. to mask the IP addresses for a group of Internet users within an organization

    b. to allow employees traveling across the country to remotely log onto the LAN

    c. to filter incoming packets and guard against IP spoofing and denial of service attacks

    d. to subdivide a LAN into smaller groups of users (in other words, to create a smaller LAN within a LAN)

    e. to encrypt data transmissions between private and public networks

27. What is a critical difference between network attached storage (NAS) and RAID?

    a. NAS is specific to one particular NOS, while RAID can be used with any file server, independent of the NOS it runs.

    b. NAS uses its own network interface and file system, while RAID relies on a file server to connect to the network and manage files.

    c. NAS relies on a mesh topology, while RAID connects to the network in a star configuration.

    d. NAS must be shut down in order to replace a faulty disk or interface, while RAID arrays can be expanded without any interruption in service.

    e. NAS exists as a distinct storage network, separate from the LAN, while RAID is part of the LAN.

28. What type of network uses the connector shown in the figure below?

BNC T-connector

a. 10Base2

b. 10Base5

c. 10BaseT

d. 100BaseTX

e. 100BaseFX

29. Which of the following figures illustrates a VPN WAN?

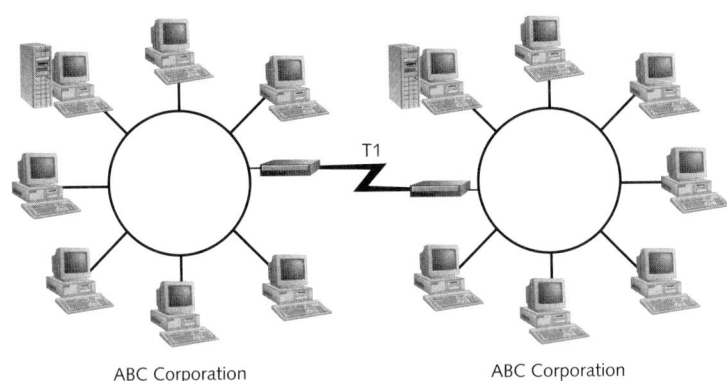

T1

ABC Corporation
Phoenix office

ABC Corporation
Dallas office

a.

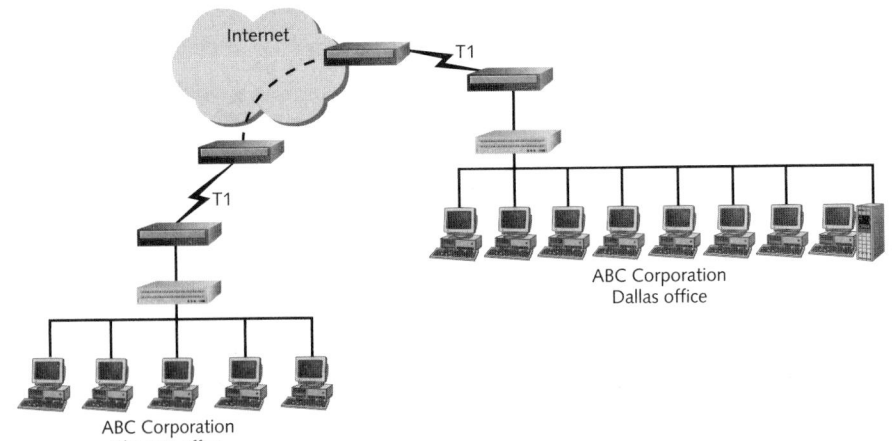

Internet

T1

T1

ABC Corporation
Dallas office

ABC Corporation
Phoenix office

b.

B

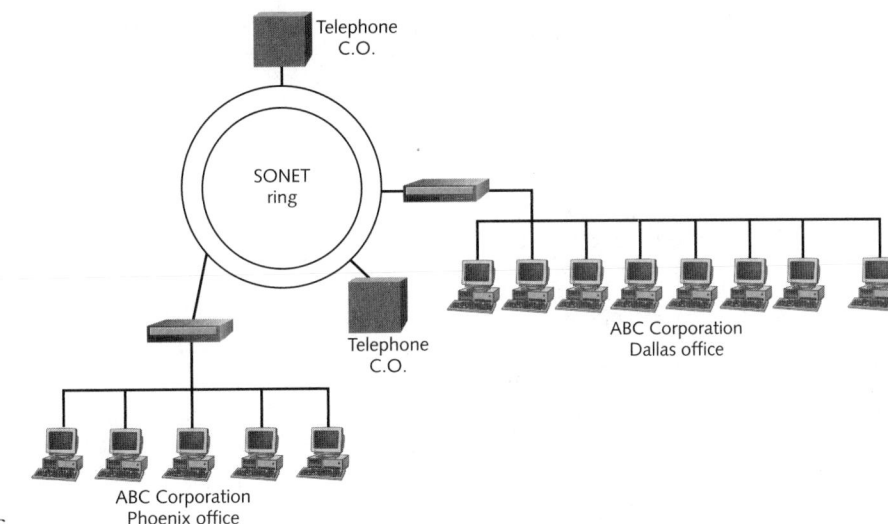

Telephone
C.O.

SONET
ring

Telephone
C.O.

ABC Corporation
Dallas office

ABC Corporation
Phoenix office

c.

T1

T1

DKZ Corporation
Los Angeles office

ABC Corporation
Phoenix office

ABC Corporation
Dallas office

d.

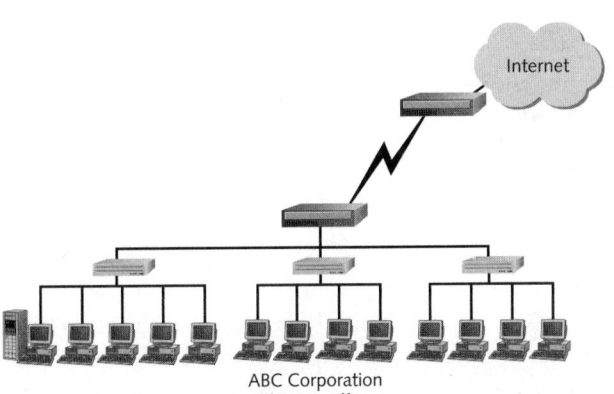

Internet

ABC Corporation
Phoenix office

e.

30. If you have an AUI cable connected to your workstation's NIC, and you need to connect this workstation to your Thicknet network, what would you connect the cable's opposite end to?

    a. MAU

    b. hub

    c. BNC T-connector

    d. transceiver

    e. LAM

31. What security measure ensures that your user name and password are contained in the NOS directory when you attempt to log onto a server?

    a. remapping

    b. obfuscation

    c. authentication

    d. caching

    e. redirection

32. You are a network administrator for a WAN that connects two regional insurance company offices—one main office and one satellite office—to each other by a T1. The main office is also connected to the Internet using a T1. This T1 provides Internet access for both offices. To ensure that your private network is not compromised by unauthorized access through the Internet connection, you install a firewall between the main office and the Internet. Shortly thereafter, users in your satellite office complain that they cannot access the file server in the main office, but users in the main office can still access the Internet. What two things should you check?

    a. whether the firewall has been configured to run in promiscuous mode

    b. whether the firewall is placed in the appropriate location on the network

    c. whether the firewall has been configured to allow access from IP addresses in the satellite office

    d. whether the firewall has been configured to receive and transmit UDP-based packets

    e. whether the firewall has been configured to allow Internet access over the main office's T1

33. What TCP/IP utility was used to generate the following output, and what piece of information does it tell you about the machine on which the utility shown below was used?

```
Windows 2000 IP Configuration

    Host Name . . . . . . . . . . . . : STUDENT1
    Primary DNS Suffix  . . . . . . . :
    Node Type . . . . . . . . . . . . : Broadcast
    IP Routing Enabled. . . . . . . . : No
    WINS Proxy Enabled. . . . . . . . : No

Ethernet adapter Local Area Connection:

    Connection-specific DNS Suffix  . :
    Description . . . . . . . . . . . : Winbond W89C940 PCI Ethernet Adapter
    Physical Address. . . . . . . . . : 00-20-78-12-77-04
    DHCP Enabled. . . . . . . . . . . : No
    IP Address. . . . . . . . . . . . : 203.188.65.109
    Subnet Mask . . . . . . . . . . . : 255.255.255.0
    Default Gateway . . . . . . . . . : 203.188.65.1
    DNS Servers . . . . . . . . . . . : 144.32.92.48

C:\>
```

   a. ipconfig; the output indicates that the machine has a MAC address of 002078127704

   b. PING; the output indicates that the machine cannot communicate with any external hosts

   c. ARP; the output indicates that the machine resolves to a name of STUDENT1

   d. winipcfg; the output indicates that the machine does not rely on DHCP

   e. nbtstat; the output indicates that it is currently connected to the machine with a NetBIOS name of STUDENT1

34. While troubleshooting a workstation connectivity problem, you type the following command: `ping 127.0.0.1`. The response you get indicates that the test failed. What can you determine about that workstation?

   a. Its network cable is faulty or not connected to the wall jack.

   b. Its TCP/IP protocol is not installed properly.

   c. Its IP address has been prevented from transmitting data past the default gateway.

   d. Its DHCP settings are incorrect.

   e. Its DNS name server specification is incorrect.

35. You are a support technician working in a telecommunications closet in a remote office. You suspect that a connectivity problem is related to a broken RJ-45 plug on a patch cable that connects a hub's uplink port to a router. You need to replace that connection, but you have forgotten to bring an extra patch cable. You decide to install a new RJ-45 connector to replace the broken RJ-45 connector. What two tools should you have in order to successfully accomplish this?

   a. punch-down tool

   b. crimping tool

   c. wire stripper

   d. cable tester

   e. multimeter

36. In the IP version 6 addressing scheme, which of the following IP addresses equals the loopback address?

    a. 1.0.0.1

    b. 127:0:0:0:0:0:0:1

    c. 0.0.0.0.0.0.0.1

    d. ::1

    e. 127.0.0.1

37. Which two of the following devices operate only at the Physical layer of the OSI model?

    a. hub

    b. switch

    c. router

    d. bridge

    e. repeater

38. What is the primary purpose for subnetting?

    a. to facilitate easier migration from IPv4 to IPv6 addressing

    b. to enable a network to use DHCP

    c. to make more efficient use of limited numbers of legitimate IP addresses

    d. to reduce the likelihood for user error when modifying TCP/IP properties

    e. to limit the number of addresses that can be assigned to one network interface

39. In which two of the following switching techniques must multiple data packets that make up the same transmission use identical paths to reach their destination?

    a. circuit switching

    b. layer 2 switching

    c. packet switching

    d. message switching

    e. layer 3 switching

40. What is unique about ATM transmission, as compared with Ethernet and Token Ring?

    a. ATM does not require CSMA/CD, making it more efficient.

    b. ATM uses a fixed packet size, making it more efficient.

c. ATM can run over SONET, making it more reliable.

d. ATM allows data to travel in both directions over a connection, making it more fault-tolerant.

e. ATM has longer network length limits, making it more economical.

41. In the network diagram shown below, which network nodes belong to a private network?

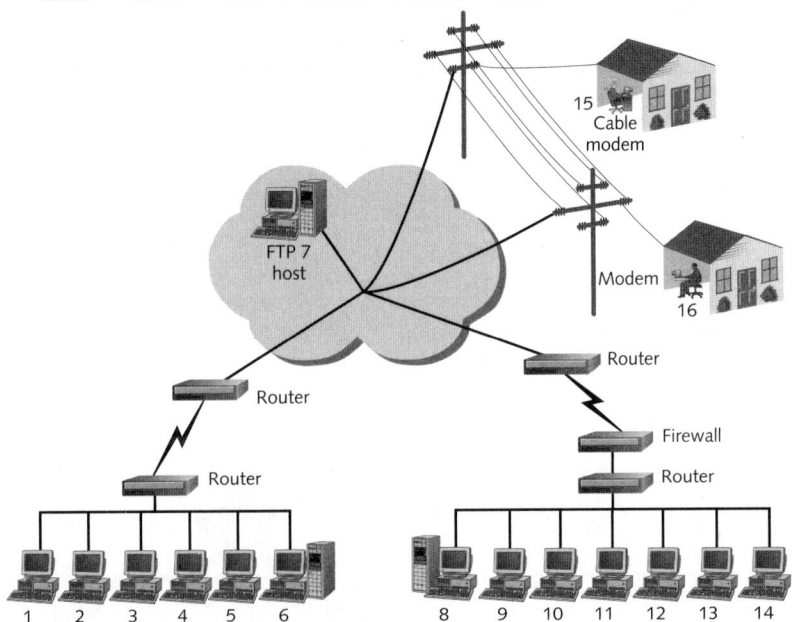

a. nodes 1 through 6 and nodes 8 through 14

b. nodes 1 through 6

c. nodes 8 through 14

d. nodes 1 through 7, plus 15 and 16

e. all of the nodes

42. You are the network administrator for a law firm whose two primary offices are located five blocks apart in the center of a large city. The two offices have different specialties, and therefore keep separate file servers. Each file server runs the Windows 2000 Server NOS. A T1 connects the two offices so employees at each office can communicate and share files. In order to protect the lawyer's records, you currently make regular backups of all the data on both file servers and store the backup tapes in an off-site warehouse. However, one of the firm's partners has asked you to do more than simply

back up data. In addition, she requests that you implement this added measure within the next week. Which of the following solutions is the best choice to ensure greater data protection in the given time frame?

a. contract with an online backup provider to back up data over the Internet using the T1

b. upgrade your version of Windows 2000 Server to Windows 2000 Advanced Server so that you can implement clustering

c. establish mirroring between the two servers using the T1

d. add a RAID 5 device to one of the file servers

e. connect the T1 to a third office across town and backup files from the two other locations to the third location

43. By default, an IPX address contains what other type of address?

a. IP address

b. SPX address

c. MAC address

d. Logical address

e. NetBIOS address

44. Which transport protocol and TCP/IP port does the Telnet utility use?

a. UDP, port 23

b. TCP, port 21

c. UDP, port 22

d. TCP, port 23

e. UDP, port 21

45. Which two of the following will guarantee that a server continually has power, even if a building's electrical service is interrupted?

a. RAID 3

b. RAID 5

c. online UPS

d. NAS

e. diesel-powered generator

46. What protocol is used to transfer mail between two UNIX mail servers?

a. SMTP

b. SNMP

  c. IMAP

  d. POP3

  e. TFTP

47. What type of fiber-optic cabling is most likely to be used for a LAN backbone?

  a. single-mode fiber

  b. dual-mode fiber

  c. duplex fiber

  d. half duplex fiber

  e. multimode fiber

48. Which two of the following technologies use two pairs of twisted-pair wiring?

  a. 10Base2

  b. 10Base5

  c. 10BaseT

  d. 100BaseTX

  e. 100BaseT4

49. You are a support technician at an organization that uses a NetWare 5.11 LAN with a mixture of Windows 98 and Windows 2000 workstations. You are asked to help a user in the Accounting Department who can retrieve files from the network, but suddenly can't print to the same printer he uses every day. You have determined that he is the only person in his area affected by this problem. Further, if you log onto the LAN with his user name and password, you can successfully print to the same printer. Which of the following might be the cause of this user's problem?

  a. He has inadvertently deleted the network printer object from his workstation's Printers window.

  b. His network password has expired.

  c. His user name has accidentally been deleted from the group that has rights to print to that printer.

  d. His workstation's client software configuration is missing the print server specification.

  e. His network adapter is loose or improperly installed.

50. What is the function of the Network layer of the OSI Model?

   a. to manage the flow of communications over a channel

   b. to add segmentation and assembly information

   c. to encode and encrypt data

   d. to add logical addresses and properly route data

   e. to apply electrical pulses to the wire

51. Which of the following utilities would you use to log onto a UNIX host?

   a. NTP

   b. ARP

   c. PING

   d. Telnet

   e. SNMP

52. You are a networking consultant helping a local TV station establish a video broadcast Web server. The station has unlimited funding to broadcast their news and feature stories over the Web. However, they currently only have a DSL connection to an ISP. This DSL connection is used to provide Internet and e-mail access to their employees. Which two of the following solutions would be good choices for the TV station to broadcast programs to the Web from their station?

   a. a SONET ring that links the local station with an Internet service provider and uses ATM for transmitting video broadcasts over the Internet

   b. a satellite uplink to a Webcasting service provider

   c. a VPN that uses the Internet and transmits video broadcasts via IPSec

   d. a fractional T1 connection to a local Internet service provider

   e. a T1 connection to the station's national broadcasting affiliate that uses ATM for transmitting video broadcasts

53. What is the default subnet mask for the following IP address: 193.13.44.87?

   a. 255.255.255.255

   b. 255.255.255.0

   c. 255.255.0.0

   d. 255.0.0.0

   e. 0.0.0.0

54. Which of the following diagrams illustrates a FDDI network?

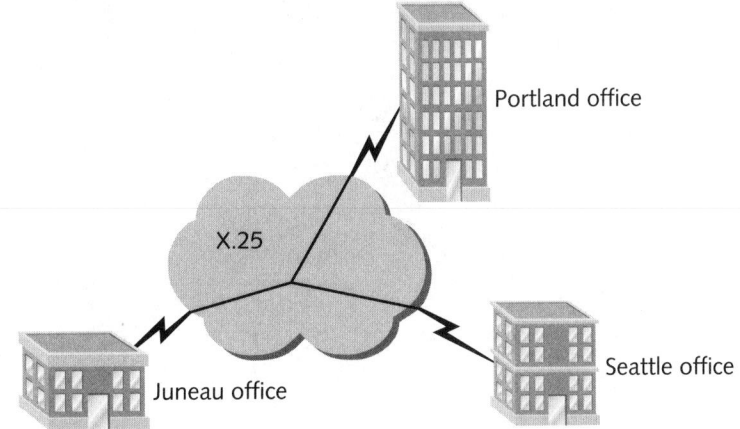

a.

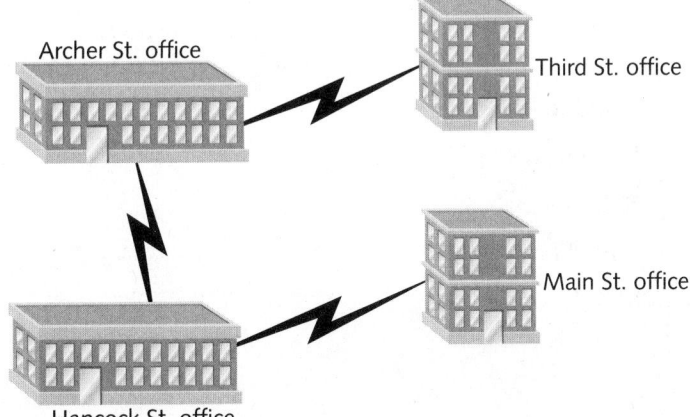

b.

c.

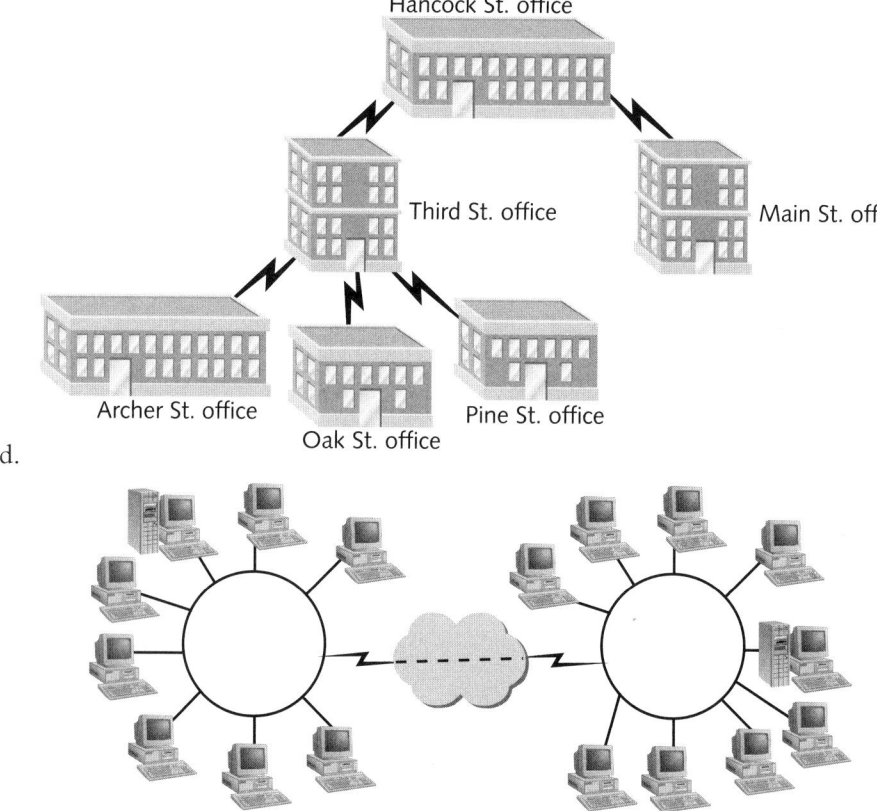

d.

e. Juneau office   Portland office

55. You are a support technician installing 13 new Windows 2000 Professional workstations on your company's network, which relies on several Windows 2000 Servers for authentication and file sharing, one UNIX e-mail server, and one UNIX proxy server. The network runs the TCP/IP protocol over 100BaseTX Ethernet technology. It also uses DHCP and NAT. Which two of the following settings must you make sure to specify on each workstation so that their users can pick up their Internet e-mail from the UNIX e-mail server.

a. Windows domain name

b. IP address

c. WINS server

d. NNTP server

e. SMTP server

56. Which of the following IEEE committees designs standards for Token Ring networks?

    a. 802.3

    b. 802.3au

    c. 802.3z

    d. 802.5

    e. 802.11

57. You are a network administrator for a LAN that includes three NetWare 5.11 file servers and 235 users. You are installing a new application on one of the file servers. This application must be accessible to 50 of the users, but not to all users. What tool would you use to create a group of users that has permission to access and run this application?

    a. NWAdmin

    b. NDS Manager

    c. NDSconfig

    d. NDS eDirectory

    e. MMC

58. What is the name of the file on a UNIX server that contains a list of host names and the IP address associated with each name?

    a. net_host

    b. hosts

    c. hostid

    d. lmhosts

    e. hostnames

59. What types of files does an incremental backup save?

    a. data that changed prior to the previous backup

    b. data that changed since the previous backup

    c. all data, regardless of whether it has changed

    d. data that were backed up exactly a week previously

    e. data that users have flagged for backup since the last backup occurred

60. What software will enable Windows 2000 domains to appear as container objects within a NetWare NDS tree?

    a. Gateway services for NetWare

    b. NDS eDirectory

    c. NWAdmin

    d. Client services for NetWare

    e. IPX/SPX-compatible Services

61. You are a support technician installing a new NIC on a Windows 98 workstation. After physically installing the NIC, then installing the appropriate device driver for the NIC, you restart the workstation. Upon restarting, an error indicates that the NIC is attempting to use an IRQ already in use by another device. The workstation's Device Manager window indicates that both the NIC and the sound card are attempting to use IRQ 11. Of the following IRQs, which one could you most likely assign to the new NIC so that it will not conflict with another device?

    a. 4

    b. 6

    c. 9

    d. 12

    e. 13

62. Which three of the following components must be installed on a Windows 2000 Professional workstation in order for it to successfully connect to a Windows 2000 file server over the network?

    a. NIC

    b. Client for Microsoft Networks

    c. file sharing services

    d. protocol(s)

    e. Microsoft Family Logon

63. Which one of the following media is most resistant to EMI/RFI?

    a. coaxial cable

    b. UTP cable

    c. STP cable

    d. fiber-optic cable

    e. microwaves

64. In the following figure, if router B suffers a failure, what will be the effect of this failure on nodes 1 through 9?

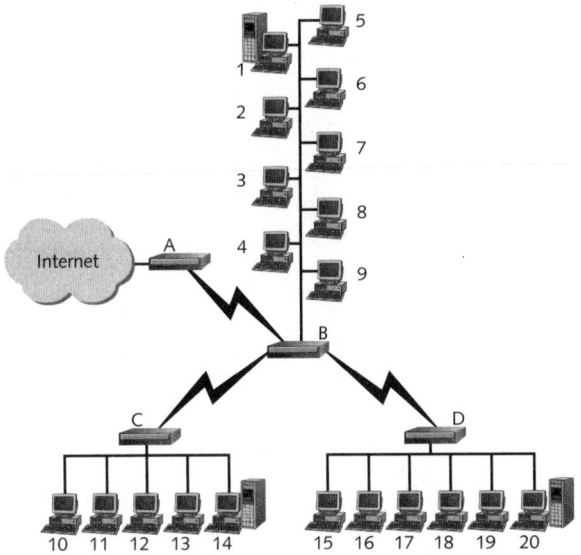

a. They will only be unable to access the Internet.

b. They will be unable to access the Internet and either nodes 9 through 14 or 15 through 20.

c. They will be unable to access the Internet, other nodes on the WAN, and other nodes on the LAN.

d. They will be unable to access the Internet and nodes 10 through 20.

e. Their connectivity will not be affected.

65. What command would you use to view the online help for the chmod utility on a UNIX server?

a. man chmod

b. chmod help

c. help chmod

d. chmod /q

e. chmod list

VISUAL GUIDE TO CONNECTORS

Throughout this book you have learned about several different cabling and connector options that may be used on networks. Some, such as RJ-45, are very common, while others, such as AUI, are nearly obsolete. So that you can compare such connectors and ensure that you understand their differences, this Appendix compiles drawings of the connectors and a brief summary of their application in a simple table. You will need to be familiar with the most popular types of connectors in order to qualify for Network+ certification. You can find more detail about these connectors and the networks on which they are used in Chapters 4 and 6.

Table C-1   Network connectors and their uses

Specification .	Male Connector (front view)	Male Connector (side view)	Female Receptacle (front view)	Application
AUI (DB-15)				Used on coaxial cabling for Thicknet (10Base5 Ethernet).
N-series Connector				Used on coaxial cabling for Thicknet (10Base5 Ethernet) networks.
BNC				Used on coaxial cabling for Thinnet (10Base2 Ethernet) networks.
Type 1 IBM Data Connector				Used on older Token Ring networks; has been replaced by RJ-45 connectors on newer Token Ring networks.
DB-9				Used on older Token Ring networks; has been replaced by RJ-45 connectors on newer Token Ring networks.
RJ-11				Used on twisted-pair cabling for telephone systems (and some older twisted-pair networks).
RJ-45				Used on twisted-pair cabling for modern networks.
ST				Used on fiber-optic cabling (for example, on 10BaseF or 100BaseF networks).
SC				Used on fiber-optic cabling (for example, 10BaseF or 100BaseF networks).
USB				Used to connect external peripherals such as modems, mice, audio players, and NICs.

STANDARD NETWORKING FORMS

Throughout this book you have learned about various operating procedures and policies that help your IT operations, upgrades, and installations run more smoothly. This appendix offers examples of forms you can use when planning and maintaining a network. Recognize that you may need to change the forms slightly to suit your environment. However, having a form template can help you remember steps you may otherwise have forgotten.

This appendix provides the following forms:

- Server Installation Checklist – Windows 2000
- Server Installation Checklist – NetWare
- Server Installation Checklist – RedHat Linux
- User Account Creation Form
- Technical Support Contacts Form
- Incident Report Form
- Network Security Checklist

Server Installation Checklist – Windows 2000

Installer: _____ Date:_____

Model and Serial Number: _____

RAM: _____ Processor: _____ Hard Disk: _____

Server is a: ❏ Domain Controller   ❏ Member Server

Server Name: _____

Domain Name: _____

NIC 1 Type: _____ IRQ:_____ Base I/O: _____ DMA: _____

NIC 2 Type: _____ IRQ:_____ Base I/O: _____ DMA: _____

Protocols:

    ❏ NetBEUI   ❏ TCP/IP

    ❏ NWLink IPS/SPX-Compatible Protocol   IP Address: _____

    ❏ Other: _____   Gateway: _____

                                                               DNS Server:_____

Disk Controller Type(s): _____

Partitions:

    1: Type: Size: Name:

    2: Type: Size: Name:

    3: Type: Size: Name:

    4: Type: Size: Name:

Registration Key:_____

Licensing Mode: ❏ Per Server   ❏ Per Seat

D

Server Installation Checklist – NetWare

Installer: _____ Date:_____

Model and Serial Number: _____

RAM: _____ Processor: _____ Hard Disk: _____

Server Name: _____

Disk Controller Types(s): _____

NIC 1 Type: _____ IRQ:_____ Base I/O: _____ DMA: _____

NIC 2 Type: _____ IRQ:_____ Base I/O: _____ DMA: _____

Partitions:

      1: Type: Size: Name:

      2: Type: Size: Name:

      3: Type: Size: Name:

      4: Type: Size: Name:

NDS Tree: _____ NDS Container:_____

Licensing Number:_____

Protocols:

      ❑ NetBEUI   ❑ TCP/IP

      ❑ NWLink IPX/SPX Compatible Protocol   IP Address: _____

      ❑ Other: _____   Gateway: _____

                                                  DNS Server:_____

Server Installation Checklist – RedHat Linux

Installer: _____ Date:_____

Model and Serial Number: _____

RAM: _____ Processor: _____ Hard Disk: _____

Keyboard Type: _____ Monitor: _____

Packages to Install: _____

_____

Mouse Type: _____

Video Card Type: _____

TCP/IP Settings:

    IP Address: _____   Netmask: _____

    Default Gateway: _____   Primary Nameserver: _____

    Domain Name: _____   Hostname: _____

User Account Creation Form

User Name: _____

Department/Location: _____ Phone: _____

Date Created: _____ By: _____

Requested By: _____

Approved By: _____

User ID: _____

Context (NetWare) or Domain (Windows 2000): _____

Group Memberships: _____

Home Directory: _____

Password Restrictions:

    Minimum password length: _____   Require unique passwords? ❏ Yes   ❏ No

    Days before password expires: ____   Grace logins: _____

Login Restrictions:

    Valid login times: _____   Maximum connections: _____

    Address restrictions: _____   Location restrictions: _____

Technical Support Contacts Form

Vendor Name: _____

Address: _____

General Phone Number: _____   Tech. Support Phone Number: _____

General Web Page: _____   Tech. Support Web Page: _____

Contact Name: _____

Products Supported:

        Product Name: _____   Product License Number: _____

        Product Name: _____   Product License Number: _____

        Product Name: _____   Product License Number: _____

        Product Name: _____   Product License Number: _____

Support Agreement Specifies:

Support Experiences with Vendor:

        Date: Reason for call: Resolution:

        Date: Reason for call: Resolution:

        Date: Reason for call: Resolution:

        Date: Reason for call: Resolution:

        Date: Reason for call: Resolution:

D

Incident Report Form

User Name: _____

User ID: _____

Location: _____ Phone: _____

Date: _____ Time: _____

Received By: _____

Nature of the problem:

Resolution:

    Date: _____ By: _____

    Notes:

Follow-up Call:

    Date: _____ By: _____

    Notes:

Network Security Checklist

❑ Write and enforce security policy

❑ Communicate security policy to all employees

❑ Identify vulnerabilities

❑ Enforce use of passwords

❑ Require minimum password length

❑ Require frequent password changes

❑ Disable Administrator user on servers (use another ID with equivalent privileges)

❑ Implement virus scanning on servers and workstations

❑ Implement firewalls between private and public networks

❑ Restrict logins to TCP/IP ports

❑ Properly configure firewall and router access

❑ Review remote access links for security threats

❑ Implement enterprise-wide intrusion detection

❑ Encrypt sensitive data in transit (for example, use digital certificates)

❑ Implement automated, enterprise-wide virus detection

❑ Implement badge access for equipment and telecommunications rooms

❑ Use security cameras to monitor entrances and equipment rooms

❑ Perform background checks on prospective employees

❑ Plan for security breaches by having a trained response team

A NETWORKING PROFESSIONAL'S TOOLKIT

Throughout this book you have learned about the variety of tools you may use while implementing, analyzing, and troubleshooting a network. Although it is simple to find information on networking devices or software packages, it is not always easy to find details about the tools used by networking professionals. This appendix provides pictures of networking tools, some familiar and some probably unfamiliar, along with their proper names and uses. You can often find these tools together in toolkits with carrying cases. Some toolkit providers include: Aven Tools, Black Box, Curtis, Hawking Technologies, Paladin, and Siemon. Toolkits are sold in many computer supply stores, such as CompUSA and J and R Computer World, and through many computer supply Web sites, such as *www.cdw.com*, *www.computers4sure.com*, *www.buycomp.com*, and *www.c-source.com*.

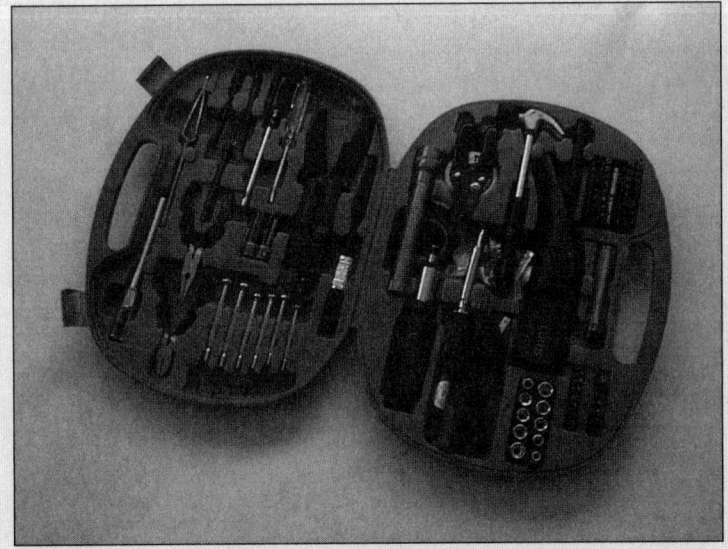

Figure E-1 A networking professional's toolkit

Many of the tools used by networking professionals are similar or identical to tools used by electricians. Tools pictured in the following figures fall into this category.

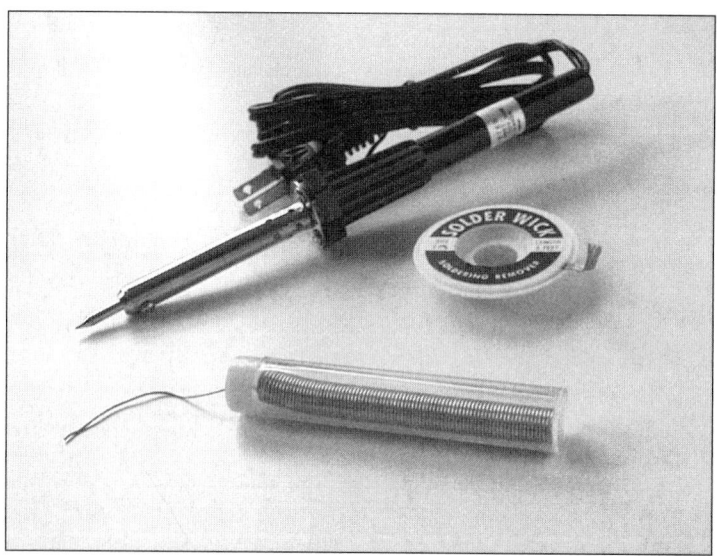

Figure E-2 Soldering iron, solder, and solder wick; used for repairing connections

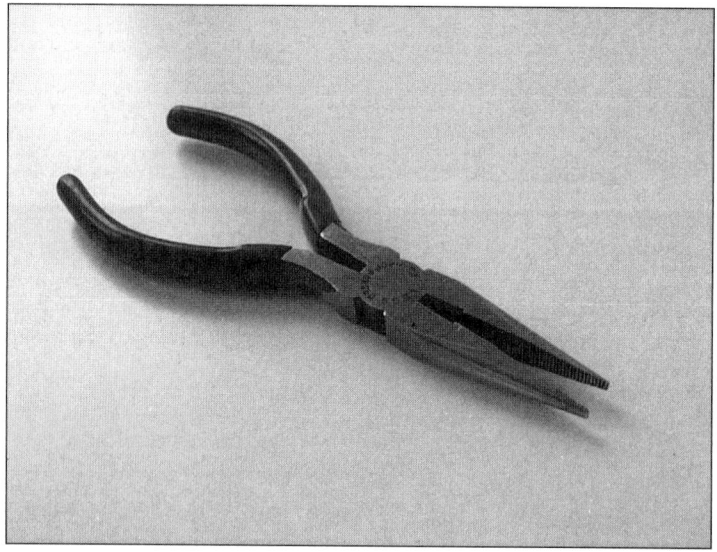

Figure E-3 Pliers; used for bending cable or components or working in tight spaces

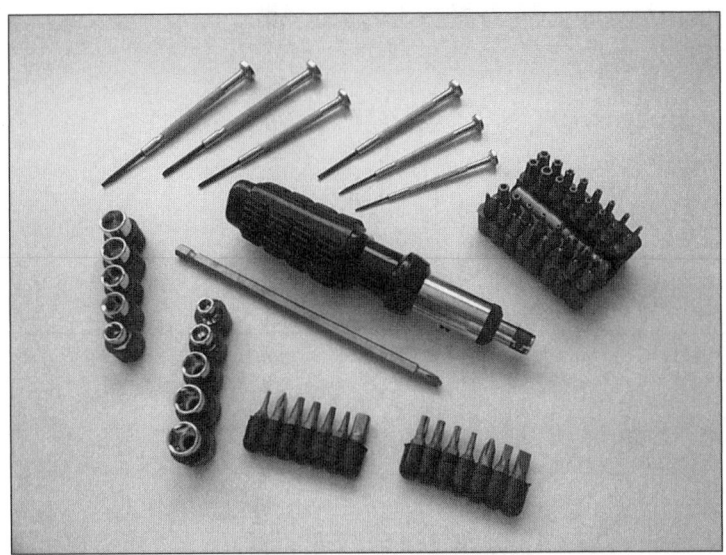

Figure E-4   Screwdriver with several different head types; used for installing and uninstalling components

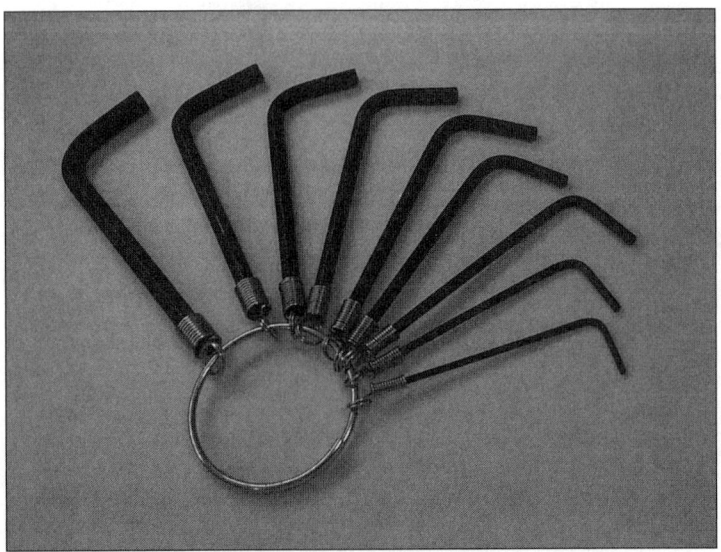

Figure E-5   Hex keyset; used for removing computer covers or components

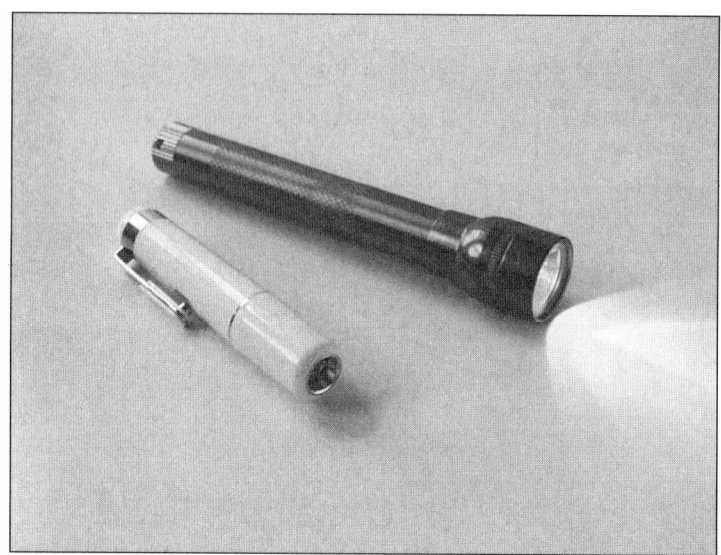

Figure E-6   Pocket flashlights; used to illuminate the interior of devices

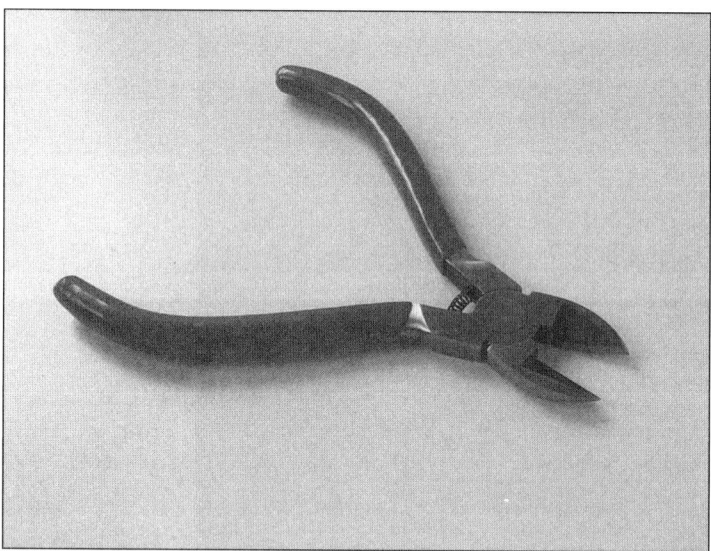

Figure E-7   Wire cutters

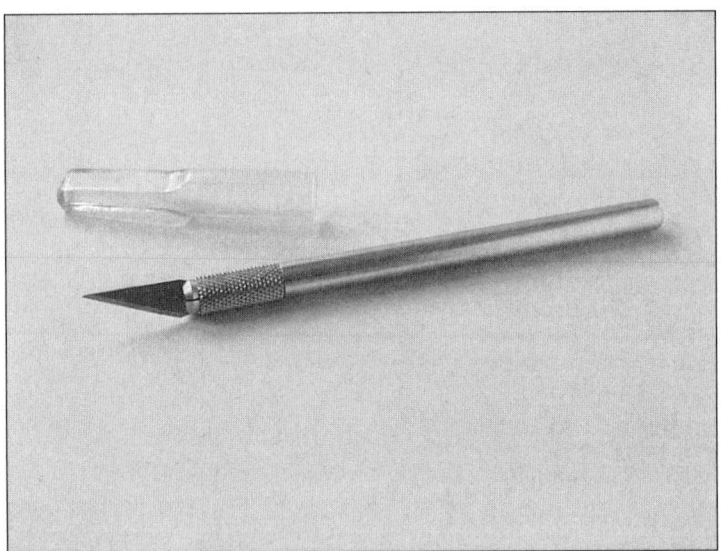

Figure E-8   Precision knife

Other tools used by networking professionals are unique to computer repair or telephony technicians. Tools pictured in the following figures fall into this category.

Figure E-9   Cable preparation tool, including wire stripper and cutter; used for preparing cable for termination

E

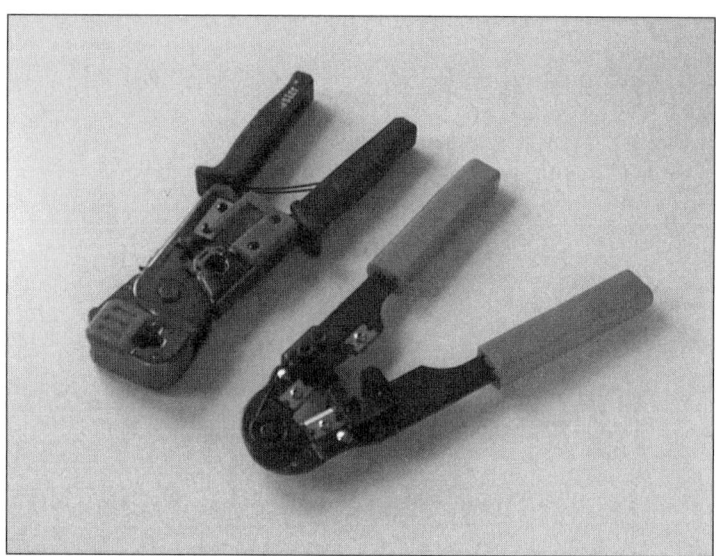

Figure E-10   Crimping tool; used for crimping wires into terminators

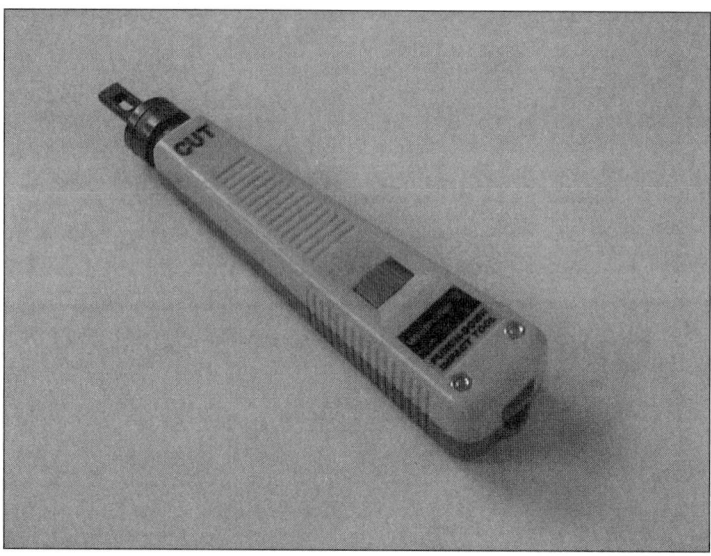

Figure E-11   Punch-down block tool; used for crimping wires into punch-down blocks

E

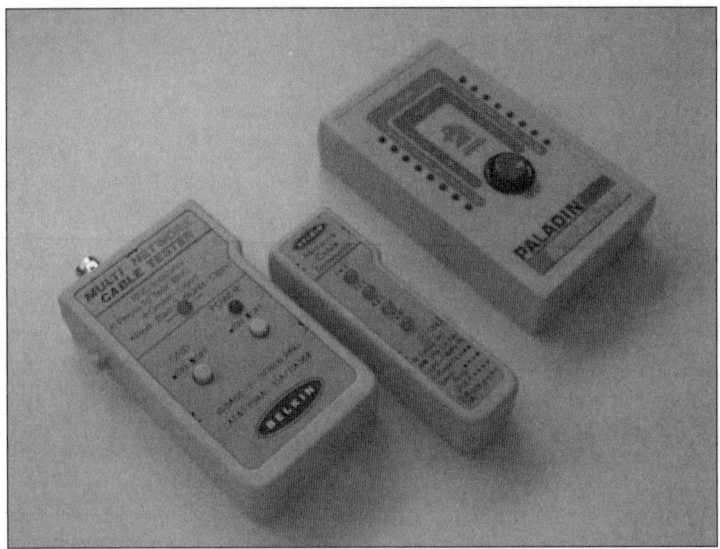

Figure E-12   Cable testing tools; used for verifying cable integrity

Figure E-13   Cable ties; used for holding bundles of cables together

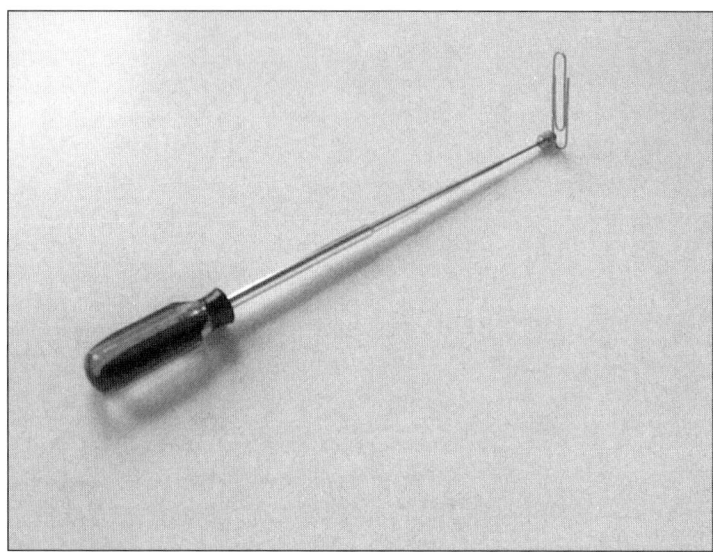

Figure E-14   Magnetic extractor; used for retrieving small components

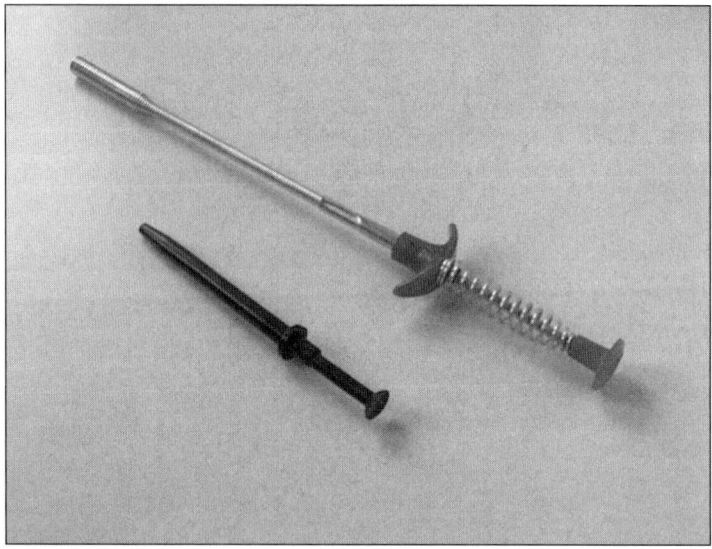

Figure E-15   Extractors; used for retrieving small components

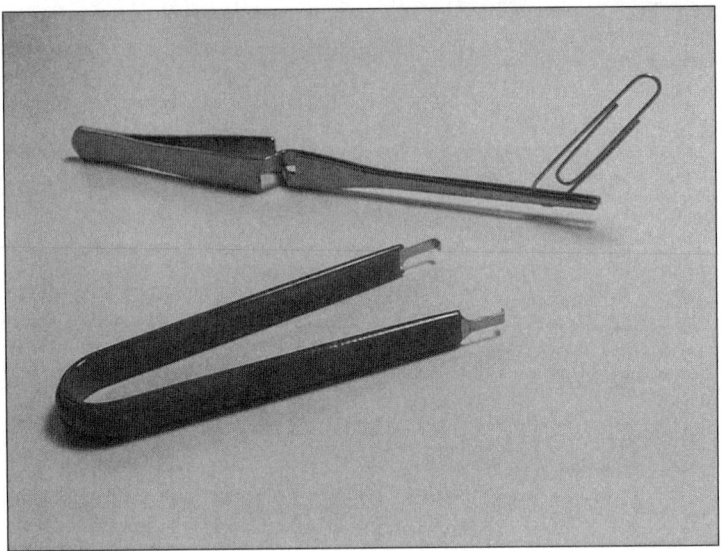

Figure E-16   Tweezers; used for holding and maneuvering small components

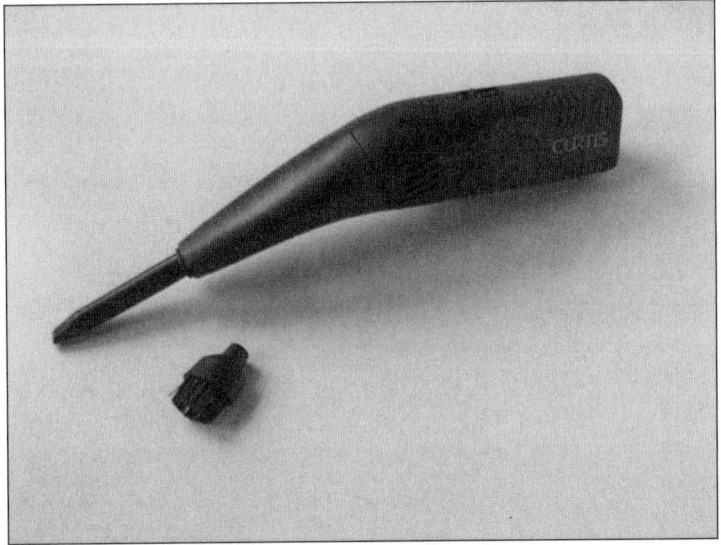

Figure E-17   Anti-static vacuum; used for cleaning electronic devices

Glossary

gigabit Ethernet — An Ethernet standard for networks that achieve 1-Gbps maximum throughput. 1 Gigabit Ethernet runs (preferably) on fiber, but may also run over twisted pair. It is primarily used for network backbones.

gigabit per second (Gbps) — 1,000,000,000 bits per second.

kilobit per second (Kbps) — 1000 bits per second.

megabit per second (Mbps) — 1,000,000 bits per second.

terabit per second (Tbps) — 1,000,000,000 bits per second.

tier architecture — A client/server environment that uses middleware to translate requests between the client and server.

Gigabit Ethernet — A standard currently being defined by the IEEE 802.3ae committee. 10 Gigabit Ethernet will allow 10-Gbps throughput and will include full-duplexing and multimode fiber requirements.

00BaseFX — A Physical layer standard for networks that specifies baseband transmission, multimode fiber cabling, and 100-Mbps throughput. 100BaseFX networks have a maximum segment length of 400 meters. 100BaseFX may also be called "Fast Ethernet."

00BaseT — A Physical layer standard for networks that specifies baseband transmission, twisted-pair cabling, and 100-Mbps throughput. 100BaseT networks have a maximum segment length of 100 meters and use the star topology. 100BaseT is also known as Fast Ethernet.

00BaseT4 — A type of 100BaseT network that uses all four wire pairs in a twisted-pair cable to achieve its 100-Mbps throughput. 100BaseT4 is not capable of full-duplex transmission and requires CAT3 or higher media.

00BaseTX — A type of 100BaseT network that uses two wire pairs in a twisted-pair cable, but uses faster signaling to achieve 100-Mbps throughput. It is capable of full-duplex transmission and requires CAT5 or higher media.

00BaseVG (100VG-AnyLAN) — A Physical layer standard for networks that specifies baseband transmission, twisted-pair media, and 100-Mbps throughput. 100BaseVG uses a different and more efficient method than 100BaseT for allowing nodes to transmit data on the media. However, 100BaseVG is rarely used.

0Base2 — See *Thinnet.*

0Base5 — See *Thicknet.*

0BaseF — A Physical layer standard for networks that specifies baseband transmission, multimode fiber cabling, and 10-Mbps throughput. 10BaseF networks have a maximum segment

length of 1000 or 2000 meters, depending on the version, and employ a star topology.

10BaseT — A Physical layer standard for networks that specifies baseband transmission, twisted pair media, and 10-Mbps throughput. 10BaseT networks have a maximum segment length of 100 meters and rely on a star topology.

802.3 — The IEEE standard for Ethernet networking devices and data handling.

802.3 Raw — See *Novell proprietary 802.3 frame.*

802.4 — The IEEE standard for Token Bus networking devices and data handling.

802.5 — The IEEE standard for Token Ring networking devices and data handling.

802.6 — The IEEE standard for Metropolitan Area Network (MAN) networking.

802.10 — The IEEE standard that describes network access controls, encryption, certification, and other security topics.

802.11 — The IEEE standard for wireless networking.

A+ — Professional certification established by CompTIA that verifies knowledge about PC operation, repair, and management.

access method — A network's method of controlling how network nodes access the communications channel. CSMA/CD is the access method used by Ethernet networks.

access server — See *communications server.*

account — A record of a user that contains all of his or her properties, including rights to resources, password, username, and so on.

acknowledgment (ACK) — A response generated at the Transport layer of the OSI Model that confirms to a sender that its frame was received.

Active Directory — Windows 2000 Server's method for organizing and managing objects associated with the network.

active monitor — On a Token Ring network, the workstation that maintains timing for token passing, monitors token and frame transmission, detects lost tokens, and corrects problems when a timing error or other disruption occurs. Only one workstation on the ring can act as the active monitor at any given time.

active topology — A topology in which each workstation participates in transmitting data over the network.

adapter card — See *expansion board.*

address — A number that uniquely identifies each workstation and device on a network. Without unique addresses, computers on the network could not reliably communicate.

address management — Centrally administering a finite number of network addresses for an entire LAN. Usually this task can be accomplished without touching the client workstations.

Address Resolution Protocol (ARP) — A core protocol in the TCP/IP suite that belongs in the Internet layer. It obtains the MAC (physical) address of a host, or node, and then creates a local database that maps the MAC address to the host's IP (logical) address.

address resource record — A type of DNS data record that maps the IP address of an Internet-connected device to its domain name.

addressing — The scheme for assigning a unique identifying number to every workstation and device on the network. The type of addressing used on a network depends on its protocols and network operating system.

Administrator — A user account that has unlimited privileges to resources and objects managed by a server or domain. The administrator account is created during NOS installation.

AIX — IBM's proprietary implementation of the UNIX system.

alias — A nickname for a node's host name. Aliases can be specified in a local host file.

alien crosstalk — A type of interference that occurs when signals from an adjacent cable interfere with another cable's transmission.

amplifier — A device that boosts, or strengthens, an analog signal.

amplitude — A measure of a signal's strength.

amplitude modulation (AM) — A modulation technique in which the amplitude of the carrier signal is modified by the application of a data signal.

analog — A signal that uses variable voltage to create continuous waves, resulting in an inexact transmission.

ANSI (American National Standards Institute) — An organization composed of more than 1000 representatives from industry and government who together determine standards for the electronics industry in addition to other fields, such as chemical and nuclear engineering, health and safety, and construction.

anycast address — A type of address specified in IPv6 that represents a group of interfaces, any one of which (and usually the first available of which) can accept a transmission. At this time, anycast addresses are not designed to be assigned to hosts, such as servers or workstations, but rather to routers.

Apache — A popular open source software Web server application often used on Linux Internet servers.

AppleTalk — The protocol suite used to interconnect Macintosh computers. Although AppleTalk was originally designed to support peer-to-peer networking among Macintoshes, it can now be routed between network segments and integrated with NetWare- or Microsoft-based networks.

AppleTalk network number — A unique 16-bit number that identifies the network to which an AppleTalk node is connected.

AppleTalk node ID — A unique 8-bit or 16-bit (if you are using extended networking, in which a network can have multiple addresses and support multiple zones) number that identifies a computer on an AppleTalk network.

AppleTalk zone — Logical groups of computers defined on an AppleTalk network.

Application layer — The seventh layer of the OSI Model. The Application layer provides interfaces to the software that enable programs to use network services.

application programming interface (API) — A routine (or set of instructions) that allows a program to interact with the operating system. APIs belong to the Application layer of the OSI Model.

application switch — Another term for a Layer 3 or Layer 4 switch.

ARP table — The database that lists MAC addresses and their associated IP addresses used for ARP queries.

array — A group of hard disks.

asset management — A system for collecting and storing data on the quantity and types of software and hardware assets in an organization's network.

asymmetric encryption — A type of encryption (such as public key encryption) that uses a different key for encoding data than is used for decoding the cipher text.

asymmetric multiprocessing — A multiprocessing method that assigns each subtask to a specific processor.

asymmetrical — The characteristic of a transmission technology that affords greater bandwidth in one direction (either from the customer to the carrier, or vice versa) than in the other direction.

asymmetrical DSL — A variation of DSL that offers more throughput when data travels downstream—downloading from a local carrier's POP to the customer—than when it travels upstream—uploading from the customer to the local carrier's POP.

asynchronous — A transmission method in which data being transmitted and received by nodes do not have to conform to any timing scheme. In asynchronous communications, a node can transmit at any time and the destination node must accept the transmission as it comes.

Asynchronous Transfer Mode (ATM) — A technology originally conceived in 1983 at Bell Labs, but standardized only in the mid-1990s. It relies on a fixed packet size to achieve data transfer rates up to 9953 Mbps. The fixed packet consists of 48 bytes of data plus a 5-byte header. The fixed packet size allows ATM to provide predictable traffic patterns and better control over bandwidth utilization.

attenuate — To lose signal strength as a transmission travels farther away from its source.

attenuation — A signal's loss of strength as it travels farther from its source.

attribute — A variable property associated with a network object. For example, a restriction on the time of day a user can log on is an attribute associated with that user object.

AUI (Attachment Unit Interface) — An Ethernet standard for connecting coaxial cables with transceivers and networked nodes.

authentication — The process whereby a network operating system verifies that a client's user name and password are valid and allows the client to log onto the network.

authentication header (AH) — In the context of IPSec, a type of encryption that provides authentication of the IP packet's data payload through public key techniques.

authentication service (AS) — In Kerberos terminology, the process that runs on a key distribution center (KDC) to initially validate a client who's logging in. The authentication service issues session keys to the client and the service the client wants to access.

authenticator — In Kerberos authentication, the user's timestamp encrypted with the session key. The authenticator is used to help the service verify that a user's ticket is valid.

autosense — A feature of modern NICs that enables a NIC to automatically sense what types of frames are running on a network and set itself to that specification.

availability — How consistently and reliably a file, device, or connection can be accessed by authorized personnel.

B channel — In ISDN, the "bearer" channel, so named because it bears traffic from point to point.

backbone — The cabling or part of a network that connects separate LAN segments. Backbone wiring provides interconnection between telecommunications closets, equipment rooms, and entrance facilities.

backleveling — The process of reverting to a previous version of a software program after attempting to upgrade it.

back up — A copy of data or program files created for archiving or safekeeping purposes.

backup — The process of copying critical data files to a secure storage area. Often backups are performed according to a formulaic schedule.

backup rotation scheme — A plan for when and how often backups occur, and which backups are full, incremental, or differential.

bandwidth — A measure of the difference between the highest and lowest frequencies that a medium can transmit.

bandwidth overhead — The burden placed on the underlying network to support a routing protocol.

base I/O port — A setting that specifies, in hexadecimal notation, which area of memory will act as a channel for moving data between the network adapter and the CPU. Like its IRQ, a device's base I/O port cannot be used by any other device.

baseband — A form of transmission in which digital signals are sent through direct current pulses applied to the wire. This direct current requires exclusive use of the wire's capacity, so baseband systems can transmit only one signal, or one channel, at a time. Every device on a baseband system shares a single channel.

baseline — A record of how well the network operates under normal conditions (including its performance, collision rate, utilization rate, and so on). Baselines are used for comparison when conditions change.

baselining — The practice of measuring and recording a network's current state of operation.

bend radius — The radius of the maximum arc into which you can loop a cable before you will cause data transmission errors. Generally, a twisted-pair cable's bend radius is equal to or greater than four times the diameter of the cable.

best path — The most efficient route from one node on a network to another. Under optimal network conditions, the best path is the most direct path between two points.

binary — A system founded on using 1s and 0s to encode information.

binding — The process of assigning one network component to work with another.

bio-recognition access — A method of authentication in which a device scans an individual's unique physical characteristics (such as the color patterns in his or her eye's iris or the geometry of his or her hand) to verify the user's identity.

BIOS (basic input/output system) — Firmware attached to the system board that controls the computer's communication with its devices, among other things.

bit — Short for binary digit. A bit equals a single pulse in the digital encoding system. It may have only one of two values: 0 or 1.

blackout — A complete power loss.

block — A unit of disk space and the smallest unit of disk space that can be controlled by the NetWare system. Smaller blocks require more server memory.

block ID — The first set of six characters that make up the MAC address and that are unique to a particular vendor.

block suballocation — A NetWare technique for using hard disk space more efficiently. Files that don't fit neatly into a whole number of blocks can take up fractions of blocks, leaving the remaining fractions free for use by other data.

BNC barrel connector — A connector used on Thinnet networks with two open ends used to connect two Thinnet coaxial cables.

BNC T-connector — A connector used on Thinnet networks with three open ends. It attaches to the Ethernet interface card at the base of the "T" and to the Thinnet cable at its two sides so as to allow the signal in and out of the NIC.

bonding — The process of combining more than one bearer channel of an ISDN line to increase throughput. For example, BRI's two 64-Kbps B channels are bonded to create an effective throughput of 128 Kbps.

boot sector virus — A virus that resides on the boot sector of a floppy disk and is transferred to the partition sector or the DOS boot sector on a hard disk. A boot sector virus can move from a floppy to a hard disk only if the floppy disk is left in the drive when the machine starts up.

Bootstrap Protocol (BOOTP) — A service that simplifies IP address management. BOOTP maintains a central list of IP addresses and their associated devices' MAC addresses, and assigns IP addresses to clients when they request it.

Border Gateway Protocol (BGP) — The routing protocol of Internet backbones. The router stress created by Internet growth has driven the development of BGP, the most complex of the routing protocols. The developers of BGP had to contend with the prospect of 100,000 routes as well as the goal of routing traffic efficiently and fairly through the hundreds of Internet backbones.

braiding — A braided metal shielding used to insulate some types of coaxial cable.

BRI (Basic Rate Interface) — A variety of ISDN that uses two 64-Kbps bearer channels and one 16-Kbps data channel, as summarized by the following notation: 2B + D. BRI is the most common form of ISDN employed by home users.

bridge — A connectivity device that operates at the Data Link layer of the OSI Model and reads header information to forward packets according to their MAC addresses. Bridges use a filtering database to determine which packets to discard and which to forward. Bridges contain one input and one output port and separate network segments.

bridge router (brouter) — A router capable of providing Layer 2 bridging functions.

broadband — 1) A form of transmission in which signals are modulated as radiofrequency analog pulses with different frequency ranges. Unlike baseband, broadband technology does not involve binary encoding. The use of multiple frequencies enables a broadband system to operate over several channels and therefore carry much more data than a baseband system. 2) A group of network connection types or transmission technologies that are generally capable of exceeding 1.544 Mbps throughput. Examples of broadband include DSL and SONET.

broadcast — A transmission that involves one transmitter and multiple receivers.

broadcast domain — In a virtual local area network (VLAN), a combination of ports that make up a Layer 2 segment and must be connected by a Layer 3 device, such as a router or Layer 3 switch.

brouter — See *bridge router*.

brownout — A momentary decrease in voltage, also known as a *sag*. An overtaxed electrical system may cause brownouts, recognizable as a dimming of the lights.

browser — Software that provides clients with a simple, graphical interface to the Web.

BSD (Berkeley Software Distribution) — A UNIX distribution that originated at the University of California at Berkeley. The BSD suffix differentiates these distributions from AT&T distributions. No longer being developed at Berkeley, the last public release of BSD UNIX was version 4.4.

bug — A flaw in software or hardware that causes it to malfunction.

bus — 1) The single cable connecting all devices in a bus topology. 2) The type of circuit used by the system board to transmit data to components. Most new Pentium computers use buses capable of exchanging 32 or 64 bits of data. As the number of bits of data a bus handles increases, so too does the speed of the device attached to the bus.

bus topology — A topology in which a single cable connects all nodes on a network without intervening connectivity devices.

byte — Eight bits of information. In a digital signaling system, broadly speaking, one byte carries one piece of information.

cable checker — A simple handheld device that determines whether cabling can provide connectivity. To accomplish this task, a cable checker applies a small voltage to each conductor at one end of the cable, then checks whether that voltage is detectable at the other end. It may also verify that voltage cannot be detected on other conductors in the cable.

cable drop — Fiber-optic or coaxial cable that connects a neighborhood cable node to a customer's house.

cable modem — A device that modulates and demodulates signals for transmission and reception via cable wiring.

cable plant — The hardware that constitutes the enterprise-wide cabling system.

cable tester — A handheld device that not only checks for cable continuity, but also ensures that the cable length is not excessive, measures the distance to a cable fault, measures attenuation along a cable, measures near-end crosstalk between wires, measures termination resistance and impedance for Thinnet cabling, issues pass/fail ratings for wiring standards, and stores and prints cable testing results.

caching — The process of saving frequently used data to an area of the physical memory so that it becomes more readily available for future requests. Caching accelerates the process of accessing the server because the operating system no longer needs to search for the requested data on the disk.

call tracking system — A software program used to document problems (also known as help desk software). Examples of popular call tracking systems include Clientele, Expert Advisor, Professional Help Desk, Remedy, and Vantive.

capacity — See *throughput*.

Carrier Sense Multiple Access/Collision Avoidance (CSMA/CA) — A network access method used on LocalTalk networks in which nodes on a shared communication channel signal their intent to transmit data before doing so, thus avoiding collisions.

Carrier Sense Multiple Access/Collision Detection (CSMA/CD) — Rules for communication used by shared Ethernet networks. In CSMA/CD each node waits its turn before transmitting data, to avoid interfering with other nodes' transmissions.

CAT — Abbreviation for the word "category" when describing a type of twisted-pair cable. For example, Category 3 unsheilded twisted-pair cable may also be called CAT3. See *Category 1, Category 2, Category 3, Category 4, Category 5, Enhanced Category 5, Category 6,* and *Category 7.*

Category 1 (CAT1) — A form of UTP that contains two wire pairs. CAT1 is suitable for voice communications, but not for data. At most, it can carry only 128 Kbps of data.

Category 2 (CAT2) — A form of UTP that contains four wire pairs and can carry up to 4 Mbps of data. CAT2 is rarely found on modern networks, because most require higher throughput.

Category 3 (CAT3) — A form of UTP that contains four wire pairs and can carry up to 10-Mbps, with a possible bandwidth of 16 MHz. CAT3 has typically been used for 10-Mbps Ethernet or 4-Mbps Token Ring networks. Network administrators are gradually replacing CAT3 cabling with CAT5 to accommodate.higher throughput. CAT3 is less expensive than CAT5.

Category 4 (CAT4) — A form of UTP that contains four wire pairs and can support up to 16-Mbps throughput. CAT4 may be used for 16-Mbps Token Ring or 10-Mbps Ethernet networks. It is guaranteed for data transmission up to 20 MHz and provides more protection against crosstalk and attenuation than CAT1, CAT2, or CAT3.

Category 5 (CAT5) — The most popular form of UTP for new network installations and upgrades to Fast Ethernet. CAT5 contains four wire pairs and supports up to 100-Mbps throughput and a 100 MHz signal rate. In addition to 100-Mbps Ethernet, CAT5 wiring can support other fast networking technologies, such as Asynchronous Transfer Mode (ATM) and Fiber Distributed Data Interface (FDDI).

Category 5 enhanced (CAT5e) — See *enhanced Category 5.*

Category 6 (CAT6) — A twisted-pair cable that contains four wire pairs, each wrapped in foil insulation. Additional foil insulation covers the bundle of wire pairs, and a fire-resistant plastic sheath covers the second foil layer. The foil insulation provides excellent resistance to crosstalk and enables CAT6 to support at least six times the throughput supported by regular CAT5.

Category 7 (CAT7) — A twisted-pair cable that contains multiple wire pairs, each separately shielded then surrounded by another layer of shielding within the jacket. CAT7 can support up to a 1-GHz signal rate. But because of its extra layers, it is less flexible than other forms of twisted-pair wiring.

CD-ROM File System (CDFS) — The read-only file system used to access resources on a CD. Windows 2000 supports this file system to allow CD-ROM file sharing.

cell — A packet of a fixed size. In ATM technology, a cell consists of 48 bytes of data plus a 5-byte header.

certification — The process of mastering material pertaining to a particular hardware system, operating system, programming language, or other software program, then proving your mastery by passing a series of exams.

Certified NetWare Engineer (CNE) — Professional certification established by Novell that demonstrates an in-depth understanding of Novell's networking software, including NetWare.

change management system — A process or program that provides support personnel with a centralized means of documenting changes made to the network. In smaller organizations, a change management system may be as simple as one document on the network to which networking personnel continually add entries to mark their changes. In larger organizations, it may consist of a database package complete with graphical interfaces and customizable fields tailored to the particular computing environment.

channel — A distinct communication path between two or more nodes, much like a lane is a distinct transportation path on a freeway. Channels may be separated either logically (as in multiplexing) or physically (as when they are carried by separate wires).

child domain — A domain found beneath another domain in a Windows 2000 domain tree.

cipher text — The unique data block that results when an original piece of data (such as text) is encrypted (for example, by using a key).

CIR (committed information rate) — The guaranteed minimum amount of bandwidth selected when leasing a frame relay circuit. Frame relay costs are partially based on CIR.

circuit switching — A type of switching in which a connection is established between two network nodes before they begin transmitting data. Bandwidth is dedicated to this connection and remains available until users terminate the communication between the two nodes.

cladding — The glass shield around the fiber core of a fiber-optic cable. Cladding acts as a mirror, reflecting light back to the core in patterns that vary depending on the transmission mode. This reflection allows fiber to bend around corners without impairing the light-based signal.

class — A type of object recognized by an NOS directory and defined in an NOS schema. Printers and users are examples of object classes.

client — A computer on the network that requests resources or services from another computer on a network. In some cases, a client could also act as a server. The term "client" may also refer to the user of a client workstation.

Client Services for NetWare (CSNW) — A Microsoft program that can be installed on Windows 2000 clients to enable them to access NetWare servers and make full use of the NetWare Directory System (NDS), its objects, files, directories, and permissions.

client/server architecture — The model of networking in which clients (typically desktop PCs) use a central server to share data, data storage space, and devices.

client/server network — A network based on the client/server architecture.

client_hello — In the context of SSL encryption, a message issued from the client to the server that contains information about what level of security the client's browser is capable of accepting and what type of encryption the client's browser can decipher (for example, RSA or Diffie-Hellman). The client_hello message also establishes a randomly generated number that uniquely identifies the client plus another number that identifies the SSL session.

clustering — See *server clustering.*

CMOS (complementary metal oxide semiconductor) — Firmware on a PC's system board that enables you to change its devices' configurations.

coaxial cable — A type of cable that consists of a central copper core surrounded by an insulator, a braided metal shielding, called braiding, and an outer cover, called the sheath or jacket. Coaxial cable, called "coax" for short, was the foundation for Ethernet networks in the 1980s and remained a popular transmission medium for many years.

collapsed backbone — A type of enterprise-wide backbone in which a router or switch acts as the single central connection point for multiple subnetworks.

collision — In Ethernet networks, the interference of one network node's data transmission with another network node's data transmission.

collision domain — A portion of a LAN encompassing devices that may cause and detect data collisions during transmission. Bridges and switches can logically define the boundaries of a collision domain.

command interpreter — A (usually text-based) program that accepts and executes system programs and applications on behalf of users. Often it includes the ability to execute a series of instructions that are stored in a file.

communications server — A server that runs communications services such as Windows NT's RAS or NetWare's NAS, also known as an access server or remote access server.

CompTIA — See *Computing Technology Industry Association.*

Computing Technology Industry Association (CompTIA) — An association of computer resellers, manufacturers, and training companies that sets industry-wide standards for computer professionals. CompTIA established and sponsors the A+ and Network+ (Net+) certifications.

conduit — Pipeline used to contain and protect the cabling. Conduit is usually made from metal.

connection-oriented — A feature of some protocols that requires the establishment of a connection between communicating nodes before the protocol will transmit data.

connectionless — A feature of some protocols that allows the protocol to service a request without requiring a verified session and without guaranteeing delivery of data.

connectors — The pieces of hardware that connect the wire to the network device, be it a file server, workstation, switch, or printer.

container — A logical receptacle for holding like objects in an NOS directory. Containers form the branches of the directory tree.

container objects — See *container.*

context — A kind of road map for finding an object in an NDS tree. A context is made up of an object's organizational unit names, arranged from most specific to most general, plus the organization name. Periods separate the organizational unit names in context.

contingency planning — The process of identifying steps that will minimize the risk of unforeseen circumstances endangering the quality or timeliness of the project's goals.

Controlled Access Unit (CAU) — A connectivity device used on a Token Ring network. In addition to passing data between nodes, a CAU provides more flexibility and easier management of connected nodes than a MAU.

convergence — The use of networks to carry data, plus video and voice signals.

convergence time — The time it takes for a router to recognize a best path in the event of a change or network outage.

core — The central component of a fiber-optic cable, consisting of one or several pure glass fibers.

core gateways — Gateways that make up the Internet backbone. The Internet Network Operations Center (INOC) operates core gateways.

cracker — A person who uses his or her knowledge of operating systems and utilities to intentionally damage or destroy data or systems.

crossover cable — A twisted-pair patch cable in which the termination locations of the transmit and receive wires on one end of the cable are reversed.

crosstalk — A type of interference caused by signals traveling on nearby wire pairs infringing on another pair's signal.

CSU (channel service unit) — A device used with T-carrier technology that provides termination for the digital signal and ensures connection integrity through error correction and line monitoring.

CSU/DSU — A combination of a CSU (channel service unit) and a DSU (data service unit) that serves as the connection point for a T1 line at the customer's site.

cut-through mode — A switching mode in which a switch reads a frame's header and decides where to forward the data before it receives the entire packet. Cut-through mode is faster, but less accurate, than the other switching method, store and forward mode.

Cyclic Redundancy Check (CRC) — An algorithm used to verify the accuracy of data contained in a data frame.

D channel — In ISDN, the "data" channel used to carry information about the call, such as session initiation and termination signals, caller identity, call forwarding, and conference calling signals.

daisy chain — A linked series of devices.

data encryption standard (DES) — A popular private key encryption technique that was developed by IBM in the 1970s.

Data Link layer — The second layer in the OSI Model. The Data Link layer bridges the networking media with the Network layer. Its primary function is to divide the data it receives from the Network layer into frames that can then be transmitted by the Physical layer.

Data Link layer address — See *MAC address*.

data packet — A discreet unit of information sent from one computer on a network to another.

data propagation delay — The length of time data take to travel from one point on the segment to another point. On Ethernet networks, CSMA/CD's collision detection routine cannot operate accurately if the data propagation delay is too long.

daughter board — See *expansion board*.

daughter card — See *expansion board*.

DB-15 — A general term for connectors that use 15 metal pins to complete a connection between devices. "DB" stands for Data bus, while the number "15" indicates how many pins are used to make the connection.

DB-9 connector — A connector containing nine pins that is used on STP-based Token Ring networks.

dedicated circuit — A continuously available link between two access points that is leased from a communications provider, such as an ISP or telephone company.

default gateway — The gateway that first interprets a device's outbound requests, and then interprets its inbound requests to and from other subnets. In the postal service analogy, the default gateway is similar to a local post office.

demand priority — A method for data transmission used by 100BaseVG Ethernet networks. Each device on a star or hierarchical network sends a request to transmit to the central hub, which grants the requests one at a time. The hub examines incoming data packets, determines the destination node, and forwards the packets to that destination. Because demand priority runs on a star topology, no workstations except the source and destination can "see" the data. Data travel from one device to the hub, then to another device.

demultiplexer (demux) — A device that separates multiplexed signals once they are received and regenerates them in their original form.

denial-of-service attack — A security attack caused by a deluge of traffic that disables the victimized system.

device driver — Software that enables an attached device to communicate with the computer's operating system.

device ID — The second set of six characters that make up a network device's MAC address. The Device ID, which is added at the factory, is based on the device's model and manufacture date.

dial-up — A type of connection that uses modems at the transmitting and receiving ends and PSTN or other lines to access a network.

dial-up networking — The process of dialing into a LAN's access server or into an ISP. Dial-up Networking is also the name of the utility that Microsoft provides with its operating systems to achieve this type of connectivity.

differential backup — A backup method in which only data that have changed since the last backup are copied to a storage medium, and that information is marked for subsequent backup, regardless of whether it has changed.

digital — As opposed to analog signals, digital signals are composed of pulses that can have a value of only 1 or 0.

digital certificate — A password-protected and encrypted file that holds an individual's identification information, including a public key and a private key. The individual's public key is used to verify the sender's digital signature, and the private key allows the individual to log onto a third-party authority who administers digital certificates.

DIP (dual inline package) switch — A small plastic toggle switch on a circuit board that can be flipped to indicate either an "on" or "off" status, which translates into a parameter setting.

direct infrared transmission — A type of infrared transmission that depends on the transmitter and receiver being within the line of sight of each other.

directory — In general, a listing that organizes resources and correlates them with their properties. In the context of network operating systems, a method for organizing and managing objects.

Directory Services Migration Tool (DSMIGRATE) — A tool provided with Windows 2000 Server that enables network administrators to migrate accounts, files, and permissions from a NetWare NDS directory to the Windows 2000 Active Server Directory.

disaster recovery — The process of restoring critical functionality and data to a network after an enterprise-wide outage that affects more than a single system or a limited group of users.

disk mirroring — A RAID technique in which data from one disk are automatically copied to another disk as the information is written.

disk striping — A simple implementation of RAID in which data are written in 64 KB blocks equally across all disks in the array.

diskless workstations — Workstations that do not contain hard disks, but instead rely on a small amount of read-only memory to connect to a network and to pick up their system files.

distinguished name (DN) — A long form of an object's name in Active Directory that explicitly indicates the object name, plus the names of its containers and domains. A distinguished name includes a domain component (DC), organizational unit (OU), and common name (CN). A client uses the distinguished name to access a particular object, such as a printer.

distributed backbone — A type of enterprise-wide backbone that consists of a number of hubs connected to a series of central hubs or routers in a hierarchy.

DIX (Digital, Intel, and Xerox) — A type of AUI connector used on Thicknet networks.

domain — (1) A group of networked devices that share a symbolic name according to Internet standards. For example, workstations used in the Whitehouse share the whitehouse.gov domain name. (2) In the context of Windows NT and Windows 2000 networking, a group of users, servers, and other resources that share account and security policies.

domain account — A type of user account on a Windows 2000 network that has privileges to resources across the domain onto which it is logged.

domain controller — A Windows 2000 server that contains a replica of the Active Directory database.

domain local group — A group on a Windows 2000 network that allows members of one domain to access resources within that domain only.

domain name — The symbolic name that identifies a domain and identifies a group of network nodes. Usually, a domain name is associated with a company or other type of organization, such as a university or military unit.

Domain Name System (DNS) — A hierarchical way of tracking domain names and their addresses, devised in the mid-1980s. The DNS database does not rely on one file or even one server, but rather is distributed over several key computers across the Internet to prevent catastrophic failure if one or a few computers go down. DNS is a TCP/IP service that belongs to the Application layer of the OSI Model.

domain tree — A group of hierarchically arranged domains that share a common namespace in the Windows 2000 Active Directory.

doskey — A command used on MS-DOS and Windows systems that enables the user to recall (using the keyboard's arrow keys) and edit previously entered commands.

dotted decimal notation — The shorthand convention used to represent IP addresses and make them more easily readable by humans. In dotted decimal notation, a decimal number between 1 and 254 represents each binary octet. A period, or dot, separates each decimal.

downstream — A term used to describe data traffic that flows from a local carrier's POP to the customer. In asymmetrical communications, downstream throughput is usually much higher than upstream throughput. In symmetrical communications, downstream and upstream throughputs are equal.

drop cable — The cable that connects a device's Ethernet interface to a transceiver in a Thicknet network.

0 (digital signal, level 0) — The equivalent of one data or voice channel in T-carrier technology, as defined by ANSI physical layer standards. All other signal levels are multiples of DS0.

SL (digital subscriber line) — A dedicated remote connectivity or WAN technology that uses advanced data modulation techniques to achieve extraordinary throughput over regular phone lines. DSL currently comes in seven different varieties, the most common of which is Asymmetric DSL (ADSL).

SL access multiplexer (DSLAM) — A connectivity device located at a carrier's office that aggregates multiple DSL subscriber lines and connects them to a larger carrier or to the Internet backbone.

SL modem — A device that demodulates an incoming DSL signal, extracting the information and passing it on to the data equipment (such as telephones and computers) and modulates an outgoing DSL signal.

SU (data service unit) — A device used in T-carrier technology that converts the digital signal used by bridges, routers, and multiplexers into the digital signal used on cabling. Typically, a DSU is combined with a CSU in a single box, a CSU/DSU.

uplex — See *full-duplex*.

ynamic IP address — An IP address that is assigned to a device through DHCP and may change when the DHCP lease expires or is terminated.

ynamic ARP table entry — A record (of an IP address and its associated MAC address) created in an ARP table when a client makes an ARP request that cannot be satisfied by data already in the ARP table.

ynamic Host Configuration Protocol (DHCP) — An application layer protocol in the TCP/IP suite that manages the dynamic distribution of IP addresses on a network. Using DHCP to assign IP addresses reduces the effort required to assign addresses and helps prevent duplicate-addressing problems.

ynamic routing — A method of routing that automatically calculates the best path between two nodes and accumulates this information in a routing table. If congestion or failures affect the network, a router using dynamic routing can detect the problems and reroute data through a different path. Most modern networks primarily use dynamic routing.

-commerce — A means of conducting business over the Web — be it in retailing, banking, stock trading, consulting, or training. Any buying and selling of products or services that occurs over the Internet belongs in the e-commerce category.

cho reply — The response signal sent by a device after another device pings it.

cho request — The request for a response generated when one device pings another device on the network.

EIA (Electronic Industries Alliance) — A trade organization composed of representatives from electronics manufacturing firms across the United States.

electrically erasable programmable read-only memory (EEPROM) — A type of ROM that is found on a circuit board and whose configuration information can be erased and rewritten through electrical pulses.

electromagnetic interference (EMI) — A type of interference that may be caused by motors, power lines, televisions, copiers, fluorescent lights, or other sources of electrical activity.

encapsulation security payload (ESP) — In the context of IPSec, a type of encryption that provides authentication of the IP packet's data payload through public key techniques. In addition, ESP also encrypts the entire IP packet for added security.

encrypted virus — A virus that is encrypted to prevent detection.

encryption — The use of an algorithm to scramble data into a format that can be read only by reversing the algorithm—decrypting the data—to keep the information private. The most popular kind of encryption algorithm weaves a key into the original data's bits, sometimes several times in different sequences, to generate a unique data block.

enhanced CAT5 (CAT5e) — A higher-grade version of CAT5 wiring that contains high-quality copper, offers a high twist ratio, and uses advanced methods for reducing crosstalk. Enhanced CAT5 can support a signaling rate of up to 200 MHz, double the capability of regular CAT5.

Enhanced Interior Gateway Routing Protocol (EIGRP) — A routing protocol developed in the mid-1980s by Cisco Systems that has a fast convergence time and a low network overhead, but is easier to configure and less CPU-intensive than OSPF. EIGRP also offers the benefits of supporting multiple protocols and limiting unnecessary network traffic between routers.

enterprise — An entire organization, including local and remote offices, a mixture of computer systems, and a number of departments. Enterprise-wide computing takes into account the breadth and diversity of a large organization's computer needs.

enterprise-wide network — A network that spans an entire organization and often services the needs of many diverse users. It may include many locations (as a WAN), or it may be confined to one location but include many different departments, floors, and network segments.

Ethernet — A networking technology originally developed at Xerox in 1970 and improved by Digital Equipment Corporation, Intel, and Xerox. Today, four types of Ethernet technology are used on LANs, with each type being governed by a set of IEEE standards.

Ethernet 802.2 frame — See *IEEE 802.3 frame*.

Ethernet 802.3 frame — See *Novell proprietary 802.3 frame*.

Ethernet II frame —The original Ethernet frame type developed by Digital, Intel, and Xerox, before the IEEE began to standardize Ethernet. Ethernet II lacks Logical Link Control layer information but contains a 2-byte type field to identify the upper-layer protocol contained in the frame. It supports TCP/IP, AppleTalk, IPX/SPX, and other higher layer protocols.

expansion board — A circuit board used to connect a device to a computer's system board.

expansion card — See *expansion board*.

expansion slots — Openings on a computer's system board that contain multiple electrical contacts into which the expansion board can be inserted.

explicit one-way trust — A type of trust relationship in which two domains that belong to different NOS directory trees are configured to trust each other.

extended attributes — Attributes beyond the basic Read, Write, System Hidden, and Archive attrevutes supported by FAT. HPFS supports extended attributes.

Extended Industry Standard Architecture (EISA) — A 32-bit bus that is compatible with older ISA devices (because it shares the same length and pin configuration as the ISA bus), but that uses an extra layer of pins (resulting in a deeper, two-layered slot connector) for a second 16 bits to achieve faster throughput. The EISA bus was introduced in the late 1980s to compete with IBM's MCA bus.

extended network prefix — The combination of an address's network and subnet information. By interpreting an address's extended network prefix, a device can determine the subnet to which an address belongs.

external network number — Another term for the network address portion of an IPX/SPX address.

fail-over — The capability for one component (such as a NIC or server) to assume another component's responsibilities without manual intervention.

failure — A deviation from a specified level of system performance for a given period of time. A failure occurs when something doesn't work as promised or as planned.

Fast Ethernet — A type of Ethernet network that is capable of 100-Mbps throughput. 100BaseT and 100BaseFX are both examples of Fast Ethernet.

FAT32 (32-bit File Allocation Table) — An enhanced version of FAT that accommodates the use of long filenames and smaller allocation units on a disk. FAT32 makes more efficient use of disk space than the original FAT and is therefore faster and can handle larger files.

FAT16 (16-bit File Allocation Table) — A file system designed for use with early DOS- and Windows-based computers that allocates file system space in 16-bit units. Compared to FAT32, FAT16 is less desirable because of its partition size, file naming, fragmentation, speed, and security limitations.

fault — The malfunction of one component of a system. A fault can result in a failure.

fault tolerance — The capacity for a system to continue performing despite an unexpected hardware or software malfunction.

feasibility study — A study that determines the costs and benefits of a project and attempts to predict whether the project will result in a favorable outcome (for example, whether it will achieve its goal without imposing excessive cost or time burdens on the organization).

Federal Communications Commission (FCC) — The regulatory agency that sets standards and policy for telecommunications transmission and equipment in the United States.

Fiber Distributed Data Interface (FDDI) — A networking standard originally specified by ANSI in the mid-1980s and later refined by ISO. FDDI uses a dual fiber-optic ring to transmit data at speeds of 100 Mbps. It was commonly used as a backbone technology in the 1980s and early 1990s, but lost favor as fast Ethernet technologies emerged in the mid-1990s. FDDI provides excellent reliability and security.

fiber-optic cable — A form of cable that contains one or several glass fibers in its core. Data are transmitted via pulsing light sent from a laser or light-emitting diode through the central fiber (or fibers). Outside the central fiber, a layer of glass called cladding acts as a mirror, reflecting light back to the core in patterns that vary depending on the transmission mode. Outside the cladding, a plastic buffer protects the core and absorbs any light that might escape. Outside the buffer, strands of Kevlar provide further protection from stretching and damage. A plastic jacket surrounds the Kevlar strands.

fiber-optic modem (FOM) — A demultiplexer used on fiber networks that employ wave division multiplexing. The fiber-optic modem separates the multiplexed signals into individual signals according to their different wavelengths.

Fibre Channel — A distinct network transmission method that relies on fiber-optic media and its own, proprietary protocol. Fibre Channel is capable of 1-Gbps (and soon, 2-Gbps) throughput.

file server — A specialized server that enables clients to share applications and data across the network.

file services — The function of a file server that allows users to share data files, applications, and storage areas.

file system — An operating system's method of organizing, managing, and accessing its files through logical structures and software routines.

File Transfer Protocol (FTP) — An application layer protocol in the TCP/IP protocol suite that manages file transfers between TCP/IP hosts.

-infected virus — A virus that attaches itself to executable files. When the infected executable file runs, the virus copies itself to memory. Later, the virus will attach itself to other executable files.

ering database — A collection of data created and used by a bridge that correlates the MAC addresses of connected workstations with their locations. A filtering database is also known as a forwarding table.

ewall — A specialized device (typically a router, but possibly only a PC running special software) that selectively filters or blocks traffic between networks. A firewall may be strictly hardware-based, or it may involve a combination of hardware and software.

mware — A combination of hardware and software. The hardware component of firmware is a read-only memory (ROM) chip that stores data established at the factory and possibly changed by configuration programs that can write to ROM.

shing — A security attack in which an Internet user sends commands to another Internet user's machine that cause the screen to fill with garbage characters. A flashing attack will cause the user to terminate his or her session.

vor — Term used to refer to the different implementations of a particular UNIX-like system. For example, the different flavors of Linux include Red Hat, Caldera, and Mandrake.

w control — A method of gauging the appropriate rate of data transmission based on how fast the recipient can accept data.

rest — In the context of Windows 2000 Server, a collection of domain trees that use different namespaces. A forest allows for trust relationships to be established between trees.

ormat Prefix — A variable-length field at the beginning of an IPv6 address that indicates what type of address it is (for example, unicast, anycast, or multicast).

rwarding table — See *filtering database*.

x and hound — Another term for the combination of devices known as a tone generator and a tone locator. The tone locator is considered the hound because it follows the tone generator (the fox).

actional T1 — An arrangement that allows organizations to use only some channels on a T1 line and pay for only the channels actually used.

ame — A package for data that includes not only the raw data, or "payload," but also the sender's and receiver's network addresses and control information.

rame Check Sequence (FCS) — The field in a data frame responsible for ensuring that data carried by the frame arrives intact. FCS uses an algorithm, such as CRC, to accomplish this verification.

ame relay — An updated, digital version of X.25 that relies on packet switching. Because it is digital, frame relay supports higher bandwidth than X.25, offering a maximum of 45-Mbps

throughput. It provides the basis for much of the world's Internet connections. On network diagrams, the frame relay system is often depicted as a cloud.

FreeBSD — An open source software implementation of the Berkeley Software Distribution version of the UNIX system.

freely distributable — A term used to describe software with a very liberal copyright. Often associated with open source software.

frequency — The number of times that a signal's amplitude changes over a fixed period of time, expressed in cycles per second, or hertz (Hz).

frequency modulation (FM) — A method of data modulation in which the frequency of the carrier signal is modified by the application of the data signal.

full backup — A backup in which all data on all servers are copied to a storage medium, regardless of whether the data are new or changed.

full-duplex — A type of transmission in which signals may travel in both directions over a medium simultaneously. May also be called, simply, "duplex."

fully qualified domain name (FQDN) — In TCP/IP addressing, the combination of a host and domain name that together uniquely identify a device.

Gantt chart — A popular method of depicting when projects begin and end along a horizontal timeline.

gateway — A combination of networking hardware and software that connects two dissimilar types of networks. Gateways perform connectivity, session management, and data translation, so they must operate at multiple layers of the OSI Model.

Gateway Services for NetWare (GSNW) — A Windows 2000 service that acts as a translator between the Windows 2000 and NetWare client redirector services. With GSNW installed, a Windows 2000 server can access files and other shared resources on any NetWare server on a network.

General Public License — The copyright that applies to freely distributable versions of UNIX and specifies that the source code must be made available to anyone receiving the system.

ghosts — Frames that are not actually data frames, but rather aberrations caused by a repeater misinterpreting stray voltage on the wire. Unlike true data frames, ghosts have no starting delimiter.

giants — Packets that exceed the medium's maximum packet size. For example, any Ethernet packet that is larger than 1518 bytes is considered a giant.

global group — A group on a Windows 2000 network that allows members of one domain to access resources within that domain as well as resources from other domains in the same forest.

globally unique identifier (GUID) — A 128-bit number generated and assigned to an object upon its creation in the Windows 2000 Active Directory. Network applications and services use an object's GUID to communicate with it.

globbing — A form of filename substitution, similar to the use of wildcards in Windows and DOS.

GNU — The name given to the free software project to implement a complete source code implementation of UNIX, the collection of UNIX-inspired utilities and tools that are included with Linux distributions and other free software UNIX systems. The acronym within an acronym stands for "GNUs Not UNIX."

gopher — A text-based utility that allows you to navigate through a series of menus to find and read specific files.

grandfather-father-son — A backup rotation scheme that uses daily (son), weekly (father), and monthly (grandfather) backup sets.

graphical user interface (GUI) — A pictorial representation of computer functions and elements that, in the case of network operating systems, enables administrators to more easily manage files, users, groups, security, printers, and other issues.

group — A means of collectively managing users' permissions and restrictions applied to shared resources. Groups form the basis for resource and account management for every type of network operating system, not just Windows 2000 Server. Many network administrators create groups according to department or, even more specifically, according to job function within a department.

Guest — A user account with very limited privileges that is created during the installation of a network operating system.

hacker — A person who masters the inner workings of operating systems and utilities in an effort to better understand them. A hacker is distinguished from a cracker in that a cracker will attempt to exploit a network's vulnerabilities for malicious purposes.

half-duplex — A type of transmission in which signals may travel in both directions over a medium, but in only one direction at a time.

handshake protocol — One of several protocols within SSL, and perhaps the most significant. As its name implies, the handshake protocol allows the client and server to authenticate (or introduce) each other and establishes terms for how they will securely exchange data during an SSL session.

hard disk redundancy — See *Redundant Array of Inexpensive Disks (RAID)*.

Hardware Compatibility List (HCL) — A list of computer components proven to be compatible with Windows 2000 Server. The HCL appears on the same CD as your Windows 2000 Server software and on Microsoft's Web site.

head-end — A cable company's central office, which connects cable wiring to many nodes before it reaches customers' sites.

hertz (Hz) — A measure of frequency equivalent to the number of amplitude cycles per second.

heuristic scanning — A type of virus scanning that attempts to identify viruses by discovering "virus-like" behavior.

hierarchical file system — The organization of files and directories (or folders) on a disk partition in which directories may contain files and other directories. When displayed graphically, this organization resembles a tree-like structure.

hierarchical hybrid topology — A network topology in which devices are divided into separate layers according to their priority or function.

High-Performance File System (HPFS) — A file system designed for IBM's OS/2 operating system that offers greater efficiency and reliability than does FAT. HPFS is rarely used but can be supported by Windows 2000 servers.

High-Speed Token Ring (HSTR) — A standard for Token Ring networks that operate at 100 Mbps.

hop — A term used to describe each trip data take from one connectivity device to another.

host — 1) A computer connected to a network that uses the TCP/IP protocol. 2) A type of computer that enables resource sharing by other computers on the same network.

host file — A text file that associates TCP/IP host names with IP addresses. On Windows 9x, NT, and 2000 platforms, the host file is called "lmhosts." On UNIX platforms the file is called "hosts" and is located in the /etc directory.

host name — A symbolic name that describes a TCP/IP device.

hosts — Name of the DNS host file found on a UNIX computer. The hosts file is usually found in the /etc directory.

hot swappable — A characteristic that enables identical components to be interchanged (or swapped) while a machine is still running (hot). Once installed, hot swappable components automatically assume the functions of their counterpart if it suffers a fault.

HOWTO — A series of brief, highly focused documents giving Linux system details. The people responsible for the Linux Documentation Project centrally coordinate the HOWTO papers (see *www.linuxhq.com/ldp/howto/HOWTO-INDEX/howtos.html*).

HP-UX — Hewlett-Packard's proprietary implementation of the UNIX system.

HTTPS — The URL prefix that indicates that a Web page requires its data to be exchanged between client and server using SSL encryption. HTTPS uses the TCP port number 443, rather than port 80 (the port that normal HTTP uses).

hub — A multiport repeater containing multiple ports to interconnect multiple devices. Unless they are used on a peer-to-peer network, hubs also contain an uplink port, one port that connects to a network's backbone. Hubs regenerate digital signals.

rd — The kernel in the GNU operating system. While many UNIX and Linux systems include GNU utilities such as the EMACS editor or the GNU C compiler, the Hurd is the only operating system kernel that can currently be called a GNU kernel.

rid fiber-coax (HFC) — A link that consists of fiber cable connecting the cable company's offices to a node location near the customer and coaxial cable connecting the node to the customer's house. HFC upgrades to existing cable wiring are required before current TV cable systems can serve as WAN links.

rid topology — A complex combination of the simple physical topologies.

pertext Markup Language (HTML) — The language that defines formatting standards for Web documents.

pertext Transport Protocol (HTTP) — The language that Web clients and servers use to communicate. HTTP forms the backbone of the Web.

ode — A UNIX file system information storage area that holds all details about a file. This information includes the size, access rights, date and time of creation, and a pointer to the actual contents of the file.

A (Independent Computing Architecture) client — A remote access client developed by Citrix Systems, Inc. that enables remote users to use virtually any LAN application over any type of connection, public or private. The ICA client is especially well suited to slower connections, as it exchanges only keystrokes, mouse clicks, and screen updates with the server. The ICA client requires that Citrix's server software run on the access server."

EE (Institute of Electrical and Electronic Engineers) — An international society composed of engineering professionals. Its goals are to promote development and education in the electrical engineering and computer science fields.

EE 802.3 frame — A popular Ethernet frame type used on IPX/SPX networks. The defining characteristics of its data portion are the source and destination service access points that belong to the Logical Link Control layer, a sublayer of the Data Link layer. Also called LLC or, in Novell lingo, Ethernet 802.2.

EE 802.3 SNAP frame — A rarely used Ethernet frame type that is an adaptation of IEEE 802.3 and Ethernet II. SNAP stands for Sub-Network Access Protocol. The SNAP portion of the frame contains the three Logical Link Control fields (DSAP, SSAP, and Control). The Organization ID (OUI) field provides a method of identifying the type of network on which the frame is running. In addition, Ethernet SNAP frames carry Ethernet type information, just as an Ethernet II frame does.

onfig — A TCP/IP configuration and management utility used with UNIX systems (similar to the ipconfig utility used on Windows NT and 2000 systems).

incremental backup — A backup in which only data that have changed since the last backup are copied to a storage medium.

indirect infrared transmission — A type of infrared transmission in which signals bounce off walls, ceilings, and any other objects in their path. Because indirect infrared signals are not confined to a specific pathway, they are not very secure.

Industry Standard Architecture (ISA) — The original PC bus, developed in the early 1980s to support an 8-bit and later 16-bit data transfer capability. Although an older technology, ISA buses are still used to connect serial devices, such as mice or modems, in new PCs.

infrared — A type of data transmission in which infrared light signals are used to transmit data through space, similar to the way a television remote control sends signals across the room. Networks may use two types of infrared transmission: direct or indirect.

integrity — The soundness of a network's files, systems, and connections. To ensure integrity, you must protect your network from anything that might render it unusable, such as corruption, tampering, natural disasters, and viruses.

integrity checking — A method of comparing the current characteristics of files and disks against an archived version of these characteristics to discover any changes. The most common example of integrity checking involves a checksum.

intelligent hub — A hub that possesses processing capabilities and can therefore interpret and manage data traffic, rather than simply regenerating signals as a simple hub would do.

Internet — A complex WAN that connects LANs around the globe.

Internet Assigned Numbers Authority (IANA) — A nonprofit, U.S. government-funded group that was established at the University of Southern California and charged with managing IP address allocation and the domain name system. The oversight for many IANA's functions was given to ICANN in 1998; however, IANA continues to perform Internet addressing and domain name system administration.

Internet Control Message Protocol (ICMP) — A core protocol in the TCP/IP suite that notifies the sender that something has gone wrong in the transmission process and that packets were not delivered.

Internet Corporation for Assigned Names and Numbers (ICANN) — The non-profit corporation currently designated by the U.S. government to maintain and assign IP addresses.

Internet Key Exchange (IKE) — The first phase of IPSec authentication, which accomplishes key management. IKE is a service that runs on UDP port 500. Once IKE has established the rules for the type of keys two nodes will use, IPSec invokes its second phase, encryption.

Internet Mail Access Protocol (IMAP) — A mail storage and manipulation protocol that depends on SMTP's transport system and improves upon the shortcomings of POP. The most current version of IMAP is version 4 (IMAP4). IMAP4 can (and eventually will) replace POP without the user having to change e-mail programs. The single biggest advantage IMAP4 has relative to POP is that it allows users to store messages on the mail server, rather than always having to download them to the local machine.

Internet Protocol (IP) — A core protocol in the TCP/IP suite that belongs to the Internet layer of the TCP/IP model and provides information about how and where data should be delivered. IP is the subprotocol that enables TCP/IP to internetwork.

Internet services — Services that enable a network to communicate with the Internet, including World Wide Web servers and browsers, file transfer capabilities, Internet addressing schemes, security filters, and a means for directly logging on to other computers.

Internet telephony — The provision of telephone service over the Internet.

internetwork — To traverse more than one LAN segment and more than one type of network through a router.

Internetwork Packet Exchange (IPX) — A core protocol of the IPX/SPX suite that operates at the Network layer of the OSI Model and provides routing and internetwork services, similar to IP in the TCP/IP suite.

Internetwork Packet Exchange/Sequenced Packet Exchange (IPX/SPX) — A protocol originally developed by Xerox, then modified and adopted by Novell in the 1980s for the NetWare network operating system.

interrupt — A wire through which a device issues voltage, thereby signaling a request for the processor's attention.

interrupt request (IRQ) — A message sent to the computer that instructs it to stop what it is doing and pay attention to something else. IRQ is often used (informally) to refer to the interrupt request number.

interrupt request number (IRQ number) — The unique number assigned to each interrupt request in a computer. Interrupt request numbers range from 0 to 15, and many PC devices reserve specific numbers for their use alone.

IntraNetWare — Another term for NetWare version 4.11, the version in which support for Internet services was first introduced.

intrusion detection — The process of monitoring the network for unauthorized access to its devices.

IP address — A logical address used in TCP/IP networking. This unique 32-bit number is divided into four groups of octets, or 8-bit bytes, that are separated by periods.

IP datagram — The IP portion of a TCP/IP frame that acts as an envelope for data, holding information necessary for routers to transfer data between subnets.

IP next generation (IPng) — See *IP Version 6.*

IP Security Protocol (IPSec) — A Layer 3 protocol that defines encryption, authentication, and key management for TCP/IP transmissions. IPSec is an enhancement to IPv4 and native to IPv6. IPSec is unique among authentication methods in that it adds security information to the header of all IP packets.

IP spoofing — A security attack in which an outsider obtains internal IP addresses, then uses those addresses to pretend that he or she has authority to access a private network from the Internet.

IP version 6 (IPv6) — A new standard for IP addressing that will replace the current IP version 4 (IPv4). Most notably, IPv6 uses a newer, more efficient header in its packets and allows for 128-bit source and destination IP addresses. The use of longer addresses will allow for more total IP addresses to be in circulation.

ipconfig — The TCP/IP configuration and management utility for use with Windows NT or Windows 2000 systems.

IPX address — An address assigned to a device on an IPX/SPX network.

ISDN (Integrated Services Digital Network) — An international standard, established by the ITU, for transmitting data over digital lines. Like PSTN, ISDN uses the telephone carrier's lines and dial-up connections, but it differs from PSTN in that it exclusively uses digital lines and switches.

ISO (International Organization for Standardization) — A collection of standards organizations representing 130 countries with headquarters located in Geneva, Switzerland. Its goal is to establish international technological standards to facilitate the global exchange of information and barrier-free trade.

ITU (International Telecommunication Union) — A United Nations agency that regulates international telecommunications, including radio and TV frequencies, satellite and telephony specifications, networking infrastructure, and tariffs applied to global communication. It also provides developing countries with technical expertise and equipment to advance these nations' technological bases.

jabber — A device that handles electrical signals improperly, usually affecting the rest of the network. A network analyzer will detect a jabber as a device that is always retransmitting, effectively bringing the network to a halt. A jabber usually results from a bad NIC. Occasionally, it can be caused by outside electrical interference.

jamming — A part of CSMA/CD in which, upon detecting a collision, a station issues a special 32-bit sequence to indicate to all nodes on an Ethernet segment that its previously transmitted frame has suffered a collision and should be considered faulty.

nper — A small, removable piece of plastic that contains a metal receptacle that fits over a pair of pins on a circuit board to complete a circuit between those two pins. By moving the jumper from one set of pins to another set of pins, you can modify the board's circuit, thereby giving it different instructions on how to operate.

rberos — A cross-platform authentication protocol that uses key encryption to verify the identity of clients and to securely exchange information once a client logs onto a system. It is an example of a private key encryption service.

rnel — The core of an operating system, such as UNIX or NetWare. The kernel, which is loaded into memory as the computer starts, oversees all critical server processes.

rnel modules — Portions of the Linux kernel that you can load and unload to add or remove functionality on a running Linux system.

y — A series of characters that is combined with a block of data during that data's encryption. In order to decrypt the resulting data, the recipient must also possess the key.

y distribution center (KDC) — In Kerberos terminology, the server that runs the authentication service and the ticket granting service in order to issue keys and tickets to clients. On a Windows 2000 network, a user's domain controller serves as his KDC.

y management — The method whereby two nodes using key encryption agree on common parameters for the keys they will use in order to encrypt data.

y pair — The combination of a public and private key used to decipher data that has been encrypted using public key encryption.

AN — See *local area network*.

AN Emulation (LANE) — A method for transporting Token Ring or Ethernet frames over ATM networks. LANE encapsulates incoming Ethernet or Token Ring frames, then converts them into ATM cells for transmission over an ATM network.

AN topology — The physical layout, or pattern, of nodes on a local area network (LAN).

ANalyzer — Novell's network monitoring software package. LANalyzer can act as a standalone program on a Windows 9x or 2000 workstation or as part of the ManageWise suite of network management tools on a NetWare server. LANalyzer offers the following capabilities: discovery of all network nodes on a segment, continuous monitoring of network traffic, alarms that are tripped when traffic conditions meet preconfigured thresholds (for example, if usage exceeds 70%), and the capturing of traffic to and from all or selected nodes.

te collisions — Collisions that take place outside the normal window in which collisions are detected and redressed. Late collisions are usually caused by a defective station (such as a card, or transceiver) that is transmitting without first verifying line status or by failure to observe the configuration guidelines for cable length, which results in collisions being recognized too late.

latency — The delay between the transmission of a signal and its receipt.

layer — (1) In the context of hierarchical topologies, the division between one set of devices and another set of devices on a network; (2) A portion of the OSI Model that corresponds to specific processes involved in data communication between two computers.

Layer 2 Forwarding (L2F) — A Layer 2 protocol similar to PPTP that provides tunneling for other protocols and can work with the authentication methods used by PPP. L2F was developed by Cisco Systems and requires special hardware on the host system end. It can encapsulate protocols to fit more than just the IP format, unlike PPTP.

Layer 2 Tunneling Protocol (L2TP) — A Layer 2 tunneling protocol developed by a number of industry consortia. L2TP is an enhanced version of L2F. Like L2F, it supports multiple protocols; unlike L2F, it does not require costly hardware upgrades to implement. L2TP is optimized to work with the next generation of IP (IPv6) and IPSec (the Layer 3 IP encryption protocol).

Layer 3 switch — A switch capable of interpreting data at Layer 3 (Network layer) of the OSI Model.

Layer 4 switch — A switch capable of interpreting data at Layer 4 (Transport layer) of the OSI Model.

lease — The agreement between a DHCP server and client on how long the client will borrow a DHCP-assigned IP address. As network administrator, you configure the duration of the lease (in the DHCP service) to be as short or long as necessary, from a matter of minutes to forever.

leased lines — Permanent dedicated connections established through a public telecommunications carrier and billed to customers on a monthly basis.

license tracking — Determining how many copies of a single application are currently in use on the network.

Lightweight Directory Access Protocol (LDAP) — A standard protocol for accessing network directories.

line noise — Fluctuations in voltage levels caused by other devices on the network or by electromagnetic interference.

Linux — A freely distributable implementation of the UNIX system. Finnish computer scientist Linus Torvalds originally developed it.

LLC frame — See *IEEE 802.3 frame*.

lmhosts — A host file on a Windows-based computer that maps IP addresses to host names and aliases.

load balancing — An automatic distribution of traffic over multiple links, hard disks, or processors intended to optimize responses.

Lobe Attachment Module (LAM) — A device that attaches to a CAU to expand the capacity of that device. LAMs typically allow up to 20 devices to plug into each CAU receptacle.

local account — A type of user account on a Windows 2000 network that has rights to the resources managed by the server the user has logged onto.

local area network (LAN) — A network of computers and other devices that is confined to a relatively small space, such as one building or even one office.

local collisions — Collisions that occur when two or more stations are transmitting simultaneously. Excessively high collision rates within the network can usually be traced to cable or routing problems.

local computer — The computer on which you are actually working (as opposed to a remote computer).

local loop — The part of a phone system that connects a customer site with a public carrier's POP. Some WAN transmission methods, such as ISDN, are suitable for only the local loop portion of the network link.

LocalTalk — A logical topology designed by Apple Computer, Inc. especially for networking Macintosh computers. LocalTalk uses the CSMA/CA network access method, and its throughput is limited to a maximum of 230 Kbps. Because of its throughput limitations, LocalTalk has been replaced by Ethernet on most modern Macintosh-based networks.

logical address — See *Network layer addresses*.

Logical Link Control (LLC) sublayer — The upper sublayer in the Data Link layer. The LLC provides a common interface and supplies reliability and flow control services.

logical topology — A networking technology defined by its Data Link layer data packaging and Physical layer signaling techniques.

loopback address — An IP address reserved for communicating from a node to itself (used mostly for testing purposes). The value of the loopback address is always 127.0.0.1.

loopback plug — A connector used for troubleshooting that plugs into a port (for example, a serial, parallel, or RJ-45 port) and crosses over the transmit line to the receive line, allowing outgoing signals to be redirected back into the computer for testing.

MAC address — A number that uniquely identifies a network node. The manufacturer hard-codes the MAC address on the NIC. This address is composed of the Block ID and Device ID.

macro viruses — A newer type of virus that takes the form of a word-processing or spreadsheet program macro, which may execute when a word-processing or spreadsheet program is in use.

MacTCP – A version of the TCP/IP protocol supplied with LocalTalk.

mail services — Network services that manage the storage and transfer of e-mail between users on a network. In addition to sending, receiving, and storing mail, mail services can include intelligent e-mail routing capabilities, notification, scheduling, indexing, document libraries, and gateways to other mail servers.

MAN — See *metropolitan area network*.

managed hub — See *intelligent hub*.

management services — Network services that centrally administer and simplify complicated management tasks on the network. Examples of management services include license tracking, security auditing, asset management, addressing management, software distribution, traffic monitoring, load balancing, and hardware diagnosis.

manual pages (man pages) — UNIX online documentation. This documentation describes the use of the commands and the programming interface to the UNIX system.

Media Access Control (MAC) sublayer — The lower sublayer of the Data Link layer. The MAC appends the physical address of the destination computer onto the frame.

media access unit (MAU) — The type of transceiver used on a Thicknet network to connect network nodes to the backbone.

media filter — A device that enables two types of cables or connectors to be linked.

member server — A type of server on a Windows 2000 network that does not hold directory information and therefore cannot authenticate users.

memory range — A hexadecimal number that indicates the area of memory that the network adapter and CPU will use for exchanging, or buffering, data. As with IRQs, some memory ranges are reserved for specific devices—most notably, the system board.

mesh network — An enterprise-wide topology in which routers are interconnected with other routers so that at least two pathways connect each node.

mesh WAN topology — A WAN topology that consists of many directly interconnected locations forming a complex mesh.

message switching — A type of switching in which a connection is established between two devices in the connection path; one device transfers data to the second device, then breaks the connection. The information is stored and forwarded from the second device once a connection between that device and a third device on the path is established.

metropolitan area network (MAN) — A network that connects clients and servers in multiple buildings within a limited geographic area. For example, a network connecting multiple city government buildings around the city's center.

MIB (management information base) — A collection of data used by management programs (which may be part of the network operating system or a third-party program) to analyze network performance and problems.

MicroChannel Architecture (MCA) — IBM's proprietary 32-bit bus for personal computers, introduced in 1987 and later replaced by the more standard EISA and PCI buses.

crosoft Certified Systems Engineer (MCSE) — A professional certification established by Microsoft that demonstrates in-depth knowledge about Microsoft's products, including Windows 98 and Windows 2000.

crosoft Management Console (MMC) — A graphical network management interface used with Windows 2000 Server.

crosoft Message Queueing (MSMQ) — An API used in a network environment. MSMQ stores messages sent between nodes in queues then forwards them to their destination based on when the link to the recipient is available.

ddleware — Software that sits between the client and server in a 3-tier architecture. Middleware may be used as a messaging service between clients and servers, as a universal query language for databases, or as means of coordinating processes between multiple servers that need to work together in servicing clients.

lestone — A reference point that marks the completion of a major task or group of tasks in a project and contributes to measuring the project's progress.

rroring — See *server mirroring*.

dem — A device that modulates analog signals into digital signals at the transmitting end for transmission over telephone lines, and demodulates digital signals into analog signals at the receiving end.

dular hub — A type of hub that provides a number of interface options within one chassis. Similar to a PC, a modular hub contains a system board and slots accommodating different adapters. These adapters may connect to other types of hubs, routers, WAN links, or to both Token Ring and Ethernet network backbones. They may also connect the modular hub to management workstations or redundant components, such as an extra power supply.

dular router — A router with multiple slots that can hold different interface cards or other devices so as to provide flexible, customizable network interoperability.

dulation — A technique for formatting signals in which one property of a simple, carrier wave is modified by the addition of a data signal during transmission.

nitor — An NLM that enables the system administrator to view server parameters such as protocols, bindings, system resources, and loaded modules. In many cases, it also allows the system administrator to modify these parameters.

lti-master replication — The technique of replicating an Active Directory database to multiple domain controllers so they each have the same data and the same privileges to modify that data. Multi-master replication is used within a domain tree.

lticast address — A type of address in the IPv6 that represents multiple interfaces, often on multiple nodes. An IPv6 multicast address begins with the following hexadecimal field: FF0x, where x is a character that identifies the address's group scope.

multicasting — A means of transmission in which one device sends data to a specific group of devices (not the entire network segment) in a point-to-multipoint fashion. Multicasting can be used for teleconferencing or videoconferencing over the Internet, for example.

multimeter — A simple instrument that can measure multiple characteristics of an electric circuit, including its resistance and voltage.

multimode fiber — A type of fiber-optic cable that contains a core with a diameter between 50 and 100 microns, over which many pulses of light generated by a light emitting diode (LED) travel at different angles. Because light is being reflected many different ways in a multimode fiber cable, the waves become less easily distinguishable the longer they travel. Thus, multimode fiber is best suited for shorter distances than single-mode fiber.

multiplexer (mux) — A device that separates a medium into multiple subchannels and issues signals to each of those subchannels.

multiplexing — A form of transmission that allows multiple signals to simultaneously travel over one medium.

multiprocessing — The technique of splitting tasks among multiple processors to expedite the completion of any single instruction.

multiprotocol network — A network that uses more than one protocol.

Multistation Access Unit (MAU) — A device on a Token Ring network that regenerates signals; equivalent to a hub.

multitasking — The ability of a processor to perform multiple activities in a brief period of time (often seeming simultaneous to the user).

n-series connector (n connector) — A type of connector used on Thicknet networks in which a screw-and-barrel arrangement securely connects coaxial cables to devices.

name server — A server that contains a database of TCP/IP host names and their associated IP addresses. A name server supplies a resolver with the requested information. If it cannot resolve the IP address, the query passes to a higher-level name server.

name space — The database of Internet IP addresses and their associated names distributed over DNS name servers worldwide.

narrowband — A type of radiofrequency transmission in which signals travel over a single frequency. The same method is used by radio and TV broadcasting stations, and signals can be easily intercepted and decoded.

nbtstat — A TCP/IP troubleshooting utility that provides information about NetBIOS names and their addresses. If you know the NetBIOS name of a workstation, you can use nbtstat to determine its IP address.

NDS eDirectory — Novell's integration tool for Windows 2000 networks. It works with the NetWare 5.x operating systems and Windows 2000 servers to enable the Windows 2000 domains to appear as container objects in NWAdmin.

NDS tree — A logical representation of how resources are grouped by NetWare in the enterprise.

needs assessment — The process of clarifying the reasons and objectives for a proposed change so as to determine whether the change is worthwhile and necessary and to elucidate the scope and nature of the proposed change.

negative frame sequence checks — The result of the cyclic redundancy checksum (CRC) generated by the originating node not matching the checksum calculated from the data received. It usually indicates noise or transmission problems on the LAN interface or cabling. A high number of (non-matching) CRCs usually results from excessive collisions or a station transmitting bad data.

NetBIOS — See *Network Basic Input Output System*.

NetBIOS Enhanced User Interface (NetBEUI) — Microsoft's adaptation of the IBM NetBIOS protocol. NetBEUI expands on NetBIOS by adding an Application layer component. NetBEUI is a fast and efficient protocol that consumes few network resources, provides excellent error correction and requires little configuration.

netstat — A TCP/IP troubleshooting utility that displays statistics and the state of current TCP/IP connections. It also displays ports, which can signal whether services are using the correct ports.

NetWare 3.x — The group of NetWare versions that includes versions 3.0, 3.1, and 3.2.

NetWare 4.x — The group of NetWare versions that includes versions 4.0, 4.1, and 4.11.

NetWare 5.x — The group of NetWare versions that includes versions 5.0, 5.1, and 5.11.

NetWare Administrator utility (NWAdmin) — The graphical NetWare utility that allows administrators to manage objects in the NDS tree from a Windows workstation.

NetWare Core Protocol (NCP) — One of the core protocols of the IPX/SPX suite. NCP handles requests for services, such as printing and file access, between clients and servers.

NetWare Directory Services (NDS) — A system of managing multiple servers and their resources, including users, volumes, groups, profiles, and printers. The NDS model is similar to Active Directory in Windows 2000. In NDS, every networked resource is treated as a separate object with distinct properties.

NetWare loadable modules (NLMs) — Routines that enable the server to run programs and services. Each NLM consumes some of the server's memory and processor resources (at least temporarily). The kernel requires many NLMs to run NetWare's core operating system.

network — A group of computers and other devices (such as printers) that are connected by some type of transmission media, usually wire or cable.

network access method — See *access method*.

network adapter — A synonym for NIC (network interface card). The device that enables a workstation, server, printer, or other node to connect to the network. Network adapters belong to the Physical layer of the OSI Model.

network address — See *Network layer addresses*.

network address translation (NAT) — A technique in which private (or hidden) IP addresses are assigned a public IP address by an IP gateway, thus masking their true origin.

network analyzer — A portable, hardware-based tool that a network manager connects to the network expressly to determine the nature of network problems. Network analyzers can typically interpret data up to Layer 7 of the OSI Model.

network architect — A professional who designs networks, performing tasks that range from choosing basic components (such as cabling type) to figuring out how to make those components work together (by, for example, choosing the correct protocols).

network attached storage (NAS) — A device or set of devices attached to a client/server network that is dedicated to providing highly fault-tolerant access to large quantities of data. NAS depends on traditional network transmission methods such as Ethernet.

Network Basic Input Output System (NetBIOS) — A protocol designed by IBM to provide Transport and Session layer services for applications running on small, homogeneous networks.

network interface card (NIC) — The device that enables a workstation to connect to the network and communicate with other computers. NICs are manufactured by several different companies and come with a variety of specifications that are tailored to the workstation's and the network's requirements.

Network layer — The third layer in the OSI Model. The Network layer translates network addresses into their physical counterparts and decides how to route data from the sender to the receiver.

Network layer addresses — Addresses that reside at the Network level of the OSI Model, follow a hierarchical addressing scheme, and can be assigned through operating system software.

Network Monitor (NetMon) — A software-based network monitoring tool that comes with Windows NT Server 4.0 or Windows 2000. Its capabilities include capturing network data traveling from one or many segments, capturing frames sent by or to a specified node, reproducing network conditions by transmitting a selected amount and type of data, detecting any other running copies of NetMon, and generating statistics about network activity.

etwork monitor — A software-based tool that continually monitors traffic on the network from a server or workstation attached to the network. Network monitors typically can interpret up to Layer 3 of the OSI Model.

etwork News Transfer Protocol (NNTP) — The protocol that supports the process of reading newsgroup messages, posting new messages, and transferring news files between news servers.

etwork operating system (NOS) — The software that runs on a server and enables the server to manage data, users, groups, security, applications, and other networking functions. The most popular network operating systems are Microsoft's Windows NT, Windows 2000, UNIX, and Novell's NetWare.

etwork Termination 1 (NT1) — A device used on ISDN networks that connects the incoming twisted-pair wiring with the customer's ISDN terminal equipment.

etwork Termination 2 (NT2) — An additional connection device required on PRI to handle the multiple ISDN lines between the customer's network termination connection and the local phone company's wires.

etwork Time Protocol (NTP) — A simple TCP/IP protocol that is used to synchronize the clocks of computers on a network. NTP belongs to the Application layer of the TCP/IP Model and depends on UDP.

etwork virus — A type of virus that takes advantage of network protocols, commands, messaging programs, and data links to propagate itself. Although all viruses could theoretically travel across network connections, network viruses are specially designed to attack network vulnerabilities.

Network+ (Net+) — Professional certification established by CompTIA that verifies broad, vendor-independent networking technology skills such as an understanding of protocols, topologies, networking hardware, and network troubleshooting.

ew Technology File System (NTFS) — A file system developed by Microsoft for use with its Windows NT and Windows 2000 operating systems. NTFS integrates reliability, compression, the ability to handle massive files, system security, and fast access. Most Windows 2000 Server partitions employ either FAT32 or NTFS.

ewsgroups — An Internet service similar to e-mail that provides a means of conveying messages, but in which information is distributed to a wide group of users at once rather than from one user to another.

FS — Network File System. A client/server application that allows you to view, store and update files on a remote computer as though they were on your own computer. Can be used to install Linux.

ode — A computer or other device connected to a network which has a unique address and is capable of sending or receiving data.

noise — Unwanted signals, or interference, from sources near network cabling, such as electrical motors, power lines and radar.

NOS — See *network operating system*.

Novell proprietary 802.3 frame — The original NetWare Ethernet frame type and the default frame type for networks running NetWare versions lower than 3.12. It supports only the IPX/SPX protocol. Sometimes called 802.3 "raw," because its data portion contains no control bits.

nslookup — A TCP/IP utility on Windows NT, Windows 2000, and UNIX systems that allows you to look up the DNS host name of a network node by specifying its IP address, or vice versa. This ability is useful for verifying that a host is configured correctly and for troubleshooting DNS resolution problems.

NWConv — A utility provided with Windows 2000 that converts (migrates) an existing NetWare server's user account, file, and other information to a Windows 2000 server.

object — A representation of a thing or person associated with the network that belongs in the NOS directory. Objects include users, printers, groups, computers, data files, and applications.

object class — See *Class*.

octet — One of the four 8-bit bytes that are separated by periods and together make up an IP address.

ohmmeter—A device used to measure resistance in an electrical circuit.

online backup — A technique in which data are backed up to a central location over the Internet.

online UPS — A power supply that uses the A/C power from the wall outlet to continuously charge its battery, while providing power to a network device through its battery.

open shortest path first (OSPF) — A routing protocol that makes up for some of the limitations of RIP and can coexist with RIP on a network.

open source software — Term used to describe software that is distributed without any restriction and whose source code is freely available. See also *freely distributable*.

Open Systems Interconnection (OSI) Model — A model for understanding and developing computer-to-computer communication developed in the 1980s by ISO. It divides networking architecture into seven layers: Physical, Data Link, Network, Transport, Session, Presentation, and Application.

optical loss — The degradation of a light signal on a fiber-optic network.

optical time domain reflectometer (OTDR) — A time domain reflectometer specifically made for use with fiber optic networks. It works by issuing a light-based signal on a fiber-optic cable and measuring the way in which the signal bounces back (or reflects) to the OTDR.

Orange Book — A rigorous security specification for computer operating systems published in 1985 by the U.S. Department of Defense.

Organizational unit (OU) — A container within an NOS directory used to group objects wih similar characteristics or priviledges.

OSI Model — See *Open Systems Interconnection Model*.

overhead — The nondata information that must accompany data in order for a signal to be properly routed and interpreted by the network.

owner — The person who takes responsibility for ensuring that project tasks are completed on time and within budgetary guidelines.

Packet Internet Groper (PING) — A TCP/IP troubleshooting utility that can verify that TCP/IP is installed, bound to the NIC, configured correctly, and communicating with the network. PING uses ICMP to send echo request and echo reply messages that determine the validity of an IP address.

packet switching — A type of switching in which data are broken into packets before they are transported. In packet switching, packets can travel any path on the network to their destination, because each packet contains a destination address and sequencing information.

packet-filtering firewall — A router that operates at the Data Link and Transport layers of the OSI Model, examining the header of every packet of data that it receives to determine whether that type of packet is authorized to continue to its destination. Packet-filtering firewalls are also called screening firewalls.

padding — Bytes added to the data (or information) portion of an Ethernet frame to make sure this field is at least 46 bytes in size. Padding has no effect on the data carried by the frame.

page file — A file on the hard disk that is used for virtual memory.

paging — The process of moving blocks of information, called pages, between RAM and into a page file on disk.

parallel backbone — The most robust enterprise-wide topology. This variation on the collapsed backbone arrangement consists of more than one connection from the central router or switch to each network segment.

parity — The mechanism used to verify the integrity of data by making the number of bits in a byte sum to either an odd or even number.

parity error checking — The process of comparing the parity of data read from a disk with the type of parity used by the system.

passive hub — A hub that simply amplifies and retransmits signals over the network.

patch — A correction, improvement, or enhancement to part of a software program, often distributed at no charge by software vendors to fix a bug in their code or to add slightly more functionality.

patch cable — A relatively short section (usually between 3 and 50 feet) of twisted-pair cabling, with connectors on both ends, that connects network devices to data outlets.

patch panel — A wall-mounted panel of data receptors into which cross-connect patch cables from the punch-down block are inserted.

PC Card — See *PCMCIA*.

PCMCIA — An interface developed in the early 1990s by the Personal Computer Memory Card International Association to provide a standard interface for connecting any type of device to a portable computer. PCMCIA slots may hold modem cards, network interface cards, external hard disk cards, or CD-ROM cards. PCMCIA cards are also known as PC Cards or credit card adapters.

peer-to-peer communication — A simple means of networking computers using a single cable. In peer-to-peer communication, no single computer has more authority than another and each computer can share its resources with other computers.

peer-to-peer network — A network in which computers communicate directly with other computers on a single segment of cable and share each others' data and devices. By default, no computer in a peer-to-peer network has more authority than another, and every computer can use resources from every other computer.

peer-to-peer topology — A WAN with single interconnection points for each location.

per seat — A Windows 2000 Server licensing mode that requires a license for every client capable of connecting to the Windows 2000 server.

per server — A Windows 2000 Server licensing mode that allows a limited number of clients to access the server simultaneously. (The number is determined by your Windows 2000 Server purchase agreement.) The restriction applies to the number of concurrent connections, rather than specific clients. Per server mode is the most popular choice for installing Windows 2000 Server.

Peripheral Component Interconnect (PCI) — A 32-, 64-, or 128-bit bus introduced in its original form in the 1990s. The PCI bus is the network adapter connection type used for nearly all new PCs. It's characterized by a shorter length than ISA, MCA, or EISA cards, but a much faster data transmission capability.

phase — A point or stage in a wave's progress over time.

physical address — See *MAC address*.

Physical layer — The lowest, or first, layer of the OSI Model. The Physical layer contains the physical networking media, such as cabling and connectors.

physical memory — The RAM chips installed on the computer's system board that provide dedicated memory to that computer.

ysical topology — The physical layout of a network. A physical topology depicts a network in broad scope; it does not specify devices, connectivity methods, or addresses on the network. Physical topologies are categorized into three fundamental geometric shapes: bus, ring, and star. These shapes can be mixed to create hybrid topologies.

ot network — A small-scale network that stands in for the larger network. A pilot network may be used to evaluate the effects of network changes or additions.

NG — See *Packet Internet Groper.*

ging — The process of sending an echo request signal from one node on a TCP/IP network to another, using the PING utility.

e — The facility in a UNIX system that enables you to combine commands to form new commands. It is one of the most powerful facilities of the UNIX system.

eline — A series of two or more UNIX commands connected together with pipe symbols.

in old telephone service (POTS) — See *PSTN.*

num — The area above the ceiling tile or below the subfloor in a building.

int of presence (POP) — The place where the two telephone systems meet—either a long-distance carrier with a local telephone company or a local carrier with an ISP's facility.

int-to-point — A data transmission that involves one transmitter and one receiver.

int-to-Point Protocol (PPP) — A communications protocol that enables a workstation to connect to a server using a serial connection. PPP can support multiple Network layer protocols, can use both asynchronous and synchronous communications, and does not require much (if any) configuration on the client workstation.

int-to-Point Tunneling Protocol (PPTP) — A Layer 2 protocol developed by Microsoft that encapsulates PPP so that any type of data can traverse the Internet masked as pure IP transmissions. PPTP supports the encryption, authentication, and LAN access services provided by RAS. Instead of users having to dial directly into an access server, they can dial into their ISP using PPTP and gain access to their corporate LAN over the Internet.

lymorphic virus — A type of virus that changes its characteristics (such as the arrangement of its bytes, size, and internal instructions) every time it is transferred to a new system, making it harder to identify.

)P — See *Post Office Protocol* or *point of presence.*

rt — The address on a host where an application makes itself available to incoming data.

port number — A unique number associated with a process running on a computer. For example, 23 is the standard port number associated with the Telnet utility.

Post Office Protocol (POP) — A TCP/IP subprotocol that provides centralized storage for e-mail messages. In the postal service analogy, POP is like the post office that holds mail until it can be delivered.

predecessors — Tasks in a project that must be completed before other tasks can begin.

preemptive multitasking — The type of multitasking supported by NetWare, UNIX, and Windows 2000 Server that actually performs one task at a time, allowing one program to use the processor for a certain period of time, then suspending that program to allow another program to use the processor.

Presentation layer — The sixth layer of the OSI Model. The Presentation layer serves as a translator between the application and the network. Here data are formatted in a schema that the network can understand, with the format varying according to the type of network used. The Presentation layer also manages data encryption and decryption, such as the scrambling of system passwords.

Pretty Good Privacy (PGP) — A key-based encryption system for e-mail that uses a two-step verification process.

PRI (Primary Rate Interface) — A type of ISDN that uses 23 bearer channels and one 64-Kbps data channel as represented by the following notation: 23B + D. PRI is less commonly used by individual subscribers than BRI, but it may be used by businesses and other organizations needing more throughput.

principal — In Kerberos terminology, a user.

print services — The network service that allows printers to be shared by several users on a network.

printer queue — A logical representation of a networked printer's functionality. To use a printer, clients must have access to the printer queue.

private key encryption — A type of key encryption in which the sender and receiver have private keys, which only they know. Data encryption standard (DES), which was developed by IBM in the 1970s, is a popular example of a private key encryption technique. Private key encryption is also known as symmetric encryption.

process — A routine of sequential instructions that runs until it has achieved its goal. For example, a spreadsheet program is a process.

process management — Planning for and handling the steps involved in accomplishing a goal in a systematic way. Processes that might be managed during a project's implementation include change, support, training, transitioning, delegation, and problem resolution.

project management — The practice of managing resources, staff, budget, timelines, and other variables so as to complete a specific goal within given bounds.

project plan — The way in which details of a managed project (for example, the timeline and the significant tasks) are organized. Some project plans are created via special project planning software, such as Microsoft Project.

promiscuous mode — The feature of a network adapter card that allows a device driver to direct it to pick up all frames that pass over the network—not just those destined for the node served by the card.

proprietary UNIX — Any implementation of UNIX for which the source code is either unavailable or available only by purchasing a licensed copy from Caldera International and Tarantella, Inc. (costing as much as millions of dollars).

protected mode — A manner in which NetWare runs services in a separate memory area from the operating system. Running services in protected mode prevents one rogue routine from taking the server down. As a result, the service and its supporting routines cannot harm critical server processes.

protocol — The rules a network uses to transfer data. Protocols ensure that data is transferred whole, in sequence, and without error from one node on the network to another.

protocol analyzer — See *network analyzer*.

proxy server — A network host that runs a proxy service. Proxy servers may also be called gateways.

proxy service — A software application on a network host that acts as an intermediary between the external and internal networks, screening all incoming and outgoing traffic and providing one address to the outside world, instead of revealing the addresses of internal LAN devices.

PSTN (Public Switched Telephone Network) — The network of typical telephone lines that has been evolving for 100 years and still services most homes.

public key encryption — A form of key encryption in which data are encrypted using two keys: one is a key known only to a user, and the other is a key associated with the user and can be obtained from a public source, such as a public key server. Some examples of public key algorithms include RSA (named after its creators, Rivest, Shamir, and Adleman), Diffie-Hellman, and Elliptic-curve cryptography. Public key encryption is also known as asymmetric encryption.

public-key server — A publicly available host (such as an Internet host) that provides free access to a list of users' public keys (for use in public key encryption).

punch-down block — A panel of data receptors into which horizontal cabling from the workstations is inserted.

PVC (permanent virtual circuit) — A point-to-point connection over which data may follow any number of different paths, as opposed to a dedicated line that follows a predefined path. X.25, frame relay, and some forms of ATM use PVCs.

quality of service (QoS) — The result of standards for delivering data within a certain period of time after their transmission. For example, ATM networks can supply four QoS levels, from a "best effort" attempt for noncritical data to a guaranteed, real-time transmission for time-sensitive data.

radiofrequency (RF) — A type of transmission that relies on signals broadcast over specific frequencies, in the same manner as radio and TV broadcasts. RF may use narrowband or spread spectrum technology.

radiofrequency interference (RFI) — A kind of interference that may be generated by motors, power lines, televisions, copiers, fluorescent lights, or broadcast signals from radio or TV towers.

RAID — See *Redundant Array of Inexpensive Disks*.

RAID Level 0 — An implementation of RAID in which data are written in 64 KB blocks equally across all disks in the array.

RAID Level 1 — An implementation of RAID that provides redundancy through disk mirroring, in which data from one disk are automatically copied to another disk as the information is written.

RAID Level 3 — An implementation of RAID that uses disk striping for data and parity error correction code on a separate parity disk.

RAID Level 5 — The most popular, highly fault-tolerant, data storage technique in use today, RAID Level 5 writes data in small blocks across several disks. At the same time, it writes parity error checking information among several disks.

real-time — The term used to describe an operating system that at least one of the following includes two characteristics: the ability to respond to external events (for example, a change in temperature), and an ability to respond to those events deterministically—with predictable response time (for example, turning on a heating element within three microseconds).

reassembly — The process of reconstructing data units that have been segmented.

redirector — A service that runs on a client workstation and determines whether the client's request should be handled by the client or the server.

redundancy — The use of more than one identical component for storing, processing, or transporting data.

Redundant Array of Inexpensive Disks (RAID) — A server redundancy measure that uses shared, multiple physical or logical hard disks to ensure data integrity and availability. Some RAID designs also increase storage capacity and improve performance. See also *disk striping*, and *disk mirroring*.

regeneration — The process of retransmitting a digital signal. Regeneration, unlike amplification, repeats the pure signal, with none of the noise it has accumulated.

Regional Internet Registry (RIR) — A not-for-profit agency that manages the distribution of IP addresses to private and public entities. ARIN is the RIR for North, Central, and South America and sub-Saharan Africa. APNIC is the RIR for Asia and the Pacific region. RIPE is the RIR for Europe and North Africa.

relative distinguished name (RDN) — An attribute of the object that identifies an object separately from its related container(s) and domain. For most objects, the relative distinguished name is the same as its common name (CN) in the distinguished name convention.

release — The act of terminating a DHCP lease.

remote access — A method for connecting and logging onto a LAN from a workstation that is remote, or not physically connected, to the LAN. Remote access can be accomplished one of three ways: by using a modem to dial directly into the LAN; by using a modem to dial directly to a workstation; or by using an Internet connection with a Web interface. Remote access may complete a connection via public or private lines.

remote access server — A combination of software and hardware that provides a central access point for multiple users to dial into a network.

Remote Access Service (RAS) — One of the simplest dial-in servers. This software is included with Windows 2000 Server. Note that "RAS" is pronounced *razz*.

Remote Authentication Dial-In User Service (RADIUS) — A server that offers authentication services to the network's access server (which may run the Windows NT or 2000 RAS or Novell's NAS, for example). RADIUS provides a single, centralized point of authentication for dial-in users and is often used by ISPs.

remote computer — The computer that you are controlling or working on via a network connection.

remote control — A remote access method in which the remote user dials into a workstation that is directly attached to a LAN. Software running on both the remote user's computer and the LAN computer allows the remote user to "take over" the LAN workstation.

remote node — A client that has dialed directly into a LAN's remote access server. The LAN treats a remote node like any other client on the LAN, allowing the remote user to perform the same functions he or she could perform while in the office.

remote user — A person working on a computer in a different geographical location from the LAN's server.

repeater — A device used to regenerate a digital signal.

replication — The process of copying Active Directory data to multiple domain controllers. This ensures redundancy so that in case one of the domain controllers fails, clients can still log onto the network, be authenticated, and access resources.

resistance — The opposition to an electric current. Resistance of a wire is a factor of its size and molecular structure.

resolver — Any host on the Internet that needs to look up domain name information.

resource record — The element of a DNS database stored on a name server that contains information about TCP/IP host names and their addresses.

resources — 1) In project management, a term used to refer to staffing, materials, and money. 2) The devices, data, and data storage space provided by a computer, whether standalone or shared.

restore — The process of retrieving files from a backup if the original files are lost or deleted.

Reverse Address Resolution Protocol (RARP) — The reverse of ARP. RARP allows the client to send a broadcast message with the MAC address of a device and receive the device's IP address in reply.

RFI — See *radiofrequency interference*.

ring topology — A network layout in which each node is connected to the two nearest nodes so that the entire network forms a circle. Data are transmitted unidirectionally around the ring. Each workstation accepts and responds to packets addressed to it, then forwards the other packets to the next workstation in the ring.

ring WAN topology — A WAN topology in which each site is connected to two other sites so that the entire WAN forms a ring pattern. This architecture is similar to the LAN ring topology, except that a WAN ring topology connects locations rather than local nodes.

risers — The backbone cabling that provides vertical connections between floors of a building.

RJ-45 — The standard connector used with shielded twisted-pair and unshielded twisted-pair cabling. "RJ" stands for registered jack.

root — A highly privileged user ID that has all rights to create, delete, modify, move, read, write, or execute files on a system. This term may specifically refer to the administrator on a UNIX-based network.

root domain — In Windows 2000 networking, the single domain from which child domains branch out in a domain tree.

root server — A DNS server maintained by ICANN and IANA that is an authority on how to contact the top-level domains, such as those ending with .com, .edu, .net, .us, and so on. ICANN oversees the operation of 13 root servers around the world.

routable — Protocols that can span more than one LAN segment because they carry Network layer and addressing information that can be interpreted by a router.

route — To direct data between networks based on addressing, patterns of usage, and availability of network segments.

router — A multiport device that can connect dissimilar LANs and WANs running at different transmission speeds and using a variety of protocols. In addition, a router can determine the best path for data transmission and perform advanced management functions. Routers operate at the Network layer (Layer 3) or higher of the OSI Model. They are intelligent, protocol-dependent devices.

Routing Information Protocol (RIP) — The oldest routing protocol that is still widely used. RIP does not work in very large network environments where data may have to travel through more than 16 routers to reach their destination (for example, on the Internet). And, compared to other routing protocols, RIP is slower and less secure.

routing protocols — Protocols that assist routers in efficiently managing information flow. For instance, routing protocols determine the best path for data to take between nodes.

routing switch — Another term for a Layer 3 or Layer 4 switch. A routing switch is a hybrid between a router and a switch and can therefore interpret data from Layer 2 and either Layer 3 or Layer 4.

runts — Packet fragments.

runts — Packets that are smaller than a logical topology's minimum packet size. For instance, any Ethernet packet that is smaller than 64 bytes is considered a runt.

sag — See *brownout*.

Samba — An open source software package that provides complete Windows 2000-style file and printer sharing facility.

schema — The description of object types, or classes, and their required and optional attributes that are stored in an NOS's directory.

screening firewall — See *packet-filtering firewall.*

SDH (Synchronous Digital Hierarchy) — The international equivalent of SONET.

security audit — An assessment of an organization's security vulnerabilities. A security audit should be performed at least annually and preferably quarterly or sooner if the network has undergone significant changes. For each risk found, it should rate the severity of a potential breach, as well as its likelihood.

segment — A part of a LAN that is logically separated from other parts of the LAN and that shares a fixed amount of traffic capacity.

segmentation — The process of decreasing the size of data units when moving data from a network segment that can handle larger data units to a network segment that can handle only smaller data units.

self-healing — A characteristic of dual-ring topologies that allows them to automatically reroute traffic along the backup ring if the primary ring becomes severed.

Sequenced Packet Exchange (SPX) — One of the core protocols in the IPX/SPX suite. SPX belongs to the Transport layer of the OSI Model and works in tandem with IPX to ensure that data are received whole, in sequence, and error free.

sequencing — The process of assigning a placeholder to each piece of a data block to allow the receiving node's Transport layer to reassemble the data in the correct order.

serial backbone — The simplest kind of backbone, consisting of two or more hubs connected to each other by a single cable.

Serial Line Internet Protocol (SLIP) — A communications protocol that enables a workstation to connect to a server using a serial connection. SLIP can support only asynchronous communications and IP traffic, and requires some configuration on the client workstation.

server — A computer on the network that manages shared resources. Servers usually have more processing power, memory, and hard disk space than clients. They run network operating software that can manage not only data, but also users, groups, security, and applications on the network.

server clustering — A fault-tolerance technique that links multiple servers together to act as a single server. In this configuration, clustered servers share processing duties and appear as a single server to users. If one server in the cluster fails, the other servers in the cluster will automatically take over its data transaction and storage responsibilities.

server console — The network administrator's primary interface to a NetWare server. Unlike Windows NT, the NetWare server interface is not entirely graphical. NetWare 4.x offers only text-based server menus at the console. NetWare 5.0 allows you to access commands through either a text-based or graphical menu system.

server mirroring — A fault-tolerance technique in which one server duplicates the transactions and data storage of another, identical server. Server mirroring requires a link between the servers and software running on both servers so that the servers can continually synchronize their actions and take over in case the other fails.

server-based network — A network that uses special computers, known as servers, to process data for and facilitate communication between the other computers on the network. See *client/server network.*

server_hello — In the context of SSL encryption, a message issued from the server to the client that confirms the information the server received in the client_hello message and agrees to certain terms of encryption based on the options the client supplied. Depending on the Web server's preferred encryption method, the server may choose to use issue your browser a public key or a digital certificate at this time.

rvice Access Point (SAP) — A feature of Ethernet networks that identifies a node or internal process that uses the LLC protocol. Each process between a source and destination node on the network may have a unique SAP.

rvice Advertising Protocol (SAP) — A core protocol in the IPX/SPX suite that works in the Application, Presentation, Session, and Transport layers of the OSI Model and runs directly over IPX. NetWare servers and routers use SAP to advertise to the entire network which services they can provide.

rvice pack — A significant patch to Windows NT or 2000 Server software.

rvices — The features provided by a network.

ssion — A connection for data exchange between two parties. The term "session" is most often used in the context of terminal and mainframe communications.

ssion key — In the context of Kerberos authentication, a key issued to both the client and service by the authentication service that uniquely identifies their session.

ession layer — The fifth layer in the OSI Model. The Session layer establishes and maintains communication between two nodes on the network. It can be considered the "traffic cop" for network communications.

ared Ethernet — A version of Ethernet in which all the nodes share a common channel and a fixed amount of bandwidth.

eath — The outer cover, or jacket, of a cable.

ell — Another term for command interpreter.

ielded twisted-pair (STP) — A type of cable containing twisted wire pairs that are not only individually insulated, but also surrounded by a shielding made of a metallic substance such as foil. The shielding acts as an antenna, converting the noise into current (assuming that the wire is properly grounded). This current induces an equal, yet opposite current in the twisted pairs it surrounds. The noise on the shielding mirrors the noise on the twisted pairs, and the two cancel each other out.

ignal bounce — A phenomenon caused by improper termination on a bus network in which signals travel endlessly between the two ends of the network, preventing new signals from getting through.

ignal level — An ANSI standard for T-carrier technology that refers to its Physical layer electrical signaling characteristics. DS0 is the equivalent of one data or voice channel. All other signal levels are multiples of DS0.

ignature scanning — The comparison of a file's content with known virus signatures (unique identifying characteristics in the code) in a signature database to determine whether the file is a virus.

imple installation — A NetWare installation option in which the most popular installation options are chosen for you, and the installation takes less time than if you had chosen a custom installation.

Simple Mail Transfer Protocol (SMTP) — A protocol within the TCP/IP suite that is responsible for moving e-mail messages between one mail server and another.

Simple Network Management Protocol (SNMP) — A communication protocol used to manage devices on a TCP/IP network.

simplex — A type of transmission in which signals may travel in only one direction over a medium.

single point of failure — A device or connection on a network that, were it to fail, could cause the entire network to stop functioning.

single-mode fiber — A type of fiber-optic cable with a core of less than 10 microns in diameter that carries light pulses along a single data path from one end of the cable to another. Single-mode fiber can carry data faster and farther than multimode fiber. However, single-mode fiber is more expensive than multimode fiber.

site license — A type of software license that, for a fixed price, allows any number of users in one location to legally access an application.

snap-in — An administrative tool, such as Computer Management, that can be added to the Microsoft Management Console (MMC).

sneakernet — The only means of exchanging data without using a network. Sneakernet requires that data be copied from a computer to a floppy disk, carried (presumably by someone wearing sneakers) to another computer, then copied from the floppy disk onto the second computer.

sniffer — A laptop equipped with a special network adapter and software that performs network analysis. Unlike laptops that may have a network monitoring tool installed, sniffers typically cannot be used for other purposes, because they don't depend on a desktop operating system such as Windows.

Sniffer Portable — Network analyzer software from Network Associates that provides data capture and analysis, node discovery, traffic trending, history, alarm tripping, and utilization prediction.

social engineering — Manipulating relationships to circumvent network security measures and gain access to a system.

socket — A logical address assigned to a specific process running on a computer. A socket forms a virtual connection between the host and client.

soft skills — Skills such as customer relations, leadership ability, and dependability, which are not easily measured, but are nevertheless important in a networking career.

software distribution — The process of automatically transferring a data file or program from the server to a client on the network.

Solaris — Sun Microsystems' proprietary implementation of the UNIX system.

SONET (Synchronous Optical Network) — A WAN technology that provides data transfer rates ranging from 64 Kbps to 39.8 Gbps, using the same time division multiplexing technique used by T-carriers. SONET is the best choice for linking WANs between North America, Europe, and Asia, because it can link directly using the different standards used in different countries.

source code — Computer instructions written in a programming language that is readable by humans. Source code must be translated into a form that is executable by the machine, typically called binary code (for the sequence of zeros and ones) or target code.

source-route bridging — A type of bridging in which the bridge polls the network to determine the best path for data between two points. Source-route bridging is not susceptible to circular routing and, for this reason, is particularly well-suited to WANs.

spanning tree algorithm — A technique used in bridging that can detect circular traffic patterns and modify the way multiple bridges work together in order to avoid such patterns.

spike — A single (or short-lived) jump in a measure of network performance, such as utilization.

sponsors — People in positions of authority who support a project and who can lobby for budget increases necessary to complete the project, appeal to a group of managers to extend a project's deadline, assist with negotiating vendor contracts, and so on.

spread spectrum — A type of radiofrequency transmission in which lower-level signals are distributed over several frequencies simultaneously. Spread spectrum RF is more secure than narrowband RF.

SSL (Secure Sockets Layer) — A method of encrypting TCP/IP transmissions—including Web pages and data entered into Web forms—en route between the client and server using public key encryption technology.

SSL session — In the context of SSL encryption, an association between the client and server that is defined by an agreement on a specific set of encryption techniques. An SSL session allows the client and server to continue to exchange data securely as long as the client is still connected to the server. SSL sessions are established by the SSL handshake protocol.

stackable hub — A type of hub designed to be linked with other hubs in a single telecommunications closet. Stackable hubs linked together logically represent one large hub to the network.

stakeholder — Any person who may be affected by a project, for better or for worse. A stakeholder may be a project participant, user, manager, or vendor.

standalone computer — A computer that uses programs and data only from its local disks and that is not connected to a network.

standalone hub — A type of hub that serves a workgroup of computers that are separate from the rest of the network. A standalone hub may be connected to another hub by a coaxial, fiber-optic, or twisted-pair cable. Such hubs are not typically connected in a hierarchical or daisy-chain fashion.

standards — Documented agreements containing technical specifications or other precise criteria that are used as guidelines to ensure that materials, products, processes, and services suit their intended purpose.

standby UPS — A power supply that provides continuous voltage to a device by switching virtually instantaneously to the battery when it detects a loss of power from the wall outlet. Upon restoration of the power, the standby UPS switches the device to use A/C power again.

star topology — A physical topology in which every node on the network is connected through a central device, such as a hub. Any single physical wire on a star network connects only two devices, so a cabling problem will affect only two nodes. Nodes transmit data to the hub, which then retransmits the data to the rest of the network segment where the destination node can pick it up.

star WAN topology — A WAN topology that mimics the arrangement of star LANs. A single site acts as the central connection point for several other locations.

star-wired bus topology — A hybrid topology in which groups of workstations are connected in a star fashion to hubs that are networked via a single bus.

star-wired ring topology — A hybrid topology that uses the physical layout of a star and the token-passing data transmission method.

static ARP table entry — A record (of an IP address and its associated MAC address) that is manually entered in the ARP table using the ARP utility.

static IP address — An IP address that is manually assigned to a device and remains constant until it is manually changed.

static routing — A technique in which a network administrator programs a router to use specific paths between nodes. Since it does not account for occasional network congestion, failed connections, or device moves, static routing is not optimal.

statistical multiplexing — A method of multiplexing in which each node on a network is assigned a separate time slot for transmission, based on the node's priority and need.

stealth virus — A type of virus that hides itself to prevent detection. Typically, stealth viruses disguise themselves as legitimate programs or replace part of a legitimate program's code with their destructive code.

storage area network (SAN) — A distinct network of multiple storage devices and servers that provides fast, highly available, and highly fault-tolerant access to large quantities of data for a client/server network. SAN uses a proprietary network transmission method (such as Fibre Channel) rather than a traditional network transmission method such as Ethernet.

..re and forward mode — A method of switching in which a switch reads the entire data frame into its memory and checks it for accuracy before transmitting it. While this method is more time-consuming than the cut-through method, it allows store and forward switches to transmit data more accurately.

..aight-through cable — A twisted-pair patch cable in which the wire terminations in both connectors follow the same scheme.

..uctured cabling — A method for uniform, enterprise-wide, multivendor cabling systems specified by the TIA/EIA 568 Commercial Building Wiring Standard. Structured cabling is based on a hierarchical design using a high-speed backbone.

..bchannel — One of many distinct communication paths established when a channel is multiplexed or modulated.

..bnet mask — A special 32-bit number that, when combined with a device's IP address, informs the rest of the network as to what kind of subnet the device is on.

..bnets — In an internetwork, the individual networks that are joined together by routers.

..bnetting — The process of subdividing a single class of network into multiple, smaller networks.

..bprotocols — Small, specialized protocols that work together and belong to a protocol suite.

..pported services list — A document (preferably online) that lists every service and software package supported within an organization, plus the names of first- and second-level support contacts for those services or software packages.

..rge — A momentary increase in voltage due to distant lightning strikes or electrical problems.

..C (switched virtual circuit) — Logical, point-to-point connections that rely on switches to determine the optimal path between sender and receiver. ATM technology uses SVCs.

..ap file — See *page file*.

..itch — 1) A connectivity device that logically subdivides a network into smaller, individual segments. Most switches operate at the Data Link layer of the OSI Model. They interpret MAC address information to determine whether to filter (discard) or forward packets they receive. 2) The letters or words added to a command that allow you to customize a utility's output. Switches are usually preceded by a hyphen or a forward slash character.

..itched Ethernet — An Ethernet model that enables multiple nodes to simultaneously transmit and receive data and individually take advantage of more bandwidth because they are assigned separate logical network segments through switching.

..itching — A component of a network's logical topology that manages how packets are filtered and forwarded between nodes on the network.

symmetric encryption — A method of encryption that requires the same key to encode the data as is used to decode the cipher text.

symmetric multiprocessing — A method of multiprocessing that splits all operations equally among two or more processors. Windows 2000 Server supports this type of multiprocessing.

symmetrical — A characteristic of transmission technology that provides equal throughput for data traveling both upstream and downstream and is suited to users who both upload and download significant amounts of data.

symmetrical DSL — A variation of DSL that provides equal throughput both upstream and downstream between the customer and the carrier.

synchronous — A transmission method in which data being transmitted and received by nodes must conform to a timing scheme.

System V — The proprietary version of UNIX, originally developed at AT&T Bell Labs, currently distributed by Caldera International and Tarantella, Inc.

T-carriers — The term for any kind of leased line that follows the standards for T1s, fractional T1s, T1Cs, T2s, T3s, or T4s.

T1 — A T-carrier technology that provides 1.544-Mbps throughput and 24 channels for voice, data, video, or audio signals. T1s may use shielded or unshielded twisted-pair, coaxial cable, fiber-optic, or microwave links. Businesses commonly use T1s to connect to their ISP, and phone companies typically use at least one T1 to connect their central offices.

T3 — A T-carrier technology that can carry the equivalent of 672 channels for voice, data, video, or audio, with a maximum data throughput of 44.736 Mbps (typically rounded up to 45 Mbps for purposes of discussion). T3s require either fiber-optic or microwave transmission media.

TCP segment — The portion of a TCP/IP packet that holds TCP data fields and becomes encapsulated by the IP datagram.

TCP/IP core protocols — The subprotocols of the TCP/IP suite.

teleconnector — A transceiver used on LocalTalk networks. The teleconnector is linked to the node's serial port on one side, and to the wall jack on the other side.

Telnet — A terminal emulation protocol used to log on to remote hosts using the TCP/IP protocol. Telnet resides in the Application layer of the TCP/IP suite.

terminal — A device with little (if any) of its own processing or disk capacity that depends on a host to supply it with applications and data-processing services.

Terminal Access Controller Access Control System (TACACS) — A centralized authentication system for remote access servers that is similar to RADIUS.

terminal adapter (TA) — Devices used to convert digital signals into analog signals for use with ISDN phones and other analog devices. Terminal adapters are sometimes called ISDN modems.

terminal equipment (TE) — Devices that connect computers to the ISDN line. Terminal equipment may include standalone devices or cards (similar to the network adapters used on Ethernet and Token Ring networks) or ISDN routers.

Thicknet — A type of coaxial cable, also known as thickwire Ethernet, that is a rigid cable approximately 1-cm thick. Thicknet was used for the original Ethernet networks. Because it is often covered with a yellow sheath, Thicknet is also called "yellow Ethernet." IEEE has designated Thicknet as 10Base5 Ethernet, with the "10" representing its throughput of 10 Mbps, the "Base" standing for baseband transmission, and the "5" representing the maximum segment length of a Thicknet cable, 500 m.

thickwire Ethernet — See *Thicknet.*

thin client — A type of software that enables a client to accomplish functions over a network while utilizing little of the client workstation's resources and, instead, relying on the server to carry the processing burden.

thin Ethernet — See *Thinnet.*

Thinnet — A type of coaxial cable, also known as thin Ethernet, that was the most popular medium for Ethernet LANs in the 1980s. Like Thicknet, Thinnet is rarely used on modern networks. IEEE has designated Thinnet as 10Base2 Ethernet, with the "10" representing its data transmission rate of 10 Mbps, the "Base" representing the fact that it uses baseband transmission, and the "2" roughly representing its maximum segment length of 185 m.

thread — A well-defined, self-contained subset of a process. Using threads within a process enables a program to efficiently perform related, multiple, simultaneous activities. Threads are also used to enable processes to use multiple processors on SMP systems.

throughput — The amount of data that a medium can transmit during a given period of time. Throughput is usually measured in megabits (1,000,000 bits) per second, or Mbps. The physical nature of every transmission medium determines its potential throughput.

ticket — In Kerberos terminology, a temporary set of credentials that a client uses to prove that its identity has been validated by the authentication service.

ticket granting service (TGS) — In Kerberos terminology, an application that runs on the key distribution center that issues ticket granting tickets to clients so that they need not request a new ticket for each new service they want to access.

ticket granting ticket (TGT) — In Kerberos terminology, a ticket that enables a user to be accepted as a validated principal by multiple services.

tiered WAN topology — A WAN topology in which sites are connected in star or ring formations and interconnected at different levels with the interconnection points organized into layers.

time division multiplexing (TDM) — A method of multiplexing that assigns a time slot in the flow of communications to every node on the network and in that time slot, carries data from that node.

time domain reflectometer (TDR) — A high-end instrument for testing the qualities of a cable. It works by issuing a signal on a cable and measuring the way in which the signal bounces back (or reflects) to the TDR.

time-dependent virus — A virus programmed to activate on a particular date. This type of virus, also known as a "time bomb," can remain dormant and harmless until its activation date arrives.

time-sharing system — A computing system to which users must attach directly so as to use the shared resources of the computer.

TLS (Transport Layer Security) — A version of SSL being standardized by the Internet Engineering Task Force (IETF). With TLS, IETF aims to create a version of SSL that will encrypt UDP as well as TCP transmissions. TLS, which will likely be supported by new Web browsers, uses slightly different encryption algorithms than SSL, but otherwise is very similar to the most recent version of SSL.

token — A special control frame that indicates to the rest of the network that a particular node has the right to transmit data.

token passing — A means of data transmission in which a 3-byte packet, called a token, is passed around the network in a round-robin fashion.

Token Ring — A networking technology developed by IBM in the 1980s. It relies upon direct links between nodes and a ring topology, using tokens to allow nodes to transmit data.

Token Ring media filter — A device that enables a DB-9 cable and a type 1 IBM cable to be connected.

tone generator — A small electronic device that issues a signal on a wire pair. When used in conjunction with a tone locator, it can help locate the termination of a wire pair.

tone locator—A small electronic device that emits a tone when it detects electrical activity on a wire pair. When used in conjunction with a tone generator, it can help locate the termination of a wire pair.

top-level domain (TLD) — The highest-level category used to distinguish domain names—for example, .org, .com, .net. A TLD is also known as the domain suffix.

topology — The physical layout of a computer network.

traceroute (or tracert) — A TCP/IP troubleshooting utility that uses ICMP to trace the path from one networked node to another, identifying all intermediate hops between the two nodes. Traceroute is useful for determining router or subnet connectivity problems.

traffic — The data transmission and processing activity taking place on a computer network at any given time.

fic monitoring — Determining how much processing activity is taking place on a network or network segment and notifying administrators when a segment becomes overloaded.

nsceiver (transmitter/receiver) — A device that both transmits and receives signals. Since a transceiver is concerned with applying signals to the wire, it belongs in the Physical layer of the OSI Model. Many different types of transceivers exist in networking.

nslational bridging — A type of bridging in which bridges can not only forward packets, but also translate packets between one logical topology and another. For instance, translational bridging can connect Token Ring and Ethernet networks.

nsmission — In networking, the application of data signals to a medium or the progress of data signals over a medium from one point to another.

ansmission Control Protocol (TCP) — A core protocol of the TCP/IP suite. TCP belongs to the Transport layer and provides reliable data delivery services.

nsmission media — The means through which data are transmitted and received. Transmission media may be physical, such as wire or cable, or atmospheric (wireless), such as radio waves.

nsparent bridging — The method of bridging used on most Ethernet networks.

ansport layer — The fourth layer of the OSI Model. The Transport layer is primarily responsible for ensuring that data are transferred from point A to point B (which may or may not be on the same network segment) reliably and without errors.

e — A logical representation of multiple, hierarchical levels in a directory. It is called a tree because the whole structure shares a common starting point (the root) and from that point extends branches (or containers), which may extend additional branches, and so on.

ivial File Transfer Protocol (TFTP) — A TCP/IP Application layer protocol that enables file transfers between computers. Unlike FTP, TFTP relies on UDP at the Transport layer and does not require a user to log onto the remote host.

ojan horse — A program that disguises itself as something useful but actually harms your system.

ıst relationship — The relationship between two domains on a Windows 2000 or Windows NT network that allows a domain controller from one domain to authenticate users from the other domain.

nneling — The process of encapsulating one protocol to make it appear as another type of protocol.

ist ratio — The number of twists per meter or foot in a twisted-pair cable.

isted-pair (TP) — A type of cable similar to telephone wiring that consists of color-coded pairs of insulated copper wires, each with a diameter of 0.4 to 0.8 mm, twisted around each other and encased in plastic coating.

two-way transitive trust — The security relationship between domains in the same domain tree in which one domain grants every other domain in the tree access to its resources and, in turn, that domain can access other domains' resources. When a new domain is added to a tree, it immediately shares a two-way trust with the other domains in the tree.

type 1 IBM connector — A type of Token Ring connector that uses interlocking tabs that snap into an identical connector when one is flipped upside-down, making for a secure connection. Type 1 IBM connectors are used on STP-based Token Ring networks.

typeful — A way of denoting an object's context in which the Organization and Organizational Unit designators ("O" and "OU," respectively) are included. For example, OU=Inv.OU=Ops.OU=Corp.O=Sutkin.

typeless — A way of denoting an object's context in which the Organization and Organizational Unit designators ("O" and "OU," respectively) are omitted. For example, Inv.Ops.Corp.Sutkin.

unicast address — A type of IPv6 address that represents a single interface on a device. An IPv6 unicast address begins with either FFC0 or FF80.

Uniform Resource Locator (URL) — A standard means of identifying every Web page, which specifies the service used, its server's host name, and its HTML page or script name.

uninterruptible power supply (UPS) — A battery-operated power source directly attached to one or more devices and to a power supply (such as a wall outlet), which prevents undesired features of the power source from harming the device or interrupting its services.

Universal Disk Format (UDF) — A file system used on CD-ROMs and digital video disc (DVD) media.

universal group — A group on a Windows 2000 network that allows members from one domain to access resources in multiple domains and forests.

unqualified host name — A TCP/IP host name minus its prefix and suffix.

unshielded twisted-pair (UTP) — A type of cabling that consists of one or more insulated wire pairs encased in a plastic sheath. As its name implies, UTP does not contain additional shielding for the twisted pairs. As a result, UTP is both less expensive and less resistant to noise than STP.

upgrade — A major change to the existing code in a software program, which may or may not be offered free from a vendor and may or may not be comprehensive enough to substitute for the original program.

upstream — A term used to describe data traffic that flows from a customer's site to the local carrier's POP. In asymmetrical communications, upstream throughput is usually much lower than downstream throughput. In symmetrical communications, upstream and downstream throughputs are equal.

USB (universal serial bus) port — A standard external bus that can be used to connect multiple types of peripherals, including modems, mice, and network adapters, to a computer. The original USB standard was capable of transmitting only 12 Mbps of data; a new standard is capable of transmitting 480 Mbps of data.

user — A person who uses a computer.

User Datagram Protocol (UDP) — A core protocol in the TCP/IP suite that sits in the Transport layer, between the Internet layer and the Application layer of the TCP/IP model. UDP is a connectionless transport service.

user principal name (UPN) — The preferred Active Directory naming convention for objects when used in informal situations. This name looks like a familiar Internet address, including the positioning of the domain name after the @ sign. UPNs are typically used for e-mail and related Internet services.

user principal name (UPN) suffix — The portion of a universal principal name (in Windows 2000 Active Directory's naming conventions) that follows the @ sign.

vampire tap — A connector used on Thicknet MAUs that pierces a hole in the coaxial cable, thus completing a connection between the metal tooth in the vampire tap and the copper core of the cable.

vault — A large tape storage library.

virtual circuits — Connections between network nodes that, while based on potentially disparate physical links, logically appear to be direct, dedicated links between those nodes.

virtual local area network (VLAN) — A network within a network that is logically defined by grouping its devices' switch ports in the same broadcast domain. A VLAN can consist of servers, workstations, printers, routers, or any other network device you can connect to a switch.

virtual memory — Memory that is logically carved out of space on the hard disk and added to physical memory (RAM).

virtual private network (VPN) — A logically constructed WAN that uses existing public transmission systems. VPNs can be created through the use of software or combined software and hardware solutions. This type of network allows an organization to carve out a private WAN on the Internet (or, less commonly over leased lines) that serves only its offices, while keeping the data secure and isolated from other (public) traffic.

virus — A program that replicates itself so as to infect more computers, either through network connections or through floppy disks passed among users. Viruses may damage files or systems or simply annoy users by flashing messages or pictures on the screen or by causing the keyboard to beep.

virus hoax — A rumor, or false alert, about a dangerous, new virus that could supposedly cause serious damage to your workstation.

Voice over IP (VoIP) — The provision of telephone service over a TCP/IP network. (Pronounced "voyp".) One form of VoIP is Internet telephony.

volt — Measurement used to describe the degree of pressure an electrical current exerts on a conductor.

volt-amp (VA) — A measure of electrical power. A volt-amp is the product of the voltage and current (measured in amps) of the electricity on a line.

voltage — The pressure (sometimes informally referred to as the strength) of an electrical current.

voltmeter — Device used to measure voltage (or electrical pressure) on an electrical circuit.

WAN — See *wide area network*.

WAN link — The line that connects one location on a WAN with another location.

WAN topology — The physical layout, or pattern, of locations on a wide area network (WAN).

wavelength — The distance between corresponding points on a wave's cycle. Wavelength is inversely proportional to frequency.

wavelength division multiplexing (WDM) — A multiplexing technique in which each signal on a fiber-optic cable is assigned a different wavelength, which equates to its own subchannel. Each wavelength is modulated with a data signal. In this manner multiple signals can be simultaneously transmitted in the same direction over a length of fiber.

Webcasting — A broadcast transmission from one Internet-attached node to multiple other Internet-attached nodes.

well-known ports — TCP/IP port numbers 0 to 1023, so called because they were long ago assigned by Internet authorities to popular services (for example, FTP and Telnet), and are therefore well known and frequently used.

wide area network (WAN) — A network connecting geographically distinct locations, which may or may not belong to the same organization. The Internet is an example of a very large WAN.

Windows Internet Naming Service (WINS) — A service that resolves NetBIOS names with IP addresses. WINS is used exclusively with systems that use NetBIOS—therefore, it is usually found on Windows-based systems.

winipcfg — The TCP/IP configuration and management utility for use with Windows 9x systems. Winipcfg differs from ipconfig in that it supplies a graphical user interface.

wireless — Networks that transmit signals through the atmosphere via infrared or RF signaling.

wizard — A simple graphical program that assists the user in performing complex tasks, such as configuring a NIC on a server.

workgroup — A group of interconnected computers that share each others' resources without relying on a central file server.

workstation — A computer that typically runs a desktop operating system and connects to a network.

orld Wide Web (WWW or Web) — A collection of inter-networked servers that share resources and exchange information according to specific protocols and formats.

orm — An unwanted program that travels between computers and across networks. Although worms do not alter other programs as viruses do, they may carry viruses.

X.25 — An analog packet switched WAN technology optimized for long-distance data transmission and standardized by the ITU in the mid-1970s. X.25 can support 2-Mbps throughput. It was originally developed and used for communications between mainframe computers and remote terminals.

xDSL — Term used to refer to all varieties of DSL.

zone — The group of machines managed by a DNS server.

Index

Internetwork Packet Exchange/Sequenced Packet Exchange (IPX/SPX), 80–86

addressing, 85–86

core protocols, 81–84

OSI Model compared, 81

interrupt(s), 256

interrupt requests (IRQs), 256–259

IntraNetWare, 438

intrusion detection, 703

IP. *See* Internet Protocol (IP)

IP addresses, 75, 520–522

static, 78

viewing current information, 78–79

ipconfig utility, troubleshooting TCP/IP, 565–566

IP next generation (IPng), 549

IPSec (Internet Protocol Security), 787–788

IP spoofing, 764

IP version 6 (IPv6), 524, 549–551

IPX (Internetwork Packet Exchange), 81–82

IPX addresses, 85, 86

IPX/SPX. *See* Internetwork Packet Exchange/Sequenced Packet Exchange (IPX/SPX)

IRQ(s) (interrupt requests), 256–259

IRQ numbers, 256–257

ISA (Industry Standard Architecture), 241

ISDN (Integrated Services Digital Network), 315–317

ISO (International Organization for Standardization), 38

ITU (International Telecommunication Union), 36, 38–39

J

jabbers, 632

jamming, 200

job searches, 20–21

jumpers, 252, 253

K

KDCs (key distribution centers), 784–785

Kerberos, 784–785

kernel

Linux, 488–489

NetWare, 444–445

kernel modules, Linux, 488

key(s), encryption, 781–782

key distribution centers (KDCs), 784–785

key management, 787

key pairs, 783

L

LADP (Lightweight Directory Access Protocol), 399

LAMs (Lobe Attachment Modules), 213

LAN(s). *See* local area networks (LANs)

LANalyzer, 633–634

LAN Emulation (LANE), 218

LAN gateway, 286

late collisions, 632

latency, 125

Layer 2 Forwarding (L2F), 789

Layer 3 switches, 280

Layer 4 switches, 280

Layer 2 Tunneling Protocol (L2TP), 789

leadership abilities of networking professionals, 18

leaf objects, 370, 450–451

leasing DHCP. *See* Dynamic Host Configuration Protocol (DHCP)

L2F (Layer 2 Forwarding), 789

license tracking, 15

Lightweight Directory Access Protocol (LADP), 399

line noise, 715

Linux, 483, 487–503

commands, 491–495

configuring for network administration, 500–503

directory structure, 489

file services, 490

file structure, 489

installing, 496–500

Internet services, 490

kernel, 488–489

memory model, 488

multiprocessing, 488

processes, 490

P

packet-filtering firewalls, 773

Packet Internet Groper (PING), 569–570

packet switching, 198–199, 313–315

padding, 205

page files, 379

paging, 379

parallel backbones, 190–191

parallel port network adapters, 245

parity, 729

distributed, 730

parity error checking, 729

passive hubs, 267

password(s), 769–770

Password Restrictions dialog box, 462

patch(es), 671–673

patch cables, 149

patch panels, cable plants, 148

PC Cards, 243–244

PCI (Peripheral Component Interconnect), 242

PCMCIA (Personal Computer Memory Card International Association) interfaces, 243–244

PC-to-PC VoIP, 576

PC-to-phone VoIP, 576

peer-to-peer topologies, 2–3, 7, 193

people. *See* networking professionals; security risks associated with people; staff people

performance requirements, needs assessment, 825

Peripheral Component Interconnect (PCI), 242

permanent virtual circuits (PVCs), 314

Personal Computer Memory Card International Association (PCMCIA) interfaces, 243–244

PGP (Pretty Good Privacy), 786

phase of analog signals, 110

phone-to-phone VoIP, 575–576

physical connectivity, verifying, 613–617

Physical layer

networking standards, 145–146

OSI Model, 40–41, 636–639

problems and symptoms, 636–639

physical memory, 378

physical plant changes. *See* hardware and physical plant changes

physical security, 770–772

physical topologies

hybrid, 184–187

simple, 178–183

pilot networks, 829–830

PING (Packet Internet Groper), 569–570

pinging, 569

pipe (|), Linux commands, 491

pipelines, 491

plain old telephone service (POTS), 310

plenum, 154

pliers, 888

pocket flashlights, 890

point of presence (POP), 311–312

Point-to-Point Protocol (PPP), 338–339

point-to-point transmission, 118

Point-to-Point Tunneling Protocol (PPTP), 789

polymorphic viruses, 708

POP. *See* point of presence (POP); Post Office Protocol (POP)

ports, 72–73

TCP/IP, 531–533

Post Office Protocol (POP), 554–555

POTS (plain old telephone service), 310

power, fault tolerance, 714–718

PPP (Point-to-Point Protocol), 338–339

PPTP (Point-to-Point Tunneling Protocol), 789

precision knives, 891

predecessors in project plans, 811

preemptive multitasking, 379

Presentation layer of OSI Model, 44–45

Pretty Good Privacy (PGP), 786

Primary Rate Interface (PRI), 315, 316–317

principals, Kerberos, 785

printer(s)

adding to network, 681

misbehaving, 641–642

sharing, 375–378

printer network adapters, 248

Network+ CoursePrep ExamGuide

Tamara Dean

THOMSON
COURSE TECHNOLOGY

Australia • Canada • Mexico • Singapore • Spain • United Kingdom • United States

TABLE OF CONTENTS

PREFACE

The *Network+ CoursePrep ExamGuide* is the very best tool to use to prepare for exam day. It provides thorough preparation for the CompTIA Network + exam.

COURSEPREP EXAMGUIDE

The *Network + CoursePrep ExamGuide* provides the essential information you need to master each exam objective. The ExamGuide devotes an entire two-page spread to each certification objective for the Network+ exam, helping you understand the objective, and giving you the bottom line information—what you *really* need to know. Memorize these facts and bulleted points before heading into the exam. In addition, there are seven practice-test questions for each objective on the right-hand page—that's over 600 questions total! CoursePrep ExamGuide provides the exam fundamentals and gets you up to speed quickly. If you are seeking even more opportunity to practice and prepare, we recommend that you consider our total solution, CoursePrep StudyGuide, which is described below.

COURSEPREP STUDYGUIDE

For those really serious about certification, we offer an even more robust solution—the *Network+ CoursePrep StudyGuide, Second Edition*, ISBN 0-619-12132-7. This offering includes all of the same great features you get with the CoursePrep ExamGuide, including the unique two page spread, the bulleted memorization points and the practice questions. In addition, you receive a password valid for six months of practice on CoursePrep, a dynamic test preparation tool. The password is found in an envelope in the back cover of the CoursePrep StudyGuide. CoursePrep is a Web-based pool of hundreds of sample test questions. CoursePrep exam simulation software mimics the exact exam environment. The CoursePrep software is flexible and allows you to practice several ways as you master the material. Choose from Certification Mode to experience actual exam-day conditions or Study Mode to request answers and explanations to practice questions. Custom Mode lets you set the options for the practice test, including number of questions, content coverage, and ability to request answers and explanation. Follow the instructions on the inside back cover to access the exam simulation software. To see a demo of this dynamic test preparation tool, go to *www.courseprep.com*.

FEATURES

The *Network+ CoursePrep ExamGuide* includes the following features:

Description of domains taken from the CompTIA Web site Each exam objective belongs to one of four domains (or broad areas) of networking knowledge. CompTIA's description of these domains helps you plan your course of study and explains the percentage of the exam devoted to each domain. For more information about Network+ exams, visit the CompTIA Web site at *www.comptia.org*.

Detailed coverage of the certification objectives in a unique two-page spread Study strategically by really focusing in on the Network+ certification objectives. To enable you to do this, each certification objective is explained in a two-page format. The left-hand page provides the critical facts you need, while the right-hand page features practice questions relating to that objective. You'll find the certification objective(s) and sub-objectives(s) at the top of each left-hand page.

An overview of the objective is provided in the ***Understanding the Objective*** section. Next, ***What You Really Need to Know*** lists bulleted, succinct facts, skills, and concepts about the objective. Memorizing these facts will be important for your success when taking the exam. ***Objectives on the Job*** places the objective in an industry perspective and tells you how you can expect to incorporate the objective on the job. This section also provides troubleshooting information.

Practice Test Questions Each right-hand page contains seven practice test questions designed to help you prepare for the exam by testing your skills, identifying your strengths and weaknesses, and demonstrating the subject matter you will face on the exam and how it will be tested. These questions are written in a similar fashion to real Network+ exam questions. The questions test your knowledge of the objectives described on the left-hand page. You can find answers to the practice test questions in the answer key at the back of the book and on the CoursePrep Web site (*www.courseprep.com*), where you can also find additional Web-based exam preparation questions.

Glossary Boldfaced terms used in the book and other terms that you need to know for the exams are listed and defined in the glossary.

ACKNOWLEDGMENTS

I could not have completed this guide without the support and planning of the ever-capable and efficient Course Technology staff, especially Amy Lyon, Product Manager, Lisa Egan, Senior Product Manager, and all those who contributed to further refining the text and creating the finished product. Many thanks to Ann Shaffer, the Developmental Editor, for doing a superb job of ensuring clarity and consistency and always being a joy to work with. Thanks also to the technical editor, James Conrad, who scrutinized the content and helped to make the guide more accurate and complete, and to Karen Jacot, Course Technology Production Editor, for helping to transform the manuscript into a published book. For additional help with technical material, I'm grateful to my smart, generous colleagues, Peyton Engel, Michael Grice, and David Klann. Thanks to Paul and Jan Dean, Nancy Dale, Sara, Bridget, Sandhya, Ann, Stacy, Jen, Lea, Kris, Susan, Carol, Paula, Alicia, and Sandy for being strong and good-humored allies.

Network+ Objectives

The following descriptions of the Network+ Objective domains are taken from the CompTIA Web site at *www.comptia.org*. Each objective belongs to one of four domains (or broad areas) of networking knowledge. For example, the objective of recognizing an RJ-45 connector belongs to the "Media and Topologies" domain, which accounts for 20 percent of the exam's content.

Domain 1.0: Media and Topologies — 20 percent of examination

This domain requires knowledge of cabling and connector types, physical topologies (such as the star topology), and logical topologies (such as Ethernet and Token Ring) that make up a network. It also includes an understanding of network connectivity devices such as hubs, routers, switches, and gateways. Many of the topics in this domain comply with industry standards, such as IEEE's working group standards for Physical and Data Link layer network access. Although the topics in this domain are highly technical, they are also relatively straightforward.

Domain 2.0: Protocols and Standards — 25 percent of examination

This domain requires knowledge of protocols and standards, the means by which two computers communicate. Given that the most popular network protocol currently used on networks is TCP/IP, this domain pays particular attention to the protocols and subprotocols in the TCP/IP suite. In addition to protocols, this domain covers the OSI Model, a popular theoretical construct used to describe computer-to-computer communication. Much of the knowledge in this domain refers to networking at the most fundamental, data-bit level.

Domain 3.0: Network Implementation — 23 percent of examination

This domain requires understanding of the most popular networking clients and network operating systems (NOSs). It covers not only the features of each, but also how to integrate different clients with different NOSs. In addition, this domain requires knowledge of good networking practices to ensure that data is safe and always available and that network access is never interrupted.

Domain 4.0: Network Support — 32 percent of examination

This domain requires the ability to diagnose and troubleshoot common network problems relating to client connectivity, remote connectivity, topology, hardware, and media. It requires knowledge of troubleshooting utilities and methodology. This domain emphasizes practical knowledge that will prove invaluable in a networking career.

1.1 Recognize the following logical or physical network topologies given a schematic diagram or description:

STAR/HIERARCHICAL PHYSICAL TOPOLOGY

UNDERSTANDING THE OBJECTIVE

Every network depends on a physical layout, or topology. The **physical topology** describes how servers, workstations, printers, and other devices are physically connected in a **local-area network (LAN)** or **wide-area network (WAN)**. While most modern networks contain a combination of topologies, all combinations rely on a few fundamental topologies: bus, star, and ring. Because each individual topology has particular advantages and disadvantages, different situations may require different topologies. The most common physical topology used on modern networks is a star, or hierarchical, topology.

WHAT YOU REALLY NEED TO KNOW

◆ In a **star topology**, every node on the network is connected through a central device, such as a hub, in a star configuration, as shown in the following diagram:

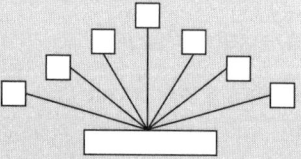

◆ In a star topology network, each device transmits its data to the hub, which repeats the data to all other devices on the segment. The recipient node then picks up the data addressed to it.

◆ Any single physical wire on a star network only connects two devices, so a cabling problem will only affect two nodes. Devices such as workstations or printers transmit data to the hub, which then retransmits the data to the network segment where the destination node is located, so the destination node can pick it up.

◆ Star topologies are more fault-tolerant and provide better performance than bus or ring topologies. On Ethernet networks, a single cable or node fault will not immobilize a star-wired network. However, star networks require more cabling and devices and are generally more expensive than bus or ring networks.

◆ Star networks can be easily upgraded, moved, and interconnected with other networks.

◆ Star topology networks that divide workstation groups and connectivity devices into layers are known as **hierarchical**.

OBJECTIVES ON THE JOB

The star topology forms the basis of the most popular type of network in use today. Because it is so popular, you should be familiar with the way connectivity devices and nodes are arranged in this topology. As your experience with star topology networks increases, you will also learn how to troubleshoot and add to them.

PRACTICE TEST QUESTIONS

1. **Which of the following is an advantage to using star topology networks over using bus or ring topology networks?**
   a. Star topology networks are more scalable.
   b. Star topology networks are less expensive to install.
   c. Star topology networks are easier to install.
   d. Star topology networks are more secure.

2. **What would happen if a node in a star-wired Ethernet network failed?**
   a. Performance over the entire network would suffer slightly.
   b. Only the failed node would be unable to transmit or receive data.
   c. Data could no longer be transmitted or received at any point in the network.
   d. The failed node would broadcast errors to the rest of the network.

3. **What is the function of a hub in a star-wired network?**
   a. to reduce RF emissions that may result in security breaches
   b. to increase available bandwidth by sending multiplexed signals
   c. to arbitrate addressing conflicts between sending nodes
   d. to repeat signals to all nodes on the segment

4. **In a network using the star topology, five workstations and a hub would be connected via how many physical cables?**
   a. three
   b. four
   c. five
   d. six

5. **In which of the following networks would it make the most sense to implement a hierarchical topology?**
   a. a LAN that connects two local lumber yards
   b. a WAN that connects freelance writers across the nation
   c. a LAN that connects multiple departments, offices, and employees in an insurance company
   d. a WAN that connects multiple churches within a city

6. **What would happen to a star network if one of its workgroup hubs failed?**
   a. All nodes connected to that hub would be unable to communicate with nodes on other segments, but they could communicate with each other.
   b. All nodes connected to that hub would be unable to communicate with nodes on other segments as well as nodes on their own segment.
   c. Nodes would be able to communicate with the network, as they would automatically connect to an alternate hub on the backbone.
   d. Communication on the entire LAN would halt.

7. **What type of terminator is used on a star-wired network?**
   a. 20-ohm resistor
   b. 50-ohm resistor
   c. 100-ohm resistor
   d. Terminators are not used on star-wired networks.

OBJECTIVES

1.1 Recognize the following logical or physical network topologies given a schematic diagram or description (continued):

BUS PHYSICAL TOPOLOGY

UNDERSTANDING THE OBJECTIVE

A bus topology is one in which multiple nodes share a single channel. By sharing that channel, they also share a fixed amount of bandwidth. Bus topologies are used on 10Base5 and 10Base2 Ethernet networks.

WHAT YOU REALLY NEED TO KNOW

◆ A **bus topology** consists of a single cable connecting all nodes on a network without intervening connectivity devices and appears as follows in a network diagram:

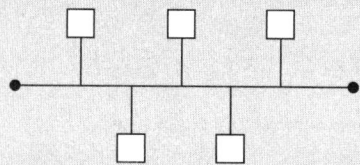

◆ Since every node on a bus topology network shares the same channel for data transmission, adding nodes on a bus network impairs performance.

◆ A bus topology can be considered a peer-to-peer topology because every device on the network shares the responsibility for getting data from one point to another.

◆ Bus topologies require 50-ohm resistors known as **terminators** at each end of the bus to prevent **signal bounce**, a phenomenon in which data travels endlessly between the two ends of the network.

◆ The bus topology is the least fault-tolerant of any topology, because one break in the cable can take down the entire network, and bus topology faults are difficult to find.

◆ A bus topology is the least expensive and simplest topology to install.

OBJECTIVES ON THE JOB

If you use a bus topology, chances are you are working on a Thinnet (10Base2) network. Bear in mind that if one of the nodes fails, the entire network will lose connectivity. For this reason, and because the addition of more nodes will cause performance problems, it may be wise to upgrade a bus topology network to a star topology network.

PRACTICE TEST QUESTIONS

1. On a bus topology, terminators eliminate the possibility of:
   a. crosstalk.
   b. noise.
   c. signal bounce.
   d. EMI.

2. How many nodes share a single channel on a bus topology?
   a. all connected nodes
   b. one
   c. two
   d. four

3. Which two of the following types of networks use a bus topology?
   a. 10BaseT
   b. 100BaseT
   c. 10Base5
   d. 10Base2

4. What is one advantage of using a network based on the bus topology over a network based on the star or mesh topologies?
   a. Bus topologies are more fault tolerant.
   b. Bus topologies allow faster throughput.
   c. Bus topologies are more secure.
   d. Bus topologies are simpler to install and maintain.

5. What type of terminator is used on a bus network?
   a. 20-ohm resistor
   b. 50-ohm resistor
   c. 20-ohm transistor
   d. 50-ohm transistor

6. You are the administrator for a LAN that uses the bus topology to connect seven workstations. Each workstation runs Windows 2000 Professional. What would you need to do if you wanted to add a workstation to the network and enable other workstations to read data from the new workstation's hard disk?
   a. Apply shared access to the appropriate folders on the new workstation.
   b. Modify the sharing services parameters in the domain controller's operating system.
   c. Modify the file sharing properties on each workstation on the network so that each can read from the added workstation.
   d. Add the new workstation's account to a folder-sharing group on the network.

7. What would happen to the entire network if one of the nodes in a bus-wired network failed?
   a. Performance would suffer slightly.
   b. The failed node could not transmit data, but other nodes would be fine.
   c. Data would no longer be transmitted to or from any node.
   d. Errors would be broadcast to every node.

1.1 Recognize the following logical or physical network topologies given a schematic diagram or description (continued):

MESH PHYSICAL TOPOLOGY

UNDERSTANDING THE OBJECTIVE

In a LAN, a mesh topology is one in which at least some of the nodes are connected via more than one link. In a WAN, a mesh topology is one in which some of the locations are connected via more than one link. Mesh topologies are most commonly used in WANs.

WHAT YOU REALLY NEED TO KNOW

◆ A **mesh topology** is one in which nodes or locations are directly interconnected with multiple other nodes or locations on the network.

◆ A network may use a **full-mesh topology**, in which each node is connected directly to each other node, as shown in the following diagram:

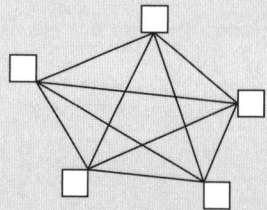

◆ Full-mesh topologies are the most expensive physical topologies because they require the most equipment, connectivity, setup, and maintenance. However, they are also the most fault-tolerant physical topologies.

◆ A less expensive, yet still fault-tolerant alternative to full-mesh topologies is a **partial-mesh topology**, in which only some of the nodes on a network are directly connected to other nodes, as shown in the following diagram:

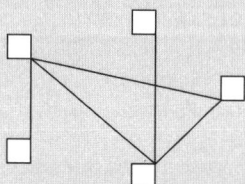

◆ Mesh topologies are typically used in the context of wide-area networks (WANs). A location in a WAN topology is equivalent to a node in a LAN topology.

OBJECTIVES ON THE JOB

If you are designing a WAN that must be fault tolerant, a mesh topology is a wise choice. In designing a partial mesh, arrange the redundant links so that they connect the most critical locations on the network.

PRACTICE TEST QUESTIONS

1. **Which of the following advantages does a partial-mesh topology provide?**
   a. All nodes have multiple connections to the network.
   b. At least some nodes have multiple connections to the network.
   c. Any node can be taken down without affecting network performance.
   d. Network performance will be similar, no matter what kind of link is used between nodes.

2. **Which of the following is the most fault-tolerant WAN topology?**
   a. partial mesh
   b. full mesh
   c. ring
   d. hierarchical

3. **If a full-mesh WAN consists of four locations, how many separate connections does it contain?**
   a. two
   b. four
   c. six
   d. eight

4. **If a partial-mesh WAN consists of four locations, how many separate connections might it contain? (Choose all that apply.)**
   a. two
   b. three
   c. four
   d. five

5. **Which of the following organizations is most likely to use a full-mesh WAN?**
   a. a school district
   b. a regional charitable organization
   c. a regional power company
   d. a local chain of grocers

6. **What would happen to the entire network if one of the nodes in a full-mesh WAN failed?**
   a. Performance for all locations on the WAN would suffer.
   b. The failed location would be unable to transmit or receive data, but other locations could communicate without a problem.
   c. Data would no longer be transmitted to or from any of the locations.
   d. The failed location would broadcast errors to every other location.

7. **A mesh WAN could connect LANs that use the bus topology. True or false?**

1.1 Recognize the following logical or physical network topologies given a schematic diagram or description (continued):

RING PHYSICAL TOPOLOGY

UNDERSTANDING THE OBJECTIVE

A ring topology connects nodes using a single channel in a ring. In order to determine which node can transmit data at any given time, ring networks use tokens that circulate on the network and are reserved by the transmitting node.

WHAT YOU REALLY NEED TO KNOW

♦ In a **ring topology**, each node is connected to the two nearest nodes so that the entire network forms a circle, as shown in the following diagram:

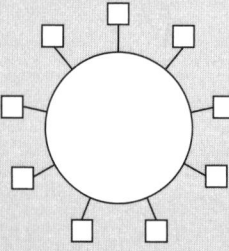

♦ Data is transmitted in one direction (unidirectionally) around the ring. Each workstation accepts and responds to packets addressed to it, then forwards the other packets to the next workstation in the ring.

♦ Because there are no ends to a ring network and because data stop at their destination, ring networks do not require terminators.

♦ Ring topologies often use the **token passing** technique, in which a node that wants to send data picks up the constantly circling token, adds its data, sends the packet, and when the recipient accepts the packet, releases the token so that other nodes can transmit.

♦ A disadvantage of the ring topology is that one defective node can take down the network.

♦ Another disadvantage with the ring topology is that, as with a bus topology, adding more nodes to a ring network can detract from performance.

♦ A popular hybrid topology used on Token Ring networks is the star-ring hybrid topology.

OBJECTIVES ON THE JOB

If you work with a Token Ring network, bear in mind that it will use the star-ring hybrid topology, not a simple ring topology. Still, you must be aware of the scalability limitations of this type of topology.

PRACTICE TEST QUESTIONS

1. **In which two of the following topologies will the addition of more nodes detrimentally affect the network's performance?**
   a. bus
   b. star
   c. ring
   d. mesh

2. **At any given time, how many tokens circulate on a simple ring network?**
   a. one
   b. five
   c. ten
   d. There are no limits on the number of tokens that may circulate.

3. **What is the function of a token on a token-passing ring network?**
   a. It signals to the rest of the network to listen for traffic.
   b. It signals to the rest of the network that the MAU is receiving an excessive number of errors.
   c. It enables multiple nodes on the network to transmit data simultaneously.
   d. It enables one node on the network to transmit data at any one time.

4. **A modern day Token Ring network actually uses which of the following hybrid topologies?**
   a. star-bus
   b. ring-bus
   c. ring-tree
   d. star-ring

5. **In how many directions is data transmitted on a ring network?**
   a. one
   b. two
   c. It depends on the number of nodes on the network.
   d. It depends on the location of the nodes on the network.

6. **What would happen to the entire network if one of the nodes in a simple ring network failed?**
   a. Performance over the entire network would suffer slightly.
   b. The failed node would be affected, but other nodes would be fine.
   c. Data would no longer be transmitted to or from any nodes.
   d. Errors would be broadcast to every node.

7. **What type of terminator is used on a ring network?**
   a. 20-ohm resistor
   b. 50-ohm resistor
   c. 20-ohm transistor
   d. Terminators are not used on ring networks.

1.1 Recognize the following logical or physical network topologies given a schematic diagram or description (continued):

WIRELESS PHYSICAL TOPOLOGY

UNDERSTANDING THE OBJECTIVE

Wireless network devices, which can interconnect with wire-bound networks, are represented on a network diagram by an antenna radiating concentric waves from one point to many points.

WHAT YOU REALLY NEED TO KNOW

◆ Nodes on a wireless network use special NICs with infrared or radio frequency transmitters (typically internal antennae) to issue signals to a base station.

◆ A wireless device's base station, or access point, allows it to connect and communicate with wire-bound devices on a LAN, such as servers and hubs.

◆ The use of base stations allows clients with wireless NICs to roam. Thus, the client does not have a static physical location on the network, as a node on a wire-bound network would have.

◆ When a large number of mobile clients are used, or when clients must communicate over a large geographical range, the number of access points must increase.

◆ When using base stations, nodes transmit signals in a broadcast fashion in order to ensure that the base station receives them. On a network diagram, this may be represented by an antenna radiating concentric waves from one point to many other points.

◆ Broadcast transmission is susceptible to eavesdropping. Thus, security is a concern in wireless networking. Using spread-spectrum radio frequency transmission is one way of improving wireless communications security.

◆ In some cases, wireless nodes may communicate directly with each other. By communicating directly, the nodes avoiding having to transmit first to a base station, then relying on the base station to repeat signals to another access point on the LAN.

◆ Wireless standards currently support data throughput at both 1 Mbps and 2 Mbps. At the 1 Mbps wireless data rate, it is possible to transmit over a greater range with less total throughput. At the 2 Mbps wireless data rate, it is possible to achieve greater throughput within a smaller range.

OBJECTIVES ON THE JOB

If you are installing or maintaining a wireless network, be certain to understand the nature of atmospheric transmission as well as the type of mobility your clients will require. This will help you determine the quantity and positioning of base stations in the network's topology.

PRACTICE TEST QUESTIONS

1. **Which of the following networks could integrate wireless devices?**
   a. Token Ring
   b. 10BaseT
   c. 100BaseT
   d. all of the above

2. **What is required for a NIC to transmit to a base station?**
   a. RJ-45 connector
   b. vampire tap
   c. antenna
   d. multiplexer

3. **As the distance between wireless mobile users and a wire-bound connectivity device increases,**
   a. the necessary quantity of base stations also increases.
   b. the possibility for eavesdropping on its signals also increases.
   c. the power required by the wireless node's NIC also increases.
   d. the possibility for incorrect data delivery also increases.

4. **What is another term for a base station?**
   a. antenna
   b. RF generator
   c. CSU/DSU
   d. access point

5. **Rather than using a base station, a wireless node may communicate directly with another wireless node. True or false?**

6. **Which of the following data transmission methods does a wireless NIC use?**
   a. duplex
   b. point-to-point
   c. broadcast
   d. unicast

7. **Which IEEE committee has specified standards for wireless LANs?**
   a. 802.2
   b. 802.3
   c. 802.10
   d. 802.11

1.2 Specify the main features of networking technologies, including speed, access, method, topology, and media:

802.2 (LLC)

UNDERSTANDING THE OBJECTIVE

Everything in the networking field, from hardware to protocols, relies on standards to ensure that components from different manufacturers can be easily integrated. IEEE is the body that sets standards at the Physical and Data Link layers of the OSI Model for computer networking. The most well-known IEEE standards are those set by the 802 Committee.

WHAT YOU REALLY NEED TO KNOW

◆ The **Institute of Electrical and Electronic Engineers (IEEE)**, or "I-triple-E," is an international society composed of engineering professionals. It maintains a standards board that establishes its own standards for the electronics and computer industry and contributes to other standards-setting bodies, such as ANSI.

◆ IEEE's committees set standards that apply to different layers of the OSI Model, including the Physical and Data Link layers, and therefore correspond to different network access methods and network media.

◆ The most well-known IEEE committee is the 802 committee. Among its popular standards are 802.3, which governs Ethernet networks; 802.5, which governs Token Ring networks; and 802.11, which governs wireless networks.

◆ To accommodate shared access for multiple network nodes (as opposed to simple point-to-point communication), the IEEE expanded the OSI Model by separating the Data Link layer into two sublayers: the Logical Link Control (LLC) sublayer and the Media Access Control (MAC) sublayer.

◆ The 802.2 standards apply to the **Logical Link Control sublayer (LLC)**, the upper sublayer in the Data Link layer, which provides a common interface and supplies reliability and flow control services.

◆ The **Media Access Control (MAC)** sublayer, the lower sublayer within the Data Link layer, appends the physical address of the destination to data frames.

◆ IEEE's specifications for Ethernet (802.3) and Token Ring (802.5) technology apply to the MAC sublayer of the Data Link layer. Thus, the 802.2 standards are independent but work in tandem with the 802.3 and 802.5 specifications.

OBJECTIVES ON THE JOB

All modern networks rely on the foundation of 802.2 LLC standards in order to frame data and ensure reliable delivery. You should be aware of how these standards are applied in your particular network, whether it uses Ethernet or Token Ring MAC sublayer standards.

PRACTICE TEST QUESTIONS

1. **The 802.2 standards apply to what sublayer of the Data Link layer?**
   a. the MAC sublayer
   b. the Logical Link Control sublayer
   c. the Access Method sublayer
   d. the Network Transmission sublayer

2. **To which other standards body does IEEE contribute its recommendations?**
   a. ISO
   b. OSI
   c. ITU
   d. ANSI

3. **In what year was the IEEE 802 committee formed?**
   a. 1980
   b. 1990
   c. 1995
   d. 1998

4. **Which of the following MAC sublayer specifications can work with the 802.2 sublayer specification? Choose all that apply.**
   a. 802.2
   b. 802.3
   c. 802.5
   d. 802.15

5. **Which of the following functions is handled by the 802.2 sublayer?**
   a. issuing electrical signals onto the wire
   b. appending a physical address to a data frame
   c. appending a logical address to a data frame
   d. ensuring appropriate flow control for a group of data frames

6. **The 802.2 specifications apply to the lower sublayer of the Data Link layer of the OSI Model. True or false?**

7. **What was the primary reason the IEEE divided the OSI Model's Data Link layer into two sublayers?**
   a. to account for the variety of functions required for point-to-point data communication
   b. to simplify the process of ensuring proper addressing between sending and receiving nodes
   c. to better articulate the difference between transmission and reception
   d. to accommodate evolving encryption techniques

1.2 Specify the main features of networking technologies, including speed, access, method, topology, and media (continued):

802.3 (ETHERNET)

UNDERSTANDING THE OBJECTIVE

IEEE 802.3 standards specify the MAC sublayer requirements for Ethernet standards, including its network access method, Carrier Sense Multiple Access/Collision Detection (CSMA/CD), which allows multiple nodes to share a single channel on an Ethernet network.

WHAT YOU REALLY NEED TO KNOW

◆ The 802.3 standards define elements of Ethernet networks in the MAC sublayer (of the Data Link layer)

◆ 802.3 specifies the **Carrier Sense Multiple Access/Collision Detection (CSMA/CD)** method of network access, allowing multiple nodes to share a single Ethernet channel.

◆ The term "Carrier Sense" refers to the fact that Ethernet NICs listen on the network and wait until they detect (or sense) that no other nodes are transmitting data over the signal (or carrier) on the communications channel before they begin to transmit. The term "Multiple Access" refers to the fact that several Ethernet nodes can be connected to a network and can monitor traffic, or access the media, simultaneously.

◆ In CSMA/CD, when a node wants to transmit data, it must first access the transmission media and determine whether the channel is free. If the channel is not free, it waits and checks again after a random (but brief) amount of time. If the channel is free, the node transmits its data.

◆ If two nodes simultaneously check the channel, determine that it's free, and begin to transmit, their two transmissions will interfere with each other; this is known as a **collision**. In this event, the network performs a series of steps known as the collision detection routine. If a station's NIC determines that its data has been involved in a collision, it will first propagate the collision throughout the network by using a **jamming** signal, ensuring that no other station attempts to transmit. Then the NIC remains silent for a random period of time. After waiting, the node will determine if the line is again available; if it is available, the line will retransmit its data.

◆ IEEE's 802.3 standards apply to all wire-based Ethernet network types, including 10Base2, 10Base5, 10BaseT, 100BaseT, and Gigabit Ethernet. These networks may use bus, star, or star-wired bus physical topologies.

OBJECTIVES ON THE JOB

Since the IEEE 802.3 standard forms the basis of the most popular networks in use today, you should be thoroughly familiar with its specifications. In particular, you should understand CSMA/CD, its advantages and disadvantages, and how it pertains to network performance on both 10BaseT and Fast Ethernet networks.

PRACTICE TEST QUESTIONS

1. **Which network access method is defined by IEEE 802.3?**
   - a. CSMA/CA
   - b. demand priority
   - c. token passing
   - d. CSMA/CD

2. **A network that follows 802.3 specifications would use which of the following topologies? Choose all that apply.**
   - a. bus
   - b. star
   - c. ring
   - d. cube

3. **At what sublayer of the Data Link layer do 802.3 standards operate?**
   - a. MMC sublayer
   - b. LLC sublayer
   - c. MAC sublayer
   - d. Ethernet sublayer

4. **In the network access method specified by 802.3, which of the following are likely to occur?**
   - a. collisions
   - b. sags
   - c. multiplexing
   - d. token arbitrations

5. **What network component is responsible for applying 802.3 standards to an electrical signal?**
   - a. RJ-45 connector
   - b. AUI connector
   - c. NIC
   - d. multimeter

6. **Which of the following networks would use 802.3 standards? Choose all that apply.**
   - a. 10BaseT
   - b. 10Base5
   - c. 100BaseVG-AnyLAN
   - d. 100BaseT

7. **At what data transmission speed is a modern 802.3-based network likely to run?**
   - a. 1 Mbps
   - b. 4 Mbps
   - c. 16 Mbps
   - d. 100 Mbps

OBJECTIVES

1.2 Specify the main features of networking technologies, including speed, access, method, topology, and media (continued):

802.5 (TOKEN RING)

UNDERSTANDING THE OBJECTIVE

IEEE 802.5 specifications describe the MAC sublayer elements of Token Ring networks, including its network access method known as token passing.

WHAT YOU REALLY NEED TO KNOW

◆ The 802.5 standards define the MAC sublayer (of the Data Link layer) elements of networks using the Token Ring transmission method.

◆ Traditional Token Ring networks transmit data at either 4 Mbps or 16 Mbps over shielded or unshielded twisted-pair wiring.

◆ The 100 Mbps Token Ring standard, finalized in 1999, is known as **high-speed Token Ring (HSTR)**. HSTR can use either twisted-pair or fiber-optic cable as its transmission medium. While it is as reliable and efficient as Fast Ethernet, it is less common because of its more costly implementation.

◆ Token Ring networks use the token-passing network access method and a star-ring hybrid physical topology.

◆ According to the 802.5 standards, on a Token Ring network, one workstation, called the active monitor, acts as the controller for token passing. Specifically, the **active monitor** maintains the timing for ring passing, monitors token and frame transmission, detects lost tokens, and corrects errors when a timing error or other disruption occurs. Only one workstation on the ring can act as the active monitor at any given time.

◆ In token passing, a 3-byte token circulates around the network. When a station has something to send, it picks up the token, changes it to a frame, and then adds the header, information, and trailer fields. Each node reads the frame as it traverses the ring to determine whether it is the intended recipient. If a node is the recipient, it picks up the data, then retransmits the frame to the next node on the ring. When the frame reaches the originating station, it reissues a free token that can then be reused.

◆ The token-passing control scheme ensures high data reliability (no collisions) and an efficient use of bandwidth. It also does not impose distance limitations on the length of a LAN segment, unlike CSMA/CD.

OBJECTIVES ON THE JOB

In the early 1990s, the Token Ring architecture competed strongly with Ethernet to be the most popular logical topology. Since that time, the economics, speed, and reliability of Ethernet have greatly improved, making Token Ring seem less desirable. Thus, you are much more likely to work with Ethernet networks than Token Ring networks.

PRACTICE TEST QUESTIONS

1. **Which of the following data transmission speeds would be used on 802.5 networks? Choose all that apply.**
   - a. 1 Mbps
   - b. 4 Mbps
   - c. 10 Mbps
   - d. 16 Mbps

2. **What network access method is specified by the 802.5 standard?**
   - a. CSMA/CA
   - b. demand priority
   - c. token-passing
   - d. CSMA/CD

3. **What type of media could be used by a network that relies on the 802.5 standard? Choose all that apply.**
   - a. coaxial cable
   - b. UTP
   - c. STP
   - d. single-mode fiber

4. **At which sublayer of the Data Link layer do 802.5 standards operate?**
   - a. MMC sublayer
   - b. MAC sublayer
   - c. LLC sublayer
   - d. TMC sublayer

5. **What network component is responsible for applying 802.5 standards to an electrical signal?**
   - a. RJ-45 connector
   - b. AUI connector
   - c. cabling
   - d. NIC

6. **Why is the 802.3 standard more popular than the 802.5 standard?**
   - a. The 802.3 standard is more reliable than the 802.5 standard.
   - b. The 802.3 standard is not subject to collisions and, therefore, suffers less data corruption than the 802.5 standard.
   - c. The 802.3 standard can offer greater speed at lower overall cost than can the 802.5 standard.
   - d. The 802.3 standard is more compatible with evolving security standards than the 802.5 standard.

7. **What type of topology would be used on an 802.5 network?**
   - a. bus
   - b. star-wired bus
   - c. star-wired ring
   - d. cube

1.2   Specify the main features of networking technologies, including speed, access, method, topology, and media (continued):

802.11B (WIRELESS)

UNDERSTANDING THE OBJECTIVE

The purpose of the IEEE 802.11b standard is to provide a wireless connectivity system that standardizes access to one or more frequency bands for LAN communications. Wireless standards were first proposed by IEEE in 1997 with the aim of facilitating interoperability between different manufacturers' wireless networking devices.

WHAT YOU REALLY NEED TO KNOW

◆ The IEEE 802.11b standard defines protocols necessary for atmospheric-based transmission between nodes on a LAN. As with 802.3 and 802.5, the 802.11b specifications apply to data transmissions between the MAC sublayer and the LLC sublayer of the Data Link layer.

◆ Typically, wireless LAN communication is issued by a radio NIC to an access point, such as a base station. Application of the 802.11b standard takes place at the NIC.

◆ The 802.11b standard supports the continuation of service according to other MAC sublayer standards, such as Ethernet (802.3). This enables those parts of a LAN that rely on wireless transmission to connect with a wire-based Ethernet LAN, for example.

◆ Wireless standards are designed to be used within buildings, such as warehouses, hospitals, office buildings, malls, and residences. The 802.11b specifications are particular to LANs, but may be used in small WANs, such as outdoor parks.

◆ Wireless LANs transmit data across a broad area (unlike wire-bound LANs). Therefore, data privacy is a concern with this type of transmission. Using spread-spectrum radio frequency and standard security measures addresses this concern.

◆ The 802.11b standard uses the **Carrier Sense Multiple Access/Collision Avoidance (CSMA/CA)** network access method, not CSMA/CD, as in Ethernet. Nodes using CSMA/CA signal their intent to transmit before actually doing so. In this way, collisions and the need for data retransmittals are (mostly) avoided.

◆ A spectrum range of 2.4 gigahertz (GHz) is used for 802.11b spread spectrum transmission. This band was selected because it is available license-free in most parts of the world.

◆ Data are transmitted at either 1, 2, or 11 Mbps using the 802.11b standards.

OBJECTIVES ON THE JOB

Although IEEE's 802.11 standards have been established for some years, wireless networking equipment is still evolving. When specifying or purchasing such equipment, be certain that it is 802.11b-compliant and interoperable with your existing network components.

PRACTICE TEST QUESTIONS

1. **What networking component is responsible for applying 802.11b standards to an electrical signal?**
   a. NIC
   b. portal
   c. base station
   d. antenna

2. **Which of the following media is the least secure?**
   a. fiber-optic cable
   b. UTP
   c. direct infrared
   d. spread-spectrum RF

3. **A modern wireless LAN is most likely to transmit data at which of the following speeds?**
   a. 2 Mbps
   b. 25 Mbps
   c. 16 Mbps
   d. 100 Mbps

4. **Which radio frequency band is specified for use by the 802.11b standard?**
   a. 1.5 GHz
   b. 2.4 GHz
   c. 5.5 GHz
   d. 6.2 GHz

5. **Which of the following network access methods do 802.11b devices use?**
   a. CSMA/CA
   b. demand priority
   c. token-passing
   d. CSMA/CD

6. **In which of the following situations would the use of 802.11b standards be most appropriate?**
   a. a WAN that connects 25 university department buildings
   b. a LAN that connects 50 inventory control personnel in a warehouse to a database server
   c. a WAN that connects 120 mobile sales people with their corporate headquarters
   d. a MAN that connects four bank branches across a large metropolitan area

7. **At what layer of the OSI Model do 802.11b standards operate?**
   a. Physical layer
   b. Data Link layer
   c. Network layer
   d. Transport layer

1.2   Specify the main features of networking technologies, including speed, access, method, topology, and media (continued):

FDDI

UNDERSTANDING THE OBJECTIVE

Fiber Distributed Data Interface (FDDI) is a logical topology whose standard was originally specified by ANSI in the mid-1980s. It uses a double fiber-optic ring to transmit data at speeds of up to 100 Mbps.

WHAT YOU REALLY NEED TO KNOW

- ◆ **FDDI (Fiber Distributed Data Interface)** is a logical topology whose standard was originally specified by ANSI in the mid-1980s and later refined by ISO.
- ◆ FDDI (pronounced "fiddy") uses a double ring of multimode or single-mode fiber to transmit data at speeds of up to 100 Mbps.
- ◆ FDDI was developed in response to the throughput limitations of Ethernet and Token Ring technologies used at the time. In fact, FDDI was the first network transport system to reach the 100 Mbps threshold. For this reason, you will frequently find it supporting network backbones that were installed in the late 1980s and early 1990s.
- ◆ A popular implementation of FDDI involves connecting LANs located in multiple buildings, such as those on college campuses. FDDI links can span distances as large as 62 miles.
- ◆ Because Ethernet technologies have developed faster transmission speeds and are more compatible with other existing network technologies, FDDI is no longer the much-coveted technology that it was in the 1980s.
- ◆ Its reliance on fiber-optic cable ensures that FDDI is more reliable and more secure than transmission methods that depend on copper wiring. Another advantage of FDDI is that it works well with Ethernet 100BaseTX technology.
- ◆ One drawback to FDDI technology is its high cost relative to Fast Ethernet (costing up to 10 times more per switch port than Fast Ethernet).
- ◆ FDDI is based on a ring physical topology similar to a Token Ring network. It also relies on the same token-passing routine that Token Ring networks use. However, unlike Token Ring technology, FDDI runs on two complete rings. During normal operation, the primary FDDI ring carries data, while the secondary ring is idle. The secondary ring will assume data transmission responsibilities should the primary ring experience Physical layer problems.

OBJECTIVES ON THE JOB

If you work on a university or other campus-wide network, you may be required to work with FDDI technology. FDDI is a separate standard from Ethernet or Token Ring, and as such, it uses different network access methods, connectivity equipment, and signaling techniques.

PRACTICE TEST QUESTIONS

1. **On what type of physical topology is a FDDI network based?**
   - a. star
   - b. ring
   - c. bus
   - d. tree

2. **Why is FDDI considered more reliable than Ethernet or Token Ring?**
   - a. It uses more sophisticated error-checking protocols.
   - b. It uses more reliable sequencing and flow-control techniques.
   - c. It is designed to better withstand data collisions.
   - d. It uses duplicate sets of transmission media.

3. **On which of the following networks is FDDI most likely to be found today?**
   - a. a VPN that connects 120 satellite sales offices with a company's headquarters
   - b. a LAN that connects 200 workstations, 5 servers, and 15 printers within an office building
   - c. a WAN that connects seven manufacturing plants across the nation
   - d. a WAN that connects 18 buildings on a college campus

4. **Which of the following agencies originally specified the FDDI standard?**
   - a. ANSI
   - b. IEEE
   - c. ISO
   - d. ITU

5. **Which of the following network technologies is the most compatible with FDDI?**
   - a. 10Base2
   - b. 10Base5
   - c. 10BaseT
   - d. 100BaseFX

6. **Why is Ethernet preferred over FDDI for modern networks?**
   - a. It can achieve faster throughput at lower overall cost.
   - b. It works better with today's popular TCP/IP protocol.
   - c. It is more reliable.
   - d. It is better suited for evolving security measures.

7. **Which of the following would be found on a FDDI network?**
   - a. collisions
   - b. tokens
   - c. amplifiers
   - d. vampire taps

1.3 Specify the characteristics (e.g., speed, length, topology, cable type, etc.) of the following technologies:

802.3 (ETHERNET) STANDARDS

UNDERSTANDING THE OBJECTIVE

The Ethernet (802.3) standard, including the specification of CSMA/CD as a network access method, applies to several types of networks, including 10Base2, 10Base5, 10BaseT, 100BaseT, and 100BaseF.

WHAT YOU REALLY NEED TO KNOW

- ◆ All types of wire-bound Ethernet use the CSMA/CD network access method.
- ◆ 10Base2 (Thinnet) and 10Base5 (Thicknet) versions of Ethernet use coaxial cable and rely on the bus physical topology. Both are capable of transmitting data up to 10 Mbps.
- ◆ 10BaseT is a standard that uses unshielded twisted-pair wiring, uses a star-based physical topology, and is capable of transmitting data at a maximum speed of 10 Mbps.
- ◆ 10BaseT networks may connect up to five network segments with up to four connectivity devices. Only three of the connected segments can contain hosts. The maximum segment length on a 10BaseT network is 100 meters.
- ◆ 100BaseT is a standard that uses unshielded twisted-pair or fiber-optic cable in a star-wired bus physical topology and is capable of transmitting data at a maximum speed of 100 Mbps. 100BaseT comes in at least two varieties: 100BaseTX and 100Base4.
- ◆ **100BaseTX** achieves its speed by sending the signal 10 times faster and condensing the time between digital pulses as well as the time a station must wait and listen for a signal. 100BaseTX requires Category 5 or higher unshielded twisted-pair cabling. 100BaseTX is capable of full duplexing.
- ◆ **100BaseT4** is different from 100BaseTX in that it uses all four pairs of wires in a UTP cable, and therefore it can use Category 3 wiring. It breaks the 100 Mbps data stream into three streams of 33 Mbps each. These three streams are sent over three wire pairs. The fourth wire pair is used for signaling. Because 100BaseT4 technology uses all four wire pairs for unidirectional signaling, it cannot support full duplexing.
- ◆ **100BaseFX** is a version of Ethernet that uses fiber-optic cable as its transmission medium. 100BaseFX and 100BaseT, both of which are considered **Fast Ethernet**, may coexist on the same network.

OBJECTIVES ON THE JOB

On any modern network, you will probably find some type of Ethernet technology. You should be familiar with the differences between Ethernet versions, and most importantly, which versions are incompatible with one another.

PRACTICE TEST QUESTIONS

1. **Which of the following Ethernet technologies can transmit data at no more than 10 Mbps? Choose all that apply.**
   a. 10BaseT
   b. 100BaseT
   c. 10Base2
   d. 100BaseFX

2. **Which of the following Ethernet technologies uses CSMA/CD?**
   a. 10Base5
   b. 10BaseT
   c. 100BaseTX
   d. all of the above

3. **Which of the following share the same maximum segment length?**
   a. 10Base2 and 10Base5
   b. 10BaseT and 10BaseF
   c. 10BaseT and 100BaseT
   d. 100BaseT and 100BaseFX

4. **Which of the following Ethernet technologies uses coaxial cable? Choose all that apply.**
   a. 10Base2
   b. 10Base5
   c. 10BaseT
   d. 100BaseFX

5. **Which of the following Ethernet technologies uses a star-wired bus physical topology? Choose all that apply.**
   a. 10Base2
   b. 10Base5
   c. 10BaseT
   d. 100BaseFX

6. **Which of the following IEEE standards specifies CSMA/CD?**
   a. 802.2
   b. 802.3
   c. 802.5
   d. 802.11

7. **Which of the following differentiate 100BaseTX and 100BaseT4? Choose all that apply.**
   a. their network access method
   b. their maximum throughput
   c. the number of wire pairs they utilize
   d. their method of achieving faster throughput

1.3 Specify the characteristics (e.g., speed, length, topology, cable type, etc.) of the following technologies (continued):

10BASET

UNDERSTANDING THE OBJECTIVE

10BaseT is an Ethernet specification that uses baseband transmission and enables data rates of up to 10 Mbps. 10BaseT networks can use unshielded or shielded twisted-pair cable, both of which require RJ-45 connectors. 10BaseT is limited to a maximum segment length of 100 meters and uses a star topology.

WHAT YOU REALLY NEED TO KNOW

- ◆ **10BaseT** uses baseband transmission (thus the "Base" in its name) and twisted-pair cabling (thus, the letter "T" in its name) and a star topology to transmit data at 10 Mbps (thus, the "10" in its name).

- ◆ As with all Ethernet networks, 10BaseT follows a set of communication rules called Carrier Sense Multiple Access with Collision Detection (CSMA/CD). CSMA/CD allows multiple nodes to share one data channel while minimizing the possibilities for data collisions.

- ◆ 10BaseT networks use unshielded twisted pair, including Category 3, 4, 5, and higher cables. Unshielded twisted pair is the same kind of wiring used for telephone connections, and for this reason, 10BaseT networks historically fit well into an organization's existing physical infrastructure.

- ◆ Nodes on a 10BaseT Ethernet network connect to a central hub or repeater in a star fashion. Typical of a star topology, a single network cable only connects two devices. This characteristic makes 10BaseT networks more fault tolerant than 10Base2 or 10Base5, which use the bus topology.

- ◆ Because 10BaseT networks use a star topology, they are easier to troubleshoot than 10Base2 or 10Base5 networks, because you can better isolate problems.

- ◆ Each node on a 10BaseT network uses RJ-45 connectors to connect the network cable with the NIC at the workstation end and with the hub at the network end.

- ◆ The maximum distance a 10BaseT segment can traverse is 100 meters.

- ◆ 10BaseT networks can contain up to five sequential segments connected by four hubs or switches.

OBJECTIVES ON THE JOB

Modern networks often can use both 10BaseT and 100BaseT on the same network. Bear in mind that all NICs and ports on such connectivity devices as routers or hubs must be compatible with the transmission technology your network uses (such as 10BaseT). Even if your network runs only 10BaseT now, it is wise to purchase devices that can automatically sense whether the network is running 10BaseT or 100BaseT and then adjust to that rate.

PRACTICE TEST QUESTIONS

1. **What is the maximum segment length for a 10BaseT network?**
   - a. 100 meters
   - b. 85 meters
   - c. 10 meters
   - d. 10 feet

2. **Which two of the following types of wiring might a 10BaseT network use?**
   - a. CAT5
   - b. CAT3
   - c. CAT2
   - d. CAT1

3. **What does the "Base" in 10BaseT represent?**
   - a. basic
   - b. basal
   - c. base 10
   - d. baseband

4. **What kind of connector is used in a 10BaseT network?**
   - a. BNC
   - b. AUI
   - c. RJ-45
   - d. RJ-52

5. **On what topology are 10BaseT networks based?**
   - a. bus
   - b. star
   - c. ring
   - d. mesh

6. **What other technology can run on the same network with 10BaseT technology?**
   - a. 10Base2
   - b. 10Base5
   - c. 100BaseT
   - d. Gigabit Ethernet

7. **What is the maximum throughput of a 10BaseT network?**
   - a. 10 Kbps
   - b. 10 Mbps
   - c. 10 Gbps
   - d. 10 Tbps

1.3   Specify the characteristics (e.g., speed, length, topology, cable type, etc.) of the following technologies (continued):

100BASET AND 100BASETX

UNDERSTANDING THE OBJECTIVE

100BaseT is an Ethernet transmission technology that can achieve data rates up to 100 Mbps. The most popular version of 100BaseT is the 100BaseTX specification, which can be easily added to an existing 10BaseT network and can take advantage of full duplexing.

WHAT YOU REALLY NEED TO KNOW

◆ **100BaseT** is specified in the IEEE 802.3 (Ethernet) standard. It uses baseband transmission (thus the "Base" in its name) and twisted-pair cabling (thus, the letter "T" in its name) and transmits data at 100 Mbps (thus, the "100" in its name).

◆ 100BaseT relies on a star-wired bus or hierarchical topology, just like 10BaseT.

◆ For best performance, 100BaseT requires CAT5 or better twisted-pair cabling with RJ-45 data connectors.

◆ 100BaseT upgrades can be easy and inexpensive to accomplish for an organization that currently uses the popular 10BaseT technology.

◆ The length between a node and its hub for 100BaseT networks cannot exceed 100 meters.

◆ Because of the speed on a 100BaseT network, the window of time for the NIC to detect and compensate for errors is very small. To minimize undetected collisions, 100BaseT buses can only practically support a maximum of three network segments connected with two hubs.

◆ **100BaseTX** is the most popular version of 100BaseT, largely because it is compatible with technology used for 10BaseT and therefore requires little investment to upgrade.

◆ 100BaseTX uses two of the four wire pairs in a CAT5 or better cable and is capable of full-duplexing.

◆ 100BaseTX sends signals 10 times faster than a 10BaseT network and condenses the time between digital pulses, as well as the time a station is required to wait and listen in CSMA/CD.

◆ 100BaseT and 100BaseTX may also be called **Fast Ethernet**.

OBJECTIVES ON THE JOB

The most popular form of fast LAN transmission technology in use today is 100BaseTX, a variation of the 100BaseT Ethernet standard. It is likely that 100BaseTX will continue to be preferred. Eventually, Fast Ethernet technologies will likely be replaced by Gigabit Ethernet, which is capable of data transmission rates up to 1 Gbps.

PRACTICE TEST QUESTIONS

1. **What is the maximum number of segments that can be connected in serial on a 100BaseT network?**
   a. two
   b. three
   c. four
   d. five

2. **Why has 100BaseTX become the most popular form of Fast Ethernet?**
   a. Its transmission methods are more sophisticated than other forms of Fast Ethernet.
   b. It provides better security than other forms of Fast Ethernet.
   c. It requires minimal investment to upgrade to 100BaseTX from the popular 10BaseT technology.
   d. It relies on the ring topology, which is already popular in most organizations.

3. **What is the maximum segment length on a 100BaseTX network?**
   a. 10 meters
   b. 85 meters
   c. 100 meters
   d. 185 meters

4. **Which of the following network access methods is used by 100BaseT?**
   a. demand priority
   b. CSMA/CA
   c. CSMA/CD
   d. token-passing

5. **What type of connector is used on a 100BaseT network?**
   a. RJ-11
   b. RJ-45
   c. AUI
   d. SC

6. **Which two of the following cable types could be used for a 100BaseTX network?**
   a. CAT7
   b. CAT5e
   c. CAT3
   d. CAT1

7. **How many wire pairs does the 100BaseTX standard require?**
   a. one
   b. two
   c. four
   d. eight

OBJECTIVES

1.3   Specify the characteristics (e.g., speed, length, topology, cable type, etc.) of the following technologies (continued):

10BASE2

UNDERSTANDING THE OBJECTIVE

10Base2 is a form of Ethernet network that provides 10 Mbps throughput over coaxial cabling. Also known as Thin Ethernet, or "Thinnet," 10Base2 was popular for LANs in the 1980s but has largely been replaced by more modern Ethernet technologies (such as 10BaseT or 100BaseT) that require less expense, afford simpler installation, and rely on more scalable topologies.

WHAT YOU REALLY NEED TO KNOW

◆ IEEE has designated **Thinnet** as **10Base2** Ethernet. The "10" represents its data transmission rate of 10 Mbps, "Base" stands for baseband transmission, and "2" represents its maximum segment length of 185 (or roughly 200) meters.

◆ Thinnet's sheath is typically black, and its cable diameter is approximately 0.64 cm. It is more flexible and easier to handle than Thicknet.

◆ Because of its black sheath, Thinnet may also be called "black Ethernet."

◆ Thinnet usually connects the wire to network devices with BNC T connectors. A BNC connector with three open ends attaches to the NIC at the base of the "T" while attaching to the Thinnet cable at its two sides. BNC barrel connectors (with only two open ends) are used to join two Thinnet cable segments.

◆ Like Thicknet, Thinnet relies on the bus topology and therefore requires terminators to avoid signal bounce.

◆ Thinnet can accommodate a maximum of 30 nodes per segment. Its total maximum network length is just over 550 meters.

◆ To minimize interference, devices on a Thinnet network should be separated by at least 0.5 m.

◆ Because of its insulation and shielding, Thinnet is more resistant to noise than twisted-pair wiring. However, it is not as resistant as Thicknet.

◆ Thinnet is less expensive than Thicknet and fiber-optic cable, but it is more expensive than twisted-pair wiring. For this reason, Thinnet is sometimes called "cheapernet."

OBJECTIVES ON THE JOB

Thinnet is occasionally used on modern networks, but more often you will see it on networks installed in the 1980s. The major advantages to Thinnet are its very low cost and ease of use. If you work with Thinnet, pay particular attention to the restrictions of its bus topology, including the need for terminators and the practical drawbacks of having all nodes share a single channel.

PRACTICE TEST QUESTIONS

1. **In the IEEE designation 10Base2, what does the 2 represent?**
   - a. 2 feet
   - b. 2 Mbps
   - c. 200 feet
   - d. 185 meters

2. **What color is typically used for the sheath of a Thinnet cable?**
   - a. yellow
   - b. black
   - c. green
   - d. red

3. **What is a BNC barrel connector used for?**
   - a. connecting a Thinnet workstation to the network
   - b. connecting a Thicknet workstation to the network
   - c. connecting two Thinnet cable segments
   - d. connecting a Thinnet segment to a Thicknet segment

4. **What is the maximum throughput on a Thinnet network?**
   - a. 1 Mbps
   - b. 4 Mbps
   - c. 10 Mbps
   - d. 100 Mbps

5. **On what physical topology does 10Base2 depend?**
   - a. bus
   - b. ring
   - c. star
   - d. mesh

6. **Why is the maximum segment length for Thicknet longer than for Thinnet?**
   - a. Thicknet is more noise-resistant than Thinnet.
   - b. Thicknet is more flexible than Thinnet.
   - c. Thicknet has a higher throughput than Thinnet.
   - d. Thicknet is more heat-resistant than Thinnet.

7. **On a 10Base2 network, how many nodes share one signal channel?**
   - a. one
   - b. two
   - c. four
   - d. all connected nodes

1.3 Specify the characteristics (e.g., speed, length, topology, cable type, etc.) of the following technologies (continued):

10BASE5

UNDERSTANDING THE OBJECTIVE

10Base5 is another form of Ethernet that provides 10 Mbps throughput over coaxial cabling. Prior to the acceptance of Thinnet, many LANs used the 10Base5 standard, also known as Thick Ethernet, or Thicknet.

WHAT YOU REALLY NEED TO KNOW

◆ **Thicknet** cabling is a rigid coaxial cable, approximately 1 cm thick, used for the original Ethernet networks. Because it is often covered with a yellow sheath, it may be called "yellow Ethernet."

◆ IEEE designates Thicknet as **10Base5** Ethernet. The "10" represents its throughput of 10 Mbps, the "Base" stands for baseband transmission, and the "5" represents the maximum segment length of a Thicknet cable, 500 meters.

◆ To minimize the possibility of interference between stations, network devices on a Thicknet network should be separated by at least 2.5 m.

◆ Thicknet is less expensive than fiber-optic cable but more expensive than twisted-pair cable. It is also more expensive than other types of coaxial cabling, such as Thinnet, because it contains more materials.

◆ Thicknet requires a combination of a vampire tap to connect to a transceiver on the backbone plus a drop cable to connect network devices.

◆ In Thicknet, the port on the device's NIC is connected with the drop cable via either an AUI connector or an n-series connector (or n-connector).

◆ **AUI (Attachment Unit Interface)** is an Ethernet standard that establishes physical specifications for connecting coaxial cables with transceivers and networked nodes.

◆ An **n-connector** uses a screw-and-barrel arrangement to securely connect coaxial cable segments and devices.

◆ Thicknet can accommodate a maximum of 100 nodes per segment. Its total maximum network length is 1500 meters. Thicknet's high resistance to noise allows its transmissions to travel longer distances without repeating than Thinnet.

OBJECTIVES ON THE JOB

If you are working with Thicknet, you should be familiar with its unique connectors, including AUI connectors, vampire taps, and n-connectors. You should also be aware that Thicknet is the least flexible networking medium, and as a result, it may present unique installation challenges. However, Thicknet is rarely used on modern networks, and it is unlikely that you will ever need to work with it.

PRACTICE TEST QUESTIONS

1. **What is the maximum throughput on a Thicknet network?**
   a. 1 Mbps
   b. 10 Mbps
   c. 100 Mbps
   d. 1 Gbps

2. **In the IEEE designation 10Base5, what does the "5" represent?**
   a. 5 meters
   b. 5 feet
   c. 50 meters
   d. 500 meters

3. **What two elements of a Thicknet network does a drop cable connect?**
   a. a network node and a transceiver
   b. a transceiver and the backbone
   c. a transceiver and a MAU
   d. a network node and another network node

4. **Based on its required medium, which of the following Ethernet technologies is the most expensive to install and maintain?**
   a. 10Base2
   b. 10Base5
   c. 10BaseT
   d. 100BaseFX

5. **On what type of physical topology does Thicknet depend?**
   a. bus
   b. star
   c. ring
   d. mesh

6. **Which of the following media is the most expensive?**
   a. Thicknet
   b. Thinnet
   c. UTP
   d. STP

7. **According to IEEE standards, what is the maximum number of nodes that can be connected to a Thicknet segment?**
   a. 10
   b. 50
   c. 100
   d. No limit is specified.

OBJECTIVES

1.3   Specify the characteristics (e.g., speed, length, topology, cable type, etc.) of the following technologies (continued):

100BASEFX

UNDERSTANDING THE OBJECTIVE

100BaseFX is another form of Fast Ethernet, or Ethernet that is capable of 100 Mbps throughput. Unlike 100BaseT, which uses unshielded twisted-pair cabling, 100BaseFX uses fiber-optic cable. It is an expensive but highly reliable and noise-resistant networking technology.

WHAT YOU REALLY NEED TO KNOW

◆ The **100BaseFX** standard specifies a network capable of 100 Mbps throughput that uses baseband transmission and fiber-optic cabling.

◆ 100BaseFX requires multimode fiber containing at least two strands of fiber. One strand is used for data transmission, while the other strand is used for reception, making 100BaseFX a full-duplex technology.

◆ 100BaseFX networks require one of several types of connectors, including the two most popular connectors: SC and ST.

◆ Its maximum segment length is 400 meters, with a maximum of two repeaters allowed to connect segments.

◆ The 100BaseFX standard uses a star topology, with its repeaters connected through a bus. The use of a star topology makes this standard highly scalable and fault-tolerant.

◆ 100BaseFX, like 100BaseT, is also considered "Fast Ethernet."

◆ Organizations converting from UTP to fiber media can combine 100BaseTX and 100BaseFX within one network. For this to occur, connectivity devices must have both RJ-45 and SC or ST ports. Alternately, a 100BaseTX to 100BaseFX media converter may be used at any point in the network to interconnect the different media and convert the signals of one standard to signals that work with the other standard.

◆ Since fiber does not conduct electrical current to transmit signals, 100BaseFX is unaffected by either EMI or RFI.

◆ 100BaseFX is significantly more expensive than 100BaseT. Not only is the cable itself more expensive than twisted pair, but fiber-optic NICs and hubs can cost as much as five times more than NICs and hubs designed for UTP networks. In addition, hiring skilled fiber cable installers costs more than hiring twisted-pair cable installers.

OBJECTIVES ON THE JOB

If you work on a network that uses 100BaseFX, chances are that some of the network (such as the backbone) uses this fiber-based technology, while other parts of the network (such as workstation connections) use the UTP-based 100BaseT technology. Thus, you should be familiar with integrating the different types of hardware required for these different Fast Ethernet standards.

PRACTICE TEST QUESTIONS

1. **On what physical topology does the 100BaseFX standard depend?**
   a. bus
   b. ring
   c. star
   d. mesh

2. **Which of the following connectors could be used on a 100BaseFX network?**
   a. AUI
   b. RJ-11
   c. RJ-45
   d. SC

3. **What is the maximum segment length for a 100BaseFX network?**
   a. 200 meters
   b. 400 meters
   c. 1200 meters
   d. 2 miles

4. **How does a 100BaseFX network achieve full duplexing?**
   a. It multiplexes a single channel on one strand of fiber into multiple subchannels.
   b. It uses two fiber strands, one for transmission and one for reception.
   c. It relies on switching and routing equipment to arbitrate sessions and avoid collisions.
   d. It uses different encoding for each transmission, so multiple signals can be issued over the same strand of fiber.

5. **100BaseFX is most likely to coexist with what other Ethernet technology on the same network?**
   a. 10Base2
   b. 10Base5
   c. 10BaseT
   d. 100BaseT

6. **What is the single greatest disadvantage to using 100BaseFX?**
   a. It is expensive.
   b. It is not highly scalable.
   c. Its standards are not stable.
   d. It is less secure than other types of Ethernet networks.

7. **What type of fiber-optic cable is specified for use with 100BaseFX?**
   a. single-mode
   b. duplex-mode
   c. reverse-mode
   d. multimode

1.3 Specify the characteristics (e.g., speed, length, topology, cable type, etc.) of the following technologies (continued):

GIGABIT ETHERNET

UNDERSTANDING THE OBJECTIVE

As you would probably guess, the evolution of Ethernet has not stopped with the development of the 100 Mbps standard. Through its 802.3z project, IEEE established specifications for an Ethernet version that runs at 1000 Mbps, called 1 Gigabit Ethernet.

WHAT YOU REALLY NEED TO KNOW

♦ **1 Gigabit Ethernet** can technically run over unshielded twisted-pair (UTP) cable, but it performs much better over multimode fiber.

♦ 1 Gigabit Ethernet is defined by IEEE's 802.3z committee.

♦ Though UTP is rare on 1 Gigabit Ethernet networks, a segment of 1 Gigabit Ethernet running on UTP can span a maximum of 100 meters.

♦ A segment of 1 Gigabit Ethernet running on fiber-optic cable can span a maximum of 550 meters.

♦ A Gigabit Ethernet network that uses fiber-optic cable requires either SC or ST connector types.

♦ Like Fast Ethernet, a fiber-based, 1 Gigabit Ethernet network uses the CSMA/CD network access method, relies on the star physical topology, and is capable of full duplexing.

♦ In March 1999, representatives from the networking industry began discussing a **10 Gigabit Ethernet** standard, which would provide 10,000 Mbps throughput. The standards for 10 Gigabit are currently being defined by the IEEE 802.3ae committee and will include full duplexing and multimode fiber requirements.

♦ IEEE aims to make the 10 Gigabit standard compatible with the Physical layer standards for 1 Gigabit Ethernet to allow organizations to easily upgrade their networks.

♦ The 1- and 10-Gigabit technologies compete directly with other fast networking solutions, such as Asynchronous Transfer Mode (ATM).

OBJECTIVES ON THE JOB

You will most likely encounter 1 Gigabit Ethernet as part of a network's backbone. It is well suited to connecting multiple buildings on a single campus, for example. Currently, this scheme would not be appropriate for connecting workstations to hubs, for example, because workstations' NICs and CPUs could not process data fast enough to make the cost worthwhile. In the near future, however, PCs will be equipped with adequate hardware and processing power to take advantage of 1 Gigabit Ethernet.

PRACTICE TEST QUESTIONS

1. **Which of the following media is preferred for 1 Gigabit Ethernet?**
   a. coaxial cable
   b. UTP
   c. STP
   d. fiber-optic cable

2. **Which of the following IEEE committees is responsible for establishing 1 Gigabit Ethernet standards?**
   a. 802.3a
   b. 802.3z
   c. 802.5
   d. 802.11b

3. **Which of the following network access methods does a 1 Gigabit Ethernet network use?**
   a. CSMA/CD
   b. CSMA/CA
   c. demand priority
   d. token-passing

4. **Which of the following technologies compete directly with 1 Gigabit Ethernet?**
   a. FDDI
   b. Token Ring
   c. 100VG-AnyLAN
   d. ATM

5. **What is the maximum segment length for a 1 Gigabit Ethernet network running over fiber-optic cable?**
   a. 50 meters
   b. 55 meters
   c. 500 meters
   d. 550 meters

6. **What part of a network is most likely to use 1 Gigabit Ethernet?**
   a. work area
   b. horizontal wiring
   c. backbone
   d. drop cables

7. **Which of the following types of connectors could be used on a 1 Gigabit Ethernet network?**
   a. BNC
   b. AUI
   c. n-connector
   d. SC

1.4 Recognize the following media connectors and/or describe their uses:

RJ-11, RJ-45, AUI, AND BNC

UNDERSTANDING THE OBJECTIVE

Different Ethernet technologies require different connectors, such as RJ-11, RJ-45, AUI, and BNC. The most common is the RJ-45 connector, used on 10BaseT and 100BaseT LANs.

WHAT YOU REALLY NEED TO KNOW

◆ **RJ-11**, which stands for **registered jack-11**, is the standard interface for phone (or modem) connections and is illustrated below.

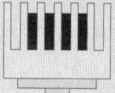 

◆ An RJ-11 jack contains four or six wires. Prior to the advent of CAT5 cabling, RJ-11 plugs and jacks could be used for LAN communications as well as phone communications.

◆ **RJ-45**, which stands for **registered jack-45,** identifies the Ethernet 10BaseT and 100BaseT interfaces.

◆ An RJ-45 jack, illustrated below, typically contains eight wires (four wire pairs) and looks like a large telephone jack.

◆ Common network interfaces are BNC or RJ-45 connectors. **BNC**, which stands for **British Naval Connector**, identifies the Ethernet 10Base2 interface and is illustrated below.

◆ An **AUI (Attachment Unit Interface)** connector is a type of data bus connector that contains 15 pins, as illustrated below, and is an Ethernet 10Base5 standard for connecting coaxial cables with transceivers and networked nodes.

OBJECTIVES ON THE JOB

On most modern networks, you will work with RJ-45 connectors. Not only should you be able to recognize these plugs, you should also be able to terminate a UTP patch cable with one, using the proper networking tools.

PRACTICE TEST QUESTIONS

1. **What type of network would use an AUI interface?**
   a. 10Base2
   b. 10Base5
   c. 10BaseT
   d. 100BaseFX

2. **What type of UTP could be used on a LAN that had RJ-11 connectors on the ends of its patch cables?**
   a. CAT3
   b. CAT5
   c. CAT6
   d. CAT7

3. **How many wire pairs are typically terminated in an RJ-45 connector?**
   a. two
   b. three
   c. four
   d. five

4. **What kind of connector would you find on the end of a CAT5 patch cable?**
   a. RJ-11
   b. RJ-45
   c. AUI
   d. BNC

5. **What type of connector would be found on a Thinnet cable?**
   a. RJ-11
   b. RJ-45
   c. AUI
   d. BNC

6. **What is another term for an AUI connector?**
   a. vampire tap
   b. DB-15
   c. n-connector
   d. barrel connector

7. **Which of the following connectors is often used to connect a modem to a phone jack?**
   a. RJ-11
   b. RJ-45
   c. AUI
   d. BNC

1.4 Recognize the following media connectors and/or describe their uses (continued):

ST AND SC

UNDERSTANDING THE OBJECTIVE

Networks that use fiber-optic cabling may use any of 10 different types of connectors. Currently, the two most popular connector types for fiber-optic–based networks are ST and SC connectors.

WHAT YOU REALLY NEED TO KNOW

◆ An ST connector terminates multimode fiber media and is illustrated below.

◆ An SC connector terminates multimode fiber media and is illustrated below.

 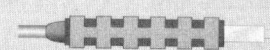

◆ ST and SC connectors are used with fiber-based networks, such as 10BaseF or 100BaseF.

◆ When used with 10BaseF or 100BaseF networks, each cable is terminated with a pair of SC or ST connectors, as illustrated below. One of the connectors handles data transmission while the other handles data reception, allowing for a full-duplex connection.

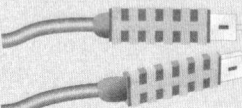

◆ Although fiber-optic cable may be terminated with one of several different types of connectors, SC or ST connectors are the most popular ones in use on modern LANs.

OBJECTIVES ON THE JOB

Bear in mind that most networks currently use fiber-based technologies only on parts of their networks, and 100BaseF is likely to coexist with 100BaseT on the same network. When combining 100BaseF and 100BaseT technologies on the same network, you must use equipment capable of accepting both SC or ST connectors and RJ-45 connectors.

PRACTICE TEST QUESTIONS

1. **Why do ST connectors terminate in pairs?**
   a. Half of the pair is used for transmission, while the other half is used for reception.
   b. Half of the pair is used for transmission and reception, while the other half is used as a fail-over cable for greater reliability.
   c. Both connectors in the pair are used to transmit and receive data simultaneously, resulting in higher throughput.
   d. One-half of the pair is used for CSMA/CD network access and the other half is used for CSMA/CA network access.

2. **Which of the following types of networks might use an SC connector?**
   a. 10BaseT
   b. 10Base5
   c. 100BaseTX
   d. 100BaseFX

3. **Which of the following connectors is most likely to be found on a network that uses ST connectors?**
   a. RJ-11
   b. RJ-45
   c. BNC
   d. AUI

4. **A network could use both ST and SC connectors. True or False?**

5. **What kind of fiber-optic cable is likely to be found inside an ST connector?**
   a. duplex-mode
   b. single-mode
   c. iso-mode
   d. multimode

6. **Which of the following physical topologies would most likely be used with SC and ST connectors?**
   a. bus
   b. star-wired bus
   c. star-wired ring
   d. ring

7. **ST and SC connectors are the only types of connectors that may be used on 100BaseF networks. True or false?**

1.5 Choose the appropriate media type and connectors to add a client to an existing network.

UNDERSTANDING THE OBJECTIVE

Understanding the type of medium and connector required by a network technology is fundamental to understanding how to install and maintain networks.

WHAT YOU REALLY NEED TO KNOW

◆ **Connectors** are the pieces of hardware that connect the wire to the network device, be it a file server, workstation, switch, or printer. Every networking medium requires a specific kind of connector. The types of connectors you use will affect the cost of installing and maintaining the network, the ease of adding new segments or nodes to the network, and the technical expertise required to maintain the network.

◆ BNC connectors are used with Thinnet, or 10Base2 Ethernet networks, which rely on coaxial cabling as their transmission medium.

◆ AUI connectors are used with Thicknet, or 10Base5 Ethernet networks, which rely on coaxial cabling as their transmission medium.

◆ The AUI standard calls for male connectors with 15 pins to connect to the MAU and female connectors with openings for 15 pins to connect to the network node's Ethernet interface.

◆ AUI connectors may also be called DB-15 or DIX connectors. **DIX** stands for Digital, Intel, and Xerox, the three companies that together pioneered Thicknet technology. **DB-15** is a more general term for connectors that use 15 metal pins to complete a connection between devices. "DB" stands for "Data bus," while the number 15 indicates how many pins are used to make the connection.

◆ RJ-11 connectors may be used with older Ethernet networks that rely on twisted-pair cabling, such as 10BaseT. However, since they are not compatible with newer UTP cable types, they are rarely found on modern networks.

◆ RJ-45 connectors are the most popular type of network connector. They may be used on both Token Ring and Ethernet networks that rely on twisted-pair cabling, including different types of 10BaseT and 100BaseT technology.

◆ ST and SC connectors are the two most popular types of connectors used with fiber-based networks, such as 10BaseF and 100BaseF.

OBJECTIVES ON THE JOB

The type of connector and medium type required by a particular network will be obvious once you begin working on the network. However, if you are designing a network from scratch, you should be careful to specify the proper medium and connector types. The most popular combination in use on modern networks is unshielded twisted-pair cabling with RJ-45 connectors.

PRACTICE TEST QUESTIONS

1. **Which of the following connectors could be used with CAT3 cable? Choose all that apply.**
   a. BNC
   b. AUI
   c. RJ-11
   d. RJ-45

2. **Which of the following connectors could be used on a 100BaseFX network?**
   a. ST
   b. AUI
   c. RJ-45
   d. DIX

3. **What type of medium is used with BNC connectors?**
   a. coaxial cable
   b. unshielded twisted-pair cable
   c. shielded twisted-pair cable
   d. fiber-optic cable

4. **Which of the following connectors would be used on a 10Base5 network?**
   a. BNC
   b. AUI
   c. RJ-11
   d. RJ-45

5. **What type of medium does a 10BaseT network use?**
   a. coaxial cable
   b. unshielded twisted-pair cable
   c. shielded twisted-pair cable
   d. fiber-optic cable

6. **On a 100BaseTX network, how many wire pairs within the cable are used?**
   a. one
   b. two
   c. four
   d. six

7. **What type of topology would a network that requires RJ-45 cabling use? Choose all that apply.**
   a. bus
   b. star-wired ring
   c. star-wired bus
   d. ring

1.6 Identify the purpose, features, and functions of the following network components:

HUBS

UNDERSTANDING THE OBJECTIVE

Hubs are simple connectivity devices that belong to the Physical layer of the OSI Model. Their primary purpose is to regenerate (or repeat) digital signals from one node to the rest of a network segment. Because they do not perform sophisticated functions, such as those that a router performs, hubs are less intricate and less expensive than higher-layer connectivity devices.

WHAT YOU REALLY NEED TO KNOW

- ◆ At its most primitive, a **hub** is a multiport repeater, or a device that regenerates the digital signals it receives from one node to the rest of the nodes on a network segment. A hub often connects multiple workstations to each other and to the network's backbone.

- ◆ Hubs belong to the Physical layer of the OSI Model.

- ◆ On Ethernet networks, hubs typically serve as the central connection point for branches of a star or star-based hybrid topology.

- ◆ On Token Ring networks, hubs are called **Multistation Access Units (MAUs)** and are used to connect nodes in a star-based ring topology.

- ◆ Hubs come in many different varieties and are specific to the type of technology a network uses—for example, 10BaseT versus Token Ring.

- ◆ On a hub, the **uplink port** is the receptacle used to connect one hub to another hub in a daisy chain or hierarchical fashion.

- ◆ On a hub, the **backbone port** is the receptacle used to connect a hub to the network's backbone, and it should only be used for this purpose.

- ◆ Some hubs have internal processing capabilities that allow them to process data, provide troubleshooting information, and monitor traffic. Such hubs are known as **intelligent hubs** or **managed hubs**.

- ◆ On Ethernet networks, hubs have collision lights (or LEDs), which can indicate the volume of collisions that segment is experiencing by blinking.

- ◆ The **link LED** is the light on a port that indicates whether it is in use. If a connection is live, this light should be solid or blinking green.

OBJECTIVES ON THE JOB

Hubs can be found on even the smallest networks, and they certainly perform critical functions on larger networks. While working as a networking professional, you should be familiar with specifying, installing, maintaining, and troubleshooting hubs. As with all network equipment, hub functionality varies from one model and manufacturer to another, so be certain to read the documentation that ships with the hub in order to properly perform these functions.

PRACTICE TEST QUESTIONS

1. **What is the main difference between a hub and a multistation access unit (MAU)?**
   a. Hubs can extend a network, while MAUs cannot.
   b. MAUs can be used in a star-bus topology, while hubs cannot.
   c. Hubs are typically used with Ethernet networks, while MAUs are used with Token Ring networks.
   d. Because of their multiport design, hubs are more fault-tolerant than MAUs.

2. **What can you view to determine whether a hub port is receiving information from a workstation's NIC?**
   a. the uplink LED
   b. the collision LED
   c. the link LED
   d. the backbone LED

3. **Which of the following characteristics do hubs and MAUs share?**
   a. Both can connect multiple workstations to the network's backbone.
   b. Both can translate between IPX and IP traffic.
   c. Both forward and/or filter frames based on their MAC address.
   d. Both interpret Network layer addresses to determine where to deliver data.

4. **Which of the following is probably the least expensive connectivity device?**
   a. switch
   b. router
   c. bridge
   d. hub

5. **What is used to connect one hub to another hub in a daisy-chain fashion?**
   a. their uplink ports
   b. their backbone ports
   c. their punch-down ports
   d. their collision ports

6. **In which two of the following types of networks would viewing a hub's collision LED be useful for troubleshooting?**
   a. 10BaseT
   b. 100BaseVG-AnyLAN
   c. Token Ring
   d. 100BaseFX

7. **What is the maximum number of hubs that can be connected in serial on a 10BaseT network?**
   a. two
   b. three
   c. four
   d. five

1.6 Identify the purpose, features, and functions of the following network components (continued):

SWITCHES AND BRIDGES

UNDERSTANDING THE OBJECTIVE

Bridges are devices that connect two LANs or LAN segments using one port per segment. Bridges listen to all network traffic and, based on the packets' MAC addresses, determine whether to forward the packets to another segment or discard them. Bridges keep track of which MAC addresses should be forwarded to which port in a filtering database.

WHAT YOU REALLY NEED TO KNOW

- ◆ **Bridges** are devices that move frames between two LANs or LAN segments.
- ◆ Bridges are similar to repeaters in that they do not modify the contents of a packet. But they are more sophisticated than repeaters, because they interpret addressing information and filter packets.
- ◆ Because they can selectively filter packets, bridges can be useful for separating LAN segments, thus reducing the possibility that errors on one segment will affect transmission on the other segment.
- ◆ Bridging occurs at the Data Link layer of the OSI Model, which encompasses flow control, error handling, and physical addressing.
- ◆ Bridges read the destination MAC address of each frame and decide whether to forward (retransmit) the packet to another segment on the network or, if it belongs to the same segment as the source address, filter (discard) it.
- ◆ As nodes on a network transmit data through the bridge, the bridge establishes a **filtering database** of known MAC addresses and their location on the network. (This filtering database is also known as a **forwarding table**.) The bridge uses its filtering database to determine whether a packet should be forwarded or filtered.
- ◆ **Switches**, which subdivide a network into smaller logical pieces (or collision domains), can be described as multiport bridges. Switches operate at the Data Link layer of the OSI Model and interpret MAC address information.
- ◆ Both switches and bridges can connect networks that use dissimilar network access methods, such as Token Ring and Ethernet.
- ◆ Because they have multiple ports, switches can make better use of limited bandwidth and prove more cost-efficient than bridges. Each port on the switch acts like a bridge, and each device connected to a switch effectively receives its own dedicated channel.

OBJECTIVES ON THE JOB

Since bridges and switches only interpret addressing information at the Data Link layer of the OSI Model, they can connect networks that use different Network layer protocols (for example, IPX and IP). Both can be useful for extending and interconnecting multiple LAN segments.

PRACTICE TEST QUESTIONS

1. **Which of the following do bridges and hubs have in common?**
   a. Both operate at the Physical layer of the OSI Model.
   b. Both can interpret MAC addresses and forward or filter frames based on this information.
   c. Both repeat signals in order to allow data to reach their destination.
   d. Both can interpret Network layer addresses to efficiently forward data to their destination.

2. **Which of the following is associated with a MAC address in a bridge's filtering database?**
   a. bridge port number
   b. IP address
   c. protocol
   d. subnet mask

3. **Why is a switch generally faster than a router?**
   a. because it does not interpret Data Link layer information
   b. because it does not acknowledge data transmission errors
   c. because it accepts only connectionless protocols
   d. because it does not pay attention to Network layer information

4. **What IEEE standard describes bridging?**
   a. 802.1
   b. 802.2
   c. 802.3
   d. 802.5

5. **What is one advantage of using a switch over a bridge?**
   a. Since switches have multiple ports, fewer are necessary to make the same number of connections between multiple segments.
   b. Switches are less expensive to install and maintain.
   c. Switches are inherently more secure than bridges.
   d. Since switches can interpret Network layer addresses, they can more efficiently forward data to their destination.

6. **Under what conditions will a bridge filter a packet?**
   a. when it detects an incorrect checksum
   b. when it detects a damaged header
   c. when the packet's destination MAC address belongs to the port on which the bridge received it
   d. when the packet's source MAC address belongs to the port on which the bridge received it.

7. **Switches provide the foundation for which of the following types of networks?**
   a. VPNs
   b. VLANs
   c. MANs
   d. WANs

1.6 Identify the purpose, features, and functions of the following network components (continued):

ROUTERS

UNDERSTANDING THE OBJECTIVE

Routers use Network layer addressing information to intelligently route data between LANs. They are used to connect dissimilar LANs in the case of WANs or LAN segments in the case of LANs.

WHAT YOU REALLY NEED TO KNOW

◆ **Routers** are devices that connect multiple LANs or LAN segments and direct data between nodes using the best possible route. A router has multiple ports and can connect dissimilar LANs and WANs running at different transmission speeds and using a variety of protocols.

◆ Routers belong to the Network layer of the OSI Model. In order for a protocol to be routable, it must contain Network layer information. IPX/SPX, TCP/IP, and AppleTalk are routable protocols, while SNA and NetBEUI are nonroutable.

◆ The best path between nodes on a network depends on the number of hops between nodes, the current network activity, unavailable links, varying network transmission speeds, and topology.

◆ When used in networking, the term **route** means to intelligently direct data based on addressing, patterns of usage, quality of service, and network availability.

◆ Unlike bridges, routers are protocol-dependent. They must be designed or configured to recognize protocols on the network.

◆ A typical router has an internal processor, its own memory and power supply, input and output jacks for different types of network connectors (depending on the network type), and usually, a management console interface.

◆ To determine the best path between two nodes, routers communicate with each other through **routing protocols**. Examples of routing protocols are EIGRP and BGP.

◆ In **static routing**, a router contains routing tables (instructions on how to forward packets) that are manually programmed by a network administrator. Since the location of devices on a network and the best paths between them can change often, static routing is not a flexible or efficient technique.

◆ In **dynamic routing**, a router calculates the best path between nodes and automatically updates its routing tables if it detects network congestion or failures. Dynamic routing is faster and more reliable than static routing.

OBJECTIVES ON THE JOB

Routers are common devices used to connect two different LANs. They are sophisticated and flexible. However, the more sophisticated the device, the more complex it is to install, configure, and maintain. Careful thought must be put into designing a network with routers.

PRACTICE TEST QUESTIONS

1. **What resource does a router use to help it determine the best path between two nodes?**
   a. filtering database
   b. routing table
   c. SNMP database
   d. DNS records

2. **What is one advantage of dynamic routing over static routing?**
   a. It is more reliable.
   b. It is more secure.
   c. It prevents network administrators from having to configure the router.
   d. It can interpret both IP and IPX addresses.

3. **Which of the following addresses could a router interpret?**
   a. 506.78.34.110
   b. AE:09:35:00:BF:34
   c. AA:01:01:46:34:29:80
   d. 128.92.35.117

4. **Which two of the following factors do routers consider when selecting the best path for data to travel between two nodes?**
   a. network transmission type
   b. network congestion
   c. network protocol
   d. data priority

5. **What is the function of a routing protocol?**
   a. to enable communications between routers
   b. to facilitate translation between the Network and Transport layers of the OSI Model
   c. to convert nonroutable protocols into routable protocols
   d. to ensure that encapsulated protocols are routed properly

6. **Which of the following cannot forward NetBEUI packets?**
   a. repeater
   b. bridge
   c. brouter
   d. router

7. **What is one of a router's primary functions?**
   a. to determine the best path for forwarding data to its destination
   b. to regenerate attenuated signals
   c. to separate groups of network devices into broadcast domains
   d. to filter traffic according to subnet

1.6 Identify the purpose, features, and functions of the following network components (continued):

GATEWAYS AND CSU/DSU

UNDERSTANDING THE OBJECTIVE

Gateways connect two dissimilar networks or subnetworks. Gateways are combinations of software and hardware, and as such, they operate at multiple layers of the OSI Model. CSU/DSUs form the terminating equipment for a T-carrier, connecting the incoming line and the multiplexer.

WHAT YOU REALLY NEED TO KNOW

- ◆ In general, a **gateway** is a computer running special software or a connectivity device that acts as a translator between two dissimilar systems. It may connect networks running different protocols, architecture, or formatting.

- ◆ Gateways operate at multiple layers of the OSI Model, including Application, Session, Transport, and Network. They repackage incoming information so the destination network can read it. They may also perform security and filtering functions.

- ◆ Gateways can exist on servers, PCs, or mainframes. In the case of connecting two large networks, a gateway is often a specialized router or router interface.

- ◆ Gateways are much slower than bridges or normal routers because of the complex translations they conduct. Because they are slow, gateways have the potential to cause extreme network congestion.

- ◆ The most common type of gateway is the e-mail gateway, which translates messages from one type of system to another.

- ◆ An Internet gateway allows and manages access between LANs and the Internet. It can restrict the kind of access LAN users have to the Internet and vice versa.

- ◆ A LAN gateway allows segments of a LAN running different protocols or network access methods to communicate with each other.

- ◆ A **CSU/DSU** is the termination point for a T-carrier line at the customer's site, connecting the line with a multiplexer.

- ◆ Although CSUs (channel service units) and DSUs (data service units) are actually two separate devices, they are typically combined into a single box called a CSU/DSU.

- ◆ The **CSU** provides termination for the digital signal and ensures connection integrity through error correction and line monitoring. The **DSU** converts the digital signal used by bridges, routers, and multiplexers into the digital signal sent via the cabling.

OBJECTIVES ON THE JOB

Chances are, if you work on a LAN that connects to the Internet (two dissimilar networks), you will need to understand gateways. Since gateways can be very different, you must be certain to understand the functions and requirements of your particular gateway before installing, configuring, or maintaining it.

PRACTICE TEST QUESTIONS

1. **Why are gateways slower than bridges?**
   a. because they must read the source and destination MAC addresses
   b. because they must manage sessions, translate encoded data, and interpret logical and physical addresses
   c. because they must assign new IP addresses to every packet
   d. because they must interpret application programming interface output

2. **What type of gateway would connect Token Ring and Ethernet networks within one building?**
   a. e-mail gateway
   b. IBM host gateway
   c. LAN gateway
   d. Internet gateway

3. **Which two of the following could be considered gateways?**
   a. router
   b. switch
   c. bridge
   d. firewall

4. **Which two of the following could host an e-mail gateway?**
   a. server
   b. PC
   c. bridge
   d. hub

5. **When acting as an e-mail gateway, in which OSI Model layers does a gateway perform most of its functions?**
   a. Data Link and Physical
   b. Transport and Network
   c. Transport and Session
   d. Application and Presentation

6. **What does "CSU" stand for?**
   a. communications service unit
   b. channel service unit
   c. communications session unit
   d. cable session unit

7. **A CSU/DSU connects an incoming T-carrier line with which of the following devices?**
   a. router
   b. modem
   c. multiplexer
   d. laser

1.6   Identify the purpose, features, and functions of the following network components (continued):

NETWORK INTERFACE CARDS/ISDN ADAPTERS/SYSTEM AREA NETWORK CARDS AND WIRELESS ACCESS POINTS

UNDERSTANDING THE OBJECTIVE

Network interface cards, wireless access points, and ISDN adapters are components of a network that connect individual devices to media and perform data transmission and reception.

WHAT YOU REALLY NEED TO KNOW

◆ A **transceiver** is a device that receives and transmits signals. In most modern networks, a transceiver can only be found in the network interface card (NIC), ISDN adapter, or wireless access point, depending on the type of network.

◆ **Network Interface Cards (NICs)** are connectivity devices that enable a workstation, server, printer, or other node to receive and transmit data over the network media. NICs are also sometimes called **network adapters**.

◆ All network adapters have their own circuitry, a system board interface, and at least one receptacle for a connection to the network. They may be external or internal to a device.

◆ NICs belong to the Physical layer of the OSI Model because they transmit data signals but do not (in general) analyze the data from higher layers.

◆ NICs come in a variety of types depending on network transport system (Ethernet vs. Token Ring), network transmission speed (for example, 10 Mbps vs. 100 Mbps), connector interfaces (for example, BNC vs. RJ-45), type of system board (for example, PCI or ISA) or device (for example, workstation or printer) they suit, and of course, manufacturer.

◆ Typically, a wireless NIC uses an antenna to exchange signals with a base station transceiver or other wireless NIC adapters. This type of connectivity suits environments where cabling cannot be installed or clients who need to be mobile.

◆ From the telephone company's lines, the ISDN channels connect to a Network Termination 1 device at the customer's site. The **Network Termination 1 (NT1)** device connects the twisted-pair wiring at the customer's building with the ISDN terminal equipment via RJ-11 or RJ-45 data jacks. The ISDN **terminal equipment (TE)** may include cards or standalone devices used to connect computers to the ISDN line (similar to a network adapter used on Ethernet or Token Ring networks).

◆ So that the ISDN line can connect to analog equipment, the signal must first pass through a terminal adapter. An **ISDN adapter** converts digital signals into analog signals for use with ISDN phones and other analog devices.

OBJECTIVES ON THE JOB

It's a good idea to use the same NIC vendor, if not the same make and model, for all devices on a network. This makes support and maintenance easier. Because Token Ring networks are becoming rare and because modern Token Ring NICs include RJ-45 receptacles, it is unlikely that you will need to use Token Ring media filters unless you are working on an older network.

PRACTICE TEST QUESTIONS

1. **Which of the following do all NICs have in common?**
   a. antenna
   b. RJ-11 receptacle
   c. RJ-45 receptacle
   d. a means for connecting to the system board

2. **What type of NIC is best suited for inventory control personnel who must quickly travel through a large warehouse entering data into their networked workstation?**
   a. PCMCIA
   b. PCI
   c. infrared
   d. USB

3. **Which two of the following features that can be found on a sophisticated NIC (such as one found in a server) improves the performance of the NIC?**
   a. diagnostic LEDs
   b. Direct Memory Access (DMA)
   c. SNMP capabilities
   d. on-board CPU

4. **Which of the following is one function of an ISDN adapter?**
   a. to convert incoming digital signals into analog signals
   b. to convert outgoing digital signals into analog signals
   c. to convert outgoing baseband signals into broadband signals
   d. to convert incoming baseband signals into broadband signals

5. **What types of receptacles would be found on an ISDN adapter?**
   a. BNC and AUI
   b. RJ-11 and RJ-45
   c. AUI and n-connector
   d. RJ-45 and RJ-52

6. **Which of the following types of NICs are you most likely to find on a modern desktop computer?**
   a. PCI
   b. PCMCIA
   c. infrared
   d. parallel port

7. **Which two of the following might be terminating equipment connected to an ISDN adapter?**
   a. fax machine
   b. multiplexer
   c. media filter
   d. telephone

1.6 Identify the purpose, features, and functions of the following network components (continued):

MODEMS

UNDERSTANDING THE OBJECTIVE

Like a NIC, a modem must have unique and appropriate IRQ, I/O address, and memory address range settings. Among other parameters, a modem's maximum port speed can be configured through the operating system. The throughput of modern modems is limited to 56 Kbps.

WHAT YOU REALLY NEED TO KNOW

◆ The word **modem** is derived from its function as a MODulator/DEModulator. A modem converts a computer's digital pulses into analog signals for the PSTN (because not all of the PSTN is necessarily capable of digital transmission), then converts the analog signals back into digital pulses at the receiving computer's end.

◆ On modern computers, modems are typically connected to the machine's system board through an expansion slot. However, if an external modem is used, it may connect to the PC's serial port, PCMCIA slot, or USB port.

◆ Often the default values assigned when the modem is installed are correct. However, the ISP a user dials might prefer different port settings (including parity, data bits, and stop bits). You can configure these values through the operating system of any personal computer.

◆ To use FIFO buffers, a modem must have a 16550 UART compatible chip. The higher the buffer settings, the faster data will be transmitted; however, less data correction will be employed.

◆ The IRQ, I/O base address, and memory range for a modem on a modern PC is initially assigned in the BIOS, but it can be modified through the operating system. IRQ 4 is commonly assigned to the COM1 or COM3 serial ports, which are used for modem connections.

◆ A modem's speed is measured in bits per second. The fastest modem transmission possible with current technology is 56 Kbps.

◆ A **dial-up** connection uses a PSTN or other line to access a remote server via modems at both the source (for example, the salesperson's computer) and destination (for example, the office's LAN server).

OBJECTIVES ON THE JOB

For networking professionals, knowledge of modems is often required when establishing or troubleshooting remote connectivity. In such a situation, it is necessary to understand how the modem interacts with the operating system and how to fine-tune a modem connection. Fortunately, however, all types of modems are similar and not nearly as complex as other connectivity devices, such as routers.

PRACTICE TEST QUESTIONS

1. **What IRQ number is commonly assigned to a computer's internal modem?**
   a. 1
   b. 3
   c. 4
   d. 9

2. **What is the most likely means for a modem to connect to a desktop computer's system board?**
   a. serial port
   b. PCMCIA slot
   c. parallel port
   d. expansion slot

3. **If a user configures her modem's maximum port speed to 115,200 bps in her operating system, at what speed is she most likely to connect to her ISP?**
   a. 576,000 bps
   b. 115,200 bps
   c. 52,600 bps
   d. 11,520 bps

4. **In a remote networking situation, who or what dictates the proper connection preferences, including data bits and parity bit?**
   a. the remote access server
   b. the client's modem
   c. the LAN manager
   d. the client's operating system

5. **From what two words does the term "modem" originate?**
   a. modulator/demodulator
   b. modifier/demodifier
   c. moderate/demoderate
   d. modiplexer/demodiplexer

6. **What type of chip is needed for a modem to support FIFO buffering?**
   a. 3000 UART or better
   b. 10000 UART or better
   c. 16550 UART or better
   d. 56000 UART or better

7. **Which of the following is one function of a modem?**
   a. to convert incoming digital signals into analog signals
   b. to convert outgoing digital signals into analog signals
   c. to convert outgoing baseband signals into broadband signals
   d. to convert incoming baseband signals into broadband signals

2.1 Given an example, identify a MAC address.

UNDERSTANDING THE OBJECTIVE

A MAC address is the unique hexadecimal number assigned to a NIC at the manufacturer's factory. The MAC address operates in the MAC sublayer of the Data Link layer of the OSI Model. It provides the interface between the Physical layer and the Logical Link Control sublayer of the Data Link layer.

WHAT YOU REALLY NEED TO KNOW

◆ The Data Link layer is subdivided into the Logical Link Control and the MAC sublayers.

◆ The **MAC sublayer** appends the physical address of the destination to the data frame, thus creating a connection between the Physical layer and the Logical Link Control sublayer of the Data Link layer.

◆ **Data Link layer addresses** are fixed numbers associated with the networking hardware and are usually assigned to the network adapter at the factory. These addresses are also called **MAC addresses**, after the Media Access Control (MAC) sublayer, or **physical addresses**.

◆ MAC addresses are 12-digit hexadecimal numbers guaranteed to be unique because industry standards govern what numbers each manufacturer can use.

◆ As an example, NICs manufactured by the 3Com Corporation begin with the following sequence of six characters: 00608C. The part of the MAC address unique to a particular vendor is called the **Block ID**. The remaining six characters in the sequence are added at the factory, based on the NIC's model and manufacture date, and together are called the **Device ID**. An example of a Device ID assigned by a manufacturer might be 005499. Together, this Block ID and Device ID would result in a unique MAC address of 00608C005499.

◆ You can view the MAC address of a device or client's NIC through the NIC diagnostic utility, or on a Windows 9x computer through the WINIPCFG utility, or on a Windows NT or 2000 computer through the IPCONFIG utility, or on a UNIX computer through the IFCONFIG utility. It may also be printed on the NIC's circuit board.

◆ MAC addresses are used by some connectivity devices, such as bridges, to determine how to forward data over the network.

OBJECTIVES ON THE JOB

MAC addresses, which are key pieces of information in troubleshooting, should never be changed (and it is difficult to do so). For example, you need to know how to recognize and interpret MAC addresses to resolve other addressing conflicts (such as IP or IPX conflicts).

PRACTICE TEST QUESTIONS

1. **Which of the following is an example of a valid MAC address?**
   a. 128.7.99.24
   b. AE:09:33:00:23:B5
   c. 92:CG:50:28:K3:48
   d. 247.34.188.203

2. **What part of a MAC address would all like-model Ethernet NICs have in common?**
   a. Port ID
   b. Node ID
   c. Block ID
   d. Host ID

3. **Which of the following devices depends on MAC addresses to forward packets?**
   a. bridges
   b. routers
   c. hubs
   d. firewalls

4. **How can an end user discover a Windows 2000 workstation's MAC address?**
   a. by checking the TCP/IP properties
   b. by running WINIPCFG /all at the command prompt
   c. by running IPCONFIG /all at the command prompt
   d. by checking the network adapter properties in the Devices tab of the System properties dialog box

5. **Which of the following terms is used interchangeably with "MAC address"?**
   a. LLC sublayer address
   b. Physical address
   c. Logical address
   d. Network address

6. **What does MAC stand for?**
   a. median axis channel
   b. multiple access carrier
   c. media access control
   d. multiple arbitrator channel

7. **Which of the following occurs at the MAC sublayer?**
   a. An address is appended to the data packet.
   b. Checksum data is added to the data packet.
   c. Flow control data is added to the data packet.
   d. Packets are padded if they do not meet the minimum packet size.

OBJECTIVES

2.2 Identify the seven layers of the OSI Model and their functions:

LAYERS 1 THROUGH 3

UNDERSTANDING THE OBJECTIVE

The Open Systems Interconnection (OSI) Model is a theoretical construct that separates the functions of a network into seven layers. Each layer is associated with different protocols, hardware, or software. Layers 1 through 3 include the Physical, Data Link, and Network layers. Services that operate at these layers include electrical pulses (Physical layer), physical addressing (Data Link layer), and logical addressing and routing (Network layer).

WHAT YOU REALLY NEED TO KNOW

- ◆ The OSI Model is a theoretical representation of what happens between two nodes on a network. It does not stipulate hardware or software.
- ◆ The **Physical layer** is the lowest, or first, layer of the OSI Model. This layer contains the physical networking medium, such as cabling, connectors, and repeaters. Protocols at the Physical layer are responsible for generating and detecting voltage in order to transmit and receive signals carrying data.
- ◆ The Physical layer handles the data transmission rate and monitors data error rates, but does not handle error correction.
- ◆ The second layer of the OSI Model, the **Data Link layer**, controls communication between the Network layer and Physical layer. Its primary function is to divide data it receives from the Network layer into distinct frames that can then be transmitted by the Physical layer.
- ◆ Bridges and switches work in the Data Link layer, because they decode frames and use the frame information to transmit data to its correct recipient.
- ◆ The primary function of the **Network layer**, the third layer, is to translate network addresses into their physical counterparts and decide how to route data from the sender to the receiver.
- ◆ The Network layer determines the best route between nodes by considering delivery priorities, network congestion, quality of service, and cost of alternative routes.
- ◆ Services that work in the Network layer include IP and IPX.

OBJECTIVES ON THE JOB

Knowledge of the OSI Model helps you identify and fix errors on a network. It also helps you understand higher-level networking concepts such as addressing. A deep understanding of what functions occur at each layer of the OSI Model helps you install, configure, and troubleshoot routers, switches, bridges, and other networking equipment.

PRACTICE TEST QUESTIONS

1. **At what layer of the OSI Model would a network be affected if a coaxial cable were severed?**
   a. Physical
   b. Data Link
   c. Network
   d. Transport

2. **Which of the following functions belongs to the Network layer of the OSI Model?**
   a. bridging
   b. repeating
   c. routing
   d. error correction

3. **At what layer of the OSI Model are MAC addresses interpreted?**
   a. Physical
   b. Data Link
   c. Network
   d. Transport

4. **If a printer can interpret physical addresses but cannot interpret an IP address, at what layer is it failing?**
   a. Physical
   b. Data Link
   c. Network
   d. Transport

5. **Which of the following is not considered when a router chooses the best path from one node to another on a network?**
   a. network congestion
   b. quality of service
   c. time to send data
   d. geographical distance between nodes

6. **At which layer of the OSI Model is data packaged into frames?**
   a. Physical
   b. Data Link
   c. Network
   d. Transport

7. **Which of the following functions belongs to the Physical layer?**
   a. applying electrical charges to a wire
   b. determining which segment a node is on, based on its MAC address
   c. determining which segment a node is on, based on its IPX address
   d. determining whether a packet has been damaged between its source and target

2.2 Identify the seven layers of the OSI Model and their functions (continued):

LAYERS 4 THROUGH 7

UNDERSTANDING THE OBJECTIVE

Layers 4 through 7 deal with higher-level functions, such as managing traffic on a network, encoding and encrypting data, and establishing a user interface. Examples of these functions include HTTP and e-mail (the Application layer), data encryption (the Presentation layer), session negotiation (the Session layer), and error correction (Transport layer).

WHAT YOU REALLY NEED TO KNOW

◆ The **Transport layer**, the fourth layer of the OSI Model, is responsible for ensuring that data is transferred from point A to point B reliably, in the correct sequence, and without errors.

◆ Transport protocols also handle **flow control**, the method of gauging the appropriate rate of transmission based on how fast the recipient can accept data.

◆ Services that work in the Transport layer include TCP and SPX.

◆ The **Session layer**, the fifth layer of the OSI Model, is responsible for establishing and maintaining communication between two nodes on the network for the session's duration. Other Session layer functions include synchronizing the dialog between the two nodes, determining whether communication has been cut, and if it has been cut, where to restart transmission.

◆ The Session layer also sets the terms of communication by deciding which node communicates first and how long a node can communicate.

◆ The **Presentation layer**, the sixth layer in the OSI Model, serves as a translator between the application and the network. At the Presentation layer, data is formatted in a schema that the network can understand.

◆ The Presentation layer also takes care of data encryption and decryption, such as the scrambling of system passwords.

◆ The top, or seventh, layer of the OSI Model is the Application layer. The **Application layer** provides interfaces to the software that enable programs to use network services, but it does not refer to a particular program.

◆ Some of the services provided by the Application layer include file transfer, file management, and message handling for electronic mail.

OBJECTIVES ON THE JOB

Problems that occur in the higher layers of the OSI Model are more apt to be related to software than hardware or firmware. For example, if you have ruled out physical connectivity problems when you are unable to dial in to your ISP's modem pool, you might find a problem at the Session layer (which handles communication).

PRACTICE TEST QUESTIONS

1. **Which layer of the OSI Model is also known as the traffic cop because it manages communication between nodes?**
   - a. Transport
   - b. Session
   - c. Presentation
   - d. Application

2. **Which of the following is a true statement?**
   - a. MS Word resides at the Application layer.
   - b. The MSMQ API resides at the Application layer.
   - c. The network operating system resides at the Application layer.
   - d. The MAC address resides at the Application layer.

3. **At which layer of the OSI Model does data encryption take place?**
   - a. Transport
   - b. Session
   - c. Presentation
   - d. Application

4. **Which layer of the OSI Model is responsible for sequencing?**
   - a. Transport
   - b. Session
   - c. Presentation
   - d. Application

5. **With which layer of the OSI Model is a programmer likely to be most familiar?**
   - a. Transport
   - b. Session
   - c. Presentation
   - d. Application

6. **Which layer of the OSI Model takes care of error correction?**
   - a. Transport
   - b. Session
   - c. Presentation
   - d. Application

7. **Which of the following is an example of a Transport layer protocol?**
   - a. IP
   - b. IPX
   - c. TCP
   - d. FTP

2.3 Differentiate between the following network protocols in terms of routing, addressing schemes, interoperability, and naming conventions:

TCP/IP

UNDERSTANDING THE OBJECTIVE

Transmission Control Protocol/Internet Protocol (TCP/IP) is the most popular protocol in use today and is used exclusively by Internet services. IP in the TCP/IP suite contains addressing information; therefore, it belongs to the Network layer of the OSI Model and is routable.

WHAT YOU REALLY NEED TO KNOW

◆ **TCP/IP** is a routable protocol (or suite of protocols). It is the protocol of choice for most modern networks, including the Internet.

◆ Two core protocols of TCP/IP are the Transmission Control Protocol (TCP) and the Internet Protocol (IP).

◆ **TCP**, a connection-oriented protocol, belongs to the Transport layer of the OSI Model and ensures that data is received whole, in sequence, and error-free. **Connection-oriented** means that TCP verifies that a connection is sound before it transmits data.

◆ **IP** operates at the Network layer of the OSI Model and provides information about how and where data should be delivered. IP is the subprotocol that enables TCP/IP to **internetwork**—that is, to traverse more than one LAN segment and more than one type of network through a router—and thus, makes it routable.

◆ In the currently used version of IP, **IP version 4 (IPv4),** each IP address is a unique 32-bit number, divided into four groups of **octets**, or 8-bit bytes, that are separated by periods.

◆ IP address data is sent across the network in binary form. For example, the IP address 131.127.3.22 (in **dotted-decimal notation**) is the same as the binary number 10000011 01111111 00000011 00010110.

◆ In order to communicate via the Internet, organizations must register for a group of IP addresses that are associated with their domain name. Available IP addresses belong to one of three classes: A, B, or C.

◆ TCP/IP is compatible with every modern desktop and network operating system, including Macintosh, NetWare, Windows 9x, Windows 2000, Windows NT, and UNIX.

OBJECTIVES ON THE JOB

Since the Internet and many different applications rely on TCP/IP and probably will for a long time, the need to understand this protocol will continue to be critical. You should know the addressing conventions of this protocol, as well as the addresses that have special meaning, such as the loopback address. You should also know how to recognize addressing conflicts and to help avoid them.

PRACTICE TEST QUESTIONS

1. **Which protocol in the TCP/IP suite is responsible for addressing?**
   a. UDP
   b. TCP
   c. ARP
   d. IP

2. **At what layer of the OSI Model does TCP reside?**
   a. Data Link
   b. Network
   c. Transport
   d. Session

3. **Which of the following is not a valid IP address?**
   a. 127.0.0.1
   b. 10.10.10.10
   c. 199.220.37.18
   d. 392.89.32.5

4. **Which of the following is a connection-oriented subprotocol of the TCP/IP suite?**
   a. TCP
   b. IP
   c. UDP
   d. ICMP

5. **Which of the following subprotocols allows TCP/IP to be routable?**
   a. TCP
   b. IP
   c. UDP
   d. ICMP

6. **On a UNIX server, what command could you type to determine the IP address of your network interface?**
   a. ipconfig /all
   b. ifconfig /all
   c. winipcfg /all
   d. inetcfg /all

7. **On what version of TCP/IP does most of the Internet currently rely?**
   a. 2
   b. 4
   c. 6
   d. 8

2.3 Differentiate between the following network protocols in terms of routing, addressing schemes, interoperability, and naming conventions (continued):

IPX/SPX

UNDERSTANDING THE OBJECTIVE

The Internetwork Packet Exchange/Sequenced Packet Exchange (IPX/SPX) protocol suite was originally designed by Xerox. Novell modified it in the 1980s for its NetWare NOS. IPX contains Network layer addressing information; therefore, the IPX/SPX protocol is routable.

WHAT YOU REALLY NEED TO KNOW

- IPX operates at the Network layer of the OSI Model and provides routing and internetwork services.

- IPX is a **connectionless** service. It does not require that a session be established before transmitting, and it does not guarantee that data will be delivered error-free.

- SPX is a connection-oriented protocol that belongs to the Transport layer of the OSI Model. It verifies that data is received whole, error-free, and in sequence.

- Because it contains addressing information, IPX/SPX is routable.

- IPX/SPX is required for Novell NetWare versions 3.x and lower. In versions 4.x and higher, IPX/SPX is optional, and it has often been replaced by TCP/IP.

- Other operating systems, such as Windows 2000, Windows 9x, Macintosh, and UNIX, can use IPX/SPX to internetwork with Novell NetWare systems.

- IPX addresses contain two parts: the network address and the node address.

- An IPX network address must be an 8-bit hexadecimal address, which means that each of its bits can have a value of either 0–9 or A–F. An example of a valid network address is 000008A2. The network address then becomes the first part of the IPX address on all nodes that use that server as their primary server.

- An IPX node address is equal to a device's MAC (or physical) address. Because MAC addresses are preassigned to all NICs, using IPX/SPX means a network administrator does not need to manually assign node addresses to each device.

OBJECTIVES ON THE JOB

If you are establishing or maintaining an IPX/SPX network, become familiar with the addressing conventions of this protocol. Node addresses depend on MAC addresses (which should never change), but network addresses are assigned manually. If they are improperly assigned, the server and all of its clients will be unable to communicate on the network.

PRACTICE TEST QUESTIONS

1. **What company originally designed the IPX/SPX protocol?**
   a. IBM
   b. Xerox
   c. Microsoft
   d. Cisco

2. **Which of the following protocols belonging to the IPX/SPX suite verifies that data is received error-free?**
   a. IPX
   b. SAP
   c. SPX
   d. NCP

3. **Two workstations on the same network running IPX/SPX will have the same**
   a. host address.
   b. network address.
   c. node address.
   d. MAC address.

4. **To what layer of the OSI Model does IPX belong?**
   a. Data Link
   b. Network
   c. Transport
   d. Session

5. **Which of the following is not a valid network address when using the IPX/SPX protocol?**
   a. 11111111
   b. AB0045099
   c. ABCABCAB
   d. F29FF034

6. **Which of the following is a connectionless protocol?**
   a. IPX
   b. SPX
   c. SAP
   d. RIP

7. **Which of the following network operating systems requires the use of IPX/SPX?**
   a. IntraNetWare
   b. NetWare 5.0
   c. NetWare 4.11
   d. NetWare 3.11

2.3 Differentiate between the following network protocols in terms of routing, addressing schemes, interoperability, and naming conventions (continued):

NETBEUI

UNDERSTANDING THE OBJECTIVE

Network Basic Input Output System (NetBIOS) is a protocol designed by IBM to provide Transport and Session layer services for applications running on small, homogenous networks. Microsoft adopted NetBIOS as its foundation protocol and added an Application layer component on top of NetBIOS called the NetBIOS Enhanced User Interface (NetBEUI).

WHAT YOU REALLY NEED TO KNOW

- ◆ Microsoft adopted IBM's NetBIOS as its foundation protocol, initially for networks using Windows for Workgroups, and added an Application layer component on top of NetBIOS called the NetBIOS Enhanced User Interface (NetBEUI).
- ◆ **NetBEUI** is a fast and efficient protocol that consumes few network resources, provides excellent error correction, and requires little configuration. NetBEUI is the easiest type of protocol to set up.
- ◆ Neither NetBIOS nor NetBEUI provides services at all the OSI Model layers, though NetBEUI roughly corresponds to the Presentation and Session layers.
- ◆ NetBEUI can only support up to 254 connections and does not allow for good security. It is therefore not appropriate for use on large networks. In practice, using the maximum of 254 nodes would result in very poor performance. Therefore, NetBEUI networks usually contain many fewer nodes.
- ◆ Because NetBEUI lacks network addressing information, it is not routable by itself.
- ◆ NetBIOS does not contain a Network layer with addressing information, but to transmit data between network nodes, NetBIOS needs to know how to reach each workstation. Network administrators must assign each workstation a NetBIOS name.
- ◆ The NetBIOS name can be any combination of 16 or fewer alphanumeric characters, including special characters.
- ◆ Once NetBIOS has found a workstation's NetBIOS name, it discovers the workstation's MAC address and uses it for further communication with the workstation.
- ◆ If you are running both TCP/IP and NetBIOS on your network, it's a good policy to make the NetBIOS name identical to the TCP/IP host name.

OBJECTIVES ON THE JOB

Today, NetBEUI is most commonly used in small Microsoft-based networks to integrate legacy, peer-to-peer networks. In newer networks, TCP/IP has become the protocol of choice because it is routable and more flexible and scalable than NetBEUI. Therefore, mastering NetBEUI is useful for administrators working on older Microsoft networks, but it is a skill rarely needed when administering modern networks.

PRACTICE TEST QUESTIONS

1. **What is the relationship between NetBIOS and NetBEUI?**
   a. NetBEUI encrypts NetBIOS on the network.
   b. NetBEUI enables NetBIOS to be routed.
   c. NetBEUI adds an Application layer to NetBIOS.
   d. NetBEUI is the IBM version of NetBIOS.

2. **To which layers of the OSI Model does NetBEUI correspond?**
   a. Physical and Network
   b. Session and Transport
   c. Transport and Network
   d. Presentation and Session

3. **What does NetBEUI use to identify workstations on the network?**
   a. host name
   b. node address
   c. network address
   d. NetBIOS name

4. **What company originally designed NetBIOS?**
   a. IBM
   b. Microsoft
   c. Sun
   d. Cisco

5. **Why is NetBEUI not suitable for large networks?**
   a. It can only support dumb terminals.
   b. It suffers poor performance when more than a hundred nodes are connected.
   c. It cannot support shared devices such as printers.
   d. It can only support up to 512 NetBIOS names.

6. **Under what circumstances can NetBIOS be routed?**
   a. if it's encapsulated by another protocol
   b. if it's bound to multiple NICs
   c. if it traverses LAN segments
   d. if it's assigned appropriate node addresses

7. **What is the maximum number of characters in a NetBIOS name?**
   a. 8
   b. 16
   c. 32
   d. 64

2.3 Differentiate between the following network protocols in terms of routing, addressing schemes, interoperability, and naming conventions (continued):

APPLETALK

UNDERSTANDING THE OBJECTIVE

AppleTalk is the protocol designed by Apple, Inc. to network Macintosh computers. It has largely been replaced by newer, more flexible protocols such as TCP/IP.

WHAT YOU REALLY NEED TO KNOW

◆ **AppleTalk** is the protocol suite used to interconnect Macintosh computers. AppleTalk is a complete protocol suite containing services that fit into each layer of the OSI Model. Since it contains Network layer addressing information, AppleTalk is routable.

◆ Although AppleTalk was originally designed to support peer-to-peer networking among Macintoshes, it can now be routed between network segments and integrated with NetWare- or Microsoft-based networks.

◆ An AppleTalk network is separated into logical groups of computers called **AppleTalk zones**. Each network can contain multiple zones, but each node can belong to only one zone.

◆ AppleTalk zones enable users to share file and printer resources on one another's Macintoshes.

◆ Zone names are not subject to the same strict naming conventions that TCP/IP and IPX/SPX networks must follow. Instead, zone names typically describe a department or other group of users who share files. An example of a zone name is "Sales and Marketing."

◆ **AppleShare** is the AppleTalk subprotocol that provides file sharing services, print queuing services, password access to files or folders, and user accounting information.

◆ An **AppleTalk node ID** is a unique 8-bit or 16-bit number that identifies a computer on an AppleTalk network. AppleTalk assigns a node ID to each workstation when the workstation first connects to the network. The ID is randomly chosen from a group of currently available addresses. Once a device has obtained an address, it stores it for later use.

◆ An **AppleTalk network number** is a unique 16-bit number that identifies the network to which a node is connected. Its use allows nodes from several different networks to communicate.

OBJECTIVES ON THE JOB

Although Apple has improved AppleTalk's ability to use different network models and span network segments, it remains unsuited to large LANs or WANs. Even Apple has begun supporting the TCP/IP protocol to integrate Macintoshes with other networks, including the Internet.

PRACTICE TEST QUESTIONS

1. **What is a logical group of computers on an AppleTalk network called?**
   - a. a workgroup
   - b. a zone
   - c. a share
   - d. a segment

2. **An AppleTalk network number is similar to what IPX/SPX number?**
   - a. host address
   - b. node ID
   - c. network address
   - d. login ID

3. **What company developed the AppleTalk suite of protocols?**
   - a. Apple
   - b. Macintosh
   - c. Microsoft
   - d. IBM

4. **Which of the following protocols are routable? Choose all that apply.**
   - a. AppleTalk
   - b. TCP/IP
   - c. IPX/SPX
   - d. NetBEUI

5. **Which of the following AppleTalk subprotocols provides print queuing functions?**
   - a. AppleTalk Transaction Protocol
   - b. Zone Information Protocol
   - c. AppleTalk Filing Protocol
   - d. AppleShare

6. **AppleTalk can be used with which of the following network operating systems? Choose all that apply.**
   - a. Windows NT
   - b. NetWare 3.11
   - c. Windows 98
   - d. DOS

7. **Which of the following networks is most likely to use AppleTalk?**
   - a. a WAN that connects 25 departments on a university campus
   - b. a group of three Macintosh graphics computers in a home-based business
   - c. a LAN that connects 120 mobile salespeople with their corporate headquarters
   - d. a MAN that connects 50 city and county government offices across a large city

2.4   Identify the OSI layers at which the following network components operate: HUBS, SWITCHES, BRIDGES, ROUTERS, NETWORK INTERFACE CARDS

UNDERSTANDING THE OBJECTIVE

The higher the OSI Model layer at which a network component operates, the more sophisticated its functions. Hubs and repeaters, which simply regenerate signals, operate at the Physical layer. NICs operate at both the Physical and Data Link layers. Bridges and traditional switches operate at the Data Link layer. Routers and Layer 3 switches, which interpret logical addressing information, operate at the Network layer. Gateways operate at multiple layers of the OSI Model.

WHAT YOU REALLY NEED TO KNOW

◆ Network devices operate at the Physical layer of the OSI Model, which handles voltage detection and signaling. Such devices include hubs and repeaters.

◆ Hubs and repeaters are not capable of interpreting any type of address—either physical or logical—but instead simply regenerate a signal on a network segment.

◆ Network Interface Cards (NICs) operate at both the Physical and Data Link layers of the OSI Model, because they are responsible for both applying signals to a network medium and packaging data into frames.

◆ Bridges operate at the Data Link layer of the OSI Model. Because of this, they are only capable of interpreting MAC (or physical) addresses, not logical addresses.

◆ Most switches also operate at the Data Link layer of the OSI Model. Like bridges, switches rely on MAC address information to determine how to direct packets to their destination.

◆ **Layer 3 switches**, so called because they can function at Layer 3 of the OSI Model (the Network layer) are capable of interpreting logical as well as physical addresses.

◆ Routers, because they rely on logical addresses to determine how to forward data to their destination, belong to the Network layer of the OSI Model.

◆ Gateways operate at several layers of the OSI Model, since they are a combination of hardware and software. Gateways are most likely to operate in the Network, Transport, Session, and Presentation layers.

OBJECTIVES ON THE JOB

Understanding the layers at which each component of a network operates is vital to properly designing a network. It is also very important in troubleshooting. For example, you may recognize errors on a network that are due to late collisions on an Ethernet network, leading you to realize that at some point on the network, data signals are not being timed properly. Because signaling belongs to the Physical layer of the OSI Model, you can then begin to examine hubs, repeaters, and NICs for the source of the problem.

PRACTICE TEST QUESTIONS

1. **Which of the following perform functions that belong to the Network layer of the OSI Model? Choose all that apply.**
   a. hubs
   b. routers
   c. gateways
   d. NICs

2. **Which of the following is responsible for assigning Data Link layer information to a packet?**
   a. hub
   b. repeater
   c. NIC
   d. router

3. **At what layer of the OSI Model do bridges operate?**
   a. Physical
   b. Data Link
   c. Network
   d. Transport

4. **If a workstation on a network that relies solely on TCP/IP begins issuing IPX/SPX-based data packets, what device will recognize this problem?**
   a. hub
   b. bridge
   c. switch
   d. router

5. **Which of the following devices could perform functions at the Session layer of the OSI Model?**
   a. hub
   b. switch
   c. gateway
   d. router

6. **A Layer 3 switch is capable of performing functions at what two layers of the OSI Model?**
   a. Physical and Data Link
   b. Data Link and Network
   c. Physical and Network
   d. Network and Transport

7. **What kind of addresses does a traditional switch interpret?**
   a. MAC addresses
   b. IP addresses
   c. logical addresses
   d. static addresses

2.5 Define the purpose, function and/or use of the following protocols within TCP/IP:

IP, TCP, AND UDP

UNDERSTANDING THE OBJECTIVE

IP, TCP, and UDP are all core protocols in the TCP/IP protocol suite. IP resides at the Network layer, while TCP and UDP are Transport layer protocols.

WHAT YOU REALLY NEED TO KNOW

◆ The **Internet Protocol (IP)** is a core protocol in the TCP/IP suite that resides at the Network layer of the OSI Model. Its primary purpose is to add logical addresses to data frames, providing information on how and where data should be delivered.

◆ Because IP provides addressing, logical addresses in the TCP/IP suite are known as **IP addresses**.

◆ IP is considered connectionless because it does not require that a session be established before it begins transmission, and it does not guarantee that data will be delivered in sequence or error-free.

◆ The **Transport Control Protocol (TCP)** belongs to the Transport layer of the TCP/IP suite and provides reliable data delivery services. TCP sits on top of the IP subprotocol and makes up for IP's reliability deficiencies with its checksum, flow control, and sequencing information.

◆ TCP is a connection-oriented subprotocol, which means it requires that a connection be established between communicating nodes before it transmits data.

◆ A TCP segment contains several components that ensure data reliability, including acknowledgment, code, urgent pointer, and flow control fields.

◆ The **User Datagram Protocol (UDP)**, like TCP, also sits in the Transport layer of the OSI Model and relies on IP. Unlike TCP, UDP is a connectionless transport service. UDP offers no assurance that packets will be received in the correct sequence. In fact, this protocol does not guarantee that the packets will be received at all.

◆ UDP's lack of sophistication is an advantage in situations where data must be transferred quickly, such as live audio or video transmissions over the Internet. In these cases, TCP, with its acknowledgments, checksums, and flow control mechanisms, would add too much overhead to the transmission and bog it down.

OBJECTIVES ON THE JOB

In optimizing and troubleshooting networks, it is critical to understand that TCP is connection-oriented, while UDP is connectionless. Different higher-level TCP/IP subprotocols rely on either TCP or UDP, using UDP when efficiency is their primary criterion or TCP when reliability is more important. For example, TCP should never be used to send live video feeds over the Internet, because its error-correction and flow control mechanisms will cause transmission delays.

PRACTICE TEST QUESTIONS

1. **Which of the following protocols is responsible for providing information on where data should be delivered?**
   - a. TCP
   - b. IP
   - c. HTTP
   - d. UDP

2. **What is the function of the Acknowledgment field in the TCP datagram?**
   - a. It confirms receipt of the data in a return message to the sender.
   - b. It confirms the size of the datagram to the recipient, proving that the datagram was not corrupted en route.
   - c. It confirms the sequence of the datagrams to the recipient.
   - d. It confirms the length of the datagram's header in a return message to the sender.

3. **What is an advantage of using UDP over TCP?**
   - a. It is more reliable.
   - b. It is more secure.
   - c. It is more widely compatible.
   - d. It is more efficient.

4. **Which of the following protocols are connectionless? Choose all that apply.**
   - a. TCP
   - b. IP
   - c. UDP
   - d. HTTP

5. **Which of the following fields would be found in both a UDP and a TCP datagram? Choose all that apply.**
   - a. Acknowledgment
   - b. Source Port
   - c. Sequence Number
   - d. Destination Port

6. **What Transport layer protocol does Telnet use?**
   - a. TCP
   - b. IP
   - c. UDP
   - d. ICMP

7. **What Network layer protocol does TCP use?**
   - a. TCP
   - b. UDP
   - c. IP
   - d. ICMP

2.5 Define the purpose, function and/or use of the following protocols within TCP/IP (continued):

FTP AND TFTP

UNDERSTANDING THE OBJECTIVE

FTP is the basic file transfer utility used most often to download programs and data from the Internet, and to upload data to Web pages or other TCP/IP hosts. FTP relies on TCP at the Transport layer. TFTP also transfers files but relies on the UDP protocol at the Transport layer.

WHAT YOU REALLY NEED TO KNOW

◆ The **File Transfer Protocol (FTP)** is an Application layer protocol in the TCP/IP suite that enables a client and server to directly exchange data through a series of commands. FTP manages file transfers between TCP/IP hosts.

◆ At the Transport layer, FTP depends on the TCP protocol, and is, therefore, connection-oriented.

◆ FTP is a popular way to distribute files over the Internet. Some software sites allow users to download programs through a process called "anonymous FTP" in which their FTP host does not require a secure log on.

◆ FTP transfers are separated into two channels: one for data and one for control information. FTP data is exchanged over TCP port 20, and the FTP control commands are sent and received through TCP port 21.

◆ Although FTP is simple, it lets you show file and directory structures, manage files and directories, send data in binary or ASCII format, compress files, and append files.

◆ The **Trivial File Transfer Protocol (TFTP)** is similar to FTP in that it is a TCP/IP Application layer protocol that enables file transfers between computers. TFTP, however, relies on UDP at the Transport layer. Its use of UDP means that TFTP is connectionless and does not guarantee reliable delivery of data.

◆ TFTP does not actually log on to the remote host before enabling file transfers. Instead, when using TFTP, a computer issues a read request or a write request to the remote host. The remote host responds with an acknowledgment, after which the two computers begin transferring data. Each time a packet of data is transmitted to the host, the local workstation waits for an acknowledgment from the host before issuing another packet.

◆ TFTP uses port 69.

OBJECTIVES ON THE JOB

Before the Web provided an easier means of transferring files, FTP commands were regularly used to exchange data between machines. You can still use FTP commands without using browser software or special client software, that is, from the operating system's command prompt. As a network professional, you may need to use these commands to download software (such as NOS patches or client updates) from hosts.

PRACTICE TEST QUESTIONS

1. **To connect to the Netscape FTP site (ftp.netscape.com) from an FTP> prompt, what command would you type?**
   - a. `ftp netscape.com`
   - b. `login ftp.netscape.com`
   - c. `ftp.netscape.com`
   - d. `open ftp.netscape.com`

2. **What Transport layer protocol does TFTP rely on?**
   - a. TCP
   - b. IP
   - c. UDP
   - d. ICMP

3. **What port is used by FTP for data transfer?**
   - a. 20
   - b. 21
   - c. 22
   - d. 23

4. **What can you type at the FTP prompt to see a list of available commands?**
   - a. ?
   - b. query
   - c. list commands
   - d. commands/H

5. **If an FTP site allows unrestricted access, what user name can you probably type to log in to the site?**
   - a. your e-mail address
   - b. anonymous
   - c. guest
   - d. anyone

6. **Which of the following functions cannot be performed via FTP?**
   - a. sending a file to a server
   - b. changing to another directory
   - c. retrieving a file from a server
   - d. changing the permissions on a file

7. **What port does TFTP use?**
   - a. 21
   - b. 23
   - c. 45
   - d. 69

2.5   Define the purpose, function and/or use of the following protocols within TCP/IP (continued):

SMTP, POP3, AND IMAP

UNDERSTANDING THE OBJECTIVE

Together, POP3 and SMTP form the routine that enables clients to pick up e-mail from a server. While SMTP transfers mail between servers, POP3 accepts the mail from SMTP and holds it until e-mail clients retrieve it. A newer subprotocol, Internet Mail Access Protocol (IMAP), is replacing POP3 in many cases.

WHAT YOU REALLY NEED TO KNOW

- ◆ The **Simple Mail Transfer Protocol (SMTP)** moves messages from one e-mail server to another over TCP/IP networks. SMTP is a subprotocol of the TCP/IP suite.

- ◆ SMTP provides the basis for Internet e-mail service and relies on higher-level programs for its instructions. Such services as the UNIX sendmail software provide a more user-friendly and sophisticated mail interface while using SMTP for transport.

- ◆ Requests to receive and send mail go through port 25 on SMTP servers.

- ◆ The **Post Office Protocol (POP)** relies on SMTP. POP is a subprotocol of the TCP/IP suite that provides centralized storage for e-mail messages. POP also assigns error messages in the case of undeliverable mail.

- ◆ The current and most widely used version of POP is POP3.

- ◆ A POP server is necessary to store messages because users are not always logged on to the network and available for receiving messages from the SMTP server.

- ◆ Both SMTP and a service such as POP3 are necessary for a mail server to receive, store, and forward messages.

- ◆ When configuring clients to use Internet e-mail, the SMTP and POP3 server names must be specified within the e-mail client.

- ◆ A small organization can use one POP server for all its users' mail. Very large corporations can have several POP servers, one for each department. Internet service providers typically have one large POP server for all their clients.

- ◆ POP3 does not let users keep the mail on the server after they retrieve it, which can be a disadvantage for users who move from machine to machine. A newer protocol that is replacing POP3, **Internet Mail Access Protocol (IMAP)**, does let users read messages and keep them on the mail server.

OBJECTIVES ON THE JOB

If a company's SMTP server is down, mail cannot leave the organization, but it can be exchanged within the organization. If a POP3 server is down, clients cannot pick up mail because the SMTP server cannot transfer mail to it. Most companies have one SMTP server and one or more POP3 servers for storing mail.

PRACTICE TEST QUESTIONS

1. **If all users in a multinational organization can send and receive mail to and from colleagues, except for those in the Marketing department, what is probably the source of the problem?**
   a. the company's SMTP server
   b. the company's POP server
   c. the Marketing department's SMTP server
   d. the Marketing department's POP server

2. **What port does SMTP use?**
   a. 20
   b. 21
   c. 25
   d. 28

3. **Which of the following is one advantage of using POP over IMAP?**
   a. It requires fewer resources on the server.
   b. It allows clients to save unread messages on the server.
   c. It allows clients to selectively delete messages on the server before downloading them.
   d. It is more reliable.

4. **What does the S in SMTP stand for?**
   a. system
   b. selective
   c. secure
   d. simple

5. **Where must a client identify its SMTP server to properly send and receive mail?**
   a. within the e-mail client software
   b. within the operating system's TCP/IP configuration
   c. within the NIC device settings
   d. within the CMOS settings

6. **Which protocol is responsible for interpreting the following type of address: user@mailserver.com?**
   a. SMTP
   b. POP
   c. IMAP
   d. SNMP

7. **Which of the following is one advantage of using IMAP over POP?**
   a. It requires fewer resources on the server.
   b. It is simpler for a client to use.
   c. It allows clients to selectively delete messages on the server before downloading them.
   d. It can be more easily integrated into environments with multiple SMTP servers.

2.5 Define the purpose, function and/or use of the following protocols within TCP/IP (continued):

HTTP AND HTTPS

UNDERSTANDING THE OBJECTIVE

HTTP and HTTPS are Application layer protocols in the TCP/IP suite that translate information from Web servers into a user-friendly format. The main difference between HTTP and HTTPS is that HTTPS uses measures to secure information in transit.

WHAT YOU REALLY NEED TO KNOW

◆ **Hypertext Transport Protocol (HTTP)**, an Application layer protocol, is the language that Web clients and servers use to exchange commands and control information.

◆ When a Web user types the Uniform Resource Locator (URL) or IP address of a Web page in the Web browser's address field, HTTP transports the information about the request to the Web server and returns the Web server's information in **Hypertext Markup Language (HTML)**, the Web document formatting language.

◆ HTTP is also the mechanism that displays a Web page after a user clicks a link.

◆ The original version of HTTP, HTTP/0.9, was released in 1990. This version provided only the simplest means of transferring data over the Internet. Since then, HTTP has been improved to make Web client/server connections more efficient, reliable, and secure.

◆ Simple HTTP information is not secured in transit. To make the HTTP exchange secure, a version of HTTP called S (Secure)-HTTP must be used. Alternately, regular HTTP can be used with an encryption program, such as SSL (Secure Sockets Layer).

◆ When Web page URLs begin with the prefix **HTTPS**, they are requiring that their data be transferred from server to client and vice versa using SSL encryption.

◆ HTTPS uses the TCP port number 443, rather than port 80. To indicate that an SSL connection has been established between a Web server and client, the client's browser displays a padlock in the lower-right corner of the screen (this applies to Internet Explorer and Netscape Communicator versions 4.0 and higher).

OBJECTIVES ON THE JOB

You should understand the differences between HTTP and HTML for troubleshooting purposes. In addition, you should understand the security limitations of HTTP in case your clients are attempting to transmit secure data. You should also understand when using HTTPS is more appropriate. For example, e-commerce sites or other sites that require financial transactions almost always use HTTPS.

PRACTICE TEST QUESTIONS

1. **To which layer of the OSI Model does HTTPS belong?**
    a. Data Link
    b. Network
    c. Session
    d. Application

2. **Which of the following is a valid HTTP address?**
    a. 205.23.88.71:80
    b. 267.12.11.89
    c. AE:56:0F:C3:88
    d. 12:80:01:CF

3. **In what year was HTTP first released?**
    a. 1989
    b. 1990
    c. 1991
    d. 1993

4. **Which of the following can be interpreted by HTTP (and result in the display of a Web page)? Choose all that apply.**
    a. http://www.whitehouse.gov
    b. html://www.ibm.net
    c. tcp://www.loc.gov
    d. www.microsoft.net

5. **Which of the following is a secure Web site?**
    a. http://www.ebay.com
    b. www.microsoft.net
    c. https://www.schwab.com/login
    d. html://www.secure.ibm.net

6. **What port does HTTPS use?**
    a. 80
    b. 88
    c. 160
    d. 443

7. **What Transport layer protocol does HTTP rely on?**
    a. TCP
    b. IP
    c. UDP
    d. ICMP

2.5 Define the purpose, function and/or use of the following protocols within TCP/IP (continued):

TELNET

UNDERSTANDING THE OBJECTIVE

Telnet is a popular terminal emulation utility that enables clients to log on to TCP/IP hosts and perform tasks as if the user were sitting at the device's console.

WHAT YOU REALLY NEED TO KNOW

◆ **Telnet** is a terminal emulation program that facilitates connections between hosts on a TCP/IP network. Prior to the World Wide Web, Telnet provided the primary means of connecting to other hosts over the Internet.

◆ Often, Telnet is used to connect two dissimilar systems. For example, a remote network administrator could use telnet to log in to a UNIX server from her Windows 2000 PC.

◆ Once connected, a user who has telnetted and logged on to a host can perform any authorized function on that host, just as if she were directly connected to the host.

◆ You can initiate a Telnet session simply by typing `telnet Y`, where `Y` is the host name or IP address of the remote host. For example, `telnet lib.dartmouth.edu` will connect you to the Dartmouth library system.

◆ Many options can be used in conjunction with Telnet, including an echo function, flow control, and the selection of full- or half-duplex communication.

◆ Connecting to a host through Telnet requires an authorized logon ID and password. Telnet is a common way to send commands to a server or network device. Routers, for example, can be controlled and managed remotely using the telnet command.

◆ Telnet relies on TCP; thus, it is a connection-oriented service and waits for a receiving node to acknowledge that the connection is sound before transmitting data.

◆ The Telnet service uses port 23 by default.

OBJECTIVES ON THE JOB

Telnet is the primary method of connecting to network devices, such as routers. It is quick and efficient but does not come with a GUI interface. For this reason, if you are charged with managing routers and other devices, you should memorize the Telnet command options and syntax.

PRACTICE TEST QUESTIONS

1. **Which of the following could not be controlled through the Telnet utility?**
   a. router
   b. workstation
   c. switch
   d. hub

2. **What port does the Telnet utility use by default?**
   a. 20
   b. 21
   c. 22
   d. 23

3. **In what layer of the OSI Model does Telnet reside?**
   a. Application
   b. Session
   c. Transport
   d. Network

4. **Which of the following utilities allow you to view the directory contents on a remote host, given the proper authority? Choose all that apply.**
   a. PING
   b. Tracert
   c. TFTP
   d. Telnet

5. **Which of the following is a good use for Telnet?**
   a. to browse the contents of an online store
   b. to assess network performance between hosts on the Internet
   c. to send commands to a router
   d. to reconfigure a client whose TCP/IP stack has been damaged

6. **Which of the following is an example of proper Telnet command syntax?**
   a. `telnet 134.45.66.78`
   b. `telnet 134.45.66.78:20`
   c. `tlnt 134.45.66.78:21`
   d. `t 134.45.66.78:23`

7. **Which of the following is a potential disadvantage to using Telnet to remotely log in to a router?**
   a. It is not very secure.
   b. It requires a high-bandwidth connection.
   c. It not very efficient.
   d. It is not compatible with all types of router operating systems.

2.5 Define the purpose, function and/or use of the following protocols within TCP/IP (continued):

ICMP, ARP, AND NTP

UNDERSTANDING THE OBJECTIVE

ICMP is a protocol that ensures packets arrive at their destination. ARP is a utility that can obtain the MAC address of a device on a TCP/IP network based on its IP address. NTP is a protocol that synchronizes the clocks of all computers on a network.

WHAT YOU REALLY NEED TO KNOW

- ◆ Whereas IP ensures that packets reach the correct destination, **Internet Control Message Protocol (ICMP)** notifies the sender when something goes wrong in the transmission process and the packets are not delivered.

- ◆ ICMP sits between IP and TCP in the Internet layer of the TCP/IP model and does not provide error control. It simply reports which networks are unreachable and which packets have been discarded because the allotted time for their delivery expired.

- ◆ ICMP is used by diagnostic utilities, such as PING and TRACERT.

- ◆ **Address Resolution Protocol (ARP)** is a TCP/IP protocol that translates IP addresses into MAC (physical) addresses. ARP accomplishes this translation by broadcasting a packet to the entire network. This packet contains the IP address of the host for which the MAC address needs to be known. When the host whose IP address is being broadcast receives the packet, it responds. Other hosts on the network ignore the broadcast.

- ◆ Hosts often keep a cache of ARP results, which enable them to respond more quickly to ARP requests (this works as long as IP addresses don't often change). This cache is known as an **ARP table**.

- ◆ ARP can be a valuable troubleshooting tool for discovering the identity of a machine whose IP address you know or for troubleshooting two machines that are trying to use the same IP address.

- ◆ **NTP**, the **Network Time Protocol**, is used to synchronize the clocks of computers on a network. It is a very simple protocol that belongs to the Application layer of the TCP/IP Model and depends on UDP.

- ◆ Time synchronization is necessary on a network (particularly one as large as the Internet) because computers may keep time at slightly different rates. Time discrepancies can adversely affect applications that depend on timed responses.

OBJECTIVES ON THE JOB

ICMP, ARP, and NTP are important protocols within the TCP/IP suite. You should practice using ARP to determine the MAC address of machines whose IP address you already know, as it may prove to be a valuable troubleshooting tool.

PRACTICE TEST QUESTIONS

1. **Which of the following utilities make use of ICMP? Choose all that apply.**
   a. TRACERT
   b. winipcfg
   c. PING
   d. inetcfg

2. **What kind of information will an ARP command return? Choose all that apply.**
   a. an IP address
   b. a socket address
   c. an IPX address
   d. a MAC address

3. **What do network hosts do to improve the speed of ARP responses?**
   a. hold ARP tables in cache
   b. keep ARP numbers in their TCP/IP configuration
   c. reassign MAC addresses if a response is not received quickly enough
   d. issue multiple broadcasts to ensure prompt responses

4. **Why is it important that the clocks of all computers on a network are synchronized?**
   a. to ensure that data are delivered to the correct recipient
   b. to ensure that time-dependent applications function properly
   c. to ensure that packets arrive at their destination in the proper order
   d. to ensure that access to shared resources is fairly arbitrated

5. **What type of transmission does ARP use to find a host with a specific IP address?**
   a. multicast
   b. unicast
   c. broadcast
   d. loopback

6. **What Transport layer protocol does NTP rely on?**
   a. TCP
   b. IP
   c. UDP
   d. ICMP

7. **Which of the following devices makes use of ARP tables?**
   a. hub
   b. bridge
   c. router
   d. NIC

2.6 Define the function of TCP/UDP ports. Identify well-known ports.

UNDERSTANDING THE OBJECTIVE

Sockets depend on the assignment of port numbers to different processes. When one computer attempts to communicate with another, it alerts the socket address of the desired process on the other computer. The second computer recognizes the request and establishes the virtual circuit between the two computers so that data exchange can begin.

WHAT YOU REALLY NEED TO KNOW

♦ A **socket** is a logical address assigned to a specific process running on a host computer. It forms a virtual connection between the host and client.

♦ A **port** is a number assigned to a process running on a host. Port numbers can have any value. Some software programs choose their own port numbers by default.

♦ The socket's address is a combination of the host computer's IP address and the port number associated with a process. For example, the Telnet service on a Web server with an IP address of 10.43.3.87 might have a socket address of 10.43.3.87:23, where 23 is the standard port number for the Telnet service.

♦ Port numbers in the range of 0 to 1023 are also called **well-known ports**, because they were long ago assigned by Internet authorities to popular services (for example, FTP and Telnet), and are, therefore, well-known and frequently used.

♦ Some well-known ports are Telnet - 23, HTTP - 80, FTP - 20 (for data transfer), FTP - 21 (for commands), SMTP - 25, and POP3 - 101.

♦ The use of port numbers simplifies TCP/IP communications. When a client requests communications with a server and specifies port 23, for example, the server knows immediately that the client wants a Telnet session. No extra data exchange is necessary to define the session type, and the server can initiate the Telnet service without delay. The server connects to the client's Telnet port, which by default is also port 23, and establishes a virtual circuit.

♦ Port numbers can be configured through software. Most servers maintain a text-based file of port numbers and their associated services, which is editable. Changing a default port number is not usually a good idea, though, because it goes against the standard. However, some network administrators who are preoccupied with security may change their servers' port numbers in an attempt to confuse potential hackers.

OBJECTIVES ON THE JOB

You most often use port numbers when networking with the Internet. For example, if you install Web server software, you must identify some ports on that server. You can then leave ports at their defaults (for example, port 80 for the HTTP server) or change them to another number not already reserved by a process.

PRACTICE TEST QUESTIONS

1. **The socket address 204.113.19.80:23 probably belongs to which of the following services?**
   - a. FTP
   - b. HTTP
   - c. Telnet
   - d. SMTP

2. **In which of the following situations does it make sense to use a port number other than the default assigned by the software?**
   - a. when configuring an FTP server for users of freeware to download a patch
   - b. when configuring a Web server that hosts an online clothing store
   - c. when configuring an FTP server for employees within an organization to download their payroll information
   - d. when configuring the SNMP interface on a server inside an organization's firewall

3. **A socket allows two computers to establish what kind of circuit?**
   - a. virtual
   - b. closed
   - c. transitory
   - d. application

4. **Which of the following processes probably uses the socket address 135.67.99.118:80?**
   - a. HTTP
   - b. Telnet
   - c. FTP
   - d. SNMP

5. **How many ports can be assigned on one server?**
   - a. only one
   - b. no more than 10
   - c. no more than 100
   - d. over 65,000

6. **What is the default port for POP3?**
   - a. 10
   - b. 21
   - c. 90
   - d. 101

7. **Port numbers in the range of 0 to 1023 are called**
   - a. default ports.
   - b. well-known ports.
   - c. constrained ports.
   - d. reserved ports.

2.7   Identify the purpose of the following network services:

DHCP AND BOOTP

UNDERSTANDING THE OBJECTIVE

DHCP replaced BOOTP as an easier and more accurate method of assigning IP addresses to clients on a network. Both arose from the need to streamline the IP addressing process when networks became large and relied mostly on TCP/IP. DHCP is ubiquitous on modern networks, and because of its popularity, the software that controls DHCP is part of all network operating systems and client software.

WHAT YOU REALLY NEED TO KNOW

◆ The **Bootstrap Protocol (BOOTP)** uses a central list of IP addresses and their associated devices' MAC addresses to dynamically assign IP addresses to clients.

◆ When a client that relies on BOOTP first connects to the network, it sends a broadcast message to the network asking to be assigned an IP address. This broadcast message includes the MAC address of the client's NIC. The BOOTP server recognizes a BOOTP client's request, looks up the client's MAC address in its BOOTP table, and responds to the client with the client's IP address, the IP address of the server, the host name of the server, and the IP address of a default router.

◆ **Dynamic Host Configuration Protocol (DHCP)** is an automated means of assigning a unique IP address to every device on a network.

◆ DHCP centrally manages IP allocation from a DHCP server on the network. It leases IP addresses to a client when the client requests a DHCP response via UDP broadcast.

◆ DHCP leases last for a time period that the network administrator specifies, from minutes to forever. The IP address assigned to a node will remain in effect (even after rebooting) until the lease has expired.

◆ DHCP leases can be manually forced to expire or renew at any time from either the client's TCP/IP configuration or the server's DHCP configuration. In Windows terms, the act of terminating a DHCP lease is called a **release**.

◆ DHCP reduces the possibility for error in IP assignment. Nodes cannot be assigned invalid addresses, and two nodes will rarely experience addressing conflicts.

◆ DHCP limits the amount of time that networking staff have to spend managing IP addresses. The opposite of DHCP, static addressing, necessitates manually configuring an IP address on each node.

OBJECTIVES ON THE JOB

Because it can be easily established and managed, DHCP is a popular method of IP address allocation on large and small networks alike. Client and server operating systems make DHCP even easier by making it part of their TCP/IP software. In fact, DHCP is typically selected as the default method of obtaining IP addresses on client machines.

PRACTICE TEST QUESTIONS

1. **By what means does a newly connected client find the DHCP server?**
    a. It issues a TCP request to which the DHCP server responds.
    b. It issues an ARP request to which the DHCP server responds.
    c. It issues a UDP broadcast to which the DHCP server responds.
    d. It issues a NETSTAT request to which the DHCP server responds.

2. **What older TCP/IP utility does DHCP replace?**
    a. nbtstat
    b. netstat
    c. RARP
    d. BOOTP

3. **What is the best course of action if a Windows 98 client receives a message upon booting up, indicating that another workstation has reserved the IP address it previously leased from the DHCP server?**
    a. Click OK and ignore the error.
    b. Click OK, click Release, and then click Renew in the TCP/IP Properties dialog box.
    c. Write down the MAC address of the other workstation and reboot that workstation before continuing.
    d. Click OK, then select Release All in the TCP/IP Properties dialog box.

4. **Which two of the following are advantages to using DHCP over older IP addressing methods?**
    a. DHCP uses fewer server resources.
    b. DHCP requires less time to manage.
    c. DHCP reduces the possibility for duplicate addresses.
    d. DHCP requires a much shorter host file.

5. **Which of the following is made easier because of DHCP?**
    a. workstation naming
    b. subnetting
    c. cabling
    d. client moves

6. **What is the opposite of DHCP?**
    a. static addressing
    b. limited-term addressing
    c. octet addressing
    d. physical addressing

7. **If it is not manually terminated, how long does a DHCP lease last?**
    a. two days
    b. one week
    c. as long as the network administrator specifies
    d. 24 hours

2.7 Identify the purpose of the following network services (continued):

DNS AND WINS

UNDERSTANDING THE OBJECTIVE

DNS associates IP addresses with domains on the Internet to allow clients to transfer information more easily. DNS, which replaces the older method of resolving names via a single host file, is a hierarchical system in which multiple servers across the Internet share the burden of finding machines belonging to specific domains.

WHAT YOU REALLY NEED TO KNOW

♦ In the mid-1980s a hierarchical way of resolving host and domain names with their IP addresses was developed. This system was called the **Domain Name System (DNS)**. The DNS database does not rely on one file or even one server, but is distributed over key computers on the Internet to prevent catastrophic failure if one or a few computers go down.

♦ DNS is a TCP/IP service that belongs to the Application layer of the OSI Model.

♦ A TCP/IP host is typically associated with a **domain**, a group of computers that have part of their IP addresses in common. Often, this group of computers belongs to the same organization.

♦ A domain is identified by its **domain name**. Usually, a domain name is associated with a company or other type of organization, such as a university or military unit. For example, IBM's domain name is ibm.com.

♦ While some organizations use only one name server, large organizations often maintain two or more name servers. When more than one name server exists, a primary name server is the ultimate naming authority on the network.

♦ Each device on the network relies on the name server and, therefore, must be able to find it. The IP address of the client's primary and secondary DNS servers must be specified in the client's TCP/IP properties.

♦ The **Windows Internet Naming Service (WINS)** provides a means of resolving NetBIOS names with IP addresses. WINS provides for the NetBIOS protocol what DNS provides for the TCP/IP protocol.

♦ WINS can be implemented on servers running Windows NT Server version 3.5 or above. The WINS server maintains a database that accepts requests from Windows or DOS clients to register with a particular NetBIOS name.

♦ WINS does not assign names or IP addresses; it only keeps track of NetBIOS names and their addresses.

OBJECTIVES ON THE JOB

Every client on the network must be able to access a DNS server to resolve host names to addresses.

PRACTICE TEST QUESTIONS

1. **Which of the following best describes the relationship between IP addresses and domains?**
   a. Each domain is associated with a single IP address.
   b. Each IP address is associated with a single domain.
   c. Each domain is associated with a range of IP addresses.
   d. Each IP address is associated with a group of domains.

2. **To what layer of the OSI Model does DNS belong?**
   a. Application
   b. Presentation
   c. Session
   d. Transport

3. **Which two of the following domain names could belong to a business?**
   a. ferrari.edu
   b. ferrari.mil
   c. ferrari.com
   d. ferrari.it

4. **Where on a client workstation is WINS configured?**
   a. in the network adapter properties
   b. in the modem settings
   c. in the TCP/IP properties
   d. in the Microsoft client settings

5. **Which one of the following is most likely to use WINS?**
   a. a Windows 3.11 workstation
   b. a Linux server
   c. a Novell server
   d. a Windows 2000 workstation

6. **What is a significant difference between the domain name system and local host files?**
   a. DNS is hierarchical, while a host file is flat.
   b. A host file is easier to maintain than DNS.
   c. A host file is more efficient than DNS.
   d. DNS represents a single point of failure while a host file ensures redundancy.

7. **How many different organizations can use the same domain name?**
   a. one
   b. no more than two
   c. no more than two, as long as they are located in the same country
   d. no more than four

2.7   Identify the purpose of the following network services (continued):

NAT/ICS

UNDERSTANDING THE OBJECTIVE

Network address translation (NAT) is a method of using an IP gateway to associate Internet-recognized IP addresses with a client. Each time the client accesses the Internet, the NAT gateway assigns the client's data a new source IP address.

WHAT YOU REALLY NEED TO KNOW

◆ IP gateways can be used to "hide" the IP numbers assigned within an organization and, or keep its devices' IP addresses secret from any public network (such as the Internet). Clients behind the gateway may use any IP addressing scheme, whether or not it is recognized or sanctioned by the Internet authorities. Once those clients need to connect to the Internet, however, they must have an Internet-recognizable IP address in order to exchange data. When the client's transmission reaches the IP gateway, the gateway assigns the client's transmission a publicly recognized IP address. This process is known as **network address translation (NAT)**.

◆ One reason for using NAT is to add a marginal amount of security to a private network when it is connected to a public network (such as the Internet). Because the transmission is assigned a new IP address when it reaches the public sphere, others outside the organization cannot trace the transmission to the client.

◆ NAT also enables a network administrator to develop her own network addressing scheme that does not conform with a scheme dictated by ICANN. This can make network management and troubleshooting easier.

◆ Yet another reason for using NAT is to share a limited number of publicly recognized IP addresses among multiple machines.

◆ **Internet Connection Sharing (ICS)** is a service found on Microsoft Windows PC operating systems, such as Windows 98 and Windows ME, that allows multiple, networked computers to share a single Internet connection and a single IP address.

◆ ICS assigns one computer to process Internet requests from each connected machine. This computer, or the host, issues each of the connected computers an IP address but that address is only for use within the home network. When the host computer accesses the Internet, it uses just the one IP address, its own.

◆ ICS is similar to NAT in that it prevents multiple nodes from having to reveal their IP addresses when connecting to a public network (such as the Internet).

OBJECTIVES ON THE JOB

Chances are that you will encounter NAT in an environment where IP addresses are scarce or where the IP addresses of clients on a private network need to be protected from outside detection.

PRACTICE TEST QUESTIONS

1. **Which of the following computers would use ICS?**
   - a. a NetWare 5.x server
   - b. a Windows 98 workstation
   - c. a Macintosh workstation
   - d. a Windows NT server

2. **What type of connectivity device manages NAT?**
   - a. bridge
   - b. hub
   - c. switch
   - d. gateway

3. **What does "ICS" stand for?**
   - a. Internet connection sharing
   - b. Internet configuration system
   - c. Intermittent communications session
   - d. Integrated communication system

4. **Which of the following are reasons for using NAT? Choose all that apply.**
   - a. to share a limited number of valid IP addresses among multiple clients
   - b. to automatically assign IP addresses to clients when they log on to a LAN
   - c. to mask the real IP addresses of clients on a private network
   - d. to increase the speed with which Web pages are retrieved from the Internet

5. **Which of the following is a reason for using ICS?**
   - a. to allow remote users to securely log in to a private LAN via the Internet
   - b. to cache frequently used Web pages so that they can be subsequently accessed faster
   - c. to share a single Internet connection among multiple clients
   - d. to detect the presence of suspicious files, such as viruses, in Internet downloads

6. **Which of the following is most likely to use ICS?**
   - a. a small nonprofit organization that uses the Internet to solicit contributions
   - b. a regional insurance company whose salespeople dial into the corporate LAN each night from their homes
   - c. an Internet Service Provider that needs to ensure connectivity between multiple data centers and telecommunications carriers
   - d. a local architectural firm that sends drawings to and receives drawings from various clients across the nation

7. **How does NAT compare to firewalls, in terms of securing data between public and private networks?**
   - a. NAT offers more security for data in transit.
   - b. NAT offers more security for resources on a server.
   - c. NAT offers less security for data in transit.
   - d. NAT offers more security for private client identification.

2.7   Identify the purpose of the following network services (continued):

SNMP

UNDERSTANDING THE OBJECTIVE

SNMP is the underlying mechanism through which network devices and connections are managed. It can detect whether a device is responding under certain predefined conditions.

WHAT YOU REALLY NEED TO KNOW

◆ The **Simple Network Management Protocol (SNMP)** collects information (such as up/down status) about computers, including network components, such as servers and routers. Network administrators rely on SNMP to monitor and manage networks.

◆ As its name implies, SNMP is a very simple subprotocol. Its functionality is limited to determining whether a device is responding under specified conditions.

◆ SNMP is a subprotocol of the TCP/IP suite that resides in the Application layer of the OSI Model.

◆ SNMP relies on the Transport layer subprotocol UDP; therefore, it does not verify that a connection has been established before it attempts to discover information about a device.

◆ Information gathered via SNMP is stored in a **Management Information Base (MIB)** by a network management system. MIBs are then interpreted by sophisticated network management software packages, such as HP OpenView.

◆ In order for devices to submit information to a MIB, they must be SNMP-compliant. Most modern routers, switches, bridges, and managed hubs have this capability.

◆ One drawback to SNMP is that it may generate a large volume of potentially superfluous information along with useful information (for example, it may report each time a NIC is disconnected from the network).

OBJECTIVES ON THE JOB

Network administrators often use SNMP to determine the health of the network. For example, a Web server's HTTP port can be monitored through SNMP to determine if it is responding. If SNMP doesn't detect a response, a program can use that information to alert the network administrator that the Web page is down. Thanks to SNMP, problems can be detected and addressed quickly.

PRACTICE TEST QUESTIONS

1. **On which of the following Transport layer subprotocols does SNMP rely?**
    a. TCP
    b. IP
    c. UDP
    d. ICMP

2. **What stores information collected by the SNMP protocol?**
    a. MIP
    b. MIB
    c. SMIP
    d. SMB

3. **Which of the following programs could be considered a network management system?**
    a. Netscape Navigator
    b. Microsoft SQL Server
    c. Microsoft Exchange Server
    d. HP OpenView

4. **In addition to detecting whether a device is running, what other two functions can SNMP help provide? Choose all that apply.**
    a. LAN topology mapping
    b. traffic route optimization
    c. broadcast transmission filtering
    d. notification of network problems

5. **At what layer of the OSI Model does SNMP operate?**
    a. Application
    b. Session
    c. Transport
    d. Data Link

6. **Which of the following network components are likely to issue SNMP data? Choose all that apply.**
    a. server
    b. repeater
    c. router
    d. tape backup drive

7. **Which of the following conditions would SNMP be able to report?**
    a. A Web server is responding to requests at half of its normal speed.
    b. Half of the ports on a switch are not accepting data.
    c. A NIC is issuing broadcast error messages to the rest of the nodes on its segment.
    d. A user is prevented from logging in to the network because he has entered an invalid password three times.

2.8   Identify IP addresses (IPv4 and IPv6) and their default subnet masks.

UNDERSTANDING THE OBJECTIVE

IPv4 is the version of TCP/IP addressing used on most hosts today. Addresses in this scheme are represented by four eight-bit bytes (for a total of 32 bits) separated by periods. In IPv6, the new addressing scheme, addresses are composed of eight 16-bit fields and total 128 bits.

WHAT YOU REALLY NEED TO KNOW

◆ The current version of IP addressing used by most of the Internet, as well as most private networks, is **IP version 4 (IPv4)**.

◆ In the IPv4 convention, each IP address is a unique 32-bit number, divided into four **octets**, or 8-bit bytes, that are separated by periods. An example of a valid IP address is 144.92.43.178.

◆ Valid octet numbers range from 0 to 255 and represent a binary address. For example, an octet with the value of 68 equals 01 00 01 00 in an 8-bit binary pattern.

◆ In the IPv4 convention, each IP address contains two types of information: network and host. The first octet identifies the network class: A, B, or C.

◆ All nodes on a Class A network share the first octet of their IP numbers, a number between 1 and 126. Nodes on a Class B network share the first two octets, and their IP addresses begin with a number between 128 and 191. Class C network IP numbers share the first three octets, with their first octet being a number between 192 and 223.

◆ Because only 126 Class A networks are available on the Internet, most Class A networks have already been reserved by large corporations, educational institutions, or governments.

◆ To respond to a demand for more IP addresses, a new addressing scheme has been developed, called **IP version 6 (IPv6)**.

◆ IPv6 addresses are composed of eight 16-bit fields and total 128 bits. The added fields and the larger address size results in an increase of 2^{128} (or 4 billion times 4 billion times 4 billion) available IP addresses in the IPv6 addressing scheme.

◆ While each octet in an IPv4 address contains binary numbers separated by a period, each field in an IPv6 address contains hexadecimal numbers separated by a colon. An example of a valid IPv6 address is F:F:0:0:0:0:3012:0CE3.

◆ Because many IPv6 addresses will contain multiple fields that have values of 0, shorthand for representing these fields has been established. This shorthand substitutes "::" for any number of adjacent multiple zero-value fields.

OBJECTIVES ON THE JOB

Even if your network uses DHCP to automatically assign IP addresses to network nodes, you still need to be able to identify, interpret, and manually assign both IP addresses and subnet masks.

PRACTICE TEST QUESTIONS

1. **What is one of the primary reasons for switching from the IPv4 to the IPv6 addressing scheme?**
   a. IPv6 offers many more IP addresses than IPv4.
   b. IPv6 is more universally accepted and used than IPv4.
   c. IPv6 is more compatible with newer networking hardware and software.
   d. IPv6 offers a simpler management solution to assigning IP addresses.

2. **Which of the following best describes the convention for representing IPv4 addresses?**
   a. eight 16-bit fields separated by periods
   b. 16 eight-bit fields separated by colons
   c. four 8-bit fields separated by periods
   d. four 16-bit fields separated by colons

3. **Which of the following types of IPv4 networks has the most available networks (assuming that subnetting is not in use)?**
   a. Class A
   b. Class B
   c. Class C
   d. They all have the same number of available networks.

4. **Which of the following is a valid IPv6 address?**
   a. AE::00::DC
   b. 124.55.89.112:80
   c. 177.9.3.58
   d. AE:03:FF:00:16:CE:C6:00E2

5. **Which of the following IPv4 addressing techniques is rendered obsolete by IPv6?**
   a. NAT
   b. IPSec
   c. RAS
   d. WINS

6. **On a Class A network in the IPv4 addressing scheme, all nodes have which octet(s) in common?**
   a. the first only
   b. the first and second
   c. the second only
   d. the second and third

7. **To which class of network does the following IPv4 address belong (assuming subnetting is not in use): 198.34.61.207?**
   a. A
   b. B
   c. C
   d. D

OBJECTIVES

2.9 Identify the purpose of subnetting and default gateways.

UNDERSTANDING THE OBJECTIVE

To efficiently use a limited number of IP addresses, the concept of subnetting was devised in the 1980s. Subnetting separates networks into smaller subnets that can use more IP addresses, as long as a subnet mask is specified. On TCP/IP networks, the gateways that connect subnets are called default IP gateways. These gateways are usually interfaces on routers.

WHAT YOU REALLY NEED TO KNOW

◆ **Subnetting** is the process of subdividing a single class of network into multiple, smaller networks. It results in a more efficient use of limited IP addresses.

◆ In subnetting, one of the address's octets is used to indicate how the network is subdivided. Rather than consisting simply of network and host information, a subnetted address consists of network, subnet, and host information.

◆ Devices in a subnetted network are assigned a **subnet mask**, a special 32-bit number that, combined with a device's IP address, tells the rest of the network the network class to which the device is attached.

◆ If a subnet mask is not specified, the default subnet mask for a Class A network is 255.0.0.0. For a Class B network, the default subnet mask is 255.255.0.0, and for a Class C network, the default subnet mask is 255.255.255.0.

◆ Every device on a TCP/IP network that connects to other networks has a **default gateway**, the gateway that first interprets its outbound requests to other subnets and last interprets its inbound requests from other subnets.

◆ In the TCP/IP configuration of every device, the address of a default gateway has to be specified before the device can communicate with devices on other TCP/IP networks.

◆ Each default gateway is assigned its own IP address. Typically, the IP address of a default gateway contains only the number "1" in its last octet.

◆ Default gateways may connect more than one internal network or connect an internal network with external networks, such as WANs or the Internet.

OBJECTIVES ON THE JOB

You should suspect an IP gateway problem when TCP/IP traffic travels properly within a subnet but not outside the subnet. Conversely, if traffic travels beyond the subnet (but has problems elsewhere), you can assume that the problem lies outside the IP default gateway.

PRACTICE TEST QUESTIONS

1. **Which of the following IP addresses probably belongs to an IP default gateway?**
   a. 161.57.89.110
   b. 161.57.89.10
   c. 161.57.89.0
   d. 161.57.89.1

2. **What is the default subnet mask for a Class B network?**
   a. 0.0.0.0
   b. 255.0.0.0
   c. 255.255.0.0
   d. 255.255.255.255

3. **In which of the following situations would an IP default gateway be necessary (assuming default subnet masks are in use)?**
   a. A printer with an IP address of 159.45.22.144 receives a print job from a server with an IP address of 159.45.22.39.
   b. A client with an IP address of 144.92.104.82 sends an e-mail message to a client with an IP address of 144.92.39.82.
   c. A client with an IP address of 144.92.104.56 downloads a Web page from an HTTP server with an IP address of 10.12.10.13.
   d. A client with an IP address of 144.92.104.56 retrieves a file from a Windows 2000 server with an IP address of 144.92.104.20.

4. **What is the main purpose for subnetting a network?**
   a. to create a more systematic way of tracking addresses on the network
   b. to more equitably allocate addresses to all devices on a network
   c. to make more efficient use of a limited number of addresses
   d. to make TCP/IP client and server configuration easier

5. **What types of information are contained in the IP address of a device on a network that has not been subnetted?**
   a. host, subnet, and network
   b. host, server, and network
   c. protocol and network
   d. host and network

6. **To what type of network does the default subnet mask 255.255.255.0 belong?**
   a. Class A
   b. Class B
   c. Class C
   d. Class D

7. **How many gateways are required to transfer information across the Internet from a client with the IP address 122.09.83.67 to a client with the IP address 155.67.28.30?**
   a. at least one
   b. at least four
   c. at least six
   d. at least eight

2.10 Identify the differences between public vs. private networks.

UNDERSTANDING THE OBJECTIVE

Public networks are accessible to multiple users and can be accessed without credentials. Data traveling over public networks is often susceptible to eavesdropping and, therefore, should be protected. Private networks are accessible only to authorized users.

WHAT YOU REALLY NEED TO KNOW

◆ A **public network** is one that allows access from any node that has the capability to connect to it. Certain resources of a public network may be restricted but access to the network is not.

◆ Most public networks rely at least in part on public transmission systems, such as the PSTN.

◆ Because they rely on public transmission methods, public networks are more susceptible to eavesdropping. Data transmitted over a public network should be protected through encryption or another technique to secure data.

◆ The Internet is the largest and most familiar example of a public network.

◆ A **private network** is one that allows only authorized users to connect to it and access its resources. Examples of private networks are corporate LANs and WANs.

◆ Private networks use private transmission systems, such as wiring inside a corporation's building, or a T-1 line leased from a telecommunications carrier that is solely dedicated to carrying one organization's network traffic.

◆ When private networks connect to public networks (for example, a corporate LAN that allows its users to connect to the Internet), measures must be taken to protect the private network from public access. NAT, data encryption (such as IPSec), and the use of firewalls can protect a private network and its data from public access.

◆ **Virtual private networks (VPNs)** are secured tunnels that protect data in transit. VPNs are often used to create private WANs over over public transmission systems.

◆ When created across public transmission systems, VPNs serve an organization's users but isolate that organization's traffic from other users of the same public lines. They provide a way of constructing a private WAN from less-expensive public transmission systems.

OBJECTIVES ON THE JOB

Chances are you will work on a private network that connects to the Internet (a public network) at some point in your career. You should be aware of current techniques for preventing unauthorized users from accessing your private network through the public network. Because these techniques change frequently, a large organization may dedicate an employee or a whole team of people to managing security between the private and public networks.

PRACTICE TEST QUESTIONS

1. **Which of the following is an example of a public network?**
   - a. PSTN
   - c. VLAN
   - b. VPN
   - d. SONET ring

2. **What kind of private WAN uses a public network's transmission systems?**
   - a. PSTN
   - c. VLAN
   - b. VPN
   - d. SONET ring

3. **On which of the following networks would the security of data in transit be of the greatest concern?**
   - a. a MAN that connects two buildings on a corporate campus via fiber-optic cable
   - b. a WAN that connects 25 buildings of an insurance company through dedicated T-1 lines in a partial mesh topology
   - c. a LAN that connects 56 customer service representatives at a company's headquarters and allows access to the Internet through a gateway and firewall
   - d. a WAN that allows its 250 salespeople to access their company's server over the Internet from hotel rooms around the country

4. **Which of the following is a good way of encrypting data in transit?**
   - a. NAT
   - b. firewalls
   - c. IPSec
   - d. HTTP

5. **Which one of the following networks would be the most expensive to install?**
   - a. a MAN that connects two office buildings on a corporate campus via fiber optic cable
   - b. a WAN that connects 25 buildings of an insurance company through dedicated T-1 lines in a partial mesh topology
   - c. a LAN that connects 56 customer service representatives at a catalog company's headquarters and allows employees to access the Internet through a gateway and firewall
   - d. a WAN that allows its 250 salespeople who work for a pharmaceutical company to dial in to a remote access server from their hotel rooms around the country

6. **Which of the following is characteristic of private networks but not public networks?**
   - a. restricted access to resources
   - b. the use of routers to interconnect dissimilar network types
   - c. the use of gateways
   - d. the use of leased WAN lines

7. **The Internet is an example of a public network. True or false?**

2.11 Identify the basic characteristics (e.g., speed, capacity, media) of the following WAN technologies:

PACKET SWITCHING VS. CIRCUIT SWITCHING

UNDERSTANDING THE OBJECTIVE

Circuit switching is a transmission technology used by the PSTN and by T-carriers. In circuit switching, a channel is dedicated to a certain transmission until the transmission is completed. In packet switching, which is used by Ethernet and FDDI, data are divided into packets. The packets may then take any route to their destination, where they are reassembled in their original order.

WHAT YOU REALLY NEED TO KNOW

- ◆ In **circuit switching**, a connection is established between two network nodes before they begin transmitting data. Bandwidth is dedicated to this connection and remains available until the users terminate communication between the two nodes. While the nodes remain connected, all data follow the same path initially selected by the switch.

- ◆ The PSTN uses circuit switching. When you place a telephone call, your call goes through a circuit-switched connection. Similarly, when you connect your home PC via modem to your ISP's access server, that connection uses circuit switching.

- ◆ Because circuit switching monopolizes its allotted bandwidth while the two stations remain connected (even when no actual communication is taking place), it is not an economical technology.

- ◆ Some network applications that cannot tolerate the time delay it takes to reorganize data packets, such as live audio or video conferencing, benefit from circuit switching's dedicated path.

- ◆ Some WAN technologies, such as ISDN and T-1 service, also use circuit switching.

- ◆ **Packet switching** breaks data into packets before they are transported. Packets can travel any path on the network to their destinations, because each packet contains the destination address and sequencing information. Consequently, packets can attempt to find the fastest circuit available at any instant. They need not follow each other along the same path, nor must they arrive at their destination in the same sequence they left the transmitting node.

- ◆ The destination node on a packet-switched network reassembles the packets based on the packets' control information. Because of the time it takes to reassemble the packets into a message, packet switching is not suited to live audio or video transmission. Nevertheless, it is a fast and efficient mechanism for transporting typical network data, such as word-processing or spreadsheet files.

- ◆ Examples of packet-switched networks include Ethernet and FDDI.

OBJECTIVES ON THE JOB

If you work on packet-switched LANs, such as those that use the Ethernet network access method, you must understand how the disassembly, sequencing, and reassembly of packets works.

PRACTICE TEST QUESTIONS

1. **Which of the following is characteristic of a packet-switched network, but not a circuit-switched network?**
   - a. sequencing
   - b. transceivers
   - c. star topology
   - d. shared channels

2. **Which of the following technologies uses packet switching?**
   - a. PSTN
   - b. Ethernet
   - c. T-1
   - d. ISDN

3. **Which of the following best describes a packet?**
   - a. a collection of data discarded by a router
   - b. a discreet unit of data
   - c. a means to translate packet-switched data into circuit-switched data
   - d. a continuous stream of data

4. **Which of the following is best suited for video conferencing over the network?**
   - a. packet switching
   - b. circuit switching
   - c. Ethernet
   - d. Token Ring

5. **Which of the following networks would certainly use a combination of packet switching and circuit switching?**
   - a. a MAN that connects two office buildings using 100BaseFX
   - b. a WAN that connects 25 buildings of an insurance regional company through dedicated T-1s
   - c. a LAN that connects 200 users within a large bank
   - d. a WAN that connects multiple office buildings using FDDI and allows remote employees to connect by dialing their ISP and logging on to a VPN

6. **What is the single greatest disadvantage to using packet switching?**
   - a. It is expensive.
   - b. It is not highly scalable.
   - c. Its standards are not stable.
   - d. It is ill suited to time-sensitive transmissions.

7. **Which of the following best describes circuit switching?**
   - a. A dedicated connection is established between two network nodes and remains available until the users terminate communication.
   - b. A connection is established between two network nodes and may allow other nodes to use and share the same channel while the first two nodes communicate.
   - c. No dedicated connection is established between two network nodes, but a best path between them is dynamically discovered as they begin transmitting data.
   - d. No connection is established between two network nodes, but data are separated into units that may follow separate paths.

OBJECTIVES

2.11 Identify the basic characteristics (e.g., speed, capacity, media) of the following WAN technologies (continued):

ISDN

UNDERSTANDING THE OBJECTIVE

ISDN was developed in the mid-1980s to send digital data over public transmission lines. ISDN can be a dial-up connection or dedicated solution. It has been a popular choice for individuals and small businesses who want a faster and more secure connection than the PSTN can offer.

WHAT YOU REALLY NEED TO KNOW

◆ **Integrated Services Digital Network (ISDN)** is a standard established by the International Telecommunications Union (ITU) for transmitting data over digital lines.

◆ ISDN is a circuit-switched technology that uses the telephone carrier's lines and dial-up connections, like PSTN. Unlike PSTN, ISDN travels exclusively over digital connections and can carry data and voice simultaneously.

◆ All ISDN connections are based on two types of channels: B channels and D channels.

◆ The **B channel**, which is the bearer channel, uses circuit-switching techniques to carry voice, video, audio, and data over the ISDN connection. A single B channel has a maximum throughput of 64 Kbps, although it is sometimes limited to 56 Kbps by the ISDN provider. The number of B channels in an ISDN connection can vary.

◆ The **D channel** is the data channel that uses packet-switching techniques to carry information about the call, such as session initiation and termination signals, caller identity, call forwarding, and conference calling signals.

◆ A single D channel has a maximum throughput of 16 Kbps.

◆ North American users commonly use two types of ISDN connections: Basic Rate Interface (BRI) or Primary Rate Interface (PRI).

◆ **BRI** uses two B channels and one D channel, as summarized by this notation: 2B+D. The two B channels are treated as separate connections and can carry voice and data or two data streams simultaneously and separately.

◆ Through a process called **bonding**, two 64-Kbps B channels can be combined to achieve an effective throughput of 128 Kbps, the maximum throughput for BRI.

◆ **PRI** uses 23 B channels and one 64-Kbps D channel, which, when combined, can offer 1.54 Mbps throughput. PRI is less commonly used by individual subscribers than BRI but can be used by organizations needing more throughput.

OBJECTIVES ON THE JOB

ISDN lines have been a popular choice for small businesses for moderately fast connections to the Internet. Due to their ability to transmit voice and data simultaneously, ISDN lines can also eliminate the need to pay for separate phone lines to support faxes, modems, and voice.

PRACTICE TEST QUESTIONS

1. **How much throughput is optimally available through BRI?**
   a. 1.455 Mbps
   b. 56 Kbps
   c. 128 Kbps
   d. 768 Kbps

2. **Which of the following is an advantage of ISDN over PSTN?**
   a. It's less expensive.
   b. It provides greater throughput.
   c. It is easier to configure.
   d. It doesn't depend on public transmission lines.

3. **Which of the following is an advantage of DSL over BRI?**
   a. It provides greater throughput.
   b. It's easier to configure.
   c. It doesn't require any special hardware.
   d. It doesn't depend on public transmission lines.

4. **In the context of ISDN services, what does "2B+D" stand for?**
   a. two basic and one denominator
   b. basic, broadband, and digital
   c. two bearer and one data
   d. bearer, broadband, and digital

5. **What is the maximum throughput of one B channel?**
   a. 8 Kbps
   b. 16 Kbps
   c. 64 Kbps
   d. 128 Kbps

6. **What is the Physical layer difference between PSTN and ISDN?**
   a. ISDN uses all digital lines, while PSTN may use analog lines.
   b. ISDN can encapsulate IP packets, while PSTN cannot.
   c. ISDN uses Ethernet NICs, while PSTN uses Token Ring NICs.
   d. ISDN lines can handle 128 Kbps while, PSTN lines can handle only 56 Kbps.

7. **In which of the following situations might ISDN be the best selection?**
   a. for a small nonprofit organization that needs a connection to the Internet to pick up mail every other day
   b. for a multinational insurance company that expects its salespeople to dial in each night from their hotel rooms
   c. for a large software development company that needs to transmit and receive programs all day and all night
   d. for a small, rural architectural firm that needs to pick up e-mail frequently and occasionally send and receive drawings

2.11 Identify the basic characteristics (e.g., speed, capacity, media) of the following WAN technologies (continued):

FDDI AND ATM

UNDERSTANDING THE OBJECTIVE

FDDI and ATM are technologies whose network access methods differ from Ethernet and Token Ring. FDDI relies on a double ring of fiber-optic cable, making it very reliable. ATM relies on fixed-size packets called cells and virtual circuits to make it fast and well suited to time-sensitive data.

WHAT YOU REALLY NEED TO KNOW

- ◆ FDDI (Fiber Distributed Data Interface) is a logical topology that uses a double ring of multimode or single-mode fiber to transmit data at speeds of 100 Mbps.

- ◆ FDDI was the first network transport system to reach the 100 Mbps threshold. For this reason, you will frequently find it supporting network backbones that were installed in the late 1980s and early 1990s.

- ◆ FDDI's double-ring topology makes it especially reliable. Normally, data circulate on the primary ring, but if the primary ring is severed, data are carried by the secondary ring.

- ◆ **ATM (Asynchronous Transfer Mode)** is a circuit-switched logical topology that relies on a fixed packet size to achieve data transfer rates up to 9953 Mbps.

- ◆ ATM may run over specific types of fiber or copper networks, such as SONET or T-carriers. It is typically used on WANs, particularly by large data carriers, such as telephone companies and Internet Service Providers.

- ◆ What sets ATM apart from Token Ring and Ethernet is its fixed packet size. The fixed packet in ATM, which is called a **cell**, consists of 48 bytes of data plus a 5-byte header. This fixed packet size allows ATM to provide predictable traffic patterns and better control over bandwidth utilization.

- ◆ ATM's smaller packet size decreases its potential throughput, but the efficiency of using cells compensates for that loss. ATM has a maximum throughput of 9953 Mbps.

- ◆ ATM relies on virtual circuits. **Virtual circuits** are connections between network nodes that, while based on potentially disparate physical links, logically appear to be direct, dedicated links between those nodes.

- ◆ The significant benefit to using circuit switching is that it allows ATM to guarantee a specific **quality of service (QoS)**. QoS is a standard that specifies that data will be delivered within a certain period of time after their transmission.

OBJECTIVES ON THE JOB

You may work with ATM on networks that carry audio or video data over fiber media. Because ATM is significantly different from the more popular Ethernet, be certain to understand its use of cells and how that technique affects the media and other components on the network.

PRACTICE TEST QUESTIONS

1. **What is the maximum throughput of an ATM network?**
   a. 9.95 Mbps
   b. 99.5 Mbps
   c. 995 Mbps
   d. 9.95 Gbps

2. **What is one primary difference between ATM and Ethernet?**
   a. ATM uses the token passing network access method, while Ethernet uses CSMA/CD.
   b. ATM uses fixed-sized packets, while Ethernet uses variable-sized packets
   c. ATM relies on connection-oriented protocols, while Ethernet relies on connectionless protocols.
   d. ATM uses permanent virtual circuits, while Ethernet uses temporary virtual circuits.

3. **What kind of switching does ATM use?**
   a. packet switching
   b. circuit switching
   c. message switching
   d. terminal switching

4. **What is the maximum throughput of a FDDI network?**
   a. 1 Mbps
   b. 10 Mbps
   c. 100 Mbps
   d. 1 Gbps

5. **What type of connector might be found on a FDDI network?**
   a. RJ-11
   b. RJ-45
   c. SC
   d. BNC

6. **What does QoS stand for?**
   a. quality of service
   b. quantity of sessions
   c. quick online status
   d. question or solution

7. **What medium does FDDI require?**
   a. coaxial cable
   b. UTP
   c. single-mode fiber
   d. multimode fiber

OBJECTIVES

2.11 Identify the basic characteristics (e.g., speed, capacity, media) of the following WAN technologies (continued):

FRAME RELAY

UNDERSTANDING THE OBJECTIVE

Frame Relay is a packet-switched technology capable of transmitting data at 1.544 or 45 Mbps throughput using public transmission systems.

WHAT YOU REALLY NEED TO KNOW

◆ **Frame Relay** is a digital, packet-switched WAN technology. The name is derived from the fact that data is separated into frames which are then relayed from one node to another without any verification or processing.

◆ Frame Relay offers a maximum of either 1.544 Mbps or 45 Mbps throughput. It is similar to X.25 packet switching technology, but because it does not perform the same error checking routines, it is faster.

◆ Frame Relay was standardized in 1984 and became popular in the United States and Canada for reliable long-distance WAN connections. However, now Frame Relay is being replaced by newer, faster technologies.

◆ On networking diagrams, packet-switched networks, such as X.25 and Frame Relay, are depicted as clouds because of the indeterminate nature of their traffic patterns. Because the early version of the Internet relied on such technologies, the Internet is still depicted as a cloud on networking diagrams.

◆ Both X.25 and Frame Relay may be configured as switched virtual circuits (SVCs) or more often, as permanent virtual circuits (PVCs).

◆ **SVCs** are connections that are established when parties need to transmit. They are dismantled once the transmission is complete.

◆ **PVCs** are connections that are established before data needs to be transmitted and maintained after the transmission is complete. Note that in a PVC, the connection is established only between the two points (the sender and receiver); the connection does not specify the exact route the data will travel. Thus, in a PVC, data may follow any number of different paths to move from point A to point B

◆ When you lease an X.25 or Frame Relay circuit from your local carrier, your contract reflects the endpoints you specify and the amount of bandwidth you require between those endpoints. The service provider guarantees a minimum amount of bandwidth, called the **committed information rate (CIR)**.

OBJECTIVES ON THE JOB

Frame Relay is usually found on WANs as an alternative to T-carrier services. Because Frame Relay is not dedicated, and data may follow any path from point A to point B, it is less expensive than (dedicated) T-carrier lines that offer comparable throughput.

PRACTICE TEST QUESTIONS

1. **How is a Frame Relay network depicted on a networking diagram?**
    a. as a full-mesh
    b. as a cloud
    c. as a single bus
    d. as a star

2. **What does "CIR" stand for?**
    a. communications inter-relay
    b. connection interface register
    c. communicating internal repeater
    d. committed information rate

3. **Frame Relay is most similar to which of the following types of WAN technologies?**
    a. T-carrier
    b. FDDI
    c. SONET
    d. cable modem technology

4. **What type of switching does a Frame Relay network use?**
    a. circuit switching
    b. packet switching
    c. message switching
    d. terminal switching

5. **What is the difference between an SVC and a PVC?**
    a. An SVC can accept only data cells, while a PVC can accept both frames and cells.
    b. An SVC remains even after a transmission is complete, while a PVC exists only for the duration of a transmission
    c. An SVC can accept only data frames, while a PVC can accept both frames and cells.
    d. An SVC exists only for the duration of a transmission, while a PVC remains in existence even after a transmission is complete.

6. **In what year was the Frame Relay standard established?**
    a. 1975
    b. 1980
    c. 1984
    d. 1991

7. **Frame Relay can reach a maximum throughput of 45 Mbps. True or false?**

2.11 Identify the basic characteristics (e.g., speed, capacity, media) of the following WAN technologies (continued):

SONET/SDH AND OCX

UNDERSTANDING THE OBJECTIVE

SONET is a fast, highly reliable WAN technology that relies on a double fiber-optic ring topology, similar to FDDI. It can provide data transfer rates as high as 39.8 Gbps.

WHAT YOU REALLY NEED TO KNOW

◆ **SONET (Synchronous Optical Network)** is a WAN technology that depends on fiber-optic transmission media to achieve its extraordinary quality of service and throughput. It was developed in the 1980s to link phone systems around the world.

◆ SONET can provide data transfer rates from 64 Kbps to 39.8 Gbps using the same TDM technique used by T-carriers. Like T-carriers, it also uses multiplexers and terminal equipment to connect at the customer's end.

◆ A typical SONET network takes the form of a ring topology, similar to FDDI, in which one ring acts as the primary route for data and the other ring acts as a backup. If, for example, a backhoe operator severs one of the rings, SONET technology would automatically reroute traffic along the backup ring. This characteristic, known as **self-healing**, makes SONET very reliable.

◆ Companies can lease an entire SONET ring from their local or long distance carrier, or they can lease part of a SONET, a circuit that offers T1 throughput, to take advantage of SONET's reliability.

◆ SONET has emerged as the best choice for linking WANs between North America, Europe, and Asia, because it can work directly with the different standards used in different countries.

◆ Internationally, SONET is known as **SDH (Synchronous Digital Hierarchy)**.

◆ SONET integrates well with T-carriers, making it a good choice for connecting WANs and LANs over long distances (even within the same country). In fact, SONET is often used to aggregate multiple T1s or T3s. SONET is also used as the underlying technology for ATM transmission.

◆ The data rate of a particular SONET ring is indicated by its **Optical Carrier (OC) level**, a rating that is internationally recognized by networking professionals and standards organizations. For example, **OC1** provides 51.84 Mbps throughput.

OBJECTIVES ON THE JOB

SONET technology is used by large global companies, long distance companies linking metropolitan areas and countries, or ISPs that want to guarantee fast, reliable access to the Internet.

PRACTICE TEST QUESTIONS

1. **Which of the following media does SONET require?**
   - a. coaxial cable
   - b. UTP
   - c. STP
   - d. fiber-optic cable

2. **What does "SONET" stand for?**
   - a. self-organizing network
   - b. system originating network
   - c. synchronous optical network
   - d. session overlay network

3. **What is the European equivalent of SONET?**
   - a. SNT
   - b. SON
   - c. SNS
   - d. SDH

4. **What technique does SONET use to increase the throughput it can sustain over a medium?**
   - a. time division multiplexing
   - b. frequency division multiplexing
   - c. wave division multiplexing
   - d. amplitude modulation

5. **How are OC levels related to SONET technology?**
   - a. They describe SONET's quality of service levels.
   - b. They indicate SONET's data rate.
   - c. They represent SONET's maximum distance.
   - d. They describe SONET's type of path between nodes.

6. **What was the original reason for developing SONET technology?**
   - a. to provide the U.S. Defense Department with a secure, national network
   - b. to provide U.S. individuals and businesses with a low-cost method of Internet access
   - c. to link phone systems around the world
   - d. to link international military bases

7. **Which of the following environments would SONET best suit?**
   - a. a small nonprofit organization that uses the Internet to solicit contributions
   - b. a regional insurance company whose salespeople dial into the corporate LAN each night from their homes to upload sales figures
   - c. an Internet Service Provider that needs to ensure connectivity between multiple data centers and telecommunications carriers
   - d. an architectural firm that sends and receives drawings from various clients across the nation

2.11 Identify the basic characteristics (e.g., speed, capacity, media) of the following WAN technologies (continued):

T1/E1 AND T3/E3

UNDERSTANDING THE OBJECTIVE

T1s and T3s (known as E1s and E3s in Europe) use time division multiplexing to achieve high throughput over public transmission systems. A T1 has a maximum throughput of 1.544 Mbps, while a T3 has a maximum throughput of 44.736 Mbps (or 45 Mbps).

WHAT YOU REALLY NEED TO KNOW

◆ T1s, fractional T1s, and T3s are collectively known as **T-carriers**.

◆ T-carrier transmission uses time division multiplexing over two wire pairs (one for transmitting and one for receiving) to divide a single channel into multiple channels. Multiplexing enables a single T1 circuit to carry 24 channels, each capable of 64 Kbps throughput. Each channel may contain data, voice, or video signals.

◆ AT&T developed T-carrier technology in 1957 in an effort to digitize voice signals, thereby enabling such signals to travel long distances. In the 1970s, many businesses installed T1s to obtain more voice throughput per line.

◆ The most common T-carrier implementations are T1 and T3.

◆ A **T1** circuit can carry the equivalent of 24 voice or data channels, giving a maximum data throughput of 1.544 Mbps.

◆ A **T3** can carry the equivalent of 672 voice or data channels, giving a maximum data throughput of 44.736 Mbps (its throughput is typically rounded up to 45 Mbps for the purposes of discussion).

◆ The speed of a T-carrier depends on its signal level. The **signal level** refers to the T-carrier's Physical layer electrical signaling characteristics as defined by ANSI standards in the early 1980s. **DS0** (which stands for "Data Signals 0") is the equivalent of one data or voice channel. All other signal levels are multiples of DS0.

◆ Technically, T1 is the North American implementation of the international DS1 standard. In Europe, the DS1 standard is implemented as **E1** and offers a slightly higher throughput than T1, while the DS3 standard is implemented as **E3**.

OBJECTIVES ON THE JOB

As a networking professional, you are most likely to work with T1 or T3 lines. In addition to knowing their capacity, you should be familiar with their costs and uses. T1s are commonly used by businesses to connect branch offices or to connect to a carrier, such as an ISP. Telephone companies also use T1s to connect their smaller central offices. ISPs may use one or more T1s or T3s to connect to their Internet carriers.

PRACTICE TEST QUESTIONS

1. **How many data channels does a T1 carry?**
   a. 1
   b. 16
   c. 24
   d. 45

2. **How do E1s and E3s achieve high throughput?**
   a. time division multiplexing
   b. frequency division multiplexing
   c. wave division multiplexing
   d. amplitude modulation

3. **What is the difference between an E1 and a T1?**
   a. An E1 has 10 times the capacity of a T1.
   b. An E1 is the European equivalent of the American T1.
   c. An E1 offers better quality of service than a T1.
   d. An E1 uses circuit switching, while a T1 uses packet switching.

4. **What type of device is used to terminate a T-carrier?**
   a. modem
   b. CSU/DSU
   c. bridge
   d. hub

5. **What is the maximum throughput of a T3?**
   a. 1.5 Mbps
   b. 22.5 Mbps
   c. 45 Mbps
   d. 99 Mbps

6. **What company developed T-carrier technology?**
   a. AT&T
   b. Microsoft
   c. IBM
   d. Cisco

7. **What is the capacity of each channel in a T-carrier?**
   a. 64 Kbps
   b. 128 Kbps
   c. 64 Mbps
   d. 128 Mbps

2.12 Define the function of the following remote access protocols and services:

RAS AND ICA

UNDERSTANDING THE OBJECTIVE

Microsoft's RAS (Remote Access Service) and Citrix System, Inc.'s ICA (Independent Computing Architecture) client are two methods of remotely accessing private networks.

WHAT YOU REALLY NEED TO KNOW

◆ The most common type of remote access involves dial-up networking. **Dial-up networking (DUN)** typically refers to a modem connection to a server through the PSTN. It is also the name of the utility that Microsoft provides with its operating systems to achieve this type of connectivity.

◆ A **remote access server** is a combination of software and hardware that provides a central access point for multiple users to dial in to a LAN or WAN.

◆ Once connected to the remote access server, the LAN treats the direct-dial remote client like any other client on the LAN. The computer dialing into the LAN becomes a **remote node** on the network.

◆ Many different software and hardware combinations can provide remote connectivity.

◆ A simple dial-in solution is provided by Microsoft Windows NT and Windows 2000. The software that allows remote clients to dial into these access servers is known as **Remote Access Service (RAS)**.

◆ Another method for remotely accessing LANs by using Citrix System, Inc.'s **ICA (Independent Computing Architecture)** client to connect to a remote access server.

◆ Once installed on a remote user's workstation, the client can connect to a Citrix server via any type of connection, public or private. The ICA client supplies the user with a standard desktop, then exchanges only keystrokes, mouse clicks, and screen updates with the server.

◆ Because all of the processing burden is placed on the server, this type of remote access is well suited to slower connections, such as dial-up PSTN connections.

◆ Citrix's ICA client can work with virtually any operating system or application. Its ease of use and broad compatibility has made the ICA client one of the most popular methods for supplying widespread remote access across an organization.

◆ In order to function properly, the ICA requires Citrix's remote access software running on the access server. Potential drawbacks to this method include cost of Citrix's products and the complex nature of its server software configuration.

OBJECTIVES ON THE JOB

Remote access is a particular concern for mobile users, such as telecommuters and employees who frequently travel. Companies that purchase remote access servers must carefully evaluate the server options for cost, ease of installation, ease of maintenance, and ease of client use.

PRACTICE TEST QUESTIONS

1. **In order for a Windows 9x machine to exchange data with a Windows 2000 server via DUN, to which of the following should the DUN software be bound? Choose all that apply.**
   a. TCP/IP
   b. IPX/SPX
   c. Client for Novell Networks
   d. Client for Microsoft Networks

2. **What does RAS stand for?**
   a. remote authentication service
   b. remote access server
   c. remote accounting service
   d. remote addressing server

3. **What transmission media does DUN typically use?**
   a. PSTN
   b. ISDN
   c. T1
   d. T3

4. **What company developed ICA?**
   a. Microsoft
   b. Citrix Systems
   c. IBM
   d. Cisco

5. **Which of the following best describes the type of data transmission that occurs while a user works on a spreadsheet via an ICA connection?**
   a. The server issues a copy of the program to the client's RAM, then the client workstation is responsible for processing program functions.
   b. The server issues pieces of the program to the client's RAM as they are needed, while the client workstation is responsible for processing program functions.
   c. The server issues screenshots of the program to the client, while the client workstation is responsible for processing program functions.
   d. The server issues screenshots of the program to the client, while the client workstation issues keystroke commands to run the program on the server.

6. **What is the maximum throughput of a typical DUN connection?**
   a. 53 Kbps
   b. 1 Mbps
   c. 1.544 Mbps
   d. 10 Mbps

7. **ICA provides encryption for sensitive data in transit. True or false?**

2.12 Define the function of the following remote access protocols and services (continued):

PPP AND PPTP

UNDERSTANDING THE OBJECTIVE

PPP and PPTP are communications protocols that enable remote access servers and remote clients to network via a dial-up connection.

WHAT YOU REALLY NEED TO KNOW

◆ **Point-to-Point Protocol (PPP)** is a communications protocol that enables a workstation to connect to a server using a serial connection (in the case of dial-up networking, "serial connection" refers to a modem). Once connected via PPP, a remote workstation can act as a client on the local LAN, with its modem and serial port serving the purpose of a NIC.

◆ Such protocols are necessary to transport Network layer traffic over serial interfaces, which belong to the Data Link layer of the OSI Model. PPP encapsulates higher-layer networking protocols in its lower-layer data frames.

◆ PPP can carry many different types of Network layer packets, such as IPX or AppleTalk.

◆ PPP can support both asynchronous and synchronous transmission.

◆ **Asynchronous** refers to a communications method in which data being transmitted and received by nodes do not have to conform to any timing scheme. In asynchronous communications, a node can transmit at any time and the destination node has to accept the transmission as it comes.

◆ **Synchronous** refers to a communications method in which data being transmitted and received by nodes must conform to a timing scheme.

◆ **Point-to-Point Tunneling Protocol (PPTP)** provides a secure tunnel for data by encapsulating PPP, so any type of PPP data can traverse the Internet masked as pure IP transmissions.

◆ PPTP supports the encryption, authentication, and LAN access services provided by RASs (remote access servers).

◆ Users typically establish a dial-up networking connection with their ISP using PPP. Once that connection is established, they make a PPTP connection (that relies on the PPP connection) to their organization's LAN.

◆ The process of encapsulating one protocol to make it appear as another type of protocol is known as **tunneling**. Tunneling secures data in transit and makes a protocol fit a type of network that the protocol wouldn't normally accommodate.

OBJECTIVES ON THE JOB

If you are supporting remote clients, you should be familiar with how your access server handles PPP and PPTP connections so that you can assist users in configuring their dial-up software.

PRACTICE TEST QUESTIONS

1. **By what mechanism does PPP enable Network layer data transmission over a serial interface?**
   a. segmentation
   b. padding
   c. flow control
   d. encapsulation

2. **Which of the following can support IPX transmission? Choose all that apply.**
   a. PPP
   b. SLIP
   c. PPTP
   d. DLC

3. **On a Windows 9x workstation, what options would you choose to select PPP as the remote networking communication protocol?**
   a. Control Panel, Modems, General
   b. Control Panel, Network, Adapter
   c. Dial-Up Networking, Connection Properties, Server Type
   d. Control Panel, System Properties, Device Manager

4. **What type of operating system can be used to supply a PPTP server?**
   a. Banyan VINES
   b. Novell NetWare 3.12 or higher
   c. Windows NT Server 4.0 or higher
   d. Novell NetWare 4.11 or higher

5. **What is the main difference between PPP and PPTP?**
   a. PPP can handle only asynchronous transmission, while PPTP can handle both asynchronous and synchronous transmission.
   b. PPP encapsulates traffic according to its original Network layer protocol, while PPTP encapsulates PPP traffic as IP-based data.
   c. PPP cannot carry Network layer protocols other than TCP/IP, while PPTP can carry any Network layer protocol.
   d. PPP is compatible with only NetWare servers, while PPTP is compatible with both NetWare and Windows NT/2000 servers.

6. **In the context of remote access, what does the term "serial connection" refer to?**
   a. modem
   b. NIC
   c. ISDN adapter
   d. router

7. **What does the "T" in "PPTP" stand for?**
   a. transmission
   b. telecommunications
   c. traffic
   d. tunneling

2.13 Identify the following security protocols and describe their purpose and function:

IPSEC AND L2TP

UNDERSTANDING THE OBJECTIVE

IPSec and L2TP are two ways of encrypting data in transit between clients and servers. Both are useful for virtual private networks (VPNs).

WHAT YOU REALLY NEED TO KNOW

◆ The **IPSec (Internet Protocol Security)** protocol defines encryption, authentication, and key management for TCP/IP transmissions.

◆ IPSec is an enhancement to IPv4 and is native to the newer, IPv6 standard.

◆ IPSec is somewhat different from other methods of securing data in transit. Rather than applying encryption to a stream of data, IPSec actually encrypts data by adding security information to the header of all IP packets. In effect, IPSec transforms the data packets. To do so, IPSec operates at the Network layer of the OSI Model.

◆ IPSec accomplishes authentication in two phases. The first phase is key management, and the second phase is encryption. **Key management** refers to how two nodes agree on common parameters for the keys they will use. IPSec relies on **Internet Key Exchange (IKE)** for its key management. A **key** is a series of characters that is combined with a block of data during that data's encryption. IKE is a service that runs on UDP port 500. Once IKE has established the rules for the type of keys two nodes will use, IPSec invokes its second phase, encryption. In this phase two types of encryption may be used: **authentication header (AH)** and **encapsulation security payload (ESP)**.

◆ IPSec can be used with any type of TCP/IP transmission. However, it most commonly runs on routers or other connectivity devices in the context of VPNs. Because VPNs are used to transmit private data over public networks, they require strict encryption and authentication to ensure that data are not compromised.

◆ **Layer 2 Tunneling Protocol (L2TP)** was developed by a number of industry consortia. L2TP is a remote access protocol that supports encryption and can encapsulate multiple Network layer protocols.

◆ L2TP will likely replace PPTP as the protocol of choice for remote access services.

OBJECTIVES ON THE JOB

If you work on VPNs, you should understand how to install, maintain, and troubleshoot the type of encryption your network requires. IPSec is the latest type of VPN encryption, and it is more sophisticated than L2TP.

PRACTICE TEST QUESTIONS

1. **IPSec is native to what version of IP?**
   a. 2
   b. 4
   c. 6
   d. 8

2. **Which of the following environments would be best suited to L2TP?**
   a. a small nonprofit organization that uses the Internet to solicit contributions
   b. a regional insurance company whose salespeople dial into the corporate LAN each night from their homes to upload sales figures
   c. an Internet Service Provider that needs to ensure connectivity between multiple data centers and telecommunications carriers
   d. an architectural firm that sends drawings to and receives drawings from various clients across the nation

3. **At what layer of the OSI Model does IPSec operate?**
   a. Physical
   b. Data Link
   c. Network
   d. Transport

4. **How does IPSec achieve encryption?**
   a. by scrambling the payload of packets between the source and destination
   b. by inserting false CRC fields into each packet
   c. by appending security information to the header of each packet
   d. by breaking packets into multiple, smaller packets and scrambling the payload of each smaller packet

5. **In the term "L2TP," what does the "2" represent?**
   a. layer 2 of the OSI Model
   b. the use of two encapsulation techniques
   c. a maximum of two channels within a tunnel
   d. the second generation of this type of encryption

6. **What organization developed L2TP?**
   a. Cisco
   b. Microsoft
   c. Xerox
   d. an industry consortium

7. **What type of device applies IPSec encryption to data?**
   a. router
   b. modem
   c. multiplexer
   d. laser

2.13 Identify the following security protocols and describe their purpose and function (continued):

SSL

UNDERSTANDING THE OBJECTIVE

SSL is an alternative to interpreting Web-based information via HTTP. In SSL, data exchanged between the client and the Web server are encrypted to protect their privacy.

WHAT YOU REALLY NEED TO KNOW

- ◆ **SSL (Secure Sockets Layer)** is a method of encrypting TCP/IP transmissions—including Web pages and data entered into Web forms—en route between the client and server using public key encryption technology.

- ◆ SSL is popular in part because it is widely accepted. The most recent versions of Web browsers, such as Netscape Communicator and Internet Explorer, include SSL client support in their software.

- ◆ Web page URLs that begin with the prefix **HTTPS** require that data be transferred from server to client and vice versa using SSL encryption. HTTPS uses the TCP port number 443, rather than port 80.

- ◆ Once an SSL connection has been established between a Web server and client, the client's browser displays a padlock in the lower-right corner of the screen (this applies to Internet Explorer and Netscape Communicator versions 4.0 and higher).

- ◆ Each time a client and server establish an SSL connection, they also establish a unique **SSL session**, or an association between the client and server defined by an agreement on a specific set of encryption techniques.

- ◆ An SSL session allows the client and server to continue to exchange data securely as long as the client is still connected to the server.

- ◆ SSL was originally developed by Netscape. Since that time, the Internet Engineering Task Force (IETF) has attempted to standardize SSL in a protocol called **TLS (transport layer security)**.

- ◆ Besides standardizing SSL for use with software from multiple vendors, IETF also aims to create a version of SSL that will encrypt UDP, as well as TCP transmissions. TLS, which will likely be supported by new Web browsers, uses slightly different encryption algorithms than SSL but otherwise is very similar to the most recent version of SSL.

OBJECTIVES ON THE JOB

If you are the administrator for an e-commerce Web site, you will most likely use SSL to transmit customer order and payment information. Before specializing in SSL, be certain to understand the concepts behind public key cryptography.

PRACTICE TEST QUESTIONS

1. **What port does HTTPS use?**
   a. 8
   b. 80
   c. 43
   d. 443

2. **What type of cryptography does SSL use?**
   a. private key
   b. public key
   c. pretty good privacy
   d. PHP

3. **What company developed SSL?**
   a. Microsoft
   b. Symantec
   c. Netscape
   d. Cisco

4. **How can a user tell whether her Web transmissions are using SSL?**
   a. Her browser displays a padlock in the lower-right corner of the screen.
   b. Her browser displays a window indicating that SSL is in use before displaying the SSL-based screen.
   c. The title bar on her browser displays an "SSL" prefix.
   d. There is no sure way to tell.

5. **Which of the following Web sites would probably use SSL?**
   a. a portal site that allows users to obtain stock quotes for free
   b. a family genealogy site that allows users to view pictures of relatives
   c. an art museum site that allows users to view current exhibitions
   d. a travel agency site that allows users to book flight reservations online

6. **What Transport layer protocol does HTTPS rely on?**
   a. TCP
   b. IP
   c. UDP
   d. ICMP

7. **Which of the following software programs interprets HTTPS data?**
   a. Microsoft Excel
   b. Lotus Notes
   c. Netscape Communicator
   d. Apple Quicktime

2.13 Identify the following security protocols and describe their purpose and function (continued):

KERBEROS

UNDERSTANDING THE OBJECTIVE

Kerberos is a private key encryption service that requires clients to verify their credentials for each service they request from a server. Kerberos also encrypts information exchanged between client and server.

WHAT YOU REALLY NEED TO KNOW

◆ **Kerberos** is a cross-platform authentication protocol that uses key encryption to verify the identity of clients to servers (and vice versa) and to provide secure information exchange once a client logs on to a system.

◆ Kerberos is an example of **private key encryption**, a type of key encryption in which the sender and receiver have private keys, that only they know.

◆ Kerberos provides significant security advantages over simple network operating system authentication. During a typical client/server logon, the NOS assumes that the client is using a rightfully assigned username and only verifies the user's name against the password in the NOS database. By contrast, Kerberos does not automatically trust the client. Instead, it requires the client to prove its identity through a third party. In addition, it requires the server to provide its identity to the client.

◆ In addition to checking the validity of clients and servers, Kerberos communications are encrypted and unlikely to be deciphered by any device on the network other than the client.

◆ In Kerberos terminology, the server that issues keys to clients during initial client authentication is known as the **key distribution center (KDC)**. In order to authenticate a client, the KDC runs an **authentication service (AS)**. An AS issues a **ticket**, which is a temporary set of credentials that a client uses to prove that its identity has been validated (note that a ticket is not the same as a key, which is used to initially validate its identity). A Kerberos client, or user, is known as a principal.

◆ Kerberos, which is named after the three-headed dog in Greek mythology who guarded the gates of Hades, was designed at Massachusetts Institute of Technology (MIT). MIT still provides free copies of the Kerberos code. In addition, many software vendors have developed their own versions of Kerberos.

OBJECTIVES ON THE JOB

Kerberos may be found on large private networks where security is a prime concern. For example, a government agency may use Kerberos to ensure that users accessing its research databases are authorized to view the information.

PRACTICE TEST QUESTIONS

1. **What type of cryptography does Kerberos use?**
   - a. private key
   - b. public key
   - c. pretty good privacy
   - d. PHP

2. **With which of the following network operating systems could Kerberos be used? Choose all that apply.**
   - a. NetWare
   - b. Windows
   - c. UNIX
   - d. MS-DOS

3. **What does Kerberos use to verify the validity of a client?**
   - a. L2TP
   - b. IPSec
   - c. SSL
   - d. tickets

4. **With what type of client software could Kerberos be used? Choose all that apply.**
   - a. Novell NetWare
   - b. Novell Client 32
   - c. Microsoft Windows 98
   - d. Apple Macintosh

5. **Which of the following environments is most likely to use Kerberos?**
   - a. an online retailer
   - b. a local animal shelter with 6 permanent employees and 18 volunteers
   - c. a research university with 30,000 students and 2300 faculty
   - d. a home network

6. **What characteristic do all key encryption schemes share?**
   - a. The more steps required to encrypt data using the key, the easier the key is to discover.
   - b. The longer the key, the more difficult the encryption will be to crack.
   - c. The more routers a key-encrypted packet must traverse, the more difficult the encryption will be to crack.
   - d. The shorter the key, the more difficult the encryption will be to crack.

7. **At what layer of the OSI Model does Kerberos primarily operate?**
   - a. Physical
   - b. Data Link
   - c. Transport
   - d. Presentation

OBJECTIVES

3.1 Identify the basic capabilities (i.e., client support, interoperability, authentication, file and print services, application support, and security) of the following server operating systems:

UNIX/LINUX

UNDERSTANDING THE OBJECTIVE

The term "UNIX" refers to a group of network operating systems that share similar kernels, directory structures, commands, and processing characteristics. UNIX comes in two varieties: proprietary and open source. Linux is the most popular open source version of UNIX.

WHAT YOU REALLY NEED TO KNOW

- A **network operating system (NOS)** is a software package that enables one machine to act as a server in a client-server network.
- NOSs differ in many ways, but all perform file- and print-sharing functions, plus provide mail, remote connectivity, security, network management, and Internet services.
- UNIX was developed in the 1960s concurrently with the TCP/IP protocol and was used on the first Internet host machines. UNIX still relies on the TCP/IP protocol.
- **UNIX** is a general term for a group of network operating systems that share similar kernels, directory structures, commands, and processing characteristics.
- UNIX versions may be proprietary (such as IBM's AIX or Sun's Solaris) or open source software. **Linux** is the most popular open source software version of UNIX.
- The advantage to using a proprietary version of UNIX is its stability and vendor support. However, open source versions are becoming more standard and more easily supported.
- UNIX uses a hierarchical file system, in which the uppermost level is called the root. Standard directories under the root include home, dev, usr, bin, var, and lib.
- UNIX software relies on a kernel, which contains the core set of instructions for the operating system.
- The creators of UNIX introduced techniques for multiprocessing; thus, UNIX supports multiple processors, as well as multiple NICs and virtual memory.
- UNIX servers can access FAT, NTFS, and HPFS file systems, as well as shared drives on Windows or NetWare servers.
- A UNIX server can support multiple types of clients, including Microsoft and Novell network clients, because it is based on the standard TCP/IP protocol stack.

OBJECTIVES ON THE JOB

As the oldest and arguably still the most efficient NOS, some form of UNIX is found in virtually every organization. Often, UNIX is used for HTTP, Telnet, FTP, DNS, or other Internet-related services, as well as robust database servers. While some UNIX systems have GUI interfaces, most network administrators still use the command-line interface, forcing administrators to memorize commands.

PRACTICE TEST QUESTIONS

1. **Which of the following is true about open source UNIX?**
   a. Open source versions of UNIX typically do not supply as many Internet services as proprietary versions of the software.
   b. Open source versions of UNIX are less accepted in the marketplace for use with robust applications.
   c. Open source versions of UNIX use a different file system than proprietary versions of the software.
   d. Open source versions of UNIX typically do not come with the same amount of vendor support as proprietary versions.

2. **What will typing `man ls` and pressing Enter at the command line of a UNIX server do?**
   a. display the help text for the file list command
   b. display the server's error log
   c. display a list of users currently logged on to the system
   d. display a list of available printers

3. **What is the uppermost level of a UNIX file system called?**
   a. branch
   b. leaf
   c. root
   d. tree

4. **What protocol is native to the UNIX environment?**
   a. IPX/SPX
   b. NetBEUI
   c. TCP/IP
   d. SNA

5. **Which of the following is a popular use for a UNIX server, even in an environment dominated by Windows 2000 or NetWare?**
   a. print server
   b. graphics server
   c. remote access server
   d. HTTP server

6. **Which of the following is a popular version of open source UNIX?**
   a. Linux
   b. VINES
   c. AIX
   d. AnyLAN

7. **What is IBM's proprietary version of UNIX called?**
   a. IBX
   b. AIX
   c. SNAX
   d. INOS

3.1 Identify the basic capabilities (i.e., client support, interoperability, authentication, file and print services, application support, and security) of the following server operating systems (continued):

NETWARE

UNDERSTANDING THE OBJECTIVE

In 1983, Novell introduced its NetWare network operating system. NetWare quickly became the standard operating system for LANs and WANs, providing reliable file- and print-sharing services for millions of users. Since then, Novell has refined NetWare to include support for TCP/IP, intranet services, a graphical user interface, and better integration with other operating systems.

WHAT YOU REALLY NEED TO KNOW

◆ The original version of Novell NetWare was based on the IPX/SPX protocol. Novell has expanded its compatibility with other protocols. NetWare 5.x is based on the TCP/IP protocol.

◆ Versions 4.x and higher of NetWare support multiple processors, multiple NICs, 32-bit addressing, and can use both physical and virtual memory.

◆ NetWare's kernel oversees all critical server functions. The program SERVER.EXE runs the kernel from a DOS prompt and is run from the server's AUTOEXEC.BAT file.

◆ NetWare uses **NetWare Loadable Modules (NLMs)** to load necessary functions or applications (such as the printer console) into memory on the server.

◆ In NetWare versions 4.x and lower, the **server console**, a text-based menu system, is the network administrator's main interface with the server. In NetWare 5.x, administrators may use a GUI interface called **ConsoleOne**.

◆ In NetWare versions 4.x and higher, the NetWare Directory System (NDS) describes how a network's volumes, resources, users, and groups are arranged. The terms "root," "tree," and "leaf" are used to describe different elements of NDS. **NWAdmin** is used to create and administer the NDS.

◆ A NetWare server can accept many different types of clients, including UNIX, Macintosh, Windows 9x, 2000, and NT, MS-DOS, and OS/2.

◆ The NDS for NT tool enables Windows 2000 domains to appear as container objects in NWAdmin. In Novell's terminology, NDS **eDirectory** extends the schema to include Windows 2000 resources. Windows 2000 servers appear as server objects, and groups and users from Windows 2000 domains appear as NDS group and user objects, respectively.

OBJECTIVES ON THE JOB

The NetWare NOS is favored by many veteran network administrators. To succeed as a network technician or administrator in a NetWare shop, you must be especially familiar with the concepts of NDS, NWAdmin, protocols, and interconnecting with other NOSs.

PRACTICE TEST QUESTIONS

1. **What does NDS stand for?**
   - a. NetWare Direct System
   - b. NetWare Distributed System
   - c. NetWare Digital Services
   - d. NetWare Directory Services

2. **From what file on a NetWare server is the SERVER.EXE program launched?**
   - a. CONFIG.SYS
   - b. AUTOEXEC.BAT
   - c. SERVER.BAT
   - d. NLM.BAT

3. **On which protocol was the first version of NetWare based?**
   - a. TCP/IP
   - b. NetBEUI
   - c. SNA
   - d. IPX/SPX

4. **What program is used to administer NDS?**
   - a. GSNW
   - b. NWAdmin
   - c. NTFS
   - d. NWConsole

5. **A user is an example of what type of NDS object?**
   - a. root
   - b. branch
   - c. leaf
   - d. stem

6. **What is the main purpose of NLMs?**
   - a. to load applications or services into memory on the server
   - b. to install the NetWare operating system on the server
   - c. to connect NetWare servers with Windows NT servers
   - d. to optimize memory usage on the server

7. **What volume does NetWare create by default upon installation?**
   - a. SYS
   - b. VOL1
   - c. USERS
   - d. DATA

3.1 Identify the basic capabilities (i.e., client support, interoperability, authentication, file and print services, application support, and security) of the following server operating systems (continued):

WINDOWS

UNDERSTANDING THE OBJECTIVE

Some of the most popular network operating systems are Microsoft's Windows NT and Windows 2000. Microsoft's NOSs have grown in popularity due to their simple-to-use graphical user interface and their similarity to the Windows desktop operating systems.

WHAT YOU REALLY NEED TO KNOW

◆ Windows 2000 Server relies on a **graphical user interface (GUI)**, a pictorial representation of computer functions that makes it easy for the network administrator to manage files, users, groups, security, printers, and so on.

◆ Windows 2000 Server uses 32-bit addressing, which helps to process instructions twice as fast as 16-bit addressing and assigns each application its own 32-bit memory area.

◆ Windows 2000 Server can use multiple processors, multiple NICs, and both physical and virtual memory. In order to determine what components can be used in a Windows 2000 server, refer to Microsoft's **Hardware Compatibility List (HCL)**. The HCL lists all the computer components proven to be compatible with Windows 2000 Server.

◆ Windows 2000 uses **Active Directory**, its directory service, for organizing and managing objects on the network.

◆ Windows 2000 can support the following file systems: CDFS, FAT, FAT32, and NTFS. Microsoft developed the **New Technology File System (NTFS)** expressly for Windows NT, the precursor to Windows 2000. NTFS integrates reliability, compression, speed, and the ability to handle large files. The main benefit to NTFS, however, is its superior security. NTFS is the preferred file system for servers running Windows 2000.

◆ A Windows 2000 server can communicate with almost any kind of client. Often, a network dominated by Windows 2000 servers uses Windows 9x, NT, or 2000 workstations.

◆ To communicate with a NetWare server running IPX/SPX, a Windows 2000 server must have the Gateway Services for NetWare (GSNW) installed in addition to the IPX/SPX protocols. To communicate with a UNIX server, a Windows 2000 server need only have the TCP/IP protocols and services installed.

OBJECTIVES ON THE JOB

Many organizations run the Windows 2000 Server network operating system, even if their network is dominated by other NOSs. Windows 2000 Server is a popular system for Web services (those running Internet Information Server), as well as file and print services.

PRACTICE TEST QUESTIONS

1. **What server resource does the Windows 2000 NOS use for virtual memory?**
   a. hard disk
   b. RAM
   c. CPU
   d. system board

2. **What protocol must be installed for a Windows 2000 server to communicate with a UNIX server?**
   a. NetBEUI
   b. IPX/SPX
   c. TCP/IP
   d. SNA

3. **What is the name of Windows 2000 Server's directory service?**
   a. Windows Directory Service
   b. Active Directory
   c. Hierarchical Directories
   d. Managed Directory Service

4. **What is the main advantage of assigning each application its own 32-bit memory area?**
   a. The application is less likely to freeze up.
   b. The application is less likely to interfere with other applications.
   c. The application executes with priority over other applications.
   d. The application can be executed from multiple workstations.

5. **Which of the following file systems must be present on a Windows 2000 server so it can communicate with Macintosh workstations?**
   a. NTFS
   b. CDFS
   c. HPFS
   d. FAT

6. **What resource can you use to determine whether your server's NIC works with the Windows 2000 Server NOS?**
   a. the server resource kit
   b. the hardware compatibility list
   c. the Microsoft NT users forum
   d. the emergency repair disk

7. **Which of the following must a Windows 2000 Server have installed in order to communicate with a NetWare server running IPX/SPX?**
   a. IntraNetWare
   b. eDirectory
   c. NDS for 2000
   d. Gateway Services for NetWare

3.1 Identify the basic capabilities (i.e., client support, interoperability, authentication, file and print services, application support, and security) of the following server operating systems (continued):

MACINTOSH

UNDERSTANDING THE OBJECTIVE

Macintosh is an operating system developed by Apple Computer, Inc. While it is used as a network operating system in small, limited environments, it is still a popular desktop operating system and can be connected to most any type of network.

WHAT YOU REALLY NEED TO KNOW

◆ The Macintosh operating system was developed by Apple Computer, Inc. as an intuitive, graphical interface for personal computers. Businesses and institutions involved in art or education, such as advertising agencies, elementary schools, and graphic designers, often use Apple Macintosh computers.

◆ AppleTalk is the protocol suite used to interconnect Macintosh computers. Although it was originally designed to support peer-to-peer networking among Macintoshes, it can now be routed between network segments and integrated with NetWare or Windows networks.

◆ Although Apple has improved AppleTalk's ability to use different network models and span network segments, it remains unsuited to large LANs or WANs. Even Apple has begun supporting the TCP/IP protocol to integrate Macintoshes with other networks, including the Internet.

◆ **LocalTalk** is a network access method designed by Apple Computer, Inc. specifically for networking Macintosh computers. It was included with the Macintosh operating system since 1984, and it provided a simple, cost-effective way of interconnecting Macintosh devices.

◆ However, LocalTalk is only capable of 230 Kbps maximum throughput—much less than the 10 Mbps or 100 Mbps throughput of an Ethernet network.

◆ LocalTalk is not easily supported by non-Macintosh devices. Since Macintosh computers are capable of using Ethernet as a network access method, Ethernet is usually preferred over LocalTalk.

◆ LocalTalk uses a transmission method called **Carrier Sense Multiple Access/Collision Avoidance (CSMA/CA)**. It is similar to the CSMA/CD used in Ethernet networks, except a node on a LocalTalk network signals its intent to transmit before it actually does so. In this way, collisions and the need for data retransmittals are (mostly) avoided.

OBJECTIVES ON THE JOB

Chances are good that you will never need to build a LocalTalk network, though occasionally you may need to troubleshoot one. LocalTalk might still be appropriate for a home network that requires simple configuration and does not require high throughput.

PRACTICE TEST QUESTIONS

1. **With which of the following network operating systems can a Macintosh computer act as a client? Choose all that apply.**
   a. MS-DOS
   b. NetWare
   c. Macintosh
   d. Windows

2. **What type of network access method does a Macintosh-based network use?**
   a. CSMA/CD
   b. CSMA/CA
   c. token-passing
   d. demand priority

3. **What logical topology does AppleTalk rely on?**
   a. LocalTalk
   b. AppleNet
   c. Ethernet
   d. Token Ring

4. **Which of the following environments is most likely to use a Macintosh-based network?**
   a. an online retailer
   b. a regional insurance company with 7 locations and 4500 employees
   c. a research university with 30,000 students and 2300 faculty
   d. a home network

5. **AppleTalk is a routable protocol. True or false?**

6. **What is the default protocol used by Macintosh clients on a network?**
   a. AppleTalk
   b. NetBEUI
   c. TCP/IP
   d. IPX/SPX

7. **What is the maximum throughput of a LocalTalk network?**
   a. 56 Kbps
   b. 230 Kbps
   c. 560 Kbps
   d. 1 Mbps

3.2 Identify the basic capabilities (i.e., client connectivity, local security mechanisms, and authentication) of the following clients:

UNIX/LINUX

UNDERSTANDING THE OBJECTIVE

A UNIX or Linux client is very similar to a UNIX or Linux server. Both rely on the TCP/IP protocol, both require username and password authentication to log on, and both assign read, write, or execute permissions according to files and groups.

WHAT YOU REALLY NEED TO KNOW

- ◆ UNIX systems may be implemented as clients or as servers. Unlike Windows 2000, in which the server and client operating systems vary considerably, the difference between a UNIX server and a UNIX client lies only in the set of optional packages included during installation. A UNIX system configured as a server has the necessary software to enable sharing of resources such as print queues, file systems, and processor time. A UNIX client typically does not have these resource sharing services installed.

- ◆ UNIX systems rely on the TCP/IP protocol. If necessary, they can also run other protocols such as IPX/SPX or AppleTalk.

- ◆ UNIX clients require users to log on with a username and password. UNIX clients use 56-bit DES encrypted passwords.

- ◆ During installation, you must supply a root password. Once installation has completed, you will be prompted to log onto the system as root, using the password you specified.

- ◆ Files and directories on a UNIX client are available only to those users who are logged on to the client and who have sufficient rights to access those files.

- ◆ Each file and directory on a UNIX client can be assigned read, write, and execute rights. Such rights can be associated with individual users, groups, or all users.

- ◆ **Samba** is a software program that runs on UNIX-based systems and allows it to supply file and printer sharing services to Windows-based clients. Samba is freely available under the same license as the Linux operating system.

OBJECTIVES ON THE JOB

It is important to have a plan for securing resources on clients and servers before beginning to configure the systems. For instance, on shared UNIX workstations, you may create separate data directories for each user's files and assign permissions so that only the directory's owner can access the directory's contents.

PRACTICE TEST QUESTIONS

1. **After you install a UNIX client according to the operating system's default options, what protocol will the client attempt to use to connect to the network?**
   - a. NetBEUI
   - b. TCP/IP
   - c. SAMBA
   - d. SNA

2. **What command would you use to add a new user called "morton" to a Linux client?**
   - a. `chmod -a morton`
   - b. `usadd morton`
   - c. `useradd morton`
   - d. `chmod +add morton`

3. **What command will enable you to view all the users currently logged onto a UNIX system?**
   - a. `nslookup`
   - b. `who`
   - c. `whois`
   - d. `ifconfig`

4. **Assuming you have rights to read the contents of a UNIX client's directory, what command would you use to do so?**
   - a. `hup files`
   - b. `list files`
   - c. `listdir`
   - d. `ls`

5. **If you wanted to learn more about the command that allows you to change the file and directory privileges on a UNIX client, what would you type at the shell prompt?**
   - a. `help config`
   - b. `mkdir /?`
   - c. `chdir -?`
   - d. `man chmod`

6. **What is one primary difference between the UNIX client operating system and the UNIX server operating system?**
   - a. The server operating system is capable of multiprocessing, while the client operating system is not.
   - b. The client operating system typically doesn't have services such as print queue sharing installed.
   - c. The server operating system can support multiple users, while the client operating system cannot.
   - d. The client operating system installs multiple Network layer protocols by default.

7. **In order to be able to use FTP on a Linux client, you must first install the FTP software. True or false?**

3.2 Identify the basic capabilities (i.e., client connectivity, local security mechanisms, and authentication) of the following clients (continued):

WINDOWS

UNDERSTANDING THE OBJECTIVE

Windows clients rely on a graphical user interface to supply functionality. They can support many types of protocols, including TCP/IP, NetBEUI, IPX/SPX, and AppleTalk. The Windows NT and Windows 2000 Professional versions require local users to log onto the client, supplying a username and password.

WHAT YOU REALLY NEED TO KNOW

♦ Windows operating systems vary considerably, not only between different versions of the operating system, but also between client and server software within each version.

♦ By default, Windows 98, NT, and 2000 operating systems rely on the TCP/IP protocol. All of the Windows operating systems can also run other protocols, such as IPX/SPX or AppleTalk.

♦ Windows clients can connect to NetWare and UNIX servers as well as servers running a version of the Windows NOS.

♦ Windows NT Workstation and Windows 2000 Professional clients provide more local file security than Windows 3.1, 9x, or ME clients. Windows NT and 2000 Professional clients require users to log onto the system with a username and password.

♦ During installation of the Windows NT Workstation and 2000 Professional client operating systems, you must supply an Administrator password. Once installation has completed, you will be prompted to log onto the system as Administrator, using the password you specified.

♦ Local access to files and directories on Windows NT Workstation and Windows 2000 Professional clients is available only to those users who are logged on to the client and who have sufficient rights to access those files.

♦ Each file and directory on such clients can be assigned full control, modify, read & execute, list folder contents, read, or write rights. Such rights can be associated with individual users, groups, or all users.

♦ Files and directories on Windows 3.1, Windows 9x, and Windows ME clients are not secured by assigning rights to users and groups. Other means (such as encryption) must be used to secure files on these versions of the Windows client operating system.

OBJECTIVES ON THE JOB

Windows clients are popular choices for many organizations because they are well-supported and well-understood. When working with Windows clients, be certain to understand the significant differences between multiple versions, including Windows 3.1, 95, 98, NT, 2000, and ME.

PRACTICE TEST QUESTIONS

1. **On which of the following Windows clients are you most likely to use NetBEUI?**
   a. Windows 2000 Professional
   b. Windows NT Workstation 4.0
   c. Windows 3.1
   d. Windows 98

2. **What is the name of the account that is created when you install Windows 2000 Professional on a workstation?**
   a. Root
   b. admin
   c. Master
   d. Administrator

3. **In order for a Windows 98 client to log onto a NetWare 4.11 server running IPX/SPX, which of the following must be installed on the client? Choose all that apply.**
   a. NWLink IPX/SPX protocol
   b. Client for NetWare Networks
   c. TCP/IP
   d. NDS eDirectory

4. **Which of the following is the most secure client operating system?**
   a. Windows ME
   b. Windows 95
   c. Windows 98
   d. Windows NT Workstation

5. **What would be the best way to secure files on your Windows 98 workstation so that only you could read them?**
   a. Modify the local file sharing properties so that only your user account has access to the files.
   b. Encrypt the files.
   c. Assign file scan rights only to those files.
   d. Compress the files and put them in an unnamed folder.

6. **Which of the following would a Windows 98 computer require in order to log onto a UNIX server?**
   a. TCP/IP
   b. IPX/SPX
   c. NetBEUI
   d. SAMBA

7. **What options would you choose to enable clients on a peer-to-peer network to read from your Windows 2000 Professional workstation's C:\MyPrograms directory?**
   a. My Computer, Folder properties, File Sharing tab
   b. Network Neighborhood, Network Properties, Security tab
   c. My Network Places, Network Properties, Access tab
   d. My Network Places, Users and Groups, Access tab

OBJECTIVES

3.2 Identify the basic capabilities (i.e., client connectivity, local security mechanisms, and authentication) of the following clients (continued):

MACINTOSH

UNDERSTANDING THE OBJECTIVE

Macintosh clients can connect to Windows, NetWare, UNIX/Linux, or Macintosh clients, using AppleTalk or TCP/IP protocols.

WHAT YOU REALLY NEED TO KNOW

- ◆ Network connections for a Macintosh client can be viewed and enabled by selecting the Chooser option from the Apple menu.
- ◆ Older Macintosh clients used LocalTalk on AppleTalk networks. However, most modern Macintosh clients rely on TCP/IP to connect to a network, whether they are directly connected to a LAN or dial in to a remote access server.
- ◆ The original version of TCP/IP used on Macintosh clients is called **MacTCP**. However, since System 7.5.2, Apple has used newer TCP/IP version for Macintosh clients called **Open Transport**.
- ◆ Open Transport provides support for DHCP, IP Multicast, and the use of multiple simultaneous TCP connections, among other features.
- ◆ The current implementation of Open Transport has two components, AppleTalk and TCP/IP, each managed and configured through a separate Control Panel. Once the software is installed, you need to configure AppleTalk and TCP/IP services through their respective Control Panels.
- ◆ In the TCP/IP Control Panel, you can specify whether or not the client uses DHCP. You can also specify the client's host and domain name, subnet mask, IP address (if static addressing is used), name server, and the gateway (or router) address. Using the "Connect via" drop-down list in the TCP/IP Control Panel, you can choose whether the client will connect to the network via Ethernet or AppleTalk.
- ◆ If you choose AppleTalk as the network type, you will be prompted to indicate what zone your Macintosh client belongs to.
- ◆ Using TCP/IP, Macintosh clients can connect to Windows, NetWare, UNIX/Linux, and Macintosh servers.
- ◆ The latest Macintosh operating system, OS X, supports multiple encryption techniques, including Kerberos and SSL. It also supports file-based permissions (similar to those on a UNIX client) that can be tailored according to user or group. Further, OS X allows users to fully encrypt all or part of their Macintosh hard disks.

OBJECTIVES ON THE JOB

Macintosh clients are popular among educational and creative organizations (such as advertising agencies). Their TCP/IP configuration is similar to that of a Windows or UNIX client.

PRACTICE TEST QUESTIONS

1. **What version of TCP/IP was standard on Macintosh clients prior to System 7.5?**
   a. AppleTalk
   b. MacTCP
   c. Open Transport
   d. NWLink

2. **What option would you choose to configure your Macintosh workstation to use DHCP rather than static IP addressing?**
   a. Apple, TCP/IP Control Panel, Configure "Using DHCP"
   b. Apple, Chooser, Network Properties, TCP/IP Controls, DHCP
   c. Apple, Chooser, Networks, Protocols, TCP/IP, Use DHCP
   d. Apple, TCP/IP Control Panel, IP Addressing tab, Use DHCP

3. **What network type would you probably choose for a Macintosh client that is connecting to a NetWare 5.0 server?**
   a. AppleTalk
   b. LocalTalk
   c. Ethernet
   d. Token Ring

4. **The router address prompt in the Macintosh TCP/IP Control Panel refers to what?**
   a. the client's core Internet router
   b. the client's IP gateway
   c. the client's closest router
   d. the client's closest connectivity device of any type

5. **What is one advantage of Open Transport over MacTCP?**
   a. It can connect to Windows servers as well as UNIX and Macintosh servers.
   b. It uses less temporary memory.
   c. It offers the option of running over LocalTalk or Ethernet.
   d. It supports DHCP.

6. **Setting file and directory permissions on a Macintosh client running the new OS X would be very similar to setting file and directory permissions on what other OS?**
   a. Windows 2000 Professional
   b. Windows 2000 Server
   c. NetWare 5.1
   d. UNIX

7. **If you didn't want anyone to read the contents of your Macintosh hard disk, even if they sat down at your computer, what type of security technique should you use?**
   a. Kerberos
   b. SSL
   c. IPSec
   d. encrypt the hard disk data

3.3 Identify the main characteristics of VLANs.

UNDERSTANDING THE OBJECTIVE

A virtual local area network (VLAN) is a network of nodes logically created by configuring ports on a switch or multiple switches. VLANs are useful for isolating traffic, either with the aim of improving performance or increasing data privacy.

WHAT YOU REALLY NEED TO KNOW

- A **virtual local area network (VLAN)** is a logically separate network within a network.
- To create a VLAN, you use a switch (or switches) to group a number of ports into a broadcast domain. The ports do not have to reside on the same switch or even on the same network segment.
- A **broadcast domain** (also known as a **collision domain**) is a combination of ports that make up a Layer 2 segment and must be connected by a Layer 3 device, such as a router or Layer 3 switch.
- A VLAN can include servers, workstations, printers, routers, or any other network device you can connect to a switch.
- One great advantage of VLANs is their ability to link geographically distant users and create small workgroups from large LANs.
- VLANs are also helpful if you are interested in keeping one workgroup's network traffic separate from another workgroup's network traffic for improved security or performance.
- To create a VLAN, you must configure the switch properly. In addition to identifying the ports that belong to each logical network, you can specify security parameters, filtering instructions (if the switch should not forward any frames from a certain segment, for example), performance requirements for certain users, and network management options.
- In setting up a VLAN, you are not merely including a certain group of nodes—you are also excluding another group. As a result, you can potentially cut a group off from the rest of the network. VLAN implementation requires careful planning to ensure that all the groups of users who need to communicate can do so after the VLAN is in operation.

OBJECTIVES ON THE JOB

If you are charged with designing a network or installing switches, you should research VLANs further. Some trade publications (and many switch manufacturers) have touted VLANs as the most advanced approach to networking—and the wave of the future.

PRACTICE TEST QUESTIONS

1. **What connectivity device is responsible for creating VLANs?**
   a. hub
   b. router
   c. switch
   d. gateway

2. **Why couldn't bridges be used to create a VLAN?**
   a. because they cannot interpret Layer 3 information
   b. because they do not contain multiple ports
   c. because they do not work with the Ethernet network access method
   d. because they cannot determine the MAC addresses of connected nodes

3. **Which of the following parameters can you specify for a VLAN when configuring a switch? Choose all that apply.**
   a. performance requirements for certain nodes
   b. the method of signaling required by certain nodes
   c. security parameters
   d. filtering instructions based on segment

4. **What is one potential pitfall when creating VLANs?**
   a. You could inadvertently forget to assign a port to a node, thus disabling all traffic on that node's segment.
   b. You could inadvertently assign one node to more than one port, thus disabling traffic to and from that node.
   c. You could inadvertently connect a segment to itself, thus causing a loop in traffic.
   d. You could inadvertently cut off network access to some nodes.

5. **Which of the following nodes could belong to a single broadcast domain? Choose all that apply.**
   a. workstation
   b. router
   c. server
   d. printer

6. **In order for two workstations to belong to the same VLAN, they must connect to the same switch. True or false?**

7. **In which of the following situations would a VLAN be most useful and appropriate?**
   a. an office of eight users connected via a peer-to-peer LAN for file and printer sharing
   b. a startup company of 18 computer scientists using a Gigabit Ethernet LAN to share data and programs
   c. a university WAN dedicated to offering long distance education to all students
   d. a pharmaceutical company's headquarters with 530 employees from various departments connected to a Fast Ethernet LAN

3.4 Identify the main characteristics of network attached storage.

UNDERSTANDING THE OBJECTIVE

Network attached storage (NAS) is a highly fault-tolerant method of storing shared data and programs on a network. Because NAS devices use their own file system and server hardware, they can access and transmit data to clients very quickly.

WHAT YOU REALLY NEED TO KNOW

◆ **Network attached storage (NAS)** is a specialized storage device or group of storage devices that provides centralized fault-tolerant data storage for a network.

◆ NAS differs from RAID in that it maintains its own interface to the LAN rather than relying on a separate server to connect it to the network and control its functions.

◆ The advantage to NAS as compared to a typical file server is that a NAS device contains its own file system that is optimized to read and write files (as opposed to also running a full-service operating system, managing printing, authenticating logon IDs, and so on). Because of this optimization, NAS reads and writes from its disk significantly faster than other types of servers could.

◆ Another advantage to using NAS is that it can easily be expanded without interrupting service. For instance, if you purchased a NAS device with 40 GB of disk space, then six months later realized you need three times as much storage space, you could add the new 80 GB to the NAS device without requiring users to log off the network or taking down the NAS device. After physically installing the new disk space, the NAS device would recognize the added storage and add it to its pool of available disk space.

◆ Although NAS is a separate device with its own file system, it still cannot communicate directly with clients on the network. When using NAS, the client requests a file from its usual file server (such as a Windows, UNIX/Linux, or NetWare server) over the LAN. The server then requests the file from the NAS device on the network. In response, the NAS device retrieves the file and transmits it to the server, which transmits it to the client.

◆ NAS is appropriate for small or medium sized enterprises that require fault tolerance, and fast access to data. Since NAS devices can store and retrieve data for any type of client (providing it can run TCP/IP), NAS is also appropriate for organizations that use a mix of different operating systems on their desktops.

OBJECTIVES ON THE JOB

If your organization relies on data or programs that must always be available, network attached storage might be an excellent way to store and serve these resources. If you work with NAS, remember that it uses its own software and hardware. Thus, installing, configuring, and maintaining NAS can be quite different from installing, configuring, and maintaining off-the-shelf servers using the Windows, NetWare or UNIX/Linux operating systems.

PRACTICE TEST QUESTIONS

1. **What is one advantage of using NAS compared to using a Windows 2000 server running RAID level 3?**
   a. It is directly attached to the file server.
   b. It can read and write data faster.
   c. It is easier to configure.
   d. It is less expensive.

2. **What type of operating system do NAS devices use?**
   a. Linux
   b. NetWare
   c. Windows 2000 Server
   d. a unique, proprietary O/S that depends on the NAS vendor

3. **On a 100BaseTX network, what type of access method would a group of NAS devices use?**
   a. demand priority
   b. CSMA/CA
   c. CSMA/CD
   d. token passing

4. **What is one advantage of NAS devices compared to a Pentium file server running NetWare 5.x?**
   a. They are easier to install and maintain.
   b. They are capable of multiprocessing.
   c. They can accept new hard disks without interruption of service.
   d. They can provide Internet services, remote access services, and management services, as well as file and print sharing services.

5. **NAS devices cannot communicate directly with clients on the same network. True or false?**

6. **Which of the following protocols do the majority of NAS devices use?**
   a. TCP/IP
   b. NetBEUI
   c. NetBIOS
   d. IPX/SPX

7. **Which of the following clients would be compatible with NAS? Choose all that apply.**
   a. MS-DOS
   b. Macintosh
   c. Windows 95
   d. Windows 98

3.5 Identify the purpose and characteristics of fault tolerance.

UNDERSTANDING THE OBJECTIVE

Fault tolerance is the capacity for a system to withstand faults. On a network, many techniques, including redundancy, backups, mirroring, clustering, and disk striping can ensure fault tolerance.

WHAT YOU REALLY NEED TO KNOW

- ◆ **Fault tolerance** is the capacity for a system to continue performing despite an unexpected hardware or software malfunction. A **fault** is the malfunction of one component of a system. A fault can result in a **failure**, or a deviation from a specified level of system performance for a given period of time.

- ◆ The aim of fault tolerance is to employ as many techniques as is prudent to prevent faults from becoming failures. Most of these techniques address single points of failure, or places in the network where one fault could immobilize the entire network.

- ◆ **Redundancy** is the use of duplicate components or machines on a network. The aim of redundancy is to eliminate single points of failure. Networks often include redundant power sources, cabling, server hard disks, NICs, and data links.

- ◆ **Server mirroring** is a fault-tolerance technique in which one server duplicates the transactions and data storage of another. The servers must be identical machines.

- ◆ Another fault-tolerance technique is **disk mirroring**, in which data are simultaneously written to two (usually) identical disks attached to a computer.

- ◆ A simple implementation of disk mirroring on a server is also known as **redundant array of inexpensive disks (RAID) level 1**.

- ◆ **RAID level 0** is the simplest implementation of disk striping. In RAID level 0, data is written in 64K blocks equally across all disks (or partitions) in the array.

- ◆ Disk striping alone does not ensure availability because if one of the disks fails, its data will be inaccessible. Thus, RAID level 0 does not provide true redundancy.

- ◆ **RAID level 3** involves disk striping with a special type of ECC (error correction code) known as parity error correction code. It writes parity information to a single disk.

- ◆ **RAID level 5** is the most common, highly fault-tolerant technique for data storage. In RAID level 5, data are written in small blocks across several disks. At the same time, parity error checking information is also distributed among the disks.

OBJECTIVES ON THE JOB

Of all fault tolerance techniques, RAID level 5 is most common on modern networks. You should understand how your server handles RAID and what kind of hardware it requires. Consider having RAID components installed by the manufacturer. That way, you are certain to get RAID components that are compatible with your hardware.

PRACTICE TEST QUESTIONS

1. **Which of the following is the least expensive method of ensuring availability on a network of 100 nodes?**
   a. using redundant NICs on all servers
   b. using redundant fiber links to the ISP
   c. using a SONET ring to connect to the local telecommunications facility
   d. leasing off-site facilities for data backup storage

2. **Which of the following will definitely render a network unusable?**
   a. failure
   b. fault
   c. redundancy
   d. security breach

3. **Which of the following components should be redundant in a fault-tolerant network?**
   a. the servers' NICs
   b. the root password
   c. the NOS software installation
   d. the SYS volume

4. **What is the aim of fault tolerance?**
   a. to eliminate faults
   b. to ensure that faults don't result in failures
   c. to address the least severe faults
   d. to create potential faults for testing purposes

5. **Which of the following could be a single point of failure for an entire network? Choose all that apply.**
   a. a server
   b. a router
   c. a hub
   d. a workstation

6. **Which of the following statements is true about mirroring?**
   a. Mirrored servers must connect to the network at the same speed.
   b. Mirrored servers must have identical NICs.
   c. Mirrored servers must be in the same computer room.
   d. Mirrored servers must use the same backup scheme.

7. **Which of the following is most likely to be implemented on a modern network?**
   a. RAID level 0
   b. RAID level 1
   c. RAID level 3
   d. RAID level 5

3.6   Identify the purpose and characteristics of disaster recovery.

UNDERSTANDING THE OBJECTIVE

Disaster recovery will allow your organization and, in particular, its computer systems to regain functionality after a disaster (such as a tornado, flood, or terrorist attack) affects you.

WHAT YOU REALLY NEED TO KNOW

◆ **Disaster recovery** is the process of restoring critical functionality and data after an enterprise-wide outage that affects more than a single system or a limited group of users.

◆ When planning for disaster recovery, you must take into account the possible extremes, rather than considering only relatively minor outages, failures, security breaches, or data corruption. In a disaster recovery plan, you should consider the worst-case scenarios, from a catastrophic hurricane to a terrorist attack.

◆ Disaster recovery should also address what might happen if your typical networking staff isn't available. The plan should outline multiple contingencies, in case your best options don't pan out. It should also specify alternate sites that can be used to supply temporary functionality.

◆ Every organization should have a disaster recovery team (with an appointed coordinator) and a disaster recovery plan. This plan should address not only computer systems, but also power, telephony, and paper-based files.

◆ The computer systems part of a disaster recovery plan should address the following issues:

- Contact names for emergency coordinators who will execute the disaster recovery response, as well as roles and responsibilities of other staff.

- Details on which data and servers are backed up, how frequently backups occur, where backups are kept (off-site), and, most importantly, how backed-up data can be recovered in full.

- Details on network topology, redundancy, and agreements with national service carriers, in case vendors fall prey to the same disaster.

- Strategies for regularly testing the disaster recovery plan.

- A plan for managing the crisis, including regular communications with employees and customers. Consider the possibility that regular communications modes (such as phone lines) might be unavailable.

OBJECTIVES ON THE JOB

Having a comprehensive disaster recovery plan not only lessens the risk of losing critical data in case of extreme situations, but also makes potential customers and your insurance providers look more favorably on your organization.

PRACTICE TEST QUESTIONS

1. **Which of the following details should be recorded in a disaster recovery plan? Choose all that apply.**
   a. where backup tapes are kept
   b. home telephone number of the network administrator
   c. what type of disaster might occur
   d. how the plan will be tested

2. **Which of the following are disasters that would be addressed by a disaster recovery plan?**
   a. a vendor going out of business
   b. a hurricane demolishing the organization's headquarters
   c. a riot in a nearby city
   d. a hacker gaining access to your Web server

3. **Which of the following would be the person most likely to coordinate an organization's computer systems disaster recovery effort?**
   a. help desk technician
   b. company CFO
   c. database programmer
   d. IT manager

4. **Besides computer systems, what other resources must be addressed by a disaster recovery plan? Choose all that apply.**
   a. paper files
   b. power
   c. IP address reservations with ICANN
   d. employees' cars

5. **Why would it be necessary to include details about an organization's service agreements with telecommunications carriers in a disaster recovery plan?**
   a. They will have to supply the organization with new equipment.
   b. The carriers may also be affected by the disaster and may owe the organization compensation for downtime.
   c. The agreements may change as a result of the disaster.
   d. The carriers may decide to void their agreement after the disaster.

6. **The computer systems part of a good disaster recovery plan should assign duties to the IT department personnel only. True or false?**

7. **A disaster recovery plan should contain several different approaches for recovering from a disaster. True or false?**

OBJECTIVES

3.7 Given a remote connectivity scenario (e.g., IP, IPX, dial-up, PPPoE, authentication, physical connectivity, etc.), configure the connection.

UNDERSTANDING THE OBJECTIVE

Many utilities, software programs, protocols, and hardware combinations are used to establish a remote connection. The modem on the client must be properly installed and configured. For Windows clients, the dial-up networking (DUN) software must be configured; then the DUN software and the TCP/IP protocol must be bound to both TCP/IP and the Client for Microsoft Networks.

WHAT YOU REALLY NEED TO KNOW

- ◆ The most common type of remote access involves dial-up networking. **Dial-up networking (DUN)** typically refers to a modem connection to a server through the PSTN. It is also the name of the utility that Microsoft provides with its operating systems to achieve this type of connectivity. To use dial-up networking, the modem and the networking client software must be properly installed and configured.

- ◆ Nearly all dial-up networking connections rely on TCP/IP network protocols. Most Windows-based clients use the PPP protocol.

- ◆ To connect to a Windows-based remote access server from a Windows workstation, the Client for Microsoft Networks and the TCP/IP protocol must be installed. Also, the dial-up networking utility must be installed and bound to TCP/IP and the Client for Microsoft Networks.

- ◆ Settings you can identify through the DUN connection properties include the server type, network and remote access protocols that will be transmitted, whether data must be encrypted, IP address, and default gateway. Most modern dial-up connections rely on DHCP to assign IP addresses.

- ◆ If incomplete or incorrect information is entered into this configuration, a session can be established, but the client might be unable to send or receive data. If the client is dialing into an ISP's server, the ISP must provide client configuration information.

- ◆ A remote access server is a combination of software and hardware that provides a central access point for multiple users to dial into a LAN or WAN.

- ◆ Different software and hardware combinations can provide remote connectivity. One example is the Windows 2000 Server's **Routing and Remote Access Service (RRAS)**.

OBJECTIVES ON THE JOB

Knowing how to establish and troubleshoot a dial-up networking connection is a basic skill related to knowing how to establish and troubleshoot any other connection to the LAN. Be sure to verify that a proper Physical layer connection exists, that appropriate protocols and clients have been correctly bound to the hardware, and that dial-up networking software and address settings are correct.

PRACTICE TEST QUESTIONS

1. Which of the following must be specified by an ISP for its clients to establish DUN connections to its remote access server?
   - a. default gateway address
   - b. TCP/IP version
   - c. maximum modem port speed
   - d. modem IRQ

2. In order for a Windows 9x machine to send and receive data via DUN to a Windows 2000 Server running RRAS and TCP/IP, to which of the following should the DUN software be bound? Choose all that apply.
   - a. TCP/IP
   - b. IPX/SPX
   - c. Client for NetWare Networks
   - d. Client for Microsoft Networks

3. What option would you choose to create a DUN connection on a Windows 2000 Professional workstation?
   - a. Network and Dial-up Connections, Make New Connection
   - b. Control Panel, Modems, General
   - c. Dial-Up Networking, Make New Connection
   - d. Dial-Up Networking, Properties

4. What does RAS stand for?
   - a. remote authentication service
   - b. remote access service
   - c. remote accounting service
   - d. remote addressing server

5. After you have created a Dial-up Networking connection on a Windows 2000 workstation, how would you indicate that PPP should be used?
   - a. Network Neighborhood, Connection properties, Network, Protocol Type
   - b. Network and Dial-up Connections, Dial-up Connection Properties, Network, Type of dial-up server I am calling
   - c. Network and Dial-up Connections, Options, Security, Protocol
   - d. Network Neighborhood, Dial-up networking, Server type

6. Which of the following transmission systems are commonly used for dial-up networking? Choose all that apply.
   - a. ISDN
   - b. PSTN
   - c. T-1
   - d. SONET

7. Which two of the following can be supported through the Windows DUN connection?
   - a. SNA
   - b. IPX
   - c. IP
   - d. DLC

3.8 Identify the purpose, benefits, and characteristics of using a firewall.

UNDERSTANDING THE OBJECTIVE

Firewalls are combinations of hardware and software that operate at the Network and Transport layers of the OSI model to filter traffic coming in and going out of a network. Firewalls most often run on router hardware, though they can also work on PCs.

WHAT YOU REALLY NEED TO KNOW

◆ A **firewall** is a specialized device (typically a router, but possibly only a PC running special software) that selectively filters or blocks traffic between networks.

◆ A firewall typically involves a combination of hardware (for example, a router) and software (for example, the router's operating system and configuration). It can be placed between two interconnected private networks or between a private network and a public network.

◆ The simplest and most common form of a firewall is a **packet filtering firewall**, which is a router that operates at the Network and Transport layers of the OSI model, examining the data headers to determine whether each packet is authorized to continue to its destination. Packet filtering firewalls are also called **screening firewalls**.

◆ You must customize a packet filtering firewall to make it effective. Specifically, you must configure the firewall to accept or deny certain types of traffic. Some of the criteria a firewall can use to accept or deny data include: source and destination IP addresses; source and destination ports (such as ports that supply TCP/UDP connections, FTP, Telnet, SNMP, and RealAudio); TCP, UDP, or ICMP protocol; whether a packet is the first packet in a new data stream or a subsequent packet; whether the packet is inbound or outbound to or from a private network; whether the packet came from or is destined for an application on your private network.

◆ Because firewalls must be tailored to your network's needs, you cannot simply purchase a firewall and install it between your private LAN and the Internet and expect it to offer much security.

◆ Packet filtering routers cannot distinguish which user is trying to get through the firewall, nor can they determine whether that user is authorized to do so.

OBJECTIVES ON THE JOB

It can take weeks to configure a firewall properly so that it is not so strict that it prevents authorized users from transmitting and receiving necessary data, and not so lenient that you risk security breaches. Also plan to create exceptions to the rules.

PRACTICE TEST QUESTIONS

1. **On which two of the following devices could a firewall run?**
   - a. server
   - b. printer
   - c. hub
   - d. router

2. **At what layers of the OSI model do firewalls operate?**
   - a. Application and Session
   - b. Data Link and Physical
   - c. Transport and Network
   - d. Presentation and Session

3. **Which two of the following criteria could be used to filter traffic on a firewall?**
   - a. IP address
   - b. login ID
   - c. password
   - d. destination port

4. **Which of the following types of networks necessarily uses more than one firewall?**
   - a. WAN
   - b. VPN
   - c. LAN
   - d. MAN

5. **Which of the following protocols can be interpreted by a firewall?**
   - a. SNA
   - b. DLC
   - c. TCP/IP
   - d. NetBEUI

6. **Before a firewall can effectively filter unwanted traffic anywhere on a network, it must be**
   - a. placed between a private and public network.
   - b. configured according to an organization's security needs.
   - c. combined with a proxy server.
   - d. attached to switch on the internal LAN.

7. **A type of firewall that masks the IP addresses of internal devices by replacing them with its own is called a**
   - a. gateway.
   - b. proxy.
   - c. packet filtering firewall.
   - d. screening firewall.

3.9 Identify the purpose, benefits, and characteristics of using a proxy.

UNDERSTANDING THE OBJECTIVE

A proxy service is one that acts on behalf of another service. Typically, a proxy server is used in networking at the border between an internal LAN and an outside WAN (such as the Internet). A proxy server can filter outgoing and incoming requests for data, cache frequently used Web pages, and obscure the specific IP addresses of devices on an internal LAN. Proxy servers are typically used in conjunction with a firewall.

WHAT YOU REALLY NEED TO KNOW

◆ In networking, the term **proxy** means a device or service that acts on behalf of another device or service.

◆ Using a proxy for a server or network device can improve security and the performance of servers, or simplify addressing on a local network.

◆ Proxy servers situated between internal LAN clients and the Internet can improve performance by caching requests and saving them on local disks for future retrieval. This saves subsequent clients who request the same data from having to connect to a remote host on the Internet, thus expediting the retrieval.

◆ A proxy device may determine what type of traffic can be exchanged between clients on an internal LAN and the Internet. The proxy may filter requests to the Internet, for example, or allow only specific IP addresses to send traffic through while denying transmission attempts from other IP addresses.

◆ A proxy server also acts as a way to obscure internal IP addresses. After a client sends its data to the proxy server, the proxy server repackages the data frames that make up the message so that, rather than the workstation's IP address being the source, the proxy server inserts its own IP address as the source.

◆ A proxy server may also allow or deny transmission requests depending on the type of protocol. For instance, a proxy server can prevent outside clients from reaching a server's FTP service, but allow outside clients to access its HTTP service.

◆ If a network uses a proxy server for Web access, each client's browser must be configured to point to the proxy server. All major Internet browser programs contain a space for the proxy server's IP address in their properties or preferences options.

◆ While proxy servers do provide some measure of security, they are usually placed on the network together with a firewall.

OBJECTIVES ON THE JOB

To use a proxy server, clients must be configured to point to the server. This is accomplished by entering a parameter into the client's Web browser. All network operating systems can supply some type of proxy server software, either as part of their program or as an add-on program.

PRACTICE TEST QUESTIONS

1. **How does a proxy server improve Web performance for clients on a private LAN?**
   a. It expedites incoming data to clients because it replaces client IP addresses.
   b. It enables incoming requests to bypass the firewall.
   c. It holds Web requests in a cache so that subsequent requests for those pages can be fulfilled locally.
   d. It enables users to save frequently used bookmarks in a shared location.

2. **Which of the following can a proxy server use as criteria to filter incoming traffic? Choose all that apply.**
   a. IP address
   b. MAC address
   c. protocol
   d. TTL

3. **Which of the following IP ranges is most likely to be found on a small, private network that uses a proxy server to share limited IP addresses?**
   a. 10.09.1.1 – 10.10.1.254
   b. 124.89.33.1 – 124.89.33.230
   c. 222.45.112.1 – 222.45.113.1
   d. 188.30.10.1 – 188.30.10.10

4. **Which of the following is a potential disadvantage to Web caching?**
   a. It takes more time to initially retrieve the Web pages for the cache.
   b. It requires clients to configure an additional parameter in their Web browsers.
   c. It does not guarantee that the cached Web pages are the most current.
   d. It is difficult to configure.

5. **If a client on a local LAN uses an IP address of 100.100.10.2 and the LAN's proxy server uses an IP address of 205.66.127.88, what will the remote host regard as the client's IP address when the client connects to a remote host on the Internet?**
   a. 100.100.10.2
   b. 100.100.10.1
   c. 205.66.127.1
   d. 205.66.127.88

6. **What device is usually found near a proxy server on the network?**
   a. modem
   b. firewall
   c. switch
   d. protocol analyzer

7. **Where in Netscape Communicator could you enter the IP address of a proxy server?**
   a. Edit, Preferences, Advanced, Proxies
   b. Tools, Internet Options, Proxy Server
   c. Tools, Internet Options, Connections, Settings
   d. Edit, Preferences, Advanced, Cache

3.10 Given a scenario, predict the impact of a particular security implementation on network functionality (e.g., blocking port numbers, encryption, etc.).

UNDERSTANDING THE OBJECTIVE

Security is a necessary part of network management. However, with each new access restriction, a network administrator risks limiting authorized access to resources and reducing network performance.

WHAT YOU REALLY NEED TO KNOW

◆ Nearly all data security measures affect network performance and access to network resources. Firewalls add another device through which data must travel, as well as another potential point of failure in the network. Authentication takes a few extra seconds of a user's time. Encryption adds time to the process of assembling and disassembling data frames.

◆ To improve network security, a network administrator could disable—or block—certain well-known ports, such as the FTP ports (20 and 21) in a device's configuration. Blocking ports prevents *any* user from connecting to and completing a transmission through those ports. This technique is useful to further guard against unauthorized access to the network.

◆ One danger of blocking ports is that the administrator may also block communication for authorized users as well. This peril can be avoided by using alternate ports, specifying access restrictions (for example, according to source address) for certain ports, or separating private and public network devices.

◆ **Authentication** is the process of verifying a user's validity and authority on a system; it generally takes place during the login process and, when properly configured, helps keep a network secure. When improperly configured, the authentication process can restrict authorized access. (For example, if you inadvertently limit the time of day an authorized user can log on to the network, the user won't be able to log in.)

◆ **Encryption** is the use of an algorithm to scramble data into a format that can be read only by reversing the algorithm—that is, by decrypting the data. The purpose of encryption is to keep information private. Many forms of encryption exist, with some being more secure than others.

◆ Encryption can limit authorized access if the recipient of encrypted data does not have the proper software, system, credentials, or configuration to decrypt the data.

OBJECTIVES ON THE JOB

The benefits of security measures must be weighed against their impact on authorized network access and network performance. For example, if you have secured the perimeter of a private LAN from outside access, you may decide that your need for data encryption within the organization is insignificant and forego encryption in favor of faster data transmission.

PRACTICE TEST QUESTIONS

1. Which of the following security measures would slow transmissions between two workstations on the same segment? Choose all that apply.
   - a. private key encryption
   - b. firewall
   - c. NOS authentication
   - d. public key encryption

2. Which of the following would potentially prevent authorized users from accessing their LAN resources while they travel?
   - a. private key encryption
   - b. firewall
   - c. NOS authentication
   - d. public key encryption

3. What port(s) should you block in order to prevent insecure FTP transmissions from going to or from your Web server? Choose all that apply.
   - a. 20
   - b. 21
   - c. 22
   - d. 23

4. What is the name of the most highly privileged account on a UNIX or Linux system?
   - a. tree
   - b. admin
   - c. root
   - d. master

5. When using a firewall to guard a private LAN from Internet-based intrusion, how can you still allow authorized users to access the network from home?
   - a. open access to all the router's ports
   - b. allow access to select ports based on incoming IP address
   - c. allow some users to bypass the firewall
   - d. apply time of day restrictions to some of the firewall's ports

6. What pieces of information do all modern NOSs require for authentication?
   - a. user name and password
   - b. first name, last name, and date of birth
   - c. username, IP address, and password
   - d. last name, IP address, and location

7. Ensuring that authorized users have appropriate access to the resources they need is part of an effective security policy. True or false?

OBJECTIVES

3.11   Given a network configuration, select the appropriate NIC and network configuration settings (DHCP, DNS, WINS, protocols, NetBIOS/host name, etc.).

UNDERSTANDING THE OBJECTIVE

Several elements contribute to the proper configuration of a network interface card and network connection. The manufacturer encodes some configuration information on the NIC. The computer's BIOS, if it is Plug and Play compatible, assigns more information such as the IRQ, DMA channel, and I/O address, which can be later changed through the operating system. Network protocols and services are also specified through the O/S.

WHAT YOU REALLY NEED TO KNOW

◆ **Plug and Play (PnP)** technology automatically attempts to configure newly inserted devices such as NICs, monitors, sound cards, etc. In order for PnP to work, the BIOS, hardware, and operating system must all be PnP compatible.

◆ Plug and Play technology can assign IRQ addresses, DMA channels, and I/O addresses. However, even if PnP is used, **device drivers**, the software unique to each component that allows it to communicate with the operating system, must be installed and configured properly through the O/S.

◆ Before a node on a TCP/IP network can exchange data with another node, it must have an IP address, client software, and TCP/IP services bound to its network interface.

◆ **WINS (Windows Internet Naming Service)** translates NetBIOS names into IP addresses, and is only used on NetBIOS networks. If WINS is used, the IP address of the WINS server must be specified in the clients' TCP/IP configuration.

◆ **Dynamic Host Configuration Protocol (DHCP)** automatically assigns IP addresses to clients on a TCP/IP network. Once the DHCP service is specified in an interface's TCP/IP properties, no individual TCP/IP addresses or servers must be specified.

◆ A **host name** is the unique name of a TCP/IP node that adheres to DNS naming conventions. **DNS (Domain Name System)** is a hierarchical way of identifying IP addresses with easily readable names. You can specify DNS server names as well as the node's host name in a client's TCP/IP configuration.

◆ A **domain name** is the name assigned to a group of hosts. A client's domain name should also be specified in that client's TCP/IP properties.

◆ If a client uses NetBIOS, that client will also require a NetBIOS name to uniquely identify it on the network.

OBJECTIVES ON THE JOB

Modifying a network interface's settings, from protocols to host names to services, is one of the most common tasks a network technician performs. It should become second nature.

PRACTICE TEST QUESTIONS

1. Which of the following will allow a networked workstation to obtain an IP address automatically once it logs onto the network?
   a. DNS
   b. WINS
   c. NetBIOS
   d. DHCP

2. What service allows a Windows computer to automatically recognize newly added hardware?
   a. SNMP
   b. PnP
   c. DHCP
   d. WINS

3. What service associates NetBIOS names with IP addresses?
   a. DNS
   b. WINS
   c. NetBIOS
   d. DHCP

4. Which of the following do not have to be specified if a workstation uses DHCP? Choose all that apply.
   a. subnet mask
   b. host name
   c. frame type
   d. IP address

5. What options would you select to configure the TCP/IP protocol on a Windows 2000 server?
   a. Local Area Connection Properties, Network Interface, Internet Protocol (TCP/IP) Properties
   b. Network Neighborhood, Properties, General, TCP/IP
   c. Network Neighborhood, Local Area Connection Properties, TCP/IP protocol Properties
   d. Network and Dial-up Connections, Local Area Connection, Properties, Protocol (TCP/IP)

6. DHCP is selected by default when you install the Windows 2000 Professional operating system. True or false?

7. Which of the following might allow a workstation to exchange data within a private, TCP/IP-based LAN, but prevent it from exchanging data with the Internet?
   a. Its TCP/IP protocol is not bound to its NIC.
   b. Its DHCP settings are incorrect.
   c. Its DNS settings are incorrect.
   d. Its WINS settings are incorrect.

4.1 Given a troubleshooting scenario, select the appropriate TCP/IP utility from among the following:

TRACERT, NETSTAT, AND NBTSTAT

UNDERSTANDING THE OBJECTIVE

Tracert is a utility that sends a packet to a specified host and retrieves information on the path the packet took to reach the host. netstat is a similar utility, but provides information about all connected TCP/IP hosts, including the connections' port numbers and status. Nbtstat is a utility that reveals the NetBIOS names and status of connected devices running NetBIOS over TCP/IP (NBT).

WHAT YOU REALLY NEED TO KNOW

◆ **Tracert** (or traceroute on UNIX systems) is a TCP/IP utility that traces the path of a packet from the originating host to another host. In its simplest form, it displays the number of router hops the packet traverses, those routers' addresses, and how long the packet took to go from one router to the next.

◆ Tracert is most useful for determining where network bottlenecks are occurring. It also indicates whether a host is unreachable.

◆ The most commonly used expression of the tracert command is `tracert Y`, where Y is the IP address or host name of a system.

◆ **Netstat** is a utility that displays specifics about active inbound and outbound TCP/IP connections on a host. When used in its most basic form, netstat displays the address (or host name) of connected systems, and the connected port, the type of Transport layer protocol in use, and the connection status.

◆ Netstat can be used with numerous parameters that supply more information about a host's connections, including statistics for network interfaces and routing tables for active connections.

◆ **Nbtstat** displays information about connected devices running NetBIOS over TCP/IP (NBT). Thus, nbtstat is useful only on Windows-based networks.

◆ Nbtstat can be used with several parameters to discover, for example, the workgroup and domain to which the NetBIOS machine belongs, MAC addresses, IP addresses, and sessions with connected hosts.

◆ Nbtstat is most commonly used with the following syntax to determine the NetBIOS name of a machine: `nbtstat -a X` (where X is the machine's IP address)

OBJECTIVES ON THE JOB

Nbtstat, netstat, and tracert are important utilities included with the TCP/IP software provided with every modern operating system. Although many software developers have created updated versions of these utilities, they are so easy to use that many network administrators don't bother with newer, modified versions.

PRACTICE TEST QUESTIONS

1. Which of the following can reveal the time it takes a packet to reach a host? Choose all that apply.
   - a. Telnet
   - b. PING
   - c. tracert
   - d. netstat

2. Which of the following can reveal hackers connected to a TCP/IP host?
   - a. PING
   - b. Telnet
   - c. tracert
   - d. netstat

3. Which of the following can reveal the number of router hops a packet has taken on its way to a remote host?
   - a. netstat
   - b. PING
   - c. tracert
   - d. Telnet

4. If you are working on the help desk when a user calls and complains about slow connection times to a particular Web site, what utility would you recommend using to locate the performance problem?
   - a. SNMP
   - b. netstat
   - c. nbtstat
   - d. tracert

5. What parameter should be used with the nbtstat command when attempting to determine the NetBIOS name of a machine whose IP address you know?
   - a. -a
   - b. -s
   - c. -i
   - d. -l

6. Suppose you are logged on to the Internet and have accessed the www.yahoo.com Web site. What utility would you use to determine which port on your machine is being used to connect to the Web site?
   - a. nbtstat
   - b. netstat
   - c. Telnet
   - d. tracert

7. The nbtstat utility can easily show whether an IP gateway to the Internet is down. True or false?

4.1 Given a troubleshooting scenario, select the appropriate TCP/IP utility from among the following (continued):

PING

UNDERSTANDING THE OBJECTIVE

The PING command is one of the most commonly used troubleshooting tools. PING sends at least one packet to the specified host and waits for a response. If there is no response, you can assume that the device or its TCP/IP stack is not functioning properly. If there is a response, information about the packets' return, such as the time it took the packets to reach the host, helps in discovering network performance problems.

WHAT YOU REALLY NEED TO KNOW

◆ **Packet Internet Groper (PING)** is a TCP/IP utility that sends at least one packet to a specified address and waits for a response.

◆ PING is a powerful troubleshooting tool. It is primarily used to help determine whether a node on a TCP/IP-based network is connected and responding.

◆ PING assigns a sequence number and time stamp on the packets it sends. Thus, if the response from the device is positive, PING can also detect how long the packets took to return and whether any were damaged in transmission. This can be helpful in troubleshooting network performance problems.

◆ PING is often the first troubleshooting tool used when a client cannot communicate with a server or vice versa.

◆ The syntax of a simple PING command is `ping X`, where X is the IP address or host name of the device. If the host responds, the output contains the following message: `reply from X: bytes=32 time=100 ms TTL=252`, where X is the IP address or host name. The other numbers may vary.

◆ One of the first PING commands to try is ping `127.0.0.1`. This IP address is reserved for the **loopback address**. Use this command to attempt to contact your own device's TCP/IP stack. If this command results in a negative response, chances are your TCP/IP protocol is corrupted or improperly installed.

◆ If the loopback PING test results in a positive response, the next devices to ping include another local host, the default IP gateway, the DNS server, or other critical devices on the network. Pinging different devices can uncover a network bottleneck.

OBJECTIVES ON THE JOB

PING is perhaps the most useful and frequently used utility in the network technician's troubleshooting repertoire. In a situation where a client cannot access a server, PING can help determine where the problem is occurring. In most cases, sufficient information about a downed node or bottleneck can be obtained from the simple PING command. However, in some cases, using one of the many PING parameters provides a necessary troubleshooting clue.

PRACTICE TEST QUESTIONS

1. **What Application layer TCP/IP protocol does PING use to request responses from devices?**
    a. SNMP
    b. SMTP
    c. ICMP
    d. RARP

2. **Which of the following is the loopback address in the IP version 4 addressing scheme?**
    a. 100.100.100.100
    b. 01.01.01.01
    c. 122.0.0.7
    d. 127.0.0.1

3. **What does TTL stand for?**
    a. time to live
    b. time to link
    c. transfer time load
    d. transfer time lost

4. **Which of the following can a PING test indicate? Choose all that apply.**
    a. what type of device is being contacted
    b. whether a packet has been damaged in transit
    c. how many routers a packet has to traverse on its way to a host
    d. how long it takes for a packet to reach a host

5. **In a response to a PING command, which of the following might point to a network congestion problem?**
    a. widely fluctuating TTL values
    b. excessive damaged packets
    c. a hostname listed as the responding node, rather than the IP address you typed
    d. a different host name than that listed in the original PING command

6. **Suppose that a client on a private LAN is connected to the Internet but cannot reach the www.microsoft.com Web page. However, the client's loopback PING test is positive, and the client can reach www.netscape.com. What should you ping next?**
    a. the LAN's gateway router
    b. the nearest core Internet gateway
    c. the ISP's DNS server
    d. www.microsoft.com

7. **What Transport layer protocol does PING rely on?**
    a. TCP
    b. UDP
    c. ARP
    d. FTP

4.1 Given a troubleshooting scenario, select the appropriate TCP/IP utility from among the following (continued):

ARP AND NSLOOKUP

UNDERSTANDING THE OBJECTIVE

ARP can be used as a diagnostic utility to provide information about a computer's ARP table. Nslookup provides information about a network's DNS database.

WHAT YOU REALLY NEED TO KNOW

◆ The ARP utility provides a way of manipulating and obtaining information from a device's ARP table. It can be a valuable troubleshooting tool for discovering the identity of a machine whose IP address you know, or for solving the problem of two machines trying to use the same IP address.

◆ Typing the ARP command alone from a Windows system will display the proper syntax and list of switches available for this command. To return useful data, the ARP command requires at least one switch. For example, typing arp -a provides the entire ARP table for your host. Following is a list of the most popular ARP switches:

-a Displays the ARP table for the host from which you issue the command.

-d Removes an entry from the ARP table; this switch must be followed by the hostname corresponding to the ARP entry that you wish to remove.

-s Adds an entry to the ARP table—in other words, creates a static ARP table entry. This switch must be followed by the hostname and MAC address of the device you wish to add.

◆ The **nslookup** utility allows you to query the DNS database from any computer on the network. Using nslookup, you can find the DNS host name of a device by specifying its IP address, or vice versa. This ability is useful for verifying that a host is configured correctly or for troubleshooting DNS resolution problems.

◆ The nslookup command returns not only the host's IP address, but also provides the primary DNS server name and address that holds the record for this name. To find the host name of a device whose IP address you know, type nslookup *ip_address* and press Enter.

◆ Many other nslookup options exist, and as with other UNIX-based commands, you can find the complete list of them in the nslookup man pages.

◆ The nslookup utility is available on UNIX and Windows 2000 systems.

OBJECTIVES ON THE JOB

Nslookup is a particularly useful tool for determining the IP address of a computer or network whose DNS information you already know.

PRACTICE TEST QUESTIONS

1. **Which of the following commands would you use to add an entry to a computer's ARP table?**
   a. `arp -a`
   b. `arp -d`
   c. `arp -s`
   d. `arp -n`

2. **On which of the following computers could you successfully use the nslookup command to determine the IP address of a host? Choose all that apply.**
   a. a Windows 98 workstation
   b. a Linux workstation
   c. a Windows 2000 Professional workstation
   d. a Macintosh workstation

3. **What command would you type to find out more about the nslookup command on a UNIX server?**
   a. `man nslookup`
   b. `help nslookup`
   c. `nslookup /?`
   d. `type nslookup`

4. **Which of the following pieces of information would you obtain from a simple nslookup command? Choose all that apply.**
   a. the host's IP address
   b. the host's location on the network
   c. the host's primary DNS server
   d. the last time the host successfully responded to an nslookup command

5. **Which of the following commands would display the ARP table for a Windows 2000 server?**
   a. `arp -a`
   b. `arp -d`
   c. `arp -s`
   d. arp -n

6. **What type of output will you receive if you type the ARP command alone at a Windows 2000 command prompt?**
   a. the computer's complete ARP table
   b. information on proper syntax for the ARP command
   c. information on the computer's ARP configuration
   d. nothing

7. **You would type the command `arp student1.class.com` to view the ARP table entry for a computer whose hostname was student1.class.com. True or false?**

4.1 Given a troubleshooting scenario, select the appropriate TCP/IP utility from among the following (continued):

IPCONFIG AND WINIPCFG

UNDERSTANDING THE OBJECTIVE

When run from the command prompt on a Windows 2000 computer, ipconfig displays the IP address, subnet mask, and default gateway address. When run from the command prompt on a Windows 9x machine, winipcfg displays the workstation's MAC address, IP address, subnet mask, and default gateway in the IP Configuration dialog box.

WHAT YOU REALLY NEED TO KNOW

◆ **Ipconfig** is a utility that comes with the Windows NT and Windows 2000 operating systems. When run from a machine's command prompt, it displays the TCP/IP configuration information.

◆ In its simplest form, ipconfig displays only the IP address, subnet mask, and default gateway for each adapter bound to TCP/IP.

◆ To display all the current TCP/IP configuration values, including the IP address, subnet mask, default gateway, and WINS and DNS configuration, use the following command: `ipconfig /all`.

◆ The command `ipconfig /?` displays a help message describing the ipconfig utility.

◆ On systems that use DHCP, you can use the `/release` or `/renew` options with ipconfig to release or renew the IP address of a network adapter.

◆ **Winipcfg** utility, when run from the command prompt, displays TCP/IP settings on Windows 9x workstations.

◆ In its simplest form, winipcfg displays the workstation's MAC address, IP address, subnet mask, and default gateway in the IP Configuration dialog box.

◆ Winipcfg can be used with many different switches to reveal more information about a workstation's TCP/IP settings.

◆ The command `winipcfg /?` displays a help message describing the use of the winipcfg utility.

◆ For more information about TCP/IP settings on a Windows 9x workstation, click the More Info button in the lower-right corner of the IP Configuration dialog box. Other settings you can view include DHCP server IP address, node type, and NetBIOS ID.

◆ On systems that use DHCP, you can use the `/release` or `/renew` options with winipcfg to release or renew the IP address of a network adapter.

OBJECTIVES ON THE JOB

Ipconfig and winipcfg should be familiar to network technicians and even end users. When a user is having connectivity problems, a help desk analyst will often ask the user to type one of these commands to determine basic TCP/IP information.

PRACTICE TEST QUESTIONS

1. Which two of the following can be displayed by typing `ipconfig` at the command prompt of a Windows 2000 Professional workstation?
   a. subnet mask
   b. NIC MAC address
   c. DHCP server address
   d. default gateway address

2. Which command displays the DHCP server address on a Windows 98 computer?
   a. `ipconfig /all`
   b. `ipconfig /?`
   c. `winipcfg /all`
   d. `winipcfg`

3. A user calls and complains of receiving the following error message after trying unsuccessfully to log into the network: "This address in use by station AC:05:20:41:CC:2D." Once you find the Windows 2000 workstation with this MAC address, what do you do to determine its IP address?
   a. Type `ipconfig /release` at the command prompt.
   b. Type `ipconfig /all` at the command prompt.
   c. Type `winipcfg /renew` at the command prompt.
   d. Type `winipcfg /all` at the command prompt.

4. What command would you use to discover the NetBIOS ID of a Windows 98 workstation?
   a. `ipconfig /all`
   b. `winipcfg /all`
   c. `ipconfig /NB`
   d. `winipcfg /NB`

5. How can you determine if a Windows 98 workstation is using DHCP?
   a. Type the `winipcfg` command at the command prompt.
   b. Start, Settings, Control Panel, Network, TCP/IP, DHCP Settings tab.
   c. Start, Settings, Control Panel, Network, TCP/IP, IP Address tab.
   d. Type the `ipconfig /all` command at the command prompt.

6. What is the fastest way to view the IP address of a Windows 2000 workstation?
   a. Type `winipcfg` at the command prompt.
   b. Type `ping 127.0.0.1` at the command prompt.
   c. Type `ipconfig` at the command prompt.
   d. Type `winipcfg /all` at the command prompt.

7. If a Windows NT server has two NICs bound to the TCP/IP protocol, how many subnet masks will be displayed when you type the `ipconfig /all` command?
   a. one
   b. two
   c. three
   d. none

4.1 Given a troubleshooting scenario, select the appropriate TCP/IP utility from among the following (continued):

IFCONFIG

UNDERSTANDING THE OBJECTIVE

Ifconfig is the utility used to reveal and modify TCP/IP properties on a UNIX or Linux computer.

WHAT YOU REALLY NEED TO KNOW

◆ **Ifconfig** is the TCP/IP configuration and management utility used on UNIX systems.

◆ As with ipconfig on Windows 2000 systems and winipcfg on Windows 9x systems, ifconfig enables you to modify TCP/IP settings for a network interface, release and renew DHCP-assigned addresses, or simply check the status of your machine's TCP/IP settings.

◆ Ifconfig also runs when a UNIX system starts in order to establish the TCP/IP configuration for that system.

◆ As with the other operating systems' TCP/IP configuration utilities, ifconfig can be used alone, or it can be used with switches to reveal more customized information. For example, if you wanted to view the TCP/IP information associated with every interface on a device, you could type: `ifconfig -a`. Notice that the syntax of the `ifconfig` command uses a hyphen (-) before some of the switches and no preceding character for other switches.

◆ The following list describes some of the popular switches you may use with ifconfig. To view a complete list of options, you can read the ifconfig man pages:

`-a` Applies the command to all interfaces on a device

`auto-dhcp` Automatically obtains an IP address from a DHCP server for an interface (as a shortcut, you can type simply `dhcp`).

`auto-dhcp release` Releases the DHCP-assigned address from an interface.

`auto-dhcp status` Displays the status of an interface's DHCP configuration.

`down` Marks the interface as unavailable to the network.

`up` Reinitializes the interface after it has been "taken down," so that it is once again available to the network.

OBJECTIVES ON THE JOB

If you work with UNIX or Linux-based servers or clients, you will need to be familiar with the ifconfig command, not only to view the computer's TCP/IP settings, but also to modify them.

PRACTICE TEST QUESTIONS

1. **Which of the following commands would list the TCP/IP settings for all network interfaces on a UNIX server?**
   a. `ifconfig /all`
   b. `ifconfig_renew`
   c. `ifconfig -a`
   d. `ifconfig -?`

2. **Which of the following commands makes a UNIX or Linux computer's network interface unavailable to the rest of the network?**
   a. `ifconfig down`
   b. `ifconfig_release`
   c. `ifconfig -stop`
   d. `ifconfig -disable`

3. **In addition to its use for reporting TCP/IP information, ifconfig also**
   a. initializes TCP/IP services when a UNIX or Linux computer boots up.
   b. releases all DHCP-assigned IP addresses for a UNIX or Linux computer's network interfaces.
   c. responds to BOOTP requests from clients attached to the same segment.
   d. updates the local ARP cache.

4. **Which of the following pieces of information would the `ifconfig-a` command reveal? Choose all that apply.**
   a. subnet mask
   b. MAC address
   c. DHCP server address
   d. username

5. **What is the name of the Windows 2000 utility that provides the same type of information that the UNIX/Linux ifconfig utility provides?**
   a. winipcfg
   b. ifconfig
   c. ipconfig
   d. netipcfg

6. **Which of the following commands would re-enable a network interface on a Linux server after it has been disabled?**
   a. `ifconfig on`
   b. `ifconfig_renew`
   c. `ifconfig -start`
   d. `ifconfig up`

7. **To find out more about using ifconfig, you could type `help ifconfig` at the UNIX shell prompt. True or false?**

4.2 Given a troubleshooting scenario involving a small office/home office network failure (e.g., xDSL, cable, home satellite, wireless, POTS), identify the cause of the failure.

UNDERSTANDING THE OBJECTIVE

Many connectivity options exist for home or small office users, including DSL, ISDN, POTS, cable modem, and home satellite. Each has different throughput and security characteristics and requires different connectivity equipment.

WHAT YOU REALLY NEED TO KNOW

♦ **PSTN**, which stands for **Public Switched Telephone Network**, refers to the network of typical telephone lines and carrier equipment that service most homes. PSTN may also be called **plain old telephone service (POTS)**.

♦ PSTN was originally composed of analog lines and developed to handle voice-based traffic. Now, however, most of the PSTN uses digital transmission through fiber-optic and copper twisted-pair cable, microwave, and satellite connections.

♦ The term **xDSL** refers to all DSL varieties, of which at least eight currently exist. The types of DSL vary in terms of their capacity and maximum line length.

♦ Once inside the customer's office or home, the DSL line must pass through a **DSL modem**, a device that demodulates the signal, extracting the information and passing it on to the computer. The DSL modem may also contain a splitter to separate the line into multiple channels for voice and data signals. The DSL modem may be external to the computer and connect to a computer's Ethernet NIC via UTP cable or to the computer's USB port. Newer DSL modems come in the form of PCI expansion boards. If the DSL bandwidth is to be shared on a LAN, the DSL modem could connect to a connectivity device, such as a hub or router, rather than just one computer.

♦ Cable technology relies on the coaxial cable wiring used for TV signals, which could transmit as much as 36 Mbps downstream and as much as 10 Mbps upstream.

♦ Cable connections require a special **cable modem**, a device that modulates and demodulates signals for transmission and reception via cable wiring. The cable modem then connects to a customer's PC via its USB port or through a UTP cable to a (typically Ethernet) NIC. Alternatively, the cable modem could connect to a connectivity device, such as a hub or router, to supply bandwidth to a LAN rather than just one computer. Before customers can subscribe to cable modem service, their local cable company must have the necessary infrastructure.

OBJECTIVES ON THE JOB

If you are troubleshooting a home or small office connection, be certain to understand the type of service to which the user has subscribed and the carrier's policies on equipment and maintenance.

PRACTICE TEST QUESTIONS

1. **If you subscribed to cable modem service and wanted to connect three PCs to your cable data line, which of the following would you require?**
   a. hub
   b. multiplexer
   c. time domain reflectometer
   d. CSU/DSU

2. **Which of the following offers the lowest throughput for a home office Internet connection?**
   a. ADSL
   b. cable modem
   c. POTS
   d. ISDN

3. **A technology in which the downstream throughput is greater than the upstream throughput is known as:**
   a. symmetrical
   b. asymmetrical
   c. high voltage
   d. frequency modulated

4. **What technique do DSL providers use to achieve extraordinary throughput over typical POTS lines?**
   a. time division multiplexing
   b. frequency division multiplexing
   c. wave division multiplexing
   d. data modulation

5. **Why do cable TV providers have to upgrade their infrastructure before they can provide Internet connectivity to their customers?**
   a. because cable TV infrastructure is not available everywhere
   b. because cable TV infrastructure is not typically capable of bi-directional signaling
   c. because cable TV infrastructure relies at least in part on the PSTN
   d. because cable TV infrastructure is subject to short distance limitations between the customer and the cable company's POP

6. **Which of the following technologies allow data and voice signals to simultaneously share the same line to a home or business? Choose all that apply.**
   a. xDSL
   b. ISDN
   c. cable modem
   d. POTS

7. **Cable modem technology is asymmetrical. True or false?**

4.3 Given a troubleshooting scenario involving a remote connectivity problem (e.g., authentication failure, protocol configuration, physical connectivity), identify the cause of the problem.

UNDERSTANDING THE OBJECTIVE

Remote connectivity requires proper configuration on both the remote client and remote access server. Connectivity can fail due to incompatible protocols, Physical layer (or line) problems, or improper or insufficient authentication.

WHAT YOU REALLY NEED TO KNOW

- ◆ Dial-up networking (DUN) is the most common type of remote access. It typically involves a modem connection to a server through the PSTN.

- ◆ Because dial-up networking requires configuration on both the server and the client side, and relies on public transmission systems, many opportunities for failed or unsatisfactory connectivity arise.

- ◆ A dial-up networking connection may fail due to a Physical layer problem such as a faulty modem, missing or faulty lines or terminators, improperly configured Network layer protocols, improperly configured remote access protocols, typing an incorrect username or password, or a hardware or software failure on the server end of the connection.

- ◆ A dial-up networking connection may suffer poor performance due to a poor quality phone cable connecting the modem to the wall jack (causing crosstalk, for example), loose connections between the modem and the wall jack, the use of Y adapters, splitters, and similar equipment in the path between the modem and the wall jack, or twisted or partially damaged cable. To ensure the fastest connection, configure phone wiring for the most direct path from the computer to the point where the telephone line enters the house. Remove devices from the path to see if something else is causing the problem. Answering machines, Caller ID boxes, cordless phones, and other equipment can create enough interference to impair connectivity.

- ◆ The following settings must be specified in order to ensure remote access connectivity: server type, network and remote access protocols that will be transmitted, whether data must be encrypted, IP address, and default gateway. Most modern dial-up connections rely on DHCP to assign IP addresses.

- ◆ If incomplete or incorrect configuration information is supplied, a session may be established, but the client might be unable to send or receive data.

OBJECTIVES ON THE JOB

If you work on the help desk of a large corporation, chances are you will be asked to help remote users dial into your network. In order to provide the best support, have the specific dial-in configuration parameters for your network close at hand.

PRACTICE TEST QUESTIONS

1. **Which of the following can prevent a dial-up user from connecting to a remote access server? Choose all that apply.**
   a. using a different operating system from the remote access server's operating system
   b. the incorrect hostname specified in the client's TCP/IP properties
   c. a damaged phone line
   d. improper modem configuration

2. **Which of the following remote access protocols is most likely to be used by a Windows 98 client connecting to a Windows NT remote access server?**
   a. L2TP
   b. PPP
   c. PPTP
   d. EIGRP

3. **If you attempt to initiate a dial-up connection from your Windows 2000 Professional workstation and you receive an error saying "There is no dial tone," what should you check?**
   a. the connection between the modem and the wall jack
   b. the quality of the cabling between the carrier's access point to your home and your wall jack
   c. the remote access protocol configuration in your dial-up software
   d. the DHCP server specification in your TCP/IP settings

4. **What is the function of a modem?**
   a. to negotiate the Session layer protocols necessary to establish a connection between a dial-up client and a remote access server
   b. to separate data into frames as it is transmitted from the computer to the PSTN, then strip data from frames as it is received from the PSTN
   c. to encrypt data as it is transmitted from the computer to the PSTN, then decrypt data as it is received from the PSTN
   d. to convert a source computer's digital pulses into analog signals for the PSTN, then convert analog signals back into digital pulses for the destination computer

5. **Why is the maximum capability of a 56 Kbps telephone line never achieved when dialing into a network over the PSTN?**
   a. The PSTN is a shared network, and therefore no single user can reserve its entire bandwidth.
   b. Every telecommunications carrier throttles the amount of bandwidth it will allow consumers, after meeting its own bandwidth needs first.
   c. The FCC limits the use of PSTN lines to 53 Kbps in order to reduce the effects of crosstalk.
   d. At that speed the client and server would not have enough time to complete the authentication process.

6. **If you did not specify your workstation's IP address in your TCP/IP configuration when dialing into your Internet Service Provider, you could not complete a connection. True or false?**

7. **A dial-VPN is a private network that relies on the PSTN. True or false?**

4.4   Given specific parameters, configure a client to connect to the following servers:

UNIX/LINUX, NETWARE, WINDOWS, AND MACINTOSH

UNDERSTANDING THE OBJECTIVE

Each client must have Physical layer components, protocols, and client software appropriate for the network and server that they're logging onto.

WHAT YOU REALLY NEED TO KNOW

- ◆ Most modern servers, including UNIX, Linux, NetWare 5.x, Windows NT and Windows 2000 Server, and Macintosh support and prefer the use of the IP as a Network layer protocol for client connections.

- ◆ In order to connect to a UNIX or Linux server, clients must have a NIC compatible with the network type, the TCP/IP protocol installed, a physical connection to the LAN where the server is located, plus a username and password valid on the server.

- ◆ In order to connect to a Windows 2000 server, clients must have the TCP/IP protocol installed and bound to the network interface, client software (such as Client for Microsoft Networks) appropriate for the server's network operating system, a physical connection to the LAN where the server is located, the appropriate domain controller specified, plus a username and password valid on the server.

- ◆ In order to connect to a NetWare 4.x or 5.x server, clients must have the TCP/IP or IPX/SPX protocol installed and bound to the network interface, client software (such as Novell's Client for NetWare Networks) appropriate for the server's NOS, a physical connection to the LAN, the appropriate NDS context specified, plus a username and password that are valid on the server.

- ◆ Most clients on modern networks run some form of the Windows operating system. If a client runs Windows 9x, the network parameters can be specified by choosing Start/ /Settings/Control Panel/Network. The Network Properties dialog box appears.

- ◆ If a client runs Windows 2000 Professional, the network parameters can be specified by choosing Start/Settings/Network and Dial-up Connections/Local Area Connection Properties. The Local Area Connection Properties dialog box appears.

- ◆ If a client runs the Macintosh operating system, the type of network it uses can be specified by selecting Chooser through the Apple menu.

- ◆ On a UNIX client, network interface and TCP/IP parameters are specified through use of the ifconfig command. A UNIX client logs onto a server from the shell prompt using the `login` command.

OBJECTIVES ON THE JOB

Both novice and experienced networking professionals have to configure clients frequently. Be certain to understand all the configuration requirements for your network, as well as any exceptions to those configurations (for example, settings for older clients).

PRACTICE TEST QUESTIONS

1. **Which of the following would be required for a Windows 2000 Professional workstation to connect to a NetWare 5.1 server? Choose all that apply.**
   a. TCP/IP
   b. IPX/SPX
   c. Client for NetWare Networks
   d. Client for Microsoft Networks

2. **What type of NIC would a Windows 2000 Professional workstation require to connect to a NetWare 5.1 server?**
   a. 10Base2
   b. 10BaseT
   c. 100BaseT
   d. NIC type depends on the network access method and speed, not the server NOS.

3. **When logging onto a Windows 2000 server, what, besides username and password, must the user supply?**
   a. NDS context
   b. domain
   c. workgroup
   d. segment

4. **When logging on to a NetWare 5.1 server, what, besides username and password, must the user supply?**
   a. NDS context
   b. domain
   c. workgroup
   d. segment

5. **What networking component is responsible for prompting the user for his username and password, then communicating this information to a server?**
   a. Network layer protocols
   b. NIC driver
   c. client software
   d. NOS

6. **What menu options would you choose on a Macintosh client to modify its IP address?**
   a. Apple, TCP/IP Control Panel, IP Address
   b. Apple, Network Properties, IP Address
   c. Apple, Chooser, TCP/IP Services, IP Address
   d. Apple, Chooser, Network Properties, TCP/IP Address

7. **A UNIX server can accept connections from any client that can run TCP/IP. True or false?**

4.5 Given a wiring task, select the appropriate tool (e.g., wire crimper, media tester/certifier, punch down tool, tone generator, optical tester, etc.).

UNDERSTANDING THE OBJECTIVE

In order to ensure connectivity and optimal network performance, cables must be constructed and installed properly. Many tools are available to ensure that these two conditions are met.

WHAT YOU REALLY NEED TO KNOW

- ◆ It is important to follow both the manufacturer's installation guidelines and the TIA/EIA standards for making and installing cable to ensure proper connectivity.

- ◆ Many network problems can be traced to poor cable installation techniques. For example, if you don't crimp twisted-pair wires in the correct position in an RJ-45 connector, the cable will fail to transmit or receive data (or both).

- ◆ Installing the wrong grade of cable can either cause your network to fail or render it more susceptible to damage (for example, using typical, inexpensive twisted-pair cable in areas that might be susceptible to fire damage).

- ◆ A **crimper** (or crimping tool) is used to terminate wires in a connector, such as an RJ-45 plug.

- ◆ Basic **cable checkers** determine whether your cabling can provide connectivity. To accomplish this task, they apply a small voltage to each conductor at one end of the cable, and then check whether that voltage is detectable at the other end.

- ◆ A **cable tester** performs the same continuity and fault tests as a cable checker, but may also ensure that the cable is not too long, measure the distance to a fault, measure attenuation, resistance, and crosstalk, and issue pass/fail ratings for different cabling standards.

- ◆ A **time domain reflectometer (TDR)** is a high-end instrument for testing wire cable and connector imperfections.

- ◆ **Optical time domain reflectometers (OTDRs)** issue a light-based signal over a fiber-optic cable. Based on the type of return light signal, the OTDR can gauge the length of the fiber, attenuation, and the location of faulty splices, breaks, connectors, or bends.

- ◆ A **tone generator** is a small electronic device that issues a signal on a wire pair. A **tone locator** is a device that emits a tone when it detects electrical activity on a wire pair. By placing the tone generator at one end of a wire and attaching a tone locator to the other end, you can verify the location of the wire's termination.

OBJECTIVES ON THE JOB

Before leaving the area in which you were working, clean it up. For instance, if you created a new patch cable in a telecommunications room, remove the debris created while splicing the cable.

PRACTICE TEST QUESTIONS

1. **Which of the following tools could determine the location of a faulty splice in a fiber optic link?**
   - a. cable checker
   - b. multimeter
   - c. TDR
   - d. OTDR

2. **What tool is used to terminate wires in an RJ-11 plug?**
   - a. crimper
   - b. pliers
   - c. wire stripper
   - d. allen wrench

3. **Which of the following tools could issue a pass/fail rating for a Category 5 cable?**
   - a. cable checker
   - b. cable tester
   - c. multimeter
   - d. tone generator

4. **If a patch cable allows a workstation to receive data, but not to transmit data, which of the following could be at fault? Choose all that apply.**
   - a. The cable may not have the proper plenum rating.
   - b. The cable may not have a sufficiently high twist ratio for the network on which it is being used.
   - c. The wires responsible for data transmission may not be properly terminated in one of the patch cable's connectors.
   - d. The transmit wire pair may be physically damaged.

5. **Which of the following can be used to determine the location of a particular wire in a bundle of wires?**
   - a. cable checker
   - b. cable tester
   - c. multimeter
   - d. tone generator

6. **What organization has established standards for structured cabling?**
   - a. IEEE
   - b. TIA/EIA
   - c. IETF
   - d. ISO

7. **Which of the following can test whether a UTP cable is transmitting an electrical signal? Choose all that apply.**
   - a. multimeter
   - b. cable checker
   - c. TDR
   - d. OTDR

4.6 Given a network scenario, interpret visual indicators (e.g., link lights, collision lights, etc.) to determine the nature of the problem.

UNDERSTANDING THE OBJECTIVE

Without performing sophisticated diagnostics, you can sometimes tell at a glance whether a hub port is faulty or a server is processing incoming data. On hubs, routers, and NICs of every sort, LEDs indicate whether they are live and accepting/sending transmissions, experiencing excessive errors, or receiving no power.

WHAT YOU REALLY NEED TO KNOW

◆ Viewing the link LEDs on hub ports, NICs, router ports, and other devices can reveal transmission problems.

◆ In general, a steady or blinking green link light (the LED next to a data port) or on a NIC indicates that data is being transmitted to or received from that network interface.

◆ In general, a steady or blinking amber LED next to a port or on a NIC indicates that a problem exists, such as excessive errors.

◆ If an LED next to a port or on a NIC is not lit, the port, NIC, or device is not in use or it is not receiving power.

◆ In general, hubs have another light called the collision LED that will indicate, by blinking, the volume of collisions the hub's (Ethernet) segment is experiencing.

◆ The front of a server or workstation often has a blinking green LED to indicate that data is being written to or read from the hard disk. In addition, another LED indicates in solid green whether the machine is receiving power.

◆ Many types of software, including network operating systems, maintain error logs to indicate whether errors have been generated through the use or attempted use of the software.

◆ While some software programs save error logs as text files, NOSs provide an interface where you can easily view error logs. In Windows 2000 Server, you can display this error log by choosing Event Viewer in the Administrative Tools submenu.

◆ Network operating system logs provide information about attempted security breaches as well as about errors in loading drivers, recognizing hardware, authenticating users, launching applications, and maintenance operations.

OBJECTIVES ON THE JOB

The LED indicator guidelines above are only generalizations. Many models and types of hardware differ. Be sure to read your manuals and understand the meaning of LED lights for your particular equipment.

PRACTICE TEST QUESTIONS

1. **How would a NIC indicate that a workstation is properly connecting to the network?**
   a. Its LED is steady amber.
   b. Its LED is blinking green.
   c. Its LED remains unlit.
   d. Its LED is steady blue.

2. **If the LED on the front of a router is not lit, what can you assume about the router?**
   a. It is properly transmitting and receiving data.
   b. It has at least one faulty port.
   c. It is waiting for incoming data.
   d. It is not receiving power.

3. **Viewing your server's resource statistics, you notice a sudden 50% decrease in a server's available hard disk resources. What might be the cause?**
   a. A user has attempted to back up his workstation to the network.
   b. The server's statistics display program has failed.
   c. The server's RAM has failed and it is relying entirely on virtual memory.
   d. The server is caching large requests for data from the Internet.

4. **How could you determine, by looking at a hub, whether an excessive number of collisions is occurring on that hub's segment?**
   a. Its uplink port LED is rapidly blinking amber.
   b. Its collision LED is rapidly blinking red.
   c. Some of its data port LEDs are rapidly blinking green.
   d. Some of its data port LEDs are not lit.

5. **What tool would you use on a Windows 2000 Server to discover trends in the amount of CPU utilization on the server over the last week?**
   a. Event Viewer
   b. Performance Monitor
   c. Account Utility
   d. Volumes Utility

6. **If one of the LEDs on the front of a server is blinking green, which of the following might be occurring?**
   a. The server is experiencing significant data errors.
   b. The server's hard disk is failing.
   c. The server's hard disk is being written to.
   d. The server's NIC is overtaxed.

7. **Which of the following could help you diagnose a server performance problem? Choose all that apply.**
   a. percent of disk space left on the DATA volume
   b. percent of CPU resources utilized
   c. percent of total users currently logged in
   d. ratio of IP traffic to IPX traffic

4.7 Given output from a diagnostic utility (e.g., tracert, ping, ipconfig, etc.), identify the utility and interpret the output.

UNDERSTANDING THE OBJECTIVE

Each diagnostic utility results in different output that is most useful in different situations. Tracert can help determine the path packets take and how much network congestion is present. Ping can determine whether a TCP/IP host is responding. Ipconfig, winipcfg, and ifconfig can reveal TCP/IP settings for a host.

WHAT YOU REALLY NEED TO KNOW

- The simplest form of the `traceroute` command is `traceroute ip_address`. On computers that use the Windows-based operating system, the proper syntax is `tracert ip_address`. This command will include lines similar to following:

  10   140 ms   114 ms   129 ms   p1-0.chcgil2-cr1.bbnplanet.net [4.24.7.134]

  11   118 ms   131 ms   114 ms   p.xchcgil26-att.bbnplanet.net [4.24.202.6]

- The output of a successful ping command resembles the following:

  Reply from 216.119.103.72: bytes=32 time=173ms TTL=114

  Reply from 216.119.103.72: bytes=32 time=175ms TTL=114

  Reply from 216.119.103.72: bytes=32 time=2240ms TTL=114

  Reply from 216.119.103.72: bytes=32 time=178ms TTL=114

  Ping statistics for 216.119.103.72:

    Packets: Sent = 4, Received = 4, Lost = 0 (0% loss),

  Approximate round trip times in milli-seconds:

    Minimum = 173ms, Maximum = 2240ms, Average = 691ms

- The output of an unsuccessful ping command resembles the following:

  Request timed out.

  Request timed out.

  Request timed out.

  Request timed out.

- The `ipconfig` command on a Windows 2000 computer reveals information about that computer's TCP/IP settings. The `winipcfg` command does the same on a Windows 9x computer, while the `Ifconfig` command does the same on a UNIX or Linux computer.

OBJECTIVES ON THE JOB

In order to properly diagnose network problems using common utilities, you must not only know their syntax, but also be able to interpret their output. For instance, when using a traceroute command, requests between the source and destination may time out, indicating network congestion, but that congestion may be so distant from your network that it is inconsequential.

PRACTICE TEST QUESTIONS

1. **Which of the following would be included in the output of an unsuccessful ping test?**
   a. `Reply from 127.0.0.1: bytes=32 time=173ms TTL=114`
   b. `Packets: Sent = 4, Received = 4, Lost = 0 (0% loss)`
   c. `Request timed out.`
   d. `Host not responding.`

2. **What command would reveal the DHCP server address for a Windows 2000 server?**
   a. `winipcfg /all`
   b. `ifconfig -a`
   c. `ifconfig dhcp`
   d. `ipconfig /all`

3. **How many packets does a simple `ping` command, when used on a Microsoft Windows 2000 Professional client, issue?**
   a. 1
   b. 2
   c. 3
   d. 4

4. **What is the maximum number of router hops a simple traceroute command will traverse?**
   a. 5
   b. 15
   c. 30
   d. 64

5. **Which of the following commands would indicate the number of Ethernet interfaces installed on a UNIX server?**
   a. `ifconfig`
   b. `ipconfig /all`
   c. `ipconfig -a`
   d. `ipnetcfg -a`

6. **What does it mean when lines 15 through 20 of a traceroute command's response read, "Request timed out"?**
   a. The client's traceroute command is not functioning properly.
   b. The network between the source and destination is experiencing congestion.
   c. The destination host is not connected to the network.
   d. The client used improper traceroute command syntax.

7. **How large are the packets issued by the default `ping` command?**
   a. 4 bytes
   b. 16 bytes
   c. 32 bytes
   d. 64 bytes

4.8 Given a scenario, predict the impact of modifying, adding, or removing network services (e.g., DHCP, DNS, WINS, etc.) on network resources and users.

UNDERSTANDING THE OBJECTIVE

Each network requires different services and settings for those services. In order to properly connect to the network, clients must use correct protocol, service, and client software settings.

WHAT YOU REALLY NEED TO KNOW

- ◆ On a TCP/IP network, each device is assigned a host name that is associated with its IP address. Together with its domain name, a host name uniquely identifies that device to other devices on the TCP/IP network.

- ◆ Every TCP/IP network that wants to communicate with the Internet must have a DNS server at its disposal (whether the server is local or remote).

- ◆ DNS is organized hierarchically for the worldwide Internet. If an organization's DNS server does not know the IP address of a requested host, it queries a higher-level DNS server. If that DNS server also doesn't know the IP address of the host, it queries a higher-level DNS server, and so on.

- ◆ In order to communicate over the Internet, clients must specify their DNS server address and hostname in their TCP/IP settings.

- ◆ In order to use the Windows Internet Naming Service (WINS), a client must specify the address or name of its WINS server in its network interface configuration, and the WINS service must be bound to the network interface.

- ◆ DHCP (Dynamic Host Configuration Protocol) is a service that automatically assigns IP addresses to network nodes, as well as other TCP/IP parameters such as default gateway and DNS server addresses. DHCP runs on a server, which may be a dedicated DHCP server or may also act as another type of server.

OBJECTIVES ON THE JOB

Before modifying the network or protocol properties on a client, be certain to understand how your changes might affect service. For example, if you change a workstation's TCP/IP settings from using a static IP address to using DHCP, remember that you no longer need to specify that client's default gateway address, for example, because the DHCP server will supply that information.

PRACTICE TEST QUESTIONS

1. **What options would you choose to configure a Windows 9x client to use DHCP?**
   a. Control Panel, Network, TCP/IP Properties, IP Address tab, Obtain IP address automatically
   b. Network and Dial-up Connections, Local Area Network Properties, Internet Protocol (TCP/IP) Properties
   c. Network Neighborhood Properties, Network Adapter Properties, TCP/IP Properties, DHCP tab
   d. Network and Dial-up Connections, Network Adapter Properties, Internet Protocol (TCP/IP) Properties, DHCP tab

2. **What is the function of a DNS server?**
   a. to supply hosts with a host name when they first log onto the network
   b. to request MAC address information based on a client's IP address
   c. to indicate which hosts are not responding to server requests at any given time
   d. to resolve hostnames with their IP addresses as requested by network nodes

3. **What options would you choose to add an additional DNS server to your Windows 2000 server's DNS settings?**
   a. Start, Settings, Control Panel, Network, TCP/IP Protocol
   b. Network and Dial-up Connections, Local Area Network Properties, Internet Protocol (TCP/IP) Properties, DNS tab
   c. Network and Dial-up Connections, Local Area Network, Properties, Internet Protocol (TCP/IP)
   d. Control Panel, Network, Properties, IP Address tab

4. **On a network that relies on NetWare 5.1 servers, clients need not specify a DNS server address in their TCP/IP configuration. True or false?**

5. **What would probably happen if you removed the binding between the Client for Microsoft Networks and the network adapter on a client that connected to a Windows 2000 server?**
   a. The client would be unable to log onto the network.
   b. The client would be able to log on, but not communicate with the network.
   c. The client would be able to log onto the network and communicate only with nodes running TCP/IP.
   d. The client's network connectivity would not be affected.

6. **What would happen if you uninstalled File and Printer Sharing for Microsoft Networks on a workstation that belonged to a Windows 2000 peer-to-peer network?**
   a. The workstation would not be able to access shared files on any other computer.
   b. Other workstations couldn't access that workstation's shared folders.
   c. No workstations could access another workstation's shared folders.
   d. The workstation would not be able to access its own shared folders.

7. **In addition to the TCP/IP protocol, DHCP services must be bound separately to a client's network interface. True or false?**

4.9 Given a network problem scenario, select an appropriate course of action based on a general troubleshooting strategy that includes the following steps:

ESTABLISH THE SYMPTOMS, IDENTIFY THE AFFECTED AREA, ESTABLISH WHAT HAS CHANGED, AND SELECT THE MOST PROBABLE CAUSE

UNDERSTANDING THE OBJECTIVE

Successful troubleshooters proceed logically and methodically. The steps listed below are the first four steps in the process: identify the symptoms, identify the scope of the problem, establish what has changed in the network, and determine the most likely cause of the problem.

WHAT YOU REALLY NEED TO KNOW

- ◆ Following a logical progression of steps in troubleshooting can help you solve problems faster and more thoroughly than a haphazard approach.
- ◆ Steps to troubleshooting network problems include:
  - Identify the symptoms. Carefully document what you learn from people or systems that alerted you to the problem and keep that documentation handy.
  - Identify the scope of the problem. Is it universal? That is, are all users on the network experiencing the problem at all times? Or is the problem limited to a specific geographic area of the network, to a specific group of users, or to a particular period of time? In other words, is the problem subject to geographic, organizational, or chronological constraints?
  - Establish what has changed on the network. Recent hardware or software changes may be causing the symptoms.
  - Determine the most probable cause of the problem. This determination may include the following techniques:

    Verify user competency

    Recreate the problem and ensure that you can reproduce it reliably.

    Verify the physical integrity of the network connection (such as cable connections, NIC installations, and power to devices), starting at the affected nodes and moving outward toward the backbone.

    Verify the logical integrity of the network connection (such as addressing, protocol bindings, software installations, and so on).

OBJECTIVES ON THE JOB

In addition to the organized method of troubleshooting described above, a general rule for troubleshooting is "Pay attention to the obvious!" While some questions sound too simple to bother asking, don't discount them. If a problem is caused by an obvious error, such as a cable being disconnected, you can save yourself a lot of time by checking cable connections first.

PRACTICE TEST QUESTIONS

1. **You receive a call from a remote user who says the network won't accept her password. How can you determine whether this problem is due to user error or client software?**
   a. Ask her to reboot and try again.
   b. Ask her to change her password.
   c. Try logging in under her user ID from your workstation.
   d. Ask her when the problem began.

2. **Suppose a user can't log on to the network, and you have verified that she is using the right password, that her protocols are correctly installed and bound to the NIC, and that the client software is correctly installed and configured. What should you check next?**
   a. the connection between the hub and the file server
   b. the connection between the workstation's NIC and the wall jack
   c. the connection between the patch panel and the hub
   d. the connection between the hub and the router

3. **A user can retrieve files from the network but cannot print to her usual printer. When you attempt to replicate the problem from a nearby workstation using her login ID, you find that you can print to that printer. What is the most likely cause of her problem?**
   a. The problem is caused by insufficient print server permissions for her user ID.
   b. The problem lies with her workstation's printer drivers.
   c. The problem lies with her workstation's NIC.
   d. The problem lies with her workstation's protocol bindings.

4. **What is a common reason for users typing in an incorrect password?**
   a. They wrote it down wrong.
   b. They have Caps Lock on and the password is case sensitive.
   c. They think they have changed the password when they actually haven't.
   d. They don't believe that it matters what password they enter.

5. **What can testing a problem with a test ID reveal that testing with an administrative ID cannot?**
   a. a problem related to rights
   b. an operator error
   c. a file corruption problem
   d. a network connectivity problem

6. **You try to reproduce a user's inability to launch the MS Excel program from the file server by logging in as the same user on a nearby workstation. Which two of the following could cause misleading results? Choose all that apply.**
   a. The nearby workstation was not identical to the user's workstation.
   b. The nearby workstation was not on the same LAN segment.
   c. The user's profile was different on the nearby workstation.
   d. The nearby workstation did not have an icon for MS Excel on its desktop.

7. **In following the proper series of troubleshooting steps, you should attempt to verify the user's competency before checking his physical and logical connections. True or false?**

4.9   Given a network problem scenario, select an appropriate course of action based on a general troubleshooting strategy that includes the following steps (continued):

IMPLEMENT A SOLUTION, TEST THE RESULT, RECOGNIZE THE POTENTIAL EFFECTS OF THE SOLUTION, AND DOCUMENT THE SOLUTION

UNDERSTANDING THE OBJECTIVE

The next four steps in troubleshooting are to implement a solution, test the solution, determine whether the solution might cause other problems or repercussions, then document the solution so that you and other staff will have a record of your troubleshooting efforts.

WHAT YOU REALLY NEED TO KNOW

- ◆ Once you have followed the first four troubleshooting steps in order to find the cause of a problem, you can follow the next four steps to remedy the problem and help assure that it doesn't happen again or that your solution doesn't cause other problems. These next four troubleshooting steps are listed below.

- ◆ Implement a solution. The following steps will help you implement a safe and reliable solution:
  - Collect all the documentation you have about a problem's symptoms from your investigation and keep it handy while solving the problem.
  - If you're reinstalling software, make a backup of the device's existing software installation. If you're changing hardware, keep the old parts handy. If you are changing the configuration of a program or device, take the time to print out the current configuration.
  - Perform the change, replacement, move, or addition that you believe will solve the problem. Record your actions in detail.

- ◆ Test the solution.

- ◆ Recognize the potential effects of the solution. For example, if you have to reassign IP addresses, how will the change of an IP address on a server affect its clients? Or in another case, if you upgrade the type of client software used on a workstation, how will that affect a user's daily routine?

- ◆ Document the solution. Make sure that both you and your colleagues understand the cause of the problem and how you solved it. This information should be kept in a centrally available repository.

OBJECTIVES ON THE JOB

The logical troubleshooting steps provided here are only guidelines. Experience in your network environment may prompt you to follow the steps in a different order or to skip certain steps entirely.

PRACTICE TEST QUESTIONS

1. **What should you be certain to do as you replace a faulty memory chip on a server?**
   a. Call the server manufacturer to notify your vendor about the faulty chip.
   b. Keep the faulty chip in a safe place in case the solution doesn't work.
   c. Keep the server powered on.
   d. Write the date and the nature of the problem on the chip.

2. **What facts should always be recorded in the documentation of a network problem? Choose all that apply.**
   a. when the problem occurred
   b. the user's password
   c. the user's date of hire
   d. how the problem was resolved

3. **You solved a user's problem by modifying his client's ODBC driver properties. When he asks you to explain why it wasn't working before, how do you respond?**
   a. Tell him that he was missing a driver.
   b. Tell him that he wasn't logging on correctly.
   c. Tell him that it didn't matter because it's fixed now.
   d. Tell him that you had to modify a parameter in his database connection.

4. **While troubleshooting a campus network performance problem, you discover that the Music Hall's wiring consists of largely CAT3 cables. What do you do?**
   a. Tell users that they will always have poor network performance.
   b. Verify the extent of the problem, notify your colleagues that this building contains older wiring, and schedule a time to upgrade it.
   c. Modify all client software to run only at lower transmission rates.
   d. Check the hubs in the building to make sure they are compatible.

5. **What is the name for the type of software that holds information about technical support requests, problems, and solutions?**
   a. network management software
   b. clustering software
   c. call tracking software
   d. network monitoring software

6. **What should you have in hand when trying to reproduce a difficult NIC problem?**
   a. the network operating system CDs
   b. the disaster recovery plan
   c. the backup schedule
   d. the NIC documentation

7. **What should you do just before applying a patch to your NOS software? Choose all that apply.**
   a. backup the current NOS installation
   b. call the NOS manufacturer to ensure that you have the latest patch
   c. evaluate other NOS options
   d. prevent users from logging into the server

4.10   Given a troubleshooting scenario involving a network with a particular physical topology (i.e., bus, star/hierarchical, mesh, ring, or wireless) and including a network diagram, identify the network area affected and the cause of the problem.

UNDERSTANDING THE OBJECTIVE

Each physical topology has different cabling requirements and access methods, thus presenting different potential failures. Simple bus and ring physical topologies are the least fault tolerant.

WHAT YOU REALLY NEED TO KNOW

- ◆ A bus topology consists of a single channel shared by all nodes on the network.
- ◆ The bus topology is the least fault-tolerant of any topology, because one break in the cable can take down the entire network, and bus topology faults are difficult to find.
- ◆ In a ring topology each node is connected to the two nearest nodes so that the entire network forms a circle. Data are transmitted in one direction (unidirectionally) around the ring. Each workstation accepts and responds to packets addressed to it, then forwards the other packets to the next workstation in the ring.
- ◆ A disadvantage of the ring topology is that, as with the bus topology, one defective node can take down the network.
- ◆ Star topologies are more fault-tolerant and provide better performance than bus or ring topologies. A single cable or node fault will not immobilize a star-wired network.
- ◆ Full mesh topologies are the most expensive physical topologies because they require the most equipment, connectivity, setup, and maintenance. However, they are also the most fault-tolerant physical topologies.
- ◆ A less expensive, yet still fault-tolerant alternative to full-mesh topologies is a partial mesh topology, in which only some of the nodes on a network are directly connected to other nodes.
- ◆ Nodes on a wireless network use special NICs with infrared or radio frequency transmitters to issue signals to a base station.
- ◆ When a large number of mobile clients are used, or when clients must communicate over a large geographical range, the number of access points must increase.
- ◆ Broadcast transmission is susceptible to eavesdropping. Thus, security is a concern in wireless networking. Using spread-spectrum radio frequency transmission is one way of improving wireless communications security.

OBJECTIVES ON THE JOB

Because star-based physical topologies are the most fault tolerant, these form the basis of most modern LANs. When working with such LANs, bear in mind segment and network length restrictions.

PRACTICE TEST QUESTIONS

1. **Which of the following physical topologies is the most fault-tolerant?**
   a. bus
   b. ring
   c. wireless
   d. full mesh

2. **On which of the following networks could a single node failure disable an entire segment? Choose all that apply.**
   a. bus
   b. ring
   c. wireless
   d. full mesh

3. **In general, which of the following topologies is most expensive?**
   a. bus
   b. ring
   c. wireless
   d. full mesh

4. **What type of symptom might indicate that a bus network has not been properly terminated?**
   a. Users cannot log onto the network.
   b. Network performance is very slow.
   c. New nodes cannot be added to the network.
   d. Data in shared folders is corrupted.

5. **A user on a wireless network complains that he occasionally cannot log onto the network. Which of the following might be at fault?**
   a. His laptop is not running the proper protocols.
   b. He is roaming out of range of network access points.
   c. His NIC is not bound to the client services.
   d. He is using an incompatible version of the client software.

6. **If all of the workstations in a workgroup on a star network lose connectivity to the network, which of the following is the most likely cause?**
   a. The workgroup hub has failed.
   b. The workstation NICs have all failed.
   c. One workstation in the workgroup has failed.
   d. One patch cable in the workgroup has failed.

7. **What would happen on a simple ring network if one of the users turned off her workstation?**
   a. Only her workstation would lose network connectivity.
   b. None of the workstations would lose network connectivity.
   c. The workstations on either side of hers in the ring would lose network connectivity.
   d. The entire network would fail.

OBJECTIVES

4.11   Given a network troubleshooting scenario involving a client connectivity problem (e.g., incorrect protocol/client software/authentication configuration, or insufficient rights/permissions), identify the cause of the problem.

UNDERSTANDING THE OBJECTIVE

Client connectivity depends on many factors: a physical connection to the network, proper protocols, proper network interface configuration, logon rights and permissions to resources.

WHAT YOU REALLY NEED TO KNOW

◆ It's important to understand the login process for troubleshooting purposes. Both the client software and the network operating system participate in logging a client on to the server.

◆ First, the user launches the client software from his desktop. Then he enters his user name and password and presses the Enter key. At this point a service on the client workstation (called the **redirector**) intercepts the request to determine whether it should be handled by the client or by the server. Once the client's redirector decides that the request is meant for the server, the client transmits this data over the network to the server. At the server, the network operating system receives the client's request and attempts to match the user name to a name in its user database. If it is successful, it then compares the password associated with that user name to the password supplied by the user. If the passwords match, the NOS responds to the client by granting it access to resources on the network, according to limitations specified for this client.

◆ Insufficient permissions will result in a client being unable to access certain resources on the server.

◆ Account errors will result in a client being unable to log onto the network (for example, if a user's account has been disabled).

◆ Physical connection faults, such as a severed cable or missing cable, will result in an inability to connect to the network.

◆ NIC configuration errors may manifest as an inability to log onto the network or an inability to exchange data with certain parts of a network.

◆ Many client connectivity problems can be traced to user errors. Before changing software or hardware, verify that the user is performing operations correctly.

OBJECTIVES ON THE JOB

Perhaps one of the most common problems you'll address as a network troubleshooter is an inability to access the network. This problem can be caused by a variety of failures (either hardware or software) and situations (for example, user error or changes in the network infrastructure). Asking the right questions will help you find the problem and solve it faster.

PRACTICE TEST QUESTIONS

1. **A user complains that she can log onto the network, but cannot retrieve a spreadsheet file in a colleague's data directory. Which of the following might be the cause of the problem?**
   a. The patch cable between her workstation and the wall jack is faulty.
   b. Her user account has been disabled.
   c. She does not have sufficient rights to access the file.
   d. Her network interface's protocol settings are incorrect.

2. **A user complains that suddenly, this morning, he cannot log onto the network at all. Which of the following might be the cause of the problem? Choose all that apply.**
   a. The patch cable between his workstation and the wall jack has been removed.
   b. His user account does not have sufficient privileges.
   c. His protocols have been uninstalled.
   d. His client software is suffering performance problems.

3. **What is the name of the service that determines whether a request should be handled by a client or the server in client/server networking?**
   a. redirector
   b. reflectometer
   c. requestor
   d. reflexor

4. **A user complains that he receives a "password incorrect" message when he attempts to log onto the network. Which of the following might be the cause of the problem? Choose all that apply.**
   a. He is typing his password incorrectly.
   b. He is using an incompatible version of the client software.
   c. His NIC is experiencing intermittent packet loss.
   d. He is attempting to log onto the wrong server.

5. **Using the wrong frame type on an Ethernet network would not prevent a client from logging onto the network. True or false?**

6. **If you are on the phone helping a user with a problem, what should you do to gain more information that will allow you to diagnose her problem?**
   a. ask her to reboot
   b. attempt to replicate the problem at your workstation
   c. ask her to read the error message that appears on her screen
   d. modify her user account properties so that she has increased privileges

7. **If all users within your organization are unable to log onto the network, what can you probably conclude about the scope of the problem?**
   a. It is limited to one network segment.
   b. It affects the entire network.
   c. It is limited to a particular time of day.
   d. It is a result of a regional Internet failure.

OBJECTIVES

4.12 Given a network troubleshooting scenario involving a wiring/infrastructure problem, identify the cause of the problem (e.g., bad media, interference, network hardware).

UNDERSTANDING THE OBJECTIVE

Wiring and infrastructure problems occur at or below the Physical layer of the OSI Model. Because most LANs are dependent on many different lengths of wiring scattered across a building and installed and maintained by different people, the potential for wiring errors is great.

WHAT YOU REALLY NEED TO KNOW

♦ If a segment or network length exceeds the IEEE maximum standards for a particular network type, the segment or network will experience an excessive number of late collisions, resulting in difficulty connecting to the network or exchanging data over the network. The solution is to reconfigure the topology so that the network and segment lengths comply with IEEE maximums.

♦ Noise affecting a signal (from EMI or RFI sources, improper grounding, or crosstalk) will result in an excessive number of packet errors such as runts, giants, and damaged frame check sequence fields. Users recognize this problem as intermittent difficulty in connecting to the network or exchanging data over the network. The solution is to remove sources of EMI or RFI from cabling areas, encase cables in conduit, or reroute cabling if necessary. If this is not possible, consider changing cable types to one with better resistance to noise. Ensure proper grounding on coaxial cable networks. Reduce crosstalk on twisted pair networks by using wires with a higher twist ratio and making sure cables are not bundled too tightly.

♦ Damaged cables (for example, crimped, bent, nicked, or partially severed cables) will result in an excessive number of normal collisions or packet errors (such as giants and runts), but few late collisions. Users recognize this problem as frequent difficulty connecting to or exchanging data with the network, very poor network response time, or a complete inability to connect to the network. Replace the faulty cable.

♦ Improper terminations, faulty connectors, loose connectors, or poorly crimped connections result in an excessive number of normal collisions and packet errors (such as giants and runts), but few late collisions. Users will recognize this as frequent problems connecting to or exchanging data with the network, very poor network response time, or a complete inability to connect to the network. Replace the connector with a good connector, reseat the loose connector, or correct the termination error.

OBJECTIVES ON THE JOB

By some estimates, more than half of all network problems occur at the Physical layer of the OSI Model, which includes cabling, network adapters, repeaters, and hubs. Because Physical layer faults are so common, you should be thoroughly familiar with the symptoms of such problems.

PRACTICE TEST QUESTIONS

1. **Which of the following symptoms could point to a faulty terminator? Choose all that apply.**
   a. garbled data in a spreadsheet or document file
   b. slow network response to requests for data
   c. an excessive number of late collisions
   d. inability to log onto the network

2. **What is the most practical way to resolve a problem with a network segment that exceeds the IEEE maximum length?**
   a. Move the connectivity devices to different telecommunications closets so the segment length is reduced.
   b. Separate the segment into two shorter segments by adding a connectivity device in between.
   c. Move the nodes on the segment closer to their central connectivity device.
   d. Recable the entire network to make certain no segments exceed the IEEE maximum length.

3. **Which of the following problems could result in excessive number of damaged packets on an Ethernet network?**
   a. excessive network lengths
   b. a severed patch cable
   c. a hub that is not powered on
   d. crosstalk

4. **At what layer of the OSI Model does EMI affect a signal?**
   a. Physical layer
   b. Data Link layer
   c. Network layer
   d. Transport layer

5. **A poorly crimped RJ-45 connector on a workstation's patch cable could result in the inability for a user to log onto the network. True or false?**

6. **What type of tool can help determine at what point in a cable a physical fault has occurred?**
   a. multimeter
   b. cable checker
   c. tone locator
   d. time domain reflectometer

7. **Which of the following is the best way to shield cables from EMI if they cannot be rerouted or replaced?**
   a. wrap them in electrician's tape
   b. encase them in a conduit
   c. erect aluminum shields between the cable runs and the EMI source(s)
   d. increase the temperature of the area through which the cables are routed

Domain 1.0 Media and Topologies
Objective 1.1 - Star/hierarchical topology
Practice Questions:
1. a
2. b
3. d
4. c
5. c
6. b
7. d

Objective 1.1 - Bus topology
Practice Questions:
1. c
2. a
3. c and d
4. d
5. b
6. a
7. c

Objective 1.1 - Mesh topology
Practice Questions:
1. b
2. b
3. c
4. c and d
5. c
6. b
7. true

Objective 1.1 - Ring topology
Practice Questions:
1. a and c
2. a
3. d
4. d
5. a
6. c
7. d

Objective 1.1 - Wireless topology
Practice Questions:
1. d
2. c
3. a
4. d
5. true
6. c
7. d

Objective 1.2 - 802.2 (LLC) standards
Practice Questions:
1. b
2. d
3. a
4. b and c
5. d
6. false
7. a

Objective 1.2 - 802.3 (Ethernet) standards
Practice Questions:
1. d
2. a and b
3. c
4. a
5. c
6. a, b, and d
7. d

Objective 1.2 - 802.5 (Token Ring) standards
Practice Questions:
1. b and d
2. c
3. b, c, and d
4. b
5. d
6. c
7. c

Objective 1.2 - 802.11b – Wireless standards
Practice Questions:
1. a
2. c
3. a
4. b
5. a
6. b
7. b

Objective 1.2 - FDDI
Practice Questions:
1. b
2. d
3. d
4. a
5. d
6. a
7. b

Objective 1.3 - Ethernet (802.3) standards
Practice Questions:
1. a and c
2. d
3. c
4. a and b
5. c and d
6. b
7. c and d

Objective 1.3 - 10BaseT
Practice Questions:
1. a
2. a and b
3. d
4. c
5. b
6. c
7. b

Objective 1.3 - 100BaseT and 100BaseTX
Practice Questions:
1. b
2. c
3. c
4. c
5. b
6. a and b
7. b

Objective 1.3 - 10Base2
Practice Questions:
1. d
2. b
3. c
4. c
5. a
6. a
7. d

Objective 1.3 - 10Base5
Practice Questions:
1. b
2. d
3. a
4. d
5. a
6. a
7. c

Objective 1.3 - 100BaseFX
Practice Questions:
1. c
2. d
3. b
4. b
5. d
6. a
7. d

Objective 1.3 - Gigabit Ethernet
Practice Questions:
1. d
2. b
3. a
4. d
5. d
6. c
7. d

Objective 1.4 - RJ-11, RJ-45, AUI, and BNC connectors
Practice Questions:
1. b
2. a
3. c
4. b
5. d
6. b
7. a

Objective 1.4 - SC and ST connectors
Practice Questions:
1. a
2. d
3. b
4. true
5. d
6. b
7. false

Objective 1.5 - Media type and connectors
Practice Questions:
1. c and d
2. a
3. a
4. b
5. b
6. b
7. b and c

Objective 1.6 - Hubs

Practice Questions:

1. c
2. c
3. a
4. d
5. a
6. a and d
7. c

Objective 1.6 - Switches and Bridges

Practice Questions:

1. c
2. a
3. d
4. b
5. a
6. c
7. b

Objective 1.6 - Routers

Practice Questions:

1. b
2. a
3. d
4. b and d
5. a
6. d
7. a

Objective 1.6 - Gateways and CSU/DSUs

Practice Questions:

1. b
2. c
3. a and d
4. a and b
5. d
6. b
7. c

Objective 1.6 - Network Interface Cards/ISDN adapters/system area network cards and wireless access points

Practice Questions:
1. d
2. c
3. b and d
4. a
5. b
6. a
7. a and d

Objective 1.6 - Modems

Practice Questions:
1. c
2. d
3. c
4. a
5. a
6. c
7. b

Domain 2.0 Protocols and Standards

Objective 2.1 - Identify a MAC address

Practice Questions:
1. b
2. c
3. a
4. c
5. b
6. c
7. a

Objective 2.2 - Layers 1 through 3 of the OSI Model

Practice Questions:
1. a
2. c
3. b
4. c
5. d
6. b
7. a

Objective 2.2 - Layers 4 through 7 of the OSI model
Practice Questions:
1. b
2. b
3. c
4. a
5. d
6. a
7. c

Objective 2.3 - TCP/IP
Practice Questions:
1. d
2. c
3. d
4. a
5. b
6. b
7. b

Objective 2.3 - IPX/SPX
Practice Questions:
1. b
2. c
3. b
4. b
5. b
6. a
7. d

Objective 2.3 - NetBEUI
Practice Questions:
1. c
2. d
3. d
4. a
5. b
6. a
7. b

Objective 2.3 - AppleTalk

Practice Questions:

1. b
2. c
3. a
4. a, b, and c
5. d
6. a and b
7. b

Objective 2.4 - OSI layers for hubs, switches, bridges, routers, network interface cards

Practice Questions:

1. b and c
2. c
3. b
4. d
5. c
6. b
7. a

Objective 2.5 - IP, TCP, and UDP

Practice Questions:

1. b
2. a
3. d
4. b and c
5. b and d
6. a
7. c

Objective 2.5 - FTP and TFTP

Practice Questions:

1. d
2. c
3. a
4. a
5. b
6. d
7. d

Objective 2.5 - SMTP, POP3, and IMAP4
Practice Questions:
1. c
2. c
3. a
4. d
5. a
6. a
7. c

Objective 2.5 - HTTP and HTTPS
Practice Questions:
1. d
2. a
3. b
4. a and d
5. c
6. d
7. a

Objective 2.5 - TELNET
Practice Questions:
1. d
2. d
3. a
4. c and d
5. c
6. a
7. a

Objective 2.5 - ICMP, ARP, and NTP
Practice Questions:
1. a and c
2. a and d
3. a
4. b
5. c
6. c
7. b

Objective 2.6 - TCP/UDP ports
Practice Questions:
1. c
2. c
3. a
4. a
5. d
6. d
7. b

Objective 2.7 - DHCP and BOOTP
Practice Questions:
1. c
2. d
3. b
4. b and c
5. d
6. a
7. c

Objective 2.7 - DNS and WINS
Practice Questions:
1. c
2. a
3. c and d
4. c
5. a
6. a
7. a

Objective 2.7 - NAT/ICS
Practice Questions:
1. b
2. d
3. a
4. a and c
5. c
6. a
7. d

Objective 2.7 - SNMP
Practice Questions:

1. c
2. b
3. d
4. a and d
5. a
6. a and c
7. b

Objective 2.8 - IP addresses and their default subnet masks
Practice Questions:

1. a
2. c
3. c
4. d
5. a
6. a
7. c

Objective 2.9 - Subnetting and default gateways
Practice Questions:

1. d
2. c
3. c
4. c
5. d
6. c
7. a

Objective 2.10 - Public vs. private networks
Practice Questions:

1. a
2. b
3. d (It could be argued that answer c is also correct; however, if the company has a firewall, it is likely that public access is restricted.)
4. c
5. b
6. a
7. true

Objective 2.11 - Packet switching vs. circuit switching
Practice Questions:
1. a
2. b
3. b
4. b
5. d
6. d
7. a

Objective 2.11 - ISDN
Practice Questions:
1. c
2. b
3. a
4. c
5. c
6. a
7. d

Objective 2.11 - FDDI and ATM
Practice Questions:
1. d
2. b
3. b
4. c
5. c
6. a
7. d

Objective 2.11 - Frame Relay
Practice Questions:
1. b
2. d
3. a
4. b
5. d
6. c
7. true

Objective 2.11 - SONET/SDH and OCx
Practice Questions:
1. d
2. c
3. d
4. a
5. b
6. c
7. c

Objective 2.11 - T1/E1 and T3/E3
Practice Questions:
1. c
2. a
3. b
4. b
5. c
6. a
7. a

Objective 2.12 - RAS and ICA
Practice Questions:
1. a and d
2. b
3. a
4. b
5. d
6. a
7. false

Objective 2.12 - PPP and PPTP
Practice Questions:
1. d
2. a and c
3. c
4. c
5. b
6. a
7. d

Objective 2.13 - IPSec and L2TP
Practice Questions:
1. c
2. b
3. c
4. c
5. a
6. d
7. a

Objective 2.13 - SSL
Practice Questions:
1. d
2. b
3. c
4. a
5. d
6. a
7. c

Objective 2.13 - Kerberos
Practice Questions:
1. a
2. a, b, and c
3. d
4. b, c, and d
5. c
6. b
7. d

Domain 3.0 Network Implementation

Objective 3.1 - UNIX/Linux server operating system
Practice Questions:
1. d
2. a
3. c
4. c
5. d
6. a
7. b

Objective 3.1 – NetWare server operating system

Practice Questions:
1. d
2. b
3. d
4. b
5. c
6. a
7. a

Objective 3.1 – Windows server operating systems

Practice Questions:
1. a
2. c
3. b
4. b
5. a
6. b
7. d

Objective 3.1 – Macintosh server operating systems

Practice Questions:
1. b, c, and d
2. b
3. a
4. d
5. true
6. c
7. b

Objective 3.2 - UNIX/Linux clients

Practice Questions:
1. b
2. c
3. b
4. d
5. d
6. b
7. false

Objective 3.2 – Windows clients
Practice Questions:

1. c
2. d
3. a and b
4. d
5. b
6. a
7. a

Objective 3.2 – Macintosh clients
Practice Questions:

1. b
2. a
3. c
4. b
5. d
6. d
7. d

Objective 3.3 - VLANs
Practice Questions:

1. c
2. b
3. a, c, and d
4. d
5. a, b ,c and d
6. false
7. d

Objective 3.4 - Network attached storage
Practice Questions:

1. b
2. d
3. c
4. d
5. true
6. a
7. a, b, c, and d

Objective 3.5 - Fault tolerance
Practice Questions:
1. a
2. a
3. a
4. b
5. a, b, c, and d
6. b
7. d

Objective 3.6 - Disaster recovery
Practice Questions:
1. a, b, and d
2. b
3. d
4. a and b
5. b
6. false
7. true

Objective 3.7 - Configure a remote connectivity connection
Practice Questions:
1. a
2. a and d
3. a
4. b
5. b
6. a and b
7. b and c

Objective 3.8 - Firewalls
Practice Questions:
1. a and d
2. c
3. a and d
4. a
5. c
6. b
7. b

Objective 3.9 - Proxies

Practice Questions:

1. c
2. a and b
3. a
4. b
5. d
6. b
7. c

Objective 3.10 - Impact of a security implementation

Practice Questions:

1. a and d
2. b
3. a and b
4. c
5. b
6. a
7. true

Objective 3.11 - NIC and network configuration settings

Practice Questions:

1. d
2. b
3. b
4. a and d
5. d
6. true
7. c

Domain 4.0 Network Support

Objective 4.1 - Tracert, netstat, and nbtstat

Practice Questions:

1. b and c
2. d
3. c
4. d
5. a
6. b
7. false

Objective 4.1 - Ping
Practice Questions:
1. c
2. d
3. a
4. b and d
5. a
6. d
7. b

Objective 4.1 - Arp and nslookup
Practice Questions:
1. c
2. b and c
3. a
4. a and c
5. a
6. b
7. a

Objective 4.1 - Ipconfig and winipcfg
Practice Questions:
1. a and d
2. c
3. b
4. b
5. c
6. c
7. b

Objective 4.1 - Ifconfig
Practice Questions:
1. c
2. a
3. a
4. a and b
5. c
6. d
7. false

Objective 4.2 - Cause of a small office/home office network failure
Practice Questions:
1. a
2. c
3. b
4. d
5. b
6. a, b, and c
7. true

Objective 4.3 - Cause of a connectivity problem
Practice Questions:
1. c and d
2. b
3. a
4. d
5. c
6. false
7. true

Objective 4.4 - Configure clients for UNIX/Linux, NetWare, Windows, and Macintosh
Practice Questions:
1. a and c
2. d
3. b
4. a
5. c
6. a
7. true

Objective 4.5 - Select the appropriate tool
Practice Questions:
1. d
2. a
3. b
4. c and d
5. d
6. b
7. a, b, and c

Objective 4.6 - Interpret visual indicators

Practice Questions:

1. b
2. d
3. a
4. b
5. b
6. c
7. a, b, and c

Objective 4.7 - Diagnostic utilities

Practice Questions:

1. c
2. d
3. d
4. c
5. a
6. b
7. c

Objective 4.8 - Modifying, adding, or removing network services

Practice Questions:

1. a
2. d
3. c
4. false
5. a
6. b
7. false

Objective 4.9 - Establish a problem's symptoms and affected area, establish what has changed, and select a probable cause

Practice Questions:

1. c
2. b
3. b
4. b
5. a
6. a and b
7. true

Objective 4.9 - Implement, test, recognize effects of, and document a solution

Practice Questions:

1. b
2. a and d
3. d
4. b
5. c
6. d
7. a and d

Objective 4.10 - Identify network area affected and cause of the problem

Practice Questions:

1. d
2. a and b
3. d
4. b
5. b
6. a
7. d

Objective 4.11 - Identify the cause of a connectivity problem

Practice Questions:

1. c
2. a and c
3. a
4. a and d
5. false
6. c
7. b

Objective 4.12 - Identify the cause of a wiring/infrastructure problem

Practice Questions:

1. b and d
2. b
3. d
4. a
5. true
6. d
7. b

GLOSSARY

1 gigabit Ethernet — An Ethernet standard for networks that achieve 1-Gbps maximum throughput. 1 Gigabit Ethernet runs (preferably) on fiber, but may also run over twisted pair. It is primarily used for network backbones.

1 gigabit per second (Gbps) — 1,000,000,000 bits per second.

1 kilobit per second (Kbps) — 1000 bits per second.

1 megabit per second (Mbps) — 1,000,000 bits per second.

1 terabit per second (Tbps) — 1,000,000,000 bits per second.

10 Gigabit Ethernet — A standard currently being defined by the IEEE 802.3ae committee. 10 Gigabit Ethernet will allow 10-Gbps throughput and will include full-duplexing and multimode fiber requirements.

100BaseFX — A Physical layer standard for networks that specifies baseband transmission, multimode fiber cabling, and 100-Mbps throughput. 100BaseFX networks have a maximum segment length of 400 meters. 100BaseFX may also be called "Fast Ethernet."

100BaseT — A Physical layer standard for networks that specifies baseband transmission, twisted-pair cabling, and 100-Mbps throughput. 100BaseT networks have a maximum segment length of 100 meters and use the star topology. 100BaseT is also known as Fast Ethernet.

100BaseT4 — A type of 100BaseT network that uses all four wire pairs in a twisted-pair cable to achieve its 100-Mbps throughput. 100BaseT4 is not capable of full-duplex transmission and requires CAT3 or higher media.

100BaseTX — A type of 100BaseT network that uses two wire pairs in a twisted-pair cable, but uses faster signaling to achieve 100-Mbps throughput. It is capable of full-duplex transmission and requires CAT5 or higher media.

100BaseVG (100VG-AnyLAN) — A Physical layer standard for networks that specifies baseband transmission, twisted-pair media, and 100-Mbps throughput. 100BaseVG uses a different and more efficient method than 100BaseT for allowing nodes to transmit data on the media. However, 100BaseVG is rarely used.

10Base2 — See *Thinnet*.

10Base5 — See *Thicknet*.

10BaseF — A Physical layer standard for networks that specifies baseband transmission, multimode fiber cabling, and 10-Mbps throughput. 10BaseF networks have a maximum segment length of 1000 or 2000 meters, depending on the version, and employ a star topology.

10BaseT — A Physical layer standard for networks that specifies baseband transmission, twisted pair media, and 10-Mbps throughput. 10BaseT networks have a maximum segment length of 100 meters and rely on a star topology.

802.3 — The IEEE standard for Ethernet networking devices and data handling.

802.4 — The IEEE standard for Token Bus networking devices and data handling.

802.5 — The IEEE standard for Token Ring networking devices and data handling.

802.6 — The IEEE standard for Metropolitan Area Network (MAN) networking.

802.10 — The IEEE standard that describes network access controls, encryption, certification, and other security topics.

802.11 — The IEEE standard for wireless networking.

A

A+ — Professional certification established by CompTIA that verifies knowledge about PC operation, repair, and management.

access method — A network's method of controlling how network nodes access the communications channel. CSMA/CD is the access method used by Ethernet networks.

access server — See *communications server*.

account — A record of a user that contains all of his or her properties, including rights to resources, password, username, and so on.

acknowledgment (ACK) — A response generated at the Transport layer of the OSI Model that confirms to a sender that its frame was received.

Active Directory — Windows 2000 Server's method for organizing and managing objects associated with the network.

active monitor — On a Token Ring network, the workstation that maintains timing for token passing, monitors token and frame transmission, detects lost tokens, and corrects problems when a timing error or other disruption occurs. Only one workstation on the ring can act as the active monitor at any given time.

active topology — A topology in which each workstation participates in transmitting data over the network.

adapter card — See *expansion board*.

address — A number that uniquely identifies each workstation and device on a network. Without unique addresses, computers on the network could not reliably communicate.

address management — Centrally administering a finite number of network addresses for an entire LAN. Usually this task can be accomplished without touching the client workstations.

Address Resolution Protocol (ARP) — A core protocol in the TCP/IP suite that belongs in the Internet layer. It obtains the MAC (physical) address of a host, or node, and then creates a local database that maps the MAC address to the host's IP (logical) address.

address resource record — A type of DNS data record that maps the IP address of an Internet-connected device to its domain name.

addressing — The scheme for assigning a unique identifying number to every workstation and device on the network. The type of addressing used on a network depends on its protocols and network operating system.

Administrator — A user account that has unlimited privileges to resources and objects managed by a server or domain. The administrator account is created during NOS installation.

AIX — IBM's proprietary implementation of the UNIX system.

alias — A nickname for a node's host name. Aliases can be specified in a local host file.

amplifier — A device that boosts, or strengthens, an analog signal.

amplitude — A measure of a signal's strength.

amplitude modulation (AM) — A modulation technique in which the amplitude of the carrier signal is modified by the application of a data signal.

analog — A signal that uses variable voltage to create continuous waves, resulting in an inexact transmission.

ANSI (American National Standards Institute) — An organization composed of more than 1000 representatives from industry and government who together determine standards for the electronics industry in addition to other fields, such as chemical and nuclear engineering, health and safety, and construction.

anycast address — A type of address specified in IPv6 that represents a group of interfaces, any one of which (and usually the first available of which) can accept a transmission. At this time, anycast addresses are not designed to be assigned to hosts, such as servers or workstations, but rather to routers.

AppleTalk — The protocol suite used to interconnect Macintosh computers. Although AppleTalk was originally designed to support peer-to-peer networking among Macintoshes, it can now be routed between network segments and integrated with NetWare- or Microsoft-based networks.

AppleTalk network number — A unique 16-bit number that identifies the network to which an AppleTalk node is connected.

AppleTalk node ID — A unique 8-bit or 16-bit (if you are using extended networking, in which a network can have multiple addresses and support multiple zones) number that identifies a computer on an AppleTalk network.

AppleTalk zone — Logical groups of computers defined on an AppleTalk network.

Application layer — The seventh layer of the OSI Model. The Application layer provides interfaces to the software that enable programs to use network services.

application programming interface (API) — A routine (or set of instructions) that allows a program to interact with the operating system. APIs belong to the Application layer of the OSI Model.

application switch — Another term for a Layer 3 or Layer 4 switch.

ARP table — The database that lists MAC addresses and their associated IP addresses used for ARP queries.

array — A group of hard disks.

asset management — A system for collecting and storing data on the quantity and types of software and hardware assets in an organization's network.

asymmetric encryption — A type of encryption (such as public key encryption) that uses a different key for encoding data than is used for decoding the cipher text.

asymmetric multiprocessing — A multiprocessing method that assigns each subtask to a specific processor.

asymmetrical — The characteristic of a transmission technology that affords greater bandwidth in one direction (either from the customer to the carrier, or vice versa) than in the other direction.

asymmetrical DSL — A variation of DSL that offers more throughput when data travels downstream — downloading from a local carrier's POP to the customer — than when it travels upstream — uploading from the customer to the local carrier's POP.

asynchronous — A transmission method in which data being transmitted and received by nodes do not have to conform to any timing scheme. In asynchronous communications, a node can transmit at any time and the destination node must accept the transmission as it comes.

Asynchronous Transfer Mode (ATM) — A technology originally conceived in 1983 at Bell Labs, but standardized only in the mid-1990s. It relies on a fixed packet size to achieve data transfer rates up to 9953 Mbps. The fixed packet consists of 48 bytes of data plus a 5-byte header. The fixed packet size allows ATM to provide predictable traffic patterns and better control over bandwidth utilization.

attenuate — To lose signal strength as a transmission travels farther away from its source.

attenuation — A signal's loss of strength as it travels farther from its source.

attribute — A variable property associated with a network object. For example, a restriction on the time of day a user can log on is an attribute associated with that user object.

AUI (Attachment Unit Interface) — An Ethernet standard for connecting coaxial cables with transceivers and networked nodes.

authentication — The process whereby a network operating system verifies that a client's user name and password are valid and allows the client to log onto the network.

authentication header (AH) — In the context of IPSec, a type of encryption that provides authentication of the IP packet's data payload through public key techniques.

authentication service (AS) — In Kerberos terminology, the process that runs on a key distribution center (KDC) to initially validate a client who's logging in. The authentication service issues session keys to the client and the service the client wants to access.

authenticator — In Kerberos authentication, the user's timestamp encrypted with the session key. The authenticator is used to help the service verify that a user's ticket is valid.

autosense — A feature of modern NICs that enables a NIC to automatically sense what types of frames are running on a network and set itself to that specification.

availability — How consistently and reliably a file, device, or connection can be accessed by authorized personnel.

B

B channel — In ISDN, the "bearer" channel, so named because it bears traffic from point to point.

backbone — The cabling or part of a network that connects separate LAN segments. Backbone wiring provides interconnection between telecommunications closets, equipment rooms, and entrance facilities.

backleveling — The process of reverting to a previous version of a software program after attempting to upgrade it.

back up — A copy of data or program files created for archiving or safekeeping purposes.

backup — The process of copying critical data files to a secure storage area. Often backups are performed according to a formulaic schedule.

backup rotation scheme — A plan for when and how often backups occur, and which backups are full, incremental, or differential.

bandwidth — A measure of the difference between the highest and lowest frequencies that a medium can transmit.

base I/O port — A setting that specifies, in hexadecimal notation, which area of memory will act as a channel for moving data between the network adapter and the CPU. Like its IRQ, a device's base I/O port cannot be used by any other device.

baseband — A form of transmission in which digital signals are sent through direct current pulses applied to the wire. This direct current requires exclusive use of the wire's capacity, so baseband systems can transmit only one signal, or one channel, at a time. Every device on a baseband system shares a single channel.

baseline — A record of how well the network operates under normal conditions (including its performance, collision rate, utilization rate, and so on). Baselines are used for comparison when conditions change.

baselining — The practice of measuring and recording a network's current state of operation.

bend radius — The radius of the maximum arc into which you can loop a cable before you will cause data transmission errors. Generally, a twisted-pair cable's bend radius is equal to or greater than four times the diameter of the cable.

best path — The most efficient route from one node on a network to another. Under optimal network conditions, the best path is the most direct path between two points.

binary — A system founded on using 1s and 0s to encode information.

binding — The process of assigning one network component to work with another.

bio-recognition access — A method of authentication in which a device scans an individual's unique physical characteristics (such as the color patterns in his or her eye's iris or the geometry of his or her hand) to verify the user's identity.

BIOS (basic input/output system) — Firmware attached to the system board that controls the computer's communication with its devices, among other things.

bit — Short for binary digit. A bit equals a single pulse in the digital encoding system. It may have only one of two values: 0 or 1.

blackout — A complete power loss.

block — A unit of disk space and the smallest unit of disk space that can be controlled by the NetWare system. Smaller blocks require more server memory.

block ID — The first set of six characters that make up the MAC address and that are unique to a particular vendor.

block suballocation — A NetWare technique for using hard disk space more efficiently. Files that don't fit neatly into a whole number of blocks can take up fractions of blocks, leaving the remaining fractions free for use by other data.

BNC barrel connector — A connector used on Thinnet networks with two open ends used to connect two Thinnet coaxial cables.

BNC T-connector — A connector used on Thinnet networks with three open ends. It attaches to the Ethernet interface card at the base of the "T" and to the Thinnet cable at its two sides so as to allow the signal in and out of the NIC.

bonding — The process of combining more than one bearer channel of an ISDN line to increase throughput. For example, BRI's two 64-Kbps B channels are bonded to create an effective throughput of 128 Kbps.

boot sector virus — A virus that resides on the boot sector of a floppy disk and is transferred to the partition sector or the DOS boot sector on a hard disk. A boot sector virus can move from a floppy to a hard disk only if the floppy disk is left in the drive when the machine starts up.

Bootstrap Protocol (BOOTP) — A service that simplifies IP address management. BOOTP maintains a central list of IP addresses and their associated devices' MAC addresses, and assigns IP addresses to clients when they request it.

Border Gateway Protocol (BGP) — The routing protocol of Internet backbones. The router stress created by Internet growth has driven the development of BGP, the most complex of the routing protocols. The developers of BGP had to contend with the prospect of 100,000 routes as well as the goal of routing traffic efficiently and fairly through the hundreds of Internet backbones.

braiding — A braided metal shielding used to insulate some types of coaxial cable.

BRI (Basic Rate Interface) — A variety of ISDN that uses two 64-Kbps bearer channels and one 16-Kbps data channel, as summarized by the following notation: 2B + D. BRI is the most common form of ISDN employed by home users.

bridge — A device that looks like a repeater, in that it has a single input and a single output, but is different from a repeater in that it can interpret the data it retransmits.

bridge router (brouter) — A router capable of providing Layer 2 bridging functions.

broadband — 1) A form of transmission in which signals are modulated as radiofrequency analog pulses with different frequency ranges. Unlike baseband, broadband technology does not involve binary encoding. The use of multiple frequencies enables a broadband system to operate over several channels and therefore carry much more data than a baseband system. 2) A group of network connection types or transmission technologies that are generally capable of exceeding 1.544 Mbps throughput. Examples of broadband include DSL and SONET.

broadcast — A transmission that involves one transmitter and multiple receivers.

broadcast domain — In a virtual local area network (VLAN), a combination of ports that make up a Layer 2 segment and must be connected by a Layer 3 device, such as a router or Layer 3 switch.

brouter — See *bridge router*.

brownout — A momentary decrease in voltage, also known as a *sag*. An overtaxed electrical system may cause brownouts, recognizable as a dimming of the lights.

browser — Software that provides clients with a simple, graphical interface to the Web.

BSD (Berkeley Software Distribution) — A UNIX distribution that originated at the University of California at Berkeley. The BSD suffix differentiates these distributions from AT&T distributions. No longer being developed at Berkeley, the last public release of BSD UNIX was version 4.4.

bug — A flaw in software or hardware that causes it to malfunction.

bus — 1) The single cable connecting all devices in a bus topology. 2) The type of circuit used by the system board to transmit data to components. Most new Pentium computers use buses capable of exchanging 32 or 64 bits of data. As the number of bits of data a bus handles increases, so too does the speed of the device attached to the bus.

bus topology — A topology in which a single cable connects all nodes on a network without intervening connectivity devices.

byte — Eight bits of information. In a digital signaling system, broadly speaking, one byte carries one piece of information.

C

cable checker — A simple handheld device that determines whether cabling can provide connectivity. To accomplish this task, a cable checker applies a small voltage to each conductor at one end of the cable, then checks whether that voltage is detectable at the other end. It may also verify that voltage cannot be detected on other conductors in the cable.

cable drop — Fiber-optic or coaxial cable that connects a neighborhood cable node to a customer's house.

cable modem — A device that modulates and demodulates signals for transmission and reception via cable wiring.

cable plant — The hardware that constitutes the enterprise-wide cabling system.

cable tester — A handheld device that not only checks for cable continuity, but also ensures that the cable length is not excessive, measures the distance to a cable fault, measures attenuation along a cable, measures near-end crosstalk between wires, measures termination resistance and impedance for Thinnet cabling, issues pass/fail ratings for wiring standards, and stores and prints cable testing results.

caching — The process of saving frequently used data to an area of the physical memory so that it becomes more readily available for future requests. Caching accelerates the process of accessing the server because the operating system no longer needs to search for the requested data on the disk.

call tracking system — A software program used to document problems (also known as help desk software). Examples of popular call tracking systems include Clientele, Expert Advisor, Professional Help Desk, Remedy, and Vantive.

capacity — See *throughput*.

Carrier Sense Multiple Access/Collision Avoidance (CSMA/CA) — A network access method used on LocalTalk networks in which nodes on a shared communication channel signal their intent to transmit data before doing so, thus avoiding collisions.

Carrier Sense Multiple Access/Collision Detection (CSMA/CD) — Rules for communication used by shared Ethernet networks. In CSMA/CD each node waits its turn before transmitting data, to avoid interfering with other nodes' transmissions.

CAT — Abbreviation for the word "category" when describing a type of twisted-pair cable. For example, Category 3 unsheilded twisted-pair cable may also be called CAT3. See *Category 1*, *Category 2*, *Category 3*, *Category 4*, *Category 5*, *Enhanced Category 5*, *Category 6*, and *Category 7*.

Category 1 (CAT1) — A form of UTP that contains two wire pairs. CAT1 is suitable for voice communications, but not for data. At most, it can carry only 20 Kbps of data.

Category 2 (CAT2) — A form of UTP that contains four wire pairs and can carry up to 4 Mbps of data. CAT2 is rarely found on modern networks, because most require higher throughput.

Category 3 (CAT3) — A form of UTP that contains four wire pairs and can carry up to 10-Mbps, with a possible bandwidth of 16 MHz. CAT3 has typically been used for 10-Mbps Ethernet or 4-Mbps Token Ring networks. Network administrators are gradually replacing CAT3 cabling with CAT5 to accommodate higher throughput. CAT3 is less expensive than CAT5.

Category 4 (CAT4) — A form of UTP that contains four wire pairs and can support up to 16-Mbps throughput. CAT4 may be used for 16-Mbps Token Ring or 10-Mbps Ethernet networks. It is guaranteed for data transmission up to 20 MHz and provides more protection against crosstalk and attenuation than CAT1, CAT2, or CAT3.

Category 5 (CAT5) — The most popular form of UTP for new network installations and upgrades to Fast Ethernet. CAT5 contains four wire pairs and supports up to 100-Mbps throughput and a 100 MHz signal rate. In addition to 100-Mbps Ethernet, CAT5 wiring can support other fast networking technologies, such as Asynchronous Transfer Mode (ATM) and Fiber Distributed Data Interface (FDDI).

Category 5 enhanced (CAT5e) — See *enhanced Category 5*.

Category 6 (CAT6) — A twisted-pair cable that contains four wire pairs, each wrapped in foil insulation. Additional foil insulation covers the bundle of wire pairs, and a fire-resistant plastic sheath covers the second foil layer. The foil insulation provides excellent resistance to crosstalk and enables CAT6 to support at least six times the throughput supported by regular CAT5.

Category 7 (CAT7) — A twisted-pair cable that contains multiple wire pairs, each separately shielded then surrounded by another layer of shielding within the jacket. CAT7 can support up to a 1-GHz signal rate. But because of its extra layers, it is less flexible than other forms of twisted-pair wiring.

CD-ROM File System (CDFS) — The read-only file system used to access resources on a CD. Windows 2000 supports this file system to allow CD-ROM file sharing.

cell — A packet of a fixed size. In ATM technology, a cell consists of 48 bytes of data plus a 5-byte header.

certification — The process of mastering material pertaining to a particular hardware system, operating system, programming language, or other software program, then proving your mastery by passing a series of exams.

Certified NetWare Engineer (CNE) — Professional certification established by Novell that demonstrates an in-depth understanding of Novell's networking software, including NetWare.

change management system — A process or program that provides support personnel with a centralized means of documenting changes made to the network. In smaller organizations, a change management system may be as simple as one document on the network to which networking personnel continually add entries to mark their changes. In larger organizations, it may consist of a database package complete with graphical interfaces and customizable fields tailored to the particular computing environment.

channel — A distinct communication path between two or more nodes, much like a lane is a distinct transportation path on a freeway. Channels may be separated either logically (as in multiplexing) or physically (as when they are carried by separate wires).

child domain — A domain found beneath another domain in a Windows 2000 domain tree.

cipher text — The unique data block that results when an original piece of data (such as text) is encrypted (for example, by using a key).

CIR (committed information rate) — The guaranteed minimum amount of bandwidth selected when leasing a frame relay circuit. Frame relay costs are partially based on CIR.

circuit switching — A type of switching in which a connection is established between two network nodes before they begin transmitting data. Bandwidth is dedicated to this connection and remains available until users terminate the communication between the two nodes.

cladding — The glass shield around the fiber core of a fiber-optic cable. Cladding acts as a mirror, reflecting light back to the core in patterns that vary depending on the transmission mode. This reflection allows fiber to bend around corners without impairing the light-based signal.

class — A type of object recognized by an NOS directory and defined in an NOS schema. Printers and users are examples of object classes.

client — A computer on the network that requests resources or services from another computer on a network. In some cases, a client could also act as a server. The term "client" may also refer to the user of a client workstation.

Client Services for NetWare (CSNW) — A Microsoft program that can be installed on Windows 2000 clients to enable them to access NetWare servers and make full use of the NetWare Directory System (NDS), its objects, files, directories, and permissions.

client/server architecture — The model of networking in which clients (typically desktop PCs) use a central server to share data, data storage space, and devices.

client/server network — A network based on the client/server architecture.

client_hello — In the context of SSL encryption, a message issued from the client to the server that contains information about what level of security the client's browser is capable of accepting and what type of encryption the client's browser can decipher (for example, RSA or Diffie-Hellman). The client_hello message also establishes a randomly generated number that uniquely identifies the client plus another number that identifies the SSL session.

clustering — See *server clustering.*

CMOS (complementary metal oxide semiconductor) — Firmware on a PC's system board that enables you to change its devices' configurations.

coaxial cable — A type of cable that consists of a central copper core surrounded by an insulator, a braided metal shielding, called braiding, and an outer cover, called the sheath or jacket. Coaxial cable, called "coax" for short, was the foundation for Ethernet networks in the 1980s and remained a popular transmission medium for many years.

collapsed backbone — A type of enterprise-wide backbone in which a router or switch acts as the single central connection point for multiple subnetworks.

collision — In Ethernet networks, the interference of one network node's data transmission with another network node's data transmission.

collision domain — A portion of a LAN encompassing devices that may cause and detect data collisions during transmission. Bridges and switches can logically define the boundaries of a collision domain.

command interpreter — A (usually text-based) program that accepts and executes system programs and applications on behalf of users. Often it includes the ability to execute a series of instructions that are stored in a file.

communications server — A server that runs communications services such as Windows NT's RAS or NetWare's NAS, also known as an access server or remote access server.

CompTIA — See *Computing Technology Industry Association.*

Computing Technology Industry Association (CompTIA) — An association of computer resellers, manufacturers, and training companies that sets industry-wide standards for computer professionals. CompTIA established and sponsors the A+ and Network+ (Net+) certifications.

conduit — Pipeline used to contain and protect the cabling. Conduit is usually made from metal.

connection-oriented — A feature of some protocols that requires the establishment of a connection between communicating nodes before the protocol will transmit data.

connectionless — A feature of some protocols that allows the protocol to service a request without requiring a verified session and without guaranteeing delivery of data.

connectors — The pieces of hardware that connect the wire to the network device, be it a file server, workstation, switch, or printer.

container — A logical receptacle for holding like objects in an NOS directory. Containers form the branches of the directory tree.

container objects — See *container.*

context — A kind of road map for finding an object in an NDS tree. A context is made up of an object's organizational unit names, arranged from most specific to most general, plus the organization name. Periods separate the organizational unit names in context.

Controlled Access Unit (CAU) — A connectivity device used on a Token Ring network. In addition to passing data between nodes, a CAU provides more flexibility and easier management of connected nodes than a MAU.

convergence — The use of networks to carry data, plus video and voice signals.

convergence time — The time it takes for a router to recognize a best path in the event of a change or network outage.

core — The central component of a fiber-optic cable, consisting of one or several pure glass fibers.

core gateways — Gateways that make up the Internet backbone. The Internet Network Operations Center (INOC) operates core gateways.

cracker — A person who uses his or her knowledge of operating systems and utilities to intentionally damage or destroy data or systems.

crossover cable — A twisted-pair patch cable in which the termination locations of the transmit and receive wires on one end of the cable are reversed.

crosstalk — A type of interference caused by signals traveling on nearby wire pairs infringing on another pair's signal.

CSU (channel service unit) — A device used with T-carrier technology that provides termination for the digital signal and ensures connection integrity through error correction and line monitoring.

CSU/DSU — A combination of a CSU (channel service unit) and a DSU (data service unit) that serves as the connection point for a T1 line at the customer's site.

cut-through mode — A switching mode in which a switch reads a frame's header and decides where to forward the data before it receives the entire packet. Cut-through mode is faster, but less accurate, than the other switching method, store and forward mode.

Cyclic Redundancy Check (CRC) — An algorithm used to verify the accuracy of data contained in a data frame.

D

D channel — In ISDN, the "data" channel used to carry information about the call, such as session initiation and termination signals, caller identity, call forwarding, and conference calling signals.

daisy chain — A linked series of devices.

data encryption standard (DES) — A popular private key encryption technique that was developed by IBM in the 1970s.

Data Link layer — The second layer in the OSI Model. The Data Link layer bridges the networking media with the Network layer. Its primary function is to divide the data it receives from the Network layer into frames that can then be transmitted by the Physical layer.

Data Link layer address — See *MAC address*.

data packet — A discreet unit of information sent from one computer on a network to another.

data propagation delay — The length of time data take to travel from one point on the segment to another point. On Ethernet networks, CSMA/CD's collision detection routine cannot operate accurately if the data propagation delay is too long.

daughter board — See *expansion board*.

daughter card — See *expansion board*.

DB-15 — A general term for connectors that use 15 metal pins to complete a connection between devices. "DB" stands for Data bus, while the number "15" indicates how many pins are used to make the connection.

DB-9 connector — A connector containing nine pins that is used on STP-based Token Ring networks.

dedicated circuit — A continuously available link between two access points that is leased from a communications provider, such as an ISP or telephone company.

default gateway — The gateway that first interprets a device's outbound requests, and then interprets its inbound requests to and from other subnets. In the postal service analogy, the default gateway is similar to a local post office.

demand priority — A method for data transmission used by 100BaseVG Ethernet networks. Each device on a star or hierarchical network sends a request to transmit to the central hub, which grants the requests one at a time. The hub examines incoming data packets, determines the destination node, and forwards the packets to that destination. Because demand priority runs on a star topology, no workstations except the source and destination can "see" the data. Data travel from one device to the hub, then to another device.

demultiplexer (demux) — A device that separates multiplexed signals once they are received and regenerates them in their original form.

denial-of-service attack — A security attack caused by a deluge of traffic that disables the victimized system.

device driver — Software that enables an attached device to communicate with the computer's operating system.

device ID — The second set of six characters that make up a network device's MAC address. The Device ID, which is added at the factory, is based on the device's model and manufacture date.

dial-up — A type of connection that uses modems at the transmitting and receiving ends and PSTN or other lines to access a network.

dial-up networking — The process of dialing into a LAN's access server or into an ISP. Dial-up Networking is also the name of the utility that Microsoft provides with its operating systems to achieve this type of connectivity.

differential backup — A backup method in which only data that have changed since the last backup are copied to a storage medium, and that information is marked for subsequent backup, regardless of whether it has changed.

digital — As opposed to analog signals, digital signals are composed of pulses that can have a value of only 1 or 0.

digital certificate — A password-protected and encrypted file that holds an individual's identification information, including a public key and a private key. The individual's public key is used to verify the sender's digital signature, and the private key allows individual to log onto a third-party authority who administers digital certificates.

DIP (dual inline package) switch — A small plastic toggle switch on a circuit board that can be flipped to indicate either an "on" or "off" status, which translates into a parameter setting.

direct infrared transmission — A type of infrared transmission that depends on the transmitter and receiver being within the line of sight of each other.

directory — In general, a listing that organizes resources and correlates them with their properties. In the context of network operating systems, a method for organizing and managing objects.

Directory Services Migration Tool (DSMIGRATE) — A tool provided withWindows 2000 Server that enables network administrators to migrate accounts, files, and permissions from a NetWare NDS directory to the Windows 2000 Active Server Directory.

disaster recovery — The process of restoring critical functionality and data to a network after an enterprise-wide outage that affects more than a single system or a limited group of users.

disk mirroring — A RAID technique in which data from one disk are automatically copied to another disk as the information is written.

disk striping — A simple implementation of RAID in which data are written in 64 KB blocks equally across all disks in the array.

diskless workstations — Workstations that do not contain hard disks, but instead rely on a small amount of read-only memory to connect to a network and to pick up their system files.

distinguished name (DN) — A long form of an object's name in Active Directory that explicitly indicates the object name, plus the names of its containers and domains. A distinguished name includes a domain component (DC), organizational unit (OU), and common name (CN). A client uses the distinguished name to access a particular object, such as a printer.

distributed backbone — A type of enterprise-wide backbone that consists of a number of hubs connected to a series of central hubs or routers in a hierarchy.

DIX (Digital, Intel, and Xerox) — A type of AUI connector used on Thicknet networks.

domain — (1) A group of networked devices that share a symbolic name according to Internet standards. For example, workstations used in the Whitehouse share the whitehouse.gov domain name. (2) In the context of Windows NT and Windows 2000 networking, a group of users, servers, and other resources that share account and security policies.

domain account — A type of user account on a Windows 2000 network that has privileges to resources across the domain onto which it is logged.

domain controller — A Windows 2000 server that contains a replica of the Active Directory database.

domain local group — A group on a Windows2000 network that allows members of one domain to access resources within that domain only.

domain name — The symbolic name that identifies a domain and identifies a group of network nodes. Usually, a domain name is associated with a company or other type of organization, such as a university or military unit.

Domain Name System (DNS) — A hierarchical way of tracking domain names and their addresses, devised in the mid-1980s. The DNS database does not rely on one file or even one server, but rather is distributed over several key computers across the Internet to prevent catastrophic failure if one or a few computers go down. DNS is a TCP/IP service that belongs to the Application layer of the OSI Model.

domain tree — A group of hierarchically arranged domains that share a common namespace in the Windows 2000 Active Directory.

doskey — A command used on MS-DOS and Windows systems that enables the user to recall (using the keyboard's arrow keys) and edit previously entered commands.

dotted decimal notation — The shorthand convention used to represent IP addresses and make them more easily readable by humans. In dotted decimal notation, a decimal number between 1 and 254 represents each binary octet. A period, or dot, separates each decimal.

downstream — A term used to describe data traffic that flows from a local carrier's POP to the customer. In asymmetrical communications, downstream throughput is usually much higher than upstream throughput. In symmetrical communications, downstream and upstream throughputs are equal.

drop cable — The cable that connects a device's Ethernet interface to a transceiver in a Thicknet network.

DS0 (digital signal, level 0) — The equivalent of one data or voice channel in T-carrier technology, as defined by ANSI physical layer standards. All other signal levels are multiples of DS0.

DSL (digital subscriber line) — A dedicated remote connectivity or WAN technology that uses advanced data modulation techniques to achieve extraordinary throughput over regular phone lines. DSL currently comes in seven different varieties, the most common of which is Asymmetric DSL (ADSL).

DSL access multiplexer (DSLAM) — A connectivity device located at a carrier's office that aggregates multiple DSL subscriber lines and connects them to a larger carrier or to the Internet backbone.

DSL modem — A device that demodulates an incoming DSL signal, extracting the information and passing it on to the data equipment (such as telephones and computers) and modulates an outgoing DSL signal.

DSU (data service unit) — A device used in T-carrier technology that converts the digital signal used by bridges, routers, and multiplexers into the digital signal used on cabling. Typically, a DSU is combined with a CSU in a single box, a CSU/DSU.

duplex — See *full-duplex.*

dynamic IP address — An IP address that is assigned to a device through DHCP and may change when the DHCP lease expires or is terminated.

dynamic ARP table entry — A record (of an IP address and its associated MAC address) created in an ARP table when a client makes an ARP request that cannot be satisfied by data already in the ARP table.

Dynamic Host Configuration Protocol (DHCP) — An application layer protocol in the TCP/IP suite that manages the dynamic distribution of IP addresses on a network. Using DHCP to assign IP addresses reduces the effort required to assign addresses and helps prevent duplicate-addressing problems.

dynamic routing — A method of routing that automatically calculates the best path between two nodes and accumulates this information in a routing table. If congestion or failures affect the network, a router using dynamic routing can detect the problems and reroute data through a different path. Most modern networks primarily use dynamic routing.

E

e-commerce — A means of conducting business over the Web — be it in retailing, banking, stock trading, consulting, or training. Any buying and selling of products or services that occurs over the Internet belongs in the e-commerce category.

echo reply — The response signal sent by a device after another device pings it.

echo request — The request for a response generated when one device pings another device on the network.

EIA (Electronic Industries Alliance) — A trade organization composed of representatives from electronics manufacturing firms across the UnitedStates.

electrically erasable programmable read-only memory (EEPROM) — A type of ROM that is found on a circuit board and whose configuration information can be erased and rewritten through electrical pulses.

electromagnetic interference (EMI) — A type of interference that may be caused by motors, power lines, televisions, copiers, fluorescent lights, or other sources of electrical activity.

encapsulation security payload (ESP) — In the context of IPSec, a type of encryption that provides authentication of the IP packet's data payload through public key techniques. In addition, ESP also encrypts the entire IP packet for added security.

encrypted virus — A virus that is encrypted to prevent detection.

encryption — The use of an algorithm to scramble data into a format that can be read only by reversing the algorithm—decrypting the data—to keep the information private. The most popular kind of encryption algorithm weaves a key into the original data's bits, sometimes several times in different sequences, to generate a unique data block.

enhanced CAT5 (CAT5e) — A higher-grade version of CAT5 wiring that contains high-quality copper, offers a high twist ratio, and uses advanced methods for reducing crosstalk. Enhanced CAT5 can support a signaling rate of up to 200 MHz, double the capability of regular CAT5.

Enhanced Interior Gateway Routing Protocol (EIGRP) — A routing protocol developed in the mid-1980s by Cisco Systems that has a fast convergence time and a low network overhead, but is easier to configure and less CPU-intensive than OSPF. EIGRP also offers the benefits of supporting multiple protocols and limiting unnecessary network traffic between routers.

enterprise — An entire organization, including local and remote offices, a mixture of computer systems, and a number of departments. Enterprise-wide computing takes into account the breadth and diversity of a large organization's computer needs.

enterprise-wide network — A network that spans an entire organization and often services the needs of many diverse users. It may include many locations (as a WAN), or it may be confined to one location but include many different departments, floors, and network segments.

Ethernet — A networking technology originally developed at Xerox in 1970 and improved by Digital Equipment Corporation, Intel, and Xerox. Today, four types of Ethernet technology are used on LANs, with each type being governed by a set of IEEE standards.

Ethernet 802.2 frame — See *IEEE 802.3 frame.*

Ethernet 802.3 frame — See *Novell proprietary 802.3 frame.*

Ethernet II frame — The original Ethernet frame type developed by Digital, Intel, and Xerox, before the IEEE began to standardize Ethernet. Ethernet II lacks Logical Link Control layer information but contains a 2-byte type field to identify the upper-layer protocol contained in the frame. It supports TCP/IP, AppleTalk, IPX/SPX, and other higher layer protocols.

expansion board — A circuit board used to connect a device to a computer's system board.

expansion card — See *expansion board.*

expansion slots — Openings on a computer's system board that contain multiple electrical contacts into which the expansion board can be inserted.

explicit one-way trust — A type of trust relationship in which two domains that belong to different NOS directory trees are configured to trust each other.

extended attributes — Attributes beyond the basic Read, Write, System Hidden, and Archive attrevutes supported by FAT.HPFS supports extended attributes.

Extended Industry Standard Architecture (EISA) — A 32-bit bus that is compatible with older ISA devices (because it shares the same length and pin configuration as the ISA bus), but that uses an extra layer of pins (resulting in a deeper, two-layered slot connector) for a second 16 bits to achieve faster throughput. The EISA bus was introduced in the late 1980s to compete with IBM's MCA bus.

extended network prefix — The combination of an address's network and subnet information. By interpreting an address's extended network prefix, a device can determine the subnet to which an address belongs.

external network number — Another term for the network address portion of an IPX/SPX address.

F

fail-over — The capability for one component (such as a NIC or server) to assume another component's responsibilities without manual intervention.

failure — A deviation from a specified level of system performance for a given period of time. A failure occurs when something doesn't work as promised or as planned.

Fast Ethernet — A type of Ethernet network that is capable of 100-Mbps throughput. 100BaseT and 100BaseFX are both examples of Fast Ethernet.

FAT32 (32-bit File Allocation Table) — An enhanced version of FAT that accommodates the use of long filenames and smaller allocation units on a disk. FAT32 makes more efficient use of disk space than the original FAT and is therefore faster and can handle larger files.

FAT16 (16-bit File Allocation Table) — A file system designed for use with early DOS- and Windows-based computers that allocates file system space in 16-bit units. Compared to FAT32, FAT16 is less desirable because of its partition size, file naming, fragmentation, speed, and security limitations.

fault — The malfunction of one component of a system. A fault can result in a failure.

fault tolerance — The capacity for a system to continue performing despite an unexpected hardware or software malfunction.

Federal Communications Commission (FCC) — The regulatory agency that sets standards and policy for telecommunications transmission and equipment in the United States.

Fiber Distributed Data Interface (FDDI) — A networking standard originally specified by ANSI in the mid-1980s and later refined by ISO. FDDI uses a dual fiber-optic ring to transmit data at speeds of 100 Mbps. It was commonly used as a backbone technology in the 1980s and early 1990s, but lost favor as fast Ethernet technologies emerged in the mid-1990s. FDDI provides excellent reliability and security.

fiber-optic cable — A form of cable that contains one or several glass fibers in its core. Data are transmitted via pulsing light sent from a laser or light-emitting diode through the central fiber (or fibers). Outside the central fiber, a layer of glass called cladding acts as a mirror, reflecting light back to the core in patterns that vary depending on the transmission mode. Outside the cladding, a plastic buffer protects the core and absorbs any light that might escape. Outside the buffer, strands of Kevlar provide further protection from stretching and damage. A plastic jacket surrounds the Kevlar strands.

fiber-optic modem (FOM) — A demultiplexer used on fiber networks that employ wave division multiplexing. The fiber-optic modem separates the multiplexed signals into individual signals according to their different wavelengths.

Fibre Channel — A distinct network transmission method that relies on fiber-optic media and its own, proprietary protocol. Fibre Channel is capable of 1-Gbps (and soon, 2-Gbps) throughput.

file server — A specialized server that enables clients to share applications and data across the network.

file services — The function of a file server that allows users to share data files, applications, and storage areas.

file system — An operating system's method of organizing, managing, and accessing its files through logical structures and software routines.

File Transfer Protocol (FTP) — An application layer protocol in the TCP/IP protocol suite that manages file transfers between TCP/IP hosts.

file-infected virus — A virus that attaches itself to executable files. When the infected executable file runs, the virus copies itself to memory. Later, the virus will attach itself to other executable files.

filtering database — A collection of data created and used by a bridge that correlates the MAC addresses of connected workstations with their locations. A filtering database is also known as a forwarding table.

firewall — A specialized device (typically a router, but possibly only a PC running special software) that selectively filters or blocks traffic between networks. A firewall may be strictly hardware-based, or it may involve a combination of hardware and software.

firmware — A combination of hardware and software. The hardware component of firmware is a read-only memory (ROM) chip that stores data established at the factory and possibly changed by configuration programs that can write to ROM.

flashing — A security attack in which an Internet user sends commands to another Internet user's machine that cause the screen to fill with garbage characters. A flashing attack will cause the user to terminate his or her session.

flavor — Term used to refer to the different implementations of a particular UNIX-like system. For example, the different flavors of Linux include Red Hat, Caldera, and Mandrake.

flow control — A method of gauging the appropriate rate of data transmission based on how fast the recipient can accept data.

forest — In the context of Windows 2000 Server, a collection of domain trees that use different namespaces. A forest allows for trust relationships to be established between trees.

Format Prefix — A variable-length field at the beginning of an IPv6 address that indicates what type of address it is (for example, unicast, anycast, or multicast).

forwarding table — See *filtering database*.

fox and hound — Another term for the combination of devices known as a tone generator and a tone locator. The tone locator is considered the hound because it follows the tone generator (the fox).

fractional T1 — An arrangement that allows organizations to use only some channels on a T1 line and pay for only the channels actually used.

frame — A package for data that includes not only the raw data, or "payload," but also the sender's and receiver's network addresses and control information.

Frame Check Sequence (FCS) — The field in a data frame responsible for ensuring that data carried by the frame arrives intact. FCS uses an algorithm, such as CRC, to accomplish this verification.

frame relay — An updated, digital version of X.25 that relies on packet switching. Because it is digital, frame relay supports higher bandwidth than X.25, offering a maximum of 45-Mbps throughput. It provides the basis for much of the world's Internet connections. On network diagrams, the frame relay system is often depicted as a cloud.

FreeBSD — An open source software implementation of the Berkeley Software Distribution version of the UNIX system.

freely distributable — A term used to describe software with a very liberal copyright. Often associated with open source software.

frequency — The number of times that a signal's amplitude changes over a fixed period of time, expressed in cycles per second, or hertz (Hz).

frequency modulation (FM) — A method of data modulation in which the frequency of the carrier signal is modified by the application of the data signal.

full backup — A backup in which all data on all servers are copied to a storage medium, regardless of whether the data are new or changed.

full-duplex — A type of transmission in which signals may travel in both directions over a medium simultaneously. May also be called, simply, "duplex."

fully qualified domain name (FQDN) — In TCP/IP addressing, the combination of a host and domain name that together uniquely identify a device.

G

gateway — A combination of networking hardware and software that connects two dissimilar types of networks. Gateways perform connectivity, session management, and data translation, so they must operate at multiple layers of the OSI Model.

Gateway Services for NetWare (GSNW) — A Windows 2000 service that acts as a translator between the Windows 2000 and NetWare client redirector services. With GSNW installed, a Windows 2000 server can access files and other shared resources on any NetWare server on a network.

General Public License — The copyright that applies to freely distributable versions of UNIX and specifies that the source code must be made available to anyone receiving the system.

ghosts — Frames that are not actually data frames, but rather aberrations caused by a repeater misinterpreting stray voltage on the wire. Unlike true data frames, ghosts have no starting delimiter.

giants — Packets that exceed the medium's maximum packet size. For example, any Ethernet packet that is larger than 1518 bytes is considered a giant.

global group — A group on a Windows 2000 network that allows members of one domain to access resources within that domain as well as resources from other domains in the same forest.

globally unique identifier (GUID) — A 128-bit number generated and assigned to an object upon its creation in the Windows 2000 Active Directory. Network applications and services use an object's GUID to communicate with it.

globbing — A form of filename substitution, similar to the use of wildcards in Windows and DOS.

GNU — The name given to the free software project to implement a complete source code implementation of UNIX, the collection of UNIX-inspired utilities and tools that are included with Linux distributions and other free software UNIX systems. The acronym within an acronym stands for "GNUs Not UNIX."

gopher — A text-based utility that allows you to navigate through a series of menus to find and read specific files.

grandfather-father-son — A backup rotation scheme that uses daily (son), weekly (father), and monthly (grandfather) backup sets.

graphical user interface (GUI) — A pictorial representation of computer functions and elements that, in the case of network operating systems, enables administrators to more easily manage files, users, groups, security, printers, and other issues.

group — A means of collectively managing users' permissions and restrictions applied to shared resources. Groups form the basis for resource and account management for every type of network operating system, not just Windows 2000 Server. Many network administrators create groups according to department or, even more specifically, according to job function within a department.

Guest — A user account with very limited privileges that is created during the installation of a network operating system.

H

hacker — A person who masters the inner workings of operating systems and utilities in an effort to better understand them. A hacker is distinguished from a cracker in that a cracker will attempt to exploit a network's vulnerabilities for malicious purposes.

half-duplex — A type of transmission in which signals may travel in both directions over a medium, but in only one direction at a time.

handshake protocol — One of several protocols within SSL, and perhaps the most significant. As its name implies, the handshake protocol allows the client and server to authenticate (or introduce) each other and establishes terms for how they will securely exchange data during an SSL session.

hard disk redundancy — See *Redundant Array of Inexpensive Disks (RAID)*.

Hardware Compatibility List (HCL) — A list of computer components proven to be compatible with Windows 2000 Server. The HCL appears on the same CD as your Windows 2000 Server software and on Microsoft's Web site.

head-end — A cable company's central office, which connects cable wiring to many nodes before it reaches customers' sites.

hertz (Hz) — A measure of frequency equivalent to the number of amplitude cycles per second.

heuristic scanning — A type of virus scanning that attempts to identify viruses by discovering "virus-like" behavior.

hierarchical file system — The organization of files and directories (or folders) on a disk partition in which directories may contain files and other directories. When displayed graphically, this organization resembles a tree-like structure.

hierarchical hybrid topology — A network topology in which devices are divided into separate layers according to their priority or function.

High-Performance File System (HPFS) — A file system designed for IBM's OS/2 operating system that offers greater efficiency and reliability than does FAT. HPFS is rarely used but can be supported by Windows 2000 servers.

High-Speed Token Ring (HSTR) — A standard for Token Ring networks that operate at 100 Mbps.

hop — A term used to describe each trip data take from one connectivity device to another.

host — 1) A computer connected to a network that uses the TCP/IP protocol. 2) A type of computer that enables resource sharing by other computers on the same network.

host file — A text file that associates TCP/IP host names with IP addresses. On Windows 9x, NT, and 2000 platforms, the host file is called "lmhosts" On UNIX platforms the file is called "hosts" and is located in the /etc directory.

host name — A symbolic name that describes a TCP/IP device.

hosts — Name of the DNS host file found on a UNIX computer. The hosts file is usually found in the /etc directory.

hot swappable — A characteristic that enables identical components to be interchanged (or swapped) while a machine is still running (hot). Once installed, hot swappable components automatically assume the functions of their counterpart if it suffers a fault.

HOWTO — A series of brief, highly focused documents giving Linux system details. The people responsible for the Linux Documentation Project centrally coordinate the HOWTO papers (see *www.linuxhq.com/ldp/ howto/HOWTO-INDEX/ howtos.html*).

HP-UX — Hewlett-Packard's proprietary implementation of the UNIX system.

HTTPS — The URL prefix that indicates that a Web page requires its data to be exchanged between client and server using SSL encryption. HTTPS uses the TCP port number 443, rather than port 80 (the port that normal HTTP uses).

hub — A multiport repeater containing multiple ports to interconnect multiple devices. Unless they are used on a peer-to-peer network, hubs also contain an uplink port, one port that connects to a network's backbone. Hubs regenerate digital signals.

Hurd — The kernel in the GNU operating system. While many UNIX and Linux systems include GNU utilities such as the EMACS editor or the GNU C compiler, the Hurd is the only operating system kernel that can currently be called a GNU kernel.

hybrid fiber-coax (HFC) — A link that consists of fiber cable connecting the cable company's offices to a node location near the customer and coaxial cable connecting the node to the customer's house. HFC upgrades to existing cable wiring are required before current TV cable systems can serve as WAN links.

hybrid topology — A complex combination of the simple physical topologies.

Hypertext Markup Language (HTML) — The language that defines formatting standards for Web documents.

Hypertext Transport Protocol (HTTP) — The language that Web clients and servers use to communicate. HTTP forms the backbone of the Web.

I

i-node — A UNIX file system information storage area that holds all details about a file. This information includes the size, access rights, date and time of creation, and a pointer to the actual contents of the file.

ICA (Independent Computing Architecture) client — A remote access client developed by Citrix Systems, Inc. that enables remote users to use virtually any LAN application over any type of connection, public or private. The ICA client is especially well suited to slower connections, as it exchanges only keystrokes, mouse clicks, and screen updates with the server. The ICA client requires that Citrix's server software run on the access server.

IEEE (Institute of Electrical and Electronic Engineers) — An international society composed of engineering professionals. Its goals are to promote development and education in the electrical engineering and computer science fields.

IEEE 802.3 frame — A popular Ethernet frame type used on IPX/SPX networks. The defining characteristics of its data portion are the source and destination service access points that belong to the Logical Link Control layer, a sublayer of the Data Link layer. Also called LLC or, in Novell lingo, Ethernet 802.2.

IEEE 802.3 SNAP frame — A rarely used Ethernet frame type that is an adaptation of IEEE 802.3 and Ethernet II. SNAP stands for Sub-Network Access Protocol. The SNAP portion of the frame contains the three Logical Link Control fields (DSAP, SSAP, and Control). The Organization ID (OUI) field provides a method of identifying the type of network on which the frame is running. In addition, Ethernet SNAP frames carry Ethernet type information, just as an Ethernet II frame does.

ifconfig — A TCP/IP configuration and management utility used with UNIX systems (similar to the ipconfig utility used on Windows NT and 2000 systems).

incremental backup — A backup in which only data that have changed since the last backup are copied to a storage medium.

indirect infrared transmission — A type of infrared transmission in which signals bounce off walls, ceilings, and any other objects in their path. Because indirect infrared signals are not confined to a specific pathway, they are not very secure.

Industry Standard Architecture (ISA) — The original PC bus, developed in the early 1980s to support an 8-bit and later 16-bit data transfer capability. Although an older technology, ISA buses are still used to connect serial devices, such as mice or modems, in new PCs.

infrared — A type of data transmission in which infrared light signals are used to transmit data through space, similar to the way a television remote control sends signals across the room. Networks may use two types of infrared transmission: direct or indirect.

integrity — The soundness of a network's files, systems, and connections. To ensure integrity, you must protect your network from anything that might render it unusable, such as corruption, tampering, natural disasters, and viruses.

integrity checking — A method of comparing the current characteristics of files and disks against an archived version of these characteristics to discover any changes. The most common example of integrity checking involves a checksum.

intelligent hub — A hub that possesses processing capabilities and can therefore interpret and manage data traffic, rather than simply regenerating signals as a simple hub would do.

Internet — A complex WAN that connects LANs around the globe.

Internet Control Message Protocol (ICMP) — A core protocol in the TCP/IP suite that notifies the sender that something has gone wrong in the transmission process and that packets were not delivered.

Internet Corporation for Assigned Names and Numbers (ICANN) — The non-profit corporation currently designated by the U.S. government to maintain and assign IP addresses.

Internet Key Exchange (IKE) — The first phase of IPSec authentication, which accomplishes key management. IKE is a service that runs on UDP port 500. Once IKE has established the rules for the type of keys two nodes will use, IPSec invokes its second phase, encryption.

Internet Mail Access Protocol (IMAP) — A mail storage and manipulation protocol that depends on SMTP's transport system and improves upon the shortcomings of POP. The most current version of IMAP is version 4 (IMAP4). IMAP4 can (and eventually will) replace POP without the user having to change e-mail programs. The single biggest advantage IMAP4 has relative to POP is that it allows users to store messages on the mail server, rather than always having to download them to the local machine.

Internet Protocol (IP) — A core protocol in the TCP/IP suite that belongs to the Internet layer of the TCP/IP model and provides information about how and where data should be delivered. IP is the subprotocol that enables TCP/IP to internetwork.

Internet services — Services that enable a network to communicate with the Internet, including World Wide Web servers and browsers, file transfer capabilities, Internet addressing schemes, security filters, and a means for directly logging on to other computers.

Internet telephony — The provision of telephone service over the Internet.

internetwork — To traverse more than one LAN segment and more than one type of network through a router.

Internetwork Packet Exchange (IPX) — A core protocol of the IPX/SPX suite that operates at the Network layer of the OSI Model and provides routing and internetwork services, similar to IP in the TCP/IP suite.

Internetwork Packet Exchange/Sequenced Packet Exchange (IPX/SPX) — A protocol originally developed by Xerox, then modified and adopted by Novell in the 1980s for the NetWare network operating system.

interrupt — A wire through which a device issues voltage, thereby signaling a request for the processor's attention.

interrupt request (IRQ) — A message sent to the computer that instructs it to stop what it is doing and pay attention to something else. IRQ is often used (informally) to refer to the interrupt request number.

interrupt request number (IRQ number) — The unique number assigned to each interrupt request in a computer. Interrupt request numbers range from 0 to 15, and many PC devices reserve specific numbers for their use alone.

IntraNetWare — Another term for NetWare version 4.11, the version in which support for Internet services was first introduced.

intrusion detection — The process of monitoring the network for unauthorized access to its devices.

IP address — A logical address used in TCP/IP networking. This unique 32-bit number is divided into four groups of octets, or 8-bit bytes, that are separated by periods.

IP datagram — The IP portion of a TCP/IP frame that acts as an envelope for data, holding information necessary for routers to transfer data between subnets.

IP next generation (IPng) — See *IP Version 6.*

IP Security Protocol (IPSec) — A Layer 3 protocol that defines encryption, authentication, and key management for TCP/IP transmissions. IPSec is an enhancement to IPv4 and native to IPv6. IPSec is unique among authentication methods in that it adds security information to the header of all IP packets.

IP spoofing — A security attack in which an outsider obtains internal IP addresses, then uses those addresses to pretend that he or she has authority to access a private network from the Internet.

IP version 6 (IPv6) — A new standard for IP addressing that will replace the current IP version 4 (IPv4). Most notably, IPv6 uses a newer, more efficient header in its packets and allows for 128-bit source and destination IP addresses. The use of longer addresses will allow for more total IP addresses to be in circulation.

ipconfig — The TCP/IP configuration and management utility for use with Windows NT or Windows 2000 systems.

IPX address — An address assigned to a device on an IPX/SPX network.

ISDN (Integrated Services Digital Network) — An international standard, established by the ITU, for transmitting data over digital lines. Like PSTN, ISDN uses the telephone carrier's lines and dial-up connections, but it differs from PSTN in that it exclusively uses digital lines andswitches.

ISO (International Organization for Standardization) — A collection of standards organizations representing 130 countries with headquarters located in Geneva, Switzerland. Its goal is to establish international technological standards to facilitate the global Exchange of information and barrier-free trade.

ITU (International Telecommunication Union) — A United Nations agency that regulates international telecommunications, including radio and TV frequencies, satellite and telephony specifications, networking infrastructure, and tariffs applied to global communication. It also provides developing countries with technical expertise and equipment to advance these nations' technological bases.

J

jabber — A device that handles electrical signals improperly, usually affecting the rest of the network. A network analyzer will detect a jabber as a device that is always retransmitting, effectively bringing the network to a halt. A jabber usually results from a bad NIC. Occasionally, it can be caused by outside electrical interference.

jamming — A part of CSMA/CD in which, upon detecting a collision, a station issues a special 32-bit sequence to indicate to all nodes on an Ethernet segment that its previously transmitted frame has suffered a collision and should be considered faulty.

jumper — A small, removable piece of plastic that contains a metal receptacle that fits over a pair of pins on a circuit board to complete a circuit between those two pins. By moving the jumper from one set of pins to another set of pins, you can modify the board's circuit, thereby giving it different instructions on how to operate.

K

Kerberos — A cross-platform authentication protocol that uses key encryption to verify the identity of clients and to securely exchange information once a client logs onto a system. It is an example of a private key encryption service.

kernel — The core of an operating system, such as UNIX or NetWare. The kernel, which is loaded into memory as the computer starts, oversees all critical server processes.

kernel modules — Portions of the Linux kernel that you can load and unload to add or remove functionality on a running Linux system.

key — A series of characters that is combined with a block of data during that data's encryption. In order to decrypt the resulting data, the recipient must also possess the key.

key distribution center (KDC) — In Kerberos terminology, the server that runs the authentication service and the ticket granting service in order to issue keys and tickets to clients. On a Windows 2000 network, a user's domain controller serves as his KDC.

key management — The method whereby two nodes using key encryption agree on common parameters for the keys they will use in order to encrypt data.

key pair — The combination of a public and private key used to decipher data that has been encrypted using public key encryption.

L

LAN — See *local area network*.

LAN Emulation (LANE) — A method for transporting Token Ring or Ethernet frames over ATM networks. LANE encapsulates incoming Ethernet or Token Ring frames, then converts them into ATM cells for transmission over an ATM network.

LAN topology — The physical layout, or pattern, of nodes on a local area network(LAN).

LANalyzer — Novell's network monitoring software package. LANalyzer can act as a standalone program on a Windows 9x or 2000 workstation or as part of the ManageWise suite of network management tools on a NetWare server. LANalyzer offers the following capabilities: discovery of all network nodes on a segment, continuous monitoring of network traffic, alarms that are tripped when traffic conditions meet preconfigured thresholds (for example, if usage exceeds 70%), and the capturing of traffic to and from all or selected nodes.

late collisions — Collisions that take place outside the normal window in which collisions are detected and redressed. Late collisions are usually caused by a defective station (such as a card, or transceiver) that is transmitting without first verifying line status or by failure to observe the configuration guidelines for cable length, which results in collisions being recognized too late.

latency — The delay between the transmission of a signal and its receipt.

layer — (1) In the context of hierarchical topologies, the division between one set of devices and another set of devices on a network; (2) A portion of the OSI Model that corresponds to specific processes involved in data communication between two computers.

Layer 2 Forwarding (L2F) — A Layer 2 protocol similar to PPTP that provides tunneling for other protocols and can work with the authentication methods used by PPP. L2F was developed by Cisco Systems and requires special hardware on the host system end. It can encapsulate protocols to fit more than just the IP format, unlike PPTP.

Layer 2 Tunneling Protocol (L2TP) — A Layer 2 tunneling protocol developed by a number of industry consortia. L2TP is an enhanced version of L2F. Like L2F, it supports multiple protocols; unlike L2F, it does not require costly hardware upgrades to implement. L2TP is optimized to work with the next generation of IP (IPv6) and IPSec (the Layer 3 IP encryption protocol).

Layer 3 switch — A switch capable of interpreting data at Layer 3 (Network layer) of the OSI Model.

Layer 4 switch — A switch capable of interpreting data at Layer 4 (Transport layer) of the OSI Model.

lease — The agreement between a DHCP server and client on how long the client will borrow a DHCP-assigned IP address. As network administrator, you configure the duration of the lease (in the DHCP service) to be as short or long as necessary, from a matter of minutes to forever.

leased lines — Permanent dedicated connections established through a public telecommunications carrier and billed to customers on a monthly basis.

license tracking — Determining how many copies of a single application are currently in use on the network.

Lightweight Directory Access Protocol (LDAP) — A standard protocol for accessing network directories.

line noise — Fluctuations in voltage levels caused by other devices on the network or by electromagnetic interference.

Linux — A freely distributable implementation of the UNIX system. Finnish computer scientist Linus Torvalds originally developed it.

LLC frame — See *IEEE 802.3 frame*.

lmhosts — A host file on a Windows-based computer that maps IP addresses to host names and aliases.

load balancing — An automatic distribution of traffic over multiple links, hard disks, or processors intended to optimize responses.

Lobe Attachment Module (LAM) — A device that attaches to a CAU to expand the capacity of that device. LAMs typically allow up to 20 devices to plug into each CAU receptacle.

local account — A type of user account on a Windows 2000 network that has rights to the resources managed by the server the user has logged onto.

local area network (LAN) — A network of computers and other devices that is confined to a relatively small space, such as one building or even one office.

local collisions — Collisions that occur when two or more stations are transmitting simultaneously. Excessively high collision rates within the network can usually be traced to cable or routing problems.

local computer — The computer on which you are actually working (as opposed to a remote computer).

local loop — The part of a phone system that connects a customer site with a public carrier's POP. Some WAN transmission methods, such as ISDN, are suitable for only the local loop portion of the network link.

LocalTalk — A logical topology designed by Apple Computer, Inc. especially for networking Macintosh computers. LocalTalk uses the CSMA/CA network access method, and its throughput is limited to a maximum of 230 Kbps. Because of its throughput limitations, LocalTalk has been replaced by Ethernet on most modern Macintosh-based networks.

logical address — See *Network layer addresses*.

Logical Link Control (LLC) sublayer — The upper sublayer in the Data Link layer. The LLC provides a common interface and supplies reliability and flow control services.

logical topology — A networking technology defined by its Data Link layer data packaging and Physical layer signaling techniques. Also known as network transport system or access method.

loopback address — An IP address reserved for communicating from a node to itself (used mostly for testing purposes). The value of the loopback address is always 127.0.0.1.

loopback plug — A connector used for troubleshooting that plugs into a port (for example, a serial, parallel, or RJ-45 port) and crosses over the transmit line to the receive line, allowing outgoing signals to be redirected back into the computer for testing.

M

MAC address — A number that uniquely identifies a network node. The manufacturer hard-codes the MAC address on the NIC. This address is composed of the Block ID and Device ID.

macro viruses — A newer type of virus that takes the form of a word-processing or spreadsheet program macro, which may execute when a word-processing or spreadsheet program is in use.

MacTCP — A version of the TCP/IP protocol supplied with LocalTalk.

mail services — Network services that manage the storage and transfer of e-mail between users on a network. In addition to sending, receiving, and storing mail, mail services can include intelligent e-mail routing capabilities, notification, scheduling, indexing, document libraries, and gateways to other mail servers.

MAN — See *metropolitan area network*.

managed hub — See *intelligent hub*.

management services — Network services that centrally administer and simplify complicated management tasks on the network. Examples of management services include license tracking, security auditing, asset management, addressing management, software distribution, traffic monitoring, load balancing, and hardware diagnosis.

manual pages (man pages) — UNIX online documentation. This documentation describes the use of the commands and the programming interface to the UNIX system.

Media Access Control (MAC) sublayer — The lower sublayer of the Data Linklayer. The MAC appends the physical address of the destination computer onto the frame.

media access unit (MAU) — The type of transceiver used on a Thicknet network to connect network nodes to the backbone.

media filter — A device that enables two types of cables or connectors to be linked.

member server — A type of server on a Windows 2000 network that does not hold directory information and therefore cannot authenticate users.

memory range — A hexadecimal number that indicates the area of memory that the network adapter and CPU will use for exchanging, or buffering, data. As with IRQs, some memory ranges are reserved for specific devices—most notably, the system board.

mesh network — An enterprise-wide topology in which routers are interconnected with other routers so that at least two pathways connect each node.

mesh WAN topology — A WAN topology that consists of many directly interconnected locations forming a complex mesh.

message switching — A type of switching in which a connection is established between two devices in the connection path; one device transfers data to the second device, then breaks the connection. The information is stored and forwarded from the second device once a connection between that device and a third device on the path is established.

metropolitan area network (MAN) — A network that connects clients and servers in multiple buildings within a limited geographic area. For example, a network connecting multiple city government buildings around the city's center.

MIB (management information base) — A collection of data used by management programs (which may be part of the network operating system or a third-party program) to analyze network performance and problems.

MicroChannel Architecture (MCA) — IBM's proprietary 32-bit bus for personal computers, introduced in 1987 and later replaced by the more standard EISA and PCI buses.

Microsoft Certified Systems Engineer (MCSE) — A professional certification established by Microsoft that demonstrates in-depth knowledge about Microsoft's products, including Windows 98 and Windows 2000.

Microsoft Management Console (MMC) — A graphical network management interface used with Windows 2000 Server.

Microsoft Message Queueing (MSMQ) — An API used in a network environment. MSMQ stores messages sent between nodes in queues then forwards them to their destination based on when the link to the recipient is available.

middleware — Software that sits between the client and server in a 3-tier architecture. Middleware may be used as a messaging service between clients and servers, as a universal query language for databases, or as means of coordinating processes between multiple servers that need to work together in servicing clients.

mirroring — See *server mirroring*.

modem — A device that modulates analog signals into digital signals at the transmitting end for transmission over telephone lines, and demodulates digital signals into analog signals at the receiving end.

modular hub — A type of hub that provides a number of interface options within one chassis. Similar to a PC, a modular hub contains a system board and slots accommodating different adapters. These adapters may connect to other types of hubs, routers, WAN links, or to both Token Ring and Ethernet network backbones. They may also connect the modular hub to management workstations or redundant components, such as an extra power supply.

modular router — A router with multiple slots that can hold different interface cards or other devices so as to provide flexible, customizable network interoperability.

modulation — A technique for formatting signals in which one property of a simple, carrier wave is modified by the addition of a data signal during transmission.

Monitor — An NLM that enables the system administrator to view server parameters such as protocols, bindings, system resources, and loaded modules. In many cases, it also allows the system administrator to modify these parameters.

multi-master replication — The technique of replicating an Active Directory database to multiple domain controllers so they each have the same data and the same privileges to modify that data. Multi-master replication is used within a domain tree.

multicast address — A type of address in the IPv6 that represents multiple interfaces, often on multiple nodes. An IPv6 multicast address begins with the following hexadecimal field: FF0x, where x is a character that identifies the address's group scope.

multicasting — A means of transmission in which one device sends data to a specific group of devices (not the entire network segment) in a point-to-multipoint fashion. Multicasting can be used for teleconferencing or videoconferencing over the Internet, for example.

multimeter — A simple instrument that can measure multiple characteristics of an electric circuit, including its resistance and voltage.

multimode fiber — A type of fiber-optic cable that contains a core with a diameter between 50 and 100 microns, over which many pulses of light generated by a light emitting diode (LED) travel at different angles. Because light is being reflected many different ways in a multimode fiber cable, the waves become less easily distinguishable the longer they travel. Thus, multimode fiber is best suited for shorter distances than single-mode fiber.

multiplexer (mux) — A device that separates a medium into multiple subchannels and issues signals to each of those subchannels.

multiplexing — A form of transmission that allows multiple signals to simultaneously travel over one medium.

multiprocessing — The technique of splitting tasks among multiple processors to expedite the completion of any single instruction.

multiprotocol network — A network that uses more than one protocol.

Multistation Access Unit (MAU) — A device on a Token Ring network that regenerates signals; equivalent to a hub.

multitasking — The ability of a processor to perform multiple activities in a brief period of time (often seeming simultaneous to the user).

N

n-series connector (n connector) — A type of connector used on Thicknet networks in which a screw-and-barrel arrangement securely connects coaxial cables to devices.

name server — A server that contains a database of TCP/IP host names and their associated IP addresses. A name server supplies a resolver with the requested information. If it cannot resolve the IP address, the query passes to a higher-level name server.

name space — The database of Internet IP addresses and their associated names distributed over DNS name servers worldwide.

narrowband — A type of radiofrequency transmission in which signals travel over a single frequency. The same method is used by radio and TV broadcasting stations, and signals can be easily intercepted and decoded.

nbtstat — A TCP/IP troubleshooting utility that provides information about NetBIOS names and their addresses. If you know the NetBIOS name of a workstation, you can use nbtstat to determine its IP address.

NDS eDirectory — Novell's integration tool for Windows 2000 networks. It works with the NetWare 5.x operating systems and Windows 2000 servers to enable the Windows 2000 domains to appear as container objects in NWAdmin.

NDS tree — A logical representation of how resources are grouped by NetWare in the enterprise.

negative frame sequence checks — The result of the cyclic redundancy checksum (CRC) generated by the originating node not matching the checksum calculated from the data received. It usually indicates noise or transmission problems on the LAN interface or cabling. A high number of (non-matching) CRCs usually results from excessive collisions or a station transmitting bad data.

NetBIOS — See *Network Basic Input Output System*.

NetBIOS Enhanced User Interface (NetBEUI) — Microsoft's adaptation of the IBM NetBIOS protocol. NetBEUI expands on NetBIOS by adding an Application layer component. NetBEUI is a fast and efficient protocol that consumes few network resources, provides excellent error correction and requires little configuration.

netstat — A TCP/IP troubleshooting utility that displays statistics and the state of current TCP/IP connections. It also displays ports, which can signal whether services are using the correct ports.

NetWare 3.x — The group of NetWare versions that includes versions 3.0, 3.1, and 3.2.

NetWare 4.x — The group of NetWare versions that includes versions 4.0, 4.1, and 4.11.

NetWare 5.x — The group of NetWare versions that includes versions 5.0, 5.1, and 5.11.

NetWare Administrator utility (NWAdmin) — The graphical NetWare utility thatallows administrators to manage objects in the NDS tree from a Windows workstation.

NetWare Core Protocol (NCP) — One of the core protocols of the IPX/SPX suite. NCP handles requests for services, such as printing and file access, between clients and servers.

NetWare Directory Services (NDS) — A system of managing multiple servers and their resources, including users, volumes, groups, profiles, and printers. The NDS model is similar to Active Directory in Windows 2000. In NDS, every networked resource is treated as a separate object with distinct properties.

NetWare loadable modules (NLMs) — Routines that enable the server to run programs and services. Each NLM consumes some of the server's memory and processor resources (at least temporarily). The kernel requires many NLMs to run NetWare's core operating system.

network — A group of computers and other devices (such as printers) that are connected by some type of transmission media, usually wire or cable.

network access method — See *access method*.

network adapter — A synonym for NIC (network interface card). The device that enables a workstation, server, printer, or other node to connect to the network. Network adapters belong to the Physical layer of the OSI Model.

network address — See *Network layer addresses*.

network address translation (NAT) — A technique in which private (or hidden) IP addresses are assigned a public IP address by an IP gateway, thus masking their true origin.

network analyzer — A portable, hardware-based tool that a network manager connects to the network expressly to determine the nature of network problems. Network analyzers can typically interpret data up to Layer 7 of the OSI Model.

network architect — A professional who designs networks, performing tasks that range from choosing basic components (such as cabling type) to figuring out how to make those components work together (by, for example, choosing the correct protocols).

network attached storage (NAS) — A device or set of devices attached to a client/server network that is dedicated to providing highly fault-tolerant access to large quantities of data. NAS depends on traditional network transmission methods such as Ethernet.

Network Basic Input Output System (NetBIOS) — A protocol designed by IBM to provide Transport and Session layer services for applications running on small, homogeneous networks.

network interface card (NIC) — The device that enables a workstation to connect to the network and communicate with other computers. NICs are manufactured by several different companies and come with a variety of specifications that are tailored to the workstation's and the network's requirements.

Network layer — The third layer in the OSI Model. The Network layer translates network addresses into their physical counterparts and decides how to route data from the sender to the receiver.

Network layer addresses — Addresses that reside at the Network level of the OSI Model, follow a hierarchical addressing scheme, and can be assigned through operating system software.

Network Monitor (NetMon) — A software-based network monitoring tool that comes with Windows NT Server 4.0 or Windows 2000. Its capabilities include capturing network data traveling from one or many segments, capturing frames sent by or to a specified node, reproducing network conditions by transmitting a selected amount and type of data, detecting any other running copies of NetMon, and generating statistics about network activity.

network monitor — A software-based tool that continually monitors traffic on the network from a server or workstation attached to the network. Network monitors typically can interpret up to Layer 3 of the OSI Model.

Network News Transfer Protocol (NNTP) — The protocol that supports the process of reading newsgroup messages, posting new messages, and transferring news files between news servers.

network operating system (NOS) — The software that runs on a server and enables the server to manage data, users, groups, security, applications, and other networking functions. The most popular network operating systems are Microsoft's Windows NT, Windows 2000, UNIX, and Novell's NetWare.

Network Termination 1 (NT1) — A device used on ISDN networks that connects the incoming twisted-pair wiring with the customer's ISDN terminal equipment.

Network Termination 2 (NT2) — An additional connection device required on PRI to handle the multiple ISDN lines between the customer's network termination connection and the local phone company's wires.

Network Time Protocol (NTP) — A simple TCP/IP protocol that is used to synchronize the clocks of computers on a network. NTP belongs to the Application layer of the TCP/IP Model and depends on UDP.

network transport system — See *logical topology*.

network virus — A type of virus that takes advantage of network protocols, commands, messaging programs, and data links to propagate itself. Although all viruses could theoretically travel across network connections, network viruses are specially designed to attack network vulnerabilities.

Network+ (Net+) — Professional certification established by CompTIA that verifies broad, vendor-independent networking technology skills such as an understanding of protocols, topologies, networking hardware, and network troubleshooting.

New Technology File System (NTFS) — A file system developed by Microsoft for use with its Windows NT and Windows 2000 operating systems. NTFS integrates reliability, compression, the ability to handle massive files, system security, and fast access. Most Windows 2000 Server partitions employ either FAT32 or NTFS.

newsgroups — An Internet service similar to e-mail that provides a means of conveying messages, but in which information is distributed to a wide group of users at once rather than from one user to another.

NFS — Network File System. A client/server application that allows you to view, store and update files on a remote computer as though they were on your own computer. Can be used to install Linux.

node — A computer or other device connected to a network which has a unique address and is capable of sending or receiving data.

noise — Unwanted signals, or interference, from sources near network cabling, such as electrical motors, power lines and radar.

NOS — See *network operating system*.

Novell proprietary 802.3 frame — The original NetWare Ethernet frame type and the default frame type for networks running NetWare versions lower than 3.12. It supports only the IPX/SPX protocol. Sometimes called 802.3 "raw," because its data portion contains no control bits.

nslookup — A TCP/IP utility on Windows NT, Windows 2000, and UNIX systems that allows you to look up the DNS host name of a network node by specifying its IP address, or vice versa. This ability is useful for verifying that a host is configured correctly and for troubleshooting DNS resolution problems.

NWConv — A utility provided with Windows 2000 that converts (migrates) an existing NetWare server's user account, file, and other information to a Windows 2000 server.

O

object — A representation of a thing or person associated with the network that belongs in the NOS directory. Objects include users, printers, groups, computers, data files, and applications.

object class — See *Class*.

octet — One of the four 8-bit bytes that are separated by periods and together make up an IP address.

ohmmeter—A device used to measure resistance in an electrical circuit.

online backup — A technique in which data are backed up to a central location over the Internet.

online UPS — A power supply that uses the A/C power from the wall outlet to continuously charge its battery, while providing power to a network device through its battery.

open shortest path first (OSPF) — A routing protocol that makes up for some of the limitations of RIP and can coexist with RIP on a network.

open source software — Term used to describe software that is distributed without any restriction and whose source code is freely available. See also *freely distributable.*

Open Systems Interconnection (OSI) Model — A model for understanding and developing computer-to-computer communication developed in the 1980s by ISO. It divides networking architecture into seven layers: Physical, Data Link, Network, Transport, Session, Presentation, and Application.

optical loss — The degradation of a light signal on a fiber-optic network.

optical time domain reflectometer (OTDR) — A time domain reflectometer specifically made for use with fiber optic networks. It works by issuing a light-based signal on a fiber-optic cable and measuring the way in which the signal bounces back (or reflects) to the OTDR.

Orange Book — A rigorous security specification for computer operating systems published in 1985 by the U.S. Department of Defense.

Organizational unit (OU) — A container within an NOS directory used to group objects wih similar characteristics or priviledges.

OSI Model — See *Open Systems Interconnection Model.*

overhead — The nondata information that must accompany data in order for a signal to be properly routed and interpreted by the network.

P

Packet Internet Groper (PING) — A TCP/IP troubleshooting utility that can verify that TCP/IP is installed, bound to the NIC, configured correctly, and communicating with the network. PING uses ICMP to send echo request and echo reply messages that determine the validity of an IP address.

packet switching — A type of switching in which data are broken into packets before they are transported. In packet switching, packets can travel any path on the network to their destination, because each packet contains a destination address and sequencing information.

packet-filtering firewall — A router that operates at the Data Link and Transport layers of the OSI Model, examining the header of every packet of data that it receives to determine whether that type of packet is authorized to continue to its destination. Packet-filtering firewalls are also called screening firewalls.

padding — Bytes added to the data (or information) portion of an Ethernet frame to make sure this field is at least 46 bytes in size. Padding has no effect on the data carried by the frame.

page file — A file on the hard disk that is used for virtual memory.

paging — The process of moving blocks of information, called pages, between RAM and into a page file on disk.

parallel backbone — The most robust enterprise-wide topology. This variation on the collapsed backbone arrangement consists of more than one connection from the central router or switch to each network segment.

parity — The mechanism used to verify the integrity of data by making the number of bits in a byte sum to either an odd or even number.

parity error checking — The process of comparing the parity of data read from a disk with the type of parity used by the system.

passive hub — A hub that simply amplifies and retransmits signals over the network.

patch — A correction, improvement, or enhancement to part of a software program, often distributed at no charge by software vendors to fix a bug in their code or to add slightly more functionality.

patch cable — A relatively short section (usually between 3 and 50 feet) of twisted-pair cabling, with connectors on both ends, that connects network devices to data outlets.

patch panel — A wall-mounted panel of data receptors into which cross-connect patch cables from the punch-down block are inserted.

PC Card — See *PCMCIA.*

PCMCIA — An interface developed in the early 1990s by the Personal Computer Memory Card International Association to provide a standard interface for connecting any type of device to a portable computer. PCMCIA slots may hold modem cards, network interface cards, external hard disk cards, or CD-ROM cards. PCMCIA cards are also known as PC Cards or credit card adapters.

peer-to-peer communication — A simple means of networking computers using a single cable. In peer-to-peer communication, no single computer has more authority than another and each computer can share its resources with other computers.

peer-to-peer network — A network in which computers communicate directly with other computers on a single segment of cable and share each others' data and devices. By default, no computer in a peer-to-peer network has more authority than another, and every computer can use resources from every other computer.

peer-to-peer topology — A WAN with single interconnection points for each location.

per seat — A Windows 2000 Server licensing mode that requires a license for every client capable of connecting to the Windows 2000 server.

per server — A Windows 2000 Server licensing mode that allows a limited number of clients to access the server simultaneously. (The number is determined by your Windows 2000 Server purchase agreement.) The restriction applies to the number of concurrent connections, rather than specific clients. Per server mode is the most popular choice for installing Windows 2000 Server.

Peripheral Component Interconnect (PCI) — A 32-, 64-, or 128-bit bus introduced in its original form in the 1990s. The PCI bus is the network adapter connection type used for nearly all new PCs. It's characterized by a shorter length than ISA, MCA, or EISA cards, but a much faster data transmission capability.

phase — A point or stage in a wave's progress overtime.

physical address — See *MAC address*.

Physical layer — The lowest, or first, layer of the OSI Model. The Physical layer contains the physical networking media, such as cabling and connectors.

physical memory — The RAM chips installed on the computer's system board that provide dedicated memory to that computer.

physical topology — The physical layout of a network. A physical topology depicts a network in broad scope; it does not specify devices, connectivity methods, or addresses on the network. Physical topologies are categorized into three fundamental geometric shapes: bus, ring, and star. These shapes can be mixed to create hybrid topologies.

PING — See *Packet Internet Groper*.

pinging — The process of sending an echo request signal from one node on a TCP/IP network to another, using the PING utility.

pipe — The facility in a UNIX system that enables you to combine commands to form new commands. It is one of the most powerful facilities of the UNIX system.

pipeline — A series of two or more UNIX commands connected together with pipe symbols.

plain old telephone service (POTS) — See *PSTN*.

plenum — The area above the ceiling tile or below the subfloor in a building.

point of presence (POP) — The place where the two telephone systems meet—either a long-distance carrier with a local telephone company or a local carrier with an ISP's facility.

point-to-point — A data transmission that involves one transmitter and one receiver.

Point-to-Point Protocol (PPP) — A communications protocol that enables a workstation to connect to a server using a serial connection. PPP can support multiple Network layer protocols, can use both asynchronous and synchronous communications, and does not require much (if any) configuration on the client workstation.

Point-to-Point Tunneling Protocol (PPTP) — A Layer 2 protocol developed by Microsoft that encapsulates PPP so that any type of data can traverse the Internet masked as pure IP transmissions. PPTP supports the encryption, authentication, and LAN access services provided by RAS. Instead of users having to dial directly into an access server, they can dial into their ISP using PPTP and gain access to their corporate LAN over the Internet.

polymorphic virus — A type of virus that changes its characteristics (such as the arrangement of its bytes, size, and internal instructions) every time it is transferred to a new system, making it harder to identify.

POP — See *Post Office Protocol* or *point of presence*.

port — The address on a host where an application makes itself available to incoming data.

port number — A unique number associated with a process running on a computer. For example, 23 is the standard port number associated with the Telnet utility.

Post Office Protocol (POP) — A TCP/IP subprotocol that provides centralized storage for e-mail messages. In the postal service analogy, POP is like the post office that holds mail until it can be delivered.

preemptive multitasking — The type of multitasking supported by NetWare, UNIX, and Windows 2000 Server that actually performs one task at a time, allowing one program to use the processor for a certain period of time, then suspending that program to allow another program to use the processor.

Presentation layer — The sixth layer of the OSI Model. The Presentation layer serves as a translator between the application and the network. Here data are formatted in a schema that the network can understand, with the format varying according to the type of network used. The Presentation layer also manages data encryption and decryption, such as the scrambling of system passwords.

Pretty Good Privacy (PGP) — A key-based encryption system for e-mail that uses a two-step verification process.

PRI (Primary Rate Interface) — A type of ISDN that uses 23 bearer channels and one 64-Kbps data channel as represented by the following notation: 23B + D. PRI is less commonly used by individual subscribers than BRI, but it may be used by businesses and other organizations needing more throughput.

principal — In Kerberos terminology, a user.

print services — The network service that allows printers to be shared by several users on a network.

printer queue — A logical representation of a networked printer's functionality. To use a printer, clients must have access to the printer queue.

private key encryption — A type of key encryption in which the sender and receiver have private keys, which only they know. Data encryption standard (DES), which was developed by IBM in the 1970s, is a popular example of a private key encryption technique. Private key encryption is also known as symmetric encryption.

process — A routine of sequential instructions that runs until it has achieved its goal. For example, a spreadsheet program is–a process.

promiscuous mode — The feature of a network adapter card that allows a device driver to direct it to pick up all frames that pass over the network—not just those destined for the node served by the card.

proprietary UNIX — Any implementation of UNIX for which the source code is either unavailable or available only by purchasing a licensed copy from Caldera International and Tarantella, Inc. (costing as much as millions of dollars).

protected mode — A manner in which NetWare runs services in a separate memory area from the operating system. Running services in protected mode prevents one rogue routine from taking the server down. As a result, the service and its supporting routines cannot harm critical server processes.

protocol — The rules a network uses to transfer data. Protocols ensure that data is transferred whole, in sequence, and without error from one node on the network to another.

protocol analyzer — See *network analyzer*.

proxy server — A network host that runs a proxy service. Proxy servers may also be called gateways.

proxy service — A software application on a network host that acts as an intermediary between the external and internal networks, screening all incoming and outgoing traffic and providing one address to the outside world, instead of revealing the addresses of internal LAN devices.

PSTN (Public Switched Telephone Network) — The network of typical telephone lines that has been evolving for 100 years and still services most homes.

public key encryption — A form of key encryption in which data are encrypted using two keys: one is a key known only to a user, and the other is a key associated with the user and can be obtained from a public source, such as a public key server. Some examples of public key algorithms include RSA (named after its creators, Rivest, Shamir, and Adleman), Diffie-Hellman, and Elliptic-curve cryptography. Public key encryption is also known as asymmetric encryption.

public-key server — A publicly available host (such as an Internet host) that provides free access to a list of users' public keys (for use in public key encryption).

punch-down block — A panel of data receptors into which horizontal cabling from the workstations is inserted.

PVC (permanent virtual circuit) — A point-to-point connection over which data may follow any number of different paths, as opposed to a dedicated line that follows a predefined path. X.25, frame relay, and some forms of ATM use PVCs.

Q

quality of service (QoS) — The result of standards for delivering data within a certain period of time after their transmission. For example, ATM networks can supply four QoS levels, from a "best effort" attempt for noncritical data to a guaranteed, real-time transmission for time-sensitive data.

R

radiofrequency (RF) — A type of transmission that relies on signals broadcast over specific frequencies, in the same manner as radio and TV broadcasts. RF may use narrowband or spread spectrum technology.

radiofrequency interference (RFI) — A kind of interference that may be generated by motors, power lines, televisions, copiers, fluorescent lights, or broadcast signals from radio or TV towers.

RAID — See *Redundant Array of Inexpensive Disks*.

RAID Level 0 — An implementation of RAID in which data are written in 64 KB blocks equally across all disks in the array.

RAID Level 1 — An implementation of RAID that provides redundancy through disk mirroring, in which data from one disk are automatically copied to another disk as the information is written.

RAID Level 3 — An implementation of RAID that uses disk striping for data and parity error correction code on a separate parity disk.

RAID Level 5 — The most popular, highly fault-tolerant, data storage technique in use today, RAID Level 5 writes data in small blocks across several disks. At the same time, it writes parity error checking information among several disks.

real-time — The term used to describe an operating system that at least one of the following includes two characteristics: the ability to respond to external events (for example, a change in temperature), and an ability to respond to those events deterministically—with predictable response time (for example, turning on a heating element within three microseconds).

reassembly — The process of reconstructing data units that have been segmented.

redirector — A service that runs on a client workstation and determines whether the client's request should be handled by the client or the server.

redundancy — The use of more than one identical component for storing, processing, or transporting data.

Redundant Array of Inexpensive Disks (RAID) — A server redundancy measure that uses shared, multiple physical or logical hard disks to ensure data integrity and availability. Some RAID designs also increase storage capacity and improve performance. See also *disk striping*, and *disk mirroring*.

regeneration — The process of retransmitting a digital signal. Regeneration, unlike amplification, repeats the pure signal, with none of the noise it has accumulated.

relative distinguished name (RDN) — An attribute of the object that identifies an object separately from its related container(s) and domain. For most objects, the relative distinguished name is the same as its common name (CN) in the distinguished name convention.

release — The act of terminating a DHCP lease.

remote access — A method for connecting and logging onto a LAN from a workstation that is remote, or not physically connected, to the LAN. Remote access can be accomplished one of three ways: by using a modem to dial directly into the LAN; by using a modem to dial directly to a workstation; or by using an Internet connection with a Web interface. Remote access may complete a connection via public or private lines.

remote access server — A combination of software and hardware that provides a central access point for multiple users to dial into a network.

Remote Access Service (RAS) — One of the simplest dial-in servers. This software is included with Windows 2000 Server. Note that "RAS" is pronounced *razz*.

Remote Authentication Dial-In User Service (RADIUS) — A server that offers authentication services to the network's access server (which may run the Windows NT or 2000 RAS or Novell's NAS, for example). RADIUS provides a single, centralized point of authentication for dial-in users and is often used by ISPs.

remote computer — The computer that you are controlling or working on via a network connection.

remote control — A remote access method in which the remote user dials into a workstation that is directly attached to a LAN. Software running on both the remote user's computer and the LAN computer allows the remote user to "take over" the LAN workstation.

remote node — A client that has dialed directly into a LAN's remote access server. The LAN treats a remote node like any other client on the LAN, allowing the remote user to perform the same functions he or she could perform while in the office.

remote user — A person working on a computer in a different geographical location from the LAN's server.

repeater — A device used to regenerate a digital signal.

replication — The process of copying Active Directory data to multiple domain controllers. This ensures redundancy so that in case one of the domain controllers fails, clients can still log onto the network, be authenticated, and access resources.

resistance — The opposition to an electric current. Resistance of a wire is a factor of its size and molecular structure.

resolver — Any host on the Internet that needs to look up domain name information.

resource record — The element of a DNS database stored on a name server that contains information about TCP/IP host names and their addresses.

resources — The devices, data, and data storage space provided by a computer, whether standalone or shared.

restore — The process of retrieving files from a backup if the original files are lost or deleted.

Reverse Address Resolution Protocol (RARP) — The reverse of ARP. RARP allows the client to send a broadcast message with the MAC address of a device and receive the device's IP address in reply.

RFI — See *radiofrequency interference.*

ring topology — A network layout in which each node is connected to the two nearest nodes so that the entire network forms a circle. Data are transmitted unidirectionally around the ring. Each workstation accepts and responds to packets addressed to it, then forwards the other packets to the next workstation in the ring.

ring WAN topology — A WAN topology in which each site is connected to two other sites so that the entire WAN forms a ring pattern. This architecture is similar to the LAN ring topology, except that a WAN ring topology connects locations rather than local nodes.

risers — The backbone cabling that provides vertical connections between floors of a building.

RJ-45 — The standard connector used with shielded twisted-pair and unshielded twisted-pair cabling. "RJ" stands for registered jack.

root — A highly privileged user ID that has all rights to create, delete, modify, move, read, write, or execute files on a system. This term may specifically refer to the administrator on a UNIX-based network.

root domain — In Windows 2000 networking, the single domain from which child domains branch out in a domain tree.

root server — A DNS server maintained by ICANN (in North America) that is an authority on how to contact the top-level domains, such as those ending with .com, .edu, .net, .us, and so on. ICANN maintains 13 root servers around the world.

routable — Protocols that can span more than one LAN segment because they carry Network layer and addressing information that can be interpreted by a router.

route — To direct data between networks based on addressing, patterns of usage, and availability of network segments.

router — A multiport device that can connect dissimilar LANs and WANs running at different transmission speeds and using a variety of protocols. In addition, a router can determine the best path for data transmission and perform advanced management functions. Routers operate at the Network layer (Layer 3) or higher of the OSI Model. They are intelligent, protocol-dependent devices.

Routing Information Protocol (RIP) — The oldest routing protocol that is still widely used. RIP does not work in very large network environments where data may have to travel through more than 16 routers to reach their destination (for example, on the Internet). And, compared to other routing protocols, RIP is slower and less secure.

routing protocols — Protocols that assist routers in efficiently managing information flow. For instance, routing protocols determine the best path for data to take between nodes.

routing switch — Another term for a Layer 3 or Layer 4 switch. A routing switch is a hybrid between a router and a switch and can therefore interpret data from Layer 2 and either Layer 3 or Layer 4.

runts — Packets that are smaller than a logical topology's minimum packet size. For instance, any Ethernet packet that is smaller than 64 bytes is considered a runt.

S

sag — See *brownout*.

Samba — An open source software package that provides complete Windows 2000-style file and printer sharing facility.

schema — The description of object types, or classes, and their required and optional attributes that are stored in an NOS's directory.

screening firewall — See *packet-filtering firewall*.

SDH (Synchronous Digital Hierarchy) — The international equivalent of SONET.

security audit — An assessment of an organization's security vulnerabilities. A security audit should be performed at least annually and preferably quarterly or sooner if the network has undergone significant changes. For each risk found, it should rate the severity of a potential breach, as well as its likelihood.

segment — A part of a LAN that is logically separated from other parts of the LAN and that shares a fixed amount of traffic capacity.

segmentation — The process of decreasing the size of data units when moving data from a network segment that can handle larger data units to a network segment that can handle only smaller data units.

self-healing — A characteristic of dual-ring topologies that allows them to automatically reroute traffic along the backup ring if the primary ring becomes severed.

Sequenced Packet Exchange (SPX) — One of the core protocols in the IPX/SPX suite. SPX belongs to the Transport layer of the OSI Model and works in tandem with IPX to ensure that data are received whole, in sequence, and error free.

sequencing — The process of assigning a placeholder to each piece of a data block to allow the receiving node's Transport layer to reassemble the data in the correct order.

serial backbone — The simplest kind of backbone, consisting of two or more hubs connected to each other by a single cable.

Serial Line Internet Protocol (SLIP) — A communications protocol that enables a workstation to connect to a server using a serial connection. SLIP can support only asynchronous communications and IP traffic, and requires some configuration on the client workstation.

server — A computer on the network that manages shared resources. Servers usually have more processing power, memory, and hard disk space than clients. They run network operating software that can manage not only data, but also users, groups, security, and applications on the network.

server clustering — A fault-tolerance technique that links multiple servers together to act as a single server. In this configuration, clustered servers share processing duties and appear as a single server to users. If one server in the cluster fails, the other servers in the cluster will automatically take over its data transaction and storage responsibilities.

server console — The network administrator's primary interface to a NetWare server. Unlike Windows NT, the NetWare server interface is not entirely graphical. NetWare 4.x offers only text-based server menus at the console. NetWare 5.0 allows you to access commands through either a text-based or graphical menu system.

server mirroring — A fault-tolerance technique in which one server duplicates the transactions and data storage of another, identical server. Server mirroring requires a link between the servers and software running on both servers so that the servers can continually synchronize their actions and take over in case the other fails.

server-based network — A network that uses special computers, known as servers, to process data for and facilitate communication between the other computers on the network. See *client/server network*.

server_hello — In the context of SSL encryption, a message issued from the server to the client that confirms the information the server received in the client_hello message and agrees to certain terms of encryption based on the options the client supplied. Depending on the Web server's preferred encryption method, the server may choose to use issue your browser a public key or a digital certificate at this time.

Service Access Point (SAP) — A feature of Ethernet networks that identifies a node or internal process that uses the LLC protocol. Each process between a source and destination node on the network may have a unique SAP.

Service Advertising Protocol (SAP) — A core protocol in the IPX/SPX suite that works in the Application, Presentation, Session, and Transport layers of the OSI Model and runs directly over IPX. NetWare servers and routers use SAP to advertise to the entire network which services they can provide.

service pack — A significant patch to Windows NT or 2000 Server software.

services — The features provided by a network.

session — A connection for data exchange between two parties. The term "session" is most often used in the context of terminal and mainframe communications.

session key — In the context of Kerberos authentication, a key issued to both the client and service by the authentication service that uniquely identifies their session.

Session layer — The fifth layer in the OSI Model. The Session layer establishes and maintains communication between two nodes on the network. It can be considered the traffic "cop" for network communications.

shared Ethernet — A version of Ethernet in which all the nodes share a common channel and a fixed amount of bandwidth.

sheath — The outer cover, or jacket, of a cable.

shell — Another term for command interpreter.

shielded twisted-pair (STP) — A type of cable containing twisted wire pairs that are not only individually insulated, but also surrounded by a shielding made of a metallic substance such as foil. The shielding acts as an antenna, converting the noise into current (assuming that the wire is properly grounded). This current induces an equal, yet opposite current in the twisted pairs it surrounds. The noise on the shielding mirrors the noise on the twisted pairs, and the two cancel each other out.

signal bounce — A phenomenon caused by improper termination on a bus network in which signals travel endlessly between the two ends of the network, preventing new signals from getting through.

signal level — An ANSI standard for T-carrier technology that refers to its Physical layer electrical signaling characteristics. DS0 is the equivalent of one data or voice channel. All other signal levels are multiples of DS0.

signature scanning — The comparison of a file's content with known virus signatures (unique identifying characteristics in the code) in a signature database to determine whether the file is a virus.

Simple Mail Transfer Protocol (SMTP) — A protocol within the TCP/IP suite that is responsible for moving e-mail messages between one mail server and another.

Simple Network Management Protocol (SNMP) — A communication protocol used to manage devices on a TCP/IP network.

simplex — A type of transmission in which signals may travel in only one direction over a medium.

single point of failure — A device or connection on a network that, were it to fail, could cause the entire network to stop functioning.

single-mode fiber — A type of fiber-optic cable with a core of less than 10 microns in diameter that carries light pulses along a single data path from one end of the cable to another. Single-mode fiber can carry data faster and farther than multimode fiber. However, single-mode fiber is more expensive than multimode fiber.

site license — A type of software license that, for a fixed price, allows any number of users in one location to legally access an application.

snap-in — An administrative tool, such as Computer Management, that can be added to the Microsoft Management Console (MMC).

sneakernet — The only means of exchanging data without using a network. Sneakernet requires that data be copied from a computer to a floppy disk, carried (presumably by someone wearing sneakers) to another computer, then copied from the floppy disk onto the second computer.

sniffer — A laptop equipped with a special network adapter and software that performs network analysis. Unlike laptops that may have a network monitoring tool installed, sniffers typically cannot be used for other purposes, because they don't depend on a desktop operating system such as Windows.

Sniffer Portable — Network analyzer software from Network Associates that provides data capture and analysis, node discovery, traffic trending, history, alarm tripping, and utilization prediction.

social engineering — Manipulating relationships to circumvent network security measures and gain access to a system.

socket — A logical address assigned to a specific process running on a computer. A socket forms a virtual connection between the host and client.

software distribution — The process of automatically transferring a data file or program from the server to a client on the network.

Solaris — Sun Microsystems' proprietary implementation of the UNIX system.

SONET (Synchronous Optical Network) — A WAN technology that provides data transfer rates ranging from 64 Kbps to 39.8 Gbps, using the same time division multiplexing technique used by T-carriers. SONET is the best choice for linking WANs between North America, Europe, and Asia, because it can link directly using the different standards used in different countries.

source code — Computer instructions written in a programming language that is readable by humans. Source code must be translated into a form that is executable by the machine, typically called binary code (for the sequence of zeros and ones) or target code.

source-route bridging — A type of bridging in which the bridge polls the network to determine the best path for data between two points. Source-route bridging is not susceptible to circular routing and, for this reason, is particularly well-suited to WANs.

spanning tree algorithm — A technique used in bridging that can detect circular traffic patterns and modify the way multiple bridges work together in order to avoid such patterns.

spike — A single (or short-lived) jump in a measure of network performance, such as utilization.

spread spectrum — A type of radiofrequency transmission in which lower-level signals are distributed over several frequencies simultaneously. Spread spectrum RF is more secure than narrowband RF.

SSL (Secure Sockets Layer) — A method of encrypting TCP/IP transmissions—including Web pages and data entered into Web forms—en route between the client and server using public key encryption technology.

SSL session — In the context of SSL encryption, an association between the client and server that is defined by an agreement on a specific set of encryption techniques. An SSL session allows the client and server to continue to exchange data securely as long as the client is still connected to the server. SSL sessions are established by the SSL handshake protocol.

stackable hub — A type of hub designed to be linked with other hubs in a single telecommunications closet. Stackable hubs linked together logically represent one large hub to the network.

standalone computer — A computer that uses programs and data only from its local disks and that is not connected to a network.

standalone hub — A type of hub that serves a workgroup of computers that are separate from the rest of the network. A standalone hub may be connected to another hub by a coaxial, fiber-optic, or twisted-pair cable. Such hubs are not typically connected in a hierarchical or daisy-chain fashion.

standards — Documented agreements containing technical specifications or other precise criteria that are used as guidelines to ensure that materials, products, processes, and services suit their intended purpose.

standby UPS — A power supply that provides continuous voltage to a device by switching virtually instantaneously to the battery when it detects a loss of power from the wall outlet. Upon restoration of the power, the standby UPS switches the device to use A/C power again.

star topology — A physical topology in which every node on the network is connected through a central device, such as a hub. Any single physical wire on a star network connects only two devices, so a cabling problem will affect only two nodes. Nodes transmit data to the hub, which then retransmits the data to the rest of the network segment where the destination node can pick it up.

star WAN topology — A WAN topology that mimics the arrangement of star LANs. A single site acts as the central connection point for several other locations.

star-wired bus topology — A hybrid topology in which groups of workstations are connected in a star fashion to hubs that are networked via a single bus.

star-wired ring topology — A hybrid topology that uses the physical layout of a star and the token-passing data transmission method.

static ARP table entry — A record (of an IP address and its associated MAC address) that is manually entered in the ARP table using the ARP utility.

static IP address — An IP address that is manually assigned to a device and remains constant until it is manually changed.

static routing — A technique in which a network administrator programs a router to use specific paths between nodes. Since it does not account for occasional network congestion, failed connections, or device moves, static routing is not optimal.

statistical multiplexing — A method of multiplexing in which each node on a network is assigned a separate time slot for transmission, based on the node's priority and need.

stealth virus — A type of virus that hides itself to prevent detection. Typically, stealth viruses disguise themselves as legitimate programs or replace part of a legitimate program's code with their destructive code.

storage area network (SAN) — A distinct network of multiple storage devices and servers that provides fast, highly available, and highly fault-tolerant access to large quantities of data for a client/server network. SAN uses a proprietary network transmission method (such as Fibre Channel) rather than a traditional network transmission method such as Ethernet.

store and forward mode — A method of switching in which a switch reads the entire data frame into its memory and checks it for accuracy before transmitting it. While this method is more time-consuming than the cut-through method, it allows store and forward switches to transmit data more accurately.

straight-through cable — A twisted-pair patch cable in which the wire terminations in both connectors follow the same scheme.

structured cabling — A method for uniform, enterprise-wide, multivendor cabling systems specified by the TIA/EIA 568 Commercial Building Wiring Standard. Structured cabling is based on a hierarchical design using a high-speed backbone.

subchannel — One of many distinct communication paths established when a channel is multiplexed or modulated.

subnet mask — A special 32-bit number that, when combined with a device's IP address, informs the rest of the network as to what kind of subnet the device is on.

subnets — In an internetwork, the individual networks that are joined together by routers.

subnetting — The process of subdividing a single class of network into multiple, smaller networks.

subprotocols — Small, specialized protocols that work together and belong to a protocol suite.

surge — A momentary increase in voltage due to distant lightning strikes or electrical problems.

SVC (switched virtual circuit) — Logical, point-to-point connections that rely on switches to determine the optimal path between sender and receiver. ATM technology uses SVCs.

swap file — See *page file*.

switch — 1) A connectivity device that logically subdivides a network into smaller, individual segments. Most switches operate at the Data Link layer of the OSI Model. They interpret MAC address information to determine whether to filter (discard) or forward packets they receive. 2) The letters or words added to a command that allow you to customize a utility's output. Switches are usually preceded by a hyphen or a forward slash character.

switched Ethernet — An Ethernet model that enables multiple nodes to simultaneously transmit and receive data and individually take advantage of more bandwidth because they are assigned separate logical network segments through switching.

switching — A component of a network's logical topology that manages how packets are filtered and forwarded between nodes on the network.

symmetric encryption — A method of encryption that requires the same key to encode the data as is used to decode the cipher text.

symmetric multiprocessing — A method of multiprocessing that splits all operations equally among two or more processors. Windows 2000 Server supports this type of multiprocessing.

symmetrical — A characteristic of transmission technology that provides equal throughput for data traveling both upstream and downstream and is suited to users who both upload and download significant amounts of data.

symmetrical DSL — A variation of DSL that provides equal throughput both upstream and downstream between the customer and the carrier.

synchronous — A transmission method in which data being transmitted and received by nodes must conform to a timing scheme.

System V — The proprietary version of UNIX, originally developed at AT&T Bell Labs, currently distributed by Caldera International and Tarantella, Inc.

T

T-carriers — The term for any kind of leased line that follows the standards for T1s, fractional T1s, T1Cs, T2s, T3s, or T4s.

T1 — A T-carrier technology that provides 1.544-Mbps throughput and 24 channels for voice, data, video, or audio signals. T1s may use shielded or unshielded twisted-pair, coaxial cable, fiber-optic, or microwave links. Businesses commonly use T1s to connect to their ISP, and phone companies typically use at least one T1 to connect their central offices.

T3 — A T-carrier technology that can carry the equivalent of 672 channels for voice, data, video, or audio, with a maximum data throughput of 44.736 Mbps (typically rounded up to 45 Mbps for purposes of discussion). T3s require either fiber-optic or microwave transmission media.

TCP segment — The portion of a TCP/IP packet that holds TCP data fields and becomes encapsulated by the IP datagram.

TCP/IP core protocols — The subprotocols of the TCP/IP suite.

teleconnector — A transceiver used on LocalTalk networks. The teleconnector is linked to the node's serial port on one side, and to the wall jack on the other side.

Telnet — A terminal emulation protocol used to log on to remote hosts using the TCP/IP protocol. Telnet resides in the Application layer of the TCP/IP suite.

terminal — A device with little (if any) of its own processing or disk capacity that depends on a host to supply it with applications and data-processing services.

Terminal Access Controller Access Control System (TACACS) — A centralized authentication system for remote access servers that is similar to RADIUS.

terminal adapter (TA) — Devices used to convert digital signals into analog signals for use with ISDN phones and other analog devices. Terminal adapters are sometimes called ISDN modems.

terminal equipment (TE) — Devices that connect computers to the ISDN line. Terminal equipment may include standalone devices or cards (similar to the network adapters used on Ethernet and Token Ring networks) or ISDN routers.

Thicknet — A type of coaxial cable, also known as thickwire Ethernet, that is a rigid cable approximately 1-cm thick. Thicknet was used for the original Ethernet networks. Because it is often covered with a yellow sheath, Thicknet is also called "yellow Ethernet." IEEE has designated Thicknet as 10Base5 Ethernet, with the "10" representing its throughput of 10 Mbps, the "Base" standing for baseband transmission, and the "5" representing the maximum segment length of a Thicknet cable, 500 m.

thickwire Ethernet — See *Thicknet*.

thin client — A type of software that enables a client to accomplish functions over a network while utilizing little of the client workstation's resources and, instead, relying on the server to carry the processing burden.

thin Ethernet — See *Thinnet*.

Thinnet — A type of coaxial cable, also known as thin Ethernet, that was the most popular medium for Ethernet LANs in the 1980s. Like Thicknet, Thinnet is rarely used on modern networks. IEEE has designated Thinnet as 10Base2 Ethernet, with the "10" representing its data transmission rate of 10 Mbps, the "Base" representing the fact that it uses baseband transmission, and the "2" roughly representing its maximum segment length of 185 m.

thread — A well-defined, self-contained subset of a process. Using threads within a process enables a program to efficiently perform related, multiple, simultaneous activities. Threads are also used to enable processes to use multiple processors on SMP systems.

throughput — The amount of data that a medium can transmit during a given period of time. Throughput is usually measured in megabits (1,000,000 bits) per second, or Mbps. The physical nature of every transmission medium determines its potential throughput.

ticket — In Kerberos terminology, a temporary set of credentials that a client uses to prove that its identity has been validated by the authentication service.

ticket granting service (TGS) — In Kerberos terminology, an application that runs on the key distribution center that issues ticket granting tickets to clients so that they need not request a new ticket for each new service they want to access.

ticket granting ticket (TGT) — In Kerberos terminology, a ticket that enables a user to be accepted as a validated principal by multiple services.

tiered WAN topology — A WAN topology in which sites are connected in star or ring formations and interconnected at different levels with the interconnection points organized into layers.

time division multiplexing (TDM) — A method of multiplexing that assigns a time slot in the flow of communications to every node on the network and in that time slot, carries data from that node.

time domain reflectometer (TDR) — A high-end instrument for testing the qualities of a cable. It works by issuing a signal on a cable and measuring the way in which the signal bounces back (or reflects) to the TDR.

time-dependent virus — A virus programmed to activate on a particular date. This type of virus, also known as a "time bomb," can remain dormant and harmless until its activation date arrives.

time-sharing system — A computing system to which users must attach directly so as to use the shared resources of the computer.

TLS (Transport Layer Security) — A version of SSL being standardized by the Internet Engineering Task Force (IETF). With TLS, IETF aims to create a version of SSL that will encrypt UDP as well as TCP transmissions. TLS, which will likely be supported by new Web browsers, uses slightly different encryption algorithms than SSL, but otherwise is very similar to the most recent version of SSL.

token — A special control frame that indicates to the rest of the network that a particular node has the right to transmit data.

token passing — A means of data transmission in which a 3-byte packet, called a token, is passed around the network in a round-robin fashion.

Token Ring — A networking technology developed by IBM in the 1980s. It relies upon direct links between nodes and a ring topology, using tokens to allow nodes to transmit data.

Token Ring media filter — A device that enables a DB-9 cable and a type 1 IBM cable to be connected.

tone generator — A small electronic device that issues a signal on a wire pair. When used in conjunction with a tone locator, it can help locate the termination of a wire pair.

tone locator—A small electronic device that emits a tone when it detects electrical activity on a wire pair. When used in conjunction with a tone generator, it can help locate the termination of a wire pair.

top-level domain (TLD) — The highest-level category used to distinguish domain names—for example, .org, .com, .net. A TLD is also known as the domain suffix.

topology — The physical layout of a computer network.

traceroute (or tracert) — A TCP/IP troubleshooting utility that uses ICMP to trace the path from one networked node to another, identifying all intermediate hops between the two nodes. Traceroute is useful for determining router or subnet connectivity problems.

traffic — The data transmission and processing activity taking place on a computer network at any given time.

traffic monitoring — Determining how much processing activity is taking place on a network or network segment and notifying administrators when a segment becomes overloaded.

transceiver (transmitter/receiver) — A device that both transmits and receives signals. Since a transceiver is concerned with applying signals to the wire, it belongs in the Physical layer of the OSI Model. Many different types of transceivers exist in networking.

translational bridging — A type of bridging in which bridges can not only forward packets, but also translate packets between one logical topology and another. For instance, translational bridging can connect Token Ring and Ethernet networks.

transmission — In networking, the application of data signals to a medium or the progress of data signals over a medium from one point to another.

Transmission Control Protocol (TCP) — A core protocol of the TCP/IP suite. TCP belongs to the Transport layer and provides reliable data delivery services.

transmission media — The means through which data are transmitted and received. Transmission media may be physical, such as wire or cable, or atmospheric (wireless), such as radio waves.

transparent bridging — The method of bridging used on most Ethernet networks.

Transport layer — The fourth layer of the OSI Model. The Transport layer is primarily responsible for ensuring that data are transferred from point A to point B (which may or may not be on the same network segment) reliably and without errors.

tree — A logical representation of multiple, hierarchical levels in a directory. It is called a tree because the whole structure shares a common starting point (the root) and from that point extends branches (or containers), which may extend additional branches, and so on.

Trivial File Transfer Protocol (TFTP) — A TCP/IP Application layer protocol that enables file transfers between computers. Unlike FTP, TFTP relies on UDP at the Transport layer and does not require a user to log onto the remote host.

Trojan horse — A program that disguises itself as something useful but actually harms your system.

trust relationship — The relationship between two domains on a Windows 2000 or Windows NT network that allows a domain controller from one domain to authenticate users from the other domain.

tunneling — The process of encapsulating one protocol to make it appear as another type of protocol.

twist ratio — The number of twists per meter or foot in a twisted-pair cable.

twisted-pair (TP) — A type of cable similar to telephone wiring that consists of color-coded pairs of insulated copper wires, each with a diameter of 0.4 to 0.8mm, twisted around each other and encased in plastic coating.

two-way transitive trust — The security relationship between domains in the same domain tree in which one domain grants every other domain in the tree access to its resources and, in turn, that domain can access other domains' resources. When a new domain is added to a tree, it immediately shares a two-way trust with the other domains in the tree.

type 1 IBM connector — A type of Token Ring connector that uses interlocking tabs that snap into an identical connector when one is flipped upside-down, making for a secure connection. Type 1 IBM connectors are used on STP-based Token Ring networks.

typeful — A way of denoting an object's context in which the Organization and Organizational Unit designators ("O" and "OU," respectively) are included. For example, OU=Inv.OU=Ops.OU=Corp.O=Sutkin.

typeless — A way of denoting an object's context in which the Organization and Organizational Unit designators ("O" and "OU," respectively) are omitted. For example, Inv.Ops.Corp.Sutkin.

U

unicast address — A type of IPv6 address that represents a single interface on a device. An IPv6 unicast address begins with either FFC0 or FF80.

Uniform Resource Locator (URL) — A standard means of identifying every Web page, which specifies the service used, its server's host name, and its HTML page or script name.

uninterruptible power supply (UPS) — A battery-operated power source directly attached to one or more devices and to a power supply (such as a wall outlet), which prevents undesired features of the power source from harming the device or interrupting its services.

Universal Disk Format (UDF) — A file system used on CD-ROMs and digital video disc (DVD) media.

universal group — A group on a Windows 2000 network that allows members from one domain to access resources in multiple domains and forests.

unqualified host name — A TCP/IP host name minus its prefix and suffix.

unshielded twisted-pair (UTP) — A type of cabling that consists of one or more insulated wire pairs encased in a plastic sheath. As its name implies, UTP does not contain additional shielding for the twisted pairs. As a result, UTP is both less expensive and less resistant to noise than STP.

upgrade — A major change to the existing code in a software program, which may or may not be offered free from a vendor and may or may not be comprehensive enough to substitute for the original program.

upstream — A term used to describe data traffic that flows from a customer's site to the local carrier's POP. In symmetrical communications, upstream throughput is usually much lower than downstream throughput. In symmetrical communications, upstream and downstream throughputs are equal.

USB (universal serial bus) port — A standard external bus that can be used to connect multiple types of peripherals, including modems, mice, and network adapters, to a computer. The original USB standard was capable of transmitting only 12 Mbps of data; a new standard is capable of transmitting 480 Mbps of data.

user — A person who uses a computer.

User Datagram Protocol (UDP) — A core protocol in the TCP/IP suite that sits in the Transport layer, between the Internet layer and the Application layer of the TCP/IP model. UDP is a connectionless transport service.

user principal name (UPN) — The preferred Active Directory naming convention for objects when used in informal situations. This name looks like a familiar Internet address, including the positioning of the domain name after the @ sign. UPNs are typically used for e-mail and related Internet services.

user principal name (UPN) suffix — The portion of a universal principal name (in Windows 2000 Active Directory's naming conventions) that follows the @ sign.

V

vampire tap — A connector used on Thicknet MAUs that pierces a hole in the coaxial cable, thus completing a connection between the metal tooth in the vampire tap and the copper core of the cable.

vault — A large tape storage library.

virtual circuits — Connections between network nodes that, while based on potentially disparate physical links, logically appear to be direct, dedicated links between those nodes.

virtual local area network (VLAN) — A network within a network that is logically defined by grouping its devices' switch ports in the same broadcast domain. A VLAN can consist of servers, workstations, printers, routers, or any other network device you can connect to a switch.

virtual memory — Memory that is logically carved out of space on the hard disk and added to physical memory (RAM).

virtual private network (VPN) — A logically constructed WAN that uses existing public transmission systems. VPNs can be created through the use of software or combined software and hardware solutions. This type of network allows an organization to carve out a private WAN on the Internet (or, less commonly over leased lines) that serves only its offices, while keeping the data secure and isolated from other (public) traffic.

virus — A program that replicates itself so as to infect more computers, either through network connections or through floppy disks passed among users. Viruses may damage files or systems or simply annoy users by flashing messages or pictures on the screen or by causing the keyboard to beep.

virus hoax — A rumor, or false alert, about a dangerous, new virus that could supposedly cause serious damage to your workstation.

Voice over IP (VoIP) — The provision of telephone service over a TCP/IP network. (Pronounced "voyp".) One form of VoIP is Internet telephony.

volt — Measurement used to describe the degree of pressure an electrical current exerts on a conductor.

volt-amp (VA) — A measure of electrical power. A volt-amp is the product of the voltage and current (measured in amps) of the electricity on a line.

voltage — The pressure (sometimes informally referred to as the strength) of an electrical current.

voltmeter — Device used to measure voltage (or electrical pressure) on an electricalcircuit.

W

WAN — See *wide area network*.

WAN link — The line that connects one location on a WAN with another location.

WAN topology — The physical layout, or pattern, of locations on a wide area network (WAN).

wavelength — The distance between corresponding points on a wave's cycle. Wavelength is inversely proportional to frequency.

wavelength division multiplexing (WDM) — A multiplexing technique in which each signal on a fiber-optic cable is assigned a different wavelength, which equates to its own subchannel. Each wavelength is modulated with a data signal. In this manner multiple signals can be simultaneously transmitted in the same direction over a length of fiber.

Webcasting — A broadcast transmission from one Internet-attached node to multiple other Internet-attached nodes.

well-known ports — TCP/IP port numbers 0 to 1023, so called because they were long ago assigned by Internet authorities to popular services (for example, FTP and Telnet), and are therefore well known and frequently used.

wide area network (WAN) — A network connecting geographically distinct locations, which may or may not belong to the same organization. The Internet is an example of a very large WAN.

Windows Internet Naming Service (WINS) — A service that resolves NetBIOS names with IP addresses. WINS is used exclusively with systems that use NetBIOS—therefore, it is usually found on Windows-based systems.

winipcfg — The TCP/IP configuration and management utility for use with Windows 9x systems. Winipcfg differs from ipconfig in that it supplies a graphical user interface.

wireless — Networks that transmit signals through the atmosphere via infrared or RF signaling.

wizard — A simple graphical program that assists the user in performing complex tasks, such as configuring a NIC on a server.

workgroup — A group of interconnected computers that share each others' resources without relying on a central file server.

workstation — A computer that typically runs a desktop operating system and connects to a network.

World Wide Web (WWW or Web) — A collection of internetworked servers that share resources and exchange information according to specific protocols and formats.

worm — An unwanted program that travels between computers and across networks. Although worms do not alter other programs as viruses do, they may carry viruses.

X

X.25 —An analog packet switched WAN technology optimized for long-distance data transmission and standardized by the ITU in the mid-1970s. X.25 can support 2-Mbps throughput. It was originally developed and used for communications between mainframe computers and remote terminals.

xDSL — Term used to refer to all varieties of DSL.

Z

zone — The group of machines managed by a DNS server.

INDEX